Beginning Cherokee

ᏔᎳᏗ ᏍᏫᏅᏯ ᏗᏍᏆᎥᏗ
ᏣᏫᎧ ᎯᎠᎹᏟ

Second Edition

Beginning Cherokee

ᏪᎵᏎᎭ ᏚᏟᎥᏴᎩ ᏗᏍᏆᏘᎾᏫᏗ ᏣᎳᎩ ᏗᎪᏪᎵ

By Ruth Bradley Holmes and Betty Sharp Smith

UNIVERSITY OF OKLAHOMA PRESS : NORMAN

Library of Congress Cataloging in Publication Data

Holmes, Ruth Bradley, 1924-
    Beginning Cherokee.

    Cherokee title follows English title.
    Bibliography: p. 331
    1. Cherokee language--Grammar. I. Smith, Betty Sharp, 1931-joint author.
    II. Title.
PM782.H6   497'.5   76-16498
ISBN: 0-8061-1463-0

13 14 15 16 17 18 19 20 21 22 23 24 25 26

INTRODUCTION

Beginning Cherokee is arranged in twenty-seven lessons with accompanying exercises. Appendices and alphabetical vocabulary lists appear in the back. This textbook combines an everyday vocabulary of words and phrases, gradual familiarity with the Cherokee syllabary, and an introduction to Cherokee verb-and-noun-building methods. Although a 36-week school year was kept in mind, these lessons can be divided or repeated according to convenience. An industrious class with a fluent Cherokee teacher meeting three times a week can occupy themselves for a school year. It is intended to be a teaching book; each lesson is a semi-independent unit that can be mastered by an interested student working alone. When you have finished this course you will be able to say many useful things in Cherokee, you will know and understand Cherokee letters, and you will have a start toward putting together sentences of your own in Cherokee conversation.

A Study Guide serves as the table of contents. We have used appendices to enlarge on subjects of unusual interest or difficulty. Verb structure required several appendices. One appendix is an annotated bibliography for closer study of related topics. Indian names for plants, flowers and animals always attract special interest, so we have scattered them throughout the lessons and devoted appendices to them in the back.

Cherokee is a meticulous language, marvelously economical in structure. Much of it is simple. There are no cases to memorize, no articles, no need for many English prepositions or explanatory phrases and clauses. The verbs are difficult, but logical and fascinating. Cherokee contains no f, v, p, b, th, r or z, and m is relatively rare. Despite this limited choice of consonants, amazingly enough, the language is extremely flexible. The Cherokee language does not employ many individual words, but it has a concise and versatile system for combining and amplifying each word nucleus (word base). English has a large rote vocabulary, but the system by which these many separate words are combined is often ambiguous and unwieldy. Cherokee may be said to tax the ingenuity and English the memory. English often has to pile on terms and clauses to straighten out what Cherokee makes plain with a neatly placed syllable or two. English speakers often choose to be imprecise in order to avoid long awkward sentences, while the terse efficiency of the Cherokee system provides for inclusion of details often omitted by the English speaker.

Examples:

I have some (living things).	da-gi-ka-ha
I have some (things of indefinite shape).	da-gi-ha
I have some (liquid).	da-gi-ne-a
I have some (flexible things).	da-gi-na-a
skin (of an animal still on the living animal)	u-ne-ga-lv
skin (of an animal off the animal)	ga-ne-ga
head (still in use)	a-s-go-li
head (off body)	u-s-ga

v

English verbs are surrounded by a cluster of modifying words, but Cherokee verbs consist of the verb nucleus and one-or-two-syllable particles attached in designated positions before and after the nucleus. The Cherokee verb is itself a mini-sentence. (See Appendices) Cherokee verbs describe not only <u>when</u> something happens, but also <u>how</u>. Cherokee has time tenses equivalent to those of English, but then it branches out into descriptive tenses. The addition of certain suffixes to the verb nucleus can indicate whether something is being done continuously, momentarily, by mistake, habitually, for no special reason, uselessly, repetitively, on purpose, permanently, for many combinations of these. There is also a thought-provoking suffix to separate hearsay from personal observation.

Examples:

He was speaking. (I heard him myself) ka-ne-<u>gunh-gi</u>
He was speaking. (Someone told me so) ka-ne-<u>ge-i</u>

Verbs, nouns and adjectives or adverbs are more closely related to one another in Cherokee than in English. The addition of prefixes and/or suffixes to a verb root can form not only many tenses and moods of a verb, but related adjectives, nouns and adverbs as well.

Example:

The doors are shut tight.   S-da-ya da-s-du-ha di-s-du-di.
(Closely closed closers)

Taking apart or analyzing Cherokee nouns will be helpful in your study of the language. The average Cherokee noun, unlike the average English noun, has a literal or 'inside' meaning. A Cherokee noun is often a short description of the thing designated and could pass for a sentence since the description usually contains a verb, as in the English nouns: a 'pick-me-up', an 'I-owe-you', a 'johnny-jump-up', or a 'hush-puppy'.

Examples:

horse	so-qui-li	burden-bearer (he-carries-heavy-things)
California	a-del'-tsu-hdlunh	where they find money (money-they-get-from-out-of-there)
flag	ga-da-di	place to be taken care of (this-place-is-treasured, <u>or</u> guarded)
cemetery	tsu-na-da-ni-soh-di	they are laid there by others, not finally
attorney	di-ti-yo-hi-hi	he argues repeatedly and on purpose with a purpose
policeman	di-da-ni-yi-s-gi	final catcher (he-catches-them-finally and conclusively)

Graphic terms such as these constitute a delightful spontaneous artform. They occur much oftener in Cherokee than in English.

Notice the resemblances between translations of English terms derived from Latin or Greek, and common Cherokee nouns:
Examples:
<pre>
From Greek - pterodactyl   wing-fingered, winged-fingers
             brontosaurus   thunder-lizard

From Latin - nasturtium   it-wrings-the nose
             convolvulus   it-twists, rolls, it-is-twining
                            (morning-glory)

Cherokee   - a-di-toh-di   to-sip-with (a spoon)
             si-kwa-u-tse-ts smiling-pig (possum)
</pre>

Cherokee nouns are concise, vivid and factual. The language is well adapted to express sardonic humor, poetic insight and stark simplicity, often all three at once.

Cherokees enjoy making irreverent half-puns on foreign words, whether the words are of English or Amerindian origin. Bartlesville is called 'Gu-gu' (Bottle) in Cherokee, sometimes 'Gu-gu-di-ga-du-hunh', (Bottletown).

Wa-sha-shi (belonging to waterways, originating in waters) is the Osage name for themselves. Cherokees call an Osage tribal member Ak-sa-si, which is mischievously close to 'sa-si', the Cherokee word for 'goose'; he/she is a goose.

'Nowata', the name for a town and a county in Oklahoma, originated from a Delaware word meaning 'welcome' or 'friendly' and was more correctly pronounced 'nu-wi-ta'. Remnants of the formerly powerful Delaware tribe chose this name for the railroad stop in Oklahoma where they were brought from the East, and near which they had been allotted land for re-settlement. Cherokees, noting how the name came to be pronounced by white settlers, call Nowata 'A-ma-di-ka-ni-gunh-gunh', or 'water-is-all-gone'.

Cherokees borrowed relatively few words whole from English. Even when the article or function was entirely new to them they usually, especially at first, made up one of the epithet action nouns so characteristic of their language. Some words were borrowed, however, such as 'ka-wi' for 'coffee' and 'wa-tsi' for 'watch', which led to 'u-ta-na wa-tsi' (big watch), or 'clock'.

The word for car or automobile has gone through some interesting changes. In the early 1900's it was called 'di-tu-le-na' (it-stares), then changed to 'a-dla-di-tla' (it-goes-on-rubber-coverings), most likely as a result of changes in car styles. Now its commonest Cherokee name is 'a-tso-do-di' (to-ride-along-in), the same word that was formerly used for a horse-drawn carriage. It is also called 'owtombil', with a soft l, or 'car', even in the middle of a Cherokee sentence. Notice that the last two English words contain sounds not present in the Cherokee language (b and r), and do not end in vowels, whereas older borrowings such as wa-tsi and ka-wi were adapted by the Cherokees to suit their own speech habits. This illustrates the invasion of Cherokee by the English language. Formerly uncongenial sounds now come as naturally as those of rote nomenclature. These more recent changes noticeable in Cherokee illustrate not only a gradual invasion of the language, but also the weakening of its adaptive vitality. The Cherokee language might not survive much longer without the present renewed enthusiasm on the part of Cherokees.

Some English words, such as 'parade' have almost replaced several Cherokee epithet action nouns that stressed the marching, the music, or the entertainers. 'Store' is now taking over from the well-established Cherokee equivalent, 'a-da-na-nv' (arranged-in-rows), although both the words 'store' and 'parade' would have sounded barbaric to Cherokees of the past because of the p, r, and consonant endings. Cherokees now oftener call their mothers 'Momma' than 'E-tsi'. Notice, though, that Momma's syllables end in vowels and its consonants are phonetically congenial to Cherokee!

Cherokee is a branch of the Iroquoian language family, related to Cayuga, Seneca, Onondega, Wyandot-Huron, Tuscarora, Oneida, and Mohawk. Due to a prehistoric migration of the Cherokees southeastward from the Great Lakes region to North Carolina, Tennessee, and Georgia, Cherokee is not very closely related to the other Iroquoian languages. Linguists have computed that this split between the Cherokee tribe and the rest of the Iroquois took place at least three thousand years ago.

Cherokee is the native tongue of about 20,000 people, although most who now speak it use it only as a second language. It has had several recognized dialects. One of these, now extinct, contained an 'r' sound. This dialect is probably responsible for the name in English, 'Cherokee'. There is no 'r' in the language now. The present Cherokee word for both the language and the people is 'Tsa-la-gi'.

The two main dialects today are the North Carolina, spoken on the Qualla Reservation by about 3,000 people (although that dialect itself is divided into two), and the Oklahoma, or Western, which is a consensus of the different ways of speech among Cherokees mingled there after their forcible removal from the East under President Jackson's admin-istration in the 1830's. Our lessons use the Oklahoma dialect.

The North Carolina Cherokees are descendants of those who managed to hold out against removal in inaccessible mountains near their homes. They were later granted amnesty and their mountain refuge became the present Qualla Reservation. The North Carolina and Oklahoma dialects can be mutually understood, but the North Carolina has changed less because its isolation sheltered it from many of the conflicts encountered by Oklahoma Cherokees. The differences among Oklahoma native speakers are not great, and usually amount to mannerisms of pitch, speed of talking, retention or omission of some vowels, and pronunciation of some consonants. (See Lesson III)

From the 1830's until after the Civil War, Cherokees in Oklahoma were an independent nation with their own Constitution, boundaries, laws, and system of self-government. Since the Cherokee language was universally spoken in the Cherokee Nation, white missionaries, ranchers and merchants who wished to deal with Cherokees applied themselves to learning it. During this time many books and papers were published in the Cherokee syllabary and voluminous personal correspondence was carried on using Cherokee letters. The Cherokee Nation maintained well financed public schools and encouraged higher learning. They recruited teachers from among men and women graduates of exacting eastern universities and young Cherokees from wealthier homes went East to attend college or to travel before coming home to Oklahoma to settle down.

The Civil War was disastrous for the Cherokee Nation. A number of prominent Cherokees were planters and owned black slaves whom they had brought with them from the eastern Cherokee territories. Because of slavery, the Cherokee Nation was not allowed to remain neutral, but was maneuvered into siding with the Confederacy. The Cherokee regiment under Stand Watie acquitted themselves well as soldiers. Stand Watie was the last Confederate general to surrender, but the Nation was torn and in ruins. Dissension, poverty and repression followed, even the eventual loss of their independence. Cherokees neglected or destroyed much of their written material in the struggle to survive, but the language has continued to be spoken.

Recent increased interest has created a demand for Amerindian language courses. Many Cherokees who ignored past opportunities to learn the language from their families are now regretting the loss. Parents who used to believe that such knowledge would only be a disadvantage to their children have changed their minds. Youths who have now concluded that their ancestors had much to offer are anxious to investigate the language for themselves. Those who do not have time to spare for organized sutdy would often like to have a convenient source book on the Cherokee language and its syllabary. Beginning Cherokee was written to fill these needs. We hope it will help everyone who uses this book, whether Cherokee or not, to understand that Indian tribes are contemporary peoples with an enduring heritage. The Cherokee language frames an outlook and an intellect that can contribute much to civilization.

These lessons grew out of a series of Indian language classes sponsored by the Bartlesville Indian Women's Club. Mrs. Betty Smith has been the Cherokee teacher of this series for five years. We would like to thank Will Rogers Rider, Jr., for his generous gift of the Cherokee letter sheets which were used to insert the Cherokee letters in this book. We would also like to thank Dee Denbo, Mr. and Mrs. John Brasher and their children Mary, Lisa, John, and Bob; Mary Crow, Fondanell Edwards, Lena Watkins, Bernis Hamlin, Betsy Grissom; Duronda, Darla and Dora Smith, Wynena Montgomery, Joan Eroncel, and all other members of the Cherokee class. They have made putting these lessons together over the past several years a pleasant task.

The staff of the Bartlesville Public Library, the late Mrs. Wilma Berry, Mr. Gene Winn and Mrs. Rosalia Purdum in particular, have made every effort to obtain helpful material both in and outside their library. Mrs. Jean Winkler and Mrs. Virginia Frobel typed the difficult manuscript, assisted in part by Mrs. Vicki Doughty. Mr. Cleo Beougher drafted the diagrams of Appendix VIII; Gilcrease Museum in Tulsa provided Appendices I, II and III from documents in their archives.

Dr. C. N. Holmes spent many toilsome hours reading all versions of the manuscript and offering invaluable suggestions that were incorporated into the text.

Durable, first-quality language tapes containing all Cherokee words, phrases, and songs that appear in the first sixteen lessons of Beginning Cherokee are available from Ruth Bradley Holmes, 1431 Valley Road, Bartlesville, Oklahoma 74003 (telephone: [918] 336-8738). The tapes contain 184 minutes of material spoken by Betty Sharp Smith.

Ruth Bradley Holmes

Betty Sharp Smith

Bartlesville, Oklahoma

x

STUDY GUIDE

Lessons & Pages	Syllabary Rows	Phrase Numbers	Verbs	Subject Matter
Lesson 1 3 - 6	none	1 - 8	none	O-si-yo phrases
Lesson 2 7 - 10	none	none	none	Syllabary Part 1
Lesson 3 11 - 15	none	none	none	Syllabary Part 2, Hymns
Lesson 4 16 - 21	2	9 - 12	ga-di?-a	Numbers 1 - 10, Ordinals
Lesson 5	3	13 - 19	ge:-ga a?-wa-du'-li-(a) ga-l'-s-ta-yv-hv'-s-ga DE-S-KV-SI (5)	Thanksgiving, Classifying verbs
Lesson 6 32 - 38	4	20 - 34	ga-li-e:-li-ga a-qua'-n'-ta go-li:-ga	Classroom phrases
Lesson 7 39 - 46	5	35 - 37	ga-dv'-ne?-a	Pitch, It-is-cold
Lesson 8 47 - 57	6	38 - 43	a-gi-wa'-s-ga GV-NE-HA (5) A-GI-HA (5)	Kenuche, Christmas
Lesson 9 58 - 67	7	44 - 50	none	Hymns, Months, Plural of human nouns, 3rd-person verbs and living adjectives
Lesson 10 68 - 72	8	51 - 59	ga-di-ta-s-ga	Hospitality phrases
Lesson 11 73 - 80	9	60 - 74	tsi-yv-wi-(ya) ga-wo:-ni-a	Forming questions, Tribal origin phrases
Lesson 12 81 - 90	10	75 - 84	tsi-lu?-gi ga-tv'-gi-(a) ni-tsi-we?-a	Interrogatives, Numbers to 1,000
Lesson 13 91 - 97	11	85 - 92	ga-da-nv?-a	Pronouns, Part 1, Birds
Lesson 14 98 - 106	12	93 - 99	ga-tv'-s-ga tsi-hwi-sv'-s-ga ga-l'-tso?-v'-s-ga TSI-GI-A (4)	Pronouns, Part 2, Fruits and plants
Lesson 15 107 - 120	all	100 - 108	tsi-tla-hv'-(s)-ga tsi-go'-ti?-(a) a-quo:-tla ga-l'-s-du-tlv'-ga	Days of the week, Ni- and di- plurals, Household objects
Lesson 16 121 - 128		none	none	Cherokee verb, Part 1 (bound pronouns)

APPENDICES

First referred to in Lesson:	Appendix Number:	Appendix Subject:
3	I	Original Cherokee syllabary and Modified (Present) Cherokee syllabary
3	II	Sequoyah's numeral system
3	III	Numeral system and alphabet (syllabary) signed by Sequoyah
3	IV	Biographical sketch of Sequoyah
5	V	I pass you - Classifying verbs
15	VI	Supplementary tree and plant list
16	VII	Verbs up to Lesson 15 with all ten personal pronouns
16	VIII	Diagrams of Cherokee and English pronominal systems
18	IX	Supplementary list of animals, snakes, insects, birds
22	X	Subject-object pronouns - Gv-ge-yu, gv-yo-li-ga
23	XI	Infinitives, future and past tenses for all verbs so far
26	XII	Structure of a Cherokee verb - Prefixes
26	XIII	Structure of a Cherokee verb - Suffixes
	XIV	Reading List

Beginning Cherokee

ᏩᎾ ᏍᏢᎥᎩ ᏗᏍᏛᎥᏗ ᎠᏬᎻᎹ
ᏣᏫ ᏣᎳᎩ

Cherokee Alphabet.

D a	R e	T i	Ꮂ o	Ꮕ u	i v
S ga Ꮖ ka	Ꮄ ge	Ꮗ gi	A go	J gu	E gv
Ꮣ ha	Ꮅ he	Ꮙ hi	F ho	Ꮈ hu	Ꮚ hv
W la	Ꮆ le	Ꮈ li	Ꮊ lo	M lu	Ꮠ lv
Ꮉ ma	Ꮇ me	H mi	Ꮖ mo	Ꮋ mu	
Ꮎ na Ꮏ hna G nah	Ꮑ ne	Ꮒ ni	Z no	Ꮔ nu	Ꮕ nv
Ꮖ qua	Ꮗ que	Ꮖ qui	V quo	Ꮘ quu	Ꮛ quv
Ꮜ sa Ꮝ s	4 se	Ꮟ si	Ꮞ so	Ꮢ su	R sv
Ꮣ da Ꮤ ta	Ꮝ de Ꮤ te	Ꮧ di Ꮨ ti	Ꮩ do	Ꮪ du	Ꮫ dv
Ꮬ dla Ꮭ tla	L tle	C tli	Ꮯ tlo	Ꮰ tlu	P tlv
G tsa	Ꮳ tse	Ꮷ tsi	K tso	Ꮴ tsu	Ꮶ tsv
G wa	Ꮺ we	Ꮻ wi	Ꮼ wo	Ꮽ wu	6 wv
Ꮿ ya	B ye	Ꭰ yi	Ꭶ yo	G yu	B yv

Sounds Represented by Vowels

a, as <u>a</u> in <u>father</u>, or short as <u>a</u> in <u>rival</u>

e, as <u>a</u> in <u>hate</u>, or short as <u>e</u> in <u>met</u>

i, as <u>i</u> in <u>pique</u>, or short as <u>i</u> in <u>pit</u>

o, as <u>o</u> in <u>note</u>, approaching <u>aw</u> in <u>law</u>

u, as <u>oo</u> in <u>fool</u>, or short as <u>u</u> in <u>pull</u>

v, as <u>u</u> in <u>but</u>, nasalized

Consonant Sounds

<u>g</u> nearly as in English, but approaching to <u>k</u>. <u>d</u> nearly as in English but approaching to <u>t</u>. <u>h</u> <u>k</u> <u>l</u> <u>m</u> <u>n</u> <u>q</u> <u>s</u> <u>t</u> <u>w</u> <u>y</u> as in English. Syllables beginning with <u>g</u> except Ꮖ (ga) have sometimes the power of <u>k</u>. A (go), S (du), Ꮫ (dv) are sometimes sounded <u>to</u>, <u>tu</u>, <u>tv</u> and syllables written with tl except Ꮭ (tla) sometimes vary to dl.

TEᏏT ᏩᎩ ᎪᏯᎿT

I-gv-yi:-iꞌ Tsa-la-giꞌ Go-hwe-lv:ꞌ-i

FIRST CHEROKEE LESSON

Lesson I is an exercise in five steps.

1. Read the paragraphs on the syllabary page opposite entitled "Sounds represented by vowels" and "Consonant sounds".

2. Examine the Cherokee words and phrases under Phrases on page 6, then turn back to this page.

3. Slowly read the explanations below of the special punctuation marks to be used in these Cherokee lessons:

   a. <u>Brackets ( ) around a letter or letters in a Cherokee word</u> in the Pronunciation column mean that the bracketed part is omitted in everyday talk by some Cherokees.

      Examples:
      (Oꞌ)-si-yoꞌ (hello) may be pronounced Oꞌ-si-yoꞌ or Si-yoꞌ
      ko:-g(a)(i) (crow)   may be: ko:-g, ko:-ga or ko:-gi
      a-geꞌ-(h(y(v)a) (woman) may be: a-geꞌ, a-geꞌ-ya, a-geꞌ-yv,
                                        a-ge-hya or a-ge-hyvꞌ

   b. <u>Brackets around English words</u> in the Translation column enclose a word-for-word translation of the Cherokee that we would not normally say in English.

      Examples: Goodbye (Weꞌll see one another again)
                 No   (Not so)

   c. <u>A colon (:) after a vowel</u> means that this vowel is long. It is doubled and takes twice as long to say.

      Examples:
      O:-s-daꞌ   O: is pronounced like the
      ko:-ga   o in an emphatic No!

3

d. <u>An apostrophe (') after a Cherokee syllable</u> in the Pronunciation column means that this syllable is accented, as in English be-fore', Che'-ro-kee, or in-tend'-ed. Cherokee words quite often have more than one stressed syllable.

    Examples: Hello   (O')-si-yo'

e. <u>An apostrophe after the consonant</u> of a Cherokee syllable means the vowel has been left out.

    Examples: hi'-s-g'   five, for hi'-s-gi'
               go'-l'ga   he knows, for go'-li-ga

f. <u>A question mark (?) between the syllables of a word</u> in the Pronunciation column indicates a pause called a 'glottal stop'. This means that you stop dead momentarily between these syllables, then go on, as in English 'apple is' or 'blood owner'. These two phrases contain one glottal stop between 'apple' and 'is', and one between 'blood' and 'owner'.

    Examples: Wa?-do   Thank you
               V?-tla   No

When two vowels fall together in English, w or y is often unconscious-ly slipped between them. Say "Goodbye again" and "Hello again", listening to yourself as you say them.

Notice that a y sound slips into "Goodbye again", making it sound like 'goodbye yagain', and a w sound slips into "Hello again", making it sound like 'hello wagain'.

Now repeat these two phrases, this time omitting any w or y as a bridge between the words. The result will be a glottal stop where the w or y was before. In Cherokee, a glottal stop often occurs between two vowels so that each vowel is pronounced individually.

    Examples: go?-i   grease, machine oil
               hi?-a   this

In English it is not noticeable whether you glide from vowel to vowel, forming a slight w or y, or whether you separate each vowel and form a glottal stop. In Cherokee it makes a difference.

Glottal stops are extremely common in Cherokee. In English, glides (unconscious w or y) are the most common way of separating vowels. In Cherokee, quick little glottal stops are the most common vowel bridge. A slight pause between each word, as though a comma might be there, is also characteristic of Cherokee.

Practice saying the following two columns:

go on, go?on	fly?up, fly up
go?in, go in	fly away, fly?away
go up, go?up	see?it, see it
go?away, go away	see out, see?out
do it, do?it	say?ah! say ah!

Glottal stops in Cherokee can begin a statement, separate words or syllables, and can end a statement. Use of the glottal stop is becoming haphazard and declining in Cherokee today, but it is still very obvious to a fluent Cherokee speaker when you omit it. Listen closely to your teacher; since the glottal stop is not a recognized sound of English it will be easy for you to miss it entirely.

g. <u>The only diphthong</u> (combination vowel) in Cherokee is the sound of 'i' in 'sight' or 'die'. This will be written <u>a-i</u> to show that it is made up of the sounds of 'a' and 'i' in the Cherokee syllabary, spoken together.

Example: a-l'-s-<u>ta-i</u>-d(i)   a meal   (rhymes with tide or tidy)

h. <u>Partial underlinings</u> will also be used for emphasis.

i. <u>When two a's</u> happen to fall together they are slurred into one another and pronounced 'v'. They will be underlined.

Example: gv:-<u>na a</u>?-wa-du'-li   I want a turkey
Pronounced: gv:-nv?-wa-du'-li

j. An asterisk (*) beside a word means that this word must be very carefully pronounced, as <u>tone</u> affects the meaning. See Lesson 7.

k. All vowels at the end of a statement are slightly nasalized, or spoken with a short 'ng' on the end. <u>A slash mark through a vowel</u> means that this vowel is nasalized more crisply, whether near the end of a statement or not. Ding-dong in English might be written dḷ-dø̸.

Example: tsi-yḷ   copper

4. Carefully pronounce the column in the Phrases on the next page labelled Pronunciation, using the paragraphs on the Syllabary labelled "Sounds representing vowels" and "Consonant sounds", and paying attention to the punctuation marks explained above in Step 3 of this lesson.

5. Learn all the Cherokee words and phrases below and try to use them often.

PHRASES

Translation	Syllabary	Pronunciation
1. Hello.	ᎣᏏᏲ	(O')-si-yo'
2. How are you?	ᏙᎯᏧ	Dto-hi:'-tsu?
3. Fine.	ᎣᏍᏓ	O:-s-da', or, a little more emphatically,
	ᎣᏍᏓᏅ	O:-s-da-dv'
4. It's all right.	ᎣᏍᏓ ᎣᏍᏓᏅ	O:-s-d(a) or O:-s-da-dv', exactly as above in P.N.3 (Phrase Number 3)
5. Goodbye. (We'll see one another again)		
one talking to one	ᏙᎾᏓᎪᎲᎢ	Do-na-da'-go-hv-(i').
one talking to several	ᏙᏓᏓᎪᎲᎢ	Do'-da-da-go'-hv-(i').
6. Thank you.	ᏩᏙ	Wa?-do'.
7. Yes.	ᎥᎥ	V:-v'.
8. No (not so), not		Tla', Tla-hv', V?-tla

When the answer is just "No", Cherokees usually don't say "Tla" alone, but use "Tla-hv'" or V?-tla".

ᏔᎵᏁ ᏣᎳᎩ ᎠᏍᏆᏙᏗ

Ta?-li:'-ne Tsa-la-gi' Go-hwe-lv:'-i

SECOND CHEROKEE LESSON

Syllabary - Part 1
          a. Background information
          b. What is a syllabary?
          c. The Cherokee syllabary

a. Background information

Cherokees are probably best known to most people as the only American Indians with their own system of writing. In the past, many other tribes in both North and South America invented systems for recalling important events, but only the Cherokees possess a writing system equivalent to the European alphabet.

The Maya and Aztecs engraved picture-writing on stone and developed a fine numeral system. The Delawares, Chippewa and others kept records on wood, stone, leather, or in bead belts. These systems relied on coded symbols, the meaning of which was known and memorized by only a few special tribal members. Their purpose was historic. They 'kept in memory' a sequence of events important to the tribe, such as migrations, spiritual crises, wars, degrees of prosperity, and terms of treaties. Keeping possession of these picture-archives was regarded as important to group survival in the same way that the Ark of the Covenant in the Bible was important to the Israelites. These records played no part in daily communication as alphabets do. They were coded aids to memory, not writing as we know it. As Sequoyah realized, a man who can write does not need to use his memory.

The Cherokee syllabary is also the only alphabet in history known to be the work of one man. The Cyrillic alphabet now used in Russian and other Slavic languages has been attributed to St. Cyril, but his authorship of it is in doubt. Other writing systems have legendary or semi-legendary authors, like Emperor Fu-Hsi of China and his Eight Trigrams, or Ts'ang Chieh and his Notched-Stick letters. Alphabets have arisen in only a few places throughout world history and have always involved centuries of

7

adaptation and thought. The European alphabet now used in English is a result of four thousand years of development, from Egypt to a Semitic tribe named the Seirites, to the Phoenicians, to the Greeks, to the Romans, to our own day. Only one man, Sequoyah, has undoubtedly invented his own alphabet. He alone accomplished in his lifetime what it has taken whole nations of people hundreds of years to do. His syllabary, though not perfect, is as well adapted to the sounds of the Cherokee language as the European alphabet is to the sounds of the English language.

b. What is a syllabary?

A syllabary is a variety of alphabet in which each letter in a word stands for a whole syllable (such as 'na'), instead of a brief sound (such as 'n-'). English is an alphabet, while Japanese and Sanskrit are modified syllabaries. Cherokee is completely a syllabary, except for one letter, ꮝ or s-s-s. The small number of consonants (lack of f, v, p, b, th, r or z) in the Cherokee language, and the fact that almost all Cherokee syllables end in a vowel, make it convenient to express the language in this way. A syllabary would be a poor system for English, since English is just the opposite of Cherokee in this respect. English has many consonants, and most English words end in consonants. Test this for yourself by examining a paragraph in English. Then examine either the Phrases you have had in Cherokee, or any other Cherokee material.

An alphabet's efficiency is judged according to how accurately each letter can represent each sound in the language, without uncertainty or duplication. Sanskrit has been called the most perfect alphabet ever devised. The English alphabet is accurate, but contains much duplication.

Examples:
    Same letters, different sounds: cough, bough, through, though, rough
    Same sounds, different letters: coffee, kawphy

Cherokee spelling is easy though it is not standardized. Each person spells as the word sounds to him. The words can almost always be spelled exactly as they are pronounced. The exceptions will be mentioned in Lesson III, but there are very few, and they consist of omitting some vowels, not of a complete change.

The syllables you say when you spell in English are actually just the names of the letters, not necessarily the sound they represent at all. Sometimes the name is the sound, as 'a' in 'ate'. However, notice that in the same word, 't' is not pronounced 'tee', but 't-', and 'e' is not pronounced at all!

When you recite the alphabet in English or spell out a word letter by letter, you <u>say</u> syllables: ay, bee, see, dee, ee, eff, jee, aitch, or see-ay-tee, bee-ay-tee, bee-oh-wye.

After these same English letters have been placed in words, however, each letter <u>counts</u> only as a short sound, not a whole syllable. For instance, see-ay-tee is pronounced cat, bee-ay-tee, bat, bee-oh-wye, boy, and so on.

c. The Cherokee syllabary

<u>Cherokee letters make the same sound as their name.</u> ꮖ , ya, is pronounced ya, whether you are reciting the alphabet, spelling, or reading words from a book. Every time a letter appears it makes the same sound, and each letter except ꮖ , s-s, stands for an entire syllable.

Example: Examine the title of this lesson on page 7 and below:

Syllabary: **W ꮅ Ꭿ Ꮹ Ꮍ Ꭺꮻ Ꭶ Ꭲ**

Pronunciation: Ta?-li:'-ne Tsa-la-gi' Go-hwe-lv:'-i

Translation: SECOND   CHEROKEE   LESSON

Hyphens are used in these lessons to divide words into syllables in such a way that each division represents one Cherokee letter when written in Cherokee. Match up each Cherokee syllable above with its Cherokee letter.

Notice that 'hwe' in the pronunciation is written as ꮻ , we, in Cherokee. This illustrates one of the flaws of Sequoyah's alphabet. He did not account for a sound in the Cherokee language called the 'intrusive h', except in the letters Ꮏ , hna, and Ꮐ , nah. The intrusive h is a barely hissed 'h' sound pronounced by breathing out through the nose just <u>as</u> you pronounce the consonant that follows it.

Examples:

Translation	Syllabary	Pronunciation
maple	Ᏸ Ꭷ Ꮆ Ᏻ	tlv-hwa-l(i)-ga'
here	D Ꮏ	a'-hni'
cold	Ꭴ Ᏸ Ꮃ Ꮆ	u-hyv'-dla(dlv)

9

Notice that 'hwe' in the pronunciation is written 'we' in the syllabary, 'hwa' is written 'wa', 'hni', 'ni', 'hyv', 'yv', and so on. Intrusive h causes no difficulty in choosing a Cherokee letter, and appears in the Pronunciation column only.

The 'h' sound before a vowel in the third row of the syllabary (ha, he, hi, ho, hu, hv), is pronounced just like 'h' in English.

Sometimes you will see ki, ko, ke, or to in the Pronunciation column, and the Cherokee letters for 'gi', 'go', 'ge', and 'do' in the Syllabary column. This illustrates another oversight on Sequoyah's part, related to his omission of intrusive h.

Intrusive h does not only occur before n, y or w. It is actually a symptom of the Cherokee habit of often breathing slightly while speaking. The amount of intrusive h used varies from speaker to speaker and from community to community.

As a native Cherokee speaker Sequoyah was of course accustomed to varying some g's toward k and some t's toward d, so he evidently did not notice enough difference to create a special letter for those sounds with each vowel. There is a difference, however, so be sure to observe it when the Pronunciation doesn't tally with the Syllabary.

It is characteristic of a Cherokee speaker to keep his lips still and his upper lip tightened slightly across his teeth in a faint Mona Lisa smile, keeping his mouth unnoticeably open. He can breathe slightly either inward or outward during speech, and sometimes breathes outward through nose and mouth at the same time, giving an extra h sound to some consonants, a t sound to the d's or a k sound to g's. In Cherokee speaking position the tongue never wags. It fits along the bottom of the mouth pressed against the lower teeth. The nasalization at the end of Cherokee phrases is added to by the resettling of the tongue along the bottom of the mouth at the end of speech. S and l sounds billow out from under the tongue, which remains in place as much as possible. L comes from beside the tongue tip and s from between the center of the tongue tip and the lower teeth. Don't bother about breathing any special way, but do try to keep your tongue against your lower jaw and your lips still to help your pronunciation.

Now go over the words and phrases you learned in Phrases in Lesson I, matching up each syllable with the proper Cherokee letter. Write each letter in Cherokee as you say it out loud. You will sometimes notice variations in the English spelling of the same word in these lessons. (ha'-tlv & ha:-dlv, da & ta, ku & gu, etc.) In doubtful cases, rather than pick one spelling and constantly adhere to it, we have spelled each word as it seems to sound in the sentence where it occurs. You will find that this will not cause you any confusion if you remember the pronunciation tips in this lesson.

ᎣᎢᎾ ᏣᎳᎩ ᎠᏈᎥᎢ

Tso-i:-ne Tsa-la-gi' Go-hwe-lv:-i

THIRD CHEROKEE LESSON

The Syllabary - Part 2 - Pronunciation and arrangement

After the hymns on this page, this lesson consists of seven steps to be taken in order to use and understand the Cherokee syllabary.

AMAZING GRACE

U-ne-la-nv-hi U-we-tsi
I-ga-gu-yv-he-yi
Hna-quo-tso-sv Wi-yu-lo-se
I-ga-gu-yv-ho-nv.

A-se-no Yi-u-ne-tse-yi
I-yu-no Du-le-nv
Ta-li-ne-dv Tse-lu-tse-li
U-dv-ne Yu-ne-tsv.

JUST AS I AM

Na-qua-s-dv-quo Ga-tsi-s-ga-ni
Tsa-gi-gv-a-qua-li-s-ga-s-do-dv,
A-le s-gi-ya-ni-s-gv Tsi-sa
Wi-gv-lu-tsi, wi-gv-lu-tsi.

Na-qua-s-dv-quo S-gi-s-de-li-s-gi
Ni-tsi-gu-ti-di S-gv-na-no
Tsi-s-ga-nv a-gi-hv s-di-yi
Wi-gv-lu-tsi, wi-gv-lu-tsi.

Most Cherokee meetings include either a prayer or a song. These are two of the hymns translated into Cherokee by Dr. Samuel A. Worcester, a missionary among the Cherokees, and a Cherokee assistant, Elias Boudinot. The Rev. Stephen Foreman, a Cherokee pastor, collaborated with Dr. Worcester on

11

many hymns also. The New Testament and the Cherokee Hymnbook by these men are both still available in print. They are entirely in the Cherokee syllabary.

Amazing Grace is especially loved. It has been sung so often, on the Trail of Tears and since, that it has become almost a Cherokee national song.

Let's sing.   **ᏓᏗᏴ**   Di-di-hno'-gi.

The Syllabary - Part 2 - Pronunciation and arrangement

1.
Examine the whole syllabary page carefully. The Cherokee letters are the large ones in boldface. The smaller lower-case letters beside each boldface one indicate pronunciation.

When Sequoyah first invented the syllabary he avoided copying from other alphabets (See Appendices I and II), but his original letters were later modified to make them easier to print.

Dr. Samuel A. Worcester designed the font from which to print Cherokee material. He evidently assigned a number of English letters to the Cherokee alphabet, drawing on fonts he happened to have available at his printing press. Between 1821 and 1861, his press printed 13,980,000 pages of Indian-language texts, most of it Cherokee. With the help of his Cherokee assistants, first Elias Boudinot and then the Rev. Stephen Foreman, he translated hymns, prayers, and the whole New Testament into Cherokee, besides his daily work as a missionary doctor.

Changing the syllabary in this way made Cherokee material immediately available to large numbers of Cherokees. Unfortunately, however, using English-looking letters has given many people the completely mistaken idea that Sequoyah imitated other alphabets extensively. He cooperated in this remodelling of his syllabary, no doubt to help realize his dream of complete literacy for the Cherokee Nation.

2.
Resolve to put out of your mind as much as possible the sounds you now associate with any of the Cherokee letters. Almost <u>none</u> of the Cherokee letters are pronounced at all like the sounds of the same or similar English

letters. The only exceptions to this are **L** , pronounced 'tle', and
C , pronounced 'tla'.

Examples:

R	e(eh)
R	sv(sunh)
y	mu
G	tsa
A	go
Z	no

Learn the Cherokee alphabet as though you had never seen any of the
letters before.

3.

Re-read carefully the paragraphs on sounds on the face of the syllabary.

The Cherokee 'l' sound is soft, as in English 'leaf' or 'liquid'.
English 'l' is rarely soft, so you will have to be careful to curl your
tongue into position to say 'liquid' before each syllable that begins
with 'l'. Some native speakers occasionally drop the vowel after 'l',
and pronounce the syllable like the 'l' and 'y' together in 'roll your own'.

Native speakers pronounce the seventh horizontal row from the top (qua,
que, qui, quo, quu, quv), in one of several ways. Some pronounce it as
written, which sounds like kwa, kway, kwee, kwoe, kwoo, kwunh. Some say
it more like gwa, gwe, gwi, etc., and some say it further back in the
throat, ghwa, ghwe, ghwi, ghwo, ghwu, ghwv.

The letters 'si' and 'se' (see and say), but not the other letters
in the 'sa' horizontal row (Row 8 from the top) are pronounced by some
as 'sh', omitting the vowel, when they are at the end of a word.

Example: wa-lo'-s(i)   frog   sometimes pronounced wa-lo'-sh'

Some pronounce the eleventh horizontal row, beginning with 'tsa', as
written. Some pronounce it dza, dze, dzi, etc. Others say ja, je, ji, etc.,
or tsha, tshe, tshi, etc. You, of course, will follow the preference of
your teacher, the custom of your community, or your own choice.

Variation from t toward d or k toward g are influenced by other sounds
in the word or phrase. This will be indicated without explanation in the
Pronunciation column.

4.
    Read the Cherokee letters out loud carefully, going across horizontally from left to right.

Examples: Reading across the top row
        D   is pronounced a(ah) as in father
        R   is pronounced e(eh)
        T   is pronounced i(ee)
        ꭳ   is pronounced o(aw)
        Ᏺ   is pronounced u(ooh)
        i   is pronounced v(unh)

    Cherokee is written all in block capitals, even in private correspondence. There is no cursive (long-hand) or lower-case in Cherokee.

5.
    Read the Cherokee letters out loud again, row by row, this time writing each one. A fine-tipped felt pen makes handsome letters. Write each one several times, till you can dash them off easily. Don't attempt to memorize them yet. Concentrate on feeling comfortable with the syllabary.

    The order of the syllabary is easy to understand and to remember. It was devised by the missionary, Dr. S. A. Worcester, for his convenience in printing Cherokee material.

    Worcester placed the vowels first, arranged across the top in <u>English</u> alphabetical order, a, e, i, o, u. He then adopted an English letter he would not need in printing Cherokee, lower-case v, to represent the Cherokee vowel not contained in English, unh, or nasal u. He placed v on the top horizontal row beside the other vowels.

    Next, he arranged the consonant groups from top to bottom in what would be English alphabetical order if Cherokee contained all of the same consonants as English. He began with ga and all the syllables with a g- sound, then ha, and all the syllables beginning with a strong h- sound, and so on through la, ma, na, qua, sa, ta (with da), tla (with dla), tsa, wa, and ya. B, f, j, p, q, r, v, and z are missing since Cherokee does not need those letters. C and k are also unnecessary since the qua row (Row 7), takes care of that sound as it is used in Cherokee. Dr. Worcester chose to include d with t, probably because d does not combine with all vowels in Cherokee, and d and t are often interchangeable.

Run your eye down each syllabary column (not across each row), and you will notice all the <u>consonants</u> in each column are in modified English alphabetical order.

Run your eye across each row, one row at a time, and you will notice the <u>vowels</u> are alphabetical.

This is a great help in memorizing the Cherokee letters.

6.
Cut out the extra syllabary page at the end of the lessons and paste it to a cardboard or have it laminated. Some places of business have laminating machines. Use your extra syllabary as a bookmark in this textbook so you can consult it constantly.

Cut up filing cards to a convenient size for use as flash cards. Write the Cherokee letter on one side of each card with your felt pen, and its pronunciation on the other side of the card. The cards must be heavy enough so that the felt pen writing does not come through. Flash cards are useful for Cherokee words and phrases as well as for learning the syllabary. If you wish you can simply write a Cherokee word or phrase in both Cherokee syllabary and English pronunciation on one side of the card, and the English translation on the other.

Examine the commercial flash card sets available in stationery stores for French, Spanish, etc. and create your own Cherokee flash card set as you go along through the lessons.

Drill yourself by going through your flash cards every day.

7.
Cover the pronunciation columns in Lesson I, P.N. 1 - 8 (<u>P</u>hrase <u>N</u>umbers 1 through 8), then sound out the Cherokee letters, looking them up in the Syllabary.

ᏅᎩᏁ ᏣᎳᎩ ᎪᏪᎸᎢ

Nv:-gi-ne Tsa-la-gi' Go-hwe-lv:-i'

FOURTH CHEROKEE LESSON

PHRASES

Translation	Syllabary	Pronunciation
9.		
Let's say the letters. (The-letters let-us-them-say)	ᏗᎪᏪᎳ ᏂᏗᏗᏩ	Di-go-hwe:-la' ni-di-di:wa.
10.		
Let's say the numbers (The-numbers let-us-them-say)	ᏗᏎᏍᏗ ᏂᏗᏗᏩ	Di-se-s-di ni-di-di'-wa.
11.		
one	ᏌᏊ	sa'-wu
two	ᏔᎵ	ta?-l(i')
three	ᏦᎢ	tso:'-(i')
four	ᏅᎩ	nv:-g(i')
five	ᎯᏍᎩ	hi:-s-g(i')
six	ᏑᏓᎵ	su'-da-l(i')
seven	ᎦᎵᏉᎩ	ga-l(i)-quo:'-g(i')
eight	ᏣᏁᎳ	tsu-ne:-l(a')
nine	ᏐᏁᎳ	so'-ne:-l(a')
ten	ᏍᎪᎯ	s-go'-(hi')
12.		
first (also 'early' & 'soon as possible')	ᎢᎬᏱᎢ	i-gv'-yi'-(i')
second (also means again)	ᏔᎵᏁᎢ	ta?-li:-ne-(i)
third	ᏦᎢᏁᎢ	tso'-i-ne'-(i)
fourth	ᏅᎩᏁᎢ	nv'-gi-ne'-(i)
fifth	ᎯᏍᎩᏁᎢ	hi-s-gi:-ne'-(i)
sixth	ᏑᏓᎵᏁᎢ	su-da-li-ne'-(i)
seventh	ᎦᎵᏉᎩᏁᎢ	ga-li-quo-gi-ne'-(i)
eighth	ᏣᏁᎵᏁᎢ	tsu-ne'-li-ne'-(i)
ninth	ᏐᏁᎵᏁᎢ	so'-ne'-li-ne'-(i)
tenth	ᏍᎪᎯᏁᎢ	s-go'-hi-ne'-(i)

16

Ordinary numbers such as the ones in P.N. 11 (Phrase Number 11) are called cardinal numbers.

Cardinals are numbers which answer the question: How many are there?

The answer must be a cardinal number such as one, two, a hundred, a thousand, and so on.

Cardinals tell the total

Ordinal numbers answer the question: Where does it fit in a numbered set?

The answer to this question must be an ordinal, such as first, second, tenth, millionth, etc.

Ordinals tell the order

Ordinal numbers are used more carefully in Cherokee than in English. English often uses cardinals in place of ordinals, but Cherokee does not.

Examples: In English:
Row 1 (the actual meaning is First Row, not a total of one row)
Book 8 (actual meaning is Eighth Book, not a total of 8 books)
Lesson 2 (actual meaning is Second Lesson, not two lessons)

In Cherokee:
I-gv'-yi'-i A-da'-nv-nv (first row)
Tsu-ne'-li-ne'-(i) Go-hwe'-la (eighth book)
Ta?-li:-ne-(i) Go-hwe-lv:-i (second lesson)

In the Cherokee heading of each lesson so far, you will notice that ordinal numbers (first, second, third) are used. In the body of the lessons, in English, we follow the usual English usage and use cardinals (Lesson I, Lesson II, Lesson III).

It is possible but not preferred in Cherokee to use cardinals and say Row 1, Book 8, Lesson 2, but this practice may have been adopted from the English language. Cherokee does not usually use cardinal numbers (one, seven, nine) in speaking of members of a numbered series until after the tenth of any series. Ordinals are preferred up to ten, and by many speakers, beyond ten also. Many careful native speakers frown on the use of any cardinal numbers where ordinals belong, whether speaking of high or low numbers.

Notice the title of this lesson: Ꭴ ᏳᏗ Ꮆ Ꮃ Ᏹ Ꭰ Ꮽ Ꭷ Ꭲ

Nv:-gi-ne Tsa-la-gi' Go-hwe-lv:-i
Fourth   Cherokee   Lesson

Look back and examine the lesson headings you have had, then learn each
lesson heading as you continue with the lessons.

CORE VOCABULARY

Core Vocabulary will contain words from the Phrases in each lesson that
you can use independently from then on to form your own Cherokee sentences.
Words in lists (e.g. P.N. 11 and 12) can also be used by you independently
without requiring any change, but they will not appear again in the Core
Vocabulary unless they have more than one possible meaning. Core Vocabulary words are arranged in English alphabetical order.

again, second (in a series) P.N. 12   tali:ne

letter (it-has-been-written)   go hwe lv
  (only a <u>letter of the alphabet</u>)
letters (they-have-been-written)   de-go-hwe'-lv

number (it-has-been-counted)   a-se:-s-di'

numbers (they-have-been-counted)   di-se'-s-di'

Verbs:

say, repeat, state (P.N. 9 & 10)

  I say, am saying   ga-di?-a
  you (one person) say, are saying   ha-di?-a
  he <u>or</u> she says, is saying   a-di?-a
  they say, are saying   a-n'-di?-a

Memorize each verb carefully. In Cherokee, personal pronouns (I, you,
he, she, etc.) are attached to the verb and change according to sounds
found in the verb. You, speaking to one person, is different from you,
speaking to two persons, or you, more than two. Until Lesson XVI 'you'
will mean only you, singular (talking to one person only).

There is no distinction of sex in Cherokee verbs. He says and she says
are exactly the same.

Du-da-nv:-hnv?-i Di-ga-lo?-qua-s-toh'-di

Rows of the Alphabet (they-have-been-arranged-in-rows (things) to-be-
                      guided-by)

Learn to recognize, to pronounce, and to write the first two rows of the
Syllabary, shown below:

Da | **R**e | **T**i | ⍺o | O'u | **i**v
Sga ⊕ka | **Ƒ**ge | **y**gi | **A**go | **J**gu | **E**gv

The Cherokee words in the syllabary section of the lessons below are
arranged in <u>Cherokee</u> alphabetical order.

There are two ways to do this. One is to go vertically down each
column (a, ga, ka, ha, la, ma, hna, nah, qua, sa, da, ta, dla, tla, tsa,
wa, ya, e, ge, he, le, and so on). The other way is to go horizontally
across the rows. Since you are learning the letters row by row it seems
more convenient to use that system (a, e, i, o, u, v, ga, ka, ge, gi, etc.).
This is also the order in which Cherokee children have traditionally recited
their alphabet in the past.

These Cherokee words use only the first two rows of the syllabary.
Fill in the blanks below with the correct Cherokee letters.

e-e-e!	_____	What a shame! Too bad! (exclamation of sadness, pronounced going downward in pitch)
E:-gi'	_____	Cherokee form of Maggie
i-i-i!	_____	Oh, my goodness! Good heavens! (exclamation of surprise and excitement, going upward in pitch)
v:-v	_____	yes
ge?-i:'	_____	far off, a long way from here, in time or space
go?-i'	_____	grease, cooking or machine oil
go:-g(i')	_____	summer
gu:-gu	_____	bottle or Bartlesville

19

EXERCISES

Exercises 1, 2 and 3 use the phrases as they have appeared in the lessons. Exercise 4 encourages you to form new combinations, and Exercise 5 gives you practice in the syllabary.

Exercise 1: Columns A and B contain the same material, A in Cherokee pronunciation and B in English. Match them up with one another.
Exercise 2: Cover Column B and translate Column A orally. This is easier than trying to think of the Cherokee first.
Exercise 3: Cover Column A and translate orally into Cherokee from English.

A.
1. ga-1(i)-quo:'-g(i')
2. di-se-s-di
3. nv'-g(i')
4. tso:'-i-ne
5. de-go-hwe:-1v
6. di-se-s-di ni-di-di'-wa
7. nv:-gi-ne tsa-la-gi' go-hwe-1v:-i
8. tsu-ne:-1(a') so-ne:-1(a')
9. s-go'-(hi)
10. i-gv:-yi-i

B.
1. Let's say the numbers.
2. letters
3. numbers
4. third
5. Fourth Cherokee Lesson
6. first
7. eight, nine
8. ten
9. four
10. seven

Exercise 4: The columns below are identical, one English, one Cherokee pronunciation. Cover the right column without looking at it and try to translate from English to Cherokee, thinking out how to use all the Cherokee you have had so far. Then check yourself by the right-hand column.

1. Count to ten by two's, short style

2. How are you, Maggie?
3. I say ten
4. You say three
5. He says five.
6. They say nine bottles (In Cherokee you say 'nine bottle', as 'bottle' doesn't change in the plural)
7. three bottles (three bottle)
8. She says (same as he says)
9. First Lesson (ordinal)
10. one lesson (cardinal)

1. ta:-1', nv:-g', su'-da-1', tsu-ne:-1', s-go
2. Do-hi:-tsu, E:-gi'?
3. Ga-di?-a s-go-hi'
4. Ha-di?-a tso'-i
5. A-di?-a hi'-s-g'.
6. A-n'-di?-a so-ne:-la gu:-gu

7. Tso'-i gu:-gu
8. A-di?-a
9. I-gv-yi-i go-hwe-1v:-i
10. sa'-wu go-hwe-1v-i

Exercise 5:
   Concealing the lower part of this page, write the Cherokee for the
syllables and words, then check yourself.

A.
1. a
2. o
3. i
4. gv
5. v
6. gi
7. go
8. u
9. ge
10. gu

B.
1. summer
2. yes
3. Maggie
4. grease
5. bottle
6. far away
7. ABC in Cherokee (1st 3 letters
   of alphabet)
8. Bartlesville is far away.
   'is' is not necessary in Cherokee,
   so it would be:
   Bartlesville far away.

A.
1. D
2. Ꮼ
3. Ꭲ
4. Ꭱ
5. ꭲ
6. Ꮿ
7. Ꭺ
8. Ꮻ
9. Ꮅ
10. Ꭻ

B.
1. ᎪᎩ
2. ꭵꭵ
3. ᏒᎩ
4. ᎪᏔ
5. ᏣᏣ
6. ᏛᏔ
7. DᏒᏔ
8. ᏛᏔ ᏣᏣ   ᏣᏣ ᏛᏔ

21

ᏔᎯᏯᏁ ᏣᎳᎩ ᎪᏪᎸᎢ

Hi'-s-gi-ne Tsa-la-gi' Go-hwe-lv:-i

FIFTH CHEROKEE LESSON

PHRASES

Translation	Syllabary	Pronunciation
13.		
Minister	ᎠᏟᏣᏙᎲᏍᎩ	a-l(i)-tsa-do'-hv'-s-gi
church service	ᏓᏂᎳᏫᎦ	da-ni-la'-wi-ga
church (where they gather to study)	ᏧᏂᎳᏫᏍᏗ	tsu-ni-la-wi'-s-di
14.		
I go (am going now)	ᎨᎦ	ge:-ga
you go	ᎮᎦ	he'-ga
he/she/it goes	ᎡᎦ	e:-ga
they go	ᎠᏁᎦ	a-ne:-ga
15.		
I am going to church. (now)	ᏧᏂᎳᏫᏍᏗᎢ ᎨᎦ	Tsu-ni-la-wi'-s-di-(i) ge:-ga.
16.		
I am going home.	ᏗᏇᏅᏒᎢ ᎨᎦ	Di-que-nv'-sv-(i) ge:-ga.
You are going home.	ᏗᏤᏅᏒᎢ ᎮᎦ	Di-tse-nv-ꜱv-(i) he'-ga.
He/she is going home.	ᏧᏪᏅᏒᎢ ᎡᎦ	Tsu-we-nv-sv-i-e:-ga.
They are going home.	ᏧᏁᏅᏒ ᎠᏁᎦ	Tsu-ne-nv-sv a-ne:-ga.
17.		
Thanksgiving menu (Thanksgiving meal)	ᎤᏃᎵᎮᎵᏍᏗ ᎠᏟᏍᏔᎢᏗ	U-(na)-li-he-li'-s-di a-l(i)-s-ta-i-di
bread (baked)	ᎦᏚ	ga-du
butter (made-of-milk)	ᎪᏕᎸᎲ	go:-tlv-hnv
corn	ᏎᎷ	se'-lu
cornbread	ᏎᎷᎦᏚ	se'-lu ga'-du
turkey	ᎬᎾ	gv:-n(a)
meat	ᎭᏫᏯ	ha-wi'ya

22

Translation	Syllabary	Pronunciation

17.(cont.)

stuffing (mixed, chosen)	DᏭᏇᎾᎢ	a-su-ya-na-(i)
gravy	DᏭᏇᎫ	a-su:-s-d(i)
potatoes	ᏅᎾ	nu:-n(a)(i)
sweet potatoes (long potatoes)	ᏅᎾ DᎯᏅᎤᏓ	nu:-n(a) a-ni'-nv-hi'-d(a)
pumpkin pie	TᏇ ᏧᏟᏇᎩ	i'-ya ge-li:-s-gi
cream	ᎤᏓᏢᏓ	u-da-tlv:-d(a)(i)
tea (leaves it-is-made-of)	ᎤᏎᎦᏍ ᎪᏢᏔ	u-ga-lo'-ga go-tlv'-ta-nv

18.

Please pass me the turkey. (Turkey I-want)	ᎬᎾ DᏫᏓᏟᎮᎠ	Gv:-n(a) a?-wa-du:-li-(a).
Please pass me the stuffing. (Stuffing I-want)	DᏭᏇᎾᎢ DᏫᏓᏟᎮᎠ	A-su-ya-na-(i) a?-wa-du:-li-(a).
Please pass me the gravy. (Gravy I-want)	DᏭᏇᎫ DᏫᏓᏟᎮᎠ	A-su:-s-di a?-wa-du:-li-(a).

19.

Please pass me the turkey. (Turkey hand-me)	ᎬᎾ ᏍᏇᎬᏏ	Gv:-n(a) de-s-kv:'-s(i).
Please pass me the stuffing. (Stuffing hand-me)	DᏭᏇᎾᎢ ᏍᏇᎬᏏ	A-su-ya-na-(i) de-s-kv:-s(i).
Please pass me the gravy. (Gravy hand-me)	DᏭᏇᎫ ᏍᏇᎩᏢᏌᏏ	A-su:-s-di de-s-gi-ne-hv:-s(i).

Notice two things in these Phrases:

1. Cherokee often does not say 'please' when you would say 'please' in English. Making your wishes known can be called an automatic 'please' in Cherokee.

2. The word for 'I-want' is the same all through P.N. 18, but in P.N. 19 the verb 'hand-me' changes in the last sentence.

   This is because something fairly solid of indefinite shape is asked for in the first two examples in P.N. 19 (turkey and stuffing), but something liquid (gravy) in the last example.

   In English you would not say 'Pour me some turkey' or 'Cut me some tea'. Cherokee does not use different verbs as English does to deal with different shapes and textures. Instead, Cherokee places little <u>shape</u>

markers (classifiers) in the middle of some very common verbs to describe what is being spoken of. These common verbs cannot be used without shape markers (classifiers) in the middle of the verb to describe the direct object of the verb.

P.N. 19 could also be translated like this: (Shape markers are underlined)

Turkey it-solid-hand-me.	Gv:-na de-s-kv:'-si
Stuffing it-solid-hand-me.	A-su-ya-na-i de-s-kv:'-s-i.
Gravy it-liquid-hand-me.	A-su:-s-di de-s-gi-ne-hv:-si.

To ask for the gravy as a solid would be an insult to the cook, of course. It is a form of Cherokee joke to re-classify things in fun.

Only about twenty Cherokee verbs need classifiers, but they are some of the most necessary ones in everyday use. Some other classifying verbs are: pick up, put down, remove, wash, hide, eat, drag, have (in your immediate possession), put in the water, put in the fire, hang up, be placed, pull along, carry, fetch, hold.

Notice that the classifying verbs above all deal with direct personal contact. They speak of active situations in which the class of object being handled makes a great difference to everyone concerned. Linguists believe that these are some of the oldest verbs in the Cherokee language. Classificatory verbs probably reflect the time when perfect accuracy and speed in description were very helpful to other members of the tribe. Though this might not be quite as necessary today, it is still marvelous to observe how much information Cherokee verbs can pack into a few syllables. Think of these classifying verbs as telegrams of compressed information.

The information in classifying verbs is divided first into two categories, Living and Non-living. Living things are not classified at all as to shape. They form classification one:

1. Live

Non-living things, however, are sub-divided into four more classifications.

2. Flexible - the commonest classification. Lightweight in proportion to size. (rope, clothing including shoes, thin stick, sheet of paper, ship's sail, garden hose)

3. Long - narrow, not flexible (gun, cigar, heavy stick, table utensils)

4. Indefinite - solid, heavy in proportion to its size (bed, most food, dishes, refrigerator, book, sand, rock)

5. Liquid - or container of liquid

Remember that only classifying verbs contain classifiers. All other verbs do not. Classifying verbs will be capitalized in Core Vocabulary.

Notice that in Cherokee the object comes <u>before</u> the verb, unlike English.

CORE VOCABULARY

Verbs:

HAND OR PASS ME (P.N. 19) Speaking to one person: (See Appendix V for all persons)

Live:
Hand me the baby.   U:-s-di de'-s-ki-ka'-si.
Hand him/her the baby.   U:-s-di hi-ka'-si.
Hand them the baby.   U:-s-di ga-hi-ka'-si.

Flexible:
Hand me the (piece of)   Go-hwe'-la de-s-gi-nv'-si.
paper.
Hand him/her the paper.   Go-hwe'-la hi-nv'-si.
Hand them the paper.   Go-hwe'-la di-ga-hi-nv'-si.

Long:
Pass me the broom.   Gv-no-sa'-s-di de-s-ge-di'-si.
Pass him/her the broom.   Gv-no-sa'-s-di hi-di'-si.
Pass them the broom.   Gv-no-sa'-s-di ti-di'-si.

Indefinite:
Pass me the turkey. (In the form of food. A live turkey would be classified like the baby, and a dead one would be flexible.)
                           Gv:-na de-s-kv'-si.
Pass him/her the turkey.   Gv:-na   hi?-v'-si.
Pass them the turkey.   Gv:-na ga-hi?-v'-si.

Liquid:
Pass me the cream.   U-da-tlv:-da de-s-gi-ne-hv'-si.

Pass him/her the cream.   U-da-tlv:-da hi-ne?-v'-si.
Pass them the cream.   U-da-tlv:-da ga-hi-ne?-v'-si.

25

eat (have a meal)
  I am eating, having a meal   ga-1(i)-s-ta-yv-hv'-s-ga
  you are having a meal   ha-1'-s-ta-yv-hv'-s-ga
  he/she is having a meal   a-1'-s-ta-yv-hv'-s-ga
  they are having a meal   a-na-1'-s-ta-yv-hv'-s-ga

  my-wife (meal-maker-for-me)   a-g(w')-s-ta'-yv-hv-s-gi'

want, wish to have
  I want   a?-wa-du'-li-(a)
  you want   tsa-du'-li-(a)
  he/she wants   u-du'-li-(a)
  they want   u-na-du'-li-(a)

Du-da-nv:-hnv?-i Di-ga-lo?-qua-s-toh'-di: (alphabet rows)

Da		**R**e	**T**i	**Ꝺ**o	**O**u	**i**v
Sga **O**ka		**F**ge	**y**gi	**A**go	**J**gu	**E**gv
ᏉTha		**P**he	**Ꭹ**hi	**F**ho	**Γ**hu	**Ꝺ**hv

Words using the first three rows of the syllabary:

a-gi:-ga-ge   _____   red

u-gu:-gu   _____   owl

gi-ga'   _____   blood

go:-hi: _____   a long time ago

go-hi   _____   this (in time) go-hi i:-ga' (this daylight)
                             means today.

ko:-g(a)(i)   _____   crow

hi?-a'   _____   this (with a concrete noun) as: hi?-a' ko:-ga,
                             this crow

Write the Cherokee words in the blanks.

EXERCISES

Exercise 1: Columns A and B contain the same material. Match them up with one another, writing out each pair together. Look up answers in Phrases on p. 21 & 22.

Exercise 2: Cover Column B and translate Column A orally.

Exercise 3: Cover Column A and translate into Cherokee from English.

A.
1. gv:-n(a)
2. di-que-nv'-sv-(i) ge:-ga.
3. tsu-ni-la-wi'-s-di(i)
4. nu:-n(a) a-ni'-nv-hi'-d(a)
5. ha-wi'-ya
6. a-1(i)-s-ta-i-di
7. i'-ya ge-li:-s-gi
8. u-(na)-li-he-li'-s-di
9. se'-lu ga'-du
10. a-1(i)-tsa-do'-hv'-s-gi

B.
1. Minister
2. Thanksgiving
3. meat
4. pumpkin pie
5. turkey
6. cornbread
7. I am going home.
8. church
9. sweet potatoes
10. a meal

Exercise 4: Translate into English orally and explain each Cherokee verb below, telling whether it has a classifier, and if so, which classifier. Tell what each classifier used implies about the headword of each sentence. Answers are on the bottom of the next page, titled EXERCISE 4.

1. Gv:-n(a) de-s-kv:-s(i).
2. U-ga-lo'-ga go-tlv'-ta-nv de-s-gi-ne-hv:-s(i).
3. Ha-wi'-ya de-s-kv:-s(i).
4. Gv:-n(a) de-s-ki-ka'-si.
5. Tsu-ni-la-wi'-s-di a-ne:-ga U-na-li-he-li'-s-di.
6. Go:-tlv-hnv u-du'li.
7. Ga-du de-s-kv:-si.
8. U-da-tlv:-da de-s-gi-ne-hv'-si.
9. Gv-no-sa'-s-di de-s-gi-di'-si.
10. U:-s-di ga-hi-ka'-si.

Exercise 5: Translate from English to Cherokee, writing the answers out in English letters. Then go over the exercise again putting each Cherokee letter you know over the English syllable. Answers are on the bottom of this page, titled EXERCISE 5.

1. Pass him the tea.
2. You want some stuffing.
3. Pass them the gravy.
4. They want pumpkin pie.

5. This crow wants (some) cornbread.
6. Pass me a bottle of blood.
7. The red owl says 'Hoo, hoo'.
8. He wants (some) potatoes.
   (Same as 'potato')

EXERCISE 4:

1. Hand me the turkey.	Indefinite classifier, implies that the object is of indefinite shape, solid, weighty in relation to size.
2. Pass me the tea.	Liquid classifier, implying that the object is a liquid.
3. Pass me the meat.	Indefinite classifier, implies that the object is of indefinite shape, solid or lumpish, weighty in relation to size.
4. Hand me the turkey.	Live classifier, so the object is a living animal or human.
5. They are going to church on Thanksgiving.	No classifier, as 'go' is not a classifying verb.
6. He wants some butter.	No classifier, as 'wants' is not a classifying verb.
7. Hand me the bread.	Indefinite classifier, implies that the object is of indefinite shape, lumpish, solid.
8. Pass me the cream.	Liquid classifier, so the object must be a liquid.
9. Pass me the broom.	Long classifier, so the object must be elongated in shape, not flexible.
10. Pass me the baby.	Live classifier, so the object must be living, either an animal or human.

EXERCISE 5:

1. U-da-tlv:-da hi-ne?-v'-si.
2. A-su-ya-na-(i) tsa-du'-li-(a).
3. A-su:-s-di ge-hi-ne?-v'-si.
4. I'-ya ge-li:-s-gi u-na-du'-li-(a).
5. Hi?-a ko:-g(a)(i) se'-lu ga'-du u-du'-li
6. Gi-ga' gu:-gu de-s-gi-ne-hv'-si.
7. A-gi:-ga-ge u-gu:-ku 'Hu, hu' a-di?-a.
8. Nu:-n(a) u-du'-li-(a).

Exercise 6:   Cherokees often omit the noun when using classifying verbs.
In Column B you will find English nouns and in Column A Cherokee verbs
from Lesson V. Go down Column A, translate the verbs and indicate what
items in Column B could be used with each Cherokee verb from Column A.

Examples: 1. tsa-du'li, you want, all items
            2. hi-di'-si, pass him something long, gun, hammer, rake, cigar

Check your written answers by turning back to p. 25.

A.	B.
1. a?-wa-du'li	1. a sweater, Flexible
2. de-s-ge-di'-si	2. a whip, Flexible
3. de-s-ki-ka'-si	3. a gun, Long
4. de-s-gi-ne-hv'-si	4. a brick, Indefinite shape
5. de-s-kv'-si	5. a chair, Indefinite
6. di-ga-hi-nv'-si	6. a hammer, Long
7. hi-nv'-si	7. a rake, Long
8. hi-ne?-v'-si	8. a puppy, Live
9. hi-di'-si	9. a snake, Live
10. ga-hi?-v'-si	10. a tigerskin, Flexible
11. ti-di'-si	11. a cigar, Long
12. hi-ka'-si	12. a potato, Indefinite
13. ga-hi-ka'-si	13. a pillow case, Flexible
14. tsa-du'-li	14. a pillow, Flexible
15. u-na-du-li-a	15. a sack of potatoes, Indefinite

Exercise 7:   These are Cherokee nouns from previous lessons.
1. Translate them. 2. Classify them. 3. Use the correct form of 'Hand
me' to go with each.   Answers are on the next page, titled EXERCISE 7.

1. a-su-ya-na-i
2. ga-du
3. se'-lu
4. gv:-na
5. u-da-tlv:-d'
6. nu:-n'
7. a-su:-s-d'
8. ha-wi'-ya
9. u-gu:-ku
10. ko:-ga
11. gi-ga'
12. ko:-gi
13. gu:-gu
14. go-hwe-lv-i
15. go-hwe'-la

29

EXERCISE 7:

1. Stuffing, indefinite, de-s-kv'-si.
2. Bread, indefinite, de-s-kv'-si.
3. Corn, sometimes long, usually indefinite, de-s-kv'-si (indefinite) or de-s-ge-di'-si (long).
4. Turkey, if live, then live classifier, de'-s-ki-ka'-si; if food, then indefinite classifier, de-s-kv'-si; if dead, then flexible classifier, de-s-gi-nv'-si.
5. Cream, liquid classifier, de-s-gi-ne-hv'-si.
6. Potato, potatoes, indefinite classifier, de-s-kv'-si.
7. Gravy, liquid classifier, de-s-gi-ne-hv'-si.
8. Meat, indefinite classifier, de-s-kv'-si.
9. Owl, if live, live classifier, de-s-ki-ka'-si; if stuffed, indefinite, de-s-kv'-si; if dead, flexible classifier, de-s-gi-nv'-si. If a cigar, long classifier, de-s-ge-di'-si.
10. Crow, if live, live classifier, de-s-ki-ka'-si; if dead, flexible classifier, de-s-gi-nv'-si.
11. Blood, liquid, de-s-gi-ne-hv'-si.
12. Crow, if live, live classifier, de-s-ki-ka'-si; if dead, flexible classifier, de-s-gi-nv'-si.
13. Bottle, if empty, indefinite classifier, de-s-kv'-si; if full, or partly full, liquid classifier, de-s-gi-ne-hv'-si.
14. Lesson, flexible classifier, de-s-gi-nv'-si.
15. Piece of paper, flexible classifier, de-s-gi-nv'-si.

Exercise 8: Columns A and B contain almost the same material. Match them up correctly and check the answers by page 24.

A.

1. Hand them the (sheet of) paper.
2. Hand them the baby.
3. Hand her the broom.
4. Hand them the broom.
5. Hand him the cream.
6. Pass them the (roast) turkey.
7. Pass him the baby.
8. Hand me the cream.
9. Hand him the (sheet of) paper.
10. Hand me the broom.

B.

1. U:-s-di hi-ka'-si.
2. Go-hwe'-la hi-nv'-si.
3. Gv-no-sa-s-di de-s-gi-di'-si.
4. Gv:-na de-s-kv'-si.
5. Gv:-na ga-hi?-v'-si.
6. U-da-tlv:-da hi-ne?-v'-si.
7. U:-s-di ga-hi-ka'-si.
8. Gv:-no-sa'-s-di hi-di'-si.
9. Gv-no-sa'-s-di ti-di'-si.
10. Gv:-na hi?-v'-si.

Exercise 9: Practice with three rows of the syllabary. If you do not have the whole syllabary on flash cards yet, make a habit of making new cards for each row as the lessons continue.

Column A is Cherokee for Column B, and Column C is the Cherokee pronunciation in English letters. Cover Column C and try to make your own pronunciation in English letters, using both Cherokee Column A and English translation Column B. Next, cover the Cherokee letters of Column A and use Column C to reconstruct Column A correctly.

A.
1. RR RY
2. AY A.Ə
3. DYSⱵ OJJ
4.
5. DYSⱵ OJJ
6. ꝺ
7. Ᏻ
8.
9.
10.

Aꝶ ⱵT
DYSⱵ OJJ
ꝺiYSⱵ JJ
ii RY
.Ə

B.
1. Too bad, Maggie!
2. The crow is far away.
3. Summer (was) long ago.
4. A red owl
5. The red owl
6. This red bottle
7. First and last letters of 'Hello'
8. Yes, Maggie.
9. First letter of 'which'?
10. First letter of 'five'.

Exercise 10: Become more observant of shapes and consistencies around your home. Use the Cherokee verb for 'hand me' ten times each day, discussing with your family the right classification to use.

C.
1. E-e-e, E:-gi'!
2. Ko:-ga ge?-i:.
3. Go:-gi' go:hi:'.
4. A-gi'-ga-ge u-gu:-ku
5. A-gi'-ga-ge u-gu:-ku
6. Hi?-a a-gi-ga-ge gu:-gu.   (two a's make v)
7. O
8. V:-v, E:-gi
9. Ga
10. Hi

31

ᏎᏕᎵᏅ ᏣᎳᎩ ᎠᏲᎵᎢ

Su-da:-li:-ne Tsa-la-gi' Go-hwe-lv:-i

SIXTH CHEROKEE LESSON

PHRASES

Translation	Syllabary	Pronunciation
20. Teacher	ᏗᏕᏲᎲᏍᎩ	Di-de-yo-hv:-s-gi
21. Let's begin.	ᏔᏕᎾ	I-da-le:-n(a)
22. Where do you (1 person) live?	ᎭᎵ ᎯᏁᎳ	Ha'-tlv hi-ne:1(a)?
23. What is your name? (What are you called?)	ᎦᏙ ᏕᏣᏙᏓ	Ga-do' de-tsa-dǿ:-(a')
24. My name is _____. (_____ I am called.)	_ _ ᏛᏩᏙᏓ	_____ da-wa?-do:-(a').
25. Please speak slowly. (Slowly speak)	ᎤᏍᎦᏃᎵ ᎯᏬᏂᎯ	U-s-ga-no*-1(i) hi-wo:-ni-(hi).
26. I don't understand.	ᏝᏳᎪᎵᎦ	Tla yi-go-li:-g(a).
27. What did you (just) say?	ᎦᏙᎩ ᎭᏗᎠ	(Ga)-do-gi ha-di?-a?
28. What is your address? (Where written-material it-you-get?)	ᎭᎵ ᎪᏪᎵ ᏗᏣᏁᏍᏗ	Ha'-tlv go-(h)we-1(i)(a) di-tsa-ne:-s-di?

29.
My address is ____.
(Written-material it-I-
get-at ____.)

ᎠᏍᎵ ᏗᎩᏁᏍᏗ

Go-(h)we:-li di-gi-ne:-s-di ____.

30.
What is it?

ᎦᏙ ᎤᏍᏗ

(Ga)-do? u:-s-d(i)?

31.
What do you want?

ᎦᏙ ᎤᏍᏗ ᏣᏚᎵ

Ga-do u:-s-di tsa-du:-li?-(a')?

32.
How about you? (to 1 or
to more than one)

ᏂᎯᎾᎥ

Ni-hi-na-(hv)?

33.
I don't know.

ᏝᏯᏆᏂᏔ

Tla-ya-qua-n(i)-ta.

34.
Let's adjourn.
  one speaking to one person ᏗᏂᏰᎵᎯ
  one speaking to several ᏗᏗᏰᎵᎯ

Di-ni-ye'-li-hi.
Di-di-ye'-li-hi.

In studying the Phrases, do not omit learning the material inside brackets, thinking you can do without it. Cherokees like to abbreviate, but there are definite rules about this, so the entire word (what Cherokees call the 'long') <u>must be learned</u>. Later you can do as many Cherokees do -- think long and speak short.

Form the habit of reviewing previous material every time you are about to study. These four steps will sharpen your memory in less than ten minutes:

Quickly review Phrases 1 - 19 in Lessons I, III, IV, and V in this way:
1. Cover the Cherokee Pronunciation column with a card and try to remember each phrase or word, uncovering the answers one at a time. It is important to speak your choice about the answer for each phrase <u>before</u> looking at the written answer.

2. With all columns uncovered, read all columns out loud, going across the three columns, one Phrase Number at a time.

3. Cover the English Translation column and translate the Cherokee Pronunciation column into English, uncovering one at a time as before, and pronouncing your answer <u>before</u> looking.

4. Read all three columns again, noticing your errors, if any.

To learn new material, use the same steps but repeat until you are certain of the answers. Don't study memory-work for more than one hour at a time. It is helpful to work with another person. Phrases must be learned in their entirety until you are more familiar with Cherokee verbs.

CORE VOCABULARY

fine, good or well (well as in 'well done') P.N. 3	o:-s-da
healthy, serene, peaceful (or health, peace, serenity)	do'-hi' or to'-hi
slowly P.N. 25	u-s-ga-no:-l(i)
teacher P.N. 20	di-de-yo-hv:-s-gi
what?, which? P.N. 23	ga-do'
what kind of? P.N. 30	ga-do' u:-s-di
where? P.N. 22	ha:-tlv
written material, personal letter	go-hwe-(la)(li)

Verb:

know (a fact, not a person)	
I know	a-qua'-n(i)-ta
you know	tsa:-n'-ta
he/she knows	u:-n'-ta
they know	u-na?-ta

Learn all the phrases and words above and use them whenever possible. Never say anything in English in class if you know the Cherokee for it.

34

Du-da-nv:-hnv?-i di-ga-lo?-qua-s-toh'-di:
Rows of the alphabet:

D a	**R** e	**T** i	**Ꮼ** o	**Ꝺ** u	**i** v
Ꮨ ga **Ꝺ** ka	**Ꝼ** ge	**Ᏽ** gi	**A** go	**J** gu	**E** gv
Ꮧ ha	**Ꮲ** he	**Ꮗ** hi	**F** ho	**Ꮁ** hu	**Ꮙ** hv
W la	**Ꮣ** le	**Ꮲ** li	**Ꮐ** lo	**M** lu	**Ꮂ** lv

Cherokee words using the first four rows of the syllabary:

a-ho:-li'	_____	mouth
a-hu'-li	_____	drum
a'-le'	_____	and, or, but *DᎧ*
v?-le	_____	locust, locusts *iᎧ*
ka:-ga	_____	who? *$ Ꮝ Ꮝ*
ki-lo'-(i)	_____	somebody *Ᏸ Ꝺ*
hv	_____	what did you say? *Ꮟ*
Lu:-ga	_____	Luke *M Ꮝ*

Verbs:

ga-li?-e:-li-ga   _____   I am happy, rejoice, am grateful, delighted

ha-li-he:-li-ga   _____   you are happy, delighted, grateful, you rejoice

a-li-he:-li-ga   _____   he/she is happy, delighted, grateful, rejoices

a-na-li-he'-li-ga _____   they are happy, delighted, grateful, they rejoice

Notice Thanksgiving, P.N. 17, U-(na)-li-he-li'-s-di, which means:
                   u-li-he-li'-s-di   for him/her to be thankful
                   u-na-li-he-li'-s-di   for them to be thankful

go'-li:-g(a)   _____   I know, understand (information, not a person) P.N. 26

ho'-l'-ga   _____   you know

go:-l'-ga   _____   he/she knows

a-no'-l'-ga   _____   they know

    Remember that when a vowel after l is omitted, the l is pronounced like the l and y of ro<u>ll y</u>our own.

    Write the proper Cherokee letters in the blanks above. Leave 'no', 'na' and 'ni' blank if you wish.

EXERCISES

Exercise 1: Columns A and B contain almost the same phrases, A in Cherokee pronunciation, and B in English. Match them up with one another. (not all will fit)

Exercise 2: Cover Column B and translate Column A orally.

Exercise 3: Cover Column A and translate orally into Cherokee.

Exercise 4: Pick out the questions in both columns and give a reasonable answer in Cherokee, translating orally both question and answer.

A.

1. Dto-hi:'-tsu?
2. Da-wa?-do:-a
3. Do-na-da-go-hv-i
4. Ni-hi-na-hv?
5. Ga-do' u:-s-di'?
6. O:-s-da-dv.
7. O:-s-da.
8. Ga-do-gi ha-di?-a?
9. Ha-tlv go-hwe-lv:-i di-tsa-ne:-s-di?
10. I-da-le:-na'
11. Di-de-yo-hv:-s-gi'
12. Do-da-da-go'-hv-i'
13. Wa?-do'.
14. Tla ya-qua-n'-ta

15. Tla yi-go-li:-g'
16. U-s-ga-no-li hi-wo:-ni-hi.
17. Ha-tlv hi-ne:-la?
18. Di-se-s-di ni-di-di-wa.
19. Ga-do' de-tsa-do:'-(a)?
20. V:-v

B.

1. Teacher
2. Let's begin.
3. Thank you.
4. Let's say the numbers.
5. Where do you live?
6. What is your name?
7. My name is ...
8. How are you?
9. Very fine.
10. What is it?
11. What did you say?
12. How about you?
13. I don't know.
14. Goodbye (speaking to one person)
15. I don't understand.
16. Please speak slowly.
17. Yes.
18. No.
19. What is your mailing address?
20. My mailing address is ...

If you are studying with someone, try doing both columns, one speaking in English, the other answering in Cherokee, then vice versa. Put some of the phrases together in your own combinations.

37

Exercise 5: First, cover the whole lower half of the page. Without looking, translate the English sentences orally into Cherokee, then write your answers in Cherokee pronunciation (English letters). Next, translate the Cherokee pronunciation into Cherokee letters, writing all the letters.

1. Who is going today?
2. Luke, Maggie and Summer are going.
3. This drum is red. (This red drum)
4. Somebody understands this Cherokee lesson.
   (Somebody this Cherokee lesson understands.)
5. I understand the drum.

1. Ka:-ga e:-ga go'-hi' i'-ga?*
2. Lu:-ga E:-gi a'-le' Go:-gi
   a-ne:-ga.
3. Hi?-a a-gi:-ga-ge a-hu'-li.
4. Ki:-lo hi?-a Tsa-la-gi' go-hwe-lv:
   go-l'-ga.
5. Go'-li:-ga a-hu'-li.

1. ᎤᏛ ᏒᏡ ᎪᎯ ᏔᏛ
2. ᎷᏛ ᎡᏗ ᎪᏍ ᎪᎩ ᎠᏁᏛ
3. ᎯᎠ ᎠᏘᏍᎨ ᎠᎻᎵ
4. ᏯᎶ ᎯᎠ ᏣᎳᎩ ᎪᏪᎸ ᎪᎵᏛ
5. ᎪᎵᏛ ᎠᎻᎵ

Blackboard drill: Fill in the rest of the word or phrases. First in English letters, then write out the Cherokee. Column B is the answer to Column A. Column B is the answer to Column A. Look up these words in this lesson.

1. di-de-___hv-___gi
2. i-da-le-___
3. ___yi-go-li-ga
4. ga-___u-s-di?
5. di-ni-ye-___ ___
6. ni-___na-hv?
7. tla-ya-___n'-ta
8. a-___li (mouth)
9. a-___li (drum)
10. ki-___lo-i

1. ᏗᏕᎶᏫᎩ
2. ᎢᏓᎴᎾ
3. ᏣᏂᎪᎵᏛ
4. ᎦᏘ ᎤᏍᏗ
5. ᏗᏂᏱᎴᎧ
6. ᏂᎠᎾᎥ
7. ᏣᎶᏘᏂᏆ
8. ᎠᎵ
9. ᎠᎵ
10. ᎩᏫᏎᏃᎵ

38

ᏚᎵᏉᎩᏁ ᏣᎳᎩ ᎪᏪᎸ

Ga-li-quo-gi:-ne Tsa-la-gi' Go-hwe-lv:-i

SEVENTH CHEROKEE LESSON

a. Pitch
b. It is cold - It (articles
c. It is cold - Is
d. It is cold - Cold (conversion)

a. Pitch

Cherokee has a musical or pitch accent which makes it sound like Chinese. However, the differences in tone do not usually change the meaning as they do in Chinese. Pitch in Cherokee seems to behave more like the musical pitch of Swedish, which depends largely on the length of syllables and surrounding consonants. Each Cherokee syllable can be spoken on one of four pitch levels, or can slide from one level to one or two others within the same syllable. The tones can be numbered as follows:

1. Low 2. Normal 3. Raised 4. High 5. Scalloped or sliding

The fifth tone is a combination of one or more of the others. Scalloped or swooping syllables often start at one level, go down and up in the same syllable, and end this same syllable higher or on the same level as the tone on which it began, often with changes in volume.

All Cherokee words are pronounced at differing tone levels, but the pitch of a syllable changes the meaning only in certain words, some of them very common ones. Such words will be marked with an asterisk (*). Stressed syllables (marked ') and/or long syllables (marked :) are especially likely to be scalloped.
Examples:

*i:-ga'	noon	scalloped long i, up on ga
*i-ga'	day	both syllables even and low
*a:-m(a')	salt	scalloped a, end the word fading upward
*a-m(a')	water	more like am-a (not a-ma); tones low & even
*u-hyv:-dla	he/she/it-is-cold	Tones 212 (one tone for each syllable)
*u-hyv:-dla	he/she-is-a-Republican	Tones 232
*u-ga'-no-wa'	he/she/it-is-warm	Tones 1123
*u-ga'-no-wa'	he/she-is-a-Democrat	Tones 2412

It-is-cold refers to the weather or to the temperature of a thing. If the same word is used referring to a person, it means 'cold-hearted'. This cannot mean 'He/she feels cold' or a different word (the word for 'shiver') would be used.

Learning the Cherokee tones requires constant contact with fluent Cherokee speech. The tone numbers above serve only as general indicators and are not included in other lessons.

39

Not all pitch twins differentiate between a short and a long syllable, like the above examples. Sometimes both syllables are long. An asterisk is a warning that a twin word exists, different only in pitch, which might easily be confused with the one you are pronouncing.

Consonants and vowels, especially the last vowel of a word or sentence, are often pronounced nasally. These nasal last vowels of a word or statement are often also scalloped. They start abruptly, tail off upward in pitch, and end abruptly after being tailed off. All vowels, as well as v, can be nasalized. If you form the habit of ending words and sentences on an up-tone instead of, as in English, on a down, you will sound more proficient. Taper your voice's volume.

Move your lips as little as possible. If you try you will find you can keep them almost still. You can only hope to learn these details by very attentive imitation of a fluent native Cherokee speaker.

PHRASES

Translation	Syllabary	Pronunciation
35.		
What am I doing? (What I-do?)	ᏌᏫ ᎦᎤᎾᎢ	(Ga-)do' ga-dv:'-ne-(v') (a')?
What are you doing? (What you-do?)	ᏌᏫ ᎮᎤᎾᎢ	(Ga-)do' ha-dv:'-ne-(v') (a')?
What is he/she doing? (What he/she do?)	ᏌᏫ ᎠᎤᎾᎢ	(Ga-)do' a-dv:-ne-(v')(a')?
What (are) they doing?	ᏌᏫ ᎠᏁᎤᎾᎢ	(Ga-)do' a-na-dv:-ne-(v') (a')?
36.		
It is cold. (Cold, or Coldness)	ᎤᎯᏴᏜ	U-hyv:-dl(a)
37.		
It is warm. (Warm, or Warmth.)	ᎤᎦᏃᏩ	U-ga?'-no-wa'

40

b. <u>It</u> is cold - It (articles)

Cherokee has no articles ('a', 'an' or 'the'), and only uses 'it' referring to some concrete thing the speaker has in mind.

Therefore, 'It is cold' and 'It is warm' in P.N. 36 and 37, speaking of the weather, contain no 'it' in Cherokee. If a person or animal feels chilly the word for 'shiver' is used.

c. It <u>is</u> cold - Is

Cherokee does not need the verb 'to be' in simple statements of fact, so 'It is cold' in English, is simplified into 'Cold' or 'Coldness' in Cherokee.

d. It is <u>cold</u> - Cold (conversion)

In Cherokee a single word, unchanged or with affixes, is frequently <u>converted</u> and used as a noun, verb, adjective, adverb, or function word.

Changing a word's usual class (conversion) is limited in English. Many words are not convertible, or are only partly convertible.

Examples:

<u>Dark</u> used as an adjective: He has dark hair.
         as a verb: Dark(en) the room.
         as a noun: She was afraid of the dark.
    as an adverb: He smiled dark(ly).

         BUT NOT: He has long hair.
                 Long(en) the room.
                 She was afraid of the long.
                 He smiled long(ly).

<u>Up</u> as a function word: He jumped up.
         as a verb: They up(ped) the price.

         BUT NOT: He jumped above.
                 They aboved the price.

Conversion that is not part of everyday usage has always been practiced by poets in the English language in order to give common words fresh force:

Examples:

G. Chaucer:	"... a steed of Lombardy, So <u>horsely</u> and so quick of eye."	(noun used as adjective)
A.E. Housman:	"The day you won your town the race, We <u>chaired</u> you through the market-place."	(noun used as verb)
T. Roethke:	"... in the <u>rivery</u> air I walk with my true love."	(noun used as adjective
R. Wilbur:	"...The long numbers that <u>rocket</u> the mind."	(noun used as verb)
Rod McKuen:	"Listen to the <u>warm</u>"	(adjective used as noun)

Cherokee converts extensively all the time, especially from verbs to other word classes.

In order to convert words from one class to another (change them from one part of speech to another) English has many affixes whose use must be memorized separately.

Examples:

Converting adjectives into nouns:

long	length (change vowel and add 'th)
short	shortness (add -ness)
healthy	health (subtract -y)

Cherokee makes constant use of a few affixes, so little memorizing of forms is necessary.
Examples:
*u-ga-no-w<u>v</u>   South; it was warm; warmed (equivalent of warm, past tense)
*u-hyv:-dl<u>v</u>   North; it was cold; chilled (equivalent of cold, past tense)

-v is a Cherokee affix meaning 'past', equivalent of -en, -ed in English. It occurs with words that in English would be called adjectives, adverbs, verbs or nouns.

CORE VOCABULARY

cold (adj.), coldness (noun), Republican (noun   *u-hyv:-dla
    or adj.), it-is-cold (verb)

day   *i-ga'

noon   *i:-ga'

North (noun, preposition, adj.), it-was-cold (verb)   *u-hyv:-dlv

salt   *a:-m(a')

South, it-was-warm, warmed (adj.)   *u-ga'-no-wv'

warm, warmth, a Democrat, it-was-warm   *u-ga'-no-w(a;)(i)

water   *a-m(a')

The mountains are in the North.	U-hyv:-dlv do?-da-la.	(Tones 213)
The mountains are cold.	Do?-da-la tsu-hyv:-dla.	(T. 132)
The mountains are in the South.	U-ga'-no-wv do?-da-la.	(T. 1123)
The mountains are warm.	Do:-da-la tsu-ga'-no-wi.	(2312)
It is cold in the North.	U-hyv:-dla u-hyv:-dlv.	(c212N114)
It was cold in the North.	U-hyv:-dlv u-hyv:-dlv.	(c212N114)
It is warm in the South.	U-ga-no-wa u-ga-no-wv.	(w1123S2114)
It was warm in the South.	U-ga-no-wv u-ga-no-wv.	(w1123S2114)
He/she is from the North, a northerner.	U-hyv:-dlv e-hi.	(213)
He/she is from the South, a southerner.	U-ga'-no-wv e-hi.	(2113)
I am in the North.	U-hyv:-dlv ge-do:?-a.	(123)
I am in the South.	U-ga-no-wv ge-do:?-a.	(1123)
I am a Republican.	A-gi-hyv:-dla.	(2232)
I am a Democrat.	A-gi-ga'-no-wa.	(22412)

The tones above are marked for the words 'u-hyv:-dla(dlv)' and 'u-ga-no-wa(wv)' only.

A-gi is a form of 'I'. 'You are a Republican' or 'You are cold' would be 'Tsa-hyv-dla', 'They are Republicans', 'They are cold: U-ni-hyv:-dla'. The close resemblance of the terms for 'cold-hearted', 'North', and 'Republican' is a characteristically Cherokee joke, since the Cherokees fought for the Confederacy and were all Democrats for many years afterward.

Du-da-nv:-hnv?-i di-ga-lo?-qua-s-toh'-di:
Rows of the alphabet:

Da	**R**e	**T**i	⍵o	Ơu	i v
Sga Ꮳka	**F**ge	**Ᏹ**gi	**A**go	**J**gu	**E**gv
Ꮬha	**Ꮖ**he	Ꭶhi	**F**ho	**Ᏻ**hu	**Ꮎ**hv
Wla	**Ꮤ**le	**Ꮅ**li	**Ꮹ**lo	**M**lu	**Ꮑ**lv
Ꮉma	**Ꭽ**me	**H**mi	**Ꮕ**mo	**Ꮽ**mu	

Cherokee words using letters you already know:

e-lo-hi'	_____	earth, world (repeatedly along place)
u-ga-lo:-g(a')	_____	leaf
u-ga-ma	_____	soup (water prepared to eat)
ga-lv'-lo:-(hi)	_____	(continuously above place) (sky)
ka-ma'-ma	_____	butterfly or elephant (!)
Ma:-ga	_____	Mark
Me:-li	_____	Mary

All translations of Cherokee nouns are approximate, but as close as we could manage.

Exercises 1, 2 and 3 use the phrases as they have appeared in the
lessons. Exercise 4 encourages you to form new combinations, and Exercise
5 gives you practice in the first 4 rows of the syllabary.

Exercise 1: Columns A and B contain almost the same material directly
from the Phrases. Match them up with one another. (Some are used more
than once)

A.
1. O:-s-da.
2. O'-si:-yo'.
3. A?-wa-du'-li-(a)
4. U-na-du'-li-(a)
5. Do-da-da-go'-hv-(i)
6. O:-s-da-dv.
7. U-ga?-no-wa'.
8. U-hyv:-dl(a)(v)
9. E:-ga.
10. (Ga)-do ha-dv:'-ne-(v)(a)?

B.
1. (I am) fine.
2. Goodbye (one to several)
3. (It is) cold.
4. Warm.
5. (It is) warm.
6. (It's) fine.
7. What are you doing?
8. I want.
9. He is going.
10. They want.
11. (I am) very fine.
12. North.

Exercise 2: Cover Column B and translate Column A orally.

Exercise 3: Cover Column A and translate orally into Cherokee.

Exercise 4: The columns below are identical, one English, one Cherokee
pronunciation. Cover the right column without looking at it and try to
translate from English to Cherokee, thinking out how to use all the
Cherokee you have had so far. Then check yourself by the right-hand
column.

1. My name is Maggie.
2. Summer is warm.
3. Too bad it's cold!
4. Fine, let's begin.
5. Good heavens, where is the machine
   oil?
6. Yes, it's definitely all-right.
7. Hello, Maggie, what are you doing?
8. Bartlesville is far away.

9. My name is Summer North.
10. Oh, that bottle is cold!
11. Maggie is going.
12. Luke is happy today.

1. E:-gi' da-wa?-do:-a'.
2. Go:-gi' u-ga?-no-wa'.
3. E-e-e, u-hyv:-dla!
4. O:-s-da', i-da-le:-na'.
5. I-i-i, ha:-tlv go?-i?

6. V:-v, o:-s-da-dv'.
7. Si-yo', E:-gi, do-ha-dv:-ne-a?
8. Gu:-gu' ge:?-i or Ge:?-i
   Gu:-gu'.
9. Go:-gi' U-hyv:-dla da-wa-do:.
10. I-i-i, u-hyv:-dla gu:-gu'!
11. E:-gi e:-ga.
12. Lu:-ga' go'-hi' *i-ga'
    a-li-he:-li-ga.

Exercise 5: Below are words and verbs directly from the Cherokee-letter word lists from Lesson IV through Lesson VII.

First, cover the bottom half of the page. Translate the English into Cherokee pronunciation (English letters), then write all the answers in Cherokee letters. Check your answers by the Cherokee in the lower half of the page. If you need to look any words up, remember Lesson IV has only 2 rows, Lesson V, 3 rows, Lesson VI, 4 rows, and Lesson VII, 5 rows.

1. sky
2. locust
3. summer
4. owl
5. world
6. leaf
7. salt
8. mouth
9. I am happy
10. you understand
11. today
12. soup
13. he/she is going
14. water
15. long ago and far away

1. RGᎧ
2. iᎧ
3. AᎩ
4. ᎣJJ
5. RGᎧ
6. ᎣᏓGᏓ
7. DᏛ
8. DᏢᏞ

9. ᏚᏞRᏞᏓ
10. ᏞᏞᏄ
11. AᎧ TᏛ
12. ᎣᏓᏙ
13. RᏛ
14. DᏙ
15. AᎧ DᏛ ᏞT

ᏧᏁᎵᏁ ᏣᎳᎩ ᎪᏪᎸᎢ

Tsu-ne:-li-ne Tsa-la-gi' Go-hwe-lv:-(i)

EIGHTH CHEROKEE LESSON

Kenuche (pronounced kanutch or kanutch'i) is the usual way to spell ᎦᎾᏥ (ga-na'-ts(i)) in English. There are many favorite ways to make it for holiday occasions. It has a delicious mapleish flavor and is rich, nourishing and digestible. This is Mrs. Betty Smith's mother's recipe.

Kenuche

Allow two days to make kenuche.
Ingredients: 2 lbs of full-grain dry white hominy. Use the kind in a bag like dried beans, not the kind in a can or box.
hickory nuts, unshelled. Enough to completely fill a 2-lb potato-sack.

1. Boil hominy in unsalted water till soft. Simmer approximately all day, cover and leave standing overnight.

2. Prepare hickory nuts. Put into a deep bowl and pound till shells can be picked out of nutmeats. The high, deep wooden bowls traditionally used will waste less nut juice, but it can be done well in a large mixing bowl, a few nuts at a time. Mold damp nutmeats into tomato-sized balls. Nutmeats may not stick together well, but this will not ruin your kenuche. Nut-balls can be wrapped and frozen for future use.

3. Line a colander with muslin cloth and place it over a deep bowl. Gradually place nut-balls into colander and run very hot water over them, mashing down to extract the flavor. Throw away nutmeat mush and keep liquid.

4. Combine nut liquid and hominy and simmer together for some hours, so flavors are thoroughly blended. Do not boil hard. Sugar can be added toward the end of cooking if everyone likes sweet kenuche. Some prefer it salted instead.

5. Serve as thick soup with either sugar or salt. This makes 20 servings. Finished kenuche can be frozen for future use. Do not keep longer than overnight without refrigeration.

47

PHRASES

Translation	Syllabary	Pronunciation
38.		
Merry Christmas!	ᏓᏂᏍᏔᏲᎯᎲ	Da-ni'-s-ta-yo'-hi-hv!
39.		
Christmas (when they fire off firecrackers)	ᏓᏂᏍᏔᏲᎯᎲᎢ	Da-ni'-s-ta-yo'-hi-hv:-(i)
Santa Claus (he fires off fire-crackers)	ᏗᏍᏔᏲᎯ	di-s-ta-yo:-hi
gift	ᎠᏓᏁᏗ	a-da-hne'-d(i)
gifts	ᏗᏓᏁᏗ	di-da-hne:-d(i)
silver (shiner)	ᎤᏥᏍᏔᎷᎩᏍᎩ	u-tsi-s-ta-lu:-gi-s-gi
star	ᏃᏈᏏ	no-q(ui)-s(i)
ribbon	ᎠᏇᏡᏍᏗ	a-que-tlu'-s-d(i)
wrapping paper	ᎦᏇᏂᏙᏗ ᎪᏪᎵ	ga-que:-n(i)-doh'-d(i) go-hwe'-li
bell (it resounds)	ᎤᎭᎸᎾ	u-ha-lv:-n(a)(i)
cedar tree	ᎠᏥᎾ	a'-tsi'-n(a')
angel or Wise Man (he/she is extraordinarily wise)	ᎠᏓᏪᎯ	a-da-we'-hi
40.		
That cedar tree is very pretty.	Ꮎ ᏙᏳ ᎤᏬᏚ ᎠᏥᎾ	Na do:-yu u-wo'-du a-tsi'-n(a)
41.		
Look at that shining star. (Lo, shines-much star)	Ꮒ ᎤᏥᏍᏔᎷᎩ ᏃᏈᏏ	Ni u-tsi-s-ta-lu:-gi no'-q(ui)-s(i).
42.		
How many gifts are you going to buy?	ᎭᎳ ᏙᏓᏣᏩᏏ ᏗᏓᏁᏗ	Ha-la' do-da-tsa-wa'-s(i) di-da-ne'-di?
43.		
I have some red and green lights.	ᏗᎩᎦᎨ ᎠᎴ ᏗᏤᏳᏍᏗ ᏓᎩ ᏗᏨᏍᏗ	Di-gi'-ga-ge a-le di-tse-yu:-s-d(i) da:-gi di-tsv-s-di.

CORE VOCABULARY

certainly, truly,   do:'-yu
very, to a great extent

firecracker   a-sta-yo'-s-toh'-di

green (the new kind)   i'-tse-yu'-s-di
  i'-tse alone is green
  or new

light-bulb   a-tsv'-s-di
light-bulbs   di-tsv'-s-di
  (it is to be lit   (or a-tsv-s-toh'-di
    they are to be lit)   di-tsv'-s-toh-di)

look, see, lo   ni

pretty, beautiful   u-wo'-du

Verbs:

buy
I buy(am buying now)   a-ki-wa-s-ga
you buy   tsi-wa'-s-ga
he/she buys   u-hwa'-s-ga
they buy   u-ni-hwa'-s-ga

give (as a gift, <u>not</u> hand me, pass me etc.
I give, am giving   gv'ne-ha
you give, are giving   hi'-ne-ha
he/she gives, is giving   a-hne-ha
they give, are giving   a-ni-hne-ha

HAVE (in immediate possession nearby. Not necessarily same as 'to own')
Live: I have   a-gi-ka'-ha
          you have   tsa-ka-ha
          he/she has   u-we-ka-ha
          they have   u-ni-ka-ha

Flexible: I have   a-gi-na-(a)
          you have   tsa-na-(a)
          he/she has   u-na-(a)
          they have   u-ni-na-(a)

49

```
                HAVE (something of indefinite shape)
Indefinite:     I have                                    a-gi-ha'
                you have                                  tsa-ha
                he/she has                                u-ha
                they have                                 u-ni-ha

Long:           I have (something long)                   a-quv-ya
                you have                                  tsv-ya
                he/she has                                u-wa-ya
                they have                                 u-nv-ya

Liquid:         I have some liquid                        a-gi-ne-ha
                you have                                  tsa-ne-ha
                he/she has                                u-ne-ha
                they have                                 u-ni-ne-ha
```

Du-da-nv:-hnv?-i di-ga-lo?-qua-s-toh'-di

Rows of the Syllabary:

Da	**R**e	**T**i	**Ꮩ**o	**O**u	**i**v
Sga **Ꭴ**ka	**Ꮛ**ge	**y**gi	**A**go	**J**gu	**E**gv
ᏉᏡha	**Ꭾ**he	**Ꮧ**hi	**Ꮂ**ho	**Γ**hu	**ᏋᏢ**hv
Wla	**Ꮝ**le	**Ꮲ**li	**Ꮆ**lo	**M**lu	**ᏟᏢ**lv
ᏠᏡma	**Ꮼ**me	**H**mi	**ᏙᏜ**mo	**ᏴᏢ**mu	
Ꮭna **ᏔᏢ**hna **G**nah	**Λ**ne	**ᏔᏢ**ni	**Z**no	**ᏔᏢ**nu	**ᏙᏚ**nv
```
```

Words using the first six rows of the Syllabary:

a-gv:-ni-ge   _____ black

a-ha-le:-n(i)(a)   _____ loudmouth

a-hni'   _____ here

u-ha-lv'-n(i)(a)   _____ bell

u-ne:-g(a)   _____ white

go?-l(a)(i)   _____ winter

ko-l(a)(i)   _____ bone, bony (Notice that go?-la and ko-la
look alike written in Cherokee)

gv:-n(a)   _____ turkey

na   _____ that

na?-v?-i   _____ close, near

nah-na?-i   _____ over there, into, at that place
(only about living beings)

Ni-hi-na-hv?   _____ how about you? P.N. 32

Fill in the blanks above.

Exercise 1: Match up Columns A and B.

Exercise 2: Cover Column B and write Column A in English.

Exercise 3: Cover Column A and write the answers in Cherokee pronunciation (English letters). Check your answers by Column A, or have a classmate check your answers.

A.	B.
1. a-tsi-na'	1. Santa Claus
2. di-da-hne:-di	2. ribbon
3. di-s-ta-yo:-hi	3. gift
4. u-tsi-s-ta-lu:-gi-s-gi	4. gifts
5. u-ha-lv:-n	5. Christmas
6. a-da-we'-hi	6. cedar tree
7. a-da-hne'-di	7. angel
8. no:-qui-si	8. wise-man
9. da-ni-s-ta-yo'-hi-hv:-i	9. star
10. a-que:-tlu-s-di	10. silver

Exercise 4: Wrapped presents are under the tree. Each member of the family picks his up. Translate the part outside brackets:

1. I have something (perhaps it's a gun?)
2. I have something (some fluffy bedroom slippers?)
3. I have something (what can it be?)
4. I have something (looks like a book.)
5. I have something (a check, I hope.)
6. I have something (is it a sweater or a blouse?)
7. Look what I have (a puppy!) (In Cherokee: Look, (puppy) it-I-have!)
8. Look what I have, a new (bike)! (In Cherokee: Look, new (bike) it-I-have!)
9. Look what I have, a green (bike)! (In Cherokee: Look, green (bike) it-I-have!)
10. Again I have (a necktie!) See Lesson IV for 'again')
11. I have some kenuche (from Grandma).
12. I have it (the clarinet I wanted.)

Answers are on the following page, titled EXERCISE 4.

EXERCISE 4:

1. A-quv'-ya, (long, inflexible)
2. A-gi-na-(a), (flexible)
3. A-gi-ha, (indefinite, solid)
4. A-gi-na-(a), (flexible)
5. A-gi-na-(a), flexible
6. A-gi-na-(a), flexible
7. Ni, (puppy) a-gi-ka'-ha! (live)
8. Ni, i:-tse (bike) a-gi-ha! (indefinite)
9. Ni, i'-tse-yu'-s-di (bike) a-gi-ha! (indefinite)
10. Ta-li:-ne (necktie) a-gi-na-(a)! (flexible)
11. Ga-na'-tsi a-gi-ne?-a, (liquid)
12. A-quv'-ya, (long, inflexible)

Exercise 5: Translate the following sentences into Cherokee. Answers are on the next page.

1. I have a piece of paper.
2. You have a lightbulb.
3. He/she has a bottle. (half full)
4. They have an owl. (a pet)
5. I have some ribbon.
6. You have some soup.
7. He has a potato.
8. They have a pretty white butterfly.
9. He has a bottle. (empty)
10. Teacher, I know the numbers well today!

Exercise 6: Reviewing classifiers. Translate into Cherokee. Answers are on the next page.

1. Hand him a lightbulb.
2. Hand him a firecracker.
3. I want a present.
4. I am buying a present.   (a bottle of cologne)
5. Hand Luke the broom.
6. I am going to church on Thanksgiving and Christmas.
7. They are giving Luke a bottle. (of aftershave)
8. They are buying Mark a book.
9. The minister, the teacher, Mary, Maggie, and Summer are having dinner here.
10. He says Mark wants a sheet of paper.
11. He wants (some) lightbulbs today.
12. (Please) hand him the book, Pastor.
13. (Please) pass the salt.
14. (Please) pass the water.
15. (Please) pass the bread and butter.

EXERCISE 5:

1. Go-hwe'-lv a-gi-na(a).
2. A-tsv'-s-toh'-di tsa-ha.
3. Gu:-gu u-ne?-a.
4. U-gu:-gu u-ni-ka-ha.
5. A-que-tlu:-s-di a-gi-na:.
6. U-ga-ma tsa-ne?-a.
7. Nu:-n u-ha.
8. U-wo'-du:-ne'-ga ka-ma'-ma u-ni-ka'-ha.
9. Gu:-gu u-ha.
10. Di-de-yo:-hv-s-gi, ko-hi *i-ga' o:-s-da-dv di-se:-s-di de-go-li-gi'

EXERCISE 6:

1. Hi?-v'-si a-tsv-s-toh'-di.
2. Hi-di:-si a-s-ta-yo:-s-toh'-di.
3. A-da-hne:-di a?-wa-du'-li(a).
4. A-da-hne?-di a-ki-hwa-s-ga.
5. Gv-no-sa'-s-di hi-di'-si Lu:-ga. (or Gv-no-sa'-s-di lu:-ga hi-di'-si)
6. Tsu-ni-la'-wi-s-di ge:-ga U-na-li-he'-li-s-di.
7. Gu:-gu a-ni'-hne Lu:-ga.
8. Go-hwe'-li a-ni-wa'-se Ma:-ga.
9. A-l'-tsa-do'-hv-s-gi, di-de-yo:-hv-s-gi, Me:-li, E:-gi, Go:-gi a-hni a-na-l'-s-ta-yv-hv:-s-ga.
10. Go-hwe'-li u-du'-li Ma:-ga, a-di?-a.
11. Di-tsv:-s-toh'-di du-du'-li ko-hi *i-ga'.
12. A-l'-tsa-do'-hv-s-gi, go-hwe'li hi-nv'-si.
13. *A:-m(a') ga-hi?-v'-si.
14. *A-m(a') ga-hi-ne?-v'-si.
15. Ga-du (a'-le') go:-tlv-hnv de-s-kv'-si.

Exercise 7: Translate the English into Cherokee but don't write it down in English letters. Write the answers down directly in Cherokee letters, looking them up if necessary. Answers are on the next page.

1. That locust is a loudmouth.

2. Winter in the north is cold.

3. I am going over there.

4. I understand -- how about you?

5. This butterfly is black and white.

EXERCISE 7:

1. Ꮎ ᎥᎴ ᎠᎱᎵ
2. ᎪᎵ ᎤᏴᏢ ᎤᏴᏜ ᎠᎴ ᎤᏴᏢ ᎪᎵ ᎤᏴᏜ
3. ᎤᎾᎢ ᎨᎦ
4. ᎪᎵᎦ - ᏂᎯᎾᏂ
5. ᎤᏁᎦ -ᎠᎴ- ᎬᏂᎨ ᎯᎠ ᎧᎹᎹ

Exercise 8: Translate the Cherokee below into English. First cover the answers on the bottom of this page, then sound the letters out, write them down (in English letters) and translate. If there are any classifying verbs, name the classification.

1. Ꮒ ᎹᎦ
2. ᎤᏁᎦᎬᏂᎨ ᎬᎾ ᎾᎥᎢ
3. ᎥᎴ ᎠᎾᎵᎮᎵᎦ ᎪᎯ -ᎢᎦ-
4. ᎤᎦᎹ ᎤᏁᎠ
5. ᏄᎾ ᎤᎭ
6. ᎠᎩᎦᎨ ᎤᎦᎶᎦ ᎤᎾᎠ
7. ᎤᎭᎸᎾ ᎨᎢ
8. ᎠᎭᏂ ᎠᎬᏂᎨ ᎫᎫ
9. ᎦᎸᎶᎯ ᎩᎦᎨ
10. ᏅᎩ ᎧᎹᎹ ᎠᎾᎵᏍᏔᏴᎲᏍᎦ

EXERCISE 8:

1. Look at Mark!
2. A black and white turkey is near.
3. The locusts are rejoicing today.
4. He/she has (some) soup. (liquid)
5. He/she has a potato. (indefinite)
6. He/she has a red leaf. (flexible)
7. (There is a) bell over there.
8. Here (is the) black bottle.
9. The sky is red.
10. Four butterflies are feeding.

Blackboard Drills

Exercise 9: Cases of unidentical twins. Mark each True or False. Answers are on the next page.

1. *a:-ma   water   3. a-hu-li   drum
   *a-ma'   salt   a-ho-li   mouth
2. *i:-ga   day   4. v-le   and
   *i-ga   noon   a-le   locust

5. The mountains are in the south.   U-ga'-no-wa' do?-da-la.
6. The mountains are cold.   Do:-da-lv tsu-hyv:-dla.
7. The mountains are warm.   U-ga'-no-wa' do?-da-la.
8. The mountains are in the north.   Do:-da-lv tsu-hyv:-dla.

Exercise 10: Vocabulary test. Fill in the blanks with 1. English syllables 2. Cherokee letters. Answers on the next page.

1. ga-lv-___ ___   - sky   16. ___-wa-s-ga - you are buying

2. e-___ ___   - earth   17. ___-hwa-s-ga - he/she is buying

3. u-___ ___-ga   - leaf   18. ___ ___-ya-na-i - stuffing

4. u-ga-___   - soup   19. ___ ___s-di - gravy

5. no-q'-___   - star   20. a-gi-___-a - I have (something
                                              flexible)
6. ___-da-hne-di   - gifts

7. i-tse-yu-___ ___   - green

8. di-de-yo-___-s-gi   - teacher

9. a-g'-s-ta___ ___-s-gi - wife (meal-maker)

10. a-l'-tsa-do-hv-___ ___ - preacher

11. u-tsi-s-ta-___ ___-s-gi - silver, shining (shiner)

12. ___-da-hne-di - gift

13. a-___-ga-ge - red

14. ___-gi - summer

15. u-da-___-da - cream

56

EXERCISE 9:   1.F, 2.F, 3.T, 4.F, 5.T, 6.T, 7.F, 8.F.

EXERCISE 10:

1. lo, hi

2. lo, hi

3. ga, lo

4. ma

5. si

6. di

7. s, di

8. hv

9. yv, hv

10. s, gi

11. lu, gi

12. a

13. gi

14. go

15. tlv

16. tsi

17. u

18. a, su

19. a, su

20. na

ᏛᏞᏑᎶᎢ   ᏣᎳᎩ   ᎠᏫᎦᎢ

So?-ne:-li'-ne-i Tsa-la-gi' Go-hwe-lv:-i

NINTH CHEROKEE LESSON

AT THE CROSS

U-ne-tla-nv-hi U-we-tsi
I-ga-gu-yv-he-yi
Hna-quo-tso-sv Wi-yu-lo-se
I-ga-gu-yv-ho-nv.

A-se-no-yi U-ne-tse-yi
I-yu-no Du-le-nv
Ta-li-ne-dv Tse-lu-tse-li
U-dv-ne Yu-ne-tsv.

Chorus: U-tsa-ti yu-wo-du
Na-ni-we Na-nah-i
I-ga Do-tsu-lv-sa-dv
Tso-sv-i Tso-sv-i
Ge-na-ni-wi-ga Ga-nv-go-gv-yi
Tsu-wo-du-hi do-di-da-ne-lv.

GUIDE ME O THOU GREAT JEHOVAH

S-qua-ti-ni-se-s-di, Ye-ho-wa
E-la-di Ga-i-sv-i;
Tsi-wa-na-ga-li-yu A-yv
Tsa-li-ni-gi-di Ni-hi.

Nv-wo-ti Ga-nv-go-gv-yi
A-nu-wo S-gi-s-du-i-si
A-tsi-lv-no U-lo-gi-lv
I-gv-i A-i-se-s-di.

Ni-go-hi-lv, ni-go-hi-lv
S-gi-s-de-li-s-ge-s-di yo-go
Ni-go-hi-lv, ni-go-hi-lv
S-gi-s-de-li-s-ge-s-di yo-go.

S-gi-s-de-li-s-gi
S-gi-s-de-li-s-gi
Di-s-gi-ga-hna-wa-di-da.
(Repeat above three
lines)

"At the Cross" uses the words of "Amazing Grace" except for the chorus.
The tune of "There is a Fountain" is often sung to the words of "Amazing
Grace" also. Many of today's most popular hymns do not exist in Cherokee
translation, so Cherokees use words of old hymns with favorite newer tunes.

The words of "Guide Me O Thou Great Jehovah" are usually sung to the
tunes of "What a Friend We Have in Jesus", "Precious Memories" or "Tell It
Everywhere You Go".

PHRASES

Translation	Syllabary	Pronunciation
44. Happy New Year!	Dₚₚₒₔⱼⱼⱼ ₜⱽₜ OₛⱼBUⱼRT	A-li-he-li'-s-di I-tse?-(i) U-de-ti-yv'-sa-di'-sv:?-i!
45. This month is ____	_ _ ⱰW	____ ka?la.
46. January	OⱿZₐWO	U-no-lv'-ta-(nv) or (ni)
February	ⱰSₚ	Ka-ga?-li
March	DOⱼₔ	A-nv:-yi
April	Ɒ℮ₕ	Ka-wo-ni
May	Dₕₒₑⱼ	A-n(i)-s-gv'-ti
June	ⱼₒₘ.ₔₔ	De-ha-lu-yi
July	ⱼβⱽ^ₕ	Gu-ye-quo:-ni
August	₅Gₕ	Ga-lo'-ni
September	Sₚₒⱼ	Du-li:-s-di
October	SₕOⱼ	Du-ni-nv:-di
November	OⱡSG	Nv-da-de:-wa
December	iₒYₔ	V'-s-gi-yi
47. What (which) shall we sing?	₅V Oₒⱼ ⱡⱼZYₕ	(Ga)-do u:-s-d(i) da-di-hno-gi:-si?
48. Let's sing it.	ₜⱼZY	I-di-hno:-gi.
49. You're right. Certainly. Right!	ₕG	Ho:-wa'.
50. baby (also means small, a baby animal, or 'of-that-kind')	Oₒⱼ	u:-s-d(i)
babies	ₔₕₒⱼ	tsu:-n'-s-di
boy	DⱼG	a-tsu'-ts(a)(i)
boys	DₕⱼG	a-ni-tsu'-ts(a)(i)

59

50.(cont.)

girl	DⰏGꞬ	a-ge-(h)yuꞌ-ts(a)
girls	DhⰏGꞬ	a-ni-ge-(h)yuꞌ-ts(a)
young boy or man, youth	DөΘ	a-(h)wi:-n(a)
young boys or men	DhөΘ	a-ni-(h)wi:-n(a)
young girl, ꞌteen	DꞶ	a:-t(a)
young girls	DΘꞶ	a-na-ta
man	DⱷᏚⱷ	a-s-ga-(h)y(a)(v)
men	DhⱷᏚⱷ	a-ni-s-ga-y(a)(v)
woman	DⰏⱷ	a-ge-(h)ya
women	DhⰏⱷ	a-ni-ge-(h)ya
old man	ꝊᎶꞋⱷᏫᏋ	uꞌ-tv-hiꞌ-s-t(v)
old men	ᏧhᎶꞋⱷᏫᏋ	tsuꞌ-n(i)-ta-hiꞌ-s-t(v)
old woman	DᏚBⰏⰊ	a-ga-yvꞌ-li-(ge)
old women	DhᏚBⰏⰊ	a-ni-ga-yvꞌ-li-(ge)

-Ni- is an important Cherokee affix, used to change words from singular
to plural.

Examples: a-tsuꞌ-tsa   boy
           a-ni-tsu-tsa   boys

The plural of nouns meaning human beings is always formed by adding
-ni- right after the first vowel.

When the human noun begins with ꞌuꞌ, ꞌtsꞌ is often added before ꞌuꞌ.

Examples: u:-s-di, tsu:-nꞌ-s-di
           uꞌ-tv-hiꞌ-s-tv, tsuꞌ-nꞌ-tv-hiꞌ-s-tv   old man, old men

Some human nouns add ꞌdi-ꞌ before ꞌniꞌ to form the plural.

Example: a-(h)yo:-tli, di-ni-yo:-tli   child, children

-Ni- is often shortened to -n-.

Verbs also use the affix -ni-.

Verbs are often discussed using the terms 1st person, 2nd person, 3rd person. These terms mean this:

	Singular	Plural
person speaking - 1st person	I want	We want
person spoken to - 2nd person	you want	You want
person spoken of - 3rd person	he or she wants	They want

They (3rd person plural) of an active Cherokee verb contains -ni- added right after the first vowel of he/she (3rd person singular) of that verb.

If the verb for he/she does not begin with a vowel, a-ni is added instead.

Example: go'-l'-ga, a-no'-l'-ga   he/she knows, they know

A-ni is also added in some other verbs:

Example: e:-ga, a-ne'-ga   he/she goes, they go, are going

Study the examples below, which include all the verbs you have had so far and nouns from this lesson. Nouns are marked N and verbs V.

Examples:

a-di?-a	V he/she says	a-n'-di?-a	They are saying
u:-s-di	N baby	tsu:-n'-s-di	babies
e:-ga	V he/she goes	a-ne'-ga	they are going
a-tsu'-tsa	N boy	a-ni-tsu'-tsa	boys
u-du'-li	V he/she wants	u-na-du'-li	they want
a-ge-hyu:-ts(a)	N little girl	a-ni-ge-hyu'tsa	little girls
a-l'-s-ta-yv-hv'-s-ga	V h/sh eat	a-na-l'-s-ta-yv-hv'-s-ga	they eat (a meal)
a-s-ga-ya'	N man	a-ni'-s-ga-ya'	men
u:-n'-ta	V he/she knows	u-na?-ta	they know
a-ge-hya	N woman	a-ni-ge'-hya	women
a-li-he:-li-ga	V he/she is glad	a-na-li-he'-li-ga	they are glad, thankful
a-hwi:-n(a)	N young man	a-ni-(h)wi'-na	young man
go:-l'-ga	V he/she knows	a-no'-l'-ga	they know, understand
a:-t(a)	N young girl	a-n(i)-a:-t(a)	young girls
a-dv:-ne-(v)(a)	V he/she does	a-na-dv:-ne-(v)(a)	they are doing
u'-tv hi'-s-t(v)	N old man	tsu'-n'-tv hi'-s-t	old men
u-hwa'-s-ga	V he/she buys	u-ni-hwa'-s-ga	they buy, are buying

Examples (cont.)

a-ga-yv'-li-(ge)	N old woman	a-ni-ga-yv'-li-(ge)	old women
a-hne-ha	V he/she gives	a-ni-hne-hv	they give, are giving
u-we-ka-ha	V HE/SHE HAS	u-ni-ka'-ha	THEY HAVE (live)
u-na-a	V HE/SHE HAS	u-ni-na-a	THEY HAVE (flexible)
u-ha	V HE/SHE HAS	u-ni-ha	THEY HAVE (indefinite)
u-ne?-a	V HE/SHE HAS	u-ni-ne'-ha	THEY HAVE (liquid)
u-wa'-ya	V HE/SHE HAS	u-nv-ya	THEY HAVE (long)
u-hyv:-dla	he/she-is-a-Republican	u-ni-hyv:-dla	they-are-Republicans
u-ga'-no-wa'	he/she-is-a-Democrat	u-ni-ga'-no-wa'	they-are-Democrats

CORE VOCABULARY

Right! certainly,   ho:-wa
(after thanks)
You're welcome.

There are many situations when v:-v (yes), o:-s-da (fine) or ho:-wa
(right) may be used. It may help you to remember that v:-v is closest to
meaning 'It is a fact', 'It is so'. O:-s-da is closest to 'It (some
specific thing) is fine'. Ho:-wa is closest to 'Agreed', or 'We are in
agreement.

old (only living things)   a-ga-yv:-li

old woman, old women   a-ga-yv:-li(ge),
                                                        a-ni-ga-yv:-li-ge

old people   a-ni-ga-yv:-li

In speaking of old people, 'the old' (men and women together), the
plural of women instead of men is used. The word for 'old men' means something like 'past progenitors', and so is unsuitable for both sexes. A-ga-
yv:-li has a complimentary meaning, 'completely grown up, growing to a
maximum, very mature'.

A-ga-yv:-li is also an adjective meaning 'old'. It can be used only
for living things (humans, animals, plants). For non-living things
Cherokee uses an entirely different adjective for old, 'u-we:-ti. This
means 'used up, worn out, dilapidated'.

Adjectives used for living things use -ni- right after the first vowel to form the plural, just like verbs and nouns.

Example of -ni- in a sentence with a <u>human noun</u> as subject (headword):

Singular: The pretty little-girl is happy.
           U-wo'-du a-ge-hyu'-tsa a-li-he:-li-ga.

Plural: The pretty little-girls are happy.
           Tsu-<u>no</u>'-du a-<u>ni</u>-ge-hyu'-tsa a-<u>na</u>-li-he'-li-ga.

The plural of 'pretty' in the sentence above has -ni- added after the first vowel because it is an <u>adjective</u> describing a <u>living</u> (not necessarily human) noun.

The plural of 'little-girls' contains a -ni- after the first vowel because 'little-girl' is a <u>human noun</u>.

'Are happy' in Cherokee contains a -ni- after the first vowel because 'rejoice, be happy' is an active <u>verb in the 3rd person plural</u> (they). A literal translation of the plural sentence would read 'Pretty little-girls they-are-happy.'

Example of -ni- with a <u>living noun</u> (not human):

Singular: The black butterfly is feeding. (having a meal)
           A-gv'-ni-ge ka-ma'ma a-l'-s-ta-yv-hv'-s-ga.

Plural: The black butterflies are feeding.
           A-ni-gv'-ni-ge ka-ma'-ma a-na'-l'-s-ta-yv-hv-s-ga

Notice that the plural of 'black' (a-ni-gv'-ni-ge) has a -ni- because it is an <u>adjective</u> describing a <u>living noun</u>.

'Are feeding' contains a -ni- because it is an active <u>verb in the 3rd person plural</u>. (Black butterflies (or elephants) they-are-feeding.)

Summary: -Ni-, (often shortened to -n-), marks the plural of:

1. Human nouns
2. Adjectives dealing with living nouns
3. Active verbs dealing with he/she, they (3rd person plural)

<u>Living human nouns</u> in the plural contain three kinds of -ni- (on the adjective, noun and verb). <u>Living non-human nouns</u> usually have only two kinds of -ni- (on the adjective and on the verb). <u>Non-living nouns</u> (things) are treated differently from either human or living nouns.

63

Du-da-nv:-hnv?-i Di-ga-lo?-qua-s-toh'-di
Rows of the syllabary:

Ꭰ a	Ꭱ e	Ꭲ i	Ꭳ o	Ꭴ u	Ꭵ v
Ꭶ ga Ꭷ ka	Ꭸ ge	Ꭹ gi	Ꭺ go	Ꭻ gu	Ꭼ gv
Ꭽ ha	Ꭾ he	Ꭿ hi	Ꮀ ho	Ꮁ hu	Ꮂ hv
Ꮃ la	Ꮄ le	Ꮅ li	Ꮆ lo	Ꮇ lu	Ꮈ lv
Ꮉ ma	Ꮊ me	Ꮋ mi	Ꮌ mo	Ꮍ mu	
Ꮎ na Ꮏ hna Ꮐ nah	Ꮑ ne	Ꮒ ni	Ꮓ no	Ꮔ nu	Ꮕ nv
Ꮖ qua	Ꮗ que	Ꮘ qui	Ꮙ quo	Ꮚ quu	Ꮛ quv

Some words using the first seven rows of the syllabary:

e-qua(quv) ________ big

hna-quu ________ right now!

qua-na̸ ________ peach

Qua-quu ________ Robert, Bob

Que-ni ________ Benny

Fill in the blanks. There are relatively few Cherokee words using the 'qua' row of the syllabary.

Exercises 1, 2 and 3 use the phrases as they have appeared in the lessons. Exercise 4 encourages new combinations, and Exercise 5 gives you practice in the first 7 rows of the syllabary.

Exercise 1: Match up all the material in A with the material in B.

A.	B.
1. a-hwi:n'	1. men
2. a-ni-s-ga-yv	2. a young man
3. a-ni-s-ga-ya	3. a (little) girl
4. a-ge-hyu:-ts'	4. (little) girls
5. a-ni-ge-yu:-tsa	5. a baby (a small one)
6. u-no-lv'-ta-ni	6. September
7. nv-da-de:-wa	7. January
8. ka-wo-ni	8. March
9. du-li:-s-di	9. May
10. a-nv:-yi	10. November

Exercise 2: Cover Column B and translate Column A orally.

Exercise 3: Cover Column A and translate Column B into Cherokee pronunciation (English letters). Write your answers.

Exercise 4: Translate the sentences below into Cherokee, writing them in English letters (Cherokee pronunciation).

1. What do you want, little girl? (In Cherokee it is more natural to say the name of the person spoken to at the beginning of the sentence.)

2. Hello, teacher, how are you?

3. Mark, you are speaking slowly.

4. The little baby wants a small bottle. (baby little bottle little he/she wants)

5. What is this thing? (What sort-of-thing this?)

6. Thank you, Bob, goodbye.

7. You're welcome. Goodbye, boys.

8. I am going-- how about you?

9. One, two, three, four, five --- five girls (teenagers) are going.

10. This is the month of February.

EXERCISE 4:

1. A-ge-hyu:-tsa, ga-do u:-s-di (tsa-du'-li)?
   (can be with or without verb--P.N. 30 & 31)

2. O'-si-yo', di-de-yo-hv:-s-gi, dto-hi-tsu?

3. Ma:-ga u-s-ga-no'-li hi-wo:-ni(a)

4. U:-s-di u:-s-di gu:-gu u:-s-di u-du'-li-a.

5. Ga-do u-s-di hi?-a?

6. Qua'-quu, wa?-do. Do-na-da-go'-hv?-i.

7. Ho:-wa. Do-da-da-go-hv a-ni-tsu-tsi.

8. Ge:-ga -- ni-hi-na-hv?

9. Sa'-wu, ta?-li, tso?-i, nv:-gi, hi-s-gi -- hi-s-g' a-ni-ge-yu'-tsa
   a-ne:-ga.

10. Ka-ga?-li ka?-la.

Exercise 5: Translate from English directly into the Cherokee syllabary.

1. old women

2. old people

3. This is the month of August.

4. February

5. he/she knows

6. they are glad

7. This peach is big.

8. he/she gives, they are giving

9. he/she has (something flexible), they have (something flexible)

10. he/she has (something liquid), they have (something liquid)

One letter needed above to translate the answers is not in the first seven
rows of the syllabary: the letter yv **B** . Answers are on the next page.

EXERCISE 5:

1. DhSBℙℙ

2. DhSBℙ

3. ꝦGh ꝹW

4. ꝹSℙ

5. AℙꝦ

6. DꝹℙℙℙꝦ

7. ꝺD ꞮꝹ Rꜫ

8. DΛⱦ DhΛꝹ

9. ꝹꝹD ꝹhꝹD

10. ꝹΛD ꝹhΛⱦ

ᏍᎪᎯᏁᎢ ᏣᎳᎩ ᎠᏍᏫᎸᎢ

S-go-hi:-ne-i Tsa-la-gi' Go-hwe-lv:-i

TENTH CHEROKEE LESSON

PHRASES

Translation	Syllabary	Pronunciation

51.
Let's say some new words.

ᏗᎢᏴ ᏗᎧᎾᏣ ᏗᏙᏣ

Di-i'-tse di-ka-ne'-tsv di-do'-tsa.

52.
What page is it on? (Where is it written?)

ᎭᏢ ᎠᏍᏫᎸᎢ

Ha'tlv go-hwe:-lv-(i)?

53.
It is on page ___.

_ _ ᎠᏍᏫᎸᎢ

_____ go-hwe:-lv-(i).

54.
Let's have some coffee. (Coffee let-us-be-about-to-drink.)

ᎧᏫ ᎢᎾᏗᏝ

Ka?-wi' i-na-di:-ta'.

55.
Do you take sugar? (Sugar do-you-mix-with?)

ᎤᎵᏎᏥᏍ ᎭᏚᏴᏍᎪ

Ka-l(i)-se:-ts(i')-s ha-su-yv'-s-go?

56.
Do you take cream? (Cream do-you-mix-with?)

ᎤᏓᏢᏛᏍ ᎭᏚᏴᏍᎪ

U?-da-tlv:'-d(a)-s ha-su-yv'-s-go?

57.
Do you take milk? (Milk do-you-mix-with?)

ᎤᏅᏗᏍ ᎭᏚᏴᏍᎪ

U-nv:-d(i')-s ha-su-yv'-s-go?

68

Translation	Syllabary	Pronunciation

58.
Would you like a cold drink?　ᎤᏝᏈᎯ ᎠᏗᏔᏍ ᏣᏚᎵᎠ　U-hyv:-dla-ke a-di-ta-s tsa-du:-li-(a)?

59.
Would you like a cookie (cup-cake, piece of cake, coffee-cake)? (baked-sweet)　ᎤᎦᎾᏍᏓᏈ ᏣᏚᎵᎠ　U:-ga-na'-s-da-ke tsa-du:-li-(a)?

CORE VOCABULARY

cake, cookie, coffee-cake (as an adjective: delicious)	u-ga-na:-s-da
coffee	ka?-wi'
cream	u?-da-tlv:-d(a or i)
milk	u-nv:-d(i)
sugar or candy	ka-l(i)-se:-ts(i)
this	hi?-a
word, words (spoken)	ka-ne'-tsv, di-ka-ne'-tsv

Verbs:

drink	
I am drinking	ga-di-ta:-s-ga'
You are drinking	ha-di:-ta-s-ga'
he/she is drinking	a-di:-ta-s-ga'
they are drinking	a-na-di:-ta-s-ga'

Du-da-nv:-hnv?-i di-ga-lo?-qua-s-toh'-di
Rows of the syllabary:

Ꭰ a	Ꭱ e	Ꭲ i	Ꭳ o	Ꭴ u	Ꭵ v
Ꭶ ga Ꭷ ka	Ꭸ ge	Ꭹ gi	Ꭺ go	Ꭻ gu	Ꭼ gv
Ꭽ ha	Ꭾ he	Ꭿ hi	Ꮀ ho	Ꮁ hu	Ꮂ hv
Ꮃ la	Ꮄ le	Ꮅ li	Ꮆ lo	Ꮇ lu	Ꮈ lv
Ꮉ ma	Ꮊ me	Ꮋ mi	Ꮌ mo	Ꮍ mu	
Ꮎ na Ꮏ hna Ꮐ nah	Ꮑ ne	Ꮒ ni	Ꮓ no	Ꮔ nu	Ꮕ nv
Ꮖ qua	Ꮗ que	Ꮘ qui	Ꮙ quo	Ꮚ quu	Ꮛ quv
Ꮜ sa Ꮝ s	Ꮞ se	Ꮟ si	Ꮠ so	Ꮡ su	Ꮢ sv

Words for eight rows of the syllabary:

a-la-su'-lo ________ shoe

ga-so'-qua-lv ________ round

sa-ko'-ni-ge ________ blue

sa:-sa ________ goose, swan

si-qua ________ pig

si-quv ________ more

Exercise 1: Match the sentences in Columns A and B with one another.

Exercise 2: Read each sentence out loud and make an answer to each sentence, either quoting directly from the lessons or a suitable Cherokee combination of your own.

Exercise 3: Without using any phrases from Columns A and B on this page, write down five phrases from anywhere in the lessons. If you cannot write them in English letters (Cherokee pronunciation), see how many Cherokee phrases you can speak correctly, with correct knowledge of their meaning.

A.
1. Ha:-tlv go-hwe:-lv-i?
2. U?-da-tlv:'-d(a)-s ha-su-yv'-sgo?
3. U-hyv:-dla-ke a-di-ta-s tsa-du'-li?
4. A-gi-lv?-dv hi?-a.
5. Ga-do' de-tsa-dø:?
6. Ka?-wi' i-na-di:-ta'.
7. Ka-l'-se:-ts'-s ha-su-yv'-s-go?
8. Dto-hi'-tsu?
9. Do-da-da-go'-hv?-i.
10. O'-si-yo'.

B.
1. I would like that. (this)
2. What page is it on?
3. Do you take cream?
4. Do you take sugar?
5. Would you like a cold drink?
6. How are you?
7. What is your name?
8. Let's have some coffee.
9. Hello.
10. Goodbye.

Exercise 4: Count from one to ten in Cherokee.

Exercise 5: Say six of the months correctly.

Exercise 6: Name ten foods in Cherokee.

Exercise 7: Take any verb you have had and give all the forms of it you know. You have had four forms so far, in only the present tense. (I, you, he/she, and they)

Exercise 8: Tell how many classifications there are in Cherokee classifying verbs. Explain what each classification means and give one example of each from the two classifying verbs you know, 'pass or hand me' and 'have'. Look up the answers of Exercises 1 through 8 in the lessons.

Exercise 9: Fill in the blanks with Cherokee letters from the first eight rows of the syllabary. Answers on next page.

1. __ __ __ __   red

2. __ __ __ tsi   sugar, candy

3. __ __ __ __ da   cookie, sweet baked goods

4. __ __ tlu-__ di   ribbon

5. __ __ __ __ di   broom

71

EXERCISE 9: 1. a,**D** gi,**Y** ga,**Ꮝ** ge,**Ꮆ** . 2. ka,**Ꮼ** li,**Ꮏ** se,**Ꮞ** . 3. u,**Ꮳ** ga,**Ꮝ** na,**Ꮎ** s,**Ꮰ** . 4. a,**D** que,**Ꮾ** s,**Ꮰ** . 5. gv,**Ꭱ** no,**Z** sa,**Ꮀ** s,**Ꮰ** .

Syllabary Test
(top eight rows, a through sv)

1. se_____   11. o_____   21. i_____

2. qui_____   12. u_____   22. a_____

3. go_____   13. lv_____   23. ha_____

4. gu_____   14. ga_____   24. i_____

5. ka_____   15. si_____   25. la_____

6. ne_____   16. hv_____   26. quv_____

7. v_____   17. ni_____   27. quu_____

8. ma_____   18. lu_____   28. lo_____

9. hna_____   19. na_____   29. ge_____

10. nah_____   20. sa_____   30. s_____

Fill in the blanks above. The answers are below, the third column first.
21.**T** 22.**D** 23.**Ᏼ** 24.**T** 25.**W** 26.**Ɛ** 27.**Ꮽ** 28.**Ꮒ** 29.**Ꮆ** 30.**Ꮰ** 11.**Ꮣ** 12.**Ꮼ**
13.**Ꭹ** 14.**Ꮝ** 15.**Ꮆ** 16.**Ꮂ** 17.** h** 18.**M** 19.**Ꮎ** 20.**U** 1.**Ꮞ** 2.**Ꮖ** 3.**Ꭺ** 4.**J** 5.
6.**Ꮠ** 7.**i** 8.**Ꮉ** 9.**Ꮏ** 10.**Ꮐ**

Exercise 10: Cover the right-hand column and translate the left column into Cherokee.

1. Hello.   1. (Oꞌ)-si-yoꞌ. P.N.1
2. Goodbye. a. to one   2. Do-na-daꞌ-go-hv?-(i) P.N.5
            b. to several   Doꞌ-da-da-goꞌ-hv?-(i).
3. Thank you.   3. Wa?-do. P.N.6
4. Youꞌre welcome.   4. Ho:-waꞌ. P.N.49
5. My name is ___.   5. _____ da-wa?-do:-(a). P.N.24
6. Where is ___?   6. Ha:-tlv_____? P.N.22
7. I want _____.   7. _____ a?-wa-duꞌ-li-(a). P.N.18
8. Today is Thanksgiving.   8. U-(na)-li-he-liꞌ-s-di go-hiꞌ. P.N.17
9. Merry Christmas!   9. Da-niꞌ-s-ta-yoꞌ-hi-hv! P.N.38
10. Happy New Year!   10. A-li-he-liꞌ-s-di I-tse?-(i)
                                       U-de-ti-yvꞌ-sa-diꞌ-sv:?-i! P.N.44

ᎤᏍᏗᎾ ᏣᏫᏱ ᎠᏬᎦᏔ

Sa-du-i:-ne Tsa-la-gi' Go-hwe-lv:-(i)

ELEVENTH CHEROKEE LESSON

How to form questions

Forming a question in both English and Cherokee is very simple. Their methods are similar.

In English

1. In English, besides just raising the voice, there are two ways to form questions.

   a. Change of word order plus a questioning word (interrogative word):

      Example:
      Statement: You are going home.
      Question: <u>Where</u> <u>are</u> <u>you</u> going?

      Questions formed by using an interrogative (questioning word) cannot be answered with yes or no.

   b. Change of word order alone:

      Example:
      Statement: You are going.
      Question: <u>Are</u> <u>you</u> going?

      Questions formed by change of word order alone can always be answered with yes or no.

In Cherokee

2. In Cherokee, besides using a questioning tone of voice as in English, there are also two ways to treat a statement to make it a question.

   a. Add an interrogative word, such as ka:-ga (who?), ha:-tlv (where), ga?-do' u:-s-di (what? or which?) onto the beginning of the state-ment. This is exactly like English method (a.) except that Cherokee does not change word order.

73

Example:
Statement: You are going home.   Di-tse-nv-sv-(i) he:-ga.
                                     (To-your-home you-are-going.)
Question: Where are you going?   Ha:-tlv he:-ga.
                                     (Where you-are-going?)

You have already had many Cherokee questions formed in this way.
See Phrase Numbers 22, 23, 27, 28, 30, 31, 32, 35, 42, 47, 52.

b. In order to ask questions whose answer can be yes or no, Cherokee uses questioner particles instead of changing the verb as English does. Questioner particles are used in the following way:

Step 1. Put the questioned idea first in the sentence. If you are wondering whether it is cold, put cold first. If you are asking whether John did it (instead of somebody else) put John first, and so on.

Step 2. Place one of the following questioner particles directly after the first Cherokee word:
-ke
-tsu
-tsv
-s-go
-s-go-hv
It is not necessary to add another questioner particle, but Cherokees often do, usually a quiet -s or -sk in an ascending tone after important nouns or adjectives, and/or -s-go or -tsu at the end of the sentence. You will hear many variations. -Ke is usually used only right after the first word.

Examples of Cherokee questions that can have a yes or no answer:

Statement: It is cold outside.   U-hyv:-dla do'-yi.
Question: Is it cold outside?   U-hyv:-dla-ke do'-yi?

Statement: It's all right.   O:-s-da-dv'.
Question: Is it all right?   O:-s-da-tsu?

Statement: You want some oil.   Go?-i tsa-du:-li(a).
Questions: Do you want some oil? Go?-i:-s tsa-du:-li-s-(go)?
                                  Go?-i-ke tsa-du'-li?

Statement: You are going.   He:-ga.
Questions: Are you going?   He:-ga-tsu?
                                  He:-ga'-s-(go-(hv))?
                                  He:-ga-ke?

74

You have had the following Cherokee yes-and-no answer questions:
P.N. 2, 55, 56, 57, 58, 59.

PHRASES

Translation	Syllabary	Pronunciation
60. It is certainly a beautiful evening.	VG ᎤᏬS R.ᎧᏰ	Do-yu'-u-wo'-du sv-hi:-ye.
61. Is it a beautiful evening this evening?	ᎤᏬSᏒ ᎠᎧ R.ᎧᏰ	U-wo'-du-ke go-hi' sv-hi:-ye?
62. It is raining and cold outdoors.	DᏎᏬᎾ ᎤBᎥZ VᏍ	A:-ga:-s-ka u-hyv:-dla-hno do-yi
63. Is it raining?	DᏎᏬᎾᏬᎠ	A:-ga:-s-ka'-s-k'?
64. It is cloudy this morning. (It was cloudy.)	ᎤGᎩᏒ ᎠᎧ RᎾᎧT	U:-lo'-gi-li' go-hi' sv-na:-le?-(i). (U-lo-gi-lv.)
65. I speak Cherokee a little. (Little I-speak Cherokee)	ᏎᏂC ᏒᎤᎻD GᏫᎩ	Ga-yo:-(tli) tsi-wo:-(ni)a) Tsa-la-gi'.
66. Do you speak Cherokee a little?	ᏎᏂCᏒ ᎩᎤᎻD GᏫᎩ	Ga-yo:-tli-ke hi-wo:-ni-(a) Tsa-la-gi'?
67. He speaks Cherokee well. (Well-indeed Cherokee he-speaks.)	ᏎᎾᏟᎧ GᏫᎩ ᏎᎤᎻD	O:-s-da-dv Tsa-la-gi' ga-wo:-ni-(a).
68. I am an Indian. (I originate of the real people.)	ᏒBᎾᏬᎧ	Tsi-yv'-wi-ya-(dv).

75

69.
You are an Indian.   ꭴᏴꭳꮣꭹ   Hi-yvꞌ-wi-ya-(dvꞌ).

70.
Are you an Indian?   ꭴᏴꭳꮣꮢꭺꮓ   Hi-yvꞌ-wi-yaꞌ-s-(g-(o(hv)?

71.
He is an Indian.   ᎠᏴꭳꮣꭹ   A-yvꞌ-wi-ya-(dvꞌ).

72.
What tribe of Indian   ᏍᏙ ꭳꮲꮧ ᎠᏴꭳꮣ   Ga-doꞌ u:-s-d(iꞌ) a-yvꞌ-wi-
does he belong to?   yaꞌ?

73.
Do you speak English? ᏋᏄꭶᏉ ꭴꮎꮂᎠ   Yu-neꞌ-ga-ke hi-wo:-n(i)-(a)?

74.
I am of Osage origin. ᎠꭴᏏ ꭿᏴꭳ   A?-saꞌ-si tsi-yvꞌ-wi.
(I originate as an ...)
...as a Delaware   Ꭰꮖꮕꭹ ꭿᏴꭳ   A-qua-nv:-gi tsi-yvꞌ-wi.
...as a Creek   ᎠᏧꮜ ꭿᏴꭳ   A-gu:-sa tsi-yvꞌ-wi.
...as a White   ꭿᏋꭕᏍ ꭿᏴꭳ   Tsi-yu-neꞌ-ga tsi-yvꞌ-wi.

CORE VOCABULARY

American Indian   a-yvꞌ-wi-yaꞌ
(yv-wi means a people,
-ya means basic, real,
true, essential)

and (placed on the end   -hno, -hnv
of the last in a series-
see P.N. 62)

child, children   a-hyoꞌ-tli
(still-sprouting)   di-ni-yoꞌ-tli

as an adjective-
childish, immature,
uncompleted

cloud, cloudy   u:-loꞌ-gi-l(a) or l(i)

English language   yo:-neꞌ-ga
(according-to-white)

76

evening	sv-hi:-ye
little bit, small amount insufficient amount	ga-yo:-tli
morning, to-morrow	sv-na:-le(i)
out-of-doors	do'-yi
people, tribe	yv'-wi
rain (always a verb) it-rains	a-ga:-s-ga'
truly, indeed, very (placed before what is emphasized) See P.N. 61	do-yu
truly, indeed (placed on the end of what is emphasized)	-dv

-Dv is often put on the end of an affirmative reply to a question. It can't be used alone. (Are you an Indian? Indeed I am. (Tsi-yv-wi-ya-dv.)

Verbs:

originate, be of a certain origin (with ya, to originate, truly, be an Indian)

I originate (truly)	tsi-yv'-wi-(ya)
you originate (truly)	hi-yv-wi-(ya)
he/she originates (truly)	a-yv'-wi-(ya)
they originate (truly)	a-ni-yv'-wi-(ya)

speak

I speak, am speaking	tsi-wo'-ni-a
you speak	hi-wo:-ni-(a)
he/she speaks	ga-wo:-ni-(a)
they speak	a-ni-wo:-ni-(a)

think, be of the opinion

I think	ge'-li-a
you think	he-li-a
he/she thinks	e'-li-a
they think	a-ne'-li-a

Du-da-nv:-hnv?-i Di-ga-lo?-qua-s-toh'-di:
Rows of the syllabary:

Ꭰ a	Ꭱ e	Ꭲ i	Ꭳ o	Ꭴ u	Ꭵ v
Ꭶ ga Ꭷ ka	Ꭸ ge	Ꭹ gi	Ꭺ go	Ꭻ gu	Ꭼ gv
Ꭽ ha	Ꭾ he	Ꭿ hi	Ꮀ ho	Ꮁ hu	Ꮂ hv
Ꮃ la	Ꮄ le	Ꮅ li	Ꮆ lo	Ꮇ lu	Ꮈ lv
Ꮉ ma	Ꮊ me	Ꮋ mi	Ꮌ mo	Ꮍ mu	
Ꮎ na Ꮏ hna Ꮐ nah	Ꮑ ne	Ꮒ ni	Ꮓ no	Ꮔ nu	Ꮕ nv
Ꮖ qua	Ꮗ que	Ꮘ qui	Ꮙ quo	Ꮚ quu	Ꮛ quv
Ꮜ sa Ꮝ s	Ꮞ se	Ꮟ si	Ꮠ so	Ꮡ su	Ꮢ sv
Ꮣ da Ꮤ ta	Ꮥ de Ꮦ te	Ꮧ di Ꮨ ti	Ꮩ do	Ꮪ du	Ꮫ dv

Some words using the first nine rows of the syllabary:

du-da-nv:-hnv?-i	____________________	rows
di-ga-lo?-qua-s-toh'-di	____________________	alphabet
Que-di	__________	Betty
Ge-li-a-da or (dv)	__________	I think I do, I think so.
u-ta-na	__________	big, big around
ga-do-hi	__________	soil
ga-da	__________	dirt
ga-da-ha	__________	dirty

Exercise 1:   Match up Columns A and B.
Exercise 2:   Cover Column B and write Column A in English.
Exercise 3:   Cover Column A and write the answers in Cherokee pronunciation.
Exercise 4:   Take all questions in Column A and change them into statements.
Exercise 5:   Take all statements in Column A and change them into questions.

A.
1. Yu-ne'-ga-ke hi-wo:-ni?
2. Ga-do' u:-s-d' a-yv'-wi-ya'?
3. O:-s-da Tsa-la-gi' ga-wo:-ni.
4. A-gu:-sa tsi-yv'-wi.
5. Tsi-yu-ne'ga tsi-yv'-wi.
6. A:-ga:-s-ka'-s-k?
7. Do-yu u-wo'-du sv-hi:-ye.
8. Ga-yo:-tli-ke hi-wo:-ni Tsa-la-gi'?
9. U:-lo'-gi-li' go-hi sv-na:-le-i.
10. Hi-yv'-wi-ya'-s-k'?

B.
1. Do you speak English?
2. I am of Delaware origin.
3. Are you an Indian?
4. He speaks Cherokee well.
5. Is it raining?
6. It is a very beautiful evening.
7. Do you speak Cherokee a little?
8. It is cloudy this morning.
9. What tribe does he belong to?
10. I am of white origin.

Exercise 6: Translate the sentences below into Cherokee and write them down in Cherokee pronunciation. Answers are on the next page.

1. Is it cloudy this morning? (Write it three ways.)
2. Do you have the broom?
3. You take sugar.
4. You take cream.
5. You take milk.
6. You want some cake.
7. Is your name Bob?
8. Are the old men going?
9. Is the woman drinking coffee and sugar? (mixed with sugar)
10. Do the men think so?

Exercise 7: Translate the Cherokee words and phrases below into English.

1. ᏊᎵ ᎠᏗᏔᏍᎦ Ꮎ ᎠᏫᏬ

6. ᎤᏣᏗᏬ ᏪᎦᎥᏬᎯ

2. ᎬᏃᎤᏍᏗ ᏣᏬ

7. ᎠᏁᏉ ᎠᏂᏬᏍᏬ

3. ᎤᏣᏪᏗᏬ ᏪᎦᎥᏬᎯ

8. ᎤᏁᏎᏍᏬ ᏪᎦᎥᏬᎯ

4. ᎤᎦᏴᏩᏬ Ꭰ.Ꭴ

9. ᎠᏂᏝᏗᏫ ᏣᏂᏔᏬᎤᏍ

5. ᎤᏍᎣᏬᏗᏫ ᏣᏍᏫ

10. ᏔᏔᏫ ᏎᏣᎥᎠ

Some of the above are questions, so put question marks onto your translation on the correct sentences.

EXERCISE 6:

1. ᎤᏣᏴᏍ ᎠᏗ. ᎤᏣᏲᎵ ᎠᏗ. ᎠᏗᎵ ᎤᏣᏴ.
2. ᎡᏃᎠᎫ ᏣᏍ
3. ᎤᏓᏂᏆ ᏔᎾᏃᏍᎠ
4. ᎤᏟᎫ ᏔᎾᏃᏍᎠ
5. ᎤᏣᎫ ᏔᎾᏃᏍᎠ
6. ᎤᏍᎤᎠᎫ ᏣᏏᎵ
7. ᏔᏍᎵ ᏍᏣᏙᎠ
8. ᏥᎭᏫᎠᏍᎾᏍ ᎠᎳᏍ
9. ᎤᎤᎵ ᎠᏗᏫᎠᏍ Ꮎ ᎠᎵᏍ ᎤᏟᎫ ᎠᏴᏍ
10. ᎠᎵᏙᎵ ᎠᎵᏍᏍᏍ

EXERCISE 7:

1. Ka-wi-ke a-di-ta-s-ga na a-ge-ya?
2. Gv-no-sa-s-di tsv-ya.
3. U-da-tlv-di-s ha-su-yv-s-go?
4. U-lo-gi-la-s ko-hi?
5. U-ga-na-s-da-ke tsa-du-li?
6. U-nv-di-s ha-su-yv-s-go?
7. A-ne-ga-ke a-ni-s-ga-ya?
8. Ka-li-s-e-tsi-s ha-su-yv-s-go?
9. A-ne-li-s-ke tsu-ni-ta-hi-s-tv?
10. Qua-qua-ke de-tsa-do-a?

Exercise 8: Fill in the blanks below:

1. ___ li-a   I think   6. ga- ___ hi   soil

2. ___ li-a   you think   7. ga- ___   dirt

3. ___ ___ ___   he thinks   8. ga-___ ___   dirty

4. ___ ___ nv-hnv-i rows (of things) 9. ___ na-le-i   morning

5. u- ___ na   big   10. ___ hi:-ye   evening

EXERCISE 8: Second column first:

6. 7. 8.   9.   10. 1.   2.   3.   4.   5.

ᏔᎳᏚᎢ ᏣᎳᎩ ᎪᏪᎸᎢ

Ta-la-du-i' Tsa-la-gi' Go-hwe-lv:'-i

CHEROKEE LESSON TWELVE

Some Common Question Words in Cherokee (Interrogatives)

Lesson XI outlined the two ways questions are formed in Cherokee:

1. <u>Question words</u> on the beginning of a sentence (answer cannot be yes or no).
2. <u>Question particles</u> on the end of some words in the sentence (answer can be yes or no).

This lesson will add some common question words (interrogatives) to those you already know.

a. The difference between Cherokee and English interrogatives -

There is an important difference between Cherokee and English question words such as who, where, which, etc.

In English, the <u>same</u> word can be used for either a question <u>or</u> a description (as an interrogative <u>or</u> as a relative).

In Cherokee, such words ask questions. Cherokee uses <u>interrogatives</u> to <u>interrogate</u>.

Examples:
            In English:
1. As part of a description - The boy <u>who</u> came today is not coming back.
2. In a question   - <u>Who</u> is that boy?

            In Cherokee:
1. Same sentence,(description)-Na a-tsu'-tsa tsu-lu'-tsv ko-hi' tla-i-
                                dv-ga-lu?-tsi. (That boy he-came today
                                not-he-will-return. Notice no word
                                for 'who' (Ka:-ga)
2. Same sentence,(question) -<u>Ka'-ga</u> na a-tsu'-tsa?

81

	In English:		In Cherokee:

1. Description - I know <u>where</u> it is.   A-qua'-n'-ta u-hna-ge:-sv. (I know its-location)
   Notice <u>no</u> 'where' (ha:tlv)
2. Question -   <u>Where</u> is it?   <u>Ha:-tlv</u>?-i'? (Where-place?)

	In English:		In Cherokee:

1. Description - He heard <u>what</u>   A-tv'-ga-nv nu-we:-sv. (It-was-
                was said.   heard that-he-said.) (<u>no</u> ga-do')
2. Question -   <u>What</u> did he say?   Ga-do' a:da?

b. Interrogatives you have already had -

You already know the following question words (interrogatives):
Ga-do'   what? which? P.N. 23, 35, 48
Ga-do' u'-s-di what? what kind of? (resembling what?)
                P.N. 31, 32
Ha:-tlv   where? where to? P.N. 22, 28, 53
Ka:-ga   who?

Review the references where these interrogatives are found. Notice how they are used, and whether each means exactly the same thing every time.

You will notice that: 1. Each time they are used, a question is intended.
                      2. The English meaning is not always exactly the same, but close enough not to cause difficulty.

c. The following Cherokee interrogatives can be counted on to mean the same thing every time they are used:

Ha:-tlv   where? where to?
Ka:-ga   who?
Do'-hv   why?
Hv   (by itself only) what? What did you say?

d. Uses of <u>ha-la'</u> -

<u>Ha-la'</u>   is another useful question word. It is used in asking the time:

Example: Ha-la' a-tli'-gi-li'   What time is it?

If the time should be right on the hour, such as eight o'clock, three o'clock, the answer is:

Tsu-ne:-l' a-tli'-gi-li'.	Eight o'clock.
Tso?-i a-tli'-gi-li'.	Three o'clock.

Ha-la'-yv means when, how far? (i.e., how far in time or space?)

Examples:

What time is the parade? (When will they pass?)	Ha-la'-yv a-tli'-gi-li-sv dv-ni-lo'-si?
How far is the river?	Ha-la'-yv e-quo'-ni?
How long is the river? (How-far in-length river?)	Ha-la'-yv wu'-s-ta e-quo'-ni?

Some more combinations of ha-la':

ha-la' i-ga?-(i)?	how much, what amount, how many?
ha-la' ni-ka'?	how big?
ha-la'-dv?	how many are there? Can refer to humans, living beings, or non-living beings (things)
ha-la'-na-ni?-a?	How many are there? Can only refer to living beings, human or not. (notice a-ni embedded in na)

e. Weak interrogatives -

In Cherokee, besides outright questions, formed in the two ways already explained in Lesson XI, there are also slightly questioning particles. These can be added onto words in sentences that are already questions or onto statements. They add to or create a doubtful, hesitant atmosphere.

-gi   Means something like 'Did you say?', 'Isn't it?', 'Wasn't it?', as: 'Three, did you say?', Tso?-i-gi?

-na   Added onto nouns it means approximately 'How about?', as: 'Ni-hi-na-hv?' How about you? 'Hi?-a-na?' How about this? Added on verbs it means 'Let's', 'Shall we', 'If it's all right with you'. It is used to soften an order or a request, and to make an invitation politely tentative. Its literal meaning is roughly 'about to'. (See P.N. 55)

-le   'Possibly', 'maybe'. It is added onto living nouns.

PHRASES

Translation	Syllabary	Translation
75.		
eleven	ᏌᏚᎢ	sa-du-(i)
twelve	ᏔᎳᏚᎢ	ta-l(a')-du-(i)
thirteen	ᏦᎦᏚᎢ	tso-ga-du-(i)
fourteen	ᏂᎦᏚᎢ	ni-ga-du-(i)
fifteen	ᏍᎩᎦᏚᎢ	s-gi'-ga-du-(i)
sixteen	ᏓᎳᏚᎢ	da-la-du-(i)
seventeen	ᎦᎵᏉᏚᎢ	ga-l(i)-qua'-du-(i)
eighteen	ᏁᎳᏚᎢ	ne-la-du-(i)
nineteen	ᏐᏁᎳᏚᎢ	so-hne-la-du-(i)
twenty	ᏔᎵᏍᎪᎯ	ta'-l'-s-go-(hi)
76.		
twenty-one	ᏔᎵᏍᎪᏌᏉ	ta'-l'-s-go-sa'-w(u)
twenty-two	ᏔᎵᏍᎪᏔᎵ	ta'-l'-s-go-ta'-l(i)
thirty	ᏦᏍᎪᎯ	tso'-s-go-(hi)
forty	ᏅᎩᏍᎪᎯ	nv'-g'-s-go-(hi)
fifty	ᎯᏍᎪᎯ	hi'-s-go-(hi)
sixty	ᏑᏓᎵᏍᎪᎯ	su'-da-l'-s-go-(hi)
seventy	ᎦᎵᏉᏍᎪᎯ	ga-l'-qua'-s-go-(hi)
eighty	ᏁᎵᏍᎪᎯ	ne'-l'-s-go-(hi)
ninety	ᏐᏁᎵᏍᎪᎯ	so-ne'-l'-s-go-(hi)
a hundred	ᏍᎪᎯᏍᏈ	s-go-hi'?-s-qua
a hundred and one	ᏍᎪᎯᏍᏈᏌᏉ	s-go-hi'?-s-qua-sa'-w(u)
two hundred	ᏔᎵᏍᎪᎯᏍᏈ	ta'-l'-s-go-hi'?-s-(qua)
a thousand	ᏌᏉ ᎢᏯᎦᏴᎵ	sa'-wu i-ya-ga-yv'-li
77.		
What time is it?	ᎭᎳ ᎠᏟᎩᎵ	Ha-la' a-tli'-gi-li'?
78.		
How much does it cost?	ᎭᎳ ᏧᎬᏩᎵᏗ	
What are the stakes?		Ha-la' tsu-gv-hwa'-l'-di?
79.		
What size do you want? (What written do you want?)	ᎭᎳ ᎪᏪᎵ ᏣᏚᎵ	Ha-la' go-hwe-li tsa-du'-li-(a)?
80.		
How many do you want? or How much do you want?	ᎭᎳ ᎢᎦᎢ ᏣᏚᎵ	Ha-la' i-ga?-i tsa-du'-li-(a)?

84

81.
When are you coming   **ᏉᎳᏴ ᏫᎤᎻᏓ**   Ha-la'-yv dv-hi-lu-tsi'?
back (re-arriving)?

82.
He heard what was said.   **ᎠᏛᎦᏃ ᎤᏬᏒ**   A-tv'-ga-nv u-we:-sv.

83.
How far is the river?   **ᏉᎳᏴ ᎡᏉᏂ**   Ha-la'-yv e-quo'-ni?

84.
How long is the river?   **ᏉᎳᏴ ᎩᏏᏝ ᎡᏉᏂ**   Ha-la'-yv wu'-s-ta e-quo'-ni?
(How-far in-length river?)

CORE VOCABULARY

goods, merchandise   tsu-gv-hwa-hl'-di
(to-be-bought-by-them)
This word can also mean things of value in the home; removable, salable
personal property.

river   e-quo'-ni

Verbs:

arrive, get there, return, come back
  I (just) arrived   tsi-lu?-gi
  you (just) arrived   hi-lu?-gi
  he/she (just) arrived   ga-lu-gi
  they (just) arrived   a-ni-lu-gi

hear
  I (just) heard, I hear   ga-tv-gi
  you (just) heard   ha-htv-gi
  he/she (just) heard   a-tv-gi
  they (just) heard   a-n'-tv-gi

say (that, it, this)
  I say (it, that, this)   ni-tsi-we?-a
  you say it   hni-we?-a
  he/she says it   ni-ga-we?-a
  they say it   na-ni-we?-a

D a	**R** e	**T** i	**ꭴ** o	**O** u	**i** v
S ga **O** ka	**F** ge	**Y** gi	**A** go	**J** gu	**E** gv
T ha	**P** he	**ꭴ** hi	**F** ho	**Γ** hu	**Ꮁ** hv
W la	**Ꮣ** le	**P** li	**G** lo	**M** lu	**Ꮑ** lv
ꮳ ma	**Ol** me	**H** mi	**ꭺ** mo	**y** mu	
Ꮻ na **t** hna **G** nah	**Λ** ne	**ꮒ** ni	**Z** no	**ꮔ** nu	**O** nv
Ꮖ qua	**ꮿ** que	**P** qui	**ꮹ** quo	**ꮕ** quu	**E** quv
U sa **ꭴ** s	**4** se	**b** si	**ꬶ** so	**ꮀ** su	**R** sv
ꮮ da **W** ta	**S** de **ꭲ** te	**ꭱ** di **ꭲ** ti	**V** do	**S** du	**ꮜ** dv
ꮣ dla **ꮮ** tla	**L** tle	**C** tli	**ꭴ** tlo	**ꮯ** tlu	**P** tlv

Some Cherokee words using these rows:

tlv-tlv-yv   later on, soon, after awhile _____

a-s-du:-di   _____ to close (verb), and door (noun)

di-tla-no-he?-di-i   _____ telephone

tla-me'-ha   _____ bat (as in vampire) or tla-ma-ha

tla-nu'-si   _____ leech

tlu-tlu   _____ martin (bird)

Exercise 1: Match up the numbers from this lesson in Columns A and B:
Check by looking up the answers.

1. ga-l'-qua'-s-go	1. one hundred
2. ga-li-qua'-du-i	2. one thousand
3. ne-la-du	3. fourteen
4. sa-du-i	4. twenty-two
5. s-go-hi'?-s-qua	5. eighteen
6. ta'-l'-s-go-hi'?-s	6. seventeen
7. da-la-du-i	7. two hundred
8. ta'-l'-s-go-ta'-l'	8. sixteen
9. sa-wu-i-ya-ga-yv'-li	9. seventy
10. ni-ga-du-i	10. eleven

Exercise 2: Translate the following questions from earlier lessons and
this lesson into English. Answers are on the next page, EXERCISE 2.

1. Ga-do' de-tsa-dø:-(a)?
2. Ga-do' u:-s-di' tsa-du:-li?-a?
3. Ni-hi-na-hv?
4. Ga-do' ha-dv:'-ne?
5. Ha-la' Tsu-gv-wa'-l'-di?
6. Ha-la' do-da-tsa-wa'-si di-da-hne'-di?
7. Ha-la' a-tli'-gi-li'?
8. Ha-la'ni-ka'?
9. Ha:-tlv he:-ga?
10. Ha-la' i-ga?-i tsa-du'-li?
11. Ha-la' go-hwe'-li tsa-du'-li-a?
12. Dto-hi'-tsu?
13. Ga-do'-gi ha-di?-a?
14. Ha'-tlv hi-ne:-la?
15. Ha'-tlv go-we'-li di-tsa-ne:-s-di?

Exercise 3: Translate into Cherokee. Answers are on the next page.

1. How many children are there in church today?
2. Who is that (this)?
3. Why are you going?
4. I hear the telephone.
5. How far is the church? (church-place)
6. Twenty, forty, sixty, eighty.
7. I want a lot of household goods.
8. Who is that man?

EXERCISE 2:

    1. What is your name?
    2. What do you want?
    3. How about you?
    4. What are you doing?
    5. How much does it cost?
    6. How many presents are you going to buy?
    7. What time is it?
    8. How big (is it)?
    9. Where are you going?
   10. How many or how much do you want?
   11. What size do you want?
   12. How are you? (Healthy??)
   13. What did you (just) say? (What are you saying?)
   14. Where do you live?
   15. What is your address?

EXERCISE 3:

    1. Ha-la'na-ni?-a di-ni-yo'-tli tsu-ni-la'-wi-s-di-i ko-hi i-ga?
    2. Ka:-ga hi?-a?
    3. Do'-hv he:-ga?
    4. Di-tla-no-he?di-i ga-tv'-gi-(a).
    5. Ha-la'-yv tsu-ni-la'-wi-s-di-(i)?
    6. Ta'-1'-s-go, nv'-g'-s-go, su-da-1'-s-go, ne'-1'-s-go.
    7. S-qui:-s-di tsu-gv-wa-1'-di a?-wa-du'-li.
    8. Ka:-ga na a-s-ga-y (a) or (v)?

Exercise 4: Fill in the blanks in these numbers from this lesson with the proper syllables.

1. sa ___ i

2. hi-___ ___ hi

3. s-___ ga-du-i

4. ___ ___ hi?-s-qua

5. tso ___ ___ hi

6. so-ne-___ s ___ ___

7. ga-___ qua-___i

8. ga-___ ___-s-___hi

9. ___ hne-la-___ ___

10. ta'-1(i)- ___ ___ sa ___

11. ta'-___ s-go-hi?-___

12. tso-__go-___

88

Exercise 5: Translate the following words and phrases from this lesson from Cherokee to English:

1. ᏌᏓ ᎠᏓᏏᎩ
2. ᏌᏓᏰ ᎣᏍᏃᎵᎯ
3. ᎠᏇᏍᏊ ᎣᎴᎲ
4. ᏌᏓᏰ ᏍᏎᏪ ᏪᎤᏂ
5. Ꮎ ᎠᏦᎦ ᏧᎷᏣ ᎠᏍ ᏓᎶᏍᏃᎵᎯ
6. ᏔᏪᏍᏔ
7. ᎶᎴᎲᎠᏍ
8. ᏁᏪᏍᏔ
9. ᏁᏩᏍᎠᏍ
10. ᏪᎴᏍᎠᏍᏍᎤ
11. ᏁᏩᏍᎠᏍᏍᎤ
12. ᏧᏁᎴᏍᏍᏃᎥᎴᏍ

Exercise 6: Write Nos. 1-20 below in Cherokee letters. Write the Cherokee pronunciation of Nos. 21-24 in English letters.

1. this	21. 2, 4, 6, 8, 10, 12, 14, 16, 18, 20
2. crow	
3. owl	22. 5, 10, 15, 20, 25, 30, 35, 40, 45, 50
4. martin	
5. leech	23. 10, 20, 30, 40, 50, 60, 70, 80, 90, 100
6. locust	
7. a long time ago	24. 100, 200, 300, 400, 500, 600, 700, 800,
8. and, or, but	900, 1,000
9. what did you say?	
10. drum	
11. sky	
12. soup	
13. earth, world	
14. leaf	
15. Luke	
16. soon	
17. George	
18. bat	
19. telephone	
20. who?	

EXERCISE 4:

1.du 2.s, go 3.gi 4.s, go 5.s, go 6.la, go, hi 7.li, du 8.li, qua, go 9.so, du, i 10.s, go, wu 11.li, s 12.s, hi

89

EXERCISE 5:

  1. What time is it?
  2. When are you coming back?
  3. I heard what he said.
  4. How long is the river?
  5. The boy who came today is not coming back.
  6. sixteen
  7. sixty
  8. eighteen
  9. eighty
10. two hundred
11. eight hundred
12. eight thousand

EXERCISE 6:

  1. ᎥD
  2. AႱ
  3. ᎣJJ
  4. ᏸᏸ
  5. ᏞᏈᏏ
  6. iᏯ
  7. A.Ꮩ
  8. DᏯ
  9. Ꮷ
10. DᎢᎱ
11. ᏚᏈᏨᎥ
12. ᎣᏎᏇ
13. RᏨᎥ
14. ᎣᏎᏨᏎ
15. MᏎ
16. PPB
17. ᏩᏝ
18. ᏞᎠᏫ
19. ᎫᏞᏃᏝᎢ
20. ᎣᏎ
21. ta?-li, nv?-gi, su'-da-li, tsu-ne-la, s-go:-hi, ta-la-du-i, ni-ga-du-i,
    da-la-du-i, ne-la-du-i, ta-l'-s-go-hi
22. hi-s-g', s-go, s-gi-ga-du-i, ta-l'-s-go, ta-l'-s-go-hi-s-g', tso'-s-go,
    tso'-s-go-hi-s-g', nv-g'-s-go, nv-g'-s-go-hi'-s-g', hi'-s-go.
23. s-go:-hi, ta-l'-s-go, tso'-s-go, nv-g'-s-go, hi'-s-go, su'-da-l'-s-go,
    ga-l'-qua-s-go, ne'-l'-s-go, so-hne-l'-s-go, s-go-hi'?-s-qua
24. s-go-hi'?-s-qua, ta'-l'-s-go-hi'?-s-, tso'-s-go-hi?-s, nv-g'-s-go-hi?-s,
    hi'-s-go-hi?-s, su-da-l'-s-go-hi?-s, ga-l'-qua-s-go-hi?-s, ne-l'-s-go-
    hi?-s, so-hne-l'-s-go-hi?-s, sa'-wu i-ya-ga-yv'-l'

ᏦᏍᏗ ᏣᏬᏯ ᎪᏩᏁᏔ
Tso-ga-du-i' Tsa-la-gi' Go-hwe-lv:-i

CHEROKEE LESSON THIRTEEN

Pronouns in Cherokee - Part I

a. Attached personal pronouns (bound pronouns)

Look closely at the verbs below:

<u>a</u>:?-<u>wa</u>-du:-li-(a)	I want	<u>tsa</u>-du:-li-(a)	you want
<u>tsi</u>-wo:-ni-(a)	I speak (am speaking)	<u>hi</u>-wo:-ni-(a)	you speak
<u>ge</u>:-ga	I go (am going)	<u>he</u>:-ga	you go

The underlined parts in the first group all mean 'I', and in the second group 'you', singular. (i.e., addressing one person)

On page 18 you learned that the personal pronouns (I, you, he/she, we, they) in Cherokee are attached to the verb and change form according to sounds in the verb. Personal pronouns attached to the verb in Cherokee are called <u>bound pronouns</u>. Bound pronouns are by far the commonest personal pronouns in the Cherokee language. They also can be attached to nouns and adjectives. Bound pronouns will be described further in Lesson XVI.

b. Detached personal pronouns

Only two Cherokee personal pronouns do not change form and do not attach themselves to verbs, though they can be used with verbs. These are a-hyv, **ᎠᏴ** and ni-hi', **ᏂᎯ** . A-hyv' means 'I' and ni-hi' means 'you' speaking to one person, two people, or more than two. A-hyv and ni-hi are used for emphasis.

Examples:

<u>I</u> am going (even if nobody else is).	A-hyv' ge:-ga. (I I-go)
Is that <u>you</u> (the one or ones I am expecting)?	Ni-hi'-tsu? (You-??)
	(Notice no 'is' is necessary in Cherokee)

91

One person could reply to 'Ni-hi'-tsu?': A-hyv'. (I) Again notice no 'is'.
                                     or: A-hyv-dv. (I-indeed.)

There is no separate word for 'we' in Cherokee. In Cherokee, 'we' must
be attached to a verb. Therefore, in the situation above, if several
people wished to reply to 'Ni-hi'-tsu?', they would have to use a verb,
such as:

    Yes, we-have-arrived. (Yes, we-arrive) V:-v, o-tsi-lu-gi'.

A-hyv' alone is often used in Cherokee in situations where a verb would
usually be included in English.

Examples:
  Who did that?   Answer in English: I did it. In Cherokee: A-hyv'.
  Who wants to go?   I do.   A-hyv'.
  Who is next?   I am.   A-hyv',
                                          or: A-hyv' hi?-a.
                                          (I this, I am he/she)

Ni-hi' is used to single people out from a group.

Examples:
  I'm telling you this.   Ni-hi' ga-di?-a hi?-a.
  The phone is for you.   Ni-hi' di-tla-no-he?-di-i.
  You three come here.   Ni-hi' tso?-i di-tse:-na. (Notice -na)

Re-examine this sentence, which also appeared on the previous page:

  A-hyv' ge:-ga.   I am going. (I I-am-going or I I-go)

Notice that a-hyv' and g- both mean I. A-hyv' is optional, for emphasis,
but g- is necessary. In Cherokee the detached personal pronouns, a-hyv'
and ni-hi' are only used in addition to the correct attached personal
pronouns, such as g- above.

PHRASES

Translation	Syllabary	Pronunciation

85.
Spring is coming.   ᎪᎨᎣ ᎠᏟᎩᎶᎦ   Go-ge:-ya a-tli-gi-lo:-ga.
(Becoming-summer time-now)

87.
The birds are flying back from the South. (Birds south-from coming-on-their-way are-flying)

ᏥᏍᏆ ᎤᎦᏃᎥ ᏓᏳᏂᎶᏒ ᎠᏂᏃᎯᎶᎦ

Tsiꞌ-s-qua u-gaꞌ-no-wv da-yuꞌ-ni-lo:-sv a-ni-no-hi-lo:-ga.

88.
Birds are migrating south.

ᏥᏍᏆ ᎤᎦᏃᎥ ᎾᏂᏛᏂᏗ

Tsiꞌ-s-qua u-gaꞌ-no-wvꞌ na:-nꞌ-dv:-nꞌ-ti

89.
Birds are building their nests. (nesting)

ᏥᏍᏆ ᎠᏂᎲᏍᎩᎸᏍᎦ

Tsiꞌ-s-qua a-ni-hne:-s-gi-lv:-s-ga.

90.
Birds are laying their eggs.

ᏥᏍᏆ ᏧᏪᏥ ᏓᏂᎲᏍᎦ

Tsiꞌ-s-qua tsu-we:-tsi da-ni-hvꞌ-s-ga.

91.
Baby birds are hatching.

ᏥᏍᏆ ᎠᏂᏓ ᎠᎾᏣᎢᎠ

Tsiꞌ-s-qua a-ni:-da a-na-tsa-i-a.

92.
bluejay	ᏛᎢᏝ	tla-i?-ga
buzzard	ᏒᎵ	su-li
cardinal	ᏙᏧᎳ	to-tsuꞌ-hwa
dove	ᏬᏯ	wo:-ya
duck	ᎧᏬᏂ	ka-wo:-n(i)
eagle	ᏬᏩᎵ	wo-haꞌ-li
hawk	ᏙᏬᏗ	to-woꞌ-d(i)
hummingbird	ᏩᎴᎳ	wa-leꞌ-la
nightingale	ᏍᏆᎴᏩᎵ	s-qua-leꞌ-wa-liꞌ
pigeon	ᎬᎴ	gv:-le
quail	ᎫᏇ	gu-que
raven	ᎪᎳᏅ	go-la-nvꞌ
robin	ᏥᏍᏉᎦ	tsi-s-quoꞌ-ga
woodpecker	ᏓᎳᎳ	da-laꞌ-la

93

CORE VOCABULARY

baby bird   a:-da-(ge)
Also, baby: fox,
rabbit, bear, pig,
possum, wolf, dog
Not: baby deer,
cow, sheep, goat, horse
Plural:
baby birds, foxes   a-ni:-da-(ge)
a-ni:-da also means
a little or nestful of
birds, foxes, rabbits
a-ni:-da a?-da means
'a single pup of a litter'

bird, birds   tsi'-s-qua

egg, eggs   u-we:-tsi, tsu-
(comes out of him/her)   we:-tsi
same word means son or
daughter of humans

Verbs:

migrate, move out, leave in a body for some length of time
I am moving out   ga-da-nv?-a
you are moving out   ha-da-nv?-a
he/she is moving out   a-da-nv?-a
they are moving out   a-n'-da-nv-a

Interesting Connected Words:

a-ni-no-hi-li   they are flying
a-ni-no'-hi-lo:-ga   they are flying plus long o (as in toe), means 'habitu-
                       ally, repeatedly'. -Ga means present time.
u-no-le   air
u-no-le'-hi   wind. -Hi means 'active', something like -er (dan<u>cer</u>)
                       in English.
u-no-lv'-ta-nv   blown
di-tla-no-he?-di-i   telephone. Approximately, 'they (words) made of (or
                       placed on) the wind (or air) have been brought to one
                       place to be used'.
ga-no-hi-li-to'   He is out hunting. (he-is-flying-around) Ga-no-hi-li
                       he-is-flying, plus -to, movement with no single
                       destination.

94

D a			**R** e		**T** i		**Ꮰ** o		**Ꮳ** u	**i** v
Ꮝ ga	**Ꭷ** ka		**Ꮆ** ge		**Ꭹ** gi		**A** go		**J** gu	**E** gv
Ꮗ ha			**Ꭾ** he		**Ꭿ** hi		**Ꮂ** ho		**Ꭸ** hu	**Ꮚ** hv
W la			**Ꮄ** le		**Ꮅ** li		**Ꮉ** lo		**Ꮇ** lu	**Ꮕ** lv
Ꮉ ma			**Ꮉ** me		**Ꮋ** mi		**Ꮽ** mo		**Ꮽ** mu	
Ꮒ na	**Ꮓ** hna	**Ꮕ** nah	**Ʌ** ne		**Ꮒ** ni		**Z** no		**Ꮔ** nu	**Ꮕ** nv
Ꮖ qua			**Ꮗ** que		**Ꮙ** qui		**Ꮚ** quo		**Ꮚ** quu	**Ꮜ** quv
Ꮜ sa	**Ꮢ** s		**4** se		**Ꮝ** si		**Ꮰ** so		**Ꮞ** su	**R** sv
Ꮣ da	**Ꮤ** ta		**S** de	**Ꮦ** te	**Ꮧ** di	**Ꮨ** ti	**V** do		**S** du	**Ꮫ** dv
Ꮬ dla	**Ꮭ** tla		**L** tle		**C** tli		**Ꮱ** tlo		**Ꮲ** tlu	**P** tlv
Ꮳ tsa			**Ꮴ** tse		**Ꮵ** tsi		**K** tso		**Ꮷ** tsu	**Ꮳ** tsv

Same words using eleven rows of syllabary:

Tsa-tsi   _____   George

Exercise 1: Match up these birds from this lesson:

1.	a:-da	1.	buzzard
2.	wa-le'-la	2.	litter of young
3.	wo-ha'-li	3.	hawk
4.	tsi-s-qua	4.	eagle
5.	tlai?-ga	5.	baby bird
6.	tsi-s-quo'-ga	6.	bird
7.	go-la-nv'	7.	bluejay
8.	da-la'-la	8.	robin
9.	ka-wo:-ni	9.	martin
10.	to-tsu'-hwa	10.	cardinal
11.	to-wo'-di	11.	red-headed woodpecker
12.	wo:-ya	12.	hummingbird
13.	su-li	13.	dove
14.	a-ni:-da	14.	owl
15.	s-qua-le'-wa-li	15.	crow
16.	gv:-le	16.	nightingale
17.	gu'-que	17.	pigeon
18.	u-gu:-ku	18.	quail
19.	tlu-tlu	19.	duck
20.	ko:-gi	20.	raven

Exercise 2: Match up these verb forms from lessons IX through XIII:

1.	ga-di-ta:-s-ga	1.	they have something (long)
2.	u-ha	2.	I think, am of the opinion
3.	u-nv-ya	3.	they think, are of the opinion
4.	ha-di:-ta-s-ga	4.	I am an Indian
5.	a-ni-hne-hv	5.	he/she is moving out
6.	a-qua'-n(i)-ta	6.	you are drinking
7.	go:-l'-ga	7.	they are giving
8.	go'-li:-g'	8.	he/she is an Indian
9.	ha-li-he:-li-ga	9.	you are speaking
10.	hi-wo:-n(i)	10.	I know
11.	ge-li-a	11.	he/she has something of indefinite
12.	a-ne'-li-a	12.	I am drinking
13.	ga-da-nv?-a	13.	he/she has something (liquid)
14.	a:-da-nv?-a	14.	he/she has something (live)
15.	ha-da-nv?-a	15.	You are moving out
16.	u-we-ka-ha	16.	you are happy
17.	a-gi-ka-ha	17.	he understands
18.	tsi-yv'-wi-ya'	18.	I understand
19.	a-yv'-wi-ya'	19.	I have something (live)
20.	u-ne?-a	20.	I am moving out

EXERCISE 2:

1. I am drinking.
2. He has it.(something with weight, of indefinite shape)
3. They have it. (something long)
4. You are drinking.
5. They are giving.
6. I know.
7. He/she understands
8. I understand.(Notice one has a long first syllable, the other has a long second syllable.)
9. You are happy.
10. You are talking.
11. I think.
12. They think.
13. I am moving out.
14. He/she is moving out.
15. You are moving out.
16. He has something live.
17. I have something live.
18. I am an Indian.
19. He is an Indian.
20. He/she has something liquid.

Exercise 3: Pronounce the Cherokee correctly and translate into English:

1. ᎠᏫᎧ
2. ᏂᏬᎥᏍ
3. ᎠᎮᏬ
4. ᎬᎧ
5. ᏣᎥᎯ
6. ᎤᎵ
7. ᎠᏬᏚᎫ
8. ᏂᎷᎩ

EXERCISE 4: 1. tla, i, ga 2. gu, que 3. a, ni, hne, s, gi, lv, s, ga
4. Tsi, s, qua, a, le, a, ni, da 5. ni, hi, tso, i, i, de, tse, na

EXERCISE 3: 7. a-s-du:-di, door 8. tsi-lu-gi, I arrive 5. e-quoʼ-ni, river
6. su-li, buzzard 3. go-ge:ya, Spring 4. gv:-le, pigeon 1. go-la-nv, raven
2. tsi-s-quoʼ-ga, robin

Exercise 4: Fill in the blanks: 1. ___ ___ ___, bluejay 2. ___ ___, quail
3. ___ ___ ___ ___ ___ ___ ___ ___, they-are-nesting 4. ___ ___ ___ ___
___ ___ ___, birds and baby-birds. 5. ___ ___ ___ ___ ___ ___ ___, you
three come here.

ᏂᎦᏚᎢ ᏣᎳᎩ ᎪᏪᎸᎢ

Ni-ga-du-iꞌ Tsa-la-giꞌ Go-hwe-lv:-i

CHEROKEE LESSON FOURTEEN

Pronouns in Cherokee - Part II

a. Some useful pronouns:

na	<u>that</u>, <u>those</u>, <u>of that</u>, <u>of those</u>. Can be used of human, living or non-living things.
na-s-gi	<u>that</u>, <u>those</u>, of human, living or non-living.
na?-ni	<u>those</u>, can only be used for living things, human or non-human.
s-gi-naꞌ	<u>that same</u>, <u>this same</u> (previously mentioned) person, animal or thing.
hi-lv:-s-gi	<u>several</u>, living or non-living. ꞌLivingꞌ includes human unless otherwise specified. ꞌHumanꞌ is reserved for people.
hi-lv:-s-gi-ni	<u>several unspecified humans</u> (several somebodies)
hi?-a	<u>this</u>, <u>that</u>. Usually a thing, nearby or previously mentioned, but can also be living.
ki-lo?ꞌ-i	<u>somebody</u>
tla-ki-loꞌ-yi-(gi)	<u>nobody</u>
s-qui:-s-di	<u>many</u>, <u>much</u>, living or non-living things.
s-qui-ya	<u>very many</u>, <u>very much</u>, <u>too many</u>, <u>too much</u>, living or non-living things.

b. Importance of Cherokee bound pronouns:

In English, a pronoun is often defined as "A word that takes the place of a noun". English sentences use <u>either</u> a noun <u>or</u> a personal pronoun.

98

Examine these two sentences in English and in Cherokee:

They are speaking.	A-ni-wo:-ni-a. (They-speak)
Men are speaking.	A-ni'-s-ga-ya a-ni-wo:-ni-a.
	(Men they-speak)

In Cherokee, as you see, there is <u>both</u> a noun and a personal pronoun. ('men' and 'they', referring to the same people). These attached personal pronouns in Cherokee are called bound pronouns.

In Cherokee, bound pronouns are a necessary part of every verb.

Detached personal pronouns (a-hyv' and ni-hi'), other pronouns (na, s-gi-na', etc.), nouns and modifiers are added as desired.

Examples:
Bound pronoun only:

Ga-wo:-ni-a.	He or she is speaking.
A-ni-wo:-ni-a.	They are speaking.

Bound pronoun plus noun:

A'-s-ga-ya ga-wo:-ni-a.	(The or a) man is speaking.
	(Man he-speaks.)

Bound pronoun plus pronoun:

Ki-lo?'-i ga-wo:-ni-a.	Someone is speaking. (Someone he-speaks)

Bound pronoun plus noun plus pronoun:
Hi-lv:-s-gi a-ni-s-ga-ya a-ni-wo:-ni-a.
Several men are speaking. (Several-of-them men they-speak.)

Bound pronoun plus noun plus pronoun plus other modifiers:
Hi-lv:-s-gi a-ni-ga-lv-la-di a-ni-s-ga-ya a-ni-wo:-ni s-ge:-s-di
ga-lv'-la-di di-de'-l'-qua'-s-di ko'-sv-hi-ye-i (i)(a)-tse'
tsu-na-de'-l'-qua-s-di a-da-ne'-lv?-i.

Several prominent men are speaking about college education this
evening in the new school building.

In English, subject and predicate are separate halves of the sentence, dependent on one another. Bound pronouns make every Cherokee verb a complete sentence in itself containing both a subject and predicate in the same word.

A Cherokee verb is the independent core of a Cherokee sentence. Other modifiers cluster around this independent core.

99

PHRASES

Translation	Syllabary	Pronunciation
93.		
I am planting (burying) many seeds.	ᏍᏘᏍᏗ ᎤᎦᏔ ᏥᏫᏒᏍᎦ	S-qui:-s-di u'-g(a)-ta tsi-wi-sv:-s-ga.
94.		
I am planting (setting out) several seedlings.	ᎯᎸᏍᎩ ᏗᎦᎪᏗ ᏕᏥᎧᎲᏍᎦ	Hi-lv:-s-gi di-ga-koh'-di de-tsi-ka-hv:-s-ga.
95.		
The peach trees are growing.	ᏆᏅ ᏕᏢᎬ ᏓᏂᏛᏍᎦ	Qua-nv de:-tl'-kv da:-n'-tv-s-ga.
96.		
That peach tree is beginning to bloom.	Ꮎ ᏆᎾ ᏢᎬ ᎠᏥᎸᏍᎦ	Na qua-na tlu-kv a-tsi-lv'-s-ga.
97.		
That (same) peach tree has pink blossoms. (is pinkly blooming)	ᏍᎩᎾ ᏆᎾ ᎩᎦᎨ ᎤᏍᎪᎸᎢ ᎤᏥᎸᎠ	S-gi-na qua-na gi'-ga-ge u-s-go'-lv:-i u-tsi-lv-a.
98.		
fruit (grown ready-to eat)	ᎤᏓᏔᏅ ᎠᎩᏍᏗ	u-da-ta-nv a-gi:-s-di
fruits	ᎤᏂᏓᏔᏅ ᎠᎩᏍᏗ	u'-n'-da-ta-nv a-gi:-s-di
tree, trees	ᏢᎬ ᏖᏢᎬ	tlu'-kv, te-tlu'-kv or:
	ᎢᏢᎬ ᏕᏢᎬ	i'-tl'-kv, de:-tl'-kv
apple	ᏒᏔ	sv?-ta
berry	ᎤᏓᏔᏅᎯ	u-da-ta-nv-hi
blackberry, briar	ᎧᏄᎦᏟ	ka-nu'-ga-tli'
cherry	ᎩᏔᏯ	gi-ta'-ya
grape	ᏖᎸᎳᏗ	te-lv'-la-di
mulberry	ᎫᏩ	ku:-wa
peach	ᏆᎾ	qua:-n(∤)
pear	ᏗᎦᏛᏗ	di-ga-dv:-d(i)
plum (little peaches)	ᏆᏅᏳᏂᏍᏗ	qua-nv'-yu:-n'-s-di
raspberry	ᏒᏗᏩᎵ	sv-di'-wa-li'
strawberry	ᎠᏂ	a?-ni
99.		
blossom, flower (it opens out)	ᎠᏥᎸᏍᎩ	a-tsi-lv'-s-gi
bush	ᎤᏓᏯᏢ	u-da'-ya-tlv

99. (cont.)

dry (ripe, of a nut)	ᏊᎶᏥᎭ	u-ka-yo:-d(i)(v)(a)
pit, stone, seed, grain	ᏊᏍᏪ	u'-g(a)-ta
soft (ripe, of a fruit)	ᏊᎬᎾᎲ	u-wa'-n(a)-sv
unripe, raw	ᎠᎪᏍᎢ	a-go:-s-di
vine (twining-along)	ᏊᏛᎤᎳᏥ	u-te-lv'-la-di
vines	ᏊᏂᏛᎤᎳᏥ	u-ni-te-lv'-la-di'

CORE VOCABULARY

Most Cherokee plant and animal names do not change in the plural, just like 'sheep', 'fish' or 'deer' in English. There are exceptions.

Many Cherokee nouns, like fruit, berry, blossom, or grape & vine in this lesson, are in the form of verbs. -Ni is added to them in the plural because active verbs form their plural with -ni. (See Lesson IX)

blossom, flower (it-opens out, blooms)	a-tsi-lv'-s-gi
blossoms, flowers (they-open-out, they-bloom)	a-ni-tsi-lv'-s-gi

As a verb:
it is blooming	a-tsi-lv'-s-ga
they are blooming	a-ni-tsi-lv'-s-ga

This verb is used only for plants, not things, animals or humans. No other persons exist, just 3rd person, singular and plural.

grape, grapes (twined along)	te-lv-la-di', u-ni-te-lv'-la-di
high, prominent	ga-lv'-la-di'
school	tsu-na-de'-l(i)-qua-s-di(i)
vine, vines (twiny, twining along)	u-te-lv'-la-di', u-ni-te-lv'-la-di

Notice that the plural of 'grape' and 'vine' is the same.

101

Verbs:

eat (something)
  I eat, am eating ...   TSI-GI?-A
  you eat   HI-GI?-A
  he/she eats   A-GI?-A
  they eat   A-NI-GI?-A

grow taller
  I am growing taller   ga-tv'-s-ga
  you are growing   ha-tv'-s-ga
  he/she is growing   a-tv'-s-ga
  they are growing   da-n'-tv'-s-ga

grow fatter
  I am growing fatter   ga-l'-tso?-v'-s-ga
  you are growing fatter   ha-l'-tso-hv'-s-ga
  he/she is growing fatter   a-l'-tso-hv'-s-ga
  they are growing fatter   a-na-l'-tso-hv'-s-ga

plant (bury) seeds
  I am planting   tsi-wi-sv:-s-ga
  you are planting   hi-wi-sv'-s-ga
  he/she is planting   a-hwi-sv'-s-ga
  they are planting   a-ni-wi-sv'-s-ga

TSI-GI?-A is a classifying verb. Each classification has come to have a meaning of its own centered around 'consume', 'grasp and consume'. Examples:

TSI-GI?-A   I am eating it, I am picking up and using it up, a solid thing of indefinite shape. (most foods)

TSI-HYE?-A   I am devouring my prey, a recently killed live thing. Prey is being eaten by the animal or person who caught it. Others use 'TSI-GI?-A' of the same meat.

TSI-S-DI-GI?-A   I am eating something long, such as an ear of corn or some carrots either sliced or whole, cooked or uncooked.

TSI-NE-GI?-A   I am acquiring a liquid for immediate use, as gassing up a car, fetching water. Cannot be used instead of 'drinking'. Also, wa-ga' tsi-ne-gi-ye, I am milking a cow.

(DE)-TSI-HYA-GA I am eating small, longish tidbits. (e.g., green beans, mushrooms, raisins, grapes, not peas, kidney-shaped beans). Of an animal, GA-HYA-GA, It (just) swallowed something whole.

GV-GI-S-DI   (for-them-to-eat) watermelon.

Ꭰ a	Ꭱ e	Ꭲ i	Ꭳ o	Ꭴ u	Ꭵ v
Ꭶ ga Ꭷ ka	Ꭸ ge	Ꭹ gi	Ꭺ go	Ꭻ gu	Ꭼ gv
Ꭽ ha	Ꭾ he	Ꭿ hi	Ꮀ ho	Ꮁ hu	Ꮂ hv
Ꮃ la	Ꮄ le	Ꮅ li	Ꮆ lo	Ꮇ lu	Ꮈ lv
Ꮉ ma	Ꮊ me	Ꮋ mi	Ꮌ mo	Ꮍ mu	
Ꮎ na Ꮏ hna Ꮐ nah	Ꮑ ne	Ꮒ ni	Ꮓ no	Ꮔ nu	Ꮕ nv
Ꮖ qua	Ꮗ que	Ꮘ qui	Ꮙ quo	Ꮚ quu	Ꮛ quv
Ꮜ sa Ꮝ s	Ꮞ se	Ꮟ si	Ꮠ so	Ꮡ su	Ꮢ sv
Ꮣ da Ꮤ ta	Ꮥ de Ꮦ te	Ꮧ di Ꮨ ti	Ꮩ do	Ꮪ du	Ꮫ dv
Ꮬ dla Ꮭ tla	Ꮮ tle	Ꮯ tli	Ꮰ tlo	Ꮱ tlu	Ꮲ tlv
Ꮳ tsa	Ꮴ tse	Ꮵ tsi	Ꮶ tso	Ꮷ tsu	Ꮸ tsv
Ꮹ wa	Ꮺ we	Ꮻ wi	Ꮼ wo	Ꮽ wu	Ꮾ wv

Words using twelve rows of the syllabary:

u-wa'n'-ga-tlv	___________	branch ᎤᏩᎦᏢ
u-wa'-n'-sv	___________	soft, ripe ᎤᏩᏒ
ga-lo-we:-di	___________	redbud
da-wa-tsi:-la	___________	elm
tlv?-hwa'-l'-ga	___________	maple
wa:-ne?-i	___________	hickory tree

Exercise 1: Match up Columns A and B: Check by consulting the lesson.

A.
1. Qua-nv de:-tl'-kv da:-n'-tv'-s-ga.
2. Qua-na tlu-kv a-tsi-lv'-s-ga.
3. a?-ni
4. di-ga-dv:-di
5. ku:-wa
6. Qua-na gi'-ga-ge u-s-go'-lv-i
   u-tsi-lv-a.
7. u'-g'-ta
8. a-tsi-lv'-s-gi
9. a-tsi-lv'-s-ga
10. u-da-ta-nv a-gi:-s-di
11. tlu-kv, i'-tl'-kv
12. Di-ga-koh'-di de-tsi-ka-hv:-s-ga.
13. sv-di-wa-li
14. u-da-ya-tlv
15. u-wa'-n'-sv
16. sv?-ta
17. gi?-ta-ya
18. u-da-ta-nv-hi
19. ki-lo?'-i
20. tla-ki-lo'-yi-gi

B.
1. fruit
2. tree, 2 ways
3. The peach trees are growing.
4. mulberry or mulberries
5. strawberry or strawberries
6. The peach tree is blooming.
7. pear or pears
8. The peach tree has pink blossoms.
9. apple or apples
10. cherry or cherries
11. seed or seeds
12. I am setting out seedlings.
13. blossom, flower
14. it is blooming
15. berry
16. raspberry or raspberries
17. bush
18. ripe (fruit), soft
19. nobody
20. somebody

Exercise 2: Translate:

1. I am eating a cookie.
2. They are eating too many strawberries. (strawberry)
3. Nobody wants those.
4. The blossoms of that tree (are) red.
5. Several vines are in bloom over here. (here)
6. Somebody is going home.
7. Several people (I don't know just who) are buying fruit today.
8. How much are the plums and raspberries?
9. Why are you happy today?
10. Do you want this little seedling?

EXERCISE 2:
1. U-ga-na-s-da tsi-gi?-a.
2. S-qui-ya a?-ni' a-ni-gi?-a.
3. Tla-ki-lo'-yi-du-na-du'-li.
4. Na tlu-kv a-tsi-lv'-s-gi a-gi'-ga-ge.
5. Hi-lv-s-gi u-ni-te-lv'-la-di a-hni a-ni-tsi-lv'-s-ga.
6. Ki-lo?'-i u-nv'-sv-i e:-ga.
7. Hi-lv'-s-gi-ni u'-n'-da-ta-nv ko-hi u-ni-hwa'-s-ga a-gi:-s-di.
8. Qua-nv'-yu:-n'-s-di a-le sv-di'-wa-li ha-la' tsu-gv-wa-l'-di?
9. Do'-hv ko:-hi ha-li-he'-li-gi?
10. Hi?-a-ke u'-s-di di-ga'-koh-di tsa-du'-li-a-s-k?

Exercise 3:
Write the following words in Cherokee and translate into English.

A.
1. Tsi'-s-qua a-ni-no-hi-li-ga.
2. tlu-tlu
3. ko:-ga
4. u-gu'-gu
5. tla-i-ga
6. gu'-que
7. ka-wo:-n
8. sa:-sa
9. s-qua-le'-wa-li'
10. to-wo'-d'

B.
1. U-n'-da-ta-nv-hi da:-n'-tv'-s-ga.
2. ka-nu'-ga-tli
3. ku:-wa
4. sv-di'-wa-li'
5. a?-ni
6. U'-n'-da-ta-nv a-gi:-s-di da:-n'-tv'-s-ga.
7. gi-ta'-ya
8. di-ga-dv:-di
9. qua:-na
10. te-lv'-la-di

C.
1. Hi-lv'-s-gi-ni te-tlu'-kv
2. wa:-ne?-i
3. ga-lo-we:-di
4. tlv-hwa'-l'-ga
5. sv?-ta
6. da-wa-tsi:-la
7. ku:-wa
8. a-tsi'-n(a)

Exercise 4:
Translate directly from English into Cherokee writing.

1. Right now.
2. Soon, later on.
3. What time is it?
4. Twenty, forty, sixty, eighty (short)
5. six, sixteen, sixty, six hundred
6. Bob is out hunting.
7. Many prominent men are Indians.
8. The sky is blue today.
9. That mountain is high.
10. What did you say?

EXERCISE 3:

A.
1. The birds are flying.
2. martin
3. crow
4. owl
5. bluejay
6. quail
7. duck
8. goose
9. nightingale
10. hawk

B.
1. Berries grow
2. blackberry(ies)
3. mulberry(ies)
4. raspberry(ies)
5. strawberry(ies)
6. Fruits grow
7. cherry(ies)
8. pear(s)
9. peach(es)
10. one grape

C.
1. several trees
2. hickory tree
3. redbud
4. maple
5. apple
6. elm
7. mulberry
8. cedar

EXERCISE 4:

1. ᏛᏬ

2. ᏈᏈᏴ

3. ᏝᎳ ᎠᏟᏴᏓ

4. ᏔᎮᏬᎠ ᏟᏴᏬᎠ ᏰᏝᏬᎠ ᏝᎳᏬᎠ

5. ᏰᏝᏗ ᎳᏓᏍᏔ ᏰᏝᏬᎠᏅ ᏰᏝᏬᏓᏬᏛ

6. ᏟᏬ ᏍᏃᏅᏛᎷ

7. ᏬᏈᏬᏓ ᎠᎯᏕᏔᎳᏛ ᎠᎯᏬᏕᏬ ᎠᎯᏴᎾᏬ

8. ᎥᏊ ᎤᎠᎯᏛ ᏍᎾᎬᏅ ᎠᏅ

9. Ꮎ ᏰᏝᏃ ᏕᏔᎳᏛ

10. ᏕᎥ ᏛᎠᏙ

ᏍᎩᎦᏚᎢ ᏣᎳᎩ ᎣᏪᎸᎢ

S-gi-ga-du-i Tsa-la-gi' Go-hwe-lv:?-i

CHEROKEE LESSON FIFTEEN

100.
Today is Sunday.
ᎪᎯ ᎤᎾᏙᏓᏆᏍᎬᎢ
Ko-hi' (u-na)-do'-da-quas-gv?-(i).

101.
Monday
ᎤᎾᏙᏓᏉᎲᎢ
(u-na)-do'-da-quo'-hnv?-(i)

Tuesday (2nd day)
ᏔᎵᏁ ᎢᎦ
ta-li:-ne *i-ga'

Wednesday (3rd day)
ᏦᎢᏁ ᎢᎦ
tso?-i-ne *i-ga'

Thursday (4th day)
ᎤᏴᎩᏁ ᎢᎦ
nv?-gi-ne *i-ga'

Friday (for-them-to-wash)
ᏧᏅᎩᎶᏍᏗ
tsu'-n'gi-lo:-s-di

Saturday (they-go-out)
ᎤᎾᏙᏓᏫᏕᎾ
(u-na) do-da-wi-de:-na

Sunday
ᎤᎾᏙᏓᏆᏍᎬᎢ
(u-na)-do-da-qua'-s-gv?-(i)

102.
What day of the week is it today?
ᎦᏙ ᎤᏍᏗ ᎢᎦ ᎠᏟᎩᎵ
(Ga)-do?' u'-s-di *i:-ga' a-tli:-gi-li'?

103.
What date is it today?
ᎦᏙ ᎤᏍᏗ ᎠᏎᏍᏗ ᎪᎯ
(Ga)-do?' u'-s-di a-se-s-di ko:-hi?

104.
I am glad you all came.
ᎦᎵᎡᎵᎩ ᏂᎦᏓ ᏥᏥᎷᎩ
Ga-li?-e'-li-gi ni-ga-da' tsi-tsi-lu-gi'.

105.
Won't you sit down?
(anywhere you choose)
To one person: (Bend yourself on something)
ᎭᎵᏍᏚᏢᎦ
Ha'-l(i)-s-du-tlv'-ga.

To several: (Let's all be sitting around)
ᏗᏓᏅᏂᏓ
I-da-nv'-ni-da.

106.
Everybody be seated. (in a certain place, such as at the dinner table)
ᏂᎦᏓ ᎢᏣᏅᏂᏓ
Ni-ga'-d(a) i-tsa-nv'-ni-da'.

107

107.

Let's lay the table. (Dishes let-us-place-upon-it)	ᎫᏕᏟᎥ ᏗᏗᏟᎶᏍ	Di-te'-li-do di-di-tla-hv'-ga.

108.

knife (to-cut-with)	ᎠᏴᎵᏬᏗ	a-ye'-l(i)-s-di
knives	ᏗᏴᎵᏬᏗ	

fork (sticks-in)	ᎥᏴ	yv'-gi
forks	ᏗᏴᏴ	di-yv'-gi

spoon (to-sip-from)	ᎠᏗᏙᏗ	a-di-toh'-di
spoons	ᏗᏗᏙᏗ	di-di-toh'-di

plate	ᎤᎵᏙ	te'-li-do
plates	ᏗᎤᎵᏙ	di-te'-li-do

cup	ᎠᎫᎩᏬᏗ	a-ku-gi'-s-di
cups	ᏗᎫᎩᏬᏗ	di-ku-gi'-s-di

glass	ᎤᎸᏌᏗ	u-lv'-sa-di
glasses	ᏧᎸᏌᏗ	tsu-lv'-sa-di

pitcher, soup or serving bowl (anything into which the contents are poured) It can also be a gas tank, cattle trough, etc. It means 'to-be-poured-into', from 'a-tli'-s-di', to pour.

	ᎠᏟᏍᏙᏗ ᏗᏟᏍᏙᏗ	a-tli-s-toh'-di di-tli-s-toh'-di

tablecloth	ᎦᏍᎩᎸ ᎠᏴᏍᏒᏗ	ga-s-ki'-lv a-ye'-s-tv'-di
tablecloths	ᏕᎦᏍᎩᎸ ᏗᏴᏍᏒᏗ	de-ga-s-ki'-lv di-ye'-s-tv'-di

ice water (no plural) (water-made-of-ice)	ᎠᎹ ᎤᏁᏍᏔᎵ ᎦᏟᏅᏴᎢ	*a-m(a') u-ne:-s-ta-li ga-tlv-nv?-i

pepper & salt (no pl.)	ᏗᏆᏲᏗ ᎠᎴ ᎠᎹ	di-qua-yo'-d(i) a-le *a:-m(a')

table or chair, also sofa, bench, but sofa and bench are oftener 'ga-nv'-hi-da' ga'-s-ki-lo' (long furniture). 'Long furniture' does not include a bed, however, which is 'ga-ni'-tlv, de-ga-ni-tlv' (to be reclined on).

table, chair	ᎦᏍᎩᎶ	ga'-s-ki-lo'
tables, chairs	ᏗᎦᏍᎩᎶ	di-ga'-s-ki-lo'

Examine the singular and plural nouns above. Notice the plural of each one is formed by adding di- or de-.

Di- is an important Cherokee prefix used, like -ni-, to change words
from singular to plural. (See Lesson IX for explanation of -ni)

In general, words forming plurals with -ni- are thought of as potent,
capable of independent movement.

Words forming their plurals with di- are thought of as passive,
incapable of independent movement.

If a non-living (inanimate) noun begins with a-, the plural is formed
by taking off the a- and substituting di-:

Example: a-ye'-l'-s-di   knife
             di-ye'-l'-s-di   knives

If the non-living noun begins with a consonant, di- is added before the
whole word:

Example: yv'-gi   fork
             di-yv'-gi   forks

Neighboring sounds often change di- to d-, de-, ti-, or te-. Before
e- or u-, di- is usually ts- (di- plus e- or u- equals ts-).

Examples: o:-da-lv, do:-da-lv   mountain, mountains
             e-quo'-ni, tse-quo-ni   river, rivers
             u-lv'-sa-di, tsu-lv'-sa-di   glass, glasses

Some natural objects take a non-living passive plural on the noun (di-),
but living, active plural (-ni-), on the adjectives. (Plurals underlined)

Example: sa-ko'-ni-ge u-gi-tv-tli   a blue feather
             a-ni-sa-ko'-ni-ge tsu-gi-tv-tli blue feathers

             u-ne:-g' u-lo'-gi-l(a)(i)   a white cloud
             u-ni-ne:-ga tsu-lo'-gi-l(a)(i) white clouds

             u'-ta-na tlu'-kv   a big tree
             tsu'-n'-ta-na te-tlu-kv   big trees

Remember that all plants take living plural adjectives (-ni-), though
they may form the plural of the noun in several ways.

109

Different ways of forming the <u>plural</u> of <u>plant nouns</u>:

1. -ni- plural on the noun because an active verb-form is used as the plant name:

<table>
<tr><td>a red flower</td><td>a-gi'-ga-ge a-tsi-lv'-s-gi (it-opens-out, blooms, it-is-a-bloomer)</td></tr>
<tr><td>red flowers</td><td>a-<u>ni</u>-gi'-ga-ge a-<u>ni</u>-tsi-lv'-s-gi</td></tr>
</table>

2. no plural on the noun:

<table>
<tr><td>a red cherry</td><td>a-gi'-ga-ge gi-ta'-ya</td></tr>
<tr><td>red cherries</td><td>a-<u>ni</u>-gi'-ga-ge gi-ta'-ya</td></tr>
</table>

3. di- plural on the noun because a passive verb-form is used as the plant name:

<table>
<tr><td>a red tree</td><td>a-gi'-ga-ge tlu'-kv ((it-has-been-)pushed-out-of-it-upward-but-not-all-the-way-out-on-it (on the earth))</td></tr>
<tr><td>red trees</td><td>a-<u>ni</u>-gi'-ga-ge <u>te</u>-tlu'-kv</td></tr>
</table>

Notice the identical -ni- living plural on all <u>adjectives</u> above.

Learn the following table. You will be using it constantly.

-Ni-	Di-
-Ni- is used to form the plurals of:	Di- is used form the plurals of:
1. Human nouns	1. Non-living (inanimate) nouns
2. Adjectives dealing with living (animate) nouns	2. Adjectives dealing with non-living (inanimate) nouns
3. Active verbs in 3rd person (he/she/it) to show the verb has a <u>plural subject</u>. In Cherokee, the <u>subject</u> (head-word) of an active verb is always living.	3. Di- is added onto all persons (1st I, 2nd you, 3rd he/she/it etc. of active verbs if the verb has a <u>plural direct object</u>. The plural direct object may be living or non-living.

See next page for examples of Nos. 1, 2 and 3 in the -ni- and di-columns above.

Sentences that illustrate the use of -ni- and di- plurals -

Notice that the sentences below beginning with 'They' have <u>both</u> a -ni-
plural and a di-plural on the verb. The di- shows that there is a <u>plural</u>
<u>direct object</u> non-living (plates) or living (pears). The -Ni- shows that
there is <u>plural subject</u> (must be living). Plural markers are underlined.
Remember 'pear(s)' has no plural on the noun. (See Lesson XIV)

Examples of di- plurals:

I just put the best plates on.　　　　Tso:-s-da <u>di</u>-te'-li-do <u>de</u>-tsi-tla-
　　　　　　　　　　　　　　　　　　　　hv'-ga.

You just put the best plates on.　　　Tso:-s-da <u>di</u>-te'-li-do <u>de</u>-hi-tla-
　　　　　　　　　　　　　　　　　　　　hv'-ga.

He/she just put the best plates on.　Tso:-s-da <u>di</u>-te'-li-do <u>da</u>'-tla-hv'-
　　　　　　　　　　　　　　　　　　　　ga.

They just put the best plates on.　　Tso:-s-da <u>di</u>-te'-li-do <u>da</u>-<u>ni</u>-tla-hv'-
　　　　　　　　　　　　　　　　　　　　ga.

Example of Nos. 2 and 3 in the -ni- column and No. 3 in the di- column:

They are eating yellow pears.　　　　A-<u>ni</u>-da-hlo'-<u>ni</u>-ge di-ga-dv'-di
　　　　　　　　　　　　　　　　　　　　<u>da</u>-<u>ni</u>'-gi?-(4)

As you have seen, in Cherokee there are differences in the treatment of
words that refer to something as human, living or non-living. These
differences show up <u>only</u> when the word, which can be either a noun,
adjective or verb, is <u>plural</u>.

Examples:

　　A. Singular

The brown baby sees a big eagle.　　　U-wo'-di-ge u:-s-di u-ta-na wo-ha'-
　　　　　　　　　　　　　　　　　　　　li a-go:-ti?-a.

The big eagle sees a brown squirrel.　U-ta-na' wo-ha'-li a-go:-ti?-a
　　　　　　　　　　　　　　　　　　　　u-wo'-di-ge sa-lo'-li.

The black dog sees a brown shoe.　　　A-gv'-hni-ge gi:-tli u-wo'-di-ge
　　　　　　　　　　　　　　　　　　　　a-la-su'-lo a-go:-ti?-a.

Notice that the adjectives, verb and nouns above do not change, whether
they refer to something human, living or non-living.

111

Now examine the sentences below, noticing how the changes agree with the -ni- and di- table on page 111. Changes are underlined.

Examples:

B. Plural subjects and plural objects:

The brown babies see (some) big eagles.
U-ni-wo'-di-ge tsu:-n'-s-di da-ni-go:-ti?-a
tsu'-n'-ta-na' wo-ha'-li.

The big eagles see (some) brown squirrels.
Tsu-n'-ta-na wo-ha'-li da-ni-go:-ti?-a
u-ni-wo'-di-ge sa-lo'-li.

The black dogs see (some) brown shoes.
A-ni-gv'-hni-ge ge'-tli da-ni-go:-ti?-a tsu-wo'-di-ge
di-la-su'-lo.

C. Single subject, plural object:

The brown baby sees some big eagles.
U-wo'-di-ge u'-s-di tsu'-n'-ta-na wo-ha'-li
da-go:-ti?-a.

D. Plural subjects, single object:

The brown babies see a big eagle.
U-ni-wo'-di-ge tsu'-n'-s-di u'-ta-na wo-ha'-li
a-ni-go:-ti?-a

Examine sentences A.B.C. and D. till you can tell exactly why each underlined change took place.

You have had many examples of -ni- and di- plurals in previous lessons. Now you can analyze Cherokee plurals of nouns and adjectives, although the verbs have not been fully discussed yet.

P.N. 43 is a good example of the main topic of this lesson:

I have some red and green lights.   Di-gi'-ga-ge a-le di-tse-yu:-s-d(i)
da:-gi-(ha) di-tsv'-s-di.
(Plural-non-living-red and plural-non-living-green them-I-of-indefinite-shape-have non-living-to-be-turned-on-with)

Notice the 'indefinite-shape' classifier because 'have' is a classifying verb. This would still be present if 'light(bulb)' were singular.

112

If P.N. 43 were to be changed to refer to something live:

I have (some) red and (some) green birds.

A-<u>ni</u>-gi'-ga-ge a-le a-ni-tse-yu:-s-di <u>da</u>:-gi-ka'-ha tsi'-s-qua.

(Plural-living-red and plural-living-green them-I-living-have bird(s))

Notice the -ka-, live classifier, which would still be present if 'bird' were singular because 'have' is a classifying verb. Look at Lessons 5 & 8 to review discussions of the two classifying verbs you have had.

CORE VOCABULARY

all ni-ga'-d(a)

dog(s) gi:-tli
(s) on the end of a noun means the noun does not change in the plural

feather, feathers u-gi-tv-tli, tsu-gi-tv-tli
1-a (living adjective)

fork, awl, needle, or yv'-gi, di-yv'-gi
pitchfork (sticks-in)

glad, pleased, P.N. 105 ga-li?-e'-li-g<u>i</u>'

Notice the -i ending on 'Ga-li?-e'-li-gi'' (instead of -a, present time). This means it has <u>just</u> happened. See tsi-lu-gi' in Lesson 13. Putting -i on the end of this verb implies that it is the arrival of the guests that has <u>made</u> the host or hostess glad, i.e., 'I have just been gladdened by your recent arrival'.

squirrel(s) sa-lo:-l(i)(a)

Verbs:

put or set dishes on a <u>raised surface</u>, such as any piece of furniture, the
                                    drainboard or a shelf

I just put dishes on it   di-te'-li-do de-tsi-tla-hv'-
                                           ga

you just put dishes on it   di-te'-li-do de-hi-tla-hv'-ga
he/she just put dishes on   di-te'-li-do da'-tla-hv'-ga
    it
they just put dishes on it   di-te'-li-do da-ni-tla-hv'-ga

see some definite thing. (Not 'understand')

I see   tsi-go:-ti?-(ł)
you see   hi-go:-ti?-(ł)
he/she sees   a-go:-ti?-(ł)
they see   a-ni-go:-ti?-(ł)

set the table (for a meal). Literally, 'I am putting dishes on a raised
                                    surface.'

I am putting dishes   di-te'-li-do de-tsi-tla-hv'-
    on it   s-ga
you are putting dishes   di-te'-li-do de-hi-tla-hv'-s-
    on it   ga
they are putting dishes   di-te'-li-do da-ni-tla-hv'-s-
    on it   ga

sit down
    I just sat down   ga-li-s-du-tlv'-ga
    you just sat down   ha'-l'-s-du-tlv'-ga
    he/she just sat down   a'-l'-s-du-tlv-ga
    they just sat down   a-na'-l'-s-du-tlv'-ga <u>or</u>
                                           a-na-nv'-ni-da'

    See P.N. 105 and notice that 'Ha'-l'-s-du-tlv'-ga' means <u>both</u> 'You just
sat down' and 'Please won't you sit down'.

    'Al'- in the verb for 'sit down' means 'self'.

Other examples:

    <u>ga'-l'</u>-s-ta-yv-hv'-s-ga   I am having a meal (literally, feeding-myself)
    <u>ga-li</u>?-e'-li-ga   I am happy (literally, gladdening myself)

114

Cherokee Alphabet.

D a	**R** e	**T** i	**Ꮹ** o	**Ꝍ** u	**i** v
Ꮝ ga **Ꝍ** ka	**Ᏺ** ge	**Ᏺ** gi	**A** go	**J** gu	**E** gv
Ꮤ ha	**Ꝑ** he	**Ᏸ** hi	**F** ho	**Ᏻ** hu	**Ꝍ** hv
W la	**Ꮄ** le	**Ꮅ** li	**Ꮐ** lo	**M** lu	**Ꮕ** lv
Ꮉ ma	**Ꮋ** me	**H** mi	**Ꮆ** mo	**Ᏻ** mu	
Ꮎ na **Ꮏ** hna **G** nah	**Ʌ** ne	**ħ** ni	**Z** no	**Ꮕ** nu	**Ꮕ** nv
Ꮖ qua	**ꮤ** que	**Ꮚ** qui	**Ꮴ** quo	**Ꮗ** quu	**Ꮄ** quv
Ꮕ sa **Ꮝ** s	**4** se	**Ᏼ** si	**Ꝑ** so	**Ꮗ** su	**Ꭱ** sv
Ꮃ da **W** ta	**Ꮝ** de **Ꮃ** te	**Ꮧ** di **Ꮨ** ti	**V** do	**Ꮥ** du	**Ꮴ** dv
Ꮪ dla **Ꮭ** tla	**L** tle	**C** tli	**Ꮧ** tlo	**Ꮵ** tlu	**P** tlv
Ꮳ tsa	**Ꮴ** tse	**Ꭿ** tsi	**K** tso	**Ꮧ** tsu	**Ꮳ** tsv
Ꮹ wa	**Ꮿ** we	**Ꮻ** wi	**Ꮼ** wo	**Ꮽ** wu	**Ꮾ** wv
Ꮿ ya	**Ᏸ** ye	**Ꮵ** yi	** Ꮁ** yo	**Ꮎ** yu	**B** yv

Sounds Represented by Vowels

a, as _a_ in _father_, or short as _a_ in _rival_ ‖ o, as _o_ in _note_, approaching _aw_ in _law_

e, as _a_ in _hate_, or short as _e_ in _met_ ‖ u, as _oo_ in _fool_, or short as _u_ in _pull_

i, as _i_ in _pique_, or short as _i_ in _pit_ ‖ v, as _u_ in _but_, nasalized

Consonant Sounds

_g_ nearly as in English, but approaching to _k_.   _d_ nearly as in English but approaching
to _t_.   _h k l m n q s t w y_ as in English. Syllables beginning with _g_ except **Ꮝ** (ga)
have sometimes the power of _k_. **A** (go), **Ꮪ** (du), **Ꝍ** (dv) are sometimes sounded _to, tu,
tv_ and syllables written with tl except **Ꮭ** (tla) sometimes vary to dl .

-Tla- in P.N. 105 and 106 means 'on a raised level' on a raised place, such as a platform, furniture, etc.

Examples:

di-<u>tla</u>-no-he?-di?i	telephone (words placed on the wind, see Lesson 13)
de-tsi-<u>tla</u>-hv'-s-ga	I am putting them on a raised place
ga'-l'-s-du-tlv'-ga	I just bent myself on a raised place

It is the custom in Cherokee to use two different verbs when inviting guests to sit down -- one verb for a single guest, and another verb for several. (P.N. 105) A-na-nv-ni-da' (They are sitting around) also means 'They are loafing'.

sit

I am sitting	a-quo'-tla
you are sitting	tso'-tla
he/she is sitting	u-wo'-tla
they are sitting	a-ni:-na

O-tsi:-na (We are sitting) also means 'We are staying home', or 'We are at home'.

Syllabary Test

You now know the whole Cherokee syllabary and can read any Cherokee material out loud so that a Cherokee speaker will understand you. You won't necessarily be able to understand all you are reading.

Sound out the Cherokee writing below, write out each syllable in English letters, and turn to the next page for the answers. For a translation, see Luke 24:1-6.

Tsi-sa' Du-le-hi'-sa-nv (Jesus' Resurrection, the commonest Cherokee term for Easter)

ᎠᏯᏙᎸᎢ 24

1 ᎢᎬᏱᏱᏃ ᎢᎦ ᏑᎾᏙᏓᏆᏍᏗ ᎨᏒ
ᎩᎳ ᎢᎦ ᏥᏂᎦᎵᏍᏗᏍᎪᎢ, ᎤᏂᎷᏤ Ꭰ-
ᏤᎵᏍᏛᎢ, ᏚᏂᏲᎴ ᏗᎦᏩᏒᎩ ᎾᏍᎩ ᏧᎾ-
ᏓᏁᏔᏅᎯ, ᎠᎴ ᎩᎶ ᎢᏳᎾᏍᏗ ᎠᏁᎮᎢ.
2 ᎤᏂᏩᏛᎮᏃ ᏅᏯ ᎢᏴᏛ ᏫᎦᏌᏆᎴ-
ᎸᏍᏔᏅᎯ ᎨᏎ ᎠᏤᎵᏍᏛᎢ.
3 ᎤᏂᏴᎸᏃ ᎥᏝ ᏳᏂᎾᏩᏛᎮ ᎠᏰᎸ
ᎤᎬᏫᏳᎯ ᏥᏌ.
4 ᎯᎠᏃ ᏄᎵᏍᏔᏁᎢ ᎾᏍᎩ ᎤᏣᏘ
ᎤᎾᏕᏯᏔᏁᎮ ᎾᏍᎩ ᏅᏗᎦᎵᏍᏙᏗ-
ᏍᎨᎢ, ᎬᏂᏳᏉ ᎠᏂᏔᎵ ᎠᏂᏍᎦᏯ ᎾᎥ
ᏚᎾᎴᏂᎴ ᏗᎬᏩᏔᎷᎩᏍᎩ ᏧᎾᏄᏩᎢ;
5 ᎠᏂᏍᎦᎢᎮᏃ ᎠᎴ ᎡᎳᏗ ᏂᏚᏅᏁ
ᏚᎾᎧᏛᎢ, ᎾᏍᎩ ᎯᎠ ᏂᎬᏩᏂᏪᏎᎴᎢ,
ᎦᏙᏃ ᎬᏃᏛ ᎢᏒᏥᏲᎰ ᏧᏂᏲᎱᏒᎯ ᏄᎾ-
ᏛᏅᎢ?
6 ᎥᏝ ᎠᏂ ᏱᎦᎾ, ᏚᎴᏅᏰᏃ; ᎢᏳᏅᏓᏓ
ᏂᏥᏪᏎᎸᎢ ᎠᏏᏉ ᎨᎵᎵ ᎢᏤᏙᎲᎩ,

Translate the following sentences from the first fifteen lessons.

1.(L.7) ᎠᎩᏴᏯ
2.(L.7) ᎤᎦᏃᏩ ᎨᎢ
3.(L.6) Ꮩ ᎤᏍᏗ
4.(L.6) ᏗᏗᏰᎵᎯ
5.(L.3) ᏗᏗᏃᎩ
6.(L.6) ᎤᏍᎦᏃᎵ ᎯᏬᏂᎯ
7.(L.6) ᎭᏢ ᎪᏪᎵ ᏗᏣᏁᏍᏗ
8.(L.4) ᏗᏎᏍᏗ ᏂᏗᏗᏩ
9.(L.5) ᎬᎾ ᎯᎥᏏ
10.(L.5) ᎤᏓᏢᏓ ᎦᎯᏁᎥᏏ
11.(L.5) ᏄᎾ ᎠᏂᏅᎯᏓ ᎦᏍᎬᏏ
12.(L.1) ᏙᎾᏓᎪᎲᎢ
13.(L.10) ᎭᏢ ᎪᏪᎸᎢ
14.(L.11) ᎠᏴᎾᏍᏛ
15.(L.8) ᎭᏔ ᏙᏓᏳᏩᏏ ᏗᏓᏁᏍᏗ
16.(L.8) ᎤᏪᏫᎭ ᎤᎾᎠ ᎤᎭ ᎤᏁᎭ
17.(L.9) ᎠᏅᎼ ᏫᏔ
18.(L.9) ᎤᏃᎸᏔᏅ ᏫᎦᎵ ᏫᏬᏂ
19.(L.13) ᎫᏇ ᎪᎳᏅ ᏓᎳᎳ ᏬᏍ
20.(L.14) ᎠᏖᎵᏙ ᏗᎫᎩᏍᏗ ᏧᎸᏌᏗ ᎠᏰᎵᏍᏗ

REVIEW EXERCISES

Exercise 1:   Match the sentences in Columns A and B with one another.
Exercise 2:   Without consulting a syllabary, write as many of these
sentences as you can in Cherokee.
Exercise 3:   Consulting a syllabary, complete the sentences below in Cherokee.

A.
 1. Di-se-s-di ni-di-di'-wa.
 2. Ga-yo'-tli tsi-wo:-ni Tsa-la-gi'.
 3. Ga-do' u-s-di' a-yv'-wi-ya
 4. Yu-ne'-ga-ke hi-wo:-ni-a?
 5. Ha-la' tsu-gv-hwa-hl'-di?
 6. Do-na-da-go'-hv-i.
 7. Hi-yv'-wi-ya-s-go-hv?
 8. Ha-l'-s-du-tlv'-ga.
 9. Ha-la' i-ga?-i tsa-du:-li-a?
10. Ha:-tlv hi-ne:-la?

B.
 1. How much does it cost?
 2. Let's say the numbers.
 3. Goodbye (speaking to one person)
 4. Are you an Indian?
 5. I speak a little Cherokee.
 6. How many do you want?
 7. Do you speak English?
 8. What tribe of Indian is he of?
 9. Where do you live?
10. Won't you sit down?

Exercise 3:   Translate these sentences from several lessons orally and
change them into questions in Cherokee, writing your answers. Look up the
answers in Lesson XI.

 1. Do'-yu u-wo'-du sv-hi:-ye.
 2. A:-ga:-s-ka a-le u-hyv:-dla ko:-hi.
 3. U:-lo'-gi-li' ko-hi' sv-na:-le?-i.
 4. O:-s-da-dv Tsa-la-gi' ga-wo:-ni.
 5. U-ni-wo'-di-ge tsu'-n'-s-di u'-ta-na wo-ha'-li da-ni-go:-ti?-(a)
 6. Na qua-na tlu-kv a-tsi-lv'-s-ga.
 7. Tsi'-s-qua a-ni-hne:-s-gi-lv-s-ga.
 8. Tsi'-s-qua u-ga'-no-wv na:-n'-dv:-n'-ti.

Exercise 4:   Count from 10 to 20 in Cherokee.
Exercise 5:   Name five birds correctly and write their names in Cherokee.
Exercise 6:   Name five fruits or plant parts correctly and write their names
in Cherokee.
Exercise 7:   Translate the following Cherokee verbs into English. Answers
are on the next page.

 1. ge'-li-a
 2. a-ni-yv'-wi-ya
 3. ga-da-nv?-a
 4. a-da-nv?-a
 5. ga-dv-ne-ʌ
 6. ha-dv-ne-ʌ
 7. a-tsi-lv'-s-ga
 8. tsi-wi-sv'-s-ga

 9. tsi-gi?-ʌ
10. a-ni-gi?-a
11. a-ne:-ga
12. i-da-nv'-ni-da
13. ga-lu-gi
14. a-tv-gi
15. hni-we?-a
17. ni-tsi-we?-a

118

EXERCISE 7:
1. I think, am of the opinion
2. they are Indian
3. I am moving out, migrating
4. he/she is moving out, migrating
5. I am doing (something)
6. you are doing (something)
7. it is blooming
8. I am planting
9. I am eating (something)
10. they are eating (something)
11. they are going
12. let's all be sitting around (Won't you (all) sit down?)
13. he/she just arrived
14. he/she hears
15. you say it
16. I say it

Exercise 8: Translate the following Cherokee phrases and change them from singular to plural. Explain why you chose each plural form. Answers are on the next page.

1. qua-na tlu-kv
2. a-gv'-hni-ge ge:-tli
3. a-gi'-ga-ge u-da'-ta-nv-hi
4. da-hlo'-ni-ge di-ga-dv'-di
5. u-wo'-di-ge ga'-s-ki-lo'
6. sa-ko'-ni-ge te'-li-do
7. u-wo'-du u'-s-di
8. u'-ta-na wo-ha'-li
9. u-wa'-n'-sv a?-ni ('u-wa'-n'-sv' forms the plural like 'u-wo'-du')
10. o:-s-da u-lv'-sa-di

Tsi-sa' Du-le-hi'-sa-nv A-ya-do-lv-i 24 Asterisks mark end of Cherokee lines.
1. I-gv-yi-yi-no i-ga su-na-do-da-qua-s-di ge-sv* gi-la i-ga tsi-ni-ga-li-s-di-s-go-i, u-ni-lu-tse a-*tse-li-s-dv-i, du-ni-yo-le di-ga-wa-sv-gi na-s-gi tsu-na-*da-ne-la-nv-hi, a-le gi-lo i-yu-na-s-di a-ne-he-i.
2. U-ni-wa-dv-he-no nv-ya i-yv-dv wi-ga-sa-qua-le-*lv-s-ta-nv-hi ge-se a-tse-li-s-dv-i.
3. U-ni-yv-lv-no v-tla yu-ni-na-wa-dv-he a-ye-lv U-gv-wi-yu-hi Tsi-sa.
4. Hi-a-no nu-li-s-ta-ne-i na-s-gi u-tsa-ti* u-na-de-ya-ta-ne-he na-s-gi nv-di-ga-li-s-do-di-* s-ge-i, gv-ni-yu-quo a-ni-ta-li a-ni-s-ga-ya na-v du-na-le-ni-le di-gv-wa-ta-lu-gi-s-gi tsu-na-nu-wa-i;
5. A-ni-s-ga-i-he-no a-le e-la-di ni-du-nv-ne* du-na-wo-dv-i, na-s-gi hi-a ni-gv-wa-ni-we-se-le-i,* Ga-do-no gvno-dv i-e-tsi-yo-ha tsu-ni-yo-hu-sv-hi nu-na-*dv-nv-i?
6. V-tla a-ni yi-ga-na, du-le-nv-ye-no; I-tsa-nv-da-da ni-tsi-we-se-lv-i a-si-quo Ge-li-li tse-do hv-gi,

119

EXERCISE 8:

1. peach tree; qua-na te-tlu-kv, peach trees. Qua-na has no change in the plural. Te- is a form of di-, plural direct object of a verb. Tlu-kv is a passive participle, meaning approximately 'Thrust out upward'. formed from a verb.

2. black dog; a-ni-gv-ni-ge ge:-tli, black dogs. A-ni-gv-ni-ge is a living plural adjective (adds -ni- right after the first vowel) because it refers to 'dog', a living being.

3. red berry; a-ni-gi-ga-ge u-n'-da-ta-nv-hi, red berries. A-ni-gi-ga-ge is a living plural adjective (adds -ni- right after initial vowel) because it refers to 'berries'. In Cherokee, living plants take living adjectives. U-n(i)-da-ta-nv-hi takes a -ni- plural because the word 'berry' in Cherokee is made up of a verb. Ni is shortened to n'.

4. yellow pear; a-ni-da-hlo-ni-ge di-ga-dv-di, yellow pears. A-ni-da-hlo-ni-ge is a living plural adjective because it refers to 'pears', and plants (or plant parts) take living adjectives in Cherokee. Di-ga-dv-di does not change in the plural.

5. brown chair; tsu-wo-di-ge di-ga-s-ki-lo, brown chairs. Tsu-wo-di-ge is a non-living plural adjective (adds di- instead of -ni-) because it refers to chairs, which are non-living objects. Di-ga-s-ki-lo has a di- placed before it because chair is a non-living object.

6. blue plate; di-sa-ko-ni-ge di-te-li-do, blue plates. Di-sa-ko-ni-ge is a non-living plural adjective because it refers to plates, which are non-living objects. Di-te-li-do has di- added to the noun base because plates are non-living plural objects.

7. pretty baby; tsu-no-du tsu-n'-s-di, pretty babies. Tsu-no-du contains di - u-ni-wo-du. di is on the plural of almost every word that begins with u- (di plus u equals tsu). Ni- marks a living plural adjective because babies are living beings. W- drops out because w- always drops out in Cherokee after plural marker u-ni-. Tsu-n'-s-di contains di-u-ni-s-di. Di is attached to the plural of almost every Cherokee noun or adjective beginning with u- and di plus u equals tsu. Ni- marks the plural of baby because babies are living human nouns. It is shortened to n'.

8. big eagle; tsu'-n'-ta-na wo-ha'-li, big eagles. Tsu-n'-ta-na contains di-u-ni-ta-na. Di is attached to the plural of almost every Cherokee word that begins with u- whether it is living or not and di plus u equals tsu-. Ni- marks a living plural adjective, referring to eagles which are living beings. Ni is shortened to n'. Wo-ha'-li does not change in the plural.

9. A ripe strawberry; tsu-nv-sv a?-ni, ripe strawberries. Tsu-nv-sv contains di-u-ni-wa-ne-sv. Di is attached to the plural of almost every Cherokee noun or adjective that begins with u- and di plus u equals tsu-. Ni marks the plural of an adjective that refers to a living being, such as a human, animal or plant, in this case some strawberries. Strawberry does not change in the plural. W drops out after u-ni.

10. a fine glass; tso:-s-da tsu-lv-sa-di, fine glasses. These words both have di- added in the plural because glasses are non-living (inanimate). They contain di-o-s-da di-u-lv-sa-di. Di plus o often becomes tso- but not as frequently as di plus u becomes tsu.

ᏔᎳᏗᏛ ᏣᎳᎩ ᎪᏪᎸ

Ta-la'-du-i' Tsa-la-gi' Go-hwe-lv:-i

CHEROKEE LESSON SIXTEEN

Cherokee Verbs -- Part I

Each Cherokee <u>verb</u> is a complete sentence, since it always contains both a noun (actually, a bound pronoun) and a verb. (both a subject and a predicate). See Lesson XIV.

Cherokee personal pronouns (I, you, he, we, you, they) are different from those of English in three ways, two of which have already been mentioned.

1. They are attached to the beginning of the verb (prefixed) and change according to the sounds in the verb. (bound pronouns)

2. There is no distinction of sex. To distinguish I (1st person singular) and You (2nd person singular) from He or She (3rd person singular) Cherokee uses a single pronoun which can be called Another.

3. There are ten bound personal pronouns which deal with the following situations:

Singular (one person acting)
1. I
2. You
3. Another (he or she)

Dual (two acting)
4. You-and-I (excluding Another)
5. You-and-Another (excluding I)
6. Another-and-I (excluding You)

Plural (three or more are acting)
7. Others-and-I (excluding You), or Exclusive We
8. Others-and-You (excluding I), or You, plural
9. Others-and-Another (excluding You and I), or They

Comprehensive plural (three or more are acting)
10. You-Another-or-Others-and-I, or Comprehensive We

You are familiar with Nos. 1, 2, 3, and 9.

There is no new Cherokee material in Lesson XVI except the two sets of bound pronouns on the next page.

These extra personal pronouns are <u>not</u> a complication. They are a solution. They clarify vague areas of possible misunderstanding that every English speaker notices at one time or another.

If a friend should say to you in English "We are going downtown.", you have no way of knowing without asking whether this means:

a. We two (the friend and another, but not including you)
b. We several (the friend and others, but not including you)
c. We two, you and the friend.
d. We all, several others or someone else and the friend, including you

The various possibilities above are lumped together and ignored in English, but Cherokee has a specific pronoun for each of them. When you have mastered Cherokee bound pronouns you will find yourself missing them in English!

There are basically two different sets of Cherokee bound pronouns:

Singular	A.	B.
1. I	ts-, g-	a?-w-, a-ki, a-gi, a-qua
2. You	h-	ts-
3. Another (he/she)	ga-, any vowel but u	u-

Dual		
4. You and I	in-	gi-n-
5. You two	s-d-	s-d-
6. Another and I	o-s-d-	o-gi-n-

Plural		
7. Others & I (Exclusive We)	o-ts-	o-g-
8. You, plural	i-ts-	i-ts-
9. They	a-n(i)	u-n(i)

Comprehensive Plural		
10. You Another or Others & I	i-d-	i-g-

Notice that:
    Number 5 above, You-and-Another, or You two, is s-d- for all verbs.
    Number 8 above, You-and-Others, or You plural, is i-ts- for all verbs.
    O- in front of any verb form means 'excluding you'. (Nos. 6 & 7)

On the next page you will find four sample verbs you already know with all ten bound pronouns, dealing with present time (in the present tense).

As you know (Lesson 13), the ending -a on Cherokee verbs means the action is happening now. Although this -a is often left off, a native Cherokee speaker can still tell the present time is meant because of the lack of features that would indicate other tenses. Future and past of ten verbs are in Appendix XI.

Groups I, II and III below use bound pronouns from Set A in speaking of the present time.

Group IV uses bound pronouns from Set B in speaking of the present time.

	Group I ts-ga	Group II ts-a	Group III g-	Group IV a-
	speak	eat	say	want

Singular - 1 person is acting

1. I	tsi-wo:-ni-a	tsi'-gi?-a	ga-di?-a	a?-wa-du'-li-(a)
2. You	hi-wo:-ni-a	hi'-gi?-a	ha-di?-a	tsa-du'-li-(a)
3. A (h/sh)	ga-wo:-ni-a	a'-gi?-a	a-di?-a	u-du'-li-(a)

Dual - 2 persons are acting

4. Y-&-I	i-ni-wo:-ni-a	i-ni'-gi?-a	i'-n(a)-di?-a	gi-na-du'-li-(a)
5. Y-&-A	s-di-wo:-ni-a	s-di'-gi?-a	s-da-di?-a	s-da-du'-li-(a)
6. A-&-I	o-s-di-wo:-ni-a	o'-s-di-gi?-a	o-s-da-di?-a	o'-gi-na-du'-li-(a)

Plural - 3 or more are acting

7. O-&-I (Excl. We)	o-tsi-wo:-ni-a	o-tsi-gi?-a	o-tsa-di?-a	o'-ga-du'-li-(a)
8. You pl.	i-tsi-wo:-ni-a	i-tsi'-gi?-a	i'-tsa-di?-a	i'-tsa-du'-li-(a)
9. They	a-ni-wo:-ni-a	a-ni'-gi?-a	a-n'-di?-a	u-na-du'-li-(a)

Comprehensive plural - 3 or more are acting

10. Cmp. We (Y-A-or-O-&-I)	i-di-wo:-ni-a	i-di-gi?-a	i'-da-di?-a	i'-ga-du'-li-(a)

Group I verbs use ts- to mean 'I' and ga- for Another or he/she.(Nos. 1&3)
Group II uses ts- to mean I and a- for Another or he/she. (Nos. 1&3)
Group III uses g- for I and almost always forms Another or he/she (3rd person singular) by leaving off g-. (Nos. 1&3)
Otherwise Groups I, II and III are exactly alike.
In Group IV, I begins with a-, 3rd person singular and plural begin with u-, and You singular is ts-. (Nos. 1, 3, 9 & 2)

PHRASES

Translation	Syllabary	Pronunciation

109. From Lesson IV

say, tell, repeat

I say	ᏩᏗ	ga-di?-a
you say	ᎭᏗ	ha-di?-a
he/she says	ᎠᏗ	a-di?-a
you & I say	ᎢᏂᏗ	i'-n'-di?-a
you two say	ᏍᏓᏗ	s-da-di?-a
another & I say	ᎣᏍᏓᏗ	o'-s-da-di?-a
others & I say	ᎣᏣᏗ	o-tsa-di?-a
you plural say	ᎢᏣᏗ	i-tsa-di?-a
they say	ᎠᏂᏗ	a-n'-di?-a
you, another or others	ᎢᏓᏗ	i-da-di?-a
& I say		

110. From Lesson V

want

I want	ᎠᏩᏚᎵ	a?-wa-du'-li-(a)
you want	ᏣᏚᎵ	tsa-du'-li-(a)
he/she wants	ᎤᏚᎵ	u-du'-li-(a)
you & I want	ᎩᎾᏚᎵ	gi-na-du'-li-(a)
you two want	ᏍᏓᏚᎵ	s-da-du'-li-(a)
another & I want	ᎣᎩᎾᏚᎵ	o'-gi-na-du'-li-(a)
others & I want	ᎣᎦᏚᎵ	o'-ga-du'-li-(a)
you plural	ᎢᏣᏚᎵ	i'-tsa-du'-li-(a)
they want	ᎤᎾᏚᎵ	u'-na-du'-li-(a)
you, another or others	ᎢᎦᏚᎵ	i'-ga-du'-li-(a)
& I want		

111. From Lesson XI

speaking, make a speech

I am speaking	ᎭᏫᏂᎠ	tsi-wo'-ni-(a)
you are speaking	ᏗᏫᏂᎠ	hi-wo:-ni-(a)
he/she is speaking	ᎦᏫᏂᎠ	ga-wo:-ni-(a)
you & I are speaking	ᎢᏂᏫᏂᎠ	i-ni-wo'-ni-a
you two are speaking	ᏍᏗᏫᏂᎠ	s-di-wo'-ni-a
another & I are speaking	ᎣᏍᏗᏫᏂᎠ	o'-s-di-wo:-ni-a
others & I are speaking	ᎣᏥᏫᏂᎠ	o-tsi-wo:-ni-a
you plural are speaking	ᎢᏥᏫᏂᎠ	i-tsi-wo:-ni-a
they are speaking	ᎠᏂᏫᏂᎠ	a-ni-wo:-ni-a
you another or others & I are speaking	ᎢᏗᏫᏂᎠ	i-di-wo"-ni-a

112. From Lesson XIV

eat (something)

I am eating	ᎭᏯᎠ	tsi-gi?-a
you are eating	ᏗᏯᎠ	hi-gi?-a
he/she is eating	ᎠᏯᎠ	a-gi?-a
you & I are eating	ᎢᏂᏯᎠ	i-ni-gi?-a
you two are eating	ᏍᏗᏯᎠ	s-di-gi?-a
another & I are eating	ᎣᏍᏗᏯᎠ	o'-s-di'-gi?-a
others & I are eating	ᎣᏥᏯᎠ	o'-tsi-gi?-a
you plural are eating	ᎢᏥᏯᎠ	i-tsi-gi?-a
they are eating	ᎠᏂᏯᎠ	a-ni-gi?-a
you another or others & I are eating	ᎢᏗᏯᎠ	i-di-gi?-a

Remember that eating in general or having a meal is 'ga-l'-s-ta-yv-hv'-s-ga'. Tsi-gi?-a is used whenever some specific thing is being eaten.

Learn all the bound pronouns thoroughly by reviewing the verbs you have had so far. These are shown in full in Appendix VIII.

Exercise 1: Match up these two columns, then check from Phrases in Lesson XV and Lesson XVI.

A.   1. gi-na-du'-li-a
     2. s-da-du'-li-a
     3. i-n'-di'?-a
     4. i-tsa-di?-a
     5. tsi-gi?-a
     6. i-tsi'-gi?-a
     7. o'-s-di-wo:-ni-a
     8. i-ni-wo:-ni-a
     9. o-tsi-wo:-ni-a
    10. i-ga-du'-li-a
    11. i-da-di?-a
    12. hi-wo:-ni?-a
    13. ha'-l'-s-du-tlv'-ga
    14. ha'-l'-s-du-tlv'-ga
    15. o-tsi:-na

B.   1. You just sat down. (You)
     2. Won't you sit down. (You)
     3. Others and I (We) are staying home.
     4. You and I are speaking. (We)
     5. Another and I are speaking. (We)
     6. You and I want ... (We)
     7. You two want ... (You)
     8. You (plural) say ... (You)
     9. I am eating ...
    10. You (plural) are eating ...
    11. You and I say ... (We)
    12. Others and I are speaking. (We)
    13. You, another or others and I say...
        (We all)
    14. You, another or others and I want...
        (We all)

The pronouns in brackets above are common English pronouns that can be used instead of the ones outside brackets in the same sentence.
Notice how specific Cherokee is in comparison.

Exercise 2: Match Column C below with either column above. Column C is in a different order from either Column A or Column B, but the material is the same.

C.   1. ᎫᏩᏂᎢ

     2. ᏍᏓᎵᎢ

     3. ᎩᎾᏛᎵᎢ

     4. ᏗᏣᏛᎵᎢ

     5. ᏗᎾᏝᎢ

     6. ᏗᎦᏝᎢ

     7. ᎭᎩᎢ

     8. ᏗᏂᎩᎢ

     9. ᏍᏛᏛᎵᎢ

    10. ᏤᎵᏬᏕᏒ

    11. ᏃᏬᏠᏩᏂᎢ

    12. ᏍᎩᎾ

    13. ᏍᎩᏩᏂᎢ

    14. ᏤᎵᏬᏕᏒ

    15. ᏗᏂᏩᏂᎢ

Exercise 3: Translate the sentences below from Cherokee into English and check the correct answer or answers below each sentence.

1. Tsa-li a-le Me-li a-n'-di?-a:

        a. o'-s-da-di?-a
        b. ga-di?-a
        c. i-da-di?-a

2. Lu-ga, Ma-ga, E-gi a-le Go-la-nv a-na-l'-s-ta-yv-hv-s-ga. Ni-ga-d' a-n'-di?-a:

        a. Ka-l'-se-ts' i-ga-du-li.
        b. Ka-l'-se-ts' i-tsa-du-li.
        c. Ka-l'-se-ts' i-di-gi?-a.

3. Tsa-ni su-da-l'-s-go sv?-ta du-ha. Ha-la i-ga?-i sv?-ta du-ha Tsa-ni?

        a. twenty
        b. forty
        c. sixty

4. Ha-la na-ni?-a? (a. sa-wu b. ta?-li c. hi-lv-s-gi)

        1. i-ni-wo-ni-a
        2. a?-wa-du-li
        3. o-gi-na-du-li
        4. hi-wo-ni
        5. o-tsi-wo-ni-a
        6. a-gi?-a
        7. i-di-gi?-a
        8. s-di-gi?-a
        9. s-da-di?-a
       10. i-ga-du-li-a

Exercise 4: Write Exercise 3, sentences and correct answers, in Cherokee, then read the Cherokee to someone out loud.

Exercise 5: Translate the following from Cherokee to English, reading it out loud in Cherokee as you go. Write the English translation down, then check on pages 6, 9 and 12 for pronunciation and translation.

ᎣᏏᏳ. ᎤᏙᎵ. ᎤᏣᎳᏍᏗ. ᏔᎵᏁ ᎠᏣᏗᏗ. ᎤᏎᎦ ᎠᏂ. ᏓᏗᏴᏮ.

EXERCISE 3:

1. Charlie <u>and</u> Mary say: a. Another and I say ... (Remember that <u>two</u> people have a special pronoun that means 'another-and-I-(excluding you'), saying 'we' as a unit.)

2. Luke, Mark, Maggie, and Raven are having a meal. <u>All of them</u> say: a. or c.

    a. Another-or-others-and-I want (some) sugar.
    c. Another-or-others-and-I are eating sugar.

Remember that there is a special Cherokee pronoun to be used when several people are speaking on behalf of all of them together.

3. John has sixty apples. How many apples does John have? c. sixty

4. How many are there? (a.one b.two c.several) 1.b.2 2.a.1 3.b.2 4.a.1 5.c. 6.a.1 7.c. 8.b.2 9.b.2 10.c.

It is helpful to think of Cherokee pronouns in groups, according to how many actors are involved.

EXERCISE 4:

1.GᎮ DᏊ ᏃᎮ DⴰᎭⅠⅮ ᎥⵌᎿⅠⅮ

2.MᏍ ᎦᎦ RᎩ DᏊ AWꙆ DⴰᎮꙆWBᎦᏬᎦ. ᎯᏚᏖ DⴰᎭⅠⅮ 'ᎤᎮ4Ꮒ TᏍᏚᎮⅠⅮ' DᏊ 'ᎤᎮ4Ꮒ T.ⅠᎩⅮ'

3.GᎯ ᎧᏖᎮꙆᎠ RW SᏊ. ᏊW TᏚT SᏊ GᎯ

4.ᏊW ⴰᎯⅠⅮ - ᎤᎩ WᎮ ᎤᎿᏬᎩ

          TᎯⵌᎯⅠⅮ - WᎮ
          DGSᎮⅠⅮ - ᎤᎩ
          ᎥᎩⴰSᎮⅠⅮ - WᎮ
          ᎤⵌᎯ - ᎤᎩ
          ᎥᏇⵌᎯⅠⅮ - ᎤᎿᏬᎩ
          DᎩⅠⅮ - ᎤᎩ
          T.ⅠᎩⅮ - ᎤᎿᏬᎩ
          ⴰⅠᎩⅮ - WᎮ
          ⴰⅬⅠⅮ - WᎮ
          TᏍSᎮⅠⅮ - ᎤᎿᏬᎩ

ᏉᏟᏍᏔ ᏣᏫᏴ ᎠᏫᎦᏔ

Ga'-li-qua'-du-i' Tsa-la-gi' Go-hwe-lv"-i

CHEROKEE LESSON SEVENTEEN

Read out loud and translate the following table conversation. The words new to you are underlined and defined below. Accents, glottal stops and length marks are omitted so you can try your own rhythm, imitating the Cherokee pronunciation you have heard.

I-da-l(i)-s-ta-yv-hv-ga, i-tse-li-s-gv i-tsa-nv-ni-da.

O-s-da a-l(i)-s-ta-i-di, ga-du a-le a-su-s-di, ha-wi-ya, se-lu di-hu-dv!

Do-yu u-te-di ha-da-s-ta-yo-hv-ga.

Do-yu-ka s-qui-s-di a-ga-na ko-hi.

Sv-ta-ke ge-li-s-gi tsa-du-li?

V-v u-s-di a-gv-ha-lv-da.

Ka-wi-ke si-wu?

Ho-wa.

i-tse-li-s-gv - (your choice) wherever you want

di-hu-dv - (boiled whole) on the cob

129

ka - -ka on the end of a word means you are counting on a 'yes' answer, if any, or at least agreement from whoever you are speaking with. The meaning of -ka is similar to but much more definite than -gi on page 83. Do-yu-ka is made up of do-yu (certainly) plus -ka (you-second-my-opinion don't-you?) Do-yu-ka is often shortened to Do-ka, and both expressions are used often.
Ka! followed by a pause and a serious statement means 'Listen to this.' Cherokee personal letters often begin with Ka instead of 'Dear So-and-so.'

u-te?-di - delicious
a-gv-ha-lv-da - (piece-cut-off) slice
si-wu - again, more

Translation of table conversation:

Let's all start our meal, you all sit down wherever you want to.
It's a fine meal, bread and gravy, meat, corn on the cob!
It certainly rained a lot today, didn't it!
Would you like some apple pie?
Yes, a tiny slice.
Some more coffee?
Yes, please. (literally, Fine, or Agreed)

Notes:

As you know, most Cherokee words contain some optional, meaningfully arranged syllables. Each optional syllable contributes something specific to the total meaning of the word.

Examine the explanations in Notes carefully and thoughtfully, so you can look below the surface of more and more Cherokee words.

i-da-l'-s-ta-yv-hv'-ga   1. When a verb ends with:
a.-hv-ga (without s) - the action just happened
b.-hv-s-ga action is taking place now
c.-hv-s-go - it happens habitually
d.-hv-s-gi - it is made to happen repeatedly
through personal effort
Examples: a-l'-s-ta-yv-hv'-s-gi
(he/she is) a big eater
di'-de-yo'-hv-s-gi'
(he/she is) a teacher

2. Saying something just happened is a Cherokee way of inviting, or of saying 'Let's.'

130

i-da-l'-s-ta-yv-hv'-ga, i-tsa-nv'-ni-da'
   1. Notice the switch in the first sentence of the table conversation
      <u>from</u> i-da-l'-s-ta-yv-hv'-ga (We all)
      <u>to</u>   i-tsa-nv'-ni-da'   (You plural)

      Since it is the host or hostess speaking, he or she naturally
      <u>excludes</u> self when inviting guests to sit down (You plural sit down
      wherever you plural wish), but includes self among those about to
      eat (You-another or-others-and-I just started our meal).

   2. Bound pronouns of Group A (see page 122 of Lesson 16) are being used.
      You can tell this because bound pronouns No. 10 (you-another-or-
      others-and-I) is <u>i-d-</u> here (i-da-l'-s-ta-yv-hv'-ga) instead of i-g-
      (Group B) You plural is the <u>same</u> in both bound pronoun groups,
      (<u>i-ts-</u>)

a-l'-s-ta-i?-d(i) (pronounced alstite. D(i) varies to ti or t') This means
      'feeding of oneself', 'a meal' (see page 22) In Cherokee, meals
      are named for the times of day:
                     sv-na'-l(e) a-l'-s-<u>ta</u>-<u>i</u>?-d(i)   morning meal
                     i:?-a-l'-s-<u>ta</u>-<u>i</u>-t(i)   noon meal
                     sv-hi'-ye a-l'-s-<u>ta</u>-<u>i</u>-t(i)   evening or late afternoon
                                                        meal
                     u'-sv?-a-l'-s-<u>ta</u>-<u>i</u>-t(i)   night meal

i-tse-li'-s-gv is a combination of 'i-tse'-li' (belonging to you plural)
      and 's-gv' (capable, able). Together these two elements add up to
      'your capability' or 'your choice'.

                              PHRASES

   Underlinings in the Cherokee job titles show the -ni- that marks the
plural of these human nouns. To find the singular, read the word <u>omitting</u>
the underlined letters.
Example:
carpenter di-<u>na</u>-ne'-s-ge:-s-gi means that carpenter, singular, is:
           di-ne'-s-ge:-s-gi   and carpenters, plural is:
           di-na-ne'-s-ge:-s-gi
   Some nouns make greater changes in the plural. They are written
separately.

113.
Some jobs   ᎫᏂᎶᏫᎥᎵ   tsu-ni-lv:-w(i)-s-ta'-n(e)-ti
carpenter   ᎫᎾᎾᎶᎨᏍᎩ   di-na-ne'-s-ge:-s-gi
clerk in a store   ᎠᏂᏓᎦᏘᏕᎯ   a-<u>n(a)</u>-da-ga-ti-de-hi
doctor   ᎠᏂᎦᎾᏘ   a-<u>ni</u>-ga-na'?-t?(i)

113. (cont.)

lawyer (arguer for a goal)	ᎫᏂᏘᎾᎠ	di-n(i)-ti-yo'-hi-hi'
marine (on-deep-water-goer)	ᎠᎹᏱᎭᏫᏂᎠᏁᏙᎯ	a-ma-yi-ha-wi-ni-a-ne-do-hi
minister	ᎠᏁᎵᏣᏙᎲᏍᎩ	a-na-l'-tsa-do'-hv-s-gi'
musician	ᎫᏂᎧᏃᎩᏍᏗᏍᎩ	di-ni-ka-no-gi:-s-di'-s-gi
nurse (caretaker of the ill)	ᏧᎾᏢᎩ ᎫᏂᎩᏔᏯ	tsu'-n'-tlv'-gi di-ni-g'-ti'-ya
poet	ᏗᎪᏪᎵᏍᎩ ᎧᏃᎮᏢᏍᎩ	di-go-we-li'-s-gi ka-(h)no-he-(t)lv'-s-gi
poets	ᏗᏃᏪᎵᏍᎩ ᎧᏃᎮᏢᏍᎩ	di-no-we-li'-s-gi ka-(h)no-he-(t)lv'-s-gi
policeman (final catcher)	ᎫᏂᏓᏂᏱᏍᎩ	di-n(i)-da-ni-yi-s-gi
repairman (makes it good again)	ᎣᏍᏓ ᎢᎬᏁᎯ	o'-s-da i-gv-ne'-hi
repairmen	ᎣᏍᏓ ᎢᏯᏅᏁᎯ	o:-s-da i-ya-nv-ne-hi
sailor (on-water-goer)	ᎠᎹᎢᎠᏁᏙᎯ	a-ma'-i-a-n(e)-do'-hi
secretary (writer-down)	ᏗᎪᏪᎵᏍᎩ ᏗᎪᏪᎵᏍᎩ	di-go-we-li'-s-gi
secretaries	ᏗᏃᏪᎵᏍᎩ ᏗᏃᏪᎵᏍᎩ	di-no-we-li'-s-gi
soldier	ᎠᏂᏲᏍᎩ	a-ni-yo:-s-gi
teacher	ᏗᏕᏲᎲᏍᎩ	di-n(a)-de-yo-hv-s-gi'
typist	ᏗᏂ ᏍᏙᏍᏗᏍᎩ	di:-n(i)-sø-s-ti:-s-(gi)

114.

When do they get off work? (each day)	ᎭᎳᏴ ᎠᏂᏑᎳᎪᎪ ᏧᏂᏢᏫᏍᏔᏁᎯ	Ha-la'-yv a-ni-su-la'-go-go tsu-ni-lv'-wi-s-ta-ne'-hi?

115.

When do you stop work? (temporarily, for time off or for vacation)	ᎭᎳᏴ ᏙᏦᏖᏙᎵ	Ha-la'-yv toh'-te-do:-li?

116.

John has a new job.	ᏣᏂ ᎠᏤᏧᎳᎲᏍᏓᏂᏘ ᎤᎭ	Tsa'-ni a'-tse tsu-lv-hwi'-s-da'-n'-ti u'-ha.

117.

I hear he is working very hard.	ᎦᏛᎩ ᏍᏔᏲᏒ ᏚᎸᏫᏍᏔᏁᎲ	Ga-tv'-gi s-ta-yo:-sv du-lv'-w'-s-ta-ne'-hv.

118.

They say Mark has been transferred.	ᎤᏣᏘᎾ ᏚᎸᏫᏍᏔ ᏁᎠᏂ ᎦᏗ	U-tsa-ti'-n(a)(a) du-lv'-w'-s-ta'-ne a-n'-di Ma:-ga.

119.
(Yes), and several
workers in his plant
have lost their jobs.

Dꭷ ᎤᎭᏫᎩ ᏧᏂᎰᏬᏓᎢᎾ
ᏏᏂᎦᏟᏎ
ᏧᏂᎭᏫᎾᎢ

A-le hi-lv'-s-gi tsu-ni-lv'-w'-
s-ta-ne'-hi du'-ni-yo-hu:-si'
tsu-ni-lv-s-ta'-n'-ti.

120.
David quit his job.

ᏛᎢ ᎤᏌᎳᎪ ᏚᎳᏬᏬᏓᎾ

Da-wi-di u-su-la-go'-tse du-
lv'-w'-s-ta-ne'-hv.

121.
That's the way it is!

ᏍᎩᎦ ᏄᏍᏗᎢ

S-gi-dv' nu-s-di'!

CORE VOCABULARY

again, more   si'-wu

delicious   u-te?-di

different place,   u-tsa-ti'-n(i)(a)
elsewhere
job, work (Noun)   tsu-lv-hwi-s-ta'-n'-ti

smart   a-sa-ma'-ti

your, yours, pl.   i-tse'-li

Ownership of personal property is shown in Cherokee by the following
possessive adjectives:

        a'-qua-tse'-li   my or mine
        tsa'-tse-li'   you, yours, sing.
        u-tse-li   his/her

        gi-na'-tse-li'   yours-and-mine
        s-da-tse-li   belonging to you two
        o'-gi-na-tse-li   another's-and-mine

        o'-ga-tse-li   others'-and-mine (not yours)
        i-tse-li   your, yours, plural
        u-na-tse-li   their, theirs

        i-ga-tse-li   yours-another-or-others'-and-my/mine

Notice that the possessive adjectives in Cherokee use bound pronouns
from Group B. (Lesson 16, page 120)

There is no difference in Cherokee between 'my' and 'mine', 'your' and 'yours', so Cherokee possessive adjectives a-qua-tse'-li, tsa'-tse-li', and so on can be translated as either 'my' or 'mine', 'your' or 'yours', etc., according to convenience in English:

Examples:

That dog is mine.	Na gi:-tli a-qua-tse'-li.
or:	A-qua-tse'-li na gi:-tli.
That is my dog.	Na ge:-tli a-qua-tse'-li.
or:	A-qua-tse'-li na gi:-tli.
My dog is smart.	A-sa-ma'-ti a-qua-tse'-li gi:-tli.
or:	A-qua-tse'-li ge:-tli a-sa-ma'-ti.

If more than one possession is referred to, the plural is formed by adding di- just before each possessive adjective, since these are <u>plural direct objects</u> grammatically in Cherokee. The literal meaning of 'my', 'your' is 'possessed by me','possessed by you', and so on.

Examples:

Those dogs are mine.	(Those dogs belong to me, Those dogs are-my-belongings, Those dogs are-possessed-by-me-personally)
	Na gi:-tli <u>di</u>-qua-tse'-li.
Those are your dogs.	Na gi:-tli <u>di</u>-tsa'-tse-li'.
His dogs are smart.	A-sa-ma'-ti <u>tsu</u>-tse-li gi:-tli.
or:	A-ni-sa-ma'-ti <u>tsu</u>-tse-li gi:-tli.
or:	<u>T</u>su-tse-li gi:-tli a-ni-sa-ma'-ti.

Notice three additional things about the sentences above:

1. 'Those dogs' looks exactly the same in Cherokee as 'That dog', but there can be no misunderstanding because of the di- plural direct object on <u>di</u>-qua-tse'-li(instead of a-qua-tse'-li) and <u>di</u>-tsa'-tse-li' (instead of tsa'-tse-li'.

2. The -ni- for plural living adjective (a-sa-ma'-ti, a-ni-sa-ma'-ti) can be left off.

3. A-sa-ma'-ti is an obvious borrowing from English. Notice the changes 'smart' was put through to take off the rough edges before it was adopted into the Cherokee language:

'A' was added to the beginning of the word because almost all Cherokee adjectives start with a vowel, and 'a' rhymed with the vowel already there.
Another 'a' was added between s and m because Cherokee does not contain the combination 'sm'.
'R' was eliminated. When borrowing, if the 'r' stands alone between two vowels it is usually changed to 'l' (Mary to Me:-li). If it stands beside another consonant it is just left out. (Charlie to Tsa:-li)
Another vowel was added at the end so it would flow better.

The dual forms of a-qua-tse'-li (two possessors for plural objects) are not much used, of course, except when the two owners are a social unit (e.g., husband and wife, partners, etc.). They have become optional.

Yours-and-my dogs are smart.   A-ni-sa-ma'-ti di-gi-na-tse'-li gi:-tli.
You-two's dogs are smart.   A-ni-sa-ma'-ti di-s-da-tse'-li gi:-tli.
His/her-and-my dogs are smart.   A-ni-sa-ma'-ti tso'-gi-na-tse'-li gi:-tli.

The four plural forms below are often used instead of the dual forms above, even when only two possessors are concerned. The dual possessive verb-adjective is still kept up between husband and wife.

Our (but not your) dogs are smart.   A-ni-sa-ma'-ti tso'-ga-tse'-li gi:-tli.
You-all's dogs are smart.   A-ni-sa-ma'-ti di-tsa-tse-li' gi:-tli.
Their dogs are smart.   A-ni-sa-ma'-ti tsu-na-tse-li' gi:-tli.

All-of-us' dogs are smart.   A-ni-sa-ma'-ti di-ga-tse'-li gi:-tli.
(The dogs possessed by you, me,
 and another or others are smart)

Verbs:

lose

    I am losing   a-gi-yo-hu'-se
    you are losing   tsa-yo-hu'-se
    he/she is losing   u-yo-hu'-se

    you and I are losing   gi-ni-yo-hu'-se
    you two are losing   s-di-yo-hu'-se
    another and I are losing   o-gi-ni-yo-hu'-se

others & I are losing   o-gi-yo-hu'-se
you plural are losing   i-tsi-yo-hu'-se
they are losing   u-ni-yo-hu'-se

you, another or others   i-gi-yo-hu'-se
   and I are losing

quit

I am quitting   tsi:-su-la-go'-ga
you are quitting   hi-su-la-go'-ga
he/she is quitting   a-su-la-go'-ga

you and I are quitting   i-ni-su-la-go'-ga
you two are quitting   s-di-su-la-go'-ga
another and I are quitting   o'-s-di-su-la-go'-ga

others and I are quitting   o-tsi-su-la-go'-ga
you plural are quitting   s-di-su-la-go'-ga
they are quitting   a-ni-su-la-go'-ga

you another or others   i-di-su-la-go'-ga
   and I are quitting

stop for awhile, take time out (from a task)

I take time out   to:-da-ge-do'-li
you take time out   to'-te-do:-li
he/she takes time out   toh-da-ye-do:-li

you and I are taking time out   to-da-ne-do'-li
you two are taking time out   to-da-s-de-do'-li
another and I are taking time out   to-da-yo:-s-de-do'-li

others and I are taking time out   to-da-yo:-tse-do'-li
you plural are taking time out   to-da:-tse-do:-li
they are taking time out   to:-dv-ne-do'-li

you, another or others and I   to-da:-de-do'-li
   are taking time out

136

work

I am working   da-gi-lv-hwi-s-ta'-ne?-ᴅ
you are working   de-tsa-lv-s-da-ne?-a
he/she is working   du-lv'-w(i)-s-ta-ne?-a

you and I are working   de-gi-ni'-lv-hwi-s-ta-ne?-ᴅ
you two are working   de-s-di'-lv-hwi-s-ta-ne?-ᴅ
another and I are working   do-ga-ni'-lv-hwi-s-ta-ne?-ᴅ

others and I are working   do-gi-lv-hwi-s-ta-ne?-ᴅ
you plural are working   de-tsi-lv-hwi-s-ta-ne?-ᴅ
they are working   du-ni-lv-hwi-s-ta-ne?-ᴅ

you another or others   de-gi-lv-hwi-s-ta-ne?-ᴅ
   and I are working

Exercise 1: Match up Column A with Column B from this lesson.

A.
1. Ha-la'-yv toh-te-do:-li?
2. U-su-la-go'-tse du-lv'-w'-s-ta-ne-hv.
3. sv-na'-le a-l'-s-ta-i-di
4. tsu-ni-lv:-w'-s-ta'-n'-ti
5. da-gi-lv-hwi-s-ta'-ne?-ᴣ
6. to-da:-de-do'-li
7. i-di-su-la-go'-ga
8. i-gi-yo-hu'-se
9. o-gi-yo-hu'-se
10. Na gi:-tli di-qua-tse-li.

B.
1. others & I (we, not you) are losing
2. you, another or others & I (we all) are taking time out
3. When do you take time off?
4. breakfast
5. some jobs
6. I am working
7. He has quit his job.
8. you, another or others & I (we all) are losing
9. you, another or others & I (we all) are quitting
10. Those dogs are mine.

Exercise 2: Match up Columns C and D then check by looking them up in the Phrases section of this lesson.

C.
1. doctor
2. doctors
3. poet
4. poets
5. marine
6. sailor
7. sailors
8. carpenters
9. John has a new job.
10. That's the way it is!

D.
1. ᏕᎾᏗ
2. ᎠᏂᏕᎾᏗ
3. ᎢᎠᏬᎮᏅᏯ ᎤᏃᎮᏗᏴᏯ
4. ᎢᏃᏬᎮᏅᏯ ᎠᏂᏃᎮᏗᏴᏯ
5. ᏅᏯᏛ ᎾᎶᏗ
6. ᎠᏦᏴᏙᎥᎧ
7. ᏤᎾᎳᏙᎮᏅᏯ
8. ᏣᏂ ᎠᏫ ᏣᎾᏍᏩᎻᎫ ᎤᏫ
9. ᎠᏦᎢᏊᎣᎥᎥᎧ
10. ᎠᏦᎢᎠᎳᎥᎧ

Exercise 3: Translate the following verbs into English, stating how many are acting in each case, and giving the commonest English equivalent. (i.e. o-gi-, we, i-gi-, we all, i-ts-, you, etc.) Answers are on the next page.

1. o-tsi-wo:-ni
2. toh-da-ye-do:-li
3. hi-su-la-go-ga
4. tsi-gi?-a
5. a-gi?-a
6. A-GI-HA
7. ga-wo:-ni-a
8. do-ga-ni;-lv-hwi-s-ta-ne?-a
9. du-ni-lv-hwi-s-ta-ne?-a
10. to:-da-ge-do:-li

11. tsi-su-la-go-ga
12. a-gi-yo-hu'-se
13. o-gi-ni-yo-hu'-se
14. gi-ni-yo-hu'-se
15. i-di-su-la-go'-ga
16. i-ga-du'-li-a
17. gi-na-du'-li-a
18. s-di-gi?-a
19. de-tsi-lv-hwi-s-ta-ne?-ᴣ
20. a-go:-ti?-a

138

EXERCISE 3:

1. we are speaking, several, others-&-I or we, not you, or we, exclusive
2. he or she is taking time out, one, he/she or another, 3rd person singular
3. you are quitting, one, you singular, 2nd person singular
4. I am eating (something), one, 1st person singular
5. he or she is eating (something), one, another, 3rd person singular
6. he or she has (something solid of indefinite shape), one, he/she, another, 3rd person singular
7. he or she is speaking, one, he/she, another, or 3rd person singular
8. he or she and I are working, two, another-&-I
9. they are working, several, 3rd person plural
10. I am taking time out, one, 1st person singular
11. I am quitting, one, 1st person singular
12. I am losing, one, 1st person singular
13. he or she and I are losing, two, another-&-I
14. you and I are losing, two
15. we are all quitting, several, you,-another-or-others-and-I
16. we all want, several, you, another or others and I
17. you and I want, two
18. you two are eating (something), two, you, or 2nd person plural
19. you are working, several, or 2nd person plural
20. he or she sees, one, he/she, another or 3rd person singular

Exercise 4: Translate the following from Cherokee to English, reading it out loud in Cherokee as you go. Write the English translation down, then check on page 16 for a translation and the pronunciation.

ᎦᎵᏉᎩᏁ	ᏧᏁᎵᏁᎢ
ᏑᏓᎵ	ᏗᏎᏍᏗ
ᏐᏁᎵᏁᎢ	ᎢᎬᏱᎢ
ᏍᎪᎯ	ᎯᏍᎩ
ᏦᎢ	ᏍᎪᎯᏁ
ᏅᎩ	ᏌᏊ
ᏔᎵ	ᎦᎵᏉᎩᏁᎢ
ᏗᎪᏪᎳ	ᏧᏁᎳ

ᏁᎳᏜᏔ ᏣᎳᎩ ᎠᏈᏱᎢ

Ne-la'-du-i Tsa-la-gi' Go-hwe:-lv-i

CHEROKEE LESSON EIGHTEEN

PHRASES

Translation	Syllabary	Pronunciation
122.		
A wolf is crossing the road.	ᎦᏃ ᏕᎦᏃᏗᏍᎦ ᏅᏃᎯ	Wa-hya' de-ga-n(a)-di'-s-ga nv-no'-hi.
A rabbit is jumping along the road.	ᏥᏍᏚ ᏓᎵᏔᏕᎦ ᏅᏃᎯ	Tsi'-s-du da-l'-ta-de-(ga) nv-no'-hi.
123.		
A hawk is eating a chicken (he just killed).	ᏚᏬᏗ ᏥᏔᎦ ᎦᎭᎠ	Tu-wo:-di tsi-ta:-ga ga-hye?-ⱥ.
A hawk is eating grain.	ᏚᏬᏗ ᎤᏍᏔ ᎠᎩᎠ	Tu-wo:-d' u'-g'-ta a-gi?-ⱥ.
124.		
A beaver is swimming toward (us). (Beaver by-water toward-comes)	ᏙᏯ ᎠᎹᏱ ᏓᏯᎢ	Do-ya a-ma-yi da-ya?-i.
A beaver is swimming away (from us). (Beaver by-water away-goes)	ᏙᏯ ᎠᎼᏩᎢ	Do-ya a-mo:-wa?-i.
125.		
I hear a fox barking. (Fox just-spoke it-I-am-hearing)	ᏧᏝ ᏂᏓᏪᏍᎬ ᏓᏟᎩᎠ	Tsu'-tla ni-ga-we:-s-gv ga-tv'-gi?-(a).

140

126.

domestic animals (pro- duced, or gentled they-live-on-it)	ᏆᎭᏓᏯᎫ ᏍᎤᏟᏔ	u-nʼ-da-nʼ-ti ga-na-tla-i
cat(s)	ᏪᏒ	we-s(a)(i)
chicken(s)	ᏥᏔᎦ	tsi-ta:-ga
cow, cattle	ᎦᏊ	wa-ga
donkey (long-eared)	ᏗᎦᎵᏅᎢᎯᏙ	di-ga-li-nvʼ-hi-dv
donkeys	ᏗᏂᎦᎵᏅᎢᎯᏙ	di-ni-ga-li-nvʼ-hi-dv
goat	ᎤᎾᏉᏣᏁᏙ	uʼ-k(a)-so?-tsa-ne-dv
goats	ᎤᎾᎾᏉᏣᏁᏙ	u-na-k(s)-so-tsa-ne-dv
horse(s) (carries burdens)	ᏐᏈᎵ	soʼ-qui-liʼ
pig(s)	ᏏᏆ	siʼ-qua
rooster (male)	ᎠᏨᏯ	a-tsvʼ-ya
roosters	ᎠᏂᏨᏯ	a-ni-tsvʼ-ya
sheep (woolly)	ᎤᏃᏕᎾ	u-no-de:-n(a)
sheep (plural)	ᎤᏂᏃᏕᎾ	u-ni-no-de:-n(a)

127.

wild animals (in-the- wilderness they-belong they-live-on-it)	ᏔᎶᎢ ᎠᏁᎲ ᏍᎤᏟᏔ	iʼ-na-ge a-ne:-hi ga-naʼ- tla-i
bear(s)	ᏲᏅ	yo-n(v)(a)
beaver(s)	ᏙᏯ	do-ya
bobcat(s)	ᎬᎮ	gv-he
buffalo(es)	ᏯᎾᏍᏏ	yaʼ-n(a)-s-s(iʼ)(aʼ)
deer(sing. & plural)	ᎠᎿ	aʼ-hwiʼ
fox(es)	ᏧᎳ	tsuʼ-(t)laʼ
panther(s)	ᏟᏓᏥ	tlv-da-tsiʼ
possum (smiling pig)	ᏏᏉᏤᏣ	si-quu:-tse-tsʼ
rabbit(s)	ᏥᏍᏚ	tsiʼ-s(a)-du
raccoon(s)	ᎬᏟ	kv-tli
skunk(s)	ᏗᎵ	di?-li
wolf(ves)	ᎦᏯ	wa-hya
groundhog(s)	ᎤᎦᎾ	oʼ-ga-naʼ

Notes:

P.N. 122 and 123 - There are many verbs that sketch wild animals' habits.

The verb used above for a rabbit (da'-l'-ta-de) cannot be used in the same sense for a wolf, since 'da-l'-ta-de-(ga)' refers to the way a rabbit jumps along. It is used for 'run' when speaking of rabbits.

'Da-l'-ta-de-(ga)' means 'jump' (not jump along) when it is used for a wolf, human or other animal that does not habitually double up when walking.

'De-ga-n'-di'-s-ga' does not describe the wolf's gait. It simply means 'cross over, traverse' (a road, a mountain, a river, etc.). It can refer to most animals and to people.

Notice that different Cherokee verbs are used for 'eat' in P.N. 123. 'Ga-hye?-a' is the term used for an animal eating its prey. 'A-gi?-a' can be used for vegetable food, such as grain, and for raw or cooked meat that was killed and taken apart by someone else.
Examples:

Tlv-da-tsi a-ni-ta?-li u-ni-no-de:-na de-ga-hye?-a.
The panther is eating two sheep (he killed).
Tu-wo:-di ha-wi'-ya a-gi?-a.
The hawk is eating some meat (someone fed him).

P.N. 124 - Notice the differences in the verb, depending on whether the beaver is coming closer or going away. In this case, unlike P.N. 123, English uses different verbs ('come' and 'go') while Cherokee uses the same verb, but with different prefixes.

Da- is placed before the bound pronoun of some Cherokee verbs if the action is coming closer to the speaker at the exact moment of which the speaker is speaking. The person or animal spoken of is usually already in sight, but can be just about to come into sight of the speaker and whoever he or she is speaking to.
Examples:

Da-ya?-i	He/she is coming this way
Da-s-da?-i	You two are coming this way
Da-tsa?-i	You plural are coming this way
Dv-na?-i	They are coming this way
Wo-ha'-li da-ga-no'-hi-li.	The eagle is flying this way.

Wi- can be placed before the bound pronoun if the action is going further away, if the animal or person spoken of is facing away from the speaker, or if the animal or person spoken of is temporarily gone from the speaker's presence at the exact moment of which the speaker is speaking.
Examples:

Wi-ga:?-i	I am on my way (already in motion)
Wa:?-i	He/she is going further away
Wi-na:?-i	You and I are outward bound, on our way, leaving for somewhere
Ge-wa-ne:-ga	They are near the horizon walking away
Wi-da'-l'-ta-de-(ga)	He is jumping away (from me)
Wi-ga-no'-hi-li-do'	He is out hunting.

Notice that 'da-ya-i' <u>cannot</u> mean 'He is coming-them' (i.e., d-cannot be a plural direct object marker) because 'go' and 'come' <u>cannot have a direct object</u>; that is, they are <u>intransitive</u>. Therefore, only <u>intransitive</u> verbs can use da- in this way.

P.N. 125 - The sounds that undisturbed animals habitually make can all be covered in Cherokee by saying 'Ni-ga-we?-a', (he/she/it says it, speaks, utters its usual sound, gives tongue, etc.)

'Ni-ga-we?-a' is usually not used if the animal's frame of mind becomes dangerous.

Examples:

A horse is snorting (he feels good)	So'-qui-li' ni-ga-we?-a.
A buffalo is snorting (threateningly)	Ya'-n(a)-s-si' da-tso-ta-s-ga. (Buffalo is blowing through his nose)
A bear is snorting (while eating)	Yo'-nv ni-ga-we?-a.
A bear is snorting (and weaving his head)	Yo'-nv u-hna-lv?-a (Bear is angered)

In English, there are many special words for the individual cries of domestic animals (mew, bleat, bray, crow, low, neigh) and few reserved for wild animals.

In Cherokee, the opposite is true. The only words specifically for domestic animal noises are 'crow' for rooster and several words dealing with dogs, but there are many descriptive terms for wild animals.

Examples:

A rooster is crowing.	A-tsv'-ya <u>a-i'</u>-hga'.
A dog is barking.	Gi:-tli da-si-hwi'-s-ga.
A fox is barking.	Tsu'-tla a-to-hi'-ya. (Also someone whooping, calling out out-of-doors)
A wolf howled.	Wa-hya' u-we-(t)lu?-gv. (Also someone in trouble calling for help)

Comparisons are made between human and wild animal behavior.

Example:

A woman/man is flirting. (is being foxlike)	A-ge'-hyv/a'-s-ga-yv tsu-la-s-gi?-a.

There are some descriptive nicknames for animals.

Example:

my horse	u-yo a-tsu:-ts' (the poor boy)

P.N. 125 - Notice 'ni-ga-we:-s-kv'. This is the <u>past</u> tense. 'Ga-tv'-gi?-a' is in the <u>present</u> tense. Cherokee uses this construction where in English one would say:

I hear a fox barking.	Cherokee: I hear a fox just-barked.
	Tsu'-tla a-to-hi'-<u>s-gv</u> ga-tv'-gi?-<u>a</u>.

P.N. 126 and 127 - Notice that wild-animal names, the names which have
been in the Cherokee language the longest, need no plural. Perhaps
at one time these names were descriptive like the ones for so many
domestic animals now, and needed a -ni- plural. If so, the original
meanings of the wild-animal names have been lost.

    A-ni- can be added to animal names that do not need any plural to
form group plurals.

1. Speaking of animals -in general or as a group:

    Examples:

A-ni-yo-nv u-ni-s-ka:-se?-ti.	Bears are fierce.
A-ni-ko:-ga na-ni-we?-a.	The crows are calling.

    A-ni-ko:-g(a)(i) means 'crow tribe', 'of the crow kind', 'they who
are crows'.

2. Speaking of people who are members of a clan, tribe, nationality or
type.

    Examples:

A-ni-wa-hyɑ'	members of the Wolf Clan, they (who) are wolves
a-ni-su:-li	jurors, a jury, they (who) are buzzards
A'-ni?-sa'-sa	the Osages, the Osage tribe, they who are Osages
A'-ni-tsa-la-gi'	the Cherokees
A-ni-ga-lv'-tsi	the French
A-n'-da'-tsi	Germans ('deutsch' is the German word for German)
A-ni-gv'-ni-ge	Blacks
A-ni-da-lo'-ni-ge	Orientals

The seven Cherokee clan names are:

A-ni-tsi'-s-qua	Bird Clan
A-ni-sa'-ha-ni	Blue Clan
A-ni?-a-hwi'	Deer Clan
A-ni-gi-du'-hw(a)(i)	Ki-tu'-wa Clan
A-ni-gi-(t)la-hi	Hair Clan
A-ni-wo:-d(i)	Paint Clan
A-ni-wa-hya'	Wolf Clan

    The meaning of some of the group names above is not apparent any
more, but you can make sense of many of them.

    See the Introduction for 'Osage' in Cherokee.

    There are several theories about the origin of the word for
'Cherokee' but they are only educated guesses.

A-ni- can also be added to ta?-li (two) and tso-i (three), but not to
any other numbers, when referring to living beings.
Examples:

    a-ni-ta?-li tsu-no'-du a-na:-t'   two pretty young-girls
    a-ni-tso-i (a)-ni-gv'-hni-ge we:-si   three black cats

CORE VOCABULARY

road	nv-no-hi
big highway	u-ta'-n'-ga-nv'-hnv

Verbs:

be angry

I am angry	a-ki-na-lv'-(ga)
you are angry	tsa-na-lv'-(ga)
he/she is angry	u-hna-lv:-(ga)
you & I are angry	gi-ni-han-lv'-(ga)
you two are angry	s-di-hna-lv'-(ga)
another & I are angry	o-gi-ni-hna-lv'-(ga)
others & I are angry	o-gi-hna-lv'-(ga)
you plural are angry	i-tsi-hna-lv'-(ga)
they are angry	u-ni-hna-lv'-(ga)
you another or others & I are angry	i-gi-hna-lv'-(ga)

cross over

I am crossing over	de-tsi-n'-di'-s-ga
you are crossing	de-hi-n'-di'-s-ga
he/she is crossing	de-ga-n'-di'-s-ga
you & I are crossing	de-ni-n'-di'-s-ga
you two are crossing	de-s-di-n'-di'-s-ga
another & I are crossing	do'-s-di-n'-di-s-ga
others & I are crossing	do-tsi-n'-di'-s-ga
you plural are crossing	de-tsi-n'-di'-s-ga
they are crossing	da-ni-n'-di'-s-ga
you another or others & I are crossing	de-di'-n'-di'-s-ga

jump along, jump

I am jumping	de-ga-li?-ta-de:-(ga)
you are jumping	de-ha'-hl'-ta-ge:-(ga)
he/she is jumping	da-hl'-ta-de-(ga)
you & I are jumping	de-na-hl'-ta-de'-(ga)
you two are jumping	de-s-da-hl'-ta-de'-(ga)
another & I are jumping	do-s-da-hl'-ta-de'-(ga)
others & I are jumping	do-tsa-l'-ta-de'-(ga)
you plural are jumping	de-tsa-l'-ta-de:-(ga)
they are jumping	da-na-l'-ta-de:-(ga)
you, another or others	de'-da-l'-ta-de:-(ga)
& I are jumping	

Exercise 1: Match up the two columns, then check from Phrases in Lesson XVIII.

A. 1. u-no-de:-na
2. yo-nv
3. o'-ga-na'
4. si'-qua
5. nv-no-hi
6. u-na-k'-so-tsa-ne-dv
7. wa-ga
8. wa-hya'
9. a-hwi'
10. kv-tli

B. 1. ᎠᏫ
2. ᏩᎦ
3. ᏏᏅ
4. ᎬᏟ
5. ᎤᏃᏕᎾ
6. ᎣᎦᎾ
7. ᏲᏆ
8. ᏅᏃᎯ
9. ᏩᏯ
10. ᎤᎾᎧᏐᏣᏁᏛ

Exercise 2: Match up the two columns A and B, then on next page.

A. 1. The beaver is coming this way.
2. The buffalo is going that way.
3. The raccoon is crossing the road.
4. A panther is eating a deer.
5. The cattle are going further away.(over there)
6. A rabbit is jumping away (from us).
7. I am on my way (starting a minute ago).
8. Why is your dog angry?
9. Several horses are crossing the river.
10. I hear a wolf.

X. 1. They live in the wilderness.
2. martin(s)
3. bluejay(s)
4. squirrel(s)
5. leaf(ves)
6. raspberries
7. wasp(s)
8. fox(es)
9. bobcat(s)
10. nightingales.

B. 1. Tlv-da-tsi a-hwi ga-hye?-a.
2. Wa-ga ge-wa-ne:-ga.
3. Hi-lv'-s-gi so'-qui-li' da-ni-n'-di'-s-ga e-quo-ni.
4. Do-ya da-ya?-i.
5. Tsi-s-du wi-da'-l'-ta-de.
6. Kv-tli de-ga-n'-di'-s-ga nv-no'-hi.
7. Ya'-n'-s-si' wa:?-i.
8. Wi-ga:?-i.
9. Wa-hya ni-ga-we:-s-kv ga-tv'-gi.
10. Do-hv tsa-tse-li gi:-tli u-hna-lv:-ga?

Exercise 3: Translate the sentences below from Cherokee into English and check the correct answer or answers below each sentence.

1. Ga-do' u-n'-s-di u-n'-da-n'-ti ga-na-tla-i?
a. di-ga-li-nv-hi-dv
b. wa-hya'
c. tsi-ta:-ga
d. tlv-da'-tsi

2. Ga-do' u-n'-s-di i-na-ge a-ne:-hi?
   a. a-tsv'-ya
   b. do-ya
   c. ya'-n'-si'
   d. wa-ga

3. Ga-do' u-n'-s-di ga-na'-tla-i u-n'-da-n'-ti a-le i-na-ge a-ne:-hi?
   a. so'-qui-li'
   b. tsi'-s-du
   c. di?-li
   d. yo-nv

4. Tsi-mi, Ke-ni a-le Tsa-ni du-ni-lv-hwi-s-ta-ne?-~~i~~ tsu-na-de-l'-qua-s-di-i. Tsa-ni a-su'-la-go'-ga a-le u-we-nv-sv-i e:-ga. Tsi-mi a-di?-a Ke-ni:
   a. Tsa-ni wa:?-i.
   b. Tsa-ni do-ya.
   c. Tsa'-ni da-ya?-i.
   d. Tsa'-ni to-da ye-do:li.

EXERCISE 2:

C. 1. ᏢᏓᏥ ᎠᏫ ᎦᏰᎠ
   2. ᏩᎦ ᎨᏩᏁᎦ
   3. ᎯᏄᏍᎩ ᎰᏈᎵ ᏓᏂᎾᏗᏍᎦ ᎡᏉᏂ
   4. ᏩᏍ ᏂᎦᏛᏍᎬ ᎦᏅᎩ
   5. ᏙᏍ ᏓᏍᎢ
   6. ᏥᏍᏚ ᏫᏓᎵᏔᎦ
   7. ᎬᏟ ᎦᎦᎾᏗᏍᎦ ᎤᏃᎯ
   8. ᏯᎾᏍᏏ ᏩᎢ
   9. ᏫᎦᎢ
   10. ᏙᎶ ᏩᏤᎵ ᎩᏟ ᎤᎾᏄᎦ

EXERCISE 3:

1. Which are domestic animals? a.donkey c.chicken
2. Which are wild animals? b.beaver c.buffalo
3. Which are domestic and wild animals? a.horse b.rabbit
4. Jim, Ken and John are working at school. John quits and goes home. Jim says to Ken: a.John is going away. d.John is taking time out.

Exercise 4: Write Exercise 3, sentences and multiple choice answers, in Cherokee, then read the Cherokee to someone out loud.

Exercise 5: Translate from Cherokee to English, reading slowly and distinctly out loud, then faster. Write your answers down in English pronunciation <u>and</u> translation. Answers in Column X on page 147.

1. ᎢᎾᎨ ᎠᏁᎯ
2. ᏊᏊ
3. ᏝᎢᎦ
4. ᏌᏩᎵ
5. ᎤᎦᏩᎦ
6. ᎡᏗᏩᎵ
7. ᎤᏓᏄᏔᏗ
8. ᏧᏝ
9. ᎬᎮ
10. ᏍᏆᏐᏩᎵ

ᏓᎳᏟᏍᏗ ᏣᏫᏯ ᎠᏫᏒᏗ

So'-hne-la'-du-i Tsa-la-gi' Go-hwe:-lv-i

CHEROKEE LESSON NINETEEN

Possessive forms in Cherokee - Part I
    a. Differences between ownership and relationship in Cherokee
    b. How to impersonalize Cherokee relationship nouns
    c. Broad outline of possessive forms in Cherokee
    d. Summary of outline

a. Differences between ownership and relationship in Cherokee:

    In English, 'my father' and 'my basket' have the same word, 'my', placed before each of them, although in one case <u>relationship</u> and in the other case <u>ownership</u> is being shown.

    In Cherokee, ownership and relationship are expressed differently. <u>Several ways to say 'my', 'your', 'his', etc. are used.</u> You are familiar with the 'my' of ownership, 'a-qua-tse'-li', (Lesson 17). 'My' in Cherokee is underlined below.
Examples:
    Ownership -

my basket	<u>a-qua-tse'-li</u> ta-lu'-tsi
my dog	<u>a-qua-tse'-li</u> gi:-tli
my cat	<u>a-qua-tse'-li</u> we'-sa
my shoes	<u>di-qua-tse'-li</u> di-la-su'-lo
my farm	<u>a-qua-tse'-li</u> ga-lo-ge:-sv

    Relationship -

my hand	<u>a?-</u>wo-ye:-n(a)(i)
my finger	<u>tsi-</u>ye'-sa-dv
my fingers	<u>de-tsi-</u>ye'-sa-dv
my father	<u>a-gi-</u>do'-da
my cousin	gu'-s-di <u>o'-</u>s-da-da'-dv-hni
my friend	<u>o'-gi-</u>na-li-i
my teacher	di-<u>que-</u>yo'-hv-s-gi'
my teachers	di-<u>gv-que-</u>yo'-hv-s-gi'

149

As you know, Cherokee is a logical and tightly organized language that classifies subjects of discussion in great detail. Since ownership is simple and relationship is complex, it is logical that there is one 'my' of ownership in Cherokee (a-qua-tse'-li) and several 'my's' of relationship.

Relationship and ownership are different in a number of ways. A relationship cannot be taken away from its possessor, but personal property can be sold, stolen or exchanged. Relationship alters living beings internally, but property is externa.. and can change ownership without altering the former owner, the new owner or owners, or the piece of property itself. Relationship must have mutuality while ownership is onesided.

The following four kinds of relationship are separately provided for in Cherokee:
1. A finger cannot exist fully without the person of whom it is a part.
2. A father is only called a father if he has a child.
3. One must be a cousin to have a cousin.
4. A teacher must have a student to complete his or her function as a teacher.

Remember that the idea of ownership or possession in relationships is alien to the Cherokee language. It is only in English translation that possessives such as 'my', 'your' are customarily used with nouns which, in Cherokee, are not considered 'owned' at all. It would be more faithful to the Cherokee meaning to say 'father-to-me', 'teacher-to-me', 'hand-to-me', 'we-two-are-cousins-to-one-another' or 'father-for-me', 'father-in-regard-to-me'.

If a noun needs a possessive in English, when translating it into Cherokee ask yourself if you can give it away. If it can be given away, it is a case of ownership; use a-qua-tse'-li. If not, it is a case of relationship and must come under one of the four kinds of mutuality outlined on page 152. Articles of clothing are an exception to this. It is optional whether to use a-qua-tse'-li or a-gi- with clothes. If the clothing is on, a-gi- is usually used. If it is off, either a-qua-tse'-li or a-gi- may be used.

The relationship terms in Lessons 19 and 20 all describe kinds and degrees of mutual participation. It is important to think of this while learning to use:
1. Cherokee relationship terms
2. The dual of Cherokee verbs
3. Subject-object pronouns

b. How to impersonalize Cherokee relationship nouns:

It is impossible in Cherokee to say 'a hand' or 'a father' without mentioning some person (e.g. my-hand, your-father). If one does not wish to specify whose hand, father, etc., the 3rd person singular or plural is used.

Examples:
    u-wo-ye:-n'   his-hand (the equivalent of 'someone's hand', 'a hand')
    tsu-no-ye:-n'   their-hands (the equivalent of 'several people's hands', 'several hands')

In situations where the meaning of a verb is impersonal with no particular subject noun in mind, English has a choice of 'we', 'one', 'they' or 'you'.

Examples:
    We must love one another.
    One doesn't do that.
    What would they say?
    What you don't know won't hurt you.

Cherokee uses 3rd person singular or plural for this situation also, more often plural. This device is used in many compound nouns.

Examples:
    Thanksgiving   U-(na)-li-he-li-s-di   When we, one, they, or you are thankful

    Saturday   (U-na)-do-da-wi-de:-n(a) When we, one, they or you go out

151

c. Broad outline of possessive forms used in Cherokee: (Expanded outline of Relationships 2 and 3 appears at end of Lesson 20.)

OWNERSHIP

How to show ownership:	Group B bound pronouns prefixed to '-tse'-li' are used as possessive adjectives. (a-qua-tse'-li)
my basket	a-qua-tse'-li ta-lu'-tsi
my dog	a-qua-tse'-li gi:-tli
my shoes	di-qua-tse'-li di-la-su'-lo
my farm	a-qua-tse'-li ga-lo-ge:-sv

If it could be given away, it is owned.

RELATIONSHIP

1. Dependent relationship - (body parts)

How to show dependent relationship:	Bound pronouns from either Group A or Group B are prefixed to the noun. (a-gi-, tsi- or g-)
my hand	a?-wo-ye:-n(a)(i)
my finger	tsi-ye'-sa-dv
my fingers	de-tsi-ye'-sa-dv

A hand cannot exist without the body of which it is a part.

2. Family relationship - (close relatives)

How to show family relationship:	Group B bound pronouns are prefixed to the noun, with the addition of a direct address form, e-.	
my father	a-gi-do'-da	father-to-me, or father-of-mine
	e-do'-da	Father!

A father is only called a father because he has a child.

3. Duplicated relationship - (two-of-a-kind)

How to show duplicated relationship:	Dual bound pronouns of either Group A or Group B are prefixed to relationship phrases. (o-s-d-, o-gi-n-)	
my cousin	gu-s-di o'-s-da-da-dv'-hni	kindred-we-two-are-born
my friend	o'-gi-na'-li-i	we-two-are-friends (to one another)

One must be a cousin to have a cousin and be a friend to have a friend.

4. Subject-object relationship - (verb-phrase nouns)

How to show subject-object relationship:	Bound pronoun changes take place within the verb-phrase. (ni, gv, qu-)	
my teacher	di-que-yo'-hv-s-gi'	maker-of-things-known-to-me
my teachers	di-gv-que-yo'-hv-s-gi'	makers of things known to me
a teacher	di-de-yo'-hv-s-gi'	maker of things known to them
teachers	di-n(i)-de-yo'-hv-s-gi'	makers of things known to them
I teach	de-ga-de-yo'-hv-s-ga	Notice the internal changes of subject-object pronouns.

152

d. Summary of outline:

   After studying the outline on page 152, re-examine the list of examples on the first page of this lesson, noticing how they were formed.

   Now study the following examples and be sure you understand how each one is put together, so that you could change prefixed pronouns yourself:

his/her basket	u-tse'-li ta-lu'-tsi
his/her dog	u-tse'-li gi:-tli
his/her cat	u-tse'-li we'-sa
his/her shoes	tsu-tse-li di-la-su'-lo
his/her farm	u-tse'-li ga-lo-ge:-sv
his-&-his-wife's farm	u-na-tse'-li ga-lo-ge:-sv (Only a very few Cherokee verbs have a 3rd person dual (they-two). Plural is used instead.)
their farm	u-na-tse'-li ga-lo-ge:-sv (Notice it is the same as above.)
my-wife's-&-my farm	o'-gi-na-tse'-li ga-lo-ge:-sv (Bound pronoun 6)
his home	u-we-nv-sv-(i) (occupied-by-him/her) (Since it is made up of a verb phrase that makes the occupant clear, a possessive pronoun would be superfluous - 'his or her occupied-by-him/her'.)
his hand	u-wo-ye:-n'
his hands	tsu-wo-ye:-n'
his finger	ga-ye'-sa-dv
his fingers	de-ga-ye'-sa-dv
his father	u-do'-da
his grandmother	u-li'-si (Also can mean 'grandchild')
his uncle	u-du'-tsi
his cousin	gu'-s-di a-n'-da-dv'-hni (they-are-cousins)
his friend	u-na'-li-i (they-are-friends)
his teacher	tsu-we-hyo'-hv-s-gi'
his teachers	di-gv-we-hyo'-hv-s-gi'

   Body parts and two-of-a-kind relationships can take bound pronouns from either Group A (ts-, g-) or Group B (a?-w-, a-ki, a-gi-), but two-of-a-kind relationships omit the singular bound pronouns.

   Other close relatives (Relationship No. 2) <u>must</u> use Group B bound pronouns.

   Verb-phrase nouns use <u>subject-object bound pronouns</u>, which are shown in Appendix XI. You are familiar with <u>subject bound pronouns</u>.

   Now go over this page again, changing each example to 'their'. (e.g. their basket, u-na-tse-li ta-lu'-tsi) Answers on page 158.

PHRASES

Translation	Syllabary	Pronunciation
128. How many children do you have?	ᏎᎳ ᏕᏣᏓᏘᎿᎠ ᏎᎳ ᏉᏂ ᏗᏪᏥ	Ha-la' de-tsa'-da-ti-hna?-a? or: Ha-la' na-ni di-tse'-tsi?
129. All girls and a single boy.	ᏂᎦᏓ ᎠᏂᎨᏳᏌ ᏌᎤ ᎤᏧᏯ ᎠᏧᏌ	Ni-ga'-da a-ni-ge-hyu:-tsa, sa'-wu u-tsu'-ya a-tsu'-tsa.
130. All boys and one girl.	ᏂᎦᏓ ᎠᏂᏧᏌ ᏌᎤ ᎤᏂᏙ	Ni-ga'-da a-ni-tsu'-tsa sa'-wu u-ni-do'.
131. We are all sisters and brothers.	ᎣᏣᏝᏅᏝᎢ	O-tsa-tla-nv'-dlv-i.
132. We are all sisters (in our family).	ᎣᏣᏓᎸᎩ	O-tsa-da-lv:-gi.
133. We are all brothers (in our family).	ᎣᏣᏝᏅᏝᎢ	O-tsa-tla-nv:-dl(v)(a)-i.
134. Have you heard Ginny is expecting a baby?	ᏍᏨᎦᏁᎨ ᏥᏂ ᎠᎩᏖᏃᏁᎤᏍᏗ	S-tv'-ga-ne-ke Tsi-ni' a-g'-te:-no-h4'-u'-s-di?
135. I hear everything!	ᎦᏨᎦ ᏅᎱᏍᎦ	Ga-tv-ga' ny-hv-s-ga'!
136. Lucy is expecting a visit from her mother.	ᎷᏏ ᎠᎩᏖᏃ ᎤᏥᎢ	Lu-si' a-g'-te:-no u'-tsi-i.
137. Lucy is looking for her children.	ᎷᏏ ᏓᎩᏖᏃ ᏧᏪᏥ	Lu-si' da-g'-te:-no tsu-we'-tsi.
138. Really?	ᏙᎨ	Do'-ke?

154

CORE VOCABULARY

farm   ga-lo-ge:-sv

singleton (single   u-tsu'-ya
  example of one type
  mixed in with some
  of another type)

Verbs:

be born
  I was born   a-qua-de:-hne
  you were born   tsa-de:-hne
  he/she was born   u-de:-hne

  you & I were born   gi-n'-de:-hne
  you two were born   s-da-de:-hne
  another & I were born   o-gi-n'-de:-hne

  others & I were born   o-ga-de'-hne
  you plural were born   i-tsa-de:-hne
  they were born   u-n'-de:-hne

  you, another or others   i-ga-de:-hne
  and I were born

Notice that 'your children' means 'those that were born to you'
                                        de-tsa-da-ti-hna?-a

expect, look for, await
  I am expecting   tsi-ga-te:-no-ha'
  you are expecting   hi-g'-te:-no-ha'
  he/she is expecting   a-k'-te:-no-ha'

  you & I are expecting   i-ni-k'-te:-no-ha'
  you two

  others & I are expecting   o-tsi-k'-te-no-ha'
  you plural are expecting   i-tsi-k'-te'-no-ha'
  they are expecting   a-ni-k'-te-no-ha

  you, another or others   i-di-k'-te'-no-ha'
  and I are expecting

155

be married

```
    I am married                    tsi-ne:-li
    you are married                 hi-ne:-li
    he/she is married               ga-ne:-li

    you and I are married           di-ni-ne:-li
    you and I are married           i-ni-ne:-li
      (to each other)
    you two are married             s-di-ne:-li
    another & I are married         o'-s-di-ne'-li
    my spouse                       o'-s-di-ne'-li

    others & I are married          o-tsi-ne'-li
    you plural are married          i-tsi-ne'-li
    they are married                a-ni-ne'-li

    you, another or others          di-di-ne'-li
    and I are married
    we live here                    i-di-ne'-la
```

Exercise 1: Match up the sentences below. Then write Column A in Cherokee.

A. 1. A-gʼ-te:-noha uʼ-s-di.
   2. A-gʼ-te:-no   uʼ-tsi-i.
   3. A-gʼ-te:-no   u-weʼ-tsi.
   4. A-gʼ-te:-no   uʼ-s-di.

B. 1. She is looking for her children.
   2. She is expecting a baby.
   3. She is looking for her baby.
   4. She is expecting her mother.
   5. She is looking for her child.

Exercise 2: Verb drill. Translate, and state a. how many are acting and b. which set of subject bound pronouns (A or B) is being used.

1. a?-wa-duʼ-li
2. i-ga-duʼ-li
3. i-ni-gi-a
4. ga-wo:-ni-a
5. o-s-di-gi-a
6. gi-ni-yo-huʼ-se
7. o-gi-ni-yo-huʼ-se
8. tsi-su-la-goʼ-ga
9. hi-su-la-goʼ-ga
10. to-da:-de-doʼ-li
11. to:-da-ge-doʼ-li
12. da-gi-lv-hwi-s-taʼ-ne?-a
13. do-gi-lv-hwi-s-taʼ-ne?-a
14. de-gi-lv-hwi-s-ta-ne?-a
15. s-di-ne:-li
16. i-tsi-kʼ-teʼ-no-haʼ
17. u-nʼ-de:-hne
18. tsi-ga-te:-no-haʼ
19. ha-di?-a
20. a-nʼ-di?-a

Exercise 3: Match up the columns below, then write them in Cherokee first, without looking at the syllabary, second, consulting the syllabary.

1. u-tsuʼ-ya
2. ga-lo-ge:-sv
3. gi-nʼ-de:-hne
4. i-ni-kʼ-te:-no-haʼ
5. o-gi-doʼ-da
6. u-duʼ-tsi
7. a-gi-duʼ-da
8. e-liʼ-si
9. u-de:-hne
10. oʼ-gi-ni-tloʼ-gi
11. tsi-ga-te:-no-haʼ
12. di-ni-ne:-li
13. di-di-neʼ-li
14. o-tsa-da-lvʼ-gi
15. do-ke
16. o-tsa-tla-nv:-dla-i
17. a-giʼ-tsi
18. eʼ-tsi
19. uʼ-tsi
20. u-weʼ-tsi

1. my mother
2. others and I are sisters
   (we, excluding you, are sisters)
3. others and I are brothers (we,
   excluding you, are brothers)
4. a single among many of another kind
5. my grandfather
6. a farm
7. you and I are expecting (something)
8. you and I were born
9. really?!
10. his or her uncle
11. he or she was born
12. grandmother!
13. his or her child
14. his or her mother
15. mother!
16. our father(Johnʼs, Maryʼs and mine,
    not yours)
17. our aunt (Johnʼs and mine, not yours)
18. I am expecting (something)
19. you and I are (each) married(people)
20. we are all married (you, another
    or others and I)

157

EXERCISE 1: A.1 -B.2 A.2 -B.4 A.3 -B.5 A.4 -B.3
  A. 1.DᏚᏛZᏤ ᎤᎾᎠᎫ
      2.DᏚᏛZ ᎤᎯᎢ
      3.ᛁ ᛁ ᎤᏫᎯ
      4.ᛁ ᛁ ᎤᎾᎫ

EXERCISE 2: 1.Iwant, one, B 2.you, another or others & I(we all) want, three or more, B 3.you and I are eating, 2, A 4.he is speaking, one, A 5.Another and I are eating, 2, A 6.you and I are losing (something), 2, B 7.Others and I(we but not you) are losing, three or more, B 8.I am quitting, one, A 9.you are quitting, one, A 10.you, another or others and I (we all) are taking time out, three or more, A 11.I am taking time out, one, A 12.I am working, one, B 13.others and I (we but not you), are working, three or more, B 14.you, another or others and I (we all) are working, three or more, B 15.you (two) are married, two, can't tell by this pronoun which group of pronouns is being used, A or B. 16.you (plural) are expecting (something or someone), three or more, can't tell by this pronoun whether A or B group of pronouns is being used. 17.they were born, three or more, B 18.I am expecting, one, A 19.you are saying, one, A 20.they are saying, three or more, A

EXERCISE 3:

1.4 ᎤᎫᎠ		11.18 ᎯᏚᏛZᏤ
2.6 ᏚᏉᎮ		12.19 ᏒᎯᎲᏞ
3.8 ᎩᎾᏚᏫ		13.20 TᏞᏫᏞ
4.7 TᎲᎧᏛZᏤ		14.2 ᏙᏍᏞᏯ
5.16 ᏙᎩᎥᏓ		15.9 ᎥᏞ
6.10 ᎤᏚᎯ		16.3 ᏙᏍᏓᏓᎤᏚT
7.5 DᎩᏚᏓ		17.1 DᎩᎯ
8.12 ᏣᏞᏴ		18.15 ᏣᎯ
9.11 ᎤᏚᏞ		19.14 ᎤᎯ
10.17 ᏙᎩᎯᏯᏯ		20.13 ᎤᏫᎯ

EXAMPLES FROM PAGE 153:
their basket, u-na-tsi'-li ta-lu'-tsi
their dog, u-na-tse'-li gi::-tli (his dogs - tsu-tse-li gi::-tli, their dogs -
        tsu-na-tse-li gi::-tli, why?)
their cat u-na-tse'-li we:-sa
their shoes tsu-na-tse-li' di-la-su'-lo
their home u-ne-nv-sv-(i) (made of a verb)
their hands tsu-no-ye:-n' ('their hand' would be a logical impossibility)
their fingers da-ni-ye'-sa-dv
their father u-ni-do'-da
their grandmother u-ni-li'-si
their uncle u-ni-du'-tsi
their cousin gu-s-di a-n'-da-dv'-hni
their friend u-na'-li-i
their teacher tsu-ne-yo-hv'-s-gi'

ᏔᎵᏍᎪᎯᏁ ᏣᎳᎩ ᎪᏪᎸᎢ

Ta-lʼ-s-go-hi:-ne Tsa-la-giʼ Go-hwe:-lv-i

TWENTIETH CHEROKEE LESSON

Relationship terms in Cherokee - I
     Cherokee social life revolves around relatives to a great extent,
so some familiarity with relationship terms is more necessary in
Cherokee than in English conversation.

a. Direct address and close relatives of an older generation
b. Same-generation relatives
c. Expanded outline of Relationships 2 and 3 from page 152

a. Direct address and close relatives of an older generation:

     In addition to the usual ten bound pronouns of Group B (approximately
a-gi, ts-, u-, gi-n-, s-d-, o-gi-n-, o-g-, i-ts-, u-n-, i-g-), all the
words in Cherokee for close relatives of an older generation have an
eleventh form that is used when speaking directly <u>to</u> older-generation
relatives.
Examples:
     Sit down, Father.   E-doʼ-da, ha-lʼ-s-du-tlvʼ-ga.
     My father just sat down.   A-gi-doʼ-da ki-loʼ-wu a-lʼ-s-du-tlvʼ-ga.

     The a-gi-doʼ-da form is used <u>only</u> when speaking <u>about</u> a close
     relative.

     These Cherokee direct-address forms are primarily for direct address
within the family and are the equivalent of capitalizing in English (as
in ʼFatherʼ above), or pet names such as ʼAuntieʼ or ʼSisʼ. They are
used when speaking <u>to</u> your own relatives, but, like their equivalent in
English, (see ʼFatherʼ above), they can also be used when speaking <u>about</u>
close relatives.
Examples:
     Auntie is coming (she is in sight).   E:-tlo-gi da-ya?-i.
     My aunt is coming (she is in sight).   A-gi-tlo-giʼ da-ya?-i.

     Mother is not at home.   E:-tsi tla yu-wo:-dla.
     My mother is not at home.   A-giʼ-tsi tla yu-wo:-dla.

In the past, direct address forms of relationship terms were more extensively used than they are today, both in and out of the family. Strangers also might be addressed by relationship terms in order to express cordial courtesy. The term used depended on the approximate ages of the Cherokee speaker and the male stranger: e.g. 'Brother' to someone of like age, 'Child' to someone obviously younger, 'Father' or 'Uncle' to someone obviously older, or 'Grandfather' to someone much older. To female strangers, 'Cousin' (Kinswoman) was often preferred. Elderly tribal members, most of whom were blood relatives, were frequently addressed as 'Uncle' or 'Aunt'. A chief was apt to be called 'Father' by many of his constituents. He, in speeches to them, might say: 'My children' (da-qua-da-ti-hna?v-(i), 'Kindred' (gu'-s-di i-da-da-dv-hni), 'Brothers' (i-da-tla-nv'-tlv-i), or we-Cherokees (i-di-tsa-la-gi') or you-Cherokees (i-tsi-tsa-la-gi'). Notice which bound pronouns are used in the previous Cherokee words: Bound pronoun No. 1 for 'my children', bound pronoun No. 10 (we all) for the next three, and bound pronoun No. 8 (you plural) for the last example.

The Cherokee language used to contain a larger variety of relationship terms, such as special words for grandparents, aunts and uncles on the mother's or father's side, and for older or younger brothers. These have dropped out of use.

Probably under the influence of English, Cherokee now uses terms for only the same close relations of an older generation that are commonly used in English, as follows:

| grandfather | father | uncle |
| grandmother | mother | aunt |

In Cherokee, terms for these relatives all have Group B bound pronouns prefixed and the eleventh prefix, e-, for direct address. Bound pronouns below are varied to illustrate how they are used.
Examples:

a-gi-du'-da	my-grandfather
tsa-li'-si	your-grandmother
u-do'-da	his-or-her-father (another's father)
gi-ni'-tsi	yours-and-my mother, the mother of you and me (our mother, said by one sibling speaking to another sibling. Siblings are persons who share the same mother and father, i.e. a brother or a sister.)
s-di-du'-tsi	the-uncle-of-you-two (your uncle, speaking to two siblings)
o-gi-ni-tlo'-gi	his-or-her-and-my-aunt, speaking to someone outside the family

Older generation relationship terms are shown below with the prefix e-
for direct address, so that you can see the base of each word. The base
is that part of the word which remains the same whatever else is added.
As you know, however, in Cherokee some sounds change when they come in
contact with one another. Therefore, in Cherokee, word bases can change
slightly.

E-du'-da	Grandfather	E-do'-da	Father
E-li'-si	Grandmother	E:-tsi	Mother

E-du'-tsi	Uncle	
E:-tlo-gi'	Aunt	

	grandfather	grandmother	father	mother
1. my	a-gi-du'-da	a-gi-li:-si	a-gi-do'-da	a-gi'-tsi
2. your	tsa-du'-da	tsa-li'-si	tsa-do'-da	tsa'-tsi
3. his or her	u-du'-da	u-li:-si	u-do'-da	u'?-tsi
4. yours & my	gi-ni-du'-da	gi-ni-li'-si	gi-ni-do'-da	gi-ni:-tsi
5. of you two	s-di-du'-da	s-di-li'-si	s-di-do'-da	s-di:-tsi
6. h/h & my	o'-gi-ni-du'-da	o-gi-ni-li'-si	o'-gi-ni-do-da	o-gi'ni'-tsi
7. our(not yr)	o-gi-du-da	o-gi-li'-si	o-gi-do'-da	o-gi'-tsi
8. your(plural)	i-tsi-du'-da	i-tsi-li'-si	i-tsi-do'-da	i-tsi'-tsi
9. their	u-ni-du'-da	u-ni-li-si	u-ni-do'-da	u-ni:-tsi
10. yr h/h or their & my	i-gi-du'-da	i-gi-li'-si	i-gi-do'-da	i-gi:-tsi
11. direct address	E-du'-da	E-li'-si	E-do'-da	E:-tsi

	uncle	aunt
1. my	a-gi-du'-tsi	a-gi-tlo-gi'
2. your	tsa-du'-tsi	tsa'-tlo-gi'
3. his or her	u-du'-tsi	u:-tlo-gi
4. yours & my	gi-ni-du'-tsi	gi-ni:-tlo-gi'
5. of you two	s-di-du'-tsi	s-di-tlo-gi'
6. his or her & my	o'-gi-ni-du'-tsi	o'-gi-ni'-tlo-gi'
7. our (not your)	o'-gi-du'-tsi	o-gi-tlo-gi
8. your (plural)	i-tsi-du'-tsi	i-tsi-tlo-gi
9. their	u-ni-du'-tsi	u-ni'-tlo-gi'
10. your, his/her or their & my	i-gi-du'-tsi	i-gi'-tlo-gi'
11. direct address	E-du'-tsi	E:-tlo-gi

b. Same-generation relatives:

Cherokee terms for relatives of the same generation are arranged differently from those of English. Review Relationship 2 and Relationship 3 on page 152, then read on below.

In English, the word chosen for a sibling (the word 'brother' or the word 'sister') depends only on the sex of one sibling: the sibling being spoken of. Examine the sentences below:

> Leslie's brother is tall.
> Leslie's sister is tall.

> The doctor's sister just arrived.
> The doctor's brother just arrived.

From the English sentences above we cannot tell whether Leslie and the doctor are male or female. They could be of either sex. All that can be told from the sentences above in English, is that Leslie (whether he or she) and the doctor (whether he or she) each has a male sibling in one sentence, and a female sibling in the other sentence.

In Cherokee, the word chosen for 'brother' or 'sister' changes according to whose brother or sister is being spoken of, as well as according to the sex of each sibling.

If reference is made to the brother of a female or to the sister of a male, a-gi-do'-i (my-sibling-of-the-opposite-sex) is used, and the usual Group B bound pronouns: tsa-do'-i (your-sibling-of-the-opposite-sex), u-do'-i (his/her sibling-of-the-opposite-sex), etc. Examples:

(If Leslie is a female):
  Leslie's brother is tall.   Le-s-li u'-do i-ni'-ga-ti'.

(If the doctor is a male):
  The doctor's sister just arrived. Ga-na?-ti u'-do ga-lu?-gi.

Notice that since 'u'-do-(i)' means 'sibling-of-the-opposite-sex', u'-do above means 'brother' in one sentence and 'sister' in the other. The Cherokee word means: 'of-the-same-ancestry-as-myself-(of-the-opposite-sex)'.

Remember that in English, in order to use the correct relationship term, who is tall and who arrived (a male or a female sibling) must be known to choose the correct term. In Cherokee, whose sibling is tall and whose sibling arrived must be known also, not only to choose the correct term but also to understand what the term (u-do-(i)) means.

If reference is made to the <u>sister of a female</u> (fellow-sister),
a-gi-lv:-gi (my-fellow-sister) is used.
Examples:
    (If Leslie is a female):

Leslie's brother is tall.	Le-s-li u'-do i-ni'-ga-ti'.
Leslie's (fellow)sister is tall.	Le-s-li u-lv:-g' i-ni'-ga-ti'.

    (If the doctor is a female):

The doctor's (fellow)sister just arrived.	Ga-na?-ti u-lv:-gi ga-lu?-gi.
The doctor's brother just arrived.	Ga-na?-t' u-do'-i ga-lu?-gi.

If reference is made to the <u>brother of a male</u> (fellow-brother), dual
verb forms are used.
Examples:
    (If Leslie is a male):

Leslie's (fellow)brother is tall.	Le-s-li di-n'-da-hnv'-tli i-ni'-ga-ti'.
Leslie's sister is tall.	Le-s-li u'-do i-ni-ga-ti'.

    (If the doctor is a male):

The doctor's sister just arrived.	Ga-na?-ti u-do'-i ga-lu?-gi.
The doctor's (fellow)brother just arrived.	Ga-na?-ti di-n'-da-hnv'-tli ga-lu?-gi.

Same-generation terms are a mixture of Relationship 2 and Relationship
3 on page 152:

Sibling-of-the-opposite-sex	Group B bound pronouns are attached to the word base. Direct address form is s-gi- or e-, more often s-gi-.
Fellow-sister	Group B bound pronouns prefixed, but dual verb form for direct address.
Fellow-brother	Dual verb forms throughout.
Fellow-cousin of either sex	Dual verb forms and Group B bound pronouns.

A brother speaking of his sister and a sister speaking of her
brother both use the same word, a-gi-do'-(i) (also A-gi-do'-(i)),
meaning 'sibling-of-the-opposite-sex'. The word for 'fellow-brother',
(brother spoken of in reference to his brother), means 'we-two were born
alike', i.e., alike in both sex and ancestry.
Examples:
  A brother speaks <u>to</u> his sister:
        Sibling-of-the-opposite-sex, come here.
                S-gi-do'-i or E-do'-i, e-he:-na.
He speaks <u>of</u> her: My sister is going (will go) to town.
             (A)(A)-gi-do'-(i) di-ga-du'-hv da-ye:-si.

Brother speaks <u>to</u> brother:
      Born-like-me, come here.
                  Di-n'-da-hnv'-tli, e-he:-na.

He speaks <u>of</u> him: Mark is my brother. (Mark he-and-I are fellow-brothers)
                Ma:-ga tso'-s-da-da-hnv'-tli.

A sister speaks <u>to</u> her brother:
      Sibling-of-the-opposite-sex, come here.
                S-gi-do'-i or E-do'-i, e-he:-na.

She speaks <u>of</u> him: My brother (my-sibling-of-the-opposite-sex) is playing
              baseball.
                A-gi-do'-i s-qua-tle:-s-di da-ne-lo-hv-s-ga.

Sister speaks <u>to</u> her sister:
      You-(<u>who</u>)-are-my-fellow-sister, come here.
                Di-n'-da-lv:-gi, e-he:-na.

She speaks <u>of</u> her: Mary is my (fellow)-sister.
                Me:-li a-gi-lv:-gi.

Notice that a sister speaking of her sister uses the form 'a-gi-lv:-gi', but speaking to her uses the dual, or two-of-a-kind form, 'di-n'-da-lv:-gi', meaning 'we-two (you-and-I)-are-sisters).

	sibling-of-the-opposite-sex	siblings-of-the-opposite-sex
1. my	(ᴁ)(a)-gi-do'-(i)	di-gi:-do <u>or</u> tsv-gi-do'-i
2. your	tsa-do'-(i)	di-ge:-tsa-do
3. his/her	u-do'-i or u'-do	tsu-do'-i or tsu'-do
4. yrs. & my	gi-ni-do'-i	di'-gi-ni'-do-(i)
5. of you two	s-di-do'-i	di-s-di:-do-(i)
6. h/h & my	o-gi-ni-do'-i	tso'-gi-ni-do'-(i)
7. our (not yr)	o-gi-do-i	tsu-ni-do-i
8. yr plural	i-tsi-do-i	di-tsa-do'-i
9. their	u-ni-do'-i	tsu-ni:-do-(i)
10. yr, h/h or their & my (of all of us)	i-gi-do-i	di-gv'-gi-do'-i
11. direct address	S-gi-do'-i or E-do'-i	

e. Expanded outline of Relationships 2 and 3 from page 150:

Family relationship	close relatives	Group B pronouns are prefixed to the base of each noun
a. older generation	my grandfather	a-gi-du'-d(a)(i)
	my grandmother	a-gi-li'-si
	my father	a-gi-do'-da
	my mother	a-gi'-tsi-i
	my uncle	a-gi-du'-tsi
	my aunt	a-gi-tlo'-gi
b. same generation	my sibling-of-the-opposite-sex	a-gi-do'-i
	my fellow-sister	a-gi-lv:-gi
	my cousin	gu'-s-di a-qua-hni
c. younger generation	my child	a-que'-tsi
	my grandchild	u-li'-si
d. by marriage	my in-law (includes any in-law plus the parents and siblings of your child's spouse	a-gi-lo-si:-yv
	my in-laws	da-gi-lo-si:-yv

Duplicated relationship	two-of-a-kind	Dual verb phrases
a. by family origin (always the same generation)	my cousin	gu'-s-di o'-s-da-da-dv'-hni (kindred we two were born)
	my fellow-brother	tso'-s-da-da-hnv'-tli
	my fellow-sister	tso'-s-da-da-lv:-gi
b. by choice	my friend	o'-gi-na'-li-i (we two are friends)
	my spouse (usually husband but can also be wife)	o'-s-di-ne'-1(i) (we two, he or she and I, live together)

165

CORE VOCABULARY

aunt(my)	a-gi-tlo-gi'
ball	s-qua-tle:-s-di

'playing ball' usually means baseball.

If someone should ask: 'Ga-do u'-s-di s-qua-tle:-s-di di-ne-lo-hv:-s-gi?' (What kind of ball are they playing?) the answer would be either: 'Go'-s-dv-ni-ha' (hitting, i.e., baseball) or: 'A-hyv-te:-s-gi' (kicking, i.e., football)

cousin (my)	gu-s-di a-qua'-hni
father (my)	a-gi-do'-da
fellow-brother (my)	tso'-s-da-da-hnv'-tli
fellow-sister (my)	a-gi-lv:-gi
friend (my)	o-gi-na'-li-i
grandfather (my)	a-gi-du'-da
grandmother (my)	a-gi-li:-si
in-law (my)	a-gi-lo:-si
just, already	ki-lo'-wu
mother (my)	a-gi:-tsi
sibling-of-the-opposite-sex (my)	(a)(ɑ)-gi-do'-i
spouse (my)	o-s-di-ne'-l(i)
tall	i-ni'-ga-ti'
town	ga-du'-hv
uncle (my)	a-gi-du'-tsi

166

Verbs:
    E-he:-na (pp. 162 and 163) in this lesson is the same verb as wa:?-i
and da-ya:?-i in Lesson 18. E-he:-na and de-he:-na mean come.
               Hwe:-na   means go.

    Notice that da-, de-, di-, d- at the beginning of the verb 'go in no
particular direction' turns it into 'go-here, come-here, come', while wi-,
often reduced to w- at the beginning of this same verb changes it to 'go-
there, go-away, go'.
    '----' in the columns below means that the form you might expect in that
space does not occur.

Come! and Go! (requesting that it be done - imperative)

1. (I) ----		----	(I)	----	----
2. (you) come!	e-he:-na or de-he:-na		(you)	go!	hwe:-na
3. have him or her come	tse:-na		have h/he go	we:-na	
4. let's (y-&-I) come	----		let's y-&-I go	----	
5. you two come!	s-de:-na		you two go!	wi-s-de:-na	
6. let's (a-&-I) come	----		let's a-&-i go	----	
7. (others-&-I)	----		----	----	
8. you plural come!	di-tse:-na		you plural go!	wi-tse:-na	
9. have them come	di-ne:-na		have them go	wa-ne:-na	
10. let's all of us come	----		----	----	

Go away! (Go more!) U-tli he:-na! or U-tli hwe:-na!

play
    I am playing   de-ga-ne-lo-hv'-s-ga
    you are playing   de-ha-ne-lo-hv'-s-ga
    he or she is playing   da-ne-lo-hv'-s-ga

    you-&-I are playing   de-na-ne-lo-hv'-s-ga
    you two are playing   de'-s-da-ne-lo-hv'-s-ga
    he or she-&-I are playing   do-s-da-ne-lo-hv'-s-ga

    others-&-I are playing   do-tsa-ne-lo-hv'-s-ga
    you plural are playing   de-tsa-ne-lo-hv'-s-ga
    they are playing   da-na-ne-lo-hv'-s-ga

    you, another or others and I are playing de-da-ne-lo-hv'-s-ga

167

Notice that many verbs with meanings that involve movement from one place to another have di- or de- prefixed. This can show either that the action is taking place some distance from the speaker or that the verb's action involves movement from one place to another.
Examples:

de-tsi-n'-di'-s-ga	I am crossing over
de-ga-l'-ta-de:-ga	I jump, lope
de-ga-ne-lo-hv'-s-ga	I am playing

Di- or de-, often reduced to d- can also be added to nouns, where it means that the noun is some distance away, out of sight of the speaker, around the edge of his or her usual horizon.
Examples:

di-ga-du'-hv	a town (some distance away)
ga-du'-hv	a town (here or nearby)
da-da'-nv-nv	a store (some distance away)
a-da'-nv-nv	a store (here or nearby)

Exercise 1: Translate into English. Answers on next page.
1. A-gi-du'-da i-ni'-ga-ti.
2. Gi-ni'-tsi tla yu-wo:-dla.
3. S-di-du'-tsi ga-no-hi-li-to'.
4. O-gi-ni-tlo-gi' wa?-i.
5. Tsa-li'-si do-yu u-da-n'-ti.
6. Ni o:-s-da tsa-lv-gi squa-tle:-s-di da-ne-lo-hv'-s-gi!
7. E:-tsi, tsu-ni-la-wi-s-di-i i-ne:-na.
8. U-tli he:-na, ge:-tli! Di-tse-nv:-sv-i w'-he:-na!
9. Na a-ge-hyv a-hyv tsa-ni-hno o-gi-ni-tsi.
10. Tsa-ni u'-do o:-s-da di-ka-no-gi-s-gi.
11. Me:-li u'-do a-l'-s-ta-yv-hv'-s-ga a-ha-ni'.
12. Gu'-s-di a-quv'-hni di-ga-du'-hv da-ye:-si sv-hi:-ye?-i

Exercise 2: Write Exercise 1 in Cherokee letters. Answers on next page.

Exercise 3: Review test. Answers are on page 170. Write the answers in
            English letters.
1. our (not your) sibling of the opposite sex
2. your (plural, i.e. speaking to several men) sister
3. Sister, pass me the broom.
4. Your brother is buying several seedlings, Mark.
5. Our uncle is coming pretty soon. (Write 'our uncle' three ways)
6. My aunt has five ducks.
7. My husband works hard on the farm. (present tense or habitual)
8. You two girls' grandmother just put some delicious cornbread on the table.
9. Pass me a knife and fork.
10. They are quitting their jobs.
11. This book is mine.
12. My mother's flowers are growing well.
13. When does the pretty typist quit work?
14. That's the way it is! The repairman will not come today.
15. Brother, hand me your smart little squirrel. (spoken by a female)
16. I am angry. I am becoming angry. I become angry habitually. I am an
    ill-tempered person.
17. My brother and I were born in Texas. (spoken by a female)
18. Mark and his brother are playing ball elsewhere.
19. I work on Monday and Wednesday. Saturday I play. (habitual)
20. I have a pet (gentled) nightingale.

Exercise 4: Write the numbers from one to fifteen in Cherokee letters.
Answers are on the next page.

Exercise 5: Name three birds, three fruits, three plant parts, three days
of the week, three colors, three months, and three household articles.
Write them all in Cherokee letters.

Exercise 6: Check your answers to Exercise 5 by examining previous lessons.
Birds - L. 13 Fruit - L. 14 Plants 14 Days of week 15 Months L. 9

169

EXERCISE 1:
1. My grandfather is tall.
2. Yours-and-my mother is not at home.
3. The uncle of you two is hunting.
4. His-or-her-and-my aunt is walking away.
5. Your grandmother is very kind.
6. See how well your sister plays ball! (Talking to a girl)
7. Mother, let's be on our way to church. (you and I)
8. Get out of here, dog! Go home!
9. That woman is John's and my mother.
10. John's sister sings well.
11. Mary's brother is eating here.
12. My cousin is going to town this evening.

EXERCISE 2:
1. ᎠᎩᏍᏛ ᏔᏂᏍᎫ
2. ᏲᏂᏟ ᏣᏀᏫᎥ
3. ᏬᎶᏏᏈ ᎦᏃᎠᏛᎤ
4. ᏬᏴᏂᏦᎩ ᏣᎢ
5. ᏣᎴᏃ ᏚᏣ ᎤᏬᎴ
6. Ꮂ ᏚᎣᏟ ᏣᎠᎩ ᏬᏔᏞᎠᏗ ᏞᎠᏧᎤᏔᎩ
7. ᎳᎢ ᏧᎭᏫᎣᏬᏗᏔ ᎢᏫᎠᎾ
8. ᎤᏟ ᏊᎾ ᎩᏟ! ᏗᏫᏟᏔ ᎤᏊᎾ
9. Ꮎ ᎠᏝᏰ ᎠᏈ ᏣᎲᏃ ᏚᏲᏂᏟ
10. ᏣᏂ ᎤᎥ ᏚᎣᏟ ᏞᎣᏃᏳᎠᎩ
11. ᎠᏞ ᎤᎥ ᎠᏞᏬᏫᏈᎠᏉ ᎠᏘᏂ
12. ᏛᎠᏗ ᎠᎬᏂ ᏛᏍᏉ ᏔᎴᏋ

EXERCISE 4:

Exercise 7: Name five animals and their plurals. Write them in singular and plural in Cherokee letters. Check answers from Lesson 18 or others.

Exercise 8: Translate the verbs below into English. Tell how many (approximately) are acting, and put down additional English equivalent translations if there are any.

1. o-tse:-ga
2. s-da-l'-tso-hv'-s-ga
3. hi-wi-sv'-s-ga
4. de-tsi-tla-hv'-ga
5. do:-s-di-tla-hv'-ga
6. a-quo'-tla
7. A-GI-NA-A
8. O-GI-HA
9. i-gi-hwa'-s-ga
10. U-NV-YA
11. a-di-ta'-s-ga
12. U-WA-YA
13. ge'-li-a
14. o-s-de'-li-a
15. o:-ts'-tv'-gi
16. a-ni-lu'-gi

170

EXERCISE 3:
1. o-gi-do'-i
2. i-tsi-do'-i
3. Di-n'-da-lv:-gi, gv-no-sa'-s-di di-s-gi-di'-si.
4. Ma:-ga, di'-s-da-da-hnv:-tli (hi-lv'-s-gi) di-ga'-koh-di tsu-hwa'-s-ga.
5. O-gi-ni-du'-tsi(our, the uncle of him and me) tlv-tlv-yv da-ye:-si.
   O-gi-du'-tsi(our, the uncle of several of us, excluding you) tlv-tlv-yv
   da-ye:-si.
   I-gi-du'-tsi(our, the uncle of all of us) tlv-tlv-yv da-ye:-si.
6. A-gi'-tlo-gi' hi'-s-gi du-we'-ka-ha' ka-wo-ni.(na).
7. O'-s-di-ne'-l ga-lo-ge:-s-gv-i s-ta-yo:-sv du-lv'-wi-s-ta-ne'-hv.
8. S-di-ge-hyu'-tsi(tsa) s-di-li'-si u-te?-di se-lu ga-du ga-s-ki-lv-i
   a-tla-hv-ga.
9. A-ye'-l'-s-di yv-gi-hno do-di-s-ge-di:-si.
10. U-ni-su-la-go'-tse tsu-ni-lv:-w'-s-ta-n'-ti.
11. Hi?-a di-go-hwe'-li a-qua-tse'-li.
12. A-gi-tsi-i a-ni-tsi-lv'-s-gi (o:-s-da) (d)a-n'-tv-s-ga.
13. Ha-la'-yv u-wo'-du di-sØ'-s-ti:-s a-su-la-go-go?-i (or toda ye-do:-li-i)?
14. S-gi-dv nu-s-di! O'-s-da-i-gv-ne'-hi tla ga-lu-tsi ko-hi'.
15. S-gi-do'-i, tsa-tse-li' a-sa-ma'-ti u'-s-di sa-lo'-li de-s-ki-ka'-si.
16. A-ki-na-lv-ga. A-ki-na-lv:-s-ga. A-ki-na-lv-s-go. A-ki-na-lv-gi'-s-gi.
17. (A)A-gi-do Nv-da:-gi o-gi-n'-de:-hne.
18. U-tsa-ti-ni Ma:-ga a-le di-n'-da-hnv'-tli s-qua-tle:-s-di da-na-ne-lo-
    hv'-s-ga.
19. Do'-da-quo'-hnv-i a-le Tso?-i-ne i-ga da-gi-lv'-w'-s-ta-ne'-ho. Do-da-
    wi-de:-na de-ga-ne-lo-hv'-s-go.
20. U-da'-n'ti s-qua-le'-wa-li a-gi-ka-ha.

Exercise 9: Translate into English. Answers are on the next page.
1. u'-tsi
2. E-li'-si!
3. u-do'-i
4. u-na-tse'-li s-qua-tle:-s-di
5. tsu-tse-li sv?-ta
6. a-qua-tse'-li we:-si u-tse'-li ta-lu'-tsi
7. tsi'-s-du wi-da'-l'-ta-de'-ga
8. o'-gi-tlo-gi (not dual because she is the aunt of three in all)
9. gi-ni'-tlo-gi (dual as she is the aunt of a total of two, yours-&-mine)
10. nv-no-hi da-ni-n'-di-s-ga

Exercise 10: Translate into English. Answers are on the next page.
ᏕᎠᏈᏫ ᎲᏍᏛ ᏈᎲᎷᏯ. ᎢᏞᎣᎲᏓ. ᏤᏸᏊ. ᏊᏣᏃᎷ ᎶᎲ. ᎤᎤ ᎢᎣᏗᏫ. ᎦᏫ.
ᎤᎮᏣᎲᏬ ᏠᎯᏴᎢᎠ. Ꮈ ᎬᏫ. ᎤᏞᎵᏈ ᏠᎯᏴᎢᎠ. ᎪᎪ ᎬᏫ. ᏗᏫᏟᎡᎢ ᎨᏕ.
ᎥᏢᎯᏃᎢ.

171

EXERCISE 8:

1. we are going, several, others-&-I, we excluding you
2. you two are getting fatter, two, 2nd person plural
3. you are planting, one, 2nd person singular
4. I just put them on it, 1st person singular, plural object
5. he or she and I are putting them on it, two, another-and-I, plural object
6. I am sitting down, staying home, one, 1st person singular
7. I have something flexible, one, 1st person singular, classifying verb
8. we have it (something flexible), others-&-I, we exclusive, we not you
9. we all are buying, several, we all, you-another-or-others-&-I, we, inclusive
10. they have it (something long, inflexible), several, 3rd person plural
11. he or she is drinking, one, 3rd person singular
12. he or she has it (something long, inflexible), one, 3rd person sing.
13. I think so, one, 1st person singular
14. we think so, two, he or she and I think so, another-and-I
15. we hear, several, others-&-I, we exclusive
16. they just arrived, several, 3rd person plural

EXERCISE 9:

1. his or her mother
2. Grandmother!
3. her brother
4. their ball
5. his apples
6. my cat's basket (my cat his or her basket)
7. the rabbit is jumping away
8. our aunt (speaking to two people)
9. our aunt (speaking to one person)
10. they are crossing the road

EXERCISE 10:

I'm glad you all came. Won't you sit down?
How are you?
Very fine, George. Let's have some coffee.
Yes, thank you.
Do you take sugar?
No, thank you.
Do you take cream?
Yes, thank you.
I am going home now. Goodbye.

ᎤᏟᎶᏍᏗ ᏣᎳᎩ ᎪᏪᎸᎢ

Ta-l'-s-go-sa'-wu Tsa-la-gi' Go-hwe:-lv-i

CHEROKEE LESSON TWENTY-ONE

Relationship terms in Cherokee - II
    a. Two-of-a-kind relationship terms
    b. Fellow-brother, fellow-sister, fellow-cousin
    c. Younger-generation relatives - child and grandchild

a. Two-of-a-kind relationship terms:

It is useful to remember that in two-of-a-kind relationship terms in Cherokee the dual can be the <u>singular</u> of the two-of-a-kind term, since the two-of-a-kind pair are thought of as a <u>set</u>, like a pair of shoes.

Relationship terms are only one of the several situations that can have a <u>singular</u> form in English and a <u>dual</u> or even <u>plural</u> form in Cherokee.

For instance, in Cherokee it is not customary to say 'I talked with John.'(singular), unless you actually did all the talking. 'John he-and-I talked.'(<u>dual</u>), is the natural Cherokee form. You do not say 'I saw him yesterday.'(singular), unless this is literally true. 'We (another-and-I) saw one another yesterday.'(<u>dual</u>) is the natural form in Cherokee. More than two people can also be acting in an English singular sentence, as in 'I walked home with them.' The Cherokee form would be 'Others-and-I (excluding you) walked home together.'(plural). These English sentences can be called false singulars since, though they are singular in form (I talked.., I saw.., I walked..), they are plural in meaning.

Make a practice of noticing these false singulars in English and you will have no trouble with the Cherokee forms. Ask yourself: How many are acting? (one, two, more) If the answer is two or more, ask yourself: What combination is acting? (you-&-I, another-&-I, others-&-you, etc.) The answer to this will give you the proper bound subject pronoun to use on any Cherokee word.

173

b. Fellow-brother, fellow-sister, fellow-cousin:

There is a singular of 'fellow-sister' and 'fellow-cousin', but
no Cherokee singular of 'fellow-brother'. The left-hand columns below
describe the situations when each Cherokee term is usually used. Literal
English meanings of the Cherokee terms are in brackets. Alternate
English meanings are listed just before each Cherokee term. It is
common in Cherokee for a phrase that could be translated as a full sentence in English to be used as a Cherokee noun. Each of the relationship terms below is both a noun and a whole sentence in Cherokee and
can be used as either in Cherokee.

Remember, possession in regard to relatives is not a Cherokee concept.
In Cherokee, no relative is said to possess any other relative, but the
whole set of fellow-brothers, fellow-sisters, fellow-cousins, or siblings
is thought of as a unit. Because of this, many Cherokee terms have
several English equivalents.

Fellow-brother

Dual

A brother speaks to his brother:	(you-&-I are brothers to one another) Brother! di-n'-da-hnv'-tli
A brother speaks of his brother:	(he-&-I-excluding you are brothers to one another) my brother he is my brother I am his brother tso'-s-da-da-hnv'-tli
Anybody speaks to a male:	(you-two are brothers to one another) your brother (speaking to one person) you(singular) are his brother he is your (singular) brother di'-s-da-da-hnv'-tli
Anybody speaks to anybody about two brothers:	
	(two-born-alike, same term as 'Brother!') his brother he is his brother they are brothers (total of two brothers) di-n'-da-hnv'-tli

Notice that in the plural forms of fellow-sister, fellow-brother and
fellow-cousin, the Cherokee forms overlap with singular and plural forms
in English. The situations covered are:
1. speaking to one of several brothers about his brothers
2. speaking to two or more brothers about an additional brother
3. speaking to two or more brothers about two or more additional
   brothers

Plural
A brother speaks to an outsider: (we-excluding you are several brothers)
      my brothers (two or more brothers besides
           the speaker)
      our (not your) brother
      our (not your) brothers (total three or
           more brothers)
          o'-tsa-tla-nv'-tlv-i

Anybody speaks to one of several brothers:
          (you-plural are several brothers)
  Speaking to one person: your brothers
  To more than one: your brother or brothers
      you (singular) are their brother
      you (plural) are his brothers
      you (plural) are their brothers
         i-tsa-tla-nv'-tlv-i

Anybody speaks to anybody about several brothers:
         (they are several brothers)
      his brothers (total of three or more)
      he is their brother
      their brother
      their brothers (total of four or more)
      they are his brothers
      they are their brothers (four or more)
         a-na-tla-nv'-tlv-i

    A-na-tla-nv'-tlv-i can also mean 'brothers and sisters' when speaking of a specific entire family.

Comprehensive plural
Several brothers talking among themselves -
A brother speaks to at least one of his own brothers about another brother
or brothers:
      (we-(including everyone addressed or
       referred to) are brothers)
      our brother
      our brothers
      my brothers
      you (singular) are our brother
      you (plural) are my brothers
      we are your brothers
      they are our brothers
      he is our brother
      I am the brother of all of you
      we are all brothers
         i-da-tla-nv'-tlv-i

Fellow-sister

<u>Dual</u>
A sister speaks to her sister: (you and I are fellow-sisters)
                                   Sister!
                                       Di-n'-da-lv:-gi
                                   You are my sister - S-gi-lv:-gi

<u>Singular</u>
A sister speaks of her sister: (this person is a fellow-sister to me)
                                   my sister
                                       a-gi-lv:-gi
Anybody speaks to a female: (this person is a fellow-sister to you)
                                   your sister
                                       tsa-lv:-gi
Anybody speaks to anybody about two sisters: (this person is a fellow-
                                   sister to that person)
                                   her sister (<u>can't</u> mean 'his sister' or
                                   'u-do'-i' would be used)
                                       u-lv:-gi
                                   I am her sister - tsi-lv:-gi

<u>Dual</u>
A sister speaks to her sister: (you and I are fellow-sisters)
                                   you are my sister
                                   I am your sister
                                       di-n'-da-lv:-gi
Anybody speaks to one <u>or</u> two sisters about the two of them:
                                       (you two are sisters to one another)
                                   your sister
                                   you are her sister
                                   she is your sister
                                       di'-s-da-da-lv:-gi
A sister speaks to an outsider about herself and her sister:
                                       (we two (she and I) are sisters)
                                   my sister
                                   she is my sister
                                   I am her sister
                                       o'-s-da-da-lv:-gi
A sister speaks to an outsider about herself-and-a-sister, speaking about
a <u>third</u> sister:
                                       (she is the sister of the <u>two</u> of us)
                                   my sister (total three sisters)
                                   my sisters (total three sisters)
                                   our sister (total three sisters)
                                   she is our sister (total three sisters)
                                   we two are her sisters (total three sisters)
                                       (o')-gi-ni-lv:-gi

Fellow-sister, continued

In English, speaking to several females <u>about their sister</u>, you would say 'Your sister,'. Speaking to one sister out of a family of several sisters about her sisters, you would say 'Your sisters'.

In Cherokee, addressing either one or more out of a family of several sisters, speaking <u>of</u> either one or more of them, the <u>same</u> word is used: I-tsa-da-lv:-gi (you are several sisters to one another)
Therefore, I-tsa-da-lv:-gi is the equivalent of <u>both</u> these English phrases: Your (plural, i.e. speaking to several) sister
            Your (plural, i.e. speaking to several) sisters

The same reasoning applies to fellow-brother plurals also. (see pp. 173 and 174).
Examples:
    our (not your) sister
    our (not your) sisters <u>both</u> are o-gi-lv:-gi

    their sister
    their sisters <u>both</u> are u-ni-lv:-gi

Notice that there is an extra form below that deals with several sisters which means 'my (several) sisters'.

<u>Plural</u>
A sister speaks to an outsider referring to her sisters:
                Form 1. (my several fellow-sisters)
                        I am their sister (total four or more)
                        they are my sisters (total four or more)
                                o'-tsa-da'-lv:-gi
                Form 2. (we (excluding you) are several sisters)
                        our sister (total four or more)
                        our sisters (total four or more)
                                o'-gi-lv:-gi

Anybody speaks to one or more of several sisters about one or more additional sisters:
                        (you are several sisters)
                        your (speaking to one person) sisters (two or more
                            additional sisters)
                        your (plural) sister
                        your (plural) sisters
                        you are their sister
                        you are their sisters
                                i-tsa-da-lv:-gi

177

Fellow-sister (continued)

Plural, cont.
Anybody speaks to anybody about several sisters:
> (they are several sisters)
> their sister
> they are their sisters
> she is their sister
> they are her sisters
> > u-ni-lv:-gi

Comprehensive plural
Several sisters talking among themselves:
> Form 1. (she is the sister of all of us)
> > i-gi-lv:-gi
> Form 2. (we-(including everyone addressed or
> > referred to) are sisters)
> > our sisters
> > my sisters
> > you (one person) are our sister
> > you (plural) are my sisters
> > we are your sisters
> > they are our sisters
> > I am the sister of all of you
> > we are all sisters
> > > i-da-da'-lv:-gi

Fellow-cousin

Use of the term cousin is simplified because there is no distinction of sex.

One person has one cousin:
    Redbird is my cousin.   To-tsu-hwa gu'-s-di a-qu∤-hni.
    Redbird is your cousin.   To-tsu-hwa gu'-s-di ts∤-hni.
    Redbird is his or her cousin. To-tsu-hwa gu'-s-di u-wa'-hni.
    Dual
    Redbird and I are cousins.   To-tsu-hwa gu'-s-di o'-s-da-da-dv'-hni.
    You and I are cousins.   Gu-s-di i-n'-da-dv'-hni.

One person has more than one cousin:
    My cousins   gu'-s-di di-quv'-hni <u>or</u>
                          gu'-s-di o'-tsa-da:-dv-hni

Two people have one cousin:
    Your-&-my cousin   gu'-s-di gi-nv'-hni
    A cousin of you two   gu'-s-di s-dv'-hni
    His or her-&-my cousin gu'-s-di o-gi-nv'-hni

Two people have more than one cousin:
    Your-&-my cousins   gu'-s-di tso'-s-da-da:-dv-hni
    The cousins of you two gu'-s-di s-da-dv'-hni
    His or her-&-my cousins gu'-s-di o-tsa-da:-dv-hni

Several or many people are cousins to one another:
    we(excluding you) are cousins gu'-s-di o-gv'-hni or gu'-s-di tso-gv-hni
    you plural are all cousins   gu'-s-di i-tsa-da-dv-hni
    they are cousins   gu'-s-di a-n'-da-dv'-hni

All of us present or referred to are cousins:
                          gu'-s-di i-da-da:-dv-hni

The plural forms of fellow-cousin (bottom four forms above) include the same various English meanings as the plurals of fellow-brother and fellow-sister:
Examples:
    we(excluding you) are cousins means both our cousin and our cousins
    you plural are cousins means both your (speaking to several) cousin
      and your cousins
    they are cousins means both their cousin and their cousins
    we are all cousins includes the same variety of meanings as we are all
      fellow-brothers and we are all fellow-sisters

Fellow-cousin (continued)

Since cousin means 'kindred' it can cover any blood or marriage relationship in the general sense of 'being related'.
Examples:

Are you any relation to him/her?	Gu'-s-di-ke s-da-da-dv'-hni?
	Gu'-s-di-ke s-quv'-hni?
Are you any relation to John?	Gu'-s-di-ke s-da-da-dv'-hni Tsa'-ni?

Sample answers to questions of relationship:

John and I are cousins.	Tsa'-ni gu'-s-di o'-s-da-da:-dv'-hni.
John is my fellow-brother.	Tsa'-ni tso'-s-da-da-hnv'-tli.
I am a sister to John.	Tsa'-ni a-gi-do'-i. or A-hyv' Tsa'-ni tsi-do'-i.
John is an in-law of mine.	Tsa'-ni a-gi-lo-si:-yv.
John is my uncle.	Tsa'-ni a-gi-du'-tsi.
I am John's uncle.	A-hyv' Tsa'-ni tsi-du'-tsi.
John and I go to the same church.	Tsa'-ni i-tsu-la-ha tso-s-di-la-wi-tsi-do'-hi.
John and I work at the same place.	Tsa'-ni i-tsu-la-ha tso-gi-ni-lv'-wi-s-ta-ne'-hi.
John and I went to school together.	Tsa'-ni tso-gi-n'-de-l'-gwa?-v?-i.
John and I grew up together.	Tsa'-ni i-tsu-la-ha tso-gi-n'-tv'-sv?-i.
John and I are old friends.	Tsa'-ni o-gi-na-li-i. or:
(... for a long time friends already were and still habitually are.)	Tsa'-ni go-hi-gi o-gi-na-li ni-ge:-so.

c. Younger-generation relatives: child and grandchild

Terms for younger-generation relatives in Cherokee are simple. Relationship terms mean only 'child, children'. There is no word for 'son'
or 'daughter'. To specify, the words a-ge-hyu:-tsa, a-ni-ge-hyu:-tsa
(girl, girls) or a-tsu:-tsa, a-ni-tsu:-tsa (boy, boys) are used, but
usually no mention is made of the sex of one's children.

The words for 'child' are made up of passive verb forms such as
'issued', 'sprouted', 'born' so the words for 'children' have di-
plurals.
Examples:

u-we'-tsi, tsu-we'-tsi	(issued from him or her)
(di plus u-)	his or her child, his or her children also means 'an egg, eggs' (Lesson 13)
a-hyo'-tli, di-ni-yo'-tli	(sprouted, being grown) a child, children

Terms for 'child, children' are of two kinds: Those that need bound
pronouns and those that do not. The two terms above (u-we'-tsi and
a-hyo'-tli) are examples of each.

180

a. Terms that have bound pronouns must refer to one's own offspring, i.e. to children actually born to the person or persons mentioned in the bound pronoun. Since there can be no such thing as a child born to more than two people, plural bound pronouns cannot be used.

my child	a-que'-tsi	my children	di-gwe'-tsi
your child	tse'-tsi	yr. children	di-tse'-tsi
his or her-&-my child	o-gi-ne'-tsi	h/h&-my children	tso-gi-ne-tsi
child of you two	s-de'-tsi	children of our	di-gi-ne'-tsi
our (your & my) child	gi-ne'-tsi	(yr.&my) plural	
their (of a pair)	u-ne'-tsi	their children	tsu-ne'-tsi

my children	da:-gwa-da-ti-hna?-v	(those-born-to-me) There
your children	de-tsa-da'-ti-hna?-v	is no singular.
his or her children	du-da-ti-han?-a	
their children	du-n'-da-ti-hna?-a	
I have children	da-gi-ka'-ha	(I have live things; classifying verb with 'live' classifier)

b. Terms that do not need bound pronouns can refer to either one's own or to any other children. With a-qua-tse'-li, one's own children are usually intended. A-hyo'-tli, di-ni-yo'-tli is the commonest Cherokee word for 'child, children'.

Examples:

na a-hyo'-tli   that child (might be your own or a completely unknown child)

tsa'-tse-li' a-hyo'-tli your child (probably your own but perhaps only in your care permanently or for a few hours)

Calling to any child one might say 'A-hyo'-tli!' or 'Hi-yo'-tli!' (Child!) in the singular and 'Di-ni-yo'-tli!' or 'Di-tsi-yo'-tli!' (Children!) in the plural.

The bound pronoun term, a-que'-tsi, has no term for direct address except 'S-que'-tsi', which means 'you-are-my-child', as S-gi-do'-i means 'you-are-my-sibling (of-the-opposite-sex)' and S-gi-li'-si (see below) means 'you-are-my-grandchild'. S-gi-do'-i is used to call to a sibling, but S-que'-tsi and S-gi-li'-si are not used to call a child or grandchild. S-que'-tsi is used only occasionally when giving a child firm instructions or advice.

Examples:

I am telling you, my daughter...   S-que'-tsi, gv-yo-se?-a...
Son, be back before dark.   S-que'-tsi, n'-u'-l'-se-hnv-no
                                     i-hi-lu?-tsv?-i'.

The term for 'his or her grandchild' is 'u-li'-si'. Since this same word can mean <u>both</u> 'his or her grandmother' <u>and</u> 'his or her grandchild', the inner meaning of the term must be something like 'skipped-generation-to-him-or-her'. (A-gi-li'-si, skipped generation to me, tsa-li'-si, skipped generation to you, etc.) All grandmother terms except E-li'-si can refer equally well to a grandmother or a grandchild. E-li'-si can mean only 'Grandmother!', and 'S-gi-li'-si' refers only to a grandchild. Both grandfather and grandmother address their grandchild as 'S-gi-li'-si' if they wish to say 'Grandchild!'. However, Cherokees do not call one another by relationship terms nearly as much as formerly.

Again probably under the influence of English, only older-generation relationship terms are habitually used today to address someone within the family.

The terms in this lesson are correct as far as they go, but in practice the use of dual relationship terms is tricky. For situations not explicitly covered here, we recommend that you use non-dual terms as much as possible ('a-gi-lv-gi', 'tsa-lv-gi', etc. and 'gu-s-di a-quv-hni', etc.) unless you live where you can get individual correction from a fluent native speaker.

Exercise 1: What relation are they? Fill the blanks below with Cherokee letters, translating the English material in brackets. Answers on next page.

1. Powhatan was the father (his/her-father) ___ ___ ___ of Pocahontas.

2. Pocahontas was the daughter (his/her-child) ___ ___ ___ of Powhatan.

3. Pocahontas said: "(Father) ___ ___ ___, John Smith is a good man."

4. Tecumseh and Tenskwatawa the Shawnee Prophet were brothers (brother-to-one-another) ___ ___ ___ ___ ___.

5. Sequoyah and George Lowry were cousins (kindred-to-one-another) ___ ___ ___ ___ ___ ___ ___ ___.

6. Sequoyah was the son (his/her-child) ___ ___ ___ of Wurteh. He called her ("Mother") ___ ___ because she was his mother (his/her-mother) ___ ___.

7. Hansel speaks about Gretel, saying: (My sister and I are eating a cookie.) ___ ___ ___ ___ ___ ___ ___ ___ ___.

8. Gretel speaks to Hansel, saying: (Brother, that witch is very wicked!) ___ ___ ___ ___ na s-gi-li' do-yu u-yo!

9. The witch speaks of Hansel and Gretel: (Those children are becoming fatter!) ___ ___ ___ ___ ___ ___ ___ ___ ___ ___ ___ ___!

10. Orville Wright says to Wilbur Wright: (Brother, we are really flying!) ___ ___ ___ ___ ___, ___ ___ ___ ___ ___ ___ ___!

11. Maria Tallchief speaks to Marjorie Tallchief: Sister, we are both dancers. (Fellow-sister, we-two-are-dancers) ___ ___ ___ ___ ___, o-s-da-l'-sgi:-s-gi.

12. Baby Bear speaks to Big Bear: (Father, I want a new chair!) ___ ___ ___, ___ ___ ___ ___ ___ ___ ___ ___!

13. Big Bear speaks to Middle-sized Bear: Our child's chair is worn out. (The-two-of-us's child his/her chair is old (inanimate)). ___ ___ ___ ___ ___ ___ ___ ___ ___ ___.

14. Red Riding Hood was called ___ ___ ___ ___ by her grandmother.

15. Hiawatha was a Mohawk, but Longfellow put Chippewa and Dakota terms into his poem, "Hiawatha". Nokomis means 'my-grandmother' in Chippewa. If Hiawatha had been a Cherokee he would have called his grandmother (___ ___!) She would have called him (___ ___ ___!) (Grandchild!). Speaking about her Hiawatha might have said (My-grandmother is old) (Old (animate)(is) my-grandmother.) ___ ___ ___ ___ ___ ___ ___ ___.

183

16. Laurie, who is no relation, speaks to Meg, Jo, Beth, and Amy: Girls, (you-are-several-sisters), it is very cold here.

17. Meg and Jo speak to a stranger: We two are sisters and we have two more sisters. (She-and-I are sisters and we-are-several-sisters.)

18. Doc speaks to Dopey, Sleepy, and Grumpy: Hi ho, hi ho, (home from work we go, Brothers.)

19. The two ugly sisters say: (We two(she-and-I)-are sisters and Cinderella (Go-s-du?-e:-li) is our sister (the sister of the two of us))

20. Wurteh said of Sequoyah: a. ga-yo-tli b. a-que-tsi c. di-ni-yo-tli

EXERCISE 1:
1. u-do-da
2. u-we'-tsi
3. E-do-da
4. di-n'-da-hnv'-tli
5. gu-s-di a-n'-da-dv'-hni
6. u-we'-tsi, E:-tsi, u:-tsi

7. A-gi-do-i u-ga-na-s-da o-s-di-gi-a
8. S-gi-do-i, na s-gi-li do-yu u-yo.
9. Na di-ni-yo-tli a-na-li-tso-hv-s-ga.
10. Di-n'-da-hnv-tli, do-yu i-ni-no-hi-li.
11. Di-ni-da-lv-gi o-s-da-li-s-gi-s-gi.
12. E-do-da, i-tse ga-s-ki-lo a-wa-du-li.

13. U-we-ti gi-ne-tsi u-tse-li ga-s-ki-lo.
14. S-gi-li-si
15. E-li-si, S-gi-li-si, A-gi-li-si a-ga-yv-li or a-ga-yv-li a-gi-li-si.
16. I-tsi-da-lv-gi, do yu u-hyv-dla a-ha-ni.
17. O-s-da-da-lv-gi a-le (ta-li a-ne-ha) o-tsa-da-lv-gi.
18. I-da-tla-nv'-dla di-ge-nv-sv tsi-de:-na.
19. O'-s-da-da-lv:gi a-le o-gi-ni-lv-gi.
20. b.

Exercise 2: Match the meanings in the columns below. More than one English meaning goes with every Cherokee relationship term. Look up the answers in the fellow-sister, fellow-brother and fellow-cousin tables in this lesson.

A.
1. he is their brother
2. he is my brother
3. our (not your) brother
4. our (not your) brothers
5. my brother
6. their brothers
7. their brother
8. his brothers
9. I am your brother
10. we are your brothers
11. Brother
12. Brothers

B.
1. di-n'-da-hnv'-tli
2. o'-tsa-tla-nv'-tlv-i
3. i-tsa-tla-nv'-tlv-i
4. di-s-da-da-hnv'-tli
5. tso'-s-da-da-hnv'-tli
6. i-da-tla-nv'-tlv-i
7. a-na-tla-nv'-tlv-i

Exercise 3: Column D is a duplicate of Column C. Most are fellow-sister terms. First, cover Column D, and see how many you can answer correctly. Next, examine the answers and reason out the answer to each relationship term as you do so. For the purposes of this exercise, all concerned are females.

C.	D.
1. you are her sister	1. di-s-da-da-lv:-gi
2. Sister!	2. di-n'-da-lv:-gi
3. your sister (to 1 person)	3. tsa-lv:-gi
4. her sister	4. u-lv:-gi
5. she is my sister	5. a-gi-lv:-gi, o-s-da-da-lv:-gi, tso:-s-da-da-lv:gi
6. she is your sister (to 1 person)	6. di-s-da-da-lv:-gi
7. you are their sister	7. i-tsa-da-lv:-gi
8. you are their sisters	8. i-tsa-da-lv:-gi
9. you are her sisters	9. i-tsa-da-lv:-gi
10. you are my sister	10. di-n'-da-lv:-gi
11. you are our sister	11. i-s-gi-lv:-gi
12. you are our sisters	12. i-gi-lv:-gi
13. you all are my sisters	13. i-gi-lv:-gi
14. I am her sister	14. tsi:-lv'-gi, o-s-da-da-lv:-gi
15. I am their sister	15. tso-tsa-da-lvv-gi, di-gi-lv:-gi
16. they are my sisters	16. tso-tsa-da-lv:-gi, di-gi-lv:-gi
17. she is their sister	17. u-ni-lv:-gi
18. her brother	18. u-do-i
19. my cousin	19. gu'-s-di a-quv'-hni
20. he and I are cousins	20. gu'-s-di o'-s-da-da-dv'-hni
21. we are all related	21. gu'-s-di i-da-da-dv'-hni
22. we (not you) are cousins	22. gu'-s-di o-gv'-hni
23. you are my sister	23. s-gi-lv:-gi
24. your-and-my-cousin (the cousin of the two of us)	24. gu'-s-di di-gi-nv'-hni
25. she is our sister	25. i-gi-lv:-gi
26. they are sisters (several)	26. a-n(a)-da-lv:-gi
27. they are sisters (two)	27. di-n'-da-lv:-gi

Exercise 4: Reread this lesson and Lesson XX from beginning to end. Try Exercise 3 assuming one, then both, are males. Look up the answers.

185

ᏔᎵᏦᏁ ᏣᎳᎩ ᎪᏪᎸᎢ

Ta-li'-tso:-ne Tsa-la-gi' Go-hwe:-lv-i

CHEROKEE LESSON TWENTY-TWO

PHRASES

Translation	Syllabary	Pronunciation
139. Fannie and Betty are friends.	ᏥᎨᏳ ᎠᎴ ᏇᏗ ᎤᎾᎵᎢ	Tsi-ge'-yu a-le Que'-di u-na'-li-i.
140. I would like you to meet my friend Daniel. He lives in Tulsa now.	ᎯᎠ ᎣᎩᎾᎵ ᏕᏂᎵ. ᏔᎵᏏᏛ ᎦᏁᎳ	Hi?-a o-gi-na'-li De:-ni-li. Ta-l'-si'-dv ga-ne'-la.
141. I am very happy to meet you, Daniel. Where are you from?	ᎦᎵᎡᎵᎩ ᏥᏕᏂᏓᎪᏩᏛ ᏕᏂᎵ. ᎭᏢ ᏖᎬᎢ	Ga-li-e'-li-gi tsi-de'-n'-da-go-wa?-tv, De:-ni-li. Ha'-tlv te-gv-i?
142. I was born in Texas, but have lived here for two years. (..two already-years)	ᏅᏓᎩ ᎠᏆᏕᏅ ᎠᏎᏃ ᏔᎵᎾᏕᏘ ᏂᎨᎣ ᎠᎭᏂ	Nv-da:-gi a'-qua-de:-hnv, a-se:-hno ta?-li na-de:-ti ni-ge?-o a'-ha-ni'.
143. I have two sisters. One of them lives in Texas. Yesterday I met a friend of my sister's from Texas, Ken Hummingbird.	ᏔᎵ ᎠᏁᎭ ᏗᎩᎸᎩ. ᏌᏭ ᏅᏓᎩ ᏫᎦᏁᎳ. ᏒᎯ ᏙᎩᏂᏢᏒ ᎠᎩᎸᎩ ᎤᎾᎵ ᏅᏓᎩ ᎡᎯ ᎨᏂ ᏩᎴᎳ	Ta?-li a-ne'-ha di-gi-lv:-gi. Sa'-wu Nv-da:-gi wi-ga-ne'-la. Sv'-hi do-gi-n'-dlo:-sv a-gi-lv:-g u-na'-li, Nv-da:-g' e'-hi, Ke-ni Wa-le'-la.
144. I think I know him. How old is he? (How many years may have occurred for him?)	ᏥᏲᎵᎦ ᎨᎵᎠ. ᎭᎳᏱᏳ ᏕᏘ ᏴᏓ	Tsi-yo-li:-ga ge'-li-a. Ha-la'(i)-yu de:-ti yv'-da?

144. (cont.) Is he married?	ᎦᏁᎵᎨ	Ga-ne'-li-ke?
145. I believe he is about twenty-five. He is not married, but he and Mary are going around together.	ᎯᏍᎩᏦᏁᏛ ᎢᏳᏕᏗᏴᏓ ᎨᎵᎠ. Ꮭ ᎦᏁᎵ ᏱᎩ ᎠᏎᏅ ᎺᎵ ᎠᎾᎵᎪᎲᏍᎦ	Hi'-s-gi-tso'-ne-dv i-yu de:-ti-yv:-da ge'-li-a. Tla ga-ne'-li-yi-gi', a-se'-hnv Me:-li a-na-li-go-hv'-s-ga.
146. How long have you lived here, Betty?	ᎭᎳ ᎾᏕᏗ ᏂᏁᎶ ᎠᎭᏂ ᏇᏗ	Ha-la' na-de:-ti hni-ne-lo a'-ha-ni', Que'-di?
147. I've lived here a long time. My oldest (child), who is eight, was born here.	ᎪᎯᏓ ᏂᎨᎣ ᎠᎭᏂ. ᎤᏓᏂᎳᎨ ᏧᏁᎳ ᎢᏳᏕᏗ ᏴᏓ ᎠᎭᏂ ᎤᏕᏅ	Go-hi'-d ni-ge?-o a'-ha-ni'. U-da-hni'-la-ge tsu-ne'-la i-yu de:-ti yv'-da a'-ha-ni' u-de:-hnv.
148. How old is your youngest now, Betty?	ᎭᎳ ᎢᏳ ᏕᏗᏴᏓ ᎣᏂ ᎡᎯ ᏇᏗ	Ha-la- i-yu de:-ti-yv'-da o:-hni e-hi, Que'-di?
149. He/she turned four on the 26th of this month. (26th just-past it-was)	ᏅᎩ ᏄᏕᏗᏯ ᏑᏓᎵᏦᏁ ᏏᏅ ᏥᎨᏒ	Nv-hgi nu-de:-ti'-ya su-da-l'-tso'-ne si'-nv tsi-ge:-sv.
150. Did you hear Sally and Jim got married ... last week? (just-past at-this-time) ... a month ago? (a-month it-was) ... two years ago? (two years it-was) ... last May? (May month it-was) ... in May? (any May)	ᏍᏓᏛᎦᏁᎨ ᏌᎵ ᎠᎴ ᏥᎻ ᏕᎨᎦᏨᏍᏔᏅ . . ᏐᏥᏛ ᏟᎩᎵᏒ . . ᏏᏅᏓ ᏥᎨᏒ . . ᏔᎳ ᎾᏕᏗ ᏥᎨᏒ . . ᎠᏂᏍᎬᏗ ᎧᎸ ᏥᎨᏒ . . ᏌᎵ ᎠᎴ ᏥᎻ ᎠᏂᏍᎬᏗ ᎧᎸ ᏕᎨᎦᏨᏍᏔᏅᎢ	S-da-tv'-ga-ne-ke Sa-li (a-le) Tsi-mi de-ge-ga-tsv'-s-ta-nv... so?-tsi-dv tli-gi-li'-sv? ...si-nv'-da tsi-ge:-sv? ... ta?-la na-de:-ti tsi-ge:-sv? ... a-n(i)-s-gv'-ti ka?-lv tsi-ge:-sv? ... a-n'-s-kv'-ti ka?-lv de-ge'-ga-tsv'-s-ta-nv-i.
151. That's wonderful!	ᏙᏳ ᏲᎪ ᎣᏍᏓ!	Do-yu yo-go'? o:-s-da!

152.

Maggie and George are	RⱯ Dↄ Gⱶ	E:-gi (a-le) Tsaʼ-tsi
... getting a divorce. (taking-out papers)	. . AⱮⱢ ⱢhLD	... go-hwe-li da-ni-tle?-a.
... separating. (separating themselves)	. . ⱢOⱢSↄhD	... da-n(a)-lʼ-ga-le-ni?-a.

153.

That's a surprise!	ⱭⱮhↃⱱ	S-qua-ni?-di-wu!
That's a shame!	LOↃ	Tlaʼ-u?-kaʼ!
How surprising.	ⱭⱮhⱵ	S-qua-ni?-di-i.
Does that surprise you?	ⱭⱮhAⱭSↃ	S-qua-nʼ-go:-s-ga-tsu?

Notes:

P.N. 139 - Tsi-geʼ-yu - English baptismal names and their nicknames were introduced to Cherokees by missionaries from New England. In the Cherokee versions of these names, consonants were substituted and vowels were often added to make them sound more natural in Cherokee. These names usually do not mean anything in Cherokee. Examples:

Quidaʼ Peter Tsa:-ni John Qua-quu Bob Wi:?-li Bill/Will
We:-g(i) Becky E-li-niʼ Ellen Queʼ-tsi Betsy Me:-l(i) Mary

Tsi-geʼ-yu is unusual since it means 'Beloved', 'I love him/her' in Cherokee. Frances, nicknamed Fannie, means 'Free', but Cherokee girls who are called Frances or Fannie in English (Fannie is more common), are consistently called Tsi-geʼ-yu in Cherokee.

P.N. 140 - 148 - As you know, Cherokee verb forms contain optional particles that help to describe the action of the verb. There are <u>four</u> sections in a Cherokee verb. Every optional particle belongs in one of these sections. Each section can contain answers to certain questions that might be asked about the action of the verb. Each section must occur in the following order:

1. <u>Prefixes</u>, if any. This section can answer or help to answer the questions where? where-to?, one or more objects?, when?
2. <u>Pronouns</u> who?, whom? Of things: what-kind-of?
3. <u>Verb base</u> what is happening?
4. <u>Suffixes</u> when?, how?, how often?, for how long?, how hard?, to or for anyone? why? with what result? Of things: from or on what level?

1. <u>Prefixes</u> - Cherokee verb forms often begin with prefixes such as wi-, da-, di-. and ni-, that set the stage for the action of the verb. Cherokee prefixes, if any, occur just before the pronoun section of a verb form. Sometimes more than one prefix is used in the same verb form, and when this is the case, they must be arranged in a certain order, as shown in Appendix 12.

188

2. <u>Pronouns</u> - The pronoun section of Cherokee verb forms can contain subject bound pronouns, subject-object bound pronouns and classifiers. You are familiar with all the subject pronouns.

   See Appendix X for the subject-object pronouns of 'Gv-ge-yu-i, I love you', and 'Gv-yo-li:-ga, I know you'.

   Classifying verbs are described in Lessons 5 and 8 and in Appendices V and VIII. The classifiers of classifying verbs can be called <u>precision pronouns</u> dealing mostly with non-living things, as contrasted with <u>bound pronouns</u> dealing exclusively with living things.

3. <u>Verb base</u> - This is the part of the verb form that does not change, or changes very slightly. It tells what is happening.

4. <u>Suffixes</u> - These tell primarily when and how the action of the verb takes place. Suffixes, like prefixes, must be added in a certain order. At least one suffix is necessary in every Cherokee verb form. Sometimes a prefix and a suffix together form a unit of meaning. Example:

   Da- on the beginning (prefixed), and -i on the end (suffixed) in a Cherokee verb form mean that the action of this verb <u>will</u> take place in the future:

Prefixes	Pronouns & Verb Base	Suffixes	
da-	ge:-s <u>or</u> ye:-s	-i	means 'I will go.'

   See Appendices XII and XIII. Several Cherokee suffixes are now dropping out of use, becoming shorter, or changing in meaning.

In Cherokee, as you know, sounds on the edges (i.e. ends and beginnings) of neighboring words often shift or become absorbed. In the same way, sounds on the edges of prefixes, pronouns, verb bases and suffixes within Cherokee verb forms often alter one another at the points where each section adjoins. This can create puzzling changes that appear as submerged and half-submerged particles. For examples, see Notes below concerning P.N. 146, hni-ne-lo and P.N. 147, te-gv-i. Brackets around Cherokee particles in the verb forms below mean that the usual form of this particle is not present. It has been changed by contact with neighboring sounds.

The verb forms on the following page have been divided into four sections, one for prefixes, one for pronouns, one for the verb base and one for the suffixes. The sections have then been arranged in columns <u>like numbers to be added up</u> so that you can follow what a Cherokee verb contains. Every Cherokee verb form can be partitioned in this way.

P.N. 140 - <u>Verb form: ga-ne'-la</u>
   1. Prefixes   none in this verb form
   2. Pronouns   g-   Shows that the subject of this verb form is <u>he or she</u>. Also shows that this verb form uses bound pronouns of Group A, ts-ga.
   3. Verb base   -a-ne-1-   Shows that the action of the verb concerns <u>living with or in, inhabiting.</u>
   4. Suffixes   -a   Shows that the action of the verb is happening at the present time.
Total meaning is: he or she is living in some particular place now

P.N. 143 - <u>Verb form: wi-ga-ne'-la</u>
   1. Prefixes   wi-   Shows that the action of this verb points <u>away</u>, or involves action directed away from where the speaker is at this moment.
   2. Pronouns   -g-   Shows that <u>he or she</u> is the subject, using bound pronouns of Group A, ts-ga.
   3. Verb base   -a-ne-1-   Shows that this verb is about <u>living with or in, inhabiting.</u>
   4. Suffixes   -a   Shows that the verb is happening now.
Total meaning is: he or she is living away from where the speaker is
                   (speaker is in Tulsa, her sister is in Texas)

P.N. 144 - <u>Verb form: ga-ne'-li-ke</u>
   1. Prefixes   none in this verb form
   2. Pronouns   g-   Shows that <u>he or she</u> is the subject of this verb form, using bound pronouns of Group A, ts-ga.
   3. Verb base   -a-ne-1-   Shows that this verb has to do with <u>living with, in or among, inhabiting.</u>
   4. Suffixes   -i   <u>Recent past</u>, changes the meaning of the word for 'inhabit' into 'cohabit', 'be married'. Some Cherokee verbs mean different things according to what tense is used.
              -ke   Shows that this verb is interrogative, <u>asks a question.</u>
Total meaning is: Is he or she married?

P.N. 145 - <u>Verb form: tla ga-ne'-li yi-gi'</u>

1. Prefixes	tla-	Not, shows that this is a negative statement about the action of the verb.
2. Pronouns	-g-	Shows that <u>he or she</u> is the subject of this verb form, using bound pronouns from Group A, ts-ga.
3. Verb base	-a-ne-1-	Shows that the action of this verb has to do with living with or in, inhabiting.
4. Suffixes	-i	Recent past, changes the verb for living with, in or among into that for <u>being</u> married.

yi-gi' - yi-gi is not a suffix. 'Tla yi-gi' is a whole sentence
<u>   meaning 'He/she is not.'</u>
Total meaning: He or she is not married, is unmarried

    Usually a verb is made negative by placing 'tla yi-' in the prefix section of a verb form. However, 'Tla yi-ga-ne'-li' would mean 'He/she does not live there', 'He/she has not lived there recently.', since 'ga-ne'-la' and 'ga-ne'-li' have interlocking meanings. (i.e., different tenses of the same verb have different, though allied, meanings.)

    Normally, Tla yi-gi' is used with nouns and adjectives, or with some verbs for emphasis.
Examples:

Tla i-ni'-ga-ti' yi-gi'.	He/she isn't tall.
Tla ga-na?-ti yi-gi'.	He/she is not a doctor.
Tla u-hna-lv-a yi-gi'.	He/she isn't angry.
Tla u-we-da'-s-di yi-gi'.	He/she doesn't go there.
Tla ga-ne'-li yi-gi'.	He/she isn't married, is unmarried.
Tla di-ka-no-gi'-s-gi yi-gi'	He/she isn't a singer. (... is not a them-singer, not a singer of songs.)

P.N. 146 - <u>Verb form: hni-ne'lo</u>

1. Prefixes	ni-	'Already'. Ni-shows that the action of this particular verb form started before the time referred to in the suffix section. Time is pinpointed in the suffix section.
2. Pronouns	(-hi-)	ni-hi-a-n- has become hni-n. He- is the bound pronoun meaning <u>you</u>, speaking to one person, from Group A, ts-ga.
3. Verb base	(-a-)ne-1-	Shows that this verb form has to do with inhabiting, living with, in or among. -A- of the verb base has been dropped along with -i- from the pronoun, 'hi-'.
4. Suffixes	-o	Shows that the action of this verb is happening now, habitually.

Total meaning: you already were and still are living in a particular
               place

P.N. 141 - <u>Verb form: te-gv-i</u>

1. Prefixes	(da-)	Shows that the action of this verb form is at a distance, facing or coming this way.
2. Pronouns	(hi-)	Shows that the subject of this verb form is you, singular, Group A, g-vowel. Da- next to -hi- becomes t-.
3. Verb base	-e-	Shows that this verb form deals with coming, going, existing, sometimes having.
4. Suffixes	-gv-i	Shows that the action of this verb form happened continuously in the past.

Total meaning is: you are from a certain place, you used to live there

P.N. 142 - <u>Verb form: ni-ge?-o</u>

1. Prefixes	ni-	'Already'. Shows that the action of this verb started before the time indicated in the suffix section.
2. Pronouns	-g-	Shows that the subject of this verb form is <u>I</u>, bound pronoun from Group A, g-vowel.
3. Verb base	-e-	Shows that this verb form has to do with coming, going, existing, perhaps having.
4. Suffixes	-o-	Shows that this verb form takes place now, habitually.

Total meaning is: I have existed (lived) for some time and still live in some particular place

P.N. 143 - <u>Verb form: a-ne-ha</u>

1. Prefixes	none in this verb form	
2. Pronouns	a-n(i)-	Shows that the subject of this verb form is they, Group A.
3. Verb base	-e-	Shows that this form has to do with being, existing, or (particularly in reference to relatives or immovable objects), having.
4. Suffixes	-ha	Shows that the action of this verb form is taking place now.

Total meaning is: they exist, live

Example: I have two sisters.   Ta?-li a-ne-ha di-gi-lv:-gi.
                                  (Two fellow-sisters exist to me.)

Also used in speaking of trees and plants, meaning to grow, stand, have existence.
  Example: Several hickory trees are standing or growing by the water.
        Hi-lv'-s-gi wa:-ne?-i te-tlu-kv a-ma-yu'-hl'-di a-ne-ha.

  Trees, bushes, etc. cannot 'stand' in Cherokee since they can't change position and 'sit' or 'lie'. They also do not 'grow' unless they are thought of as changing in size.

192

P.N. 143 - <u>Verb form: e-hi</u>
1. Prefixes   none in this verb form.
2. Pronouns   none in this verb form. In verbs that take bound pro-
                                nouns of Group A, g-vowel-, <u>no pronoun</u>
                                means that the subject of this particular
                                verb is <u>he or she</u>. (e.g., ge-li-a, e-li-a,
                                I think, he or she thinks, ga-li-he-li-ga,
                                a-li-ge-li-ga, I am glad, he or she is glad)
3. Verb base   -e-   Shows that the action of this verb form
                                has to do with being, existing, perhaps
                                having.
4. Suffixes   -hi   Shows that the action of this verb took
                                place in the recent past.
Total meaning is: he or she just came from where he or she formerly
                       existed

P.N. 147 - <u>Verb form: ni-ge?-o</u>   'I've lived here for...', See 142 above.

P.N. 148 - <u>Verb form: e-hi</u>
1. Prefixes   none in this verb form.
2. Pronouns   none in this verb form. (See P.N. 143 above) Subject
                                is he or she.
3. Verb base   -e-   Shows that the action has to do with being,
                                existing, living, perhaps having.
4. Suffixes   -hi   Shows that the action took place recently.
Total meaning is: he or she recently existed, came into existence

o:-hni e-hi (last existing, last who came to be) means 'youngest', speaking
     usually of one's own child, but also can refer to a relative, as
     my youngest aunt, cousin, etc., but in this case the relationship
     would have to be mentioned. O:hni (last) can be used without e-hi
     to mean 'youngest child' if the meaning is obvious.

u-da-hni'-la-ge, with or without e-hi, means 'oldest', usually one's own
     child, but can be any other relative. For children's ages, ta?-li:-ne
     e-hi, tso-i-ne e-hi (2nd existing, 3rd existing) is often used.

P.N. 144 - tsi-yo-li-ga - I know him. This is a subject-object pronoun.
Remember go-li:-ga in Lesson 6, 'I know (it). In English, the object
is separated from the subject. (I know him). In Cherokee, the subject
and object of a verb are placed together in the pronoun section of the
verb form, just before the verb base.
Example:
1. Prefixes   none in this verb form
2. Pronouns   tsi-yo   I-him
3. Verb base   o-li-g-   know
4. Suffixes   -a   present tense
Total meaning: I know him

P.N. 145 and 149 - hi'-s-gi-tso'-ne-(dv), su-da-l'-tso'-ne   Also see the
heading of this lesson, Ta-li'-tso:-ne for 'twenty-two' instead of 'Ta-
l'-s-go-ta-l''.

In Cherokee, there are eight special numbers from twenty-two through
twenty-nine that are used only when speaking of a numbered set, such as
dates of the month between 22 and 29, total age if it is between 22 and
29, or total lessons so far when there are between 22 and 29. A 22 rifle
is called 'ta-li-tso'-ne'. These numbers mean roughly 'two of the third
ten', 'three of the third ten', etc. They are:

22	ta-li'-tso:-ne	25	hi'-s-gi-tso'-ne
23	tso'-i-tso'-ne	26	su'-da-l'-tso'-ne
24	nv-hgi-tso:-ne	27	ga-hl'-quo'-i-tso'-ne

28 ne:-l'-tso:-ne
29 so-hne-l'-tso'-ne

P.N. 145 -dv, usually means 'indeed, certainly', but it cannot always be
translated this way and sound natural in English. It can also mean 'approximately', 'surely', 'probably'. Sometimes, as in P.N. 140, Tu-l'-
si-dv, it sounds awkward in English to translate it at all. Here, in
P.N. 145, it shows that the speaker is not sure of the exact age. It
means the same as the English 'He must certainly be twenty-five', 'He
is surely twenty-five'.

P.N. 145 - Me:-li a-na-li-go-hv'-s-ga - Notice that though in English it
means 'he and Mary are going around together', it actually says in
Cherokee, 'Mary they are going around together'. Since there is no
Cherokee pronoun for 'he' separate from a verb (see Lesson 13), and since
there is no need to repeat Ken's name, a plural third person bound pronoun on the verb makes the meaning clear. See P.N. 146 and 148 below.

P.N. 150 - Sa-li (a-le) Tsi-mi, P.N. 152 - E:-gi (a-le) Tsa'-tsi - In Cherokee,
if it is obvious or well known that 'and' is meant, it can be omitted.
(Sally, Jim got married; Maggie, George are getting a divorce, and so on.)

P.N. 152 - da-n(a)-<u>l</u>'-ga-le-ni?-a - Notice that this is a reflexive verb (Reflexives are pronouns that <u>reflect back</u> onto the subject (e.g., 'separating <u>themselves</u>.' More verbs in Cherokee use reflexives than in English.

Examples:

a-<u>l</u>'-s-ta-yv-hv'-s-ga	he is having a meal (feeding himself)
ga-<u>li</u>-eh-li-ga	I am rejoicing (I am rejoicing myself)
ha-<u>l</u>'-s-du-tlv'-ga	you just sat down (you just seated yourself)
gu'-s-di s-<u>da-da</u>-dv'-hni	you two are cousins (you two are related to one another)

You are familiar with the Cherokee reflexives, -l' (-self) and -a-da- (-self or one another), which are object pronouns (see Appendix X). Quite often, as you see above, it sounds odd or unnecessary to translate the Cherokee reflexives into English.

In most Cherokee verbs that routinely contain a reflexive, the reflexive must be used, but in da-na-l'-ga-le'-ni-a above, l' is optional in the dual and plural. In the singular, this verb means 'starting' rather than 'starting to separate'. I.e., ga-le'-ni-a, I am starting (myself), ha-le'-ni-a, you are starting yourself, a-le'-ni-a, he/she is starting (him or herself).

CORE VOCABULARY

but	a-se:-(h)n(v)(o)
month	si-nv-d(a)(o)

Si-nv'-da is usually used for a length of time (duration, and cannot be used if a particular month is mentioned. (see May-month, P.N. 150) If the name of a particular month is mentioned, ka?-1(a)(v) must be used, whether speaking of a length of time (durative) or an event at a certain time (punctual).

Texas	Nv-da:-gi
last	o:-hni

week Notice that 'a-tli-gi-li'-svi' (time-past) was used for 'week' in P.N. 150. 'Sv-do'-da-qua'-s-di' (division of a month) is used when the duration of a week instead of an event within the week is referred to.

year
    ((times) a year has occurred)   (i-yu) de:-ti-yv-da

Verbs:

associate with, go around together, approach nearer to one another
    (Can't be in the singular)
    you-&-I go around together   i-na-li-go-hv'-s-ga
    you-two go around together   s-da-li-go-hv'-s-ga
    another-&-I go around together   o'-s-da-li-go-hv'-s-ga

    others-&-I go around together   o-tsa-li-go-hv'-s-ga
    you plural go around together   i'-tsa-li-go-hv'-s-ga
    they go around together   a'-na-li-go-hv'-s-ga

    we all go around together   i-da-li-go-hv-s-ga

be, exist, live somewhere
    I have lived for a period of time and still live there   ni-ge?-o
    you have lived for some time and still live there   hne-ho
    he/she/it has lived for some time and still lives there   ne:-ho

    you-&-I have lived and still live there   ni-ne:-ho
    you-two have lived and still live there   ni-s-de-ho
    another-&-I have lived and still live there   no-s-de'-ho

    others-&-I have lived and still live there   no-tse:-ho
    you plural have lived and still live there   ni-tse'-ho
    they have lived and still live there   na-ne:-ho

    we all have lived and still live there   ni-de;-ho

be married, be a married person
    I am married   tsi-ne'-li
    you are married   hi-ne'-li
    he/she is married   ga-ne'-li

    you-&-I are married people   di-ni-ne'-li
    you-&-I are married to each other   i-ni-ne'-li
    you-two are married people   di-s-di-ne'-li
    you-two are married to each other   s-di-ne'-li
    another-&-I are married people   tso-tsi-ne-li
    another-&-I are married to each other   o-s-di-ne'-li

others-&-I (we, not you) are married	tso-tsi-ne-li
you plural are married	di-tsi-ne'-li
they are married (they are married people)	di-ni-ne'-li
they are married (to one another)	a-ni-ne'-li
they live there	a-ni-ne'-la
we are all married people	di-di-ne'-li

get married
I got married	a-gwa-ne'-l'-dv-i
they got married	u-na-ne'-l'-dv-i

The commonest term for getting married is:
I got married	dv-gwa-tsv'-s-ta-nv-i
you got married	de-tsa-tsv-s-ta-nv-i
he/she got married	da-ga-tsv'-s-ta-nv-i
you-&-I got married	de-gi-n'-tsv'-s-ta-nv-i
you-two got married	de-s-da-tsv'-s-ta-nv-i
another-&-I got married	do-gi-n'-tsv'-s-ta-nv-i
we (others-&-I, not you) got married	do-ga-tsv'-s-ta-nv-i
you plural got married	de-tsa-tsv'-s-ta-nv-i
they got married	de-ge-ga-tsv'-s-ta-nv-i
we all got married	de:-ga-tsv'-s-ta-nv-i

Although the verb for being married is so close to living with or among, inhabiting, etc., it cannot be used of a couple who are living together without having had a marriage ceremony. To describe that situation, only joking remarks are used.

In describing a permanently separated couple, whether there has been a divorce decree or not, the same terms are used:i.e.

They used to be married: U-na-ne-l'-dv **or** A-ni-ne'-li tsi-ge:-sv.

'Tsi-ge:-sv', (formerly existing, used-to-be), is used often. When speaking of someone who is now dead, it is usual in Cherokee to mention this fact. (Mary who used to be, who formerly existed). Tsi-ge:-sv can mean either **'former'** or **'late'**.

Examples:
Me:-li tsi-ge:-sv a-gi-tlo-gi ge:-sv	The late Mary (now dead) was my aunt.
Me:-li a-da-s-da-yv'-hv-s-gi	Mary used to be a cook.
tsi-ge:-sv	

Tsi-ge:-sv is used often in expressions dealing with time. (See P.N. 149 and 150).

Examples:
Tsi-ge:-sv, Nv-no-hi a-ha-ni	There used to be a path here.
E:-ti tsi-ge:-sv	Last year (the year that was)

meet by chance, happen to see
    Dual and plural:

you-&-I met	de-gi-n'-dlo:-sv
you-two met	de-s-da-dlo:-sv
another-&-I met	do-gi-n'-dlo:-sv
others-&-I (we, not you) met	do-ga-dlo:-sv
you plural met	de:-tsa-dlo:-sv
they met	du-n'-dlo:-sv
you, another or others & I met	do-ga-dlo:-sv

separate, start to part
    Dual and plural:

I am separating from you	de-n(a-1')-ga-le'-ni-a
you two are separating	de-s-da-(1')-ga-le'-ni-a
I am separating from him	do-s-da-(1')-ga-le'-ni-a
several of us are separating from one another	do:-tsa-(1')-ga-le-ni-a
you are separating from one another	de'-tsa-(1')-ga-le-ni-a
they are separating	da-n(a-1')-ga-le-ni-a
you, another or others and I are separating	de-da-(1')-ga-le-ni-a

surprise

I am surprised	a?-s-qua-n'-go:-s-ga
you are surprised	s-qua-n'-go:-s-ga
he/she is surprised	u-s-qua-n'-go:-s-ga
you-&-I are surprised	gi-ni-s-qua-n'-go:-s-ga
you-two are surprised	s-di-s-qua-n'-go:-s-ga
another-&-I are surprised	o'-gi-ni-s-qua-n'-go:-s-ga
others-&-I are surprised	o'-gi-s-qua-n'-go:-s-ga
you plural are surprised	i'tsi-s-qua-n'-go:-s-ga
they are surprised	u-ni-s-qua-n'-go:-s-ga
we are all surprised	i-gi-s-qua-n'-go:-s-ga
(we, another or others & I)	

    Notice that 'you are surprised', s-qua-n'-go:-s-ga, seems to have no bound pronoun for 'you', which you would expect to be ts-, since the other subject pronouns are in Group B. Ts- next to s- is too much hissing for Cherokee ears, so ts- plus s- becomes s-.
    If you wish to use a direct object in English, for instance, 'I surprised him', 'she surprised them', a different Cherokee verb must be used, as 's-qua-n'-go:-s-ga' does not combine with subject-object pronouns. S-qua-n'-go:-s-ga in Cherokee is intransitive (i.e., cannot have a direct object.)

Exercise 1: Match up the following sentences from this lesson, then check by looking up the answers.

1. ᎤᎴᎯᏯᏍᏗ
2. ᎠᏛ ᎦᏂ ᎶᎤᎿ
3. ᎠᏗᏱ ᏥᏍᎦ ᎠᏫᎭ
4. ᎤᏛᏫᏏ ᎠᏫᎭ ᎤᎦᏅ
5. De:-ni-li ga-li-e'-li-gi
   tsi-de'-n'-da go-wa?-tv.
6. Tsi-yo-li:-ga ge'-li-a.
7. Ha-la' yu-de:-ti yv'-da?
8. Ta?-li na-de:-ti ni-ge?-o a'-ha-ni'
9. Ta?-li a-ne'-ha di-gi-lv:-gi.
10. ᎡᏏᏊ ᏪᎻ ᏔᎤᏍᏓᏪᎥᎠ
11. ᎦᎳᏫᏫ
12. ᎢᏫᎦ ᎠᏓ ᎤᎤᏂᎢ
13. ᎤᏟᏱ ᎠᏣᏏᎾ
14. Nv-hgi nu-de:-ti'-ya su-da-li'-
    tso'-ne si'-ne tsi-ge:-sv.
15. Tla'-u?-ka
16. Sa-li Tsi-mi de-ge-ga-tsv'-s-ta-
    nv ta?-la na-de:-ti tsi-ge:-sv.
17. Sa-li a-le Tsi-mi de-ge-ga-tsv'-
    s-ta-nv so?-tsi-dv tli-gi-li'-sv.
18. ᎤᏫᎦᏟᏫ ᎤᏢ ᏥᎯ ᎦᏞᏍᏣᎤᏪᎤᏔ
    ᏆᎤᏓ ᏥᏫᎡ

1. That's wonderful!
2. I've lived here a long time.
3. Is she married?
4. Sally & Jim got married two years ago.
5. Sally & Jim got married last week.
6. Did you hear Sally & Jim got married
   a month ago:
7. I am very happy to meet you, Daniel.
8. He turned four on the 26th of this month.
9. Are you surprised?
10. I have two sisters.
11. Fannie and Betty are friends.
12. I think I know her.
13. I was born in Texas.
14. Where are you from?
15. My oldest daughter was born here.
16. Maggie and George are separating.
17. That's a shame!
18. I have lived here for two years.

Exercise 2: Answers are on the next page.

1. Translate this old riddle into Cherokee:
      Brothers and sisters have I none
      But that boy's father is my father's son.

2. Who is that boy? (Translate this question and the answer into Cherokee.)
3. Write the riddle, the question and the answer in Cherokee letters.
4. As you sit in the bus station, a man comes up to you and says: Hi-yo'-
   tli, a-hyv di-ga-de-yo'-hv-s-gi', ha'-tlv dide-lo-qua-s-di-i?
   He wants you to: a. show him the telephone
                      b. show him the school
                      c. direct him to your farm
5. According to sentence 4, you are:
                      a. a child
                      b. a marine
                      c. a farmer
6. According to sentence 4, the man is:
                      a. a new student
                      b. a new teacher
                      c. a repairman

7. You try to chat with a little boy and a little girl in a waiting room. The woman with them smiles and says: 'A-na-tla-nv:-dla.' Does she mean:

> a. They don't speak English.
> b. They are my cousins.
> c. They are my brother and sister.
> d. They are my sister's children.

8. Nancy is the sister of Bob and George.

> a. Na-n'-si' u-do Qua-quu a-le Tsa-tsi.
> b. Na-n'-si' a-gi-do-i Qua-quu Tsa-tsi.
> c. Na-n'-si' u-ni-do Qua-quu a-le Tsa-tsi.

Exercise 3. Review this lesson, then translate the following English sentences directly into written Cherokee. If you wish to simplify this exercise, translate into English letters first, then put the English syllables into Cherokee letters. Answers are on the following page. If necessary, review classifiers in Lessons 5 and 8.

1. I have a brother who lives (off) in Washington. (spoken by a woman)
2. John and Mary are not married, but they are going around together.
3. Daniel, my sister's friend, is from Texas. (spoken by a man)
4. Daniel, my sister's friend, is from Texas. (spoken by a woman)
5. Where are you from, Jim?
6. How old is Fannie?
7. Betty and Sally have lived in Texas for three years now.
8. George and Maggie got married a month ago.
9. George and Maggie got married in the month of May.
10. George and Maggie got married last May.
11. I believe John is about twenty-seven.
12. I think I know him.
13. I think I know Maggie. (Maggie I think I know her.)
14. I have a 22.
15. I met Betty's friend yesterday. (yesterday that was)
16. I met his friend last night. (last night that was)
17. I happened to meet the doctor downtown yesterday. (I am not in town now)
18. One of my brothers lives here in town. (spoken by a man)
19. Hand me my cousin's 22.
20. John and Leslie are at the minister's home.

EXERCISE 2:

1. Tla ya-ne-hv o-tsa-dla-nv-dlv-i, a-se:-hnv na a-tsu'-tsi u-do-da a-gi-do-da u-we-tsi.
2. Ka-ga na a-tsu'-tsa? Na a-tsu-tsa a-gwe'-tsi.
3. Ꮪ ꮿꮅꭹ ꭶꮎꮆꮃꮨ Ꭰꮄꮣ Ꮐ ꭰꮵꭶ ꮩꮅꭲ ꭰꮻꮅꭲ ꮳꮻꮢ. Ꭴꮝ Ꮐ ꭰꮵꭶ. Ꭰꮻꮢ.
4. b, 5.a, 6.b, 7.c, 8.c.

EXERCISE 3:

1. Sa'-wu e-ha a-gi-do(i) Wa-sv-da-no?-i wi-ga-ne'-la.
2. Tsa-ni (a-le) Me:-li tla a-ni-ne-li yi-gi' a-se-hnv a-na-li-go-hv'-s-ga.
3. De-ni:-li a-gi-lv-gi u-na-li-i Nv-da-gi e-hi.
4. De-ni:-li a-gi-do-i u-na-li-i Nv-da:-gi e-hi.
5. Tsi-mi' ha-tlv te-gv-i?
6. Ha-la' i-yu de-ti-yv-da Tsi-ge-yu-i?
7. Que-di (a-le) Sa-li tso-i na-de-ti-ya Nv-da-gi na-ne-ho.
8. Tsa-tsi (a-le) E-gi si-nv-da tsi-ge-sv de-ge-ga-tsv-s-ta-nv-i.
9. Tsa-tsi (a-le) E-gi a-n'-s-kv-ti ka?-lv de-ge-ga-tsv-s-ta-nv-i.
10. Tsa-tsi (a-le) E-gi a-n'-s-kv-ti ka?-lv tsi-ge:-sv de-ge-ga-tsv-s-ta-nv-i.
11. Tsa-ni ga-li-quo-i-tso-ne (ta-l'-s-go ga-li-quo) i-yu-de-ti-yv-da ge-li-a.
12. Tsi-yo-li-ga ge-li-a.
13. E-gi tsi-yo-li-ga ge-li-a.
14. Ta-li-tso-ne a-quv-ya.
15. Sv-hi tsi-ge-sv Que-di u-na-li-i do-gi-n'-dlo-sv.
16. U-sv tsi-ge-sv u-na-li-i do-gi-n'-dlo-sv.
17. Di-ga-du-hv do-gi-n'-dlo-sv ga-na?-ti sv-hi tsi-ge-sv.
18. Sa-wu tso'-s-da-da-hnv:-tli a-ha-ni ga-du-hv-i (ga-ne-la or e-ha).
19. Ta-li-tso-ne de-s-ki-di-si gu-s-di a-quv-hni u-tse-li. or: De-s-ki-di-si ta-li-tso-ne gu-s-di aquv-hni u-tse-li-i.
20. Tsa-ni (a-le) Le-s-li a-l'-tsa-do-hv-s-gi-i tsu-we-nv-sv-(i)((w)a-ne-do).

1. ᏌᏊ ᎡᎭ ᎠᎩᏙᎢ ᏩᏒᏓᏃᎢ ᏫᎦᏁᎳ
2. ᏣᏂ ᎠᎴ ᎺᎵ Ꮭ ᎠᏂᏁᎵ ᏱᎩ ᎠᏎᏅ ᎠᎾᎵᎪᎲᏍᎦ
3. ᏕᏂᎵ ᎠᎩᎸᎩ ᎤᎾᎵᎢ ᏅᏓᎩ ᎡᎯ
4. ᏕᏂᎵ ᎠᎩᏙᎢ ᎤᎾᎵᎢ ᏅᏓᎩ ᎡᎯ
5. ᏥᎻ ᎭᏢ ᏖᎬᎢ
6. ᎭᎳ ᎢᏳ ᏕᏘᏴᏓ ᏥᎨᏳᎢ
7. ᏇᏗ ᎠᎴ ᏌᎵ ᏦᎢ ᎾᏕᏘᏯ ᏅᏓᎩ ᎾᏁᎰ
8. ᏣᏥ ᎠᎴ ᎡᎩ ᏏᏅᏓ ᏥᎨᏒ ᏕᎨᎦᏨᏍᏔᏅᎢ
9. ᏣᏥ ᎠᎴ ᎡᎩ ᎠᏂᏍᎬᏘ ᎧᎸ ᏕᎨᎦᏨᏍᏔᏅᎢ
10. ᏣᏥ ᎠᎴ ᎡᎩ ᎠᏂᏍᎬᏘ ᎧᎸ ᏥᎨᏒ ᏕᎨᎦᏨᏍᏔᏅᎢ
11. ᏣᏂ ᎦᎵᏉᎢᏦᏁ - ᏔᎵᏍᎪ ᎦᎵᏉ - ᎢᏳ ᏕᏘᏴᏓ ᎨᎵᎠ
12. ᏥᏲᎵᎦ ᎨᎵᎠ
13. ᎡᎩ ᏥᏲᎵᎦ ᎨᎵᎠ
14. ᏔᎵᏦᏁ ᎠᏋᏯ
15. ᏒᎯ ᏥᎨᏒ ᏇᏗ ᎤᎾᎵᎢ ᏙᎩᏂᏠᏒ
16. ᎤᏒ ᏥᎨᏒ ᎤᎾᎵᎢ ᏙᎩᏂᏠᏒ
17. ᏗᎦᏚᎲ ᏙᎩᏂᏠᏒ ᎦᎾᏘ ᏒᎯ ᏥᎨᏒ
18. ᏌᏊ ᏦᏍᏓᏓᏅᏟ ᎠᎭᏂ ᎦᏚᎲᎢ ᎦᏁᎳ - ᎡᎭ
19. ᏔᎵᏦᏁ ᏕᏍᎩᏗᏏ ᎫᏍᏗ ᎠᏋᏂ ᎤᏤᎢ
20. ᏣᏂ ᎠᎴ ᎴᏍᎵ ᎠᎵᏣᏙᎲᏍᎩ

Exercise 4. Partition the following verb forms from this lesson. Add up and explain the parts as it is done in the Notes of this lesson and in the example below: Answers are on the next page.

1. Verb form: ga-li-e-li-gi
   1. Prefixes   none in this verb form
   2. Pronouns   g-   I (Set A, g-vowel)
                      -a-l'-   reflexive pronoun meaning - 'self'
   3. Verb base   -i-e-li-g- shows that the action of this verb has to
                                  do with rejoicing, being thankful
   4. Suffixes   -i   shows the action just took place
Total meaning is: I have just started rejoicing, being glad about something.

Verb forms:
   1. a-qua-de:-hnv
   2. ge-li-a
   3. do-gi-n'-dlo:-sv
   4. s-qua-n'-go:-s-ga-tsu
   5. da-na-l'-ga-le-ni-a

Exercise 5: Translate the following verb forms from Cherokee into English: Tell how many (one, two or several) are acting and when the action is taking place. If there is a prefix, identify it and tell its approximate meaning.

   1. gi-ni-s-qua-n'-go:-s-ga
   2. do-ga-dlo'-sv
   3. da-ye:-si or da-ge:-si
   4. na-ne:-ho
   5. ni-ge?-o
   6. a-ne-ha
   7. da-go'-ti-a
   8. a-go'-ti-a
   9. ga-wo:-ni-a
  10. ga-li-e'-li-ga
  11. ga-li-e'-li-gi
  12. i-ga-du'-li-a
  13. u-de:-hnv
  14. da-ya?-i
  15. tsi-gi-a
  16. ha-l'-s-du-tlv'-ga
  17. a-n'-di?-a
  18. o-tsi-su-la-go'-ga
  19. o-gi-yo-hu'-se
  20. a-i-hga

EXERCISE 4:

1. Verb form: a-qua-de:-hnv
   1. Prefixes   none in this verb   subject
   2. Pronouns   a-qu-   I (Group B bound pronouns)
   3. Verb base   a-de:-hn   shows that the action has to do with
                                       being born
   4. Suffixes   -nv   shows that the action took place in the past
Total meaning: I was born

2. Verb form: ge-li-a
   1. Prefixes   none in this verb form
   2. Pronouns   g-   I, Group A, g- vowel
   3. Verb base   -e-li-   shows that the action has to do with
                                       thinking
   4. Suffixes   -a   shows that the action is taking place now
Total meaning: I think or believe

3. Verb form: do-gi-n'-dlo:-sv
   1. Prefixes   d-   plural object
   2. Pronouns   o-gi-n'-   another-and-I, Group B subject bound pronouns
   3. Verb base   -dlo:-s   shows that the action has to do with coming
                                       together, meeting
   4. Suffixes   -sv   shows that the action took place in the past
Total meaning: another-and-I met

4. Verb form: s-qua-n'-go:-s-ga-tsu
   1. Prefixes   none in this verb form
   2. Pronouns   none in this verb form. Ts- (you singular) has
                        merged with -s- leaving 's-'.
   3. Verb base   s-qua-n'-go:- shows that this verb form has to do
                                       with surprising
   4. Suffixes   -s-g   action is progressing (not yet finished)
                        -a   action is taking place now
                        -tsu   questioner, shows the verb form is a ques-
                                       tion
Total meaning: are you surprised?

5. Verb form: da-na-l'-ga-le'-ni-a
   1. Prefixes   d-   plural object
   2. Pronouns   -an(i)-   they
                        al(i)-   -self
   3. Verb base   ga-le-n-   being parted
   4. Suffixes   -i-a   present
Total meaning: they are being parted, separating themselves

EXERCISE 5:

1. you and I are surprised, 2
2. we (several) not you, met, d- plural object
3. I will go, one, da- future (coming toward me)
4. they have lived and still live there, several, ni- already
5. I have lived and still live (there), one, ni- already
6. They exist, several
7. he sees them, one, di-, de-, plural
8. he sees (it), one
9. he is speaking, one
10. I am happy, one
11. I have just been gladdened, one
12. you, another or others and I (we all) want, several
13. he or she was born, one
14. he or she is coming this way, one, da-, movement this way
15. I am eating (it), one
16. you just sat down, one
17. they say, they are saying, several
18. we (not you) are quitting
19. we (not you) lost, are losing
20. it (a rooster) is crowing

ᏦᎢᏦᏁ ᏣᎳᎩ ᎪᏒᎸᎢ

Tso-i-tso'-ne Tsa-la-gi' Go-hwe:-lv-i

CHEROKEE LESSON TWENTY-THREE

154.

money	ᎠᏕᎳ ᎠᏕᎸᎢ	a-de-la or a-de-lv-i
one dollar	ᎤᎾᏍᏓ	u-hno'-s-da
several dollars	ᎤᏂᎾᏍᏓ	u-ni-hno'-s-da
one dollar	ᎤᎾᏍᏓ	u-hno'-s-da
two dollars	ᏔᎵᏕᎸᎢ	ta-l-de-lv-i
three dollars	ᏦᎠᏕᎸᎢ	tso?-a-de-lv-i
four dollars	ᏅᎦᏕᎸᎢ	nv-ga-de-lv-i
five dollars	ᎯᏍᎦᏕᎸᎢ	hi-s-ga-de-lv-i
six dollars	ᏑᏓᎵᏕᎸᎢ	su-da-l'-de-lv-i
seven dollars	ᎦᎵᏬᎦᏕᎸᎢ	ga-l'-wo-ga-de-lv-i
eight dollars	ᏧᏁᎳᏕᎸᎢ	tsu-ne-la-de-lv-i
nine dollars	ᏐᏁᎳᏕᎸᎢ	so-ne-la-de-lv-i
ten dollars	ᏍᎪᎭᏕᎸᎢ	s-go-ha-de-lv-i
eleven dollars	ᏌᏚᎠᏕᎸᎢ	sa-du-a-de-lv-i
twelve dollars	ᏔᎵᏚᎠᏕᎸᎢ	ta-l'-du-a-de-lv-i
thirteen dollars	ᏦᏍᏚᎠᏕᎸᎢ	tso'-ga-du-a-de-lv-i
twenty dollars	ᏔᎵᏍᎪᎠᏕᎸᎢ	ta-l'-s-go-a-de-lv-i
fifty dollars	ᎯᏍᎪᎠᏕᎸᎢ	hi'-s-go-a-de-lv-i
one hundred dollars	ᏍᎪᎯᏟᏆ ᎠᏕᎳ	s-go-hi-ts-qua' a-de'-la
a thousand dollars	ᏌᏊᎢᏯᎦᏴᎳ ᎠᏕᎳ	sa'-wu?-i'-ya-ga-yv'-la' a-de'-la
a million dollars	ᏌᏊᎢᏳᏆᏗᏅᏓ ᎠᏕᎳ	sa'-wu?-i-yu'-qua-di-nv'-da' a-de'-la

155.

one cent or one penny	ᏌᏊ ᏗᏓᏅᏕᏗ	sa'?-wu i-da-n'-te-di
two cents	ᏔᎵᏗᏅᏕᏗ	ta?-li i-da-n'-te-di
three cents	ᏦᎢᏓᏅᏕᏗ	tso-i-da'-n'-te?-di
four cents	ᏅᎩᏯᏗᏅᏕᏗ	nv-gi-i-da-n'-te?-di
five cents, a nickel	ᎯᏍᎩᏯᏗᏅᏕᏗ	hi'-s-gi-i-da'-n'-te?-di
ten cents, a dime	ᏍᎪᏓᏅᏕᏗ	s-go-da'-n'-te?-di
25 cents (quartered)	ᎩᏄᏗ	gi-nu?-di
50 cents (half, middle)	ᎠᏰᏟ	a-ye:-tli

156.
I want to buy a car,   . . ᎠᏯᏥ.ᎤᏫᎯ   Ow?tomobil' a-ki-wa-hi'-
but I don't have enough ᎠᏣᏏᎵ ᎠᏎᏪ   s-di a'?-wa-du'-li, a-se:-
money yet.   ᏟᎡᎵ ᎢᎿᎦ   hnv tla?-e:-li i-ni-gᾴ
   ᎠᏕᎳ ᏏᏗᎦᎲ   a-de-la yi-da-gi-hv.

157.
I am borrowing money.   ᎠᏕᎳ ᏕᎦᏙᎵᎤᏍᎦ   A-de-la de-ga-to'-l'-s-ga.

158.
I am putting my old   ᎤᏪᏗ . . ᎠᏯᎣᎵᏗ   U-we:-ti ow?-tomobili a-g'-
car up for sale.   s-goh'-l'-ti.
(I-just-offered...)

159.
How much do I owe you?   ᎭᎳ ᎡᏍᏕ   Ha-la' gv-tu-ga?
(How-much I-you-owe?)

160.
Will this be cash or   ᎠᏕᎳᎨ ᎡᏍᎤᎠᎢ   A-de-la-ke gv-tu-ge:-s-di-
charge? (money or I-you- ᎠᎢ   ke hi?-a?
to-owe?) or: ᎠᏕᎳᎨ ᎡᏍᎤᎠᎢ   A-de-la-ke gv-tu-ge:-s-di-ke
(Money or you-me-to-owe?).ᎠᎢ   di-ke hi?-a?

161.
Charge, please.   ᎡᏍᎤᎠᎫ   Gv-tu-ge:-s-di-wu.
(I-you-to-owe-then)

162.
It'll be cash. (I will ᎠᏕᎳ ᏙᎵᎡᎥᏂ   A-de-la (do-)da-gv-ta-ni'.
use money.) or: ᎠᏕᎳ ᎶᎾᎤᎥᎠ   A-de-la da-n'-kwi-yv?-a.
(Money them-I-will-pay.)

Notes:

P.N. 156 - Ow?tomobil' - a car or automobile, is pronounced with the 'ow'
   of 'brown cow' and a soft '1', as in roll your own'. For other common
   ways to say 'car' in Cherokee, see the Introduction.

Some common English words are used directly in Cherokee sentences.
Examples:

balloon-i	ice-cream-i	purse-i	'Bootsi' is used for cowboy boots,
bus-i	park-i	boots-i	not work boots or overshoes.
coke-i	porch-i		

Some speakers who do not like using English words when speaking Cherokee, use purposely cumbersome descriptive terms, such as (instead of 'bootsi'): wa-ga' di-ni-ke'-hi-do(hi) tsu-na-la'-su-lo
  (cattle for-the-chasing-of their-foot-coverings, cow-chasing shoes)

P.N. 156 - a-ki-wa-hi'-s-di a?-wa-du'-li - I want to buy, I-to-buy I-want. A-ki-wa-hi'-s-di is the <u>infinitive</u> form of the verb, corresponding in English to '<u>to</u> buy', '<u>to</u> eat', as shown in Appendix XI.
    In Cherokee, the infinitive form of a verb (the verb form with the meaning of 'to....') is used with almost the <u>same</u> verbs as in English. See 'modal verb' or 'modals' in a grammar or dictionary. Notice that word order below is optional.
Examples:

<u>I want to buy</u>... (I-want I-to-buy   a-gwa-du'-li a-ki-wa-hi'-s-di-i
   or: I-to-buy I-want)   or: a-ki-wa-hi'-s-di a'-gwa-du'-li

<u>I like to buy</u>... (I-like I-to-   a-gi-lv:-k'-w'-di a-ki-wa-hi'-s-di-i
   buy   or: I-to-buy I-like)   or: a-ki-wa-hi'-s-di a-gi-lv:-k'-w'-di(i)

<u>I know how to buy</u>... (I-know   a-qua'-n'-ta' a-ki-wa-hi'-s-di-i
   I-to-buy   or: I-to-buy   or: a-ki-wa-hi'-s-di a-qua'-n'-ta'
   I-know)

<u>I am afraid to buy</u>... (I-fear   tsi-s-ka'-ha a-ki-wa-hi'-s-di-i
   I-to-buy   or: I-to-buy   or: a-ki-wa-hi'-s-di tsi-s-ka-ha
   I-fear)

<u>I am thinking of buying</u>, I think   ge-li-a a-ki-wa-hi'-s-di-i
   I will buy... (I-think I-to-buy
   or: I-to-buy I-think)   or: a-ki-wa-hi'-s-di ge'-li-a

<u>I ought to buy</u> (I-to-buy)   a-ki-wa-hi'-s-di-(i)

As you see, <u>use</u> of the infinitive corresponds closely in the two languages. There is an important difference between the <u>form</u> of the infinitive in English and the form of the infinitive in Cherokee:

<u>Cherokee infinitive verb forms must have bound pronouns.</u>

Re-examine the examples above, noticing that the infinitive verb forms (a-ki-wa-hi'-s-di-(i)) have a bound pronoun from Group B for 'I', 'a-k(i)'.

Using bound pronouns on Cherokee infinitive forms is not difficult for a speaker of English to learn. Bound pronouns below are underlined.
Examples:

I want you to buy (I-want you-to-buy)

a'-gwa-du'-li tsa-wa-hi'-s-di-i

or: (you-to-buy I-want)

tsa-wa-hi'-s-di a'-gwa-du'-li

They want him to buy (They-want him-to-buy)

u-na-du-li u-hwa-hi'-s-di-i

or: (him-to-buy they-want)

u-hwa-hi-s-di u-na-du-li

There are two forms of the infinitive of 'to buy', both with the same meaning. They are shown above (a-ki-wa-hi'-s-di and a-ki-hwa'-s-di).

P.N. 156 - tla?-e:-li i-ni-ga a-de-la yi-da-gi-hv - I don't have enough money yet. The underlining shows that in Cherokee, money is plural. (D-marks a plural object) Notice also that the classifying verb, A-GI-HA, is used, and that money is classified as a solid, 'indefinite' in shape.
If you want to specify paper money, a-de-la cannot be used. Then 'u-ni-hno'-s-ta' must be used, with a 'flexible' classifier, if the money is in sight in your hand or within reach. If the money has been put away into a flexible container on your person or in reach (for instance, into a purse, sack or wallet, not into a box, trunk or drawer), a 'hidden flexible' classifier is used:
Examples:

Go-hwe'-li a-gi-la. I have a paper. (in my pocket, sack, wallet, purse or just wrapped up)

U-ni-hno'-s-da da-gi-la. I have some dollar-bills. (concealed on my person or very nearby)

If you are speaking of paper money, but are not specifying that it is paper, a-de-la with the 'indefinite' classifier of A-GI-HA in the plural is used.

P.N. 157 - a-de-la de-ga-to'-l'-s-ga - I am borrowing money, notice again that 'money' is plural. (de-, plural object in the prefix section)

P.N. 158 - a-g'-s-goh'-l'-ti - I just offered it. In Cherokee, separate verbs are used for 'offering for sale' and for 'completing a sale', or 'selling'. A-g'-s-goh'-l'-ti can mean either 'I just offered it' or 'I just offered it for sale'.

P.N. 159 - gv-tu-ga, I owe you (I-you-owe) -Gv- is a <u>subject-object</u> pronoun, a combination of two Cherokee pronouns:
    1. A <u>subject</u> pronoun for 'I' (A subject is <u>active</u>)
    2. An <u>object</u> pronoun for 'you, singular'. (An object is <u>acted upon</u>)
Subject pronouns in English are: I   you   he   she   we   they
Object pronouns in English are: me   you   him   her   us   them

In English, subject and object pronouns are placed <u>apart</u>, at opposite ends of the verb. (e.g., <u>I</u> love <u>you</u>).

In Cherokee, subject and object pronouns are placed <u>together</u>, in the pronoun section of the verb form. Compare the arrangement of Cherokee and English subject and object pronouns below.
Examples:
Cherokee: gv-ge-yu (I-you-love)   English: I love you
       gv-yo-li-ga (I-you-know)   I know you
       gv-s-te-li-a (I-you-am-helping)   I am helping you
       de-gv-ye-yo-hv'-s-ga (I-you-am-teaching)   I am teaching you

Notice the de- plural object marker in de-gv-ye-yo-hv'-s-ga', literally 'Them (things)-I make known to you)

Cherokee subject-object pronouns and their English equivalents are underlined below. Literal meanings of the Cherokee are hyphenated.
    I owe myself   ----------   This can't be literally true, so it is not used in Cherokee.

    I owe <u>you</u>   gv-tu-ga   I-you-owe
    I owe <u>him or her</u>   tsi-tu-ga   I-him/her-owe
    I owe <u>them</u>   ga-<u>tsi</u>-tu-ga I-them-owe

See Appendix X for the other subject-object pronouns that go with gv-tu-ga.

Subject-object pronouns in Cherokee clarify exactly who is doing what to whom. They also function <u>instead of passive verb forms</u>.

In English, either passive or active verbs can be used in describing the same event:
    Active - The dog <u>bit</u> the cat.   Passive - The cat <u>was bitten</u> by the dog.

Passive verb forms are used often in English (e.g., this book <u>was written</u>, our house <u>is being built</u>, etc.) This is not the case in Cherokee.

P.N. 160 - a-de-la-<u>ke</u> gv-tu-ge:-s-di-<u>ke</u> - (either) cash or charge   When the questioner word, -ke, is used twice it means 'either...or'. -Ke is placed on the end of each alternative.

CORE VOCABULARY

Verbs:

It is not necessary to learn each one of the ten subject bound pronouns for each verb tense individually as you have been doing.

Each Cherokee verb has a vowel sound that acts as a hinge or connector between the pronoun section and the verb base section. By combining the bound pronouns, which you now know, and the verb base, by means of this connector you can construct all the pronouns necessary for that tense. The connector vowel combines with the vowel of the neighboring pronoun, sometimes causing changes in pronunciation. A Cherokee speaker will understand you, however, and if you ask for help, can correct your pronunciation in the cases where local custom dictates that one sound or another should be left off. There are also connector sounds between verb bases and the suffix section as shown in Appendix XII.

The following verbs contain enough bound pronouns for you to conveniently recall the rest. Bound pronouns for review are on pages 122 and 123.

offer, offer for sale, negotiate, suggest	Pronoun	Vowel	Verb base	Suffix
I just offered (it)	a-g'	(i)	s-goh'-l'-t	i
you singular just offered (it)	ts	i	s-goh'-l'-t	i
he/she just offered (it)	u-	(i)	s-goh'-l'-t	i
you-&-I just offered (it)	gi-n	i	s-goh'-l'-t	i
they just offered (it)	u-n	i	s-goh'-l'-t	i

owe, 'owe' must be used with subject-object pronouns				
I owe (it) to him/her	ts	i	tu-g	a
you singular owe (it)	h	i	tu-g	a
he/she owes it	uda	(i)	tu-g	a
you-&-I owe (it)	e-n	i	tu-g	a
they owe (it)	u-n	da	tu-g	a

pay				
I am paying (it)	g	a	kwi:-y	i
you singular are paying (it)	h(i)	a	kwi:-y	i
he/she is paying (it)		a	kwi:-y	i
they are paying (it)	i-n(i)	(a)	kwi:-y	i

use				
I am using it	g	ɉ	n-di-	a
you singular are using (it)	h(i)	ɉ	n-di-	a
he/she is using it			-di-	a
you-&-I are using it	i-n	ɉ	n-di-	a
they are using (it)	a-n	ɉ	n-di-	a

Exercise 1: Translate from English into Cherokee. Answers are on the next page.

1. I think I owe you four dollars and fourteen cents.
2. He has several dollars. (in his pocket)
3. This costs $3.25.
4. I am giving you a quarter. Please give me five nickels.
5. $9.98
6. $1.98
7. $1.50
8. one and a half
9. $1.53
10. I want to buy some ice cream. How much is it?
11. A thousand dollars. A thousand men. A thousand children. A thousand words. (With a numeral, a di- plural omits the di-.)
12. I want him to buy a lot of cokes. He has enough money.

Exercise 2: Translate from Cherokee into English. Answers are on the next page.

1. ᏌᏚᎠᏕᏎᎢ
2. ᎯᏍᎪᎠᏕᏎᎢ
3. . . . ᎠᎩᏩᎯᏍᏗ ᎠᏆᏚᎵ
4. ᎤᏕᏕᏎᎢ ᏦᏍᎪᎯᏔᎵ ᎢᏓᏂᏛᏗ
5. ᎠᏕᎳᎰ ᎬᏚᎰᏍᏗᎰ ᎯᎠ
6. Ꮭ ᎢᏂᏕ ᎠᏕᎳ ᏯᏓᎩᎭ
7. Ꮭ ᎢᏂᏕ ᎪᎯ ᎠᏕᎳ ᏯᏓᎩᎭ
8. ᏝᎡᎵ ᎢᏂᏕ ᎠᏕᎳ ᏯᏓᎩᎭ
9. ᎬᏚᎰᏍᏗᏊ
10. . . . ᎠᎩᏍᎪᎵᏗ
11. ᏍᏈᏍᏗ ᎠᏕᏎ ᏓᏂᏙᎵᏍᏕ
12. ᏕᎵᏦᏕ ᎤᏂᏩᏍᏗᎢ ᎤᎾᏚᎵᎠ
13. ᎤᏬᏚ ᎤᏁᏅᏒ
14. ᏙᏏ ᎤᏬᏚ ᎤᏁᏅᏒ
15. Ꮎ ᎤᏅᏒ ᎠᏂᎩᏕᎰ ᎡᏗᏩᎵ ᏧᏩᎯᏍᏗ ᎤᏚᎵ
16. ᏍᎪᎯᏤᏐᏌᏊ ᏍᎪᎯᏤᏐᏔᎵ ᏍᎪᎯᏤᏐᏦ
17. ᏔᎵ ᏍᎪᎯᏤᏐᎯᏍᎪᎄᏓᎵ
18. ᏌᏊ ᎢᏳ ᏐᏗᏅᏓ ᎠᏕᎳ
19. ᏔᎵᏍᎪᏤ ᎠᏕᎳ ᎠᏰᏟ. ᎯᏍᏕᏦᏁ ᎠᏕᎳ ᎯᏍᎪᏓᏅᏛᏗ
20. ᎭᎳ ᎯᎠ ᏧᎬᏩᎵᏗ ᎠᏦᏙᏗ?

Exercise 3: Translate. For answers, see pages 16 and 68.

1. Let's say some new words.
2. Let's say the numbers.
3. Let's say the letters.
4. What page is it on?
5. 1st, 2nd, 3rd.

EXERCISE 1:
1. Nv-ga-de'-la ni-ga-du-i-da-n'-te gv-tu-ga ge'-li-a.
2. Hi-lv-s-gi u-ni-hno'-s-da du-la?-a purse-i.
3. Tso?-a-de'-lv gi-nu?-di tsu-gv-wah-l'-di. or: Tso?-a-de-la-ta-l'-s-go-hi-s-gi-da-n'-te-di.
4. Gi-nu?-di gv-ne?-a. Hi-s-gi' i-da-n'-te-di di-s-kv-si.
5. So-hne'-1 (a) a-de-lv so-hne-l'-s-go tsu-ne'-la i-da'-n'-te-di.
6. U-hno:-s-da so-hne-l'-s-go tsu-ne-la i-da-n'-te-di.
7. U-hno:-s-da hi-g'-s-go?-i-da-n'-te-di.
8. Sa-wu a-le a-ye?-li.
9. U-hno:-s-da hi-g-s-go-tso?-i-da-n'-te-di.
10. Ice-cream-i a-ki-wa-hi'-s-di a-wa-du-li. Ha-la' tsu-gv-wa-l'-di?
11. Sa-wu i-ya-ga-yv'-li a-de'-l(a). Sa-wu i-ya-ga-yv'-li na-ni a-ni'-s-ga-ya. Sa-wu i-ya-ga-yv'-li na-ni di-ni-yo:-tli. Sa-wu i-ya-ga-yv'-li ka-ne:-tsv.
12. S-qui'-s-di u-hyv-dla di-di'-ta-s-di a-wa-du'-li tsu-hwa-hi-s-di. E-li-wu a-de'-la du-ha.

EXERCISE 2:
1. $11.00
2. $50.00
3. I want to buy a car.
4. I owe you four dollars and thirty-two cents.
5. Will this be cash or charge?
6. I don't have enough money now.
7. I don't have enough money today.
8. I don't have enough money yet.
9. Charge, please.
10. I am putting a car up for sale.
11. They are borrowing a lot of money.
12. They want to buy a house. (The house is not owned by anyone in particular yet so 'ga-l'-tso-de' is used.)
13. They have a pretty home. (They live prettily)
14. They have a very pretty home. (certainly prettily they live)
15. She wants to buy those red, ripe raspberries.
16. 101, 102, 103
17. 256
18. $1,000,000
19. $25.50, (two ways)
20. How much is this car worth? or: How much does this car cost? (same thing in Cherokee)

ᏅᎦᏦᏁ ᏣᎳᎩ ᎪᏪᎸᎢ

Nvᵎ-ga-tsoᵎ-ne Tsa-la-giᵎ Go-hwe:-lv-i

CHEROKEE LESSON TWENTY-FOUR

163. May I help you? (Will I help you?)	ᏓᎬᏍᏖᎸᎯᎨ	Da-gv-s-te-lvᵎ-hi-ke?
164. I want to buy some wool material and three men's shirts.	ᎤᏭᏍᏗ ᎠᏃᏬ ᎠᎩᏩᎯᏍᏗ ᎠᏩᏚᎵ ᎠᎴ ᏦᎢ ᎠᏍᎦᏱ ᏧᏀᏬ	U-wu-ya?-ti a-hno-wo a-ki-wa-hiᵎ-s-di a?-wa-duᵎ-li, a-le tso?-i a-s-ga-yi tsuᵎ-hna-wo.
165. Certainly. There are many kinds and sizes. What color do you want?	ᎰᏩ. ᏍᏈᏍᏗᏛ ᏧᏓᎴᏅᏓ ᎠᎴ ᏗᎪᏪᎵ ᎦᏙᎤᏍᏗ ᎠᏑᏫᏔ ᏣᏚᎵ	Ho:-wa. S-quiᵎ-s-di-dv tsu-da-le-hnv:-dᵎ a-le di-go-hweᵎ-li. Ga-do?uᵎ-s-dᵎ a-su-wiᵎ-t(ᏣᏚᎵ) tsa-duᵎ-li?
166. How much is this thread?	Ꭿ ᎠᏍᏗ ᎭᎳ ᏧᎬᏩᎵᏗᎢ	Hi? a-s-di ha-laᵎ tsu-gv-hwaᵎ-lᵎ-di-(i)?
167. Fifty cents a spool (Fifty cents each thread.) We sell many of these.	ᎠᏰᏟ ᏏᏴᏫ ᎠᏍᏗ ᎤᎪᏗ ᏕᏥᎾᏕᎪᎢ	A-yeᵎ-tli si-yv-wi-ha aᵎ-s-di. U-goᵎ-d de-tsi-nᵎ-deh-go?-i
168. Do you have something less expensive?	ᎦᏲᏟᎨ ᏧᎬᎵᏗ ᏣᎭ	Ga-yoᵎ-tli-ke tsu-gv-waᵎ-hlᵎ-di tsa-ha?
169. These are 35 cents apiece.	ᎯᎢᏀ ᏦᏍᎪᎯᏍᎩᏓᏅᏖ ᏏᏴᏫᎭ	Hi-i-hna tso-s-go-hiᵎ-s-gi i-daᵎ-nᵎ-te si-yv-wi-ha.
170. I would like to buy four of them.	ᏅᎩ ᏗᎩᏩᏍᏗ ᏯᏆᏚᎳ	Nv:-gi (di)-ki-hwa(wa-hi)-s-di yaᵎ-gwa-duᵎ-la.

171. How much cloth do you want? (How many measures...)	ᎭᎳ ᎢᏳ ᏟᎶᏓ ᎠᏃᏬ ᏣᏚᎵᎠ	Ha-la' i-yu tli-lo'-da a'-hno-wo tsa-du'-li-(a)?
172. Eight yards of thirty-five-inch fabric, seven and a half yards of thirty-nine-inch fabric, or seven yards of fifty-four-inch fabric.	ᏧᏁᎳ ᏑᏟᎶᏛ ᏦᏍᎪᎯᏍᎩ ᎢᏯ ᏏᏔᏛ ᎠᏄᏬ ᎦᎵᏉ ᎠᏰᏟ ᏑᏟᎶᏛ ᏦᏍᎪᏐᏁᎵ ᎠᎴ ᎦᎵᏉᎩ ᎢᏳ ᏟᎶᏓ ᎯᏍᎪᏅᎩ ᎢᏯᏏᏔᏛ ᎠᏄᏬᎢ	Tsu-ne'-l' su-tli-lo'-dv tso'-s-go-hi'-s-k' i-ya si?-ta-dv a-hnu'-wo, ga'-l'-quo'-g' a-ye'-tli su-tli-lo-dv tso'-s-go-so-hne-li, a-le ga-l'-quo'-gi, i-yu-tli-lo-da hi'-g'-s-go-nv-gi' i-ya-si?-ta-dv a-hnu-wo-i.
173. All the fabrics on this table are very reasonable -- 1.98 a yard.	ᏂᎦᏓ ᎠᎾᏬ ᏥᏓᏜ ᎠᎭᏂ ᎦᏍᎩᎸ ᎡᎳᏗ ᏧᎬᏩᎵᏗ. ᎤᏃᏍᏓ ᏐᏁᎳᏍᎪ ᏧᏁᎳ ᏑᏟᎶᏛ	Ni-ga'-da a-hna-wo tsi-da-dla a-ha-ni' ga'-s-ki-lv, e-la-di tsu-gv'-wa-l'-di. U-hno'-s-da, so-hne'-l'-s-go tsu-ne-la su-tli-lo-dv.
174. Do you have something more expensive? (High in price...)	ᎦᎸᎳᏗᎨ ᏧᎬᏩᎵᏗ ᏣᎭ	Ga-lv:-l'-di-ke tsu-gv-wa'-l'-di tsa-ha?
175. These are the best (we have). I can order anything for you.	ᎯᎢᏛ ᏫᏙᏒ. ᎠᏴ ᏂᎦᎵᏍᏘᏍᎬ ᎠᏆᏓᏅᏍᏗ	Hi-i-dv wi-do:-sv. A-hyv ni-ga-l'-s-ti'-s-gv a-gwa-da-nv:-s-di.
176. I would like that. All my children want new clothes.	ᏯᏆᏚᎸᏭ. ᏂᎦᏓ ᏓᏆᏓᏘᏅᎥ ᏗᏤ ᏚᎾᏚᎵ ᏧᎾᏅᏬ	Ya'-gwa-du-lv-wu. Ni-ga'-da da-qua-da'-ti-hna?-v di-tse du'-n'-du'-li tsu-na'-hna-wo.
177. clothing	ᏗᏅᏬ	di'-hna-wo
belt, belts	ᎠᏓᏠᏍᏗ ᏗᏓᏠᏍᏗ	a-da'-tlo:-s-di, di-da'-tlo:-s-di
blouse, blouses <u>or</u> shirt, shirts	ᎠᏃᏬ ᏗᏅᏬ	a'-hno-wo, di'-hna-wo
coat, coats	ᎦᏌᎴᎾ ᏗᎦᏌᎴᎾ	ga-sa-le:-na, di-ga-sa-le:-na
dress, dresses <u>or</u> skirt, skirts	ᎠᏌᏃ ᏗᏌᏃ	a'-sa-no, di'-sa-no

177. (cont.)

English	Syllabary	Romanization
glove, gloves	ᎤᏕᏴᏑᎶ ᏗᏟᏴᏑᎶ	a-li-ye-su-lo, di-li-ye-su-lo
hat, hats	ᎤᎵᏍᏬᏙᏬ ᏗᎵᏍᏬᏙᏬ	a-l(i)-s-que'-t(o)-wo, di'-l'-s-que'-t(o)-wo
one bead or a pendant	ᎠᏬᎵᏗ	a'-yah-l'-di
a necklace, necklaces (beads)	ᏗᏬᎵᏗ	di-yah'-l'-di
necktie, neckties	ᎠᏬᏢᏗ ᏗᏬᏢᏗ	a-yah-tlv-di, di-yah-tlv-di
pants, 1 pr.	ᎠᏑᎶ	a-su-lo
pants, more than 1 pr.	ᏗᏑᎶ	di-su-lo
sleeve (like-a-wing, to-be-used-as-a-wing)	ᎪᏆᏛᏙᏗ ᏗᎪᏆᏛᏙᏗ	go-hya-dv-doh-di, di-go-hya-dv-doh-di
sock, socks	ᎤᎵᏲ ᏗᎵᏲ	a-li-yo-(i), di-li-yo?-(i)

178.

English	Syllabary	Romanization
I would like to try this on. (I am trying it on...)	ᏯᏆᏚᎲᏭ ᎠᏆᏁᏙᏗ ᎯᎠ. -ᎦᏁᎵᏗ-	Ya'-gwa-du-lv-wu a-qua-ne'-l'-doh-di hi?-a. (ga-neh-l'-di? a)

179.

English	Syllabary	Romanization
sewing materials	ᎦᏴᏫᏒᏙᏗ	ga-yeh'-w(i)-sv-doh'-di
button, buttons	ᎦᏗ ᏗᎦᏗ	ga?-di, di-ga?-di
cotton cloth	ᎤᏥᎸ	u-tsi-lv
leather	ᎦᏃᏥ	ga-no'-tsi
needle, needles	ᏴᎩ ᏗᏴᎩ	yv-gi, di-yv'-gi
pattern or patterns	ᏗᏟᎶᏍᏙᏗ	di-tli-lo:-s-doh-di
pin, pins	ᎤᏍᏆᏘ ᏧᏍᏆᏘ	u'-s-qua-ti', tsu'-s-qua-ti'
pin, pins (straight)	ᎤᏍᏆᏘ ᎦᏥᏃᏍᏓ ᏧᏍᏆᏘ ᏗᎦᏥᏃᏍᏓ	u'-s-qua-ti', ga-tsi-no:-s-da, tsu'-s-qua-ti di-ga-tsi-no:-s-da
satin (shiny cloth, shiner cloth)	ᎤᏥᏍᏓᎷᎩᏍᎩ ᎠᎾᏬ	u-tsi-s-da-lu-gi'-s-g(i) a-hnu-wo
scissors	ᏗᎵᏍᏙᏗ	di'-l'-s-toh-di
silk	ᏏᎵᎩ	si'-hl'-gi
thread, yarn, string	ᎠᏍᏗ	a'-s-di
velvet (slick cloth)	ᏔᏫᏍᎧᎨ ᎠᎾᏬ	da-wi'-s-ka-ge a-hnu-wo
yardstick, ruler, tape measure (to-measure-it-with)	ᎠᏟᎶᏍᏙᏗ	a-tli-lo:-s-toh'-ti (no plural)

Notes:

P.N. 163 - da-gv-s-te-lv-hi-ke - (Will I help you?) Future of gv-s-te'-li-a.
I am helping you, (I-you-am-helping), see Appendix X, plus -ke, question
marker or interrogative.

P.N. 164 - U-wu-ya-ti a-ki-wa-hi'-s-di a?-wa-du'-li (woollen I-to-buy I-want)
A-ki-wa-hi'-s-di is an infinitive, going with 'want'. See Lesson 23.

P.N. 164 - a-s-ga-yi tsu'-hna-wo - men's shirts. Notice that in Cherokee the
singular (man shirts)is used where the plural (men's shirts) is used
in English.

P.N. 170 - di-ki-hwaʼ-s-di - (them-I-to-buy) This verb form is made up of:
1. di, them, in the prefix section. 2. a-ki, I, in the pronoun section.
3. the verb base, 4. the infinitive marker in the suffix section ((s)-di-
(yi)(i)). Notice that di is optional after a numeral.

P.N. 170 - yaʼ-gwa-duʼ-la (would like) is made up of yi in the prefix section,
a-gw(a) in the pronoun section, a-du-l- in the verb base section, and -a
in the suffix section. Tla-yi in the prefix section of a Cherokee verb
form makes the statement <u>negative</u>. Yi- without the tla but with a change
in the suffix section, makes the verb's meaning tentative:

<u>Positive statement - I do want, I want</u>   a-gwa-duʼ-li-(a)

Contains: Prefix section	Pronoun section	Verb base	Suffix section
------	aʔ-w or a-gw-	a-du-l-	-i-(a)

<u>Negative statement - I do not want</u>   tla-y(i)aʼ-gwa-duʼ-li-(a)

Contains: Prefix section	Pronoun section	Verb base	Suffix section
tla-y(i)-	aʔ-w or a-gw-	a-du-l-	-i-(a)

<u>Tentative statement - I might want, I would like</u>   yaʼ-gwa-duʼ-la or
yaʼ-gwa-duʼ-lv-wu

Contains: Prefix section	Pronoun section	Verb base	Suffix section
y(i)-	aʔ-w or a-gw-	a-du-l-	-a <u>or</u> -v-wu

P.N. 173 - tsi-daʼ-dla - lying on, placed on a raised surface, such as a
porch, a table, platform, chair or shelf.
   This is a classifying verb but it has no ʼliquidʼ or ʼlivingʼ classification categories. It is one of those Cherokee verbs which can only be
used to describe inactive things, so there are no bound pronouns except
3rd person singular and plural (it and they). Since fabrics are being
spoken of here, they are classified as ʼflexibleʼ, plural. (See Lessons
5 and 8 to review classifying verbs)
Examples:
<u>Flexible</u>

a-hna-wo <u>a-tlaʔ-aʼ</u>	a fabric, some fabric is on it
a-hna-wo <u>tsi-daʼ-dla</u>	fabrics are lying on it
diʼ-hna-wo tsi-daʼ-dla	clothes are lying on it

Notice that in Cherokee, ʼfabricsʼ is not a plural <u>noun</u>, though the
<u>verb</u> is plural. In Cherokee, the plural of the noun ʼfabricʼ means
ʼclothesʼ. Think of English ʼcloth, clothesʼ.

   The other classification categories that can be used with this verb
for ʼlying on, being placed onʼ are:
<u>Long</u>

goʼ-kʼ-s-di <u>a:-tlv</u>	a cigar or cigarette is lying on it
di-goʼ-kʼ-s-di tsi-da<u>:-tlv</u>	cigars or cigarettes are lying on it

<u>Indefinite</u>

sv?-ta a-tla-h(ɑ́ʼ)(aʼ)	an apple is lying on it
sv?-ta tsi-da<u>ʼ-tla-h(ɑ́ʼ)(aʼ)</u>	apples are lying on it

P.N. 173 (cont.) - TSI-DA'-DLA - lying on, placed on

Since this classifying verb has no 'liquid' classification, in order to use this verb speaking of a liquid in a container the 'indefinite' classifier is used with the addition of the word 'poured'.

Example:
Tsu-lv'-sa-di *a-ma' da-dli'-s-dv da'-tla'hd(ha).
Poured glasses of water are on it. (standing on it, placed on it, etc.)

Other verbs, not TSI-DA-DLA, would have to be employed to describe a <u>liquid</u> lying directly on a raised surface (as a puddle, for instance), or that a <u>living thing</u> was lying on a raised surface. (a cat on the table, for instance).

P.N. 175 - ni-ga-1'-s-ti'-s-gv a-qua-da-nv:-s-di (I am able to obtain, it can happen I-to-get)

'Ni-ga-1'-s-ti-ya'', ni-ga-1'-s-ti-ha' is a common verb with the meaning of 'it is happening, he/she/it is becoming'. Something or some-one is changing from one state to another or from one form into some-thing else. This change is taking place by a natural process or through circumstances beyond immediate control, or both. 'Ni-ga-1'-s-ti-ya' (ha')' can be used impersonally, (e.g., <u>it is</u> getting dark)

As you know, suffix sections can answer the question of 'when?' about a verb form. The suffix sections below are underlined to show differences in time.

Examples:
Go:-li ni-ga-1'-s-ti-<u>(ya)</u>(ha)	Winter is coming on.
Sv-hi-ye ni-ga-1'-s-ti-<u>(ya')</u>(ha')	Darkness is falling.
Na bus-i u-we:-ti ni-ga-1'-s-ti-<u>(ya')</u>(ha')	That bus is getting old.
Qua-nd u-ni-da-lo'-ni-ge na-na'-1'-s-ti-<u>(ya')</u>(ha')	The peaches are turning yellow.
Gi-ta-ya na-na-1'-s-ti-<u>(ya')</u>(ha')	Cherries are forming (on the trees)
A-gi-wo'-di-ge ni-ga-li'-s-ti-<u>(ya)</u>(ha)	I am getting brown.
U-go:-d' ni-ga-1'-s-t<u>i</u> *a-ma'.	There is plenty of water coming in.
E:-tla-we ni-ga-1'-s-d<u>a</u> ga-wo'-ni-hv.	He has stopped talking. (His speech has become silent.)

Examine the verb forms above, noticing the underlinings on the time information from the suffix section. Notice ni- in the prefix sections, meaning 'by then, already', and telling that the action described <u>began</u> <u>before</u> the time pinpointed in the suffix section. Also notice that this is one of the verbs that contain the reflexive, -a-1'.

Examine 'ni-ga-li'-s-ti-ya(I-am-becoming)' and 'ni-ga-<u>1</u>'-s-ti-ya'(he/she/it-is-becoming). Notice that this verb resembles 'go-li:-ga, go'-<u>1</u>' -ga (I-know, he/she-knows): i.e. g-means <u>both</u> 'I' and 'he/she' in both verbs, and both verbs have a long li (underlined) in the 'I' form, and short 1' in the he/she form.

The expression 'Ni-ga-1'-s-ti'-s-gv- in P.N. 175 means 'It can hap-
pen'. It is often used with the meaning of: 'It makes no difference,',
'It doesn't matter', 'Whatever you prefer'.
Examples:
   Ni-ga-1'-s-di:-s-gv s-qua-tle:-s-di go-s-dv-ne-hi a-le a-yv-te'-s-gi.
   It makes no difference to him/her whether he/she plays baseball or
   football. (...whether he/she is a hitter or a kicker of the ball.)

   Ga-do', ni-da-ga-1'-s-ta-ni'?
   What is to happen next? (can be used for: What shall we do next?)

   Ni-ga-1'-s-ti'-s-gv.
   Whatever you like. Whatever comes up.

   Ni-ga-1'-s-ti'-s-gv is also used of happenings that were not
      intended or foreseen.
Example:
   Me:-li ni-ga-1'-s-ti'-s-gv nu-1'-s-da:-ne-(ha)!
   Things are piling up on Mary! Mary has a lot of problems'

   Since 'nu-1'-s-da:-ne-(ha') is another verb that means 'it is hap-
pening', 'Ni-ga-1'-s-ti'-s-gv nu-1'-s-da:-ne-ha.' actually means 'It
can happen it is happening'. (Whatever can happen is happening to
Mary.)
   Combining two different words with almost duplicate meanings is a
Cherokee method of intensifying both words.

P.N. 175 - a-qua-da-nv:-s-di - This is an infinitive form with a reflexive,
   -da-, in the pronoun section, after a-qua, 'I'. This is a common verb
   with many meanings. It is tied in with other verbs. Like many Cherokee
   verbs, it can change its meaning when it changes its tense. Suffixes,
   prefixes and circumstances alter its meaning also.
   Here, it means approximately 'I order myself to', or 'I-to-get',
   'I-myself-to-move'. See Lesson 13 where this verb means 'migrate, move
   out', and Lesson 23 where it means 'use, put forth'.
   Examples:
   Tsi-nv'-s-ga u-we-nv:-s-di-i.   I am ordering him to get out.
                                            (I-am-moving him-to-move)
   Notice the infinitive (he-to-depart) with tsi-nv'-s-ga, (I-am-ordering)
   See the note on P.N. 156, Lesson 23, p. 207.
   Ga-n'-di-nv:-s-di.   These things are for sale.
   (Literally, They-them(things)-to-move or: They-them(things-to-dispose-
                                                of)
   Ga-tsi-nv:-s-di a?-wa-du'-li.   I want to order them to go.
   A-gwe-nv:-s-di a?-wa-du'-li.   I want to go.
   A-qua-da-nv:-s-di a?-wa-du'-li.   I want to move out.
   A-qua-da-nv-s-toh'-di a?-wa-du'-li.   I want to get ready to go.
   (Literally, I-to-move-myself-in-order-to-depart I-want)

P.N. 176 - Ya'-gwa-du-lv-wu - I would like (that). It would please me.
I would want that. See note to P.N. 170. -Wu after -a (tentative) adds
a more decisive feeling to the verb. Also see the note to P.N. 158.

P.N. 176 - di-tse- du-n'-du'-li tsu-na-hna-wo - they want new clothes -
(new they-want clothes). Notice the word order. When a noun has a
modifier in Cherokee, the modifier is often put <u>before</u> the verb and the
noun itself <u>after</u> the verb. If the noun has more than one modifier
one of them is especially likely to be placed alone on the opposite
side of the verb to the other modifier and noun. An English sentence
such as 'I want a great, big, red, rosy apple.' would sound ridiculous
and/or fantastic to a Cherokee speaker: Cherokee uses adjectives
sparingly and series of adjectives <u>do not occur</u>. Instead, a Cherokee
speaker would be apt to use two or more verbs (see note on P.N. 175),
an emphatic particle, or one superlative adjective.

P.N. 177 - ga-sa-le:-na usually means a long coat, but it can also mean a
suit coat or sport jacket. To be specific, 's-qua-la' ga-sa-le:-na'
(short coat) and 'ga-nv'-hi-da' ga-sa-le:-na' (long coat) can be used.

P.N. 177 - di'-hna-wo - clothing In Cherokee, when you speak of putting
on, having on, or taking off articles of clothing, the clothing term
is treated as an active verb in various tenses.

English term: Literal meaning of Cherokee equivalents:
<u>Putting on:</u> I am hatting.   I am shirting.   I am gloving.
<u>Having on:</u>   I have hatted.   I have shirted.   I have gloved.
<u>Taking off:</u> I unhatted.   I unshirted.   I ungloved.

Clothing terms in Cherokee cannot be reflexive; you cannot say 'I
dressed myself.' in Cherokee. Cherokee usage resembles that in the
English phrase: I am suiting up (in a uniform to play a game). It
may help you to think of these Cherokee verbs as 'I am hatting up',
'I have shirted up', etc.

Examples:
    hat, hats - a-l(i)-s-que'-t(o)-wo, di'-l'-s=que'-t'-wo
I am putting on a hat.   Ga-li-s-que-tu-s-ga.
I have on a hat.   A-gwa-l'-s-que:-tl'-ga.
I took off my hat.   Ga-l'-s-que'-tl'-gi.

Of course the terms above can <u>only</u> be used of a hat, hatting.

Ga-ni-wo?-a can be used in some tenses when speaking of various
garments, not only a shirt or blouse. If anything <u>but</u> a shirt or
blouse is meant, it must be named.
Examples:
    I am putting on a shirt or blouse.   Ga-ni-wo?-a.
    I am putting on a coat.   Ga-sa-le:-na ga-ni-wo?-a.

Ga-ni-wo?-a in several tenses used speaking of a shirt or blouse:
Examples:

shirt or blouse, shirts or blouses - a'-hnu-wo, di'-hnu-wo
I am putting on a shirt or blouse.   Ga-ni-wo?-a.
I have on a shirt or blouse.   A'-gwa-hnu-wa.
I took off a shirt or blouse.   Ga-ni-we-gi.

Ga-ni-wo?-a used with other garments:
Examples:

I am putting on a coat.   Ga-sa-le:-na ga-ni-wo?-a.
    (Ga-sa-le:-na has no clothing verb of its own. It always goes with
     various tenses of 'ga-ni-wo?-a')
I have on a skirt.   E'-l'-di (e'-hi) a'-sa-no a-gwa-
                                          hnu-wa.
    (E-la-di means 'close to ground level', 'on a lower level')
I have on a dress or skirt.   A'-sa-no a-gwa-hnu-wa.
But: I took off a dress or skirt.   Ga-sa-no-hya. (not A'-sa-no ga-ni-
                                          we-gi)

Cherokee speakers usually prefer to use individual clothing verbs and
more often say 'A-gwa'-sa-no' than 'A'-sa-no a-gwa-hnu-wa'.
Example:

A'-sa-no-a-qua-tse'-li u'-sa-no.   She has on my dress.

Ga-ni-wo?-a with the plural object marker, d-, is used in Cherokee with
the same meaning as the English verb 'to dress'.
Examples:

De-ga-ni-wo?-a.   I am dressing. (putting on more than one garment
                          of any kind)
Da-gwa-hnu-wa.   I am dressed. (in several garments of any kind)
De-ga-ni-we-gi.   I undressed. (took off several garments of any
                          kind)

-Gi is a Cherokee suffix that often means 'un-', as in English 'undo',
'untie'.

The examples below illustrate how to use the rest of the clothing terms
in this lesson:

glove, gloves - a-li-ye'-su-lo, di-li-ye'-su-lo
I am putting on a glove   Ga-li-ye-su-li:-ya.
I am putting on gloves.   De-ga-li-ye-su-li:-ya.

I have on a glove.   A-gwa-l'-ye-su-la.
I have on gloves.   Da-gwa-l'-ye'-su-la.

I took off a glove.   Ga-li-ye-su-le-gi.
I took off my gloves.   De-ga-li-ye-su-le-gi.

Notice the plural object marker, d-, whenever there is more than one
direct object of the verb 'to glove'. (I am gloving them, etc.)

220

```
    one pair of pants, more than one pair of pants - a-su-lo, di-su-lo
        (Pants are singular in Cherokee)
I am putting on my pants.              Ga-su-li:-ya.
I have on pants.                       A-gwa-su:-la.
I took off my pants.                   Ga:-su'-le-gi. or Ga-su-le?-a.


    dress or skirt, dresses or skirts - a'-sa-no, di'-sa-no
        (It is not always necessary to specify 'e'-l'-di a'-sa-no' for skirt.)
I am putting on a dress or skirt.      Ga-sa-no-hi-ha'.
I have on a dress or skirt.            A-gwa-sa-no.
I took off a dress or skirt.           Ga-sa-no-hya.


    sock, socks - a-li-yo-(i), di-li-yo-(i)
I am putting on socks.                 De-ga-li-yo-hi-ha'.
I have on socks.                       Da-gwa-li-yo.
I took off my socks.                   De-ga-li-yo-gi.
```

There are <u>classifying verb phrases</u> in the other clothing terms in P.N.
177. A'-yah-l'-di, bead or pendant, di-yah'-l'-di, beads or a necklace,
a-yah-tlv-di, necktie, and di-yah-tlv-di, neckties contain the <u>same</u>
classifying verb as the one in P.N. 173, TSI-DA-DLA. Reread the note on
P.N. 173. Yah means 'throat'.

```
    a'-yah-l'-di      for-him/her-to-have-on-the-throat-a-solid-of-indefinite-
                          shape
    a-yah-tlv-di      for-him/her-to-have-around-the-throat-something-flexible


I am putting on a necklace.       De-ga'-ya-dlv'-s-ga.
I have on a necklace.             Da-gwa-hya?-dlv.
I am putting on a necktie.        Ga-ya-dlv?-s-gah.
I have on a necktie.              A-gwa-hya-dla.
I took off my necktie.            Ga'-hya-tle-gi.
```

    A-da-tlo:-s-di, belt, means 'to-encircle-oneself-with'. It contains
a verb that depends on <u>pitch</u> to make its meaning clear.

```
    I am putting on a belt.       *A-qua-da'-tlo:-s-di. (long, scalloped,
                                    low)
    I have on a belt.             *A-qua-da'-tlo:-s-di'.(upward in pitch)
    I took off my belt.           Ga-da'-dlo-hi.
```

Clothing terms, as you see, use either Group A or Group B bound pronouns,
depending on the bound pronoun group that goes with the time involved.
Examine the terms in this lesson and those in Appendices XI and XII, noticing
which bound pronoun group goes with which time tense.

```
    I am getting especially dressed up,   Ga-do-du-s-ti-ya.
        prettying myself up (u-wo'-du,
        pretty, beautiful) This can be said by both men and women.
    I am getting ready.               Ga-dv-nv-s-ti:-ya.
    I am all ready.                   A-gwa-dv-nv:-s-di.
```

CORE VOCABULARY

best, of the best kind, excellent - singular   wo:-sv
                                      plural   wi-do:-sv
     Both wo:-sv and wi-do:-sv can refer to things, animals or people.
<u>The</u> best (referring to one thing, animal or person),   wo:-sv-na
        or: extremely good, excellent.

color, colored - singular   a-su-hwi?-t(v)(i)
            plural things   di-su-hwi'?-t(v)
            Plural living beings   di-ni-su-hwi?-t(v)
     This can only be used of artificial colors or of artificially colored
objects and living beings. It means 'colored, dyed, painted'. Di-su-
hwi-toh-di (to-use-to-color-with) refers to crayons, coloring pencils, dry
paints, dyes, or coloring powders. Tsi-su-hwi'-s-ga means 'I am painting
or coloring.' Tsi-lo-ne?-a means 'I am painting (with liquid paint only)'.
Di-ga-lo-ne:-s-gi means 'painter', di-ni-ga-lo-ne:-s-gi, 'painters'.

different - singular, a thing, animal or person   (n)u-da-le:-(hnv:-d(a))
          plural things   tsu-da-le-(hnv:-d)a))
          plural living beings   tsu-n'-da-le-(hnv:-dₒa))
          As a verb: we differ   do-gi-n-da-le-hnv:-tsa

each (thing)   si-yv-wi-(ha)
each (living being)   si-yv-wi-ya

high   ga-lv'-la-di'
The highest or:
  extremely high   wa-ga-lv'-l'-di:-yv

inch   i-ya si?-ta-dv

yard   su-tli-lo-dv
     This actually means 'measurement'. It is used for yard, mile or gallon.

Verbs:

become, happen
  I am becoming...   ni-ga-li:-s-ti-(ya)(ha')
  you are becoming ...   na'-l'-s-ti-(ya)(ha')
  he/she/it is becoming ...   ni-ga'-l'-s-ti-(ya)(ha')
  you-&-I are becoming ...   ni-na'-l'-s-ti-(ya)(ha')
  they are becoming ...   na-na'-l'-s-ti-(ya)(ha')

a-l'-s-ti'-s-gi - (he/she repeatedly makes it happen) A name used for someone who likes to start a disagreement.

222

dress, put them on ('them' meaning 'clothes')
  I am dressing   de-ga-ni-wo?-a
  you are dressing   de-hah-na-wo?-a
  he/she is dressing   de-hna-wo?-a
  you-&-I are dressing   de-na-hna-wo?-a
  they are dressing   da-na-hna-wo?-a

have on (a coat, shirt, dress, skirt, or blouse)
  I have on ...   a-gwa-hnu'-wa   you-&-I ...   de-gi-na-hnu-wa
  you ...   tsa-hnu-wa   you-two ...   de-s-da-hnu-wa
  he/she ...   u-hnu-wa   he/she-&-I ...   do-gi-na-hnu-wa

      others-&-I ...   do-ga-hnu-wa
      you-plural ...   de-tsa-hnu-wa
      they ...   du-na-hnu-wa

      you,-another-or-others-&-I ...   de-ga-hnu-wa

Notice the plural object markers in the duals and plurals above.

sell
  ga-n'-de-gi - a seller, salesman or merchant

I sell (it) habitually or as my customary job   tsi-n'-de-gi
you sell (it)   hi-n'-de-gi
he/she sells (it)   ga-n'-de-gi
you-&-I sell (it)   i-ni-n'-de-gi
they sell (it)   a-ni-n'-de-gi

I am selling (it), some particular thing now   tsi-n'-de-ga
you are selling (it), some particular thing now hi-n'-de-ga, etc.

I sell (it) often, whenever I have the opportunity tsi-n'-de-go, etc.

I just sold (it)   tsi-n'-du-ga
you just sold (it)   hi-n'-du-ga
he/she just sold (it)   ga-n'-du-ga
you-&-I just sold it   i-ni-n'-du-ga
they just sold it   a-ni-n'-du-ga

   Notice that in tsi-n'-du-ga etc. above a vowel in the verb base changes (e changes to u) and this changes the time tense of the verb. (to recent past from several kinds of present time)

Exercise 1:   Match up the two columns below and check yourself from this
   lesson.

A.

1. I would like to buy four of them.
2. Do you have something less expensive?
3. Do you have something more expensive?
4. I would like that
5. I would like to try this on.
6. How much do I owe you?
7. These are the best (things).
8. Will this be cash or charge?
9. What color do you want?
10. There are many kinds and sizes.

B.

1. S-qui'-s-di-dv tsu-da-le-hnv:-d a-le dᴓ-go-hwe'-li.
2. Ga-do u'-s-d' a-su-wi'-tᴓ tsa-du'-li?
3. Ga-yo-tli-ke tsu-gv-wa'-hl'-di tsa-ha?
4. Nv:-gi di-ki-hwa'-s-di ya-gwa-du-la.
5. U-go:-di-ke tsu-gv-wa'-l'-di tsa-ha?
6. Ya'-gwa-du-lv-wu.
7. Hi-i-dv wi-do:-sv.
8. Ha-la' gv-tu-ga.
9. A-de'-la-ke gv-tu-ge:-s-di hi?-a?
10. Ya'-qua-du-lv-wu a-qua-ne'-l'-doh-di hi?-a.

Exercise 2:   Translate from English to Cherokee.   Answers are on the next page.

1. a blue belt
2. some safety pins
3. a long coat
4. short sleeves
5. a yardstick
6. a big black hat
7. straight pins
8. a hundred new socks
9. silk thread
10. soft gloves
11. a dress pattern
12. cotton pants
13. a short leather jacket
14. scissors
15. a wool skirt

Exercise 3:   Translate from English to Cherokee letters:

1. I would like to try on that red dress and a wool overcoat.
2. I want to buy two pair of trousers and a sport coat.
3. I like to buy a lot of pretty-colored fabrics.
4. I ought to sew the baby a shirt.
5. four yards of 54-inch material
6. eleven miles
7. The house has been painted white.
8. A glass of water is on the table.
9. A cup of milk is on the table.
10. A gallon of gasoline (ge:-sa-li-ni) is (poured) in the car.

Exercise 4: Correctly fill in and name the missing section of each verb
   below.   Example: I don't want (it) tla __ a-gwa-du'-li-(a)
          Answer : yi-, prefix section, (y- before a-)
1. I am married, __ ne'-li   3. I love you, __ ge'-uy-(i)
2. you are surprised, __ qua-n'-go:-s-g-__   4. I know you, _ _ li:-ga

224

EXERCISE 4:

1. tsi-, pronoun section (no prefix section in this verb form)
2. s-, pronoun section, no prefix section in this verb form. Ts- has changed to s-.
3. gv-, pronoun section, subject object pronoun. No prefix section in this verb form.
4. Gv-yo, pronoun section, subject-object pronoun, no prefix section in this verb form.

EXERCISE 3:

1. ᏉᏆᏚᎳᏊ ᎠᏆᏁᎵᏙᏗ ᎠᎩᎦᎨ ᎠᏌᏃ ᎠᎴ ᎤᏊᏉᎫ ᎦᏌᎴᎾ
2. ᎠᏆᏚᎵ ᏗᎩᎶᏛᏍᏗ ᎳᎵ ᏗᎸᎶ ᎠᎴ - ᏍᏆᎳ - ᎦᏌᎴᎾ
3. ᎠᎩᏄᏗ ᏗᎩᎶᏛᏍᏗ ᏍᏢᏍᏗ ᏧᏬᏚ ᏗᎸᎾᏨ ᏗᏄᏬ ᏗᎦᏰᎤᏍᏙᏗ
4. ᏥᏰᎾᏎᏗ ᎤᏍᏗᎢ ᎤᏖᏬᎢ
5. ᏅᎩ ᎢᏳᏟᎶᏓ ᏛᎩᏍᎪᏅᎩ ᎢᏉᏏᎳᏨ ᎠᏄᏬᎢ
6. ᏌᏚᎢ ᎢᏳᏟᎶᏓ
7. ᎦᎵᏦᎦ ᎤᏁᎦ ᎠᎸᎾᏓ
8. ᎤᏄᏌᏗ ᎠᏑᏟᏍᏨ ᎠᏞᏂ ᎦᏍᎩᏄᎢ
9. ᎠᏟᏍᏨ ᎠᎫᎩᏍᏗ ᎤᏅᏗ ᎠᏞᏂ ᎦᏍᎩᏄᎢ
10. ᎸᏟᎶᏓ ᎨᏌᎵᏂ ᎠᏟᏍᏨ . . .

EXERCISE 2:

1. ᏌᎪᏂᎨ ᎠᏓᏘᏍᏗ
2. ᎢᎦᏓ ᏧᏍᏆᎫ
3. ᎦᏅᏛᏓ ᎦᏌᎴᎾ
4. ᏍᏆᎳ ᏗᎪᏍᏨ
5. ᎠᏟᎶᏍᏙᏗ
6. ᎤᎳᎾ ᎬᏂᎨ ᎠᎵᏍᏇᏙᏬᎢ
7. ᏗᎦᏥᏃᏍᏓ ᏧᏍᏆᎫ
8. ᏉᎪᏛᏙᏆ ᏗᏙ ᏗᎵᏮᎢ
9. ᏏᎵᎩ ᎠᏍᏗ
10. ᏧᎶᏂᎨ ᏗᎵᏰᎸᎶᎢ
11. ᎠᏌᏃ ᏗᏟᎶᏍᏙᏗ
12. ᎠᏥᏄ ᎠᎸᎶ
13. ᏍᏆᎳ ᎦᏃᏥ ᎦᏌᎴᎾ
14. ᏗᎵᏍᏙᏗ
15. ᎤᏊᏉᎫ ᎡᎳᏗ ᎠᏌᏃᎢ

Exercise 5: Translate this conversation.

1. ᎡᏛᏰ ᏂᎦᎵᏍᏗᏉ
2. ᎠᏆᏓᏅᏍᏙᏗ ᎠᏣᏚᎵ
3. ᎦᏙ ᏂᏓᎦᎵᏍᏔᏂ
4. ᎠᏆᏓᏅᏍᏗ ᎠᏣᏚᎵ
5. ᎩᎳᏉ ᎾᎾᎵᏍᏗᏉ
6. ᎠᎩᏬᏗᎨ ᏂᎦᎵᏍᏗᏂ
7. ᎡᏓᏭ ᏂᎦᎵᏍᏓ ᎦᏬᏂᏜ
8. ᏧᏄᏌᏗ ᎠᏑ ᏓᏟᏍᏨ ᏓᏞᏂ
9. ᏥᏅᏍᎦ ᎤᏭᏅᏍᏗᎢ
10. ᎦᏙ ᏂᏓᎦᎵᏍᏔᏂ
11. ᏂᎦᎵᏍᏗᏍᎬ
12. ᎠᎩᏙᏓ ᏂᎦᎵᏍᏗᏍᎬ

EXERCISE 6: Translate from Cherokee to English. Answers are on pp. 73-76.

ᎤᏬᏚᎨ ᎡᏛᏰ
ᏧᏍᏓᏨ ᏣᎳᎩ ᎦᏬᏂ. ᎦᏮᏟᎨ ᏣᎳᎩ ᏛᏬᏂ

ᎠᎦᏍᏫ ᎤᏴᏜᏃ ᏙᎼ
ᏥᏴᎾᏉ. ᎦᏮᏟᏨ ᏣᎳᎩ ᏥᏬᏂᎠ

ᎤᎪᏍᎧᏅ ᏣᎳᎩ ᎠᏬᎦᎢ

Hi-s-ga-tso'-ne Tsa-la-gi' Go-hwe:-lv-i

CHEROKEE LESSON TWENTY-FIVE

Parts of the body -

Review Lesson 19 paying special attention to the remarks on body parts and to the outline on page 152.

If you know subject bound pronouns thoroughly as they appear on pages 122 and 123 you will have only one problem with body-parts: Do not fail to memorize which group of bound pronouns goes with each particular body-part.

In Cherokee, each body part still in its natural place (i.e. on a body) must take one of three sets of bound subject pronouns. Some body parts take Group A (ts-ga-) bound pronouns, some take Group A (ts-a-) bound pronouns, and some take Group B (a?-u-) bound pronouns. Notice underlinings below. Examples:

Group A (ts-ga-)

my-ear	tsi-le:-na	my-ears	di-tsi-le:-na
your-ear	hi-le:-na	your-ears	ti-le:-na
h/h-ear	ga-le:-na	h/h-ears	di-ga-le:-na

Group A (ts-a-)

my-eye	tsi-k(a)-to'-li	my-eyes	di-tsi-k(a)-to'-li
your-eye	hi-k(a)-to'-li	your-eyes	ti'-k'-to'-li
h/h-eye	a-k(a)-to'-li	h/h-eyes	di'-k'-to'-li

Group B (a?w-u-)

my-hand	a?-wo-ye:-n(a)	my-hands	di-gwo-ye:-n(i)(a)
your-hand	tso-ye:-n(a)	your-hands	di-tso-ye:-n(a)(a)
h/h-hand	u-wo-ye:-n(a)	h/h-hands	tsu-wo-ye:-n(a)(a)

Notice how easily many of these forms can become confused with one another unless you know: 1. Bound pronoun forms (pages 122 and 123)
2. Which group of bound pronoun forms belongs with each particular body part. (this lesson)

For instance, translate tso-ye:-na, tsi-le:-na, di-ga-le:-na, di-gwo-ye:-na. di-ka-to'-li, tsu-wo-ye:-na, looking them up in the samples above.

Notice that the plural forms on the previous page are exactly like the singular, but with di- added. The plural forms that do not have di-, are examples of submerged or half-submerged neighboring sounds.
Examples:
    ti-le:-na your-ears (di- next to hi- becomes ti-)
    ti'-k'-to'-li your-eyes (di- next to-hi- becomes ti-)
    tsu-wo-ye:-n(a) his/her-hands (di- next to -u- becomes tsu-)

A few body parts add de- instead of di-, and these must be memorized. De- next to -u becomes du-.

If you know <u>certain body part terms and their precise meanings</u> you will be able to tell what group the term belongs to, and can then tell what <u>any</u> bound pronoun for that part will be. There are exceptions, but very slight and very few. The significant body part terms are:
                    1. my ... (any body part)
                    2. his/her/its... (any body part)
                    3. a plural body part with any bound pronoun.
                        This will show whether di- or de- is added.

Re-examine the examples on the previous page and confirm this in your own mind.

Notice that only <u>one body part term</u> can be enough to diagnose a body part from Group B. If you know my-, his/her/its- <u>or</u> their- of a Group B body part term you can recognize it and tell what the other bound pronouns for that part will be. Confirm this by examining a?-wo-ye:-na on the previous page.

In Cherokee, the term for a body part usually changes according to whether the part is <u>on</u> the body (e.g., a sore foot, short legs, pretty hair), or <u>off</u> the body. (e.g., animal skins, cuts of meat, extracted teeth)

Many body part terms can be converted (see Lesson 7) from a noun into a past tense verb in the following way: Group B bound pronouns are added before the word base.

Word bases below are underlined the past tense marker below is -nv or -na.
Examples:

tsi'-<u>n'-doh</u>-gv	my-tooth (in my head)
a-wa-da-<u>n'-toh'</u>-ta-nv	my-tooth (out). This term means something like 'my-former-tooth', 'toothed-by-me'.
u-da-<u>n'-toh</u>-ta-nv	his/her/its-former-tooth, a tooth separate from its body, some un-specified human or animal's former tooth (see Lesson 19)

a-g'-<u>s-ti-g</u>v-i	my-hair, my-hairdo, my-hair-arrangement (on my head) A-g-s-ti-gv-i means a whole head of human hair. A single hair is '(u)-gi-tlv'.
a-g'-<u>s-ti-</u>ye-hnv	my-cut-off-hair (may or may not have come off my head)
u-<u>s-ti-</u>ye:-n(v)	his/her/its-cut-off-hair, some cut-off hair
a-l'-<u>s-di-</u>ye-hnv-s-doh-di	a wig (he-or-she-puts-it-onto-him-or herself-to-use-as-hair
a-gv'-hni-ge u'-<u>s-ti-g</u>i a-ge-hyu'-tsa	a black-haired girl

When body part terms are used to refer to cuts of meat, some need a past tense suffix (-nv or -na) and some do not. Notice -nv or -na below. Examples:

di-ga-nu'-la-tsi	his/her/its-ribs <u>or</u> ribs as meat. As a cut of meat, it can refer to either spare ribs or a rib roast.
u-we:-la	his/her/its-liver <u>or</u> liver as meat.
tsi-ta:-ga tsu-la'-ya-dv-n(v)(a)	chicken legs (chicken(s)-their-former-legs)
u-no-de:-na u-la'-ya-dv-n(v)(a)	leg of lamb (sheep-its-former-leg)

Notice that though the 3rd person singular of 'his/her/its-leg' (on the body), is <u>ga</u>-la'-ya-dv, a leg as meat has 'u-'. This is because 'u-' is the correct 3rd person singular bound pronoun for the <u>past tense</u>, since meat cuts <u>were</u> parts of a body but are no longer attached. Past tense uses the bound pronouns of Group B (see Appendix XI)

Not all body part terms use a past-tense suffix and Group B bound pronouns to show that the body part is detached. Some body parts use a different, though related, <u>word</u>:
Examples:

a-s-go'li	his/her/its-head (still on a living or dead human or animal)
u-s-ga, tsu-s-ga	a severed head (human or animal); also, a cabbage-head
u-ne'-ga-lv-i	his/her/its-skin, still on living or dead human or animal)
ga-ne-ga	a skin or fur (off)

If the animal is named, u-ne'-ga-lv-nv(na) is used:

do-ya tsu-ni-ne'-ga-lv-nv-i	beaver-skins
e:-tli u-ne'-ga-lv-nv-i go-tlv'-ta-nv ga-sa-le:-na	a mink coat (mink-skin-made-of coat)

Two body parts that usually do not take bound pronouns are 'gi-ga', blood, and 'ko:-li, tsu-ko:-li', bone, bones, Blood is a mass noun. That is, it has neither a singular nor a plural and is thought of as a <u>material</u> like butter, tea, meat in English, not as a <u>separate object</u>. Blood is a mass noun in English also, since we say 'some blood' in English, not 'a blood'.

In speaking of blood still circulating, Cherokee uses the classifying verb for 'have (in one's immediate possession)' with the 'liquid' classifier, but in a past tense of the verb 'have' (a-gi-ne-<u>hv</u>, not a-gi-ne-ha). See Lesson 8 and Appendices V and XI for classifying verbs.
Example:
My blood is pale.   Gi-ga a-gi-<u>ne</u>-hv u-s-go-lv:-ga.
(Blood I-have-had-<u>liquid</u> has-started-to-pale.)

The verb for 'paling', 'to pale', is in a beginning-present tense. Compare u-s-go-lv-s-ga, it is paling; u-s-go-lv-gi, it just paled; u-s-go-lv-gv, it was pale; u-s-go-lv-gv?-i, it used to pale; u-s-go-lv:-ga, it begins-to-pale,

There is no specific word for 'bleeding'. A verb meaning 'leaking, bursting out' is used with the word 'blood', with or without a body part term. This same verb can be used for air bursting from a tire or balloon, but not for other body liquids, such as tears.
Examples:
I am bleeding.   Gi-ga ga-ta'-s-gi-(a)
(I am leaking blood)
My finger is bleeding.   Tsi-ye'-sa-dv gi-ga a-ta-s-gi-(a).
(My-finger blood is leaking).
I am bleeding from a cut.   Ga-da-ye'-li-ga gi-ga a-ta-s-gi-(a).
(I-(having)-cut-myself blood is bursting out.)

The word for 'bone, bones' can be used in several ways.
Example:
My bones are hurting.
   1. 'Bone' as a mass noun (a material rather than a separate
       object: naming a body part but no plural on 'bone'.)
       a. Ko:-li du-ti'-tlv da-gwe-s-ta:-ne-(a).
          (Bone of the/his/her/someone's-joints are hurting me.)
       b. Ko:-li da-g'-ti'-tlv da-gwe-s-ta:-ne-(a)
          (Bone of my-joints are hurting me.)

   2. 'Bone' as an ordinary noun. (no bound pronoun)
       Tsu-ko:-lo da-gwe-s-ta:-ne-(a).
       (Bones-in they are hurting me.)

   3. 'Bone' as an ordinary body part, (with a bound pronoun).
       Tsi-ko:-lo (d)a-gwe-s-ta:-ne-(a).
       (My-bone(s) is or are causing me pain, hurting me.)

Notice in No. 1 above it is possible to use the word for 'joints' without naming the possessor of the joints accurately except in the verb. (i.e., to say 'du-ti-tlv da-gwe-s-ta:-ne' instead of 'da-g'-ti-tlv da-gwe-s-ta:-ne). Do not think you can sometimes do without bound pronouns for all body parts. Only 'ribs' and 'joints' of the body parts in this book can sometimes be used without the specific bound pronoun, and then only if the possessor is clear from the rest of the sentence.

A?-ti:-sa (right, toward the right) and a-k'-s-ga-ni' (left, toward the left) mean 'right hand' and 'left hand' when Group A (ts-a-) bound pronouns are added. These two words are also used as either adjectives or prepositions just as they are in English.

Examples:

Body-part:	my-right-hand	tsi?-ti:-sa
	your-left-hand	hi?-s-ka-n(a?)-i (also: 'You are left-handed.)
	he is left-handed	a?-s-ka-n(a?)-i
	he is a sinner	a-s-ka-n(a?)-i
Adjectives:	my right ear	tsi-le:-n' a?-ti:-sa
	your left ear	hi-le:-n' a?-s-ka-ni
Prepositions:	to the right	a?-ti:-si
	to the left	a?-s-ka-ni'-(i)

A sample of one body-part term from each of the three bound pronoun groups (A, ts-ga-, A, ts-a-, and B, a?-u-) is shown below with all the bound pronouns that are physically possible. (Examples of impossible body-terms: your-and-my-arm, their-leg, my-heads).

Group A (ts-ga-(includes ka-))

Singular pronoun, singular body-part:

my-arm	tsi-no-ge:-n(i)
your-arm	hi-hno-ge:-n(i)
his-or-her-arm	ka-no-ge:-n(i)

Singular pronoun, plural body-part:

my-arms	*di-tsi'?-no-ge:-ni(a)
your-arms	ti-hno-ge:-ni
his-or-her-arms	di-ka-no-ge:-ni(a)

Dual pronoun, plural body-part:

your-&-my-arms	di-ni-hno-ge:-ni
you-two's-arms	di-s-di-hno-ge:-ni
h/h-&-my-arms	tso-s-di-hno-ge:-ni

Plural pronoun, plural body part:
    our (not your) arms (several people's)   tso-tsi-no-ge:-ni
    your arms (several people's)   *di'-tsi:-no-ge:-ni
    their arms   di'-ni-hno-ge:-ni
    all of our arms, theirs and ours   di-di-hno-ge:-ni

Group A (ts-a-)
    Singular pronoun, singular body-part:
        my-eye   tsi-k(a)-to'-li
        your-eye   hi'-k'-to'-li
        his or her eye   a-k(a)-to'-li

    Singular pronoun, plural body-part:
        my-eyes   di-tsi-ga:-to'-li
        your-eyes   ti:-k'-to'-li
        his-or-her-eyes   di'-k'-to'-li

    Dual pronoun, plural body-part:
        your-and-my-eyes   di-ni-k'-to'-li
        you-two's-eyes   di-s-di-k'-to'-li
        his-or-her-&-my eyes   di-di-k'-to-li - same
                                      as below

    Plural pronoun, plural body-part:
        our (not your) eyes (several people's)   do-tsi:-k'-to'-li
        your plural eyes (several people's)   di'-tsi:-k'-to'-li
        their-eyes (several people's)   di'-ni-k'-to'-li

        eyes-of-all-of-us, their-&-our-eyes   di:-di'-k'-to'-li

Group B (a-u-)
    Singular pronoun, singular body-part:
        my-hand   a?-wo-ye:-n(a)
        your-hand   tso-ye:-na
        his-or-her-hand   u-wo-ye:-na

    Singular pronoun, plural body-part:
        my-hands   di-gwo-ye:-n(i)(a)
        your-hands   di-tso-ye:-n(i)(a)
        his-or-her-hands   tsu-wo-ye:-n(i)(a)

    Dual pronoun, plural body-part:
        your-&-my hands   di-no-ye:-ni
        hands of you-two   di-s-do-ye:-ni
        his-or-her-&-my hands   di-go-ye:-ni - same
                                      as below

    Plural pronoun, plural body-part:
        our(not your) hands (several people involved) tso-go-ye:-ni
        your plural hands (several people involved) di'-tso-ye:-ni
        their-hands (of several people)   tsu-no-ye:-ni

        hands of all of us, theirs and ours   di'-go-ye:-ni

231

CORE VOCABULARY

arm (my)   tsi-no-ge:-n(i)
arm (his or her)   ka-no-ge:-n(i)
arms (their)   di-ni-hno-ge:-ni

blood   gi-ga

bone, bones   ko:-li, tsu-ko:-li

ear (my)   tsi-le:-na
ear (his or her)   ga-le:-na
ears (their)   di-ni-le:-na

eye (my)   tsi-k(a)-to'-li
eye (his or her)   a'-k(a)-to'-li
eyes (their)   di-ni-k'-to'-li

finger (my)   tsi-ye'-sa-dv
finger (his or her)   ga-ye'-sa-dv
fingers (their)   da-ni-ye'-sa-dv

joint (my)   a'-gw'-ti'-tlv
joint (his or her)   u-ti'-tlv
joints (their)   du'-n'-ti'-tlv

   This means 'joined, knitted together'. 'De-ga-ti-tlv-s-ga' means 'I am
joining them together' (things, not living beings), as, for instance, two
boards in carpentering.

hair (my)   a-g'-s-ti-gv-i
hair (his or her)   u-s-ti-gv-i
hair (their)   du-n'-s-ti-gv-i

hand (my)   a?-wo-ye:-n(a)(i)
hand (his or her)   u-wo-ye:-n(a)(i)
hands (their   tsu-no-ye:-n(a)(i)

head (my)   tsi-s-go'-li
head (his or her)   a-s-go'-li
heads (their)   di-ni-s-go'-li

liver (my)   a-gwe:-la
liver (his or her)   u-we:-la
livers (their)   tsu-ni-we-la

232

left hand (my)　　　　　　　　　　tsi'?-s-ka-ni'
left hand (his or her)　　　　　a'-g-s-ka-ni'
left hands (their)　　　　　　　di-ni?-s-ka-ni'

rib (my)　　　　　　　　　　　　a-gi-nu'-la-tsi
rib (his or her)　　　　　　　　ga-nu'-la-tsi
ribs (their)　　　　　　　　　　tsu-ni-nu-la-tsi

right hand (my)　　　　　　　　tsi?-ti:-s(a)(i)
right hand (his or her)　　　　a?-ti:-sa
right hands (their)　　　　　　di-ni?-ti:-s(a)(i)

skin (my)　　　　　　　　　　　a-gi-ne-ga-lv-(i)
skin (his or her)　　　　　　　u-ne-ga-lv-i
skin (their)　　　　　　　　　u-ni-ne-ga-lv-i

tooth (my)　　　　　　　　　　tsi-nv-doh-gv
tooth (his or her)　　　　　　ga-n'-doh-gv
teeth (their)　　　　　　　　da-ni-n'-doh'-gv

Verbs:
　　burst out with, shed, as:　balloon a-ta-s-gi, the balloon burst or
　　　　　　　　　　　　　　gi-ga　　ga-ta-s-gi, I am shedding blood

　　　　I am shedding (it)　　　　　ga-ta-s-gi-(a)
　　　　you are shedding (it)　　　ha-ta-s-gi-(a)
　　　　he or she is shedding (it)　a-ta-s-gi-(a)
　　　　you-&-I are shedding (it)　i-n'-ta-s-gi-(a)
　　　　they are shedding (it)　　a-n'-ta-s-gi-(a)

　　be hurt (by a thing or things), feel pain (because of a thing or things)
　　Examples:
　　　　I am in pain.　　　　　　A-gwe-s-ta-ne?-(a).
　　　　My-arms are hurting me.　Di-tsi-no-ge:-n'
　　　　　　　　　　　　　　　da-gwe-s-ta'-ne?-(a).
　　　　My-arm is hurting me.　　Tsi-no-ge:-n' a-gwe-s-ta'-
　　　　　　　　　　　　　　　ne?-(a).
　　　　(My) shoes are hurting me.　Da-gwa-la-su-tlv da-gwe-s-
　　　　　　　　　　　　　　　ta'-ne?-(a).

　　join, fasten together (of two things, not living beings)
　　　Notice d- plural object (them-I am-joining)
　　　I am joining (them)　　　　　de-ga-ti-tlv'-s-ga
　　　you singular are joining (them)　de-ha-ti-tlv-s-ga
　　　he or she is joining (them)　da-ti-tlv-s-ga
　　　you-&-I are joining (them)　de-n'-ti-tlv'-s-ga
　　　they are joining (them)　　da-n'-ti-tlv'-s-ga

Exercise 1: The following body-part terms are found in the explanations, Phrases or Core Vocabulary of this lesson. Translate them into English and write them in Cherokee. Answers are on the next page.

1. di-tso-ye:-na
2. di-gwo-ye:-na
3. ga-le:-na
4. di-di-k(a)-to-li
5. di-ni-k(a)-to-li
6. tsu-no-ye:-ni
7. di-tsi-hno-ge:-ni
8. di-di-hno-ge:-ni
9. hi-k(a)-to-li
10. di-go-ye:-ni

11. tsi-no-ge:-ni
12. tsi-le:-na
13. a-k(a)-ti:-sa
14. tsu-ni-nu-la-tsi
15. tsi-s-ka-ni
16. u-ni-ne-ga-lv-i
17. da-ni-n(e)-doh-gv
18. ga-n(e)-doh-gv
19. tsi-n(v)-doh-gv
20. ga-nu-la-tsi

Exercise 2: The following body part terms are not in the lesson anywhere, but you can tell what they are from the information given. To save space, # is 'equals'.

   Example: Tsi-ho'-li means my-mouth, a-ho'-li means his/her mouth, and di-ni-ho'-li means their-mouths. What is your-mouth?
   Answer: Hi-ho'-li.

1. Tsi-le:-na#my-ear; ga-le:-na#his/her-ear; di-ni-le:-na#their ears. Your-(pl.)-ears?
2. U-we:-la means 'his-liver'. My-liver?
3. A?-wa-da-n'-to'-gi means 'my-heart'. Your-heart?
4. Tsi-ga'-v?-ga#my-tongue; ga'-v?-ga#his/her-tongue. Your-tongue?
5. A'-ka-to'-li#his/her-eye. My-eye?
6. A-qua-la'-s-de:-ni#my-foot. My-feet? Your-foot? The-feet-of-all-of-us?
7. De-ga-ye'-sa-dv#his-fingers. My-fingers? My-finger?
8. Tsu-na'-hwi#their-hearts (animal hearts). Its-heart?
9. Tsi-ye'-lv-i#my-body; a-ye-lv-i#his/her-body; di-ni-ye'-lv-i#their-bodies; Your-body?
10. Tsi-n'-doh'-gv#my-tooth; ka-n'-doh'-gv#his/her-tooth; de-ni-n'-doh-gv#their-teeth; teeth of you-two?

Exercise 3: The following body-part terms are found in this lesson. Translate from English into Cherokee using the information given.

1. Hair in Cherokee belongs to Group B. What is 'His-hair'?
2. Leg in Cherokee belongs to Group A ts-ga. Name two ways to say "Their-legs'.
3. Body in Cherokee belongs to Group A ts-a-. How would you say 'Her-body'?
4. Finger in Cherokee belongs to Group A ts-ga-. How would you say 'My-finger'?
5. Skin in Cherokee belongs to Group B a?-u-. What is 'a beaver-skin'?
6. Eye in Cherokee belongs to Group A ts-a-. What is 'your-eyes'? (to one person)
7. Stomach belongs to Group B a?-u-. What is 'Their-stomachs'?
8. Right-hand belongs to Group A ts-a-. What is 'Their right-hands'?
9. What is 'my blood' in Cherokee?
10. What is 'I have a sister and a brother' in Cherokee? (you are a male)

234

EXERCISE 1:

20. ᏚᎯᏬᎯ	his or her-rib		10. ᏗᎠᏴᎯ	his/her-&-my-hands
19. ᏆᏟᎥᎦ	my-tooth		9. ᏬᎣᎺᏉ	your-eye
18. ᏚᏑᎥᎦ	his or her-tooth		8. ᏗᏗᏃᏝᎯ	their-&-our-eyes
17. ᏔᎮᏑᎥᎦ	their-teeth		7. ᏗᏆᏃᏝᎯ	your(pl.)-arms
16. ᎤᎯᎾᏍᎠᎢ	their-skin		6. ᎫᏃᏴᎤ	their-hands
15. ᏆᏆᎣᎯ	my-left-hand		5. ᏗᎮᎣᎺᏉ	their-eyes
14. ᎫᎮᎠᏬᎯ	their-ribs		4. ᏗᏗᎠᎺᏉ	their-&-our-eyes
13. ᎠᎣᏒᎤ	my-right-hand		3. ᏚᏟᎣ	his/her-ear
12. ᏆᏟᎣ	my-ear		2. ᎫᎥᏴᎣ	my-hands
11. ᏆᏃᏝᎯ	my-arm		1. ᏗᏦᏴᎣ	your(pl.)-hands

EXERCISE 2:

1. di-tsi-le-na.
2. a?-we-la (or A-que-la, A-gwe-la)
3. tsa-da-n'-to-gi
4. hi-ga-n?-gv
5. tsi-k'-to-li
6. di-qua-la-s-de:-n(i or a), tsa-la-s-
7. de:-n(i or a), di-di-la-s-de:-n(i or a)
8. de-tsi-ye-sa-dv, tsi-ye-sa-dv
9. u-nah-wi
10. hi-ye-lv-i
10. s-dv-doh-gv

EXERCISE 3:

1. ᎤᏬᏎᎢᎢ
2. ᏗᎭᏬᏆᎯ ᏚᎲᏬᏍᏈ
3. ᎠᏴᎠᎢ
4. ᏆᏴᎤᏍᏈ
5. ᏝᏬ ᎤᎾᏍᎠᏓ
6. ᎫᏐᎺᏉ
7. ᎫᎭᏬᏕᏟ
8. ᏗᎭᎣᏒᎤ
9. ᏯᏍ ᎠᏴᎶᏓ
10. ᎠᏴᎥᎢ ᎠᏓ -Ꮑ- ᏓᏬᎵᏟᎤᏍ -ᎠᏆᏔ-

Exercise 4: Translate from Cherokee into English. Answers are on pp. 64, 70, 78 and 86.

ᎶᎶᏴ	ᎠᏪᏍᎬ	ᏚᏔᏆᏑ	ᏒᎨ
ᎤᏫᎣ	ᏚᎵᏔ	ᏚᏒ	ᏚᎥᎠ
ᏝᎠᏔ	�6Ꮢ	ᏝᏆᏏ	ᎤᏁ

ᏑᏓᎵᏦᏁ ᏣᎳᎩ ᎪᏪᎸᎢ

Su-da-l'-tso'-ne Tsa-la-gi' Go-hwe:-lv-i

CHEROKEE LESSON TWENTY-SIX

180.		
See that blood. I must have cut myself.	Ꮎ ᎩᎦ ᏄᏍᏗ. ᎦᏓᏰᎳᎦ.	Na gi-ga nu-s-di. Ga-da-ye-la-ga.
181.		
I (just) broke my leg.	ᏥᏅᏍᎨᏂ ᏥᏍᏆᎳ.	Tsi-nv-s-ge:-ni tsi:-s-qua-la'.
You (just) broke a leg.	ᎯᎳᏯᏛ ᎯᏍᏆᎳ.	Hi-la'-ya-dv hi'-s-qua-la'.
He/she (just) broke a leg.	ᎦᎳᏯᏛ ᎠᏍᏆᎳ.	Ga-la'-ya-dv a'-s-qua-la'.
182.		
Something is wrong with that boy's foot.	Ꮎ ᎠᏧᏥ ᎫᏍᏗ ᎤᎵᏍᏔᏁ ᎤᎳᏍᏕᏂ.	Na a-tsu'-tsi gu'-s-di u-l'-s-ta:-hne u-la-s-de:-ni.
183.		
My eyes are swollen. I have a headache and my bones ache. I think I have a fever. (I-think-something-is-on-my-joints)	ᏗᏥᎧᏙᎵ ᏚᏬᏘᏒ. ᏥᏍᎪᎵ ᎠᏇᏍᏔᏁᎠ ᎠᎴ ᏧᎪᎶ ᏓᏇᏍᏔᏁ. ᎠᏆᏗᏝᎲᏍᎦ ᎨᎵᎠ.	Di-tsi-k'-to'-li du:-wo-ti'-sv. Tsi-s-go'-li a-gwe-s-ta-ne?-a a-le tsu-ko:-lo da-gwe-s-ta:-ne. A-gwa-di'-tle-hv-s-ga ge'-li-a.
184.		
There is something wrong with my blood. I feel tired all the time.	ᎩᎪ ᎫᏍᏗ ᎤᏍᏗ. ᏓᎩᏯᏪᎪ ᏂᎪᎯᎸ.	Gi-go gu-s-d' u'-s-di. Da-gi-ya-we:-go ni-go-hi-lv.
185.		
I, he/she is ill.	ᎠᎩᏢᎦ. ᎤᏢᎦ.	A-g'-tlv'-ga. U-tlv'-ga.
I, he/she had a fall.	ᎠᎩᏅᏨ. ᎤᏅᏤ.	A-gi-nv'-tsv. U-nv'-tse.
I, he/she swallowed something poisonous.	ᎠᏓᎯ ᎠᎩᎩᏒ. ᎠᏓᎯ ᎤᎩᏎ.	A-da'-hi a-gi-ki'-sv. A-da'-hi u-ki'-se.
I, he/she lost consciousness (at a prior time).	ᎾᏆᏂᏔ ᎾᏄᎵᏍᏔᏅ. ᏄᏂᏛ ᏄᎵᏍᏔᏅ.	Na-qua-n?-tv'-na nu'-hl'-s-ta-nv. Nu:-n'-tv-na nu-hl'-s-ta-nv or nu-hl'-s-ta'-ne-lv(i)

185. (cont.)

He/she is unconscious.	ᏃᏂᎬ ᏤᎶᏪᏞᏘ.	Nu:-nʼ-tv-na nu-hlʼ-s-ta-hne.
I, he/she has a cough.	ᎠᏴᏊᎦᏫᎠ. ᎤᏞᎦᏫᎠ.	A-gʼ-si-hwaʼ-s-go. U-si-si-waʼ-s-go.
a cut, cuts	ᏣᏚᏑᏞᎦᏔ ᏕᏣᏚᏑᏞᏓᏔ	tsa-daʼ-hye-tla-lv?-i de-tsa-daʼ-hye-tla-lv?-i
medicine	ᏅᏬᏘ	nv-wo-ti
a pill, pills	ᎠᏱᏍᏗ ᏗᏯᏍᏗ	a-kiʼ-s-di, di-kiʼ-s-di
a sore, sores	ᏣᏍᏍᏓᏔ ᏕᏣᏍᏍᏓᏔ	tsa-dʼ-s-da-lv?-i de-tsa-dʼ-s-da-lv-i
I, he/she is hard of hearing.	ᏍᏔᏯ ᎠᏴᎢᎤᏗ. ᏍᏔᏯ ᎤᎢᎤᏗ.	S-ta-yi a-gʼ-tv-go:-di. S-ta-yi u-tv-go:-di.
I, he/she is deaf.	ᏗᎩᎵᎨᎾ ᏧᎵᎨᎾ	Di-gi-li?-e:-na. Tsu-li-e:-na.
I, he/she is blind.	ᏗᏥᎨᏆ. ᏗᎨᏫ	Di-tsi-ke:-wa. Di-ke:-wi.

186.

He/she must rest.	ᎤᏣᏪᏐᎸᏍᏙᏗ.	U-tsa-we-soʼ-lv-s-doh-di.
He/she must go to the hospital.	ᏧᏂᏓᏘ ᏧᎾᏂᏒ ᎤᏪᏅᏍᏗ.	Tsu-ni-dlv:-dʼ tsu-na-nʼ-sv-di u-we-nv:-s-di.
He/she must have a shot.	ᎠᏢᎩᏣᏫᏍᏗ.	Aʼ-tsi-tsa-yo:-s-di.
He/she must come again on this date.	ᎯᎢᏯ ᎠᏟᎩᎵᏒ ᎤᏪᏓᏍᏗ ᎨᏎᏍᏗ.	Hi-i-ya a-tli-gi-liʼ-sv u-we:-da-s-di ge-se:-s-di.
Don't worry. (Stop being about to constantly think of it.)	ᎮᏍᏗ ᏱᏣᏓᏁᎢᏕᏍᎨᏍᏗ.	He:-s-di yi-tsa-daʼ-nʼ-te-di-s-ge:-s-di.

187.

Body parts from Group A ts-ga(ka)

arm (my)	ᏥᏃᎨᎾ	tsi-no-ge:-n(a)
arm (his or her)	ᎧᏃᎨᎾ	ka-no-ge:-n(a)
arms (their)	ᏗᏂᏃᎨᎾ	di-ni-no-ge:-n(a)
ear (my)	ᏥᎴᎾ	tsi-le:-n(a)
ear (his or her)	ᎦᎴᎾ	ga-le:-n(a)
ears (their)	ᏗᏂᎴᎾ	di-ni-le:-n(a)
leg (my)	ᏥᏅᏍᎨᎾ	tsi-nv-s-ge:-n(i)(a)
leg (his or her)	ᎧᏅᏍᎨᎾ	ka-nv-s-ge:-n(i)(a)
legs (their)	ᏗᏂᏅᏍᎨᎾ	di-ni-nvʼ-s-ge:-n(i)(a)
leg (my)	ᏥᎳᏯᏛ	tsi-laʼ-ya-dv
leg (his or her)	ᎦᎳᏯᏛ	ga-laʼ-ya-dv
legs (their)	ᏕᏂᎳᏯᏛ	de-ni-laʼ-ya-dv

187. (cont.)

tooth (my)	ᏥᏂᏙᎬ	tsi-n'-doh'-gv
tooth (his or her)	ᎧᏂᏙᎬ	ka-n'-doh-gv
teeth (their)	ᏕᏂᏂᏙᎬ	de-ni-n'-doh'-gv
tongue (my)	ᏥᎦᏁᎦ	tsi-(ga)'-n?-g(a)(v)(o)
tongue (his or her)	ᎦᏁᎬ	ga'-n?-g(a)(v)(o)
tongues (their)	ᏓᏂᏁᎬ	*di-ni'-n?-g(a)(v)(o)

188.
Body parts from Group A ts-a-

body (my)	ᏥᏰᎸᎢ	tsi-ye-lv-i
body (his or her)	ᎠᏰᎸᎢ	a-ye-lv-i
bodies (their)	ᏗᏂᏰᎸᎢ	di-ni-ye'-lv-i
eye (my)	ᏥᎧᏙᎵ	tsi-k'-to'-li
eye (his or her)	ᎠᎧᏙᎵ	a'-ka-to'-li
eyes (their)	ᏗᏂᎧᏙᎵ	di-ni-k'-to'-li
mouth (my)	ᏥᎰᎵ	tsi-ho'-li
mouth (his or her)	ᎠᎰᎵ	a-ho'-li
mouths (their)	ᏗᏂᎰᎵ	di-ni-ho'-li

189.
Body parts from Group B a?-u-

foot (my)	ᎠᏆᎳᏍᏕᏂ	a-qua-la'-s-de:-n(i)
foot (his or her)	ᎤᎳᏍᏕᏂ	u-la'-s-de:-n(i)
feet (their)	ᏧᎾᎳᏍᏕᏂ	tsu-na-la-s-de:-n(i)
feet (his/her, a <u>pair</u>)	ᏚᎳᏍᎬᎢ	du-la-s-gv?-i
hair (my)	ᎠᎩᏍᏘᎬᎢ	a-g'-s-ti-gv-i
hair (his or her)	ᎤᏍᏘᎬᎢ	u-s-ti-gv-i
hair (their)	ᏚᏂᏍᏘᎬᎢ	du-n'-s-ti-gv-i
hand (my)	ᎠᏬᏰᎾ	a?-wo-ye:-n(a)(i)
hand (his or her)	ᎤᏬᏰᎾ	u-wo-ye:-n(a)(i)
hands (their)	ᏧᏃᏰᎾ	tsu-no-ye:-n(a)(i)
heart (my)	ᎠᏩᏓᏁᏙᎩ	a?-wa-da-n'-to'gi
heart (his or her)	ᎤᏓᏁᏙᎩ	u-da-n'-to'-gi
hearts (their)	ᏧᏂᏓᏁᏙᎩ	tsu-n'-da-n'-to'-gi
skin (my)	ᎠᎩᏁᎦᎸᎢ	a-gi-ne'-ga-lv-i
skin (his or her)	ᎤᏁᎦᎸᎢ	u-ne'-ga-lv-i
skins (their)	ᏚᏂᏁᎦᎸᎢ	du-ni-ne'-ga-lv-i
stomach (my)	ᎠᎩᏍᏉᏟ	a-g'-s?-wo:-tli
stomach (his or her)	ᎤᏍᏉᏟ	u'-s(h)?-wo:-tli
stomachs (their)	ᏧᏂᏍᏉᏟ	tsu-n'?-s-quo:-tli

Notes:

P.N. 180 - gi-ga nu-s-di - a blood spot (something of blood)

P.N. 182 - gu'-s-di u-l'-s-ta:-hne - something is wrong with ..., something has happened to ...

P.N. 184 - Gu'-s-di u'-s-di - something is wrong with...

These are all expressions that can be used often in connection with body parts and states of health. In general, whenever you hear 'gu'-s-di' or 'nu'-s-di', it means that something out of the ordinary is being described. A similar remark that is easy to remember because, like many Cherokee expressions, it rhymes, is:

Gu'-s-di nu'-s-di.   Something is wrong. This can also be used in the sense of: What's wrong? What's bothering you?

More examples:

Gi'-ga-ge nu'-s-di ka-lv-gv.	It is (unusually) red toward the east.
Gu'-s-di a-gi-go-tv?-di.	He/she is showing me something.
Tla-wo:-tu nu'-s-di.	It is (unusually) muddy (here). or:
	It is (unusually) muddy (today).

(It is muddier than expected for the time or the place.)

Nv-yo nu'-s-di.	It is rocky (here or today).
U'-n'-tsi nu'-s-di.	There's some snow on the ground.
Ga-du-li:-da nu:-s-di.	It's damp or wet (here or today).

P.N. 181 - tsi:-s-qua-la' - I just broke ... S-qua-la' means 'short, shortened, cut off'. As an adjective, it can be used for a short person or a short string, but not for a short period of time. It is used for clothing (see Lesson 24), also: s-qua-la' di-go-hya-da a'-hnu-wo, 'a short-sleeved shirt'.

As a verb, it is usually used for snapping off something long and inflexible such as a bone, post or axle. 'A-g'-s-qua-lo?-v' means 'I hit my head.' (I got shortened.) 'Di-da-s-qua-lv-ni-s-toh-di', a billie club, means 'tool to shorten them with'.

In speaking of something that has no length, or did not break by snapping off but by coming apart or failing to work the verb 'a-gi-yo:-s-di' is used:

Examples:

The wagon broke down.	Da-gwa-le:-lu a-yo-gi.
I am breaking a plate.	Te-li-do tsi-yo:-s-ti-ya.
I just broke a plate.	Te-li-do tsi-yo'-s-ta.
I just broke my watch.	Wa-tsi tsi-yo'-s-ta.
Jim broke my gun.	Tsi-mi a-gi-yo-s-da:-si ga-lo'-(g)we-(d(i)).

P.N. 181 - gi-go - in (my) blood

P.N. 183 - tsu-ko:-lo - in (my) bones

As you know, -i added to the end of a word means 'at', 'in that place', 'this particular one'.

-O on the end of some nouns means 'place of', 'in', or 'to'. Often -o and -i are combined, and then their meanings are combined also.

Examples:

nv-ya	rock or rocks	nv-yo	on the rock or rocks, a rocky place
		nv-yo-i	in or to a rocky place
e-quo-ni	river	e-quo-no-(i)	on, by or along the river
nv-no-hi	road	nv-no	on, by or along the road
Gu'-gu	Bartlesville	Gu-go	to Bartlesville
		Gu-go-i	in or to Bartlesville
gu'-gu	bottle or jar	gu-go	on or against a bottle or jar
gi-ta-ya	cherry or cherries	Gi-ta-yo	'a place where there are cherries', 'cherry place' (Cherry Hill, Oklahoma)
		Gi-ta-yo-i	in Cherry Hill (in or to a place where there are cherries)
A-gu:-sv	a Creek, a member of the Creek tribe	Gu:-so	'a place where there are Creeks', Creek place (Muskogee, Oklahoma, the oldest and largest town in what used to be the Creek Nation)
		Gu:-so-i	to Muskogee, in Muskogee
A?-sa:-si	an Osage, a member of the Osage tribe	A-ni?-sa'-so	'a place where there are Osages', Osage place, (Pawhuska, Oklahoma, formerly the capital of the Osage Nation)
		A-ni?-sa'-so-i	to or in Pawhuska
Wa-sv-da-nv	Washington D.C.	Wa-sv-da-no-i	to or in Washington
ka-nu'-ga-tli	blackberry or blackberries	Ka-nu-ga-tlo-yi	to or in Blackberry Patch, a community in North Carolina
u-wa-sv	alone, he/she/it is alone	O-wa-s-so	'alone place', 'place where one person lives', (Owasso, Oklahoma)
		O-wa-s-so-i	to or in Owasso
ga-lv'-la-di'	high	ga-lv-lo-(hi)	high in the sky, in heaven
a-dʌ	wooden	a-doh	woods, 'place where there is wood'
		a-do?-i	in, to or toward the woods
e-do-da	Father'	e-do-do-(i)	to/at Father's (house)

P.N. 185 - a-da'-hi - poisonous. This means 'deadly, death-causing', as: a-da'-hi ga-nu'-la, deadly grass or weed; a-da'-hi i'-na-dv, deadly snake; a-da-hi-s-toh-di, fatal weapon (to-be-used-to-kill-with).

CORE VOCABULARY

hard, loud, taut	s-ta-yi, a-s-da-ya
harder, louder, more taut	a-s-da-ya-hi-ge
hardest, loudest, tautest	wa-s-ta-yv, s-ta-yo-sv
sharp-edged, sharp-pointed	go-s-ta-yi, go-s-da-ya
sharper or sharpest	wi-go-s-ta-yv

swollen, puffed up (of things or living beings)   u-wo-ti:-sv
  go:-ti-s-ga'   it is rising (of breads, cakes)

Verbs:

break, snap off, shorten, cut a piece off the end
  I just broke (it)   tsi-s-qua-la'
  you just broke (it)   hi-s-qua-la'
  he/she just broke it or: it just broke   a-s-qua-la'
  you-&-I just broke (it)   i-ni'-s-qua-la'
  they just broke (it)   a-ni-s-qua-la'

  I just broke something of someone else's   tsi-s-qua-l'-<u>si</u>'
  you just broke something of someone else's   hi-s-qua-l'-<u>si</u>', etc.

cut (with a knife), make a cut in   tsi-ye'-hlo-h∤
  I am cutting (it)   tsi-ye'-hlo-h∤
  you are cutting (it)   hi-hye:-hlo-h∤
  he/she is cutting (it)   a-hye:-hlo-h∤
  you-&-I are cutting (it)   i-ni-hye'-hlo-h∤
  they are cutting (it)   a-ni-hye-hlo-h∤

happen to
  (something) unusual is happening to me   gu'-s-di na-gwa-l'-s-tah-ne
  (something) exciting is happening to me   a-li-he'-li-s-di na-gwa-l'-s-tah-ne
  (something) bad, evil, mean is happening   u-yo na-gwa-l'-s-tah-ne
    to me
  (something) good is happening to me   o:-s-da na-gwa-l'-s-tah-ne
  (something) is happening to you   ni-tsa-l'-s-tah-ne
  (something) is happening to him/her/it   nu-l'-s-tah-ne
  (something) is happening to you-&-me   ni-gi-na-l'-s-tah-ne
  (something) is happening to them   nu-na-l'-s-tah-ne
  something just happened to me   na-gwa-l'-s-tah-<u>si</u>'
  something just happened to you   ni-tsa-l'-s-tah-<u>si</u>'
  something just happened to him/her/it   nu-l'-<u>s</u>-tah-<u>si</u>'

rest
  I am resting   a-gwa-tsv-weh-so-lv:-s-di
  you are resting   tsa-tsa-we:-so-lv-s-di
  he/she is resting   u-tsa-we-so-lv-s-di
  you-&-I are resting   gi-n'-tsa-we-so-lv-s-di
  they are resting   u-n'-tsa-we-so-lv-s-di

swell up, become puffy
  I am swelling up   *go:-ti-s-ga (low, level tone)
  you are swelling up   ho:-ti-s-ga
  he/she is swelling up   *go:?-ti-s-ga'(scalloped, upward)
  you-&-I are swelling up   i-no-ti-s-ga
  they are swelling up   a-no-ti-s-ga

tire, be tired
 I am tired   da-gi-ya-we:-ga
 you are tired   de-tsa-ya-we:-ga
 he/she is tired   du-ya-we:-ga
 you-&-I are tired   de-gi-ni-ya-we:-ga
 they are tired   du-ni'-ya-we:-ga

dv-gi-yo:-tli   he/she will shoot me
dv-gi-tsa-yo:-tli   he/she will give me a shot

EXERCISES

Exercise 1:   Choose the appropriate answers below after translating the Cherokee sentences.

1. Your child comes in from school and says: Do-yu u-yo ge:-sv di-gwe-yo-hv-s-gi ko'-hi.   U-tlv'-ga ge'-li-a!
 You reply:
      a. Tsa-di-tle-hv-s-ga ge'-li-a.
      b. S-gi-dv' nu-s-di'. Coke-i-ke ice-cream-i-ke tsa-du'-li?
      c. Tsu-ni-dlv:-d tsu-na-n'-sv-di tse-nv:-s-di ge'-li-a.

2. A man stops your car and says: A-gi-do'-da u-nv:-tse a-le nu:-n'-tv nu-hl'-s-ta-hne'-lv.   You immediately:
      a. Get out and go with him to help.
      b. Have him lie down in the back seat while you drive him to a doctor.
      c. Tell him you haven't seen anyone of that description.

3. You work in a doctor's office. A teen-ager comes in and says: A-gi-li'-si u-tlv'-ga, do-yi automobil-i u-wo:-tla.   You tell him:
      a. The parking lot is only for patients.
      b. The doctor is busy but the nurse can give him his shot so he won't overpark.
      c. The doctor will be with him in a moment.

Exercise 2:   Translate into English from Cherokee:

1. DꟾⱢᏁᏉ DYᏬᏐᏉᎢᏟ ᏦᏰᏱ
2. ᎣᏍᏤᎢᎢ DᏢᏍᏓᏰᎣᏍᎥᏙ
3. ᎣᏟᏁᏉ ᏟᏟᏁᏉ ᏂᎣᏍᎧᎿ
4. ᎣᏁᏍᎿᎢ ᎣᏁᏍᎿᎣ
5. ᎣᏍᏂᎢᏟ DᎡᏇ ᏝᎮᎣᏉᏞ
6. ᎣᏰᏰᎧ ᎣᏰᏰᎿ
7. ᏚᏰᎧᎿ ᏚᏃᎧᎿ ᎣᎣᏍᎮᎧ
8. ᏕᏁᏫ ᎮᏕᏁᏫ ᏚᏥᏁᏫ
0. ᎮᏃᎮᎧ ᏚᏃᎧᎧ ᎣᎣᏍᎮᎧ
10. ᏕᏂᏐᏤᎢᏚ ᏕᏂᏁᏫ ᏕᏫᏐᏤᎢ
11. ᎣᏃᎮᎧ ᏕᏫᏐᏘ ᏕᎮᏫᏐᏘ
12. ᎣᏫᏐᏕᎿ ᎮᏃᎮᎮ ᏚᏕᏫᏐᎿ

EXERCISE 1:   1. My teacher was certainly mean today. I think she's sick.
a. I think you have a fever. b. That's the way things go sometimes. Do you
want a coke or ice-cream? c. I think you should go to the hospital. (b)
2. My father had a fall and is unconscious. (a) 3. My grandmother is sick;
she is sitting outside in the car. (c)

EXERCISE 2:   Notice that it is impossible to indicate some words' sounds
exactly in the syllabary.

1. a-qua-da-ne-do-gi, my-heart; a-gi-s-quo-tli, my-stomach; tso-ye:-na,
   your-hand
2. u-s-ti-gv-i, his/her-hair; a-li-s-ti-ye-hv-s-do-di, a wig
3. u-da-ne-do-gi, his/her-heart; tsa-da-ne-do-gi, your-heart; hi-ka-s-ka-ni,
   your-right-hand
4. u-ne-ga-lv-i, his/her-skin; u-ne-ga-lv-nv, a skin
5. u-s-quo-tli, his/her-stomach; a-gwe-la, my-liver; di-tsi-ka-to-li, my-eyes
6. u-wo-ye-na, his/her-hand; u-wo-ye-ni, his/her-hand
7. tsu-wo-ye-ni, his/her-hands; tsu-no-ye-ni, their hands; tsu-no-ye-na,
   their-hands
8. ga-ne-gv, his/her-tongue; tsi-ga-ne-gv, my-tongue; di-ni-ga-ne-gv,
   their-tongues
9. tsi-no-ge-na, my-arm; tsu-no-ye-na, their-hands; ka-nv-s-ge-na, his/her-leg
10. du-ni-s-ti-gv-i, their-hair; de-ni-ne-do-gv, their-teeth; du-la-s-gv-i,
    both his/her feet
11. ka-no-ge-na, his/her-arm; ga-la-ya-dv, his/her-foot; de-ni-la-ya-dv,
    their-feet
12. u-la-s-de-ni, his/her-foot; tsi-no-ge-ni, my-arm; tsu-na-la-s-de-ni,
    their-feet

Exercise 3:   Match columns A and B. Look up the answers in this lesson.

A.
1. ᏒᏣᏗᎿᏍᏙᎥᏗ
2. ᏍᏫᏃ ᎠᏯᎶᎠᏗ
3. ᏞᏲᏍᏍᎠ ᏂᎠᎦᎤ
4. ᎦᏩᏍᎣ ᎠᏍᎢᏣ
5. ᎠᏟᏣᎦᎠᏗ
6. ᏒᏒᎤ
7. ᎠᏯᏍᏗ ᏒᏫᏗ ᎦᎦᎠᏞᎤᎢ
8. ᎤᎠᏗ ᏚᎦᏞᎤᏘᏍᏒᎠᏗ
9. Ꮎ ᎠᏛ ᏚᎠᏗ ᏒᎶᏍᏩᎸ ᏒᏫᏍᏂ
10. ᎠᎢᏞᏌᏍᏛ ᎭᏒᎠ

B
1. He or she must rest.
2. I am hard of hearing.
3. I feel tired all the time.
4. He or she had a fall.
5. I think I have a fever.
6. He or she must have a shot.
7. Don't worry.
8. Something is wrong with that boy's foot.
9. He or she just broke a leg.
10. a pill, medicine, sores

Exercise 4: Compare the Cherokee spellings in this lesson with the pronunciation columns, noting the difficulties involved.(e.g., a?-wa-da-n'-to:-gi must
be spelled a-qua-(or wa-)-da-(ne-nv- or ni-)-do-(not to-)-gi.

ᏚᏡᎧᎵ ᏣᏫᏴ ᎠᏫᎥᏔ

Ga-l'-qua-tso'-ne Tsa-la-gi Go-hwe:-lv-i

CHEROKEE LESSON TWENTY-SEVEN

Driving around on country roads you might find the following sentences useful.

190.
How many miles to ...?   Ha-la' i-yu tli-lo'-da ...?
(How many times a measurement is...?)

191.
I am out of gas.   Ge-sa-li:-ni ka-ni'-gi-da' ni-ga-l'-
                                                s-ti:-ya.

Where is a gas station?   Ha'-tlv go'-tlv ge-sa-li:-ni ga-ne-
                                                gi'-s-di-i?

192.
I would like to use the telephone.   Ya-qua-du-la-wu, di-tla-no-he?-di-i
                                                a-g'-do-di-i.

193.
Where is the dance ground?   Ha'-tlv (go'-tlv) u-na-l'-s-gi-s-di-i?
Where is the ball-field?   Ha'-tlv (go'-tlv) u-no-s-dv-ni'-s-di?
                                                or: Ha'-tlv (go'-tlv) s-qua-tle:-s-di
                                                tsu-na-ne-hl'-di-yi?

194.
Turn right at the next turnoff.   A-k'-ti-sa, ha-tle:-sv-i.
Turn left at the crossroads.   A-g'-s-ka-ni', de-gi-n'-di'-s-gv-i.
Turn east at the second turnoff.   Ta-li:-ne a-tle-s-gv ka-lv'-gv ha-
                                                tle-sv-i.

Turn west...   U-de'-li-gv, ha-tle-sv-i...
Turn north...   U-yv'-tlv, ha-tle-sv-i...
Turn south...   U-ga'-no-wv, ha-tle-sv-i...

195.
What time is the meeting?   Ha-la'-ya do-dv-na-tlo:-si?
(When will they meet?)

196.
Soon. Later. Now.   Ki-lo-wa-yu'-s-di. Ko-hi-yv-i. No-wv.
The meeting is over.   A-ni-s-qua-da' da-na-tlo:-s-gv-i.

197.
How far is it to town?   Ha-la'-yv di-ga-du'-hnv?
How far is it to the highway?   Ha-la'-yv di-ga-nv-hnv?or: nv-no-hi?
How far is it to the bridge?   Ha-la'-yv di-sv-tlv?

198.
Nearby. Over there. There is a   Na?-v. Ge-na ge:-ta. Ka-no-he'-s-gi.
sign.

199.
Where is a restaurant?   Ha'-tlv tsu-nah-l(i)-s-da-(i)-di-(i)?
Where is a restroom?   Ha'-tlv, do-yi e-da-s-di-(i)?
Where is a hotel or motel?   Ha'-tlv, tsu-ni-sv'-s-di-(i)?
Where is the hospital?   Ha'-tlv, tsu-ni-tlv-gi tsu-nah-n'-tlv'-
                                  di-i?
Where is the cemetery?   Ha'-tlv, tsu-n'-da-ni-soh-di-i?
Where is a grocery store?   Ha'-tlv, a-l'-s-ta-(i)-di a-da-na-nv-i?

200.
Is this the right road to ...?   Hi-i-s-go-hv tsi-ga-nv-hna ...?

201.
This is the wrong road. (Elsewhere- U-tsa-ti-na-dv ga-nv-hnv.
(is) where-they-go.) You must turn   Tsa-go-tlv-s-doh-di-dv.
around.

202.
What time do they close?   Ha-la'-yv, a-ni-s-du-hv-s-go-i?

203.
They are closed. They are still U-ni-s-du-ha. Si-dv u-ni-s-du?-i?-da.
open.

204.
Are you sure? (Is that the truth?) Do'-he?

205.
I am not sure.   Tla-do-ya-qua-n'-ta.
(I don't know the truth.)

206.

Where is a good place to fish?   Ha'-tlv o:-s-da a-su?-di?
Where can I launch a boat?   Ha'-tlv i-tsi-u-di-ga tsi-yu?
Where can I swim?   Ha'-tlv i-ga-da-wo-tsa? also: Ha'-tlv
                                        a-gwa-da-wo:-s-di?
Where can I fish?   Ha'-tlv yi-ga-su-hv-ga?
Where can I hunt?   Ha'-tlv yi-tsi-no?-i-li-da?

207.

Where can I buy bait?   Ha'-tlv (go:tlv) ga?-di a-ki-hwa-hi'-
                                        s-di-i(i)?
Where can I weigh my deer?   Ha'-tlv (go:-tlv) a-hwi di-ga-dv'-di-(i)?
Where can I rent (borrow, use) a   Ha'-tlv tsi-yu di-to'-l'-s-di?
boat?
Where can I get a fishing license?   Ha'-tlv (go:-tlv) a-su?-di go-we'-li
                                        ga-ne-s-di-i?
Where can I get a hunting license?   Ha'-tlv (go:-tlv) ga-no-hi-li-da'-s-d(i)
                                        go-we'-li ga-ne-s-di-i?

208.

Is it all right to camp here? We   A-l(i)-s-go'-l(i)-di-ke a-sv:-s-di
have our own wood and water.   a'-ha-ni'? A-da do-gv-ya a-le a-ma'
                                        o-gi-ne-ha.

209.

You're welcome to camp but don't   I-tsi-sv:-s-di-gwu, ni-tso'-ta-nv'-na
light any fires.   yi-gi'.

210.

Is it all right to park here?   A-l'-s-go'-l'-di-ke a-le'-w(i)-s-doh-di
                                        a'-ha-ni'?
Is it all right to eat here?   A-l'-s-go'-l'-di-ke a-l'-s-ta-i?-di
                                        a'-ha-ni'?
Is it all right to fish here?   A-l'-s-go'-l'-di-ke a-su?-di a'-ha-ni'?
Is it all right to hunt here?   A-l'-s-go'-l'-di-ke ga-no-hi-li-da-s-d(i)
                                        a'-ha-ni'?

211.

Fishing is poor (here).   Tla o:-s-da yi-gi' a-su?-di.
There is good fishing across the   O:-sa-ni' u-do:-tlv a-su?-di a-ma-y(i)
lake (water).   di-ga-n'-di'-sv.
There is better fishing down the   Da-tse:-tla u-do:-tlv a-su?-di nv-no
road.   wi-ga-nv'-hnv.

212.

I can't allow you to hunt. I can't   Tla-yi-ga-gv'-ya-li-s-go'-l'-da'-si
permit firearms.   tsa-no-hi-li-da-s-di. Tla ya?-wa-l'-
                                        s-go'-l'-di' tsu-ni-s-da-yo:-s-di.

213.

I am leaving right away.

Ki-lo-wi-yu-s-di dv-ga-ni-gi:-si.
or: Ki-lo-wi-yu-s-di da-ga-hne'-la-di.

214.

Goodbye. Come again. (to one person)
  (to several people)

Do-na-da-go?-hv-i. I-he-do'-lv?-i.
Do-da-da-go?-hv?-i. I-tse-do'-lv?-i.

Notes:

P.N. 191 - Ha'-tlv (go:-tlv) ge-sa-li:-ni ga-ne-gi-s-di-i? Where can one get gas?

'Go:-tlv' is often used, as you can see from other phrases in this lesson. It means something like 'the designated place'. Notice that it is optional; the sentences would mean the same without 'go:-tlv', but 'go:-tlv' is usually included. It refers to some specific area allocated to some purpose or divided up in a certain way. As you know, 'go-tlv-nv' means 'made-of-(it)' as a modifier; as a noun, it means 'butter'.

'Ga-ne-gi-s-di-i' means 'for-them-to-get-a-liquid-place'. It is a form of the classifying verb, A-GI-S-DI, 'pick up and then use up', or 'eat'. 'Ga' means 'for-them' and 'ne' is a liquid classifier. See note on P.N. 207 below. This sentence could also be: Ha'-tlv go:-tlv ge-sa-li:-ni a-gi-ne-gi-s-di-i, (Where is the proper place for me to get gasoline?)

P.N. 194 - ha-tle-sv-i - turn off. This does not mean turn around. It means 'veer off in one direction or another'. Ga-dle:-ya means 'I am veering off, changing direction'; da-ga-dle:-si', 'I will veer off'.

P.N. 197 - Notice that all the places mentioned have 'di' prefixed, because they are all at a distance from the speaker.

'Ga-nv'-hnv' means 'gone-on-by-them', and 'nv-no-hi' means 'they habitually go on it'. 'Tsi-ga-nv'-hnv' (for-them-to-go-on), usually refers to a small road or trail; nv-no-hi and ga-nv'-hnv are larger.

P.N. 198 - Ka-no-he'-s-gi - a sign that tells directions. It is unusual for a non-living thing to have a -s-gi ending. This word means 'teller', 'announcer', and usually refers to a person who is an announcer or herald. Many words in constant use are derived from the verb, 'ka-ne-s-di', 'to speak, to address'.
Examples:

advertisement   de-ka-no'-tsa-tlv

Examples of words derived from 'ka-ne-s-di', continued:
```
  brooch, ornamental pin            a-ka-ne:-s-doh-di
     (to tell something with)
     This word takes bound pronouns like body parts:
        my brooch                   a-gi-ka-ne:-s-doh-di
        your brooch                 tsa-ka-ne:-s-doh-di
        his/her brooch              u-ka-ne:-s-doh-di
     Without bound pronouns, a-ka-ne:-s-doh-di means 'election button'.
        my election button          a-qua-tse'-li a-ka-ne:-s-doh-di
     Also:
        corsage (flower brooch)     a-tsi-lv-s-gi a-ka-ne:-s-doh-di
  compass (truth declarer)          du-yu'?-dv ka-no-he-s-gi
  declaration                       ka-ne-tsv i-ya-dv-ne-di
  discussion                        ka-no-he-lv-di
  Gospel Words of Jesus             Ka-no-hwe-da U-hno-he-da Tsi-sa'
  gossip (a thing)                  ka-no-he:-da
  gossip (a person)                 ka-no-he:-da a-hi-do-hi
  gossips (They go back and forth with announcements)
                                    ka-no-he:-da a-ni-hi-do-hi
  history, a story                  ka-no-ge:-s-di
  law(s) (proclaimed to be done)    di-ka-hna-wa-dv-s-di
  lecture, scolding, harangue,peptalk   ka-no-hwe-da
     Also:  inspired words, see Gospel above.  It means 'spoken outward'.
  music, song                       ka-no-gi-s-di
  musical instrument                di-ka-no-gi-s-di
     Also: any music-making machine, such as a radio, transistor, phonograph.
     Also: hymns, songs, especially those sung by a group.
  musician                          ka-no-gi:-s-di'-s-gi or di-ka-no-gi:-
                                       s-di'-s-gi
  musicians                         di-ni-ka-no-gi:-s-di'-s-gi
  New Testament                     I-tse Ka-no-ge:-dv Da-tlo-hi-s-tv
     New Pronouncements as He Went About
  reservation (told to stay there)  ka-no-hi-yv-hi
  singer                            ka-no-gi:-s-gi or di-ka-no-gi:-s-gi
  singers, a choir                  di-ni-hno-gi:-s-gi
  song, speech of praise, psalm     di-ka-no-gi-dv
  song, quotation                   ka-no-ge:-da
  story, poem                       ka-no-he-tlv-s-gi
  stories, poems                    di-ka-no-he-tlv-s-gi
  story-teller                      ka-no-he:-s-gi
  testimony                         ka-no-he-tlv-di
  tradition                         ka-no-ge-tlv-di
  treaty                            ka-no-ge-dv da-tlo-hi-s-tv
  tyrannical boss                   ka-ne-tsi-do-hi
  word, words (spoken, spokens)     (i)-ka-ne-tsv, u-ni-ne-tsv
  word, words (something to speak,  ka-ne-s-di, di-ka-ne:-s-di
     things to speak)
```

P.N. 199 - tsu-hna-l'-s-da-i?-di-i   where they have a meal or meals
    do-yi e-da-s-di-i   where he/she goes outside alone
             (Notice that this epithet noun
 is singular, where plural is more common, so 'alone' is implied)
    tsu-ni-sv-s-di-i   where they stay overnight
    tsu-nah-n'-tlv-di-i   where they lie on a raised surface
            all the time
    tsu-n'-da-ni-soh-di-i   where they have been buried

P.N. 201 - tsa-go:-tlv-s-doh-di-dv - You must turn around.
  '-Doh-' could be eliminated in this sentence without changing its
meaning. With -dv here, it means 'All you need to do is to turn around',
'Dv is somewhat reassuring-- 'Just turn around and you'll be headed
right, etc. -Doh- has varied meanings. Among them are 'for a little
while', 'as if', 'instead of', 'by means of'. Sometimes it changes the
meaning of the verb entirely, as: ga-no-hi-li, he/she is flying;
ga-no-hi-li-do', he/she is hunting. See Appendix XIII, Suffixes.
   Compare these forms: I must turn around. a-gwa-go-tlv:-s-di
           I am turning around ga-go-tlv?-a
           I am turning aside, ga-tle-ya
           veering off. (as in P.N. 194)

P.N. 203 - U-ni-s-du-ha - They are closed.
   Si-dv u-ni-s-du?-i?-da - They are still open (Still-surely they
are open)
  -Gi or -?i- means 'un-' in Cherokee, as in 'undressing' in Lesson 24.
Therefore, u-ni-s-du?-i?-da means 'unclosed', 'open'.
Example:
  S-da-ya da-s-du-ha di-s-du?-di. The doors are shut tight.
          (Closely closed closers)

P.N. 204 - Do-ke - Is that true?

P.N. 205 - Tla-do-ya-qua-n'-ta' - I don't know if it's true.
  Du-yu?-da (du-yu'-k'-dv) means 'truth'. (See 'compass' in the note to
P.N. 198 above.) You are familiar with the expression 'Do-he udo?',
which means 'Really?' (Truly true?) Du-yu? when spoken sometimes
emerges as 'doowoo'.
Examples:
  Du-yu?-dv ka-no-he-s-gi. He tells the truth. (habitually) (He is
          a truth-speaker.)
  Du-yu?-dv ka-no-he'-ya. He is telling the truth. (on this occasion)
  Tsi-s-ga-ha du-yu?-dv a-ki-no-he?-di. I am afraid to tell the truth.

P.N. 207 - ga-ne-s-di-i - Notice this flexible classifier appears the same
  as the liquid classifier on 'ga-ne-gi-s-di-i', P.N. 191. Liquid and
  flexible classifiers are always much alike and sometimes identical.
  (See Appendix V) -Ka- always means 'living' wherever it occurs as a
  classifier. The other classifiers may vary from verb to verb.

P.N. 208 - A-l(i)-s-go'-l(i)-di-ke - Is it permitted? Notice the reflexive, a-l(i).

P.N. 208 - A-da do-gv-ya a-le a-ma' o-gi-ne-ha'. - We have firewood and
water. Notice the classifiers, which are underlined above.

A-da   do-gv-ya   a-le   a-ma'   o-gi-ne-ha'.
Wood them-we-long-have and   water it-we-liquid-have.

The verbs underlined above both mean 'we have' and are the same
classifying verb, A-GI-HA. Referring to wood, which is long, this verb
must contain a 'long' classifier, and referring to water, which is
liquid, it must contain a 'liquid' classifier. It is impossible in
Cherokee to make the same verb for 'we-have' do for two or more classifications. When speaking of 'having' objects that are a mixture of
shapes and/or consistencies, the correct classifier must be used for
each classifiable object. Also notice that if one object is singular
and another object is plural this difference must be observed. (i.e.,
do-gv-ya and o-gi-ne-ha) 'We have' is underlined below, with other
examples of mixed classifiers.

We have coal and firewood.   Ka-no:-s-gi o-gi-ha a-le a-da do-gv-ya.
We have paper and kindling.   Go-we'-li do-gi-na?-a a-le a-da do-gv-ya.
We have a dog and a gun.   Gi:-tli o-gi-ka'-ha a-le ga-lo'-gwe
                              o-gv-ya.

But if more than one different object with the same classification is
mentioned, only one verb is used, as in English.
Example:
We have matches and wood.   A-tsi-lv-go-tlv-di a-le a-da do-gv-ya.

This is true of all classifying verbs in Cherokee. One verb can be
used only if all the items mentioned are in the same category. (i.e.,
if all of them are long, flexible, indefinite, live or liquid, as above
when matches and wood are both long.)

P.N. 211 - wi-ga-nv'-hnv - Notice wi-before ga-nv'-hnv, showing movement
away. Prefixed to 'them-to-go-on' (road), it means 'them-to-go-away-on',
or 'down the road from here'.

P.N. 212 - Tla-ya?-wa-l'-s-go'-l'-di - I will not permit, it is not permitted by me, I do not permit myself to... - Notice the infinitive here.
Without 'tla' and 'yi', an infinitive would mean 'I ought to permit...'
(See 'a-ki-wa-hi-s-di-i', 'I ought to buy') With the negatives 'tla'
and 'yi', 'A?-wa-l'-s-go'-l'-di', I ought to permit, becomes 'tla-ya?-wa-
l'-s-go'-l'-di', I ought not to permit, I cannot permit. This is a more
tactful way of saying 'I don't allow', 'I won't allow'.

P.N. 213 - dv-ga-ni-gi:-si - I am leaving, I will leave, I will un-arrive,
as in P.N. 203.

Exercise 1: Write out all the phrases in Lesson 27 in Cherokee on the following pages, checking your answers with the syllabary if necessary.

You can now appreciate the position of the Cherokees when they first learned the syllabary in 1821. You can understand how differences in Cherokee spelling come about and how the Cherokee Nation could learn to read so quickly without standardized study.

You will enjoy what you have learned so far if you continue Cherokee studies from the reading list in Appendix XIV and if you make opportunities to practice Cherokee as much as possible.

Vocabulary List -- Cherokee-English

Since the Cherokee language does not contain the same consonants as English, alphabetical order in Cherokee is as follows:

A, D, E, G, H, I, K, N, O, Q, S, T, U, V (unh), W, Y

Although Cherokee contains L and M, these letters rarely occur at the beginning of words.

P.N. - Phrase Number   p. - page   L. - lesson

a:-da-(ge), a-ni:-da-(ge)	nestling, nestlings (refers to baby birds, foxes, rabbits, bears, dogs, wolves, possums, <u>not</u> to hooved animals)
a-ni:-da	a litter
a-ni:-da a?-da	one of a litter, P.N. 91
a-da-we'-hi	Wise Man, angel, P.N. 39
a-da	wooden, L. 26
a-da'-tlo:-s-di, di-da'-tlo:-s-di	belt, belts, P.N. 177
a-de-la or a-de-lv-i	money, P.N. 154
a-di-toh-di, di-di-toh-di	spoon, spoons, P.N. 108
a-gi-ki:-sv	I have swallowed (it) whole
a-g'-si-hwa-s-go	I (habitually) cough
a-gwa-di-tle-hv-s-ga	it is on me, has settled on me, L. 26
a?-ni	strawberry, strawberries, P.N. 98
A-k-sa-s(i)	an Osage
A-ni-k-sa-s(i)	the Osages, the Osage tribe, L. 11
a?-ti:-s(i)(a)	to the right, See L. 25
a-tsv-s-toh-di	light-bulb, P.N. 43
a-tsv'-ya, a-ni-tsv'-ya	rooster, roosters, P.N. 126
a?-w- or a-gw- a-du'-li-(a), or tsa-du'-li(a)	want, wish to have, V., P.N. 18
a-?-wa-da-n'-to'-gi	my-heart, See L. 25
A-TLA-HA (3)	an object is at rest or on a raised surface, L. 24
a?-we:-la	my-liver, See L. 25
a?-wo-ye:-n(a)	my-hand, See L. 25, p. 226
a-yah'-l'-di	one bead, a pendant
di-yah'-l'-di	beads, a necklace, P.N. 177
a-ye'-l'-s-di, di-ye'-l'-s-di	knife, knives, P.N. 108
a-yo:-s-gi, a-ni-yo:-s-gi	soldier, soldiers, P.N. 113
a-doh	woods, L. 26
a-ga-s-ga'; a-ga-na'	it is raining; it just rained, P.N. 62
a-ge-(h)yu'-ts(a)	girl
a-ni-ge-(h)yu'-ts(a)	girls, P.N. 50
a-gi-do'-i	my-sibling-of-the-opposite-sex; brother of female; sister of male

a-gi-do-da; u-do-da

my-father; his/her-father

a-gi-du-da; u-du-da

my-grandfather; his/her grandfather

a-gi-du'-tsi; u-du'-tsi-
a-gi'-ga-ge or a-gi'-ya-ge
a-gi-lv:-gi

my-uncle; his/her-uncle, p. 161
red, p. 26
my-sister; spoken by a female, my
   fellow-sister, See L. 19, 20, 21

a-gi-nu-la-tsi
a-gi-nv-tse
a-gi-tlo-gi', di-gv-gi-tlo-gi
a-gi-yo-hu'-se; tsa-yo-hu'-se
a-go:-s-di
a-g'-s-go'-hl'-ti

my-rib, See L. 25
I fell, L. 26
aunt (my), aunts (my), p. 158
I am losing; you are losing, V., p. 134
raw, unripe, P.N. 99
for-me-to-permit, to put up for sale,
   to allow, See L. 24 and 27

a-g'-s-ka-ni-yi
a-g'-s-ta-yv-hv'-s-gi
a-g'-s-ti-gv-i
a-g'-s?-wo:-tli
a-gv-ha-lv-d(a)
(a)-gv'-ni-ge
a-gwe:-la
a-gwe-s-ta-ne-ha
a'-gw'-ti'-tlv
a-ha-le:-n(a)(i)
a'-ha-ni' or a'-hni'
a'-hni', a'-ha-ni'
a-hnu-wo, di-hun-wo,
   a-hna-wo, di'-hna-wo

to the left, See L. 25
wife (meal-maker for me), C.V., p. 26
my-hair, See L. 25
my-stomach, See L. 26
cut-off piece of food, p. 129
black, p. 51
my-liver, See L. 25
suffer pain, L. 26
my-joint, See L. 25 and 26
loudmouth, p. 51
here, p. 51
here, p. 9
cloth, cloths, fabric, fabrics, a
   piece of clothing, clothes,
   P.N. 164, 177, 179

a-ho:-li: tsi-ho:-li
a-hu'-li
a'-hwi'
a-(h)wi:-n(a)
   a-ni-(h)wi:-n(a)

mouth (his or her); mouth (my), p. 35
drum, p. 35
deer, P.N. 127
youth
   older boy from teen-ager through
   young manhood, P.N. 46

a-(h)yo:-tli, di-ni-yo:-tli
a-gi-lo:-si
a-ki-hwa'-s-ga, tsa-hwa'-s-ga

child, children, p. 60
my-in-law, p. 165
buy, I am buying, you are buying, V.
   P.N. 42

a-ki-na-lv'(ga)
   tsa-na-lv'-(ga)
a-ku-gi'-s-di, di-ku-gi'-s-di
a-la-su'-lo, di-la-su-lo
a-l'-s-que'-to-wo,
   di'-l'-s-que'-to-wo
a-l(i)-s-ta-i-d(i)
a-l'-s-ti'-s-gi
a-l'-tsa-do'-hv-s-gi'
   a-na-l'-tsa-do'-hv-s-gi

I am angry
   you are angry, V., p. 143
cup, cups, P.N. 108
shoe, shoes, p. 70
hat
   hats, P.N. 177
meal, menu, P.N. 17
troublemaker, p. 222
minister, P.N. 13
ministers, P.N. 113

254

a-li-ye'-su-lo, di-li-ye'-su-lo	glove, gloves, P.N. 177
a-li-yo-(i), di-li-yo?-(i)	sock, socks. P.N. 177
*a:-m(a')	salt (See pitch p. 40.)
a-ma'-yi-e-do-hi, a-ma'-yi-a-ne-do'-hi	sailor, sailors, P.N. 113
a-ma'-yi-ha-wi'-ni'-e-do-hi	marine (member of the marines)
a-ma'-yi-ha-wi-ni-a-ne-do-hi	marines (several members of the
	marines), P.N. 113
A-ni?-a-hwi'	Deer Clan, p. 144
a-ni:-da	nestlings or 'a litter of young'; can
	refer to the young of bears, pigs,
	rabbits, foxes, dogs, wolves, **not**
	to hooved animals, P.N. 91
A-ni-da-lo'-ni-ge	Orientals, p. 142
A-ni-ga-lv'-tsi	French people, p. 142
A-ni-gi-du'-hw(a)(i)	Ki-tu'-wa Clan, p. 142
A-ni-gi-(t)la-hi	Hair Clan, p. 142
A-ni-gv'-ni-ge	Blacks, negroes, p. 142
A-n'-da'-tsi	Germans, p. 142
A-ni-sa'-ha-ni	Blue Clan, members of the Blue Clan,
	p. 142
a-ni-su-li	jurors, a jury, p. 142
A-ni-tsa-la-gi'	Cherokees, the Cherokee tribe, p. 142
A-ni-tsi'-s-qua	Bird Clan, p. 142
A-ni-wah-ya	Wolf Clan, p. 142
A-ni-wo:-d(i)	Paint Clan, p. 142
A-n(v)(i)-s-gv'-ti	May, P.N. 46
A-nv:-yi	March, P.N. 46
a-qua-da-n'-to'-gi	my-heart, See L. 25
a-qua-la'-s-de:-n(i)	my-foot, See L. 26
a-qua'-n(i)-ta', tsa:-n(i)-ta'	I know it, I know how, P.N. 33
a'-qua-tse'-li	my, mine, p. 133
a-que-tlu'-s-d(i)	ribbon, P.N. 39
a-que'-tsi	my-child
u-we'-tsi	son or daughter
a-quo-ye:-n(i)(a)	my-hand, See L. 25, p. 226
a-sa-ma'-ti	smart, p. 133
a'-sa-no, di'-sa-no	dress, dresses or skirt, skirts
e'-l'-di a'-sa-no	skirt, P.N. 177
a-s-da-ya, s-ta-yi	hard, loud, taut
a-s-da-ya-hi-ge	louder, tauter, harder
wa-s-ta-yv u/a-s-ta-yo-sv-(i)	loudest, very loud, tautest,
	very taut, hardest, very hard,
	L. 26, p. 240
a'-s-di	thread, yarn, string, P.N. 179
a-se:-hno, a-se:-hnv	but, P.N. 142
a-se:-s-di, di-se'-s-di	number, numbers, P.N. 10
a'-s-ga-ya', a-ni-s-ga-ya	man, men, P.N. 50
a?-s-gua-n'-go-s-ga	I am surprised, P.N. 153

(a')

a-s-ta-yo'-s-toh-di	firecracker, p. 49
a-su:-s-di	gravy, P.N. 17
a-su?-di	to fish, L. 27
a-su-lo, di-su-lo	pants, singular and plural, P.N. 177
a-su-ya-na-(i)	stuffing of meat, P.N. 17
a:-t(a), a-na'-t(a)	young girl, teenager plus a little
A-n'-ta-nu:-ts	P.N. 50
a-tli'-gi-li'	time, P.N. 77
a-tli-gi-lo:-ga	the time is coming, a certain time
	is approaching, is about to be here
a-tli-gi-li'-sv	a week, P.N. 156
a-tli-lo:-s-toh'-t(i)	yardstick, measuring tape, ruler (to
	measure-it-with); Plural - di-tli-
	lo:-s-doh'-di, pattern or patterns
	(to-measure-them-with), P.N. 179
a-tli-s-toh'-di, di-tli-s-toh'-di	pitcher, soup or serving bowl, tank,
	anything into which the contents
	are poured, P.N. 108
a-tsa-di	fish
a-tsi-lv'-s-ga, a-ni-tsi-lv'-s-ga	it blooms, they bloom, V., P.N. 99
a-tsi-lv'-s-gi, a-ni-tsi-lv'-s-gi	flowers, blossoms (nouns)
a-tsi-lv'-s-gi	flower or blossom
a-ni-tsi-lv'-s-gi (noun)	flowers or blossoms
a-tsi-lv'-s-ga, a-ni-tsi-lv'-s-ga	it blooms, V., P.N. 99
a-tsi'-n(a'), a-ni-tsi-n(a)	cedar tree, cedar trees
a-tsu'-ts(a)(i), a-ni-tsu'-ts(a)(i)	boy, boys, P.N. 50
a-tsv'-s-di, di-tsv'-s-di	light-bulb, light-bulbs, or lamp,
	lamps, P.N. 43
da-gi-lv'-w(i)-s-ta-ne?-a,	work, V., p. 137
de-tsa-lv-s-da-ne?-a	
da-gwa-da-ti-hna?-v-i	those born to me, my-children, p. 181
da-gwa-le:-lu, do-gwa-le:-lu	wagon, wagons, See L. 26, p. 239
da-la-du-(i)	sixteen, P.N. 75
da-la'-la	woodpecker, P.N. 92
da-ni-la'-wi-ga	church service, P.N. 13
da-ni'-s-ta-yo'-hi-hv'	Christmas, P.N. 39
da-wa-tsi:-la	elm, p. 103
de-ga'-l'-ta-de:-(ga)	I am jumping
de-ha'-hl'-ta-de:-(ga)	you are jumping, V., p. 146
de-ga-ni-wo?-a	I am dressing, I amputting them
	(several garments) on, See L. 24
De-ha-lu-y(i)(a)	June
(d)e:-ti-yv'-da	year, years, P.N. 142, 144, 150
de-tsi-n'-di'-s-ga	I am crossing over
de-hi-n'-di'-s-ga	you are crossing over, V., p. 145
di-da-ni-yi:-s-gi	policeman
di-n'-da-ni-yi-s-gi	policemen, P.N. 113

di-de-yo'-hv-s-gi   teacher
    di-n(a)-de-yo'-hv-s-gi'   teachers, P.N. 113
di-ga-dv'-di   scales, a weighing machine
    pear, pears; they-weigh
di-ga-dv:-d(i)   pear, pears, P.N. 98
di-ga-li-nv'-hi-dv   donkey
    di-n(i)-ga-li-nv'-hi-dv   donkeys, P.N. 126
di-ga-lo-ne:-s-gi   painter
    di-ni-ga-lo-ne:-s-gi   painters, p. 222
di-go-we-li'-s-gi ka-no-he-(t)lv'-s-gi
    di-no-we-li'-s-gi a-ni-no-he-(t)lv'-s-gi (poets)
    poet, poets, P.N. 113
di'-hna-wo   clothing
    a'-hno-wo, di'-hna-wo   blouse, blouses or shirt, shirts
    a'-hno-wo   cloth
di-hu-dv   boiled-whole, p. 129
di-ka-no-gi'-s-gi   musician (singer-of-them, singer of
    di-ni-hno-gi'-s-gi   songs), P.N. 113
di?-li   skunk, skunks, P.N. 127
di'-l'-s-toh-di   scissors, P.N. 179
di-ne'-s-ge:-s-gi   carpenter
    di-na-ne'-s-ge:-s-gi   carpenters, P.N. 113
di-qua-yo'-d(i)   pepper, P.N. 108
di-sø'-s-ti:-s(gi)   typist
    di-ni-sø'-s-ti:-s(gi)   typists, P.N. 113
di-s-ta-yo:-hi-hi   Santa Claus, P.N. 39
di'-ti-yo'-hi-hi'   lawyer
    di'-n'-ti-yo'-hi-hi'   lawyers, P.N. 113
di-tla-no-he?-di-(i)   telephone, p. 86
di-tli-lo:-s-toh'-ti or   pattern or patterns (to-measure-them-
    di-tli-lo:-s-doh'-di   with); Singular - a-tli-lo:-s-toh-
    ti means 'yardstick, measuring tape,
    ruler' (to-measure-it-with),P.N. 179
do'-da-da-go'-hv-(i)   goodbye (to more than one person)
    P.N. 5
do'-hi   healthy, serene, or peaceful, P.N. 2
do'-hv?   why?, p. 82
do-na-da'-go-hv-(i)   goodbye (to one person), P.N. 5
do-ya   beaver, beavers, P.N. 127
do'-yi   out-of-doors, P.N. 62
do-yi e-da-s-di-i   toilet, privy, restroom, P.N. 199
do:-yu   certainly, truly, very, P.N. 40
Du-li:-s-di   September, P.N. 46
Du-ni-nv:-di   October, P.N. 46
du-yu'-k'-dv   truth, L. 27
e-lo-hi'   earth, world, p. 44
e-qua(quv)   big, p. 64
e-quo-ni, tse-quo-ni   river, rivers,P.N. 83
e:-ti-ya   year, yearing, L. 22
    u-de-ti-yv-sa-di-sv

ga-da-ha	dirty, p. 78
ga-da-nv?-a	I am moving out, migrating
ha-da-nv?-a	you are moving out, migrating, V.
	P.N. 88
ga?-di	bait, P.N. 207
ga?-di, di-ga?-di	button, buttons, P.N. 179
ga-di-ta:-s-ga, ha-di-ta:-s-ga	I am drinking, you are drinking, V.
	P.N. 54
ga-di?-a, ha-di?-a	say, repeat, state, recite, P.N. 9
ga-do'	what? which?, P.N. 23
ga-do u:-s-di	what kind of? what is it? (what do
	you want? what's the matter?)
	P.N. 30
ga-do' u'-s-di	which? what kind of?, P.N. 31
ga-du	bread, P.N. 17
ga-du'-hv	town, p. 163
ga-ge:-da	heavy, p. 103
ga-go-tlv?-a	I am turning around
ga-tle:-ya	I am veering, changing direction, L. 27
ga-l(i)-qua-du-(i)	seventeen, P.N. 75
ga-l'-qua'-s-go-(hi)	seventy, P.N. 75
ga-l(i)-quo:-g(i')	seven, P.N. 11
ga-li-quo-gi-ne'-(i)	seventh, P.N. 12
ga-li-s-ta-yv-hv-s-ga	eat
ha-l(i)-s-ta-yv-hv-s-ga	have a meal, V., C.V., p. 26
ga-lo-ge:-sv, de-ga-lo-ge:-sv	farm, farms (ga-lo-gi-a, I am hoeing)
	p. 149
Ga-lo'-ni	August, P.N. 46
ga-lo-we:-d(i)	redbud, p. 104
ga-li?-e:-li-ga, ha-li-he'-li-ga	be glad, grateful, delighted, re-
	joice; U-na-li-he-li'-s-di,
	Thanksgiving, V., p. 36
ga-l'-tso?-v'-s-ga	I am growing fatter
ha-l'-tso-hv'-s-ga	you are growing fatter, V., p. 102
ga-lv'-la-di	high, prominent, famous, honored,
	p. 101
ga-lv'-lo-(hi)	sky, p. 44
ga-n'-de-gi	seller, p. 223
ga-ni'-tlv, de-ga-ni'-tlv	bed, beds, P.N. 108
ga-nv-hnv, nv-no-hi	highway, road, trail, L. 27
ga-que:-n(i)-doh-di	wrapping paper, P.N. 39
ga'-s-ki-lo'	furniture, table, chair, bench, sofa,
	platform
ga-nv'-hi-da ga'-s-ki-lo	(long furniture) sofa, bench,
	P.N. 108
ga-s-ki'-lv a-ye'-s-tv'-di	tablecloth
de-ga-ski'-lv di-ye'-s-tv'-di	tablecloths, P.N. 108
ga-so'-qua-lv	round, p. 70
ga-tle:-ya	I am veering, changing direction,
	turning off, P.N. 194

ga-do-hi   soil, p. 78
ga-tv-gi; ha-htv-gi   I (just) heard; you (just) heard, V.
      P.N. 82

ga-tv'-s-ga; ha-tv'-s-ga   I am growing taller; you are growing
      taller, V., p. 102

ga-yeh'-w(i)-sv-doh'-di   sewing materials (to sew with) P.N. 179
ga-yo'-tli   childish, immature, scanty, uncompleted
      P.N. 65. Also, a little bit, an
      insufficient amount.

ge'-li-a; he-li-a   I think; you think, V., p. 77
ge-li:-s-gi   pie (chopped up), P.N. 17
ge?-i: far off, a long way from here in time
      or space, C.V., p. 19

ge-na?-i   over there, at some distance
gi-ga'   blood, p. 26
gi-nu?-di   a quarter, 25 cents (quartered) P.M. 154
gi-ta'-ya   cherry, cherries, P.N. 98
gi:-tla(tli)   dog, dogs, p. 111
go:-g(i)   summer, C.V., p. 19
go:-hi: tsi-ge:-sv   long ago, p. 26
go-hi   this (in time)
    go-hi i:-ga   this day, today, p. 26
go-hwe'-li, di-go-hwe'-li   letter, letters (of the alphabet) P.N. 9
go-hya-dv, di-go-hya-dv   wing, wings, P.N. 177
go?-i'   grease, shortening, oil, cooking or
      machine oil, C.V., p. 19

go?-l(a)(i)   winter, p. 51
go-la-nv'   raven, P.N. 92
go-ti:-s-ga   it is swelling, puffing up, L. 26
go:-tlv-hnv   butter, P.N. 17
go-we-li'-s-gi,   secretary, secretaries, P.N. 113
    di-no-we-li'-s-gi
gu:-gu   bottle, bottles, Bartlesville, C.V.,
      p. 19

gu'-que   quail, P.N. 92
gu'-s-di a-quv'-hni   my-cousin
    gu'-s-di a-qua'-hni   See L. 19, 20, 21
gu'-s-di o'-s-da-da-dv'-hni   my-cousin, See L. 19, 20, 21
Gu-ye-quo:-ni   July, P.N. 46
gv-he   bobcat, bobcats, P.N. 127
gv:-le   pigeon, P.N. 92
gv-n(a)   turkey, P.N. 17
gv-ne-ha, hi-ne-ha   give as a gift, V., P.N. 42
gv-no-sa'-s-di   broom, C.V., p. 25

ha-la'?   what? how much? how many?, p. 82
      see p. 83 other combinations with
      ha-la'
ha-la'-yv?   when? how far?, p. 83, see other
      combinations with ha-la'

259

ha:-tlv(dlv, dla) where? where to?, P.N. 22
ha-wi'-ya meat, P.N. 17
hi?-a this, that (with a concrete noun), p.26
hi-lv'-s-gi several (living or non-living things)
  p. 99
  hi-lv:-s-gi-ni' several unspecified humans,
  several somebodies
hi-lv'-s-gi-ni several unspecified humans, several
  somebodies, p. 99
hi:-s-gi', hi:-s-g' five, P.N. 11
hi-s-gi:-ne-(i) fifth of a series, P.N. 12
hna-quu, hno-wu right now, now, p. 64
-hno and, suffixed, P.N. 62
hv? what? what did you say?, p. 82

i-da-n'-te-di cent, cents, but cannot be used without a number, as: sa'-wu i-da-n'-
  te-di, 1 cent, P.N. 154
*i-ga' day (keep the i short and the whole
  word on an even, low tone,) p. 39
*i:-ga noon (scalloped long i, up on ga)
  p. 39
i-ni'-ga-ti' tall, p. 162
i'-tl'(u)-kv, de:-tl'-kv tree, trees, P.N. 98
i-tse'-li your, yours (plural), p. 133
i-tse-li-s-gv your choice, as you wish, p. 129
i'-tse-yu'-s-di green (of the new kind), P.N. 43
i'-ya pumpkin, P.N. 17
i-ya si?-ta-dv inch, P.N. 172

ka Attention!, p. 130
ka:-ga, ga:-ga who?, p. 35
Ka-ga?-li February, P.N. 46
ka-l(i)-se:-ts(i) sugar, candy, P.N. 55
ka?-l(v)(a) month, the month of ____, P.N. 45
ka-lv-gv east (it is risen), P.N. 194
ka-n(a)-ts(i)-s-de:-tsi hornet, wasp A. IX
ka-ne'-tsv, di-ka-ne'-tsv (spoken) word, words, P.N. 51
ka-nu'-ga-tli' blackberry, blackberries, P.N. 98
ka-wo:-n(i) duck, P.N. 92
Ka-wo-ni April, P.N. 46
ki-lo?'-i somebody, p. 98
ki-lo-wu just, already, p. 159
ko:-ga, ko:-gi crow, p. 26
ko-hi-yv-i later, P.N. 196
ko:-li, tsu-ko:li bone, bones, p. 51
ku:-wa mulberry, mulberries, P.N. 98
kv-tli raccoon, P.N. 127

na, na-s-gi — that, those, of that, of those, p. 98

nah-na?-i, nah-nv?-i — over there, into, at that place, p. 51

nah-nv?-i, nah-na?-i — over there, into, at that place, p. 51

na?-v?-(i) — close, near, p. 51

na-s-gi, na — that, those, of that, of those, p. 99

ne-la-du-(i) — eighteen, P.N. 75

ne'-l'-s-go — eighty, P.N. 75

Ni! — Look, See, Lo, P.N. 41

ni-ga-du-(i) — fourteen, P.N. 75

no'-qu(i)-si, a-ni-no'-qu(i)-si — star, stars, P.N. 39

nu-da-le tsu'-n-da-le
   tsu'-da-le — (living, plural)
   (non-living, plural)
   different, varied, P.N. 165

nu:-n(a)(i) — potato, potatoes, P.N. 17

nu:-n(a)(i) ga-nv-hi-da
   nu:-n(a)(i) a-ni-nv'-hi-da — sweet potato, yam
   sweet potatoes, yams
   (long potato), P.N. 17

Nv-da:-gi — Texas, P.N. 142

nv'-gi-ne'-(i) — fourth of a series, P.N. 12

nv?-gi-ne *i-ga' — (4th day) Thursday, P.N. 101

nv'-g'-s-go-(hi) — forty, P.N. 75

nv:-hgi', nv:-g' — four, P.N. 11

nv-no-hi, ga-nv-hnv — road, highway, P.N. 122

nv-no-hi — road; nv-no-hi has no plural. To say
   'roads', de-ga-nv-hnv must be used.
   ga-nv-hnv - road
   de-ga-nv-hnv - roads, L. 18

nv-wo-ti — medicine, L. 26

nv-ya; nv-yo — rock or rocks; on the rock or rocks,
   L. 26

o'-ga-na' — groundhog, groundhogs, P.N. 127

o:-hni — last, P.N. 148

o:-s-da — fine, P.N. 3

o'-s-da i-gv-ne'-hi
   o-sda i-ya-nv-ne'-hi — repairman
   repairmen, P.N. 113

o-s-di-ne'-l(i) — spouse, husband, p. 152

(O')-si-yo' — hello, P.N. 1

qua-na (singular and plural) — peach, peaches, p. 64

qua-nv-yu:-n'-s-ti — plum, plums, P.N. 98

sa-du-(i) — eleven, P.N. 75

sa-ko'-ni-ge — blue, p. 70

sa:-sa — goose, swan
   a?-sa:-s(a)(i), a-ni?-sa:-s(i)
   Osage, Osages, p. 76

sa'-wu or sa-quu — one, P.N. 11

se'-lu   corn, P.N. 17
se'-lu ga-du   cornbread, P.N. 17
s-gi-ga-du-(i)   fifteen, P.N. 75
s-gi-na'   that same, this same, namely, p. 98
s-go-(hi)   ten, P.N. 11
s-go-hi'?-s-qua   one hundred, a hundred, P.N. 76
   s-go-hi?-s-qua sa'-wu   101
   ta-l'-sgo-hi?-s-qua   200
   s-go-hi?-s-qua'   one hundred dollars, P.N. 154
si'-hl'-gi   silk, P.N. 179
si-nv-da, si-nv-do   month, the length of a month, P.N. 150
si-qua   pig, pigs, p. 70
si-quu:-tse-ts'-(di)   possum, P.N. 127
si-quv   more, p. 70
si-wu   again, more, p. 129
si-yv'-wi-ha   each (thing)
   si-yv'-wi-ya   each living being, P.N. 167
so-hi'   hickory nut, hickory nuts, A. VI
   wa:-ne?-i   hickory tree, hickory trees A. VI
soh-ne-l(a)   nine, P.N. 11
so-hne-la-du-(i)   nineteen, P.N. 75
so-hne'-l'-s-go-(hi)   ninety, P.N. 75
so'-qui-li'   horse, horses, P.N. 126
s-qua-le'-wa-li'   nightingale, P.N. 92
s-qua-tle:-s-di   ball, balls, p. 166
s-qua-tle:-s-di tsu-na-ne-hl'-di-yi
                                                ballfield, P.N. 193
s-qui:-s-di   many, much, very many, very much, p.98
s-qui:-ya   very many, very much, too many, too
                                                  much, p.98
s-ta-yi, a-s-da-ya   hard, loud, taut, L. 26
   a-s-da-yi:-s-di   harder, louder, tauter
   wa-s-ta-yv   hardest, loudest, tautest, very
   a/u-s-ta-yo-sv?-i   hard, very loud, very taut
su'-da-l(i')   six, P.N. 11
su-da-li-ne'-(i)   sixth, P.N. 12
su'-da-l'-s-go-(hi)   sixty, P.N. 76
su-li   buzzard, P.N. 92
sv-di'-wa-li'   raspberry, raspberries, P.N. 98
sv-hi:-ye   evening, P.N. 60
sv-na'-le(i)   morning, tomorrow, P.N. 64
sv?-ta or sv-k-ta   apple, apples, P.N. 98

ta-l(a)-du-(i)   twelve, P.N. 75
ta?-li   two, P.N. 11
ta?-li:-ne   second in a series, again (once again)
                                                  P.N. 12 (ordinals)
ta-li:-ne *i-ga'   Tuesday (2nd day), P.N. 101

262

ta'-l'-s-go-(hi)   twenty, P.N. 75
ta'-l'-s-go-sa'-w(u)   twenty-one, P.N. 76
ta'-l'-s-go-ta'-l(i)   twenty-two, P.N. 76
ta'-l'-s-go-tso(i)   twenty-three,
ta-lu'-tsi, di-ta-lu'-tsi   basket, baskets, p. 149
te'-li-do, di-te'-li-do   plate, plates, P.N. 108
te-lv'-la-di, u-ni-te-lv-la-di   grape, grapes, P.N. 98
   u-te-lv'-la-di, u-ni-te-lv'-la-di   vine, vines, P.N. 99

tla   not, no, P.N. 8
                                                        tla-yi- before a verb makes the
                                                        verb a negative; tla-yi-gi' before
                                                        an adjective means 'he, she, it
                                                        is not'
tla-hv'   no, P.N. 8
tla-i?-ga   bluejay, P.N. 92
tla-ki-lo'-yi(gi')   nobody, p. 98
tla-me'-ha   bat (as in 'vampire'), p. 86
tla-nu'-si   leech, p. 86
tlu'-kv, te-tlu'-kv   tree, trees, P.N. 98
tlu-tlu   martin (bird), p. 86
tlv-da-tsi'   panther, panthers, P.N. 127, lion, tiger
tlv-hwa'-l(i)-ga   maple, p. 9
tlv-tlv-yv   soon, later, later on, p. 86
to:-da-ge-do'-li   I am taking time out
   to'-te-do'-li   you are taking time out, V., p. 136
to-tsu'-hwa   cardinal (the bird), P.N. 92
to-wo'-d(i)   hawk, P.N. 92
tsa-da-hye-tla-lv-i   cut
   de-tsa-da-hye-tla-lv-i   cuts, P.N. 185
tsa-d'-s-da-lv?-i   a sore
   de-tsa-d'-s-da-lv?-i   sores, L. 26
tsa'-tse-li'   your, yours, (singular), p. 133
tsi-ga'-n'-ga'   my-tongue, See L. 26
TSI-GI?-A   I am eating (a single thing)
   hi-gi?-a   you are eating (a single thing), V.
                                                        p. 102
tsi-ho'-li   my-mouth, See L. 26
tsi-k'-to'-li   my-eye, See L. 25, p. 226
tsi-la'-ya-dv   my-leg, See L. 25
tsi-le:-na   my-ear, See L. 25, p. 226
tsi-lu?-gi   I (just) arrived
   hi-lu?-gi   you (just) arrived
                                                        arrive, get there, return, come
                                                        back, V., P.N. 81
tsi'-n'-doh-gv   my-tooth, See L. 25, p. 227
tsi-no-ge:n(a)(i)   my-arm, See L. 25 and 26
tsi-nv-s-ge:-n(i)(a)   my-leg, See L. 25 and 26
tsi'-s(a)-du   rabbit, rabbits, P.N. 127

tsi-s-go'-li	my-head, See L. 25 and 26
tsi?-s-ka-ni	my-left-hand, See L. 25
tsi'-s-qua	bird, birds, P.N. 87
tsi-s-qua-la	I just broke it off, snapped it, See L. 26
tsi-s-quo'-ga	robin, P.N. 92
tsi-su-la-go'-ga	I am quitting
hi-su-la-go'-ga	you are quitting, p. 136
tsi-ta:-ga	chicken, chickens, P.N. 126
tsi?-ti:-sa	my-right-hand, See L. 25
tsi-wi-sv:-s-ga	I am planting (seeds)
hi-wi-sv:-s-ga	you are planting (seeds), V., p. 102
tsi-wo'-ni-a; hi-wo:-ni-a	I am speaking; you are speaking, V., p. 77
tsi-ye'-sa-dv	my-finger, See L. 25 and 26
tsi-yu	boat, airplane, L. 27
tsi-yu-a-ma-yi e-do-hi	boat
tsi-yu ga-lv-la-di e-do-hi	plane
tso-ga-du-(i)	thirteen, P.N. 75
tso?-i	three, P.N. 11
tso'-i-ne'-(i)	third of a series, P.N. 12
tso?-i-ne *i-ga'	Wednesday (3rd day), P.N. 101
tso'-s-da-da-hnv'-tli	my brother, (spoken by a male, fellow brother), See L. 20
tso'-s-go-(hi)	thirty, P.N. 75
tsu-na-de'-l'-qua-s-di	school, p. 101
tsu-n'-da-ni-soh-di-i	cemetery, P.N. 199
tsu-ne:-l(a)	eight, P.N. 11
tsu'-n'-di-lo:-s-di	Friday (for-them-towash), P.N. 101
tsu-ni-la'-wi-s-di	church, P.N. 13
tsu-ni-lv:-w(i)-s-ta'-nti	workers, jobs, P.N. 113
tsu-ni-sv'-s-di-i	(where they spend the night) hotel, motel, P.N. 199
tsu'-n'-tlv'-gi di'-g'-ti'-ya	nurse
tsu'-n'-tlv'-gi di-ni'-g'-ti-ya	nurses, P.N. 113
tsu'-(t)la', tsu'-hli	fox, foxes, P.N. 127
u-da-ta-nv a-gi:-s-di	fruit
u'-n'-da-ta-nv a-gi:-s-di	fruits, P.N. 98
u-da-ta-nv-hi	berry
u-n'-da-ta-nv-hi	berries
u-da-ta-nv-hi, u-n'-da-ta-nv-hi	berry, berries
u-da-ta-nv a-gi:-s-di	fruit
u'-n'-da-ta-nv a-gi:-s-di	fruits, P.N. 98
u-da-tlv:-d(a)(i)	cream, P.N. 17
u-da'-ya-tlv, u-n'-da-ya-tlv(i)	bush, bushes, P.N. 99
u-de-li-gv	west, P.N. 194
u-do'-(i)	his-sister or her-brother (a sibling of the opposite sex), See L. 19, 20 21. This takes both pronouns
u-ga-lo'-ga	leaf, leaves, P.N. 17

264

u-ga-lo'-ga go-tlv'-ta-nv   tea (leaves it is made of), P.N. 17
u-ga-ma   soup (water prepared to eat), p. 44
u-ga-na:-s-d(a), u-ni-ga-na:-s-d(a)   cake, cookies, coffeecake; as an
                         adjective: delicious, P.N. 59

*u-ga'-no-w(a')(i'); u-ga-no-wv   warm, warmth, Democrat; South P.N. 37
u'-g(a)-ta', u-ni-g'-ta   seed, pit, stone of a fruit, grain, and
           plural. Like leaf, u-ni-g'ta means
           'several <u>kinds</u> of seeds, pits, etc.'
           Usually no plural is used, P.N. 99

u-gi-tlv   a single hair, L. 25 and 26
u-gu:-ku   owl, p. 26
u-ha-lv:-n(a)(i)   bell, P.N. 39
u-hno:-s-da; u-ni-hno:-s-da   one dollar; several dollars, P.N. 154
*u-hyv:-dla; u-hyv:-dlv   cold, coldness, Republican; North
           P.N. 36

u'-k(a)-so?-tsa-ne-dv   goat
   u-na-k(a)-so-tsa-ne-dv   goats, P.N. 126
u'-ka-yo:-d(a)   dry, (of a nut) ripe, P.N. 99
u-lo:-gi-l(a)(i)   cloud
   tsu-lo:-gi-l(a)(i)   cloudy, P.N. 64
u-lv:-gi   her-sister, See L. 19, 20, 21
u-lv'-sa-di, tsu-lv'-sa-di   glass, glasses, P.N. 108
u-nah-wi   heart (of an animal), See L. 25
u-na-li-i; o-gi-na'-li-i   his-friend; my-friend, See L. 19, 20,
           and 21

u-na-l'-s-gi-s-di-i   dance ground, L. 27
(u-na)-do'-da-quo'-hnv(i)   Monday, P.N. 101
(u-na)-do-da-wi-de:-na   Saturday (they go out), P.N. 101
U-(na)-li-he-li'-s-di   Thanksgiving, P.N. 17
u-na-tse-li   their, p. 133
u-ne:-g(a)   white, p. 51
u-ne:-s-ta-lv   ice, P.N. 108
u-no-de:-n(a), u-ni-no-de:-n(a)   sheep, P.N. 126
(u-no)-do'-da-qua-s-gv?(i)   Sunday, P.N. 100
u-no-lv'-ta-(nv)(ni)   January, P.N. 46
u-no-s-dv-ni'-s-di   ball-field, P.N. 193
u'-s-di, tsu'-n'-s-di   baby, babies, small, something small,
   u:-s-di, tsu'-n'-s-di   C.V., p. 25
u-s-ga   a severed head, L. 25, p. 228
u'-s-ga-no:-l(i)   slowly, P.N. 25
u'-s-qua-ti', tsu'-s-qua-ti'   pin, pins (safety pin or brooch)
           straight pin is: u'-s-qua-ti'
           ga-tsi-no:-s-da, tsu'-s-qua-ti'
           di-ga-tsi-no:-s-da, P.N. 179
u'-tv-hi-s-tv, tsu'-n'-tv-hi-s-t(v)   old man, old men, P.N. 50
u'-ta-na'   big, big around, hefty, p. 78
u'-ta-n'-ga-nv'-hnv   highway
u-te?-di   delicious, p. 129

u-te-lv'-la-di
   u-ni-te-lv'-la-di
   te-lv'-la-di, u-ni-te-la-di
u-tsa-ti'-n(i)(a)
u-tse-li
u-tsi-i
u-tsi-lv
u-tsi'-s-da-lu-gi'-s-gi a-hun-wo
   u-tsi-s-da-lu-gi'-s-gi
   a-hnu-wo
   di'-hna-wo
u-tsi-s-ta-lu:-gi'-s-gi
u-tsu-ya
u-wa'-n'-ga-tlv
u-wa'-n'-sv
u-wa-sv
u-we:-tsi, tsu-we:-tsi
u-wo'-du
u-wo-ti:-sv
   go-ti:-s-ga

u-yo
v?-le
V'-s-gi-yi
v?-tla
v:-v

wa-ga
wa-ga-lv'-l'-di:-yv
wa-ga-lv'-l'-di:-yv
wah-ya
wa-le'-la
wa:-ne?-i
wa-s-ta-yv

we-s(a)(i)
wi-do:-sv, plural of wo:-sv
wo-ha'-li
wo:-sv, wi-do"-sv

  wo:-sv
   tso:-sv-(i)
  wa-no:-sv
   wo:-sv-na

wo:-sv, wi-do:-sv

---

vine,
   vines, P.N. 99
   grape, grapes, P.N. 98
elsewhere, p. 132
his, her, its, p. 133
his/her-mother, p. 152
cotton cloth, P.N. 179
satin, P.N. 179
   shiny
   cloth
   clothes
silver (shiner), P.N. 39
singleton, P.N. 129
branch, p. 103
soft, (of a fruit) ripe, P.N. 99
alone, only, p. 240
egg, eggs or child, children, P.N. 90
pretty, beautiful, P.N. 40
swollen, puffed up
   it is swelling up, it is rising
   (of baked goods) L. 26

poor, wicked, mean, evil, miserable, p. 143
locust, locusts, p. 35
December, P.N. 46
no, P.N. 8
yes, P.N. 7

cow, cattle, P.N. 126
the highest one, extremely high
See ga-lv'-la-di, high
wolf, wolves, P.N. 127
hummingbird, P.N. 92
hickory tree, p. 10.
loudest, tautest, hardest, very loud,
   very taut, very hard, L. 26, p. 240
cat, cats, P.N. 126
best, excellent, See wo:-sv
eagle, P.N. 92
best, excellent, of the best kind,
   can be used for things, animals or
   people.
   good (singular)
   good (plural), a good place
   good, plural, living beings
   the best, can be a thing, animal
   or person, P.N. 175
best, excellent (the best, wo:-sv-na)
   P.N. 175

266

wo:-sv-n(a)(i)	the best one, the most excellent one, See wo:-sv
wo:-ya	dove, P.N. 92
ya-n(a)-s-si'	buffalo, buffaloes, P.N. 127
yo-n(v)(a)	bear, bears, P.N. 127
yv'-gi, di-yv'-gi	fork, forks, needle, needles, pitch-fork, pitchforks, P.N. 108

yv'-wi, a-ni-yv'-wi
   yv'-wi-ya', a-ni-yv'-wi-ya'
	people, a people
	   American Indian people, American Indian tribes (truly originated)
	   as a verb: originate, P.N. 74

a-yv-wi-ya'	an Indian person

again, more — si-wu, p. 129

again, second in a series — ta-li:-ne, P.N. 12

allow, permit, put up for sale — a-g'-s-go'-hl'-ti (for me to permit) L. 24, L. 27

all — ni-ga'-d(a)

alone, only — u-wa-sv, L. 26, p. 240

already, just — ki-lo-wu, p. 159

and — a-le, -hno suffixed, P.N. 62

and, or, but — a-le, p. 35

angel, Wise Man, sage — a-da-we'-hi, P.N. 39

angry, be angry — a-ki-na-lv'-(ga), I am angry; tsa-na-lv'-(ga), you are angry, V., p. 145

apple, apples — sv?-ta, P.N. 98 or sv-k-ta

April — Ka-wo-ni, P.N. 46

arm (my) — tsi-no-ge:-n(a)(i), See L. 25 & 26

arrive, get there, return, come back — tsi-lu?-gi, hi-lu?-gi, V., P.N. 81

Attention! — ka, p. 130

August — Ga-lo'-ni, P.N. 46

aunt (my), aunts (my) — a-gi-tlo-gi', di-gv-gi-tlo-gi p. 159

baby, babies; also, small, a baby animal, or 'of that kind' — u:-s-di, tsu:-n'-s-di, P.N. 50

bait — ga?-di, P.N. 207

ball, balls — s-qua-tle:-s-di, di-s-qua-tle:-s-di, p. 166

ball-field — u-no-s-dv-ni'-s-di-(yi), P.N. 193; s-qua-tle:-s-di

basket, baskets — ta-lu'-tsi, di-ta-lu'-tsi, p. 149

bat (as in vampire) — tla-me'-ha, p. 86, or tla-ma-ha

a bead, pendant — a-yah'-l'-di, P.N. 177

bear, bears — yo-n(v)(a), P.N. 127

beautiful, pretty — u-wo'-du, P.N. 40

beaver, beavers — do-ya, P.N. 127

become, happen — ni-ga-li:-s-ti-(ya)(ha), P.N. 175

bed, beds — ga-ni'-tlv, de-ga-ni'-tlv, P.N. 108

bell — u-ha-lv:-n(i)(a), p. 51

belt, belts — a-da'-tlo:-s-di, di-da'-tlo:-s-di, P.N. 177

bench, see table

best, of the best kind, excellent | wo:-sv, singular; wi-do:-sv, plural. Both can refer to things, animals, or people p. 222

big | e-qua(quv), p. 64
big, big around | u'-ta-na', p. 78
bird, birds | tsi'-s-qua, P.N. 87
Birds, (Clan) | A-tsi-s-qua
   member of | A-ni-tsi-s-qua, p. 142
black | a-gv'-ni-ge, p. 51
blackberry, blackberries | ka-nu'-ga-tli', P.N. 98
Blacks, negroes | A-ni-gv'-ni-ge, p. 142
blind | di-tsi-ke:-wa, I am blind; di-ke:-wi, L. 26
   he/she is blind
blood | gi-ga', p. 26
blossom, flower | a-tsi-lv'-s-gi, P.N. 99
blossoms, flowers | a-ni-tsi-lv'-s-gi
blouse, blouses or shirt, shirts | a'-hno-wo, di'-hna-wo, P.N. 177
blue | sa-ko'-ni-ge, p. 70
Blue Clan | A-ni-sa'-ha-ni, p. 142
bluejay | tla-i?-ga, P.N. 92
boat | tsi-yu, L. 27, P.N. 207
bobcat, bobcats | gv-he, P.N. 127
body (my) | tsi-ye-lv-i, See L. 26
bone, bones, bony | ko:-l(i)(a), p. 51, See p. 229
bottle, bottles, Bartlesville | gu:-gu, p. 19
boy, boys | a-tsu'-ts(a)(i), a-ni-tsu'-ts(a)(i), P.N. 50; older boy, teenaged to young manhood, singular and plural, a-(h)wi:-n(a), a-ni-(h)wi:-n(a)

branch | u-wa'-n'-ga-tlv, p. 103
bread | ga-du, P.N. 17
break (off) | tsi-s-qua-la, I (just) broke it, snapped it off, L. 26

broom | gv-no-sa'-s-di, C.V., p. 25
brother (my) | a-gi-do'-i, sibling-of-the opposite sex (brother spoken by a female); tso'-s-da-da-hnv-tli, fellow-brother (brother spoken by a male) L. 20

buffalo, buffaloes | ya'-n'-s-si', P.N. 127
burst out (of blood and air) | ga-ta-s-gi-(a), L. 25 and 26
bush, bushes | u-da-ya-tlv, u-n'-da-ya-tlv, P.N. 99

but, and, or | a-le, p. 35
but | a-se:-hnv, a-se:-hno-(i), p. 195
butter | go:-tlv-hnv, P.N. 17
button, buttons | ga?-di, di-ga?-di, P.N. 179

269

buy, I am buying (now)	a-ki-wa'-s'ga, tsi-hwa'-s-ga P.N. 42
buzzard	su-li, P.N. 92
cake, cookie, coffee-cake, noun	u-ga-na:-s-d(a), u-ni-ga-na:-s-d', P.N. 59; as an adjective: delicious
camp, stay overnight	a-sv:-s-di, L. 27
camp, noun or verb	Ge?i o-gi-l'-tso-da. We are camping over there. (They have a tent)
candy, sugar	ka-l(i)-se:-ts(i), P.N. 55
cardinal (the bird)	to-tsu'-hwa, P.N. 92
carpenter	di-ne'-s-ge:-s-gi
carpenters	di-na-ne'-s-ge:-s-gi, P.N. 113
cat, cats	we-s(a)(i), P.N. 126
cattle, cow, cows	wa-ga, P.N. 126
cedar tree, cedar trees	a'-tsi'-n(a), a-ni-tsi-n(a), P.N. 40
cemetery	tsu-n'-da-ni-soh-di-i, P.N. 199
cent	i-da-n'-te-di
one cent	sa?-wu i-da-n'-te-di
two cents	ta?-li i-da-n'-te-di,etc,P.N. 154
certainly, truly	do:-yu, P.N. 40
chair, see table	
Cherokees, the Cherokee tribe	A-ni-tsa-la-gi', p. 142
cherry, cherries	gi-ta'-ya, P.N. 98
chicken, chickens	tsi-ta:-ga, P.N. 126
child, children	a-(h)yo:-tli, di-ni-yo'-tli p. 60
childish, immature, uncompleted, scanty	ga-yo'-tli, P.N. 65
Christmas	da-ni'-s-ta-yo'-hi-hv' (when they shoot off firecrackers) P.N. 39
church	tsu-ni-la-wi-s-di, P.N. 13
church service	da-ni-la'-wi-ga, P.N. 13
Deer Clan	A-ni?-a-hwi', p. 142
close, V.	See L. 27, notes to P.N. 202
close, near	na?-v?-i, p. 51
clothing	di'-hna-wo, P.N. 177
cloud, cloudy	u:-lo'-gi-l(a)(i); clouds, tsu-lo'-gi-l(a)(i), P.N. 64
coffeecake, cookie, cake	u-ga-na:-s-d(a), u-ni-ga-na:-s-d(a), P.N. 59; as an adjective: delicious
cookie, cake, coffeecake	u-ga-na:-s-d(a), u-ni-ga-na:-s-d(a), P.N. 59; as an adjective: delicious

cold	u-hyv'-dla (dlv), u-yv-tla, p. 9
coldness, cold, North, Republican	u-hyv-dla (dlv), P.N. 36
color, colored (artifically)	a-su-wi-t(v), p. 222
corn	se'-lu, P.N. 17
cornbread	se'-lu ga-du, P.N. 17
cotton cloth	u-tsi-lv, P.N. 179
cough, V.	a-g'-si-hwa'-s-go, I have a cough, L. 26
cousin (my), cousins (my)	gu'-s-di, a-qua'-hni, a-quv'-hni. The usual word for 'my cousin' used by Cherokee speakers is gu'-s-di o'-s-da-da-dv'-hni, See L. 19, 20 21
cow, cattle	wa-ga, P.N. 126
cream	u-da-tlv:-d(a)(i), P.N. 17
cross over	de-tsi-n'-di'-s-ga, I am crossing over; de-hi-n'-di'-s-ga, you are crossing over, V. p. 145
crow	ko:-g(a)(i), p. 26
cup, cups	a-ku-gi'-s-di, di-ku-gi'-s-di P.N. 108
cut, V.	tsi-ye'-hlo-ha, L. 26
cut, cuts, noun	tsa-da'-hye-tla-lv-i, de-tsa-da-hye-tla-lv-i, P.N. 185
dance, noun	a-na-l'-s-gi-a, or a-l'-s-gi-a; dance hall, u-na-l'-s-gi-s-di (where they dance), or i-ga-l'-s-gi-s-di (where we all dance)
dance, V.	ga-li'-s-gi-a, I am dancing
dancing ground	u-na-l'-s-gi-s-di-i, P.N. 193
day	*i-ga' (keep the i short and the whole word on an even, low tone (see noon, *i:-ga)
deaf	di-gi-li?-e:-na, I am deaf, L.26
December	V'-s-gi-yi, P.N. 46
deer; Deer Clan	a'-hwi'; A-ni?-a-hwi', P.N. 127
be delighted, glad, happy, grateful, rejoice	
	g a-li-e:-li-ga, (h)a-li-he'-li-ga, V., p. 36
Democrat, South, warm, warmth	u-ga'-no-wa' (wi), P.N. 37
different	(n)u-da-le-(hn(v:-d)(a), P.N.165
dirt	ga-dv, p. 78
dirty	ga-da-ha, p. 78
do; I am doing; you are doing, V.	ga-dv'-ne?-a, ha-dv'-ne?-a, P.N. 35
dog, dogs	gi-tli, p. 111

dollar, dollars

u-hno:-s-da, one dollar;
u-ni-hno:-s-da, several
dollars (an approximate
amount). Any exact number
of dollars more than one
dollar is: ta-l'-de-lv-i,
$2; tso?-a-de-lv-i, $3, etc.
P.N. 154

one dollar

u-hno:-s-da; u-ni-hno:-s-da,
P.N. 154. For other numbers
of dollars, See L. 23

donkey, donkeys

di-ga-li-nv'-hi-dv, di-n(i)-ga
li-nv'-hi-dv, P.N. 126

dove
dress, V.

wo:-ya, P.N. 92
de-ga-ni-wo?-a, I am dressing
(I am putting on several
garments), See L. 24

dress, dresses or skirt, skirts
drink, V.

a'-sa-no, di'-sa-no, P.N. 177
ga-di-ta:-s-ga, I am drinking;
ha-di-ta:-s-ga, you are
drinking, P.N. 54

drum, drums
dry

a-hu'-li, p. 35
u-ka-yo:-d (of a nut), ripe,
P.N. 99

duck

ka-wo:-n(i), P.N. 92

each (thing)

si-yv'-wi-ha; each (living
being) si-yv'-wi-ya, P.N.167

eagle
ear (my)
early, first, as soon as possible
earth, world
east
eat (something), V.

wo-ha'-li, P.N. 92
tsi-le:-na, See L. 25, p. 226
i-gv-yi-i, P.N. 12
e-lo-hi, p. 44
ka-lv-gv, P.N. 194
tsi-gi?-a, I am eating (a
single thing); hi-gi?-a,
you are eating (a single
thing), p. 102

eat (have a meal), V.

ga-l(i)-s-ta-yv-hv'-s-ga
ha-l-(i)-s-ta-yv-hv'-s-ga,
C.V., p. 26

egg, eggs
eighteen
eighth
eighty
eleven
elm
elsewhere
emit, leak, burst out with
evening

u-we:-tsi, tsu-we:-tsi, P.N. 90
ne-la-du-(i), P.N. 75
tsu-ne'-li-ne'-(i), P.N. 12
ne'-l'-s-go, P.N. 75
sa-du-(i), P.N. 75
da-wa-tsi:-l(a), p. 103
u-tsa-ti'-n(i)(a), p. 132
ga-ta-s-gi-(a), L. 25 and 26
sv-hi:-ye, P.N. 60

excellent, best, of the best kind	wo:-sv, singular; wi-do:-sv, plural. Both can mean either things, animals or people, p. 222
eye (my)	tsi-k'-to'-li, See L. 25, p. 226
fabric, cloth	a-hnu-wo, di-hnu-wo; clothes, di-hnu-wo, L. 24
famous, honored, high, prominent	ga-lv'-la-di, p. 101
far off, a long way from here in time or space	ge?-i:', C.V., p. 19
farm, farms	ga-lo-ge:-sv, di-ga-lo-ge:-sv (ga-lo-gi?-s, I hoe), p. 149
father (my)	a-gi-do'-d, See L. 20 and 21
February	Ka-ga?-li, P.N. 46
fever	a-gwa-di-tle-hv-s-ga, I have a fever, L. 26
fifteen	s-gi-ga-du-(i), P.N. 75
fifth of a series	hi-s-gi:-ne-(i), P.N. 12
fifty	hi'?-s-go-(hi), P.N. 75
fine, good or well	o:-s-da, P.N. 3
finger (my)	tsi-ye'-sa-dv, See L. 25 & 26
firecracker	a-s-ta-yo'-s-toh-di, p. 49
first, early, as soon as possible	i-gv-yi-i, P.N. 12
fish, V.	a-su?-di, L. 27
fish, noun	a-tsa-di
five	hi:-s-gi', hi:-s-g', P.N. 11
flower, blossom	a-tsi-lv'-s-gi, P.N. 99
flowers, blossoms	a-ni-tsi-lv'-s-gi, P.N. 99
forest, wood, woods	a-doh, L. 26
fork, forks	yv'-gi, di-yv'-gi, P.N. 108
foot (my)	a-qua-la'-s-de:-n(i), See L. 26
four	nv:-g(i), P.N. 11
fourteen	ni-ga-du(i), P.N. 75
fourth of a series	nv-gi-ne'-(i), P.N. 12
forty	nv'-g'-s-go-(hi), P.N. 75
fox, foxes	tsu'-(t)la',(li'), P.N. 127
French (people)	A-ni-ga-lv'-tsi, p. 142
friend (my)	o-gi-na-li-i, See L. 19 & 20
Friday	tsu'-n'-gi-lo:-s-di (for them to wash), P.N. 101
fruit, fruits	u-da-ta-nv a-gi:-s-di, u'-n'-da-ta-nv a-gi:-s-di P.N. 98
furniture, see table	
Germans	A-n'-da'-tsi, p. 142
gift, gifts	a-da-hne'-d(i), di-da-hne:-d(i) P.N. 39

girl, girls	a-ge-(h)yu-tsa, a-ni-ge-(h)yu-tsa; young girl, teenager, a:-t(a), a-na-t(a); woman, women, a-ge-(h)ya, a-ni-ge'-(h)ya, P.N. 50
give (as a gift), V.	gv-ne-ha, I am giving (now); hi-ne-ha, you are giving, P.N. 42
be glad, rejoice, be happy, grateful, delighted	(g)a-li-e:-li-ga, (h)a-li-he:-li-ga, V., p. 35
glass, glasses	u-lv'-sa-di, tsu-l'-sa-di P.N. 108
glove	a-li-ye'-su-lo, P.N. 177
gloves	di-li-ye'-su-lo, P.N. 177
go, V.	ge:-ga, he'-ga, P.N. 14
goat	u'-k(a)-so?-tsa-ne-dv, P.N. 126
goats	u-na-k(a)-so-tsa-ne-dv, P.N. 126
good	o:-s-da better, wo:-sv-na best, wo:-sv; plural, wi-do:-sv, p. 222
goodbye (to one person) (to more than one person)	do-na-da'-go-hv-(i) do'-da-da-go'-hv-(i), P.N. 5
goods, merchandise, price, personal property, stake of a game	tsu-gv-hwa-hl'-di, P.N. 78
goose, swan	sa:-sa, p. 70
grain, seed, pit, stone of a fruit	u'-g'-ta, u-ni-g'-ta, P.N. 99 u-ni-g'-ta means several kinds of seeds, etc. Usually no plural is used.
grandfather (my)	a-gi-du'-da. Takes bound pronouns, p. 161
grandmother (my)	a-gi-li'-si; u-li'-si means his or her grandchild or her-grandchild, p. 161
grape, grapes	te-lv'-la-di, u-ni-te-lv-la-di P.N. 98
be grateful, happy, delighted, glad rejoice	(g)a-li-e:-li-ga, (h)a-li-he'-li-ga, V. p. 36
gravy	a-su:-s-di, P.N. 17
grease, oil (cooking or machine oil)	go?-i', C.V., p. 19
green	i'-tse-yu'-s-di (of the new kind), P.N. 43
groundhog, groundhogs	o'-ga-na', P.N. 127
grow fatter, V.	ga-l'-tso?-v'-s-ga, I am growing fatter; ha-l'-tso-hv'-s-ga, you are growing fatter, p. 102

grow taller, V.   ga-tv'-s-ga; I am growing
taller, ha-tv'-s-ga, p. 102

hair (a single hair)   u-gi:-tli, L. 25 and 26
Hair Clan   A-ni-gi-(t)la-hi, p. 142
hair (my)   a-g'-s-ti-gv-i, See L. 25
hand (my)   a?-wo-ye:-n(a), See L. 25,
p. 226

hand or pass (me), V.   DE-S-KV-'SI, P.N. 19
half, middle, 50 cents   a-ye:-tli, P.N. 154
half-dollar   (a)-ye:-tli, P.N. 154
happen, become   ni-ga-li:-s-ti-ya-(ha), p. 222
(I am becoming); nu-l'-s-ta:
-hne, it is becoming, happening, it has happened

be <u>happy</u>, rejoice, be grateful, delighted   (g)a-li-e:-li-ga, I am glad;
(h)a-li-he:-li-ga, you
are glad, V., p. 36

hard, loud, taut   s-ta-yi, a-s-da-ya, L. 26, p. 240
hat   a-l'-s-que'-to-wo, P.N. 177
hats   di'-l'-s-que'-to-wo, P.N. 177
have (in immediate possession), I have   live: a-gi-ka-ha, L. 8
     you (singular) have   tsa-ka-ha
     I have   flexible: a-gi-na-a
     you (singular) have   tsa-na-a
     I have   indefinite: a-gi-ha
     you (singular) have   tsa-ha
     I have   liquid: a-gi-ne-a
     you (singular) have   tsa-ne-a
     I have   long: a-quv-ya
     you (singular) have   tsv-ya
hawk   to-wo'-d(i), P.N. 92
head (my)   tsi-s-go'-li, See L. 25 and 26
   u-s-ga, a severed head
healthy, serene, peaceful   do-hi, P.N. 2
hear, V.   ga-tv-gi, I (just) heard;
ha-htv-gi, you (just)
heard, P.N. 82

heart (of an animal)   u-nah-wi, tsu-nah-wi
     heart (of a human)   a-gwa-da-n'-to'-gi, my-heart,
See L. 25

heavy   ga-ge:-da,
hello   (o')-si-yo', P.N. 1
here   a'-hni', a'-ha-ni', p. 9
hickory (tree) (trees)   wa:-ne?-i, A. VI
     hickory (nut) (nuts)   so-hi'
high, prominent, famous, honored   ga-lv'-la-di, p. 101

high, prominent, high-priced, noble	ga-lv'-la-di', the highest one, extremely high, wa-ga-lv'-l'-di:-yv, p. 101
high-priced, high, prominent, noble, fine	ga-lv'-la-di, the highest one, extremely highly placed, wa-ga-lv'-l'-di:-yv, p. 101
highway, road, trail	ga-nv-hnv, nv-no-hi, P.N. 197
highway	u-ta'-n'-ga-nv'-hnv,
his, hers	u-tse'-li, p. 133
home, house (my)	(di)-que-nv-sv, P.N. 16
honored, famous, high, prominent	ga-lv'-la-di, p. 101
hornet, wasp	ka-n(a)-ts(i)-s-de:-tsi, A. IX
horse, horses	so'-qui-li, P.N. 126
hospital	tsu-ni-dlv:-d' tsu-na-n'-sv-di, L. 26
hotel or motel	tsu-ni-sv'-s-di-i, P.N. 199
house, home (my)	(di)-que-nv-sv; house (not belonging to any particular person, a building), ga-l'tso-de
hummingbird	wa-le'-la or wa-le-li, P.N. 92
a hundred	s-go-hi?-s-qua, P.N. 76
ice	u-ne:-s-ta-lv, P.N. 108
immature, childish, uncompleted, scanty	ga-yo'-tli, P.N. 65
inch	i-ya si?-ta-dv, P.N. 172
in-law (my)	a-gi-lo:-si(yv), p. 165
Indian, American Indian	tsi-yv'-wi-ya', I am an Indian, I originate truly, of the real people. tribes, See p. 76 Cherokee clans, See p. 142
January	u-no-lv'-ta-n(v)(i), P.N. 46
job, workers	tsu-ni-lv:-w(i)-s-ta'-nti, p. 131
join	de-ga-ti-tlv-s-ga, I am joining them (no singular object, of course), p. 230
joint (my)	a-gw'-ti'-tlv, See L. 25 and 26
July	Gu-ye-quo:-ni, P.N. 46
jump, V.	de-ga-l'-ta-de:-(ga), I am jumping, de-ha'-hl'-ta-de:-(ga), p. 146

276

June	De-ha-lu'-yi, P.N. 46
jurors, a jury	a-ni-su-li, p. 142
just, already	ki-lo-wu, p. 158
Ki-tu'-wa Clan	A-ni-gi-du'-hwa(i), p. 144
knife, knives	a-ye'-l-s-di, di-ye'-l'-s-di
	P.N. 108
know (a fact, not a person),	a-qua'-n(i)-ta, tsa:-n'-ta,
know how to	V., P.N. 33
know, understand, V.	go'-li:-g(a)(i), ho'-l'-ga,
	P.N. 26, p. 36
lamp, light bulb	a-tsv'-s-di, di-tsv'-s-di, P.N.43;
	a-tsv'-s-doh-di, di-tsv'-s-doh-di
last	o:-hni, P.N. 148
later, later on, soon	tlv-tlv-yv, p. 86
later	ko-hi-sv-i, P.N. 196
lawyer	di'-ti-yo'-hi-hi', P.N. 113
lawyers	di'-n(i)-ti-yo'-hi-hi', P.N. 113
leaf, leaves	u-ga-lo:-g(a'), tsu-ga-lo:-ga;
	u-ga-lo:-ga can mean leaf or
	leaves; tsu-ga-lo:-ga can
	mean many leaves (of one
	kind) or many kinds of
	leaves, p. 44
leak, emit, burst out	ga-ta-s-gi-(a), L. 25 and 26
leather	ga-no'-tsi, P.N. 179
leech	tla-nu-si, p. 86
leg (my)	tsi-la'-ya-dv,
	tsi-nv-s-ge:-n(a)(i), See
	L. 25
left (toward the left)	a-g'-s-ka-ni-i; my-left-hand,
	tsi-g'-s-ka-ni, See L. 25
letter (of the alphabet)	go-hwe'-lv, di-go-hwe'-lv, P.N. 9
letter, written material	go-hwe-l(a)(i), p. 34
alphabet	du-da-nv:-hnv?-i,
	di-ga-lo?-qua-s-toh-di (They
	have been arranged in rows;
	things to be guided by)
	p. 19
license	go-hwe'-li (paper written)
divorce papers	di-da-ga-le:-n'-di-s-gi
	go-we'-li, also, di-tle:-s-
	doh-di go-(h)we'-li, L. 22
fishing license	a-su?-di go-we'-li, L. 27
hunting license	ga-no-hi-li-da-s-d' go-we'-li
marriage license	di-da-tsv'-s-doh-di go-we'-li,
	also, di-da-tsv'-s-di-s-gi
	go-hwe'-li, See L. 22 & 27

light-bulb, lamp	a-tsv'-s-di, di-tsv-s-di, P.N. 43
liver (my)	a-gwe:-li, See L. 25
locust, locusts	v?-le, p. 35
long ago	go:-hi:, p. 26
look, see Lo	ni, P.N. 41
lose, V.	a-gi-yo-hu:-se, I am losing; tsa-yo-hu'-se, you are losing, p. 135
loud, hard, taut	s-ta-yi, a-s-da-ya, L. 26
loudmouth	a-ha-le:-n(i)(a), p. 51
man, men	a'-s-ga-ya, a-ni-s-ga-ya', P.N. 50
young man, youth and plural	a-(h)wi:-n(a), a-ni-(h)wi:-n(a)
old man, old men	u'-tv-hi'-s-t(v) tsu'-n'-tv-hi-s-t(v), P.N. 50
many, much, very many, very much	s-qui:-s-di, p. 98
	very many, very much, too many, too much, s-qui:-ya
March	A-nv:-yi, P.N. 46
marine (member of the marines), singular and plural	a-ma'-yi-ha-wi'-ni'-e-do'-hi a-ma'-yi-ha-wi'-ne-a-ne-do'-hi P.N. 113
martin (a bird)	tlu-tlu, p. 86
matches	a-tsi-lv-go-tlv-di (to-make-fire), L. 27
materials, sewing	ga-yeh'-w(i)-sv-doh'-di See Appendix XII, P.N. 179
maple	tlv-hwa'-l(i)-ga, p. 9
May	A-n(v)(i)-s-gv'-ti, P.N. 46
meal	a-l'-s-ta-i-d(i), p. 131
meal, menu	a-l'-s-ta-i-d(i), P.N. 17
meat	ha-wi-'-ya, P.N. 17
medicine	nv-wo-ti, L. 26
middle, in the middle, in the midst of, half, 50 cents	(a)-ye:-tli, P.N. 154
migrate, move out, V.	ga-da-nv?-a, I am moving out; ha-da-nv?-a, you are moving out, P.N. 87
milk	u-nv:-d(i), P.N. 57
minister, pastor, reverend	a-l(i)-tsa-do'-hv-s-gi',P.N. 13
minister, ministers	a-l'-tsa-do'-hv-s-gi', a-na-l'-tsa-do'-hv-s-gi', P.N. 113
Monday	(u-na)-do'-da-quo'-hnv?(i) P.N. 101
money	a-de-la, or a-de-lv-i, P.N. 154
month	si-nv-da, si-nv-do, p. 195 ka?-la, ka?-lv, P.N. 45
more, again	si-wu, p. 129

more

morning, tomorrow

motel, hotel

mother (my)

mountain, mountains

mouth (my)

move out, migrate, V.

mulberry, mulberries

musician

my, mine

much, many, very many, very much

namely

near, close

needle, needles

negroes, blacks

nestling, also baby fox, rabbit, bear
    pig, possum, wolf, dog (born
    several at a time)

new

nightingale

nine

nineteen

ninth

no, not, not so

noon

North; cold, coldness, Republican

November

now, right now

number, numbers

nurse, nurses

si-quv, p. 70

sv-na:-le(i), P.N. 64

tsu-ni-sv'-s-di-i, P.N. 199

a-gi-tsi; his/her mother,
    u-tsi-i, p. 159

o'-da-lv(la), do:-da-lv(la),
    p. 43

tsi-ho:-li, L. 24, 25 and 26

ga-da-nv?-a, I am moving out;
    ha-da-nv?-a, you are moving
    out, P.N. 87

ku:-wa, P.N. 98

di-ka-no-gi:-s-di'-s-gi
    di-ni-ka-no-gi:-s-di'-s-gi
    P.N. 113

a'-qua-tse'-li, p. 133

s-qui:-s-di; very many, very
    much, too many, too much,
    s-qui:-ya, p. 98

s-gi-na', p. 98

na?-i, p. 51

yv-gi, di-yv'-gi, P.N. 179

A-ni-gv'-ni-ge, p. 142

a:-da-(ge), a-ni:-da-(ge)

    a-ni:-da means 'litter' or
    'nestlings'.
    a-ni:-da a?-da means 'a
    single one out of a 'litter'.
    P.N. 91

i'-tse, a'-tse, p. 49

s-qua-le'-wa-li', P.N. 92

soh-ne'-l(a), P.N. 11

so-hne-la-du-(i), P.N. 75

so'-ne-li-ne'-(i), P.N. 12

tla-hv', v?-tla, tla, P.N. 8

*i:-ga' - scalloped i, up on ga
    (*i-ga', day, i short, whole
    word on an even low tone)
    L. 7, p. 39. See day *i-ga'

*u-hyv:-dlv; *u-hyv:-dla, P.N. 36

Nv-da-de'-wa, P.N. 46

hna-quu, hno-wu, p. 64

a-se:-s-di, di-se'-s-di, P.N. 10

tsu'-n'-tlv'-gi di-g'-ti'-ya
    tsu'-n-tlv'-gi di-ni'-g'-
    ti'-ya, P.N. 113

279

October	Du-ni-nv:-di, P.N. 46
oil, grease, shortening, cooking or machine oil	go?-i, C.V., p. 19
one	sa'-wu, P.N. 11
or, and, but	a-le, p. 35
Orientals	A-ni-da-lo'-ni-ge, p. 142
originate, be of a certain origin, ancestry	tsi-yv'-wi, I am of a certain origin
	hi-yv'-wi, you are of a certain origin
	tsi-yv-wi-ya, originate truly, be an American Indian, V., P.N. 68
	tsi-yv'-wi-ya, I am an Indian
	hi-yv'-wi-ya, you are an Indian
Osage, Osages	a?-sa:-s(i)(a), a-ni?-sa:-s(i)(a), a member of the Osage tribe, the Osage tribe, P.N. 74
out-of-doors	do'-yi, P.N. 62
owl	u-gu'-ku, p. 26
Paint Clan	A-ni-wo:-d(i), p. 142
painter	di-ga-lo-ne:-s-gi,
painters	di-ni-ga-lo-ne:-s-gi, p. 222
panther, panthers	tlv-da-tsi', P.N. 127
pants	a-su-lo, one pair; di-su-lo, more than one pair, P.N. 177
pattern or patterns (to-measure-them-with)	di-tli-lo:-s-doh-di, P.N. 179
peach, peaches	qua-na, p. 64
pear, pears	di-ga-dv:-d(i), P.N. 98
a pendant, a bead	a-yah'-l-di; beads, a necklace, di-yah'-l-di, P.N. 177
people, a people	yv'-wi, a-ni-yv'-wi, P.N. 74
pepper	di-qua-yo'-d(i), P.N. 108
permit, allow, put up for sale	a-g'-s-go'-hl'-ti, L. 27
pie	ge-li:-s-gi, P.N. 17
pig, pigs	si-qua, p. 70
pigeon	gv:-le, P.N. 92
pin, pins (safety pin or brooch)	u'-s-qua-ti', tsu'-s-qua-ti', P.N. 179
	straight pin is: u'-s-qua-ti' ga-tsi-no:s-da, tsu'-s-qua-ti' di-ga-tsi-no:-s-da, P.N. 179
pit, stone (of a fruit), seed, grain	u'-g(a)-ta, P.N. 99
pitcher, soup or serving bowl, tank	a-tli-s-toh-di, di-tli-s-toh-di, P.N. 108

plant, V.   tsi-wi-sv:-s-ga, I am planting,
                                                  hi-wi-sv:-sga, you are
                                                  planting, p. 102
plate, plates   te'-li-do, di-te'-li-do, P.N. 108
platform, see table
plum, plums   qua-nv'-yu:-n'-s-di, P.N. 98
poet, poets   di-go-we-li'-s-gi ka-no-he-
                                                  lv'-s-gi, di-no-we-li'-s-gi
                                                  a-ni-hno-he-lv'-s-gi, (writer-
                                                  down of chants), P.N. 113
policeman, policemen   di-da-ni-yi'-s-gi,
                                                  di-n'-da-ni-yi-s-gi, P.N. 113
poor, wicked, wretched, bad   u-yo, p. 143
possum   si-quu:-tse-ts', P.N. 127
potato, potatoes   nu:-n(a)(i), P.N. 17
pretty, beautiful   u-wo'-du, P.N. 40
prominent, high, high-priced, noble,
   highly placed   ga-lv'-la-di'; the highest one,
                                                  wa-ga-lv'-l'di:-yv, p. 101
pumpkin   i'-ya, P.N. 17

quail   gu'-que, P.N. 92
quarter (25 cents)   gi-nu?-di, P.N. 154
                                                  quarter (one fourth)
quit, V.   tsi-su-la-go:-ga, I am quitting,
                                                  hi-su-la-go:-ga, you are
                                                  quitting, p. 136

rabbit, rabbits   tsi'-s(a)-du, P.N. 127
raccoon, raccoons   kv-tli, P.N. 127
rain (always a verb)   a-ga-s-ga', it is raining,
                                                  P.N. 62
raspberry   sv-di'-wa-li', P.N. 98
raven   go-la-nv', P.N. 92
raw, unripe   a-go:-s-di, P.N. 99
red   a-gi'-ga-ge, p. 26
redbud   ga-lo-we:-d(i), p. 103
rejoice, be glad, delighted, grateful, happy
                                               ga-li-e:-li-ga,
                                                  ha-li-he'-li-ga, V., p. 36
repairman, repairmen   o'-s-da i-gv-ne'-hi,
                                                  o'-s-da i-ya-nv-ne'-hi,
                                                  P.N. 113
Republican, cold, coldness, North   u-hyv:-dla(dlv), P.N. 36
rest, V.   a-gwa-tsv-weh-so-lv:-s-di,
                                                  I am resting, L. 26
restroom, toilet, privy   do-yi e-da-s-di-i, P.N. 199
rib (my)   a-gi-nu'-la-tsi, See L. 25
ribbon   a-que-tlu'-s-di, P.N. 39

right (toward the right)	a?k-ti:-si; my-right-hand, tsi?k-ti:sa
right-hand (my)	tsi?k-ti:-sa, See L. 25
ripe (of a fruit)	u-wa'-n'-sv (soft)
(of a nut)	u-ka-yo:-d (dry), P.N. 99
river, rivers	e-quo-ni, tse-quo-ni, P.N. 83
road	nv-no-hi, P.N. 122
robin	tsi-s-quo'-ga, P.N. 92
rock or rocks	nv-ya, L. 26
rooster, roosters	a-tsv'-ya, a-ni-tsv'-ya, P.N. 126
round	ga-so'-qua-lv, p. 70
sailor	a-ma'-yi-a-do'-hi
sailors	a-ma'-yi-a-ne-do'-hi,P.N. 113
salt	*a:-m(a'), (scalloped long a, end the word upward) See water, am-a, p. 39
same, that same, this same, previously mentioned person, animal or thing	s-gi-na', p. 98
Santa Claus	di-s-ta-yo'-hi (he shoots off firecrackers), P.N. 39
satin (shiny cloth)	u-tsi-s-da-lu-gi'-s-g(i) a-hnu-wo, P.N. 179
Saturday	(u-na)-do-da-wi-de:-na (they go out), P.N. 101
say, repeat, state, recite, V.	ga-di?-a, ha-di?-a, P.N. 9
say, utter, V.	ni-tsi-we?-a, I (just) said; hni-we?-a, you (just) said, P.N. 82
scanty, childish, immature, uncompleted	ga-yo'-tli, P.N. 65
school	tsu-na-del'-qua-s-di(i), p. 101
scissors	di'-l'-s-toh-di, P.N. 179
secretary, secretaries	go-we-li'-s-gi, a-no-we-li'-s-gi or di-no-we-li'-s-gi, P.N.113
second (of a series), once again	ta?-li:-ne-(i), P.N. 12
seed, grain, pit of a fruit	u'-g'-ta, u-ni-g'-ta, P.N. 99
sell (put up for sale)	a-g'-s-go'-hl'-ti; also permit, allow, L. 24 and 27
sell, V.	tsi-n'-de-ga, I am selling it, p. 223
seller	ga-n'-de-gi, p. 223
September	Du-li:-s-di, P.N. 46
seven	ga-l(i)-quo:-g(i'), P.N. 11
seventeen	ga-l(i)-qua-du-(i), P.N. 75
seventh	ga-li-quo-gi-ne'-(i), P.N. 12
seventy	ga-l'-qua'-s-go-(hi), P.N. 76
several (living or non-living things)	hi-lv'-s-gi, p. 98
sewing materials	ga-yeh'-w(i)-sv-doh'-di, P.N. 179

sharp-edged, sharp-pointed
    sharper or sharpest, very sharp
sheep

snell, shells

shirt, shirts or blouse, blouses
shoe, shoes
shoot, V.
shortening, grease, oil, cooking or machine oil

sibling-of-the-opposite sex (my)

silk
silver

singleton
sister (my)

six
sixteen
sixth
sixty
skin or fur (on a body)
   skin or fur (off its body)
   a kind of skin or fur (off its body)
skirt, skirts or dress, dresses

skunk, skunks
sky
sleeve, sleeves (like-a-wing, to-be-used-as-a-wing)

slowly
smart
sock, socks

sofa, see table
soft
soil
soldier, soldiers

somebody

go-s-ta-yi, go-s-da-ya
   wi-go-s-ta-yv, L. 26, p. 240
u-no-de:-n(a), u-ni-no-de:-n(a),
   P.N. 126
u-hya'-s-ga, tsu-hya'-s-ga.
   Sea shell, nut shell, turtle
   shell; not a gun shell.
a'-hno-wo, di'-hna-wo, P.N. 177
a-la-su'-lo, di-la-su-lo, p. 70
di-s-da-yo:-s-di, See L. 26, 27

go?-i', C.V., p. 19
a-gi-do'-i; his or her sibling
   of the opposite sex,
   u-do'-(i), p. 162
si'-hl'-gi, P.N. 179
u-tsi-s-ta-lu:-gi-s-gi
   (shiner), P.N. 39
u-tsu-ya, P.N. 129
a-gi-lv:-gi, my-sister spoken
   by a female, fellow-sister;
a-gi-do'-i, my-sister spoken
   by a male, sibling-of-the-
   opposite-sex, See L. 20
su'-da-l(i'), P.N. 11
da-la-du-(i), P.N. 75
su-da-li-ne'-(i), P.N. 12
su-da-l'-s-go-(hi), P.N. 76
tsi-ne-ga-lv, my-skin;
   ga-ne-ga
   tsu-ni-ne-ga-lv-nv-i, L. 25
a'-sa-no, di'-sa-no, e'-l'-di,
   a'-sa-no, P.N. 177, skirt
di?-li, P.N. 127
ga-lv'-lo:-(hi), p. 44

go-hya-dv-doh-di,
   di-go-hya-dv-doh-di, P.N.177
u'-s-ga-no:-l(i), P.N. 25
a-sa-ma'-ti, p. 131
a-li-yo-(i), di-li-yo?-i,
   P.N. 177

u-wa'-n'-sv, P.N. 99
ga-to-hi, p. 78
a-yo:-s-gi, a-ni-yo:-s-gi,
   P.N. 113
ki-lo'-(i), p. 35

soon, later on	tlv-tlv-yv, p. 86
a sore, sores	tsa-d'-s-da-lv?-i, de-tsa-d'-s-da-lv?-i, L. 26
soup	u-ga-ma, p. 44
South, warm, warmth, Democrat	u-ga'-no-wa'(wi), P.N. 37
speak, V.	tsi-wo'-ni-a, I am speaking (now); hi-wo:-ni-a, you are speaking, P.N. 65
spoon, spoons	a-di-toh-di, di-di-toh-di, P.N. 108
spouse (my)	o-s-di-ne'-l(i), usually used for 'husband', p. 152
star, stars	no'-qui-si, a-ni-no'-qu(i)-si, P.N. 39
stomach (my)	a-g'-s?-wo:-tli, See L. 26
stop (for awhile), take time out from a task	to:-da-ge-do'-li, I am taking time out; to'-te-do'-li, you are taking time out, p. 136
strawberry, strawberries	a?-ni, P.N. 98
string, thread, yarn	a'-s-di, P.N. 179
stuffing (of meat)	a-su-ya-na-(i), P.N. 17
sugar, candy	ka-l(i)-se:-ts(i), P.N. 55
summer	go:-g(i), C.V., p. 19
Sunday	(u-no)-do'-da-qua-s-gv?-i, P.N. 100
swan, goose	sa:-sa, p. 70
sweet, sugar, candy	ka-l(i)-se-tsi, P.N. 55
sweet potato, sweet potatoes	nu:-n(a)(i) ga-nv-hi-da nu:-n(a)(i) a-ni-nv-hi'-da, P.N. 17
swell, puff up	go-ti:-s-ga, it is swelling, L. 26
swollen, puffed up	u-wo-ti:-sv; go-ti:-sga, it is swelling, L. 26
table, chair, bench, platform, sofa, furniture	ga'-s-ki-lo'; plural, di-ga-s-ki-lo; sofa, bench, ga-nv'-hi-da ga'-s-ki-lo' (long furniture), <u>not bed</u>, P.N. 108
tablecloth	ga-s-ki-lv a-ye'-s-tv'-di,
tablecloths	de-ga-s-ki'-lv di-ye'-s-tv'-di P.N. 108
tall	i-ni'-ga-ti, p. 162
tank, pitcher, soup or serving bowl	a-tli-s-toh'-di, di-tli-s-toh'-di, P.N. 108
taut, hard, loud	s-ta-yi, a-s-da-ya, L. 26, p. 240

tea	u-ga-lo'-ga go-tlv'-ta-nv, P.N. 17
teacher	di-de-yo'-hv-s-gi, P.N. 20
teacher, teachers	di-de-yo'-hv-s-gi, di-n(a)-de-yo'-hv-s-gi', P.N. 113
telephone	di-tla-no-he?-di(i), p. 86
ten	s-go-(hi), P.N. 11
tenth	s-go'-hi-ne'-(i), P.N. 12
Texas	Nv-da:-gi, P.N. 142
thank you	wa-do', P.N. 6
Thanksgiving	U-(na)-li-he-li'-s-di, P.N. 17
that	na, na-s-gi, hi?-a, pp. 26, 51, 98
that, those	na, na-s-gi, pp. 51, 98
their, theirs	u-na-tse-li, p. 133
think, be of the opinion, V.	ge'-li-a, I think; he-li-a, you think, p. 77
third	tso-i-ne'-(i), P.N. 12
thirteen	tso-ga-du-(i), P.N. 75
thirty	tso'-s-go-(hi), P.N. 75
this, that	hi?-a, p. 26
those, that	na, na-s-gi, p. 51
a thousand	sa'-wu i-ya-ga-yv'-li, P.N. 75
one thousand dollars	sa'-wu i'-ya-ga-yv'-la', P.N. 154
thread, yarn, string	a'-s-di, P.N. 179
three	tso?-i, P.N. 11
Thursday	nv?-gi-ne *i-ga' (4th day), P.N. 101
time	a-tli'-gi-li', P.N. 77
tire, be tired, V.	da-gi-ya-we:-a, I am tired, L. 26
today	go-hi i:-ga or go-hi, p. 26
toilet	do-yi e-da-s-di-i, P.N. 199
tomorrow	sv-na'-le(i), P.N. 64
tongue (my)	tsi-ga'-n?-ga', See L. 26
tooth (my)	tsi'-n-doh-gv, See L. 25, p. 227
town	ga-du'-hv, p. 163
tree, trees	tlu'-kv, te-tlu'-kv or i'-tl'-kv, de:-tl'-vk, P.N. 98
troublemaker	a-l'-s-ti'-s-gi, p. 222
truly, certainly, very	do:-yu, P.N. 40
truth	du-yu'-k'-dv, L. 27
Tuesday (second day)	ta-li:-ne *i-ga', P.N. 101
turkey	gv-n(a), P.N. 17
turn around, V.	ga-go-tlv?-a, L. 27
turn in a new direction	ga-tle:ya

twelve	ta-l(a')-du(i), P.N. 75
twenty	ta'-l'-s-go-(hi), P.N. 75
twenty-one	ta'-l'-s-go-sa'-wu, P.N. 76
twenty-two	ta'-l'-s-go-ta'-l(i), P.N. 76
twenty-three	ta'-l'-s-go-tso'-(i), See p. 194
twenty-four	ta'-l'-s-go-nv:-g', See p. 194
two	ta?-li, P.N. 11
typist	di-sø'-s-ti:-s(gi)
typists	di-ni-sø'-s-ti:-s(-gi), P.N. 113
uncle (my)	a-gi-du'-tsi; his/her-uncle,
	u-du'-tsi, p. 160
uncompleted, scanty, childish, immature	ga-yo'-tli, P.N. 65
unconscious, V.	na-qua-n'-ta na-nu-hl'-s-ta-nv,
	I lost consciousness, L. 26
understand, know, V.	go'-li:-g(a)(i), ho'-l'-ga,
	P.N. 26
unripe, raw	a-go:-s-di, P.N. 99
veer off, turn in a new direction	ga-tle:-ya, L. 27
velvet (slick cloth)	da-wi'-s-ka-ge a-hnu-wo,
	P.N. 179
very, certainly, truly	do:-yu, P.N. 40
wagon, wagons	do-gwa-le:-lu, L. 26
want, wish to have	a?-wa-du'-li-(a), tsa-du'-li-(a)
	a-gwa-du'-li-(a), a-qua-du'-
	li-(a), P.N. 18, C.V., p. 26
warm, warmth, South, Democrat	u-ga'-no-wa' (i), P.N. 37
warmth, warm, South, Democrat	u-ga'-no-wa' (i), P.N. 37
wasp, hornet	ka-n(a)-ts(i)-s-de:-tsi, A. IX
water	*a-m(a'), (more like am-a on
	an even, low tone), p. 39
	see salt, *a:-m(a')
Wednesday	tso?-i-ne *i-ga' (3rd day),
	P.N. 101
week	a-tli-gi-li'-sv, P.N. 150
	sv-do'-da-qua-s-di-i
well, good or fine	o:-s-da, P.N. 3
west	u-de-li-gv (where it is hidden),
	P.N. 194
what (did you say)?	hv?, p. 82
what? which?	ga-do'
what kind of?	ga-do'-u:-s-di, P.N. 23, 30
when, how far?	ha-la'-yv?, p. 83
where	ha-tlv(tla), P.N. 22
where? where to?	ha:-tlv(dlv,tla)?, P.N. 22
which? what kind of?	ga-do' u'-s-di, P.N. 23
white	u-ne:-g(a), p. 51
who?	ka:-g(a), ga:-g(a), p. 35
why?	do'-hv?, p. 82

wife (cook for me)

wing, wings

winter
Wise Man, sage, angel
wolf, wolves
Wolf clan
woman, women
   old woman, old women

wood, wooden
woodpecker
woods, wood, forest
wool material

word, words

world, earth
work

wrapping paper

yard (a measurement)

yarn, thread, string
year

yes
your, yours (plural)
   your, yours, (singular)
youth, young man, teen-age boy

a-g'-s-ta-yv-hv'-s-gi, C.V.,
   p. 26
go-hya-dv, de-go-hya-dv,
   P.N. 177
go:-la, p. 51
a-da-we'-hi, P.N. 39
wah-ya, P.N. 127
A-ni-wah-ya, p. 142
a-ge'-(h)ya, a-ni-ge(h)ya;
a-ga-yv'-li-ge, a-ni-ga-yv'-li-
   ge, P.N. 50
a-da, L. 26
da-la'-la, P.N. 92
a-doh, L. 26
u-wu-ya-ti, or u-wu-ya-t(i)(a-hnu-wo)
   P.N. 164
ka-ne'-tsv, di-ka-ne'-tsv,
   P.N. 51
e-lo-hi', p. 44
di-gi-lv'-w(i)-s-ta-n(e)?-di
   I am working, da-gi-lv:-w(i)-
   s-da-ne?-a, p. 137
ga-que:-n(i)-doh-di, P.N. 39

su-tli-lo-dv (can also mean a
   mile or a gallon) P.N. 172
a'-s-di, P.N. 179
u-de:ti-yv-da, P.N. 142
e-ti:-y(a)(v)
tsu-de:-ti-yv-sa-di-(sv)
v:-v, P.N. 7; ho:-wa, P.N. 49
i-tsa-tse-li, p. 133
   tsa'-tse-li'
a-(h)wi:-n(a), a-ni-(h)wi:-n(a),
   P.N. 50

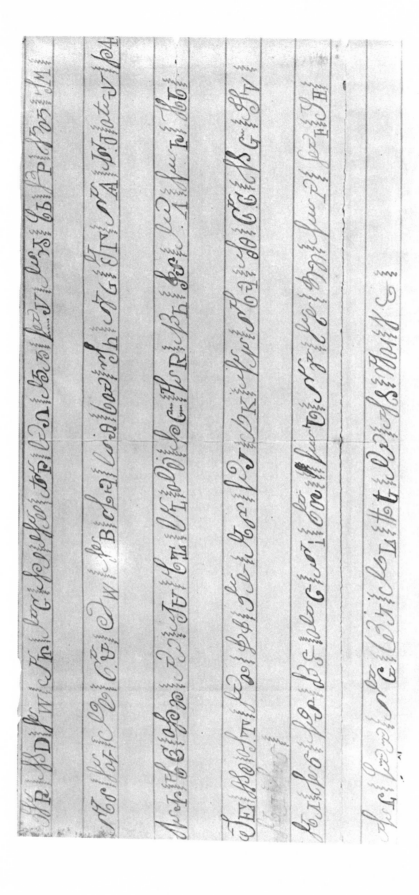

Appendix I   The original Cherokee syllabary as invented by Sequoyah with the modified or present syllabary, shown together.   From the John Howard Payne papers, The Thomas Gilcrease Institute of American History and Art, Tulsa, Oklahoma.

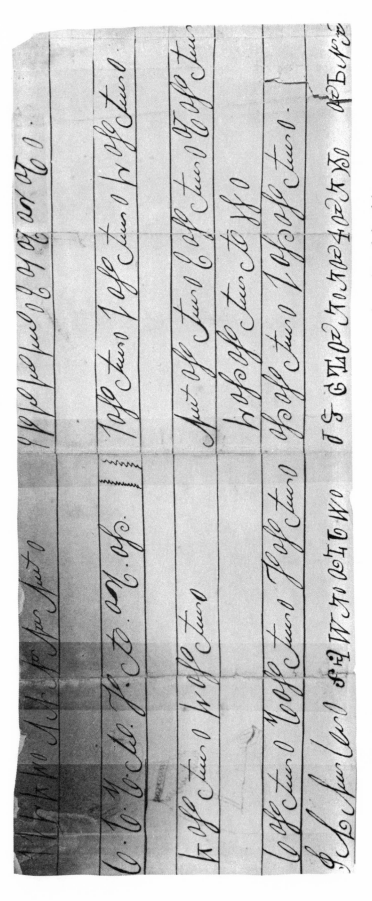

Appendix II   The symbols for numbers invented by Sequoyah, signed by him.

From the John Howard Payne papers, The Thomas Gilcrease Institute of American

History and Art, Tulsa, Oklahoma.

Appendix III   The number system and Cherokee alphabet, signed by Sequoyah.
From the John Howard Payne papers, The Thomas Gilcrease Institute of American
History and Art, Tulsa, Oklahoma.

BIOGRAPHICAL SKETCH OF SEQUOYAH

Information on some details of Sequoyah's life is fragmentary. His genius and achievements are thoroughly documented, however. He was born between 1760 and 1770 five miles from the original Cherokee capital of Chota in Tuskegee, now part of Tennessee. At that time the Cherokees were an independent nation still living on their original tribal lands. They were coexisting with the British Colonies as equal neighbors and were making separate trade agreements with the British government.

Sequoyah's mother, Wurteh, belonged to a prominent Cherokee family. Her brothers, Doublehead, Onitositah and Pumpkinhead, and a nephew, George Lowrey, were all chiefs. Sequoyah's father was probably a white shopkeeper named Nathaniel Gist with whom Wurteh lived until he went home to Virginia while Sequoyah was still a baby. Gist had nothing further to do with either Wurteh or Sequoyah and died before his son became famous.

Wurteh brought up Sequoyah in a little cabin in the Overhills country, where they were on the usual close Cherokee family terms with her prosperous relations. Sequoyah and his cousin, George Lowrey, were lifelong friends; some accounts say that he was the first person to whom Sequoyah showed the syllabary.

In Sequoyah's childhood Cherokees owned all the surrounding territory so he grew up knowing nothing but Cherokee, although he learned a few words of English in his old age in Arkansas. In appearance Sequoyah has been described as resembling a fullblood. He was dark, slight, and interested in everything, with brilliant eyes and an open, cheerful manner. He became a blacksmith and taught himself to be a silversmith. He was naturally mechanical and a gifted artist whose special talent was for drawing animals. He married, had a family of four boys, and settled on some land in the village of Tallassee not far from his birthplace.

When dealing with white men, Sequoyah used the name of George Guess or Gist. 'Guess' was possibly a Cherokee version of 'Gist'. So far as is known, 'Sequoyah' was his personal name from early youth. Its origin and meaning are uncertain; it certainly does not mean 'he guessed it' in Cherokee although many references say it does. Many Cherokees pronounce his name 'Sequoyi' but Sequoyah himself signed it in his syllabary 'S-si-quo-ya'. (See Appendix II)

As a very young man he had noticed the power that ability to read gave white men. It was at this time that Sequoyah began to think and talk, both jokingly and seriously, about creating an equivalent advantage for the Cherokees.

About 1806 he and other Cherokees were forced off their land in Tennessee by white encroachment on Cherokee trade agreements. Sequoyah moved his family to present-day Alabama just across the border from Tennessee. The Cherokee Nation, expecting to stay permanently, established another capital and named it New Echota.

In 1809 Sequoyah started work on the syllabary. He had a pair of silver spurs on which he had a friend stamp his Cherokee name in English letters. It is said that he used to sit on a log turning the spurs in his hand, thinking, and jotting down tentative ideas on wood shingles which he stored in a little work cabin he built for the purpose. He used a nephew's speller and some printed alphabets lent by missionaries for ideas as to the function of the letters. For the sounds the letters represented he had to rely only on his own powers of analysis since he knew no English at all at this time. The alphabets he saw are supposed to have included English, Hebrew and Greek. At first he hoped to make a letter for every word, but soon found this would make too many letters. He used to make his friends and family repeat words so he could try to break sounds down into their smallest parts.

During the Creek War of 1813-1814 he was a member of the Cherokee regiment commanded by another cousin, a brother of George Lowrey's. They fought under the U.S. Government against the Creeks. The injury to his leg that made him limp in later life may have happened at this time. Invalided home, he returned to the syllabary and continued to give it all his time even after his leg was healed. The shabby treatment given his Cherokee regiment by the U.S. Government after the Creek War ended may have fuelled his new determination, for Sequoyah was always agonizingly aware of the advantage written communication gave white men. His preoccupation made him neglect other work and earned him a reputation as a crank. He became so alienated from his wife and family that his work cabin was purposely burned down with his shingles in it while he was in town for the day. This was intended as a pointed hint to him to devote himself to something else.

In later life he said that the loss of all his early work turned out to be a good thing. He said that he had reached a dead end in his thinking, and the loss of his shingles made him make a fresh start. At the time he felt it was a disaster; he left home and migrated to Arkansas.

In Arkansas he continued work on his syllabary, reducing two hundred letters to eighty-six. He married again in about 1815. In 1821, possibly through George Lowrey, he was granted a hearing before the tribal council. At the council meeting Sequoyah and his little daughter wrote messages to one another in the alphabet, as proof that writing worked just as well in Cherokee as in English. The council was impressed. They then chose some Cherokee youths and instructed Sequoyah to train them in his syllabary in preparation for a final test at a designated time.

The test was passed, the council voted his syllabary in as the official

Cherokee alphabet, and Cherokees took up writing with delight. Young braves would take trips for the pleasure of writing home. Family members left notes for one another around the house and taught one another the letters. In a few months the whole nation was reading and writing. It was a triumph.

Sequoyah was now a tribal personage. Missionaries started making a font from which to print Cherokee periodicals. He helped to adapt his syllabary for printing purposes and eliminated another of the original letters. A medal was struck for him in 1825 by the U.S. Government. The government also promised him money for a printing press and for improvements on his Arkansas property most of which was never paid. He became involved in the question of removing the Cherokees to the West and visited Washington on behalf of the Cherokees in 1827. On one of these visits the only known picture of him was painted by Charles Bird King of Washington.

Sequoyah then spent much time thinking into and creating a system of numbers on the decimal system which he laid before the tribal council. They sensibly voted Sequoyah's numbers out, as Arabic numerals, which are simpler, were already in use. This invention, though it came to nothing, is as astonishing as the syllabary. Sequoyah also made some chemical experiments with paint. His later years were spent on his farm home near Fort Gibson close to the transcontinental trail where many people came for a look at the famous 'Cherokee sage'. He enjoyed meeting people and was active in tribal affairs.

In 1839 Sequoyah as President of the Western Cherokees and his cousin George Lowrey as President of the Eastern Cherokees co-signed the Act of Union uniting two previously warring factions of the Cherokee Nation: those who had migrated west earlier and those who had tried to remain in the east till they were forcibly removed.

Dreaming of reuniting all Cherokees in the new Cherokee Nation in Oklahoma, Sequoyah invited a splinter group of tribesmen in Texas to return to Oklahoma. In 1842 he set off himself to find another group of dissidents who were supposed to have gone to Mexico. He never returned; he became ill on the way and died near San Fernando, Mexico, in 1843. Friends and a son who buried him by a river were unable to find the grave again because floods had changed the riverbank and local landmarks. His grave has never been identified but a search is continuing for a small elderly skeleton with a damaged leg. Like so many traditional heroes of other nations he has vanished into legend.

CLASSIFYING VERB DE S KV SI, from Lesson 5, 'HANDING OR PASSING A CLASSIFIED OBJECT TO SOMEONE'

	..something Live (e.g. a puppy)	..something Indefinite in shape, solid (e.g. a sugar-bowl)	..something Long, inflexible (e.g. a board)	..something Flexible, light for its size (e.g. a cloth)	..something Liquid
One person is passing something classified to one person:					
I am passing you ...	gv-ka'-ne?-a	gv-ne?-a	gv-de?-a	*gv-nv-ne?-a	gv-ne?-v?-si'(se)
I am passing him/her ...	tsi-ka'-ne?-a	tsi-ne?-a	tsi-de?-a	tsi-nv'-ne?-a	tsi-ne?-v?-si'(se)
One person is passing something classified to two persons:					
I am passing you-two ...	s-dv-ka'-ne?-a	s-dv'-ne?-a	s-dv-de?-a	s-dv-nv-ne?-a	s-dv-ne?-v-hsi'
One person is passing something classified to several persons:					
I am passing you(plural) ...	i-tsv-ka'-ne?-a	i-tsv-ne?-a	i-tsv-de?-a	i-tsv-nv-ne?-a	i-tsv-ne?-v:-si'
I am passing them ...	ga-tsi-ka'-ne?-a	ga-tsi-ne?-a	ga-tsi-de?-a	ga-tsi-nv-ne?-a	ga-tsi-ne:?-v-si'
One person is passing something classified to one person:					
you are passing me ...	(d)e-s-ki-ka'-si	(d)e-s-kv-si	(d)e-s-gi-di-si	(d)e-s-ki-nv-si	(d)e-s-ki-ne-hv-si'
you are passing him/her ...	hi-ka'-ne?-a	hi-ne?-a	hi-de?-a	hi-nv-ne?-a	hi-ne?-v?-si
One person is passing something classified to two persons:					
you are passing him/her-&-me ...	s-gi-ni-ka'-ne?-a	s-gi-ni'-ne?-a	s-gi-ni-de?-a	s-gi-ni-nv-ne?-a	s-gi-neh-hv-si', a-gi-ne:-hne
One person is passing something classified to several persons:					
you are passing us(them-&-me)...	i-s-gi-ka'-ne?-a	i-s-gi-ne?-a	i-s-gi-de?-a	i-s-gi-nv-ne?-a	i-s-gi-neh-hv-si'
you are passing them ...	ga-hi-ka'-ne?-a	ga-hi-ne?-a	ga-hi-de?-a	ga-hi-nv-ne?-a	ga-hi-ne?-v?-si'

294

APPENDIX V

CLASSIFYING VERB DE S KV SI, from Lesson 5, 'HANDING OR PASSING A CLASSIFIED OBJECT TO SOMEONE'

	..something... Live (e.g. a puppy)	.. something .. Indefinite in shape, solid (e.g. a sugar-bowl)	..something.. Long, inflexible (e.g. a board)	.. something .. Flexible, light for its size (e.g. a cloth)	.. something .. Liquid
One person is passing something classified to one person:					
he/she is passing me ...	a-gi-ka'-ne	a-ki-ne?-a	a-gi-de?-a	a-gi-nv-ne?-a	a-gi-ne-hv-si'-se
he/she is passing you ...	tsa-ka-ne?-a	tsa-ne-ha	tsa-de?-a	tsa-nv-ne?-a	tsa-ne:-hv-si'-se
he/she is passing him/her ...	ga-ka'-ne	a-tsi'-ne	a'-tsi-de	a-tsi-nv:-ne	a-tsi-ne?-v?-se
One person is passing something classified to two persons:					
he/she is passing you-&-me ...	gi-ni'-ka-ne	gi-ni'-hne	gi-ni:-de	gi-ni-nv:-ne	gi-ni'-ne:-hne
he/she is passing you-two ...	s-di-ka-ne	s-di:-hne	s-di:-de	s-di?-nv:-ne	s-di-ne:-hne
he/she is passing him/her-&-me ...	gi-ni'-ka'-ne	gi-ni:-hne	gi-n:-de	gi-ni-nv'-ne	gi-ni'-nv-hne
One person is passing something classified to several persons:					
he/she is passing us(them-&-me) ...	i-gi-ka'-ne	i-gi:-hne	i-gi:-de	i-gi-nv:-ne	i-gi-nv:-hne
he/she is passing you(plural) ...	i-tsi-ka-ne	i-tsi:-hne	i-tsi:-de	i-tsi-nv'-ne	i-tsi-nv:-hne'
he/she is passing them ...	de:-ga-ka'-ne	da:-hne	da:-de	de:-ga-nv'-ne	de:-ga-nv:-hne
Two people are passing something classified to one person:					
you-&-I are passing him/her ...	eh-ni-ka'-ne	e:-ni-ne?-a	e:-ni-de?-a	e:-ni-nv-ne?-a	e:-ni-ne:-hne
Two people are passing something classified to several people:					
you-&-I are passing them ...	ge-ni-ka'-ne	ge-ni-ne?-a	ge-ni-de?-a	ge-ni-nv'-ne	ge-ni-ne?-v-se

There are no special forms for 'you-&-I' passing something classified to two other people.

295

CLASSIFYING VERB DE S KV SI, from Lesson 5

	..something.. Live (e.g.. a puppy)	.. something .. Indefinite in shape, solid (sugar bowl)	-- something .. Long, inflexible (a board)	.. something .. Flexible, light for its size	.. something .. Liquid
Two people are passing something classified to one person:					
you-two are passing me ...	s-gi-ni-ka'-ne	s-gi-ni-ne?-a	s-gi-ni-de?a	s-gi-ni-nv-ne	s-gi-ne-?-v'-si'
you-two are passing him/her ...	eh-s-di-ka'-ne	e-s-di-ne	e-s-di-de?-a	*e-s-di-nv-ne	*e-s-di-nv-ne
Two people are passing something classified to two people:					
you-two are passing him/her-&-me ...	s-gi-ni-ka-ne	s-gi-ni-ne?-a	s-gi-ni-de?-a	s-gi-ni-nv-ne	s-gi-ni-ne-v:-si'
Two people are passing something classified to several people:					
you-two are passing us(them-&-me) ...	de'-s-gi-ka'-ne	de-s-gi'-ne	de-s-gi:-de	de-s-gi-nv'-ne	de-s-gi-ni-ne?-v?-s(e)(i)
you-two are passing them ...	de-s-di-ka'-ne	de-s-di'-hne	de-s-di'-de	de-s-di-nv'-ne	de-s-di-nv-hne
Several people are passing something classified to one person:					
they are passing me ...	gv-gi-ka'-ne	gv:-ki'-ne	gv:-gi-de	gv:-gi-nv'-ne	gv:-gi-nv'-hne
they are passing you ...	ge:-tsa-ka'-ne	ge'-tsa-de	ge:-tsa-de	ge:-tsa-nv'-ne	ge:-tsa-nv:-hne
they are passing him/her	a'-ni-ka'-ne	ani:-hne	ani:-de	a-ni-nv'-ne	a-ni-nv:-hne
Several people are passing something classified to two people:					
they are passing you-&-me ...	ge'-gi-ni-ka'-ne	ge:-gi-ni'-hne	ge:-gi-ni'-de	ge:-gi-ni-nv'-ne	ge:-gi-ni-nv:-hne
they are passing you-two ...	ge-s-di-ka'-ne	ge:-s-di'-hne	ge-s-di:-de	ge:-s-di-nv'-ne	ge:-s-di-nv-hne
they are passing him/her-&-me ...	ge'-gi-ni-ka'-ne	ge-gi-ni'-hne	ge'-s-di-ni:de	ge-gi-ni-nv'-ne	ge-gi-ni-nv:-hne
Several people are passing something classified to several other people:					
they are passing us (them-&-me)	ge'-gi-ni-ka'-ne	ge:-gi-ni'-hne	ge:-gi-ni'-de	ge:-gi-ni-nv'-ne	ge:-gi-ni-nv:-hne
they are passing you (plural)	ge:-tsi-ka'-ne	ge:-tsa'-ne'	ge:-tsa-de	ge:-tsa-nv'-ne	ge:-tsa-nv-hne
they are passing them ...	da-ni-ka'-ne	da'-ni-hne	da-ni'-de	da-ni-nv'-ne	da-ni-nv-hne

SUPPLEMENTARY LIST OF PLANTS, TREES AND VEGETABLES

When there are two Cherokee forms, one is singular and the other is plural. Otherwise, singular and plural are the same, as in English 'deer'.

Trees, plants and parts of plants

acorn	gv:le
ash	dǿ:-tsu
branch (on tree)	u-wa'-n'-ga-tlv, du-wa-n'-ga-tlv-i
branch (off tree)	u-wa'-n'-ga-tlv-nv, tsu-wa'-n'-ga-tlv-nv
brush,	sa-lu-yi
bush	u-da'-tl'-gv, du-da'-tl'-gv
cedar, fir	a'-tsi-na' or a-tsi:-n'; Three plurals: a-ni-tsi-na', a-ni-tsi:-n & tsi-na' de:-tl'-ga
chestnut	u-ni-ge'-n(i)(a)
chinquapin	u-hna-gi:-n(i')(a)
dewberry, boysenberry	u-dlo'-si-nv-da
dogwood	ka-na'-si-ta'
elm	da-wa-tsi:-l(a)(i)
four o'clocks	nv-hga a-tli-gi-li'-sv a-ni-tsi-lv-s-gi
grass, weed	ga-nu-lɉ-(i)
hazelnut or hazelnut bush	yu'-gi-da'
hickory tree	wa-ne?-i
hickory nut or nut	so:-hi
honeysuckle	gv-na-gi'-hl(e)-ge-(i)
huckleberry	ku-wa-ya'
linden, basswood	i:-de-ha
mulberry	ku:-wa'
mushroom	da-wo-li
oak	a-da:-ya
pecan (long nuts)	so:-hi a-ni-nv-hi:-da'
persimmon	sa'-l(i)
pine	no:-ts(i')
redbud	ga-lo-we:-d(i)
root	u-hna-s-de:-tlv, du-hna-s-de:-tlv
sassafras	ka:-n'-s-ta-tsi'
seedling	ga'-koh-di, di-ga'-koh-di
spicebush	noh?-da-tli'
straw, hay, rye	ka-ne'-s-ga'
stump	u-hni'-hl'-g(a)(v)-i, du-hni'-hl'-gv-i
sycamore (white bark)	ko-tsu-ne:-g(a)
thorn (to-prick)	u-tsa-yo:-s-di, tsu-tsa-yo:-s-di

walnut	se:-di
wheat	u-tsa-le:-s-di
willow (it-comes-off)	di-l(i)-ga-li:-s-gi

Vegetables

beans	tu-ya
brown beans	u-ni-wo'-di-ge tu-ya
bush beans (low beans)	tu-ya e-la-di' i'-na-ti'
green beans	tu-ya a-ni-tse-i
white beans	u-ni-ne-g(a) tu-ya
carrots (yellow growers-in-the-ground)	a-ni-da-lo'-ni-ge ga:-do' a-ni'-l'di:-s-gi
cabbage	tsu-ga-de:-ni
cucumber	ga-ga-ma
lettuce	go:-s-da-gi:-s-di (a-go:-s-da a-gi:-s-di means 'something raw to eat')
onion	sv-gi
garden onions (planted they exist)	a-hwi'-sv-nv e-hi
store-bought onions	sv-gi a-da'-na-nv a-hwa-sv-i
wild onions	sv:-gi i'-na-ge e-hi
oranges	a-ni-da-lo'-ni-ge
peanuts	tu-ya ga:-do' a-ni-la-di'-s-gi (beans grown in the ground)
poke greens	dla:-ya-de
pumpkin	i-ya
radish	gi'-ga-ge ga:-do' ga-la-di'-s-gi (red it grows in the ground)
squash	s-qua:-si
tomatoes	da-ma'-tli
turnip	da'-kw'-sa-ni'
watermelon	gv-gi:-s-di
wheat biscuit (see 'wheat')	u-tsa-le:-s-di
wheat biscuits	u-ni-tsa-le:-s-di

Translation	Syllabary	Translation

Lesson IV
say, tell, repeat
  I say   ga-di?-a
  you say   ha-di?-a
  he/she says   a-di?-a

  You and I say   i'-n'-di?-a
  You two say   s-da-di?-a
  Another & I say   o'-s-da-di?-a

  Others and I say   o-tsa-di?-a
  You, plural say   i-tsa-di?-a
  They say   a-n'-di?-a

  You Another or Others
  & I say   i-da-di?-a

Lesson V
go
  I am going, I go   ge:-ga
  you go   he'-ga
  he/she goes   e:-ga

  You and I go   i-ne'-ga
  You two go   s-de:-ga
  Another & I go   o-s-de'-ga

  Others and I go   o-tse:-ga
  You, plural go   i-tse:-ga
  They go   a-ne'-ga

  You Another or Others
  & I go   i-de:-ga

Lesson V
want
  I want   a?-wa-du'-li-(a)
  you want   tsa-du'-li-(a)
  he/she wants   u-du'-li-(a)

  You and I want   gi-na-du'-li-(a)
  You two want   s-da-du'-li-(a)
  Another & I want   o'-gi-na-du'-li-(a)

  Others and I want   o'-ga-du'-li-(a)
  You plural want   i-tsa-du'-li-(a)
  They want   u'-na-du'-li-(a)

  You others & I want   i'-ga-du'-li-(a)

Lesson V
eat, have a meal
  I am eating, having a meal   ga-l'-s-ta-yv-hv'-s-ga
  you are eating   ha-l'-s-ta-yv-hv'-s-ga
  he/she is eating   a-l'-s-ta-yv-hv'-s-ga

  You and I are eating   i-na-l'-s-ta-yv-hv-s-ga
  You two are eating   s-da-l'-s-ta-yv-hv'-s-ga
  Another & I are eating   o-s-da-l'-s-ta-yv-hv'-s-ga

  Others and I are eating   o-tsa-l'-s-ta-yv-hv'-s-ga
  You plural are eating   i-tsa-l'-s-ta-yv-hv'-s-ga
  They are eating   a-na-l'-s-ta-yv-hv'-s-ga

  You others & I eat   i-da-l'-s-ta-yv-hv'-s-ga

Lesson VI
rejoice, be glad, thankful
  I am glad   ga-li-e:-l-ga(i)
  you are glad   ha-li-he'-li-ga
  he/she is glad   a-li-he'-li-ga

  You and I are glad   i-na-li-he'-li-ga
  You two are glad   s-da-li-he'-li-ga
  Another & I are glad   o'-s-da-li-he'-li-ga

  Others and I are glad   o'-tsa-li-he'-li-ga
  You plural are glad   i-tsa-li-he'-li-ga
  They are glad   a-na-li-he'-li-ga

  You others & I are glad   i-da-li-he'-li-ga

Lesson VI
know, understand
  I understand   go-li:-g(a)
  you understand   ho'-hl'-ga
  he/she understands   go'-l'-ga

  You and I understand   i-no'-hl'-ga
  You two understand   s-do'-hl'-ga
  Another & I understand   o-s-do'-hl'-ga

  Others and I understand   o:-tso'-hl'-ga
  You plural understand   i-tso'-l'-ga
  They understand   a-no'-l'-ga

  You another or others
  & I understand   i-do'-l'-ga

Lesson VI
know, know how to
  I know   a-qua'-n(i)-ta
  you know   tsa'-n'-ta
  he/she knows   u:-n'ta

  You and I know   gi-na'-n'-ta
  You two know   s-da:-n'-ta
  Another & I know   o'-gi-na:-n'-ta

  You another or others
  & I know   i-ga:-n'-ta

Lesson VII
do
  I am doing (it)   ga-dv'-ne?-ɑ̸
  you are doing (it)   ha-dv'-ne?-ɑ̸
  he/she is doing (it)   a-dv'-ne?-ɑ̸

  You & I are doing   i-na-dv'-ne?-ɑ̸
  You two are doing   s-da-dv'-ne?-ɑ̸
  Another & I are doing   o'-s-da-dv'-ne?-ɑ̸

  Others & I are doing   o-tsa-dv'-ne?-ɑ̸
  You plural are doing   i-tsa-dv'-ne?-ɑ̸
  They are doing   a-na-dv'-ne?-ɑ̸

  Others & I are doing   i-da-dv'-ne?-ɑ̸

Lesson VIII
buy
   I am buying   a-gi-wa'-s-ga
   you are buying   tsa-wa'-s-ga
   he/she is buying   u-hwa'-s-ga

   You and I are buying   gi-ni-hwa'-s-ga
   You two are buying   s-di-hwa'-s-ga
   Another & I are buying   o'-gi-ni-hwa'-s-ga

   Others & I are buying   o-gi-hwa'-s-ga
   You plural are buying   i-tsi-hwa'-s-ga
   They are buying   u-ni-hwa'-s-ga

   You another or others
   & I buy   i-gi-hwa'-s-ga

Lesson VIII
HAVE (nearby in immediate possession) something weighty of <u>indefinite</u> shape
   I HAVE IT   A-GI-HA
   YOU HAVE IT   TSA-HA
   HE/SHE HAS IT   U-HA

   YOU & I HAVE IT   GI-NI-HA
   YOU TWO HAVE IT   S-DI-HA
   ANOTHER & I HAVE IT   O-GI-NI-HA

   OTHERS & I HAVE IT   O-GI-HA
   YOU PLURAL HAVE IT   I-TSI-HA
   THEY HAVE IT   U-NI-HA

   YOU ANOTHER or OTHERS
   & I HAVE IT   I-GI-HA

HAVE something live
   I HAVE IT/HIM/HER   A-GI-KA'-HA
   YOU HAVE IT   TSA-KA-HA
   HE/SHE HAS IT   U-WE-KA-HA

   YOU & I HAVE IT   GI-NI-KA-HA
   YOU TWO HAVE IT   S-DI-KA-HA
   ANOTHER & I HAVE IT   O-GI-NI-KA-HA

   OTHERS & I HAVE IT   O-GI-KA-HA
   YOU PLURAL HAVE IT   I-TSI-KA-HA
   THEY HAVE IT   U-NI-KA-HA

   YOU ANOTHER or OTHERS
   & I HAVE IT   I-GI-KA-HA

HAVE (something <u>flexible</u>, broad in proportion to weight)

I HAVE IT	A-GI-NA-(A)
YOU HAVE IT	TSA-NA-(A)
HE/SHE HAVE IT	U-NA-(A)
YOU & I HAVE IT	GI-NI-NA-(A)
YOU TWO HAVE IT	S-DI-NA-(A)
ANOTHER & I HAVE IT	O-GI-NI-NA-(A)
OTHERS & I HAVE IT	O-GI-NA-(A)
YOU PLURAL HAVE IT	I-TSI-NA-(A)
THEY HAVE IT	U-NI-NA-(A)
YOU ANOTHER or OTHERS & I HAVE IT	I-GI-NA-(A)

HAVE (something <u>long</u>, narrow inflexible)

I HAVE IT	A-QUV'-YA
YOU HAVE IT	TSV-YA
HE/SHE HAS IT	U-WA-YA
YOU & I HAVE IT	GI-NV-YA
YOU TWO HAVE IT	S-DV-YA
ANOTHER & I HAVE IT	O-GI-NY-YA
OTHERS & I HAVE IT	O-GV-YA
YOU PLURAL HAVE IT	I-TSV-YA
THEY HAVE IT	U-NV-YA
YOU ANOTHER or OTHERS & I HAVE IT	

HAVE (something <u>liquid</u>)

I HAVE IT	A-GI-NE?-A
YOU HAVE IT	TSA-NE?-A
HE/SHE HAS IT	U-NE?-A
YOU & I HAVE IT	GI-NI-NE?-A
YOU TWO HAVE IT	S-DI-NE?-A
ANOTHER & I HAVE IT	O-GI-NI-NE?-A
OTHERS & I HAVE IT	O-GI-NE?-A
YOU PLURAL HAVE IT	I-TSI-NE?-A
THEY HAVE IT	U-NI-NE-HA
YOU ANOTHER or OTHERS & I HAVE IT	I-GI-NE-HA

Lesson X
drink

I am drinking	ga-di-ta'-s-ga
you are drinking	ha-di-ta'-s-ga
he/she is drinking	a-di-ta'-s-ga
You & I are drinking	i'-n'-di-ta'-s-ga
You two are drinking	s-da-ti-ta'-s-ga
Another & I are drinking	o'-s-da-ti-ta'-s-ga
Others & I are drinking	o-tsa-di-ta'-s-ga
You plural are drinking	i-tsa-di-ta'-s-ga
They are drinking	a-na-di-ta-s-ga
You Another or Others & I are drinking	i-da-ti-ta'-s-ga

Lesson XI
originate, be of a certain origin. With -ya, originate truly, be an Indian.
Without -ya: to be descended from, to be of a certain origin
With -ya: to originate truly, to be an Indian

I originate (truly)	tsi-yv'-wi-(ya)
you originate (truly)	hi-yv'-wi-(ya)
he/she originates (truly)	a-yv'-wi-(ya)
You & I originate (truly)	i-ni-yv'-wi-(ya)
You two originate (truly)	s-di-yv'-wi-(ya)
Another & I originate (truly)	o:-s-di-yv'-wi-(ya)
Others & I originate (truly)	o-tsi-yv'-wi-(ya)
You plural originate (truly)	i-tsi-yv-wi-(ya)
They originate (truly)	a-ni-yv-wi-(ya)
You another or others & I originate (truly)	i-di-yv-wi-(ya)

Lesson XI
speak, make a speech

I am speaking	tsi-wo'-ni-a
you are speaking	hi-wo:-ni-(a)
he/she is speaking	ga-wo:-ni-(a)
You & I are speaking	i-ni-wo'-ni-a
You two are speaking	s-di-wo'-ni-a
Another & I are speaking	o'-s-di-wo:-ni-a
Others & I are speaking	o-tsi-wo:-ni-a
You Plural are speaking	i-tsi-wo:-ni-a
They are speaking	a-ni-wo:-ni-a

304

(cont.)
You Another or Others
& I are speaking   i-di-wo'-ni-a

Lesson XI
think, think that, be of the opinion that
  I think   ge'-li-a
  you think   he-li-a
  he/she thinks   e'-li-a

  You & I think   i-ne'-li-a
  You two think   s-de'-li-a
  Another & I think   o-s-de'-li-a

  Others & I think   o-tse'-li-a
  You plural think   i-tse'-li-a
  They think   a-ne'-li-a

  You, another or others
  & I think   i-de'-li-a

Lesson XII
arrive, get there, come back, return
  I am arriving (just now)   tsi-lu?-gi
  you arrive   hi-lu?-gi
  he/she arrives   ga-lu'-gi

  You & I arrive   i-ni-lu-gi
  You two arrive   s-di-lu-gi
  Another & I arrive   o'-s-di-lu'-gi

  Others & I arrive   o-tsi-lu'-gi
  You plural arrive   i-tsi-lu-gi
  They arrive   a-ni-lu'-gi

  You, another or others
  & I arrive   i-di-lu'-gi

Lesson XII
hear
  I hear   ga-tv'-gi-(a)
  you hear   ha-tv'-gi-(a)
  he/she hears   a-tv'-gi-(a)

(cont.)
You & I hear	i-n'-tv'-gi-(a)
You two hear	s-da-tv'-gi-(a)
Another & I hear	o:-s'-tv'-gi-(a)

Others & I hear	o:-ts'-tv'-gi-(a)
You plural hear	i'-ts'-tv'-gi-(a)
They hear	a-n'-tv-gi-(a)

| You, another or others & I hear | i'-d'-tv'-gi-(a) |

Lesson XII
say something
I say it	ni-tsi-we?-a
you say it	hni-we?-a
he/she says it	ni-ga-we?-a

You & I say it	ni-ni-we?-a
You two say it	ni-s-di-we?-a
Another & I say it	no'-s-di-we?-a

Others & I say it	no-tsi-we?-a
You plural say it	ni-tsi-we?-a
They say it	na-ni-we?-a

| You, another or others & I say it | ni-di-we?-a |

Lesson XIII
Migrate, move out
I am moving out	ga-da-nv?-a'
you are moving out	ha-da-nv?-a
he/she is moving out	a-da-nv?-a

You & I are moving out	i-na-dv-nv?-a
You two are moving out	s-da-dv-nv?-a
Another & I are moving out	o-s-da-dv-nv?-a

Others & I are moving out	o'-tsa-dv-nv?-a
You plural are moving out	i-tsa-dv-nv?-a
They are moving out	a-na-dv-nv?-a

| You, another or others & I are moving out | i-da-dv-nv?-a |

306

Lesson XIV
grow, grow up, or grow taller
  I am growing   ga-tv'-s-ga
   you are growing   ha-tv'-s-ga
   he/she is growing   a-tv'-s-ga

   You & I are growing   de-na-tv'-s-ga
   You two are growing   de:-s-da-tv'-s-ga
   Another & I are growing   do'-s-da-tv'-s-ga

   Others & I are growing   do-tsa-tv'-s-ga
   You plural are growing   de:-tsa-tv'-s-ga
   They are growing   da-n(a)-tv'-s-ga

   You, another or others
   & I are growing   de-da-tv'-s-ga

Lesson XIV
plant   sv:-ga (recent past)
  I am planting   tsi-hwi-sv'-s-ga
   you are planting   hi-wi-sv'-s-ga
   he/she is planting   a-hwi-sv'-s-ga

   You & I are planting   i-ni-hwi-sv'-s-ga
   You two are planting   s-di-hwi-sv'-s-ga
   Another & I are planting   o'-s-di-hwi-sv'-s-ga

   Others & I are planting   o-tsi-hwi-sv'-s-ga
   You plural are planting   i-tsi-hwi-sv'-s-ga
   They are planting   a-ni-hwi-sv'-s-ga

   You, another or others
   & I are planting   i-di-hwi-sv'-s-ga

Lesson XIV
become fatter
  I am fattening   ga-l(i)-tso?-v'-s-ga
   you are fattening   ha-l'-tso?-v'-s-ga
   he/she is fattening   a-l'-tso-hv'-s-ga

   You & I are fattening   i-na-l'-tso-hv'-s-ga
   You two are fattening   s-da-l'-tso-hv'-s-ga
   Another & I are fattening   o:-s-da-l'-tso-hv'-s-ga

(cont.)
Others & I are fattening   o-tsa-l'-tso-hv'-s-ga
You plural are fattening   i-tsa-l'-tso-hv'-s-ga
They are fattening   a-na-l'-tso-hv'-s-ga

You, another or others
& I are fattening   i-da-l'-tso-hv'-s-ga

Lesson XIV
eat (something)
 I am eating   tsi-gi?-a
 you are eating   hi-gi?-a
 he/she is eating   a-gi?-a

 You & I are eating   i-ni-gi?-a
 You two are eating   s-di-gi?-a
 Another & I are eating   o'-s-di'-gi?-a

 Others & I are eating   o'-tsi-gi?-a
 You plural are eating   i-tsi-gi?-a
 They are eating   a-ni-gi?-a

 You, another or others
 & I are eating   i-di-gi?-a

Lesson XV
put on raised surface, such as a piece of furniture, shelf, drainboard,etc.
 I just put them on it   de-tsi-tla-hv'-ga
 you just put them on it   de-hi-tla-hv'-ga
 he/she just put them on it da'-tla-hv'-ga

 You & I just put them on it de-ni-tla-hv'-ga
 You two just put them on it de:-s-di-tla-hv'-ga
 Another & I just put them on it do:-s-di-tla-hv'-ga

 Others & I just put them on it do-tsi-tla-hv'-ga
 You plural just put them on it de-tsi-tla-hv'-ga
 They just put them on it   da-ni-tla-hv'-ga

 You, another or others
 & I just put them on it   de-di-tla-hv'-ga

Lesson XV
see (something. Not 'understand')
  I see   tsi-go:-ti?-(ɑ̸)
  you see   hi-go'-ti?-(ɑ̸)
  he/she sees   a-go:-ti-(ɑ̸)

  You & I see   i-ni-go'-ti-(a)
  You two see   s-di-go'-ti-(a)
  Another & I see   o'-s-di-go'-ti-(a)

  Others & I see   o-tsi-go'-ti-(a)
  You plural see   i-tsi-go'-ti-(a)
  They see   a-ni-go'-ti-(a)

  You, another or others
  & I see   i-di-go'-ti-(a)

Lesson XV
put on raised surface
  I am putting them on it   de-tsi-tla-hv'-s-ga
  you are putting them on it de-hi-tla-hv'-s-ga
  he/she are putting them
    on it   da'-tla-hv'-s-ga

  You & I are putting them
    on it   de-ni-tla-hv'-s-ga
  You two are putting them
    on it   de-s-di-tla-hv'-s-ga
  Another & I are putting
    them on it   do'-s-di-tla-hv'-s-ga

  Others & I are putting
    them on it   do-tsi-tla-hv'-s-ga
  You plural are putting
    them on it   de-tsi-tla-hv'-s-ga
  They are putting them
    on it   da-ni-tla-hv'-s-ga

  You, another or others
  & I are putting them
  on it   de-di-tla-hv'-s-ga

Lesson XV
sit down
   I just sat down   ga'-l'-s-du-tlv'-ga
   you   ha'-l'-s-du-tlv'-ga
   he/she   a'-l'-s-du-tlv'-ga

   You and I   di-na'-l'-s-du-tlv'-ga
   You two   di-s-da'-l'-s-du-tlv'-ga
   Another & I   do-s-da-l'-s-du-tlv'-ga

   Others & I   da-yo-tsa-nv-ni
   You plural   da-tsa-nv-ni
   They   da-tsa-nv-ni

   You, another or others
   & I   da-da-nv'-ni

Lesson XV
sit
   I am sitting   a-quo'-tla
   you are sitting   tso'-tla
   he/she is sitting   u-wo'-tla

   You & I are sitting   de-gi-no'-tla
   You two are sitting   de-s-do'-tla
   Another & I are sitting   do-gi-no'-tla

   Others & I are sitting   o-tsi:-na
   You plural are sitting   i-tsi:-na
   They are sitting   a-ni:-na

   You, another or others
   & I are sitting   i-di'-na

Diagrams of Cherokee and English personal pronouns

Re-read Lesson 16. Examine the diagrams attached to this appendix and refer to them as you read further. The Cherokee diagram represents bound personal pronouns as they are used in the average Cherokee active verb. In Cherokee, the term 'active verb' covers all transitive verbs and some that are not completely transitive.

The personal pronoun 'I' (first person singular) has a favored position in written English. It is the only personal pronoun that is always capitalized. 'I' has no special position in Cherokee.

The English pronominal system is vague in areas that concern the domain of 'I' in combination with other personal pronouns. In English, 'I' is always dominant. That is, when 'I' combines with any person or persons the result is always 'we', first person plural.

Examples:
I plus another equals we
I plus you   equals we
I plus others equals we
I plus you plus another or others equals we

In Cherokee, each person or combination of persons retains a recognizable identity. Re-examine the diagrams and confirm this in your own mind.

The English personal pronoun system has lost its distinction between 2nd person singular and 2nd person plural. Not long ago, the English language included both a singular and a plural pronoun for 'you', but 'thou' has dropped out of use.

English 3rd person singular pronouns (he, she, it) are divided according to sex, but English usage is not consistent. 'He' is always distinguished from 'she' in humans, but animals are often called 'it' like inanimate objects, and some objects, things such as boats or other machines are called 'she'. Cherokee does not recognize sex as a category, but is consistent in its divisions of 3rd person as follows:

There is no distinction of sex in Cherokee pronouns; he and she are lumped together as 'another'. There is no distinction in Cherokee between the pronoun for he, she, or it. The verb used shows whether the subject will be 'another' (an animate being of either sex, including plants and some natural objects), or 'it' (an inanimate object). In Cherokee, 'it' (an inanimate object), cannot be the <u>subject</u> of an active verb, since inanimate objects cannot act of their own volition. An inanimate object (a thing) must either be the <u>object</u> of an active verb, or it can be the <u>subject</u> of certain inactive verbs. Inactive verbs may or may not also be classifying verbs.

311

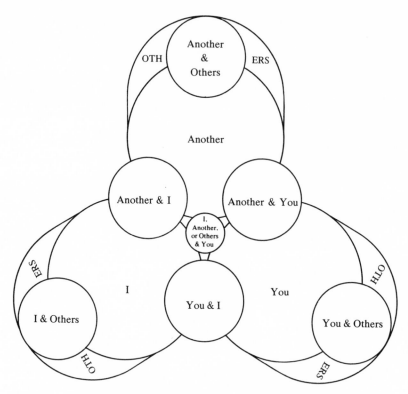

CHEROKEE PERSONAL PRONOUN SYSTEM

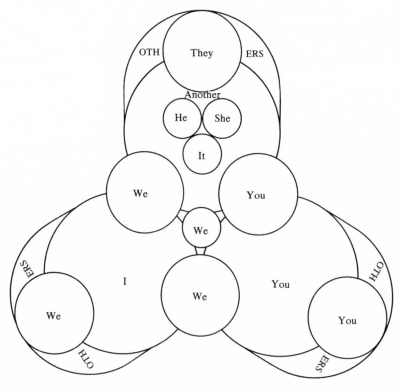

ENGLISH PERSONAL PRONOUN SYSTEM

When using classifying verbs, Cherokee distinguishes 'it-long' from 'it-liquid', 'it-solid', 'it-flexible', and 'him-or-her-live' by means of precision pronouns embedded in each classifying verb. When <u>not</u> using classifying verbs there is less development of 3rd person singular pronouns in Cherokee than in English.

English classifies number rather loosely and deals only with one (singular), and one plus another or others (plural).

Cherokee classifies one (singular), one plus another (dual), one plus others (plural), and two plus others (comprehensive plural).

Cherokee distinguishes between third person <u>plural</u> pronouns in more detail than English does. Several living beings (a-ni, u-ni-) are distinct from several inanimate objects (di-) in Cherokee, but in English both living and non-living third person plural pronouns are called 'they'.

Examples:
    it plus it equals they
    he plus she equals they
    he plus he equals they, etc.

Cherokee pronouns are divided not only according to number (1, 2 or more) but also according to person more painstakingly than English.

Examples:
    1st person plus 3rd person singular in Cherokee is   o-s-d-   or o-gi-n-
    1st person plus 3rd person plural in Cherokee is   o-ts-   or o-g-
    1st person plus 2nd person singular in Cherokee is   i-n-   or gi-n-
    1st person plus 2nd person plural in Cherokee is   i-d-   or i-g-

Cherokee personal pronouns therefore would seem to be more accurate and more comprehensive than those of English.

SUPPLEMENTARY LIST OF ANIMALS, INSECTS, REPTILES, AND BIRDS

Where there are two Cherokee forms below, one is singular and the other is plural. Otherwise, singular and plural are the same, as in English 'deer'.

Animals and parts of animals
chipmunk	ki-yu:-ga
horn, antler	yo-n(a)(i), tsu-hyo-na
horn, antler	u-lu-gv-gi, du-lu-gv-gi
set of horns, antlers	du-tl'-gv?-i
mink	e:-tli
mole	ta-ni:-qua
monkey	a-da-le-s-gi-yi'-s-gi, a-n'-da-le-s-gi-yi'-s-gi
mouse, rat	tsi-s-de-tsi
tail	ga-ni-da-dv, da-ni-ni'-da-dv
tracks	du-la-si-hnv
whisker	a-ha-nu-lv, da-ha-nu-lv-sv
weasel (yellow rat)	da-lo'-ni-ge tsi-s-de-tsi

Insects
a biting insect	di-(n')-da-tsv:-s-gi tsv-s-go'-yi
ant	do-sv-da-li
bee	wa-du-li:-si
earthworm	u-tsi:-ya, u-ni-tsi:-ya
fly	tvh?-ga
louse, lice	ti:-na'
spider	(a-ni-)ka-na-ne'-s-gi
tick	gu-ga-(i)
wasp, hornet	ka-n(a)-ts(i)-s-de-tsi, a-ni-ka-n(a)-ts(i)-s-de:-tsi
worms, grubs, insects, unpleasant bugs	s-go-yi, tsv-s-go'-yi
yellowjacket	tsa-s-ga-ya

Reptiles and Fish
alligator (also, iron pot)	tsu-la-s-gi, tsu-n'-la-s-gi
blacksnake (climber)	ga-le-gi
bullfrog	ka-nu-na
catfish	tsu-li-s-da-na:-li, tsu-n'-li-s-da-na:-li
crawfish	tsi:-s-dv-na
fish	a-tsa?-di
lizard	ti-yo'-ha-li'
perch	a-go:-li, a-ni-go:-li
rattlesnake	u-tso'-n(a)-ti', u-n'-tso'-n'-ti'
snake	i'-na-dv
toad, tadpole	teh?-ga
water mocassin	u'-ga-n'-te:-na, u-ni-ga-n'-te:-na

Birds
    bluebird   tsa-quo'-la-de
    chickadee   tsi-ga-li:-li
    fox sparrow   wa:-kv:-ta
    meadowlark (star)   no:-k'-si'
    sapsucker   kv-gwo:-ha
    winter wren   tsi-s-tsi-s or: tsi-tsi
    wren   tse-ni'
    yellow mockingbird   hu-hu

315

APPENDIX X

CAPITALS are used below for English subject pronouns; small letters for object pr.

	Love GV GE YU I	Know GV YO LI GA	Teach DE GV YE YO HV S GA	See GV GO TI A
I..me (I-myself)	a-gwa-da-ge-yu	ga-da-yo-li-ga	de-ga-da-ye-yo-hv-s-ga	ga-da-go-ti-a
I..you	gv-ge-yu-i	gv-yo-li-ga	de-gv-ye-yo-hv-s-ga	gv-goh-ti-a
I..him/her	tsi-ge-yu	tsi-yo-li-ga	de-tsi-ye-yo-hv-s-ga	tsi:-goh-ti-a
I..it		go-li:-ga		tsi-go'-ti-a
I..you-&-me	s-dv-ge'-yu	s-dv-yo-li-ga	de-s-dv-ye-yo-hv-s-ga	s-dv-go-ti-a
I..you-two				
I..another-&-me				
I..us (I-other-&-me)	i-tsv-ge-yu	i-tsv-yo-li-ga	de-tsv-ye-yo-hv-s-ga	i-tsv-go-ti-a
I..you (plural)	ga-tsi-ge-yu	ga-tsi-yo-li-ga	de-ga-tsi-ye-yo-hv-s-ga	ga-tsi-go-ti-a
I..them (live)	da-gi-ge'-yu	de-go-hl'-ga		de-tsi-go-ti-a
I..them (things)				
I-you-another-or-others-&-me				
YOU-me	s-gi-ge'-yu	s-quo'-hl'-ga	de-s-que-hyo-hv-s-ga	s-gi-go'-ti-a
YOU-you (YOU-yourself)	tsa-da-ge'-yu	a-da-do'-hl'-ga	de-ha-da-de-yo-hv-s-ga	ha-da-go'-ti-a
YOU-him/her	hi-ge'-yu	hi-yo-li-ga(h/h)	de-ga-tsi-ye-yo-hv-s-ga	hi:-goh-ti-a
YOU-it		ho:-hl'-ga(it)		hi-go-ti-a
YOU-you-&-me				
YOU-you-&-another				
YOU-another-&-me	s-gi-ni-ge'-yu	s-gi-no'-l'-ga	de-s-gi-ne-yo-hv-s-ga	s-gi-ni-go-ti-a
YOU-others-&-me (YOU-us)	i-s-gi-ge'-yu	i-s-go-hl'-ga	de-s-ge-yo-hv-s-ga	i-s-gi-go-ti-a
YOU (singular)-you-(plural)				
YOU-them (living)	de-hi-ge-yu	de-ho-hl'-ga	de-he-hyo-hv-s-ga	de-hi-go-ti-a
YOU-them (living)				ga-hi-go-ti-a
YOU-them (things)				de-tsi-go-ti-a
YOU-y-a-or-o-&-me			de-s-gi-ye-yo-hv-s-ga	

APPENDIX X

Love	Know	Teach	See	SUBJECT, object pronouns
a-gi-ge'-yu	a-gwo'-l'-ga	da-gwe-yo-hv-s-ga	a-gi-go-ti-a	HE/SHE..me
tsa-ge'-yu	tso-l'-ga	deh-tseh-yo-hv-s-ga	tsa-go-ti-a	HE/SHE..you
u-ge'-yu	a-go-li:-ga(h/h)	de-ge-yo-hv-s-ga	a-tsi-go-ti-a	HE/SHE..him/her
	go:-hl'-ga		a-go-ti-a(it)	
u-da-ge'-yu	a-da-do'-l'-ga	da-da-de-yo-hv-s-ga	a-da-go-ti-a	HE/SHE..himself/ herself
gi-ni-ge'-yu	gi-no:-tl'-ga	deh-gi-neh-yo-hv-s-ga	gi-ni-go-ti-a	HE/SHE..you-&-me
s-di-ge'-yu	s-do-hl'-ga	deh-s-de-hyo-hv-s-ga	s-di-go-ti-a	HE/SHE..you-two
o'-gi-ni-ge'-yu	o'-gi-no'-hl'-ga	do-gi-neh-hyo-hv-s-ga	o'-gi-ni-go-ti-a	HE/SHE..another-&-me
		o-gi-neh-yo-hv-s-ga		
		tso-gi-neh-yo-hv-s-ga		
o-gi-ge'-yu	o-go'-hl'-ga	do-ge?-hyo-hv-s-ga	o-tsi-go-ti-a	HE/SHE..us(them-&-me)
i-tsi-ge'-yu	i-tso-hl'-ga	de-tse-yo-hv-s-ga	i-tsi-go-ti-a	HE/SHE..you(plural)
du-ge'-yu	de-go'-hl'-ga	deh-geh-yo-hv-s-ga	da-go-ti-a	HE/SHE..them
i-gi-ge'-yu	i-go-hl'-ga	de-ge-hyo-hv-s-ga	i-gi-go-ti-a	HE/SHE..y,a-or-o-&-me
------	------	------	------	YOU-&-I..me
e:-ni-ge-yu	i-no'-hl'-ga(it)	------	------	YOU-&-I..you
	e:-no-li-ga			
	------	eh-ne-hyo-hv-s-ga	e:-ni-go-ti-a	YOU-&-I..him/her/it
di-gi-n'-da-ge'-yu	di-n'-da-do'-l'-gi	do-s-da-da-de-yo-hv-s-ga	e:-da-go-ti-a	YOU-&-I..selves
	------	do-s-da-da-de-yo-hv-s-ga	de:-n'-da-go-ti-a or: do'-sd-a-da-go-ti-a	YOU-&-I..one another
------	------	------	------	YOU-&-I..you-two
------	------	------	------	YOU-&-I..another-&-me
------	------	------	------	YOU-&-I..us(them-&-me)
------	------	------	------	YOU-&-I..you(plural)
de:-ni-ge'-yu	di-no'-hl'-gi	deh-neh-yo-hv-s-ga	de:-ni-go-ti-a (living or not) ge:ni-go-ti-a (living)	YOU-&-I..them(living)
------	------	------	------	YOU-&-I..y,a-or-o-&-me

317

Love	Know	Teach	See	
s-gi-ni-ge'-yu	s-gi-no-hl'-gi	deh-s-gi-neh-yo-hv-s-ga	s-gi-ni-go-ti-a	YOU-TWO..me
e:-s-di-ge'-yu	e-s-do'-li-gi	deh-s-de-yo-hv-s-ga	e:-s-di-go-ti-a*	YOU-TWO..you(sing..)
	s-do:-hl'-gi(it)			YOU-TWO..him/her
di-s-da-da-ge'-yu		deh-s-da-da-deh-yo-hv-s-ga	s-da-da-go-ti-a	YOU-TWO..you-&-me
s-gi-ni-ge'-yu / tsi-s-gi-ni-ge'-yu	s-gi-no-hl'-gi	deh-s-gi-ne-yo-hv-s-ga	s-gi-ni-go-ti	YOU-TWO..yourselves
s-gi-ni-ge'-yu	s-gi-no-hl'-gi(a)	deh-s-gi-ne-yo-hv-s-ga	s-gi-ni-go-ti-a	YOU-TWO...us two
de-s-di-ge'-yu	di-s-do'-hl'-gi	deh-s-de-yo-hv-s-ga	de-s-di-go-ti-a	YOU-TWO...us(o-&-me)
				YOU-TWO...you(plural)
				YOU-TWO...them
				YOU-TWO...y,a-or-o-&-me
s-tv-ge-yu	s-dv-yo'-li::-gi	deh-s-dv-ye-yo-hv-s-ga	s-dv-go'-ti-a	A-&-I..me
o-s-ti-ge'-yu	o-s-do:-hl'-gi	do-s-de-yo-hv-s-ga	o-s-di-go-ti-a	A-&-I..you
o-gi-ni-ge'-yu	o-gi-no'-l'-gi		o-s-di-go-ti-a	A-&-I..him/her
				A-&-I..it
s-dv-ge'-yu	s-dv-yo'-li-gi	de-s-dv-ye-yo-hv-s-ga	s-dv-go-ti-a	A-&-I..you-&-me
				A-&-I..you-two
tso-gi-n'-da-ge'-yu / or: do-gi-n-da-ge'-yu	tso-s-ta-da-do'-l'-gi	do-s-da-da-de-yo-hv-s-ga	do-s-da-da'-go-ti-a	A-&-I..ourselves
i-tsv-ge'-yu	i-tsv-yo-li-gi	de-tsv-ye-yo-hv-s-ga	i-tsv-go-ti-a	A-&-I..us(them-&-me)
do-s-ti-ge'-yu	tso-s-to:-li-gi (living) or: tso-s-to'-hl'-gi	do-s-de-hyo-hv-s-ga	do-s-di-go'-ti-a	A-&-I..you(plural)
				A-&-I..them
				A-&-I..y,a-or-o-&-me

APPENDIX X

Love	Know	Teach	See	
i'-s-gi-ge'-yu	i-s-go'-hl'-gi	de-s-ge-yo-hv-s-ga	i-s-gi-go-ti	YOU(PLURAL)..me
-------	e-tso'-li-gi	-------	-------	YOU(PL.)..you(sing.)
e:-tsi-ge'-yu	e:-tso-hl'-gi	de-tse-yo-hv-s-ga	e:-tsi-go-ti	YOU(PL.)..him/her
-------	-------	-------	-------	YOU(PL.)..it
-------	-------	-------	-------	
				YOU(PL.)..you-&-me
				YOU(PL.)..you-two
				YOU(PL.)..another-&-me
				YOU(PL.)..us(them-&-me)
				YOU(PL.)..you(pl.)(-selves or one another)
				YOU(PL.)..them
				YOU(PL.)..y,a-o-&-me
gv-gi-ge'-yu	gv:-gwo'-hl'-gi	de-gv-gwe-yo-hv-s-ga	gv-gi-go-ti-a	THEY..me
ge:-htsa-ge'-yu	ge-tso'-l'-gi	ge:-tse-yo-hv-s-ga	ge:-tsa-go-ti-a	THEY..you
u-ni-ge'-yu	a-no'-hl'-ga(i)	a-ne-yo-hv-s-ga	a-ni-go-ti	THEY..him/her
ge-gi-ni-ge-yu	ge-gi-no-hl'-ga	ge-gi-ne-yo-hv-s-ga	ge-gi-ni-go-ti	THEY..you-&-me
ge-s-di-ge-yu	ge:-s-do-hl'-gi	ge-s-de-yo-hv-s-ga	ge-s-di-go-ti	THEY..you-two
go-gi-ni-ge-yu	go-gi-no'-hl'-gi	go-gi-ne-yo-hv-s-ga	go-gi-ni-go-ti	THEY..another-&-me
			ge-gi-go-ti-a	
ge-tsi-ge-yu	ge-tso-l'-gi	ge-ge-yo-hv-s-ga	ge-tsi-go-ti	THEY..you(plural)
du-ni-ge'-yu	di-noh-l'-gi	de-tse-yo-hv-s-ga	da-ni-go-ti-a	THEY..them
du-n'-da-ge'-yu		da-n'-da-de-yo-hv-s-ga	a-n'-da-go'-ti	THEY..themselves or one another
-------	di-n'-do'-hl'-gi	-------		THEY..y,a-o-&-me
	We all know one another	We all know one another, see one another, love one another	i-da-da-go-ti	i-da-da-go-ti
de-ga-da-ge'-yu		de-da-da-de-hyo-hv-s-ga	di-da-da-do-l'-gi	di-da-da-do-l'-gi

319

PRESENT	FUTURE	PAST	INFINITIVE
ga-da-nv?-a I am moving out a-da-nv?-a he/she is moving out	da-ga-da-nv'-si' I will move out dv-da-nv:-si' he/she will move out	a-qua-da-nv-sv?i I moved out u-da-nv-sv?-i he/she moved out	a-gwa-da-nv:-s-di
tsi-wo:-ni?-a I am speaking ga-wo:-ni?-a he/she is speaking	da-tsi-wo'-ni-si I will speak da-ga-wo'-ni-si he/she will speak	a-gi-wo-ni:-sv?-i I spoke, was speaking u-wo-ni:-sv?-i he/she spoke	a-gi-wo-ni-hi:-s-di
ge:-li-a I think e:-li-a he/she thinks	da-ge-li:-si' I will think da-ye-li:-si' he/she will think	a-que-li:-sv?-i I thought u-we-li'-sv?-i he/she thought	a-que-li'-s-di
ga-l'-tso?-v-s-ga I am getting fatter a-l'-tso?-v'-s-ga he/she is getting fatter	da-tsi-l'-tso?-v?-si' I will get fat da-ga-l'-tso?-hv?-si' he/she will get fat	a-qua-l'-tso-hv'-sv?-i I got fat u-l'-tso-hv-sv?-i he/she got fat	a-gwa-l'-tso-hv-s-di
a-ki-hwa'-s-ga I am buying u-hwa'-s-ga he/she is buying	dv-ki-hwa:-si I will buy da-yu-hwa'-si he/she will buy	a-ki-wa'-s-sv?-i I bought u-hwa'-sv (i) he/she bought	a-ki-wa-hi:-s-di
ga-li?-e'-li-ga I am happy a-li-he'-li-ga he/she is happy	da-ga-li-e-li-tsi I will be happy dv-li-he-li-tsi he/she will be happy	a-qua-li-he-li-tsv?-i I was happy u-li-he-li-tsv?-i he/she was happy	a-gwa-li-he'-li-s-di

320

APPENDIX XI

PRESENT	FUTURE	PAST	INFINITIVE
tsi-lu?-gi I (just) arrived ga-lu?-gi he/she (just) arrived	da-tsi-lu?-tsi I will arrive da-ga-lu?-tsi he/she will arrive	a-gi-lu?-tsv?-i I arrived u-lu?-tsv?-i he/she arrived (tsi-luh-gv,	a-gi-lu-hi-s-di
go-li:-ga I know go'-l'-ga he/she knows	da-go-li'-tsi I will know da-go'-li'-tsi he/she will know	a-quo'-l'-tsv?-i I knew u-wo'-l'-tsv?-i he/she knew	a-gwo-l'-s-di or a-gwo-(t)l(i)-s-di
tsi-hwi-sv'-s-ga I am planting a-hwi-sv'-s-ga he/she is planting	da-tsi-hwi'-sv-ni I will plant dv-hwi-sv-ni he/she will plant	a-gi-hwi'-sv-nv?-i I planted, was planting u-hwi'-sv-nv?-i he/she planted, was planting	a-gi-hwi-sv:-s-di
ga-tv-gi?-a I hear a-tv'-gi?-a he/she hears	da-ga'-tv-ga'-ni I will hear dv-tv-ga'-ni he/she will hear	a-g'-tv-ga-nv?-i I heard u'-tv-ga'-nv?-i he/she heard	
ga-l'-s-ta-yv-hv'-s-ga I am feeding, having a meal a-l'-s-ta-yv-hv'-s-ga he/she is feeding, having a meal	da-ga'-l'-s-ta-yv-hni I will have a meal dv'-l'-s-ta-yv'-hni he/she will feed, have a meal	a-qua-l'-s-ta-yv-hnv?-i I had a meal, was feeding u-l'-s-ta-yv-hnv?-i he/she fed, had a meal	a-qua-l'-s-ta-i-di
de-tsi-tla-hv'-s-ga I am putting them on it da-tla-hv'-s-ga he/she is putting them on it	do-da-tsi-tla-hni I will put them on it do-dv-tla-hni he/she will put them on it	da-u-k'-tla-hvnv?-i I put them on it du'-tl'-hnv?-i he/she put them on it	di-gw'-tla-hv'-s-di

321

Present, Future, Past and Infinitives of 25 common verbs -

PRESENT	FUTURE	PAST	INFINITIVE

a-qua-duꞋ-li?-a
  I want
u-duꞋ-li?-a
  he/she wants
	dv-qua-duꞋ-lv-hi
	  I will want
	da-yu-duꞋ-lv-hi
	  he/she will want
		a-qua-du-lv-hv?-i
		  I wanted
		u-du-lv-hv?-i
		  he/she wanted	

tsi-go:-ti-a
  I see
a-go:-ti-a
  he/she sees
	da-tsi-go:?-i
	  I will see
	dv-go-hiꞋ
	  he/she will see
		a-gi-go-hv?-i
		  I saw
		u-go-hv?-i
		  he/she saw
			tsi-go-tv-di-i
			a-gi-go-tv-di

TSI-GI?-A
  I am eating it
A-GI?-A
  he/she is eating it
	DAꞋ-TSI-GIꞋ
	  I will eat it
	DV:-GIꞋ
	  he/she will eat it
		A-GI-GV?-I
		  I ate it
		U-GV?-I
		  he/she ate it
			A-GI-GIꞋ-S-DI
			  me-to-eat
			A-GIꞋ-S-DI
			  me-to-eat (a little
			    at a time)

ga-di-ta-s-ga
  I am drinking
a-di-taꞋ-s-ga
  he/she is drinking
	da-ga-di-ta-hi
	  I will drink
	dvꞋ-nꞋ-di-ta-hi
	8 he/she will drink
		a-qua-di-ta-hv?-i
		  I drank, was drinking
		u-di-ta-hv?-i
		  he/she drank, was drinking
			a-wa-di::-ta-s-di
			  to drink

ga-tvꞋ-s-ga
  I am growing
a-tvꞋ-s-ga
  he/she is growing
	da-ga-tvꞋ-si
	  I will grow
	dv-tvꞋ-s-iꞋ
	  he/she will grow
		a-qua-tvꞋ-sv?-i
		  I grew
		u-tv-sv?-i
		  he/she grew
			a-gwa-tv-hi::-s-di
			  for me-to-grow

ni-tsi-we?-a
  I say it
ni-ga-we?-a
  he/she said it
    says it
	ni-daꞋ-tsi-we::-siꞋ
	  I will say it
	ni-da-tsi-we:-siꞋ
	  he/she will say it
		na-gi-we:-sv?-i (se-hv)
		  I said it
		nu-we:-sv?-i
		  he/she said it (some time ago)
			ya-gi-we:-s-di-i
			  for-me-to-say-it

322

APPENDIX XI

PRESENT	FUTURE	PAST	INFINITIVE
a-gi-lv:-kwⁱ-di* it pleases me (I like..)	da-tsi-lv-quoⁱ-ta-niⁱ it will please me	da-gi-lvⁱ-kⁱ-ta-nv?-i it pleased me	a-gi-lv:-kwⁱ-di*
u-lvⁱ-kⁱ-di he/she likes	da-ga-lvⁱ-kⁱ-ta-niⁱ he/she will like	u-lvⁱ-kⁱ-ta-n(e)(v)?-i he/she liked	a-gi-lv:?-doh-di
a-qua-daⁱn(v)-te I am thinking of (something)	da-tsi-da-nⁱ-teh-ta-niⁱ I will think of...	a-qua-da-nⁱ-teh-ta-nv I thought of...	a-qua-da-nⁱ-teh-di
a-qua-da-n(v)-teh-di, or I am thinking of (something, infinitive form)			
a-da-n(v)-te he/she is thinking of (something)	da-v-da-nⁱ-teh-ta-niⁱ he/she will think of	u-daⁱ-nⁱ-teh-ta-nv he/she thought of	
u-da-n(v)-teh-di he/she is thinking of (something)			
a-quaⁱ-nⁱ-ta I know how	a-qua-nⁱ-te:-s-di I will know how	a-qua-nⁱ-tv I knew how	a-qua-n-ti
u:-nⁱ-ta he/she knows	u-nⁱ-te:-s-di he/she will know	u:-nⁱ-tv he/she knew	
A-GI-HA I have something solid	A-GI-HE::-S-DI I will hve it (solid)	A-GI-HV?-I I had it (solid)	A-GI-HVⁱ-S-DI
U-HA he/she has it (solid)	U-HE::-S-DI he/she has it (solid)	U-HV?-I he/she had it (solid)	
A-GI-NA-A I have it (flexible)	A-GI-NA?-E-SDI	A-GI-NA-V?-I	A-GI-NA?-I
U-NA-A he/she has it (flexible)	U-NA?-E-S-DI	U-NA?-V?-I	U-NA?-I

APPENDIX XI

PRESENT	FUTURE	PAST	INFINITIVE
A-QUV-YA I have it (long)	A-QUV-YE:S-DI I will have it (long)	A-QUV-YV-?I I had it (long)	DI-QUV-YI
U-WA-YA he/she has it (long)	U-WA-YE:S-DI he/she will have it (long)	U-WA-YV?-I he/she had it (long)	TSU-WA-YI
A-GI-NE?-A I have it (liquid)	A-GI-NE-HE:S-DI I will have it (liquid)	A-GI-NE-HV?-I I had it (liquid)	A-GI-NE-HI
U-NE?-A he/she has it (liquid)	U-NE-HE:S-DI he/she will have it (liquid)	U-NE-HV?-I he/she had it (liquid)	
A-GI-KA-HA I have it (live)	A-GI-KA-HE:S-DI I will have it (live)	A-GI-KA-HV?-I I had it (live)	
U-WE-KA-HA he/she has it (live)	U-WE-KA-HE:-S-DI he/she will have it (live)	U-WA-KA-HV?-I he/she had it (live)	
a-quo:-tla I am sitting, am home	a-quo-tle:-s-di I will be sitting	tsa-quo'-tlv I was sitting	a-qua-l'-s-du-he:-s-di
u-wo:-tla he/she is sitting, is at home	u-wo-tle:-s-di he/she will be at home	tsu-wo'-tlv he/she was sitting, was at home	
ga-dv'-ne?-a I am doing (it)	ni-da-ga-dv-ne:-li I will do it	na-qua-dv-ne-lv?-i I did it	ya?-gwa-dv:-n'-hdi
a-dv'-ne?-a he/she is doing it	ni-dv?-dv-ne:-li he/she will do it	nu-dv-ne-lv?-i he/she did it	
tsi-dli'-s-ti?-a I am pouring it	da-tsi-dli:-s-ta-ni' I will pour it	tsi-dli:-s-da-dv?-(i) I poured it	a-gi-dli:-s-di
a-dli'-s-ti?-a he/she is pouring it	dv-dli:-s-ta-ni he/she will pour it	a:dli-s-ta he/she poured it	

324

STRUCTURE OF A CHEROKEE VERB - PREFIXES

Prefixes are numbered according to the order in which they occur.

Direction and scope of the action		Action itself	When the action occurs and an assessment of the action
Living beings involved in the action	Living beings or things passively involved	Beings or things indirectly involved	Verb base	Suffixes (see Appendix XIII)
Prefixes (see below) 1. Subject pronouns 2. Subject-object pronouns	Classifiers (precision pronouns)	Indirect object		

PREFIXES - PRONOUNS - VERB - SUFFIXES

1. tla as a separate word means 'not', 'no'. As a prefix with -yi-, tla- makes the verb negative. (a-qua-n'-ta, I know, tla-ya-qua-n'-ta, I don't know.)

2. d-, plural object. (da-gi-ha, I have several solid things.)

3. da-, action is coming toward the speaker in time or space.
   a. da-, action starts at a distance and approaches the speaker. (da-ya-i, he/she is coming nearer.)
   b. da- plus the suffix -i, marks the future tense. The action is approaching the speaker in time. (da-ge:-si, I will go.)
   c. d-, action involves a change of place. (da-1'-ta-de-ga, he/she is jumping)
   d. di- on nouns, means the noun is at a distance from the speaker. (di-ga-du-hv, a town at a distance)

4. a-, 'again', 'ready to...'. (da-ga-lu-tsi, he will arrive; dv-ga-lu-tsi, he will arrive again, come back. Remember a plus a equals v: da-a-ga-lu-tsi

5. ni-, 'already', 'while', 'assuming that' or 'if'. Ni- combines with many particles. It means that the action already started before the time of this verb. (ni-ge?-o, I have already been here and am continuing to remain here) With -na, it means that the action of the verb is contradicted or ended. (nu-wo-hi-yu-sv-na, faithless (formerly-faithful) Re-examine P.N. 209; I-tsi-sv-s-di-gwu ni-tso-ta-nv-na yi-gi, Assuming that a fire is not made you may stay.

6. wi-, person acting is at a distance, going away from speaker or facing away from the speaker. (Wa?-i, he/she is walking away. Wa-go:-ti-a, He sees it over there.) With -na on an adjective, it means the quality has been carried to an extreme (wo:-sv-na, the best (formerly good, gone to an extreme of goodness)

325

APPENDIX XII

STRUCTURE OF A CHEROKEE VERB - PREFIXES

Prefixes are numbered according to the order in which they occur.

Direction and scope of the action	Action itself	When the action occurs and an assessment of the action			
Living beings involved in the action	Living beings or things passively involved		Verb base	Beings or things indirectly involved	Suffixes (see Appendix XIII)
Prefixes (see below) 1. Subject pronouns 2. Subject-object pronouns	Classifiers (precision pronouns)			Indirect object	

PREFIXES -   PRONOUNS   - VERB -   SUFFIXES

7. If a direct object has been built into the verb, it goes here. (English: fox-hunting, wrong-doing; Cherokee: firemaking I-tsi-sv'-s-di-gwu ni-tso-ta-nv-na yi-gi'. You can spend the night if you don't make a fire (fire-make)).

8. yi-, with recent past suffix -a added directly to the verb base, shows tentative action. With tla-, negative of any verb. (ya-gwa-du-la, I would like, tla-ya-gwa-du-la, I would not like)

326

STRUCTURE OF A CHEROKEE VERB - SOME COMMON SUFFIXES

	Direction and scope of the action	Action itself	When the action occurs and an assessment of the action
	Living beings involved in the action	Living beings or things passively involved		Beings or things indirectly involved
Prefixes (see App.XII)	1. Subject pronouns	Classifiers	Verb base	Suffixes (see below)
	2. Subject-object pronouns	(precision pronouns)		Indirect object

PREFIXES-   PRONOUNS   - VERB -   SUFFIXES

Suffixes are numbered beginning with the one that occurs closest to the verb base.

1. -?i, -gi, means 'un-'. Action involves doing the exact opposite of the verb base's primary meaning. (s-du?-di, to close; s-du-?i-di, to open)

2. -s-da, action is accidental, to a small extent, insignificant (gv-yv-ni-s-da, I accidentally nudged you)

3. -doh(?), -toh(?), -do, -to, the action has no single purpose, it happens on no one occasion.
   This suffix has many uses.
   With -di, infinitive, it is often used as a noun:
   u-da-n'-te-doh-di   a sigh (for-him/her-to <u>passingly-think-of-it</u>)
   a-tsv-s-doh-di   a light-bulb (for-him/her-to-light-it-with, <u>to-help-him/her-to-light-it</u>)
   -Doh can mean 'as if', 'in imitation of':
   a-l'-s-di-ye-hnv-s-doh-di a wig (he/she-puts-it-onto-him-or-herself-to-use-as-hair)
   It can replace an English passive:
   ga-l'-tso-de a-hi-l'-doh-di a house trailer (house <u>to-be-steered</u>)
   It can mean 'with difficulty', 'imperfectly':
   ga-wo-ni-hi-s-doh-di   He is <u>trying</u> to speak, but is speaking poorly or incoherently.
   tsi-ya-tv-da-s-di   I am <u>listening</u> to him (making an effort to hear him).
   -Doh can mean 'for awhile':
   a-gi-go-tv-doh-di u-du-li   He wants me to see it <u>for awhile</u> (i.e., he wants <u>to show it to me</u>)

STRUCTURE OF A CHEROKEE VERB - SOME COMMON SUFFIXES

Direction and scope of the action			Action itself	When the action occurs and an assessment of the action
Living beings involved in the action		Living beings or things passively involved	Verb base	Beings or things indirectly involved
Prefixes (see App. XII)	1. Subject pronouns 2. Subject-object pronouns	Classifiers (precision pronouns)		Indirect object	Suffixes (see below)
PREFIXES-	PRONOUNS		- VERB -	SUFFIXES

3. -doh, (continued)
-Doh can scatter the verb's force:

    ga-no-s-gi-s-gi   a thief
    ga-no-s-gi-si-do-hi   a sneak thief (he/she characteristically goes around stealing or pilfering)

.Doh can change the meaning of the verb entirely:

    ga-no-hi-li-doh, he is hunting (literally, he/she is flying around)

-Doh can mean 'as a tool with the purpose of...':

    a-di-toh-di   a spoon (to drink slightly with, to sip with)

4. -v, the action is past. (a-di-ta-s-gv, he was drinking; u-di-ta-hv, he drank (on one occasion). Ga-di-ta-s-gi tsi-ge:-sv, I used to drink (I was a drinker)) A-di-ta-s-ge:-sv, I used to drink.))

5. -e, -ne, -ye, the action has an indirect object, 'for him/her', 'because of him/her'. (de-tsi-no-gi-ye, I am singing for him/her. I-ya a-g'-s-go'-l'-ta-ne, He is selling a pumpkin to me. Gv-to-lv?-e. I am borrowing from you. Wa-ga' tsi-ne-gi-ye, I am milking the cow (getting liquid from the cow). Tsi-hwa-se, I am buying it for or from him/her. V-g'-su-hwi-se-lv, I had it painted (I caused someone else to paint it)
-si, the action has a direct and indirect object. (tsi:-s-qua-l'-si', I broke his leg (for him).

6. -ga, -la, means recent past, imperative: (Ha-di-ta, you just drank, also, Drink!, A-gwa-du-la, I just wanted. With yi-, the action is tentative: Ya-gwa-du-la, I would like. Tsi-hwi-sv-ga, I just planted.)

328

STRUCTURE OF A CHEROKEE VERB - SOME COMMON SUFFIXES

Direction and scope of the action		Action itself	When the action occurs and an assess-ment of the action	
Living beings involved in the action	Living beings or things passively involved	Verb base	Beings or things indirectly involved	Suffixes (see below)
Prefixes (see App. XII) 1. Subject pronouns 2. Subject-object pronouns	Classifiers (precision pronouns)		Indirect object	
PREFIXES- PRONOUNS		- VERB -	SUFFIXES	

7. -hi, the action is characteristic of the actor, 'often', one by one, each separately, on many separate occasions. (di-ti-yo'-hi-hi, lawyer, also see other job names in Lesson 17. A-ma' wa-ga' da-n'-di-ta-hi-hi, the cows are coming down to drink one by one. a-tv-ga-nv-hi, hearsay)

8. -s-gi, the action is done repeatedly through personal effort. (Job names in Lesson 17. A-du-la-di-s-gi, a beggar; u-du-li-s-gi, a discontented person; ga-lo-nv-he-s-gi, cheat, traitor; di-ga-lo-ne-sgi, painter)

9. -ga, on purpose to..., with an effort, on a matter of some importance. (gv-yv-ni-ga, I hit you (very much on purpose), tsi-hwi-sv-ni-ga, I came to plant (not to do anything else))

10. -o, habitual or continued action. (A-ma' wa-ga' da-n'-di-ta-hi'-hi-hø, The cows continually come down to drink one by one.)

11. -na, finished, done thoroughly, an accomplished fact (u-ne-ga·lv-na, an animal skin, (former-skin)

12. -i, with the prefix da-, the action is in the future (da-ge:-si, I will go).

STRUCTURE OF A CHEROKEE VERB - SOME COMMON SUFFIXES

	Direction and scope of the action	Action itself	When the action occurs and an assessment of the action
	Living beings involved in the action	Verb base	Beings or things indirectly involved
	Living beings or things passively involved		
Prefixes (see App. XII)	1. Subject pronouns 2. Subject-object pronouns	Classifiers (precision pronouns)	Indirect object
			Suffixes (see below)
PREFIXES-	PRONOUNS	- VERB -	SUFFIXES

13. -(s)-di-(yi), or (yi), infinitive. Always has a bound pronoun, unlike English infinitives. Has many uses, including all those of the infinitive in English, plus others. -I, in slot 12 above, plus -di, means 'about to' (u-lu-tsi-di, he is about to arrive). An ordinary Cherokee infinitive, with bound pronouns of course, can mean 'ought to'. (A-ki-wa-hi'-s-di-i, I ought to buy it, I intend to, I think I will buy it. The intention to buy is not very strong.)

14. -ge-s-di, action will be happening (stative future). (Gv-tu-ge:-s-di, I will be owing you)

15. -ga, -ha, action is happening at present. (Gv-yo-ha, I am looking for you. Gv-s-da-yv-hv-s-ga, I am cooking for you.)

16. -e-i, action has been seen by someone else and only reported to the speaker. (Ka-ne-ge-i, he spoke; I was not present)

17. -wu, -?wu, -gwu, action is unimpeded, unopposed, 'go ahead and ...' (Gv-tu-ge-s-di-wu, Go ahead and charge, go ahead and have me owe you)

18. -tsu, -s-g(o)-hv))), the action is questioned. (De-hi-no-gi-si-ga-tsu? Did you come to sing?)

330

READING LIST

For Further Study

Chafe, Wallace: Handbook of the Seneca Language, New York State
    Museum and Science Service, Bulletin No. 388, 1963.
        You will enjoy comparing Cherokee with another Iroquoian language.

Cherokee hymnal and a Cherokee New Testament are both available in
    facsimile copies from Box 948, Tahlequah, OK 74465. They are entirely
    in Cherokee.

Feeling, Durbin: Cherokee English Dictionary, edited by Wm. Pulte,
    published by the Cherokee Nation of Oklahoma, 1975. Also available
    from Box 948, Tahlequah 74465.

Haas, Mary R., Classificatory verbs in Muskogee, Internation Journal
    of Linguistics, 1948.
        A study of Muskogee (Creek) classificatory verbs, using some Cherokee
    terms for comparison. We were unable to attest the pitch variation
    described between a 'human' and a 'living' category in Cherokee. Use
    of pitch is declining rapidly. The pitch classification for 'human'
    may have disappeared, or it may occur only in certain communities.

Holmes, Ruth B., Prehistoric contacts of Cherokee and Nostratic elements
    found today in the Cherokee language, manuscripts in preparation.

Lounsbury, Floyd G., Iroquois-Cherokee linguistic relations, Bureau of
    American Ethnology, Bull. 180, Washington D.C., 1961.
        F.G. Lounsbury summarizes linguistic evidence of a prehistoric
    separation between Cherokee and the rest of the Iroquoian languages.

Michelson, Gunther, A thousand words of Mohawk, National Museum of Man,
    National Museums of Canada, Ottawa, 1973.
        Introduction to another Iroquoian language for perspective on
    Cherokee.

Reyburn, Wm., Cherokee verb morphology, Parts I, II and III, International
    Journal of American Linguistics, 1953 and 1954.
        Reyburn's many verb forms were very helpful to us. He describes
    the Eastern Cherokee (Qualla) dialect, and differences exist which
    might mislead a beginning student of Oklahoma Cherokee. These articles
    would benefit a native speaker familiar with linguistic terminology.

Siebert, Frank T., Jr., The original home of the proto-Algonquian people,
    National Museum of Canada, Bull. 214, 1967.
        This interesting study, based on animal and plant names, places
    the original home of the proto-Algonquian peoples in the same area as
    that of the proto-Iroquoians, at almost the same time.

READING LIST (continued)

Related reading:

Corkran, David H., The Cherokee Frontier: Conflict and Survival, 1740-62, University of Oklahoma Press, 1962, Norman, Oklahoma.

Josephy, Alvin M., Jr., The Indian Heritage of America, Alfred A. Knopf New York, 1970.

Kilpatrick, Jack F. and Kilpatrick, Anna G., editors, New Echota Letters. Contributions of S.A. Worcester to the Cherokee Phoenix, the first Cherokee newspaper. Southern Methodist University Press, Dallas, 1968
_____, Run Toward the Nightland: Magic Rituals of the Oklahoma Cherokees, Southern Methodist University, Dallas, 1967.
_____, The Wa-hne-na-u-hi Manuscript, Anthropological Papers No. 77, Bureau of American Ethnology Bulletin 196.
_____, Chronicles of Wolftown, Anthropological Papers No. 75, Bureau of American Ethnology Bulletin 196.

King, Duane: The Cherokee Indian Nation, a troubled history, published by the Tennessee University Press: Knoxville, 1979.

Morgan, Lewis Henry, League of the Iroquois, a paperback facsimile copy of a book that first appeared in 1851, Rochester, New York. Citadel Press, 120 Enterprise Avenue, Secaucus, N.J. 07094.

Woodward, Grace Steele, The Cherokees: A national history. University of Oklahoma Press, Norman, 1963.

INTERMEDIATE ALGEBRA

THE JOHNSTON/WILLIS
DEVELOPMENTAL MATHEMATICS SERIES

Essential Arithmetic, Fifth Edition (paperbound, 1988)
Johnston/Willis/Lazaris

Essential Algebra, Fifth Edition (paperbound, 1988)
Johnston/Willis/Lazaris

Developmental Mathematics, Second Edition (paperbound, 1987)
Johnston/Willis/Hughes

Elementary Algebra, Second Edition (hardbound, 1987)
Willis/Johnston/Steig

Intermediate Algebra, Second Edition (hardbound, 1987)
Willis/Johnston/Steig

Intermediate Algebra, Fourth Edition (paperbound, 1988)
Johnston/Willis/Lazaris

INTERMEDIATE ALGEBRA
FOURTH EDITION

C. L. JOHNSTON
ALDEN T. WILLIS
Formerly of East Los Angeles College

JEANNE LAZARIS
East Los Angeles College

Wadsworth Publishing Company
Belmont, California
A Division of Wadsworth, Inc.

This book is dedicated to our students, who inspired us to do our best to produce a book worthy of their time.

Mathematics Publisher: Kevin J. Howat
Mathematics Development Editor: Anne Scanlan-Rohrer
Assistant Mathematics Editor: Barbara Holland
Editorial Assistant: Sally Uchizono
Production Editor: Sandra Craig
Managing Designers: Julia Scannell and James Chadwick
Print Buyer: Karen Hunt
Text and Cover Designer: Julia Scannell
Copy Editor: Mary Roybal
Technical Illustrators: Carl Brown and Reese Thornton
Compositor: Composition House
Cover Illustration: Frank Miller
Signing Representative: Ken King

Printed in the United States of America   14

1 2 3 4 5 6 7 8 9 10—92 91 90 89 88

Library of Congress Cataloging-in-Publication Data

Johnston, C. L. (Carol Lee), 1911–
    Intermediate algebra.

    Includes index.
    1. Algebra.   I. Willis, Alden T.   II. Lazaris, Jeanne, 1932–   .   III. Title.
QA154.2.J63   1988   512.9   87-22983
ISBN 0-534-08148-7

Contents

4 POLYNOMIALS

5 FACTORING

6 FRACTIONS

7 EXPONENTS AND RADICALS

Preface

Intermediate Algebra, Fourth Edition, can be used in an intermediate algebra course in any community college or four-year college, in either a lecture format or a learning laboratory setting, or it can be used for self-study. This book will prepare the student for college algebra, statistics, business calculus, and science courses.

Features of This Book

The major features of this book include:

1. The book uses a one-step, one-concept-at-a-time approach. The topics are divided into small sections, each with its own examples and exercises. This approach allows students to master each step before proceeding confidently to the next section.

2. Many concrete, annotated examples illustrate the general algebraic principles covered in each section. To prevent confusion, each example ends with this symbol: ∎.

3. Important concepts and algorithms are enclosed in boxes for easy identification and reference.

4. The approach to solving word problems includes a detailed method for translating a word statement into an algebraic equation or inequality.

5. Visual aids such as shading and color guide students through worked-out problems.

6. In special "Words of Caution," students are warned against common algebraic errors.

7. The importance of checking solutions is stressed throughout the book.

8. A review section with Set I and Set II exercise sets appears at the end of each chapter, and some chapters also have a midchapter review that includes Set I and Set II exercise sets. The Set II review exercises allow space for working problems and for answers; they can be removed from the text for grading. (Removal of these pages will not interrupt the continuity of the text.)

9. This book contains more than 6,000 exercises.

   Set I Exercises. The complete solutions for odd-numbered exercises are included in the back of the book, together with the answers for all of the Set I exercises. In most cases (except in the review exercises), the even-numbered exercises are matched with the odd-numbered exercises. Thus, students can use the solutions for odd-numbered exercises as study aids for doing the even-numbered Set I exercises.

   Set II Exercises. Answers to all Set II exercises are included in the Instructor's Manual. No answers for Set II exercises are given in the text. The odd-numbered exercises of Set II are, for the most part (except in the review exercises), matched to the odd-numbered exercises of Set I, while the even-numbered exercises of Set II are *not* so matched. Thus, while students can use the odd-numbered exercises of Set I as aids for doing the odd-numbered exercises of Set II, they are on their own in doing the even-numbered exercises of Set II.

10. A diagnostic test at the end of each chapter can be used for study and review or as a pretest. Complete solutions to all problems in these diagnostic tests, together with section references, appear in the answer section of the book.

11. A set of cumulative review exercises is included at the end of each chapter except Chapter 1.

Using This Book

Intermediate Algebra, Fourth Edition, can be used in three types of instructional programs: lecture, laboratory, and self-study.

The conventional lecture course. This book has been class-tested and used successfully in conventional lecture courses by the authors and by many other instructors. It is not a workbook, and therefore it contains enough material to stimulate classroom discussion. Examinations for each chapter are provided in the Instructor's Manual, and two different kinds of computer software enable instructors to create their own tests. One software program utilizes a test bank with full graphics capability, and the other is a random-access test generator. Tutorial software is available to help students who require extra assistance.

The learning laboratory class. This text has also been used successfully in many learning labs. The format of explanation, example, and exercises in each section of the book and the tutorial software make the book easy to use in laboratories. Students may use the diagnostic test at the end of each chapter as a pretest or for review and diagnostic purposes. Because several forms of each chapter test are available in the Instructor's Manual, and because of the test generators that are available, a student who does not pass a test can review the material covered on that test and can then take a different form of the test.

Self-study. This book lends itself to self-study because each new topic is short enough to be mastered before continuing, and because more than 900 examples and over 1,500 completely solved exercises show students exactly how to proceed. Students can use the diagnostic test at the end of each chapter to determine which parts of that chapter need to be studied and can thus concentrate on those areas in which they have weaknesses. The tutorial software and the random test generator, which provides answers and cross-references to the text and permits the creation of individualized work sheets, extend the usefulness of the new edition in laboratory and self-study settings.

Changes in the Fourth Edition

The fourth edition includes changes that resulted from many helpful comments from users of the first three editions as well as the authors' own classroom experience in teaching from the book. The major changes in the fourth edition include the following:

1. The level of the text has been raised. While elementary algebra is still reviewed, some very simple examples and exercises have been deleted, and more challenging problems have been included. Most of the exercises sets include problems that require the use of techniques learned in earlier sections as well as techniques learned in the current section. The exercises on factoring and on working with fractions have been made more challenging, and more exercises have been included in the sections on using synthetic division in factoring and graphing.

2. Topics such as prime numbers, prime factorization, products of the form $(a + b)(a - b)$, squares of binomials, and so on are introduced early, along with the topics to which they are related.

3. The word problems have been updated and now include problems leading to inequalities. Word problems are included in nearly every chapter and in all cumulative review exercises after word problems are introduced.

4. The binomial theorem is introduced early in the book and is used often to provide ample practice with this difficult topic. Students have many opportunities to observe that $(x + y)^n \neq x^n + y^n$. In addition, students are, at the appropriate time, asked to solve problems such as $(x + 1)^4 = x^4 + 4x + 1$, and to solve word problems that lead to equations such as $(x + 2)^3 = 56 + x^3$.

5. There is more emphasis on finding the domain of a function and on utilizing new techniques, as they are learned, in finding the domain. Also, the concept of comparing the graphs of the functions $y = f(x)$, $y = f(x) + h$, and $y = f(x + h)$ is introduced.

6. The chapter on logarithms, Chapter 11, has been extensively revised and now includes natural logarithms. The sections covering the finding of logs by using tables and solving arithmetic problems by using logs have been moved to Appendix B. The main focus of Chapter 11 is now on solving exponential and logarithmic equations, with the calculator being used for finding the logs. There is also an entirely new section on word problems from business and the sciences that must be solved using logarithms.

7. A new section on solving systems of quadratic *inequalities* in two variables (graphically) is included.

8. Variations and proportion are moved from Chapter 3 to Chapter 8, where variations are treated as particular kinds of functions.

9. The number of problems in the Set II exercises has been increased; there is now the same number of problems in each Set II exercise set as in the corresponding Set I exercise set.

Ancillaries

The following ancillaries are available with this test:

1. The Instructor's Manual contains five different tests for each chaper, two forms of three midterm examinations, and two final examinations that can be easily removed and duplicated for class use. These tests are prepared with adequate space for students to work the problems. Answer keys for these tests are provided in the manual. The manual also contains the answers to the Set II exercises.

2. The test bank for *Intermediate Algebra*, Fourth Edition, is also available from the publisher in a computerized format entitled *Micro-Pac*© *Genie*, for use on the IBM PC or 100 percent compatible machines. This software program allows instructors to arrange items in a variety of ways and print them quickly and easily. Since *Genie* combines word processing and graphics with database management, it also permits instructors to create their own questions—even questions with mathematical notation or geometric figures—as well as to edit the questions provided in the test bank.

3. In addition, Wadsworth offers the *Johnston/Willis/Lazaris Computerized Test Generator* (JeWeL TEST) software for Apple II and IBM PC or compatible machines. This software, written by Ron Staszkow of Ohlone College, allows instructors to produce many different forms of the same test for quizzes, work sheets, practice tests, and so on. Answers and cross-references to the text provide additional instructional support.

4. An "intelligent" tutoring software system is also available for the IBM PC and compatibles. *Expert Tutor*, written by Sergei Ovchinnikov of San Francisco State University, uses a highly interactive format and sophisticated techniques to tailor lessons to the specific algebra and prealgebra learning problems of students. The result is individualized tutoring strategies with specific page references to problems, examples, and explanations in the textbook.

5. A set of videotapes and a set of audiocassettes, covering major algebraic concepts, are also available.

To obtain additional information about these supplements, contact your Wadsworth-Brooks/Cole representative.

Acknowledgments

We wish to thank the members of the editorial staff at Wadsworth Publishing Company for their help with this edition. Special thanks go to Anne Scanlan-Rohrer, Kevin Howat, Sandra Craig, Julia Scannell, Barbara Holland, Sally Uchizono, Ruthie Singer, and Mary Roybal.

We also wish to thank our many friends for their valuable suggestions. In particular, we are deeply grateful to Gale Hughes for preparing the Instructor's Manual and for checking all examples and exercises, and to the following reviewers: Bernard Belouin, North Adams State College; Mary Jean Brod, University of Montana; Barbara Buhr, Fresno City College; Payton T. Butler, J. Sargeant Reynolds Community College; Deann Christianson, University of the Pacific; Leonard Clark, San Diego City College; Chuck Edgar, Onondaga Community College; Karen A. Estes, Saint Petersburg Junior College; Leonard Fellman, College of Alameda; Jean L. Holton, Tidewater Community College; Jeannine Hugill, Highland Community College; Alma S. McKinney, North Florida Junior College; Barbara McLachlan, Mesa Community College; James W. Newsom, Tidewater Community College; Ann B. Oaks, Hobart and William Smith Colleges; Robert Pumford, Jamestown Community College; Betty Weissbecker, J. Sargeant Reynolds Community College. We would also like to thank Barbara Buhr, Fresno City College; Nancy Golar, Saint Thomas Aquinas College; and Sandy Gomez, Gavilan College, for checking the odd-numbered Set I solutions.

1 Review of Elementary Topics

Intermediate algebra is made up of two types of topics: (1) those that were introduced in beginning algebra and are expanded in this course, and (2) new topics not covered in beginning algebra. With most topics, we begin with the ideas learned in beginning algebra and then develop these ideas further.

In Chapter 1 we review sets, the properties of real numbers, integral exponents, and simplifying and evaluating algebraic expressions.

1.1 Sets

Since ideas in all branches of mathematics—arithmetic, algebra, geometry, calculus, statistics, and so on—can be explained in terms of sets, a basic understanding of sets is helpful.

1.1A Basic Definitions

Set   A **set** is a collection of objects or things.

Example 1   Examples of sets:

a. The set of students registered at your college on May 7, 1987, at 8 A.M.

b. The set of letters in our alphabet, that is, a, b, c, d, and so forth.   ■

Element of a Set   The objects or things that make up a set are called its **elements** or **members**. A set may contain just a few elements, many elements, or no elements at all.

Roster Method of Representing a Set   A **roster** is a list of the members of a group. The method of representing a set by listing its elements is called the **roster method**. Whenever the roster method is used, it is customary to put the elements inside a pair of braces, { }. We *never* use parentheses for sets. Thus, (3, 4, 5) does *not* name a set.

Example 2   Examples to show the elements of sets and the roster method:

a. Set $\{5, 7, 9\}$ has elements 5, 7, and 9.

b. Set $\{a, f, h, k\}$ has elements a, f, h, and k.   ■

NOTE   It is customary, though not necessary, to arrange numbers and letters in sets in numerical and alphabetical order (to make reading easier) and to represent elements of a set with lowercase letters.   ☑

Naming a Set   A set is usually named by a capital letter. The expression "$A = \{1, 5, 7\}$" is read "A is the set whose elements are 1, 5, and 7."

Set of Digits   One important set of numbers is the set of **digits**. This set contains the numerals 0, 1, 2, 3, 4, 5, 6, 7, 8, and 9. These symbols make up our entire number system; *any* number can be written by using some combination of these numerals.

Modified Roster Method   If the number of elements in a set is so large that it is either inconvenient or impossible to list all its members, we modify the roster notation. For example, the set of digits could be represented as follows:

$$D = \{0, 1, 2, \underline{\dots}, 9\}$$

This is read "D is the set whose elements are 0, 1, 2, and so on up to 9." The three dots to the right of the number 2 indicate that the remaining numbers are to be found in the same way we have begun, namely, by adding 1 to each number to find the next number, until we reach 9, the last number in the set.

Natural Numbers   The numbers 1, 2, 3, 4, 5, 6, and so on are called **natural nu..** or **counting numbers**. Since this set has no largest number, we represent it as follows:

$$\{1, 2, 3, 4, \dots \}$$

This is read "the set whose elements are 1, 2, 3, 4, and so on ." This set will be called N throughout this text; that is,

$$N = \{1, 2, 3, 4, \dots\}$$

Even Numbers   Natural numbers that end in 0, 2, 4, 6, or 8 are called **even natural numbers**.

Odd Numbers   Natural numbers that end in 1, 3, 5, 7, or 9 are called **odd natural numbers**.

Consecutive Numbers   Numbers that follow one another without interruption in sequence are called **consecutive numbers**. For example, 15, 16, 17, and 18 are four consecutive numbers beginning with 15.

The Meaning of the Equal Sign   The equal sign ($=$) in a statement means that the expression on the left side of the equal sign *has the same value or values as* the expression on the right side of the equal sign.

Equal Sets   Two sets are said to be equal if they both contain exactly the same elements. We will use the equal sign between such sets. If two sets are *not* equal to each other, we will use the sign $\neq$, which is read " is not equal to ."

Example 3   Examples of equal sets and unequal sets:

a. $\{1, 5, 7\} = \{5, 1, 7\}$. Notice that both sets have exactly the same elements, even though the elements are not listed in the same order.

b. $\{1, 5, 5, 5\} = \{5, 1\}$. Notice that both sets have exactly the same elements, even though 5 is repeated several times in one of the rosters.

c. $\{7, 8, 11\} \neq \{7, 11\}$. These sets are not equal because they do not both have exactly the same elements. ■

The Set-builder (or Rule) Method of Representing a Set   A set can also be represented by a *rule* describing its members in such a way that we definitely know whether a particular element is in that set or is not in that set. In this notation, the vertical bar is read "such that."

$$\{x \mid x \text{ is a natural number}\}$$

is read "the set of all x such that x is a natural number ."
The rule

Example 4   Example of changing from set-builder notation to roster notation: Write $\{x \mid x$ is an even natural number$\}$ in roster notation.
Solution   The natural numbers are 1, 2, 3, 4, 5, 6, . . .; selecting the *even* ones gives us the set $\{2, 4, 6, \dots\}$. Therefore,

$$\{x \mid x \text{ is an even natural number}\} = \{2, 4, 6, \dots\}$$ ■

Example 5   Examples of changing from roster notation to set-builder notation:

a. Write $\{1, 3, 5, \ldots\}$ in set-builder notation.

We have to find a new way of describing this set, a way that starts "The set of all x such that . . . . We should notice that all of the numbers listed are natural numbers and that they are also all odd numbers. Therefore, we can say

$$\{1, 3, 5, \ldots\} = \{x \mid x \text{ is a natural number and } x \text{ is an odd number}\}$$

or

$$\{1, 3, 5, \ldots\} = \{x \mid x \text{ is an odd natural number}\}$$

NOTE   It is important to realize that other answers could also be correct.   ☑

b. Write $\{0, 3, 6, 9\}$ in set-builder notation.

We might notice that all of the numbers are digits and that they are all divisible by 3.* We could then say

$$\{0, 3, 6, 9\} = \{x \mid x \text{ is a digit and } x \text{ is divisible by 3}\}$$

or

$$\{0, 3, 6, 9\} = \{x \mid x \text{ is a digit and } x \text{ is 0 or is a multiple of 3†}\}   ∎$$

The Symbol $\in$ If we wish to show that a number or object is a member of a given set, we use the symbol $\in$, which is read " is an element of ." Thus, the expression "$2 \in A$" is read "2 is an element of set A." If we wish to show that a number or object is *not* a member of a given set, we use the symbol $\notin$, which is read " is not an element of ."

Example 6   Examples to show the use of $\in$ and $\notin$:

a. If $A = \{2, 3, 4\}$, we can say $2 \in A$, $5 \notin A$, $3 \in A$, and $4 \in A$.

b. If $F = \{x \mid x \text{ is an even natural number}\}$, then $2 \in F$, $5 \notin F$, $12 \in F$, and $\frac{2}{3} \notin F$.   ∎

The Empty Set or Null Set   A set with *no* elements in it is said to be the **empty set** (or null set). We use the symbols $\{\ \ \}$ or ϕ to represent the empty set.

A WORD OF CAUTION $\{\phi\}$ is *not* the correct symbol for the empty set.   ☑

Example 7   Examples of empty sets:

a. The set of all people in your math class who are 10 feet tall.

b. The set of all of the digits greater than 10.   ∎

Finite Set   If, in counting the elements of a set, the counting comes to an end, the set is called a **finite set**.

---

* When we say that a number is "divisible by n," we mean that when we divide the number by n, the remainder is 0.

† When we say that a number is a "multiple of n," we mean that it is one of the numbers n, $2n$, $3n$, $4n$, $5n$, and so on.

Example 8   Examples of finite sets:

a. $A = \{5, 9, 10, 13\}$

b. $D = $ The set of digits

c. $\phi = \{\quad\}$ ∎

Infinite Set   If, in counting the elements of a set, the counting never comes to an end, the set is called an **infinite set**. A set is infinite if it is not finite.

Example 9   Examples of infinite sets:

a. $N = \{1, 2, 3, \ldots\}$ The natural numbers

b. $\{x \mid x$ is an odd natural number$\}$ ∎

Subsets   A set A is called a **subset** of set B if every member of A is also a member of B. "A is a subset of B" is written "$A \subseteq B$."

NOTE   The symbol $\subseteq$ is used to indicate that one *set* is a *subset* of another set. The symbol $\in$ is used to indicate that a particular *element* is a *member* of a particular set.   ☑

Example 10   Examples of subsets:

a. If $A = \{3, 5\}$ and $B = \{3, 5, 7\}$, then $A \subseteq B$ because every member of A is also a member of B.

b. If $C = \{10, 7, 5\}$ and $H = \{5, 7, 10\}$, then $C \subseteq H$ because every member of C is also a member of H.

NOTE   *Every set is a subset of itself.* Also, mathematicians agree that *the empty set is a subset of every set.*   ☑

c. If $E = \{4, 7\}$ and $F = \{7, 8, 5\}$, then E is not a subset of F because $4 \in E$, but $4 \notin F$. The symbol for "is not a subset of" is $\nsubseteq$. Therefore, $E \nsubseteq F$.   ∎

EXERCISES 1.1A   In all exercises, N refers to the set of natural numbers and D to the set of digits.

Set I   For Exercises 1 and 2, write "True" if the statement is always true; otherwise, write "False."

1. a. The collection consisting of *, &, $, and 5 is a set.

b. $\{x \mid x$ is a natural number$\} = \{1, 2, 3\}$

c. $\{2, 6, 1, 6\} = \{1, 2, 6\}$ d. $23 \subseteq N$

e. $0 \in N$ f. $\{2\} \in D$

g. $\{2, 6\} \subseteq N$ h. $\{\quad\} \subseteq N$

i. $10 \in D$ j. $0 \in \phi$

k. If $A = \{5, 11, 19\}$, then $11 \in A$.

l. The collection consisting of all the natural numbers between 0 and 1 is a set.

2. a. The collection consisting of a, 3, $\hat{\ }$, and # is a set.

   b. $\{0, 3, 6, \ldots\} = \{x \,|\, x$ is a natural number divisible by 3$\}$

   c. $\{2, 2, 7, 7\} = \{7, 2\}$ **d.** $2 \in N$

   e. $\{5\} \in N$ **f.** $5 \subseteq N$

   g. $\{1, 3, 5\} \subseteq N$ **h.** $\{\ \} \subseteq D$

   i. $0 \in D$ **j.** $\{3\} \in D$

   k. If $B = \{a, b, c, d, e\}$, then $\{a, b\} \subseteq B$.

   l. The collection consisting of all the digits greater than 12 is a set.

In Exercises 3 and 4, state which of the sets are finite and which are infinite.

3. a. the set of even natural numbers

   b. the set of days in the week

   c. the set of books in the Huntington Library

4. a. the set of natural numbers divisible by 7

   b. the set of months in the year

   c. the set of odd digits

5. List all the subsets of the set $\{a, b, c\}$.

6. List all the subsets of the set $\{1, 2\}$.

7. If $A = \{3, 5, 10, 11\}$, $B = \{3, 5, 12\}$, and $C = \{5, 3\}$, state which of the following statements are true and which are false:

   a. $B \subseteq A$ **b.** $C \subseteq B$ **c.** $C \nsubseteq A$

8. If $E = \{a, b, h, k\}$, $F = \{a, b, c, k\}$, and $G = \{b, k\}$, state which of the following statements are true and which are false:

   a. $F \nsubseteq E$ **b.** $G \nsubseteq F$ **c.** $G \subseteq E$

9. Write each of the given sets in roster notation:

   a. $\{x \,|\, x$ is an even digit$\}$

   b. $\{x \,|\, x$ is a natural number divisible by 5$\}$

10. Write each of the given sets in roster notation:

   a. $\{x \,|\, x$ is an odd natural number$\}$

   b. $\{x \,|\, x$ is a natural number that is a multiple of 11$\}$

11. Write each of the given sets in set-builder notation:

   a. $\{a, b, c, d, e\}$ **b.** $\{4, 8, 12\}$

   c. $\{10, 20, 30, \ldots\}$

12. Write each of the given sets in set-builder notation:

   a. $\{0, 2, 4, 6, 8\}$ **b.** $\{x, y, z\}$

   c. $\{5, 10, 15, \ldots\}$

Set II

1. Write "True" if the statement is always true; otherwise, write "False."

   a. The collection consisting of 3, w, %, and @ is a set.

   b. $\{x|x \text{ is a digit}\} = \{0, 1, 2, 9\}$

   c. $\{5, x, 5\} = \{5, x\}$ d. $\{\ \} \subseteq \{1, 3, 5\}$

   e. $\{0\} \in D$ f. $12 \in D$

   g. $0 \notin N$ h. $\{0, 5\} \nsubseteq N$

   i. $0 \notin \{\ \}$ j. $3 \subseteq D$

   k. If $C = \{a, 3, d, 5\}$, then $2 \notin C$.

   l. The collection consisting of all the digits less than 0 is a set.

2. Write all the elements of the set $\{2, a, 3\}$.

In Exercises 3 and 4, state which of the sets are finite and which are infinite.

3. a. the set of even digits

   b. the set of letters in our alphabet

   c. the set of books in the Library of Congress

4. a. the set of natural numbers divisible by 6

   b. the set of digits that are multiples of 6

   c. $\{1, 2, 3, \ldots, 100\}$

5. List all the subsets of the set $\{*, \$, \&\}$.

6. List all the subsets of the set $\{0, 1, 2, 3\}$.

7. If $A = \{2, 4, 7, 11\}$, $B = \{4, 7, 12\}$, and $C = \{4, 7, 11\}$, state which of the following statements are true and which are false:

   a. $B \subseteq A$ b. $C \subseteq A$ c. $C \nsubseteq B$

8. If $E = \{1, 2, 3, \ldots, 8\}$, $F = \{2, 3, 5\}$, and $G = \{5\}$, state which of the following statements are true and which are false:

   a. $F \subseteq E$ b. $G \nsubseteq E$ c. $E \subseteq F$

9. Write each of the given sets in roster notation:

   a. $\{x|x \text{ is a digit divisible by 4}\}$

   b. $\{x|x \text{ is a natural number that is a multiple of 8}\}$

10. Write each of the given sets in roster notation:

    a. $\{x|x \text{ is a natural number that is a multiple of 6}\}$

    b. $\{x|x \text{ is a digit that is divisible by 5}\}$

11. Write each of the given sets in set-builder notation:

    a. $\{0, 3, 6, 9\}$ b. $\{7, 14, 21, \ldots\}$ c. $\{a, b, c\}$

12. Write each of the given sets in set-builder notation:

    a. {Sunday, Monday, Tuesday, Wednesday, Thursday, Friday, Saturday}

    b. $\{0, 5\}$

    c. $\{4, 8, 12, \ldots\}$

1.1B Union and Intersection of Sets

Union of Sets   The **union** of sets A and B, written $A \cup B$, is the set that contains all the elements of set A and all the elements of set B. For an element to be in $A \cup B$, it must be in set A *or* set B or both.

Example 11   Examples of set union:

a. If $A = \{2, 3, 4\}$ and $B = \{1, 3, 5\}$, find $A \cup B$.

$A \cup B = \{1, 2, 3, 4, 5\}$ (These are the elements that are in set A or set B or both.)

b. If $C = \{3, 4, 8\}$ and $D = \{4, 3, 8\}$, find $C \cup D$.

$C \cup D = \{3, 4, 8\}$ ■

Intersection of Sets   The **intersection** of sets A and B, written $A \cap B$, is the set that contains only those elements that are in *both* A and B. For an element to be in $A \cap B$, it must be in set A *and* in set B. (The symbol $\cap$ suggests the letter A for *and*.)

Example 12   Examples of intersection of sets:

a. If $A = \{2, 3, 4\}$ and $B = \{1, 3, 5\}$, find $A \cap B$.

$A \cap B = \{3\}$ (3 is the only element in A *and* in B.)

b. If $E = \{b, c, g\}$ and $F = \{1, 2, 5, 7\}$, find $E \cap F$.

$E \cap F = \{\ \ \}$ (None of the elements of E are in F.)   ■

Example 13   If $A = \{1, 4, 7\}$, $B = \{1, 6, 9\}$, and $C = \{4, 7\}$, find $(A \cap B) \cup C$.

We first find $A \cap B$: $A \cap B = \{1\}$. We then find the union of $(A \cap B)$ with C:

$$\{1\} \cup \{4, 7\} = \{1, 4, 7\}$$

Therefore,

$$(A \cap B) \cup C = \{1, 4, 7\}\quad ■$$

EXERCISES 1.1B

Set I   **1.** Given $A = \{1, 2, 3, 4\}$ and $B = \{2, 4, 5\}$, find the following:

a. $A \cup B$ b. $A \cap B$ c. $B \cup A$ d. $B \cap A$

2. Given $C = \{2, 5, 6, 12\}$ and $D = \{7, 8, 9\}$, find the following:

a. $C \cap D$ b. $C \cup D$ c. $D \cap C$ d. $D \cup C$

3. Given $X = \{2, 5, 6, 11\}$, $Y = \{5, 7, 11, 13\}$, and $Z = \{0, 3, 4, 6\}$, find the following:

a. $X \cap Y$ b. $Y \cup Z$ c. $X \cap Z$

d. $Y \cap Z$ e. $X \cup Y$ f. $Z \cup Y$

g. $(X \cap Y) \cap Z$ h. $X \cap (Y \cap Z)$

i. $(X \cup Y) \cup Z$ j. $X \cup (Y \cup Z)$

4. Given $K = \{a, 4, 7, b\}$, $L = \{m, 4, 6, b\}$, and $M = \{n, 3, 5, t\}$, find the following:

a. $K \cap L$ b. $K \cup L$ c. $K \cup M$

d. $L \cap M$ e. $K \cap M$ f. $L \cup M$

g. $(K \cap L) \cap M$ h. $K \cap (L \cap M)$

i. $(K \cup L) \cup M$ j. $K \cup (L \cup M)$

Set II   1. Given $H = \{1, 3, 5, 7\}$ and $K = \{2, 4, 6\}$, find the following:

a. $H \cap K$ b. $H \cup K$ c. $K \cap H$ d. $K \cup H$

2. Given $S = \{1, 5, 10\}$ and $T = \{5\}$, find the following:

a. $S \cap T$ b. $S \cup T$ c. $T \cap S$ d. $T \cup S$

3. Given $A = \{a, 5, 7, b\}$, $B = \{c, 6, 7, b\}$, and $C = \{3, 4, 6\}$, find the following:

a. $A \cap B$ b. $A \cup B$ c. $A \cap C$

d. $A \cup C$ e. $B \cap C$ f. $B \cup C$

g. $(A \cap B) \cap C$ h. $A \cap (B \cap C)$

i. $(A \cup B) \cup C$ j. $A \cup (B \cup C)$

4. Given $E = \{a, b, c\}$, $F = \{c, d, e, f, g\}$, and $G = \{g\}$, find the following:

a. $E \cap F$ b. $F \cap E$ c. $E \cup F$

d. $E \cup G$ e. $E \cap G$ f. $G \cap E$

g. $E \cap (F \cup G)$ h. $(E \cap F) \cup (E \cap G)$

i. $E \cup (F \cap G)$ j. $(E \cup F) \cap (E \cup G)$

1.2 Real Numbers

We have already identified two important sets of numbers, namely, the set of *digits*, $D = \{0, 1, 2, \ldots, 9\}$, and the set of *natural numbers*, $N = \{1, 2, 3, \ldots\}$.

Whole Numbers   When 0 is included with the natural numbers, we have the set of **whole numbers**, which we call W. Therefore, $W = \{0, 1, 2, \ldots\}$. The set of natural numbers is a subset of the set of whole numbers; that is, $N \subseteq W$.

The Negative of a Number   The *negative* of a nonzero number is found by changing its sign. Thus, the negative of b is $-b$, and the negative of $-b$ is b. Zero is neither a positive nor a negative number. However, we *can* say that the negative of zero is zero; that is, $-0 = 0$.

Example 1   Examples of the negatives of numbers:

a. The negative of 4 is -4. (-4 is read as "negative four.")

b. The negative of -5 is 5. ■

Integers   The union of the set of whole numbers (W) with the set of the negatives of the natural numbers is the **set of integers**, which we will call J. In roster notation,

$$J = \{\ldots, -3, -2, -1, 0, 1, 2, 3, \ldots\}$$

The set of whole numbers is a subset of the set of integers; that is, $W \subseteq J$.

Rational Numbers   The set of **rational numbers** is the set

$$Q = \left\{ \frac{a}{b} \,\middle|\, a, b \in J, b \neq 0 \right\}$$

The set of integers is a subset of the set of rational numbers (that is, $J \subseteq Q$), because any integer can be written as a rational number, for example,

$$5 = \frac{5}{1}, \qquad 17 = \frac{17}{1}, \qquad 0 = \frac{0}{1}, \qquad -7 = \frac{-7}{1}$$

The set of *terminating decimals* (decimals that have only zeros to the right of some specific decimal place) is a subset of the set of rational numbers, because any terminating decimal can be written as a rational number, for example,

$$0.1 = \frac{1}{10}, \qquad -1.03 = -\frac{103}{100}$$

The set of *nonterminating, repeating decimals** is a subset of the set of rational numbers, because any nonterminating, repeating decimal can be written as a rational number, for example,

$$0.666\ldots = \frac{2}{3}, \qquad -0.272727\ldots = -\frac{3}{11}$$

The set of *mixed numbers* is a subset of the set of rational numbers, because any mixed number can be written as a rational number, for example,

$$2\frac{1}{3} = \frac{7}{3}, \qquad -5\frac{1}{2} = -\frac{11}{2}$$

It is also true that $N \subseteq Q$ and $W \subseteq Q$; that is, the set of natural numbers and the set of whole numbers are both subsets of the set of rational numbers.

Irrational Numbers   One very important set of numbers exists that is not a subset of any of the sets of numbers we've discussed so far. When we change any one of these numbers into its decimal equivalent, we always get a *nonterminating, nonrepeating decimal*. This set is the set of **irrational numbers**, which we will call H. A few examples of irrational numbers are $\sqrt{2}$, $\sqrt{8}$, $\sqrt[3]{55}$, and π.

$\sqrt{2} \doteq 1.414213562\ldots$,   The digits go on forever; they never terminate and never start repeating

$\doteq$ means "is approximately equal to"

$\sqrt{8} \doteq 2.828427125\ldots$

$\sqrt[3]{55} \doteq 3.802952461\ldots$

$\pi \doteq 3.141592654\ldots$

There are infinitely many more irrational numbers, each of which becomes a nonterminating, nonrepeating decimal when it is changed to its decimal equivalent.

Irrational numbers cannot be put into the form $\frac{a}{b}$ where a and b are integers and $b \neq 0$.

Real Numbers   The union of the set of rational numbers and the set of irrational numbers comprises the set of **real numbers**, which we call R. In set notation, $Q \cup H = R$. (We will be concerned only with real numbers until Chapter 7.)

The set of rational numbers is a subset of the set of real numbers, and the set of irrational numbers is a subset of the set of real numbers. *No number can be a rational number and also an irrational number.* That is, $H \cap Q = \{ \quad \}$.

---

*These repeating decimals repeat a *number* or a *block of numbers*. (In 0.666..., the 6 repeats, and in −0.272727..., the block 27 repeats.) In Chapter 12, we discuss how to change 0.272727... to $\frac{3}{11}$.

We can graph all of the real numbers on the *real number line*. There is a point on the number line that corresponds to each real number, as shown in Figure 1.2.1.

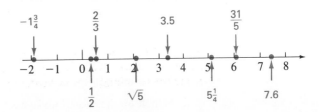

FIGURE 1.2.1   NUMBER LINE

The arrowhead at the right of the number line indicates the direction in which the numbers get larger.

Example 2   Graph the numbers -4 and $2.23606797\ldots$ on the real number line and determine which are real numbers, which are integers, which are natural numbers, which are irrational numbers, and which are rational numbers.

Solution

-4 is a rational number (it could be expressed as $-\frac{4}{1}$), a real number, and an integer. $2.23606797\ldots$ is a nonterminating, nonrepeating decimal; therefore, it is an irrational number and a real number. (Remember, every irrational number is a real number.) Therefore, the following relationships hold:

The real numbers are -4 and $2.23606797\ldots$.

The integer is -4.

Neither is a natural number.

The irrational number is $2.23606797\ldots$.

The rational number is -4. ■

The relationships between number systems discussed above are shown in Figure 1.2.2.

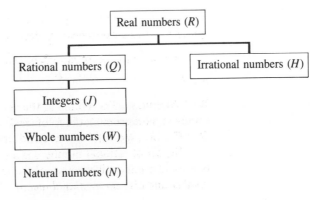

FIGURE 1.2.2

NOTE $N \subseteq W \subseteq J \subseteq Q \subseteq R$, $H \subseteq R$, and $Q \cap H = \{\ \ \}$.   ✓

EXERCISES 1.2

Set I **1.** Graph the numbers 7, 2.449489734..., -5, 10, $-\frac{3}{4}$, and 0.222... on a number line and determine the following:

a. Which are real numbers?

b. Which are integers?

c. Which are natural numbers?

d. Which are irrational numbers?

e. Which are rational numbers?

2. Graph the numbers $-2.64575131...$, -11, $\frac{5}{6}$, $3\frac{1}{3}$, 1.666..., and 4 on a number line and determine the following:

a. Which are real numbers?

b. Which are integers?

c. Which are natural numbers?

d. Which are irrational numbers?

e. Which are rational numbers?

In Exercises 3 and 4, replace the question mark with either $\subseteq$ or $\in$ to form a true statement. The letters refer to the sets defined above.

3. a. $\{1, 3\} ? J$ b. $2 ? N$ c. $N ? R$

    d. $\frac{3}{4} ? Q$ e. $\frac{3}{4} ? R$ f. $\{3\} ? R$

4. a. $J ? Q$ b. $\{2, 3, 4\} ? R$ c. $\frac{2}{3} ? R$

    d. $-4 ? J$ e. $J ? R$ f. $\{-5\} ? J$

In Exercises 5 and 6, write "True" if the statement is always true; otherwise write "False." The letters refer to the sets defined above.

5. a. Every real number is a rational number.

b. Every integer is a real number.

c. $R \subseteq W$ d. $3 \in J$

e. $3 \in H$ f. $H \subseteq R$

g. $3.31662479... \in H$ h. $-3.872983346... \in R$

6. a. Every irrational number is a real number.

b. Every rational number is an integer.

c. $5 \in H$ d. $5 \in Q$

e. $Q \subseteq R$ f. $J \subseteq Q$

g. $0.13131313... \in H$ h. $-4.123105626... \in H$

Set II **1.** Graph the numbers $-5.196152432...$, $\frac{5}{7}$, $-2\frac{4}{9}$, 4.444..., 0, and 2 on a number line and determine the following:

a. Which are real numbers?

b. Which are integers?

c. Which are natural numbers?

d. Which are irrational numbers?

e. Which are rational numbers?

2. Graph the numbers $-3, 0.12121212\ldots, 6, 2\frac{2}{3}, -1\frac{1}{2}$, and $-4.2163461\ldots$ on a number line and determine the following:

   a. Which are real numbers?

   b. Which are integers?

   c. Which are natural numbers?

   d. Which are irrational numbers?

   e. Which are rational numbers?

In Exercises 3 and 4, replace the question mark with either $\subseteq$ or $\in$ to form a true statement. The letters refer to the sets defined above.

3. a. $\{0, 5\} \, ? \, W$ b. $12 \, ? \, W$ c. $\{12\} \, ? \, N$

   d. $\frac{8}{9} \, ? \, R$ e. $W \, ? \, J$ f. $\{1, 3\} \, ? \, D$

4. a. $0 \, ? \, W$ b. $12 \, ? \, N$ c. $\{0\} \, ? \, W$

   d. $5 \, ? \, D$ e. $\{12\} \, ? \, R$ f. $\frac{1}{4} \, ? \, R$

In Exercises 5 and 6, write "True" if the statement is always true; otherwise write "False." The letters refer to the sets defined above.

5. a. Every whole number is an integer.

   b. Every integer is a rational number.

   c. $W \subseteq H$ d. $7 \in Q$

   e. $7 \in R$ f. $Q \subseteq N$

   g. $-0.232323\ldots \in H$ h. $3.741657387\ldots \in H$

6. a. Every rational number is a real number.

   b. The set of digits is a subset of the set of natural numbers.

   c. $R \subseteq Q$ d. $0 \in H$

   e. $\frac{1}{5} \in H$ f. $H \subseteq Q$

   g. $0.16513278\ldots \in H$ h. $0.16513278\ldots \in R$

1.3 Definitions and Symbols

1.3A Definitions

Constant A **constant** is an object or symbol that does not change its value in a particular problem or discussion. It is usually represented by a number symbol, but it can be represented by one of the first few letters of the alphabet. Thus, in the expression $4x + 3y - 5$, the constants are $4, 3$, and -5. In the expression $ax + by + c$, the constants are understood to be a, b, and c.

Variable A **variable** is an object or symbol that acts as a placeholder for a number that is unknown. A variable is usually represented by a letter, and it may assume different values in a particular problem or discussion. An equation or inequality (see Chapter 2) is usually, but not always, *true* for some values of the variable and *false* for other values. In the expression $ax + by + c$, it is understood that the variables are x and y.

Algebraic Expression An **algebraic expression** consists of numbers, variables, signs of operation (such as $+$, $-$, $\times$, $\div$), and signs of grouping. For example, $4x + 3y - 5$ is an algebraic expression.

Terms The plus and minus signs in an algebraic expression break it up into smaller pieces called **terms**. Each plus and minus sign is part of the term that follows it. An expression within grouping symbols is considered as a single term even though it may contain plus and minus signs. A *bar* (for example, a fraction bar) is one example of a grouping symbol.

Example 1 Identify the terms in each algebraic expression:

a. $3x - 9x(2y + 5z)$

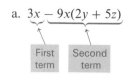

First term Second term

The part inside the parentheses is considered as a single unit or term, and since the part inside the parentheses is being multiplied by $-9x$, $-9x(2y + 5z)$ is considered to be one term. Therefore, this expression has only two terms, as shown.

b. $\dfrac{2 - x}{xy} + (2x - 1)$

This expression also has only two terms, since the fraction bar is a grouping symbol. The first term is $\dfrac{2 - x}{xy}$, and the second term is $2x - 1$. ■

Factors The numbers that are multiplied together to give a product are called the **factors** of that product. The number 1 may be considered to be a factor of any number.

Example 2 Identify the factors in each of the following expressions:

a. $3 \cdot 5 = 15$ 3 and 5 are factors of 15

b. $7abc$ 7, *a*, *b*, and *c* are the factors of 7*abc*

c. x 1 (understood) and *x* are the factors of *x*   ■

Coefficients In a term with two factors, the **coefficient** of one factor is the other factor. In a term with more than two factors, the coefficient of each factor is the product of all the other factors in the term.

Numerical Coefficients A **numerical coefficient** is a coefficient that is a *number* rather than a *letter*. When we refer to "the coefficient" of a term, it is understood that we mean the numerical coefficient of that term. If a term has no numerical coefficient showing, then the numerical coefficient is understood to be 1.

Literal Coefficients A **literal coefficient** is a coefficient that is a letter or the product of letters.

Example 3 Identify the coefficients in the following terms:

a. $12xyz$

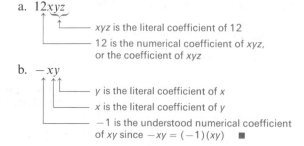

xyz is the literal coefficient of 12

12 is the numerical coefficient of *xyz*, or the coefficient of *xyz*

b. $-xy$

y is the literal coefficient of *x*

x is the literal coefficient of *y*

-1 is the understood numerical coefficient of *xy* since $-xy = (-1)(xy)$ ■

EXERCISES 1.3A

Set I   In Exercises 1 and 2, (a) list the constants and (b) list the variables.

1. $xy + 3$ 　　　　　　　　　　　**2.** $4z - 2y$

In Exercises 3–10, (a) determine the number of terms, (b) write the *second* term if there is one, and (c) list all of the factors of the *first* term.

3. $E + 5F - 3$ 　　　　　　　　　**4.** $R + 2T - 6$

5. $(R + S) - 2(x + y)$ 　　　　　　**6.** $(A + 2B) - 5(W + V)$

7. $3XYZ + 4$ 　　　　　　　　　　**8.** $4ab + 3x$

9. $2A + \dfrac{3B - C}{DE}$ 　　　　　　　**10.** $3st + \dfrac{w + z}{xyz}$

In Exercises 11–14, (a) write the numerical coefficient of the first term and (b) write the literal part of the second term.

11. $2R - 5RT + 3T$ 　　　　　　　**12.** $4x - 3xy + z$

13. $-x - y + z$ 　　　　　　　　　**14.** $-a + 2b - c$

Set II   In Exercises 1 and 2, (a) list the constants and (b) list the variables.

1. $4X - Z$ 　　　　　　　　　　　**2.** $3x - 2st$

In Exercises 3–10, (a) determine the number of terms, (b) write the *second* term if there is one, and (c) list all of the factors of the *first* term.

3. $X + 7Y - 8$ 　　　　　　　　　**4.** $3(x - 5y + 7z)$

5. $(2X - Y) - 4(a + b)$ 　　　　　　**6.** $-4x + \dfrac{1}{6st} - 3z$

7. $7st + 3uv$ 　　　　　　　　　　**8.** $x + 2(y + z + 4) - w + s$

9. $3A + \dfrac{2B - 3C}{2AB}$ 　　　　　　**10.** $6 - 3xy + \dfrac{z}{2}$

In Exercises 11–14, (a) write the numerical coefficient of the first term and (b) write the literal part of the second term.

11. $2X + Y - 3$ 　　　　　　　　　**12.** $9x - 5y + z$

13. $4(X + 2) - 5Y$ 　　　　　　　　**14.** $z - 3w$

1.3B   Inequalities and Absolute Values

"Greater Than" and "Less Than" Symbols   The symbols $>$ and $<$ are called **inequality symbols**. Let X be any number on the number line. Then numbers to the right of X on the number line are said to be *greater than* X, written "$> X$." Numbers to the left of X on the number line are said to be *less than* X, written "$< X$." The arrowhead at the right of the number line indicates the direction in which numbers get larger.

Example 4   Examples of "greater than" and "less than" symbols:

a. $-1 > -4$ is read "-1 is greater than -4"

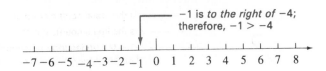

-1 is *to the right of* -4; therefore, $-1 > -4$

b. $-2 < 1$ is read "-2 is less than 1"

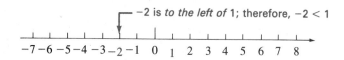

Note that $1 > -2$ and $-2 < 1$ give the same information even though they are read differently. ∎

In general,

$$a < b \text{ may always be replaced by } b > a$$

and

$$a > b \text{ may always be replaced by } b < a.$$

"Less Than or Equal to" Symbol   The inequality $a \leq b$ is read "a is less than *or* equal to b. This means that if $\begin{cases} \text{either} & a < b \\ \text{or} & a = b \end{cases}$ is true, then $a \leq b$ is true. For example, $2 \leq 3$ is true because $2 < 3$ is true (even though $2 = 3$ is *not* true). Remember, only *one* of the two statements $\begin{cases} 2 < 3 \\ 2 = 3 \end{cases}$ need be true in order that $2 \leq 3$ be true.

"Greater Than or Equal to" Symbol   The inequality $a \geq b$ is read "a is greater than *or* equal to b." This means that if $\begin{cases} \text{either} & a > b \\ \text{or} & a = b \end{cases}$ is true, then $a \geq b$ is true. For example, $5 \geq 1$ is true because $5 > 1$ is true (even though $5 = 1$ is *not* true).

Continued Inequality Symbols   A **continued inequality** has *two* valid inequality symbols in it; *they must both be "less than" symbols or both be "greater than" symbols.* If the continued inequality $a < b < c$ is to be valid, the following two inequalities must *both* be true: $a < b$ and $b < c$.*

Example 5   Examples of continued inequalities:

a. $4 < 7 < 9$ is read "4 is less than 7, which is less than 9." It can also be read "7 is greater than 4 *and* less than 9." (Remember that $4 < 7$ can be replaced by $7 > 4$.) $4 < 7 < 9$ means that 7 is *between* 4 and 9.

b. $10 > 0 > -3$ is read "10 is greater than 0, which is greater than -3," or "0 is less than 10 and greater than -3." (Remember that $10 > 0$ can be replaced by $0 < 10$.) $10 > 0 > -3$ means that 0 is between 10 and -3.

NOTE   Even though the statement $10 > 0 > -3$ is correct as written, it is customary to write such continued inequalities so that the numbers are in the same order as on the number line, that is, $-3 < 0 < 10$. ∎

---

* It must also be true that a must be less than c because of the *transitive property of inequalities*. The transitive property states that if $x < y$ and $y < z$, then $x < z$.

A WORD OF CAUTION Notice that $-3 < 0 > -2$ is *not* correct because the inequality symbols are not both less than or both greater than. $\boxed{\checkmark}$

Example 6 Determine whether each of the following is a valid or an invalid continued inequality:

a. $10 < 12 > 5$

Invalid because one symbol is $<$ and the other is $>$

b. $10 < 15 < 32$

Valid because both symbols are $<$ *and* it is true that $10 < 15$, $15 < 32$, *and* $10 < 32$

c. $2 > 5 > 8$

Invalid because $2 > 5$, $5 > 8$, and $2 > 8$ are *false* statements

d. $9 > 3 < 5$

Invalid because one symbol is $>$ and the other is $<$ ∎

The Slash Line Symbol A slash line drawn through a symbol puts a "not" in the meaning of the symbol. We've seen this already in such symbols as $\neq$, $\notin$, and $\nsubseteq$. The symbol $\not<$ is read " is not less than " and is equivalent to the symbol $\geq$. The symbol $\not>$ is read " is not greater than ."

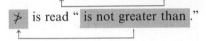

Example 7 Examples showing the use of the slash line:

a. $3 \not< -2$ is read "3 is *not* less than -2."

b. $-6 \not> -5$ is read "-6 is *not* greater than -5. It is equivalent to $-6 \leq -5$. ∎

Absolute Value The symbol for the **absolute value** of a real number x is $|x|$. The formal definition of the absolute value of a real number x is

$$|x| = \begin{cases} x \text{ if } x \geq 0 & (x \text{ is greater than zero, or } x \text{ equals zero}) \\ -x \text{ if } x < 0 & (x \text{ is less than zero}) \end{cases}$$

$-x$ is *not* a negative number in this case because x is a negative number, and the negative of a negative number is positive; for example, if $x = -2$, then $-x = -(-2) = 2$

We can think of the absolute value of a number as being the distance between that number and 0 on the number line *with no regard for direction*. See Figure 1.3.1.

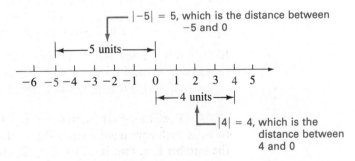

FIGURE 1.3.1 ABSOLUTE VALUE

NOTE The absolute value of a number is always positive or zero. $\boxed{\checkmark}$

Example 8   Examples of absolute values of real numbers:

a. $|9| = 9$ The distance between 0 and 9 is 9

b. $|-4| = -(-4) = 4$ The distance between -4 and 0 is 4

c. $-|-5| = -(+5) = -5$

d. $-|3| = -(+3) = -3$

e. $|0| = 0$

NOTE In (c) and (d), negative signs were located *outside* the absolute value symbols. ■

EXERCISES 1.3B

Set I   In Exercises 1 and 2, evaluate each expression.

1. a. $|7|$ b. $|-5|$ c. $-|-12|$

2. a. $|-34|$ b. $-|5|$ c. $-|-3|$

In Exercises 3 and 4, determine which of the two symbols, $<$ or $>$, should be used to make each statement true.

3. a. $-15 ? -13$ b. $-15 ? |-13|$ c. $|-15| ? -13$ d. $|2| ? |-3|$

4. a. $-19 ? -23$ b. $-19 ? |-23|$ c. $|-19| ? -23$ d. $|-19| ? |-23|$

In Exercises 5 and 6, determine whether each inequality is a valid or an invalid continued inequality. If it is invalid, state *why* the inequality is invalid.

5. a. $3 < 5 < 10$ b. $-2 > 1 > 7$ c. $0 < 4 > 2$

d. $8 > 3 > -1$ e. $8 > 5 < 9$ f. $0 > 3 > 8$

6. a. $4 > 0 > -2$ b. $-2 < 6 > 5$ c. $3 > 1 < 7$

d. $-1 < 3 < 6$ e. $4 > 7 > 11$ f. $5 < 0 < -2$

In Exercises 7 and 8, determine whether the expression is true or false.

7. $3 \not< 8$ **8.** $-4 \not> 5$

Set II   In Exercises 1 and 2, evaluate each expression.

1. a. $|-15|$ b. $|35|$ c. $-|-22|$

2. a. $-|-5|$ b. $-|13|$ c. $|-2|$

In Exercises 3 and 4, determine which of the two symbols, $<$ or $>$, should be used to make each statement true.

3. a. $-18 ? -12$ b. $-63 ? |-104|$ c. $|7| ? |-8|$ d. $|-3| ? -5$

4. a. $0 ? |-5|$ b. $|15| ? |-3|$ c. $-8 ? |-6|$ d. $|10| ? |-14|$

In Exercises 5 and 6, determine whether the inequality is a valid or an invalid continued inequality. If it is invalid, state *why* the inequality is invalid.

5. a. $-1 < 7 > 5$ b. $0 < 4 < 6$ c. $1 > 3 > 7$

d. $3 > 2 < 5$ e. $8 < 4 < 2$ f. $8 > 2 > -4$

6. a. $-3 < 5 > 4$ **b.** $18 > 5 > -6$ **c.** $2 > 0 < 8$

d. $-8 < -6 < -2$ **e.** $-3 > 1 > 5$ **f.** $8 > 5 > 1$

In Exercises 7 and 8, determine whether the statement is true or false.

7. $-2 \not> 0$ **8.** $3 \not< -5$

1.4 Operations on Signed Numbers

Addition of Signed Numbers

The answer to an addition problem is called the **sum**. The rules for addition of signed numbers can be summarized as follows:

TO ADD TWO SIGNED NUMBERS

1. When the numbers have the same sign:

  1. Add their absolute values *and*

  2. Give the sum the sign of both numbers.

2. When the numbers have different signs:

  1. Subtract the smaller absolute value from the larger absolute value *and*

  2. Give that answer the sign of the number with the larger absolute value

---

Example 1   Examples of adding signed numbers:

a. $(-7) + (-11) = -18$ Case 1
  — Sum of absolute values $(7 + 11 = 18)$
  — Same sign as both numbers

b. $(+18.3) + (-32) = -13.7$ Case 2
  — Difference of absolute values $(32 - 18.3 = 13.7)$
  — Sign of number with larger absolute value (-32)

c. $-\dfrac{1}{8} + \dfrac{3}{4} = +\dfrac{5}{8}$ Case 2
  — Difference of absolute values $\left(\dfrac{3}{4} - \dfrac{1}{8} = \dfrac{5}{8}\right)$
  — Sign of number with larger absolute value $\left(\dfrac{3}{4}\right)$ ∎

Additive Identity   Since adding 0 to a number gives the identical number we started with (for example, $7 + 0 = 0 + 7 = 7$), we call 0 the **additive identity**.

THE ADDITIVE IDENTITY IS 0

If a is any real number, then $a + 0 = 0 + a = a$

Additive Inverse When the sum of two numbers is 0, we say they are the **additive inverses** of each other. Therefore, the *negative* of a number can also be called the *additive inverse* of that number.

ADDITIVE INVERSE

The *additive inverse* of a is $-a$.

$$a + (-a) = 0$$

$$-a + a = 0$$

Subtraction of Signed Numbers

Subtraction is the *inverse* operation of addition. That is, it "undoes" addition. The answer to a subtraction problem is called the **difference**.

DEFINITION OF SUBTRACTION

$$a - b = a + (-b)$$

This definition leads to the following rules for subtracting signed numbers:

TO SUBTRACT ONE SIGNED NUMBER FROM ANOTHER

1. Change the subtraction symbol to an addition symbol *and* change the sign of the number being subtracted.

2. Add the resulting signed numbers.

Subtraction Involving Zero

If a is any real number, then

1. $a - 0 = a$ because $a - 0 = a + (-0) = a + 0 = a$.

2. $0 - a = -a$ because $0 - a = 0 + (-a) = -a$.

A WORD OF CAUTION "Subtract a from b" means $b - a$. ☑

Example 2   Examples of subtracting signed numbers:

a. Subtract -3 from 0. [This means $0 - (-3)$.]

$$0 - (-3) = -(-3) = 3 \quad or \quad 0 - (-3) = 0 + (+3) = 3$$

b. Subtract 4 from -2. [This means $(-2) - (+4)$.]

$$(-2) - (+4) = -2 + (-4) = -6$$

c. $2.345 - 11.6 = 2.345 + (-11.6) = -9.255$

d. $\dfrac{2}{3} - \left(-\dfrac{2}{5}\right) = \dfrac{2}{3} + \left(+\dfrac{2}{5}\right) = \dfrac{16}{15}$ or $1\dfrac{1}{15}$ ∎

Multiplication of Signed Numbers

The answer to a multiplication problem is called the **product**. The rules for multiplying two signed numbers are summarized as follows:

TO MULTIPLY TWO SIGNED NONZERO NUMBERS

Multiply their absolute values *and* attach the correct sign to the left of the product of the absolute values. The sign is *positive* when the numbers have the same sign and *negative* when the numbers have different signs.

Multiplicative Identity   Since multiplying any real number by 1 gives the identical number we started with (for example, $0.15 \times 1 = 1 \times 0.15 = 0.15$), we call 1 the **multiplicative identity**.

THE MULTIPLICATIVE IDENTITY IS 1

If a is any real number, then

$$a \cdot 1 = 1 \cdot a = a$$

NOTE   The *multiplicative inverse* will be discussed in Section 6.3.   ☑

Multiplication Involving Zero   Multiplying any real number by 0 gives a product of 0.

If a is any real number, then

$$a \cdot 0 = 0 \cdot a = 0$$

Example 3   Examples of multiplying signed numbers:

a. $(-0.14)(-10) = +1.40$

        — Product of the absolute values:
          $0.14 \times 10 = 1.40$

        — Positive because the numbers have
          the same sign

b. $\left(4\dfrac{1}{2}\right)\left(-1\dfrac{1}{3}\right) = \left(\dfrac{9}{2}\right)\left(-\dfrac{4}{3}\right) = -\left(\dfrac{9\cdot4}{2\cdot3}\right) = -\dfrac{6}{1} = -6$

        — Product of the absolute values:

$$\frac{9}{2} \times \frac{4}{3} = \frac{\overset{3}{\cancel{9}}\cdot\overset{2}{\cancel{4}}}{\underset{1}{\cancel{2}}\cdot\underset{1}{\cancel{3}}} = 6$$

        — Negative because the numbers
          have different signs

c. $(-7)(0) = 0$ Product of any real number and 0 is 0 ∎

Division of Signed Numbers

Division is the *inverse* of multiplication because it "undoes" multiplication. The answer to a division problem is called the **quotient**. The number we are dividing *by* is called the **divisor**, and the number we are dividing *into* is called the **dividend**. If the divisor does not divide exactly into the dividend, the part that is left over is called the **remainder**.

When the remainder is 0, we can say that the divisor and the quotient are both factors of the dividend.

Because of the inverse relation between division and multiplication, the rules for finding the sign of a quotient are the same as those used for finding the sign of a product.

TO DIVIDE ONE SIGNED NUMBER BY ANOTHER

Divide the absolute value of the dividend by the absolute value of the divisor *and* attach the correct sign to the left of the quotient of the absolute values. The sign is *positive* when the numbers have the same sign and *negative* when the numbers have different signs.

To check the answer in a division problem,

Divisor × Quotient + Remainder = Dividend

---

or, if the divisor is a *factor* of the dividend,

$$\boxed{\text{Divisor} \times \text{Quotient} = \text{Dividend}}$$

Division Involving Zero *Division of zero by a number other than zero is possible, and the quotient is always* 0. That is, $0 \div 2$ or $\frac{0}{2} = 0$ because $2 \times 0 = 0$ (divisor × quotient = dividend). Therefore,

$$2\overline{)0}^{\,0}$$

Division of a nonzero number by zero is impossible. Consider $\frac{4}{0}$ or $4 \div 0$. Suppose the quotient is some unknown number we call q. Then $4 \div 0 = q$ means we must find a number q such that $0 \times q = 4$. However, there is no such number, since any number times 0 is 0, and so $0 \times q = 0$. Therefore, $4 \div 0$ *has no answer.*

Division of zero by zero cannot be determined. Consider $0 \div 0$ or $\frac{0}{0}$. Suppose that the quotient is 1. Then $0 \div 0 = 1$. This means that 0×1 has to equal 0, and, in fact, it does. This might lead us to assume that the quotient is indeed 1. But now let us suppose that the quotient is 0. (That is, suppose $0 \div 0 = 0$.) This could be true only if 0×0 equals 0, which it does. Furthermore, we could say $0 \div 0 = 5$, since $0 \times 5 = 0$. The quotient could also be -3 or π or 156, or *any* number! Therefore, we say that $0 \div 0$ cannot be determined.

Division involving zero can be summarized as follows:

If a is any real number *except* 0, then

1. $\frac{0}{a} = 0$

2. $\frac{a}{0}$ is not possible

3. $\frac{0}{0}$ cannot be determined

Example 4   Examples of dividing signed numbers:

a. $(-5) \div (-25) = +\frac{1}{5}$

Quotient of absolute values: $5 \div 25 = \frac{1}{5}$

Positive because the numbers have the same sign

b. $\frac{3\frac{2}{5}}{-17} = \left(3\frac{2}{5}\right) \div (-17) = -\left(\frac{\overset{1}{\cancel{17}}}{5} \cdot \frac{1}{\cancel{17}}\right) = -\frac{1}{5}$ ∎

EXERCISES 1.4

Set I   Perform the indicated operations (or write "not possible" or "cannot be determined").

1. $(5) + (-9)$ **2.** $(-10) + (7)$ **3.** $(-12) + (-7)$

4. $-\dfrac{7}{8} + \left(-\dfrac{3}{8}\right)$ **5.** $-\dfrac{7}{12} + \left(-\dfrac{1}{6}\right)$ **6.** $-\dfrac{3}{4} + \left(-\dfrac{3}{8}\right)$

7. $5\dfrac{1}{4} + \left(-2\dfrac{1}{2}\right)$ **8.** $-1\dfrac{7}{10} + 3\dfrac{2}{5}$ **9.** $(-13.5) - (-8.06)$

10. $-1.5 - (-1.13)$ **11.** $2.4 - (-13)$ **12.** $7.2 - (-89)$

13. $\dfrac{1}{3} - \left(-\dfrac{1}{2}\right)$ **14.** $17\dfrac{5}{6} - \left(-8\dfrac{1}{3}\right)$ **15.** $-5\dfrac{3}{4} - 2\dfrac{1}{2}$

16. $-1.56 - 9.7$ **17.** $16.71 - (-18.9)$ **18.** $8.9 - (-3.71)$

19. $0 - 3$ **20.** $0\,(-3)$ **21.** $(-26)(-10)$

22. $(-1.1)(-7)$ **23.** $\dfrac{3}{8}\left(-\dfrac{4}{9}\right)$ **24.** $\dfrac{-150}{10}$

25. $-12 \div 36$ **26.** $\dfrac{-15}{-6}$ **27.** $7\dfrac{1}{2} \div \left(-\dfrac{1}{2}\right)$

28. $-\dfrac{5}{4} \div 0$ **29.** $0 \div \left(-\dfrac{3}{8}\right)$ **30.** $0 \div 0$

31. $-\dfrac{5}{4} \div \left(-\dfrac{3}{8}\right)$ **32.** $-25,000 \div (-100)$

33. Subtract -3 from -8.   **34.** Subtract 0.3 from -1.26.

35. Subtract $-\dfrac{2}{3}$ from 5.   **36.** $|-8| + (-15)$

37. $|-10| - (-25)$ **38.** $|-2| - |-9|$

39. $-3|-4|$ **40.** $|-15| - 4$

Set II   Perform the indicated operations (or write "not possible" or "cannot be determined").

1. $(-59) + (74)$ **2.** $(6) + (-15)$ **3.** $\dfrac{5}{8} + \left(-\dfrac{3}{4}\right)$

4. $\dfrac{1}{2} + \dfrac{1}{3}$ **5.** $-4\dfrac{1}{2} + 1\dfrac{3}{4}$ **6.** $10\dfrac{3}{8} + \left(-2\dfrac{3}{4}\right)$

7. $(-395.7) + (84.91)$ **8.** $-1\dfrac{2}{3} + \left(-3\dfrac{2}{5}\right)$ **9.** $281 - (960)$

10. $3.62 + (-1.634)$ **11.** $28.61 - (-37.9)$ **12.** $-8 - (-3.2)$

13. $-18\dfrac{3}{10} - 7\dfrac{2}{5}$ **14.** $16\dfrac{2}{3} - \left(-3\dfrac{7}{12}\right)$ **15.** $-6.483 - (-2.7)$

16. $3.28 - 7.6$ **17.** $(-26)(10)$ **18.** $-5.2 - (7.3)$

19. $0(-13)$ **20.** $0 - 13$ **21.** $(-34)(12)$

22. $-6(0)$ **23.** $\dfrac{3}{7}\left(\dfrac{-14}{15}\right)$ **24.** $\dfrac{-180}{10}$

25. $-15 \div 60$ **26.** $-4 \div 12$ **27.** $\dfrac{0}{0}$

28. $\dfrac{2}{3} \div 0$ **29.** $0 \div 7$ **30.** $1.6 \div 0$

31. Subtract -1 from -2.   **32.** Subtract 1.26 from 0.3.

33. $\dfrac{160}{-40}$ **34.** Subtract -5.2 from -1.63.

35. $|-3| + (-7)$ **36.** $|-6| - |-10|$

37. $|-5| - (-6)$ **38.** $4 - |-8|$

39. $|8| + |-18|$ **40.** $-2 - |-10|$

1.5 Commutative, Associative, and Distributive Properties of Real Numbers

Commutative Properties

Addition Is Commutative   If we change the order of the two numbers in an addition problem, we get the same sum. This property is called the **commutative property of addition**.

COMMUTATIVE PROPERTY OF ADDITION

If a and b represent any real numbers, then

$$a + b = b + a$$

Example 1

$7 + 5 = 5 + 7$ Order changed

$12 \ = \ 12$ True ∎

Subtraction is not commutative, as a single example will prove:

Example 2

$3 - 2 \neq 2 - 3$ Order changed

$1 \ \neq \ -1$ Unequal ∎

Multiplication Is Commutative   If we change the order of the two numbers in a multiplication problem, we get the same product. This property is called the **commutative property of multiplication**.

COMMUTATIVE PROPERTY OF MULTIPLICATION

If a and b are real numbers, then

$$a \cdot b = b \cdot a$$

Example 3

$$(4)(5) = (5)(4) \qquad \text{Order changed}$$
$$20 \;=\; 20 \qquad \text{True} \quad \blacksquare$$

Division is not commutative, as a single example will prove:

Example 4

$$10 \div 5 \neq 5 \div 10 \qquad \text{Order changed}$$
$$2 \neq \frac{1}{2} \qquad \text{Unequal} \quad \blacksquare$$

Associative Properties

Addition Is Associative   In adding three numbers, the sum is unchanged no matter how the numbers are grouped. This property is called the **associative property of addition**.

ASSOCIATIVE PROPERTY OF ADDITION

If a, b, and c represent any real numbers, then

$$a + b + c = (a + b) + c = a + (b + c)$$

Example 5

$$(2 + 3) + 4 = 2 + (3 + 4) \qquad \text{Grouping changed}$$
$$5 \;+ 4 = 2 +\; 7$$
$$9 \;=\; 9 \qquad \text{True} \quad \blacksquare$$

Subtraction is not associative, as a single example will prove:

Example 6

$$(7 - 4) - 8 \neq 7 - (4 - 8) \qquad \text{Grouping changed}$$
$$3 \;- 8 \neq 7 - \;(-4)$$
$$-5 \;\neq\; 11 \qquad \text{Unequal} \quad \blacksquare$$

Multiplication Is Associative   In multiplying three numbers, the product is unchanged no matter how the numbers are grouped. This property is called the **associative property of multiplication**.

ASSOCIATIVE PROPERTY OF MULTIPLICATION

If a, b, and c are real numbers, then

$$a \cdot b \cdot c = (a \cdot b) \cdot c = a \cdot (b \cdot c)$$

Example 7

$$(3 \cdot 4) \cdot 2 = 3 \cdot (4 \cdot 2) \qquad \text{Grouping changed}$$
$$12 \;\cdot 2 = 3 \cdot\; 8$$
$$24 \;=\; 24 \qquad \text{True} \quad \blacksquare$$

Division is not associative, as a single example will prove:

Example 8

$$(16 \div 4) \div 2 \neq 16 \div (4 \div 2) \qquad \text{Grouping changed}$$

$$4 \quad \div 2 \neq 16 \div \quad 2$$

$$2 \quad \neq \quad 8 \qquad \text{Unequal} \quad \blacksquare$$

How to Determine Whether Commutativity or Associativity Has Been Used In commutativity, the numbers or letters actually exchange places (commute).

$$a + b = b + a \qquad c \cdot d = d \cdot c$$

The first element occupies the second place and vice versa.

In associativity, the numbers or letters stay in their original places, but the grouping (combination) is changed.

$$a + (b + c) = (a + b) + c \qquad (d \cdot e) \cdot f = d \cdot (e \cdot f)$$

Distributive Property

The distributive rule is one of the most important and most often used rules in mathematics.

Multiplication Is Distributive over Addition The distributive rule can be verified by substituting *any* real numbers for a, b, and c. We may distribute from either the right or from the left.

MULTIPLICATION IS DISTRIBUTIVE OVER ADDITION

$$a(b + c) = ab + ac$$

$$(b + c)a = ba + ca$$

NOTE The distributive rules may be extended to include any number of terms inside the parentheses, and the terms may be subtracted as well as added. That is,

$$a(b + c - d + e) = ab + ac - ad + ae$$

and so forth.
☑

Example 9

$$3(5 + 7) = 3 \cdot 5 + 3 \cdot 7$$

$$3(\ 12 \ ) = \ 15 + 21$$

$$36 = 36 \quad \blacksquare$$

A WORD OF CAUTION A common mistake students make is to think that the distributive rule applies to expressions such as $2(3 \cdot 4)$.

The distributive rule applies only when this is an addition or subtraction ───────┐

$$2(3 \cdot 4) \neq (2 \cdot 3)(2 \cdot 4)$$

$$2(12) \neq \ 6 \ \cdot 8$$

$$24 \ \neq \ \ 48$$
☑

27

Example 10   State whether each of the following is true or false. If the statement is *true*, give the reason.

a. $(1.2 + 5) + 2.4 = 1.2 + (5 + 2.4)$ True (Addition is associative.)

b. $\dfrac{2}{3}\left(-\dfrac{5}{8}\right) = -\dfrac{5}{8}\left(\dfrac{2}{3}\right)$ True (Multiplication is commutative.)

c. $-8(1) = -8$ True (Multiplicative identity.)

d. $0.1 - 5 = 5 - 0.1$ False

e. $17 + (-17) = 0$ True (Additive inverse.)

f. $3(7 + 9) = 3(7) + 3(9)$ True (Distributive rule.)

g. $2 \div \left(\dfrac{3}{5}\right) = \left(\dfrac{3}{5}\right) \div 2$ False

h. $(y \div z) \div x = y \div (z \div x)$ False

i. $4(2 \cdot 3) = 4(2) \cdot 4(3)$ False

j. $(1 + 2) + 3 = (2 + 1) + 3$ True (Addition is commutative. Notice that the *order* was changed, not the grouping.) ■

NOTE   We will accept the commutative, associative, and distributive rules as true without proof. ☑

EXERCISES 1.5

Set I   State whether each of the following is true or false. If the statement is *true*, give the reason.

1. $5 + 10 = 10 + 5$

2. $x + y = y + x$

3. $(3)(8 + 2) = (2 + 8)(3)$

4. $(2)(5 + 6) = (6 + 5)(2)$

5. $3(8 + 2) = 3 \cdot 8 + 3 \cdot 2$

6. $2(5 + 6) = 2 \cdot 5 + 2 \cdot 6$

7. $6 - (4 - 2) = (6 - 4) - 2$

8. $(12 \div 6) \div 3 = 12 \div (6 \div 3)$

9. $14(7 \cdot 2) = 14(7) \cdot 14(2)$

10. $25(2 \cdot 6) = 25(2) \cdot 25(6)$

11. $16 - 4 = 4 - 16$

12. $\left(\frac{2}{3}\right) \div \left(\frac{1}{2}\right) = \left(\frac{1}{2}\right) \div \left(\frac{2}{3}\right)$

13. $6 + (2 \cdot 4) = 6 + (4 \cdot 2)$

14. $(6)(3) + 4 = 4 + (3)(6)$

15. $19 + 0 = 19$

16. $0 + (-5) = -5$

17. $8 + (2 + 4) = (8 + 2) + 4$

18. $(8)(2) - 10 = 10 - (2)(8)$

19. $3(0) = 3$

20. $0(-1) = -1$

21. $(7 + 5)(3) = 7(3) + 5(3)$

22. $(6 + 2)(5) = 6(5) + 2(5)$

23. $1(-6) = -6$

24. $5(1) = 5$

25. $4 \div 12 = 12 \div 4$

26. $31 + 2 = 2 + 31$

27. $-8 + 8 = 0$

28. $15 + (-15) = 0$

Set II State whether each of the following is true or false. If the statement is *true*, give t͟͟
reason.

1. $8 + 3 = 3 + 8$

2. $6 \cdot 3 + 6 \cdot 8 = 6(3 + 8)$

3. $(7)(2 + 3) = (3 + 2)(7)$

4. $\frac{7}{8} \div 8 = 8 \div \frac{7}{8}$

5. $4(9 + 3) = 4(9) + 4(3)$

6. $4(2 + 9) = 4(9 + 2)$

7. $4(9 \cdot 3) = 4(9) \cdot 4(3)$

8. $3(7) = 7(3)$

9. $(7)(8) = (8)(7)$

10. $(6 \cdot 7)5 = (6 \cdot 5) \cdot (7 \cdot 5)$

11. $16 \div 5 = 5 \div 16$

12. $2 - 8 = 8 - 2$

13. $16 - 23 = 23 - 16$

14. $(1 + 4)(5) = 1(5) + 4(5)$

15. $18 + 0 = 18$

16. $-6 + 6 = 0$

17. $5 + (4 + 2) = (2 + 4) + 5$

18. $\frac{1}{2}(6 + 7) = \frac{1}{2}(6) + \frac{1}{2}(7)$

19. $0(-6) = -6$

20. $1(-6) = -6$

21. $3(5 \cdot 7) = (3 \cdot 5)(7)$

22. $17 \div 1 = 1 \div 17$

23. $(-4)(1) = -4$

24. $-4 + 4 = 0$

25. $(4 + 9)(2) = 4(2) + 9(2)$

26. $0 \div 5 = 5 \div 0$

27. $13 + (-13) = 0$

28. $13(0) = 0$

1.6 Powers of Rational Numbers

The shortened notation for a product such as $3 \cdot 3 \cdot 3 \cdot 3$ is 3^4. That is, by definition,

$$3^4 = 3 \cdot 3 \cdot 3 \cdot 3 = 81$$

Base and Exponent

In the expression 3^4, 3 is called the **base** and 4 is called the **exponent**. The number 4 (the exponent) indicates that 3 (the base) is to be used as a *factor* 4 times. An exponent is written as a small number above and to the right of the base. The entire symbol 3^4 is called an *exponential expression* and is commonly read as "three to the fourth power" or "three to the fourth." See Figure 1.6.1.

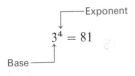

FIGURE 1.6.1

A WORD OF CAUTION When you write an exponential number, *be sure that your exponents look like exponents.* For example, be sure that 3^4 does not look like 34.

When the exponent is 2, as in b^2, we usually say "*b* squared" rather than "*b* to the second power"; likewise, when the exponent is 3, as in b^3, we usually say "*b* cubed" rather than "*b* to the third power."

A WORD OF CAUTION *The exponent always applies only to the immediately preceding symbol.* Students often think that expressions such as $(-6)^2$ and -6^2 are the same. They are *not* the same. For example, in the expression

$$(-6)^2 = (-6)(-6) = 36$$

the exponent applies to everything inside of the ( ) because the immediately preceding symbol is), part of the grouping symbol ( ), while in the expression

$$-6^2 = -6 \cdot 6 = -36$$

the exponent applies *only* to the 6. Therefore, $-6^2 \neq (-6)^2$. ☑

Even Power   If a base has an exponent that is an even number, we say that it is an **even power** of the base. For example, 3^2, 5^4, and $(-2)^6$ are even powers.

Odd Power   If a base has an exponent that is an odd number, we say that it is an **odd power** of the base. For example, 3^1, 10^3, and $(-4)^5$ are odd powers.

Example 1   Examples of powers:

a. $2^3 = 2 \cdot 2 \cdot 2 = 8$ $2^3 = 8$ is read "two cubed equals 8"; it is an odd power

b. $(-4)^2 = (-4)(-4) = 16$ $(-4)^2 = 16$ is read "negative four squared equals 16"; it is an even power

c. $(-0.2)^3 = (-0.2)(-0.2)(-0.2) = -0.008$

   NOTICE: An *odd* power of a negative real number is always negative

   NOTICE: An *even* power of a negative real number is always positive

d. $\left(-\dfrac{1}{2}\right)^2 = \left(-\dfrac{1}{2}\right)\left(-\dfrac{1}{2}\right) = \dfrac{1}{4}$

e. $1^5 = 1 \cdot 1 \cdot 1 \cdot 1 \cdot 1 = 1$

f. $(-1)^9 = -1$

g. $0^4 = 0 \cdot 0 \cdot 0 \cdot 0 = 0$ Any nonzero power of 0 equals 0   ■

In the examples above, the exponents were all natural numbers. Cases in which exponents are numbers other than natural numbers will be discussed in Section 1.11B.

NOTE   It is suggested that you memorize the squares of the first sixteen whole numbers and the cubes of the first five whole numbers. ☑

Finding Powers with a Calculator   Many calculators have an x^2 key, $\boxed{x^2}$, and some have a y^x or x^y key, $\boxed{y^x}$ or $\boxed{x^y}$.

Example 2   Find 38^2 with a calculator.

On most calculators, to find 38^2 press these keys (in order): $\boxed{3}$ $\boxed{8}$ $\boxed{x^2}$. The display shows 1444. Therefore, $38^2 = 1,444$. (If your calculator uses Reverse Polish Logic (RPL), consult your instruction manual.)   ■

Example 3   Find 4^5 with a calculator (if your calculator has a $\boxed{y^x}$ key).

Press these keys (in order): $\boxed{4}$ $\boxed{y^x}$ $\boxed{5}$. The display shows 1024. Therefore, $4^5 = 1,024$. (Again, if your calculator uses RPL, consult your manual.) ■

EXERCISES 1.6

Set I   Find the value of each of the following expressions. In Exercises 1–15, do *not* use a calculator.

1. 4^3 **2.** 7^2 **3.** $(-3)^4$ **4.** $(-2)^4$

5. -2^4 **6.** -3^4 **7.** 0^5 **8.** 0^6

9. $(-1)^{49}$ **10.** $(-1)^{50}$ **11.** $\left(\dfrac{1}{2}\right)^4$ **12.** $\left(\dfrac{7}{8}\right)^2$

13. $(-0.1)^3$ **14.** $(0.1)^4$ **15.** $\left(\dfrac{1}{10}\right)^3$ **16.** 17.3^2

17. 9.2^3 **18.** $(-1.5)^4$ **19.** $(-2.5)^4$ **20.** $(-5.3)^3$

Set II   Find the value of each of the following expressions. In Exercises 1–15, do *not* use a calculator.

1. 5^3 **2.** $(-2)^6$ **3.** -2^6 **4.** 0^4

5. $(-15)^2$ **6.** $(-3)^3$ **7.** $(-1)^{79}$ **8.** $(-1)^{64}$

9. $\left(\dfrac{1}{10}\right)^4$ **10.** $(-2)^3$ **11.** -2^7 **12.** $(-1)^{83}$

13. $(-13)^2$ **14.** -2^3 **15.** $\left(\dfrac{1}{10}\right)^5$ **16.** $(-1.4)^3$

17. $(-1.26)^4$ **18.** $(-3.8)^4$ **19.** $(3)^9$ **20.** 18^3

1.7 Roots

1.7A Square Roots

Just as subtraction is the inverse operation of addition and division is the inverse operation of multiplication, finding roots is an inverse operation of raising to powers. Thus, finding the **square root** of a number is the inverse operation of squaring a number.

Every positive number has both a positive and a negative square root. The positive square root is called the **principal square root**.

The Square Root Symbol

The notation for the principal square root of p is $\sqrt{p}$, which is read "the square root of p." When we are asked to find $\sqrt{p}$, we must find some positive number whose square is p. For example, "find $\sqrt{9}$" means we must find a positive number whose square is 9. The answer is, of course, that $\sqrt{9} = 3$.

The entire expression $\sqrt{p}$ is called a **radical expression** or, more simply, a **radical**. The parts of a radical are shown in Figure 1.7.1.

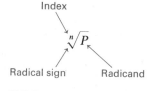

FIGURE 1.7.1

When no index is given, the index is understood to be 2, and the radical is a square root.

A WORD OF CAUTION   When the symbol $\sqrt{p}$ is used, it *always* represents the *principal square root* of *p*. Since the principal square root is positive, $\sqrt{p}$ is always positive (or zero).   ☑

In this section the radicand will always be the square of some integer.* You will find such problems easy to do if you have memorized the squares of the first sixteen whole numbers.

Example 1   Examples of finding the principal square roots:

a. $\sqrt{36} = 6$ This is true because $6^2 = 36$

b. $\sqrt{0} = 0$ This is true because $0^2 = 0$

c. $\sqrt{1} = 1$ This is true because $1^2 = 1$

d. $-\sqrt{9} = -(\sqrt{9}) = -3;$ Since $\sqrt{9} = 3, -\sqrt{9} = -3$ ■

A WORD OF CAUTION   Note that in Example 1d the negative sign was *outside* the radical sign. Had the problem been $\sqrt{-9}$, we could not have solved it at this time. No *real* number exists whose square is -9, since the square of every real number is always positive or zero. We will discuss square roots of negative numbers in Chapter 7.   ☑

EXERCISES 1.7A

Set I   Find the principal roots:

1. $-\sqrt{36}$ **2.** $\sqrt{49}$ **3.** $-\sqrt{25}$ **4.** $\sqrt{64}$ **5.** $-\sqrt{100}$

6. $-\sqrt{144}$ **7.** $\sqrt{81}$ **8.** $\sqrt{121}$ **9.** $-\sqrt{256}$ **10.** $-\sqrt{16}$

Set II   Find the principal roots:

1. $-\sqrt{169}$ **2.** $-\sqrt{49}$ **3.** $\sqrt{225}$ **4.** $\sqrt{289}$ **5.** $-\sqrt{400}$

6. $\sqrt{144}$ **7.** $-\sqrt{900}$ **8.** $-\sqrt{64}$ **9.** $\sqrt{100}$ **10.** $-\sqrt{121}$

1.7B   Finding Square Roots with a Calculator

We can easily find the square root of a number such as 762,129 by using a calculator that has a square root key, ☑ . We would simply press the following keys (in order): | 7 | | 6 | | 2 | | 1 | | 2 | | 9 | | √ | . The display shows

---

* In Section 1.7B we will consider square roots in which the radicand is *not* the square of an integer.

873. Thus, $\sqrt{762,129} = 873$. We can also use the calculator to *approximate* square roots of numbers when the radicands are not the squares of whole numbers.

Example 2   Approximating square roots with the calculator.

Find $\sqrt{2}$. Since this is an *irrational* number—that is, there is no integer whose square is 2—its decimal approximation will not terminate and will not repeat. We press these keys: ⬚ 2 ⬚ ⬚ $\sqrt{}$ ⬚. The display shows 1.414213562. (Your calculator may not show the same number of digits.) If we round off this answer to three decimal places, we see that $\sqrt{2} \doteq 1.414$ ■

EXERCISES 1.7B

Set I   Find the exact or approximate square roots, using a calculator. (Round off approximate roots to three decimal places.)

1. $\sqrt{209,764}$ **2.** $\sqrt{389,376}$ **3.** $\sqrt{12}$ **4.** $\sqrt{17}$

5. $\sqrt{184}$ **6.** $\sqrt{191}$ **7.** $\sqrt{2.8}$ **8.** $\sqrt{9.38}$

Set II   Find the exact or approximate square roots, using a calculator. (Round off approximate roots to three decimal places.)

1. $\sqrt{393,129}$ **2.** $\sqrt{395,641}$ **3.** $\sqrt{18}$ **4.** $\sqrt{23}$

5. $\sqrt{172}$ **6.** $\sqrt{1.63}$ **7.** $\sqrt{85.2}$ **8.** $\sqrt{73.2}$

1.7C   Higher Roots

Roots other than square roots are called **higher roots**.

Radicals   A **radical** is any indicated root of a number. Some examples of radicals are $\sqrt{9}, \sqrt{2}, \sqrt{8}, \sqrt[3]{8}, \sqrt[3]{55},$ and $\sqrt[5]{-32}$.

Some Symbols Used to Indicate Roots   The symbol $\sqrt[3]{p}$ indicates the *cubic root* of p. When the *index* of a radical is 3, we must find a number whose *cube* is p; for example, $\sqrt[3]{8} = 2$ because $2^3 = 8$. You will find these problems easier to do if you have memorized the cubes of the first few whole numbers.

The notation $\sqrt[4]{p}$ indicates the *fourth root* of p. When the *index* is 4, we must find a number whose *fourth power* is p. The symbol $\sqrt[5]{p}$ indicates a *fifth root*, and so forth.

When the index is an even number, we call the index an *even index*. When the index is an odd number, we call the index an *odd index*.

Principal Roots   Every even-index radical with a positive radicand has *both* a positive and a negative real root; the positive root is called the *principal root*. (An even-index radical with a negative radicand is not real.) Every odd-index radical has a single real root called the *principal root*; the principal root is *positive* when the radicand is positive and *negative* when the radicand is negative.

NOTE   Mathematicians agree that the radical symbol is to stand for the principal root. ☑

Principal roots can be summarized as follows:

PRINCIPAL ROOTS

The symbol $\sqrt[n]{p}$ always represents the principal nth root of p.

If the radicand is positive, the principal root is positive.

If the radicand is negative and the index is

1. odd, the principal root is negative.

2. even, the root is not a real number.

Example 3 Finding higher roots:

a. Find $\sqrt[4]{16}$.

We must find a positive number whose *fourth* power is 16. That is, we must solve $(?)^4 = 16$. If we have memorized that $2^4 = 16$, then this problem is easy to do. If we haven't memorized that fact, then we must use the "trial and error" method. That is, we start with 1 and check to see if $1^4 = 16$. It doesn't. Next, we check to see if $2^4 = 16$. It does. Therefore, $\sqrt[4]{16} = 2$.

b. Find $-\sqrt[3]{-343}$.

Since the index is odd and the radicand is negative, the principal root of $\sqrt[3]{-343}$ will be negative. We must find a negative number whose cube is -343. We will use the "trial and error" method. We probably know that $(-3)^3 = -27$ and that $(-4)^3 = -64$. Does $(-5)^3 = -343$? No; $(-5)^3 = -125$. Does $(-6)^3 = -343$? No; $(-6)^3 = -216$. Does $(-7)^3 = -343$? Yes! Therefore, $\sqrt[3]{-343} = -7$. But the problem was to find the *negative* of $\sqrt[3]{-343}$, that is, $-\sqrt[3]{-343}$. $-\sqrt[3]{-343} = -(-7) = 7$. Therefore, $-\sqrt[3]{-343} = 7$. ∎

All roots of positive numbers (and zero) and all odd roots of negative numbers are *real numbers* and therefore can be represented by points on the number line. See Figure 1.7.2.

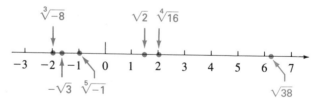

FIGURE 1.7.2

EXERCISES 1.7C

Set I   Find each indicated root either by inspection or by trial and error.

1. $\sqrt[3]{8}$ **2.** $\sqrt[5]{1}$ **3.** $-\sqrt[3]{27}$ **4.** $-\sqrt[4]{16}$

5. $\sqrt[3]{-64}$ **6.** $\sqrt[3]{-27}$ **7.** $-\sqrt[5]{32}$ **8.** $-\sqrt[3]{64}$

9. $\sqrt[3]{-1,000}$ **10.** $\sqrt[3]{-216}$ **11.** $-\sqrt[5]{-32}$ **12.** $-\sqrt[3]{-125}$

Set II   Find each indicated root either by inspection or by trial and error.

1. $\sqrt[4]{16}$ **2.** $-\sqrt[7]{-1}$ **3.** $\sqrt[5]{-243}$ **4.** $\sqrt[3]{-125}$

5. $-\sqrt[4]{81}$ **6.** $-\sqrt[6]{64}$ **7.** $-\sqrt[3]{216}$ **8.** $-\sqrt[3]{-8}$

9. $\sqrt[3]{27}$ **10.** $\sqrt[9]{1}$ **11.** $\sqrt[3]{-1}$ **12.** $\sqrt[4]{10,000}$

1.8 Order of Operations

In evaluating expressions with more than one operation, the following order of operations is used:

ORDER OF OPERATIONS

1. If there are any parentheses in the expression, that part of the expression within a pair of parentheses is evaluated first. Then the entire expression is evaluated.

2. Any evaluation always proceeds in this order:

First: Powers and roots are done.

Second: Multiplication and division are done in order from left to right.

Third: Addition and subtraction are done in order from left to right.

Example 1   Evaluate $8 - 6 - 4 + 7$.

It is important to realize that an expression such as $8 - 6 - 4 + 7$ is evaluated by doing the addition and subtraction *in order from left to right*, because subtraction is neither associative nor commutative. If the expression is considered as a *sum*—that is, as $8 + (-6) + (-4) + 7$—then the terms can be added in any order, because addition *is* commutative and associative.

Both methods correct

Evaluated left to right	*Added in any order*
$8 - 6 - 4 + 7$	$(8) + (-6) + (-4) + (7)$
$= 2 - 4 + 7$	$= (8) + (7) + (-6) + (-4)$
$= -2 + 7$	$= 15 + (-10)$
$= 5$	$= 5$ ∎

Example 2   Evaluate $7 + 3 \cdot 5$.

$$7 + 3 \cdot 5$$

Multiplication is done *before* addition

$$= 7 + 15 = 22 \quad \blacksquare$$

Example 3   Evaluate $4^2 + \sqrt{25} - 6$.

$$4^2 + \sqrt{25} - 6$$

Powers and roots are done first

$$= \underbrace{16 + 5}_{} - 6$$

$$= 21 - 6 = 15 \quad \blacksquare$$

Example 4   Evaluate $16 \div 2 \cdot 4$.

$$\underbrace{16 \div 2}_{} \cdot 4$$

Division is done first because it is on the left

$$= \underbrace{ 8 \cdot 4}_{}$$

$$= 32 \quad \blacksquare$$

Example 5   Evaluate $\sqrt[3]{-8}(-3)^2 - 2(-6)$.

$$\sqrt[3]{-8}(-3)^2 - 2(-6)$$

Roots and powers are done first

$$= -2(9) - 2(-6)$$

Multiplication is done before subtraction

$$= -18 - (-12)$$

$$= -18 + 12 = -6 \quad \blacksquare$$

Example 6   Evaluate $\dfrac{(-4) + (-2)}{8 - 5}$.

$$\frac{(-4) + (-2)}{8 - 5}$$

This bar is a grouping symbol for both $\underline{(-4) + (-2)}$ and $\overline{8 - 5}$; notice that the bar can be used either above or below the numbers being grouped $\blacksquare$

$$= \frac{-6}{3} = -2$$

Example 7   Evaluate $6 - 4(2 \cdot 3^2 - 12 \div 2)$.

$$6 - 4(2 \cdot 3^2 - 12 \div 2)$$

First, evaluate the expression inside the parentheses

$$= 6 - 4(2 \cdot 9 - 12 \div 2)$$

Do the power inside ( )

$$= 6 - 4(18 - 6)$$

Do the $\times$ and $\div$ inside ( )

$$= 6 - 4(12)$$

Do the $-$ inside ( )

$$= 6 - 48 = -42 \quad \blacksquare$$

Example 8   Evaluate $20 - [5 - (3 - 7)]$.

$$20 - [5 - (3 - 7)]$$

When grouping symbols appear within other grouping symbols, evaluate the *inner* grouping first

$$= 20 - [5 - (-4)]$$

$$= 20 - [5 + 4]$$

$$= 20 - 9 = 11 \quad \blacksquare$$

EXERCISES 1.8

Set I   In working the following exercises, be sure to perform the operations in the correct order.

1. $16 - 9 - 4$ **2.** $18 - 6 - 3$ **3.** $12 \div 6 \div 2$

4. $16 \div 4 \div 2$ **5.** $10 \div 2(-5)$ **6.** $15 \div 5(-3)$

7. $3 \cdot 2^4$ **8.** $5 \cdot 3^2$ **9.** $8 + 6 \cdot 5$

10. $3 + 2 \cdot 4$ **11.** $7 + 5 \div 3$ **12.** $5 + 3 \div 2$

13. $10 - 3 \cdot 2$ **14.** $12 - 2 \cdot 4$ **15.** $10(-15)^2 - 4^3$

16. $3(-4)^2 - 2^4$ **17.** $\frac{1}{2} - 0.02 \times 10^3$ **18.** $\frac{1}{3} - 0.04 \times 10^2$

19. $10^2\sqrt{16} \cdot 5$ **20.** $10^2\sqrt{25} \cdot 3$ **21.** $2 + 3 \cdot 100 \div 25$

22. $3 + 2 \cdot 100 \div 4$ **23.** $28 + 14/7$ **24.** $36 + 18/3$

25. $2\sqrt{9}(2^3 - 5)$ **26.** $5\sqrt{36}(4^2 - 8)$

27. $(-18) \div (-3)(-6)$ **28.** $(-16) \div (-4)(-2)$

29. $(-10)^3 - 5(10^2)\sqrt[3]{-27}$ **30.** $(-10)^2 - 5(10^3)\sqrt[3]{-8}$

31. $20 - [5 - (7 - 10)]$ **32.** $16 - [8 - (2 - 7)]$

33. $\dfrac{7 + (-12)}{8 - 3}$ **34.** $\dfrac{-14 + (-2)}{9 - 5}$

35. $8 - [5(-2)^3 - \sqrt{16}]$ **36.** $10 - [3(-3)^2 - \sqrt{25}]$

37. $(3 \cdot 5^2 - 15 \div 3) \div (-7)$ **38.** $(3 \cdot 4^3 - 72 \div 6) \div (-9)$

39. $15 - \{4 - [2 - 3(6 - 4)]\}$ **40.** $17 - \{6 - [9 - 2(7 - 2)]\}$

Set II   In working the following exercises, be sure to perform the operations in the correct order.

1. $15 - 7 - 2$ **2.** $3 + 2 \cdot 6$ **3.** $81 \div 9 \div 3$

4. $12 + 6 \div 6$ **5.** $18 \div 3(-6)$ **6.** $8 - 24 \div 8$

7. $2 \cdot 5^2$ **8.** $8 \cdot 3^2$ **9.** $9 + 6 \cdot 3$

10. $2(-5) + 6 \div 24$ **11.** $9 + 7 \div 4$ **12.** $64 \div 2 \div 2$

13. $17 - 3 \cdot 5$ **14.** $3\sqrt{64}(2^3 - 1)$ **15.** $5(-3)^2 - 3^3$

16. $6(4) - 8 \div 24$ **17.** $\frac{1}{2} - 0.2 \times 10^2$ **18.** $10^2\sqrt[3]{8} \div 10 \cdot 2$

19. $10^2\sqrt{9} \cdot 4$ **20.** $75 \div 5^2 \cdot 4 + 12 \cdot 5$ **21.** $4 + 2 \cdot 100 \div 5$

22. $100 \div 5^2 \cdot 6 + 8 \cdot 75$ **23.** $24 + 12/6$ **24.** $10^4 \cdot 4^2 + 100(15)$

25. $4\sqrt{25}(3^2 - 4)$ **26.** $8^2\sqrt{25} \div 10 \cdot 4$

27. $(-15) \div (-3)(-5)$ **28.** $10^4 \cdot 2^3 + 10(140)$

29. $(-10)^3 - 4(10^2)\sqrt[3]{-8}$ **30.** $6 + 3 \cdot 30 \div 5$

31. $18 - [9 - (3 - 8)]$ **32.** $100 \div 2^2 \cdot 5 + 9 \cdot 25$

33. $\dfrac{8 + (-16)}{12 - 4}$ **34.** $\frac{3}{5} + 72 \div 9 \cdot 2 - \frac{1}{3}$

35. $(-8)/2 \times (-4)/-1$ **36.** $18 - 11 - 3$

37. $(2 \cdot 3^3 - 63 \div 7) \div (-9)$ **38.** $10^2 \sqrt[3]{27} \div 10 \cdot 3$

39. $20 - \{5 - [9 - 3(6 - 2)]\}$ **40.** $\frac{2}{3} + 77 \div 11 \cdot 2 - \frac{1}{2}$

1.9 Prime Numbers and Factorization of Natural Numbers; LCM

Prime Numbers   A **prime number** is a natural number greater than 1 that cannot be written as a product of two natural numbers except as the product of itself and 1. (That is, a prime number has no natural number factors other than itself and 1.)

A partial list of prime numbers is 2, 3, 5, 7, 11, 13, 17, 19, 23, 29,.... There is no largest prime number.

Composite Numbers   A **composite number** is a number that is not prime; it is a natural number that can be exactly divided by some natural number besides itself and 1.

NOTE   One (1) is neither prime nor composite.   ☑

Factoring a Natural Number   A systematic method for finding all the integral factors of a number will be demonstrated in Examples 1 and 2.

Example 1   List all of the integral factors (or divisors) of 36. Is 36 prime or composite?

We know that

$$1 \cdot 36 = 36$$
$$2 \cdot 18 = 36$$
$$3 \cdot 12 = 36$$
$$4 \cdot 9 \ = 36$$

and

$$6 \cdot 6 \ = 36$$

By "pairing up" the factors in this manner,

$$\{1, 2, 3, 4, 6, 9, 12, 18, 36\}$$

you can check to see if you have omitted any factors. (Because 36 is the square of an integer, when we "pair up" the factors, there is a single, unpaired number left in the center.) The integral factors of 36 are ± 1,* ± 2, ± 3, ± 4, ± 6, ± 9, ± 12, ± 18, and ± 36. Since 36 has natural number factors other than 1 and 36, it is a composite number. ∎

Example 2   List all of the integral factors of 31. Is 31 prime or composite?

The integral factors of 31 are ± 1 and ± 31. Since the only natural number factors are 1 and 31, 31 is a prime number. ∎

---

* The symbol $\pm$ is read "plus or minus" (positive or negative). For example, ± 1 is read "plus or minus 1."

Prime Factorization of Natural Numbers The **prime factorization** of a natural number greater than 1 is the indicated product of all of its factors that are themselves prime numbers.

Example 3 Find the prime factorization of 18.

$$18 = 2 \cdot 9$$
$$18 = 3 \cdot 6$$

These are *not prime* factorizations because 9 and 6 are not prime numbers

$$18 = 2 \cdot 9 = 2 \cdot 3 \cdot 3 = \boxed{2 \cdot 3^2}$$
$$18 = 3 \cdot 6 = 3 \cdot 2 \cdot 3 = \boxed{2 \cdot 3^2}$$

These *are prime* factorizations because all the factors are prime numbers

Note that the two ways we factored 18 led to the *same* prime factorization ($2 \cdot 3^2$). The prime factorization of any positive integer (greater than 1) is unique. ■

A systematic method for finding the prime factorization will be demonstrated in Examples 4, 5, and 6.

Example 4 Find the prime factorization of 315.

We first try to divide 315 by the smallest prime, 2. Two does not divide exactly into 315, and so we try to divide 315 by the next prime number, which is 3. Three *does* divide evenly into 315 and gives a quotient of 105. We again try 3 as a divisor of the quotient, 105. Three *does* divide evenly into 105 and gives a new quotient of 35. We then try to divide *that* quotient (35) by 3. Three does not divide exactly into 35, and so we try to divide 35 by the next prime number, which is 5. Five *does* divide evenly into 35 and gives a quotient of 7. The process then ends because the quotient, 7, is itself a prime.

The work of finding the prime factorization of a number can be conveniently arranged by putting the quotients under the number we're dividing into, as follows:

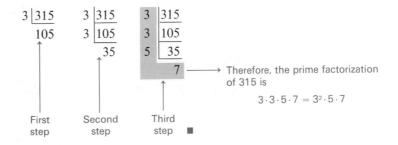

Therefore, the prime factorization of 315 is

$$3 \cdot 3 \cdot 5 \cdot 7 = 3^2 \cdot 5 \cdot 7$$

First step   Second step   Third step ■

Example 5 Find the prime factorization of 48.

$$
\begin{array}{r|r}
2 & 48 \\
2 & 24 \\
2 & 12 \\
2 & 6 \\
  & 3 \\
\end{array}
$$

Therefore, $48 = 2 \cdot 2 \cdot 2 \cdot 2 \cdot 3 = 2^4 \cdot 3$; $2^4 \cdot 3$ is the *prime factorization* of 48 ■

When trying to find the prime factors of a number, we do not need to try any prime that has a square greater than that number. (See Example 6.)

Example 6   Find the prime factorization of 97.

Primes in order of size

2	does not divide 97
3	does not divide 97
5	does not divide 97
7	does not divide 97
11	and larger primes need not be tried because $11^2 = 121$, which is greater than 97

Therefore, the prime factorization of 97 is simply 97, since 97 is a prime number. ■

Least Common Multiple   The **least common multiple (LCM)** of two or more numbers is the *smallest* (least) number that is a multiple of each of the numbers. The LCM is used in solving fractional equations and in adding and subtracting fractions. The least common multiple can be found as follows:

TO FIND THE LCM OF TWO OR MORE NUMBERS

1. Express each number in prime factored form.

2. Write down (once only) each base that appears in any of the numbers.

3. The exponent on each base must be the largest exponent that appears on that base in any of the numbers.

4. The LCM is the *product* of the exponential numbers found in step 3.

Example 7   Find the LCM of 18 and 48.

$18 = 2 \cdot 3^2$ and $48 = 2^4 \cdot 3$. The bases that appear in one or both numbers are 2 and 3. Therefore, the bases in the LCM are 2 and 3. The *largest* exponent that appears on the 2 (in either of the numbers) is 4. Therefore, the exponent on the 2 in the LCM must be 4. The *largest* exponent that appears on the 3 in either of the numbers is 2. Therefore, the exponent on the 3 in the LCM must be 2. The LCM, then, is $2^4 \cdot 3^2 = 144$.

NOTE   144 is the smallest number that is a multiple of both 18 and 48. We could also say that 144 is the smallest number that 18 and 48 both divide into. ■

Example 8   Find the LCM of 360, 378, and 108.

$360 = 2^3 \cdot 3^2 \cdot 5$, $378 = 2 \cdot 3^3 \cdot 7$, and $108 = 2^2 \cdot 3^3$. Bases in the LCM must be 2, 3, 5, and 7. The exponent on the 2 must be 3; the exponent on the 3 must be 3; the exponent on the 5 must be 1; the exponent on the 7 must be 1. The LCM, therefore, is $2^3 \cdot 3^3 \cdot 5 \cdot 7 = 7,560$. This is the smallest number that 360, 378, and 108 all divide into. ■

EXERCISES 1.9

Set I   In Exercises 1–10, state whether each of the numbers is prime or composite, and give the set of *all* integral factors for each number.

1. 5	**2.** 8	**3.** 13	**4.** 15	**5.** 12
6. 11	**7.** 51	**8.** 42	**9.** 111	**10.** 101

In Exercises 11–22, find the prime factorization of each number.

11. 28 **12.** 30 **13.** 32 **14.** 33 **15.** 43

16. 35 **17.** 84 **18.** 75 **19.** 144 **20.** 180

21. 156 **22.** 221

In Exercises 23–26, find the LCM of the numbers.

23. 144, 360 **24.** 84, 35

25. 270, 900, 75 **26.** 140, 105, 98

Set II   In Exercises 1–10, state whether each of the numbers is prime or composite, and give the set of *all* integral factors for each number.

1. 21 **2.** 23 **3.** 55 **4.** 41 **5.** 49

6. 9 **7.** 44 **8.** 30 **9.** 17 **10.** 87

In Exercises 11–22, find the prime factorization of each number.

11. 21 **12.** 31 **13.** 45 **14.** 87 **15.** 186

16. 238 **17.** 19 **18.** 40 **19.** 36 **20.** 27

21. 72 **22.** 228

In Exercises 23–26, find the LCM of the numbers.

23. 87, 58 **24.** 93, 155

25. 280, 84, 350 **26.** 85, 102, 170

1.10 Review 1.1–1.9

Sets 1.1A   A **set** is a collection of objects or things.

The *elements of a set* are the objects that make up the set.

$5 \in A$ is read "5 is an element of set A"

$9 \notin B$ is read "9 is not an element of set B"

The *roster method* of representing a set is a list of its members enclosed in braces.

The *modified roster method* is used when the number of elements in the set is so large that it is not convenient or even possible to list all its members.

The *rule (or set-builder) method* can also be used to represent a set.

Equal sets are sets having exactly the same members.

The *empty set* is a set having no elements.

ϕ is read "the empty set"

$\{\ \ \}$ is read "the empty set"

A *finite set* is one for which the counting of all its elements comes to an end.

An *infinite set* is one for which the counting of all its elements never comes to an end.

Set *A* is a *subset* of set *B* if every member of *A* is also a member of *B*.

$$P \subseteq Q \text{ is read ``}P \text{ is a subset of } Q\text{''}$$

$$P \nsubseteq Q \text{ is read ``}P \text{ is not a subset of } Q\text{''}$$

**Union and Intersection of sets
1.1B**

The union of sets A and B, written $A \cup B$, is the set that contains all the elements of *A* as well as all the elements of *B*.

The intersection of sets A and B, written $A \cap B$, is the set that contains all the elements that are in *both A* and *B*.

**Kinds of Numbers
1.2**

All the numbers that can be represented by points on the number line are **real numbers**. Some subsets of the real numbers are:

The set of digits, $D = \{0, 1, 2, 3, 4, 5, 6, 7, 8, 9\}$

The set of natural numbers, $N = \{1, 2, 3, \ldots\}$

The set of whole numbers, $W = \{0, 1, 2, \ldots\}$

The set of integers, $J = \{\ldots, -3, -2, -1, 0, 1, 2, 3, \ldots\}$

The set of rational numbers, $Q = \left\{ \dfrac{a}{b} \middle| a, b \in J; b \neq 0 \right\}$

The set of irrational numbers, $H = \{x \mid x \in R, x \notin Q\}$

**Definitions
1.3A**

Constant An object or symbol that does not change its value in a particular problem or discussion.

Variable An object or symbol that is a placeholder for a number that is unknown.

Algebraic expression An expression that consists of numbers, letters, signs of operation $(+, -, \times, \div,$ powers, roots), and signs of grouping.

Term The $+$ and $-$ signs in an algebraic expression break the expression up into smaller pieces called *terms*; an expression within grouping symbols is considered as a single term.

Factors The numbers that are multiplied together to give a product are called the *factors* of that product.

**Inequality Symbols
1.3B**

Greater than: The statement $a > b$ is read "*a* is greater than *b*."

Greater than or equal to: The statement $c \geq d$ is read "*c* is greater than or equal to *d*."

Not greater than: The statement $e \ngtr f$ is read "*e* is not greater than *f*."

Less than: The statement $g < h$ is read "*g* is less than *h*."

Less than or equal to: The statement $i \leq j$ is read "*i* is less than or equal to *j*."

Not less than: The statement $k \nless l$ is read "*k* is not less than *l*."

Not equal to: The statement $m \neq n$ is read "*m* is not equal to *n*."

Continued inequalities: The statement $a < b < c$ is a valid continued inequality only if the inequalities $a < b$, $b < c$, and $a < c$ are all true.

Absolute Value
1.3B

The absolute value of a real number x is written $|x|$, where

$$|x| = \begin{cases} x & \text{if } x \geq 0 \quad (x \text{ greater than zero, or } x = 0) \\ -x & \text{if } x < 0 \quad (x \text{ less than zero}) \end{cases}$$

Operations on
Signed Numbers
1.4

To add signed numbers:

1. When the numbers have the same sign
   1. Add their absolute values *and*
   2. Give the sum the sign of both numbers.

2. When the numbers have different signs
   1. Subtract the smaller absolute value from the larger absolute value *and*
   2. Give that answer the sign of the number with the larger absolute value.

To subtract one signed number from another:

1. Change the subtraction symbol to an addition symbol *and* change the sign of the number being subtracted.

2. Add the resulting signed numbers.

To multiply two signed numbers:

1. Multiply their absolute values *and*

2. attach the correct sign to the product. The sign is *positive* when the numbers have the same sign and *negative* when the numbers have different signs.

To divide one signed number by another:

1. Divide the absolute value of the dividend by the absolute value of the divisor *and*

2. attach the correct sign to the quotient. The sign is *positive* when the numbers have the same sign and *negative* when the numbers have different signs.

Operations with Zero
1.4

If a is any real number,

1. $a + 0 = 0 + a = a$ 2. $a - 0 = a$
3. $0 - a = 0 + (-a) = -a$ 4. $a \cdot 0 = 0 \cdot a = 0$

If a is any real number *except 0,*

5. $\dfrac{0}{a} = 0$

6. $\dfrac{a}{0}$ is not possible $\left(\dfrac{a}{0} \text{ is not a real number}\right)$

7. $\dfrac{0}{0}$ cannot be determined

Commutative Properties
(Order Changed)
1.5

$$\left. \begin{array}{ll} \textit{Addition}: & a + b = b + a \\ \textit{Multiplication}: & a \cdot b = b \cdot a \end{array} \right\} a, b \in R$$

Subtraction and *division* are not commutative.

Associative Properties (Grouping Changed) 1.5

Addition: $\qquad a + b + c = (a + b) + c = a + (b + c)$

Multiplication: $\quad a \cdot b \cdot c = (a \cdot b) \cdot c = a \cdot (b \cdot c)$ $\Big\}\, a, b, c \in R$

Subtraction and *division* are not associative.

Distributive Rule(s) 1.5

$a(b + c) = ab + ac$

$(b + c)a = ba + ca$ $\Big\}$ These rules can be extended to have any number of terms within the parentheses

Powers of Signed Numbers 1.6

Exponent

$(\underset{\text{Base}}{-2})^{\,3} = (-2)(-2)(-2) = \boxed{-8}$

Square Roots 1.7

The *square root* of a number N is a number that when squared gives N. Every positive number has both a positive and a negative square root. The positive square root is called the *principal square root*. The principal square root of N is written $\sqrt{N}$. When the symbol $\sqrt{N}$ is used, it always represents the principal square root of N.

Higher Roots 1.7C

Roots other than square roots are called *higher roots.*

Order of Operations 1.8

1. If there are parentheses in an expression, that part of the expression within a pair of parentheses is evaluated first; then the entire expression is evaluated.

2. Any evaluation always proceeds in this order:

   First: Powers and roots are done.

   Second: Multiplication and division are done in order from left to right.

   Third: Addition and subtraction are done in order from left to right.

Prime and Composite Numbers 1.9

A **prime number** is a positive integer greater than 1 that cannot be written as a product of two natural numbers except as the product of itself and 1. A prime number has no factors other than itself and 1.

A **composite number** is a positive integer that can be exactly divided by some positive integer other than itself and 1.

Prime Factorization of Positive Integers 1.9

The **prime factorization** of a positive integer is the indicated product of all its factors that are themselves prime numbers.

Least Common Multiple (LCM) 1.9

To find the LCM of two or more numbers, proceed as follows:

1. Factor each number completely; repeated factors should be expressed in exponential form.

2. Write down each different base that appears in any of the numbers.

3. Raise each base to the highest power it has in *any* of the numbers.

4. The LCM is the product of all the powers found in step 3.

Review Exercises 1.10 Set I

1. Is the set of natural numbers a finite set or an infinite set?

2. Is the set of digits a finite set or an infinite set?

3. Write the following set in roster notation:

$$\{x \mid x \text{ is a digit less than 5}\}$$

4. $P = \{5, x, z\}$. Is $y \in P$?

5. Given $A = \{5, 7, 8\}$, $B = \{2, 5, 7\}$, and $C = \{1, 3, 4, 6\}$, find the following:

  a. $A \cup B$ b. $A \cap B$ c. $C \cap B$ d. Is $\{2\}$ a subset of A?

6. Given the numbers -2, 4.53, $0.161616\ldots$, $\frac{2}{3}$, $2.6457513\ldots$, and 0, answer the following questions:

  a. Which are real numbers?

  b. Which are integers?

  c. Which are natural numbers?

  d. Which are irrational numbers?

  e. Which are rational numbers?

In Exercises 7–17, find the value of each expression or write "not possible" or "cannot be determined."

7. $|4|$ **8.** $|0|$ **9.** $|-10|$ **10.** $(-6)^2$

11. -5^2 **12.** $\dfrac{0}{5}$ **13.** $\dfrac{7}{0}$ **14.** 0^3

15. $6 + 2\sqrt{16} - 2^3$

16. $20 - \{5 - 2[-3(4 - 6) + 2] - 3\}$

17. $6 + 18 \div 6 \div 3$

18. a. Write all of the integral factors of 28.

  b. Write the prime factorization of 28.

  c. Write the prime factorization of 168.

  d. Find the least common multiple of 28 and 168.

In Exercises 19–21, state *why* if your answer is no.

19. Is $-2 < 0 < 8$ a valid continued inequality?

20. Is $1 > 5 > 7$ a valid continued inequality?

21. Is $5 < 8 > 6$ a valid continued inequality?

In Exercises 22–30, state whether each of the following is true or false. If the statement is *true*, give the reason.

22. $8 - (-15) = -15 - 8$ **23.** $7 \cdot 1 = 7$

24. $\left(\dfrac{5}{6} + \dfrac{1}{8}\right) + \dfrac{2}{3} = \dfrac{5}{6} + \left(\dfrac{1}{8} + \dfrac{2}{3}\right)$ **25.** $6 + (-6) = 0$

26. $\left(\dfrac{1}{2} \div \dfrac{3}{8}\right) \div \dfrac{2}{7} = \dfrac{1}{2} \div \left(\dfrac{3}{8} \div \dfrac{2}{7}\right)$

27. $\dfrac{1}{2} + 0 = \dfrac{1}{2}$

28. $6 + (2 + 5) = 6 + (5 + 2)$

29. $(-5) \cdot 0 = -5$

30. $\dfrac{1}{2}\left(\dfrac{5}{8} + \dfrac{1}{3}\right) = \dfrac{1}{2} \cdot \dfrac{5}{8} + \dfrac{1}{2} \cdot \dfrac{1}{3}$

Review Exercises 1.10 Set II

NAME _____

1. Is the empty set a subset of the set of integers?

2. Write the following set in roster notation:

$$\{x \mid x \text{ is a whole number less than 6}\}$$

3. Is every irrational number a real number?

4. Given $G = \{1, 4, 8\}$, is $12 \in G$?

5. Is 10 a digit?

6. Given $A = \{2, 4, 6\}$, $B = \{1, 3, 5\}$, and $C = \{3, 5, 7\}$, find the following:

   a. $A \cup B$

   b. $A \cap B$

   c. $C \cap B$

   d. Is $3 \in A$?

7. Is 0 a real number?

8. Given the numbers $6.1644140\ldots$, -3, 4.1, $\frac{3}{7}$, 5, and $0.656565\ldots$, determine the following:

   a. Which are real numbers?

   b. Which are integers?

   c. Which are natural numbers?

   d. Which are irrational numbers?

   e. Which are rational numbers?

In Exercises 9–20, find the value of each expression or write "not possible" or "cannot be determined."

9. $|-14|$

10. $-|-23|$

11. $(-11)^2$

12. $(-5)^3$

13. -4^2

14. $\dfrac{0}{7}$

ANSWERS

1. _____

2. _____

3. _____

4. _____

5. _____

6a. _____

6b. _____

6c. _____

6d. _____

7. _____

8a. _____

8b. _____

8c. _____

8d. _____

8e. _____

9. _____

10. _____

11. _____

12. _____

13. _____

14. _____

15. $\dfrac{0}{0}$ **16.** $\dfrac{8}{0}$ **17.** $10 - 2\sqrt[3]{64} - 3^2$

15. _____

16. _____

17. _____

18. $20 \div 10 \cdot 2$ **19.** $4 + 16 \div 4 \div 2$ **20.** $17 + 12 \cdot 2$

18. _____

19. _____

20. _____

21. a. Write all of the integral factors of 132.

21a. _____

21b. _____

b. Write the prime factorization of 132.

21c. _____

21d. _____

c. Write the prime factorization of 110.

22. _____

23. _____

24. _____

d. Find the least common multiple of 132 and 110.

25. _____

26. _____

22. Is $7 < 10 > 8$ a valid continued inequality? State *why* if your answer is no.

27. _____

28. _____

In Exercises 23–30, state whether each of the following is true or false. If the statement is *true*, give the reason.

29. _____

30. _____

23. $\dfrac{4}{5} \cdot \left(\dfrac{2}{3} \cdot \dfrac{6}{11}\right) = \left(\dfrac{4}{5} \cdot \dfrac{2}{3}\right) \cdot \dfrac{6}{11}$ **24.** $\dfrac{6}{7} \div \dfrac{5}{2} = \dfrac{5}{2} \div \dfrac{6}{7}$

25. $\left(\dfrac{1}{2} - \dfrac{1}{8}\right) - \dfrac{1}{3} = \dfrac{1}{2} - \left(\dfrac{1}{8} - \dfrac{1}{3}\right)$ **26.** $1 \cdot 17 = 17$

27. $3 \cdot [(-4) \cdot 6] = 3 \cdot [6 \cdot (-4)]$ **28.** $6(-2 + 6) = 6 \cdot (-2) + 6 \cdot 6$

29. $7 + (4 \cdot 5) = (5 \cdot 4) + 7$ **30.** $\dfrac{2}{3} + \dfrac{1}{6} = \dfrac{1}{6} + \dfrac{2}{3}$

1.11 Algebraic Expressions: Rules of Exponents

1.11A Positive Integer Exponents

In Section 1.6, we discussed powers of rational numbers. We now discuss powers of variables. Just as 3^4 means $3 \cdot 3 \cdot 3 \cdot 3$, x^4 means $x \cdot x \cdot x \cdot x = xxxx$. In the exponential expression x^n, the *base* is x, the *exponent* is n, and x^n means that x is multiplied by itself n times. If a variable has no exponent, then the exponent is understood to be 1.

An exponent always applies *only* to the immediately preceding symbol, as shown in the following example:

Example 1   Rewrite without exponents:

a. $x^2 y^3 = xxyyy$

b. $xy^3 = xyyy$ The exponent applies only to the y

c. $(xy)^3 = (xy)(xy)(xy)$

$\qquad = xxxyyy$

This exponent applies to whatever is inside the parentheses

d. $y^1 = y$ ■

The Rules of Exponents

The first five basic rules of exponents are

RULE 1.1

$$x^m \cdot x^n = x^{m+n}$$

RULE 1.2

$$(x^m)^n = x^{mn}$$

RULE 1.3

$$(xy)^n = x^n y^n$$

RULE 1.4

$$\frac{x^m}{x^n} = x^{m-n} \qquad (x \neq 0)$$

(In *this* section, $m > n$ also.)

RULE 1.5

$$\left(\frac{x}{y}\right)^n = \frac{x^n}{y^n} \qquad (y \neq 0)$$

NOTE   We must add the restrictions $x \neq 0$ and $y \neq 0$ to avoid dividing by 0, which is not permitted.

Example 2 Rewrite each of the following expressions with the base appearing only once, if possible:

a. $w \cdot w^7 = w^1 \cdot w^7 = w^{1+7} = w^8$ (When the base is written without an exponent, its exponent is understood to be 1.)

b. $x^3 \cdot y^2$ cannot be rewritten. (Rule 1.1 does not apply because the bases are different.)

c. $x^3 + x^2$ cannot be simplified. (Rule 1.1 does not apply to a *sum* of two exponential numbers.)

d. $2^a \cdot 2^b = 2^{a+b}$ ■

A WORD OF CAUTION A common mistake students make when the bases are constants is to multiply the bases as well as add the exponents.

Correct method	Incorrect method
$10^9 \cdot 10^4 = 10^{9+4}$	$10^9 \cdot 10^4 \neq (10 \cdot 10)^{9+4} = 100^{13}$
$= 10^{13}$	
$2^3 \cdot 2^2 = 2^{3+2}$	$2^3 \cdot 2^2 \neq (2 \cdot 2)^{3+2} = 4^5$
$= 2^5 = 32$	$= 1,024$

When multiplying powers of the same base, add the exponents; do *not* multiply the bases as well. ☑

Example 3 Rewrite each of the following without parentheses:

a. $(x)^4 = (x^1)^4 = x^{1 \cdot 4} = x^4$

b. $(10^6)^2 = 10^{6 \cdot 2} = 10^{12}$

c. $(2^a)^b = 2^{a \cdot b} = 2^{ab}$

d. $(2x)^3 = 2^3 x^3$

e. $(xy)^7 = x^7 y^7$ ■

A WORD OF CAUTION An exponent applies only to the symbol immediately preceding it. For example,

$$2x^3 \neq (2x)^3 = 2^3 x^3$$

This exponent 3 applies to *both* 2 and x

This exponent 3 applies *only* to x ☑

Throughout this book, unless otherwise noted, we do not allow any of the variables to have a value that makes a denominator zero.

Example 4 Rewrite each of the following with the base appearing only once, if possible:

a. $\dfrac{x^5}{x^3} = x^{5-3} = x^2$

b. $\dfrac{10^7}{10^3} = 10^{7-3} = 10^4$

c. $\dfrac{y^3}{y} = \dfrac{y^3}{y^1} = y^{3-1} = y^2$

d. $\dfrac{2^a}{2^b} = 2^{a-b}$

1.11 / ALGEBRAIC EXPRESSIONS: RULES OF EXPONENTS

e. $\dfrac{x^5}{y^2}$ This cannot be rewritten, since Rule 1.4 does not apply when the bases are different.

f. $x^5 - x^2$ This cannot be rewritten, since Rule 1.4 does not apply to subtraction problems.

g. $\dfrac{x^5 - y^3}{x^2}$ The expression can either be left as it is or be changed as follows:

$$\frac{x^5 - y^3}{x^2} = \frac{x^5}{x^2} - \frac{y^3}{x^2} = x^3 - \frac{y^3}{x^2} \quad \blacksquare$$

A WORD OF CAUTION   A common mistake is to divide *only* x^5 by x^2 instead of dividing *both* x^5 and y^3 by x^2 in Example 4g. However, $\dfrac{x^5 - y^3}{x^2} \neq x^3 - y^3$. Expressions such as $\dfrac{x^5 - y^3}{x^2}$ are discussed further in Section 4.5.   ☑

Example 5   Rewrite each of the following without parentheses:

a. $\left(\dfrac{a}{b}\right)^4 = \dfrac{a^4}{b^4}$

b. $\left(\dfrac{3}{z}\right)^2 = \dfrac{3^2}{z^2}$ ■

NOTE   The proofs of Rules 1.1, 1.2, 1.3, 1.4, and 1.5 are beyond the scope of this book.   ☑

EXERCISES 1.11A

Set I   Use the rules of exponents to simplify each of the following expressions, if possible.

1. $10^2 \cdot 10^4$ 2. $2^3 \cdot 2^2$ 3. $x^2 \cdot x^5$ 4. $y^6 \cdot y^3$

5. $x^4 + x^6$ 6. $y^3 + y^7$ 7. $2^x \cdot 2^y$ 8. $3^m \cdot 3^n$

9. $\dfrac{a^8}{a^3}$ 10. $\dfrac{x^5}{x^2}$ 11. $x^6 - x$ 12. $y^4 - y$

13. $(10^3)^2$ 14. $(5^2)^4$ 15. $(3^a)^b$ 16. $(2^m)^n$

17. $(xy)^5$ 18. $(uv)^4$ 19. $(2x)^6$ 20. $(3x)^4$

21. $x^8 \cdot y^5$ 22. $s^2 \cdot t^4$ 23. $3^{4x} \cdot 3^{7x}$ 24. $5^x \cdot 5^{3x}$

25. $\dfrac{a^x}{a^y}$ 26. $\dfrac{x^a}{x^b}$ 27. $\dfrac{x^4}{y^2}$ 28. $\dfrac{a^5}{b^3}$

29. $\left(\dfrac{x}{y}\right)^3$ 30. $\left(\dfrac{u}{v}\right)^7$ 31. $\left(\dfrac{3}{x}\right)^4$ 32. $\left(\dfrac{x}{5}\right)^2$

Set II   Use the rules of exponents to simplify each of the following expressions, if possible.

1. $5^2 \cdot 5^3$ 2. $y^3 + y$ 3. $X^4 \cdot X^2$ 4. $x^4 + x^3$

5. $u^4 + u^7$ 6. $4 \cdot 4^3$ 7. $5^a \cdot 5^b$ 8. $(2v)^3$

9. $\dfrac{P^5}{P^3}$ 10. $\dfrac{x^4}{y^3}$ 11. $z^7 + z^4$ 12. $y^5 - y^2$

51

13. $(4^2)^3$ **14.** xx^5 **15.** $(2^x)^y$ **16.** xy^5

17. $(ab)^7$ **18.** $(2^3)^2$ **19.** $(4x)^2$ **20.** $(xy)^5$

21. $a^4 \cdot b^2$ **22.** $3^2 \cdot 3^3$ **23.** $4^{3x} \cdot 4^{5x}$ **24.** $x^2 \cdot y^5$

25. $\dfrac{U^x}{U^y}$ **26.** $\dfrac{x^6}{y^2}$ **27.** $\dfrac{r^6}{t^2}$ **28.** $\dfrac{z^6}{z^2}$

29. $\left(\dfrac{a}{b}\right)^6$ **30.** $\left(\dfrac{3}{x}\right)^4$ **31.** $\left(\dfrac{x}{2}\right)^5$ **32.** $\dfrac{a^{14}}{a^9}$

1.11B Zero and Negative Exponents

The Zero Exponent

When we used Rule 1.4 in Section 1.11A, the exponent of the numerator was always larger than the exponent of the denominator. We now consider the case where the exponents of the numerator and the denominator are the same.

We know that $\dfrac{x^n}{x^n} = 1$ (if $x \neq 0$) because any nonzero number divided by itself is 1.

However, if we use Rule 1.4 in the same problem, we have

$$\frac{x^n}{x^n} = x^{n-n} = x^0$$

We want x^0 to equal 1; therefore, we *define* x^0 to be 1 (if $x \neq 0$).

RULE 1.6

By definition,

$$x^0 = 1 \qquad (x \neq 0)$$

NOTE $x \neq 0$ in Rule 1.6 because $0^0 = 0^{1-1} = \dfrac{0}{0}$, which cannot be determined. ☑

Example 6   Rewrite with no zero exponents:

a. $a^0 = 1$ provided $a \neq 0$.

b. $10^0 = 1$

c. $(3y)^0 = 1$ provided $y \neq 0$.

d. $6x^0 = 6 \cdot 1 = 6$ provided $x \neq 0$.

Remember: The exponent applies *only* to the x, not to the 6 ■

Negative Exponents

We now consider Rule 1.4 when the exponent of the numerator is *less than* the exponent of the denominator.

Consider the expression $\dfrac{x^3}{x^5}$.

$$\frac{x^3}{x^5} = \frac{xxx}{xxxxx} = \frac{xxx \cdot 1}{xxx \cdot xx} = \boxed{\frac{xxx}{xxx}} \cdot \frac{1}{xx} = 1 \cdot \frac{1}{xx} = \frac{1}{x^2}$$

└──── The value of this fraction is 1

If we use Rule 1.4,

$$\frac{x^3}{x^5} = x^{3-5} = x^{-2}$$

Therefore, we want x^{-2} to equal $\frac{1}{x^2}$. We then *define* x^{-n} to equal $\frac{1}{x^n}$.

RULE 1.7a

By definition,

$$x^{-n} = \frac{1}{x^n} \qquad (x \neq 0)$$

NOTE x^{-n} is not necessarily a negative number.   ☑

NOTE $x \neq 0$ in Rule 1.7a. Consider 0^{-3}: $0^{-3} = \frac{1}{0^3}$, which is undefined.   ☑

Rule 1.7a is valid whether n is a positive or a negative number.

Example 7   Rewrite with no negative exponents:

a. $6^{-2} = \frac{1}{6^2} = \frac{1}{36}$

b. $(-5)^{-3} = \frac{1}{(-5)^3} = -\frac{1}{125}$ ∎

Proofs of the following rules are provided in Appendix A.

RULE 1.7b

$$\frac{1}{x^{-n}} = x^n \qquad (x \neq 0)$$

RULE 1.7c

$$\left(\frac{x}{y}\right)^{-n} = \left(\frac{y}{x}\right)^n \qquad (x \neq 0, y \neq 0)$$

Example 8   Rewrite each of the following with positive exponents only:

a. $x^{-5} = \frac{1}{x^5}$

b. $10^{-4} = \frac{1}{10^4}$

c. $(3x)^{-1} = \dfrac{1}{3x}$

d. $\dfrac{1}{y^{-3}} = y^3$

e. $\left(\dfrac{a}{b}\right)^{-4} = \left(\dfrac{b}{a}\right)^4$

f. $x^{-6a} = \dfrac{1}{x^{6a}}$ ∎

A factor can be moved either from the numerator to the denominator or from the denominator to the numerator of a fraction simply by moving it and changing the sign of its exponent. If a factor has no exponent, then the exponent is understood to be 1.

NOTE   Moving a factor from the numerator to the denominator (or from the denominator to the numerator) by changing the sign of the exponent does *not* change the sign of the *expression*.   ☑

Example 9   Rewrite $\dfrac{a^{-2}b^4}{c^5 d^{-3}}$ with positive exponents only.

$$\frac{a^{-2}b^4}{c^5 d^{-3}} = \frac{b^4 d^3}{a^2 c^5}$$

Notice that a^{-2} (which was a factor of the numerator) was moved to the denominator and its exponent changed to $+2$, and that d^{-3} (which was a factor of the denominator) was moved to the numerator and its exponent changed to $+3$.   ∎

NOTE   If a single number or letter appears in the numerator or denominator of a fraction, that number can still be considered a factor of the numerator or denominator. For example,

$$\frac{5}{x} = \frac{1 \cdot 5}{1 \cdot x}$$

Therefore, we can say that 5 is a factor of the numerator and x is a factor of the denominator of $\dfrac{5}{x}$.   ☑

Example 10   Rewrite each of the following with no negative exponents:

a. $\dfrac{h^5}{k^{-4}} = \dfrac{h^5}{1k^{-4}} = \dfrac{h^5 \cdot k^4}{1} = h^5 k^4$

NOTE   If an expression has no denominator, then the denominator is understood to be 1. See Examples 10b and 10c.   ☑

b. $6x^{-8} = \dfrac{6x^{-8}}{1} = \dfrac{6}{1 \cdot x^8} = \dfrac{6}{x^8}$

In the expression $6x^{-8}$, the denominator is understood to be 1. The factor x^{-8} moves to the denominator, and its exponent becomes $+8$. (Remember: The exponent applies only to the x, not to the 6.)

c. $(3x)^{-5} = \dfrac{1}{(3x)^5} = \dfrac{1}{3^5 x^5}$

In this case, the -5 applies to everything inside the parentheses. ■

Example 11 Write each of the following expressions without fractions, using negative exponents if necessary:

a. $\dfrac{m^5}{n^2} = m^5 n^{-2}$

Notice that n^2 (a factor of the denominator) was moved to the numerator and its exponent changed to -2.

b. $\dfrac{y^3}{z^{-2}} = y^3 z^2$

c. $\dfrac{a}{2c^2} = 2^{-1} a c^{-2}$ ■

A WORD OF CAUTION An expression that is a term of (rather than a factor of) a numerator *cannot* be moved from the numerator to the denominator of a fraction simply by moving it and changing the sign of the exponent. For example,

$$\frac{a^{-2} + b^5}{c^4} \neq \frac{b^5}{a^2 c^4}$$

Notice that since a^{-2} is a term of rather than a factor of the numerator, we cannot move it to the denominator and change the exponent to $+2$. Instead, we proceed as follows:

$$\frac{a^{-2} + b^5}{c^4} = \frac{\dfrac{1}{a^2} + b^5}{c^4}$$

←—The expression on the right is still not simplified; such expressions will be simplified in Section 6.6 ☑

The rules from Section 1.11A for multiplying exponential numbers, raising exponential numbers to powers, and dividing exponential numbers also apply when the exponents are negative integers or zero.

Example 12 Use the rules of exponents to rewrite each of the following with positive exponents only or no exponents and with the base appearing only once:

a. $y^3 \cdot y^{-2} = y^{3-2} = y^1 = y$

b. $10^7 \cdot 10^{-3} = 10^{7-3} = 10^4$

c. $\dfrac{x^4}{x^7} = x^{4-7} = x^{-3} = \dfrac{1}{x^3}$

d. $(x^3)^{-2} = x^{-6} = \dfrac{1}{x^6}$

e. $5^4 \cdot 5^{-4} = 5^{4-4} = 5^0 = 1$

f. $(2^3)^{-1} = 2^{-3} = \dfrac{1}{2^3}$

g. $\dfrac{x^{-3}}{x^2} = x^{-3-2} = x^{-5} = \dfrac{1}{x^5}$ or $\dfrac{x^{-3}}{x^2} = \dfrac{1}{x^3 x^2} = \dfrac{1}{x^5}$ ■

Example 13   Examples of evaluating expressions with numerical bases:

a. $10^8 \cdot 10^{-3} = 10^{8-3} = 10^5 = 100{,}000$

b. $(2^{-3})^2 = 2^{-6} = \dfrac{1}{2^6} = \dfrac{1}{64}$ ∎

EXERCISES 1.11B

Set I   In Exercises 1–16, write each expression using only positive exponents or no exponents.

1. a^{-3}	**2.** x^{-2}	**3.** 10^{-3}	**4.** 10^{-5}
5. $5b^{-7}$	**6.** $3y^{-2}$	**7.** $(5b)^{-2}$	**8.** $(3y)^{-2}$
9. $x^{-3}y^2z^0$	**10.** $r^3s^{-4}t^0$	**11.** $xy^{-2}z^{-3}w^0$	**12.** $z^{-4}bc^{-5}a^0$
13. $\dfrac{a^3}{b^{-4}}$	**14.** $\dfrac{c^4}{d^{-5}}$	**15.** $\dfrac{x^{-3}}{y^{-2}}$	**16.** $\dfrac{P^{-2}}{Q^{-4}}$

In Exercises 17–40, use the rules of exponents to rewrite each expression with no parentheses, with the base appearing only once if possible, and with positive exponents or no exponents.

17. $x^{-3} \cdot x^{-4}$	**18.** $y^{-1} \cdot y^{-4}$	**19.** $(a^3)^{-2}$	**20.** $(b^2)^{-4}$
21. $x^8 \cdot x^{-2}$	**22.** $a^{-3} \cdot a^5$	**23.** $(x^{2a})^{-3}$	**24.** $(y^{3c})^{-2}$
25. $\dfrac{y^3}{y^{-2}}$	**26.** $\dfrac{x^8}{x^{-4}}$	**27.** $\dfrac{x^{3a}}{x^{-a}}$	**28.** $\dfrac{a^{4x}}{a^{-2x}}$
29. $(3^x)^0$	**30.** $(2^a)^0$	**31.** $5x^0$	**32.** $2y^0$
33. $x^{-3} + x^{-5}$		**34.** $y^{-2} + y^{-6}$	
35. $x^7 - x^{-5}$		**36.** $y^{10} - y^{-3}$	
37. $x^0 + y^0$		**38.** $a^0 + b^0 + c^0$	
39. $(x + y)^0$		**40.** $(a + b + c)^0$	

In Exercises 41–48, evaluate each expression.

41. $10^5 \cdot 10^{-2}$	**42.** $2^4 \cdot 2^{-2}$	**43.** $(3^{-2})^{-2}$	**44.** $(10^{-1})^{-3}$
45. $(10^0)^5$	**46.** $(3^0)^4$	**47.** $\dfrac{10^2 \cdot 10^{-1}}{10^{-3}}$	**48.** $\dfrac{2^{-3} \cdot 2^2}{2^{-4}}$

In Exercises 49–54, write each expression without fractions, using negative exponents if necessary.

49. $\dfrac{y}{x^3}$	**50.** $\dfrac{x}{y^2}$	**51.** $\dfrac{x}{a^{-4}}$	**52.** $\dfrac{m^2}{n^{-3}}$
53. $\dfrac{x^4y^{-3}}{z^{-2}}$	**54.** $\dfrac{a^{-1}b^3}{c^{-4}}$		

Set II   In Exercises 1–16, write each expression using only positive exponents or no exponents.

1. x^{-4}	**2.** 16^0	**3.** 10^{-2}	**4.** $(-2)^{-3}$
5. $2a^{-4}$	**6.** $6x^0$	**7.** $(2a)^{-2}$	**8.** $(-4x)^{-2}$

9. $x^0 y^{-1} z^2$ **10.** $3x^0 y^{-1}$ **11.** $x^{-3} y z^{-2}$ **12.** $y^3 z^{-1} w^0$

13. $\dfrac{a^4}{b^{-3}}$ **14.** $\dfrac{x^{-1} y}{z^{-2}}$ **15.** $\dfrac{x^{-5}}{y^{-4}}$ **16.** $\dfrac{a^0 b^{-3} c}{d^{-4}}$

In Exercises 17–40, use the rules of exponents to rewrite each expression with no parentheses, with the base appearing only once if possible, and with positive exponents or no exponents.

17. $a^{-3} \cdot a^{-5}$ **18.** $x^{-3} \cdot x^5$ **19.** $(a^{-2})^3$ **20.** $(-x^2)^{-3}$

21. $x^8 x^{-2}$ **22.** $(a^{-3})^2$ **23.** $(z^{4b})^{-4}$ **24.** $s^{-4} \cdot s^2$

25. $\dfrac{x}{y^{-3}}$ **26.** $\dfrac{a^5}{b^2}$ **27.** $\dfrac{y^{2b}}{y^{-b}}$ **28.** $\dfrac{x^4}{x^{-2}}$

29. $(3R)^0$ **30.** $6a^0$ **31.** $4X^0$ **32.** $(3xy)^0$

33. $a^{-7} + a^{-2}$ **34.** $x^{-2} - x^3$ **35.** $u^4 - u^{-5}$ **36.** $3x^{-5}$

37. $a^0 + b^0 + c^0 + d^0$ **38.** $x + 5^0$

39. $(a + b + c + d)^0$ **40.** $a^3 b^{-2}$

In Exercises 41–48, evaluate each expression.

41. $10^{-3} \cdot 10^5$ **42.** -2^{-3} **43.** $(2^{-3})^{-2}$ **44.** $(10^2)^{-4}$

45. $(7^0)^8$ **46.** $(8^0)^2$ **47.** $\dfrac{10^{-3} \cdot 10}{10^{-4}}$ **48.** $\dfrac{2^{-1}}{2^6 \cdot 2^{-4}}$

In Exercises 49–54, write each expression without fractions, using negative exponents if necessary.

49. $\dfrac{a}{b^4}$ **50.** $\dfrac{x^{-2}}{y^3}$ **51.** $\dfrac{x}{y^{-3}}$ **52.** $\dfrac{a^{-4}}{b}$

53. $\dfrac{x^2 y^{-3}}{z^{-5}}$ **54.** $\dfrac{a^{-1} b}{c^{-6}}$

1.11C   General Rule of Exponents

The combination of all of the rules of exponents gives us the following general rule:

RULE 1.8

$$\left(\frac{x^a y^b}{z^c}\right)^n = \frac{x^{an} y^{bn}}{z^{cn}}$$

None of the letters can have a value that makes the denominator zero.

In applying Rule 1.8, notice the following:

1. x, y, and z are *factors* of the expression within the parentheses. They are *not* separated by $+$ or $-$ signs.

2. The exponent of *each* factor within the parentheses is multiplied by the exponent outside the parentheses.

Example 14   Use the General Rule of Exponents (Rule 1.8) to rewrite each of the following, if possible:

$\llcorner$ 1 is understood to be the exponent of the 2, and that 1 must be multiplied by 3.

a. $\left(\dfrac{2a^{-3}b^2}{c^5}\right)^3 = \dfrac{2^{1\cdot3}a^{(-3)3}b^{2\cdot3}}{c^{5\cdot3}} = \dfrac{2^3a^{-9}b^6}{c^{15}} = \dfrac{8b^6}{a^9c^{15}}$

b. $\left(\dfrac{3^2c^{-4}}{d^3}\right)^{-1} = \dfrac{3^{2(-1)}c^{(-4)(-1)}}{d^{3(-1)}} = \dfrac{3^{-2}c^4}{d^{-3}} = \dfrac{c^4d^3}{3^2} = \dfrac{c^4d^3}{9}$

If we use Rule 1.7c,

$$\left(\frac{3^2c^{-4}}{d^3}\right)^{-1} = \frac{d^3}{3^2c^{-4}} = \frac{c^4d^3}{9}$$

c. $(x^2 + y^3)^4$

Rule 1.8 cannot be used here because the $+$ sign means that x^2 and y^3 are terms, not factors, of the expression inside the parentheses. Expressions of this kind will be simplified in Section 4.4C. ∎

Simplified Form of Expressions with Exponents.   When we wish to remove parentheses in an expression in which a *single term* is inside each set of grouping symbols, that is, as in the expression $(3x^2)(7x^3)$, we first multiply the numerical coefficients together and then use the rules of exponents to simplify the literal part of the expression. This is possible because multiplication is both associative and commutative.

Example 15   Simplify each expression:

a. $(3x^2)(7x^3) = 3\cdot7\cdot x^2\cdot x^3 = 21x^{2+3} = 21x^5$

b. $(2x^3y^2)(4xy^5z)(-3x^2) = 2(4)(-3)x^3y^2xy^5zx^2 = -24x^6y^7z$

c. $(-8a^3b^2c^6)(-5ab^3) = 40a^4b^5c^6$ ∎

An expression with exponents is considered *simplified* when (1) there are no parentheses, (2) each different base appears only once in each separate term, and (3) the exponent on each base is a single natural number.

Example 16   Simplify each expression:

a. $x^{-2}\cdot x^7 = x^{-2+7} = x^5$

b. $(83x^5)^0 = 1$

c. $\dfrac{x^5y^2}{x^3y^{-1}} = x^{5-3}y^{2-(-1)} = x^2y^3$

d. $(2x)^{-1} = \dfrac{1}{2x}$

e. $2x^{-1} = \dfrac{2}{x}$

f. $(x^3y^{-1})^5 = x^{15}y^{-5} = \dfrac{x^{15}}{y^5}$

g. $\left(\dfrac{3^{-7}x^{10}}{y^{-4}}\right)^0 = 1$

h. $\left(\dfrac{x^5 y^4}{x^3 y^7}\right)^2 = (x^2 y^{-3})^2 = x^4 y^{-6} = \dfrac{x^4}{y^6}$

⌐ Simplify the expression within the
  parentheses first whenever possible

i. $(5^0 h^{-2})^{-3} = (1 h^{-2})^{-3} = (h^{-2})^{-3} = h^6$ ∎

EXERCISES 1.11C

Set I   Write each expression in simplest form.

1. $(5x)^{-3}$ **2.** $(4y)^{-2}$ **3.** $7x^{-2}$ **4.** $3y^{-4}$

5. $\left(\dfrac{3}{x}\right)^3$ **6.** $\left(\dfrac{7}{y}\right)^2$ **7.** $\dfrac{8^2}{z}$ **8.** $\dfrac{2^3}{x}$

9. $(a^2 b^3)^2$ **10.** $(x^4 y^5)^3$ **11.** $(m^{-2} n)^4$ **12.** $(p^{-3} r)^5$

13. $(x^{-2} y^3)^{-4}$ **14.** $(w^{-3} z^4)^{-2}$ **15.** $(10^0 k^{-4})^{-2}$ **16.** $(6^0 z^{-5})^{-2}$

17. $(2x^2 y^{-4})^3$ **18.** $(3a^{-1} b^5)^2$ **19.** $(5m^{-3} n^5)^{-2}$ **20.** $(8x^8 y^{-2})^{-1}$

21. $\left(\dfrac{xy^4}{z^2}\right)^2$ **22.** $\left(\dfrac{a^3 b}{c^2}\right)^3$ **23.** $\left(\dfrac{M^{-2}}{N^3}\right)^4$ **24.** $\left(\dfrac{R^5}{S^{-4}}\right)^3$

25. $\left(\dfrac{x^{-5}}{y^4 z^{-3}}\right)^{-2}$ **26.** $\left(\dfrac{a^{-4}}{b^2 c^{-5}}\right)^{-3}$ **27.** $\left(\dfrac{r^7 s^8}{r^9 s^6}\right)^0$ **28.** $\left(\dfrac{t^5 u^6}{t^8 u^7}\right)^0$

29. $\left(\dfrac{3x^2}{y^3}\right)^2$ **30.** $\left(\dfrac{2a^4}{b^2}\right)^4$ **31.** $\left(\dfrac{4a^{-2}}{b^3}\right)^{-1}$ **32.** $\left(\dfrac{m^{-4}}{5n^3}\right)^{-2}$

33. $\left(\dfrac{x^{-1} y^2}{x^4}\right)^{-2}$ **34.** $\left(\dfrac{u^{-4} v^3}{v^4}\right)^{-3}$ **35.** $\left(\dfrac{x^{3n} x^{2n}}{x^{4n}}\right)^2$ **36.** $\left(\dfrac{x^{2n-1} y^{3n}}{x^n y^{2n+2}}\right)^2$

37. $(2x^5 y^2)(-3x^4)$ **38.** $(-4a^2 b^3)(7b^2)$

39. $(-4x^{-2} y^3)(-2xy^{-1})$ **40.** $(-5a^4 b^{-3})(-2a^{-5} b^4)$

41. $(2s^3 t^0 u^{-4})(3su^3)(-s)$ **42.** $(4xy^0 z^{-3})(-z)(2x^3 z)$

Set II   Write each expression in simplest form.

1. $(2x)^{-4}$ **2.** $2x^{-4}$ **3.** $3y^{-3}$ **4.** $(3y)^{-3}$

5. $\left(\dfrac{5}{z}\right)^2$ **6.** $\dfrac{5^2}{z}$ **7.** $\dfrac{2^4}{y}$ **8.** $\left(\dfrac{6z}{x}\right)^2$

9. $(x^4 y^6)^2$ **10.** $(2xy^5)^5$ **11.** $(x^{-3} y^4)^3$ **12.** $(xy^4)^3$

13. $(a^{-3} b^2)^{-3}$ **14.** $(2x^{-4})^{-4}$ **15.** $(x^0 y^{-3})^{-5}$ **16.** $(3x^{-6} z)^0$

17. $(4x^4 y^{-2})^4$ **18.** $(3x^4 yz^2)^0$ **19.** $(2x^{-1} y^5)^{-3}$ **20.** $(3xy^2)^{-1}$

21. $\left(\dfrac{a^3 b}{c^4}\right)^2$ **22.** $\left(\dfrac{5^0 x^4}{3^{-1} y^2}\right)^2$ **23.** $\left(\dfrac{u^{-2}}{v^4}\right)^3$ **24.** $\left(\dfrac{x^3 y^5}{z^4}\right)^{-1}$

25. $\left(\dfrac{x^{-4} y^2}{z^{-3}}\right)^{-2}$ **26.** $\left(\dfrac{5s^4 t^{-2}}{2x^2}\right)^{-2}$ **27.** $\left(\dfrac{r^5 s^9}{r^2 s^{10}}\right)^0$ **28.** $\left(\dfrac{ab^3}{b^4}\right)^2$

29. $\left(\dfrac{3a^2}{b^3}\right)^3$ **30.** $\left(\dfrac{4x^0}{y^3}\right)^2$ **31.** $\left(\dfrac{4m^{-3}}{n^5}\right)^{-2}$ **32.** $\left(\dfrac{u^3 v^{-2}}{u^5 w^{-3}}\right)^{-1}$

33. $\left(\dfrac{x^3}{x^{-2}y^{-4}}\right)^{-1}$ **34.** $\left(\dfrac{g^{-3}}{2h^4}\right)^{-2}$ **35.** $\dfrac{(x^{3n}y^{2n-1})^3}{(xy)^2}$ **36.** $\dfrac{(x^{2n}y^{3n})^3}{(xy^n)^2}$

37. $(-3x^2y^4)(8y)$ **38.** $(8x^2y)(-4xy)$ **39.** $(-4xy^3)(2x^2y^3)$

40. $(4^0a^3b^{-2})(3ab^5)$ **41.** $(5x^0y^{-4}z)(-y)(3y^2z)$ **42.** $(-3x^0y^4)(2xy^{-5})$

1.12 Scientific Notation and the Calculator

Now that we have discussed zero and negative exponents, we can introduce scientific notation, a notation used in many science courses and often seen in calculator displays.

A number written in **scientific notation** is written as the product of some number between 1 and 10 and a power of 10. That is, it must be in the form

$$a \times 10^n \text{ where } 1 \leq a < 10 \text{ and } n \text{ is an integer}$$

For example, 4.32×10^3 is written in scientific notation, because 4.32 is a number between 1 and 10 and 10^3 is a power of 10. Any decimal number can be written in scientific notation.

We will discuss first how to find the correct power of 10 and then how to find a.

FINDING THE EXPONENT OF THE 10

1. Place a caret ($_\wedge$) to the right of the first nonzero digit of the number.

2. Draw an arrow *from* the caret *to* the actual decimal point.

3. The *sign* of the exponent of 10 will be positive if the arrow points right and negative if the arrow points left.

4. The number of digits separating the caret and the actual decimal point gives us the absolute value of the exponent of the 10.

The above rules imply that if the number we're converting to scientific notation is greater than or equal to 10, the exponent of the 10 will be positive; if the number is less than 1, the exponent of the 10 will be negative.

FINDING a

Place the decimal point so that there is exactly one nonzero digit to its left. This means that the decimal point will be where the caret is in the instructions for finding the exponent of 10.

A number is then written in scientific notation by writing it in the form $a \times 10^n$.

Example 1   Write the following decimal numbers in scientific notation:

	Decimal notation	Scientific notation
a.	2,450	$2\underset{\rightarrow}{450.} = 2.45 \times 10^3$
b.	2.45	$2.45 = 2.45 \times 10^0$
c.	0.0245	$0.0\underset{\leftarrow}{245} = 2.45 \times 10^{-2}$
d.	92,900,000	$9\underset{\rightarrow}{2900000.} = 9.29 \times 10^7$
e.	0.0056	$0.005\underset{\leftarrow}{6} = 5.6 \times 10^{-3}$
f.	684.5	$6\underset{\rightarrow}{84.5} = 6.845 \times 10^2$

Number between 1 and 10 ↑   ↑ Power of 10 ∎

To change from scientific notation to decimal notation, simply multiply by the power of 10. For example,

$$4.32 \times 10^3 = 4,320$$

$$2.3 \times 10^{-3} = 0.0023$$

It is sometimes necessary to convert a number such as 0.435×10^7 or 732.4×10^3 to scientific notation or to decimal notation. Examples 2 and 3 demonstrate how to do this.

Example 2   Convert 0.435×10^7 to scientific notation.

$$0.435 \times 10^7 = (4.35 \times 10^{-1}) \times 10^7 = 4.35 \times 10^6 \quad \blacksquare$$

Example 3   Convert 732.4×10^3 to scientific notation and then to decimal notation.

$$732.4 \times 10^3 = (7.324 \times 10^2) \times 10^3 = 7.324 \times 10^5 \text{ in scientific notation}$$

$$732.4 \times 10^3 = 732,400 \text{ in decimal notation} \quad \blacksquare$$

When a *calculator* is used and answers are very large or very small, the display will most likely be in scientific notation. On the calculator, however, numbers in scientific notation are displayed in a different (and possibly misleading) way. $\boxed{2.45 \quad 04}$ or $\boxed{2.45 \quad ^{04}}$ does *not* mean 2.45 to the fourth power; it means 2.45×10^4, which is 24,500.

Example 4   Find $600,000 \times 300,000$ using a calculator.

The display probably shows $\boxed{1.8 \quad 11}$ or $\boxed{1.8 \quad ^{11}}$, which means $1.8 \times 10^{11} = 180,000,000,000$. In contrast, 1.8^{11} is approximately 642.6841007. ∎

Example 5   Find $0.00006 \div 500$ using a calculator.

The display probably shows $\boxed{1.2 \quad -07}$ or $\boxed{1.2 \quad ^{-07}}$, which means $1.2 \times 10^{-7} = 0.00000012$. ∎

EXERCISES 1.12

Set I   In Exercises 1–12, write each number in scientific notation.

1. 28.56   **2.** 375.4   **3.** 0.06184

4. 0.003056   **5.** 78,000   **6.** 1,400

7. 0.2006   **8.** 0.000095   **9.** 0.362×10^{-2}

10. 0.6314×10^{-3} **11.** 245.2×10^{-5} **12.** 31.7×10^{-4}

In Exercises 13–16, perform the indicated operations with a calculator and express each answer in scientific notation.

13. $560{,}000 \times 23{,}000$ **14.** $0.00006 \div 20{,}000$

15. $\sqrt{0.00000256}$ **16.** $\sqrt{0.00000081}$

Set II   In Exercises 1–12, write each number in scientific notation.

1. 50.48   **2.** 0.0878   **3.** 4500.9

4. 0.000505   **5.** 289.3   **6.** 2,478,000

7. 0.00612   **8.** 0.00001   **9.** 63.7×10^{4}

10. 0.0357×10^{-5} **11.** 0.492×10^{-3} **12.** 0.251×10^{4}

In Exercises 13–16, perform the indicated operations with a calculator and express each answer in scientific notation.

13. $340{,}000 \times 680{,}000$ **14.** $0.00025 \div 500$

15. $\sqrt{0.00000289}$ **16.** $\sqrt{0.00000001}$

1.13 Evaluating and Substituting in Algebraic Expressions and Formulas

1.13A Evaluating Algebraic Expressions

The process of substituting a numerical value for a variable in an algebraic expression is called *evaluating*.

    If the number being substituted is a *negative* number, it is almost always necessary to enclose the number in parentheses. In the expression $3x$, for example, if -2 is to be substituted for x, then writing $3 - 2$ is incorrect; $3x$ means 3 *times* x, and $3 - 2$ means *subtract* 2 from 3. The correct notation is $3(-2)$. Likewise, if -4 is to be substituted for x in the expression x^2, then -4^2 is *incorrect* since -4^2 means $-(4)^2 = -16$. We wish -4 to be squared; therefore, the correct substitution is $(-4)^2$.

Example 1   Find the value of $3x^2 - 5y^3$ if $x = -4$ and $y = -2$.

$$3x^2 - 5y^3$$
$$= 3(-4)^2 - 5(-2)^3$$
$$= 3(16) - 5(-8)$$
$$= 48 + 40$$
$$= 88 \quad \blacksquare$$

Example 2 Find the value of $2a - [b - (3x - 4y)]$ if $a = -3$, $b = 4$, $x = -5$, and $y = -2$.

$$2a \quad - [b \quad - (3x \quad - 4y)]$$
$$= 2(-3) - [(4) - \{3(-5) - 4(-2)\}] \longleftarrow \text{Braces are used in place of parentheses to clarify the grouping}$$
$$= 2(-3) - [4 \quad - \{-15 + 8\}]$$
$$= 2(-3) - [4 - \{-7\}]$$
$$= 2(-3) - [4 + 7]$$
$$= \quad -6 \; -[11]$$
$$= \quad -6 \; -11$$
$$= -17 \quad \blacksquare$$

Example 3 Evaluate $b - \sqrt{b^2 - 4ac}$ when $a = 3$, $b = -7$, and $c = 2$.

$$b - \sqrt{b^2 - 4ac} \qquad \qquad \text{This bar is a grouping symbol for } b^2 - 4ac$$
$$= (-7) - \sqrt{(-7)^2 - 4(3)(2)}$$
$$= (-7) - \sqrt{49 - 24}$$
$$= (-7) - \sqrt{25}$$
$$= (-7) - \quad 5 \quad = -12 \quad \blacksquare$$

A WORD OF CAUTION   In Example 3, *two* errors are made if you write

$$b - \sqrt{b^2 - 4ac} = -7 - \sqrt{-7^2 - 4(3)(2)} = -7 - \sqrt{49 - 24}.$$

It is incorrect to omit the ( ) around -7 here, and $-7^2 = -49$, not 49. $\boxed{\checkmark}$

Substitutions in Algebraic Expressions

It is sometimes desirable to make substitutions of one variable for another variable in an algebraic expression. If the expression being substituted has more than one term, *be sure to enclose the expression in parentheses.*

Example 4 Substitute x for $2a^2 - 3a$ in the following expression.

$(2a^2 - 3a)^2 + 5(2a^2 - 3a) - 15$

When we let $x = 2a^2 - 3a$ in the expression

$(2a^2 - 3a)^2 + 5(2a^2 - 3a) - 15$, we get $x^2 + 5x - 15$. $\blacksquare$

Example 5 Substitute $x^3 - 7x$ for b in the expression $2b^2 - 5$.

When we let $b = x^3 - 7x$ in the expression $2b^2 - 5$, we get $2(x^3 - 7x)^2 - 5$.* Notice that it is necessary to put $x^3 - 7x$ *inside parentheses* when we make the substitution. $\blacksquare$

---

* This expression cannot be simplified at this time.

EXERCISES 1.13A

Set I   In Exercises 1–18, evaluate the expression when $a = \frac{1}{3}$, $b = -5$, $c = -1$, $x = 5$, $y = -6$, $D = 0$, $E = -1$, $F = 5$, $G = -15$, $H = -4$, and $J = 2$.

1. $2y^2 + 3x$

2. $c^3 - y$

3. $b - 12a^2$

4. $y - 24a^2$

5. $b^2 - 4xy$

6. $y^2 - 5cx$

7. $(x + y)^2$

8. $(b + c)^2$

9. $x^2 + 2xy + y^2$

10. $b^2 + 2bc + c^2$

11. $x^2 + y^2$

12. $b^2 + c^2$

13. $\dfrac{3D}{F + G}$

14. $\dfrac{5D}{G + H}$

15. $2E - [F - (D - 5G)]$

16. $3G - [D - (F - 2H)]$

17. $-E - \sqrt{E^2 - 4HF}$

18. $-E + \sqrt{E^2 - 4GJ}$

In Exercises 19–22, make the indicated substitutions.

19. Substitute b for $x^3 - 7x$ in the expression $5(x^3 - 7x)^2 - 4(x^3 - 7x) + 8$.

20. Substitute c for $a^5 + a$ in the expression $4(a^5 + a) + 3$.

21. Substitute $x^2 - 4x$ for a in the expression $2a^2 - 3a + 7$. (Do not attempt to simplify the result.)

22. Substitute $y^4 + 2$ for b in the expression $b^2 - 2b$. (Do not attempt to simplify the result.)

Set II   In Exercises 1–18, evaluate the expression when $a = \frac{3}{4}$, $b = 5$, $c = -4$, $d = 3$, $e = -2$, and $f = -8$.

1. $4c^2 + 5e$

2. $c^2 + e$

3. $b - 14a^2$

4. $(b + c)^2$

5. $c^2 - 4bc$

6. $b^2 + c^2$

7. $(b + e)^2$

8. $b^2 + 2bc + c^2$

9. $b^2 + 2be + e^2$

10. $(f + e)^2$

11. $b^2 + e^2$

12. $f^2 + 2ef + e^2$

13. $\dfrac{5c}{e + f}$

14. $f^2 + e^2$

15. $2b - [f - (c - b)]$

16. $c - \{b - (d - f) - e\}$

17. $-e + \sqrt{e^2 - 4df}$

18. $(b + c + d)^2$

In Exercises 19–22, make the indicated substitutions.

19. Substitute d for $x^2 + 2x$ in the expression $3(x^2 + 2x)^2 + 4(x^2 + 2x) - 5$.

20. Substitute a for $x^3 - x$ in the expression $7(x^3 - x)^2 - (x^3 - x) - 3$.

21. Substitute $z^2 + 3z - 5$ for c in the expression $3c^4 - 2c + 4$. (Do not attempt to simplify the result.)

22. Substitute $a^2 + 5a$ for x in the expression $-2x^3 - 4x^2 + 3x - 2$. (Do not attempt to simplify the result.)

1.13B Evaluating Formulas

One reason for studying algebra is to prepare to use *formulas*. Students will encounter formulas in many of their courses, as well as in real-life situations. In the examples and exercises in this section, we have listed the subject areas in which the given formulas are used.

A formula is evaluated in the same way in which any expression having numbers and letters is evaluated.

Example 6 Given the formula $A = \frac{1}{2}h(a + b)$, find A when $h = 5$, $a = 3$, and $b = 7$. (Geometry—area of a trapezoid)

$$A = \frac{1}{2} h(a + b)$$

$$A = \frac{1}{2}(5)(3 + 7)$$

$$= \frac{1}{2}(5)(10)$$

$$= \frac{1}{2}(50)$$

$$= 25 \quad \blacksquare$$

Example 7 Given the formula $T = \pi\sqrt{\dfrac{L}{g}}$, find T when $\pi \doteq 3.14$, $L = 96$, and $g = 32$. (Physics)

$$T = \pi\sqrt{\frac{L}{g}}$$

$$\doteq (3.14)\sqrt{\frac{96}{32}} = (3.14)\sqrt{3} \doteq (3.14)(1.732)$$

$$\doteq 5.44 \qquad \text{Rounded off to 2 decimal places} \quad \blacksquare$$

Formulas will be discussed further in Chapter 6.

EXERCISES 1.13B

Set I Evaluate each formula, using the values of the variables given with the formula. Answers that are not exact may be rounded off to two decimal places.

For Exercises 1 and 2, evaluate this formula from nursing: $q = \dfrac{DQ}{H}$.

1. $D = 5$, $H = 30$, $Q = 420$ **2.** $D = 25$, $H = 90$, $Q = 450$

For Exercises 3 and 4, evaluate this formula from business: $A = P(1 + rt)$.

3. $P = 500$, $r = 0.09$, $t = 2.5$ **4.** $P = 400$, $r = 0.07$, $t = 3.5$

For Exercises 5 and 6, evaluate this formula from business: $A = P(1 + i)^n$.

5. $P = 600$, $i = 0.085$, $n = 2$ **6.** $P = 700$, $i = 0.075$, $n = 2$

For Exercises 7 and 8, evaluate this formula from chemistry: $C = \frac{5}{9}(F - 32)$.

7. $F = -10$

8. $F = -7$

For Exercises 9 and 10, evaluate this formula from physics: $s = \frac{1}{2}gt^2$.

9. $g = 32, t = 8\frac{1}{2}$

10. $g = 32, t = 4\frac{3}{4}$

For Exercises 11 and 12, evaluate this formula from physics: $Z = \dfrac{Rr}{R + r}$.

11. $R = 22, r = 8$

12. $R = 55, r = 25$

For Exercises 13 and 14, evaluate this formula from geometry: $S = 2\pi r^2 + 2\pi rh$. (Use $\pi \doteq 3.14$.)

13. $r = 3, h = 20$

14. $r = 6, h = 10$

Set II   Evaluate each formula, using the values of the variables given with the formula. Answers that are not exact may be rounded off to two decimal places.

For Exercises 1 and 2, evaluate this formula from nursing: $q = \dfrac{DQ}{H}$.

1. $D = 15, H = 80, Q = 320$

2. $D = 20, H = 24, Q = 300$

For Exercises 3 and 4, evaluate this formula from business: $A = P(1 + rt)$.

3. $P = 450, r = 0.08, t = 2.5$

4. $P = 1,000, r = 0.06, t = 5.5$

For Exercises 5 and 6, evaluate this formula from business: $A = P(1 + i)^n$.

5. $P = 900, i = 0.095, n = 2$

6. $P = 400, i = 0.055, n = 3$

For Exercises 7 and 8, evaluate this formula from chemistry: $C = \frac{5}{9}(F - 32)$.

7. $F = 95$

8. $F = 14$

For Exercises 9 and 10, evaluate this formula from physics: $s = \frac{1}{2}gt^2$.

9. $g = 32, t = 5\frac{1}{2}$

10. $g = 32, t = 6\frac{1}{4}$

For Exercises 11 and 12, evaluate this formula from physics: $Z = \dfrac{Rr}{R + r}$.

11. $R = 150, r = 25$

12. $R = 80, r = 35$

For Exercises 13 and 14, evaluate this formula from geometry: $S = 2\pi r^2 + 2\pi rh$. (Use $\pi \doteq 3.14$.)

13. $r = 3.6, h = 5.1$

14. $r = 6.5, h = 1.2$

1.14 Simplifying Algebraic Expressions

1.14A   Square Roots (of Perfect Squares) with Variables

We discussed the method for finding the square roots of positive numbers or zero in Section 1.7. We now extend this concept to include finding square roots of algebraic expressions that are products of factors.

The algebraic expression x^2 has *two* square roots, x and $-x$. Since x itself can be either a positive or a negative number, we don't know which is the *principal* square root. However, we do know that $|x|$ must be positive (or zero); therefore, $|x|$ is the principal square root of x^2.

NOTE   In this section, we assume that all letters represent positive numbers. For this reason, the absolute value symbol need not be used, and we will write $\sqrt{x^2} = x$. ☑

All of the radicands in this section are perfect squares. This means that any numerical coefficients are squares of integers and that the exponents on any variables are always *even* numbers. In Chapter 7, we consider simplifying radicals in which the radicands are *not* perfect squares.

TO FIND THE PRINCIPAL SQUARE ROOT OF A PRODUCT OF FACTORS

1. The principal square root of the numerical coefficient is found by inspection or by trial and error.

2. The square root of each literal factor is found by dividing its exponent by 2.

Example 1   Find the principal square root of each of the following expressions:

a. $\sqrt{9x^2} = 3x$ because $(3x)^2 = 9x^2$

b. $\sqrt{25x^2} = 5x$ because $(5x)^2 = 25x^2$

c. $\sqrt{100a^6 b^{10}} = 10a^{6/2} b^{10/2} = 10a^3 b^5$ ■

EXERCISES 1.14A

Set I   Find the principal square roots of the expressions that follow.

1. $\sqrt{4x^2}$ 2. $\sqrt{9y^2}$ 3. $\sqrt{m^4 n^2}$ 4. $\sqrt{u^{10} v^6}$

5. $\sqrt{25a^4 b^2}$ 6. $\sqrt{100b^4 c^2}$ 7. $\sqrt{x^{10} y^4}$ 8. $\sqrt{x^{12} y^8}$

9. $\sqrt{100a^{10} y^2}$ 10. $\sqrt{121a^{24} b^4}$ 11. $\sqrt{81m^8 n^{16}}$ 12. $\sqrt{49c^{18} d^{10}}$

Set II   Find the principal square roots of the expressions that follow.

1. $\sqrt{100a^8}$ 2. $\sqrt{49b^6}$ 3. $\sqrt{36e^8 f^2}$ 4. $\sqrt{81h^{12} k^{14}}$

5. $\sqrt{9a^4 b^2 c^6}$ 6. $\sqrt{144x^8 y^2 z^6}$ 7. $\sqrt{121a^4 b^8}$ 8. $\sqrt{144x^6 y^2}$

9. $\sqrt{169a^8 b^6 c^4}$ 10. $\sqrt{4s^6 t^6}$ 11. $\sqrt{16u^2 v^8}$ 12. $\sqrt{x^{12} y^{16}}$

1.14B   Using the Distributive Rules to Simplify an Expression

The distributive rules

$$a(b + c) = ab + ac \quad \text{and} \quad (b + c)a = ba + ca$$

can be used to remove parentheses when two or more terms are within the parentheses. To use the distributive rule, multiply *each term* inside the grouping symbols by the factor that is outside them.

Example 2   Use the distributive rule to remove the parentheses:

a. $4x(x^2 - 2xy + y^2) = (4x)(x^2) - (4x)(2xy) + (4x)(y^2)$
$$= 4x^3 \qquad - 8x^2y \qquad + 4xy^2$$

b. $(-2x^2 + xy^2)(-3xy) = (-2x^2)(-3xy) + (xy^2)(-3xy)$
$$= 6x^3y \qquad\qquad - 3x^2y^3 \quad \blacksquare$$

A WORD OF CAUTION $(-2x^2 + xy^2) - 3xy \neq (-2x^2 + xy^2)(-3xy)$

$3xy$ is being *subtracted* from $(-2x^2 + xy^2)$

$-3xy$ is *not* a factor following the parentheses

$-3xy$ is being *multiplied* by $(-2x^2 + xy^2)$

$(-3xy)$ *is* a factor following the parentheses

EXERCISES 1.14B

Set I   Simplify.

1. $3a(6 + x)$ **2.** $5b(7 + y)$

3. $(x - 5)(-4)$ **4.** $(y - 2)(-5)$

5. $-3(x - 2y + 2)$ **6.** $-2(x - 3y + 4)$

7. $x(xy - 3)$ **8.** $a(ab - 4)$

9. $3a(ab - 2a^2)$ **10.** $4x(3x - 2y^2)$

11. $(3x^3 - 2x^2y + y^3)(-2xy)$ **12.** $(4z^3 - z^2y - y^3)(-2yz)$

13. $(-2ab)(3a^2b)(6abc^3)$ **14.** $(5x^2y)(-2xy^3)(3xyz^2)$

15. $4xy^2(3x^3y^2 - 2x^2y^3 + 5xy^4)$ **16.** $-2x^2(5x^4y - 2x^3y^2 - 3xy^3)$

17. $(3mn^2)(-2m^2n)(5m^2 - n^2)$ **18.** $(6a^2b)(-3ab^2)(2a^2 - b^2)$

19. $(2x^2)(-4xy^2z)(3xy - 2xz + 5yz)$ **20.** $(7a^2b)(3a - 2b - c)(ab^2)$

21. $(7x + 3y) - 2x^2$ **22.** $(3a - b) - 4c$

Set II   Simplify.

1. $2R(R + S)$ **2.** $7x(x - 5)$

3. $(x - 7)(-3)$ **4.** $(x - 7) - y$

5. $-4(x - 5y + 3)$ **6.** $(a + 7b - c) - 3$

7. $u(uv - 5)$ **8.** $(a + 7b - c)(-3)$

9. $4xy^2z(3x^2 - xy)$ **10.** $2a(a^2 + 3b - c^3)$

11. $(2x^3 - 5xy + y^2)(-3xy)$ **12.** $(3x^3y - 4x + 2z) - 3y$

13. $(5xy^2z^2)(-3yz)(2xz^2)$ **14.** $(-2xy^3)(4xz)(-2yz^4)$

15. $2x^2y(-4xy^2z + 3xz - y^2z)$ **16.** $3a^2b(-2ab^2 + 8ab - 1)$

17. $(4xy^2)(-2xy)(5x^2 - xy)$ **18.** $9x^2y(2y^2)(3x^3 - y^2)$

19. $4u^2v(-3uv^2)(u - 3v - w)$ **20.** $2x^3z(-3xz)(8x^2 + 2z^2)$

21. $(8c^3 - 3bc) - b^2$ **22.** $(8c - 3bc)(-b^2)$

1.14C Removing Grouping Symbols

The common grouping symbols are

( ) Parentheses

[ ] Brackets

{ } Braces

—— Bar (generally used with fractions and radicals)

When we *simplify* an algebraic expression, we remove all grouping symbols. The distributive rule can be used to remove them if the grouping symbols contain more than one term.

**REMOVING GROUPING SYMBOLS THAT
CONTAIN MORE THAN ONE TERM**

1. If a set of grouping symbols containing more than one term is preceded by or followed by a *factor*, use the distributive rule.

2. If a set of grouping symbols containing more than one term is *not* preceded by and *not* followed by a factor and is

a. preceded by a + or − sign, insert a 1 between the sign and the grouping symbol and use the distributive rule.

b. preceded by no sign at all, drop the grouping symbols.

3. If grouping symbols occur within other grouping symbols, remove the *innermost* grouping symbols first.

Example 3   Remove the grouping symbols in $(3x - 5) + 6y$.

Applying part b of the second rule, we have

$$(3x - 5) + 6y = 3x - 5 + 6y \quad \blacksquare$$

There is one shortcut we can safely take in using part a of the second rule. If the grouping symbols are preceded by a + sign *and* if the sign of the first term inside the grouping symbols is an *understood* plus sign, then we can simply drop the grouping symbols.

Example 4   Remove the grouping symbols:

a. $5z + (4y + 7)$

Following the shortcut, we have

$$5z + (4y + 7) = 5z + 4y + 7$$

(Compare this result with the result you obtain if you use part a of the second rule.)

b. $5z + (-3y + 7)$

Following part a of the second rule, we have

> Multiplying a number by 1 does not change its value

$$5z + (-3y + 7) = 5z + 1(-3y + 7)$$
$$= 5z + 1(-3y) + 1(7)$$
$$= 5z - 3y + 7$$

c. $3x - (8y + 2z - 5w)$

Following part a of the second rule, we have

$$3x - (8y + 2z - 5w) = 3x - 1(8y + 2z - 5w)$$
$$= 3x + (-1)(8y) + (-1)(2z) + (-1)(-5w)$$
$$= 3x - 8y - 2z + 5w$$

The parentheses are preceded by a *negative* sign

If we had simply changed the sign of each term inside the parentheses and dropped the parentheses and the negative sign in front of them, we would have

$$3x - (8y + 2z - 5w) = 3x - 8y - 2z + 5w \longleftarrow \text{The correct answer}$$

The sign of 8y is an understood plus sign

d. $2x - (-8 - 6z + w)$

Following part a of the second rule, we have

$$2x - (-8 - 6z + w) = 2x - 1(-8 - 6z + w)$$
$$= 2x - 1(-8) - 1(-6z) - 1(w)$$
$$= 2x + 8 + 6z - w$$

We could have treated Example 4d as a subtraction problem. In this case, we would change the subtraction symbol to an addition symbol *and* change the sign of each term inside the parentheses, and then add:

$$2x - (-8 - 6z + w) = 2x + (+8 + 6z - w)$$
$$= 2x + 8 + 6z - w$$

e. $3 + 2[a - 5(x - 4y)]$ Grouping symbols within grouping symbols

$$3 + 2[a - 5(x - 4y)] = 3 + 2[a - 5x + 20y]$$
$$= 3 + 2a - 10x + 40y$$

Be sure to remove *inner* grouping symbols *first.* ■

A WORD OF CAUTION   The following are some common errors made in removing grouping symbols:

	Correct	*Common error*
a.	$-(x - 2y) = -x + 2y$	$-(x - 2y) \neq -x - 2y$
		$-1(-2y) = +2y$, not $-2y$
b.	$6(y - 3) = 6y - 18$	$6(y - 3) \neq 6y - 3$
		-3 was not multiplied by the 6
c.	$3 + 2(x + y) = 3 + 2x + 2y$	$3 + 2(x + y) \neq 5(x + y)$
		Order of operations was not followed ☑

EXERCISES 1.14C

Set I   Remove the grouping symbols.

1. $10 + (4x - y)$ **2.** $8 + (3a - b)$

3. $7 - (-4R - S)$ **4.** $9 - (-3m - n)$

5. $6 - 2(a - 3b)$ **6.** $12 - 3(2R - S)$

7. $3 - 2x(x - 4y)$ **8.** $2 - 5x(2x - 3y)$

9. $-(x - y) + (2 - a)$ **10.** $-(a - b) + (x - 3)$

11. $(a - b)(2) - 6$ **12.** $(x - y)(3) - 5$

13. $x - [a + (y - b)]$ **14.** $y - [m + (x - n)]$

15. $5 - 3[a - 4(2x - y)]$ **16.** $7 - 5[x - 3(2a - b)]$

17. $2 - [a - (b - c)]$ **18.** $5 - [x - (y + z)]$

19. $9 - 2[-3a - 4(2x - y)]$ **20.** $P - \{x - [y - (4 - z)]\}$

Set II   Remove the grouping symbols.

1. $5 + (2x - y)$ **2.** $7 - (a - 3b)$

3. $4 - (-3a - b)$ **4.** $8 - 5(z - w)$

5. $7 - 2(6R - S)$ **6.** $2 - 2(3x + y)$

7. $4 - 6x(3x - 2y)$ **8.** $(9 - z) - x$

9. $-(c - d) + (a - b)$ **10.** $(a + b) - (c - d)$

11. $(c - d)(5) - 4$ **12.** $(a + b)(3) - 2$

13. $z - [a + (b - c)]$ **14.** $s - \{t - (u - v) - w\}$

15. $6 - 4[x - 3(a - 2b)]$ **16.** $5 - 2(3x - [y - a])$

17. $3 - [x - (y - z)]$ **18.** $(x + y)(2) - 3z$

19. $a - \{b - [c - (2 - d)]\}$ **20.** $x - \{y - [z + w]\}$

1.14D   Combining Like Terms

Like Terms   Terms that have *equal* literal parts are called **like terms**.

Unlike Terms   Terms that do not have *equal* literal parts are called **unlike terms**.

Example 5   Examples of like terms:

a. $23x$, $5.4x$, x, $0.7x$, and $\frac{1}{2}x$ are like terms. (They can be called "x-terms.")

b. $34x^2y$, $8yx^2$, xyx, $2.8x^2y$, and $\frac{1}{5}x^2y$ are like terms. ■

Example 6   Examples of unlike terms:

a. $5x^2$ and $5x$ are unlike terms. (The literal parts, x^2 and x, are different.)

b. $4x^2$ and $10x^2y$ are unlike terms. ■

Because of the distributive rule, combining like terms is possible. For example,

—This step need not be shown

$$3x + 5x = (3 + 5)x = 8x$$

TO COMBINE LIKE TERMS

1. Identify the like terms.

2. Find the sum of each group of like terms by adding the numerical coefficients.

When we combine like terms, we are usually changing the grouping and the order in which the terms appear. The commutative and associative properties of addition guarantee that when we do this the sum remains unchanged.

Example 7   Combine like terms:

—$x^2y = 1x^2y$

a. $5x^2y - 8x^2y + x^2y = (5 - 8 + 1)x^2y = -2x^2y$

—$ba = ab$; therefore, all the terms are like terms

b. $4ab + ba - 6ab = -1ab = -ab$

c. $12a - 7b - 9a + 4b$

$= (12a - 9a) + (-7b + 4b)$ ←——Only like terms may be combined

$= 3a - 3b$

d. $7x - 2y + 9 - 11x + 3 - 4y = -4x - 6y + 12$ ■

NOTE   While it is possible to *combine* (add or subtract) only *like* terms, it is possible to *multiply* unlike terms together; for example, $3x + 3x^2$ cannot be simplified, but $(3x)(3x^2) = 9x^3$.   ☑

EXERCISES 1.14D

Set I   Simplify.

1. $5x - 8x + x$

2. $3a - 5a + a$

3. $8x^2y - 2x^2y$

4. $10ab^2 - 3ab^2$

5. $6xy^2 + 8x^2y$ **6.** $5a^2b - 4ab^2$

7. $2xy - 5yx + xy$ **8.** $8mn - 7nm + 3mn$

9. $5xyz^2 - 2(xyz)^2$ **10.** $3(abc)^3 - 4abc^3$

11. $5xyz^2 - xyz^2 - 4xyz^2$ **12.** $7a^2bc - a^2bc - 5a^2bc$

13. $7x^2y - 2xy^2 - 4x^2y$ **14.** $4xy^2 - 5x^2y - 2y^2x$

15. $3ab - a + b - ab$ **16.** $5xy - x - y + xy$

17. $2x^3 - 2x^2 + 3x - 5x$ **18.** $5y^2 - 3y^3 + 2y - 4y$

19. $4x - 3y + 7 - 2x + 4 - 6y$ **20.** $3b - 5a - 9 - 2a + 4 - 5b$

21. $a^2b - 5ab + 7ab^2 - 3a^2b + 4ab$ **22.** $xy^2 + y - 5x^2y + 3xy^2 + x^2y$

Set II   Simplify.

1. $4y + y - 10y$ **2.** $10a - 16a + a$

3. $a^2b - 3a^2b$ **4.** $2x^3y - 9yx^3$

5. $4a^2b + 6ab^2$ **6.** $12x^3y + 8xy^3$

7. $5uv - 2vu + uv$ **8.** $ab + 3ab - 18ba$

9. $3(stu)^2 - 5stu^2$ **10.** $2 + 4xy$

11. $8ab^2c - ab^2c - 4ab^2c$ **12.** $6fg^2 - 2(fg)^2$

13. $5ab^2c - 7a^2bc - 2ab^2c$ **14.** $17x(yz)^2 - 12xy^2z^2$

15. $6st + s - t - st$ **16.** $8 - 2xy - 6yx$

17. $5R^3 - 2R + 3R^2 - R$ **18.** $9x + 2y - 3z$

19. $6x - 6 + 4y - 3 + 2x - 7y$ **20.** $4 + 2a - 3b - 7 - 6b - 2a$

21. $xy - 2xy^2 - 5x^2y - 3xy + 2x^2y - 4xy^2$

22. $st^2 - 3s + 2t - s^2t - 5s + 3t$

1.14E Simplifying Algebraic Expressions

> TO SIMPLIFY AN ALGEBRAIC EXPRESSION
>
> **1.** Remove all grouping symbols.
>
> **2.** Combine powers of variables in each term.
>
> **3.** Remove all zero and negative exponents.
>
> **4.** Simplify all radicals.*
>
> **5.** Combine all like terms.

NOTE   We will add to this list in later chapters.   ☑

---

* In this section, all radical signs will be completely removed, since all radicands will be perfect squares.

Example 8 Simplify the following algebraic expressions:

a. $x(x^2 + xy + y^2) - y(x^2 + xy + y^2)$

$= x^3 + x^2y + xy^2 - x^2y - xy^2 - y^3$

$= x^3 + x^2y - x^2y + xy^2 - xy^2 - y^3$

$= x^3 + 0 + 0 - y^3$

$= x^3 - y^3$

b. $\sqrt{16} - \{8[-5(3x - 2) + 13] - 11x\}$

$= 4 - \{8[-15x + 10 + 13] - 11x\}$

$= 4 - \{8[-15x + 23] - 11x\}$

$= 4 - \{-120x + 184 - 11x\}$

$= 4 - \{-131x + 184\}$

$= 4 + 131x - 184$

$= 131x - 180$

c. $\sqrt{9x^2} + x^{-1}x^2 - 4x^0(12x) - (3x)^0$

$= 3x + x^1 - 4(1)(12x) - 1$

$= 3x + x - 48x - 1$

$= -44x - 1$ ∎

Example 9 Rewrite $-3(a - 2b) + 2(-a - 3b)$ when $a = x + y$ and $b = x - y$ and then simplify.

If $a = x + y$ and $b = x - y$, then we have

$-3(a - 2b) + 2(-a - 3b)$

$= -3([x + y] - 2[x - y]) + 2(-[x + y] - 3[x - y])$

$= -3(x + y - 2x + 2y) + 2(-x - y - 3x + 3y)$

$= -3(-x + 3y) + 2(-4x + 2y)$

$= 3x - 9y - 8x + 4y$

$= -5x - 5y$ ∎

EXERCISES 1.14E

Set I In Exercises 1-28, simplify the algebraic expressions. Assume that the variables represent positive numbers.

1. $2h(3h^2 - k) - k(h - 3k^3)$

2. $4x(2y^2 - 3x) - x(2x - 3y^2)$

3. $(3x - 4) - 5x$

4. $(5x - 7) - 8x$

5. $(3x - 4)(-5x)$

6. $(5x - 7)(-8x)$

7. $2 + 3x$

8. $5 + 8y$

9. $3x - [5y - (2x - 4y)]$

10. $2x - [7y - (3x - 2y)]$

11. $-10[-2(3x - 5) + 17] - 4x$

12. $-20[-3(2x - 4) + 20] - 5x$

13. $8 - 2(x - [y - 3x])$

14. $9 - 4(u - [t - 2u])$

15. $2x(4 + 5x) - \sqrt{16x^2}$ **16.** $5y(2 + 5y) - \sqrt{36y^2}$

17. $(3u - v) - \{2u - (10 - v) - 20\} - \sqrt{64v^2}$

18. $(5x - y) - \{3x - (8 - y) - 15\} - \sqrt{49x^2}$

19. $50 - \{-2t - [5t - (6 - 2t)]\} + 7^0$

20. $24 - \{-4x - [2x - (3 - 5x)]\} + 3^0$

21. $100v - 3\{-4[-2(-4 - v) - 5v]\}$

22. $60z - 4\{-3[-4(-2 - z) - 3z]\}$

23. $w^2(w^2 - 4) + 4(w^2 - 4)$ **24.** $x^2(x^2 - 9) + 9(x^2 - 9)$

25. $3x(5 \cdot 4x^2)(2x^3)$ **26.** $2y(2 \cdot 3y^3)(5y^4)$

27. $5X^{-4}X^6 + 3X^0$ **28.** $3Y^3Y^{-1} + 2Y^0$

In Exercises 29–32, substitute $a = x + 2y$ and $b = 3x - y$ and simplify.

29. $3a - 5b$ **30.** $4a - 2b$

31. $2(3a - b)$ **32.** $3(5b - a)$

Set II   In Exercises 1–28, simplify the algebraic expressions. Assume that the variables represent positive numbers.

1. $3x(2x^2 - y) - y(x - 4y^2)$ **2.** $5a^2(4a - ab + b^2)$

3. $(4s - 7) - 2s$ **4.** $(2x + 3y) - 9x$

5. $(4y - 7)(-2y)$ **6.** $(2x + 3y)(-9x)$

7. $4 + 5z$ **8.** $(8 + 3x)y$

9. $2s - [4t - (3s - 5t)]$ **10.** $(8 + 3x) + y$

11. $-5[-2(2x - 4) + 15] - 2x$ **12.** $\sqrt{121x^6z^4} + 3x^3z^2$

13. $6 - 4(y - [x - 3y])$ **14.** $8 + 2(x - [y - 4])$

15. $2z(3 + 7z) - \sqrt{16z^2}$ **16.** $3x + 7y - 2z$

17. $(2x - y) - \{5x - (6 - y) - 12\} - \sqrt{121y^2}$

18. $16 - 4\{6 - 2(x - 3y) + x\}$

19. $36 - \{-2x - [6x - (5 - 2x)]\} + 3x^0$

20. $(3x + 14y - 3z^2[3z + x])^0$

21. $50x - 5\{-2[-3(-3 - x) - 2x]\}$

22. $x^0 + y^0 + z^0 + 8^0$

23. $y^2(y^2 - 16) + 16(y^2 - 16)$

24. $(x + y + z + 8)^0$

25. $4x(3 \cdot 5x^2)(6x^4)$ **26.** $3x(2x^2)(-16xy^3)$

27. $4z^{-7}z^{10} + 7z^0$ **28.** $-3x^{-3}x^5 - 18x^0$

In Exercises 29–32, substitute $a = x + 3y$ and $b = 2x - y$ and simplify.

29. $7a - 2b$ **30.** $12a - b$

31. $5(2a - b)$ **32.** $b - 3a$

1.15 Review: 1.11–1.14

The Rules of Exponents 1.11

1.1 $x^m \cdot x^n = x^{m+n}$

1.2 $(x^m)^n = x^{mn}$

1.3 $(xy)^n = x^n y^n$

1.4 $\dfrac{x^m}{x^n} = x^{m-n} \quad (x \neq 0)$

1.5 $\left(\dfrac{x}{y}\right)^n = \dfrac{x^n}{y^n} \quad (y \neq 0)$

1.6 $x^0 = 1 \quad (x \neq 0)$

1.7a $x^{-n} = \dfrac{1}{x^n} \quad (x \neq 0)$

1.7b $\dfrac{1}{x^{-n}} = x^n \quad (x \neq 0)$

1.7c $\left(\dfrac{x}{y}\right)^{-n} = \left(\dfrac{y}{x}\right)^n \ (x \neq 0,\ y \neq 0)$

1.8 $\left(\dfrac{x^a y^b}{z^c}\right)^n = \dfrac{x^{an} y^{bn}}{z^{cn}} \quad (z \neq 0)$

None of the variables can have a value that makes the denominator zero.

Scientific Notation 1.12

A number written in scientific notation is written as the product of some number between 1 and 10 and a power of 10. That is, it must be of the form

$$a \times 10^n, \text{ where } 1 \leq a < 10 \text{ and } n \text{ is an integer}$$

Evaluating Algebraic Expressions 1.13

1. First replace each letter by its number value.
2. Then carry out all operations in the correct order.

Simplifying Algebraic Expressions 1.14

To simplify an algebraic expression:

1. Remove all grouping symbols.
2. Combine powers of variables in each term.
3. Remove all zero and negative exponents.
4. Simplify all radicals.
5. Combine all like terms.

Review Exercises 1.15 Set I

In Exercises 1–18, simplify each expression, using only positive exponents in your answers.

1. $x^3 \cdot x^5$
2. $x^4 + x^2$
3. $(N^2)^3$
4. $s^6 - s^2$
5. $\dfrac{a^5}{a^2}$
6. $\dfrac{x^6}{y^4}$
7. $\left(\dfrac{2a}{b^2}\right)^3$
8. $x^4 y^{-2}$
9. $\left(\dfrac{x^{-4}y}{x^{-2}}\right)^{-1}$
10. $s^0 + t^0$
11. $(s+t)^0$
12. xy^4
13. $3c^3 d^2(c - 4d)$
14. $8 - 2(3x - y)$
15. $(-10x^2 y^3)(-8x^3)(-xy^2 z^4)$
16. $(4x^3 + 2x - y)(-2x)$
17. $5 - 2[3 - 5(x - y) + 4x - 6]$
18. $(4x^3 + 2x - y) - 2x$

19. Write 148.6 in scientific notation.

20. Write 3.17×10^{-3} in decimal notation.

In Exercises 21–24, evaluate each formula, using the values of the variables given with the formula. You should use a calculator for Exercises 23 and 24.

21. $A = P(1 + rt)$ $P = 550, r = 0.09, t = 2.5$

22. $C = \frac{5}{9}(F - 32)$ $F = 104$

23. $S = R\left[\dfrac{(1 + i)^n - 1}{i}\right]$ $R = 750, i = 0.09, n = 3$

24. $S = \dfrac{a(1 - r^n)}{1 - r}$ $a = 7.5, r = 2, n = 6$

Review Exercises 1.15 Set II

NAME _____

In Exercises 1–18, simplify each expression, using only positive exponents in your answers.

1. $y^6 + y^5$

2. $x^4 \cdot x^8$

3. $(z^4)^3$

4. $\dfrac{a^5}{b^2}$

5. $\dfrac{y^6}{y^4}$

6. $s^6 - s^2$

7. $\left(\dfrac{x}{2b^2}\right)^3$

8. $\left(\dfrac{x^{-4}y}{x^{-2}}\right)^{-2}$

9. $x^4 x^{-2}$

10. $x^0 y^0$

11. $(x + y)^0$

12. $x^0 + y^0$

13. $5 - 2(x - 6y)$

14. $(3x^2 - 2) - 3x$

15. $(5ab^2)(-2a^2)(-3a^3b)$

16. $3xy^2(4x^2 - 5y^3)$

ANSWERS

1. _____

2. _____

3. _____

4. _____

5. _____

6. _____

7. _____

8. _____

9. _____

10. _____

11. _____

12. _____

13. _____

14. _____

15. _____

16. _____

17. $2x(4x^2 + 2xy + y^2) - y(4x^2 + 2xy + y^2)$

17. _____

18. _____

18. $20 - 3\{x - 2[5x - 3(x - y) - 3y] + 4x\}$

19. _____

20. _____

In Exercises 19–21, evaluate each formula, using a calculator and using the values of the variables given with the formula.

21. _____

19. $I = Prt$ $\qquad P = 1{,}250, r = 0.08, t = 3.5$

22. _____

23. _____

20. $F = \frac{9}{5}C + 32 \qquad C = 25.5$

21. $S = P(1 + i)^n \qquad P = 950, i = 0.09, n = 4$

22. Write 0.000538 in scientific notation.

23. Write 1.452×10^5 in decimal notation.

Chapter 1 Diagnostic Test

The purpose of this test is to see how well you understand the basic ideas of sets, operations with real numbers, and simplification and evaluation of algebraic expressions. We recommend that you work this diagnostic test *before* your instructor tests you on this chapter. Allow yourself about 50 minutes.

Complete solutions for all the problems on this test, together with section references, are given in the answer section at the end of the book. For the problems you do incorrectly, study the sections cited.

1. Write "true" if the statement is always true; otherwise, write "false."

   a. $\{5, 3, 3, 5\}$ and $\{3, 5\}$ are equal sets.

   b. The set of digits divisible by 3 is a finite set.

   c. 0 is a real number.

   d. Every irrational number is a real number.

   e. The empty set is a subset of every set.

   f. $\dfrac{9}{0} = 0$

   g. $(7 \cdot 5) \cdot 2 = 7(5 \cdot 2)$ illustrates the commutative property of multiplication.

   h. Division is commutative.

   i. The set of digits is a subset of the set of natural numbers.

   j. Every integer is a real number.

   k. $\dfrac{0}{9} = 0$

   l. $-2 < 7 < 10$ is a valid continued inequality.

   m. Every real number is a rational number.

   n. $4 < 8 > 12$ is a valid continued inequality.

   o. $3 \cdot (7 \cdot 2) = (3 \cdot 7) \cdot (3 \cdot 2)$

2. Write $\{x \mid x \text{ is an even whole number}\}$ in roster notation.

3. Given $A = \{x, w, k, z\}$, $B = \{x, y, z, k\}$, and $C = \{k, x\}$, state whether the following statements are true or false:

   a. $B \subseteq A$

   b. $C \subseteq B$

4. Given the numbers -3, 2.4, 0, 5, $2.8652916\ldots$, $\frac{1}{2}$, and $0.18181818\ldots$, determine the following:

   a. Which are real numbers?

   b. Which are integers?

   c. Which are natural numbers?

   d. Which are irrational numbers?

   e. Which are rational numbers?

5. Given $A = \{x, z, w\}$, $B = \{x, y, w\}$, and $C = \{y, r, s\}$, find the following:

a. $A \cup C$

b. $A \cap C$

c. $A \cap B$

d. $B \cup C$

In Problems 6–25, find the value of each expression (if it has one).

6. $|-17|$ **7.** $(-5)^2$ **8.** $30 \div (-5)$

9. $(-35) - (2)$ **10.** $(-27) - (-17)$ **11.** $(-9)(-8)$

12. $(-19)(0)$ **13.** $\dfrac{-40}{-8}$ **14.** $(-9) + (-13)$

15. -6^2 **16.** $(-2)^0$ **17.** $-|-3|$

18. $\sqrt[3]{-27}$ **19.** $\sqrt[4]{16}$ **20.** $(3^{-2})^{-1}$

21. $10^{-3} \cdot 10^5$ **22.** $\dfrac{2^{-4}}{2^{-7}}$ **23.** $16 \div 4 \cdot 2$

24. $2\sqrt{9} - 5$ **25.** $\sqrt{81}$

26. Write 0.000316 in scientific notation.

27. a. Write 78 in prime factored form.

b. Write 65 in prime factored form.

c. Find the LCM of 78 and 65.

In Problems 28–31, simplify each expression.

28. $x^2 \cdot x^{-5}$ **29.** $(N^2)^4$

30. $\left(\dfrac{2X^3}{Y}\right)^2$ **31.** $\left(\dfrac{xy^{-2}}{y^{-3}}\right)^{-1}$

In Problems 32 and 33, simplify each expression and write it with no denominator.

32. $\dfrac{1}{a^{-3}}$ **33.** $\left(\dfrac{x^{-a}}{2}\right)^{-3}$

34. Given the formula $S = \dfrac{a(1 - r^n)}{1 - r}$, find S when $a = -8$, $r = 3$, and $n = 2$.

In Problems 35–37, simplify the expressions.

35. $7x - 2(5 - x) + \sqrt{81x^2}$

36. $6x(2xy^2 - 3x^3) - 3x^2(2y^2 - 6x^2)$

37. $7x - 2\{6 - 3[8 - 2(x - 3) - 2(6 - x)]\}$

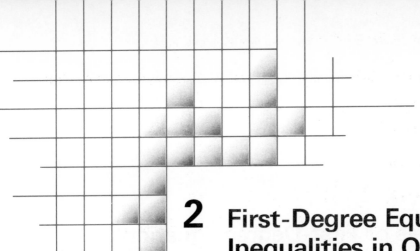

2 First-Degree Equations and Inequalities in One Unknown

Most problems in algebra are solved by the use of equations or inequalities. In this chapter, we show how to solve equations and inequalities that have only one unknown. We discuss other types of equations and inequalities in later chapters.

2.1 Types of First-Degree Equations, Their Solutions, and Their Graphs

First-Degree Equation with Only One Unknown

A **first-degree equation with only one unknown** is an equation with only one variable and in which the highest power of that variable is the first power; for example, $3x + 8 = 17$ is a first-degree equation with one unknown.

Domain The set of all the numbers that can be used in place of a variable is called the **domain** of the variable. For example, in the expression $1/x$, x cannot be 0 because we cannot allow division by 0. We would say, therefore, that 0 is not in the domain of the variable; we could also say that the domain is the set of all real numbers except 0.

In some applications, the solution set must be restricted to some subset of the set of real numbers. For example, if x were to represent the number of dimes in a collection of coins, it wouldn't make sense to say that we had 1.72 dimes. In this case, we would need to restrict the domain of the variable to the set of whole numbers.

In this chapter, if the domain of the variable is not mentioned, the domain is understood to be the set of real numbers, R.

Solutions of Equations

A **solution** of an equation is a number from the domain of the variable that, when substituted for the variable, makes the two sides of the equation equal. A solution of an equation is also called a **root** or a **zero** of the equation.

Kinds of Equations

Conditional Equations A **conditional equation** is an equation whose two sides are equal only when certain numbers (the solutions) are substituted for the variable. For example, $3x + 8 = 17$ is a conditional equation. The two sides are equal if 3 is substituted for x, but they are *not* equal if any other number is substituted for x. When we solve a first-degree conditional equation in one variable, our answer should be in the form $x = a$, where a is some number.

Identities If the two sides of an equation are equal when *any* value in the domain is substituted for the variable, then the equation is called an **identity**. For example, $2(x + 3) = 2x + 6$ is an identity. The two sides are equal if we substitute 7 for x, 0 for x, -23 for x, or any other real number for x.

Equations with No Solution If *no* number will make the two sides of an equation equal, we say that the equation is an **equation with no solution**. For example, $x + 1 = x + 2$ is such an equation; no value of x will make the two sides equal to each other.

Solution Sets of Equations

The **solution set** of an equation is the set of all numbers that are solutions of that equation. For example, the solution set of the equation $3x + 8 = 17$ is $\{3\}$. The solution set of an identity is the set of all the numbers in the domain of the variable. The solution set of an equation with no solution is the empty set.

Equivalent Equations

Equations that have the same solution set are called **equivalent equations**.

Example 1   Examples of solutions, solution sets, and equivalent equations:

The *solution* of the equation $3x + 8 = 17$ is $x = 3$, because $3(3) + 8 = 17$. The *solution set* of this equation is $\{3\}$. (Notice that 3 is written within braces, because we are discussing a set.) The equations $3x + 8 = 17$, $3x = 9$, and $x = 3$ are *equivalent equations* because they all have the same solution set. ∎

When we solve first-degree equations, we use the following principles of equality:

PRINCIPLES OF EQUALITY

To get an equation equivalent to the one you started with:

1. Add the same number to both sides of an equation.   *Addition rule*

2. Subtract the same number from both sides of an equation.   *Subtraction rule*

3. Multiply both sides of an equation by the same nonzero number.   *Multiplication rule*

4. Divide both sides of an equation by the same nonzero number.   *Division rule*

When we solve a first-degree equation with one variable using the principles of equality listed above, three outcomes are possible:

1. If the equation can be reduced to the form $x = a$, where a is some number, the equation is a *conditional equation* (see Examples 2 and 4). If there are restrictions on the domain, the equation may have *no solution* even though it reduces to the form $x = a$ (see Example 3).

2. If the two sides of the equation reduce to the same constant, so that we obtain a true statement (for example, $0 = 0$), the equation is an *identity* (see Example 5).

3. If the two sides of the equation reduce to unequal constants, so that we obtain a false statement (for example, $2 = 5$), the equation is an *equation with no solution* (see Example 6).

The procedure for solving a first-degree equation in one variable is as follows:

TO SOLVE A FIRST-DEGREE EQUATION WITH ONLY ONE UNKNOWN

Always write each new equation *under* the previous one.

1. Remove fractions by multiplying both sides of the equation by the least common multiple (LCM) of all the denominators.

2. Remove all grouping symbols.

3. Combine like terms on each side of the equal sign.

4. Move all the terms that contain the variable to one side of the equal sign (usually the *left* side) and all the constants to the other side by adding the appropriate terms to both sides of the equation.

5. Divide both sides of the equation by the coefficient of the variable.

6. Determine whether the equation is a conditional equation, an identity, or an equation with no solution.

7. If the equation is a conditional equation, check the solution.

To check the solution of an equation, perform the following steps:

1. Determine whether the (possible) solution is in the domain of the variable. If it is, continue with steps 2, 3, and 4. (If it is not, the equation has no solution.)

2. Replace the variable in the given equation by the number found in the solution.

3. Perform the indicated operations on both sides of the equal sign.

4. If the resulting numbers on both sides of the equal sign are the same, the solution is correct.

Example 2   Find the solution set for $8x - 3[2 - (x + 4)] = 4(x - 2)$ and graph it on the number line.

$$8x - 3[2 - (x + 4)] = 4(x - 2)$$

$$8x - 3[2 - x - 4] = 4x - 8 \qquad \text{Remove grouping symbols and simplify}$$

$$8x - 3[-x - 2] = 4x - 8$$

$$8x + 3x + 6 = 4x - 8$$

$$11x + 6 = 4x - 8* \qquad \text{Combine like terms}$$

$$\underline{-4x - 6 \qquad -4x - 6} \qquad \left\{ \begin{array}{l} \text{Add } -4x - 6 \text{ to both sides to} \\ \text{get the } x\text{-term on one side and} \\ \text{the constant on the other} \end{array} \right.$$

$$7x = -14 \qquad \text{Divide both sides by 7}$$

$$x = -2$$

---

* It is incorrect to write $11x + 6 = 4x - 8 = 7x = -14 = x = -2$.

An equal sign here implies that $4x - 8 = 7x$

An equal sign here implies that $-14 = -2$

The (possible) solution of the equation is $x = -2$. Since the equation reduced to the form $x = a$, the equation is a conditional equation.

Check

$$8x - 3[2 - (x + 4)] = 4(x - 2)$$

$$8(-2) - 3[2 - (\{-2\} + 4)] \overset{?}{=} 4(\{-2\} - 2)$$

$$-16 - 3[2 - (2)] \overset{?}{=} 4(-4)$$

$$-16 - 3[0] \overset{?}{=} -16$$

$$-16 = -16$$

The solution checks. Therefore, $x = -2$ is the condition necessary to make the two sides of the equation equal to each other, and $\{-2\}$ is the solution set.

The *graph* of the solution (or of the solution set) is

■

Example 3   Find $\{x \mid 2(3x + 5) = 14, x \in J\}$.

In this example, the domain is restricted by the statement $x \in J$; that is, we are interested only in integer solutions to the equation.

$$2(3x + 5) = 14$$

$$6x + 10 = 14$$

$$6x = 4$$

$$x = \frac{4}{6} = \frac{2}{3}$$

The equation has no solution that is an integer, since $\frac{2}{3}$ is not an integer. Therefore, $\{x \mid 2(3x + 5) = 14, x \in J\} = \{\ \ \}$. If we had been asked to graph the solution set, there would be no points to graph.   ■

Example 4   Solve $\dfrac{x + 3}{6} - \dfrac{2x - 3}{9} = \dfrac{13}{18}$ and graph its solution set on the number line.

To begin, multiply both sides by the LCM of 6, 9, and 18, which is 18.

$$\frac{18}{1} \cdot \left(\frac{x + 3}{6} - \frac{2x - 3}{9} \right) = \frac{18}{1} \cdot \frac{13}{18} \quad \longleftarrow \text{Use the distributive rule}$$

$$\frac{\overset{3}{\cancel{18}}}{1} \cdot \frac{x + 3}{\underset{1}{\cancel{6}}} - \frac{\overset{2}{\cancel{18}}}{1} \cdot \frac{2x - 3}{\underset{1}{\cancel{9}}} = \frac{\overset{1}{\cancel{18}}}{1} \cdot \frac{13}{\underset{1}{\cancel{18}}}$$

$$3(x + 3) - 2(2x - 3) = 13$$

$$3x + 9 - 4x + 6 = 13$$

$$-x + 15 = 13$$

$$-x = -2 \quad \longleftarrow \text{Multiply or divide both sides by } -1$$

$$x = 2$$

The solution of the equation is $x = 2$; the solution set is $\{2\}$. Since we found a single solution, the equation is a conditional equation. The graph of the solution is

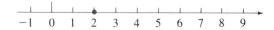

(The check of the solution will not be shown.) ■

Example 5 Solve $4(3x - 5) - 2x = 2(5x + 1) - 22$ and graph the solution set on the number line.

$$4(3x - 5) - 2x = 2(5x + 1) - 22$$
$$12x - 20 - 2x = \quad 10x + 2 - 22$$
$$10x - 20 = \quad 10x - 20$$
$$\underline{-10x + 20 \quad -10x + 20} \qquad \text{Add } -10x + 20 \text{ to both sides}$$
$$0 = 0 \qquad \text{A true statement}$$

If we had added just $-10x$ to both sides, our final statement would have been $20 = 20$, which is also a true statement. *Note that no variable appears in the last step.* Since the variable disappeared completely and we were left with a *true* statement, this equation is an identity. *Any* real number will make the two sides equal. We will show the check for two real numbers, selected at random.

Check If we substitute -1 for x, we have

$$4(3[-1] - 5) - 2[-1] \stackrel{?}{=} 2(5[-1] + 1) - 22$$
$$-30 = -30$$

If we substitute 7 for x, we have

$$4(3[7] - 5) - 2[7] \stackrel{?}{=} 2(5[7] + 1) - 22$$
$$50 = 50$$

The solution set is $\{x \mid x \in R\}$—the set of all real numbers. The graph of the solution set of this equation is

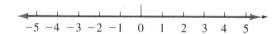

■

Example 6 Solve $4(x - 1) - 3(4 - x) = 7x - 13$.

$$4(x - 1) - 3(4 - x) = \quad 7x - 13$$
$$4x - 4 - 12 + 3x = \quad 7x - 13$$
$$7x - 16 = \quad 7x - 13$$
$$\underline{-7x \qquad \qquad -7x} \qquad \text{Add } -7x \text{ (or } -7x + 16 \text{ or } -7x + 13) \text{ to both sides}$$
$$-16 = -13 \qquad \text{A false statement}$$

Note that no variable appears in the last step. Since the variable disappeared completely and we were left with a *false* statement, this equation is an equation with *no solution*. No number can be found that will make the two sides of the equation equal.

The solution set is the empty set, { }. If we had been asked to graph the solution set, there would be no points to graph. ■

EXERCISES 2.1

Set I In each exercise, find the solution set. Identify any equation that is not a conditional equation as an identity or as an equation with no solution. Graph the solution set of each conditional equation on the real number line.

1. $4x + 3(4 + 3x) = -1$

2. $5x + 2(4 + x) = -6$

3. $7y - 2(5 + 4y) = 8$

4. $5y - 3(4 + 2y) = 3$

5. $4x + 12 = 2(6 + 2x)$

6. $6x + 15 = 3(5 + 2x)$

7. $3[5 - 2(5 - z)] = 2(3z + 7)$

8. $5[4 - 3(2 - z)] = 3(5z + 6)$

9. $\dfrac{x}{3} - \dfrac{x}{6} = 18$

10. $\dfrac{x}{4} - \dfrac{x}{8} = 16$

11. $\dfrac{y + 3}{8} - \dfrac{3}{4} = \dfrac{y + 6}{10}$

12. $\dfrac{y + 7}{12} - \dfrac{5}{6} = \dfrac{y + 4}{9}$

13. $\{z \mid 5z - 3(2 + 3z) = 6, z \in N\}$

14. $\{z \mid 8z + 6 = 2(7z + 9), z \in N\}$

15. $\{x \mid 7x - 2(5 + 4x) = 8, x \in J\}$

16. $\{x \mid 7x + 15 = 3(3x + 5), x \in J\}$

17. $\{x \mid 2(3x - 6) - 3(5x + 4) = 5(7x - 8), x \in J\}$

18. $\{z \mid 4(7z - 9) - 7(4z + 3) = 6(9z - 10), z \in J\}$

19. $\dfrac{2(y - 3)}{5} - \dfrac{3(y + 2)}{2} = \dfrac{7}{10}$

20. $\dfrac{5(x - 4)}{6} - \dfrac{2(x + 4)}{9} = \dfrac{5}{18}$

21. $6.23z + 2.5(3.08 - 8.2z) = -14.7$

22. $9.84 - 4.6x = 5.17(9.01 - 8.23x)$

Set II In each exercise, find the solution set. Identify any equation that is not a conditional equation as an identity or as an equation with no solution. Graph the solution set of each conditional equation on the real number line.

1. $6x + 3(2 + 2x) = -6$

2. $7x + 5(2 + x) = -2$

3. $8y - 3(2 + 3y) = 5$

4. $8y + 4(6 - 2y) = -2$

5. $8x + 12 = 4(2x + 3)$

6. $14x - 3(4 - x) = 2(x + 9)$

7. $3[15 - (5 - 3x)] = 9(x + 18)$

8. $3 + 5(x - 4) = 9x + 1$

9. $\dfrac{z}{9} - \dfrac{z}{2} = \dfrac{7}{3}$

10. $\dfrac{x}{5} - \dfrac{x}{10} = 8$

11. $\dfrac{x + 1}{4} - \dfrac{5}{8} = \dfrac{x - 1}{8}$

12. $\dfrac{x + 3}{5} - \dfrac{x}{2} = \dfrac{5 - 3x}{10}$

13. $\{x \mid 4x + 5(-4 - 5x) = 22,\ x \in N\}$

14. $\{x \mid 3x - 4(2 - x) = 6,\ x \in N\}$

15. $\{y \mid 10 - 7y = 4(11 - 6y),\ y \in J\}$

16. $\{y \mid -37 - 9(y + 1) = 4(2y - 3),\ y \in J\}$

17. $\{x \mid 6(3x - 5) = 3[4(1 - x) - 7],\ x \in J\}$

18. $\{x \mid 16 - 8(2x - 2) = 5(5x - 10),\ x \in N\}$

19. $\dfrac{2(x - 3)}{3} - \dfrac{3(x + 2)}{4} = \dfrac{5}{6}$

20. $\dfrac{3(x - 4)}{4} - \dfrac{5(x + 2)}{6} = \dfrac{7}{12}$

21. $7.02(5.3x - 4.28) = 11.6 - 2.94x$

22. $7.23 - 6.1x = 3.2(1.08 - 5.3x)$

2.2 Simple First-Degree Inequalities, Their Solutions, and Their Graphs

In this section, we discuss simple conditional first-degree inequalities that have the symbols $<, >, \leq,$ or $\geq$ in them. **Simple** (or **singular**) **inequalities** are inequalities that contain only *one* statement with only *one* inequality symbol.

Sense
The **sense** of an inequality symbol refers to the direction in which the symbol points.

$\left.\begin{array}{l} a > b \\ c > d \end{array}\right\}$ Same sense (both are $>$) $\qquad$ $\left.\begin{array}{l} a < b \\ c > d \end{array}\right\}$ Opposite sense (one is $>$, one is $<$)

$\left.\begin{array}{l} a \geq b \\ c \leq d \end{array}\right\}$ Opposite sense $\qquad\qquad\qquad$ $\left.\begin{array}{l} a \leq b \\ c \leq d \end{array}\right\}$ Same sense

Example 1 $\quad$ Determine whether the sense is changed in each of the following:

a. $\quad$
$$\begin{array}{cc} 10 > & 5 \\ +6 & +6 \\ \hline 16\ ?\ & 11 \end{array} \qquad 16 > 11$$

We started with "greater than"
Add 6 to both sides
Still "greater than"
Sense is not changed

b. $\quad$
$$\begin{array}{cc} 7 < & 12 \\ -2 & -2 \\ \hline 5\ ?\ & 10 \end{array} \qquad 5 < 10$$

We started with "less than"
Subtract 2 from both sides
Still "less than"
Sense is not changed

c. $\quad$
$$\begin{array}{cc} 3 < & 4 \\ \times 2 & \times 2 \\ \hline 6\ ?\ & 8 \end{array} \qquad 6 < 8$$

Multiply both sides by 2
Sense is not changed

d.

$$3 < 4 <$$

$$\times(-2) \quad \times(-2)$$

$$\overline{-6 \ ? \ -8} \qquad -6 > -8$$

We started with "less than"

Multiply both sides by -2

Now we have "greater than"

Sense is changed

e. $9 > 6 \qquad\qquad >$

$$\dfrac{9}{3} \quad \dfrac{6}{3}$$

$$3 \ ? \ 2 \qquad\qquad 3 > 2$$

Divide both sides by 3

Sense is not changed

f. $9 > 6 \qquad\qquad >$

$$\dfrac{9}{-3} \quad \dfrac{6}{-3}$$

$$-3 \ ? \ -2 \qquad\qquad -3 < -2$$

Divide both sides by -3

Sense is changed ∎

We see from Example 1 that when we multiply or divide both sides of an inequality by a *negative* number, the sense of the inequality changes.

Solutions and Solution Sets of an Inequality

A *solution* of a conditional inequality is any number that, when substituted for the variable, makes the inequality a true statement.

The *solution set* of an inequality is the set of all numbers that are solutions of the inequality. While the solution set of a first-degree conditional *equation* normally has just one element in it, the solution set of an *inequality* usually contains infinitely many numbers.

When we solve a simple first-degree inequality, we must find *all* of the values of the variable that satisfy the inequality. Therefore, our answer will be in the form $x < a$, $x > a$, $x \le a$, or $x \ge a$.

The method used to solve inequalities may be summarized as follows:

TO SOLVE AN INEQUALITY

Proceed in the same way used to solve equations, with the exception that the sense must be changed when multiplying or dividing both sides by a negative number.

A WORD OF CAUTION We solve an inequality by a method very much like the method used for solving an equation. For this reason, some students confuse the solution of an inequality with that of an equation. For example,

$$3x - 5 < 2x + 1$$
$$\underline{-2x + 5 \qquad -2x + 5}$$
$$x \ \boxed{=} \ 6 \qquad \text{whereas} \qquad x \boxed{<} 6$$

$$\underset{\text{Error}}{\uparrow}\underset{\text{Correct}}{\uparrow}$$

Remember that when we add the same number to both sides of an inequality we get an *inequality* with the sense unchanged. We do *not* get an equation. An infinite number of numbers satisfy the above inequality, since any real number less than 6 is a solution. For example, 3, -6, and -201 are all solutions. ☑

Example 2 Solve $3x - 2(2x - 7) \leq 2(3 + x) - 4$ and graph the solution set on the real number line.

$$3x - 2(2x - 7) \leq 2(3 + x) - 4$$

Note that no restrictions were put on the domain of the variable

$$3x - 4x + 14 \leq 6 + 2x - 4$$

$$-x + 14 \leq 2 + 2x$$

$$\underline{x - 2 \qquad -2 + x} \longleftarrow$$

Add $x - 2$ to both sides to get the x-term on one side and the constant on the other*

$$12 \leq 3x$$

$$\frac{12}{3} \leq \frac{3x}{3}$$

Sense is not changed if we divide both sides by 3

$$4 \leq x$$

or

$$x \geq 4 \qquad \text{Remember: } 4 \leq x \text{ can be replaced by } x \geq 4$$

Because the solution set of the inequality is the set of all real numbers *greater than or equal to* 4, when we graph the solution set we must have a solid circle at the 4 and must shade in that part of the number line that lies to the right of 4.

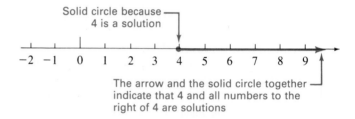

Solid circle because 4 is a solution

The arrow and the solid circle together indicate that 4 and all numbers to the right of 4 are solutions

Example 3 Solve $\dfrac{x + 2}{15} > \dfrac{x + 3}{5} - \dfrac{1}{3}$ and graph the solution set.

$$\frac{x + 2}{15} > \frac{x + 3}{5} - \frac{1}{3}$$

$$\frac{15}{1} \cdot \frac{x + 2}{15} > \frac{15}{1} \cdot \left(\frac{x + 3}{5} - \frac{1}{3} \right) \qquad \text{The LCM of 15, 5, and 3 is 15}$$

$$x + 2 > 3(x + 3) - 5$$

$$x + 2 > 3x + 9 - 5 \qquad \text{Alternate solution}$$

$$x + 2 > 3x + 4$$

$$\underline{-x - 4 \qquad -x - 4} \quad \text{or} \rightarrow \quad x + 2 > 3x + 4$$
$$\underline{\qquad\qquad -3x - 2 \quad -3x - 2}$$

$$-2 > 2x \qquad\qquad\qquad -2x \boxed{>} 2$$

$$\frac{-2}{2} > \frac{2x}{2} \qquad\qquad \frac{-2x}{-2} \boxed{<} \frac{2}{-2} \quad \leftarrow \text{Sense of inequality changes}$$

$$-1 > x \longleftarrow \text{Equivalent statements}$$

$$x < -1 \qquad\qquad\qquad x < -1$$

The solution set is $\{x \mid x < -1, x \in R\}$.

_____

* We could have added $-2x - 14$ to both sides rather than $x - 2$.

To graph the solution set on the real number line, we put a *hollow* circle at -1 to indicate that -1 itself is *not* to be included, but that numbers such as -1.1, -1.01, -1.00001, and so on *are* to be included. We heavily shade in all of the number line to the *left* of -1.

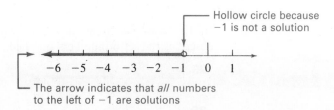

Hollow circle because -1 is not a solution

The arrow indicates that *all* numbers to the left of -1 are solutions

■

Example 4   Rewrite $\{x\mid 4(3x - 5) < 10, x \in N\}$ in roster notation and graph it on the real number line.

We must first solve $4(3x - 5) < 10$.

$$12x - 20 < 10$$

$$12x < 30$$

$$x < \frac{30}{12}$$

$$x < \frac{5}{2}$$

The *natural numbers* that are less than $5/2$ are 1 and 2. Therefore,

$$\{x\mid 4(3x - 5) < 10, x \in N\} = \{1, 2\}$$

The graph is

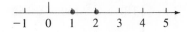

■

EXERCISES 2.2

Set I   In Exercises 1–18, solve each inequality and graph the solution set on the real number line.

1. $3x - 1 < 11$ **2.** $7x - 12 < 30$

3. $17 \geq 2x - 9$ **4.** $33 \geq 5 - 4x$

5. $2y - 16 > 17 + 5y$ **6.** $6y + 7 > 4y - 3$

7. $4z - 22 < 6(z - 7)$ **8.** $8(a - 3) > 15a - 10$

9. $9(2 - 5m) - 4 \geq 13m + 8(3 - 7m)$ **10.** $18k - 3(8 - 4k) \leq 7(2 - 5k) + 27$

11. $10 - 5x > 2[3 - 5(x - 4)]$ **12.** $3[2 + 4(y + 5)] < 30 + 6y$

13. $\dfrac{z}{3} > 7 - \dfrac{z}{4}$ **14.** $\dfrac{t}{5} - 8 > -\dfrac{t}{3}$

15. $\dfrac{1}{3} + \dfrac{w + 2}{5} \geq \dfrac{w - 5}{3}$ **16.** $\dfrac{u - 2}{3} - \dfrac{u + 2}{4} \geq -\dfrac{2}{3}$

17. $14.73(2.65x - 11.08) - 22.51x \geq 13.94x(40.27)$

18. $1.065 - 9.801x \leq 5.216x - 2.740(9.102 - 7.641x)$

In Exercises 19–22, rewrite the set in roster notation and graph it on the real number line.

19. $\{x \mid x + 3 < 10, \, x \in N\}$

20. $\{x \mid x + 5 < 8, \, x \in N\}$

21. $\{x \mid 2(x + 3) \leq 11, \, x \in N\}$

22. $\{x \mid 3(x + 1) \leq 17, \, x \in N\}$

In Exercises 23–26, write, in set-builder notation, the algebraic statement that describes the set of numbers graphed.

23.

```
  ┼───┼───●━━━━━►
 -1   0   1   2   3
```

24.

```
  ┼───┼───●━━━┼━━►
 -3  -2  -1   0   1
```

25.

```
  ◄━━━┼━━━○───┼───┼─►
      2   3   4   5   6
```

26.

```
  ◄━━━┼━━━○───┼───┼─►
      4   5   6   7   8
```

Set II In Exercises 1–18, solve the inequality and graph the solution set on the real number line.

1. $-3 \leq x + 4$

2. $3x + 2 \geq 8$

3. $18 - 7y > -3$

4. $5 - 3y \leq 8$

5. $11z - 7 < 5z - 13$

6. $3x - 8 \leq 7 - 2x$

7. $3(2 + 3x) \geq 5x - 6$

8. $4(x - 1) \leq 7x + 2$

9. $6(10 - 3t) + 25 \geq 4t - 5(3 - 2t)$

10. $6x - 4(3 - 2x) > 5(3 - 4x) + 7$

11. $6z < 2 - 4[2 - 3(z - 5)]$

12. $28 - 7x \geq [6 - 2(x - 1)]$

13. $\dfrac{w}{3} > 12 - \dfrac{w}{6}$

14. $\dfrac{x}{2} \leq 5 - \dfrac{x}{3}$

15. $\dfrac{1}{2} + \dfrac{u + 9}{5} \geq \dfrac{u + 1}{2}$

16. $\dfrac{x - 4}{2} - \dfrac{x + 4}{4} < -\dfrac{3}{2}$

17. $54.7x - 48.2(20.5 - 37.6x) \leq 81.9(60.3x - 19.1) + 97.4$

18. $3.7 - 1.06x < 8.62 - 1.4(6.2 - 3.2x)$

In Exercises 19–22, rewrite the set in roster notation and graph it on the real number line.

19. $\{x \mid x + 2 < 8, \, x \in N\}$

20. $\{x \mid x - 1 < 4, \, x \in N\}$

21. $\{x \mid 4(x + 4) \leq 42, \, x \in N\}$

22. $\{x \mid 3(x + 5) < 27, \, x \in N\}$

In Exercises 23–26, write, in set-builder notation, the algebraic statement that describes the set of numbers graphed.

23.

24.

25.

```
  ◄━━━┼━━━○───┼───┼─►
     -1   0   1   2   3
```

26.

```
  ◄━━━┼━━━┼━━━●───┼─►
      0   1   2   3   4
```

2.3 Combined Inequalities and Their Graphs

Combined Inequalities

Combined inequalities result when we connect two or more simple inequalities with the words *or* or *and*.

Example 1   Examples of combined inequalities:

  a. $x > 3$ or $x \leq -1$

  b. $x \leq -1$ and $x \geq -4$

  c. $-3 < x < 4$

A *continued inequality*, first discussed in Section 1.3B, is a combined inequality, because the statement $a < x < b$ is equivalent to the compound statement $a < x$ *and* $x < b$. If $a < b$, then $a < x < b$ is a ▢valid continued inequality, and so is $b > x > a$. ∎

Writing Combined Inequalities to Describe a Graph   When the graph to be described is an unbroken line segment, we can write the algebraic statement that describes it as a *continued inequality*.

Example 2   Write the algebraic statement that describes the set of numbers that is graphed.

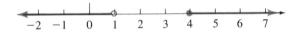

The graph is an unbroken line segment; the set is $\{x \mid -2 < x \leq 4\}$.   ∎

When the graph to be described occurs in two *separate* portions of the number line, the algebraic statement that describes it must contain two separate statements.

Example 3   Write the algebraic statement that describes the set of numbers that is graphed.

The graph occupies two separate portions of the number line, so we must write the algebraic description as two separate statements. The set graphed here is $\{x \mid x < 1\}$ ▢∪ $\{x \mid x \geq 4\}$. This set could also be written as $\{x \mid x < 1$ ▢*or* $x \geq 4\}$.   ∎

A WORD OF CAUTION   Students often write the algebraic statement for the graph of Example 3 as $\{x \mid 1 > x \geq 4\}$, which is incorrect. The statement $1 > x \geq 4$ is an *invalid* inequality, because $1 \geq 4$ is a false statement.   ☑

A WORD OF CAUTION   Students also often try to write the algebraic statement for the graph of Example 3 as $\{x \mid 1 < x \geq 4\}$ or as $\{x \mid 1 > x \leq 4\}$. These are incorrect, because in a continued inequality both inequalities must have the *same sense*.   ☑

Solution Sets and Graphs of Combined Inequalities   The solution set of a combined inequality containing the word ▢*or* is the *union* of the solution sets of the two simple inequalities.

Example 4   Find and graph the solution set for $x - 1 > 2$ ▢*or* $x - 1 \leq -2$.

We must solve each inequality:

$$x - 1 > 2 \quad \boxed{\text{or}} \quad x - 1 \leq -2$$
$$x > 3 \quad \boxed{\text{or}} \quad x \leq -1$$

The solution set is $\{x \mid x > 3$ ▢*or* $x \leq -1\}$, which can also be written $\{x \mid x > 3\}$ ▢∪ $\{x \mid x \leq -1\}$. We must graph all of the numbers greater than 3 ▢*or* less than or equal to -1.

∎

The solution set of a combined inequality containing the word *and* is the *intersection* of the solution sets of the two simple inequalities; likewise, the solution set of a continued inequality is the intersection of the solution sets of the two simple inequalities.

Example 5   Graph the solution set for $x > -2$ *and* $x < 4$.

We must find the set of all the numbers greater than -2 *and at the same time* less than 4. We find this set by graphing each inequality separately and then finding where the two graphs overlap.

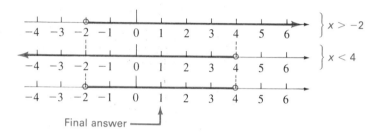

$$\{x \mid x > -2 \ and \ x < 4\} = \{x \mid x > -2\} \cap \{x \mid x < 4\}$$
$$= \{x \mid -2 < x < 4\} \quad \blacksquare$$

If $a > b$, then $a < x < b$ is an *invalid* continued inequality, and the solution set for the inequality is the empty set (see Example 6).

Example 6   Graph the set $\{x \mid 7 < x < 2\}$.

The statement $7 < x < 2$ is an *invalid* statement because $7 < 2$ is *false*. The solution set is $\{ \ \}$, and the graph has no points on it.

■

Example 7   Solve $x > 1$ *or* $x < 4$ graphically, and describe the solution set in set-builder notation.

We graph each inequality separately and then include in our final answer any number that is in one graph *or* the other *or* both.

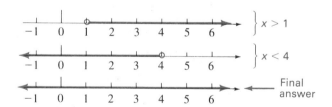

The solution set for $x > 1$ or $x < 4$ is $\{x \mid x \in R\}$.   ■

Solving Continued Inequalities

When we solve a continued inequality, we want to rewrite it so that x is all by itself between the two inequality symbols. That is, we want our answer to be in the form $a < x < b$ (if $a < b$) or $a > x > b$ (if $a > b$).

Example 8   Find the solution set for $2 < x + 5 \le 9$ and graph it on the real number line.

Notice first of all that $2 \le 9$ is a true statement, so the continued inequality is valid. Also notice that no restrictions were put on the domain of the variable.

Since $\{x | 2 < x + 5 \le 9\} = \{x | x + 5 > 2\} \cap \{x | x + 5 \le 9\}$, we could first find the solution set of each of the inequalities separately and then find the intersection of the two solution sets. However, the continued inequality may be more conveniently solved as follows:

$$
\begin{array}{cccc}
2 < & x + 5 \le & 9 & \\
-5 & -5 & -5 & \text{Add } -5 \text{ to all three parts of the inequality} \\
\hline
-3 < & x & \le 4 &
\end{array}
$$

The solution set is $\{x | -3 < x \le 4\}$. The graph will include the 4 (we will have a solid circle at 4) and the set of all points on the number line that lie between -3 and 4. We will have a hollow circle at -3.

Example 9   Solve $-7 \le 2x + 1 \le 5$ and graph the solution set on the number line.

$$-7 \le 2x + 1 \le 5 \qquad \text{Mentally add } -1 \text{ to all three parts of the inequality}$$

$$-8 \le \quad 2x \quad \le 4 \longleftarrow \text{Dividing all parts of a continued inequality by the } \textit{positive}$$
$$-4 \le \quad x \quad \le 2 \qquad \text{number 2 does } \textit{not} \text{ change the sense of the inequality}$$

The solution set is $\{x | -4 \le x \le 2\}$, and its graph is

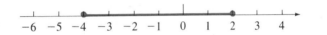

Example 10   Write $\{x | -7 \le 2x + 1 \le 5, x \in N\}$ in roster notation and graph the set.

The inequality is the same inequality as in Example 9, but now a restriction has been put on the domain. The only *natural numbers* that satisfy the inequality are 1 and 2; therefore,

$$\{x | -7 \le 2x + 1 \le 5, x \in N\} = \{1, 2\}$$

EXERCISES 2.3

Set I   In Exercises 1–8, write, in set-builder notation, the algebraic statement that describes the set that is graphed.

1.

2.

3.

4.

5.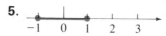

6.

7.

8.

In Exercises 9–22, solve the inequalities and graph their solution sets.

9. $5 > x - 2 \geq 3$

10. $7 > x - 3 \geq 4$

11. $-5 \geq x - 3 \geq 2$

12. $-3 \geq x - 2 \geq 4$

13. $-4 < 3x - 1 \leq 7$

14. $-6 < 4x - 2 \leq 5$

15. $x - 1 > 3$ or $x - 1 < -3$

16. $x - 2 > 5$ or $x - 2 < -5$

17. $2x + 1 \geq 3$ or $2x + 1 \leq -3$

18. $3x - 2 \geq 5$ or $3x - 2 \leq -5$

19. $x > 4$ and $x \geq 2$

20. $x < 3$ and $x < -1$

21. $x > 4$ or $x \geq 2$

22. $x < 3$ or $x < -1$

In Exercises 23–28, rewrite in roster notation and graph.

23. $\{x \mid -5 \leq x - 3 \leq 2, x \in N\}$

24. $\{x \mid -3 \leq x - 2 \leq 4, x \in N\}$

25. $\{x \mid 4 \geq x - 3 > -5, x \in J\}$

26. $\{x \mid 6 \geq x - 2 > -4, x \in J\}$

27. $\{x \mid -3 \leq 2x + 1 \leq 7, x \in N\}$

28. $\{x \mid -5 \leq 2x + 3 \leq 5, x \in N\}$

Set II   In Exercises 1–8, write, in set-builder notation, the algebraic statement that describes the set that is graphed.

1.

2.

3.

4.

5.

6.

7.

8.

In Exercises 9–22, solve the inequalities and graph their solution sets.

9. $8 > x - 1 \geq 2$

10. $-3 < x + 2 < 5$

11. $-6 \geq x - 4 \geq 3$

12. $7 > x + 3 \geq -1$

13. $-5 < 3x - 2 \leq 4$

14. $0 \leq 2x + 4 < 8$

15. $x - 3 > 4$ or $x - 3 < -4$

16. $x + 5 > 1$ or $x + 5 < -1$

17. $4x - 1 \geq 2$ or $4x - 1 \leq -2$

18. $3x + 2 > 5$ or $3x + 2 < -5$

19. $x < 6$ and $x < -2$

20. $x > 3$ and $x < 6$

21. $x < 6$ or $x < -2$

22. $x > 3$ or $x < 6$

In Exercises 23–28, rewrite in roster notation and graph.

23. $\{x \mid -4 \geq x - 2 > 1, x \in N\}$

24. $\{x \mid 2 \leq x + 4 < 8, x \in N\}$

25. $\{x \mid 5 \geq x - 2 > -3, x \in J\}$

26. $\{x \mid -2 \leq x - 1 < 4, x \in J\}$

27. $\{x \mid -2 \leq 2x + 4 \leq 10, x \in N\}$

28. $\{x \mid -6 < 2x - 3 \leq 5, x \in J\}$

2.4 Conditional Equations and Inequalities with Absolute Value Signs

In this section, we consider conditional equations and inequalities that have absolute value signs in them. Recall that the definition of $|N|$ is

$$|N| = \begin{cases} N & \text{if } N \geq 0 \\ -N & \text{if } N < 0 \end{cases}$$

Equations: $|N| = a$

We first consider equations of the form $|N| = a$, where $a \geq 0$.* Rule 2.1 (which is proved in Appendix A) permits us to rewrite such equations with no absolute value symbols in them.

RULE 2.1

If $a \geq 0$, and

$$\text{if } |N| = a, \quad \text{then} \quad N = a \quad \text{or} \quad N = -a$$

where N is any algebraic expression.

Example 1 Solve $\left| \dfrac{3 - 2x}{5} \right| = 2$ and graph its solution.

Because the equation is in the form $|N| = a$, we can use Rule 2.1. According to Rule 2.1, if

$$\left| \frac{3 - 2x}{5} \right| = 2,$$

then

$$\frac{3 - 2x}{5} = 2 \quad \text{or} \quad \frac{3 - 2x}{5} = -2$$

$$3 - 2x = 10 \quad \text{or} \quad 3 - 2x = -10$$

$$-2x = 7 \quad \text{or} \quad -2x = -13$$

$$x = -\frac{7}{2} \quad \text{or} \quad x = \frac{13}{2}$$

Therefore, the solution set is $\{-3\frac{1}{2}, 6\frac{1}{2}\}$. The graph of the solution set is

(The check is left to the student.) ■

---

* If $a < 0$, then $|N| = a$ will have no solution, because no positive number can equal a negative number.

Example 2   Solve $|x| = -3$.

We know that $|x| \geq 0$, and no number that is greater than or equal to 0 can equal -3. Therefore, there is *no solution*. ■

Inequalities: $|N| < a$

We now consider conditional inequalities of the form $|N| < a$ or $|N| \leq a$. Rule 2.2 (which is proved in Appendix A) permits us to rewrite such inequalities as continued inequalities with no absolute value symbols in them.

RULE 2.2

If a is a positive real number,* and

$$\text{if} \quad |N| < a, \quad \text{then} \quad -a < N < a$$

$$\text{if} \quad |N| \leq a, \quad \text{then} \quad -a \leq N \leq a$$

where N is any algebraic expression.

Example 3   Find the solution set for $|x| < 3$.

Using Rule 2.2, we rewrite $|x| < 3$ as $-3 < x < 3$, and this continued inequality has been solved.

If we consider the absolute value to mean the distance from a number to 0, the solution set of the inequality $|x| < 3$ will be the set of all real numbers whose distance from 0 is less than 3 units (see Figure 2.4.1).

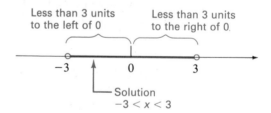

FIGURE 2.4.1

The solution set is $\{x \mid -3 < x < 3\}$. ■

Example 4   Solve $|2x - 3| \leq 5$ and graph its solution set.

We use Rule 2.2 because our inequality is in the form $|N| \leq a$. Rule 2.2 instructs us to rewrite our inequality as

$$-5 \leq 2x - 3 \leq 5$$

We then solve that inequality as follows:

$$-5 \leq 2x - 3 \leq 5$$
$$-2 \leq 2x \qquad \leq 8$$
$$-1 \leq \ x \qquad \leq 4$$

---

* If $a < 0$ in Rule 2.2, then the solution set is the empty set. For example, $|x| < -2$ has no solution, since $|x|$ is always greater than or equal to 0 and cannot be < -2.

The solution set is $\{x\,|-1 \le x \le 4\}$. The graph is

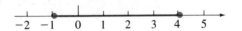

Example 5   Solve $\left|\dfrac{4-3x}{2}\right| \le 6$ and graph its solution set.

We use Rule 2.2, because the inequality is in the form $|N| \le a$.

$$-6 \le \frac{4-3x}{2} \le 6$$

$$-12 \le 4-3x \le 12$$

$$-16 \le -3x \le 8$$

$$\frac{-16}{-3} \ge \frac{-3x}{-3} \ge \frac{8}{-3} \qquad \text{Dividing all three parts by } -3 \text{ changes the } sense$$

$$\frac{16}{3} \ge x \ge -\frac{8}{3}$$

Therefore, the solution set is $\left\{x\,\middle|\,-\dfrac{8}{3} \le x \le \dfrac{16}{3}\right\}$. The graph of the solution set is

Inequalities: $|N| > a$

Now let us examine conditional inequalities of the form $|N| > a$ or $|N| \ge a$. Rule 2.3, which follows, is proved in Appendix A.

RULE 2.3

If a is a positive real number,* and

$$\text{if}\quad |N| > a, \quad \text{then}\quad N > a \quad \text{or}\quad N < -a$$

$$\text{if}\quad |N| \ge a, \quad \text{then}\quad N \ge a \quad \text{or}\quad N \le -a$$

where N is any algebraic expression.

We will use Rule 2.3 in rewriting any inequality of the form $|N| > a$ or $|N| \ge a$ as a combined inequality with no absolute value symbols in it. We will then solve the combined inequality according to the methods learned in Section 2.2.

Example 6   Find the solution set for $|x| > 3$.

Using Rule 2.3 (because the inequality is in the form $|N| > a$), we rewrite $|x| > 3$ as $x > 3$ *or* $x < -3$.

---

* If $a < 0$ in Rule 2.3, then the solution set is R. For example, if we solve $|x| > -2$, we can see that *any* real number will be a solution, since the absolute value of any real number is greater than or equal to zero, and zero is, of course, greater than -2. Thus, the solution set is the set of all real numbers.

If we consider the absolute value to mean the distance from a number to 0, then $|x| > 3$ can be interpreted as the set of points whose distance from 0 is *greater than* 3 units (see Figure 2.4.2).

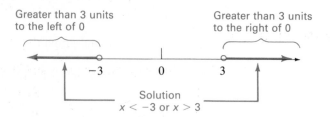

FIGURE 2.4.2

The solution set is the set of all real numbers less than -3 *or* greater than $+3$. In set-builder notation, the solution set is $\{x \mid x > 3 \text{ or } x < -3\}$, which can also be written as

$$\{x \mid x > 3\} \cup \{x \mid x < -3\} \quad \blacksquare$$

Example 7   Solve $|5 - 2x| > 3$ and graph its solution set.

We use Rule 2.3, because the inequality is in the form $|N| > a$. Rule 2.3 instructs us to rewrite the original inequality as

$$5 - 2x > 3 \quad \text{or} \quad 5 - 2x < -3$$

We then solve each of these inequalities as follows:

$$
\begin{array}{ccc}
5 - 2x > 3 & \text{or} & 5 - 2x < -3 \\
\underline{-5 \qquad -5} & & \underline{-5 \qquad -5} \\
-2x > -2 & \text{or} & -2x < -8 \\
\\
\dfrac{-2x}{-2} < \dfrac{-2}{-2} & \text{or} & \dfrac{-2x}{-2} > \dfrac{-8}{-2} \\
\\
x < 1 & \text{or} & x > 4
\end{array}
$$

Divide both sides by -2; sense is changed

The solution set is $\{x \mid x < 1 \quad \text{or} \quad x > 4\}$. The graph of the solution set is

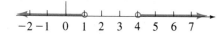

$\qquad\qquad\qquad\qquad\qquad\qquad\qquad\qquad$ $\blacksquare$

Example 8   Solve $\left| 3 - \dfrac{x}{2} \right| > 5$.

We use Rule 2.3, since the inequality is in the form $|N| > a$. Rule 2.3 instructs us to rewrite the inequality as

$$
\begin{array}{ccc}
3 - \dfrac{x}{2} > 5 & \text{or} & 3 - \dfrac{x}{2} < -5 \\
\\
2\left(3 - \dfrac{x}{2}\right) > 2(5) & \text{or} & 2\left(3 - \dfrac{x}{2}\right) < 2(-5) \\
\\
6 - x > 10 & \text{or} & 6 - x < -10 \\
\\
-x > 4 & \text{or} & -x < -16 \\
\\
x < -4 & \text{or} & x > 16
\end{array}
$$

The solution set is $\{x \mid x < -4 \text{ or } x > 16\}$. The graph of the solution set is

EXERCISES 2.4

Set I   Solve the following equations and inequalities and graph their solution sets.

1. $|x| = 3$

2. $|x| = 5$

3. $|3x| = 12$

4. $|2x| = 10$

5. $|x| < 2$

6. $|x| < 7$

7. $|4x| < 12$

8. $|3x| < 9$

9. $|5x| \leq 25$

10. $|2x| \leq 2$

11. $|x| > 2$

12. $|x| > 3$

13. $|3x| \geq 3$

14. $|4x| \geq 8$

15. $|x + 2| = 5$

16. $|x + 3| = 7$

17. $|x - 3| < 2$

18. $|x - 4| < 1$

19. $|x + 4| \leq 3$

20. $|x + 2| \leq 4$

21. $|x + 1| > 3$

22. $|x - 2| > 4$

23. $|x + 5| \geq 2$

24. $|x + 4| \geq 1$

25. $|3x + 4| = 3$

26. $|4x + 3| = 5$

27. $|2x - 3| < 4$

28. $|3x - 1| < 5$

29. $|3x - 5| \geq 6$

30. $|4x - 1| \geq 3$

31. $|1 - 2x| \leq 5$

32. $|2 - 3x| < 4$

33. $|2 - 3x| > 4$

34. $|5 - 2x| \geq 6$

35. $\left| \dfrac{5x + 2}{3} \right| \geq 2$

36. $\left| \dfrac{4x + 3}{5} \right| \geq 3$

37. $\left| \dfrac{3x - 4}{5} \right| < 1$

38. $\left| \dfrac{5x - 1}{2} \right| < 2$

39. $\left| \dfrac{1 - x}{2} \right| = 6$

40. $\left| \dfrac{3 - x}{2} \right| = 4$

41. $\left| \dfrac{5 - x}{2} \right| \leq 7$

42. $\left| \dfrac{4 - x}{3} \right| \leq 3$

43. $\left| 3 - \dfrac{x}{2} \right| > 4$

44. $\left| 4 - \dfrac{x}{3} \right| > 1$

45. $\left| 4 - \dfrac{x}{2} \right| < 3$

46. $\left| 5 - \dfrac{x}{3} \right| < 2$

Set II   Solve the following equations and inequalities and graph their solution sets.

1. $|x| = 4$

2. $|x| = -3$

3. $|4x| = 16$

4. $|x| = 0$

5. $|x| < 4$

6. $|x| < -1$

7. $|3x| < 12$

8. $|2x| \leq 4$

9. $|3x| \leq 15$

10. $|8x| < 12$

11. $|x| > 1$

12. $|x| > 0$

13. $|2x| \geq 6$

14. $|5x| < 15$

15. $|x + 7| = 5$

16. $|x - 3| = 2$

17. $|x - 5| < 3$

18. $|x + 1| \leq 1$

19. $|x + 3| \leq 2$

20. $|x - 2| < 0$

21. $|x + 3| > 5$

22. $|x + 2| \geq 3$

23. $|x + 5| \geq 2$

24. $|x - 1| > 1$

25. $|2x + 3| = 5$

26. $|3x - 1| = 2$

27. $|3x - 4| < 7$

28. $|5x + 3| \leq 3$

29. $|5x - 3| \geq 4$

30. $|4x + 2| > 2$

31. $|3 - 4x| \leq 7$ **32.** $|4 - 2x| < 1$ **33.** $|2 - 4x| \geq 5$

34. $|7 - 3x| > 0$ **35.** $\left|\dfrac{2x + 5}{5}\right| \geq 3$ **36.** $\left|\dfrac{5x - 2}{3}\right| \leq 2$

37. $\left|\dfrac{3x - 4}{2}\right| < 1$ **38.** $\left|\dfrac{4x + 7}{3}\right| \geq 1$ **39.** $\left|\dfrac{3 - x}{4}\right| = 5$

40. $\left|\dfrac{4 - x}{3}\right| = 2$ **41.** $\left|\dfrac{3 - x}{2}\right| \leq 5$ **42.** $\left|\dfrac{6 - 2x}{3}\right| \leq 4$

43. $\left|5 - \dfrac{x}{2}\right| > 1$ **44.** $\left|7 - \dfrac{x}{3}\right| > 5$ **45.** $\left|4 - \dfrac{x}{3}\right| < 1$

46. $\left|8 - \dfrac{x}{2}\right| \leq 2$

2.5 Review: 2.1–2.4

Types of Equations
2.1

A **conditional equation** is an equation whose two sides are equal only when certain numbers (called *solutions*) are substituted for the variable.

An **identity** (or *identical equation*) is an equation whose two sides are equal no matter what permissible number is substituted for the variable.

No solution exists for an equation whose two sides are unequal no matter what permissible number is substituted for the variable.

To Solve a First-Degree Equation with Only One Unknown
2.1

1. Remove fractions by multiplying both sides by the lowest common multiple (LCM) of all the denominators.

2. Remove grouping symbols.

3. Combine like terms on each side of the equation.

4. Move all the terms that contain the variable to one side of the equal sign and all constants to the other side.

5. Divide both sides of the equation by the coefficient of the variable.

6. Determine whether the equation is a conditional equation, an identity, or an equation with no solution.

7. If the equation is a conditional equation, check the solution.

To Solve a First-Degree Inequality with Only One Unknown
2.2

Proceed in the same way used to solve equations, with the exception that the *sense* must be changed when multiplying or dividing both sides by a negative number.

To Graph Solutions on the Number Line
2.2

To graph the solution $a < x \leq b$:

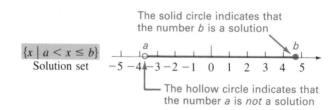

The solid circle indicates that the number *b* is a solution

$\{x \mid a < x \leq b\}$
Solution set

The hollow circle indicates that the number *a* is *not* a solution

To graph the solution $x > c$:

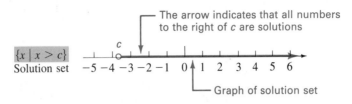

$\{x \mid x > c\}$
Solution set

The arrow indicates that all numbers to the right of c are solutions

Graph of solution set

Other types of solutions, for example, $x < c$, $x \le c$, $a \le x < b$, and so on, are graphed using the same procedures.

**To Solve an Equation with Absolute Value Signs
2.4**

An equation that has an absolute value sign is equivalent to *two* equations without absolute value signs.

If $|N| = a$, then $N = a$ or $N = -a$. (Rule 2.1)

**To Solve an Inequality with Absolute Value Signs
2.4**

If $|N| < a$, then $-a < N < a$. (Rule 2.2)

If $|N| > a$, then $N > a$ or $N < -a$. (Rule 2.3)

Review Exercises 2.5 Set I

In Exercises 1–5, find the solution set for each equation. Identify any equation that is not a conditional equation as an identity or as an equation with no solution.

1. $7 - 2(M - 4) = 5$

2. $5[-13z - 8(4 - 2z) + 20] = 15z - 17$

3. $\dfrac{3(x + 3)}{4} - \dfrac{2(x - 3)}{3} = 1$

4. $\dfrac{x - 1}{4} + \dfrac{x - 8}{2} = x - 4 - \dfrac{x + 1}{4}$

5. $2[-7y - 3(5 - 4y) + 10] = 10y - 12$

In Exercises 6–10, solve each inequality.

6. $10 - 3(x + 2) \ge 9 - 2(4 - 3x)$

7. $\dfrac{3z}{5} - \dfrac{2z}{3} < \dfrac{1}{2}$

8. $\dfrac{2w}{3} - \dfrac{5w}{6} < \dfrac{7}{12}$

9. $\dfrac{2(x + 6)}{10} + \dfrac{3x}{20} < 3$

10. $\dfrac{5(x - 3)}{7} - \dfrac{3x}{2} < 5$

In Exercises 11–25, find each set or solution set and graph it.

11. $\{x \mid 3x + 2 = 11,\ x \in J\}$

12. $|3x| = 9$

13. $|x| \le 3$

14. $|x| \ge 2$

15. $|6 - 2x| = 10$

16. $3|x - 2| \le 6$

17. $2|x - 3| \le 4$

18. $\{x \mid -3 < 2x - 1 < 8\}$

19. $\{x | -2 < x + 1 < 0, x \in J\}$

20. $\{x | -5 < 3x + 1 < 2\}$

21. $\{x | -3 < x - 1 < 0, x \in J\}$

22. $\left\{ x \left| \dfrac{2(x-1)}{6} + \dfrac{x}{9} = 1, x \in J \right. \right\}$

23. $\left\{ x \left| \dfrac{3(x-1)}{4} + \dfrac{x}{8} = 1, x \in J \right. \right\}$

24. $\left| 2 - \dfrac{x}{3} \right| \leq 1$

25. $\left| \dfrac{2x-4}{3} \right| \geq 2$

In Exercises 26–28, write in set-builder notation the algebraic statement that describes each graph.

26.

27.
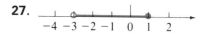

28.

Review Exercises 2.5 Set II

NAME _____

In Exercises 1–5, find the solution set for each equation. Identify any equation that is not a conditional equation as an identity or as an equation with no solution.

1. $13 = 8 - 5(2a + 13)$

2. $5(t - 3) + 1 = 3t - 2(7 - t)$

3. $3[-8x - 5(3 - 4x) + 10] = 36x + 2$

4. $\dfrac{x + 3}{4} = \dfrac{x - 2}{3} + \dfrac{1}{4}$

5. $\dfrac{3(x - 3)}{4} + 1 = \dfrac{8(x + 2)}{7}$

In Exercises 6–10, solve each inequality.

6. $2(x - 4) - 5 \geq 7 + 3(2x - 1)$

7. $15 - 4(m - 6) \leq 2(2 - 5m) + 8$

8. $\dfrac{2w}{4} - \dfrac{7}{9} < \dfrac{5w}{6}$

9. $\dfrac{5x}{3} < 11 - \dfrac{7(x - 9)}{12}$

10. $\dfrac{x}{3} - \dfrac{x + 2}{5} < 1$

In Exercises 11–25, find each set or solution set.

11. $|8x| = 12$

12. $\{x \mid 13 + 2x = 1, x \in N\}$

ANSWERS

1. _____

2. _____

3. _____

4. _____

5. _____

6. _____

7. _____

8. _____

9. _____

10. _____

11. _____

12. _____

13. $|11 - 7x| = 17$

14. $|x| > 5$

15. $\{x \mid -2 < x + 3 < 1, x \in J\}$

16. $\left\{ x \mid \dfrac{13}{15} - \dfrac{x}{5} = \dfrac{2(8 - x)}{15}, x \in J \right\}$

17. $\left| 4 - \dfrac{x}{2} \right| \le 2$

18. $8|2 - x| < 40$

19. $\left| \dfrac{3x + 2}{4} \right| > 2$

20. $\{x \mid -1 < 2x + 3 < 4\}$

21. $\{x \mid 5 < 3x - 1 < 2\}$

22. $\left| 5 - \dfrac{x}{3} \right| \ge 1$

23. $\{x \mid -3 \le 2x - 1 \le 7, x \in N\}$

24. $|x - 4| = -3$

25. $\{x \mid -4 < 3 - x < 4\}$

13. _____

14. _____

15. _____

16. _____

17. _____

18. _____

19. _____

20. _____

21. _____

22. _____

23. _____

24. _____

25. _____

26. _____

27. _____

28. _____

In Exercises 26–28, write in set-builder notation the algebraic statement that describes each graph.

26.

27.

28.

Chapter 2 Diagnostic Test

The purpose of this test is to see how well you understand the solution of first-degree equations and inequalities in one unknown. We recommend that you work this diagnostic test *before* your instructor tests you on this chapter. Allow yourself about 50 minutes.

Complete solutions for all the problems on this test, together with section references, are given in the answer section at the end of the book. For the problems you do incorrectly, study the sections cited.

In Problems 1–4, solve each equation. Identify any equation that is not a conditional equation as an identity or as an equation with no solution.

1. $8x - 4(2 + 3x) = 12$

2. $3(x - 6) = 5(1 + 2x) - 7(x - 4)$

3. $\dfrac{x}{6} - \dfrac{x + 2}{4} = \dfrac{1}{3}$

4. $2[7x - 4(1 + 3x)] = 5(3 - 2x) - 23$

In Problems 5–7, solve each inequality.

5. $5w + 2 \le 10 - w$

6. $13h - 4(2 + 3h) \ge 0$

7. $2[-5y - 6(y - 7)] < 6 + 4y$

In Problems 8–15, find each set or solution set and graph it.

8. $\{x \mid -3 < x + 1 < 5, x \in J\}$

9. $\{x \mid 4 \ge 3x + 7 > -2, x \in R\}$

10. $\left\{ x \left| \dfrac{5(x - 2)}{3} + \dfrac{x}{4} \le 12, x \in R \right. \right\}$

11. $\left\{ x \left| \left| \dfrac{2x + 3}{5} \right| = 1 \right. \right\}$

12. $|3x - 1| > 2$

13. $|7 - 3x| \ge 6$

14. $\left| \dfrac{5x + 1}{2} \right| \le 7$

15. $\{x \mid |2x - 5| < 11\}$

Cumulative Review Exercises
Chapters 1–2

In Exercises 1–28, find the value of each expression or write "Not possible" or "Cannot be determined."

1. $(-14) - (-22)$

2. $(-12)(-4)$

3. $(-1)^7$

4. $(-6) + (-8)$

5. $(-2)^4$

6. $\sqrt{64}$

7. $\dfrac{9}{0}$

8. $\dfrac{0}{-7}$

9. $\dfrac{|-20|}{-5}$

10. $(-18) - (7)$

11. $\sqrt[3]{-64}$

12. -6^2

13. $(35) \div (-7)$

14. $(-10)(0)(8)$

15. $\sqrt[9]{-1}$

16. $10^{-2} \cdot 10^5$

17. $(4^0)^3$

18. $(2^{-3})^{-1}$

19. $-3 - 2^2 \cdot 6$

20. $7 - [4 - (13 - 5)]$

21. $(-11) + 15$

22. $(14)(-2)$

23. $|0|$

24. $\sqrt{81}$

25. $\sqrt[4]{81}$

26. $3 + 2 \cdot 5$

27. $\dfrac{0}{0}$

28. $16 \div (-2)^2 - \dfrac{7-1}{2}$

In Exercises 29 and 30, simplify.

29. $y - 2(x - y) - 3(1 - y) - \sqrt{4y^2}$

30. $2x(x^2 + 1) - x(x^2 + 3x - 2)$

In Exercises 31–38, find the solution set for each equation or inequality. Identify any *equation* that is not a conditional equation as an identity or as an equation with no solution.

31. $6(3x - 5) + 7 = 9(3 + 2x) - 1$

32. $5x - 7 \leq 8x + 4$

33. $2x + 3 = 2(2x + 5)$

34. $\dfrac{x}{4} + \dfrac{x-3}{10} = \dfrac{29}{20}$

35. $-5 < x + 4 \leq 3$

36. $8\{4 + 3(x - 2)\} = 3(8x + 3) - 25$

37. $|2x + 3| > 1$

38. $|x - 4| \leq 3$

3 Word Problems

The main reason for studying algebra is to equip oneself with the tools necessary to solve problems. Most problems are expressed in words. In this chapter, we show methods for solving some traditional word problems. The skills learned in this chapter can be applied to solving mathematical problems encountered in many fields of learning as well as in real-life situations.

3.1 Method of Solving Word Problems

In this section, we show how to translate an English sentence into an algebraic equation or inequality. The resulting equation or inequality is then solved using the methods learned in Chapter 2.

METHOD FOR SOLVING WORD PROBLEMS

1. To solve a word problem, first read it very carefully and determine what *type** of problem it is, if possible. *Be sure you understand the problem.* Don't try to solve it at this point.

2. Determine what is unknown. What is being asked for is often found in the last sentence of the problem, which may begin with "What is the..." or "Find the ...."

3. Represent one unknown number by a variable, and *declare* the meaning in a sentence of the form "Let $x = ...$." Then reread the problem to see how you can represent any other unknown numbers in terms of the same variable.

4. Reread the entire word problem, translating each English phrase into an algebraic expression.

5. Fit the algebraic expressions together into an equation or inequality.

6. Using the methods described in Chapter 2, solve the equation or inequality for the variable.

7. Answer *all* of the questions asked in the problem.

8. Check the solution(s) in the word statement.

The following list of key word expressions and their corresponding algebraic operations may help you translate English sentences into an algebraic equation or inequality:

+	−	×	÷
the sum of	minus	times	divided by
added to	decreased by	the product of	the quotient of
increased by	less than	multiplied by	
plus	subtracted from		
more than	the difference of		

---

* We discuss several general types of word problems in this chapter, for example, mixture problems, distance–rate–time problems, and so on.

NOTE   Because subtraction is not commutative, care must be taken to get the numbers in a subtraction word problem in the correct order. For example, while the statements "m minus n" "m decreased by n," and "the difference of m and n" are translated as $m - n$, the expressions "m subtracted from n" and "m less than n" are translated as $n - m$. ☑

Example 1   Three times an unknown number decreased by 5 is 13. What is the unknown number?

Let x = the unknown number.

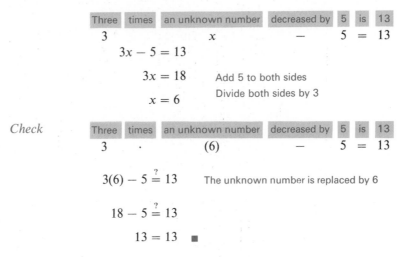

Three	times	an unknown number	decreased by	5	is	13
3		x	$-$	5	$=$	13

$$3x - 5 = 13$$

$$3x = 18 \qquad \text{Add 5 to both sides}$$

$$x = 6 \qquad \text{Divide both sides by 3}$$

Check

Three	times	an unknown number	decreased by	5	is	13
3	$\cdot$	(6)	$-$	5	$=$	13

$$3(6) - 5 \overset{?}{=} 13 \qquad \text{The unknown number is replaced by 6}$$

$$18 - 5 \overset{?}{=} 13$$

$$13 = 13 \quad \blacksquare$$

NOTE   To check a word problem, you must check the solution in the *word statement*. Any error that may have been made in writing the equation will not be discovered if you simply substitute the solution in the equation. ☑

Example 2   Find three consecutive integers such that the sum of the first two is 23 less than 3 times the third.

The domain is the set of integers. Let

$$x = \text{the first integer}$$
$$x + 1 = \text{the second integer}$$
$$x + 2 = \text{the third integer}$$

sum of first two integers	is	23 less than	3 times the third

$$x + (x + 1) = 3(x + 2) - 23$$

$$2x + 1 = 3x + 6 - 23$$

$$2x + 1 = 3x - 17$$

$$18 = x$$

$$x = 18, \quad x + 1 = 19, \quad x + 2 = 20$$

The integers are 18, 19, and 20.

Check The sum of 18 and 19 is 37, and 3 times 20 is 60; 37 is 23 less than 60. The problem checks.   ■

Example 3   Find three consecutive odd integers whose sum is 72.

The domain is the set of odd integers.

NOTE   Adding 2 to any odd integer gives the *next* odd integer; that is, $5 + 2 = 7$, $-17 + 2 = -15$, and so forth. Therefore, if x is an odd integer, the next odd integer is $x + 2$, and the one after that is $x + 4$. ☑

Let
$$x = \text{the first odd integer}$$
$$x + 2 = \text{the second odd integer}$$
$$x + 4 = \text{the third odd integer}$$

$$\boxed{\text{sum of the integers}} \;\; \boxed{\text{is}} \;\; \boxed{72}$$

$$x + (x + 2) + (x + 4) = 72$$
$$3x + 6 = 72$$
$$3x = 66$$
$$x = 22$$

Since 22 is not an odd integer, it is not in the domain. Therefore, there is no solution. ∎

When a problem deals with *inequalities* rather than with quantities that are *equal* to each other, you will almost always find more than one correct answer (see Example 4).

Example 4   Find four consecutive even integers whose sum is between 21 and 45.

The domain is the set of even integers.

Let
$$x = \text{the first even integer}$$
$$x + 2 = \text{the second even integer}$$
$$x + 4 = \text{the third even integer}$$
$$x + 6 = \text{the fourth even integer}$$

Because the sum of the integers is to be *between* 21 and 45, the algebraic statement can be written as a continued inequality.

$$21 < x + (x + 2) + (x + 4) + (x + 6) < 45$$
$$21 < 4x + 12 < 45$$
$$9 < 4x < 33$$
$$\frac{9}{4} < x < \frac{33}{4}$$

The even integers between 9/4 and 33/4 are 4, 6, and 8; therefore, we will have *three* sets of answers:

	If $x = 4$	If $x = 6$	If $x = 8$
	$x + 2 = 6$	$x + 2 = 8$	$x + 2 = 10$
	$x + 4 = 8$	$x + 4 = 10$	$x + 4 = 12$
	$x + 6 = 10$	$x + 6 = 12$	$x + 6 = 14$
Sum:	28	36	44

In all three cases, the sum of the four consecutive even integers is between 21 and 45. Therefore, four consecutive even integers whose sum is between 21 and 45 are 4, 6, 8, and 10; 6, 8, 10, and 12; *and* 8, 10, 12, and 14. ∎

EXERCISES 3.1

Set I   In *all* exercises, set up the problem algebraically. Be sure to state what your variables represent.

In Exercises 1–6, solve for the unknown number and check your solution.

1. Seven more than twice an unknown number is 23.

2. Eleven more than 3 times an unknown number is 38.

3. Four times an unknown number, decreased by 7, is 25.

4. Five times an unknown number, decreased by 6, is 49.

5. When an unknown number is decreased by 7, the difference is half the unknown number.

6. When an unknown number is decreased by 12, the difference is half the unknown number.

In Exercises 7–18, solve for the unknowns and check your solutions.

7. A 12-cm length of string is cut into two pieces. The first piece is 3 times as long as the second piece. How long is each piece?

8. A 12-m length of rope is cut into two pieces. The first piece is twice as long as the second piece. How long is each piece?

9. The sum of three consecutive integers is 19. Find the integers.

10. The sum of three consecutive integers is 40. Find the integers.

11. A 42-cm piece of wire is cut so that the first piece is 8 cm longer than the second piece. How long is each piece?

12. A 50-m piece of hose is cut so that the first piece is 6 m longer than the second piece. How long is each piece?

13. The sum of the first two of three consecutive integers less the third integer is 10. What are the integers?

14. The sum of the first two of three consecutive integers less the third is 17. What are the integers?

15. Find three consecutive odd integers such that 3 times the sum of the last two is 40 more than 5 times the first.

16. Find three consecutive odd integers such that 5 times the sum of the last two is 60 more than 5 times the first.

17. David buys 4 more cans of corn than cans of peas and 3 times as many cans of green beans as cans of peas. If he buys 24 cans of these three vegetables altogether, how many cans of each kind does he buy?

18. John buys 6 more cans of peaches than cans of pears and 3 times as many cans of cherries as cans of pears. If he buys 21 cans of these three fruits altogether, how many cans of each kind does he buy?

In Exercises 19–22, find the unknown number and check your solution.

19. Three times the sum of 8 and an unknown number is equal to twice the sum of the unknown number and 7.

20. Four times the sum of 5 and an unknown number is equal to 3 times the sum of the unknown number and 9.

21. When twice the sum of 5 and an unknown number is subtracted from 8 times the unknown number, the result is equal to 4 times the sum of 8 and twice the unknown number.

22. When 7 times the sum of 2 and an unknown number is subtracted from 4 times the sum of 3 and twice the unknown number, the result is equal to 0.

In Exercises 23–26, find *all possible solutions* for each problem.

23. Find three consecutive even integers whose sum is between 21 and 45.

24. Find three consecutive even integers whose sum is between 81 and 93.

25. In a certain mathematics class, a student needs between 560 and 640 points in order to receive a C. The final exam is worth 200 points. If Clark has 396 points just before the final, what range of scores on the final exam will give him a C for the course?

26. In a certain English class, a student needs between 720 and 810 points in order to receive a B. The final exam is worth 200 points. If Cathy has 584 points just before the final, what range of scores on the final exam will give her a B grade for the course?

Set II   In *all* exercises, set up the problem algebraically. Be sure to state what your variables represent.

In Exercises 1–6, solve for the unknown number and check your solution.

1. Nine more than 4 times an unknown number is 33.

2. Seven plus an unknown number is equal to 17 decreased by the unknown number.

3. Five times an unknown number, decreased by 8, is 12.

4. Four plus an unknown number is equal to 20 decreased by the unknown number.

5. When an unknown number is decreased by 12, the difference is one-third the unknown number.

6. Two plus an unknown number is equal to 8 decreased by the unknown number.

In Exercises 7–18, solve for the unknowns and check your solutions.

7. A 36-cm length of cord is cut into two pieces. The first piece is 5 times as long as the second piece. How long is each piece?

8. A 32-cm piece of string is cut so that the first piece is one-third the length of the second piece. How long is each piece?

9. The sum of three consecutive integers is 73. Find the integers.

10. The sum of three consecutive integers is 84. What are the integers?

11. A 52-m piece of rope is cut so that the first piece is 14 m longer than the second piece. How long is each piece?

12. A piece of pipe 60 cm long is cut so that one piece is 34 cm shorter than the other piece. How long is each piece?

13. The sum of the first two of three consecutive integers less the third is 20. What are the integers?

14. The sum of three consecutive even integers is −54. What are the integers?

15. Find three consecutive odd integers such that 4 times the sum of the last two is 48 more than 7 times the first.

16. The sum of the first two of three consecutive integers less the third is 85. What are the integers?

17. Tom buys 4 more cans of tomato soup than cans of split pea soup and 3 times as many cans of vegetable soup as cans of split pea soup. If he buys 29 cans of these three soups altogether, how many cans of each kind does he buy?

18. The total receipts for a concert were $7,120. Some tickets were $8.50 each, and the rest were $9.50 each. If 800 tickets were sold altogether, how many of each kind of ticket were sold?

In Exercises 19–22, solve for the unknown number and check your solution.

19. Four times the sum of 6 and an unknown number is equal to 3 times the sum of the unknown number and 10.

20. When an unknown number is subtracted from 42, the difference is one-sixth the unknown number.

21. When 3 times the sum of 4 and an unknown number is subtracted from 8 times the unknown number, the result is equal to 4 times the sum of 3 and twice the unknown number.

22. When an unknown number is subtracted from 16, the difference is one-third the unknown number.

In Exercises 23–26, find *all possible solutions* for each problem.

23. Find three consecutive even integers whose sum is between 39 and 51.

24. Find four consecutive odd integers whose sum is between -5 and 20.

25. In a certain history class, a student needs between 600 and 675 points in order to receive a B. The final exam is worth 150 points. If Manuel has 467 points just before the final, what range of scores on the final exam will give him a B for the course?

26. In a certain physics class, a student needs at least 450 points in order to receive an A. The final exam is worth 100 points. If Cindy has 367 points just before the final, what range of scores on the final exam will give her an A for the course?

3.2 Ratio Problems

Ratio is another word for *fraction*; in algebra fractions are often called *rational* numbers.

The ratio of a to b is written $\dfrac{a}{b}$ or $a:b$.

The ratio of b to a is written $\dfrac{b}{a}$ or $b:a$.

We call a and b the *terms* of the ratio. The terms of a ratio may be any kind of number; the only restriction is that the denominator cannot be zero.

The key to solving ratio problems is to use the given ratio to help represent the unknown numbers.

TO REPRESENT THE UNKNOWNS IN A RATIO PROBLEM

1. Multiply each term of the ratio by x.

2. Let the resulting products represent the unknowns.

Example 1   Two numbers are in the ratio 3 to 5. Their sum is -80. Find the numbers.*

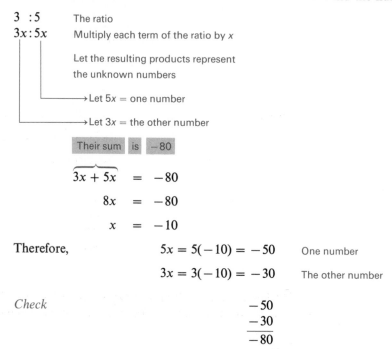

$3 : 5$ The ratio

$3x : 5x$ Multiply each term of the ratio by x

Let the resulting products represent the unknown numbers

→ Let $5x$ = one number

→ Let $3x$ = the other number

Their sum   is -80

$$\overbrace{3x + 5x} = -80$$

$$8x = -80$$

$$x = -10$$

Therefore, $5x = 5(-10) = -50$ One number

$3x = 3(-10) = -30$ The other number

Check

$$-50$$
$$-30$$
$$\overline{-80}$$

Note that we were not finished when we found that $x = -10$. ∎

Certain problems related to rectangles, squares, and triangles lead to ratio word problems in algebra. Figure 3.2.1 shows a collection of facts from geometry that are helpful in solving such problems.

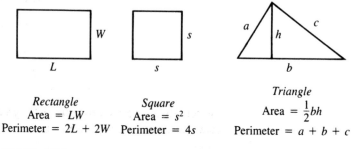

Rectangle
Area = LW
Perimeter = $2L + 2W$

Square
Area = s^2
Perimeter = $4s$

Triangle
Area = $\frac{1}{2}bh$
Perimeter = $a + b + c$

FIGURE 3.2.1

---

* The same problem could have been worded as follows: Divide (separate) -80 into two parts whose ratio is $3 : 5$.

Example 2   The three sides of a triangle are in the ratio $2:3:4$. The perimeter is 63. Find the three sides.

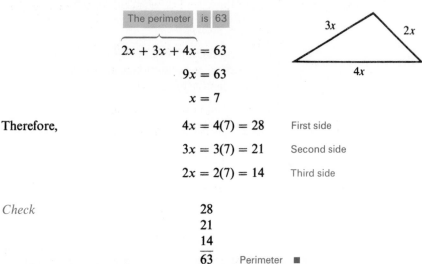

2 : 3 : 4   The ratio
$2x:3x:4x$ Multiply each term of the ratio by x

Let the resulting products represent the unknowns

→ Let $4x$ = first side
→ Let $3x$ = second side
→ Let $2x$ = third side

The perimeter is 63

$$2x + 3x + 4x = 63$$
$$9x = 63$$
$$x = 7$$

Therefore, $4x = 4(7) = 28$ First side
                  $3x = 3(7) = 21$ Second side
                  $2x = 2(7) = 14$ Third side

Check
$$
\begin{array}{l}
28 \\
21 \\
\underline{14} \\
63
\end{array}
$$
Perimeter ∎

Example 3   The length and width of a rectangle are in the ratio $5:3$. The perimeter is to be less than 48. What values can the length of the rectangle have?

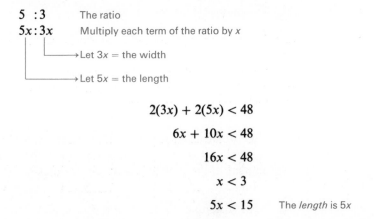

5 : 3   The ratio
$5x:3x$ Multiply each term of the ratio by x

→ Let $3x$ = the width
→ Let $5x$ = the length

$$2(3x) + 2(5x) < 48$$
$$6x + 10x < 48$$
$$16x < 48$$
$$x < 3$$
$$5x < 15$$ The *length* is $5x$

The length of the rectangle must be greater than 0, since the length of a side of a rectangle cannot be negative or zero, *and* less than 15.

Check If the length were 10, the width would be 6 and the perimeter would be 32. If the length were 8, the width would be 24/5 and the perimeter would be 128/5, or 25.6. (Check the problem using several other values between 0 and 15 for the length of the rectangle.) ∎

EXERCISES 3.2

Set I   In each exercise, set up the problem algebraically and solve. Be sure to state what your variables represent. In Exercises 1–10, check your solutions.

1. Two numbers are in the ratio of 4 to 5. Their sum is 81. Find the numbers.

2. Two numbers are in the ratio of 8 to 3. Their sum is 77. Find the numbers.

3. The three sides of a triangle are in the ratio $3:4:5$. The perimeter is 108. Find the three sides.

4. The three sides of a triangle are in the ratio $4:5:6$. The perimeter is 120. Find the three sides.

5. Fifty-four hr of a student's week are spent in study, class, and work. The times spent in these activities are in the ratio $4:2:3$. How many hours are spent in each activity?

6. Forty-eight hr of a student's week are spent in study, class, and work. The times spent in these activities are in the ratio $4:2:6$. How many hours are spent in each activity?

7. The length and width of a rectangle are in the ratio of 7 to 6. The perimeter is 78. Find the length and width.

8. The length and width of a rectangle are in the ratio of 9 to 5. The perimeter is 196. Find the length and width.

9. Divide (separate) 143 into two parts whose ratio is $7:6$.

10. Divide (separate) 221 into two parts whose ratio is $8:5$.

11. The three sides of a triangle are in the ratio $4:5:6$. The perimeter is to be less than 60. What is the range of values that the *shortest* side can have?

12. The three sides of a triangle are in the ratio $8:9:10$. The perimeter is to be less than 81. What is the range of values that the *shortest* side can have?

Set II   In each exercise, set up the problem algebraically and solve. Be sure to state what your variables represent. In Exercises 1–10, check your solutions.

1. Two numbers are in the ratio of 2 to 7. Their sum is 99. Find the numbers.

2. Three numbers are in the ratio $4:7:3$. Their sum is 56. Find the numbers.

3. The sides of a triangle are in the ratio $5:6:7$. The perimeter is 72. Find the sides.

4. The ratio of pineapple juice to orange juice to lemon juice in a punch recipe is 11 to 6 to 1. If 36 ℓ of punch are to be made (with only these three juices), how much pineapple juice should be used?

5. The formula for a particular shade of green paint calls for mixing 3 parts of blue paint with 1 part of yellow paint. Find the number of liters of blue and the number of liters of yellow needed to make 14 ℓ of the desired shade of green paint.

6. In Mrs. Aguilar's bread recipe, flour and water are to be mixed in the ratio of 3 parts water to 5 parts flour. How many parts of flour are needed to make a mixture of 64 parts of water and flour?

7. The length and width of a rectangle are in the ratio of 8 to 3. The perimeter is 88. Find the length and the width.

8. Nick needs to mix gasoline and oil in the ratio of 50 to 1 for his motorcycle. If he needs to mix 382.5 oz altogether, how much gasoline should he use? How much oil?

9. Divide (separate) 207 into two parts whose ratio is 5:4.

10. Todd has nickels, dimes, and quarters in the ratio 5:8:7. If he has 140 of these coins altogether, how many of each kind does he have?

11. The three sides of a triangle are in the ratio 4:5:8. The perimeter is to be less than 85. What is the range of values that the *shortest* side can have?

12. The three sides of a triangle are in the ratio 3:5:7. The perimeter is to be greater than 60. What is the range of values that the *longest* side can have?

3.3 Distance-Rate-Time Problems

Distance-rate-time problems are used in any field involving motion. A physical law relating distance traveled d, rate of travel r, and time of travel t is

$$d = r \cdot t$$

For example, if you are driving your car at an average speed of 50 mph, then

$$d = r \cdot t$$

you travel a distance of $\quad$ 50 mi in 1 hr $\qquad$ $50 = 50(1)$
you travel a distance of 100 mi in 2 hr $\qquad$ $100 = 50(2)$
you travel a distance of 150 mi in 3 hr $\qquad$ $150 = 50(3)$

and so on. Students often find a chart helpful in solving distance-rate-time problems.

METHOD FOR SOLVING DISTANCE-RATE-TIME PROBLEMS

1. Draw the blank chart:

	d	$=$	r	$\cdot$	t

2. Fill in as many of the boxes as possible, using the information given.

3. Let x represent an unknown. Express other unknowns in terms of x, if possible.

4. Fill in the remaining boxes, using x and the formula $d = r \cdot t$.

5. Write an equation, using the information in the chart along with any unused facts given in the problem.

6. Solve the resulting equation.

7. Answer all of the questions asked in the problem.

8. Check your solution(s) in the original word problem.

Example 1   A carload of campers leaves Los Angeles for Lake Havasu at 8:00 A.M. A second carload of campers leaves Los Angeles at 8:30 A.M. and drives 10 mph faster over the same road. If the second car overtakes the first at 10:30 A.M., what is the average speed of each car?

Let
$$x = \text{Rate of first car}$$
$$x + 10 = \text{Rate of second car}$$

	d	$=$	r	$\cdot$	t
First car			x		$\dfrac{5}{2}$
Second car			$x + 10$		2

First car leaves at 8:00 A.M. and is overtaken at 10:30 A.M.

Second car leaves at 8:30 A.M. and overtakes the first car at 10:30 A.M.

Use the formula $d = r \cdot t$ to fill in the two empty boxes.

	d	$=$	r	$\cdot$	t
First car	$x\left(\dfrac{5}{2}\right)$		x		$\dfrac{5}{2}$
Second car	$(x + 10)2$		$x + 10$		2

$d = r \cdot t$
$d = x\left(\dfrac{5}{2}\right)$

$d = r \cdot t$
$d = (x + 10)2$

Since both cars start at the same place and end at the same place, they have both traveled the same distance. Therefore,

"$=$" because the distances are equal

$$\frac{5}{2}x = 2(x + 10)$$

$$5x = 4(x + 10)$$

$$5x = 4x + 40$$

$$x = 40 \text{ mph} \qquad \text{First car}$$

$$x + 10 = 40 + 10 = 50 \text{ mph} \qquad \text{Second car}$$

Check The first car travels $(2\frac{1}{2}$ hr$)$ (40 mph) $= 100$ miles.
The second car travels (2 hr) (50 mph) $= 100$ miles. ■

Example 2   A boat cruises downstream for 4 hr before heading back. After traveling upstream for 5 hr, it is still 16 mi short of the starting point. If the speed of the stream is 4 mph, find the speed of the boat in still water.

Let
$$x = \text{Speed of boat in still water}$$
$$x + 4 = \text{Speed of boat downstream}$$
$$x - 4 = \text{Speed of boat upstream}$$

	d	$=$	r	$\cdot$	t
Downstream	$(x + 4)4$		$x + 4$		4
Upstream	$(x - 4)5$		$x - 4$		5

$d = r \cdot t$
$d = (x + 4)4$

$d = r \cdot t$
$d = (x - 4)5$

We now use the "unused fact" that the distance downstream is 16 mi plus the distance upstream, as shown in the diagram below:

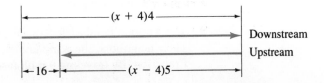

$$\boxed{\text{Distance traveled downstream}} = 16 + \boxed{\text{Distance traveled upstream}}$$

$$(x + 4)4 = 16 + (x - 4)5$$

$$4x + 16 = 16 + 5x - 20$$

$$20 = x$$

$$x = 20 \text{ mph} \qquad \text{Speed of boat in still water}$$

Check Speed downstream is 24 mph. Speed upstream is 16 mph.

$$(4 \text{ hr}) (24 \text{ mph}) \overset{?}{=} 16 \text{ mi} + (5 \text{ hr}) (16 \text{ mph})$$

$$96 \text{ mi} \overset{?}{=} 16 \text{ mi} + 80 \text{ mi} = 96 \text{ mi} \quad \blacksquare$$

Example 3   Joe drove from his home to Los Angeles to pick up his wife, Linda. He drove 45 mph. Linda, driving at 54 mph, drove on the return trip. If the total driving time for the round trip was 11 hr, how far from their home is Los Angeles?

Let $\qquad\qquad\qquad x = $ the number of hours Joe drove

$11 - x = $ the number of hours Linda drove

	d	$=$	r	$\cdot$	t
Joe drove	$45x$		45		x
Linda drove	$54(11 - x)$		54		$11 - x$

We now use the "unused fact" that their distances are equal.

$$45x = 54(11 - x)$$

$$45x = 594 - 54x$$

$$99x = 594$$

$$x = 6 \qquad \text{Number of hours Joe drove}$$

$$45x = 270 \qquad \text{Number of miles Joe lives from Los Angeles}$$

Check Hours Linda drove: $11 - 6 = 5$
       Miles Linda drove: 54 mph (5 hr) = 270 mi $\blacksquare$

EXERCISES 3.3

Set I In each exercise, set up the problem algebraically, solve, and check. Be sure to state what your variables represent.

1. The Malone family left San Diego by car at 7 A.M., bound for San Francisco. Their neighbors, the King family, left in their car at 8 A.M., also bound for San Francisco. By traveling 9 mph faster, the Kings overtook the Malones at 1 P.M.

   a. Find the average speed of each car.

   b. Find the total distance traveled by each car before they met.

2. The Duran family left Ames, Iowa, by car at 6 A.M., bound for Yellowstone National Park. Their neighbors, the Silva family, left in their car at 8 A.M., also bound for Yellowstone. By traveling 10 mph faster, the Silvas overtook the Durans at 4 P.M.

   a. Find the average speed of each car.

   b. Find the total distance traveled before they met.

3. Eric hiked from his camp to a lake in the mountains and returned to camp later in the day. He walked at a rate of 2 mph going to the lake and 5 mph coming back. If the trip to the lake took 3 hr longer than the trip back:

   a. How long did it take him to hike to the lake?

   b. How far is it from his camp to the lake?

4. Lee hiked from her camp up to an observation tower in the mountains and returned to camp later in the day. She walked up at the rate of 2 mph and jogged back at the rate of 6 mph. The trip to the tower took 2 hr longer than the return trip.

   a. How long did it take her to hike to the tower?

   b. How far is it from her camp to the tower?

5. Fran and Ron live 54 mi apart. Both leave their homes at 7 A.M. by bicycle, riding toward one another. They meet at 10 A.M. If Ron's average speed is four-fifths of Fran's, how fast does each cycle?

6. Tran and Atour live 60 mi apart. Both leave their homes at 10 A.M. by bicycle, riding toward one another. They meet at 2 P.M. If Atour's average speed is two-thirds of Tran's, how fast does each cycle?

7. Colin paddles a kayak downstream for 3 hr. After having lunch, he paddles upstream for 5 hr. At that time, he is still 6 mi short of his starting point. If the speed of the stream is 2 mph, how fast does Colin row in still water? How far downstream did he travel?

8. Jessica paddles a kayak downstream for 4 hr. After having lunch, she paddles upstream for 6 hrs. At that time, she is still 4 mi short of her starting point. If the speed of the stream is 1 mph, how fast does Jessica row in still water? How far downstream did she travel?

9. Mr. Zaleva flew his private plane from his office to his company's storage facility bucking a 20 mph head wind all the way. He flew home the same day with the same wind at his back. The round trip took 10 hr of flying time. If the plane makes 100 mph in still air, how far is the storage facility from his office?

10. Mr. Summers drove his motorboat upstream a certain distance while pulling his son Brian on a water ski. He returned to the starting point pulling his other son Derek. The round trip took 25 min of skiing time. On both legs of the trip, the speedometer read 30 mph. If the speed of the current is 6 mph, how far upstream did he travel?

Set II In each exercise, set up the problem algebraically, solve, and check. Be sure to state what your variables represent.

1. The Dent family left Chino by car at 6 A.M., bound for Lake Mojave. Their neighbor, Mr. Scott, left in his car at 7 A.M., also bound for Lake Mojave. By traveling 10 mph faster, Mr. Scott overtook the Dents at noon.

a. Find the average speed of each car.

b. Find the total distance traveled before they met.

2. Bill and Andrew live 34 mi apart. Both leave their homes at 9 A.M., walking toward each other. They meet at 1 P.M. If Andrew's average speed is $\frac{1}{2}$ mph faster than Bill's, how fast does each walk? How far from Bill's house did they meet?

3. Lori hiked from her camp to a waterfall and returned to camp later in the day. She walked at a rate of $1\frac{1}{2}$ mph going to the waterfall and 3 mph coming back. If the trip to the waterfall took 1 hr longer than the trip back:

a. How long did it take her to hike to the waterfall?

b. How far is it from her camp to the waterfall?

4. David jogged from his home to a park at the rate of 7 mph. He later walked home at the rate of 5 mph. If the trip home took 0.6 hours longer than the trip to the park, how long did it take David to get from home to the park? How far is the park from his home?

5. Matthew and Lucas live 63 mi apart. Both leave their homes at 8 A.M. by bicycle, riding toward one another. They meet at 11 A.M. If Lucas's average speed is three-fourths of Matthew's, how fast does each cycle?

6. Anthony and Mark leave a marina at the same time, traveling in the same direction. The speed of Mark's boat is $\frac{7}{8}$ the speed of Anthony's boat. In 3 hr, Anthony is 12 mi ahead of Mark. How fast is each going?

7. The Powitzsky family motors their houseboat upstream for 4 hr. After lunch, they motor downstream for 2 hr. At that time, they are still 12 mi away from the marina where they began. If the speed of the houseboat in still water is 15 mph, what is the speed of the stream? How far upstream did the Powitzskys travel?

8. Plane A can travel a distance of 630 mi in $2\frac{1}{2}$ hr. The speed of plane B is $\frac{6}{7}$ that of plane A. If both planes leave an airport at the same time and fly in opposite directions, how long will it take them to be 1,872 mi apart?

9. Mr. Lee flew his private plane from his home to a nearby recreation area, bucking a 25 mph head wind all the way. He flew back home the same day with the same wind at his back. The round trip took 8 hr. If the plane makes 100 mph in still air, how far is his home from the recreation area?

10. Two trains are traveling in the same direction, with the first train going 6 mph slower than the second train. The first train leaves a depot at 4 A.M. The second leaves the same depot at 5 A.M. and passes the first train at 10 A.M. How fast is each train going?

3.4 Mixture Problems

Mixture problems, used in business, usually involve mixing two or more dry ingredients. This type of problem is often called a *money problem*, since the cost of each item is often important.

TWO IMPORTANT RELATIONSHIPS NECESSARY TO SOLVE MIXTURE PROBLEMS

1. $\left(\begin{matrix} \text{Amount of} \\ \text{ingredient A} \end{matrix}\right) + \left(\begin{matrix} \text{Amount of} \\ \text{ingredient B} \end{matrix}\right) = \left(\begin{matrix} \text{Amount of} \\ \text{mixture} \end{matrix}\right)$

2. $\left(\begin{matrix} \text{Cost of} \\ \text{ingredient A} \end{matrix}\right) + \left(\begin{matrix} \text{Cost of} \\ \text{ingredient B} \end{matrix}\right) = \left(\begin{matrix} \text{Cost of} \\ \text{mixture} \end{matrix}\right)$

Students often find a chart helpful in solving mixture problems.

	Ingredient A	Ingredient B	Mixture
Unit cost			← This square is sometimes empty
Amount		+	=
Total cost		+	=

In each column (that is, in each vertical line), the total cost is found by multiplying the unit cost by the amount. The *bottom row* of the chart gives us the equation.

Example 1 — A wholesaler makes up a 50-lb mixture of two kinds of coffee, one costing $3.40 per pound and the other costing $3.60 per pound. How many pounds of each kind of coffee must be used if the mixture is to cost $3.54 per pound?

Let
$$x = \text{Amount of \$3.40 coffee}$$
$$50 - x = \text{Amount of \$3.60 coffee}$$

	Ingredient A		Ingredient B		Mixture
Unit cost	$3.40		$3.60		$3.54
Amount	x	+	$50 - x$	=	50
Total cost	$3.40x	+	$3.60(50 - x)$	=	$3.54(50)

Notice that

$$\boxed{\begin{matrix} \text{Amount of} \\ \text{ingredient A} \end{matrix}} + \boxed{\begin{matrix} \text{Amount of} \\ \text{ingredient B} \end{matrix}} = \boxed{\begin{matrix} \text{Amount of} \\ \text{mixture} \end{matrix}}$$

$$x \quad + \quad (50 - x) \quad = \quad 50$$

and that

Total cost of ingredient A	+	Total cost of ingredient B	=	Total cost of mixture

$$3.40x + 3.60(50 - x) = 3.54(50)$$
$$340x + 360(50 - x) = 354(50)$$
$$340x + 18,000 - 360x = 17,700$$
$$-20x = -300$$
$$x = 15 \text{ lb} \qquad \text{\$3.40 coffee}$$
$$50 - x = 35 \text{ lb} \qquad \text{\$3.60 coffee}$$

Check Total cost of \$3.40 coffee is 15(\$3.40) =   \$51.00

Total cost of \$3.60 coffee is 35(\$3.60) = +126.00
$$\overline{\qquad \$177.00}$$

Total cost of mixture is 50(\$3.54) = \$177.00 ■

Example 2 Bill has \$3.85 in nickels, dimes, and quarters. If he has twice as many nickels as quarters and 34 coins altogether, how many of each kind of coin does he have?

Let $\qquad x =$ the number of quarters

$2x =$ the number of nickels Twice as many nickels as quarters

$34 - [x + 2x] =$ the number of dimes 34 coins in all

	Quarters	Nickels	Dimes	Mixture
Value of each coin	\$0.25	\$0.05	\$0.10	XXXXXXX XXXXXXX
Number of coins	x	$2x$	$34 - 3x$	34
Total value	\$0.25x	\$0.05($2x$)	\$0.10($34 - 3x$)	\$3.85

$$0.25x + 0.05(2x) + 0.10(34 - 3x) = 3.85$$
$$25x + 5(2x) + 10(34 - 3x) = 385$$
$$25x + 10x + 340 - 30x = 385$$
$$5x = 45$$
$$x = 9 \qquad \text{The number of quarters}$$
$$2x = 18 \qquad \text{The number of nickels}$$
$$34 - 3x = 7 \qquad \text{The number of dimes}$$

Check
$$\begin{array}{rl} 9 & \text{quarters: \$2.25} \\ 18 & \text{nickels: } 0.90 \\ 7 & \text{dimes: } 0.70 \\ \hline 34 & \text{coins} \qquad \text{\$3.85} \end{array}$$

There are twice as many nickels as quarters and two more quarters than dimes ■

EXERCISES 3.4

Set I In each exercise, set up the problem algebraically, solve, and check. Be sure to state what your variables represent.

1. A dealer makes up a 100-lb mixture of Colombian coffee costing $3.90 per pound and Brazilian coffee costing $3.60 per pound. How many pounds of each kind must be used in order for the mixture to cost $3.72 per pound?

2. A dealer makes up a 50-lb mixture of cashews and peanuts. If the cashews cost $7.60 a pound and the peanuts $2.60 a pound, how many pounds of each kind of nut must be used in order for the mixture to cost $4.20 a pound?

3. A 10-lb mixture of almonds and walnuts costs $39.72. If walnuts cost $4.50 a pound and almonds $3.00 a pound, how many pounds of each kind are there?

4. Mrs. Diederich paid $15.81 for a 6-lb mixture of granola and dried apple chunks. If the granola cost $2.10 a pound and the dried apple chunks cost $4.24 a pound, how many pounds of each kind did she buy?

5. Doris has 17 coins with a total value of $1.15. If all the coins are nickels or dimes, how many of each kind of coin does she have?

6. Heather has 17 coins with a total value of $3.35. If the coins are all dimes and quarters, how many of each kind of coin does she have?

7. Dianne has $3.20 in nickels, dimes, and quarters. If she has 7 more dimes than quarters and 3 times as many nickels as quarters, how many of each kind of coin does she have?

8. Trisha has $4.15 in nickels, dimes, and quarters. If she has 5 more nickels than dimes and twice as many quarters as dimes, how many of each kind of coin does she have?

9. Mrs. Robinson mixes 15 lb of English toffee candy costing $6.60 a pound with peanut brittle costing $4.20 a pound. How many pounds of peanut brittle must she use to make a mixture costing $5.10 a pound?

10. Mrs. Reid mixes 24 lb of macadamia nuts costing $8.30 a pound with peanuts costing $3.30 a pound. How many pounds of peanuts must she use to make a mixture costing $6.30 a pound?

11. Joyce spent $108.50 for 23 tickets to a movie. Some were for children and some for adults. If each child's ticket cost $3.50 and each adult's ticket cost $5.25, how many of each kind of ticket did she buy?

12. Jerry spent $9.18 for 45 stamps. Some were 18¢ stamps and some were 22¢ stamps. How many of each kind did he buy?

Set II In each exercise, set up the problem algebraically, solve, and check. Be sure to state what your variables represent.

1. A 100-lb mixture of Delicious and Spartan apples costs 96¢ a pound. If the Delicious apples cost 99¢ a pound and the Spartan apples cost 89¢ a pound, how many pounds of each kind should be used?

2. A delicatessen makes up a 40-pt mixture of peaches and pears for a fruit salad. Peaches cost 71¢ a pint and pears cost 79¢ a pint. If the 40-pt mixture costs $29.76, how many pints of each kind of fruit must be used?

3. Mrs. Koontz paid $36.85 for a 10-lb mixture of Brand A and Brand B coffee. If Brand A cost $3.85 a pound and Brand B cost $3.60 a pound, how many pounds of each brand did she buy?

4. A 5-lb mixture of caramels and nougats costs $11.27. If nougats cost $2.30 a pound and caramels $2.20 a pound, how many pounds of each kind are there?

5. Michelle has 14 coins with a total value of $1.85. If all the coins are dimes and quarters, how many of each kind of coin does she have?

6. Joey has 18 coins consisting of nickels, dimes, and quarters. If he has 5 more dimes than quarters and if the total value of the coins is $1.90, how many of each kind of coin does he have?

7. Michael has $2.25 in nickels, dimes, and quarters. If he has 3 fewer dimes than quarters and as many nickels as the sum of the dimes and quarters, how many of each kind of coin does he have?

8. A 50-lb mixture of Delicious and Granny Smith apples costs $47.70. If the Delicious apples cost 99¢ a pound and the Granny Smith apples cost 89¢ a pound, how many pounds of each kind are there?

9. Mrs. Curtis mixes 16 lb of Brand A coffee costing $3.50 a pound with Brand B coffee costing $3.60 a pound. If the mixture is to cost $3.56 a pound, how many pounds of Brand B should she use?

10. Jennifer's piggy bank contains nickels, dimes, and quarters. She has 4 more dimes than quarters and 3 times as many nickels as dimes. The total value of the coins is $5.00. How many of each kind of coin does she have?

11. A 50-lb mixture of Red Delicious and Granny Smith apples costs $53.30. If the Red Delicious apples cost $1.29 a pound and the Granny Smith apples cost 89¢ a pound, how many pounds of each kind are there?

12. A dealer makes up a 10-lb mixture of dried tropical fruit and raisins. The tropical fruit costs $1.58 a pound, and the raisins cost $1.38 a pound. How many pounds of each should be used if the mixture is to cost $1.49 a pound?

3.5 Solution Problems

Another type of mixture problem, found in chemistry and nursing, involves the mixing of liquids. Such problems are often called *solution problems* because a mixture of two or more liquids is, under certain conditions, a solution.*

A "60% solution of alcohol" is a mixture that is 60% pure alcohol and 40% water. To find the number of milliliters of pure alcohol in, for example, 80 ml of a 60% solution of alcohol, change 60% to a decimal (0.6) and multiply that number by 80 ml (answer: 48 ml). If we add pure alcohol to a solution to get a *stronger* solution, we are adding a 100% solution of alcohol. If we add water to obtain a *weaker* solution, we are adding a 0% solution of alcohol.

An alloy of metals is often a solution, too. To find the amount of pure tin in 10 oz of a lead-tin alloy that is 18% tin, change 18% to 0.18 and multiply 0.18 by 10 oz (answer: 1.8 oz).

---

* A **solution** is a homogeneous mixture of two or more substances.

Solution problems can be solved by using a method similar to the one used for solving mixture problems. The chart is as follows:

	Ingredient A	Ingredient B	Mixture
Percent			
Amount		+	=
Total amount of pure substance		+	=

In each column (vertical line), the total amount of the substance is found by multiplying the percent (changed to a decimal or common fraction) by the amount.

TWO RELATIONSHIPS NECESSARY TO SOLVE SOLUTION PROBLEMS

1. $\left(\begin{array}{c}\text{Amount of}\\\text{ingredient A}\end{array}\right) + \left(\begin{array}{c}\text{Amount of}\\\text{ingredient B}\end{array}\right) = \left(\begin{array}{c}\text{Amount of}\\\text{mixture}\end{array}\right)$

2. $\left(\begin{array}{c}\text{Total amount of}\\\text{pure substance}\\\text{from ingredient A}\end{array}\right) + \left(\begin{array}{c}\text{Total amount of}\\\text{pure substance}\\\text{from ingredient B}\end{array}\right) = \left(\begin{array}{c}\text{Total amount of}\\\text{pure substance}\\\text{in mixture}\end{array}\right)$

Example 1

How many milliliters (ml) of water must be added to 60 ml of a 5% glycerin solution to reduce it to a 2% solution?

Let x = number of ml of water to be added

	5% solution	Water	Mixture
Percent	0.05	0.0	0.02
Amount	60 +	x =	60 + x
Total amount of pure glycerin	0.05(60) +	0.0x =	0.02(60 + x)

Amount of glycerin in 5% solution	+	Amount of glycerin in water added	=	Amount of glycerin in 2% solution
0.05(60)	+	0	=	0.02(60 + x)
5(60)	+	0	=	2(60 + x)

$$300 = 120 + 2x$$
$$180 = 2x$$
$$90 = x$$
$$x = 90 \text{ ml of water} \quad \blacksquare$$

Example 2 How many liters of a 20% alcohol solution must be added to 3 ℓ of a 90% alcohol solution to make an 80% solution?

Let x = number of liters of 20% solution

	20% solution	90% solution	Mixture
Percent	0.20	0.90	0.80
Amount	x +	3 =	$x + 3$
Total	$0.20x$ +	$0.90(3)$ =	$0.80(x + 3)$

$$\underset{\text{in 20\% solution}}{\text{Amount of alcohol}} + \underset{\text{in 90\% solution}}{\text{Amount of alcohol}} = \underset{\text{in 80\% solution}}{\text{Amount of alcohol}}$$

$$0.20x + 0.90(3) = 0.80(x + 3)$$
$$2x + 9(3) = 8(x + 3)$$
$$2x + 27 = 8x + 24$$
$$3 = 6x$$
$$\frac{1}{2} = x$$

$$x = \frac{1}{2} \ \ell \text{ of 20\% alcohol} \quad \blacksquare$$

EXERCISES 3.5

Set I   In each exercise, set up the problem algebraically, solve, and check. Be sure to state what your variables represent.

1. How many milliliters of water must be added to 500 ml of a 40% solution of hydrochloric acid to reduce it to a 25% solution?

2. How many liters of water must be added to 10 ℓ of a 30% solution of antifreeze to reduce it to a 20% solution?

3. How many liters of pure alcohol must be added to 10 ℓ of a 20% solution of alcohol to make a 50% solution?

4. How many milliliters of pure alcohol must be added to 1,000 ml of a 10% solution of alcohol to make a 40% solution?

5. How many cubic centimeters (cc) of a 20% solution of sulfuric acid must be mixed with 100 cc of a 50% solution to make a 25% solution of sulfuric acid?

6. How many pints of a 2% solution of disinfectant must be mixed with 5 pt of a 12% solution to make a 4% solution of disinfectant?

7. If 100 gal of 75% glycerin solution are made up by combining a 30% glycerin solution with a 90% glycerin solution, how much of each solution must be used?

8. Two copper alloys, one containing 65% copper and the other 20% copper, are to be mixed to produce an alloy that is 35% copper. How much of the 65% alloy should be used to obtain 1,200 g of an alloy that is 35% copper?

9. A chemist has two solutions of hydrochloric acid. One is a 40% solution, and the other is a 90% solution. How many liters of each should be mixed to get 10 ℓ of a 50% solution?

10. If whole milk contains 3.25% butterfat and nonfat milk contains 0.5% butterfat, how much whole milk should be added to 1,000 ml of nonfat milk to obtain milk with 2% butterfat?

Set II   In each exercise, set up the problem algebraically, solve, and check. Be sure to state what your variables represent.

1. How many cubic centimeters of water must be added to 600 cc of a 20% solution of potassium chloride to reduce it to a 5% solution?

2. How many milliliters of a 36% solution of hydrochloric acid should be added to 1,000 ml of a 60% solution to make a 56% solution?

3. How many liters of pure alcohol must be added to 200 ℓ of a 5% solution to make a 62% solution?

4. A 30% solution of antifreeze is to be mixed with an 80% solution of antifreeze to make 1,000 ml (1 ℓ) of a 40% solution. How many milliliters of each should be used?

5. How many cubic centimeters of a 25% solution of nitric acid must be mixed with 100 cc of a 5% solution to make a 21% solution?

6. A 30% acetic acid solution must be mixed with a 5% acetic acid solution to obtain 100 ℓ of a 25% acetic acid solution. How many liters each of the 30% solution and the 5% solution must be used?

7. A chemist has two solutions of hydrochloric acid, one a 40% solution and the other a 90% solution. How many liters of each should be mixed to get 20 ℓ of a 75% solution?

8. If 1,500 cc of a 10% dextrose solution is made up by combining a 20% solution with a 5% solution, how much of each solution must be used?

9. A certain fertilizer has a 20% nitrogen content. Another fertilizer is 40% nitrogen. How much of each should be mixed together to get a 100-kg mixture with a 32% nitrogen content?

10. How many liters of a 24% acetic acid solution must be mixed with 3 ℓ of a 32% solution to make a 28.8% solution?

3.6 Miscellaneous Word Problems

Some word problems involve the individual digits of a number. Consider the number 59. In that number, we say that 5 is the *tens digit* and 9 is the *units digit*. The number itself equals $5(10) + 9$. In general, a two-digit number equals the tens digit times ten *plus* the units digit. A three-digit number equals the hundreds digit times 100 *plus* the tens digit times 10 *plus* the units digit.

If we reverse the digits in a two-digit number, the new number will be the old units digit times 10 *plus* the old tens digit. For example, if we reverse the digits of the number 75, which is $7(10) + 5$, we get the number 57, which is $5(10) + 7$.

Example 1   The sum of the digits of a two-digit number is 8. The number formed by reversing the digits is 36 more than the original number. Find the original number.

Let $\qquad x =$ Units digit

$$\underline{8 - x = \text{Tens digit}}$$
$$8 \qquad \text{(Sum of the digits is 8)}$$

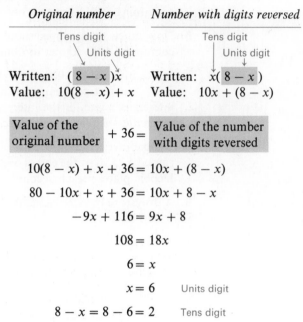

Original number	Number with digits reversed
Written: $(8 - x)x$	Written: $x(8 - x)$
Value: $10(8 - x) + x$	Value: $10x + (8 - x)$

Value of the original number $+ 36 = $ Value of the number with digits reversed

$$10(8 - x) + x + 36 = 10x + (8 - x)$$
$$80 - 10x + x + 36 = 10x + 8 - x$$
$$-9x + 116 = 9x + 8$$
$$108 = 18x$$
$$6 = x$$
$$x = 6 \qquad \text{Units digit}$$
$$8 - x = 8 - 6 = 2 \qquad \text{Tens digit}$$

Therefore, the original number is 26.

Check   Sum of digits $= 2 + 6 = 8$
Original number 26
Increased by $\quad\underline{36}$
62 Number with digits reversed ∎

The exercise sets in this section include a variety of different kinds of word problems, some of which have not been discussed. We leave it to students to devise their own solutions, guided by the general method of solving word problems given in Section 3.1.

EXERCISES 3.6

Set I   In each exercise, set up the problem algebraically, solve, and check. Be sure to state what your variables represent.

1. The sum of the digits of a two-digit number is 13. The number formed by reversing the digits is 27 more than the original number. Find the original number.

2. The sum of the digits of a two-digit number is 7. The number formed by reversing the digits is 27 less than the original number. Find the original number.

3. The units digit of a three-digit number is twice the hundreds digit. The sum of the digits is 6. If the digits are reversed, the new number is 198 more than the original number. Find the original number.

4. The units digit of a three-digit number is twice the hundreds digit. The sum of the digits is 11. If the digits are reversed, the new number is 297 more than the original number. Find the original number.

For Exercises 5 and 6, use the following: Nickel coinage is composed of copper and nickel in the ratio of 3 to 1.

5. How much pure copper should be melted with 20 lb of a copper-nickel alloy containing 60% copper to obtain the alloy for nickel coinage?

6. How much pure copper should be melted with 30 lb of a copper-nickel alloy containing 40% copper to obtain the alloy for nickel coinage?

7. Janice invested $13,000. Part of the money was placed in an account that paid 5.25% interest per year, and the rest was put into an account that paid 5.75% interest per year. If the interest Janice earned the first year was $702.50, how much did she place in each account?

8. Debbie invested $1,400. Part of the money earned 6.25% per year, and the rest earned 5.75%. At the end of one year, the interest paid was $83.50. How much did Debbie place in each account?

9. A drugstore buys 18 cameras. If it had bought 10 cameras of a higher quality, it would have paid $48 more per camera for the same total expenditure. Find the price of each type of camera.

10. A discount store buys 25 stereos. If it had bought 14 stereos of a higher quality, it would have paid $55 more per stereo for the same total expenditure. Find the price of each type of stereo.

Set II   In each exercise, set up the problem algebraically, solve, and check. Be sure to state what your variables represent.

1. The sum of the digits of a two-digit number is 12. The number formed by reversing the digits is 36 more than the original number. Find the original number.

2. The ratio of the tens digit to the units digit of a two-digit number is 3 to 2. The sum of the digits is 10. What is the number?

3. The units digit of a three-digit number is 3 times the hundreds digit. The sum of the digits is 12. If the digits are reversed, the new number is 594 more than the original number. Find the original number.

4. The tens digit of a two-digit number is 4 times the units digit. If the digits are reversed, the new number is 54 less than the original number. Find the original number.

5. How much pure copper should be melted with 50 lb of a copper-nickel alloy containing 40% copper to obtain an alloy that is 50% copper?

6. George has received exam scores of 83, 75, 62, and 87. What score must he receive on the fifth exam in order to have an average score of 80?

7. Jim invested $20,000. Some of the money was invested at 7.4% interest per year, and the rest was invested at 6.8%. The amount of interest he earned for the year was $1,469.20. How much did he invest at each rate?

8. Tickets for some seats at a concert sold for $9 each, and tickets for better seats sold for $12 each. If 1,000 tickets were sold in all and if the amount of money brought in was $10,320, how many of the $9 tickets were sold?

9. A drugstore buys 22 cameras. If it had bought 15 cameras of a higher quality, it would have paid $35 more per camera for the same total expenditure. Find the price of each type of camera.

10. Scott is 6 times as old as Sharon. In 20 years, Scott will be only twice as old as Sharon. How old is Scott now?

3.7 Review: 3.1–3.6

Method for Solving Word Problems 3.1

1. Read the problem very carefully. Try to determine what type of problem it is, if possible. *Be sure you understand the problem.* Don't try to solve it at this point.

2. Determine what is unknown. What is being asked for?

3. Represent one unknown number by a variable, and declare the meaning in a sentence of the form "Let $x = \ldots$." Then reread the problem to see how you can represent any other unknown numbers in terms of the same variable.

4. Reread the entire word problem, translating each English phrase into an algebraic expression.

5. Fit the algebraic expressions together into an equation or inequality.

6. Using the methods described in Chapter 2, solve the equation or inequality for the variable.

7. Answer all of the questions asked in the problem.

8. Check the solution in the word statement.

Review Exercises 3.7 Set I

In each exercise, set up the problem algebraically, solve, and check. Be sure to state what your variables represent.

1. When 5 times an unknown number is subtracted from 28 and the result is divided by 3, the quotient is 3 times the unknown number. Find the unknown number.

2. The sum of three consecutive integers is 23. What are the integers?

3. The sides of a triangle are in the ratio $3:7:8$. The perimeter is to be less than 36. What is the range of values that the *shortest* side can have?

4. Gwen has $2.20 in nickels, dimes, and quarters. If she has 3 more dimes than quarters and 2 fewer nickels than quarters, how many of each kind of coin does she have?

5. A dealer makes up a 15-lb mixture of different candies costing $2.20 and $2.60 a pound. How many pounds of each kind of candy must be used for the mixture to cost $2.36 a pound?

6. How many cubic centimeters of water must be added to 10 cc of a 17% solution of a disinfectant to reduce it to a 0.2% solution?

7. Mr. Sontag takes 30 min to drive to work in the morning, but he takes 45 min to return home over the same route during the evening rush hour. If his average morning speed is 10 mph faster than his average evening speed, how far is it from his home to his work?

8. The sum of the digits of a two-digit number is 11. If the digits are reversed, the new number is 45 less than the original number. What is the original number?

9. Mr. Curtis invested part of $27,000 at 12% interest and the remainder at 8%. His total yearly income from these two investments is $2,780. How much is invested at each rate?

Review Exercises 3.7 Set II

NAME _____

In each exercise, set up the problem algebraically, solve, and check. Be sure to state what your variables represent.

ANSWERS

1. Dimitri has 19 coins in her pocket with a total value of $3.10. If all the coins are dimes or quarters, how many of each does she have?

1. _____

_____

2. _____

3. _____

2. How many cubic centimeters of a 50% phenol solution must be added to 400 cc of a 5% solution to make it a 10% solution?

4. _____

5. _____

_____

3. After sailing downstream for 2 hr, it takes a boat 7 hr to return to its starting point. If the speed of the boat in still water is 9 mph, what is the speed of the stream?

4. The sum of the digits of a two-digit number is 10. If the digits are reversed, the new number is 72 less than the original number. Find the original number.

5. Mrs. McMahon paid $5.63 for a total of 12 cans of beef soup and tomato soup. If the beef soup costs 65¢ a can and the tomato soup 34¢ a can, how many cans of each kind of soup did she buy?

6. The sum of three consecutive integers is -222. Find the integers.

7. The ratio of the length to the width of a rectangle is 7 to 3. The perimeter is to be less than or equal to 40. What is the range of values that the width can have?

8. When 7 times an unknown number is subtracted from 120 and the result is divided by 2, the quotient is 46. Find the unknown number.

9. Mr. Reid had $15,000 to invest. Part of the money was invested at 7.8% interest per year, and the rest was invested at 7.2% interest per year. If the amount of money earned the first year was $1,138.80, how much was invested at each rate?

Chapter 3 Diagnostic Test

The purpose of this test is to see how well you understand solving word problems. We recommend that you work this diagnostic test *before* your instructor tests you on this chapter. Allow yourself about 50 minutes.

Complete solutions for all the problems on this test, together with section references, are given in the answer section at the end of the book. For the problems you do incorrectly, study the sections cited.

Set up each problem algebraically and solve. Be sure to state what your variables represent.

1. When 23 is added to 4 times an unknown number, the sum is 31. Find the unknown number.

2. The sum of two consecutive integers is 55. Find the integers.

3. The length and width of a rectangle are in the ratio of 5 to 4. The perimeter is 90. Find the length and the width.

4. Linda has 14 coins with a total value of $2.15. If all the coins are dimes or quarters, how many of each kind of coin does she have?

5. A grocer makes up a 60-lb mixture of cashews and peanuts. If the cashews cost $7.40 a pound and the peanuts cost $2.80 a pound, how many pounds of each kind of nut must be used for the mixture to cost $4.18 a pound?

6. How many cubic centimeters of water must be added to 600 cc of a 20% solution of potassium chloride to reduce it to a 15% solution?

7. The units digit of a two-digit number is twice the tens digit. If the digits are reversed, the value is increased by 27. Find the original number.

8. Mrs. Rice invested part of $23,000 at 8% interest and the remainder at 10%. Her total yearly income from these two investments is $2,170. How much is invested at each rate?

9. Roy hikes from his camp to a mountain lake one day and returns the next day. He walks up to the lake at a rate of 3 mph and returns to his camp at a rate of 5 mph. If the hike to the lake takes Roy 2 hr longer than the return trip:

   a. How long does it take him to hike to the lake?

   b. How far is the lake from his camp?

Cumulative Review Exercises
Chapters 1–3

1. Given the numbers -2, $\frac{1}{2}$, 4.5, 1.4142136..., 10, 0, and 0.234234234...:

   a. Which are natural numbers?

   b. Which are real numbers?

   c. Which are rational numbers?

   d. Which are integers?

   e. Which are irrational numbers?

2. Simplify. Write the answer using only positive exponents.

$$\left(\frac{a^2b^2}{a^5b}\right)^{-2}$$

3. Given the formula $s = \frac{1}{2}gt^2$, find s if $g = 32$ and $t = 2$.

In Exercises 4 and 5, remove grouping symbols and combine like terms.

4. $2xy(4xy - 5x + 2) - 3y(2x^2y - x)$

5. $6 - \{4 - [3x - 2(5 - 3x)]\}$

In Exercises 6–10, solve each equation or inequality.

6. $\dfrac{x}{2} + \dfrac{x + 3}{3} = \dfrac{1}{6}$

7. $12 - 3(4x - 5) \geq 9(2 - x) - 6$

8. $-3 < 2x + 1 < 5$

9. $\left|\dfrac{2x - 6}{4}\right| = 1$

10. $|4x - 2| < 10$

In Exercises 11 and 12, set up the problem algebraically, solve, and check. Be sure to state what your variables represent.

11. The ratio of the length of a rectangle to its width is $7:4$. The perimeter is 66 in. Find the length and the width.

12. Bud invested $12,000. Part of the money was invested at 7.4% interest per year, and the rest was invested at 6.8% interest. If the amount of money earned the first year was $861.00, how much was invested at each rate?

4 Polynomials

In this chapter, we look in detail at a particular type of algebraic expression called a *polynomial*. Polynomials have the same importance in algebra that whole numbers have in arithmetic. Most of the work in arithmetic involves operations with whole numbers. In the same way, most of the work in algebra involves operations with polynomials.

4.1 Basic Definitions

Polynomials

A **polynomial in one variable** is an algebraic expression that has only terms of the form ax^n, where a stands for any real number, n stands for any positive integer (or zero), and x stands for any variable. For example, $3x^3 - 4x^2 + 2x - 5$ is a polynomial in x, because each of its terms is of the form ax^n. Reminder: $-5 = -5x^0$.

A polynomial with only one term is called a **monomial**, a polynomial with two terms is called a **binomial**, and a polynomial with three terms is called a **trinomial**. We will not use special names for polynomials of more than three terms.

Example 1   The following algebraic expressions are all polynomials in one variable:

a. $3x$ This polynomial is a monomial in x.

b. $4z^4 - 2z^2$ This polynomial is a binomial in z.

c. $7x^2 - 5x + 2$ This polynomial is a trinomial.

d. 5 This is a monomial; it is of the form $5x^0$ ($5x^0 = 5 \cdot 1 = 5$).

e. $x^3 + \frac{1}{3}x^2 - \frac{2}{5}x + 1$ ∎

If an algebraic expression contains terms with negative (or fractional*) exponents on the variables or if it contains terms with variables in a denominator or under a radical sign, then the algebraic expression is *not* a polynomial.

Example 2   The following algebraic expressions are *not* polynomials:

a. $4x^{-2}$ This expression is *not* a polynomial because it has a negative exponent on a variable.

b. $\dfrac{2}{x - 5}$ This is *not* a polynomial because the variable is in the denominator.

c. $\sqrt{x - 5}$ This is *not* a polynomial because the variable is under a radical sign. ∎

An algebraic expression with two variables is a **polynomial in two variables** if (1) it contains no negative or fractional exponents on the variables, (2) no variables are in denominators, and (3) no variables are under radical signs.

Example 3   The following algebraic expressions are polynomials in two variables:

a. $\sqrt{5}x^2y$ This polynomial is a monomial; note that *constants* can be under radical signs.

---

* Fractional exponents are discussed in Section 7.1.

b. $-3xy^3 + \frac{2}{3}x^2y$ This polynomial is a binomial; note that *constants* can be in denominators.

c. $4u^2v^2 - 7uv + 6$ This polynomial is a trinomial in u and v.

d. $(x - y)^2 - 2(x - y) - 8$ ∎

Degree of a Term of a Polynomial

If a polynomial has only one variable, then the **degree of any term** of that polynomial is the exponent on the variable in that term. If a polynomial has more than one variable, the degree of any term of that polynomial is the *sum* of the exponents on the variables in that term.

Example 4   Find the degree of each term:

a. 5^2x^3 3rd degree (only exponents of *variables* determine the degree of the term)

b. $6x^2y$ 3rd degree because $6x^2y = 6x^2y^1$
$$2 + 1 = 3$$

c. 14 0 degree because $14 = 14x^0$

d. $-2u^3vw^2$ 6th degree because $-2u^3vw^2 = -2u^3v^1w^2$
$$3 + 1 + 2 = 6$$ ∎

Degree of a Polynomial

The **degree of a polynomial** is defined to be the degree of its highest-degree term. Therefore, to find the degree of a polynomial, first find the degree of each of its terms. The *largest* of these numbers will be the degree of the polynomial.*

Example 5   Find the degree of each polynomial:

a. $9x^3 - 7x + 5$

    0 degree term
    1st degree term
    3rd degree term ← highest-degree term

Therefore, $9x^3 - 7x + 5$ is a 3rd degree polynomial.

b. $14uv^3 - 11u^5v + 8$

    0 degree term
    6th degree term ← highest-degree term
    4th degree term

Therefore, $14uv^3 - 11u^5v + 8$ is a 6th degree polynomial.   ∎

Leading Coefficient   The **leading coefficient** of a polynomial is the numerical coefficient of its highest degree term.

Descending Powers   When polynomials must be written in **descending powers** of one of the variables, the exponents of that variable must get smaller as we read from left to right.

Example 6   Arrange $5 - 2x^2 + 4x$ in descending powers of x and name the leading coefficient.

$-2x^2 + 4x + 5$.   The leading coefficient is -2.   ∎

A polynomial with more than one variable can be arranged in descending powers of *any one* of its variables.

---

* Mathematicians define the zero polynomial, 0, as having *no* degree.

Example 7   Arrange $3x^3y - 5xy + 2x^2y^2 - 10$ (a) in descending powers of x, (b) in descending powers of y.

a. $3x^3y + 2x^2y^2 - 5xy - 10$ Descending powers of x

b. $2x^2y^2 + 3x^3y - 5xy - 10$ Descending powers of y

Since y is the same power in both terms, the higher-degree term is written first   ■

Polynomial Equations

A **polynomial equation** is an equation that has a polynomial on both sides of the equal sign. The polynomial on one side of the equal sign can be the zero polynomial, 0. The **degree of the equation** equals the degree of the term in the equation with the *highest degree*.

Example 8   Examples of polynomial equations:

a. $5x - 3 = 3x + 4$ This equation is a 1st degree polynomial equation in one variable.

b. $2x^2 - 4x + 7 = 0$ This equation is a 2nd degree equation in one variable. It is also called a *quadratic equation*.   ■

EXERCISES 4.1

Set I   In Exercises 1–16, if the expression is a polynomial, find its degree. If it is *not* a polynomial, write "Not a polynomial."

1. $2x^2 + \frac{1}{3}x$ **2.** $\frac{1}{9}y^2 - 5$ **3.** $x^{-2} + 5x^{-1} + 4$

4. $y^{-3} + y^{-2} + 6$ **5.** 10   **6.** 20

7. $\frac{4}{x} + 7x - 3$ **8.** $\frac{3}{x} - 2x + 5$ **9.** $\sqrt{5x + 6}$

10. $\sqrt{2y} - 5$ **11.** $\sqrt{x + 4}$ **12.** $\sqrt{z - 3}$

13. $\frac{1}{2y^2 - 5y} - 3y$ **14.** $\frac{1}{2x^2 + 4x} + 5x$

15. $x^3y^3 - 3^7x^2y + 3^4xy^2 - y^3$ **16.** $2^7y^2z^3 - 3yz^5 + 6z^4$

In Exercises 17–20, write each polynomial in descending powers of the indicated variable and find the leading coefficient.

17. $7x^3 - 4x - 5 + 8x^5$ Powers of x

18. $10 - 3y^5 + 4y^2 - 2y^3$ Powers of y

19. $3x^2y + 8x^3 + y^3 - y^5$ Powers of y

20. $6y^3 + 7x^2 - 4y^2 + y$ Powers of y

Set II   In Exercises 1–16, if the expression is a polynomial, find its degree. If it is *not* a polynomial, write "Not a polynomial."

1. $4x^3 - \frac{1}{2}x$ **2.** $\sqrt{3x} - 5$ **3.** $x^{-3} - 3x^2 + 3$

4. $4x^3 + 2x^2z^2 - 6$ **5.** 7   **6.** $\sqrt{8 - 3x}$

7. $\frac{3}{x} - 4x + 2$ **8.** $\frac{3}{4}x^5 - 2x^3y^3 + 3$ **9.** $\sqrt{3y} + 2$

10. $\dfrac{3}{x^3 + 2x^2 - 5x + 1}$ **11.** $\sqrt{x - 2}$ **12.** $3^5x + \sqrt{5}$

13. $5z + \dfrac{1}{3x^3 + 7x}$ **14.** $y^{-3} - 2y^{-2} + 3y$

15. $x^4y^3 + 2^8x^3y^2 - 3xy^5$ **16.** x

In Exercises 17-20, write each polynomial in descending powers of the indicated variable and find the leading coefficient.

17. $12b^2 - 14b^4 + 8 - 7b$ Powers of b

18. $8 - 2x + 13x^2y + 2x^4$ Powers of x

19. $3xy + 4y^5 - 3y^2 - 3$ Powers of y

20. $4st^2 - 9s^2t + 3s^2t^3 - 5t^6$ Powers of t

4.2 Addition and Subtraction of Polynomials

Addition

Polynomials can be added horizontally by removing the grouping symbols and combining like terms, as was done in Section 1.14. It is often helpful to underline all like terms with the same kind of line before adding.

Example 1   Add the polynomials.

$$(5x^3y^2 - 3x^2y^2 + 4xy^3) + (4x^2y^2 - 2xy^2) + (-7x^3y^2 + 6xy^2 - 3xy^3)$$

$$= 5x^3y^2 - 3x^2y^2 + 4xy^3 + 4x^2y^2 - 2xy^2 - 7x^3y^2 + 6xy^2 - 3xy^3$$

$$= -2x^3y^2 + x^2y^2 + xy^3 + 4xy^2 \quad \blacksquare$$

Vertical addition is sometimes desirable or necessary. In this case, it is important to have all like terms lined up vertically.

TO ADD POLYNOMIALS VERTICALLY

1. Arrange them under one another so that like terms are in the same vertical line.

2. Find the sum of the terms in each vertical line by adding the numerical coefficients.

Example 2   Add $(3x^2 + 2x - 1) + (2x + 5) + (4x^3 + 7x^2 - 6)$.

$$
\begin{array}{r}
3x^2 + 2x - 1 \\
2x + 5 \\
4x^3 + 7x^2 - 6 \\
\hline
4x^3 + 10x^2 + 4x - 2
\end{array}
\quad \blacksquare
$$

Subtraction

Polynomials can be subtracted horizontally by removing grouping symbols and combining like terms (see Section 1.14). Remember that "subtract 3 from 5" means $5 - 3$, *not* $3 - 5$.

Example 3　Subtract $(-4x^2y + 10xy^2 + 9xy - 7)$ from $(11x^2y - 8xy^2 + 7xy + 2)$.

$$(11x^2y - 8xy^2 + 7xy + 2) - (-4x^2y + 10xy^2 + 9xy - 7)$$
$$= 11x^2y - 8xy^2 + 7xy + 2 + 4x^2y - 10xy^2 - 9xy + 7$$
$$= 15x^2y - 18xy^2 - 2xy + 9 \quad \blacksquare$$

It is necessary to know how to subtract polynomials vertically in order to be able to use long division in dividing one polynomial by another.

TO SUBTRACT POLYNOMIALS VERTICALLY

1. Write the polynomial being subtracted *under* the polynomial it is being subtracted from. Write like terms in the same vertical line.

2. *Mentally* change the sign of each term in the polynomial being subtracted.*

3. Find the sum of the *resulting* terms in each vertical line by adding the numerical coefficients.

Example 4　Subtract $(4x^2y^2 + 7x^2y - 2xy + 9)$ from $(6x^2y^2 - 2x^2y + 5xy + 8)$ vertically.

Signs changed mentally

$$6x^2y^2 - 2x^2y + 5xy + 8$$
$$4x^2y^2 + 7x^2y - 2xy + 9$$
$$\overline{2x^2y^2 - 9x^2y + 7xy - 1}$$

Example 4—Alternate method
Sign changes shown

$$6x^2y^2 - 2x^2y + 5xy + 8$$
$$\ominus \quad \ominus \quad \oplus \quad \ominus$$
$$4x^2y^2 + 7x^2y - 2xy + 9$$
$$\overline{2x^2y^2 - 9x^2y + 7xy - 1} \quad \blacksquare$$

EXERCISES 4.2

Set I　In Exercises 1–4, perform the indicated operations.

1. $(-3x^4 - 2x^3 + 5) + (2x^4 + x^3 - 7x - 12)$

2. $(-5y^3 + 3y^2 - 3y) + (3y^3 - y + 4)$

3. $(7 - 8v^3 + 9v^2 + 4v) - (9v^3 + 6 - 8v^2 + 4v)$

4. $(3x + 7x^3 - x^2 - 5) - (3x^2 - 6x^3 + 2 - 5x)$

5. Add:　$4x^3 + 7x^2 - 5x + 4$
$2x^3 - 5x^2 + 5x - 6$

---

* Your instructor may allow or require you to *show* the sign changes. See Example 4—Alternate method.

6. Add: $\quad 3y^4 - 2y^3 + 4y + 10$
$\qquad\underline{-5y^4 + 2y^3 + 4y - 6}$

7. Subtract $(6 + 3x^5 - 4x^2)$ from $(4x^3 + 6 + x)$.

8. Subtract $(7 - 4x^4 + 3x^3)$ from $(x^3 + 7 - 3x)$.

9. Subtract $(3y^4 + 2y^3 - 5y)$ from $(2y^4 + 4y^3 + 8)$.

10. Subtract $(2y^3 - 3y^2 + 4)$ from $(7y^3 + 5y^2 - 5y)$.

In Exercises 11–14, subtract the bottom polynomial from the top polynomial.

11. $\quad -3x^4 - 2x^3 \qquad + 4x - 3$
$\qquad\underline{2x^4 + 5x^3 - x^2 \qquad - 1}$

12. $\quad -2x^4 \qquad + 3x^2 - x + 1$
$\qquad\underline{- x^3 - 2x^2 + x - 5}$

13. $\quad5x^3 - 3x^2 + 7x - 17$
$\qquad\underline{-2x^3 - 7x^2 \qquad - 6}$

14. $\quad2x^3 + 7x^2 - 3x - 12$
$\qquad\underline{-5x^3 + 9x^2 - 2x}$

15. Subtract $(-3m^2n^2 + 2mn - 7)$ from the sum of $(6m^2n^2 - 8mn + 9)$ and $(-10m^2n^2 + 18mn - 11)$.

16. Subtract $(-9u^2v + 8uv^2 - 16)$ from the sum of $(7u^2v - 5uv^2 + 14)$ and $(11u^2v + 17uv^2 - 13)$.

17. Subtract the sum of $(x^3y + 3xy^2 - 4)$ and $(2x^3y - xy^2 + 5)$ from the sum of $(5 + xy^2 + x^3y)$ and $(-6 - 3xy^2 + 4x^3y)$.

18. Subtract the sum of $(2m^2n - 4mn^2 + 6)$ and $(-3m^2n + 5mn^2 - 4)$ from the sum of $(5 + m^2n - mn^2)$ and $(3 + 4m^2n + 2mn^2)$.

In Exercises 19 and 20, perform the indicated operations.

19. $(8.586x^2 - 9.030x + 6.976) - [1.946x^2 - 41.45x - (7.468 - 3.914x^2)]$

20. $(24.21 - 35.28x - 73.92x^2) - [82.04x - 53.29x^2 - (64.34 - 19.43x^2)]$

Set II   In Exercises 1–4, perform the indicated operations.

1. $(-3x^5 + 2x^3 - 4x + 1) + (-4x^5 + 2x^2 - 4x - 6)$

2. $(-5x^4 - 2x^3 + 6x^2 - 3) - (-2x^4 + 4x^3 + 3x + 4)$

3. $(4x^5 + 3x^4 - 2x^2 + 5) - (-x^4 + x^3 - x^2 + x)$

4. $(-8y^3 - y^2 + 7y - 6) - (-8y^3 - y^2 + 7y - 6)$

In Exercises 5 and 6, add the two polynomials.

5. $\quad 13h^3 - 8h^2 + 16h - 14$
$\qquad\underline{6h^3 + 5h^2 - 18h + 9}$

6. $\quad3x^3 - 2x^2 + 5x - 3$
$\qquad\underline{-7x^3 \qquad - 9x - 4}$

7. Subtract $(22 + 8y^2 - 14y)$ from $(11y^2 - 5y - 12y^3)$.

8. Subtract $(5x^3 - 3x - x^4)$ from $(-3x^2 - x^4 + 7 - x)$.

9. Subtract $(w - 12w^3 - 15 - 18w^2)$ from $(18w^3 + 5 - 9w)$.

10. Subtract $(z^3 - 3z^2 + 2 - z)$ from $(5z - z^3 + z^2)$.

In Exercises 11–14, subtract the bottom polynomial from the top polynomial.

11. $2x^3 - 5x^2 \qquad - 3$
$\underline{5x^3 + 2x^2 - 3x + 7}$

12. $-4y^4 + 6y^3 + 2y^2 \qquad - 6$
$\underline{\quad 3y^4 \qquad + 6y^2 - y + 5}$

13. $\quad 7z^3 - 6z^2 + 4z$
$\underline{-4z^3 - 8z^2 + 8z - 2}$

14. $-2x^3 + \ x^2$
$\underline{-6x^3 - 3x^2 - 5x + 4}$

15. Subtract $(5xy - 12 + 3xy^2)$ from the sum of $(7x^2y + 4xy^2 - 5)$ and $(8xy^2 - 7x^2y + xy)$.

16. Subtract the sum of $(2x^3 - 5x + 4)$ and $(-5x^3 + 2x^2 - 2)$ from $(x^3 - 2x^2 - 3x)$.

17. Given the polynomials $(10a^3 - 8a + 12)$, $(11a^2 + 9a - 14)$, and $(-6a^3 + 17a)$, subtract the sum of the first two from the sum of the last two.

18. Subtract the sum of $(4m^3n^3 - 10mn)$ and $(-10m^2n^2 - 15mn)$ from the sum of $(5m^3n^3 - 8m^2n^2 + 20mn)$ and $(-14m^2n^2 + 5mn)$.

In Exercises 19 and 20, perform the indicated operations.

19. $(55.26x - 41.37 - 72.84x^2) - [28.10 - 19.05x - (89.91x^2 - 13.33)]$

20. $(23.1x^2 - 3.4x + 2) - [3.05x - 4.6x^2 - (5.13x^2 + 8.1)]$

4.3 Multiplication of Polynomials

When we multiply a monomial by a monomial, we use the techniques described in Section 1.11C (see Example 15 in that section). For example, $(3xy^2)(2x^3y^3) = 6x^4y^5$.

When we multiply a monomial by a polynomial with *more* than one term, we use the distributive rule (see Section 1.14B). For example, $7xy^3(3x - 1) = 21x^2y^3 - 7xy^3$.

4.3A Products of Two Binomials

Since we often need to find the product of two binomials, it is helpful to be able to find their product by inspection. First, however, the step-by-step procedure for multiplying two binomials is shown.

Example 1   Multiply $(2x + 3)(x + 5)$.

In Step 1, $(2x + 3)$ is distributed over $x + 5$.

$$(2x + 3)(x + 5) = (2x + 3)(x) + (2x + 3)(5) \qquad \text{Step 1}$$
$$= 2x^2 + 3x + 10x + 15 \qquad \text{Step 2}$$
$$= 2x^2 + 13x + 15 \qquad \text{Step 3}$$

The distributive rule is used again in Step 2; in that step, the two *middle terms* are $3x$ and $10x$. We call $3x$ (the product of the two "inside" terms) the *inner product*, and we call $10x$ (the product of the two "outside" terms) the *outer product*.

Outer product $= 10x$

$(2x + 3)(x + 5)$

Inner product $= 3x$

Product of two first terms is $(2x)(x) = 2x^2$

Product of two last terms is $3(5) = 15$ ■

When a multiplication problem is in the form $(ax + by)(cx + dy)$, as in Example 1, the multiplication can be done very quickly using the following rules:

TO MULTIPLY $(ax + by)(cx + dy)$

1. The *first term* of the product is the product of the first terms of the binomials.

2. The *middle term* of the product is the sum of the inner and outer products.

3. The *last term* of the product is the product of the last terms of the binomials.

When we use this method of multiplying binomials, we find the product of the two *First* terms, the *Outer* product, the *Inner* product, and the product of the two *Last* terms. For this reason, this procedure is often called the FOIL method.

Example 2   Multiply $(3x + 2y)(4x - 5y)$.

Product of first terms
Product of last terms

$$(3x + 2y)(4x - 5y) = 12x^2 - 7xy - 10y^2$$

Sum of inner and outer products

■

Practice this procedure until you can write the answer without having to write down any intermediate steps. We call this finding the product by inspection.

We can use the FOIL method to find the product of two binomials even when the problem is *not* in the form $(ax + by)(cx + dy)$. See Examples 3 and 4.

Example 3   Multiply $(2x + 3)(5y - 7)$.

$$(2x + 3)(5y - 7) = 10xy - 14x + 15y - 21$$ ■

Example 4   Multiply $(3x^2 + 2)(x + 5)$.

$$(3x^2 + 2)(x + 5) = 3x^3 + 15x^2 + 2x + 10$$ ■

In Examples 3 and 4, the inner and outer products are not like terms, so they cannot be combined.

EXERCISES 4.3A

Set I   Find the products.

1. $(x + 5)(x + 4)$ **2.** $(y + 3)(y + 7)$ **3.** $(y + 8)(y - 9)$

4. $(z + 10)(z - 3)$ **5.** $(3x + 4)(2x - 5)$ **6.** $(2y + 5)(4y - 3)$

7. $(4x + 5y)(4x - 5y)$ **8.** $(s - 2t)(s + 2t)$ **9.** $(2x - 3y)(5x - y)$

10. $(6u - v)(3u - 4v)$ **11.** $(7z - 2)(8w + 3)$ **12.** $(9z - 1)(4x + 5)$

13. $(8x - 9y)(8x + 9y)$ **14.** $(7w + 2x)(7w - 2x)$ **15.** $(2s^2 + 5)(s + 1)$

16. $(3u^2 + 2)(u + 1)$ **17.** $(2x - y)(2x - y)$ **18.** $(5z - w)(5z - w)$

19. $(2x + 3)(3y - 4)$ **20.** $(4u - 2)(3v - 5)$ **21.** $(7x^2 - 3)(7x^2 - 3)$

22. $(4x^2 - 5)(4x^2 - 5)$ **23.** $(3x - 4)(2x^2 + 5)$ **24.** $(5y - 2)(3y^2 + 1)$

25. $3x(2x - 4)(x - 1)$ **26.** $7x(x + 3)(2x - 5)$

Set II   Find the products.

1. $(z + 2)(z + 5)$ **2.** $(x - 9)(x + 2)$ **3.** $(z + 4)(z - 5)$

4. $(y - 6)(y - 4)$ **5.** $(6x + 2)(2x - 6)$ **6.** $(3x^2 + 3)(x - 1)$

7. $(3x + 4y)(3x - 4y)$ **8.** $(x + 8y)(x + 8y)$ **9.** $(3x - y)(5x - 7y)$

10. $(2x - 3)(5 - y)$ **11.** $(8x + 3)(3y - 2)$ **12.** $(4x + 5)(2x^2 + 7)$

13. $(6y - 5z)(6y + 5z)$ **14.** $(7x - y)(7x - y)$ **15.** $(8x^2 + 7)(x + 1)$

16. $(3x^3 - 4)(2x^3 + 3)$ **17.** $(3x - y)(3x - y)$ **18.** $(4x^2 - 1)(4x^2 + 1)$

19. $(2x - 1)(y - 4)$ **20.** $(2x - 1)(x - 4)$ **21.** $(2x^2 - 6)(2x^2 - 6)$

22. $(x - 6)(2x - 3)$ **23.** $(7x - 1)(2x^2 + 3)$ **24.** $(x + 1)(x + 1)$

25. $5x(3x + 2)(2x - 4)$ **26.** $3x^2(4x - 1)(x + 2)$

4.3B   Multiplying a Polynomial by a Polynomial

When each of the polynomials has several terms, we must apply the distributive rule at least twice.

Example 5   Multiply $(x^2 - 3x + 2)(x - 5)$.

$$(x^2 - 3x + 2)(x - 5) = \boxed{(x^2 - 3x + 2)}\, x + \boxed{(x^2 - 3x + 2)}\,(-5)$$
$$= x^3 - 3x^2 + 2x - 5x^2 + 15x - 10$$
$$= x^3 - 8x^2 + 17x - 10$$

The same work can be arranged vertically, as follows:

$$
\begin{array}{r}
x^2 - 3x + 2 \\
x - 5 \\
\hline
-5x^2 + 15x - 10 \\
x^3 - 3x^2 + 2x \\
\hline
x^3 - 8x^2 + 17x - 10
\end{array}
$$

Product $(x^2 - 3x + 2)(-5)$

Product $(x^2 - 3x + 2)(x)$

Notice that the second line is moved one place to the left so like terms are in the same vertical line ∎

Example 6   Multiply $(2m + 2m^4 - 5 - 3m^2)(2 + m^2 - 3m)$.

Note that $0m^3$ was written in to save a place for the m^3 terms that arise in the multiplication

$$
\begin{array}{r}
2m^4 + 0m^3 - 3m^2 + 2m - 5 \\
m^2 - 3m + 2 \\
\hline
4m^4 \qquad - 6m^2 + 4m - 10 \\
-6m^5 \qquad + 9m^3 - 6m^2 + 15m \\
2m^6 \qquad - 3m^4 + 2m^3 - 5m^2 \\
\hline
2m^6 - 6m^5 + m^4 + 11m^3 - 17m^2 + 19m - 10
\end{array}
$$

Multiplication is simplified by first arranging the polynomials in descending powers of m

Always be careful to line up like terms. (See Example 7.)

Example 7   Multiply $(3a^2b - 6ab^2)(2ab - 5)$.

$$
\begin{array}{r}
3a^2b - 6ab^2 \\
2ab - 5 \\
\hline
-15a^2b + 30ab^2 \\
6a^3b^2 - 12a^2b^3 \\
\hline
6a^3b^2 - 12a^2b^3 - 15a^2b + 30ab^2
\end{array}
$$

Notice that the second line is moved over far enough so only like terms are in the same vertical line

EXERCISES 4.3B

Set I   Find the products.

1. $(2h - 3)(4h^2 - 5h + 7)$ **2.** $(5k - 6)(2k^2 + 7k - 3)$

3. $(4 + a^4 + 3a^2 - 2a)(a + 3)$ **4.** $(3b - 5 + b^4 - 2b^3)(b - 5)$

5. $(4 - 3z^3 + z^2 - 5z)(4 - z)$ **6.** $(3 + 2v^2 - v^3 + 4v)(2 - v)$

7. $(3u^2 - u + 5)(2u^2 + 4u - 1)$ **8.** $(2w^2 + w - 7)(5w^2 - 3w - 1)$

9. $-2xy(-3x^2y + xy^2 - 4y^3)$ **10.** $-3xy(-4xy^2 - x^2y + 3x^3)$

11. $(a^3 - 3a^2b + 3ab^2 - b^3)(-5a^2b)$ **12.** $(m^3 - 3m^2p + 3mp^2 - p^3)(-4mp^2)$

13. $(x^2 + 2x + 3)^2$ **14.** $(z^2 - 3z - 4)^2$

15. $[(x + y)(x^2 - xy + y^2)][(x - y)(x^2 + xy + y^2)]$

16. $[(a - 1)(a^2 + a + 1)][(a + 1)(a^2 - a + 1)]$

Set II   Find the products.

1. $(4a - 3)(6a^2 - 8a + 15)$ **2.** $(3x - 5)(4x^2 - 5x + 2)$

3. $(8 + 2z^4 - z^2 - 9z)(z - 4)$ **4.** $(3x + 1)(x - 5 - 2x^3 + x^2)$

5. $(6 - k)(4k - 7 + k^4 - 5k^3)$ **6.** $(3x + 2y - 1)(3x + 2y + 1)$

7. $(5h^2 - h + 8)(h^2 + 3h - 2)$ **8.** $(2x^2 + 3x - 4)(2x^2 + 3x - 4)$

9. $-4yz(6y^3 - y^2z + 3yz^2)$ **10.** $(5xy)(-2y^2)(3x^2y)$

11. $(2e^3 - 4e^2f + 7ef^2 - f^3)(-5ef^2)$ **12.** $(2x - y - 1)(2x + y + 1)$

13. $(3p^2 - 5p + 4)^2$ **14.** $(x + 1)(x^4 - x^3 + x^2 - x + 1)$

15. $[(2a - b)(4a^2 + 2ab + b^2)][(2a + b)(4a^2 - 2ab + b^2)]$

16. $[(x + 3y)(x - 3y)][(x^2 - 3xy + 9y^2)(x^2 + 3xy + 9y^2)]$

4.4 Special Products and the Binomial Theorem

4.4A The Product of the Sum and Difference of Two Terms

RULE 4.1

$$(a + b)(a - b) = a^2 - b^2$$

Proof of Rule 4.1:

$$(a + b)(a - b) = a^2 - ab + ab - b^2 = a^2 - b^2$$

Because $a + b$ is the *sum* of two terms and $a - b$ is the *difference* of two terms, Rule 4.1 can be stated in words as follows:

The product of the sum and difference of two terms is equal to the square of the first term minus the square of the second term.

Example 1   Find the following products:

a. $(2x + 3y)(2x - 3y) = (2x)^2 - (3y)^2 = 4x^2 - 9y^2$

b. $(x + y + 2)(x + y - 2)$

At first glance, this does not appear to be the product of two binomials at all. However, if we group the variables as $[x + y]$, we then have a product of the sum and difference of two terms:

$$(x + y + 2)(x + y - 2) = ([x + y] + 2)([x + y] - 2)$$
$$= (x + y)^2 - 2^2$$
$$= (x + y)(x + y) - 4$$
$$= x^2 + 2xy + y^2 - 4 \quad \blacksquare$$

EXERCISES 4.4A

Set I   Find the products.

1. $(2u + 5v)(2u - 5v)$

2. $(3m - 7n)(3m + 7n)$

3. $(2x^2 - 9)(2x^2 + 9)$

4. $(10y^2 - 3)(10y^2 + 3)$

5. $(x^5 - y^6)(x^5 + y^6)$

6. $(a^7 + b^4)(a^7 - b^4)$

7. $(7mn + 2rs)(7mn - 2rs)$

8. $(8hk + 5ef)(8hk - 5ef)$

9. $(12x^4y^3 + u^7v)(12x^4y^3 - u^7v)$

10. $(11a^5b^2 + 9c^3d^6)(11a^5b^2 - 9c^3d^6)$

11. $(a + b + 2)(a + b - 2)$ **12.** $(x + y + 5)(x + y - 5)$

13. $(x^2 + y + 5)(x^2 + y - 5)$ **14.** $(u^2 - v + 7)(u^2 - v - 7)$

15. $7x(x - 1)(x + 1)$ **16.** $3y(2y - 5)(2y + 5)$

Set II   Find the products.

1. $(6x - 5)(6x + 5)$ **2.** $(4 + 3z)(4 - 3z)$

3. $(7u - 8v)(7u + 8v)$ **4.** $(x - 8y)(x + 8y)$

5. $(x^6 - y^5)(x^6 + y^5)$ **6.** $(x^2 + y^3)(x^2 - y^3)$

7. $(2xy + 3uv)(2xy - 3uv)$ **8.** $(3abc - ef)(3abc + ef)$

9. $(13z^2w^3 + 5v^5u^7)(13z^2w^3 - 5v^5u^7)$ **10.** $(16x^3y^2 - 11z^4)(16x^3y^2 + 11z^4)$

11. $(s + t - 1)(s + t + 1)$ **12.** $(2x - y - 3)(2x + y + 3)$

13. $(x^2 + y + 5)(x^2 + y - 5)$ **14.** $(x^2 - y + 5)(x^2 + y - 5)$

15. $3z(5z - 1)(5z + 1)$ **16.** $4ab^2(a - 2)(a + 2)$

4.4B   The Square of a Binomial

Rules 4.2 and 4.3 help us quickly square a binomial.

RULE 4.2

$$(a + b)^2 = a^2 + 2ab + b^2$$

Proof of Rule 4.2:

$$(a + b)^2 = (a + b)(a + b) = a^2 + 2ab + b^2$$

$$\underset{\underline{ab}}{\underline{ab}}$$

$$a^2 + \overline{2ab} + b^2$$

RULE 4.3

$$(a - b)^2 = a^2 - 2ab + b^2$$

Proof of Rule 4.3:

$$(a - b)^2 = (a - b)(a - b) = a^2 - 2ab + b^2$$

$$\underset{-ab}{-ab}$$

$$a^2 - \overline{2\,ab} + b^2$$

These two rules can be stated in words as follows:

TO SQUARE A BINOMIAL

1. The *first term* of the product is the square of the first term of the binomial.

2. The *middle term* of the product is twice the product of the two terms of the binomial.

3. The *last term* of the product is the square of the last term of the binomial.

Example 2 **Simplify:**

a. $(2x + 3)^2 = (2x)^2 + 2(2x)(3) + (3)^2$
$$= 4x^2 + 12x + 9$$

b. $(5m - 2n^2)^2 = (5m)^2 + 2(5m)(-2n^2) + (-2n^2)^2$
$$= 25m^2 - 20mn^2 + 4n^4$$

c. $([x + y] - 3)^2 = [x + y]^2 - 2[x + y](3) + 3^2$
$$= x^2 + 2xy + y^2 - 6x - 6y + 9 \quad \blacksquare$$

A WORD OF CAUTION   Using the rules for exponents, students remember that

$$(ab)^2 = a^2b^2$$

Here, *a* and *b* are *factors*

They try to apply this rule of exponents to the expression $(a + b)^2$, but

$(a + b)^2$ cannot be found simply by squaring *a* and *b*.

Here, *a* and *b* are *terms*

Correct method	*Incorrect method*
$(a + b)^2 = (a + b)(a + b)$	$(a + b)^2 \neq a^2 + b^2$
$\qquad = a^2 + \boxed{2ab} + b^2$	

This is the term that students sometimes leave out ✓

EXERCISES 4.4B

Set I   Simplify.

1. $(2x + 3)^2$

2. $(6x + 5)^2$

3. $(5x - 3)^2$

4. $(9x - 6)^2$

5. $(7x - 10y)^2$

6. $(4u - 9v)^2$

7. $([u + v] + 7)^2$

8. $([s + t] + 4)^2$

9. $([2x - y] - 3)^2$

10. $([3z - w] - 7)^2$

11. $(x + [u + v])^2$

12. $(s + [y + 2])^2$

13. $(y - [x - 2])^2$

14. $(x - [z - 5])^2$

15. $5(x - 3)^2$

16. $7(x + 1)^2$

Set II Simplify.

1. $(3x + 4)^2$
2. $(6x - 5y)^2$
3. $(5x - 2)^2$
4. $(8yz + 2)^2$
5. $(6x - 7y)^2$
6. $(3 - [x - y])^2$
7. $([x + y] + 5)^2$
8. $([x + y] + [a + b])^2$
9. $([7x - y] - 3)^2$
10. $(4x + [a - b])^2$
11. $(s + [x + 3])^2$
12. $3x(x - 1)^2$
13. $(z - [y - 3])^2$
14. $(3x + 4)^2 x^2$
15. $8(a + 5)^2$
16. $3x(-4x)^2(2x^3)$

4.4C The Binomial Theorem

Powers of binomials occur so frequently that it is convenient to have a method for expanding *any* power of *any* binomial. We know that $(a + b)^0 = 1$, $(a + b)^1 = a + b$, and $(a + b)^2 = a^2 + 2ab + b^2$. Let's find $(a + b)^3$ and $(a + b)^4$.

$$(a + b)^3 = (a + b)^2(a + b)$$
$$= (a^2 + 2ab + b^2)(a + b)$$
$$= (a^2 + 2ab + b^2)(a) + (a^2 + 2ab + b^2)(b)$$
$$= a^3 + 2a^2b + ab^2 + a^2b + 2ab^2 + b^3$$
$$= a^3 + 3a^2b + 3ab^2 + b^3$$

$$(a + b)^4 = \{(a + b)^2\}^2$$
$$= (a^2 + 2ab + b^2)^2$$

Let's finish the multiplication vertically:

$$
\begin{array}{r}
a^2 + 2ab + b^2 \\
a^2 + 2ab + b^2 \\
\hline
a^2b^2 + 2ab^3 + b^4 \\
2a^3b + 4a^2b^2 + 2ab^3 \\
a^4 + 2a^3b + a^2b^2 \\
\hline
a^4 + 4a^3b + 6a^2b^2 + 4ab^3 + b^4
\end{array}
$$

We see, therefore, that

$$(a + b)^0 = 1$$
$$(a + b)^1 = 1a + 1b$$
$$(a + b)^2 = 1a^2 + 2ab + 1b^2$$
$$(a + b)^3 = 1a^3 + 3a^2b + 3ab^2 + 1b^3$$
$$(a + b)^4 = 1a^4 + 4a^3b + 6a^2b^2 + 4ab^3 + 1b^4$$
$$\vdots$$

A careful examination of the above binomial expansions shows that they are always polynomials in a and b. Each term has the form Ca^rb^s, where C is the numerical coefficient. The degree of each term in $(a + b)^n$ is n, since $r + s = n$. The number of terms in each expansion is one more than n, or $n + 1$. Let's look at $(a + b)^4$ in detail:

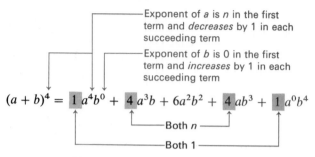

Exponent of a is n in the first term and *decreases* by 1 in each succeeding term

Exponent of b is 0 in the first term and *increases* by 1 in each succeeding term

$$(a + b)^4 = \boxed{1}\,a^4b^0 + \boxed{4}\,a^3b + 6a^2b^2 + \boxed{4}\,ab^3 + \boxed{1}\,a^0b^4$$

Both n

Both 1

Binomial coefficients are *symmetrical*

Since the binomial coefficients are symmetrical, we need only find half of them. The remaining coefficients are obtained by setting them equal to their corresponding symmetrical coefficients. The binomial coefficients are written according to the following pattern:

$$1,\ n,\ \frac{n(n - 1)}{1 \cdot 2},\ \frac{n(n - 1)(n - 2)}{1 \cdot 2 \cdot 3},\ \ldots$$

Coefficient of second term is n

Coefficient of first term is 1

Compare these coefficients with those in Examples 3a and 3b below.

Example 3 Find the binomial coefficients:

a. Coefficients for the expansion of $(a + b)^5$.

$$n + 1 = 5 + 1 = 6 \text{ terms}$$

Find the first three coefficients; then use symmetry:

1st	2nd	3rd	4th	5th	6th
1	5	$\dfrac{5 \cdot 4}{1 \cdot 2}$	10	5	1
		$= 10$			

b. Coefficients for the expansion of $(a + b)^8$.

$$n + 1 = 8 + 1 = 9 \text{ terms}$$

Find the first five coefficients; then use symmetry:

1st	2nd	3rd	4th	5th	6th	7th	8th	9th
1	8	$\dfrac{8 \cdot 7}{1 \cdot 2}$	$\dfrac{8 \cdot 7 \cdot 6}{1 \cdot 2 \cdot 3}$	$\dfrac{8 \cdot 7 \cdot 6 \cdot 5}{1 \cdot 2 \cdot 3 \cdot 4}$	56	28	8	1
		$= 28$	$= 56$	$= 70$				

You may want to verify that $\dfrac{5 \cdot 4 \cdot 3}{1 \cdot 2 \cdot 3} = \dfrac{5 \cdot 4}{1 \cdot 2}, \dfrac{8 \cdot 7 \cdot 6 \cdot 5 \cdot 4}{1 \cdot 2 \cdot 3 \cdot 4 \cdot 5} = \dfrac{8 \cdot 7 \cdot 6}{1 \cdot 2 \cdot 3}$, and so forth. ∎

The procedure for expanding a binomial is summarized in Rule 4.4.

RULE 4.4: THE BINOMIAL THEOREM

To expand $(a + b)^n$ (n a positive integer)

1. Make a blank form with $(n + 1)$ terms.

$$(\quad)(\quad) + (\quad)(\quad) + (\quad)(\quad) + (\quad)(\quad) + \cdots$$

2. Fill in the powers of a and b.

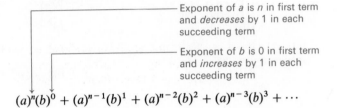

Exponent of a is n in first term and *decreases* by 1 in each succeeding term

Exponent of b is 0 in first term and *increases* by 1 in each succeeding term

$$(a)^n(b)^0 + (a)^{n-1}(b)^1 + (a)^{n-2}(b)^2 + (a)^{n-3}(b)^3 + \cdots$$

3. Write the coefficients as follows:

$$1, \frac{n}{1}, \frac{n(n-1)}{1 \cdot 2}, \frac{n(n-1)(n-2)}{1 \cdot 2 \cdot 3}, \cdots$$

Coefficient of second term is n

Coefficient of first term is 1

Calculate *half* the coefficients. The remaining coefficients are symmetrical to these.

4. $(a + b)^n = 1(a)^n(b)^0 + \dfrac{n}{1}(a)^{n-1}(b)^1 + \dfrac{n(n-1)}{1 \cdot 2}(a)^{n-2}(b)^2$

$$+ \frac{n(n-1)(n-2)}{1 \cdot 2 \cdot 3}(a)^{n-3}(b)^3 + \cdots$$

5. Rewrite the entire expansion with each term simplified.

Example 4   Expand $(a + b)^5$.

Step 1 Make a blank form with $n + 1 = 6$ terms.

$$(\quad)(\quad) + (\quad)(\quad) + (\quad)(\quad) + (\quad)(\quad) + (\quad)(\quad) + (\quad)(\quad)$$

Step 2 Fill in the powers of a and b.

$$(a)^5(b)^0 + (a)^4(b)^1 + (a)^3(b)^2 + (a)^2(b)^3 + (a)^1(b)^4 + (a)^0(b)^5$$

Steps 3 and 4 Write in the coefficients.

$$1(a)^5(b)^0 + 5(a)^4(b)^1 + \frac{5 \cdot 4}{1 \cdot 2}(a)^3(b)^2 + \frac{5 \cdot 4}{1 \cdot 2}(a)^2(b)^3 + 5(a)^1(b)^4 + 1(a)^0(b)^5$$

Step 5 Simplify the expansion.

$$(a + b)^5 = a^5 + 5a^4b + 10a^3b^2 + 10a^2b^3 + 5ab^4 + b^5 \quad \blacksquare$$

An alternate method of determining the numerical coefficients is to use Pascal's triangle, as shown below.

Pascal's Triangle

If the binomial expansions for the first five values of *n* are written, we have

$$(a + b)^0 = \quad\quad 1$$
$$(a + b)^1 = \quad\quad 1a + 1b$$
$$(a + b)^2 = \quad\quad 1a^2 + 2ab + 1b^2$$
$$(a + b)^3 = \quad\quad 1a^3 + 3a^2b + 3ab^2 + 1b^3$$
$$(a + b)^4 = 1a^4 + 4a^3b + 6a^2b^2 + 4ab^3 + 1b^4$$
$$\vdots$$

If we omit everything in the above display except the numerical coefficients, we get a triangular array of numbers known as *Pascal's triangle*:

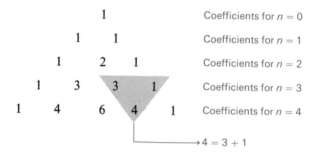

| | | | 1 | | | Coefficients for $n = 0$ |

```
              1                 Coefficients for n = 0
           1     1              Coefficients for n = 1
        1     2     1           Coefficients for n = 2
     1     3    [3]    1         Coefficients for n = 3
  1     4     6   [4]     1      Coefficients for n = 4
                                 4 = 3 + 1
```

A close examination of the numbers in Pascal's triangle reveals that

1. The first and last numbers in any row are 1.

2. Any other number in Pascal's triangle is the sum of the two closest numbers in the row above it (see shaded triangle).

Pascal's triangle can be used to find the coefficients in a binomial expansion. The triangle we have shown can be extended to any size by using the two rules given above. Try extending the triangle by one more row; you should get the coefficients we computed in Example 4.

The terms of the binomial being expanded often consist of more than the single variables *a* and *b* (see Example 5).

Example 5 Examples of binomials with terms that consist of more than a single variable:

a. $(3x^2 + 5y)^3$ In this binomial $\begin{cases} a = 3x^2 \\ b = 5y \end{cases}$

b. $(2e^3 - f^2)^5$ In this binomial $\begin{cases} a = 2e^3 \\ b = -f^2 \end{cases}$

c. $\left(\dfrac{x}{2} - 4\right)^4$ In this binomial $\begin{cases} a = \dfrac{x}{2} \\ b = -4 \quad \blacksquare \end{cases}$

Example 6   Expand $(3x^2 + 5y)^3$. Find the coefficients from the rules on page 157 *or* from Pascal's triangle.

Steps 1–4

$$1(3x^2)^3(5y)^0 + 3(3x^2)^2(5y)^1 + 3(3x^2)^1(5y)^2 + 1(3x^2)^0(5y)^3$$

Step 5

$$(3x^2 + 5y)^3 = 27x^6 + 135x^4y + 225x^2y^2 + 125y^3 \quad \blacksquare$$

Example 7   Expand $(2e^3 - f^2)^5$.

Steps 1–4   We learned from Example 4 that the coefficients are 1, 5, 10, 10, 5, and 1.

$$1(2e^3)^5 + 5(2e^3)^4(-f^2)^1 + 10(2e^3)^3(-f^2)^2$$
$$+ 10(2e^3)^2(-f^2)^3 + 5(2e^3)(-f^2)^4 + 1(-f^2)^5$$

Step 5

$$(2e^3 - f^2)^5 = 32e^{15} - 80e^{12}f^2 + 80e^9f^4 - 40e^6f^6 + 10e^3f^8 - f^{10} \quad \blacksquare$$

Example 8   Expand $\left(\dfrac{x}{2} - 4\right)^4$.

Steps 1–4

$$1\left(\frac{x}{2}\right)^4(-4)^0 + 4\left(\frac{x}{2}\right)^3(-4)^1 + \frac{4 \cdot 3}{1 \cdot 2}\left(\frac{x}{2}\right)^2(-4)^2 + 4\left(\frac{x}{2}\right)^1(-4)^3 + 1\left(\frac{x}{2}\right)^0(-4)^4$$

Step 5

$$\left(\frac{x}{2} - 4\right)^4 = \frac{x^4}{16} - 2x^3 + 24x^2 - 128x + 256 \quad \blacksquare$$

NOTE   When the binomial being expanded contains a *difference* of terms, the terms of the expansion alternate in sign (Examples 7 and 8). ✓

Example 9   Write the first five terms of the expansion of $(x + y^2)^{12}$.

Steps 1–4

$$1(x)^{12}(y^2)^0 + 12(x)^{11}(y^2)^1 + \frac{12 \cdot 11}{1 \cdot 2}(x)^{10}(y^2)^2$$

$$+ \frac{12 \cdot 11 \cdot 10}{1 \cdot 2 \cdot 3}(x)^9(y^2)^3 + \frac{12 \cdot 11 \cdot 10 \cdot 9}{1 \cdot 2 \cdot 3 \cdot 4}(x)^8(y^2)^4 + \cdots$$

Step 5

$$(x + y^2)^{12} = x^{12} + 12x^{11}y^2 + 66x^{10}y^4 + 220x^9y^6 + 495x^8y^8 + \cdots \quad \blacksquare$$

In this section, we discussed the binomial expansion for *natural number powers* only. Other numbers can be used for powers of binomials, but binomial expansions using such numbers as exponents are not discussed in this book.

EXERCISES 4.4C

Set I   In Exercises 1–16, expand each binomial.

1. $(x + y)^5$ **2.** $(r + s)^4$ **3.** $(x - 2)^5$

4. $(y - 3)^4$ **5.** $(3r + s)^6$ **6.** $(2x + y)^6$

7. $(x + y^2)^4$ **8.** $(u + v^2)^5$ **9.** $\left(2x - \dfrac{1}{2}\right)^5$

10. $\left(3x - \dfrac{1}{3}\right)^4$ **11.** $\left(\dfrac{1}{3}x + \dfrac{3}{2}\right)^4$ **12.** $\left(\dfrac{1}{5}x + \dfrac{5}{2}\right)^4$

13. $(4x^2 - 3y^2)^5$ **14.** $(3x^2 - 2y^3)^5$ **15.** $(x + x^{-1})^4$

16. $(x^{-1} - x)^4$

17. Write the first four terms of the expansion of $(x + 2y^2)^{10}$.

18. Write the first four terms of the expansion of $(x + 3y^2)^8$.

19. Write the first four terms of the expansion of $(x - 3y^2)^{10}$.

20. Write the first four terms of the expansion of $(x - 2y^3)^{11}$.

Set II   In Exercises 1–16, expand each binomial.

1. $(s + t)^6$ **2.** $(x - y)^6$ **3.** $(x + 4)^4$

4. $(2x - 3y)^3$ **5.** $(4x - y)^5$ **6.** $(s - t)^5$

7. $(x + y^2)^3$ **8.** $(x - y)^5$ **9.** $\left(2x - \dfrac{1}{2}\right)^6$

10. $(y + y^{-1})^5$ **11.** $\left(\dfrac{1}{4}x + \dfrac{3}{2}\right)^4$ **12.** $(x + x^{-1})^6$

13. $(3s^2 - 3t^3)^5$ **14.** $(x^{-1} - x)^3$ **15.** $(3x + 2y^{-1})^4$

16. $(y^{-1} - y)^7$

17. Write the first four terms of the expansion of $(2x - y^2)^{14}$.

18. Write the first four terms of the expansion of $(3x + y^2)^{12}$.

19. Write the first four terms of the expansion of $(3 - x^2)^{10}$.

20. Write the first four terms of the expansion of $(2h - k^2)^{11}$.

4.5 Division of Polynomials

4.5A Division of a Polynomial by a Monomial

> TO DIVIDE A POLYNOMIAL BY A MONOMIAL
>
> Divide *each* term in the polynomial by the monomial; then add the resulting quotients.

1 Divide:

a. $\dfrac{4x^3 - 6x^2}{2x}$

$$\frac{4x^3 - 6x^2}{2x} = \frac{1}{2x}(4x^3 - 6x^2)$$

By the distributive rule $\quad = \left(\dfrac{1}{2x}\right)(4x^3) + \left(\dfrac{1}{2x}\right)(-6x^2)$

Dividing each term of the polynomial by the monomial $\quad = \dfrac{4x^3}{2x} + \dfrac{-6x^2}{2x}$

$$= \quad 2x^2 \quad - \quad 3x$$

b. $\dfrac{4x^2y - 8xy^2 + 12xy}{-4xy}$

$$\frac{4x^2y - 8xy^2 + 12xy}{-4xy} = \frac{4x^2y}{-4xy} + \frac{-8xy^2}{-4xy} + \frac{12xy}{-4xy}$$

$$= -x + 2y - 3 \quad \blacksquare$$

EXERCISES 4.5A

Set I Perform the indicated divisions.

1. $\dfrac{18x^5 - 24x^4 - 12x^3}{6x^2}$

2. $\dfrac{16y^4 - 36y^3 + 20y^2}{-4y^2}$

3. $\dfrac{55a^4b^3 - 33ab^2}{-11ab}$

4. $\dfrac{26m^2n^4 - 52m^3n}{-13mn}$

5. $\dfrac{-15x^2y^2z^2 - 30xyz}{-5xyz}$

6. $\dfrac{-24a^2b^2c^2 - 16abc}{-8abc}$

7. $(13x^3y^2 - 26x^5y^3 + 39x^4y^6) \div (13x^2y^2)$

8. $(21m^2n^3 - 35m^3n^2 - 14m^3n^5) \div (7m^2n^2)$

Set II Perform the indicated divisions.

1. $\dfrac{24h^6 - 56h^4 - 40h^3}{8h^2}$

2. $\dfrac{5x^4 - 40x^3 + 10x^2}{-5x^2}$

3. $\dfrac{60e^5f^3 - 84e^2f^4}{12ef^2}$

4. $\dfrac{7y^5 - 35y^4 + 14y^3}{7y^2}$

5. $\dfrac{-45r^3s^2t^4 + 63r^2s^3t^3}{-9rs^2t}$

6. $\dfrac{42u^4 - 56u^2 + 28u^6}{-14u^2}$

7. $(-30m^4n^2 + 60m^2n^3 - 45m^3n^4) \div (15m^2n^2)$

8. $(32x^3y^2z - 64xy^2z + 48xy^3z^2) \div (-16xy^2z)$

4.5B Division of a Polynomial by a Polynomial

The method used to divide one polynomial (the dividend) by a polynomial (the divisor) with two or more terms is similar to the method used to divide one whole number by another (using long division) in arithmetic. The long-division procedure can be summarized as follows [Reading Hint: Read the steps in the summary, and *while you are doing so*, look also at the steps in Example 2 to see that the authors are following the step-by-step method of the summary.]:

TO DIVIDE ONE POLYNOMIAL BY ANOTHER

1. Arrange the divisor and the dividend in descending powers of one variable. In the *dividend*, leave spaces for any missing terms.

2. Find the first term of the quotient by dividing the first term of the dividend by the first term of the divisor.

3. Multiply the *entire* divisor by the first term of the quotient. Place the product under the dividend, lining up like terms.

4. Subtract the product found in step 3 from the dividend, bringing down at least one term. This difference is the *remainder*. If the degree of the remainder is not less than the degree of the divisor, continue with steps 5–8.

5. Find the next term of the quotient by dividing the first term of the remainder by the first term of the divisor.

6. Multiply the entire divisor by the term found in step 5.

7. Subtract the product found in step 6 from the polynomial above it, bringing down at least one more term.

8. Repeat steps 5 through 7 until the remainder is 0 *or* until the degree of the remainder is less than the degree of the divisor.

9. Check your answer.

Example 2 Divide $(27x + 19x^2 + 6x^3 + 10)$ by $(5 + 3x)$.

Step 1 $3x + 5 \overline{)6x^3 + 19x^2 + 27x + 10}$

First term in quotient is $\dfrac{6x^3}{3x} = 2x^2$

Step 2 $3x + 5 \overline{)\,6x^3\, + 19x^2 + 27x + 10}$ $2x^2$

Step 3
$$
\begin{array}{r}
2x^2 \\
3x + 5 \overline{)6x^3 + 19x^2 + 27x + 10} \\
6x^3 + 10x^2
\end{array}
$$
This is $2x^2(3x + 5)$

Step 4
$$
\begin{array}{r}
2x^2 \\
3x + 5 \overline{)6x^3 + 19x^2 + 27x + 10} \\
6x^3 + 10x^2 \\
\hline
9x^2 + 27x
\end{array}
$$
Subtract and bring down a term

Remainder

The division must be continued because the degree of the remainder is not less than the degree of the divisor.

Second term in quotient is $\dfrac{9x^2}{3x} = 3x$

Step 5
$$
3x + 5 \overline{)6x^3 + 19x^2 + 27x + 10} \quad 2x^2 + 3x
$$
$$
\underline{6x^3 + 10x^2}
$$
$$
9x^2 + 27x
$$

Step 6
$$
3x + 5 \overline{)6x^3 + 19x^2 + 27x + 10} \quad 2x^2 + 3x
$$
$$
\underline{6x^3 + 10x^2}
$$
$$
9x^2 + 27x
$$
$$
9x^2 + 15x \qquad \text{This is } 3x(3x + 5)
$$

Step 7
$$
3x + 5 \overline{)6x^3 + 19x^2 + 27x + 10} \quad 2x^2 + 3x
$$
$$
\underline{6x^3 + 10x^2}
$$
$$
9x^2 + 27x
$$
$$
\underline{9x^2 + 15x} \qquad \text{Subtract and bring down a term}
$$
$$
12x + 10 \qquad \text{Remainder}
$$

The degree of the remainder is *still* not less than the degree of the divisor. Therefore, we must repeat steps 5, 6, and 7.

Third term in quotient is $\dfrac{12x}{3x} = 4$

$$
3x + 5 \overline{)6x^3 + 19x^2 + 27x + 10} \quad 2x^2 + 3x + 4
$$
$$
\underline{6x^3 + 10x^2}
$$
$$
9x^2 + 27x
$$
$$
\underline{9x^2 + 15x}
$$
$$
12x + 10
$$
$$
\underline{12x + 20} \qquad \text{This is } 4(3x + 5)
$$
$$
-10 \qquad \text{Remainder}
$$

The division is finished because the degree of the remainder is less than the degree of the divisor.

Answer　$2x^2 + 3x + 4 - \dfrac{10}{3x + 5}$

or　$2x^2 + 3x + 4 + \dfrac{-10}{3x + 5}$

Check　$(3x + 5)(2x^2 + 3x + 4) + (-10) = 6x^3 + 19x^2 + 27x + 10$ ∎

Example 3   Divide $(x^3 - 3 + x^4 - 5x)$ by $(x^2 - 1 - x)$. (Notice that an x^2 term is missing from the dividend, so we wrote it as $0x^2$ and used it as a placeholder.)

$$
\begin{array}{r}
x^2 + 2x + 3 \\
x^2 - x - 1\overline{)x^4 + x^3 + 0x^2 - 5x - 3} \\
\underline{x^4 - x^3 - x^2} \\
2x^3 + x^2 - 5x \\
\underline{2x^3 - 2x^2 - 2x} \\
3x^2 - 3x - 3 \\
\underline{3x^2 - 3x - 3} \\
0
\end{array}
$$

Answer $x^2 + 2x + 3$

Check $(x^2 + 2x + 3)(x^2 - x - 1) = x^4 + x^3 - 5x - 3$ ∎

NOTE   When the final remainder is 0, we can say that the *divisor* is a *factor* of the dividend and that the *quotient* is a *factor* of the dividend. Therefore, in Example 3, we can say that $x^2 + 2x + 3$ and $x^2 - x - 1$ are factors of $x^4 + x^3 - 5x - 3$.   ☑

It is sometimes necessary to bring down more than one term from the dividend (see Example 4).

Example 4 $(6x^3 + 4x^4 - 1 + 2x) \div (3x - 1 + 2x^2)$.

$$
\begin{array}{r}
2x^2 + 1 \\
2x^2 + 3x - 1\overline{)4x^4 + 6x^3 + 0x^2 + 2x - 1} \\
\underline{4x^4 + 6x^3 - 2x^2} \\
2x^2 + 2x - 1 \\
\underline{2x^2 + 3x - 1} \\
-x
\end{array}
$$

Answer $2x^2 + 1 + \dfrac{-x}{2x^2 + 3x - 1}$

or $2x^2 + 1 - \dfrac{x}{2x^2 + 3x - 1}$

Check $(2x^2 + 1)(2x^2 + 3x - 1) - x = 4x^4 + 6x^3 + 2x - 1$ ∎

Example 5 $(17ab^2 + 12a^3 - 10b^3 - 11a^2b) \div (3a - 2b)$.

Arrange the terms of the dividend and divisor in descending powers of a before beginning the division.

$$
\begin{array}{r}
4a^2 - ab + 5b^2 \\
3a - 2b\overline{)12a^3 - 11a^2b + 17ab^2 - 10b^3} \\
\underline{12a^3 - 8a^2b} \\
-3a^2b + 17ab^2 \\
\underline{-3a^2b + 2ab^2} \\
15ab^2 - 10b^3 \\
\underline{15ab^2 - 10b^3} \\
0
\end{array}
$$

Answer $4a^2 - ab + 5b^2$

Check $(3a - 2b)(4a^2 - ab + 5b^2) = 12a^3 - 11a^2b + 17ab^2 - 10b^3$

Since the remainder is 0, we can say that the divisor and quotient are both factors of the dividend.   ∎

Example 6 $(1 - x^5) \div (1 - x)$.

$$
\begin{array}{r}
x^4 + x^3 + x^2 + x + 1 \\
-x + 1 \overline{)\, -x^5 + 0x^4 + 0x^3 + 0x^2 + 0x + 1} \\
\underline{-x^5 + x^4} \\
-x^4 + 0x^3 \\
\underline{-x^4 + x^3} \\
-x^3 + 0x^2 \\
\underline{-x^3 + x^2} \\
-x^2 + 0x \\
\underline{-x^2 + x} \\
-x + 1 \\
\underline{-x + 1} \\
0
\end{array}
$$

Answer $x^4 + x^3 + x^2 + x + 1$

Check $(1 - x)(x^4 + x^3 + x^2 + x + 1) = 1 - x^5$

Note that $x^4 + x^3 + x^2 + x + 1$ and $1 - x$ are factors of $1 - x^5$. ∎

EXERCISES 4.5B

Set I   Perform the indicated divisions.

1. $(x^2 + 10x - 5) \div (x + 7)$

2. $(x^2 + 9x - 5) \div (x + 4)$

3. $(6z^3 - 13z^2 - 4z + 15) \div (3z - 5)$

4. $(6y^3 + 7y^2 - 11y - 12) \div (2y + 3)$

5. $(v^4 - 3v^3 - 8v^2 - 9v - 5) \div (v + 1)$

6. $(w^4 - 2w^3 - 12w^2 - 13w - 10) \div (w + 2)$

7. $(8x - 4x^3 + 10) \div (2 - x)$

8. $(12x - 15 - x^3) \div (3 - x)$

9. $(17xy^2 + 12x^3 - 10y^3 - 11x^2y) \div (3x - 2y)$

10. $(13x^2y - 11xy^2 + 10x^3 - 12y^3) \div (2x + 3y)$

11. $(x^4 - 7x + 6) \div (x - 2)$

12. $(x^4 + 6x + 3) \div (x - 1)$

13. $(x + 8x^2 + 4x^4 - 3x^3 + 2) \div (x + 1 + 4x^2)$

14. $(11x^2 + 10 + 2x^4 - x^3 + 3x) \div (x + 2x^2 + 2)$

15. $(2x^4 + 7x^2 + 5) \div (x^2 + 2)$

16. $(3x^4 + 11x^2 + 1) \div (x^2 + 3)$

17. $(2x^5 - 10x^3 + 3x^2 - 15) \div (3 + 2x^3)$

18. $(3x^5 - 6x^3 + x^2 - 2) \div (1 + 3x^3)$

19. $(3x^4 + 14x^3 + 2x^2 + 3x + 2) \div (3x^2 - x + 1)$

20. $(2x^4 + 13x^3 - 10x^2 + 9x - 2) \div (2x^2 - x + 1)$

Set II   Perform the indicated divisions.

1. $(x^2 - 3x - 11) \div (x + 3)$

2. $(6x^3 + 23x^2y + 16xy^2 + 3y^3) \div (3x + y)$

3. $(20w^3 - 23w^2 - 29w + 14) \div (5w - 2)$

4. $(2x^4 + 3x^3 + 2x^2 - x + 3) \div (2x + 3)$

5. $(z^4 - 2z^3 - 4z^2 - 10z - 9) \div (z + 1)$

6. $(x^4 - 1) \div (x - 1)$

7. $(8x - x^3 + 25) \div (4 - x)$

8. $(2x^2 + 6 + 3x + x^3) \div (x + 2)$

9. $(15x^3 - 5xy^2 + 12y^3 - 23x^2y) \div (3x - 4y)$

10. $(4x + x^3 + 4 + x^2) \div (x + 1)$

11. $(x^4 - 29x + 4) \div (x - 3)$

12. $(x^5 - 1) \div (x^2 + x - 1)$

13. $(2x + 3x^4 - 2x^3 + 3 + 9x^2) \div (x + 3x^2 + 1)$

14. $(3x^4 + 2x^3 - 6x^2 - x + 5) \div (3x + 2)$

15. $(2x^4 + 7x^2 + 3) \div (x^2 + 1)$

16. $(x^3 + x^2 + x + 3) \div (x + 1)$

17. $(3x^2 + 2x + 6 + x^3) \div (x + 3)$

18. $(2x^4 + x^3 + 4x^2 - 4x - 5) \div (2x + 1)$

19. $(3x^5 - 12x^3 + 2x^2 - 8) \div (2 + 3x^3)$

20. $(2x^4 + 7x^3 + 10x^2 + x - 4) \div (2x^2 + x - 1)$

4.6 Synthetic Division

Synthetic division may be used when we divide a polynomial by a *first-degree* binomial.

Synthetic Division and Long Division

Before we show how synthetic division is done, we will show how synthetic division is derived from long division.

Example 1   Divide $(19x + 2x^3 - 5 - 11x^2)$ by $(x - 3)$, using *long division*.

$$
\begin{array}{r}
2x^2 - 5x + 4 \quad \text{R7} \\
x - 3\overline{)2x^3 - 11x^2 + 19x - 5} \\
\underline{2x^3 - 6x^2} \\
-5x^2 + 19x \\
\underline{-5x^2 + 15x} \\
4x - 5 \\
\underline{4x - 12} \\
7 \quad \blacksquare
\end{array}
$$

We note (1) that when we divide any polynomial by a *first-degree* polynomial, the degree of the quotient is *always one less than* the degree of the dividend and (2) that the quotient is in descending powers of the variable. Therefore, in order to shorten the division process, we can *temporarily* omit the variables. (We will put them back in later.) When we omit the variables, we must put in zeros for any missing terms. If we leave out the variables and the plus signs in Example 1, we have

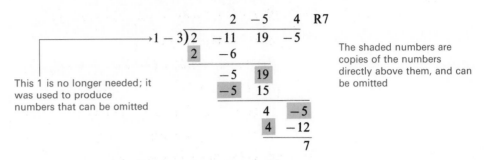

We see that most of the numerical coefficients are repeated several times. We can abbreviate the long-division process considerably by leaving out the *repetitions* of the numerical coefficients. This gives us

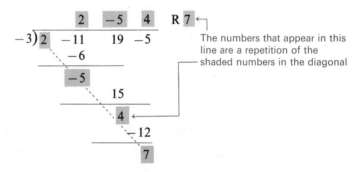

If we omit the numbers at the top and remove the empty spaces, the work is brought closer together, as follows:

$$
\begin{array}{r|rrrr}
-3 & 2 & -11 & 19 & -5 \\
   &   & -6 & 15 & -12 \\
\hline
   & 2 & -5 & 4 & 7
\end{array}
$$

Notice that if we subtract this row from the top row we get the bottom row

Also notice that if we multiply each of the first three numbers in the bottom row by the -3, we get the numbers in the second row. Changing the -3 to a $+3$ would permit us to *add* instead of *subtract*.

The Synthetic Division Process

We now demonstrate the synthetic division procedure for the division problem in Example 1. The numbers for the problem $(19x + 2x^3 - 5 - 11x^2) \div (x - 3)$ are arranged as follows when we are getting ready to use synthetic division:

$$
\begin{array}{r|rrrr}
  & 2 & -11 & 19 & -5 \\
  &   &   &   &   \\
3 &   &   &   &
\end{array}
$$

Coefficients of the dividend arranged in descending powers of the variable

Note the sign change (we are using a $+3$ instead of a -3 so we can *add* instead of subtract) and that we have moved the 3 down

We next bring down the *first* number, 2, from the top row.

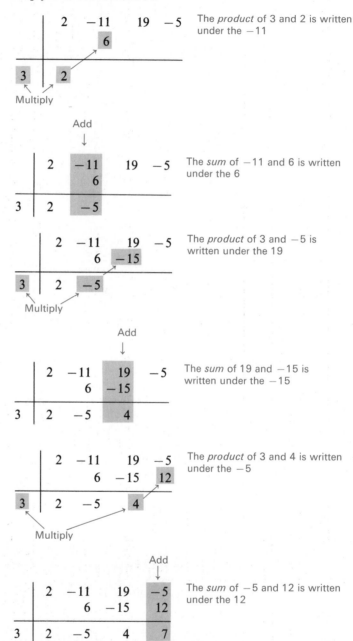

$$\begin{array}{c|cccc} & 2 & -11 & 19 & -5 \\ \hline 3 & 2 \leftarrow & & & \end{array}$$ ——— Bring down the leading coefficient

We now multiply and add as follows:

The *product* of 3 and 2 is written under the −11

The *sum* of −11 and 6 is written under the 6

The *product* of 3 and −5 is written under the 19

The *sum* of 19 and −15 is written under the −15

The *product* of 3 and 4 is written under the −5

The *sum* of −5 and 12 is written under the 12

The last number in the bottom row is the *remainder*. The other numbers in the last row are the coefficients for the quotient. We now supply the missing variables, remembering that the *degree* of the quotient is *one less than* the degree of the dividend.

Therefore, $\dfrac{2x^3 - 11x^2 + 19x - 5}{x - 3} = 2x^2 - 5x + 4 + \dfrac{7}{x - 3}$

Check $(x - 3)(2x^2 - 5x + 4) + 7 = 2x^3 - 11x^2 + 19x - 5$

Example 2   Divide $2x^4 - 3x^2 + 5$ by $x - 1$.

$$
\begin{array}{r|rrrrr}
 & 2 & 0 & -3 & 0 & 5 \\
 &   & 2 & 2 & -1 & -1 \\
\hline
1 & 2 & 2 & -1 & -1 & 4 \\
 & 2x^3 & +2x^2 & -1x & -1 & R\,4
\end{array}
$$

Zeros are used for all missing powers

Sign changed

Therefore, $\dfrac{2x^4 - 3x^2 + 5}{x - 1} = 2x^3 + 2x^2 - x - 1 + \dfrac{4}{x - 1}$.

Check $(x - 1)(2x^3 + 2x^2 - x - 1) + 4 = 2x^4 - 3x^2 + 5$ ■

Example 3   Divide $\dfrac{x^5 + 32}{x + 2}$.

Note the sign change (we're dividing by $x + 2$) ⟶

$$
\begin{array}{r|rrrrrr}
 & 1 & 0 & 0 & 0 & 0 & 32 \\
 &   & -2 & 4 & -8 & 16 & -32 \\
\hline
-2 & 1 & -2 & 4 & -8 & 16 & 0 \\
 & 1x^4 & -2x^3 & +4x^2 & -8x & +16 &
\end{array}
$$

Therefore, $\dfrac{x^5 + 32}{x + 2} = x^4 - 2x^3 + 4x^2 - 8x + 16$.

Check $(x + 2)(x^4 - 2x^3 + 4x^2 - 8x + 16) = x^5 + 32$

Since the remainder is 0, we can say that $x + 2$ and $x^4 - 2x^3 + 4x^2 - 8x + 16$ are *factors* of $x^5 + 32$.   ■

Synthetic division is a very useful tool when the divisor is a first-degree binomial, and we will use it in both *factoring* (Section 5.8) and *graphing* (Section 8.8).

Synthetic division can also be used when the divisor is of the form $ax + b$ or $ax - b$; however, in this book we use synthetic division only when the divisor is of the form $x + a$ or $x - a$.

EXERCISES 4.6

Set I   Use synthetic division to perform the divisions.

1. $(x^2 + 2x - 18) \div (x - 3)$

2. $(x^2 + 4x - 10) \div (x - 2)$

3. $(x^3 + 3x^2 - 5x + 6) \div (x + 4)$

4. $(x^3 + 6x^2 + 4x - 7) \div (x + 5)$

5. $(x^4 + 6x^3 - x - 4) \div (x + 6)$

6. $(2x^4 + 5x^3 + 10x - 2) \div (x + 3)$

7. $\dfrac{x^4 - 16}{x - 2}$

8. $\dfrac{x^7 - 1}{x - 1}$

9. $\dfrac{x^6 - 3x^5 - 2x^2 + 3x + 5}{x - 3}$

10. $\dfrac{x^6 - 3x^4 - 7x - 2}{x - 2}$

11. $(3x^4 - x^3 + 9x^2 - 1) \div \left(x - \dfrac{1}{3}\right)$

12. $(3x^4 - 4x^3 - x^2 - x - 2) \div \left(x + \dfrac{2}{3}\right)$

13. $\dfrac{x^5 + x^4 - 45x^3 - 45x^2 + 324x + 324}{x + 3}$

14. $\dfrac{x^5 + x^4 - 45x^3 - 45x^2 + 324x + 324}{x + 6}$

15. $\dfrac{4x^4 - 45x^2 + 3x + 100}{x - 2}$

16. $\dfrac{9x^4 - 13x^2 + 2x + 6}{x - 1}$

17. $(2.6x^3 + 1.8x - 6.4) \div (x - 1.5)$

18. $(3.8x^3 - 1.4x^2 - 23.9) \div (x - 2.5)$

19. $(2.7x^3 - 1.6x + 3.289) \div (x - 1.2)$

20. $(3x^3 + 1.2x^2 - 1.5) \div (x - 1.6)$

Set II   Use synthetic division to perform the divisions.

1. $(x^2 + 7x + 10) \div (x + 3)$ **2.** $(x^2 + 6x + 12) \div (x - 2)$

3. $(x^3 - 8x^2 + 11x - 14) \div (x - 6)$ **4.** $(x^4 + 5x^3 - x^2 - 4x + 7) \div (x + 5)$

5. $(2x^4 - 10x^3 - 6x + 15) \div (x - 5)$ **6.** $(2x^3 + 3x^2 + x - 15) \div \left(x - \dfrac{3}{2}\right)$

7. $\dfrac{x^4 - 81}{x - 3}$

8. $(x^5 - 4x^4 + 4x^3 + 4x^2 - 11x + 8) \div (x - 2)$

9. $(x^6 - 4x^5 - 12x^3 + 48x^2 - 15x + 43) \div (x - 4)$

10. $(x^5 - 32) \div (x - 2)$

11. $(8x^4 - 2x^3 - 6x^2 + 4x + 3) \div \left(x + \dfrac{3}{4}\right)$

12. $(2x^4 + 15x^3 + 6x^2 - 8x - 7) \div (x + 7)$

13. $\dfrac{x^5 + x^4 - 45x^3 - 45x^2 + 324x + 324}{x - 6}$

14. $(x^5 + 1) \div (x + 1)$

15. $\dfrac{4x^4 - 13x^2 + 2x + 6}{x - 2}$

16. $(2x^3 + 5x^2 + 5x - 4) \div \left(x - \dfrac{1}{2}\right)$

17. $(1.4x^3 - 2.6x^2 + 56.3) \div (x + 3.5)$

18. $(3x^3 + 8x^2 + 6x - 3) \div \left(x - \dfrac{1}{3}\right)$

19. $(2.4x^3 + 1.32x^2 - 3.6) \div (x - 1.1)$

20. $(x^5 - 5x^4 + 10x^3 - 10x^2 + 5x - 1) \div (x - 1)$

4.7 Review: 4.1–4.6

Polynomials
4.1

A **polynomial in x** is an algebraic expression that has only terms of the form ax^n, where a is any real number and n is a positive integer (or zero). A **polynomial in x and y** is an algebraic expression that has only terms of the form ax^ny^m, where a is any real number and n and m are positive integers (or zero).

A *monomial* is a polynomial of one term.

A *binomial* is a polynomial of two terms.

A *trinomial* is a polynomial of three terms.

Degree of Polynomials
4.1

The **degree of a term** in a polynomial is the sum of the exponents of its variables. The **degree of a polynomial** is the same as that of its highest-degree term.

To Add Polynomials
4.2

Add *like* terms.

To Subtract Polynomials
4.2

Change the sign of each term in the polynomial being subtracted; then add the resulting *like* terms.

To Multiply Two Binomials
4.3A

To multiply two binomials, use the FOIL method.

To Multiply a Polynomial by a Polynomial
4.3B

Multiply the first polynomial by *each term* of the second polynomial; then add the resulting products.

Special Products
4.4

$(a + b)(a - b) = a^2 - b^2$ (Section 4.4A)

$\left.\begin{array}{l}(a + b)^2 = a^2 + 2ab + b^2 \\ (a - b)^2 = a^2 - 2ab + b^2\end{array}\right\}$ Square of a binomial (Section 4.4B)

$(a + b)^n$ Use the Binomial Theorem (Section 4.4C)

To Divide a Polynomial by a Monomial
4.5A

Divide *each term* in the polynomial by the monomial; then add the resulting quotients.

To Divide a Polynomial by a Polynomial
4.5B

We use a method like that of long division of whole numbers in arithmetic.

Synthetic Division
4.6

Synthetic division can be used to divide a polynomial by a first-degree binomial.

Review Exercises 4.7 Set I

In Exercises 1–4, if the expression is a polynomial, find its degree. Otherwise, write "Not a polynomial."

1. $7x^2 - \dfrac{3}{5}xy^2 + 12$

2. $\dfrac{16}{3z - w} - 2w^2$

3. $\sqrt{7 + x}$

4. $8x^{-2} + x^{-1} - 4$

In Exercises 5 and 6, perform the indicated operations and simplify the results.

5. $(13x - 6x^3 + 14 - 15x^2) + (-17 - 23x^2 + 4x^3 + 11x)$

6. $(5x^2y + 3xy^2 - 4 + y^2) - (8 - 4x^2y + 2xy^2 - y^2)$

In Exercises 7 and 8, subtract the bottom polynomial from the top one.

7. $\begin{array}{l} x^3 \qquad - 4x + 2 \\ \overline{3x^3 + 2x^2 + \ x - 5} \end{array}$

8. $\begin{array}{l} x^4 \qquad + x^2 \qquad + 1 \\ \overline{\qquad x^3 \qquad + x} \end{array}$

9. Subtract $(3k^2 - 5k - 6)$ from the sum of $(2k^3 - 7k + 11)$ and $(4k^3 + k^2 - 9k)$.

In Exercises 10–22, find the products.

10. $(5a^2b + 3a - 2c)(-3ab^2)$

11. $(5x - 4y)(7x - 2y)$

12. $(x^2 + 3)^4$

13. $(4x^2 - 5x + 1)(2x^2 + x - 3)$

14. $(7x + 5)(7x - 5)$

15. $\left(2x^2 + \dfrac{1}{2}\right)^5$

16. $(3 + x + y)^2$

17. $(a - 5)^2$

18. $(z + 3)(z^2 - 3z + 9)$

19. $(a + b + 4)^2$

20. $(z^{-2} + z^2)^4$

21. $4x(x^2 - y^2)(x^2 + y^2)$

22. $\left(\dfrac{1}{3} + 3x^2\right)^4$

In Exercises 23–27, perform the divisions.

23. $\dfrac{-15a^2b^3 + 20a^4b^2 - 10ab}{-5ab}$

24. $(6x^2 - 9x + 10) \div (2x - 3)$

25. $(10a^2 + 23ab - 5b^2) \div (5a - b)$

26. $(3x^4 - 2x^3 + 2x^2 + 2x - 15) \div (3x^2 - 2x + 5)$

27. $\dfrac{x^4 - 81}{x + 3}$

In Exercises 28–30, use synthetic division to find the quotient and the remainder.

28. $(3x^5 + 7x^4 - 4x^2 + 4) \div (x + 2)$

29. $(5x^5 - 2x^4 + 10x^3 - 4x^2 + 2) \div \left(x - \dfrac{2}{5}\right)$

30. $(2x^5 + 6x^4 + x + 5) \div (x + 3)$

Review Exercises 4.7 Set II

NAME _____

In Exercises 1–4, if the expression is a polynomial, find its degree. Otherwise, write "Not a polynomial."

1. $\dfrac{1}{2} a^2 b^3 - 2^3 ab^2 + 5$

2. $9m^3 - \dfrac{8}{m - 5n}$

3. $\sqrt{z + 4}$

4. $x^{-3} + 2x^{-1} - 4$

In Exercises 5 and 6, perform the indicated operations and simplify the results.

5. $(7z - 20 + 11z^3 - 9z^2) + (-16z^3 + 15 - 3z^2 + 12z)$

6. $(18ef^2 - 14 - 6e^2f + 4f) - (17 + 13f - 14e^2f + 10ef^2)$

In Exercises 7 and 8, subtract the bottom polynomial from the top one.

7. $\begin{array}{l} x^3 - 2x^2 \qquad + 1 \\ \underline{5x^3 + 2x^2 - x + 3} \end{array}$

8. $\begin{array}{l} x^4 + x^3 \qquad + 1 \\ \underline{\qquad\quad x^2 + x} \end{array}$

9. Subtract $(13h^3 - 2h^2 + 7)$ from the sum of $(12h^2 - 5h - 18)$ and $(9h^3 + 10h - 6)$.

In Exercises 10–22, find the products.

10. $-4ab^2(7ab^2 - 5b + 4c)$

11. $(y^2 - 3y + 5)(2y - 3)$

12. $(3n^2 - 6n + 2)(n^2 + 4n - 5)$

13. $(w - 2x - 5)^2$

14. $(a^2 + 5b)(a^2 - 5b)$

15. $(2x - 3y)^2$

16. $(4m + 3n)(2m - 5n)$

17. $2x(x^4 + y^4)(x^4 - y^4)$

ANSWERS

1. _____

2. _____

3. _____

4. _____

5. _____

6. _____

7. _____

8. _____

9. _____

10. _____

11. _____

12. _____

13. _____

14. _____

15. _____

16. _____

17. _____

18. $(x^2 + 1)^6$

19. $(x^2 + x^{-1})^4$

18. _____

19. _____

20. $\left(4c^2 - \dfrac{1}{2}\right)^5$

21. $(m^{-1} - m^2)^6$

20. _____

21. _____

22. $(2x - 3)(4x^2 + 6x + 9)$

22. _____

23. _____

In Exercises 23–27, perform the divisions.

23. $\dfrac{24m^4n^3 - 30m^2n^2 + 18m^4n}{-6m^2n}$

24. $(21c^2 - 29c - 18) \div (3c - 5)$

24. _____

25. _____

26. _____

25. $(12a^2 - 7ab - 10b^2) \div (4a - 5b)$

27. _____

28. _____

26. $(20k^4 - 8k^3 - 39k^2 + 6k - 9) \div (5k^2 - 2k - 6)$

29. _____

30. _____

27. $\dfrac{x^6 - 64}{x - 2}$

In Exercises 28–30, use synthetic division to find the quotient and the remainder.

28. $(4x^5 - 16x^3 - 6x + 3) \div (x - 2)$

29. $(12x^5 + x^4 - 6x^3 + 8x + 11) \div \left(x + \dfrac{3}{4}\right)$

30. $(2x^5 + 10x^4 - 3x^2 - 14x + 1) \div (x + 5)$

Chapter 4 Diagnostic Test

The purpose of this test is to see how well you understand operations with polynomials. We recommend that you work this diagnostic test *before* your instructor tests you on this chapter. Allow yourself about 50 minutes.

Complete solutions for all the problems on this test, together with section references, are given in the answer section at the end of the book. For the problems you do incorrectly, study the sections cited.

1. In the polynomial $2x^2y^3 - 5^2x^2y^2 - \frac{1}{3}xy$, find:

   a. The degree of the third term
   b. The degree of the polynomial

2. Add: $-4x^3 - 3x^2 \quad\;\; + \;\; 5$
$$2x^2 + 6x - 10$$
$$3x^3 \qquad\quad - 2x + \;\; 8$$

3. Subtract the bottom polynomial from the top one.

$$3x^4 - x^3 \qquad + \; x - 2$$
$$5x^4 + x^3 + x^2 - 3x - 5$$

4. Subtract $(8 - z + 4z^2)$ from $(-3z^2 - 6z + 8)$.

5. Simplify: $(3ab^2 - 5ab) - (a^3 + 2ab) + (4ab - 7ab^2)$.

In Problems 6–12, find the products.

6. $-3ab(6a^2 - 2ab^2 + 5b)$

7. $(x - 2)(x^2 + 2x + 4)$

8. $(m^2 - 2m + 5)^2$

9. $(2x^4 + 3)(2x^4 - 3)$

10. $(5m - 2)(3m + 4)$

11. $(3R^2 - 5)^2$

12. $(2x + 1)^5$

In Problems 13–16, perform the divisions.

13. $\dfrac{9z^3w + 6z^2w^2 - 12zw^3}{3zw}$

14. $(12y^2 - 4y + 1) \div (3y + 2)$

15. $(6x^4 - 3x^3 + 2x^2 + 5x - 7) \div (2x^2 - x + 4)$

16. Use synthetic division: $(2x^4 + 3x^3 - 7x^2 - 5) \div (x + 3)$.

Cumulative Review Exercises
Chapters 1–4

1. Evaluate $10 - (\sqrt[3]{-27} - 5^2)$.

2. Simplify $\left(\dfrac{x^2 y^{-1}}{y^{-4}}\right)^{-1}$. Write your answer using only positive exponents.

3. Find the LCM of 108 and 360.

4. Simplify: $5a - \{9 - 2(3 - a) - 3a\}$.

In Exercises 5–9, solve each equation or inequality.

5. $4(x - 3) = 4 - (x + 6)$

6. $1 - x \le 2(x - 4)$

7. $|5 - x| = 6$

8. $|3x - 5| > 7$

9. $|2x - 1| \le 4$

In Exercises 10–12, perform the indicated operations and simplify the results.

10. $(3x^4 + 7x^2 - 2x)(x + 2)$

11. $(x - 1)^6$

12. $(x^3 + 2x^2 - 13x - 16) \div (x + 4)$

In Exercises 13–15, set up the problem algebraically and solve it. Be sure to state what your variables represent.

13. The three sides of a triangle are in the ratio $2 : 4 : 5$. The perimeter is 88. Find the three sides.

14. If raisins cost $1.38 per pound and granola costs $2.10 per pound, how many pounds of raisins must be mixed with 15 lb of granola for the mixture to cost $37.71?

15. A boat has a speed of 30 mph in still water. It travels downstream for 40 min and then starts back upstream. In 40 more minutes, it is still 4 mi short of its starting point. What is the speed of the stream?

5 Factoring

This chapter deals with factoring algebraic expressions. We will review the methods of factoring learned in elementary algebra and discuss additional types of factoring. We will also solve equations whose solution involves factoring and solve word problems that lead to such equations.

5.1 Greatest Common Factor (GCF)

It is essential that the techniques of factoring be mastered, because factoring is used extensively in work with algebraic fractions, in graphing, and in solving equations.

Factoring an algebraic expression means rewriting it (if possible) as a single term that is a *product of prime factors*. In Chapter 1, we used the distributive rule to rewrite a product of factors as a sum of terms, that is, $a(b + c) = ab + ac$. We now use the distributive rule to rewrite a sum of terms as a product of factors (that is, as a single term) whenever possible. When we use the distributive rule to get

$$ab + ac = a(b + c)$$

we say we are factoring out the greatest common factor. Notice that the right side of this equation has only *one term*.

Greatest Common Factor (GCF)
The **greatest common factor (GCF)** of two or more terms in an algebraic expression is the *largest* term that is a factor of all the terms. We find the GCF as follows:

TO FIND THE GREATEST COMMON FACTOR (GCF)

1. Write each numerical coefficient in prime factored form. Repeated factors must be expressed in exponential form.

2. Write down each different base, numerical or literal, that is common to all terms.

3. Raise each of the bases written down in step 2 to the *lowest* power to which it occurs in any of the terms.

4. The *greatest common factor* (GCF) is the *product* of all the powers found in step 3. It may be positive or negative.

Example 1   Find the GCF for the terms of $6y^5 - 21y^2$.

$$6y^5 - 21y^2 = 2 \cdot 3 \cdot y^5 - 3 \cdot 7 \cdot y^2$$

The bases common to both terms are 3 and y. The lowest power on the 3 is an understood 1, and the lowest power on the y is a 2. Therefore, the GCF is $3y^2$ (or $-3y^2$). ■

TO FACTOR OUT THE GCF

1. Combine like terms, if there are any.

2. Find the GCF for all of the terms. It will often, but not always, be a monomial.

3. Find the *polynomial factor** by dividing each term of the polynomial being factored by the GCF. The polynomial factor will always have as many terms as the expression in step 1. It should have only *integer* coefficients.

4. Rewrite the expression as the product of the factors found in steps 2 and 3.

5. Check the result by using the distributive rule to remove the parentheses; you should get back the polynomial you started with.

NOTE   If an expression has been factored, *it has only one term*. However, even if an expression has only one term, it still may not be factored completely. Any expression inside parentheses should always be examined carefully to see whether it could be factored further.   ☑

Example 2   Factor $6y^5 - 21y^2$.

We found in Example 1 that the GCF is $3y^2$. To find the polynomial factor, divide $6y^5$ by $3y^2$ and then divide $-21y^2$ by $3y^2$.

$$6y^5 - 21y^2 = 3y^2(2y^3 - 7)$$

This term is $\dfrac{-21y^2}{3y^2}$

This term is $\dfrac{6y^5}{3y^2}$

Notice that $3y^2(2y^3 - 7)$ has only one term and that $(2y^3 - 7)$ has no common factor left in it.

Check $3y^2(2y^3 - 7) = 6y^5 - 21y^2$

The factoring could be done using $-3y^2$ as the GCF:

$$6y^5 - 21y^2 = -3y^2(-2y^3 + 7) = -3y^2(7 - 2y^3)$$

Check $-3y^2(7 - 2y^3) = -21y^2 + 6y^5 = 6y^5 - 21y^2$ ∎

Prime (or Irreducible) Polynomials

A polynomial is said to be **prime**, or **irreducible**, over the integers if it cannot be expressed as a product of polynomials of lower degree such that all the constants in the new polynomials are integers. In this chapter, when we say to factor a polynomial, we mean to factor over the integers.

Factorization of polynomials over the integers is unique; that is, a polynomial can be completely factored over the integers in one and only one way (except for the order in which the factors are written).

---

* We call this factor the polynomial factor because it will be a polynomial and will always have more than one term.

Example 3   Factor $3x - 7y$.

Although 3 and x are factors of the first term of $3x - 7y$, they are not factors of the second term. In fact, $3x$ and $-7y$ have no common integral factor. While it is true that

$$3x - 7y = 3\left(x - \frac{7}{3}y\right)$$

and that

$$3x - 7y = 7\left(\frac{3}{7}x - y\right)$$

the parentheses now contain constants that are *not* integers. We must conclude that $3x - 7y$ is *not factorable* over the integers. It is a prime polynomial.   ∎

Example 4   Factor $21x^3y^3z^3 + 28x^2y^2z^4 - 35xy^3z^3 + 7xy^2z^3$.

$$21x^3y^3z^3 + 28x^2y^2z^4 - 35xy^3z^3 + 7xy^2z^3$$
$$= 3 \cdot 7x^3y^3z^3 + 2^2 \cdot 7x^2y^2z^4 - 5 \cdot 7xy^3z^3 + 7xy^2z^3$$

The bases common to all four terms are 7, x, y, and z. When we raise each of these bases to the lowest power that occurs in any term, we find that the GCF is $7xy^2z^3$.
    The polynomial factor is

$$\frac{3 \cdot 7x^3y^3z^3}{7xy^2z^3} + \frac{2^2 \cdot 7x^2y^2z^4}{7xy^2z^3} - \frac{5 \cdot 7xy^3z^3}{7xy^2z^3} + \frac{7xy^2z^3}{7xy^2z^3} = 3x^2y + 4xz - 5y + 1$$

Therefore $21x^3y^3z^3 + 28x^2y^2z^4 - 35xy^3z^3 + 7xy^2z^3$
$$= 7xy^2z^3(3x^2y + 4xz - 5y + 1)$$

Note that our answer has one term and that the expression within the parentheses has no common factor left in it.

Check $7xy^2z^3(3x^2y + 4xz - 5y + 1)$
$$= 21x^3y^3z^3 + 28x^2y^2z^4 - 35xy^3z^3 + 7xy^2z^3 \quad ∎$$

Sometimes an expression has a GCF that is not a monomial. Such an expression can still be factored using the same rules as above. This type of factoring is used in *factoring by grouping* (covered in Section 5.2) and is also used extensively in calculus.

Example 5   Factor $a(x + y) + b(x + y)$.

This expression has two terms and thus is *not* in factored form. The common factor, $x + y$, is not a monomial; it is a binomial. Nevertheless, $x + y$ is the GCF. We factor as follows:

Therefore, $a(x + y) + b(x + y) = (x + y)(a + b)$.

Our answer has one term, so it is in factored form.

Check $(x + y)(a + b) = (a + b)(x + y) = a(x + y) + b(x + y)$ ∎

Example 6   Factor $72x^2(m^2 + n)^2 + 36(m^2 + n)$.

The GCF is $2^2 \cdot 3^2(m^2 + n)^1$. Therefore,

$$72x^2(m^2 + n)^2 + 36(m^2 + n) = 36(m^2 + n)(2x^2[m^2 + n] + 1)$$

When we remove the inner grouping symbols, we have

$$72x^2(m^2 + n)^2 + 36(m^2 + n) = 36(m^2 + n)(2x^2m^2 + 2x^2n + 1)$$

Check $36(m^2 + n)(2x^2m^2 + 2x^2n + 1) = 36(m^2 + n)(2x^2[m^2 + n] + 1)$

$$= 72x^2(m^2 + n)^2 + 36(m^2 + n)$$ ∎

EXERCISES 5.1

Set I   Factor each of the following expressions or write "Not factorable."

1. $54x^3yz^4 - 72xy^3$ **2.** $225ab^5c - 105a^3b^2c^6$

3. $16x^3 - 8x^2 + 4x$ **4.** $27a^4 - 9a^2 + 3a$

5. $3x^3 - 4y^2 + 5z$ **6.** $7z^3 + 3y^2 - 4x$

7. $6my + 15mz - 5n - 4n$ **8.** $4nx + 8ny + 16z - 4z$

9. $-35r^7s^5t^4 - 55r^8s^9u^4 + 40p^8r^9s^8$

10. $-120a^8b^7c^5 + 40a^4c^3d^9 - 80a^5c^5$

11. $10x^2 - 21y + 11z^3$ **12.** $15a^3 + 14b^5 - 13c$

13. $-24x^8y^3 - 12x^7y^4 + 48x^5y^5 + 60x^4y^6$

14. $64y^9z^5 + 48y^8z^6 - 16y^7z^7 - 80y^4z^8$

15. $m(a + b) + n(a + b)$ **16.** $3a(a - 2b) + 2(a - 2b)$

17. $x(y + 1) - (y + 1)$ **18.** $2e(3e - f) - 3(3e - f)$

19. $5(x - y) - (x - y)^2$ **20.** $4(a + b) - (a + b)^2$

21. $8x(y^2 + 3z)^2 - 6x^4(y^2 + 3z)$

22. $12a^3(b - 2c^5)^3 - 15a^2(b - 2c^5)^2$

23. $5(x + y)^3(a + b)^5 + 15(x + y)^2(a + b)^6$

24. $14(s + t)^4(u + v)^7 + 7(s + t)^5(u + v)^6$

Set II   Factor each of the following expressions or write "Not factorable."

1. $168s^4 - 126st^3u$ **2.** $-5x^3 + 10x^5y - 15x^3y^2$

3. $25y^3 - 15y^2 + 5y$ **4.** $17 + 34x^2 - 85xy$

5. $5a^2 - 2b + 3c$ **6.** $3x(x + y) - 6x^2(x + y)^2$

7. $7xy + 3yx - 5z + z$ **8.** $7xy + 49xy^2 - 14x^2y$

9. $-36x^3y^7 - 18x^4y^5 + 27x^5y^3 - 9x^6y^2$

10. $5x^4 - 7y^3 + 3z$ **11.** $25s^2 - 28t^3 + 9u$

12. $6a(b - c)^3 - 9a^2(b - c)^2$

13. $10a^2b^4 - 15a^3c^3 - 25a^5c^7$

14. $3a^3 + 17b - 8c^2$

15. $a(a + b) + 3b(a + b)$

16. $15x^4y^3 - 18x^5y^6 + 27y^4$

17. $3x(2y - 5) - 2(2y - 5)$

18. $3x^3(y + 3z)^2 - 6x^4(y + 3z)^3$

19. $6(a - b)^2 - (a - b)$

20. $12(x + y)^3 - 3(x + y)^4$

21. $6s^4(t^3 + 2u)^3 - 9s^3(t^3 + 2u)^2$

22. $24x^3(a - 5b)^5 - 32x^4(a - 5b)^4$

23. $21(a + b)^4(c + d)^7 + 3(a + b)^5(c + d)^6$

24. $54s^4(u^2 - v^3)^3 - 36s^3(u^2 - v^3)^4$

5.2 Factoring by Grouping

If a polynomial has four or more terms, we can sometimes factor it by first separating its terms into two or more groups and factoring each group separately. Since we will still have more than one term at this point, the expression will not yet be factored. However, if we then see that each of the groups has a common factor, we will be able to factor the polynomial.

We begin by considering problems in which we can factor the expression by grouping the terms into two groups of two terms each. The rules that follow assume that any factor common to all four terms has already been factored out.

TO FACTOR AN EXPRESSION OF FOUR TERMS BY GROUPING TWO AND TWO

1. Arrange the four terms into two groups of two terms each. Each group of two terms should have a common factor.

2. Factor out the GCF from each group. You will now have two terms. *The expression will not yet be factored.*

3. Factor the two-term expression resulting from step 2, if possible.

4. If the two terms resulting from step 2 do not have a GCF, try a different arrangement of the original four terms.

Example 1   Factor $ax + ay + bx + by$.

$$\text{GCF} = a \qquad \text{GCF} = b$$

$$ax + ay + bx + by$$

$$= a(x + y) + b(x + y) \quad \leftarrow \text{This expression is not in factored form because it has two terms}$$

$$= (x + y)(a + b)$$

Therefore, $ax + ay + bx + by = (x + y)(a + b)$.

Check
$$(x + y)(a + b) = (x + y)a + (x + y)b$$
$$= ax + ay + bx + by \quad \blacksquare$$

It is often possible to group terms differently and still be able to factor the expression. *The same factors are obtained no matter what grouping is used*, because factorization over the integers is unique.

Example 2   Factor $ab - b + a - 1$.

One Grouping

$$\boxed{ab - b} + \boxed{a - 1}$$

$$= b(\boxed{a - 1}) + 1(\boxed{a - 1}) \longleftarrow \text{Not yet factored}$$

$$= (\boxed{a - 1})(b + 1)$$

If we rearrange the terms, we have

A Different Grouping

$$\boxed{ab + a} - b - 1$$

$$= a(\boxed{b + 1}) - 1(\boxed{b + 1}) \longleftarrow$$

┌ Note that when we factor -1
│ from $-b - 1$, we must change
│ the sign of each term that goes
│ *into* the parentheses

$$= (\boxed{b + 1})(a - 1)$$

Therefore, $ab - b + a - 1 = (a - 1)(b + 1) = (b + 1)(a - 1)$.

Check $(a - 1)(b + 1) = ab - b + a - 1$ ∎

Example 3   Factor $2x^2 - 6xy + 3x - 9y$.

$$\text{GCF} = 2x \longrightarrow \qquad\qquad \longleftarrow \text{GCF} = 3$$

$$\boxed{2x^2 - 6xy} + \boxed{3x - 9y}$$

$$= 2x(\boxed{x - 3y}) + 3(\boxed{x - 3y}) \qquad (x - 3y) \text{ is the GCF}$$

$$= (\boxed{x - 3y})(2x + 3)$$

Therefore, $2x^2 - 6xy + 3x - 9y = (x - 3y)(2x + 3)$.

Check $(x - 3y)(2x + 3) = 2x^2 - 6xy + 3x - 9y$ ∎

If we have an expression to factor that has six terms, we can try either three groups of two terms each *or* two groups of three terms each.

Example 4   Factor $ax^2 - ax + 5a + bx^2 - bx + 5b$.

If we try two groups of three terms each, we have

$$ax^2 - ax + 5a + bx^2 - bx + 5b$$

$$= a(\boxed{x^2 - x + 5}) + b(\boxed{x^2 - x + 5}) \qquad \text{Common } trinomial \text{ factor}$$

$$= (\boxed{x^2 - x + 5})(a + b)$$

If we try three groups of two terms each, we rearrange and have

$$ax^2 + bx^2 - ax - bx + 5a + 5b$$

$$= x^2(\boxed{a + b}) - x(\boxed{a + b}) + 5(\boxed{a + b}) \qquad \text{Common } \textit{binomial} \text{ factor}$$

$$= (\boxed{a + b})(x^2 - x + 5)$$

Check $\qquad (x^2 - x + 5)(a + b) = (a + b)(x^2 - x + 5)$

$$= ax^2 + bx^2 - ax - bx + 5a + 5b \quad \blacksquare$$

A WORD OF CAUTION An expression is *not* factored until it has been written as a single term that is a product of factors. To illustrate this, consider Example 1 again:

$$ax + ay + bx + by \qquad \text{(Example 1)}$$

$$= \boxed{a(x + y)} + \boxed{b(x + y)} \qquad \text{This expression is } \textit{not} \text{ in factored}$$
$$\text{form because it has } \textit{two} \text{ terms}$$

First   Second
term   term

$$= \boxed{(x + y)(a + b)} \qquad \textit{Factored form} \text{ of}$$
$$ax + ay + bx + by$$

Single term

☑

EXERCISES 5.2

Set I   Factor each expression or write "Not factorable."

1. $mx - nx - my + ny$ $\qquad$ **2.** $ah - ak - bh + bk$

3. $xy + x - y - 1$ $\qquad$ **4.** $ad - d + a - 1$

5. $3a^2 - 6ab + 2a - 4b$ $\qquad$ **6.** $2h^2 - 6hk + 5h - 15k$

7. $6e^2 - 2ef - 9e + 3f$ $\qquad$ **8.** $8m^2 - 4mn - 6m + 3n$

9. $x^3 + 3x^2 - 2x - 6$ $\qquad$ **10.** $a^3 - a^2 - 2a + 2$

11. $b^3 + 4b^2 + 5b - 20$ $\qquad$ **12.** $6x^3 + 3x^2 - 2x + 1$

13. $2a^3 + 8a^2 - 3a - 12$ $\qquad$ **14.** $5y^3 - 10y^2 + 2y - 4$

15. $acm + bcm + acn + bcn$ $\qquad$ **16.** $cku + ckv + dku + dkv$

17. $a^2x + 2ax + 5x + a^2y + 2ay + 5y$ $\qquad$ **18.** $ax^2 + 3ax + 7a + bx^2 + 3bx + 7b$

19. $s^2x - sx + 4x + s^2y - sy + 4y$ $\qquad$ **20.** $at^2 - at + 3a + bt^2 - bt + 3b$

21. $ax^2 + ax + a - x^2 - x - 1$ $\qquad$ **22.** $xy^2 + xy + 2x - y^2 - y - 2$

Set II   Factor each expression or write "Not factorable."

1. $hw - kw - hz + kz$ $\qquad$ **2.** $3a - 5b + 6ac - 10bc$

3. $xy - x + y - 1$ $\qquad$ **4.** $3x^3 - 7x^2 + 3x - 7$

5. $12m^2 - 6mn + 14m - 7n$ $\qquad$ **6.** $a^3m + 4a^2m - a^2n - 4an$

7. $6x^2 - 3xy - 4x + 2y$ $\qquad$ **8.** $6x + 3y - 12ax - 6ay$

9. $x^3 + x^2 - 2x - 2$

10. $7xy - 3z - 14axy + 6az$

11. $4a^3 + 8a^2 - a + 2$

12. $8x^2 - 11xy - 16x + 22y$

13. $3t^3 - 12t^2 + 2t - 8$

14. $ab - ac - bd - cd$

15. $acx + acy + bcx + bcy$

16. $x^4 + x^3 + x^2 + x$

17. $ax^2 + 3ax + 8a + bx^2 + 3bx + 8b$

18. $x^3 + x^2a + x^2 + ax + 4x + 4a$

19. $a^2x - ax + 4x + a^2y - ay + 4y$

20. $2x^3 - 2ax^2 + x^2 - ax + x - a$

21. $b^2y + 2by + 3y - b^2 - 2b - 3$

22. $a^2x + 3ax + 4x - a^2 - 3a - 4$

5.3 Factoring the Difference of Two Squares

The expression $a^2 - b^2$ is called a *difference of two squares*. In Section 4.4A, we proved that $(a + b)(a - b) = a^2 - b^2$. Therefore, it must be true that $a^2 - b^2$ *factors into* $(a + b)(a - b)$.

TO FACTOR THE DIFFERENCE OF TWO SQUARES

1. Find the principal square root of each of the terms by inspection.

2. The two binomial factors are the sum of and the difference of the square roots found in step 1.

$$a^2 - b^2 = (a + b)(a - b)$$

Example 1   Factor $49a^6b^2 - 81c^4d^8$.

Difference of two squares

$$49a^6b^2 - 81c^4d^8 = (7a^3b)^2 - (9c^2d^4)^2$$

$\sqrt{81c^4d^8}$

$$= (7a^3b + 9c^2d^4)(7a^3b - 9c^2d^4)$$

$\sqrt{49a^6b^2}$

Check $(7a^3b + 9c^2d^4)(7a^3b - 9c^2d^4) = 49a^6b^2 - 81c^4d^8$ ∎

A WORD OF CAUTION   A *sum* of two squares is *not factorable* over the integers. (Exception: If a sum of two squares is of degree four or more, it *may* be factorable by completing the square, a method of factoring covered in Section 5.7.) ☑

Example 2   Factor $a^2 + b^2$.

Since $a^2 + b^2$ has no common monomial factor and since it is a *sum* of two squares, it is not factorable. It is a *prime polynomial*. ∎

We will consider an expression to be *completely factored* when all of its factors are prime. By this we mean that no more factoring can be done by any method.

Example 3   Factor $a^4 - b^4$.

This factor can be factored again

$$a^4 - b^4 = (a^2 + b^2)(a^2 - b^2) = (a^2 + b^2)(a + b)(a - b)$$

This factor is a sum of two squares and cannot be factored

Check

$$(a^2 + b^2)(a + b)(a - b) = (a^2 + b^2)(a^2 - b^2)$$
$$= a^4 - b^4 \quad ∎$$

A WORD OF CAUTION   Always remove the GCF first whenever possible.   ☑

Example 4   Factor $27x^4 - 12y^2$.

$$27x^4 - 12y^2 = 3(9x^4 - 4y^2) \longleftarrow \text{This has been factored,}$$
but
this factor is not prime, so it factors further

$$= 3(3x^2 + 2y)(3x^2 - 2y) \quad ∎$$

Sometimes the quantities that are squares are not monomials. If the entire expression is in the form $a^2 - b^2$, we can still factor it (see Example 5).

Example 5   Factor $(x - y)^2 - (a + b)^2$.

$$(x - y)^2 - (a + b)^2 \qquad \text{Difference of two squares}$$
$$= [\qquad + \qquad][\qquad - \qquad]$$
$$= [(x - y) + (a + b)][(x - y) - (a + b)]$$
$$= (x - y + a + b)(x - y - a - b)$$

Check

$$(x - y + a + b)(x - y - a - b)$$
$$= ([x - y] + [a + b])([x - y] - [a + b])$$
$$= [x - y]^2 - [a + b]^2 \quad ∎$$

Example 6   Factor $a^2 - b^2 + a - b$.

If we group the terms into two groups of two terms each, we have

$$a^2 - b^2 + a - b$$

$$= (a + b)(\;a - b\;) + (\;a - b\;) \qquad a - b \text{ is a common binomial factor}$$

$$= (a + b)(\;a - b\;) + 1(\;a - b\;)$$

$$= (\;a - b\;)([a + b] + 1)$$

$$= (a - b)(a + b + 1)$$

Check $(a - b)(a + b + 1) = a^2 - b^2 + a - b$ ∎

EXERCISES 5.3

Set I   Factor completely or write "Not factorable."

1. $2x^2 - 8y^2$
2. $3x^2 - 27y^2$
3. $98u^4 - 72v^4$
4. $243m^6 - 300n^4$
5. $x^4 - y^4$
6. $a^4 - 16$
7. $4c^2 + 1$
8. $16d^2 + 1$
9. $4h^4k^4 - 1$
10. $9x^4 - 1$
11. $25a^4b^2 - a^2b^4$
12. $x^2y^4 - 100x^4y^2$
13. $16x^2 + 8x$
14. $25y^2 + 5y$
15. $9x^2 + 7y$
16. $36a^2 + 5b$
17. $(x + y)^2 - 4$
18. $(a + b)^2 - 9$
19. $(a + b)x^2 - (a + b)y^2$
20. $(x + y)a^2 - (x + y)b^2$
21. $9x^2 + y^2$
22. $25x^2 + y^2$
23. $x^2 - 9y^2 + x - 3y$
24. $x^2 - y^2 + x - y$
25. $x + 2y + x^2 - 4y^2$
26. $a + b + a^2 - b^2$

Set II   Factor completely or write "Not factorable."

1. $6m^2 - 54n^4$
2. $3x^2 - 27x$
3. $50a^2 - 8b^2$
4. $4x^2 - 9$
5. $x^4 - 81$
6. $x^2 + 16$
7. $16y^4z^4 + 1$
8. $1 - 25a^2b^2$
9. $16y^4z^4 - 1$
10. $81x^2 - y^2$
11. $3b^2x^4 - 12b^2y^2$
12. $y^4 - 256$
13. $4x^2 + 8x$
14. $28a^2b^2 - 7a^2$
15. $25x^2 + 3y$
16. $49a^2 - 7a$
17. $(s + t)^2 - 16$
18. $(s + t)a^2 - (s + t)b^2$
19. $(s + t)x^2 - (s + t)y^2$
20. $(a - b)^2 - 1$
21. $4 + x^2$
22. $9x^2 - 3x$
23. $s^2 - t^2 + s - t$
24. $4x + 4y + x^2 - y^2$
25. $4x + y + 16x^2 - y^2$
26. $49x^2 - a^2 + 14x - 2a$

5.4 Factoring Trinomials

5.4A Factoring a Trinomial with a Leading Coefficient of 1

While many trinomials are not factorable, many others factor into the product of two binomials. Careful examination of the following multiplication problems leads us to the *Rule of Signs for Factoring Trinomials* that follows.

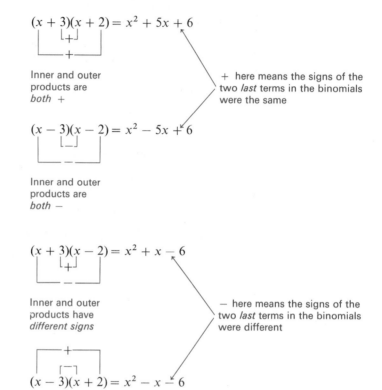

Inner and outer products are *both +*

\+ here means the signs of the two *last* terms in the binomials were the same

Inner and outer products are *both −*

Inner and outer products have *different signs*

− here means the signs of the two *last* terms in the binomials were different

---

RULE OF SIGNS FOR FACTORING TRINOMIALS

1. If the last term of the trinomial is +, the signs in the binomials are the same.

    a. If the middle term of the trinomial is +, both signs in the binomials are +.

    b. If the middle term of the trinomial is −, both signs in the binomials are −.

2. If the last term of the trinomial is −, the signs in the binomials are different, and we must put the signs in last.

The method of factoring a trinomial with a leading coefficient of 1 is summarized as follows:

TO FACTOR A TRINOMIAL WITH A LEADING COEFFICIENT OF 1

(It is assumed that like terms have been combined.)

1. Factor out the GCF.

2. Arrange the trinomial in descending powers of the variable.

3. Make a blank outline. We *assume* that the trinomial will factor into the product of two binomials. If the Rule of Signs indicates that the signs will both be positive or both be negative, insert those signs.

4. The first term inside each set of parentheses will be the square root of the first term of the trinomial. If the third term of the trinomial has a variable, the square root of *that* variable must be a factor of the second term in each binomial.

5. To find the last term of each binomial:

   a. List (mentally, at least) *all* pairs of integral factors of the coefficient of the last term of the trinomial.

   b. Select the particular pair of factors that has a sum equal to the coefficient of the middle term of the trinomial. If no such pair of factors exists, the trinomial is *not factorable*.

6. Check your result by multiplying the binomials together.

Example 1   Factor $z^2 + 8zw + 12w^2$.

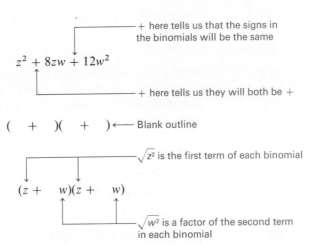

The pairs of integral factors of $+12$ are $(1)(12)$, $(-1)(-12)$, $(2)(6)$, $(-2)(-6)$, $(3)(4)$, and $(-3)(-4)$. We must select the pair whose sum is $+8$—the pair 2 and 6. We then have

$$z^2 + 8zw + 12w^2 = (z + 2w)(z + 6w) \ or \ (z + 6w)(z + 2w)$$

Check $(z + 2w)(z + 6w) = (z + 6w)(z + 2w) = z^2 + 8zw + 12w^2$ ∎

A WORD OF CAUTION *Both sets of parentheses are essential.* Note:

$$(z + 2w)z + 6w = z^2 + 2zw + 6w \neq z^2 + 8zw + 12w^2$$

$$z + 2w(z + 6w) = z + 2zw + 12w^2 \neq z^2 + 8zw + 12w^2$$

$$z + 2w \cdot z + 6w = z + 2zw + 6w \neq z^2 + 8zw + 12w^2 \qquad \boxed{\checkmark}$$

Example 2 Factor $m^2 - 6m + 8$.

+ here tells us the signs will be the *same*

$$m^2 - 6m + 8$$

− here tells us they will both be −

We must find two integers whose product is $+8$ and whose sum is -6. The integers are -2 and -4. Therefore,

$$m^2 - 6m + 8 = (m - 2)(m - 4) \ or \ (m - 4)(m - 2)$$

Check $(m - 2)(m - 4) = (m - 4)(m - 2) = m^2 - 6m + 8$ ∎

Example 3 Factor $w^2 + 8w - 20$.

$$w^2 + 8w - 20$$

− here tells us the signs in the binomial will be *different*

We must find two integers whose product is -20 and whose sum is $+8$. The integers are $+10$ and -2. Therefore,

$$w^2 + 8w - 20 = (w - 2)(w + 10) \ or \ (w + 10)(w - 2)$$

The order of the factors is unimportant

Check $(w - 2)(w + 10) = (w + 10)(w - 2) = w^2 + 8w - 20$ ∎

Example 4 Factor $x^2 + 3x - 5$.

We must find two integers whose product is -5 and whose sum is 3. The only pairs of integers whose product is -5 are $(-1)(5)$ and $(1)(-5)$. The sum of neither pair is $+3$. Therefore, this trinomial is *not factorable* over the integers; it is a prime polynomial. ∎

Example 5 Factor $2ax^2 - 14axy - 60ay^2$.

All three terms have a common factor. The GCF is $2a$. When we factor out the GCF, we have

$$2ax^2 - 14axy - 60ay^2 = 2a(x^2 - 7xy - 30y^2)$$

The trinomial has been factored, but not completely. We must now factor $x^2 - 7xy - 30y^2$. To do this, we must find two integers whose product is -30 and whose sum is -7. The only such pair of integers is (3) and (-10). Therefore,

$$2ax^2 - 14axy - 60ay^2 = 2a(x + 3y)(x - 10y)$$

Check
$$2a(x + 3y)(x - 10y) = 2a(x^2 - 7xy - 30y^2)$$
$$= 2ax^2 - 14axy - 60ay^2 \quad ∎$$

Sometimes the terms of the trinomial are not monomials (see Example 6).

Example 6   Factor $(x - y)^2 - 2(x - y) - 8$.

This problem can be solved by using a substitution. If we let $(x - y) = a$, we have

$$(x - y)^2 - 2(x - y) - 8$$

$$= a^2 - 2a - 8 = (a + 2) \cdot (a - 4) \qquad -8 = (-1)(8) = (-8)(1)$$
$$= (-2)(4) = (-4)(2)$$

Substituting
back

$$\rightarrow (x - y)^2 - 2(x - y) - 8 = [(x - y) + 2][(x - y) - 4]$$

$$= (x - y + 2)(x - y - 4) \quad \blacksquare$$

EXERCISES 5.4A

Set I   Factor completely or write "Not factorable."

1. $x^2 - 7x + 18$ 2. $x^2 - 3x + 18$ 3. $m^2 + 13m + 12$

4. $x^2 + 15x + 14$ 5. $x^2 + 7x + 1$ 6. $x^2 + 5x + 1$

7. $t^2 + 7t - 30$ 8. $m^2 - 13m - 30$ 9. $x^2 + 4x + 6x$

10. $y^2 + 7y + 3y$ 11. $u^4 - 15u^2 + 14$ 12. $y^4 - 16y^2 + 15$

13. $u^2 + 12u - 64$ 14. $v^2 - 30v - 64$ 15. $3x + x^2 + 2$

16. $7a + a^2 + 10$ 17. $x^4 - 6x^3 + 2x^2$ 18. $y^6 - 2y^4 + 2y^2$

19. $x^2 + xy - 2y^2$ 20. $x^2 + 6xy + 9y^2$

21. $(a + b)^2 + 6(a + b) + 8$ 22. $(m + n)^2 + 9(m + n) + 8$

23. $(x + y)^2 - 13(x + y) - 30$ 24. $(x + y)^2 - 10(x + y) - 24$

Set II   Factor completely or write "Not factorable."

1. $z^2 - 9z + 20$ 2. $x^3 - 6x^2 - 16x$ 3. $u^2 + 11u + 10$

4. $x^2 - 12x + 35$ 5. $x^2 + 4x + 1$ 6. $x^2 + x - 56$

7. $x^2 + 9x + 10$ 8. $x^2 + 6x + 6$ 9. $x^2 + 5x + 3x$

10. $x^2 + 12x - 13$ 11. $x^4 + 2x^2 - 3$ 12. $x^4 + 2x^3 - 3x^2$

13. $f^2 - 7f - 18$ 14. $x^2 + 8x + 7x$ 15. $10v + v^2 + 16$

16. $15 - 8x + x^2$ 17. $z^4 + 3z^3 + 5z^2$ 18. $x^4 - 21 - 4x^2$

19. $a^2 + 4ab + 3b^2$ 20. $x^2 + 5x - 24$

21. $(a + b)^2 + 9(a + b) + 14$ 22. $(x + y)^2 - (x + y) - 12$

23. $(x + y)^2 - 2(x + y) - 15$ 24. $(a - b)^2 - 6(a - b) + 5$

5.4B   Factoring a Trinomial with a Leading Coefficient Unequal to 1

Two methods will be shown for factoring a trinomial in which the leading coefficient is not 1. The first is a trial-and-error method; the second, the Master Product Method, makes use of factoring by grouping.

The Trial Method

The rules that follow assume that like terms have been combined and that any common factors have been factored out. It is also assumed that the trinomial has been arranged in descending powers of the variable and that the leading coefficient is positive. If the leading coefficient is negative but the *third* term is positive, either arrange the trinomial in ascending powers* or factor out -1 before proceeding. We will continue to use the Rule of Signs for Factoring Trinomials from Section 5.4A.

TO FACTOR A TRINOMIAL WITH A LEADING COEFFICIENT UNEQUAL TO 1

1. Make a blank outline and fill in the *literal parts* of each term of each binomial.† Fill in the signs in each binomial if they are both positive or both negative.

2. List (mentally, at least) all pairs of factors of the coefficient of the first term of the trinomial and of the last term of the trinomial.

3. By trial and error, select the pairs of factors (if they exist) from step 2 that make the sum of the inner and outer products of the binomials equal to the middle term of the trinomial. If no such pairs exist, the trinomial is *not factorable*.

4. Check the result.

Example 7   Factor $5x^2 + 13xy + 6y^2$.

Blank outline

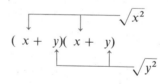

Variables are in place, and so are the signs, since the signs must both be $+$

Since the only positive factors of 5 are 5 and 1, we can put them in the blank outline also:

$$(5x + \quad y)(1x + \quad y)$$

There are two pairs of factors to try for 6, which is the coefficient of y^2—$(1)(6)$ and $(2)(3)$. Therefore, we must try the following combinations:

$$(5x + \quad y)(x + 6y)$$
$$(5x + 6y)(x + \quad y)$$
$$(5x + 2y)(x + 3y)$$
$$(5x + 3y)(x + 2y)$$

---

* A polynomial is in *ascending powers* if its exponents *increase* as we read from left to right.

† See step 4, p. 189.

In all of these combinations, the product of the two first terms is $5x^2$ and the product of the two last terms is $6y^2$. However, only in the *last* combination is the sum of the inner and outer products equal to $13xy$. Therefore,

$$5x^2 + 13xy + 6y^2 = (5x + 3y)(x + 2y)$$

Check $(5x + 3y)(x + 2y) = 5x^2 + 13xy + 6y^2$ ∎

NOTE It is not necessary to *write* all possible combinations as was done in Example 7. ☑

If the original trinomial does not have a common factor, then neither of the *binomial factors* can have a common factor. This fact can help you eliminate some combinations from consideration (see Example 8).

Example 8 Factor $6x^2 - 89x - 15$.

There is no common factor for all three terms. The pairs of positive factors of 6 are $(2)(3)$ and $(1)(6)$. The pairs of factors of -15 are $(3)(-5)$, $(-3)(5)$, $(15)(-1)$, and $(-15)(1)$. Thus, the *possible* factorizations are

$$(2x - 3)(3x + 5) \qquad (2x + 3)(3x - 5)$$
$$\star(2x - 5)(3x + 3) \qquad \star(2x + 5)(3x - 3)$$
$$\star(2x - 1)(3x + 15) \qquad \star(2x + 1)(3x - 15)$$
$$(2x - 15)(3x + 1) \qquad (2x + 15)(3x - 1)$$
$$\star(6x - 3)(x + 5) \qquad \star(6x + 3)(x - 5)$$
$$(6x - 5)(x + 3) \qquad (6x + 5)(x - 3)$$
$$\star(6x - 15)(x + 1) \qquad \star(6x + 15)(x - 1)$$
$$(6x - 1)(x + 15) \qquad \boxed{(6x + 1)(x - 15)}$$

This is the *only* combination in which the sum of the inner and outer products is $-89x$

Therefore, $6x^2 - 89x - 15 = (6x + 1)(x - 15)$.

Check $(6x + 1)(x - 15) = 6x^2 - 89x - 15$

The starred combinations all have a common factor of 3 in one of the binomials. Since the original trinomial had no common factor, these combinations need not be given any consideration. ∎

Example 9 Factor $3x^2 - x + 7$.

Possible factorizations:

$$(3x - 7)(x - 1)$$
$$(3x - 1)(x - 7)$$

In both of these factorizations, the product of the two first terms is $3x^2$ and the product of the two last terms is $+7$. However, in neither one is the sum of the inner and outer products $-x$. Therefore, $3x^2 - x + 7$ is *not factorable*. ∎

Example 10 Factor $12 + 7x - 10x^2$.

If we arranged this trinomial in *descending* powers of x, the leading coefficient would be negative. Therefore, we will leave it in *ascending* powers. Note that 12, 7, and 10 have no common factor. The pairs of positive factors of 12 are (3)(4), (2)(6), and (1)(12). The pairs of factors of -10 are (2)(-5), (-2)(5), (1)(-10), and (-1)(10).

This time, rather than write *all* possible combinations of binomials, we will stop when we find a combination that gives us $12 + 7x - 10x^2$. In each starred combination, one of the binomials has a common factor of 2.

$$\star(3 + 5x)(4 - 2x)$$
$$(3 + 2x)(4 - 5x)$$
$$\star(3 - 5x)(4 + 2x)$$
$$(3 - 2x)(4 + 5x) \leftarrow \text{The sum of the inner and outer}$$
$$\text{products is } +7x$$

Therefore: $12 + 7x - 10x^2 = (3 - 2x)(4 + 5x)$.

Check $(3 - 2x)(4 + 5x) = 12 + 7x - 10x^2$ ∎

Example 11 Factor $15x^2 - 25xy - 10y^2$.

$$5(3x^2 - 5xy - 2y^2) \qquad \text{First, remove the common factor, 5}$$

$$5(x - 2y) \quad (3x + 1y) \qquad \text{Then factor the remaining trinomial}$$
$$\underset{-6xy}{\underline{\quad\quad}}$$
$$\underset{+1xy}{\underline{\quad\quad\quad\quad}}$$
$$-5xy$$

Therefore, $15x^2 - 25xy - 10y^2 = 5(x - 2y)(3x + y)$.

Check $5(x - 2y)(3x + y) = 5(3x^2 - 5xy - 2y^2)$
$$= 15x^2 - 25xy - 10y^2 \quad ∎$$

A WORD OF CAUTION If the 5 isn't factored out first in Example 11, we will get

$$15x^2 - 25xy - 10y^2 = (5x - 10y)(3x + y)$$

or $$15x^2 - 25xy - 10y^2 = (x - 2y)(15x + 5y)$$

Neither of these binomials is completely factored. ☑

Example 12 Factor $5(2y - z)^2 + 12(2y - z) + 4$.

We can use a substitution here. Let $(2y - z) = a$. Then

$$5(2y - z)^2 + 12(2y - z) + 4 = 5a^2 + 12a + 4 = (a + \quad)(a + \quad)$$
$$\underset{+12a}{\underline{\quad\quad\quad\quad}}$$

$$5 = 1 \cdot 5 \quad | \quad 4 = 1 \cdot 4$$
$$= 2 \cdot 2$$

$$(1a + 2)(5a + 2)$$
$$\underset{+10a}{\underline{\quad\quad}}$$
$$\underset{+2a}{\underline{\quad\quad\quad\quad}}$$
$$+12a$$

Therefore, $5a^2 + 12a + 4 = (a + 2)(5a + 2)$. Substituting back $2y - z$ for a, we have

$$5(2y - z)^2 + 12(2y - z) + 4 = [(2y - z) + 2][5(2y - z) + 2]$$
$$= (2y - z + 2)(10y - 5z + 2)$$

Check $([2y - z] + 2)(5[2y - z] + 2) = 5(2y - z)^2 + 12(2y - z) + 4$ ∎

Example 13 Factor $2x^2 + 5xy - 3y^2 + 8x - 4y$.

Since this expression has more than three terms, we will have to factor by grouping. Try grouping the first three terms and the last two terms.

$$2x^2 + 5xy - 3y^2 + 8x - 4y$$

Factoring each group, we have

$$(\,2x - y\,)(x + 3y) + 4(\,2x - y\,)$$

Note that we still have two terms. The expression has not yet been completely factored. However, we now have a common *binomial* factor, namely, $2x - y$. When we factor this out we have

$$(2x - y)[(x + 3y) + 4]$$

Therefore, $2x^2 + 5xy - 3y^2 + 8x - 4y = (2x - y)(x + 3y + 4)$.

Check $(2x - y)(x + 3y + 4) = 2x^2 + 5xy - 3y^2 + 8x - 4y$ ∎

The Master Product Method

The *Master Product Method*, which makes use of factoring by grouping, is a method of factoring trinomials that eliminates some of the guesswork. It can also be used to determine whether a trinomial is factorable or not. The rules that follow assume that any common factors have been factored out.

TO FACTOR A TRINOMIAL BY THE MASTER PRODUCT METHOD

Arrange the trinomial in descending powers.

$$ax^2 + bx + c$$

1. Find the Master Product (MP) by multiplying the first and last coefficients of the trinomial being factored (MP $= a \cdot c$).

2. List the pairs of factors of the Master Product (MP).

3. Choose the pair of factors whose sum is the coefficient of the middle term (b).

4. Rewrite the given trinomial, replacing the middle term by the sum of two terms whose coefficients are the pair of factors found in step 3.

5. Factor the step 4 expression by grouping.

Check your factoring by multiplying the binomial factors to see if their product is the given trinomial.

Example 14   Factor $5x + 2x^2 + 3$.

$$\underbrace{2x^2 + 5x + 3}_{} \qquad \text{Arranged in descending powers}$$

$$\text{Master Product} = (2)(+3) = +6$$

$$6 = (+1)(+6) = (-1)(-6)$$
$$= (+2)(+3) = (-2)(-3)$$

$$(+2) + (+3) = 5 \longleftarrow \text{The middle coefficient}$$

$$\underbrace{2x^2 + 2x}_{} + \underbrace{3x + 3}_{} \longleftarrow \text{Factor by grouping}$$

$$= 2x(x + 1) + 3(x + 1)$$

Therefore, $2x^2 + 5x + 3 = (x + 1)(2x + 3)$.

Check $(x + 1)(2x + 3) = 2x^2 + 5x + 3$ ■

Example 15   Factor $3m^2 - 2mn - 8n^2$.

$$\text{Master Product} = (3)(-8) = -24$$

$$-24 = (-1)(24) = (1)(-24)$$
$$= (-2)(12) = (2)(-12)$$
$$= (-3)(8) \ = (3)(-8)$$
$$= (-4)(6) \ = (4)(-6) \qquad (+4) + (-6) = -2 \longleftarrow \text{The middle coefficient}$$

$$\underbrace{3m^2 + 4mn}_{} - \underbrace{6mn - 8n^2}_{} \longleftarrow \text{Factor by grouping}$$

$$= m(3m + 4n) - 2n(3m + 4n)$$

Therefore, $3m^2 - 2mn - 8n^2 = (3m + 4n)(m - 2n)$. (The checking is left to the student.) ■

Example 16   Factor $12x^2 - 5x + 10$.

$$\text{Master Product} = 12(10) = 120$$

$$120 = 1(120) = (-1)(-120)$$
$$= \ \ 2(60) = (-2)(-60)$$
$$= \ \ 3(40) = (-3)(-40)$$
$$= \ \ 4(30) = (-4)(-30)$$
$$= \ \ 5(24) = (-5)(-24)$$
$$= \ \ 6(20) = (-6)(-20)$$
$$= \ \ 8(15) = (-8)(-15)$$
$$= 10(12) = (-10)(-12)$$

None of the sums of these pairs is -5. Therefore, the trinomial is not factorable. ■

Factoring Trinomials That Are Perfect Squares

Associated with factoring perfect squares are the special products

$$(a + b)^2 = a^2 + 2ab + b^2$$

$$(a - b)^2 = a^2 - 2ab + b^2$$

A trinomial is a perfect square if:

1. Its first and last terms are perfect squares.

2. Its middle term is twice the product of the square roots of its first and last terms.

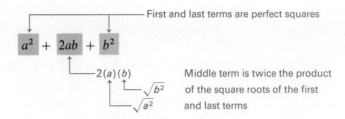

Therefore, $a^2 + 2ab + b^2 = (\sqrt{a^2} + \sqrt{b^2})^2 = (a + b)^2$.

TO FACTOR A TRINOMIAL THAT IS A PERFECT SQUARE

1. Find a, the square root of the first term, and b, the square root of the last term.

2. The trinomial is a perfect square if its middle term is either $+2ab$ or $-2ab$.

3. The factors of the trinomial are

$(a + b)^2$ if the middle term is $+2ab$

$(a - b)^2$ if the middle term is $-2ab$

NOTE   Such trinomials can *also* be factored by the trial method or by the Master Product Method.   ☑

Example 17   Factor $4x^2 - 12x + 9$.

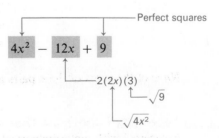

Therefore, $4x^2 - 12x + 9 = (\sqrt{4x^2} - \sqrt{9})^2 = (2x - 3)^2$.

Check $(2x - 3)^2 = 4x^2 - 12x + 9$ ∎

Example 18 Factor $36x^4 - 13x^2 + 1$.

$36x^4 - 13x^2 + 1$ *might* be a perfect square, since $36x^4 = (6x^2)^2$ and $1 = 1^2$. We check:

$$(6x^2 - 1)^2 \overset{?}{=} 36x^4 - 13x^2 + 1$$

$$\text{No;} \ (6x^2 - 1)^2 = 36x^4 - 12x^2 + 1$$

However, the expression still might be factorable. We try

$$(9x^2 - 1)(4x^2 - 1) \overset{?}{=} 36x^4 - 13x^2 + 1$$

This *does* check, and the expression has been factored. However, neither factor is prime, so we must factor again.

$$36x^4 - 13x^2 + 1 = (3x - 1)(3x + 1)(2x - 1)(2x + 1)$$

$$\textit{Check} \ (3x - 1)(3x + 1)(2x - 1)(2x + 1) = (9x^2 - 1)(4x^2 - 1)$$
$$= 36x^4 - 13x^2 + 1 \quad \blacksquare$$

In Section 5.2, we discussed factoring by grouping; in that section, we always had a common factor after factoring each group. We can *also* complete the factoring after we've grouped if we have a difference of two squares (see Example 19) or a factorable trinomial (see Example 20).

Example 19 Factor $x^2 + 4xy + 4y^2 - 9$.

We can see that if we grouped the first two terms and the last two terms, we would *not* have a common binomial factor. Let's try grouping the first *three* terms together.

$$(x^2 + 4xy + 4y^2) - (9)$$
$$= (x + 2y)^2 - 9 \longleftarrow \text{This is a difference of two squares}$$
$$= ([x + 2y] + 3)([x + 2y] - 3)$$
$$= (x + 2y + 3)(x + 2y - 3)$$

Therefore,

$$(x^2 + 4xy + 4y^2) - (9) = (x + 2y + 3)(x + 2y - 3)$$

$$\textit{Check} \ (x + 2y + 3)(x + 2y - 3) = (x + 2y)^2 - 3^2$$
$$= x^2 + 4xy + 4y^2 - 9 \quad \blacksquare$$

The type of factoring seen in Example 19 is used in Section 5.7 on factoring by completing the square.

Example 20 Factor $5x^2 - 30xy + 45y^2 - 14x + 42y - 3$.

Since the polynomial has more than three terms, we must factor by grouping. Let's look at the first three terms only:

$$5x^2 - 30xy + 45y^2 = 5(x^2 - 6xy + 9y^2) = 5(x - 3y)^2$$

That result leads us to believe that we may have a factorable trinomial. Let's try the following grouping:

$$\boxed{5x^2 - 30xy + 45y^2} - \boxed{14x + 42y} - \boxed{3}$$
$$= 5(x - 3y)^2 - 14(x - 3y) - 3$$

Double check: If we removed the parentheses, would we get back the original polynomial? Yes. Continuing, we let $a = x - 3y$. We then have

$$5a^2 - 14a - 3 = (5a + 1)(a - 3)$$

Substituting back,

$$5x^2 - 30xy + 45y^2 - 14x + 42y - 3$$
$$= (5[x - 3y] + 1)([x - 3y] - 3)$$
$$= (5x - 15y + 1)(x - 3y - 3)$$

(The checking is left to the student.) ■

EXERCISES 5.4B

Set I   Factor completely or write "Not factorable."

1. $5x^2 + 9x + 4$ **2.** $5x^2 + 12x + 4$ **3.** $7 - 22b + 3b^2$

4. $7 - 10u + 3u^2$ **5.** $x + 3x^2 + 1$ **6.** $x + 11x^2 + 1$

7. $3n^2 + 14n - 5$ **8.** $3n^2 + 2n - 5$ **9.** $3t^2 - 17tz - 6z^2$

10. $3x^2 - 7xy - 6y^2$ **11.** $-7 + 4x^2 + x$ **12.** $-13 + 6x^2 + x$

13. $8 + 12z - 8z^2$ **14.** $9 + 21z - 18z^2$ **15.** $1 + 4a^2 + 4a$

16. $1 + 9b^2 + 6b$ **17.** $2x^2 - 18$ **18.** $5y^2 - 80$

19. $4 + 7h^2 - 11h$ **20.** $4 + 7h^2 - 16h$ **21.** $24xy + 72x^2 + 2y^2$

22. $16xy + 32x^2 + 2y^2$ **23.** $x^2 - 7xy + 49y^2$ **24.** $x^2 - 5xy + 25y^2$

25. $2x^2y + 8xy^2 + 8y^3$ **26.** $3x^3 + 6x^2y + 3xy^2$ **27.** $6e^4 - 7e^2 - 20$

28. $10f^4 - 29f^2 - 21$ **29.** $12x^4 - 75x^2y^2$ **30.** $36x^4 - 16x^2y^2$

31. $a^4 + 2a^2b^2 + b^4$ **32.** $x^4 + 6x^2y^2 + 9y^4$

33. $2(a + b)^2 + 7(a + b) + 3$ **34.** $3(a - b)^2 + 7(a - b) + 2$

35. $4(x - y)^2 - 8(x - y) - 5$ **36.** $4(x + y)^2 - 4(x + y) - 3$

37. $5x^2 + 10xy + 5y^2 - 21x - 21y + 4$

38. $5x^2 - 10xy + 5y^2 - 12x + 12y + 4$

39. $(2x - y)^2 - (3a + b)^2$ **40.** $(2x + 3y)^2 - (a - b)^2$

41. $x^2 + 10xy + 25y^2 - 9$ **42.** $x^2 + 8xy + 16y^2 - 25$

43. $a^2 - 4x^2 - 4xy - y^2$ **44.** $x^2 - 9a^2 - 6ab - b^2$

45. $4x^4 - 13x^2 + 9$ **46.** $9x^4 - 13x^2 + 4$

47. $3x^2 - 7xy - 6y^2 - x + 3y$ **48.** $3t^2 - 17tz - 6z^2 - 3t - z$

49. $3n^2 + 2mn - 5m^2 + 3n + 5m$ **50.** $3n^2 + 14mn - 5m^2 + 3n - m$

Set II   Factor completely or write "Not factorable."

1. $3x^2 + 7x + 4$ **2.** $7x^2 + 13x - 2$ **3.** $2 - 9x + 4x^2$

4. $3x^2 - 5x - 8$ **5.** $x + 7x^2 + 1$ **6.** $3x^2 + 6x - 6$

7. $5k^2 + 2k - 7$ **8.** $13a^2 - 18a + 5$ **9.** $3w^2 + 7wx - 6x^2$

10. $2x^2 - 2x - 12$ **11.** $-5 + 8x^2 + x$ **12.** $29x - 5 + 6x^2$

13. $8 - 14v - 4v^2$ **14.** $64c^2 - 16c + 1$ **15.** $1 + 16m^2 + 8m$

16. $5x^2 + 5x + 1$ **17.** $3z^2 - 75$ **18.** $5k + 3k^2 - 2$

19. $6 + 7x^2 - 23x$ **20.** $21x^2 + 22x - 8$ **21.** $128x^2 + 32xy + 2y^2$

22. $2y^2 - 72$ **23.** $x^2 - 2xy + 4y^2$ **24.** $11x^2 + 32xy - 3y^2$

25. $18mn^2 - 24m^2n + 8m^3$ **26.** $5x^2 + 7xy + 3x$

27. $2e^4 + 11e^2 - 6$ **28.** $5x^4 - 17x^2 + 6$

29. $36x^4 - 81x^2y^2$ **30.** $-24 - 6x + 45x^2$

31. $w^4 + 8w^2y^2 + 16y^4$ **32.** $17u - 12 + 5u^2$

33. $3(a - b)^2 + 16(a - b) + 5$ **34.** $4x^2 + 8xy + 4y^2 + 11x + 11y + 7$

35. $6(x + y)^2 - 7(x + y) - 3$ **36.** $6a^2 + 12ab + 6b^2 + 11a + 11b + 5$

37. $5a^2 + 10ab + 5b^2 - 16a - 16b + 3$ **38.** $4a^2 - 8ab + 4b^2 + 9a - 9b + 5$

39. $(3x + y)^2 - (a - 2b)^2$ **40.** $-8 + 14v + 4v^2$

41. $x^2 + 6xy + 9y^2 - 16$ **42.** $5z^3 + 40z^2 + 15z$

43. $y^2 - 25x^2 - 10xz - z^2$ **44.** $8x^3 + 24x^2 + 8x$

45. $9x^4 - 37x^2 + 4$ **46.** $7y^3 + 28y^2 + 14y$

47. $3w^2 + 7wx - 6x^2 - w - 3x$ **48.** $5(a + b) - 2 + 12(a + b)^2$

49. $5k^2 + 2km - 7m^2 + 5k + 7m$ **50.** $-8 + 10(x - y) + 12(x - y)^2$

5.5 Review: 5.1–5.4

Several methods of factoring have been discussed so far:

5.1 *First, check for a common factor.* If there is a common factor, factor it out.

5.3 *If the expression to be factored has two terms:* Is it a *difference* of two *squares*?

If the expression to be factored has three terms:

5.4A 1. Is the leading coefficient 1?

5.4B 2. Are the first and last terms perfect squares? If so, is the trinomial a perfect square?

5.4B 3. Is the leading coefficient unequal to 1?

5.2 *If the expression to be factored has four or more terms*: Can it be factored by grouping?

Check to see if any factor can be factored again.

Check your solution.

Review Exercises 5.5 Set I

Factor completely or write "Not factorable."

1. $65x^2y^3 - 39xy^4 - 13xy$ **2.** $3xyz - 5a + 3b$ **3.** $3x^3 + 9x^2 - 12x$

4. $x^3y^6 + 5$ **5.** $x^2 + 13x + 40$ **6.** $x^2 + x - 20$

7. $8 + x^2 + 8x$ **8.** $x^2 - 11x + 18$ **9.** $x^2 - 256$

10. $x^2 - 14x + 13$ **11.** $3x^2 - x - 14$ **12.** $2x^2 - 11x - 40$

13. $3xy + 12x + 2y + 8$ **14.** $x^3 + 5x^2 - x - 5$ **15.** $5ag - 7x + 10cd - 14$

16. $x^2 - x + 12$ **17.** $8x^3 - 2x$ **18.** $x^2 + 9$

19. $4x^2 + 11x - 3$ **20.** $11a - 10 + 8a^2$

Review Exercises 5.5 Set II

NAME _____

Factor completely or write "Not factorable."

1. $14ac + 56ab - 7a$

2. $x^2 - 144$

3. $x^3 - 7x^2 + x - 4$

4. $x^2 - 14x + 48$

5. $7x^2 + 5x - 2$

6. $x^2 + 16$

7. $5x^2 + 11x - 12$

8. $6 - 15x + 6x^2$

9. $2xy + 5y + 8x + 20$

10. $4x^2 - y^2 + 2x - y$

11. $6x + 5x^2 - 8$

12. $x^3 + 8x^2 - 4x - 32$

13. $2 + 15x + 7x^2$

14. $3x^3 - x^2 + 3x - 1$

15. $5x^2 + x + 1$

16. $8x^2 + 30x - 8$

ANSWERS

1. _____

2. _____

3. _____

4. _____

5. _____

6. _____

7. _____

8. _____

9. _____

10. _____

11. _____

12. _____

13. _____

14. _____

15. _____

16. _____

17. $3x^2y^2 + 9xy^3 - 21xy^2$

18. $x^3 - x^2 - 8x + 8$

19. $11x^2 + 31x - 6$

20. $5ax - 10a + 3bx - 6b - x + 2$

5.6 Factoring the Sum or Difference of Two Cubes

A *sum of two cubes* is a binomial that fits the pattern $a^3 + b^3$. A *difference of two cubes* is a binomial that fits the pattern $a^3 - b^3$. For example, $(2x)^3 + (3y)^3$ is a sum of two cubes.

The factoring formulas for factoring $a^3 + b^3$ and $a^3 - b^3$ are based on the following special products:

Sum of two cubes	Difference of two cubes

$(a + b)(a^2 - ab + b^2) = a^3 + b^3$ $(a - b)(a^2 + ab + b^2) = a^3 - b^3$

since
$$a^2 - ab + b^2$$
$$\underline{a + b}$$
$$a^2 b - ab^2 + b^3$$
$$\underline{a^3 - a^2 b + ab^2 \qquad}$$
$$a^3 \qquad\qquad + b^3$$

since
$$a^2 + ab + b^2$$
$$\underline{a - b}$$
$$- a^2 b - ab^2 - b^3$$
$$\underline{a^3 + a^2 b + ab^2 \qquad}$$
$$a^3 \qquad\qquad - b^3$$

This shows:

Finding the product   Finding the product

$(a + b)(a^2 - ab + b^2) = a^3 + b^3$ $(a - b)(a^2 + ab + b^2) = a^3 - b^3$

—Same sign—   —Same sign—

Finding the factors   Finding the factors

$a^3 + b^3$ factors into $a^3 - b^3$ factors into
$(a + b)(a^2 - ab + b^2)$ $(a - b)(a^2 + ab + b^2)$

Note that each product of factors contains exactly one negative sign. When we're factoring a *difference* of two cubes, the negative sign is in the *binomial factor*. When we're factoring a *sum* of two cubes, the negative sign is in front of the *second term* of the *trinomial factor*.

A WORD OF CAUTION $a^3 + b^3 \neq (a + b)^3$

Remember that

$$(a + b)^3 = (a + b)(a + b)(a + b)$$
$$= a^3 + 3a^2 b + 3ab^2 + b^3$$

whereas

$$a^3 + b^3 = (a + b)(a^2 - ab + b^2) \qquad \boxed{\checkmark}$$

In order to use the factoring formulas, you must be able to find the cubic root of a term. The cubic root of the numerical coefficient is found by using the methods learned in Section 1.7C. The cubic root of the *variable* is found by dividing each exponent by 3.

Example 1   Find $\sqrt[3]{27a^6 b^3}$.

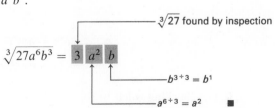

$\sqrt[3]{27}$ found by inspection

$$\sqrt[3]{27a^6 b^3} = 3\ a^2\ b$$

$b^{3 \div 3} = b^1$

$a^{6 \div 3} = a^2$ ∎

The factoring formulas are summarized as follows:

TO FACTOR THE SUM OR DIFFERENCE OF TWO CUBES

1. Find a, the cubic root of the first term, and b, the cubic root of the second term. (Express numerical coefficients in prime factored form if necessary.)

2. Substitute a and b in the factors given in the following formulas:

$$a^3 + b^3 = (a + b)(a^2 - ab + b^2)$$
$$a^3 - b^3 = (a - b)(a^2 + ab + b^2)$$

A WORD OF CAUTION   A common mistake students make is to think that the middle term of the trinomial factor is $2ab$ instead of ab.

$$a^3 + b^3 = (a + b)(a^2 - \boxed{ab} + b^2)$$

Not $2ab$

☑

NOTE   The expression $a^2 - ab + b^2$ does *not* factor further.

☑

Example 2   Factor $x^3 + 8$.

$$\sqrt[3]{x^3} = x^{3 \div 3} = x^1$$
$$\sqrt[3]{8} = 2$$

$$x^3 + 8 = (\,x\,)^3 + (\,2\,)^3$$

Same signs — Always +

$$= (\,\blacksquare + \blacksquare\,)(\,\blacksquare - \blacksquare + \blacksquare\,)$$

Always opposite signs

$$= (x + 2)[(x)^2 - (x)(2) + (2)^2]$$
$$= (x + 2)(x^2 - 2x + 4)$$

Check $(x + 2)(x^2 - 2x + 4) = x^3 - 2x^2 + 4x + 2x^2 - 4x + 8 = x^3 + 8$ ■

Example 3   Factor $27x^3 - 64y^3$.

$$27x^3 - 64y^3 = (3x)^3 - (4y)^3$$

Same signs — Always +

$$= (\,\blacksquare - \blacksquare\,)(\,\blacksquare + \blacksquare + \blacksquare\,)$$

Always opposite signs

$$= (3x - 4y)[(3x)^2 + (3x)(4y) + (4y)^2]$$
$$= (3x - 4y)(9x^2 + 12xy + 16y^2)$$

(The checking is left to the student.)   ■

Example 4   Factor $(x + 2)^3 - (y - 2z)^3$.

Let $(x + 2) = a$ and $(y - 2z) = b$. Then

$$(x + 2)^3 - (y - 2z)^3 = a^3 - b^3 = (a - b)(a^2 + ab + b^2)$$

Since $a = x + 2$ and $b = y - 2z$, substituting back gives

$(x + 2)^3 - (y - 2z)^3$
$$= [(x + 2) - (y - 2z)][(x + 2)^2 + (x + 2)(y - 2z) + (y - 2z)^2]$$
$$= [x + 2 - y + 2z][x^2 + 4x + 4 + xy + 2y - 2xz - 4z + y^2 - 4yz + 4z^2]$$

(The checking is left to the student.) ∎

EXERCISES 5.6

Set I   Factor completely or write "Not factorable."

1. $x^3 - 8$ 　　　　　　2. $x^3 - 27$ 　　　　　　3. $64 + a^3$

4. $8 + b^3$ 　　　　　　5. $125 - x^3$ 　　　　　　6. $1 - a^3$

7. $8x^3 - 2x$ 　　　　　8. $27x^3 - 3x$ 　　　　　9. $c^3 - 27a^3b^3$

10. $c^3 - 64a^3b^3$ 　　11. $8x^3y^6 + 27$ 　　　12. $64a^6b^3 + 125$

13. $125x^6y^4 - 1$ 　　14. $64a^6b^3 - 9$ 　　　15. $a^4 + ab^3$

16. $x^3y + y^4$ 　　　　17. $81 - 3x^3$ 　　　　　18. $40 - 5b^3$

19. $(x + y)^3 + 1$ 　　20. $1 + (x - y)^3$ 　　21. $64x^3 - y^6$

22. $125w^3 - v^6$ 　　23. $4a^3b^3 + 108c^6$ 　24. $5x^3y^6 + 40z^9$

25. $x^6 - 729$ 　　　　26. $y^6 - 64$ 　　　　　27. $(x + 1)^3 - (y - z)^3$

28. $(x - y)^3 - (a + b)^3$

Set II   Factor completely or write "Not factorable."

1. $a^3 - 125$ 　　　　　2. $b^3 + 1$ 　　　　　　3. $27 + c^3$

4. $16 + 2x^3$ 　　　　　5. $8 - b^3$ 　　　　　　6. $x^3y^3 + 64$

7. $64a^3 - 4a$ 　　　　8. $8a^3 + 27$ 　　　　　9. $x^3 - 64y^3z^3$

10. $x^3 - xy^2$ 　　　　11. $8a^6b^3 + 1$ 　　　　12. $250 - 2c^3$

13. $8x^9y^5 - 27$ 　　　14. $x^3 + 4x$ 　　　　　15. $x^4y^3 + x$

16. $a^4 + 8a$ 　　　　　17. $16 - 2m^3$ 　　　　18. $3x^3 - 81$

19. $(a + b)^3 - (x - y)^3$ 　20. $(x + y)^3 + (u + v)^3$ 　21. $27a^3 - b^6$

22. $(s - 2)^3 + (t - 3v)^3$ 　23. $2x^3y^3 + 16z^6$ 　24. $x^6 + 64y^6$

25. $z^6 - 1$ 　　　　　26. $6x^4 + 48x$ 　　　　27. $(a - 2)^3 - (b + c)^3$

28. $(a + x)^3 - 8(b - z)^3$

5.7 Factoring by Completing the Square of a Polynomial

Some binomials and trinomials are not factorable by any method discussed so far but *may* be factorable by a method called *completing the square*. An expression cannot be factored by completing the square unless it satisfies the following conditions:

---

1. The first and last terms of the expression to be factored must be perfect squares.

2. Any literal factor in the first and last terms must be at least *fourth* degree.

If these conditions are satisfied, we then try to find a positive perfect square term to add to the given binomial or trinomial to make it a polynomial that is a perfect square. Of course, *when a term is added, the same term must also be subtracted* so that the value of the original expression is unchanged. We will then have an expression that is a difference of two squares, and a difference of two squares is *always* factorable.

To factor a polynomial that is in the form $ax^4 + bx^2y^2 + cy^4$, where a and c are perfect squares, the following steps may be used:

1. Form the binomials $\sqrt{ax^4} + \sqrt{cy^4}$ and $\sqrt{ax^4} - \sqrt{cy^4}$.

2. Square one of the binomials found in step 1.

3. Subtract the polynomial being factored from the trinomial found in step 2.

4. If the difference found in step 3 is a positive term that is a perfect square, *add it to* and *subtract it from* the polynomial being factored, and continue with step 5. If it is not, repeat steps 2 and 3, using the other binomial from step 1. If the difference found in step 3 is still not a positive term that is a perfect square, the polynomial cannot be factored over the integers.

5. Regroup the terms to form a difference of two squares.

6. Factor the difference of two squares.

7. Determine whether any factor can be factored further.

8. Check the result.

NOTE   The polynomials found in steps 1, 2, and 3 do *not* equal the polynomial that is being factored, and steps 1, 2, and 3 need not be shown.   ☑

Example 1   Factor $x^4 + x^2 + 1$.

Step 1 The binomials are $\sqrt{x^4} + \sqrt{1} = x^2 + 1$ and $\sqrt{x^4} - \sqrt{1} = x^2 - 1$.

Step 2 We'll try $x^2 + 1$:

$$(x^2 + 1)^2 = x^4 + 2x^2 + 1$$

─ The difference is positive and is a perfect square

Step 3 $(x^4 + 2x^2 + 1) - (x^4 + x^2 + 1) = x^2$.

$$\overset{\displaystyle \overset{\rule{0pt}{0pt}}{\underset{\downarrow}{\quad}} x^2 - x^2 = 0}{}$$

Step 4 $x^4 + x^2 + 1 = x^4 + x^2 + 1 + \boxed{x^2 - x^2}$

Step 5 $\qquad\qquad = (x^4 + x^2 + 1 + x^2) - x^2$

$\qquad\qquad\qquad = (x^4 + 2x^2 + 1) - x^2$

$\qquad\qquad\qquad = (x^2 + 1)^2 - x^2 \qquad$ Difference of two squares

Step 6 $\qquad\qquad = [(x^2 + 1) + x][(x^2 + 1) - x]$

Step 7 $\qquad\qquad = (x^2 + x + 1)(x^2 - x + 1) \qquad$ Both factors are prime

Step 8 $(x^2 + x + 1)(x^2 - x + 1)$

$\qquad\qquad = x^2(x^2 - x + 1) + x(x^2 - x + 1) + 1(x^2 - x + 1)$

$\qquad\qquad = x^4 - x^3 + x^2 + x^3 - x^2 + x + x^2 - x + 1$

$\qquad\qquad = x^4 + x^2 + 1 \quad \blacksquare$

Example 2 Factor $h^4 - 14h^2k^2 + 25k^4$.

Step 1 The binomials are $\sqrt{h^4} + \sqrt{25k^4} = h^2 + 5k^2$ and $\sqrt{h^4} - \sqrt{25k^4} = h^2 - 5k^2$.

Step 2 We'll try $h^2 + 5k^2$:

$$(h^2 + 5k^2)^2 = h^4 + 10h^2k^2 + 25k^4$$

Step 3 $(h^4 + 10h^2k^2 + 25k^4) - (h^4 - 14h^2k^2 + 25k^4) = 24h^2k^2$

$24h^2k^2$ is not a perfect square. We will repeat steps 2 and 3, using the binomial $h^2 - 5k^2$.

Step 2 $(h^2 - 5k^2)^2 = h^4 - 10h^2k^2 + 25k^4$

Step 3 $(h^4 - 10h^2k^2 + 25k^4) - (h^4 - 14h^2k^2 + 25k^4) = 4h^2k^2$

$4h^2k^2$ is positive and is a perfect square.

$$\overset{\displaystyle \overset{\rule{0pt}{0pt}}{\underset{\downarrow}{\quad}} 4h^2k^2 - 4h^2k^2 = 0}{}$$

Step 4 $h^4 - 14h^2k^2 + 25k^4 = h^4 - 14h^2k^2 + 25k^4 + \boxed{4h^2k^2 - 4h^2k^2}$

Step 5 $\qquad\qquad = (h^4 - 14h^2k^2 + 25k^4 + 4h^2k^2) - 4h^2k^2$

$\qquad\qquad\qquad = (h^4 - 10h^2k^2 + 25k^4) - 4h^2k^2$

$\qquad\qquad\qquad = (h^2 - 5k^2)^2 - (2hk)^2$

Step 6 $\qquad\qquad = [(h^2 - 5k^2) + 2hk][(h^2 - 5k^2) - 2hk]$

Step 7 $\qquad\qquad = (h^2 + 2hk - 5k^2)(h^2 - 2hk - 5k^2)$

Both factors are prime.

Step 8 The checking is left to the student. $\quad \blacksquare$

Example 3 Factor $a^4 + 4$.

Step 1 The binomials are $\sqrt{a^4} + \sqrt{4} = a^2 + 2$ and $\sqrt{a^4} - \sqrt{4} = a^2 - 2$.

Step 2 We'll try $a^2 + 2$:

$$(a^2 + 2)^2 = a^4 + 4a^2 + 4$$

Step 3 $(a^4 + 4a^2 + 4) - (a^4 + 4) = 4a^2 \leftarrow$ A positive, perfect square

$$4a^2 - 4a^2 = 0$$

Step 4 $a^4 + 4 = a^4 + 4 + \boxed{4a^2 - 4a^2}$

Step 5 $= (a^4 + 4a^2 + 4) - 4a^2$

$= (a^2 + 2)^2 - (2a)^2$

Step 6 $= [(a^2 + 2) + 2a][(a^2 + 2) - 2a]$

Step 7 $= (a^2 + 2a + 2)(a^2 - 2a + 2)$

Both factors are prime.

Step 8 The checking is left to the student. ■

Example 4   Factor $h^4 - 6h^2k^2 + 25k^4$.

Step 1 The binomials are $\sqrt{h^4} + \sqrt{25k^4} = h^2 + 5k^2$ and $\sqrt{h^4} - \sqrt{25k^4} = h^2 - 5k^2$.

Step 2 We'll try $h^2 - 5k^2$:

$$(h^2 - 5k^2)^2 = h^4 - 10h^2k^2 + 25k^4$$

Step 3 $(h^4 - 10h^2k^2 + 25k^4) - (h^4 - 6h^2k^2 + 25k^4) = -4h^2k^2$

The difference is negative, not positive. We repeat steps 2 and 3, trying the binomial $h^2 + 5k^2$.

Step 2 $(h^2 + 5k^2)^2 = h^4 + 10h^2k^2 + 25k^4$

Step 3 $(h^4 + 10h^2k^2 + 25k^4) - (h^4 - 6h^2k^2 + 25k^4) = 16h^2k^2$

$$16h^2k^2 - 16h^2k^2 = 0$$

Step 4 $h^4 - 6h^2k^2 + 25k^4 = h^4 - 6h^2k^2 + 25k^4 + \boxed{16h^2k^2 - 16h^2k^2}$

Step 5 $= (h^4 - 6h^2k^2 + 25k^4 + 16h^2k^2) - 16h^2k^2$

$= (h^4 + 10h^2k^2 + 25k^4) - 16h^2k^2$

$= (h^2 + 5k^2)^2 - (4hk)^2$

Step 6 $= [(h^2 + 5k^2) + 4hk][(h^2 + 5k^2) - 4hk]$

Step 7 $= (h^2 + 4hk + 5k^2)(h^2 - 4hk + 5k^2)$

Both factors are prime.

Step 8 The checking is left to the student. ■

Example 5   Factor $x^4 - 2x^2 + 9$.

Step 1 The binomials are $\sqrt{x^4} + \sqrt{9} = x^2 + 3$ and $\sqrt{x^4} - \sqrt{9} = x^2 - 3$.

Step 2 We'll try $x^2 + 3$:

$$(x^2 + 3)^2 = x^4 + 6x^2 + 9$$

Step 3 $(x^4 + 6x^2 + 9) - (x^4 - 2x^2 + 9) = 8x^2$

$8x^2$ is not a perfect square. We repeat steps 2 and 3, using the binomial $x^2 - 3$.

Step 2 $(x^2 - 3)^2 = x^4 - 6x^2 + 9$

Step 3 $(x^4 - 6x^2 + 9) - (x^4 - 2x^2 + 9) = -4x^2$

The difference is negative, not positive. We have tried both binomials from step 1, and neither one gave us a difference that was a positive, perfect square. Therefore, $x^4 - 2x^2 + 9$ is not factorable over the integers. ■

EXERCISES 5.7

Set I   Factor completely or write "Not factorable."

1. $x^4 + 3x^2 + 4$ **2.** $x^4 + 5x^2 + 9$ **3.** $4m^4 + 3m^2 + 1$

4. $9u^4 + 5u^2 + 1$ **5.** $64a^4 + b^4$ **6.** $a^4 + 4b^4$

7. $x^4 - 3x^2 + 9$ **8.** $x^4 - x^2 + 16$ **9.** $a^4 - 17a^2b^2 + 16b^4$

10. $a^4 - 37a^2 + 36$ **11.** $x^2 + x + 1$ **12.** $x^2 + 5x + 9$

13. $a^4 - 3a^2b^2 + 9b^4$ **14.** $a^4 - 15a^2b^2 + 25b^4$ **15.** $a^4 + 9$

16. $x^4 + 25$ **17.** $50x^4 - 12x^2y^2 + 2y^4$

18. $32x^4 - 2x^2y^2 + 2y^4$ **19.** $8m^4n + 2n^5$

20. $3m^5 + 12mn^4$ **21.** $50x^4y + 32x^2y^3 + 8y^5$

22. $48x^5 + 21x^3y^2 + 3xy^4$

Set II   Factor completely or write "Not factorable."

1. $u^4 + 4u^2 + 16$ **2.** $x^4 + 7x^2 + 16$ **3.** $y^4 - 9y^2 + 16$

4. $16m^4 + 8m^2 + 1$ **5.** $4a^4 + 1$ **6.** $x^4 + 10x^2 + 49$

7. $x^4 - 21x^2 + 4$ **8.** $4x^4 - 76x^2 + 9$ **9.** $x^4 - 10x^2 + 9$

10. $x^4 - 3x^2 + 1$ **11.** $x^2 + 3x + 4$ **12.** $2x^4 - 38x^2 + 18$

13. $z^4 + z^2w^2 + 25w^4$ **14.** $x^4 - 14x^2 + 25$ **15.** $y^4 + 1$

16. $9x^4 - 7x^2y^2 + y^4$ **17.** $2x^8y - 6x^4y + 18y$ **18.** $x^2 + 7x + 16$

19. $2a^5 + 128a$ **20.** $x^4 - 17x^2y^2 + 64y^4$ **21.** $27x^4 + 6x^2y^2 + 3y^4$

22. $8x^4 - 80x^2 + 2$

5.8 Factoring Using Synthetic Division

Consider the factored polynomial $(x - r_1)(x - r_2)(x - r_3)$. If these factors are multiplied, the *constant* term in their product must be $r_1r_2r_3$, the product of the constant terms in each factor. For example,

$$(x - 5)(x + 2)(x - 3) = x^3 - 6x^2 - x + 30$$

$$(-5)(+2)(-3) = 30$$

If a polynomial *does* have a factor of the form $x - a$ or $x + a$, then a must be a factor of the constant term of the polynomial. We know that $x - 7$, for example, cannot be a factor of $x^3 - 6x^2 - x + 30$, because 7 is not a factor of 30. We recall that if the remainder in a division problem is zero, the divisor and quotient are factors of the dividend.

The rules for factoring a polynomial using synthetic division are summarized below. They assume that any common factors have been factored out and that the polynomial has been arranged in descending powers of the variable.

TO FACTOR A POLYNOMIAL BY SYNTHETIC DIVISION WHEN THE LEADING COEFFICIENT IS 1

1. Find all the positive and negative factors of the constant term of the polynomial.

2. Begin dividing the polynomial synthetically by each of the factors found in step 1. Stop when a remainder of zero is obtained.

3. If a remainder of zero is obtained for a, then $(x - a)$ and the quotient are factors of the polynomial.

4. Apply *any* method of factoring to see if the quotient can be factored further.

5. Check.

Example 1 Factor $x^3 - x^2 + 2x - 8$.

Step 1 Factors of the constant term 8 are $\pm 1, \pm 2, \pm 4, \pm 8$.

Step 2 Divide synthetically by $\pm 1, \pm 2, \pm 4, \pm 8$ until a remainder of zero is obtained.

$$1x^3 \quad -1x^2 + 2x \quad -8$$

Divide by $+1$

$$\begin{array}{c|cccc} & 1 & -1 & 2 & -8 \\ & & 1 & 0 & 2 \\ \hline 1 & 1 & 0 & 2 & -6 \end{array}$$

Remainder *not* zero; therefore, $(x - 1)$ is not a factor

Divide by -1

$$\begin{array}{c|cccc} & 1 & -1 & 2 & -8 \\ & & -1 & 2 & -4 \\ \hline -1 & 1 & -2 & 4 & -12 \end{array}$$

Remainder *not* zero; therefore, $(x + 1)$ is not a factor

Divide by $+2$

$$\begin{array}{c|cccc} & 1 & -1 & 2 & -8 \\ & & 2 & 2 & 8 \\ \hline 2 & 1 & 1 & 4 & 0 \end{array}$$

Remainder *is* zero; therefore, $(x - 2)$ is a factor

$$x^2 + x + 4$$

Quotient is another factor

Step 3 $x^3 - x^2 + 2x - 8 = (x - 2)(x^2 + x + 4)$

Step 4 Applying the methods for factoring trinomials, we see that the quotient $x^2 + x + 4$ cannot be factored further.

Step 5: Check
$$(x - 2)(x^2 + x + 4)$$
$$= x^3 + x^2 + 4x - 2x^2 - 2x - 8$$
$$= x^3 - x^2 + 2x - 8 \quad \blacksquare$$

Example 2 Factor $x^5 - 3x^4 + 2x^3 - x^2 + 3x - 2$.

Step 1 Integral factors of the constant term 2 are ± 1, ± 2.

Step 2 Divide synthetically by ± 1 and ± 2 until a remainder of zero is obtained.

$$\begin{array}{r|rrrrrr}
 & 1 & -3 & 2 & -1 & 3 & -2 \\
 &   & 1 & -2 & 0 & -1 & 2 \\
\hline
\boxed{1} & 1 & -2 & 0 & -1 & 2 & \boxed{0}
\end{array}$$
$\longleftarrow$ Remainder *is* zero; therefore, $(x - 1)$ is a factor

$$\boxed{x^4 - 2x^3 - x + 2}$$
$\uparrow$
Quotient is another factor

Step 3 $x^5 - 3x^4 + 2x^3 - x^2 + 3x - 2 = (x - 1)(x^4 - 2x^3 - x + 2)$

Step 4 To see if the quotient $x^4 - 2x^3 - x + 2$ can be factored further, we will use synthetic division again, even though this particular quotient can be factored by other methods.

Step 1 Factors of the constant term 2 are ± 1 and ± 2. *It is important to try the factor 1 again.*

Step 2
$$\begin{array}{r|rrrrr}
 & 1 & -2 & 0 & -1 & 2 \\
 &   & 1 & -1 & -1 & -2 \\
\hline
\boxed{1} & 1 & -1 & -1 & -2 & \boxed{0}
\end{array}$$
$\longleftarrow$ Remainder *is* zero; therefore, $(x - 1)$ is a factor

$$\boxed{x^3 - x^2 - x - 2}$$
$\uparrow$
Quotient is another factor

Step 3 $x^5 - 3x^4 + 2x^3 - x^2 + 3x - 2$

$$= (x - 1)(x^4 - 2x^3 - x + 2)$$
$$= (x - 1)(x - 1)(x^3 - x^2 - x - 2)$$

Step 4 To see if the quotient $x^3 - x^2 - x - 2$ can be factored further, we'll use synthetic division *again*.

Step 1 Factors of the constant term -2 are ± 1, ± 2.

Step 2
$$\begin{array}{r|rrrr}
 & 1 & -1 & -1 & -2 \\
 &   & 1 & 0 & -1 \\
\hline
\boxed{1} & 1 & 0 & -1 & \boxed{-3}
\end{array}$$
$\longleftarrow$ Remainder is *not* zero

$(x - 1)$ *is not* a factor of $x^3 - x^2 - x - 2$.

We'll try $+2$:

$$\begin{array}{r|rrrr}
 & 1 & -1 & -1 & -2 \\
 &   & 2 & 2 & 2 \\
\hline
\boxed{2} & 1 & 1 & 1 & \boxed{0}
\end{array}$$
$\longleftarrow$ Remainder *is* zero; therefore, $(x - 2)$ is a factor

The *quotient* is $\boxed{x^2 + x + 1}$. It will not factor further.

Therefore, $x^5 - 3x^4 + 2x^3 - x^2 + 3x - 2$

$$= (x - 1)(x^4 - 2x^3 - x + 2)$$
$$= (x - 1)(x - 1)(x^3 - x^2 - x - 2)$$
$$= (x - 1)^2(x - 2)(x^2 + x + 1)$$

Step 5: *Check* $(x - 1)^2(x - 2)(x^2 + x + 1)$

$$= (x^2 - 2x + 1)(x - 2)(x^2 + x + 1)$$
$$= (x^3 - 4x^2 + 5x - 2)(x^2 + x + 1)$$
$$= x^5 - 3x^4 + 2x^3 - x^2 + 3x - 2 \quad \blacksquare$$

When the leading coefficient is *not* 1, we may need to try all integer factors of the constant *divided by* all factors of the leading coefficient in addition to all integral factors of the constant (see Example 3).

Example 3   Factor $2x^4 + x^3 - x + 1$.

Integral factors of 1 are ± 1. We may also need to try $\pm \frac{1}{2}$.

$$2x^4 + x^3 - x + 1 = 2x^4 + x^3 + 0x^2 - x + 1$$

	2	1	0	−1	1	
		2	3	3	2	
1	2	3	3	2	3	←——Remainder is not 0

	2	1	0	−1	1	
		−2	1	−1	2	
−1	2	−1	1	−2	3	←——Remainder is not 0

	2	1	0	−1	1	
		1	1	1/2	−1/4	
1/2	2	2	1	−1/2	3/4	←——Remainder is not 0

	2	1	0	−1	1	
		−1	0	0	1/2	
−1/2	2	0	0	−1	3/2	←——Remainder is not 0

The polynomial is not factorable.   ■

Example 4   Factor $x^5 + 1$.

Factors of the constant term $+1$ are ± 1.

$$1x^5 + 0x^4 + 0x^3 + 0x^2 + 0x + 1$$

	1	0	0	0	0	1	
		1	1	1	1	1	
1	1	1	1	1	1	2	←—— Remainder is *not* zero; therefore, $(x - 1)$ is not a factor

	1	0	0	0	0	1	
		−1	1	−1	1	−1	
−1	1	−1	1	−1	1	0	←——Remainder *is* zero; therefore, $(x + 1)$ is a factor

$$1x^4 - 1x^3 + 1x^2 - 1x + 1$$

└——Quotient is another factor

See if the quotient can be factored further.

$$1x^4 - 1x^3 + 1x^2 - 1x + 1$$

$$
\begin{array}{r|rrrrr}
 & 1 & -1 & 1 & -1 & 1 \\
 & & -1 & 2 & -3 & 4 \\
\hline
-1 & 1 & -2 & 3 & -4 & \boxed{5}
\end{array}
$$

± 1 are the only factors of the constant term 1; since we already know that $(x - 1)$ is not a factor, the only factor we need to try is $(x + 1)$

↑——Remainder *not* zero

Therefore, $x^5 + 1 = (x + 1)(x^4 - x^3 + x^2 - x + 1)$.

Check $(x + 1)(x^4 - x^3 + x^2 - x + 1)$

$$= x^5 - \cancel{x^4} + \cancel{x^3} - \cancel{x^2} + \cancel{x} + \cancel{x^4} - \cancel{x^3} + \cancel{x^2} - \cancel{x} + 1$$

$$= x^5 + 1 \quad \blacksquare$$

EXERCISES 5.8

Set I   Factor completely or write "Not factorable."

1. $x^3 + x^2 + x - 3$ **2.** $x^3 + x^2 - 5x - 2$

3. $x^3 - 3x^2 - 4x + 12$ **4.** $x^3 - 2x^2 - 5x + 6$

5. $2x^3 - 8x^2 + 2x + 12$ **6.** $2x^3 + 12x^2 + 22x + 12$

7. $6x^3 - 13x^2 + 4$ **8.** $x^3 - 7x - 6$

9. $x^4 - 3x^2 + 4x + 4$ **10.** $x^4 - x^3 - 5x^2 + 5x + 6$

11. $x^4 + 2x^3 - 3x^2 - 8x - 4$ **12.** $x^4 + 4x^3 + 3x^2 - 4x - 4$

13. $3x^4 - 4x^3 - 1$ **14.** $2x^4 + 3x^3 + 2x^2 + x + 1$

15. $x^4 - 4x^3 + 34x - 7x^2 - 24$ **16.** $x^4 + 6x^3 + 3x^2 - 26x - 24$

17. $6x^3 + x^2 - 11x - 6$ **18.** $6x^3 - 19x^2 + x + 6$

Set II   Factor completely or write "Not factorable."

1. $x^3 + 2x^2 + 2x - 5$ **2.** $x^3 + 7x^2 + 11x + 2$

3. $x^3 + 2x^2 - 5x - 6$ **4.** $x^3 - 11x^2 - 25x + 3$

5. $2x^3 - 12x^2 + 22x - 12$ **6.** $x^3 - 2x^2 + 2x - 1$

7. $x^3 - 7x + 6$ **8.** $x^4 + x^3 - 3x^2 - 4x - 4$

9. $x^4 + 3x^3 + 3x^2 + x - 2$ **10.** $2x^3 + 8x^2 + 8x$

11. $x^4 + 6x^3 + 8x^2 - 6x - 9$ **12.** $2x^3 + x^2 + x + 1$

13. $2x^4 + 2x^3 + 3x^2 + x - 1$ **14.** $x^3 - 3x^2 - 8x - 10$

15. $x^4 + 2x^3 - 13x^2 - 38x - 24$ **16.** $x^4 + 3x^3 - 3x^2 - 7x + 6$

17. $6x^3 + 7x^2 - 7x - 6$ **18.** $x^7 + 1$

5.9 How to Select the Method of Factoring

With so many different kinds of factoring to choose from, a student is often confused as to which method of factoring to try first. The following is a procedure you can use to select the correct method for factoring a particular algebraic expression.

First, check for a common factor, no matter how many terms the expression has. If there is a common factor, factor it out. This simplifies the remaining polynomial factor.

If the expression to be factored has two terms:

1. Is it a *difference* of two *squares*? (Section 5.3)

2. Is it a *sum* of two *squares*? If so, it is *not factorable*, unless it is of at least fourth degree and can be factored by completing the square. (Section 5.7)

3. Is it a *sum* or *difference* of two *cubes*? (Section 5.6)

4. Can it be factored by completing the square? (Section 5.7)

5. Can it be factored by synthetic division? (Section 5.8)

If the expression to be factored has three terms:

1. Is the leading coefficient 1? (Section 5.4A)

2. Are the first and last terms perfect squares? If so, is the trinomial a perfect square? (Section 5.4B)

3. Is the leading coefficient unequal to 1? (Section 5.4B)

4. Can it be factored by completing the square? (Section 5.7)

5. Can it be factored by synthetic division? (Section 5.8)

If the expression to be factored has four or more terms:

1. Can it be factored by grouping? (Section 5.2)

2. Can it be factored by synthetic division? (Section 5.8)

Check to see if any factor can be factored again. When the expression is *completely factored*, the same factors are obtained no matter what method is used.

Check the result by multiplying the factors together.

Example 1   Selecting the method of factoring.

	Method
a. $6x^2y - 12xy + 4y$ $= 2y(3x^2 - 6x + 2)$	Common factor $3x^2 - 6x + 2$ is not factorable
b. $3x^3 - 27xy^2$ $= 3x(x^2 - 9y^2)$ $= 3x(x + 3y)(x - 3y)$	Common factor Difference of two squares
c. $2ac - 3ad + 10bc - 15bd$ $= a(2c - 3d) + 5b(2c - 3d)$ $= (2c - 3d)(a + 5b)$	Grouping

Method

d. $3x^3 - 17x + 10$

Synthetic division

$$\begin{array}{r|rrrr} & 3 & 0 & -17 & 10 \\ & & 6 & 12 & -10 \\ \hline 2 & 3 & 6 & -5 & \boxed{0} \end{array}$$

$= (x - 2)(3x^2 + 6x - 5)$

e. $2a^3b + 16b$

Common factor
$= 2b(a^3 + 8)$
Sum of two cubes
$= 2b(a + 2)(a^2 - 2a + 4)$

f. $6x^2 + 9x - 10$

Master Product Method shows this is not factorable

g. $1 + 4x^4$

$\boxed{1 + 4x^2 + 4x^4} - 4x^2$

Complete the square
$= (1 + 2x^2)^2 - (2x)^2$
Difference of two squares
$= [(1 + 2x^2) + 2x][(1 + 2x^2) - 2x]$
$= (1 + 2x + 2x^2)(1 - 2x + 2x^2)$

h. $12x^2 - 13x - 4$

Trinomial with a leading coefficient $\neq 1$
$= (3x - 4)(4x + 1)$

i. $2xy^3 - 14xy^2 + 24xy$

Common factor
$= 2xy(y^2 - 7y + 12)$
Trinomial with a leading coefficient of 1
$= 2xy(y - 3)(y - 4)$

j. $16x^2 - 24xy + 9y^2$

Trinomial is a perfect square
$= (4x - 3y)^2$

k. $\boxed{x^2 - y^2} + \boxed{2x - 2y}$

Grouping
$= (x + y)(x - y) + 2(x - y)$
Difference of two squares
$= (x - y)(x + y + 2)$ ∎

EXERCISES 5.9

Set I   Factor completely or write "Not factorable."

1. $12e^2 + 13e - 35$

2. $30f^2 + 17f - 21$

3. $6ac - 6bd + 6bc - 6ad$

4. $10cy - 6cz + 5dy - 3dz$

5. $2xy^3 - 4xy^2 - 30xy$

6. $3yz^3 - 6yz^2 - 24yz$

7. $3x^3 + 24h^3$

8. $54f^3 - 2g^3$

9. $9e^2 - 30ef + 25f^2$

10. $16m^2 + 56mp + 49p^2$

11. $x^3 + 3x^2 - 4x - 12$

12. $a^3 - 2a^2 - 9a + 18$

13. $a^2 - b^2 - a + b$

14. $x^2 - y^2 - x - y$

15. $x^2 + x - 10$

16. $x^2 + x + 14$

17. $x^3 - 8y^3 + x^2 - 4y^2$

18. $a^3 - b^3 + a^2 - b^2$

19. $3x^3 + x^2 + 3x + 5$

20. $5x^3 - 7x^2 - 7x + 2$

21. $4 + k^4$

22. $64 + a^4$

23. $10x^2 + 2x - 21$ **24.** $10x^2 + 10x - 21$

25. $x^2 - 4xy + 4y^2 - 5x + 10y + 6$ **26.** $x^2 - 6xy + 9y^2 - 8x + 24y + 15$

27. $x^2 - 6xy + 9y^2 - 25$ **28.** $a^2 - 8ab + 16b^2 - 1$

Set II   Factor completely or write "Not factorable."

1. $5x^2 + 12x + 4$ **2.** $2a^2mn - 18b^2mn$

3. $4ac + 4bc - 8ad - 8bd$ **4.** $15x^2 - 13x - 2$

5. $6x^3y + 4x^2y - 10xy$ **6.** $3x^2 - 18x + 15$

7. $4x^3 + 32y^3$ **8.** $4x^2 + 4x + 1 - y^2$

9. $16x^2 - 24xy + 9y^2$ **10.** $x^2 + 100$

11. $b + b^2 - 16b - 16$ **12.** $x^4 - 4x^3 - 5x^2 + x - 5$

13. $x^2 - 4y^2 - x + 2y$ **14.** $x^4 + 15x^2 + 64$

15. $x^2 + x + 3$ **16.** $27 + 12x^2 + 36x$

17. $x^3 + y^3 + x^2 - y^2$ **18.** $2x^3 - x^2 - 18x + 9$

19. $3x^3 - 5x^2 - 7x - 5$ **20.** $x^4 - 23x^2y^2 + y^4$

21. $1 + 4a^4$ **22.** $1 + 4a^2$

23. $10x^2 + 28x - 21$ **24.** $6x^2 + 7xy - 10y^2$

25. $x^2 - 2xy + y^2 - 10x + 10y + 21$ **26.** $9x^2 + 6xy + y^2 - z^2 - 2z - 1$

27. $x^2 - 10xy + 25y^2 - 16$ **28.** $25x^2 - 10xy + y^2 + 35x - 7y + 12$

5.10   Solving Equations by Factoring

In Chapter 2, we discussed solving first-degree equations. We are now ready to solve quadratic (second-degree) and higher-degree equations. The method of solving such equations is based on Rule 5.1, which is stated without proof.

RULE 5.1

If the product of two factors is zero, then one or both of the factors must be zero.

If $a \cdot b = 0$, then $\begin{cases} a = 0 \\ \text{or } b = 0 \\ \text{or both } a \text{ and } b = 0 \end{cases}$

Rule 5.1 can be extended to include more than two factors; that is, if a product of factors is zero, at least one of the factors must be zero.

Many higher-degree equations can be solved by factoring. The method is summarized below.

TO SOLVE AN EQUATION BY FACTORING

1. Get all nonzero terms to one side of the equation by adding the same expression to both sides. *Only zero must remain on the other side.* Then arrange the polynomial in descending powers.

2. Factor the polynomial completely.

3. Applying Rule 5.1, set each factor equal to zero.*

4. Solve each resulting first-degree equation.

5. Check apparent solutions in the original equation.

Example 1   Solve $4x^2 - 16x = 0$.

The polynomial must be factored first.

$$4x^2 - 16x = 0$$

$$4x(x - 4) = 0$$

$$4x = 0 \quad | \quad x - 4 = 0$$
$$x = 0 \quad | \quad x = 4$$

Solution set $= \{0, 4\}$

Check For $x = 0$: $4(0^2) - 16(0) = 0$

For $x = 4$: $4(4^2) - 16(4) = 64 - 64 = 0$ ∎

Example 2   Solve $x^2 - x = 6$.

$$x^2 - x = 6$$

$$x^2 - x - 6 = 0 \qquad \text{Add } -6 \text{ to both sides}$$

$$(x + 2)(x - 3) = 0 \qquad \text{Factor}$$

$$x + 2 = \quad 0 \quad | \quad x - 3 = 0$$
$$x = -2 \quad | \quad x = 3$$

Solution set $= \{-2, 3\}$

Check For $x = -2$: $(-2)^2 - (-2) = 4 + 2 = 6$

For $x = 3$: $(3)^2 - (3) = 9 - 3 = 6$ ∎

Sometimes, it is convenient to get all terms to the right side of the equation, leaving only zero on the left side (see Example 3).

---

* If any of the factors are not first-degree polynomials, we cannot solve the equation at this time.

Example 3   Solve $4 - x = 3x^2$.

First, add $(-4 + x)$ to both sides so that only zero remains on the left side. Then arrange the terms in descending powers. *Second,* factor the polynomial.

$$4 - x = 3x^2$$
$$0 = 3x^2 + x - 4$$
$$0 = (x - 1)(3x + 4)$$

$$
\begin{array}{c|c}
x - 1 = 0 & 3x + 4 = 0 \\
x = 1 & 3x = -4 \\
 & x = -\dfrac{4}{3}
\end{array}
$$

Solution set $= \left\{ 1, \ -\dfrac{4}{3} \right\}$

(The checking is left to the student.)   ■

A WORD OF CAUTION   The product must equal *zero*, or no conclusions can be drawn about the factors.

Suppose $(x - 1)(x - 3) =$ 8 .

— No conclusion can be drawn because the product $\neq 0$

Students sometimes think that if $(x - 1)(x - 3) = 8$, then $x - 1 = 8$ *or* $x - 3 = 8$. Both these assumptions are incorrect, because

$$
\begin{array}{c|c}
\text{if } x - 1 = 8 & \text{if } x - 3 = 8 \\
\text{then } x = 9 & \text{then } x = 11 \\
\text{Therefore, } (x - 1)(x - 3) = & \text{Therefore, } (x - 1)(x - 3) = \\
(9 - 1)(9 - 3) = & (11 - 1)(11 - 3) = \\
8 \ \cdot \ 6 \ \ = 48 & 10 \ \cdot \ 8 \ \ = 80 \\
\neq 8 & \neq 8
\end{array}
$$

The correct solution is

$$(x - 1)(x - 3) = 8$$
$$x^2 - 4x + 3 = 8$$
$$x^2 - 4x - 5 = 0 \qquad \text{Add } -8 \text{ to both sides}$$
$$(x - 5)(x + 1) = 0 \qquad \text{Factor}$$

$$
\begin{array}{c|c}
x - 5 = 0 & x + 1 = 0 \\
x = 5 & x = -1
\end{array}
$$

Example 4   Solve $2x^3 - 3x^2 = 8x + 3$.

First, we move all terms to the left side.

$$2x^3 - 3x^2 - 8x - 3 = 0$$

Second, we factor the polynomial on the left using synthetic division. The integral factors of -3 are ± 1 and ± 3. (We may also need to try $\pm 1/2$ and $\pm 3/2$.)

		2	-3	-8	-3
			2	-1	-9
Divide by $+1$	**1**	2	-1	-9	**-12**

Remainder *not* zero; therefore, $(x - 1)$ is not a factor

		2	-3	-8	-3
			-2	5	3
Divide by -1	**-1**	2	-5	-3	**0**

Remainder *is* zero; therefore, $(x + 1)$ is a factor

$$2x^2 - 5x - 3$$

Quotient is another factor

$$2x^3 - 3x^2 - 8x - 3 = (x + 1)(2x^2 - 5x - 3)$$

See if the quotient $2x^2 - 5x - 3$ can be factored further.

$$2x^2 - 5x - 3 = (x - 3)(2x + 1)$$

Therefore, $2x^3 - 3x^2 - 8x - 3 = (x + 1)(x - 3)(2x + 1)$.
We then have $2x^3 - 3x^2 - 8x - 3 = 0$
$$(x + 1)(x - 3)(2x + 1) = 0$$

Third, we use Rule 5.1 and set each factor equal to zero; *fourth*, we solve each of the resulting equations.

$x + 1 = 0$	$x - 3 = 0$	$2x + 1 = 0$
$x = -1$	$x = 3$	$2x = -1$
		$x = -\dfrac{1}{2}$

Therefore, the solution set is $\{-1, 3, -\frac{1}{2}\}$.

(The checking is left to the student.) ∎

Example 5   Solve $(x + 2)^3 = x^3 + 56$.

We first remove the grouping symbols, using the binomial theorem. We then have

$$x^3 + 3x^2(2) + 3x(2)^2 + (2)^3 = x^3 + 56$$
$$x^3 + 6x^2 + 12x + 8 - x^3 - 56 = 0 \qquad \text{All terms moved to left}$$
$$6x^2 + 12x - 48 = 0$$
$$6(x^2 + 2x - 8) = 0 \qquad \text{Divide both sides by 6}$$
$$(x + 4)(x - 2) = 0$$

$x + 4 = 0$	$x - 2 = 0$
$x = -4$	$x = 2$

The solution set is $\{-4, 2\}$.

Check

For $x = -4$: $(-4 + 2)^3 \stackrel{?}{=} (-4)^3 + 56$

$(-2)^3 \stackrel{?}{=} -64 + 56$

$-8 = -8$

For $x = 2$: $(2 + 2)^3 \stackrel{?}{=} 2^3 + 56$

$4^3 \stackrel{?}{=} 8 + 56$

$64 = 64$ ∎

EXERCISES 5.10

Set I   Solve each of the following equations.

1. $3x(x - 4) = 0$ **2.** $5x(x + 6) = 0$ **3.** $4x^2 = 12x$

4. $6a^2 = 9a$ **5.** $x(x - 4) = 12$ **6.** $x(x - 2) = 15$

7. $2x^3 + x^2 = 3x$ **8.** $4x^3 = 10x - 18x^2$ **9.** $2x^2 - 15 = -7x$

10. $3x^2 - 10 = -13x$ **11.** $4x^2 + 9 = 12x$ **12.** $25x^2 + 4 = 20x$

13. $21x^2 + 60x = 18x^3$ **14.** $68x^2 = 30x^3 + 30x$

15. $4x(2x - 1)(3x + 7) = 0$ **16.** $5x(4x - 3)(7x - 6) = 0$

17. $x^3 + 3x^2 - 4x = 12$ **18.** $x^3 + x^2 - 9x = 9$

19. $x^3 - 2x^2 - 13x - 10 = 0$ **20.** $x^3 + 4x^2 + x - 6 = 0$

21. $x^4 - 10x^2 + 9 = 0$ **22.** $x^4 - 13x^2 + 36 = 0$

23. $(x + 3)^3 = x^3 + 63$ **24.** $(x + 1)^3 = x^3 + 37$

25. $(x + 3)^4 = x^4 + 108x + 81$ **26.** $(x + 2)^4 = x^4 + 32x + 16$

Set II   Solve each of the following equations.

1. $4x(x - 2) = 0$ **2.** $16x^2 = 5x$ **3.** $x(3x - 1) = 2$

4. $x^2 + 9 = 6x$ **5.** $x(x + 1) = 12$ **6.** $(x + 2)^3 = x^3 + 8$

7. $6x^3 + 10x^2 = 4x$ **8.** $4x^3 + 10x^2 = 6x$ **9.** $3x^2 - 2 = x$

10. $4x^4 - 5x^2 + 1 = 0$ **11.** $6x^2 + 12 = 17x$ **12.** $2x^3 + 3x^2 = 2x + 3$

13. $30x - 3x^2 = 9x^3$ **14.** $x^3 - 5x^2 + 2x + 8 = 0$

15. $3x(3x - 1)(5x + 7) = 0$ **16.** $4x^3 = 20x^2 + 9x - 45$

17. $z^3 - 2z^2 + 2 = z$ **18.** $14x^4 + 41x^3 = 3x^2$

19. $x^3 - 6x^2 + 11x - 6 = 0$ **20.** $(x - 1)^4 = x^4 - 2x + 1$

21. $x^4 - 5x^2 + 4 = 0$ **22.** $(x - 2)^3 = x^3 - 2$

23. $(x + 2)^3 = x^3 + 26$ **24.** $x^3 + x^2 + 15 = 17x$

25. $(x + 1)^4 = x^4 + 4x + 1$ **26.** $7x^2 + 4 = 29x$

5.11 Word Problems Solved by Factoring

Some word problems and some problems about geometric figures lead to equations that can be solved by factoring. Several formulas relating to geometric figures were given in Section 3.2. You might want to review them at this time.

Example 1   The width of a rectangle is 5 cm less than its length. Its area is 10 more (numerically) than its perimeter. What are the dimensions of the rectangle?

NOTE   The domain is the set of positive real numbers, since the length of a rectangle cannot be negative or zero.   ☑

Let
$$L = \text{length}$$
$$L - 5 = \text{width}$$

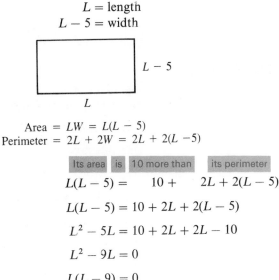

$L - 5$

L

$$\text{Area} = LW = L(L - 5)$$
$$\text{Perimeter} = 2L + 2W = 2L + 2(L - 5)$$

| Its area | is | 10 more than | its perimeter |

$$L(L - 5) = \quad 10 + \quad 2L + 2(L - 5)$$

$$L(L - 5) = 10 + 2L + 2(L - 5)$$

$$L^2 - 5L = 10 + 2L + 2L - 10$$

$$L^2 - 9L = 0$$

$$L(L - 9) = 0$$

Not in the domain ⟶ $L = 0$ | $L - 9 = 0$

$L = 9$ Length

$L - 5 = 4$ Width

Therefore, the rectangle has a length of 9 cm and a width of 4 cm.

Check   Area = 36 sq. cm

Perimeter = 26 cm

36 is 10 more than 26   ∎

Example 2   The base of a triangle is 5 cm more than the height. If the area is 33 sq. cm, find the height and the base of the triangle.

Let $h = \text{height of triangle (in cm)}$

$$5 + h = \text{base of triangle (in cm)}$$

| area of triangle | is | 33 |

$$\frac{1}{2} h(5 + h) = 33$$

$$5h + h^2 = 66$$

$$h^2 + 5h - 66 = 0$$

$$(h - 6)(h + 11) = 0$$

$h - 6 = 0$ | $h + 11 = 0$

$h = 6$ | $h = -11$ −11 is not in the domain

$$5 + h = 11$$

Therefore, the height is 6 cm and the base is 11 cm.

Check   The area is $\frac{1}{2}(6 \text{ cm})(11 \text{ cm}) = 33$ sq. cm.   ∎

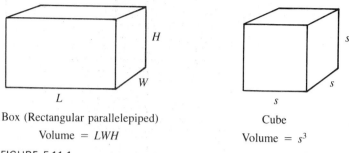

Box (Rectangular parallelepiped)
Volume $= LWH$

Cube
Volume $= s^3$

FIGURE 5.11.1

Figure 5.11.1 shows some more geometric relationships often used in word problems. The *domain* in such problems is the set of *positive* real numbers, since the length of a cube or box cannot be negative or zero.

Example 3 One cube has a side 2 cm longer than the side of a second cube. If the volume of the larger cube is 56 cc (cubic centimeters) more than the volume of the smaller cube, find the length of the side of each cube. (The domain is the set of all positive real numbers.)

Let
$$x = \text{length of the side of the smaller cube}$$
$$x + 2 = \text{length of the side of the larger cube}$$

| volume of larger cube | is | 56 more than | volume of smaller cube |

$$(x + 2)^3 = 56 + x^3$$
$$x^3 + 6x^2 + 12x + 8 = 56 + x^3$$
$$6x^2 + 12x - 48 = 0$$
$$6(x^2 + 2x - 8) = 0 \qquad \text{Divide both sides by 6}$$
$$(x - 2)(x + 4) = 0$$

$x - 2 = 0$	$x + 4 = 0$	
$x = 2$	$x = -4$	-4 is not in the domain
$x + 2 = 4$		

Length of side of smaller cube: 2 cm
Length of side of larger cube: 4 cm

Check Volume of smaller cube: 8 cc
Volume of larger cube: 64 cc
$64 = 56 + 8$ ∎

EXERCISES 5.11

Set I Set up algebraically and solve. Be sure to state what your variables represent.

1. Find three consecutive even integers such that the product of the first two is 38 more than the third number.

2. Find three consecutive odd integers such that the product of the first two is 52 more than the third number.

3. The length and width of a rectangle are in the ratio of 3 to 2. The area is 150. Find the length and width.

4. The length and width of a rectangle are in the ratio of 4 to 3. The area is 192. Find the length and width.

5. The height of a rectangular box equals the length of a side of a certain cube. The width of the box is 3 more than its height, and the length of the box is 4 times its height. The volume of the box is 8 times the volume of the cube. Find the *dimensions* of the box, and find the *volume* of the cube.

6. The height of a rectangular box equals the length of a side of a certain cube. The width of the box is twice its height, and the length of the box is 10 more than its height. The volume of the box is 6 times the volume of the cube. Find the *dimensions* of the box, and find the *volume* of the cube.

7. The width of a rectangle is 5 m less than its length. The area is 46 more (numerically) than its perimeter. What are the dimensions of the rectangle?

8. The width of a rectangle is 7 m less than its length. The area is 4 more (numerically) than its perimeter. What are the dimensions of the rectangle?

9. The base of a triangle is 7 cm more than the height. If the area is 39 sq. cm, find the height and the base of the triangle.

10. The base of a triangle is 4 m more than the height. If the area is 48 sq. m, find the height and the base of the triangle.

11. One square has a side 6 cm shorter than the side of a second square. The area of the larger square is 9 times as great as the area of the smaller square. Find the length of the side of each square.

12. One square has a side 4 cm shorter than the side of a second square. The area of the larger square is 4 times as great as the area of the smaller square. Find the length of the side of each square.

13. One cube has a side 3 cm longer than the side of a second cube. If the volume of the larger cube is 63 cc more than the volume of the smaller one, find the length of a side of each cube.

14. One cube has a side 1 cm longer than the side of a second cube. If the volume of the larger cube is 37 cc more than the volume of the smaller one, find the length of a side of each cube.

15. A box with no top is to be formed from a rectangular sheet of metal by cutting 2-in. squares from the corners and folding up the sides. The length of the box is to be 3 in. more than its width, and its volume is to be 80 cu. in.

   a. Find the dimensions of the original sheet of metal.

   b. Find the dimensions of the box.

16. A box with no top is to be formed from a rectangular sheet of metal by cutting 3-in. squares from the corners and folding up the sides. The length of the box is to be 3 in. more than its width, and its volume is to be 30 cu. in.

   a. Find the dimensions of the original sheet of metal.

   b. Find the dimensions of the box.

17. Thirty-five square yards of carpet are laid in a rectangular room. The length is 3 yd less than two times the width. Find the dimensions of the room.

18. Fifty-four square yards of carpet are laid in a rectangular room. The length is 3 yd less than two times the width. Find the dimensions of the room.

Set II   Set up algebraically and solve. Be sure to state what your variables represent.

1. Find three consecutive even integers such that the product of the first two is 16 more than the third number.

2. Find three consecutive odd integers such that the product of the first and third is 13 more than 16 times the second.

3. The length and width of a rectangle are in the ratio of 5 to 3. The area is 735. Find the length and width.

4. The base and height of a triangle are in the ratio 3:2. If the area of the triangle is 48 sq. cm, find its base and height.

5. The width of a rectangular box equals the length of a side of a certain cube. The height of the box is 2 more than its width, and the length of the box is 3 times its width. The volume of the box is 6 times the volume of the cube. Find the *dimensions* of the box, and find the *volume* of the cube.

6. A 2-cm wide mat surrounds a picture. The area of the picture itself is 286 sq. cm. If the length of the outside of the mat is twice its width, what are the dimensions of the outside of the mat? What are the dimensions of the picture?

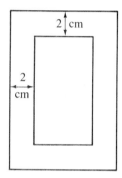

7. The width of a rectangle is 6 yd less than its length. The area is 23 more (numerically) than its perimeter. What are the dimensions of the rectangle?

8. Patricia is 3 years older than Sandra. The product of their ages is 154. How old is each?

9. The base of a triangle is 6 cm more than the height. If the area is 20 sq. cm, find the height and the base of the triangle.

10. Find three consecutive odd integers such that the product of the first and third is 9 more than 12 times the second.

11. One square has a side 2 m longer than the side of a second square. The area of the larger square is 16 times the area of the smaller square. Find the length of the side of each square.

12. The length of a rectangular box is twice its width, and its height is 2 cm less than its width. The volume of the box is 150 cc. Find the dimensions of the box.

13. One cube has a side 2 cm longer than the side of a second cube. If the volume of the larger cube is 26 cc more than the volume of the smaller one, find the length of a side of each cube.

14. Find three consecutive odd integers such that the product of the first and third is 11 more than 14 times the second.

15. A box with no top is formed from a square sheet of metal by cutting 3-in. squares from the corners and folding up the sides. The box is to have a volume of 12 cu. in.

    a. Find the dimensions of the sheet of metal.

    b. Find the dimensions of the box.

16. One cube has a side 2 cm longer than the side of a second cube. If the volume of the larger cube is 152 cc more than the volume of the smaller one, find the length of a side of each cube.

17. Forty square yards of carpet are laid in a rectangular room. The length is 2 yd less than three times the width. Find the dimensions of the room.

18. The base of a triangle is 5 m more than the height. The area is 12 sq. m. Find the base and the height.

5.12 Review: 5.6–5.11

Methods of Factoring

5.1 *First, check for a common factor.* If there is a common factor, factor it out.

If the expression to be factored has two terms:

5.3 1. Is it a *difference* of two *squares*?

2. Is it a *sum* of two *squares*? (It is not factorable unless it can be factored by completing the square.)

5.6 3. Is it a *sum* or *difference* of two *cubes*?

5.7 4. Can it be factored by completing the square?

5.8 5. Can it be factored by synthetic division?

If the expression to be factored has three terms:

5.4A 1. Is the leading coefficient 1?

5.4B 2. Are the first and last terms perfect squares? If so, is the trinomial a perfect square?

5.4B 3. Is the leading coefficient unequal to 1?

5.7 4. Can it be factored by completing the square?

5.8 5. Can it be factored by synthetic division?

If the expression to be factored has four or more terms:

5.2 1. Can it be factored by grouping?

5.8 2. Can it be factored by synthetic division?

Check to see if any factor can be factored again.

Check your solution.

To Solve an Equation by Factoring 5.10
1. Get *all* nonzero terms to one side of the equation by adding the same expression to both sides. *Only zero must remain on the other side.* Then arrange the polynomial in descending powers.

2. Factor the polynomial.

3. Set each factor equal to zero and solve for the variable.

Word Problems about Geometric Figures 5.11
In solving word problems about geometric figures, make a drawing of the figure and write the given information on it as an aid in writing the equation.

Review Exercises 5.12 Set I

In Exercises 1–33, factor completely or write "Not factorable."

1. $15u^2v - 3uv$

2. $3n^2 + 16n + 5$

3. $4x^2y - 8xy^2 + 4xy$

4. $5x^2 + 11x + 2$

5. $17u - 12 + 5u^2$

6. $4 + 21x + 5x^2$

7. $6u^3v^2 - 9uv^3 - 12uv$

8. $15a^2 + 15ab - 30b^2$

9. $81 - 9m^2$

10. $x^2 + 25$

11. $10x^2 - xy - 24y^2$

12. $28x^2 - 13xy - 6y^2$

13. $8a^3 - 27b^3$

14. $64h^3 - 125k^3$

15. $1 + 4y + 4y^2$

16. $4 + 12x + 9x^2$

17. $x^3 + 8y^3$

18. $27x^3 + y^3$

19. $x^2 + x - y - y^2$

20. $x^2 - x + y - y^2$

21. $x^3 - 2x^2 - 4x + 3$

22. $x^2 + x + 9$

23. $8a^2 - 8ab + 2b^2$

24. $18h^2 - 12hk + 2k^2$

25. $x^3 - 4x^2 - 4x + 16$

26. $9x^4 + 8x^2 + 4$

27. $x^3 - 5x^2 + 8x - 4$

28. $x^3 - 2x^2 - 9x + 18$

29. $4x^4 - 5x^2 + 25$

30. $x^2 + 8x + 16 - 25y^2$

31. $(2x + 3y)^2 + (2x + y) - 6$

32. $a^2 + 6ab + 9b^2 - 7a - 21b + 12$

33. $x^2 + 4xy + 4y^2 - 5x - 10y + 6$

In Exercises 34–44, solve each equation.

34. $5z^2 - 12z + 7 = 0$

35. $x^2 = 3(6 + x)$

36. $x^3 = 36x^2$

37. $6x^2 = 13x + 5$

38. $12x^2 = 47x - 45$

39. $x^3 + 3x^2 - 18x = 40$

40. $x^3 - 2x^2 - 9x + 18 = 0$

41. $(x + 3)^3 = x^3 + 27$

42. $4 + 5x^2 + 12x = 0$

43. $(x + 3)^4 = x^4 + 12x^3 + 81$

44. $(x + 2)^4 = x^4 + 8x^3 + 16$

In Exercises 45–50, set up algebraically and solve. Be sure to state what your variables represent.

45. Find three consecutive odd integers such that the product of the first and third is 5 more than 8 times the second.

46. The height and base of a triangle are in the ratio of 4 to 5. The area is 40. Find the height and the base.

47. The length and width of a rectangle are in the ratio of 5 to 3. The area is 240. Find the length and the width.

48. The length of a rectangle is 7 more than the width. The area is 40 more (numerically) than its perimeter. What are the dimensions of the rectangle?

49. One cube has a side 4 cm longer than the side of a second cube. If the volume of the larger cube is 316 cc more than the volume of the smaller one, find the length of a side of each cube.

50. One square has a side 3 cm longer than the side of a second square. The area of the larger square is 16 times the area of the smaller square. Find the length of a side of each square.

Review Exercises 5.12 Set II

NAME _____

In Exercises 1–33, factor completely or write "Not factorable."

1. $2a^2 - 9a + 10$

2. $a^2 - 2ab - 15b^2$

3. $5x^2 + x - 1$

4. $3x^2 + 13x - 10$

5. $6x^2 + xy - 15y^2$

6. $5a^2 + 13ab - 6b^2$

7. $2ac + bc - 3bd - 6ad$

8. $x^4 + 9x^2 + 25$

9. $64x^3 + 27y^3$

10. $64x^4 + 1$

11. $6x^2 + 29x + 20$

12. $x^2 + 100$

13. $3x^3 - 12xy^2$

14. $x^2 + x + 17$

15. $4y^2 - 5y - 6$

16. $5a^4 - 40ab^3$

ANSWERS

1. _____

2. _____

3. _____

4. _____

5. _____

6. _____

7. _____

8. _____

9. _____

10. _____

11. _____

12. _____

13. _____

14. _____

15. _____

16. _____

17. $x^3 + x^2 - 9x - 9$

18. $x^2 - 10xy + 25y^2 - 9$

19. $3x^3 - 81$

20. $3n^2 - 8n - 5$

21. $x^3 - 3x^2 - 4x + 12$

22. $y^2 + 36$

23. $6x^2 + x - 2$

24. $x^2 + x + 15$

25. $y^2 + 10y + 25 - 4x^2$

26. $(5x - 2)^2 + 8(5x - 2)y + 15y^2$

27. $a^3 + a^2b - b^2a - b^3$

28. $x^4 + 2x^2 + 9$

29. $x^2 + 6xy + 9y^2 - 2x - 6y - 24$

30. $(3x - 2y)^2 - (3x - 2y) - 6$

31. $x^3 + 2x^2 - 29x - 30$

32. $9x^4 - 4x^2 + 4$

33. $9x^2 + 12xy + 4y^2 - 4a^2 - 4ab - b^2$

In Exercises 34–44, solve each equation.

34. $x(x - 2) = 15$

35. $x^3 = 16x^2$

36. $x^2 = 4(5 + 2x)$

37. $8x^2 = 10x + 12$

38. $x^3 - 2x^2 - 5x + 6 = 0$

39. $x^3 = 9x^2$

40. $x^3 + x^2 - 22x = 40$

41. $x^3 + 4x^2 - 25x = 100$

42. $x^3 - 5x^2 - 4x + 20 = 0$

43. $(x + 4)^3 = x^3 + 64$

44. $(x - 2)^3 = x^3 - 8$

ANSWERS

34. _____

35. _____

36. _____

37. _____

38. _____

39. _____

40. _____

41. _____

42. _____

43. _____

44. _____

In Exercises 45–50, set up algebraically and solve. Be sure to state what your variables represent.

45. Find three consecutive odd integers such that the product of the first and third is 4 less than 25 times the second.

45. _____

46. _____

47. _____

48. _____

46. The length and width of a rectangle are in the ratio of 7 to 5. The area is 560. Find the length and the width.

49. _____

50. _____

47. One cube has a side 1 cm longer than the side of a second cube. If the volume of the larger cube is 91 cc more than the volume of the smaller one, find the length of a side of each cube.

48. Find three consecutive odd integers such that the product of the first and third is 7 more than 10 times the second.

49. The area of a square is 3 times its perimeter (numerically). What is the length of its side?

50. The height of a rectangular box is 2 cm less than the width, and the length is 7 times the width. The volume is 525 cc. Find the dimensions of the box.

Chapter 5 Diagnostic Test

The purpose of this test is to see how well you understand factoring and solving equations by factoring. We recommend that you work this diagnostic test *before* your instructor tests you on this chapter. Allow yourself about 50 minutes.

Complete solutions for all the problems on this test, together with section references, are given in the answer section at the end of the book. For the problems you do incorrectly, study the sections cited.

In Problems 1–11, factor the expressions completely.

1. $4x - 16x^3$

2. $43 + 7x^2 + 6$

3. $7x^2 + 23x + 6$

4. $x^2 + 81$

5. $2x^3 + 4x^2 + 16x$

6. $6x^2 - 5x - 6$

7. $y^3 - 1$

8. $3ac + 6bc - 5ad - 10bd$

9. $x^4 + 5x^2 + 9$

10. $x^3 - 8x + 3$

11. $4x^2 + 4x + 1 - y^2$

In Problems 12–15, solve the equations.

12. $2x^2 + x - 15 = 0$

13. $8y^2 = 4y$

14. $6x^2 - 15 = 27x$

15. $(x + 1)^3 = x^3 + 1$

In Problems 16 and 17, set up algebraically and solve. Be sure to state what your variables represent.

16. Find three consecutive even integers such that the product of the first two is 68 more than the third number.

17. The base of a triangle is 8 cm more than the height. If the area is 64 sq. cm, find the height and the base.

Cumulative Review Exercises
Chapters 1–5

1. Evaluate $18 \div 2\sqrt{9} - 4^2 \cdot 3$.

2. Given the formula $h = 48t - 16t^2$, find h when $t = 2$.

3. Solve $2(x - 3) - 5 = 6 - 3(x + 4)$.

4. Solve $-6 < 4x - 2 < 10$.

5. Solve $|2x - 3| \geq 7$.

6. State which of the following are real numbers: $\frac{2}{3}$, $4.7958315\ldots$, 0.

7. Solve $2x^2 = 9x + 5$

In Exercises 8 and 9, factor each expression completely or write "Not factorable."

8. $3x^3 + 81$

9. $x^3 + 6x^2 + 6x + 5$

In Exercises 10–14, perform the indicated operations and simplify.

10. $(2x^2 - 3x + 4) - (x^2 - 5x - 6) + (3 - x + 5x^2)$

11. $(a - 4)(a^2 - 2a + 5)$

12. $(3x + 5)^2$

13. $(2x - 1)^5$

14. $(x^3 - 2x^2 - 6x + 8) \div (x + 2)$

In Exercises 15 and 16, set up the problem algebraically, solve, and check.

15. How many quarts of pure antifreeze must be added to 10 qt of a 20% solution of antifreeze to make a 50% solution?

16. A motorboat crosses a lake traveling 6 mph and returns traveling 4 mph. If it takes $\frac{1}{2}$ hour longer for the return trip, what is the distance across the lake?

6 Fractions

In this chapter, we discuss what algebraic fractions are, how to perform necessary operations with them, and how to solve equations and word problems involving them. A knowledge of factoring and *arithmetic* fractions will help you in your work with *algebraic* fractions.

6.1 Algebraic Fractions

Algebraic Fraction

A **simple algebraic fraction**, also called a **rational expression**, is an algebraic expression of the form

$$\frac{P}{Q}$$

where P and Q are polynomials. P and Q are called the *terms* of the fraction; P is called the *numerator* and Q the *denominator* of the fraction. We learned in Chapter 1 that the *domain of a variable* is the set of all the numbers that can be used in place of a variable and also that we cannot divide by zero. Consequently, the domain of the variable in an algebraic fraction will be the set of all real numbers except those that would make the denominator, Q, equal to zero.

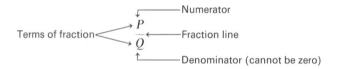

Example 1   Examples of algebraic fractions:

a. $\dfrac{x}{3}$

The domain is the set of all real numbers.

b. $\dfrac{5}{x}$

The domain is the set of all real numbers except 0.

c. $\dfrac{2x - 5}{x - 1}$

The domain is the set of all real numbers except 1.

d. $\dfrac{x^2 + 2}{x^2 - 3x - 4} = \dfrac{x^2 + 2}{(x - 4)(x + 1)}$

The domain is the set of all real numbers except 4 and -1.

e. $\dfrac{2}{3}$

The domain is the set of all real numbers. Arithmetic fractions are also algebraic fractions; here, 2 and 3 are polynomials of degree 0. ■

NOTE   After this section, whenever a fraction is written, it will be understood that the value(s) of the variable(s) that make the denominator zero are excluded.   ✓

A WORD OF CAUTION If you are accustomed to writing fractions with a *slanted bar* (/), be sure to put parentheses around any numerator or denominator that contains more than one term.

$$(x + 2)/(x - 5) = \frac{x + 2}{x - 5}$$

but

$$x + 2/x - 5 = x + \frac{2}{x} - 5 \qquad \boxed{\checkmark}$$

Equivalent fractions are fractions that have the same value. If a fraction is multiplied by 1, its value is unchanged.

$$\left.\begin{array}{l} \dfrac{2}{2} = 1 \\[2ex] \dfrac{x}{x} = 1 \\[2ex] \dfrac{x + 2}{x + 2} = 1 \end{array}\right\}$$

Multiplying a fraction by expressions like these will produce equivalent fractions

For example,

$$\frac{5}{6} = \frac{5}{6} \cdot \boxed{\frac{2}{2}} = \frac{10}{12} \qquad \text{A fraction equivalent to } \frac{5}{6}$$

$$\frac{x}{x + 2} = \frac{x}{x + 2} \cdot \boxed{\frac{x}{x}} = \frac{x^2}{x(x + 2)} \qquad \text{A fraction equivalent to } \frac{x}{x + 2}$$

$$\frac{2}{x} = \frac{2}{x} \cdot \boxed{\frac{x + 2}{x + 2}} = \frac{2x + 4}{x(x + 2)} \qquad \text{A fraction equivalent to } \frac{2}{x}$$

In algebra, as in arithmetic, we get a fraction equivalent to the one we started with if we:

1. Multiply both numerator and denominator by the same nonzero number.

2. Divide both numerator and denominator by the same nonzero number.

A WORD OF CAUTION We do *not* get a fraction equivalent to the one we started with if we *add* the same number to or *subtract* the same number from both the numerator and the denominator. $\boxed{\checkmark}$

Example 2 Determine whether the pairs of fractions are equivalent:

a. $\dfrac{x + 3}{x + 6}, \dfrac{2(x + 3)}{2(x + 6)}$

Yes; the second fraction can be obtained from the first by multiplying both numerator and denominator by 2.

b. $\dfrac{3 + x}{5 + x}, \dfrac{3}{5}$

No; the second fraction cannot be obtained from the first by multiplying or dividing both numerator and denominator by the same number. ∎

The Three Signs of a Fraction

Every fraction has three signs associated with it, even if those signs are not visible: the sign of the fraction, the sign of the numerator, and the sign of the denominator.

$$\text{Sign of fraction} \rightarrow + \underset{\uparrow\ \text{Sign of denominator}}{\overset{\text{Sign of numerator}\ \downarrow}{\frac{+8}{+4}}}$$

Let us compare three other fractions with $+\dfrac{+8}{+4}$.

$$+ \frac{-8}{-4} = +\left(\frac{-8}{-4}\right) = +(+2) = 2$$

$$\left\{\begin{array}{l}\text{Sign of numerator and sign of}\\ \text{denominator are different from } +\dfrac{+8}{+4}\end{array}\right.$$

$$- \frac{-8}{+4} = -\left(\frac{-8}{+4}\right) = -(-2) = 2$$

$$\left\{\begin{array}{l}\text{Sign of fraction and sign of}\\ \text{numerator are different from } +\dfrac{+8}{+4}\end{array}\right.$$

$$- \frac{+8}{-4} = -\left(\frac{+8}{-4}\right) = -(-2) = 2$$

$$\left\{\begin{array}{l}\text{Sign of fraction and sign of}\\ \text{denominator are different from } +\dfrac{+8}{+4}\end{array}\right.$$

Since each of these fractions equals the same number, the fractions must all equal each other. Therefore,

$$+ \frac{+8}{+4} = +\frac{-8}{-4} = -\frac{-8}{+4} = -\frac{+8}{-4} = 2$$

It can also be shown that

$$- \frac{+8}{+4} = +\frac{-8}{+4} = +\frac{+8}{-4} = -\frac{-8}{-4} = -2$$

RULE OF SIGNS FOR FRACTIONS

If any two of the three signs of a fraction are changed, the value of the fraction is unchanged.

This rule of signs is helpful in simplifying some expressions with fractions.

Example 3   Find the missing term:

a. $-\dfrac{-5}{xy} = \dfrac{?}{xy}$

Solution Since the signs of the *denominators* are both understood to be + and the signs of the *fractions* are different, the signs of the numerators must be different. Therefore,

$$-\frac{-5}{xy} = \frac{5}{xy}$$

b. $\dfrac{8}{-x} = \dfrac{-8}{?}$

Solution Since the signs of the *fractions* are both understood to be + and the signs of the *numerators* are different, the signs of the denominators must be different. Therefore,

$$\frac{8}{-x} = \frac{-8}{x} \quad \blacksquare$$

Recall from Section 1.14C that

$$-(b - a) = -1(b - a) = -b + a = a - b$$

Consequently, $a - b$ can always be substituted for $-(b - a)$, and $-(b - a)$ can always be substituted for $a - b$.

Example 4   Find the missing term:

a. $-\dfrac{1}{2 - x} = \dfrac{1}{?}$

   Solution

$$-\frac{1}{2 - x} = \boxed{+} \frac{1}{\boxed{-}(2 - x)} = \frac{1}{x - 2}$$

Here, we changed the sign of the fraction and the denominator

b. $\dfrac{y - 5}{-3} = \dfrac{?}{3}$

   Solution

$$\frac{y - 5}{-3} = \frac{\boxed{-}(y - 5)}{\boxed{-}(-3)} = \frac{5 - y}{3}$$

Here, we changed the sign of the numerator and the denominator

c. $\dfrac{x - y}{(a + b)(c - d)} = \dfrac{?}{(a + b)(d - c)}$

Solution

$$\dfrac{x - y}{(a + b)(c - d)} = \dfrac{\boxed{\ } (x - y)}{(a + b)(\boxed{\ } [c - d])}$$

Here, we changed the sign of the numerator and the denominator

$$= \dfrac{y - x}{(a + b)(d - c)} \quad \blacksquare$$

EXERCISES 6.1

Set I   In Exercises 1–8, find the domain of the variable.

1. $\dfrac{10 - 7y}{y + 4}$

2. $\dfrac{3z + 2}{5 - z}$

3. $\dfrac{5x}{9}$

4. $\dfrac{7}{2x}$

5. $\dfrac{a^2 + 1}{a^2 - 25}$

6. $\dfrac{h^2 + 5}{h^2 - h - 6}$

7. $\dfrac{4c + 3}{c^4 - 13c^2 + 36}$

8. $\dfrac{2x - 5}{x^3 - 5x^2 - 9x + 45}$

In Exercises 9–14, determine whether the pairs of fractions are equivalent.

9. $\dfrac{3}{6y}, \dfrac{1}{2y}$

10. $\dfrac{8}{4x}, \dfrac{2}{x}$

11. $\dfrac{x}{5}, \dfrac{x + 5}{10}$

12. $\dfrac{3}{z}, \dfrac{9}{z + 6}$

13. $\dfrac{2 + x}{3 - y}, \dfrac{8(2 + x)}{8(3 - y)}$

14. $\dfrac{4 - x}{y + 2}, \dfrac{3(4 - x)}{3(y + 2)}$

In Exercises 15–24, find the missing term.

15. $-\dfrac{5}{8} = \dfrac{5}{?}$

16. $-\dfrac{6}{-k} = \dfrac{?}{k}$

17. $\dfrac{-x}{5} = \dfrac{x}{?}$

18. $\dfrac{6}{-k} = \dfrac{?}{k}$

19. $\dfrac{8 - y}{4y - 7} = \dfrac{y - 8}{?}$

20. $\dfrac{w - 2}{5 - w} = \dfrac{?}{w - 5}$

21. $\dfrac{u - v}{a - b} = \dfrac{v - u}{?}$

22. $\dfrac{2 - x}{y - 5} = \dfrac{?}{5 - y}$

23. $\dfrac{a - b}{(3a + 2b)(a - 5b)} = \dfrac{?}{(3a + 2b)(5b - a)}$

24. $\dfrac{(e + 4f)(7e - 3f)}{2e - f} = \dfrac{(e + 4f)(3f - 7e)}{?}$

Set II   In Exercises 1–8, find the domain of the variable.

1. $\dfrac{4y + 5}{2y - 9}$

2. $\dfrac{x + 2}{5}$

3. $\dfrac{11}{6d}$

4. $\dfrac{3 - x}{x + 2}$

5. $\dfrac{2a^2 + 13}{a^2 + 3a - 28}$

6. $\dfrac{3x^2 - 13x + 12}{9x^2 - 24x + 16}$

7. $\dfrac{u^2 + 10u + 1}{u^3 - 16u + 2u^2 - 32}$

8. $\dfrac{5}{v^3 + 3v^2 - v - 3}$

In Exercises 9–14, determine whether the pairs of fractions are equivalent.

9. $\dfrac{12}{3y}, \dfrac{4}{y}$

10. $\dfrac{12}{3+y}, \dfrac{4}{y}$

11. $\dfrac{z}{2}, \dfrac{z+6}{8}$

12. $\dfrac{6+3y}{8+4y}, \dfrac{3}{4}$

13. $\dfrac{9-y}{x+2}, \dfrac{2(9-y)}{2(x+2)}$

14. $\dfrac{y+2}{y+4}, \dfrac{1}{2}$

In Exercises 15–24, find the missing term.

15. $-\dfrac{2}{7} = \dfrac{2}{?}$

16. $\dfrac{-8}{x} = -\dfrac{?}{x}$

17. $\dfrac{-14}{3m} = \dfrac{14}{?}$

18. $\dfrac{4-x}{x+3} = -\dfrac{?}{x+3}$

19. $\dfrac{5-x}{3y-2} = \dfrac{x-5}{?}$

20. $\dfrac{?}{x+5} = \dfrac{x+10}{-(x+5)}$

21. $\dfrac{x-y}{c-d} = \dfrac{?}{d-c}$

22. $\dfrac{y-2}{?} = \dfrac{2-y}{y+7}$

23. $\dfrac{5t-2u}{(t-4u)(3t+u)} = \dfrac{?}{(4u-t)(3t+u)}$

24. $\dfrac{(8-x)(8+x)}{?} = \dfrac{(x-8)(x+8)}{(3+x)(5+x)}$

6.2 Reducing Fractions to Lowest Terms

We reduce fractions to lowest terms in algebra for the same reason we do in arithmetic—it makes them simpler and easier to work with. After this section, it is understood that all fractions are to be reduced to lowest terms unless otherwise indicated.

TO REDUCE A FRACTION TO LOWEST TERMS

1. Factor the numerator and denominator completely.

2. Divide numerator and denominator by all factors common to both.

The new fraction will, of course, be equivalent to the original fraction.

Example 1 Reduce to lowest terms:

a. $\dfrac{4x^2y}{2xy} = \dfrac{\overset{2}{\cancel{4x^2y}}}{\underset{1}{\cancel{2xy}}} = 2x$

Here, the literal parts of the fraction are already factored; the common factors are 2, x, and y.

b. $\dfrac{3x^2-5xy-2y^2}{6x^3y+2x^2y^2} = \dfrac{(x-2y)\overset{1}{\cancel{(3x+y)}}}{2x^2y\underset{1}{\cancel{(3x+y)}}} = \dfrac{x-2y}{2x^2y}$

c. $\dfrac{2b^2 + ab - 3a^2}{4a^2 - 9ab + 5b^2}$

$$\overbrace{(-1)(b - a) = (a - b)}$$

$$= \frac{(b - a)(2b + 3a)}{(a - b)(4a - 5b)} = \frac{(-1)(b - a)\,(2b + 3a)}{(-1)(a - b)(4a - 5b)} = \frac{\overset{1}{\cancel{(a - b)}}(2b + 3a)}{(-1)\underset{1}{\cancel{(a - b)}}(4a - 5b)}$$

Changing the sign of both numerator and denominator is equivalent to multiplying each by -1

$$= \frac{(2b + 3a)}{(-1)(4a - 5b)} = \frac{2b + 3a}{5b - 4a}$$

or $\dfrac{(b - a)(2b + 3a)}{(a - b)\,(4a - 5b)} = \dfrac{(b - a)(2b + 3a)}{-(b - a)\,(4a - 5b)}$

Substituting $-(b - a)$ for $a - b$

$$= \frac{2b + 3a}{-(4a - 5b)} = \frac{2b + 3a}{5b - 4a}$$

Difference of 2 cubes

d. $\dfrac{\overbrace{x^3 - 8}}{\underbrace{x^3 - 2x^2 + 4x - 8}} = \dfrac{\overset{1}{\cancel{(x - 2)}}(x^2 + 2x + 4)}{\underset{1}{\cancel{(x - 2)}}(x^2 + 4)}$

Factor by grouping or by synthetic division

$$= \frac{x^2 + 2x + 4}{x^2 + 4}$$

Not factorable

e. $\dfrac{\overbrace{a^2 - 3ab + b^2}}{\underbrace{a^4 - 7a^2b^2 + b^4}}$

Factor by completing the square

$$= \frac{\overset{1}{\cancel{a^2 - 3ab + b^2}}}{\underset{1}{\cancel{(a^2 - 3ab + b^2)}}(a^2 + 3ab + b^2)}$$

This 1 $cannot$ be omitted

$$= \frac{1}{a^2 + 3ab + b^2}$$

A WORD OF CAUTION A common error made in reducing fractions is to forget that the number the numerator and denominator are divided by *must* be a *factor* of *both* (see Example 1f).

Error:

3 is *not* a factor of the numerator

$$\frac{3 + 2}{3} \neq 2 \qquad \text{\textit{Incorrect} reduction}$$

The above reduction is incorrect because

$$\frac{3 + 2}{3} = \frac{5}{3} \neq 2$$

☑

f. $\dfrac{x + 3}{x + 6}$

This fraction cannot be reduced, since neither x nor 3 is a *factor* of numerator or denominator. ∎

When a fraction has only one term in the denominator but several terms in the numerator, it can be reduced as a single fraction or it can be rewritten as a sum of several fractions, as was done in Section 4.5A; each of the resulting fractions can then be reduced (see Example 2).

Example 2 Reduce to lowest terms:

x is *not* a factor of the numerator

a. $\dfrac{x + y}{x}$ ← This is an acceptable answer

This fraction cannot be reduced.

If we write $\dfrac{x + y}{x}$ as a sum of fractions, we have

$$\frac{x + y}{x} = \frac{x}{x} + \frac{y}{x} = 1 + \frac{y}{x} \qquad \text{← This is an acceptable answer}$$

This is an acceptable answer ⟶

b. $\dfrac{7pqr - 21p^2r + 28qr^3}{7pqr} = \dfrac{7r(pq - 3p^2 + 4qr^2)}{7pqr} = \dfrac{pq - 3p^2 + 4qr^2}{pq}$

The same problem can also be done this way:

$$\frac{7pqr - 21p^2r + 28qr^3}{7pqr} = \frac{7pqr}{7pqr} - \frac{21p^2r}{7pqr} + \frac{28qr^3}{7pqr} = 1 - \frac{3p}{q} + \frac{4r^2}{p}$$

This is an acceptable answer ⟶

Notice that

$$\frac{pq - 3p^2 + 4qr^2}{pq} = \frac{pq}{pq} - \frac{3p^2}{pq} + \frac{4qr^2}{pq} = 1 - \frac{3p}{q} + \frac{4r^2}{p} \qquad ∎$$

EXERCISES 6.2

Set I Reduce each fraction to lowest terms.

1. $\dfrac{12m^3n}{4mn}$ 2. $\dfrac{-6hk^4}{24hk}$ 3. $\dfrac{15a^4b^3c^2}{-35ab^5c}$ 4. $\dfrac{40e^2f^2g}{16e^4fg^3}$

5. $\dfrac{40x - 8x^2}{5x^2 + 10x}$ 6. $\dfrac{16y^4 - 16y^3}{24y^2 - 24y}$ 7. $\dfrac{c^2 - 4}{4}$ 8. $\dfrac{9 + d^2}{9}$

9. $\dfrac{24w^2x^3 - 16wx^4}{18w^3x - 12w^2x^2}$ 10. $\dfrac{18c^5d + 45c^4d^2}{12c^2d^3 + 30cd^4}$ 11. $\dfrac{x^2 - 16}{x^2 - 9x + 20}$

12. $\dfrac{x^2 - 2x - 15}{x^2 - 9}$ 13. $\dfrac{2x^2 - xy - y^2}{y^2 - 4xy + 3x^2}$ 14. $\dfrac{2k^2 + 3hk - 5h^2}{3h^2 - 7hk + 4k^2}$

15. $\dfrac{2x^2 - 3x - 9}{12 - 7x + x^2}$ 16. $\dfrac{15 + 7y - 2y^2}{4y^2 - 21y + 5}$ 17. $\dfrac{2y^2 + xy - 6x^2}{3x^2 + xy - 2y^2}$

18. $\dfrac{10y^2 + 11xy - 6x^2}{4x^2 - 4xy - 15y^2}$ 19. $\dfrac{2x^2 - 9x - 5}{2x^2 + 5x + 3}$ 20. $\dfrac{3x^2 - 11x - 4}{3x^2 + 5x + 2}$

21. $\dfrac{a^3 - 1}{1 - a^2}$ 22. $\dfrac{x^3 + y^3}{y^2 - x^2}$ 23. $\dfrac{x^2 + 4}{x^2 + 4x + 4}$

24. $\dfrac{9 + y^2}{9 + 6y + y^2}$ 25. $\dfrac{4x^4 + y^4}{6x^2 + 6xy + 3y^2}$ 26. $\dfrac{x^4 + x^2y^2 + y^4}{2x^2 - 2xy + 2y^2}$

27. $\dfrac{x^3 + 8}{x^3 - 3x^2 + 6x - 4}$ 28. $\dfrac{x^3 + 4x^2 + 12x + 9}{x^3 - 27}$

29. $\dfrac{13x^3y^2 - 26xy^3 + 39xy}{13x^2y^2}$ 30. $\dfrac{21m^2n^3 - 35m^3n^2 - 14mn}{7m^2n^2}$

31. $\dfrac{6a^2bc^2 - 4ab^2c^2 + 12bc}{6abc}$ 32. $\dfrac{8a^3b^2c - 4a^2bc - 10ac}{4abc}$

Set II Reduce each fraction to lowest terms.

1. $\dfrac{15c^2d^5}{12c^2d^3}$ 2. $\dfrac{24x^4y^2}{48x^6y^3}$ 3. $\dfrac{14e^5f^2g^3}{-42e^3f^4g}$

4. $\dfrac{x^2 + 9}{x^2 - 9}$ 5. $\dfrac{32m^2 - 24m^3}{80m^3 - 60m^4}$ 6. $\dfrac{x^2 + x - 6}{x^2 + 6x + 9}$

7. $\dfrac{6}{6 - x}$ 8. $\dfrac{2x^2 - 7x - 15}{2x^2 + 7x - 15}$ 9. $\dfrac{12a^4b - 30a^3b^2}{18a^2b^2 - 45ab^3}$

10. $\dfrac{x - 4}{x^2 - 16}$ 11. $\dfrac{h^2 - 2h - 24}{h^2 - 36}$ 12. $\dfrac{5x^2 - 11x + 2}{5x^2 + 7x + 2}$

13. $\dfrac{24x^2 + 14xy - 5y^2}{3y^2 - 14xy + 8x^2}$ 14. $\dfrac{8x^3 + 1}{8x^3 + 4x^2 + 2x + 1}$ 15. $\dfrac{6x^2 + 5x - 4}{4 - 3x - 10x^2}$

16. $\dfrac{x + 4}{3x^2 + 9x - 12}$ 17. $\dfrac{21m^2 - mn - 2n^2}{4n^2 - 9nm - 9m^2}$ 18. $\dfrac{2x^3 - x^2 - 8x + 4}{2 - 3x - 2x^2}$

19. $\dfrac{5x^2 - 4x - 1}{5x^2 + 7x + 2}$ 20. $\dfrac{x^2 - x + 7}{x^4 + 13x^2 + 49}$ 21. $\dfrac{4x^2 - w^2}{w^3 - 8x^3}$

22. $\dfrac{5 - x}{9x^2 - 39x - 30}$

23. $\dfrac{x^2 + 16}{x^2 + 8x + 16}$

24. $\dfrac{x^3 + 4x^2 + x - 6}{3 - 2x - x^2}$

25. $\dfrac{5x^2 - 15x + 20}{x^4 - x^2 + 16}$

26. $\dfrac{x^4 + 4}{x^4 - 4}$

27. $\dfrac{x^3 - x^2 + x - 1}{x^3 - 2x^2 + 1}$

28. $\dfrac{6x^2 - x - 2}{8x - 10x^2 - 3x^3}$

29. $\dfrac{-30m^4n^2 + 60m^2n^3 - 45m^3n}{15m^3n^2}$

30. $\dfrac{15xyz^3 - 12xz^2 + 10y^2z}{6y^2z}$

31. $\dfrac{24abc + 18b^2c - 8bc}{12ac}$

32. $\dfrac{32x^3yz - 12xy^2 + 48xy^2z}{-16xy^2z}$

6.3 Multiplication and Division of Fractions

Multiplication of Fractions

The definition of multiplication of fractions is

$$\frac{a}{b} \cdot \frac{c}{d} = \frac{a \cdot c}{b \cdot d}$$

In practice, however, we can often reduce the resulting fraction. Therefore, we use the following rules:

TO MULTIPLY FRACTIONS

1. Factor the numerator and denominator of the fractions.

2. Divide numerator and denominator by all factors common to both.

3. The answer is the product of the factors remaining in the numerator divided by the product of the factors remaining in the denominator. A factor of 1 will always remain in both numerator and denominator (see Examples 1a and 3b).

Example 1   Multiply the fractions:

a. $\dfrac{a}{3} \cdot \dfrac{1}{a^2} = \dfrac{\overset{1}{\cancel{a}}}{3} \cdot \dfrac{1}{\underset{a}{\cancel{a^2}}} = \dfrac{1}{3a}$

b. $\dfrac{2y^3}{3x^2} \cdot \dfrac{12x}{5y^2} = \dfrac{2y^3 \cdot \overset{4}{\cancel{12x}}}{\underset{1}{\cancel{3x^2}} \cdot 5y^2} = \dfrac{8y}{5x}$

c. $\dfrac{10xy^3}{x^2 - y^2} \cdot \dfrac{2x^2 + xy - y^2}{15x^2y} = \dfrac{\overset{2}{\cancel{10xy^3}}}{\cancel{(x+y)}(x-y)} \cdot \dfrac{\cancel{(x+y)}(2x-y)}{\underset{3}{\cancel{15x^2y}}}$

$$= \dfrac{2y^2(2x - y)}{3x(x - y)}$$

d. $\dfrac{a^3 - b^3}{\underbrace{a^2 - b^2 - a + b}} \cdot \dfrac{8a^2b}{4a^3 + 4a^2b + 4ab^2}$

$\longrightarrow$ Factor by grouping: $= (a + b)(a - b) - 1(a - b) = \boxed{(a - b)(a + b - 1)}$

$$= \dfrac{\overset{1}{\cancel{(a-b)}}\overset{1}{\cancel{(a^2 + ab + b^2)}}}{\underset{1}{\cancel{(a-b)}}\,(a + b - 1)} \cdot \dfrac{\overset{2}{\cancel{8}}\cancel{a}ab}{\underset{1}{\cancel{4}}\cancel{a}\underset{1}{\cancel{(a^2 + ab + b^2)}}}$$

$$= \dfrac{2ab}{a + b - 1} \qquad \blacksquare$$

The Reciprocal of a Fraction   The *reciprocal* of a nonzero fraction can be found by interchanging the numerator and denominator of the fraction. (Zero has no reciprocal.)

Multiplicative Inverse

When the product of two numbers equals the multiplicative identity, 1, we say the numbers are the multiplicative inverses of each other. Let's consider the product of $\dfrac{a}{b}$ and its reciprocal, $\dfrac{b}{a}$:

$$\dfrac{a}{b} \cdot \dfrac{b}{a} = 1$$

The product of any nonzero fraction and its reciprocal is always 1. Therefore, the reciprocal of a fraction can also be called its *multiplicative inverse*.

Example 2   Find the product of $\dfrac{x}{6}$ and its reciprocal.

The reciprocal of $\dfrac{x}{6}$ is $\dfrac{6}{x}$.

The product is $\dfrac{\overset{1}{\cancel{x}}}{\underset{1}{\cancel{6}}} \cdot \dfrac{\overset{1}{\cancel{6}}}{\underset{1}{\cancel{x}}} = 1.$ $\blacksquare$

Division of Fractions

We know that if we multiply any fraction by its reciprocal, the product is 1, and we know from arithmetic that a division problem can be interpreted as a fraction. Therefore, $\dfrac{a}{b} \div \dfrac{c}{d}$ can be interpreted as

$$\dfrac{\dfrac{a}{b}}{\dfrac{c}{d}}$$

If we then multiply both the numerator and the denominator of this fraction by $\dfrac{d}{c}$ $\left(\text{the reciprocal of } \dfrac{c}{d}\right)$, we have

$$\frac{\dfrac{a}{b}\cdot\dfrac{d}{c}}{\dfrac{c}{d}\cdot\dfrac{d}{c}} = \frac{\dfrac{ad}{bc}}{1} = \frac{ad}{bc}$$

The rule for dividing fractions is as follows:

TO DIVIDE FRACTIONS

Multiply the dividend by the reciprocal of the divisor.

$$\frac{a}{b} \div \frac{c}{d} = \frac{a}{b} \cdot \frac{d}{c}$$

Dividend ⎽⎽⎽↑   ↑⎽⎽⎽ Divisor

Example 3   Divide the fractions:

a. $\dfrac{3y^3 - 3y^2}{16y^5 + 8y^4} \div \dfrac{y^2 + 2y - 3}{4y + 12} = \dfrac{3y^2\cancel{(y-1)}}{\underset{2}{\cancel{8}}y^4(2y + 1)} \cdot \dfrac{\overset{1}{\cancel{4}}\cancel{(y+3)}}{\cancel{(y-1)}\cancel{(y+3)}}$

$$= \frac{3}{2y^2(2y + 1)}$$

b. $\dfrac{x^2 + x - 2}{x + 2} \div \dfrac{x^2 + 2x - 3}{x + 3} = \dfrac{\overset{1}{\cancel{(x+2)}}\overset{1}{\cancel{(x-1)}}}{\underset{1}{\cancel{x+2}}} \cdot \dfrac{\overset{1}{\cancel{x+3}}}{\underset{1}{\cancel{(x+3)}}\underset{1}{\cancel{(x-1)}}} = 1$

c. $\dfrac{y^2 - x^2}{4xy - 2y^2} \div \dfrac{2x - 2y}{2x^2 + xy - y^2} = \dfrac{(y + x)(y - x)}{2y\cancel{(2x-y)}} \cdot \dfrac{(x + y)\cancel{(2x-y)}}{2(x - y)}$

$$= \frac{(x + y)^2\,(y - x)}{4y(x - y)} = \frac{(x + y)^2\,(-1)(x-y)}{4y(x-y)}$$

$$= \frac{(-1)(x + y)^2}{4y} = -\frac{(x + y)^2}{4y}$$

d. $\dfrac{x^2 + 4y^2}{\underbrace{x^4 + 4y^4}} \div \dfrac{24x^3 + 96xy^2}{3x^2 + 6xy + 6y^2}$

    ↑⎽⎽⎽ Factor by completing the square

$$= \frac{\overset{1}{\cancel{x^2 + 4y^2}}}{\cancel{(x^2 + 2xy + 2y^2)}(x^2 - 2xy + 2y^2)} \cdot \frac{\overset{1}{\cancel{3}}\cancel{(x^2 + 2xy + 2y^2)}}{\underset{8}{\cancel{24}}x\underset{1}{\cancel{(x^2 + 4y^2)}}}$$

$$= \frac{1}{8x(x^2 - 2xy + 2y^2)} \quad\blacksquare$$

EXERCISES 6.3

Set I   Perform the indicated operations.

1. $\dfrac{27x^4y^3}{22x^5yz} \cdot \dfrac{55x^2z^2}{9y^3z}$

2. $\dfrac{13b^2c^4}{42a^4b^3} \cdot \dfrac{35a^3bc^2}{39ac^5}$

3. $\dfrac{mn^3}{18n^2} \div \dfrac{5m^4}{24m^3n}$

4. $\dfrac{27k^3}{h^5k} \div \dfrac{15hk^2}{-4h^4}$

5. $\dfrac{15u - 6u^2}{10u^2} \cdot \dfrac{15u^3}{35 - 14u}$

6. $\dfrac{-22v^2}{63v + 84} \cdot \dfrac{42v^3 + 56v^2}{55v^3}$

7. $\dfrac{-15c^4}{40c^3 - 24c^2} \div \dfrac{35c}{35c^2 - 21c}$

8. $\dfrac{40d - 30d^2}{d^2} \div \dfrac{24d^2 - 18d^3}{12d^3}$

9. $\dfrac{d^2e^2 - d^3e}{12e^2d} \div \dfrac{d^2e^2 - de^3}{3e^2d + 3e^3}$

10. $\dfrac{9m^2n + 3mn^2}{16mn^2} \div \dfrac{2mn^2 - m^2n}{10mn^2 - 20n^3}$

11. $\dfrac{w^2 - 2w - 8}{6w - 24} \cdot \dfrac{5w^2}{w^2 - 3w - 10}$

12. $\dfrac{-15k^3}{8k + 32} \div \dfrac{15k^2 - 5k^3}{k^2 + k - 12}$

13. $\dfrac{4a^2 + 8ab + 4b^2}{a^2 - b^2} \div \dfrac{6ab + 6b^2}{b - a}$

14. $\dfrac{u^2 - v^2}{7u^2 - 14uv + 7v^2} \div \dfrac{2u^2 + 2uv}{14v - 14u}$

15. $\dfrac{4 - 2a}{2a + 2} \div \dfrac{2a^3 - 16}{a^2 + 2a + 1}$

16. $\dfrac{18 + 6a}{4 - 2a} \div \dfrac{2a^3 + 54}{4a - 8}$

17. $\dfrac{x^3 + y^3}{2x - 2y} \div \dfrac{x^2 - xy + y^2}{x^2 - y^2}$

18. $\dfrac{x^3 - y^3}{3x + 3y} \div \dfrac{x^2 + xy + y^2}{x^2 - y^2}$

19. $\dfrac{e^2 + 10ef + 25f^2}{e^2 - 25f^2} \cdot \dfrac{3e - 3f}{f - e} \div \dfrac{e + 5f}{5f - e}$

20. $\dfrac{3x - y}{y + x} \div \dfrac{y^2 + yx - 12x^2}{4x^2 + 5xy + y^2} \cdot \dfrac{10x^2 - 8xy}{8xy - 10x^2}$

21. $\dfrac{(x + y)^2 + x + y}{(x - y)^2 - x + y} \cdot \dfrac{x^2 - 2xy + y^2}{x^2 + 2xy + y^2} \cdot \dfrac{x + y}{x - y}$

22. $\dfrac{ac + bc + ad + bd}{ac - ad - bc + bd} \cdot \dfrac{c^2 - 2cd + d^2}{a^2 + 2ab + b^2} \cdot \dfrac{a - b}{c + d}$

23. $\dfrac{m^4 + 4}{m^2 - 4} \cdot \dfrac{m + 2}{m^2 - 2m + 2}$

24. $\dfrac{R^4 + 5R^2 + 9}{R^2 - 9} \cdot \dfrac{R - 3}{R^2 - R + 3}$

Set II   Perform the indicated operations.

1. $\dfrac{11m^4p^2}{30mn^2} \cdot \dfrac{21n^5p}{22m^3np^4}$

2. $\dfrac{65x^5y^3}{78x^2y^4} \cdot \dfrac{4y^2}{x^4}$

3. $\dfrac{5m^2n^3}{18mn^2} \div \dfrac{15n^3}{36m^2n}$

4. $\dfrac{x + 3}{6} \cdot \dfrac{1}{3x + 9}$

5. $\dfrac{7b}{24a^2b^2} \cdot \dfrac{32a^2b^3}{7 - 21a}$

6. $\dfrac{34a^3b^3}{7ab^2} \cdot \dfrac{21a^3b^2}{17a^2b}$

7. $\dfrac{-7f^2}{40f + 16f^2} \div \dfrac{28f^3}{30f^3 + 12f^4}$

8. $\dfrac{12e^2 - 18e}{25e^4} \cdot \dfrac{15e^2}{18e^2 - 27e}$

9. $\dfrac{6x^2y - 2xy^2}{9xy + 18y^2} \div \dfrac{4x^2y^2 - 12x^3y}{3x^2 + 6xy}$

10. $\dfrac{x^4 + 4}{x^2 - 2x + 2} \div \dfrac{x^2 + 2x + 2}{x^2 + 4}$

11. $\dfrac{6v^2 - 36v}{25 - 5v} \cdot \dfrac{v^2 - 11v + 30}{-12v^2}$

12. $\dfrac{x^3 + 27}{x^2 - 9} \div \dfrac{x^2 - 3x + 9}{x^2 + 9}$

13. $\dfrac{5h^2k - h^3}{9hk + 18k^2} \div \dfrac{h^2 - 7hk + 10k^2}{3h^2 - 12k^2}$

14. $\dfrac{x^2 - 2x - 3}{x^4 - 10x^2 + 9} \cdot \dfrac{x - 1}{x + 3}$

15. $\dfrac{32 + 4b^3}{b^2 - b - 6} \div \dfrac{b^2 - 2b + 4}{15b - 5b^2}$

16. $\dfrac{2a^2 - 7a + 6}{a^2 + a - 6} \cdot \dfrac{2a^2 + 13a + 15}{15a - 7a^2 - 2a^3}$

17. $\dfrac{5y^2 + 15yz + 45z^2}{9z^2 + 3zy} \div \dfrac{2y^3 - 54z^3}{9z^2 - y^2}$

18. $\dfrac{x^3 - 7x + 6}{6 - x - x^2} \div \dfrac{x^3 + 2x^2 - 13x + 10}{x^2 + 3x - 10}$

19. $\dfrac{6uv - 6v^2 + 6v}{10uv} \cdot \dfrac{(u + v) - (u + v)^2}{(u - v)^2 + (u - v)} \cdot \dfrac{5uv - 5u^2}{3v^2 + 3vu}$

20. $\dfrac{x^2 + 6x + 9 - y^2}{5x - 5y + 15} \cdot \dfrac{15x - 15y}{9x^2 - 9y^2} \cdot \dfrac{1}{6 + 2x + 2y}$

21. $\dfrac{10nm - 15n^2}{3n + 2m} \div \dfrac{9mn - 6m^2}{4m^2 + 12mn + 9n^2} \div \dfrac{4m^2 - 9n^2}{27n - 18m}$

22. $\dfrac{xs - ys + xt - yt}{sx + tx + sy + ty} \cdot \dfrac{sx + sy - ty - xt}{xs - ys - tx + yt}$

23. $\dfrac{4c^4 + 1}{36 - c^2} \cdot \dfrac{c - 6}{2c^2 - 2c + 1}$

24. $\dfrac{9x^2 - 30x + 25}{9x^2 - 25} \div \dfrac{3x^3 + 3x^2}{3x^2 - 2x - 5}$

6.4 Lowest Common Denominator (LCD)

We ordinarily use the *lowest common denominator* (*LCD*) when we add or subtract unlike fractions (unlike fractions are defined in Section 6.5). The LCD is the least common multiple (LCM) of all the denominators (see Section 1.9 for review).

TO FIND THE LCD

1. Factor each denominator completely. Repeated factors should be expressed as powers.

2. Write down each different base that appears.

3. Raise each base to the highest power to which it occurs in *any* denominator.

4. The LCD is the product of all the factors found in step 3.

Example 1   Find the LCD for $\dfrac{2}{x} + \dfrac{x}{x + 2}$.

Step 1 The denominators are already factored.
Step 2 $x, (x + 2)$ All the different bases
Step 3 $x^1, (x + 2)^1$ Highest powers of bases
Step 4 LCD $= x(x + 2)$ ∎

Example 2 Find the LCD for $\dfrac{2x-3}{x^2+10x+25} - \dfrac{5}{4x^2+20x} + \dfrac{4x-3}{x^2+2x-15}$.

Step 1 $x^2 + 10x + 25 = (x+5)^2$
$\qquad 4x^2 + 20x = 4x(x+5) = 2^2x(x+5)$ Denominators in factored form
$\qquad x^2 + 2x - 15 = (x+5)(x-3)$
Step 2 $2, x, (x+5), (x-3)$ All the different bases
Step 3 $2^2, x, (x+5)^2, (x-3)$ Highest powers of the bases
Step 4 LCD $= 4x(x+5)^2(x-3)$ ∎

Example 3 Find the LCD for $\dfrac{x+2}{x^3+8} + \dfrac{5x}{x^2-2x+4} - \dfrac{3x^2}{x^3-2x^2}$.

It happens that two of these fractions are reducible:

$$\frac{x+2}{x^3+8} = \frac{\overset{1}{\cancel{x+2}}}{\underset{1}{\cancel{(x+2)}}(x^2-2x+4)}$$

$$= \frac{1}{x^2-2x+4}$$

and

$$\frac{3x^2}{x^3-2x^2} = \frac{\overset{1}{3\cancel{x^2}}}{\underset{1}{\cancel{x^2}}(x-2)} = \frac{3}{x-2}$$

Now the denominators are $x^2 - 2x + 4$, $x^2 - 2x + 4$, and $x - 2$.

$$\text{LCD} = (x-2)^1(x^2-2x+4)^1 = (x-2)(x^2-2x+4) \quad ∎$$

EXERCISES 6.4

Set I Find the LCD in each exercise. *Do not add the fractions.*

1. $\dfrac{9}{25a^3} + \dfrac{7}{15a}$

2. $\dfrac{13}{18b^2} + \dfrac{11}{12b^4}$

3. $\dfrac{49}{60hk^3} + \dfrac{71}{90h^2k^4}$

4. $\dfrac{44}{42x^2y^2} - \dfrac{45}{49x^3y}$

5. $\dfrac{11}{2w-10} - \dfrac{15}{4w}$

6. $\dfrac{27}{2m^2} + \dfrac{19}{8m-48}$

7. $\dfrac{15b}{9b^2-c^2} + \dfrac{12c}{(3b-c)^2}$

8. $\dfrac{14e}{(5f-2e)^2} + \dfrac{27f}{4e^2-25f^2}$

9. $\dfrac{5}{2g^3} - \dfrac{3g-9}{g^2-6g+9} + \dfrac{12g}{4g^2-12g}$

10. $\dfrac{5y-30}{y^2-12y+36} + \dfrac{7}{9y^2} - \dfrac{15y}{3y^2-18y}$

11. $\dfrac{2x-5}{2x^2-16x+32} + \dfrac{4x+7}{x^2+x-20}$

12. $\dfrac{8k-1}{5k^2-30k+45} + \dfrac{3k-4}{k^2+4k-21}$

13. $\dfrac{35}{3e^2} - \dfrac{2e}{e^2-9} - \dfrac{13}{4e-12}$

14. $\dfrac{3}{8u^3} - \dfrac{5u-1}{6u^2+18u} - \dfrac{6u+7}{u^2-5u-24}$

15. $\dfrac{x^2 + 1}{12x^3 + 24x^2} - \dfrac{4x + 3}{x^2 - 4x + 4} - \dfrac{1}{x^2 - 4}$

16. $\dfrac{2y + 5}{y^2 + 6y + 9} + \dfrac{7y}{y^2 - 9} - \dfrac{11}{8y^2 - 24y}$

Set II   Find the LCD in each exercise. *Do not add the fractions.*

1. $\dfrac{17}{50c} + \dfrac{23}{40c^2}$

2. $\dfrac{83}{12x^2} + \dfrac{5}{18x^4}$

3. $\dfrac{35}{24m^2n} + \dfrac{25}{63mn^3}$

4. $\dfrac{5}{28b^3c^2} - \dfrac{8}{49bc^5}$

5. $\dfrac{50}{9z - 63} - \dfrac{16}{3z}$

6. $\dfrac{18}{5 - 25x} + \dfrac{3}{10 - 50x}$

7. $\dfrac{6uv}{9v^2 - 16u^2} + \dfrac{12u^2v}{(4u - 3v)^2}$

8. $\dfrac{13x}{x^2 - 4} - \dfrac{15x^2}{x^2 + 4}$

9. $\dfrac{3}{25h} - \dfrac{20h^3}{5h^4 - 25h^3} + \dfrac{4h - 20}{h^2 - 10h + 25}$

10. $\dfrac{9}{4x^2 - 9} - \dfrac{7x}{6x + 9} + \dfrac{5}{2x^3 - x^2 - 3x}$

11. $\dfrac{5a - 3}{3a^2 - 30a + 72} + \dfrac{7a + 2}{a^2 - 12a + 36}$

12. $\dfrac{3x - 7}{15x^2 - 55x - 20} + \dfrac{5x - 20}{6x^2 + 20x + 6}$

13. $\dfrac{15}{4m^2} - \dfrac{11m}{2m^2 - 50} + \dfrac{2m - 5}{m^2 - 2m - 35}$

14. $\dfrac{5}{6x^2 + 30x} - \dfrac{7x}{2x^2 - 50} + \dfrac{8x + 40}{3x^2 - 9x - 30}$

15. $\dfrac{17}{2z^2 - 98} - \dfrac{9z + 11}{4z^3 - 28z^2} - \dfrac{13z}{z^2 - 14z + 49}$

16. $\dfrac{x - 5}{2x^3 + 7x^2 - 15x} - \dfrac{4x^2 + 9}{4x^3 - 12x^2 + 9x} + \dfrac{9}{4x^4 - 9x^2}$

6.5 Addition of Fractions

Like Fractions
Like fractions are fractions that have the same denominator.

Example 1   Examples of like fractions:

a. $\dfrac{2}{x}, \dfrac{8}{x}, \dfrac{a}{x}, \dfrac{x + 1}{x}$

b. $\dfrac{2}{a - b}, \dfrac{5a}{a - b}, \dfrac{3ab}{a - b}, \dfrac{a + b}{a - b}$ ∎

TO ADD LIKE FRACTIONS

1. Add the numerators.

2. Write the sum of the numerators over the denominator of the like fractions.

$$\frac{a}{c} + \frac{b}{c} = \frac{a+b}{c}$$

3. Reduce the resulting fraction to lowest terms.

NOTE   Any subtraction of fractions can be done as an addition problem.

$$\frac{a}{c} - \frac{b}{c} = \frac{a}{c} + \frac{-b}{c} = \frac{a-b}{c}$$

☑

Example 2   Add the following fractions:

a. $\dfrac{3}{4a} - \dfrac{5}{4a} = \dfrac{3}{4a} + \dfrac{-5}{4a} = \dfrac{3-5}{4a} = \dfrac{-2}{4a} = -\dfrac{\overset{1}{\cancel{2}}}{\underset{2}{\cancel{4}a}} = -\dfrac{1}{2a}$

b. $\dfrac{4x}{2x-y} - \dfrac{2y}{2x-y} = \dfrac{4x-2y}{2x-y} = \dfrac{2(2x-y)}{(2x-y)} = \dfrac{2\cancel{(2x-y)}}{\cancel{(2x-y)}} = 2$

c. $\dfrac{15}{d-5} + \dfrac{-3d}{d-5} = \dfrac{15-3d}{d-5} = \dfrac{3(5-d)}{d-5}$

$$= \boxed{-\dfrac{3(d-5)}{(d-5)}} = -\dfrac{3\cancel{(d-5)}}{\cancel{(d-5)}} = -3 \quad\blacksquare$$

Changing sign of
fraction and numerator ——

A WORD OF CAUTION   Students often confuse *addition of fractions* with *solving equations*, and they multiply both fractions by the same number. This is *incorrect*.

Correct method	*Incorrect method*

$$\dfrac{6}{5a} + \dfrac{2}{5a} = \dfrac{8}{5a} \qquad \cancel{\dfrac{6}{5a} + \dfrac{2}{5a}} = (5a)\left(\dfrac{6}{5a}\right) + (5a)\left(\dfrac{2}{5a}\right) = 8$$

☑

A WORD OF CAUTION   It is *incorrect* to cancel a numerator of one fraction against a denominator of a *different* fraction when adding or subtracting. For example,

$$\dfrac{y+1}{y-2} + \dfrac{5}{y+1} \neq \dfrac{\overset{1}{\cancel{y+1}}}{y-2} + \dfrac{5}{\underset{1}{\cancel{y+1}}}$$

☑

In a subtraction problem, if the numerator of the fraction being subtracted has more than one term, you *must* put parentheses around that numerator when you rewrite the problem as a single fraction (see Example 3).

Example 3 Subtract $\dfrac{3}{x+5} - \dfrac{x+2}{x+5}$.

$$\frac{3}{x+5} - \frac{x+2}{x+5} = \frac{3-(x+2)}{x+5} = \frac{3-x-2}{x+5} = \frac{1-x}{x+5}$$

$\left(\dfrac{-x+1}{x+5}\text{ is also a correct answer.}\right)$ ■

Unlike Fractions

Unlike fractions are fractions that have different denominators.

Example 4 Examples of unlike fractions:

a. $\dfrac{2}{x}, \dfrac{6}{x^2}, \dfrac{x-1}{5x}$

b. $\dfrac{5}{x+2}, \dfrac{2x}{x-1}$ ■

Because the definition of addition of fractions is $\dfrac{a}{c} + \dfrac{b}{c} = \dfrac{a+b}{c}$, we can add fractions only when they are *like fractions*. The procedure for adding unlike fractions follows:

TO ADD UNLIKE FRACTIONS

1. Find the LCD.

2. Convert all fractions to equivalent fractions that have the LCD as denominator.

3. Add the resulting like fractions.

4. Reduce the resulting fraction to lowest terms.

A WORD OF CAUTION Students frequently *reduce* the fractions just after they have converted them to equivalent fractions with the LCD as denominator. The addition then cannot be done, because the fractions no longer have the same denominator. ☑

When denominators are not identical but are the *negatives* of each other, we can make the fractions like fractions by changing the signs of the numerator and denominator of one of the fractions.

If a numerator or denominator has more than one term in it, you *must* put parentheses around that numerator or denominator when you change its sign.

$$\frac{a+b}{c-d} \neq \frac{-a+b}{-c-d}$$

Rather,

$$\frac{a+b}{c-d} = \frac{-(a+b)}{-(c-d)} = \frac{-a-b}{d-c}$$

Example 5   Add $\dfrac{9}{x-2} + \dfrac{5+x}{2-x}$.

Changing the sign of numerator and denominator

$$\frac{9}{x-2} + \frac{5+x}{2-x} = \frac{9}{x-2} + \frac{-(5+x)}{-(2-x)}$$

$$= \frac{9}{x-2} + \frac{-5-x}{x-2}$$

$$= \frac{9-5-x}{x-2}$$

$$= \frac{4-x}{x-2}$$

$\left(\dfrac{x-4}{2-x} \text{ is also a correct answer.} \right)$

This problem could also be done by substituting $-1(x-2)$ for $2-x$:

$$\frac{9}{x-2} + \frac{5+x}{2-x} = \frac{9}{x-2} + \frac{5+x}{-1(x-2)}$$

The fractions do not yet have like denominators. We can then change the sign of the second fraction and the sign of its denominator. The problem now becomes

$$\frac{9}{x-2} - \frac{5+x}{x-2}$$

The remainder of the solution is left to the student.

We could instead change the signs of the numerator and denominator of the second fraction:

$$\frac{9}{x-2} + \frac{-(5+x)}{x-2}$$

Again, the remainder of the solution is left to the student. ∎

Example 6   Add $\dfrac{7}{18x^2y} + \dfrac{5}{8xy^4}$.

Step 1 LCD $= 72x^2y^4$

$$-4y^3 = \frac{72x^2y^4}{18x^2y} = \frac{\text{LCD}}{\text{Denominator of fraction}}$$

Step 2 $\dfrac{7}{18x^2y} = \dfrac{7\,(4y^3)}{18x^2y\,(4y^3)} = \dfrac{28y^3}{72x^2y^4}$

$$\frac{5}{8xy^4} = \frac{5\,(9x)}{8xy^4\,(9x)} = \frac{45x}{72x^2y^4}$$

$$-9x = \frac{72x^2y^4}{8xy^4} = \frac{\text{LCD}}{\text{Denominator of fraction}}$$

Step 3 $\dfrac{7}{18x^2y} + \dfrac{5}{8xy^4} = \dfrac{28y^3}{72x^2y^4} + \dfrac{45x}{72x^2y^4} = \dfrac{28y^3 + 45x}{72x^2y^4}$ ∎

Example 7 Add $3 - \dfrac{2a}{a + 2}$.

Note parentheses

Step 1 LCD $= a + 2$

Step 2 $3 = \dfrac{3}{1} \cdot \dfrac{a + 2}{a + 2} = \dfrac{3(a + 2)}{1(a + 2)} = \dfrac{3a + 6}{a + 2}$

Step 3 $3 - \dfrac{2a}{a + 2} = \dfrac{3a + 6}{a + 2} - \dfrac{2a}{a + 2} = \dfrac{3a + 6 - 2a}{a + 2} = \dfrac{a + 6}{a + 2}$ ∎

Example 8 Add $\dfrac{z + 1}{z + 2} - \dfrac{z - 1}{z - 2}$.

Step 1 LCD $= (z + 2)(z - 2)$

Note parentheses

Step 2 $\dfrac{z + 1}{z + 2} = \dfrac{z + 1}{z + 2} \cdot \dfrac{z - 2}{z - 2} = \dfrac{(z + 1)(z - 2)}{(z + 2)(z - 2)} = \dfrac{z^2 - z - 2}{(z + 2)(z - 2)}$

$\dfrac{z - 1}{z - 2} = \dfrac{z - 1}{z - 2} \cdot \dfrac{z + 2}{z + 2} = \dfrac{(z - 1)(z + 2)}{(z - 2)(z + 2)} = \dfrac{z^2 + z - 2}{(z - 2)(z + 2)}$

Step 3 $\dfrac{z + 1}{z + 2} - \dfrac{z - 1}{z - 2} = \dfrac{z^2 - z - 2}{(z + 2)(z - 2)} - \dfrac{z^2 + z - 2}{(z - 2)(z + 2)}$

$= \dfrac{z^2 - z - 2 - (z^2 + z - 2)}{(z + 2)(z - 2)}$

$= \dfrac{-2z}{(z + 2)(z - 2)} = -\dfrac{2z}{z^2 - 4}$

Changing the sign of fraction and numerator ∎

Example 9 Add $\dfrac{x + 2}{x^2 - 2x - 15} + \dfrac{x - 5}{x^2 + 5x + 6}$.

Step 1 $x^2 - 2x - 15 = (x + 3)(x - 5)$

$x^2 + 5x + 6 = (x + 2)(x + 3)$

LCD $= (x + 3)(x - 5)(x + 2)$

Step 2 $\dfrac{x + 2}{x^2 - 2x - 15} = \dfrac{(x + 2)(x + 2)}{(x + 3)(x - 5)(x + 2)}$

$\dfrac{x - 5}{x^2 + 5x + 6} = \dfrac{(x - 5)(x - 5)}{(x + 2)(x + 3)(x - 5)}$

Step 3 $\dfrac{x + 2}{x^2 - 2x - 15} + \dfrac{x - 5}{x^2 + 5x + 6}$

$= \dfrac{(x + 2)(x + 2)}{(x + 3)(x - 5)(x + 2)} + \dfrac{(x - 5)(x - 5)}{(x + 2)(x + 3)(x - 5)}$

$= \dfrac{x^2 + 4x + 4 + x^2 - 10x + 25}{(x + 3)(x - 5)(x + 2)}$

$= \dfrac{2x^2 - 6x + 29}{(x + 3)(x - 5)(x + 2)}$ ∎

EXERCISES 6.5

Set I   Add the fractions.

1. $\dfrac{5a}{a+2} + \dfrac{10}{a+2}$

2. $\dfrac{6b}{b-3} - \dfrac{18}{b-3}$

3. $\dfrac{8m}{2m-3n} - \dfrac{12n}{2m-3n}$

4. $\dfrac{21k}{4h+3k} + \dfrac{28h}{4h+3k}$

5. $\dfrac{-15w}{1-5w} - \dfrac{3}{5w-1}$

6. $\dfrac{-35}{6w-7} - \dfrac{30w}{7-6w}$

7. $\dfrac{7z}{8z-4} + \dfrac{6-5z}{4-8z}$

8. $\dfrac{8x}{6x-5} + \dfrac{10-4x}{5-6x}$

9. $\dfrac{12x-31}{12x-28} - \dfrac{18x-39}{28-12x}$

10. $\dfrac{13-30w}{15-10w} - \dfrac{10w+17}{10w-15}$

11. $\dfrac{9}{25a^3} + \dfrac{7}{15a}$

12. $\dfrac{13}{18b^2} + \dfrac{11}{12b^4}$

13. $\dfrac{49}{60h^2k^2} - \dfrac{71}{90hk^4}$

14. $\dfrac{44}{42x^2y^2} - \dfrac{45}{49x^3y}$

15. $\dfrac{5}{t} + \dfrac{2t}{t-4}$

16. $\dfrac{6r}{r-8} - \dfrac{11}{r}$

17. $\dfrac{3k}{8k-4} - \dfrac{7}{6k}$

18. $\dfrac{2}{9j} + \dfrac{4j}{18j+12}$

19. $x^2 - \dfrac{3}{x} + \dfrac{5}{x-3}$

20. $y^2 - \dfrac{2}{y} + \dfrac{3}{y-5}$

21. $\dfrac{2a+3b}{b} + \dfrac{b}{2a-3b}$

22. $\dfrac{3x-5y}{y} + \dfrac{y}{3x+5y}$

23. $\dfrac{2}{a+3} - \dfrac{4}{a-1}$

24. $\dfrac{5}{b-2} - \dfrac{3}{b+4}$

25. $\dfrac{x+2}{x-3} - \dfrac{x+3}{x-2}$

26. $\dfrac{x-4}{x+6} - \dfrac{x-6}{x+4}$

27. $\dfrac{x+2}{x^2+x-2} + \dfrac{3}{x^2-1}$

28. $\dfrac{5}{x^2-4} + \dfrac{x+1}{x^2-x-2}$

29. $\dfrac{2x}{x-3} - \dfrac{2x}{x+3} + \dfrac{36}{x^2-9}$

30. $\dfrac{m}{m+6} - \dfrac{m}{m-6} - \dfrac{72}{m^2-36}$

31. $\dfrac{x-2}{x^2+4x+4} - \dfrac{x+1}{x^2-4}$

32. $\dfrac{x-2}{x^2-1} - \dfrac{x+1}{x^2-2x+1}$

33. $\dfrac{4}{x^2+2x+4} + \dfrac{x-2}{x+2}$

34. $\dfrac{x+3}{x-9} + \dfrac{3}{x^2-3x+9}$

35. $\dfrac{5}{2g^3} - \dfrac{3g-9}{g^2-6g+9} + \dfrac{12g}{4g^2-12g}$

36. $\dfrac{5y-30}{y^2-12y+36} + \dfrac{7}{9y^2} - \dfrac{15y}{3y^2-18y}$

37. $\dfrac{2x-5}{2x^2-16x+32} + \dfrac{4x+7}{x^2+x-20}$

38. $\dfrac{8k-1}{5k^2-30k+45} + \dfrac{3k-4}{k^2+4k-21}$

39. $\dfrac{35}{3e^2} - \dfrac{2e}{e^2 - 9} - \dfrac{3}{4e - 12}$

40. $\dfrac{3}{8u^3} - \dfrac{5u - 1}{6u^2 + 18u} - \dfrac{6u + 7}{u^2 - 5u - 24}$

41. $\dfrac{x^2 + 1}{12x^3 + 24x^2} - \dfrac{4x + 3}{x^2 - 4x + 4} - \dfrac{1}{x^2 - 4}$

42. $\dfrac{2y + 5}{y^2 + 6y + 9} + \dfrac{7y}{y^2 - 9} - \dfrac{11}{8y^2 - 24y}$

43. $\dfrac{7}{3y^3 - 12y^2 + 48y} + \dfrac{y^2 + 4}{y^3 + 64} - \dfrac{y}{y^2 + 8y + 16}$

44. $\dfrac{x^2 + 9}{x^3 + 27} + \dfrac{5}{2x^3 - 6x^2 + 18x} - \dfrac{x}{x^2 + 6x + 9}$

45. $\dfrac{x - 1}{x^3 + x^2 - 9x - 9} - \dfrac{x + 3}{x^3 - 3x^2 - x + 3}$

46. $\dfrac{x + 2}{x^3 - 2x^2 - x + 2} - \dfrac{x - 1}{x^3 + x^2 - 4x - 4}$

47. $\dfrac{x + 1}{x^3 + 5x^2 + 3x - 9} - \dfrac{x - 3}{x^3 + x^2 - 5x + 3}$

48. $\dfrac{x + 5}{x^3 - x^2 - 16x - 20} - \dfrac{x - 2}{x^3 - 8x^2 + 5x + 50}$

Set II   Add the fractions.

1. $\dfrac{24}{8 + c} + \dfrac{3c}{8 + c}$

2. $\dfrac{35}{2 - x} + \dfrac{15}{2 - x}$

3. $\dfrac{30c}{4b - 5c} - \dfrac{24b}{4b - 5c}$

4. $\dfrac{16y}{4y + 5} + \dfrac{20}{4y + 5}$

5. $\dfrac{-35t}{3 - 7t} - \dfrac{15}{7t - 3}$

6. $\dfrac{x + 3}{3x - 5} - \dfrac{2x + 4}{5 - 3x}$

7. $\dfrac{5u}{6u - 15} + \dfrac{30 - 7u}{15 - 6u}$

8. $\dfrac{5 + a}{2a - 5} + \dfrac{3a - 2}{5 - 2a}$

9. $\dfrac{12x - 5}{18x - 6} - \dfrac{15x - 4}{6 - 18x}$

10. $\dfrac{16 - 3x}{2x - 7} + \dfrac{3x - 5}{7 - 2x}$

11. $\dfrac{17}{50c} + \dfrac{23}{40c^2}$

12. $\dfrac{18}{25x^2} + \dfrac{7}{30x^3}$

13. $\dfrac{35}{27m^2n} - \dfrac{25}{63mn^3}$

14. $\dfrac{13}{15x^3y} - \dfrac{41}{40xy^3}$

15. $\dfrac{6}{e} + \dfrac{3e}{5 - e}$

16. $\dfrac{8}{x + 5} + x$

17. $\dfrac{9}{12d} - \dfrac{4}{18 - 27d}$

18. $\dfrac{6}{3x + 6} - \dfrac{5}{9x + 18}$

19. $\dfrac{5}{n} - n - \dfrac{8}{n - 6}$

20. $\dfrac{3 - x}{x^2} - \dfrac{x}{4x + x^2} - \dfrac{1}{x + 4}$

21. $\dfrac{k}{h - k} + \dfrac{k + h}{k}$

22. $\dfrac{c - d}{c} - \dfrac{d}{d - c}$

23. $\dfrac{7}{x - 5} - \dfrac{13}{x + 4}$

24. $\dfrac{8}{4 + a} + \dfrac{8}{2 + a}$

25. $\dfrac{z - 3}{z - 6} - \dfrac{z + 6}{z + 3}$

26. $\dfrac{x + 5}{x + 1} - \dfrac{x - 1}{x - 5}$

27. $\dfrac{16 - 4a}{a^2 + a - 12} + \dfrac{3}{a^2 - 16}$

28. $\dfrac{2x + 4}{x^2 + 2x - 8} + \dfrac{3}{5x^2 - 7x - 6}$

29. $\dfrac{3c}{c+5} - \dfrac{3c}{c-5} + \dfrac{150}{c^2 - 25}$

30. $\dfrac{5x}{x+3} - \dfrac{5x}{x-3} + \dfrac{90}{x^2 - 9}$

31. $\dfrac{m+1}{m^2 - 9} - \dfrac{m-2}{m^2 + 4m - 21}$

32. $x - \dfrac{x}{2x^2 + x - 3} + \dfrac{4}{3x^2 - x - 2}$

33. $\dfrac{u-4}{u+8} + \dfrac{8}{u^2 + 4u + 16}$

34. $\dfrac{x}{x^3 - 8} - \dfrac{2}{x^2 - 4} + \dfrac{5}{x+2}$

35. $\dfrac{3}{25h} - \dfrac{20h^3}{5h^4 - 25h^3} + \dfrac{4h - 20}{h^2 - 10h + 25}$

36. $\dfrac{8-x}{4-x} - \dfrac{x}{x-4} + \dfrac{4x}{3x^2 - 48}$

37. $\dfrac{5a-3}{3a^2 - 30a + 72} + \dfrac{7a+2}{a^2 - 12a + 36}$

38. $\dfrac{x+3}{6x^2 - 7x - 6} - \dfrac{3x-2}{2x^2 + 5x - 3}$

39. $\dfrac{15}{4m^2} - \dfrac{11m}{2m^2 - 50} + \dfrac{2m-5}{m^2 - 2m - 35}$

40. $\dfrac{8}{3x^3 + 6x^2 - 9x} - \dfrac{4}{9x^3 - 9x^2} - \dfrac{x+2}{5x^2 + 15x}$

41. $\dfrac{17}{2z^2 - 98} - \dfrac{9z+11}{4z^3 - 28z^2} - \dfrac{13z}{z^2 - 14z + 49}$

42. $\dfrac{5}{4x^2 + 12x + 9} - \dfrac{8}{4x^2 - 9} - \dfrac{1}{6x^2 + 9x}$

43. $\dfrac{x^2 + 1}{x^3 + 1} + \dfrac{3}{5x^3 - 5x^2 + 5x} - \dfrac{x}{x^2 + 2x + 1}$

44. $\dfrac{x}{8x+4} - \dfrac{3}{8x^3 + 1} + \dfrac{5}{8x^2 - 4x + 2}$

45. $\dfrac{x+5}{x^3 - 5x^2 - x + 5} - \dfrac{x+1}{x^3 - x^2 - 25x + 25}$

46. $\dfrac{x-4}{x^3 - 5x^2 - 4x + 20} - \dfrac{x+5}{x^3 - 2x^2 - 25x + 50}$

47. $\dfrac{x+3}{x^3 - x^2 - 5x - 3} - \dfrac{x-1}{x^3 - 5x^2 + 3x + 9}$

48. $\dfrac{x-2}{x^3 + 4x^2 + x - 6} - \dfrac{x+2}{x^3 - 7x + 6}$

6.6 Complex Fractions

A **simple fraction** is a fraction that has only one fraction line.

Examples of simple fractions: $\dfrac{2}{x}, \quad \dfrac{3+y}{12}, \quad \dfrac{7a - 7b}{ab^2}, \quad \dfrac{5}{x+y}$

A **complex fraction** is a fraction that has more than one fraction line.

Examples of complex fractions: $\dfrac{\frac{2}{x}}{3}$, $\dfrac{\frac{3}{a}}{\frac{1}{c}}$, $\dfrac{\frac{3}{z}}{\frac{5}{z}}$, $\dfrac{\frac{3}{x} - \frac{2}{y}}{\frac{5}{x} + \frac{3}{y}}$

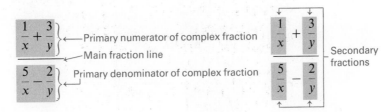

$\left.\dfrac{\frac{1}{x} + \frac{3}{y}}{\quad}\right\}$ ←——Primary numerator of complex fraction

←—Main fraction line

$\left.\dfrac{\frac{5}{x} - \frac{2}{y}}{}\right\}$ Primary denominator of complex fraction

$\dfrac{\frac{1}{x} + \frac{3}{y}}{\frac{5}{x} - \frac{2}{y}}$ — Secondary fractions

---

TO SIMPLIFY COMPLEX FRACTIONS

Method 1: Multiply both the numerator and the denominator of the complex fraction by the LCD of the secondary fractions; then simplify the results.

Method 2: First, simplify the numerator and denominator of the complex fraction so that each is a single fraction; then divide the simplified numerator by the simplified denominator.

Note that in some of the examples below, the solution by method 1 is easier than that by method 2. In others, the opposite is true.

Example 1 Simplify $\dfrac{\frac{2}{x} - \frac{3}{x^2}}{5 + \frac{1}{x}}$.

Method 1 $\dfrac{\frac{2}{x} - \frac{3}{x^2}}{5 + \frac{1}{x}}$ The LCD of the secondary denominators x and x^2 is x^2

$$\frac{x^2}{x^2}\left(\frac{\frac{2}{x} - \frac{3}{x^2}}{5 + \frac{1}{x}}\right) = \frac{\frac{x^2}{1}\left(\frac{2}{x}\right) - \frac{x^2}{1}\left(\frac{3}{x^2}\right)}{\frac{x^2}{1}\left(\frac{5}{1}\right) + \frac{x^2}{1}\left(\frac{1}{x}\right)} = \frac{2x - 3}{5x^2 + x}$$

Method 2 $\dfrac{\frac{2}{x} - \frac{3}{x^2}}{5 + \frac{1}{x}} = \left(\frac{2}{x} - \frac{3}{x^2}\right) \div \left(5 + \frac{1}{x}\right)$

$$= \left(\frac{2x}{x^2} - \frac{3}{x^2}\right) \div \left(\frac{5x}{x} + \frac{1}{x}\right)$$

$$= \frac{2x - 3}{x^2} \div \frac{5x + 1}{x}$$

$$= \frac{2x - 3}{x^2} \cdot \frac{x}{5x + 1} = \frac{2x - 3}{5x^2 + x} \quad \blacksquare$$

Example 2   Simplify $\dfrac{x - \dfrac{4}{x}}{x - \dfrac{2}{x + 1}}.$

Method 1 $\dfrac{x - \dfrac{4}{x}}{x - \dfrac{2}{x + 1}}$ The LCD of the secondary denominators x and $x + 1$ is $x(x + 1)$

$$\dfrac{x(x + 1)}{x(x + 1)}\left(\dfrac{x - \dfrac{4}{x}}{x - \dfrac{2}{x + 1}}\right) = \dfrac{\dfrac{x(x + 1)}{1} \cdot \dfrac{x}{1} - \dfrac{x(x + 1)}{1} \cdot \dfrac{4}{x}}{\dfrac{x(x + 1)}{1} \cdot \dfrac{x}{1} - \dfrac{x(x + 1)}{1} \cdot \dfrac{2}{(x + 1)}}$$

$$= \dfrac{x^2(x + 1) - 4(x + 1)}{x^2(x + 1) - 2x} = \dfrac{(x + 1)(x^2 - 4)}{x^3 + x^2 - 2x}$$

$$= \dfrac{(x + 1)\cancel{(x + 2)}(x - 2)}{x(x - 1)\cancel{(x + 2)}} = \dfrac{(x + 1)(x - 2)}{x(x - 1)}$$

Method 2   This method is left to the student.   ■

Example 3   Simplify $\dfrac{16x^{-2} - y^{-2}}{4x^{-1} - y^{-1}}.$

$$\dfrac{16x^{-2} - y^{-2}}{4x^{-1} - y^{-1}} = \dfrac{\dfrac{16}{x^2} - \dfrac{1}{y^2}}{\dfrac{4}{x} - \dfrac{1}{y}}$$ The LCD of the secondary denominators is $x^2 y^2$

$$= \dfrac{\dfrac{x^2 y^2}{x^2 y^2}\left(\dfrac{16}{x^2} - \dfrac{1}{y^2}\right)}{\dfrac{4}{x} - \dfrac{1}{y}}$$

$$= \dfrac{\dfrac{x^2 y^2}{1}\left(\dfrac{16}{x^2}\right) - \dfrac{x^2 y^2}{1}\left(\dfrac{1}{y^2}\right)}{\dfrac{x^2 y^2}{1}\left(\dfrac{4}{x}\right) - \dfrac{x^2 y^2}{1}\left(\dfrac{1}{y}\right)}$$

$$= \dfrac{16y^2 - x^2}{4xy^2 - x^2 y}$$

$$= \dfrac{\cancel{(4y - x)}(4y + x)}{xy\cancel{(4y - x)}}$$

$$= \dfrac{4y + x}{xy}$$ ■

Example 4   Simplify $\dfrac{3}{x + \dfrac{2}{x + \dfrac{1}{5x}}}.$

This type of complex fraction is sometimes called a *continued fraction*. The primary denominator itself contains a complex fraction; we will simplify this complex fraction first:

$$\cfrac{3}{x + \cfrac{2}{x + \cfrac{1}{5x}}} = \cfrac{3}{x + \cfrac{2(5x)}{\left(x + \cfrac{1}{5x}\right)(5x)}}$$

$$= \cfrac{3}{x + \cfrac{10x}{5x^2 + 1}}$$

We now simplify the main complex fraction:

$$\cfrac{3}{x + \cfrac{10x}{5x^2 + 1}} = \cfrac{3(5x^2 + 1)}{\left(x + \cfrac{10x}{5x^2 + 1}\right)(5x^2 + 1)}$$

$$= \frac{3(5x^2 + 1)}{x(5x^2 + 1) + 10x}$$

$$= \frac{15x^2 + 3}{5x^3 + 11x} \quad \blacksquare$$

EXERCISES 6.6

Set I   Simplify each of the complex fractions.

1. $\dfrac{\dfrac{21m^3n}{14mn^2}}{\dfrac{20m^2n^2}{8mn^3}}$

2. $\dfrac{\dfrac{10a^2b}{12a^4b^3}}{\dfrac{5ab^2}{16a^2b^3}}$

3. $\dfrac{\dfrac{15h - 6}{18h}}{\dfrac{30h^2 - 12h}{8h}}$

4. $\dfrac{\dfrac{9k^4}{20k^2 - 35k^3}}{\dfrac{12k}{16 - 28k}}$

5. $\dfrac{\dfrac{c}{d} + 2}{\dfrac{c^2}{d^2} - 4}$

6. $\dfrac{\dfrac{x^2}{y^2} - 1}{\dfrac{x}{y} - 1}$

7. $\dfrac{a + 2 - \dfrac{9}{a + 2}}{a + 1 + \dfrac{a - 7}{a + 2}}$

8. $\dfrac{x - 3 + \dfrac{x - 3}{x + 2}}{x + 4 - \dfrac{4x + 23}{x + 2}}$

9. $\dfrac{\dfrac{x + y}{y} + \dfrac{y}{x - y}}{\dfrac{y}{x - y}}$

10. $\dfrac{\dfrac{a - b}{a} - \dfrac{a}{a + b}}{\dfrac{b^2}{a + b}}$

11. $\dfrac{\dfrac{x}{x + 1} + \dfrac{4}{x}}{\dfrac{x}{x + 1} - 2}$

12. $\dfrac{\dfrac{4x}{4x + 1} + \dfrac{1}{x}}{\dfrac{2}{4x + 1} + 2}$

13. $\dfrac{\dfrac{x + 4}{x} - \dfrac{3}{x - 1}}{x + 1 + \dfrac{2x + 1}{x - 1}}$

14. $\dfrac{\dfrac{1}{x} + \dfrac{x}{x - 6}}{x - 1 - \dfrac{12}{x}}$

15. $\dfrac{4x^{-2} - y^{-2}}{2x^{-1} + y^{-1}}$

16. $\dfrac{x^{-2} - 9y^{-2}}{x^{-1} - 3y^{-1}}$

17. $\dfrac{\dfrac{x-2}{x+2} - \dfrac{x+2}{x-2}}{\dfrac{x-2}{x+2} + \dfrac{x+2}{x-2}}$

18. $\dfrac{\dfrac{m+3}{m-3} + \dfrac{m-3}{m+3}}{\dfrac{m+3}{m-3} - \dfrac{m-3}{m+3}}$

19. $\dfrac{\dfrac{2x+y}{x} + \dfrac{3x+y}{y-x}}{\dfrac{x+y}{y} + \dfrac{2(x+y)}{x-y}}$

20. $\dfrac{\dfrac{a+b}{b} + \dfrac{2(a+b)}{a-b}}{\dfrac{2a-b}{a} - \dfrac{5b-a}{b-a}}$

21. $\dfrac{1}{x + \dfrac{1}{x + \dfrac{1}{x+x}}}$

22. $\dfrac{2}{y + \dfrac{2}{y + \dfrac{2}{y+y}}}$

23. $\dfrac{x + \dfrac{1}{2 + \dfrac{x}{3}}}{x - \dfrac{3}{4 + \dfrac{x}{2}}}$

24. $\dfrac{x + \dfrac{5}{1 + \dfrac{x}{2}}}{x - \dfrac{4}{2 + \dfrac{x}{3}}}$

Set II Simplify each of the complex fractions.

1. $\dfrac{\dfrac{15e^3 f^3}{36e^2 f^4}}{\dfrac{5e^2 f}{33e^3 f^2}}$

2. $\dfrac{\dfrac{8x^2}{y^3}}{\dfrac{4x^3}{5y^4}}$

3. $\dfrac{\dfrac{30h^2 - 40hk}{2hk^2}}{\dfrac{54hk^2 - 72k^3}{6k^3}}$

4. $\dfrac{\dfrac{8x-16}{5x^2 - 5x - 60}}{\dfrac{4x-8}{5x+15}}$

5. $\dfrac{\dfrac{9a^2}{5b^2} - 5}{\dfrac{3a}{b} + 5}$

6. $\dfrac{\dfrac{x^2}{y^2} - 4}{\dfrac{x+2y}{y^3}}$

7. $\dfrac{z + 5 + \dfrac{z+5}{z-3}}{z - 4 - \dfrac{2}{z-3}}$

8. $\dfrac{x - 3 - \dfrac{16}{x+3}}{x - 4 - \dfrac{9}{x+4}}$

9. $\dfrac{\dfrac{5m}{n-m}}{\dfrac{m+n}{n} + \dfrac{n}{m-n}}$

10. $\dfrac{\dfrac{a+2b}{a} - \dfrac{3b}{a-2b}}{a - b - \dfrac{6b^2}{a-2b}}$

11. $\dfrac{\dfrac{1}{w} + \dfrac{9w}{6w+1}}{\dfrac{5}{6w+1} + 5}$

12. $\dfrac{\dfrac{1}{x} - \dfrac{3}{x+2}}{\dfrac{5}{x+2} - \dfrac{1}{x^2}}$

13. $\dfrac{2x - 5 - \dfrac{3}{x}}{\dfrac{1}{x} + \dfrac{x}{x-12}}$

14. $\dfrac{3x + \dfrac{9x}{x-1}}{x + 8 + \dfrac{18}{x-1}}$

15. $\dfrac{5c^{-1} + 2d^{-1}}{25c^{-2} - 4d^{-2}}$

16. $\dfrac{25a^{-2} - b^{-2}}{5a^{-1} + b^{-1}}$

17. $\dfrac{\dfrac{2t-1}{2t+1} - \dfrac{2t+1}{2t-1}}{\dfrac{2t-1}{2t+1} + \dfrac{2t+1}{2t-1}}$

18. $\dfrac{\dfrac{x+1}{x-3} - \dfrac{x-2}{x+2}}{\dfrac{x+3}{x+2} - \dfrac{x+3}{x-3}}$

19. $\dfrac{\dfrac{u-3v}{u} + \dfrac{3u-4v}{u-v}}{\dfrac{2u-7v}{v} + \dfrac{2u-v}{u-v}}$

20. $\dfrac{\dfrac{x}{x^2-1} + \dfrac{3x+3}{x-1}}{\dfrac{2x-1}{x-1} + \dfrac{x}{1-x}}$

21. $\dfrac{1}{2z + \dfrac{1}{2z + \dfrac{1}{2z}}}$

22. $\dfrac{5}{1 + \dfrac{1}{x + \dfrac{1}{x}}}$

23. $\dfrac{x - \dfrac{1}{2 + \dfrac{x}{3}}}{x + \dfrac{1}{1 + \dfrac{x}{5}}}$

24. $\dfrac{\dfrac{1}{3 + \dfrac{x}{2}} + x}{x - \dfrac{1}{2 + \dfrac{x}{3}}}$

6.7 Review: 6.1–6.6

The Domain of an Algebraic Fraction 6.1

The domain of the variable in an algebraic fraction is the set of all real numbers except those that would make the denominator equal to zero.

The Three Signs of a Fraction 6.1

Every fraction has three signs associated with it: the sign of the entire fraction, the sign of the numerator, and the sign of the denominator. If any two of the three signs of a fraction are changed, the value of the fraction is unchanged.

To Reduce a Fraction to Lowest Terms 6.2

1. Factor the numerator and denominator completely.

2. Divide numerator and denominator by all factors common to both.

To Multiply Fractions 6.3

1. Factor the numerator and denominator of the fractions.

2. Divide numerator and denominator by all factors common to both.

3. The answer is the product of factors remaining in the numerator divided by the product of factors remaining in the denominator. A factor of 1 will always remain in both numerator and denominator.

Multiplicative Inverse 6.3

When the product of two numbers is 1, the numbers are the multiplicative inverses of each other. The reciprocal of a nonzero fraction (found by interchanging its numerator and denominator) is its multiplicative inverse.

To Divide Fractions 6.3

Multiply the dividend by the reciprocal of the divisor.

$$\frac{a}{b} \div \frac{c}{d} = \frac{a}{b} \cdot \frac{d}{c}$$

Dividend ⟶   ⟵ Divisor

To Find the LCD 6.4

1. Factor each denominator completely. Repeated factors should be expressed as powers.

2. Write down each different base that appears.

3. Raise each base to the highest power to which it occurs in *any* denominator.

4. The LCD is the product of all the factors found in step 3.

To Add Like Fractions 6.5

1. Add the numerators.

2. Write the sum of the numerators over the denominator of the like fractions.

3. Reduce the resulting fraction to lowest terms.

To Add Unlike Fractions 6.5

1. Find the LCD.

2. Convert all fractions to equivalent fractions that have the LCD as denominator.

3. Add the resulting like fractions.

4. Reduce the resulting fraction to lowest terms.

To Simplify Complex Fractions
6.6

Method 1 Multiply both the numerator and the denominator of the complex fraction by the LCD of the secondary fractions; then simplify the results.

Method 2 First, simplify the numerator and denominator of the complex fraction; then divide the simplified numerator by the simplified denominator.

Review Exercises 6.7 Set I

In Exercises 1 and 2, find the domain of the variable.

1. $\dfrac{15}{20 - 45a^2}$

2. $\dfrac{7m - 10}{6m^2 - 21m - 90}$

In Exercises 3–6, reduce each fraction to lowest terms.

3. $\dfrac{4z^3 + 4z^2 - 24z}{2z^2 + 4z - 6}$

4. $\dfrac{6k^3 - 12k^2 - 18k}{3k^2 + 3k - 36}$

5. $\dfrac{a^3 - 27b^3}{a^2 - 3ab + 2a - 6b}$

6. $\dfrac{x^4 + 4}{4x^2 - 8x + 8}$

In Exercises 7–20, perform the indicated operations.

7. $\dfrac{-35mn^2p^2}{14m^3p^3} \cdot \dfrac{13m^4n}{52n^3p}$

8. $\dfrac{10b^2c}{6ab^4} \div \dfrac{15abc^2}{-12ac^3}$

9. $\dfrac{z^2 + 3z + 2}{z^2 + 2z + 1} \div \dfrac{z^2 + 2z - 3}{z^2 - 1}$

10. $\dfrac{a^2 - a - 2}{a^2 - 4a + 4} \cdot \dfrac{a^2 - 4}{a^2 + 3a + 2}$

11. $\dfrac{x^3 + y^3}{3x^2 - 3xy + 3y^2} \div \dfrac{x^2 - y^2}{x^2 + xy - 2y^2} \cdot \dfrac{15x^2y}{5x^2y + 10xy^2}$

12. $\dfrac{a^2 - 4b^2}{a^2 + 2ab + b^2} \cdot \dfrac{a^2 + 2ab + 4b^2}{a + 2b} \div \dfrac{a^3 - 8b^3}{2a^2 + 4ab + 2b^2}$

13. $\dfrac{20y - 7}{6y - 8} + \dfrac{17 + 2y}{8 - 6y}$

14. $\dfrac{23 - 22z}{30z - 24} + \dfrac{38z - 25}{24 - 30z}$

15. $\dfrac{11}{30e^3f} - \dfrac{7}{45e^2f^2}$

16. $\dfrac{3}{28u^2v^2} - \dfrac{7}{40u^4v}$

17. $\dfrac{a + 1}{a^2 - a - 2} - \dfrac{a - 2}{a^2 + a - 6}$

18. $\dfrac{x + 2}{x^2 + x - 2} - \dfrac{x - 3}{x^2 - x - 6}$

19. $\dfrac{15x}{5x^2 + 20x} - \dfrac{7}{3x^2} - \dfrac{3x + 12}{x^2 + 8x + 16}$

20. $\dfrac{4y - 20}{y^2 - 10y + 25} - \dfrac{5}{11y^3} + \dfrac{24y}{30y - 6y^2}$

In Exercises 21–24, simplify the complex fractions.

21. $\dfrac{\dfrac{x}{y + 1} + 2}{\dfrac{x}{y + 1} - 2}$

22. $\dfrac{3 - \dfrac{a}{b + 2}}{2 + \dfrac{a}{b + 2}}$

23. $\dfrac{8R^{-3} + T^{-3}}{4R^{-2} - T^{-2}}$

24. $\dfrac{m^{-2} - 16n^{-2}}{m^{-3} - 64n^{-3}}$

Review Exercises 6.7 Set II

NAME

In Exercises 1 and 2, find the domain of the variable.

1. $\dfrac{11y - 6}{6y^2 + 8y - 64}$

2. $\dfrac{3x + 9}{2x^2 + 9x - 5}$

In Exercises 3–6, reduce each fraction to lowest terms.

3. $\dfrac{x^4 + x^2 + 1}{6x^2 + 6x + 6}$

4. $\dfrac{2x^2 + 3x - 20}{x^3 + 64}$

5. $\dfrac{m^3 + 8n^3}{m^2 - 6n + 2mn - 3m}$

6. $\dfrac{6a^2 + 11ab - 2b^2}{ac + 2bc - ad - 2bd}$

In Exercises 7–20, perform the indicated operations.

7. $\dfrac{55f^5 g^3}{-8e^2 f^2} \cdot \dfrac{4e^3 g}{15ef^2 g^2}$

8. $\dfrac{39a^3 b^5}{5ac^2} \cdot \dfrac{30c^3 d^2}{65a^2 b}$

9. $\dfrac{a^2 + 4a - 21}{6a^3 + 42a^2} \div \dfrac{3a^2 - 27}{36a^3}$

10. $\dfrac{2x^2 - 11x - 21}{2x^2 + 11x + 12} \div \dfrac{3x^2 + 13x + 4}{3x^3 - 20x^2 - 7x}$

11. $\dfrac{4h^2 + 8hk + 16k^2}{15hk^2 + 30k^3} \div \dfrac{3h^3 - 24k^3}{18kh^3} \div \dfrac{16h^2 - 8hk}{5h^2 - 20k^2}$

1. _____

2. _____

3. _____

4. _____

5. _____

6. _____

7. _____

8. _____

9. _____

10. _____

11. _____

12. $\dfrac{7x^2 + 19x - 6}{2x^2 - 11x + 15} \cdot \dfrac{5x^2 - 16x + 3}{x^3 + 2x^2 - 3x} \cdot \dfrac{2x^2 - 7x + 5}{70x^2 - 34x + 4}$

12. _____

13. _____

14. _____

15. _____

16. _____

17. _____

18. _____

19. _____

20. _____

21. _____

22. _____

23. _____

24. _____

13. $\dfrac{18 - 27u}{15 - 25u} + \dfrac{23u - 12}{25u - 15}$

14. $\dfrac{4x + 2}{3x - 5} + \dfrac{6x - 1}{5 - 3x}$

15. $\dfrac{7}{20a^3b^2} - \dfrac{13}{30ab^4}$

16. $\dfrac{5}{8x^2y} - \dfrac{3}{14xy^3}$

17. $\dfrac{3w - 15}{w^2 - 3w - 10} - \dfrac{5w + 30}{w^2 + w - 30}$

18. $\dfrac{x + 1}{x^2 - x - 6} - \dfrac{x - 3}{x^2 + 3x + 2}$

19. $\dfrac{12y^2 + 18y}{4y^2 - 9} + \dfrac{18y - 12y^2}{4y^2 - 12y + 9} - \dfrac{9}{8y^2}$

20. $\dfrac{7}{5y^2} - \dfrac{y + 1}{5y^2 - 9y - 2} - \dfrac{2y - 1}{2y^2 - y - 6}$

In Exercises 21–24, simplify the complex fraction.

21. $\dfrac{\dfrac{3}{w} + \dfrac{4w}{4w + 3}}{\dfrac{6}{4w + 3} + 2}$

22. $\dfrac{3 + \dfrac{7}{x - 1}}{\dfrac{5}{x + 2} + 1}$

23. $\dfrac{8y^{-3} - 27x^{-3}}{4y^{-2} - 9x^{-2}}$

24. $\dfrac{64x^{-3} + 1}{16x^{-2} - 1}$

6.8 Solving Equations That Have Fractions

In Section 2.1, we removed fractions from simple equations by multiplying both sides by the same number. In this section, we must sometimes multiply both sides of an equation by an expression containing the variable. This procedure, however, can lead to an equation that is *not equivalent to* the original equation. (In Chapter 2, we learned that *equivalent equations* are equations with identical solution sets.)

Equivalent equations are obtained when:

1. The same number or expression is added to or subtracted from both sides of the given equation.

2. Both sides of the given equation are multiplied or divided by the same *nonzero* number.

Nonequivalent equations may be obtained when:

1. Both sides of the given equation are multiplied by an expression containing the variable. In this case, **extraneous roots** (that is, roots that are not roots of the original equation) may be introduced (see Example 1). We must, therefore, *check all roots in the given equation*.

2. Both sides of the given equation are divided by an expression containing the variable. In this case, roots of the given equation may be lost (see Example 2).

Example 1   1. $x - 1 = 0$ Solution set $= \{1\}$

   $(x + 2)(x - 1) = (x + 2) \cdot 0$ Multiply both sides by $(x + 2)$

2. $(x + 2)(x - 1) = 0$ Solution set $= \{$ -2 , $1\}$

Extraneous root ⎯⎯⎯⏋

Equations 1 and 2 are *not equivalent* because they have different solution sets.   ∎

Example 2   1. $(x - 5)(x + 4) = 0$ Solution set $= \{5, -4\}$

   $\dfrac{(x - 5)(x + 4)}{(x - 5)} = \dfrac{0}{(x - 5)}$ Divide both sides by $(x - 5)$

2. $x + 4 = 0$ Solution set $= \{-4\}$

Equations 1 and 2 are *not equivalent* because they have different solution sets. For this reason, *do not divide both sides of an equation by an expression containing the variable.*   ∎

TO SOLVE AN EQUATION THAT HAS FRACTIONS

1. Remove fractions by multiplying each term by the LCD.

2. Remove grouping symbols.

3. Combine like terms.

If a *first-degree equation* is obtained in step 3:	If the degree of the equation obtained in step 3 is *greater than one*:
4. Get all terms with the unknown on one side and the remaining terms on the other side.	**4.** Get all nonzero terms on one side and arrange them in descending powers. *Only zero must remain on the other side.*
5. Divide both sides by the coefficient of the unknown.	**5.** Factor the polynomial.
	6. Set each factor equal to zero and then solve for the variable.

Check apparent solutions in the original equation. Any value of the variable that makes any denominator in the equation equal zero is *not* a solution; it is an extraneous root. Any value of the variable that gives a false statement (such as $7 = 2$) when checked is also an extraneous root.

Example 3   Solve $\dfrac{3}{x + 1} - \dfrac{2}{x} = \dfrac{5}{2x}$.

$LCD = 2x(x + 1)$. The domain of the variable is the set of all real numbers except -1 and 0. The LCD contains the variable. Therefore, all apparent solutions must be checked.

$$2x(x + 1)\left(\frac{3}{x + 1} - \frac{2}{x}\right) = 2x(x + 1)\left(\frac{5}{2x}\right)$$

$$\frac{2x(x + 1)}{1} \cdot \frac{3}{(x + 1)} - \frac{2x(x + 1)}{1} \cdot \frac{2}{x} = \frac{2x(x + 1)}{1} \cdot \frac{5}{2x}$$

$$6x - 4(x + 1) = 5(x + 1)$$

$$6x - 4x - 4 = 5x + 5$$

$$2x - 4 = 5x + 5$$

$$-9 = 3x$$

$$-3 = x$$

The solution $x = -3$ *is* in the domain of the variable. We must, however, still check it in the original equation.

Check $\dfrac{3}{x+1} - \dfrac{2}{x} = \dfrac{5}{2x}$

$$\dfrac{3}{-2} - \dfrac{2}{-3} \overset{?}{=} \dfrac{5}{-6}$$

$$-\dfrac{9}{6} + \dfrac{4}{6} \overset{?}{=} -\dfrac{5}{6}$$

$$-\dfrac{5}{6} = -\dfrac{5}{6} \qquad \text{A true statement}$$

Therefore, the solution is $x = -3$, and the solution set is $\{-3\}$. ∎

Example 4 Solve $\dfrac{x}{x-3} = \dfrac{3}{x-3} + 4$.

The domain is the set of all real numbers except 3. LCD $= x - 3$.

$$(x-3)\left[\dfrac{x}{x-3}\right] = (x-3)\left[\dfrac{3}{x-3} + 4\right]$$

$$\dfrac{(x-3)}{1} \cdot \dfrac{x}{(x-3)} = \dfrac{(x-3)}{1} \cdot \dfrac{3}{(x-3)} + \dfrac{(x-3)}{1} \cdot \dfrac{4}{1}$$

$$x = 3 + 4(x-3)$$

$$x = 3 + 4x - 12$$

$$x = 4x - 9$$

$$9 = 3x$$

$$3 = x$$

Extraneous root ⟶ | Since 3 is not in the domain, this equation has *no solution*

If we try to check the value 3 in the original equation, we obtain numbers that are not real numbers:

$$\dfrac{x}{x-3} = \dfrac{3}{x-3} + 4$$

$$\dfrac{3}{3-3} \overset{?}{=} \dfrac{3}{3-3} + 4$$

$$\dfrac{3}{0} \overset{?}{=} \dfrac{3}{0} + 4$$

Not a real number

Therefore, 3 is not a root of the given equation. This equation has no real roots. The solution set of the equation is $\{\ \}$. ∎

Example 5 Solve $\dfrac{x+2}{x-2} = \dfrac{14}{x+1}$.

The domain is the set of all real numbers except 2 and -1. LCD $= (x - 2)(x + 1)$.

$$(x-2)(x+1)\left(\frac{x+2}{x-2}\right) = (x-2)(x+1)\left(\frac{14}{x+1}\right)$$

$$(x + 2)(x + 1) = 14(x - 2)$$
$$x^2 + 3x + 2 = 14x - 28$$
$$x^2 - 11x + 30 = 0$$
$$(x - 5)(x - 6) = 0$$
$$x - 5 = 0 \; or \; x - 6 = 0$$
$$x = 5 \; or \qquad x = 6$$

These numbers *are* in the domain of the variable.

$Check \dfrac{5+2}{5-2} \overset{?}{=} \dfrac{14}{5+1}$ $\qquad \dfrac{6+2}{6-2} \overset{?}{=} \dfrac{14}{6+1}$

$\qquad\quad \dfrac{7}{3} \overset{?}{=} \dfrac{14}{6}$ $\qquad\qquad \dfrac{8}{4} \overset{?}{=} \dfrac{14}{7}$

$\qquad\quad \dfrac{7}{3} = \dfrac{7}{3}$ $\qquad\qquad\quad 2 = 2$

The solution set is $\{5, 6\}$. ■

Example 6   Solve $\dfrac{2}{x} + \dfrac{3}{x^2} = 1$.

LCD $= x^2$. The domain is the set of all real numbers except zero.

$$x^2\left[\frac{2}{x} + \frac{3}{x^2}\right] = x^2 [1]$$

$$\frac{x^2}{1}\left(\frac{2}{x}\right) + \frac{x^2}{1}\left(\frac{3}{x^2}\right) = \frac{x^2}{1}\left(\frac{1}{1}\right)$$

$$2x + 3 = x^2 \longleftarrow \text{Second-degree term}$$
$$0 = x^2 - 2x - 3$$
$$0 = (x - 3)(x + 1)$$
$$x - 3 = 0 \; or \; x + 1 = 0$$
$$x = 3 \; or \qquad x = -1$$

Check for $x = 3$	*Check for* $x = -1$
$\dfrac{2}{x} + \dfrac{3}{x^2} = 1$	$\dfrac{2}{x} + \dfrac{3}{x^2} = 1$
$\dfrac{2}{3} + \dfrac{3}{3^2} \overset{?}{=} 1$	$\dfrac{2}{-1} + \dfrac{3}{(-1)^2} \overset{?}{=} 1$
$\dfrac{2}{3} + \dfrac{1}{3} \overset{?}{=} 1$	$-2 + 3 \overset{?}{=} 1$
$1 = 1$	$1 = 1$

The solution set is $\{3, -1\}$. ■

A WORD OF CAUTION A common mistake students make is to confuse an equation such as $\dfrac{2}{x} + \dfrac{3}{x^2} = 1$ with an addition problem such as $\dfrac{2}{x} + \dfrac{3}{x^2}$.

The equation	*The addition problem*
Both sides are multiplied by the LCD to remove fractions.	Each fraction is changed into an equivalent fraction that has the LCD for a denominator.

$$\frac{2}{x} + \frac{3}{x^2} = 1 \qquad LCD = x^2$$

$$\boxed{\frac{x^2}{1}} \cdot \frac{2}{x} + \boxed{\frac{x^2}{1}} \cdot \frac{3}{x^2} = \boxed{\frac{x^2}{1}} \cdot \frac{1}{1}$$

$$2x + 3 = x^2$$

This equation is then solved by factoring (see Example 6 above). Here, the result is two numbers (-1 and 3) that make both sides of the given equation equal.

$$\frac{2}{x} + \frac{3}{x^2} \qquad LCD = x^2$$

This is 1

$$= \frac{2}{x} \cdot \boxed{\frac{x}{x}} + \frac{3}{x^2}$$

$$= \frac{2x}{x^2} + \frac{3}{x^2} = \frac{2x + 3}{x^2}$$

Here, the result is a fraction that represents the sum of the given fractions.

Common error

The usual mistake made is to multiply both terms of *the sum* by the LCD.

$$\boxed{\frac{x^2}{1}} \cdot \frac{2}{x} + \boxed{\frac{x^2}{1}} \cdot \frac{3}{x^2} = 2x + 3$$

$$\neq \frac{2}{x} + \frac{3}{x^2}$$

The sum has been multiplied by x^2 and therefore is no longer equal to its original value. ☑

Example 7 Solve $\dfrac{x}{x-3} - \dfrac{3x}{x^2 - x - 6} = \dfrac{4x^2 - 4x - 18}{x^2 - x - 6}$.

Since $x^2 - x - 6 = (x + 2)(x - 3)$, the LCD is $(x + 2)(x - 3)$. The domain is the set of all real numbers except -2 and 3.

$$(x + 2)(x - 3)\left[\frac{x}{x - 3} - \frac{3x}{x^2 - x - 6} \right] = (x + 2)(x - 3)\left[\frac{4x^2 - 4x - 18}{x^2 - x - 6} \right]$$

$$(x + 2)(x - 3)\left[\frac{x}{x - 3} \right] - (x + 2)(x - 3)\left[\frac{3x}{(x + 2)(x - 3)} \right] = 4x^2 - 4x - 18$$

(Continued)

$$x(x + 2) - 3x = 4x^2 - 4x - 18$$
$$x^2 + 2x - 3x = 4x^2 - 4x - 18$$
$$x^2 - x = 4x^2 - 4x - 18$$
$$0 = 3x^2 - 3x - 18$$
$$0 = 3(x^2 - x - 6)$$
$$0 = 3(x + 2)(x - 3)$$
$$x + 2 = \quad 0 \text{ or } x - 3 = 0$$
$$x = -2 \text{ or } \quad x = 3$$

Neither of these numbers is in the domain of the variable. Therefore, there is no solution. The solution set is { }. ∎

Example 8   Solve $\dfrac{5}{x - 7} - \dfrac{1}{2x} = \dfrac{9x + 7}{2x^2 - 14x}$.

Since $2x^2 - 14x = 2x(x - 7)$, the domain is all real numbers except 0 and 7. The LCD is $2x(x - 7)$.

$$2x(x - 7) \left[\frac{5}{x - 7} - \frac{1}{2x} \right] = 2x(x - 7) \left[\frac{9x + 7}{2x^2 - 14x} \right]$$

$$2x(x - 7) \left(\frac{5}{x - 7} \right) - 2x(x - 7) \left(\frac{1}{2x} \right) = 2x(x - 7) \left[\frac{9x + 7}{2x^2 - 14x} \right]$$

$$10x - (x - 7) = 9x + 7$$
$$10x - x + 7 = 9x + 7$$
$$9x + 7 = 9x + 7$$
$$7 = 7$$

This is an identity; however, the solution set is *not* the set of all real numbers, since 0 and 7 are not in the domain of the variable. The solution set, therefore, is the set of all real numbers *except* 0 and 7. ∎

EXERCISES 6.8

Set I   Find the solution set for each problem.

1. $\dfrac{2}{k - 5} - \dfrac{5}{k} = \dfrac{3}{4k}$

2. $\dfrac{4}{h} - \dfrac{6}{h - 7} = \dfrac{2}{3h}$

3. $\dfrac{x}{x - 2} = \dfrac{2}{x - 2} + 5$

4. $\dfrac{x}{x + 5} = 4 - \dfrac{5}{x + 5}$

5. $\dfrac{12m}{2m - 3} = 6 + \dfrac{18}{2m - 3}$

6. $\dfrac{40w}{5w + 6} = 8 - \dfrac{48}{5w + 6}$

7. $\dfrac{2y}{7y + 5} = \dfrac{1}{3y}$

8. $\dfrac{2b}{3 - 4b} = \dfrac{1}{2b}$

9. $\dfrac{3e - 5}{4e} = \dfrac{e}{2e + 3}$

10. $\dfrac{2x - 1}{3x} = \dfrac{3}{2x + 7}$

11. $\dfrac{1}{2} - \dfrac{1}{x} = \dfrac{4}{x^2}$

12. $\dfrac{7}{4} - \dfrac{17}{4x} = \dfrac{3}{x^2}$

13. $\dfrac{4}{x + 1} = \dfrac{3}{x} + \dfrac{1}{15}$

14. $\dfrac{1}{x + 1} = \dfrac{3}{x} + \dfrac{1}{2}$

15. $\dfrac{6}{x + 4} = \dfrac{5}{x + 3} + \dfrac{4}{x}$

16. $\dfrac{7}{x + 5} = \dfrac{3}{x - 1} - \dfrac{4}{x}$

17. $\dfrac{6}{x^2 - 9} + \dfrac{1}{5} = \dfrac{1}{x - 3}$

18. $\dfrac{6 - x}{x^2 - 4} - 2 = \dfrac{x}{x + 2}$

19. $\dfrac{x + 2}{x - 2} - \dfrac{x - 2}{x + 2} = \dfrac{16}{x^2 - 4}$

20. $\dfrac{x - 5}{x + 5} - \dfrac{x + 5}{x - 5} = \dfrac{100}{x^2 - 25}$

21. $\dfrac{2}{x^2 + 5x + 6} + \dfrac{3}{x^2 - 3x - 10} = \dfrac{5x - 1}{x^3 - 19x - 30}$

22. $\dfrac{4}{x^2 + 6x + 5} + \dfrac{2}{x^2 - 2x - 3} = \dfrac{6x - 2}{x^3 + 3x^2 - 13x - 15}$

23. $\dfrac{1}{2x^2 - 11x + 15} + \dfrac{x - 1}{2x^2 + x - 15} = \dfrac{-4}{x^2 - 9}$

24. $\dfrac{1}{3x^2 - 10x + 8} + \dfrac{x + 8}{3x^2 + 2x - 8} = \dfrac{6}{x^2 - 4}$

25. $\dfrac{8}{x^3 + 64} + \dfrac{3}{x^2 - 16} = \dfrac{-1}{x^2 - 4x + 16}$

26. $\dfrac{12}{x^3 + 27} + \dfrac{1}{x^2 - 9} = \dfrac{1}{x^2 - 3x + 9}$

Set II Find the solution set for each problem.

1. $\dfrac{7}{2t - 3} - \dfrac{4}{5t} = \dfrac{3}{t}$

2. $\dfrac{6}{x} = \dfrac{7}{x - 3} - \dfrac{1}{2}$

3. $\dfrac{8}{6 + 5e} = 3 - \dfrac{15e}{6 + 5e}$

4. $5 = \dfrac{3}{x - 2} - \dfrac{8}{2 - x}$

5. $\dfrac{36}{4 - 3d} = 9 + \dfrac{27d}{4 - 3d}$

6. $\dfrac{13}{3 - x} = 8 - \dfrac{5x}{3 - x}$

7. $\dfrac{4a}{33 - 5a} = \dfrac{2}{a}$

8. $\dfrac{9}{x} = \dfrac{24 - 3x}{5}$

9. $\dfrac{3}{1 - 2x} + \dfrac{5}{2 - x} = 2$

10. $\dfrac{x}{8} = \dfrac{5}{6} - \dfrac{1}{x - 1}$

11. $\dfrac{1}{2} - \dfrac{1}{6x} = \dfrac{7}{3x^2}$

12. $\dfrac{1}{5x} + \dfrac{1}{x^2} = \dfrac{2}{4x + 5}$

13. $\dfrac{4}{3x - 1} = \dfrac{2}{x} + 1$

14. $\dfrac{3}{1 - 2x} = \dfrac{2x + 1}{x - 2}$

15. $\dfrac{11}{2 - 3x} = \dfrac{6}{x + 6} + \dfrac{3}{x}$

16. $\dfrac{x - 5}{3 + 2x} = \dfrac{2x - 1}{x - 9}$

17. $\dfrac{x + 25}{x^2 - 25} = 1 - \dfrac{12x}{x - 5}$

18. $\dfrac{x + 4}{x^2 - 16} + 1 = \dfrac{-7}{x - 4}$

19. $\dfrac{x - 4}{x + 4} - \dfrac{x + 4}{x - 4} = \dfrac{64}{x^2 - 16}$

20. $\dfrac{4}{x^2 - x - 6} - \dfrac{2}{x^2 - 2x - 3} = \dfrac{-1}{x + 1}$

21. $\dfrac{3}{x^2 + 5x + 4} + \dfrac{2}{x^2 + 3x - 4} = \dfrac{5x - 1}{x^3 + 4x^2 - x - 4}$

22. $\dfrac{6}{x^2 - 3x - 10} + \dfrac{2}{x^2 - 2x - 8} = \dfrac{1}{x - 4}$

23. $\dfrac{1}{4x^2 + 11x - 3} + \dfrac{24x - 1}{4x^2 - 13x + 3} = \dfrac{6}{x^2 - 9}$

24. $\dfrac{6}{x^2 + x - 6} - \dfrac{5}{x^2 - x - 2} = \dfrac{-1}{x + 1}$

25. $\dfrac{12}{x^3 + 8} - \dfrac{1}{x^2 - 4} = \dfrac{1}{x^2 - 2x + 4}$

26. $\dfrac{14}{x^3 + 1} + \dfrac{4}{x^2 - 1} = \dfrac{7}{x^2 - x + 1}$

6.9 Literal Equations

Literal equations are equations that contain more than one variable. Such equations are also called *equations in two (or more) variables*. **Formulas** are literal equations that have applications in real-life situations. Sometimes, literal equations have already been solved for one of the variables.

Example 1   Examples of literal equations:

a. $A = P(1 + rt)$

This is an equation in four variables; it is also a formula, because it has applications in business. It has already been solved for A; you might be asked to solve it for P, for r, or for t.

b. $\dfrac{4ab}{d} = 15$

This is an equation in three variables; it is not a formula. It has not been solved for any of its variables; you might be asked to solve for a, for b, or for d. ∎

When we are asked to *solve* a literal equation for any one of its variables, that variable must appear only once all by itself on one side of the equal sign. All other variables and all constants must be on the other side of the equal sign.

The method for solving literal equations can be summarized as follows:

TO SOLVE A LITERAL EQUATION

1. *Remove fractions* (it there are any) by multiplying both sides by the LCD.

2. *Remove grouping symbols* (if there are any).

3. *Collect like terms*, with all terms containing the variable you are solving for on one side, all other terms on the other side.

4. *Factor out the variable you are solving for* (if it appears in more than one term).

5. *Divide both sides by the coefficient of the variable you are solving for.*

Example 2   Solve $A = P(1 + rt)$ for t.

$$A = P(1 + rt)$$

$$A = P + Prt$$ Remove ( ) by using the distributive rule

$$A - P = Prt$$ Collect terms with the variable you are solving for (t) on one side and all other terms on the other side

$$\frac{A - P}{Pr} = \frac{Prt}{Pr}$$ Divide both sides by Pr

$$t = \frac{A - P}{Pr}$$ Solution ■

Example 3   Solve $\dfrac{1}{F} = \dfrac{1}{u} + \dfrac{1}{v}$ for u.

$$\text{LCD} = Fuv$$

$$\frac{Fuv}{1} \cdot \frac{1}{F} = \frac{Fuv}{1} \cdot \frac{1}{u} + \frac{Fuv}{1} \cdot \frac{1}{v}$$ Remove fractions by multiplying both sides by the LCD

$$uv = Fv + Fu$$

$$uv - Fu = Fv$$ Collect terms with the variable you are solving for (u) on one side and all other terms on the other side

$$u(v - F) = Fv$$ Remove u as a common factor

$$\frac{u(v - F)}{(v - F)} = \frac{Fv}{(v - F)}$$ Divide both sides by $(v - F)$

$$u = \frac{Fv}{v - F}$$ Solution ■

Example 4   Solve $I = \dfrac{nE}{R + nr}$ for n.

$$(R + nr)\, I = (R + nr)\, \dfrac{nE}{R + nr}$$

Multiply both sides by the LCD

$$IR + Inr = nE$$

$$IR = nE - Inr$$

Collect terms with the variable you are solving for (n) on one side and all other terms on the other side

$$IR = n(E - Ir)$$

Remove n as a common factor

$$n = \dfrac{IR}{E - Ir}$$

Divide both sides by $(E - Ir)$ ■

EXERCISES 6.9

Set I   Solve for the variable listed after each equation.

1. $2(3x - y) = xy - 12$; y

2. $2(3x - y) = xy - 12$; x

3. $z = \dfrac{x - m}{s}$; m

4. $s^2 = \dfrac{N - n}{N - 1}$; N

5. $\dfrac{2x}{5yz} = z + x$; x

6. $\dfrac{xy}{z} = x + y$; y

7. $C = \dfrac{5}{9}(F - 32)$; F

8. $A = \dfrac{h}{2}(B + b)$; B

9. $s = c\left(1 + \dfrac{a}{c}\right)$; c

10. $Z = \dfrac{Rr}{R + r}$; R

11. $A = P(1 + rt)$; r

12. $S = \dfrac{1}{2}g(2t - 1)$; t

13. $v^2 = \dfrac{2}{r} - \dfrac{1}{a}$; a

14. $\dfrac{1}{p} = 1 + \dfrac{1}{s}$; s

15. $S = \dfrac{a}{1 - r}$; r

16. $I = \dfrac{E}{R + r}$; R

17. $\dfrac{1}{F} = \dfrac{1}{u} + \dfrac{1}{v}$; F

18. $\dfrac{1}{c} = \dfrac{1}{a} + \dfrac{1}{b}$; b

19. $L = a + (n - 1)d$; n

20. $A = 2\pi rh + 2\pi r^2$; h

21. $C = \dfrac{a}{1 + \dfrac{a}{\pi A}}$; a

22. $R = \dfrac{V + v}{1 + \dfrac{vV}{c^2}}$; v

Set II   Solve for the variable listed after each equation.

1. $5(2x + y) = 2xy + 25$; x

2. $\dfrac{mn}{m + n} = 1$; m

3. $3ab - 5 = 4(2a + b)$; b

4. $\dfrac{x - y}{x} = x + y$; y

5. $\dfrac{1}{f} = \dfrac{1}{a} + \dfrac{1}{b};\ a$

6. $A = \dfrac{h}{2}(B + b);\ b$

7. $A = \dfrac{h}{2}(B + b);\ h$

8. $\dfrac{1}{f} = \dfrac{1}{a} + \dfrac{1}{b};\ f$

9. $a = b\left[1 + \dfrac{c}{b}\right];\ b$

10. $PV = nRT;\ V$

11. $\dfrac{2}{15ab - 8a^2} = \dfrac{7}{20a^2 - 12ab};\ b$

12. $x = \dfrac{y}{z + 4};\ z$

13. $v^2 = \dfrac{2}{r} - \dfrac{1}{a};\ r$

14. $\dfrac{2}{x} = \dfrac{y}{3} + \dfrac{1}{y};\ x$

15. $I = \dfrac{E}{R + r};\ r$

16. $A = P + Prt;\ P$

17. $\dfrac{1}{R} = \dfrac{1}{r_1} + \dfrac{1}{r_2};\ r_1$

18. $y = mx + b;\ x$

19. $C = \dfrac{a}{1 + \dfrac{a}{\pi A}};\ A$

20. $\dfrac{x}{a} + \dfrac{y}{b} = 1;\ b$

21. $E = \dfrac{k(1 - A)\pi R^2}{r^2};\ A$

22. $S = \dfrac{n}{2}(A + L);\ A$

6.10 Word Problems Leading to Equations That Have Fractions

All the types of word problems discussed in Chapter 3 can lead to equations that have fractions. For examples of how to solve word problems of those types, refer back to Chapter 3.

In this section, we introduce a new type of word problem called a *work problem*. One basic relationship used to solve work problems is

$$\text{Rate} \times \text{Time} = \text{Amount of work}$$

For example, suppose Jose can assemble a radio in 3 days.

$$\text{Jose's } rate = \frac{1 \text{ radio}}{3 \text{ days}} = \frac{1}{3} \text{ radio per day}$$

If his working *time* is 5 days, then

$$\text{Rate} \cdot \text{Time} = \text{Amount of work}$$

$$\frac{1}{3} \cdot 5 = \frac{5}{3} \text{ radios}$$

The other basic relationship used to solve work problems is

$$\begin{pmatrix} \text{Amount } A \\ \text{does in} \\ \text{time } x \end{pmatrix} + \begin{pmatrix} \text{Amount } B \\ \text{does in} \\ \text{time } x \end{pmatrix} = \begin{pmatrix} \text{Amount done} \\ \text{together in} \\ \text{time } x \end{pmatrix}$$

Example 1 Albert can paint a house in 6 days. Ben can do the same job in 8 days. How long would it take them to paint the same house if they work together?

$$\text{Albert's rate} = \frac{1 \text{ house}}{6 \text{ days}} = \frac{1}{6} \text{ house per day}$$

$$\text{Ben's rate} = \frac{1 \text{ house}}{8 \text{ days}} = \frac{1}{8} \text{ house per day}$$

Let x = number of days to paint the house working together. Then

Albert's rate	·	Albert's time	=	Amount Albert paints
$\frac{1}{6}$	·	x	=	$\frac{x}{6}$

Ben's rate	·	Ben's time	=	Amount Ben paints
$\frac{1}{8}$	·	x	=	$\frac{x}{8}$

Therefore,

Amount Albert paints in x days	+	Amount Ben paints in x days	=	Amount painted together in x days
$\frac{x}{6}$	+	$\frac{x}{8}$	=	1

(One house painted)

$$\text{LCD} = 24 \qquad \frac{\overset{4}{\cancel{24}}}{1} \cdot \frac{x}{\cancel{6}} + \frac{\overset{3}{\cancel{24}}}{1} \cdot \frac{x}{\cancel{8}} = \frac{24}{1} \cdot \frac{1}{1}$$

$$4x + 3x = 24$$

$$7x = 24$$

$$x = \frac{24}{7} = 3\tfrac{3}{7} \text{ days}$$

Therefore, it takes them $3\tfrac{3}{7}$ days to paint the house when they work together. ■

Example 2 Machine A can make 200 brackets in 6 hr. How long does it take machine B to make 100 brackets if the two machines working together can make 200 brackets in 5 hr?

Let x = number of hours for machine B to make 100 brackets

$$\text{A's rate} = \frac{200 \text{ brackets}}{6 \text{ hr}} = \frac{100}{3} \text{ brackets per hour}$$

$$\text{B's rate} = \frac{100 \text{ brackets}}{x \text{ hr}} = \frac{100}{x} \text{ brackets per hour}$$

The two machines working together can make 200 brackets if each machine runs for 5 hours. Therefore,

Number of brackets A does in 5 hr	+	Number of brackets B does in 5 hr	=	Number of brackets done together in 5 hr

$$\frac{100}{3}(5) \quad + \quad \frac{100}{x}(5) \quad = \quad 200$$

$$\text{LCD} = 3x \qquad \frac{3x}{1} \cdot \frac{500}{3} \quad + \quad \frac{3x}{1} \cdot \frac{500}{x} \quad = \quad \frac{3x}{1} \cdot \frac{200}{1}$$

$$500x \quad + \quad 1500 \quad = \quad 600x$$

$$1500 = 100x$$

$$15 = x$$

Therefore, it takes machine B 15 hr to make 100 brackets. ■

Example 3 It takes pipe 1 twelve minutes to fill a particular tank. It takes pipe 2 only eight minutes to fill the same tank. Pipe 3 takes six minutes to *empty* the same tank. How long does it take to fill the tank when all three pipes are open?

$$\text{Pipe 1's rate} = \frac{1 \text{ tank}}{12 \text{ min}} = \frac{1}{12} \text{ tank per minute}$$

$$\text{Pipe 2's rate} = \frac{1 \text{ tank}}{8 \text{ min}} = \frac{1}{8} \text{ tank per minute}$$

$$\text{Pipe 3's rate} = \frac{1 \text{ tank}}{6 \text{ min}} = \frac{1}{6} \text{ tank per minute}$$

Let x = time for all three together to fill the tank

Amount 1 does in time x	+	Amount 2 does in time x	−	Amount 3 does in time x	=	1 full tank

Because pipe 3 *empties* the tank

$$\frac{1}{12}x \quad + \quad \frac{1}{8}x \quad - \quad \frac{1}{6}x \quad = \quad 1$$

$$\text{LCD} = 24$$

$$\overset{2}{\frac{24}{1}} \cdot \frac{x}{12} \quad + \quad \overset{3}{\frac{24}{1}} \cdot \frac{x}{8} \quad - \quad \overset{4}{\frac{24}{1}} \cdot \frac{x}{6} \quad = \quad \frac{24}{1} \cdot \frac{1}{1}$$

$$2x \quad + \quad 3x \quad - \quad 4x \quad = \quad 24$$

$$x = 24 \text{ min}$$

Therefore, it takes 24 min to fill the tank when all three pipes are open. ■

EXERCISES 6.10

Set I Set up each problem algebraically, solve, and check. Be sure to state what your variables represent.

1. Henry can paint a house in 5 days and Jim can do the same work in 4 days. If they work together, how many days will it take them to paint the house?

2. Juan can paint a house in 6 days and Maria can do it in 9 days. How many days will it take them to paint the house if they work together?

3. Abby can type 100 pages of manuscript in 3 hr. How long does it take David to type 80 pages if he and Abby working together can type a 500-page manuscript in 10 hr?

4. Carlos can wrap 200 newspapers in 55 min. How long does it take Bernice to wrap 150 papers if she and Carlos working together can wrap 400 papers in 1 hr?

5. Machine A takes 36 hr to do a job that machine B does in 24 hr. If machine A runs for 12 hr before machine B is turned on, how long will it take both machines running together to finish the job?

6. Machine A takes 18 hr to do a job that machine B does in 15 hr. If machine A runs for 3 hr before machine B is turned on, how long will it take both machines running together to finish the job?

7. Two numbers differ by 8. One-fourth the larger is 1 more than one-third the smaller. Find the numbers.

8. Two numbers differ by 6. One-fifth the smaller exceeds one-half the larger by 3. Find the numbers.

9. It takes one plane $\frac{1}{2}$ hr longer than another to fly a certain distance. Find the distance if one plane travels 500 mph and the other 400 mph.

10. It takes Barbara 10 min longer than Ed to ride her bicycle a certain distance. Find the distance if Barbara's speed is 9 mph and Ed's is 12 mph.

11. An automobile radiator contains 14 qt of a 45% solution of antifreeze. How much must be drained out and replaced by pure antifreeze to make a 50% solution?

12. An automobile radiator contains 12 qt of a 30% solution of antifreeze. How much must be drained out and replaced with pure antifreeze to make a 50% solution?

13. The tens digit of a two-digit number is 1 more than its units digit. The product of the digits divided by the sum of the digits is $\frac{6}{5}$. Find the number.

14. The units digit of a two-digit number is 1 more than the tens digit. The product of the digits divided by the sum of the digits is $\frac{12}{7}$. Find the number.

15. Pipe 2 takes 1 hr longer to fill a particular tank than pipe 1. Pipe 3 can drain the tank in 2 hr. If it takes 3 hr to fill the tank when all three pipes are open, how long does it take pipe 1 to fill the tank alone?

16. Pipe 2 takes 2 hr more time to fill a particular tank than pipe 1. Pipe 3 can drain the tank in 4 hr. If it takes 2 hr to fill the tank when all three pipes are open, how long does it take pipe 1 to fill the tank alone?

17. Ruth can proofread 230 pages of a deposition in 4 hr. How long does it take Sandra to proofread 60 pages if, when they work together, they can proofread 525 pages in 6 hr?

18. Alice can crochet 3 sweaters in 48 hr. How long does it take Willa to crochet 2 sweaters if together they can crochet 15 sweaters in 112 hr?

19. In a film-processing lab, machine A can process 5,700 ft of film in 60 min. How long does it take machine B to process 4,300 ft of film if the two machines running together can process 15,500 ft of film in 50 min?

20. In a film-processing lab, machine C can process 3,225 ft of film in 15 min. How long does it take machine D to process 12,750 ft of film if the two machines running together can process 28,800 ft of film in 45 min?

Set II Set up each problem algebraically, solve, and check. Be sure to state what your variables represent.

1. Merwin can wax all his floors in 4 hr. His wife, June, can do the same job in 3 hr. How long will it take them if they work together?

2. The denominator of a fraction exceeds the numerator by 6. The value of the fraction is $\frac{3}{5}$. Find the fraction.

3. It takes Bert 8 hr to clean the yard and mow the lawn. He and his brother Howard can do the same job in 3 hr working together. How long does it take Howard working alone?

4. The rate of Tom's boat in still water is 30 mph. If it can travel 132 miles *with* the current in the same time that it can travel 108 miles *against* the current, find the speed of the current.

5. Machine A takes 20 hr to do a job that machine B does in 28 hr. If machine A runs for 8 hr before machine B is turned on, how long will it take both machines running together to finish the job?

6. The sum of a fraction and its reciprocal is $\frac{73}{24}$. Find the fraction and its reciprocal.

7. Two numbers differ by 22. One-eighth the larger exceeds one-sixth the smaller by 2. Find the numbers.

8. Sherma can type 15 words per minute faster than Karen. If Sherma types 3,850 words in the same time that Karen types 3,100 words, find the rate of each.

9. It takes Mina 10 min longer than Andrea to jog eight laps around the school soccer field. Find the distance around the soccer field if Mina's speed is 3 mph and Andrea's is 4 mph.

10. Machine A can make 400 bushings in 8 hr. How long does it take machine B to make 50 bushings if the two machines working together can make 800 bushings in 12 hr?

11. One-fifth of the 10% antifreeze solution in a car radiator is drained and replaced by an antifreeze solution of unknown concentration. If the resulting mixture is 25% antifreeze, what was the unknown concentration?

12. The units digit of a two-digit number is 2 more than the tens digit. The product of the digits divided by the sum of the digits is $\frac{3}{4}$. Find the two-digit number.

13. The tens digit of a two-digit number is 4 more than its units digit. The product of the digits divided by the sum of the digits is $\frac{3}{2}$. Find the number.

14. The speed of a plane in still air is 480 mph. If it can fly 3,030 miles *with* the wind in the same time that it can fly 2,730 miles *against* the wind, what is the speed of the wind?

15. A refinery tank has one fill pipe and two drain pipes. Pipe 1 can fill the tank in 3 hr. Pipe 2 takes 6 hr longer to drain the tank than pipe 3. If it takes 12 hr to fill the tank when all three pipes are open, how long does it take pipe 3 to drain the tank alone?

16. It takes Dick 30 min longer than Jonathan to walk a certain distance. Find the distance if Dick's speed is 3 mph and Jonathan's is 4 mph.

17. Lori can knit 4 scarves in 24 hr. How long does it take Anita to knit one scarf if together they can knit 21 scarves in 72 hr?

18. The speed of the current in a river is 6 mph. If a boat can travel 222 miles *with* the current in the same time it can travel 150 miles *against* the current, what is the speed of the boat in still water?

19. In a film-processing lab, machine A can process 4,275 ft of film in 45 min. How long does it take machine B to process 10,625 ft of film if the two machines running together can process 41,600 ft of film in 80 min?

20. The tens digit of a two-digit number is 2 more than the units digit. If the product of the digits divided by the sum of the digits is $\frac{12}{5}$, find the number.

6.11 Review: 6.8–6.10

To Solve an Equation That Has Fractions 6.8

1. Remove fractions by multiplying each term by the LCD.

2. Remove grouping symbols.

3. Combine like terms.

First-degree equations	*Second-degree (quadratic) equations*
4. Get all terms with the unknown on one side and the remaining terms on the other side.	4. Get all nonzero terms on one side and arrange them in descending powers. *Only zero must remain on the other side.*
5. Divide both sides by the coefficient of the unknown.	5. Factor the polynomial.
	6. Set each factor equal to zero and then solve for the variable.

Literal Equations 6.9

Literal equations are equations that have more than one variable.

To Solve a Literal Equation 6.9

Proceed in the same way used to solve an equation with one variable. The solution will be expressed in terms of the other variables given in the literal equation, as well as numbers.

Review Exercises 6.11 Set I

In Exercises 1–8, solve the equations for the variable.

1. $\dfrac{7}{2z + 5} = \dfrac{13}{3z}$

2. $\dfrac{11}{6c - 7} = \dfrac{8}{5c}$

3. $\dfrac{5a - 4}{6a} = \dfrac{-2}{3a + 10}$

4. $\dfrac{3b}{5b - 4} = \dfrac{7 - 2b}{3}$

5. $\dfrac{3}{x} - \dfrac{8}{x^2} = \dfrac{1}{4}$

6. $\dfrac{4}{x^2} - \dfrac{3}{x} = \dfrac{5}{2}$

7. $\dfrac{9}{x+1} = \dfrac{4}{x} + \dfrac{1}{x-1}$

8. $\dfrac{4}{3x-1} - \dfrac{2}{x+1} = \dfrac{1}{x}$

In Exercises 9–12, solve for the variable listed after each equation.

9. $5(x - 2y) = 14 + 3(2x - y); \ y$

10. $2(5 - 2x) = 22 - 2(y - 5x); \ x$

11. $R = \dfrac{R_1 R_2}{R_1 + R_2}; \ R_1$

12. $F = \dfrac{1}{\dfrac{1}{u} + \dfrac{1}{v}}; \ v$

In Exercises 13–16, set up the problem algebraically and solve. Be sure to state what your variables represent.

13. Using tractor A, a man can cultivate his corn in 20 hr. With tractor B, the same corn can be cultivated in 15 hr. After one man cultivates with tractor A for 5 hr, he is joined by a second man using tractor B. How long will it take both men and tractors working together to finish the job?

14. Section gang A can lay a rail in 16 min. Section gang B can lay a rail in 12 min. After gang A has been working 4 min, how long will it take both gangs working together to finish laying one rail?

15. The denominator of a fraction is 10 more than its numerator. If 1 is added to both numerator and denominator, the value of the new fraction is $\frac{2}{3}$. Find the original fraction.

16. Pipes 1 and 2 run into a tank, while pipe 3 runs out the bottom. Pipe 1 can fill the tank in 4 hr; pipe 2 can fill it in 6 hr. When pipes 1, 2, and 3 are open, the tank is filled in 5 hr. How long does it take pipe 3 to drain the tank by itself?

Review Exercises 6.11 Set II

NAME _____

ANSWERS

In Exercises 1–8, solve the equations for the variable.

1. $\dfrac{3}{5f - 2} = \dfrac{7}{12f}$

2. $\dfrac{8}{x + 5} = \dfrac{1}{13 - 2x}$

3. $\dfrac{4u + 1}{5u} = \dfrac{20}{3u + 6}$

4. $\dfrac{2x + 1}{4x + 2} = \dfrac{3x - 2}{2}$

5. $\dfrac{17}{6x} + \dfrac{5}{2x^2} = \dfrac{2}{3}$

6. $\dfrac{3}{x} - \dfrac{1}{x^2} = \dfrac{11}{16}$

7. $\dfrac{9}{2x - 1} = \dfrac{4}{x} - \dfrac{1}{x - 3}$

8. $\dfrac{6}{6 + x} - \dfrac{1}{x} = \dfrac{13}{4}$

1. _____

2. _____

3. _____

4. _____

5. _____

6. _____

7. _____

8. _____

9. _____

10. _____

11. _____

12. _____

In Exercises 9–12, solve for the variable listed after each equation.

9. $4(2y + x) = xy + 32$; x

10. $ab = \dfrac{c}{a} - \dfrac{b}{a}$; b

11. $\dfrac{1}{p} = 1 + \dfrac{1}{s}$; p

12. $\dfrac{a}{b - 3} = \dfrac{1}{a} + \dfrac{1}{4}$; b

In Exercises 13–16, set up the problem algebraically and solve. Be sure to state what your variables represent.

13. A tank is filled through pipes 1 and 2 and drained through pipe 3. Pipe 1 can fill the tank in 5 hr and pipe 2 can fill it in 3 hr. When pipes 1, 2, and 3 are open, the tank is filled in 6 hr. How long does it take pipe 3 to drain the tank by itself?

14. Machine A can produce 25 sprocket wheels in 30 min. How many sprocket wheels can machine B produce in 1 hr if both machines working together can produce 315 sprocket wheels in $3\frac{1}{2}$ hours?

15. The numerator of a fraction is 32 less than its denominator. If the numerator and denominator are each increased by 3, the new fraction has a value of $\frac{1}{2}$. Find the original fraction.

16. Machine A can produce 25 sprocket wheels in 30 min. How long does it take machine B to produce 112 sprocket wheels if both machines working together can produce 477 sprocket wheels in $4\frac{1}{2}$ hr?

Chapter 6 Diagnostic Test

The purpose of this test is to see how well you understand operations with fractions. We recommend that you work this diagnostic test *before* your instructor tests you on this chapter. Allow yourself about 50 minutes.

Complete solutions for all the problems on this test, together with section references, are given in the answer section at the end of the book. For the problems you do incorrectly, study the sections cited.

1. What is the domain of the variable?

   a. $\dfrac{2x + 3}{x^2 - 4x}$

   b. $\dfrac{y + 2}{3y^2 - y - 10}$

2. Find the missing term in each of the following expressions.

   a. $\dfrac{4}{-h} = \dfrac{-4}{?}$

   b. $\dfrac{-3}{k - 2} = \dfrac{?}{2 - k}$

3. Reduce each fraction to the lowest terms.

   a. $\dfrac{f^2 + 5f + 6}{f^2 - 9}$

   b. $\dfrac{x^4 - 2x^3 + 5x^2 - 10x}{x^3 - 8}$

In Problems 4–9, perform the indicated operations.

4. $\dfrac{z}{2z^2 - 5z - 3} \cdot \dfrac{6z^2 - 9z - 6}{6z^2}$

5. $\dfrac{x^2 - 2x - 24}{x^2 - 36} \cdot \dfrac{x^2 + 7x + 6}{x^2 + x - 12} \div (x^3 + 1)$

6. $\dfrac{3m + 3n}{m^3 - n^3} \div \dfrac{m^2 - n^2}{m^2 + mn + n^2}$

7. $\dfrac{20a + 27b}{12a - 20b} + \dfrac{44a - 13b}{20b - 12a}$

8. $\dfrac{x}{x + 4} - \dfrac{x}{x - 4} - \dfrac{32}{x^2 - 16}$

9. $\dfrac{3}{x^2 + x - 6} - \dfrac{2}{x^2 - 4} - \dfrac{3}{x^2 + 5x + 6}$

In Problems 10 and 11, simplify the complex fractions.

10. $\dfrac{\dfrac{8h^4}{5k}}{\dfrac{4h^2}{15k^3}}$

11. $\dfrac{6 - \dfrac{4}{w}}{\dfrac{3w}{w - 2} + \dfrac{1}{w}}$

In Problems 12–14, find the solution set.

12. $\dfrac{2}{3a + 5} - \dfrac{6}{a - 2} = 3$

13. $\dfrac{x}{x + 7} = 3 - \dfrac{7}{x + 7}$

14. $\dfrac{3}{2z} + \dfrac{3}{z^2} = -\dfrac{1}{6}$

15. Solve for r in terms of the other variables: $I = \dfrac{E}{R + r}$

16. Set up algebraically, solve, and check: Sidney can make 24 bushings on a lathe in 8 hr. How long does it take Ruben to make 8 bushings if he and Sidney can make 14 bushings in 4 hr when they work together?

Cumulative Review Exercises
Chapters 1–6

1. Simplify. Write your answer using only positive exponents.

$$\left(\frac{x^4 y^{-3}}{x^{-2}}\right)^{-2}$$

2. Solve $\dfrac{x-2}{4} = \dfrac{x+3}{2} + \dfrac{1}{4}$.

3. Solve $9 - 2(m - 6) \le 3(4 - m) + 5$.

In Exercises 4–9, perform the indicated operations and simplify.

4. $(2x - 5)(x^2 - 4x + 3)$

5. $(8a^2 + 6a + 1) \div (2a + 3)$

6. $(x - 2)^6$

7. $\dfrac{x+3}{2x^2 + 3x - 2} \cdot \dfrac{2x^2 - 9x + 4}{3x^2 + 10x + 3} \div \dfrac{x-4}{x+2}$

8. $\dfrac{3x}{2x^2 + 15x + 7} + \dfrac{4}{2x^2 - 5x - 3}$

9. $\dfrac{a-3}{a^3 + 27} - \dfrac{1}{a^2 - 9}$

In Exercises 10–13, factor completely.

10. $10x^2 + 3xy - 18y^2$

11. $x^4 - x^2 - 12$

12. $x^3 - 8$

13. $6ax + 3bx - 2ay - by$

In Exercises 14 and 15, set up algebraically, solve, and check.

14. The length of a rectangle is 7 in. more than the width. The area is 60 sq. in. What are its dimensions?

15. Mrs. Kishinami spent $9.70 for 50 stamps. If she bought only 18¢ and 20¢ stamps, how many of each kind did she buy?

7 Exponents and Radicals

In this chapter, we extend the rules of exponents to include rational exponents, and we define the relation between exponents and radicals. Radicals are more fully discussed in this chapter than in Chapter 1, and *complex numbers* are introduced.

7.1 Rational Exponents

Let's review the eight basic rules for integral exponents from Section 1.11 (it is understood that none of the variables can have a value that makes a denominator zero):

The rules of exponents

1.1. $x^m \cdot x^n = x^{m+n}$	1.2. $(x^m)^n = x^{mn}$
1.3. $(xy)^n = x^n y^n$	1.4. $\dfrac{x^m}{x^n} = x^{m-n}$
1.5. $\left(\dfrac{x}{y}\right)^n = \dfrac{x^n}{y^n}$	1.6. $x^0 = 1$
1.7a. $x^{-n} = \dfrac{1}{x^n}$	1.8. $\left(\dfrac{x^a y^b}{z^c}\right)^n = \dfrac{x^{an} y^{bn}}{z^{cn}}$

In this section, we define additional rules for exponents that make it possible to have exponents that are rational numbers.

7.1A The Meaning of Rational Exponents

The following discussion is not a proof; it is included to help you understand why we define rational exponents the way we do.

We know that for all $x \geq 0$, $\sqrt{x}$ is a number such that $(\sqrt{x})^2 = x$. Suppose we let $\sqrt{x} = x^p$, where p is some rational number to be determined. Then

$$(\sqrt{x})^2 = x$$
$$(x^p)^2 = x \qquad \text{Substitute } x^p \text{ for } \sqrt{x}$$
$$x^{2p} = x^1 \qquad \text{Rule 1.2}$$

If $x^{2p} = x^1$, it must be true that $2p = 1$, or

$$p = \tfrac{1}{2}$$

That is, $x^p = x^{1/2}$. Therefore, we want $x^{1/2}$ to equal $\sqrt{x}$.

Similarly, we know that $\sqrt[3]{x}$ is a number such that $(\sqrt[3]{x})^3 = x$. Suppose we let $\sqrt[3]{x} = x^r$, where r is some rational number to be determined. Then

$$(\sqrt[3]{x})^3 = x$$
$$(x^r)^3 = x \qquad \text{Substitute } x^r \text{ for } \sqrt[3]{x}$$
$$x^{3r} = x^1 \qquad \text{Rule 1.2}$$

If $x^{3r} = x^1$, it must be true that $3r = 1$, or

$$r = \tfrac{1}{3}$$

That is, $x^r = x^{1/3}$. Therefore, we want $x^{1/3}$ to equal $\sqrt[3]{x}$. Consequently, we state the following *definition*:

RULE 7.1

$$\sqrt[n]{x} = x^{1/n}, \text{ if } x \geq 0 \text{ when } n \text{ is even.}$$

A WORD OF CAUTION   When you write fractional exponents, *be sure your exponents look like exponents*! That is, be sure $2^{1/4}$ doesn't look like $2\tfrac{1}{4}$.   ☑

Before we use Rule 7.1, let's review the rules about principal roots from Chapter 1.

PRINCIPAL ROOTS

The symbol $\sqrt[n]{p}$ always represents the *principal* nth root of p.

If the *radicand is positive*, the principal root is positive.

If the *radicand is negative* and if the *index* is

1. odd, the principal root is negative.

2. even, the root is *not a real number*.*

Example 1   Use Rule 7.1 to change from radical form to exponential form:

a. $\sqrt[4]{z} = z^{1/4}$, if $z \geq 0$ b. $\sqrt[5]{y} = y^{1/5}$

c. $\sqrt[3]{-10} = -\sqrt[3]{10} = -10^{1/3}$ d. $\sqrt{14} = 14^{1/2}$

　　　　The rules about principal roots
　　　　remind us that an *odd* root of a
　　　　negative number is *negative*   ■

Example 2   Use Rule 7.1 to change from exponential form to radical form:

a. $a^{1/4} = \sqrt[4]{a}$, if $a \geq 0$ b. $x^{1/7} = \sqrt[7]{x}$ ■

Example 3   Evaluate each expression:

a. $27^{1/3} = \sqrt[3]{27} = 3$ b. $100^{1/2} = \sqrt{100} = 10$

c. $(-8)^{1/3} = \sqrt[3]{(-8)} = -2$ d. $32^{1/5} = \sqrt[5]{32} = 2$ ■

---

* Numbers that are not real numbers are discussed in Section 7.8.

Example 4   Use Rule 7.1 to change from radical form to exponential form:

a. $\sqrt[3]{x^2} = (x^2)^{1/3}$ Rule 7.1

$= x^{2/3}$ Rule 1.2

b. $(\sqrt[3]{x})^2 = (x^{1/3})^2 = x^{(1/3)2} = x^{2/3}$

Therefore, $\sqrt[3]{x^2} = (\sqrt[3]{x})^2 = x^{2/3}$ ∎

Examples 4a and 4b lead to the following rule:

RULE 7.2

$\sqrt[b]{x^a} = (\sqrt[b]{x})^a = x^{a/b}$ if $x \geq 0$ when b is even.

Example 5   Use Rule 7.2; assume that all variables represent nonnegative numbers:

a. $\sqrt[5]{m^3} = m^{3/5}$ b. $(\sqrt[4]{z})^3 = (z^{1/4})^3 = z^{3/4}$

c. $d^{4/5} = \sqrt[5]{d^4}$ or $(\sqrt[5]{d})^4$ d. $a^{2/3} = (\sqrt[3]{a})^2$

e. $8^{2/3} = (\sqrt[3]{8})^2 = (\sqrt[3]{2^3})^2 = (2)^2 = 4$ ∎

EXERCISES 7.1A

Set I   In Exercises 1–10, replace each radical by an equivalent exponential expression; assume that all variables represent nonnegative numbers.

1. $\sqrt{5}$ **2.** $\sqrt{7}$ **3.** $\sqrt[3]{z}$ **4.** $\sqrt[4]{x}$ **5.** $\sqrt[4]{x^3}$

6. $\sqrt[5]{y^2}$ **7.** $(\sqrt[3]{x^2})^2$ **8.** $(\sqrt[4]{x^3})^2$ **9.** $\sqrt[n]{x^{2n}}$ **10.** $\sqrt[n]{y^{5n}}$

In Exercises 11–16, rewrite each expression in radical form; assume that all variables represent nonnegative numbers.

11. $7^{1/2}$ **12.** $5^{1/3}$ **13.** $a^{3/5}$ **14.** $b^{2/3}$ **15.** $x^{m/n}$

16. $x^{(a+b)/a}$

In Exercises 17–24, evaluate each expression.

17. $8^{1/3}$ **18.** $27^{1/3}$ **19.** $(-27)^{2/3}$ **20.** $(-8)^{2/3}$

21. $4^{3/2}$ **22.** $9^{3/2}$ **23.** $(-16)^{3/4}$ **24.** $(-1)^{1/4}$

Set II   In Exercises 1–10, replace each radical by an equivalent exponential expression; assume that all variables represent nonnegative numbers.

1. $\sqrt{17}$ **2.** $\sqrt{31}$ **3.** $\sqrt[3]{y}$ **4.** $\sqrt[5]{x^2}$ **5.** $\sqrt[4]{x^7}$

6. $\sqrt[3]{z^4}$ **7.** $(\sqrt[3]{x})^2$ **8.** $(\sqrt{y})^3$ **9.** $\sqrt[n]{x^{3n}}$ **10.** $\sqrt[n]{x^{7n}}$

In Exercises 11–16, rewrite each expression in radical form; assume that the variables represent nonnegative numbers.

11. $13^{1/3}$ **12.** $7^{1/4}$ **13.** $x^{4/7}$ **14.** $c^{2/5}$ **15.** $y^{a/b}$

16. $z^{(a-b)/b}$

In Exercises 17–24, evaluate each expression.

17. $64^{2/3}$ **18.** $16^{3/4}$ **19.** $8^{2/3}$ **20.** $(-1)^{1/5}$ **21.** $27^{4/3}$

22. $1^{7/8}$ **23.** $25^{3/2}$ **24.** $(-64)^{2/3}$

7.1B   Using the Rules of Exponents When the Exponents Are Rational Numbers

All of the rules of exponents reviewed at the beginning of this section can be used when the exponents are *any* rational numbers, as long as the radicand is nonnegative whenever the denominator of an exponent is an even number.

Example 6   Use the rules of exponents to simplify each expression; assume that all variables represent nonnegative numbers:

a. $a^{1/2}a^{-1/4} = a^{1/2+(-1/4)} = a^{1/4}$ Rule 1.1

b. $(8)^{2/3} = (2^3)^{2/3} = 2^{3(2/3)}$ For an alternate solution, see Example 5e

$\qquad = 2^2 = 4$

c. $x^{-1/3} = \dfrac{1}{x^{1/3}}$ Rule 1.7

d. $(z^{-1/2})^4 = z^{(-1/2)4} = z^{-2} = \dfrac{1}{z^2}$ Rules 1.2 and 1.7

e. $\dfrac{y^{2/3}}{y^{1/2}} = y^{2/3-1/2} = y^{1/6}$ Rule 1.4

f. $x^{-1/2}x x^{2/5} = x^{-1/2+1+2/5}$

$\qquad = x^{-5/10+10/10+4/10} = x^{9/10}$ Rule 1.1

g. $\dfrac{b^{3/2}b^{-2/3}}{b^{5/6}} = b^{3/2-2/3-5/6}$

$\qquad = b^{9/6-4/6-5/6} = b^0 = 1$ Rules 1.1, 1.4, and 1.6

h. $(9h^{-2/5}k^{4/3})^{-3/2} = (3^2 h^{-2/5}k^{4/3})^{-3/2}$

$\qquad = 3^{2(-3/2)}h^{-2/5(-3/2)}k^{4/3(-3/2)}$

$\qquad = 3^{-3}h^{3/5}k^{-2} = \dfrac{h^{3/5}}{27k^2}$ Rules 1.7 and 1.8

i. $\left(\dfrac{xy^{-2/3}}{z^{-4}}\right)^{-3/4} = \dfrac{x^{(1)(-3/4)}y^{(-2/3)(-3/4)}}{z^{-4(-3/4)}}$

$\qquad = \dfrac{x^{-3/4}y^{1/2}}{z^3} = \dfrac{y^{1/2}}{x^{3/4}z^3}$ Rules 1.7 and 1.8

j. $\left(\dfrac{c^{5/2}d^{-3}}{c^{-1/2}}\right)^{2/3} = (c^{5/2+1/2}d^{-3})^{2/3} = \left(\dfrac{c^3}{d^3}\right)^{2/3}$

$\qquad = \dfrac{c^{3(2/3)}}{d^{3(2/3)}} = \dfrac{c^2}{d^2}$ Rules 1.4 and 1.8   ■

It is often necessary in calculus to factor algebraic expressions that are *not* polynomials. We may use the techniques of factoring learned in Chapter 5 to factor those algebraic expressions that contain fractional exponents (see Example 7) and/or negative exponents (see Examples 8 and 9).

Example 7   Factor $6x^{4/3}y^{1/5} - 12x^{1/3}y^{6/5}$.

Solution The GCF is $6x^{1/3}y^{1/5}$.

$$6x^{4/3}y^{1/5} - 12x^{1/3}y^{6/5} = 6x^{1/3}y^{1/5}(x - 2y)$$

Check $$6x^{1/3}y^{1/5}(x - 2y) = 6x^{1/3}y^{1/5}(x) - 6x^{1/3}y^{1/5}(2y)$$
$$= 6x^{4/3}y^{1/5} - 12x^{1/3}y^{6/5} \quad \blacksquare$$

Example 8   Factor $x^{-4} - x^{-2} - 6$.

Solution $x^{-4} - x^{-2} - 6$ is quadratic in form.

$$x^{-4} - x^{-2} - 6 = (x^{-2})^2 - (x^{-2})^1 - 6$$
$$= (x^{-2} - 3)(x^{-2} + 2)$$
$$= \left(\frac{1}{x^2} - 3\right)\left(\frac{1}{x^2} + 2\right)$$

Check $(x^{-2} - 3)(x^{-2} + 2) = x^{-4} - x^{-2} - 6.$ $\blacksquare$

Example 9   Factor $8x^{-1/3}y^{3/5}z^{-5/4} + 48x^{2/3}y^{-2/5}z^{-1/4}$.

Solution The GCF for $8x^{-1/3}y^{3/5}z^{-5/4} + 48x^{2/3}y^{-2/5}z^{-1/4}$ is $8x^{-1/3}y^{-2/5}z^{-5/4}$.

$$8x^{-1/3}y^{3/5}z^{-5/4} + 48x^{2/3}y^{-2/5}z^{-1/4}$$
$$= 8x^{-1/3}y^{-2/5}z^{-5/4}(y + 6xz)$$
$$= \frac{8}{x^{1/3}y^{2/5}z^{5/4}}(y + 6xz)$$

Check $$8x^{-1/3}y^{-2/5}z^{-5/4}(y + 6xz)$$
$$= 8x^{-1/3}y^{-2/5}z^{-5/4}(y) + 8x^{-1/3}y^{-2/5}z^{-5/4}(6xz)$$
$$= 8x^{-1/3}y^{3/5}z^{-5/4} + 48x^{2/3}y^{-2/5}z^{-1/4} \quad \blacksquare$$

EXERCISES 7.1B

Set I   In Exercises 1–30, perform the indicated operations. Express answers in exponential form, using positive exponents; assume that all variables represent nonnegative numbers.

1. $x^{1/2}x^{3/2}$

2. $y^{5/4}y^{3/4}$

3. $a^{3/4}a^{-1/2}$

4. $b^{5/6}b^{-1/3}$

5. $z^{-1/2}z^{2/3}$

6. $N^{-1/3}N^{3/4}$

7. $(H^{3/4})^2$

8. $(s^{5/6})^3$

9. $(x^{-3/4})^{1/3}$

10. $(y^{-2/3})^{1/2}$

11. $\dfrac{a^{3/4}}{a^{1/2}}$

12. $\dfrac{b^{2/3}}{b^{1/6}}$

13. $\dfrac{x^{1/2}}{x^{-1/3}}$

14. $\dfrac{z^{1/4}}{z^{-1/3}}$

15. $x^{2/3}xx^{-1/2}$

16. $x^{3/4}xx^{-1/3}$

17. $(x^{-1/2})^3(x^{2/3})^2$

18. $(x^{3/4})^2(x^{-2/3})^3$

19. $\dfrac{u^{1/2}v^{-2/3}}{u^{-1/4}v^{-1}}$

20. $\dfrac{u^{2/3}v^{-3/5}}{u^{-1/3}v^{-1}}$

21. $(16x^{-2/5}y^{4/9})^{3/2}$

22. $(8x^{9/8}y^{-3/4})^{2/3}$

23. $\left(\dfrac{a^6d^0}{b^{-9}c^3}\right)^{7/3}$

24. $\left(\dfrac{y^{10}z^{-5}}{x^0w^{-15}}\right)^{7/5}$

25. $\left(\dfrac{x^3y^0z^{-1}}{32x^{-1}z^2}\right)^{2/5}$ **26.** $\left(\dfrac{ab^{-1}c^0}{8a^{-4}b^4}\right)^{2/3}$ **27.** $\left(\dfrac{x^{-1}y^{2/3}}{z^{-5}}\right)^{-3/5}$

28. $\left(\dfrac{a^{3/4}b^{-1}}{c^{-2}}\right)^{-2/3}$ **29.** $\left(\dfrac{9x^{-2/3}y^{2/9}}{x^{-2}}\right)^{-3/2}$ **30.** $\left(\dfrac{27R^{3/5}S^{-5/2}}{S^{-4}}\right)^{-2/3}$

In Exercises 31–36, evaluate each expression.

31. $(8)^{-2/3}$ **32.** $(27)^{-2/3}$ **33.** $(4)^{1/2}(9)^{-3/2}$

34. $(8)^{1/3}(16)^{-3/2}$ **35.** $(100)^{-1/2}(-8)^{1/3}$ **36.** $(10^4)^{-1/2}(-27)^{1/3}$

In Exercises 37–48, factor each expression completely. Negative exponents may be left in your answers.

37. $3x^{2/3}y^{7/6} - 9x^{5/3}y^{1/6}$ **38.** $12a^{7/4}b^{3/8} - 8a^{3/4}b^{11/8}$

39. $18x^{5/2}y^{1/3} + 21x^{1/2}y^{4/3}$ **40.** $36x^{3/5}y^{5/4} + 30x^{8/5}y^{1/4}$

41. $5v^{-2} - 17v^{-1} + 6$ **42.** $5v^{-2} - 11v^{-1} + 6$

43. $35k^{-4} - 12k^{-2} + 1$ **44.** $18k^{-4} - 9k^{-2} + 1$

45. $2a^{1/4}b^{-8/3} - a^{-3/4}b^{1/3}$ **46.** $3x^{-2/5}y^{2/3} - 5x^{3/5}y^{-1/3}$

47. $8c^{-3/4}d^{-2/3}e^{1/5} + 12c^{1/4}d^{1/3}e^{-4/5}$ **48.** $15x^{1/2}y^{-1/3} + 10x^{-1/2}y^{2/3}$

Set II   In Exercises 1–30, perform the indicated operations. Express answers in exponential form, using positive exponents; assume that all variables represent nonnegative numbers.

1. $a^{1/4}a^{3/4}$ **2.** $b^{3/5}b^{1/4}$ **3.** $x^{5/6}x^{-1/3}$

4. $c^{2/3}c^{-1/4}$ **5.** $z^{-1/5}z^{2/3}$ **6.** $y^{7/8}y^{-1/3}$

7. $(x^{3/5})^2$ **8.** $(a^{2/5})^{1/3}$ **9.** $(x^{-3/7})^{1/3}$

10. $(a^{-1/4})^{-8/9}$ **11.** $\dfrac{x^{7/8}}{x^{1/4}}$ **12.** $\dfrac{y^{5/6}}{y^{1/3}}$

13. $\dfrac{p^{3/5}}{p^{-1/2}}$ **14.** $\dfrac{a^{-2/5}}{a^{-7/10}}$ **15.** $z^{2/5}z^{-3/5}z^{7/10}$

16. $x^{-1/3}x^{2/5}x^{3/4}$ **17.** $(x^{-1/3})^4(x^{2/3})^5$ **18.** $(a^{-3/4})^3(a^{5/6})^2$

19. $\dfrac{x^{1/3}y^{-4/5}}{x^{-1/4}y^{-1}}$ **20.** $\dfrac{a^{-2/5}b^{2/3}}{a^{1/2}b^{1/2}}$ **21.** $(36R^{-4/3}S^{2/5})^{1/2}$

22. $(49x^{-1/5}y^{3/4})^{1/2}$ **23.** $\left(\dfrac{s^3t^0}{u^{-6}v^9}\right)^{4/3}$ **24.** $\left(\dfrac{a^0b^4}{c^8d^{-12}}\right)^{1/4}$

25. $\left(\dfrac{y^{2/3}z^{-2/3}}{4z^{-3}}\right)^{3/2}$ **26.** $\left(\dfrac{8a^{-12}}{b^9c^3}\right)^{2/3}$ **27.** $\left(\dfrac{R^{-3/2}S^{1/2}}{8R^{-2}}\right)^{2/3}$

28. $\left(\dfrac{16x^8y^4}{x^{12}}\right)^{3/4}$ **29.** $\left(\dfrac{x^2y^{-4}z^6}{32x^{-2}y^0z}\right)^{3/5}$ **30.** $\left(\dfrac{64a^6b^8}{a^{18}b^2}\right)^{5/6}$

In Exercises 31–36, evaluate each expression.

31. $(64)^{-2/3}$ **32.** $16^{-3/4}$ **33.** $9^{1/2}(25)^{3/2}$

34. $(10^6)^{-1/2}(125)^{1/3}$ **35.** $\dfrac{(10^4)^{1/2}(10^{-2})^{3/2}}{(10^5)^{-1/5}}$ **36.** $\dfrac{(2^4)^{1/4}(2^{-8})^{1/2}}{(2^{-6})^{-1/3}}$

In Exercises 37–48, factor each expression completely. Negative exponents may be left in your answers.

37. $8a^{1/6}b^{5/4} - 4a^{7/6}b^{1/4}$

38. $3x^{7/6}y^{1/4} - 6x^{1/6}y^{5/4}$

39. $9u^{3/8}v^{8/3} + 6u^{11/8}v^{2/3}$

40. $5z^{-2} - 19z^{-1} + 12$

41. $3t^{-2} + 17t^{-1} - 6$

42. $7x^{-4/5}y^{2/3}z^{1/4} + 14x^{1/5}y^{-1/3}z^{-3/4}$

43. $3t^{-2} + 14t^{-1} - 5$

44. $3t^{-2} + 7t^{-1} - 6$

45. $5a^{3/4}b^{-1/3} - a^{-1/4}b^{2/3}$

46. $2x^{-4} - 9x^{-2} + 9$

47. $6x^{-3/4}y^{1/3}z^{-1/2} + 8x^{1/4}y^{-2/3}z^{1/2}$

48. $5x^{3/5}y^{-3/5} - 25x^{-2/5}y^{2/5}$

7.2 Simplifying Radicals

In this section, we will simplify radicals of three kinds: (1) radicals that do not involve fractions, (2) radicals that do involve fractions, and (3) radicals in which the order of the radical can be reduced.

7.2A Radicals That Do Not Involve Fractions

Recall from Section 1.14A that the rule for simplifying a square root with factors that are positive variables is to divide each exponent by 2. We can now show why this is so. If $x \geq 0$,

$$\sqrt{x^n} = (x^n)^{1/2} = x^{n/2}$$

Note that in the expression $\sqrt{x^n}$, we can consider x^n to be a *factor* of the radicand. The other factor is an understood 1.

A WORD OF CAUTION If the square root contains *two or more terms* with even exponents, we *cannot* simplify the radical by dividing each exponent by 2. That is,

$$\sqrt{x^2 + y^2} \neq x + y$$

Proof: Suppose $x = 3$ and $y = 4$. Then $\sqrt{3^2 + 4^2} = \sqrt{9 + 16} = \sqrt{25} = 5$, but $3 + 4 = 7$. Therefore, $\sqrt{3^2 + 4^2} \neq 3 + 4$. ☑

$\sqrt{x^2} = |x|$

As we mentioned in Section 1.14A, the *principal* square root of x^2 is $|x|$. If x is known or is *assumed* to be positive, we may use $\sqrt{x^2} = x$, as we did in Chapter 1. If x is *not* assumed to be positive, we must use $\sqrt{x^2} = |x|$. We can see why if we let $x = -5$: Then "$\sqrt{(-5)^2} = -5$" is a *false* statement, since $\sqrt{(-5)^2} = \sqrt{25} = 5$, and $5 \neq -5$. Therefore, if $x = -5$, $\sqrt{x^2} \neq x$. However, "$\sqrt{(-5)^2} = |-5|$" is a *true* statement and is equivalent to $\sqrt{x^2} = |x|$.

Example 1 Simplify the radicals:

a. $\sqrt{x^6y^8}$

$\sqrt{x^6y^8} = |x^{6/2}y^{8/2}| = |x^3y^4|$ *or* $|x^3|y^4$. We do not need absolute value symbols around y^4 because y^4 is positive when y is *any* real number, positive or negative.

b. $\sqrt{(a + b)^2}$. Assume that a and b are positive.

$\sqrt{(a + b)^2} = (a + b)^{2/2} = (a + b)^1 = a + b$. We do not need absolute value symbols because a and b were *assumed* positive, and the sum of two positive numbers is always positive.

c. $\sqrt{(c - d)^2}$. Assume that c and d are positive.

$\sqrt{(c - d)^2} = |(c - d)^{2/2}| = |(c - d)^1| = |c - d|$. The absolute value symbols are necessary because $c - d$ can be negative even when c and d are positive. Try $c = 1$, $d = 6$:

$$\sqrt{(1 - 6)^2} = \sqrt{(-5)^2} = \sqrt{25} = 5$$

Therefore, $\sqrt{(1 - 6)^2} \neq 1 - 6$; however, $\sqrt{(1 - 6)^2} = |1 - 6|$. ■

Higher-Order Radicals

Before we consider simplifying *higher*-order radicals, a new definition will be helpful:

PERFECT POWER

A factor (of a radicand) raised to an exponent exactly divisible by the index of the radical is called a **perfect power**.

To simplify a radical when the radicand is a product of perfect powers, first express any numerical coefficients in prime factored form; then divide the exponent of each factor by the index of the radical. If the index is an *even* number, you may need to put absolute value symbols around the result.

Because the principal root is negative if the radicand is negative and the index is odd, cubic roots of negative numbers will be negative, fifth roots of negative numbers will be negative, and so forth. This fact suggests that a negative sign can be "moved across" the radical sign *if and only if* the index of the radical is an odd number. You can verify that $\sqrt[3]{-8} = -\sqrt[3]{8}$, that $\sqrt[5]{-32} = -\sqrt[5]{32}$, and so forth.

A radical is not considered to be in *simplest radical form* if the radicand is negative.

A WORD OF CAUTION $\sqrt{-16} \neq -\sqrt{16}$. Remember, $-\sqrt{16} = -4$, but $\sqrt{-16}$ is *not a real number*. (Numbers such as $\sqrt{-16}$ will be discussed in Section 7.8.) ☑

Example 2   Simplify the radicals:

a. $\sqrt[4]{2^4}$

$\sqrt[4]{2^4} = 2^{4/4} = 2^1 = 2$. No absolute value symbols are necessary because 2 is a positive number.

b. $\sqrt[4]{z^{12}}$

$\sqrt[4]{z^{12}} = |z^{12/4}| = |z^3|$. Absolute value symbols are necessary because the index of the radical is even.

c. $\sqrt[3]{-b^6}$

The cubic root of a negative number is negative

$\sqrt[3]{-b^6} = -\sqrt[3]{b^6} = -b^{6/3} = -b^2$. Note that $-b^2$ is a *negative* number. Let's verify that this is correct by substituting 2 for b: $\sqrt[3]{-2^6} = \sqrt[3]{-64} = -4 = -2^2$, and $-\sqrt[3]{64} = -4 = -2^2$.

d. $\sqrt[7]{-2^7 y^7}$

$\sqrt[7]{-2^7 y^7} = -\sqrt[7]{2^7 y^7} = -(2^7 y^7)^{1/7} = -2^1 y^1 = -2y$. Absolute value signs would be *incorrect* here because the index is odd. $-2y$ is a positive number if y is negative and a negative number if y is positive, as it should be. ∎

A basic rule for working with radicals is

RULE 7.3

$$\sqrt[n]{ab} = \sqrt[n]{a}\sqrt[n]{b}$$

if a and b are not *both* negative when n is even.

This rule is easily proved if we change the radicals to exponential form (we assume that $a \geq 0$ and $b \geq 0$):

$$\sqrt[n]{ab} = (ab)^{1/n} = a^{1/n}b^{1/n} = \sqrt[n]{a}\sqrt[n]{b}$$

It is *also* true, of course, that $\sqrt[n]{a}\sqrt[n]{b} = \sqrt[n]{ab}$.

In this section we will use Rule 7.3 for *simplifying* radicals, and in Section 7.4 we will use it for *multiplying* radicals.

Example 3   Verify that Rule 7.3 is true:

a. $\sqrt{36} \overset{?}{=} \sqrt{4}\sqrt{9}$

$6 \overset{?}{=} 2 \cdot 3$

$6 = 6$

b. $\sqrt[3]{8}\sqrt[3]{27} \overset{?}{=} \sqrt[3]{216}$

$2 \cdot 3 \overset{?}{=} 6$

$6 = 6$ ∎

NOTE   We now have an alternate way of approaching a problem such as $\sqrt[3]{-b^6}$. We can think of it this way:

$$\sqrt[3]{-b^6} = \sqrt[3]{(-1)b^6} = \sqrt[3]{-1}\sqrt[3]{b^6} = (-1)(b^{6/3}) = -b^2 \qquad \boxed{\checkmark}$$

Simplified Form of a Radical

A number of conditions must be satisfied in order for a radical to be in *simplest radical form*. We will explore these conditions in the following sections. The *first* of these conditions is that the radicand cannot be negative. The *second* is that when the radicand is expressed in prime factored form, none of the factors can have an exponent that is greater than or equal to the index of the radical.

When any exponent *is* greater than the index of the radical, we simplify the radical as follows:

TO SIMPLIFY A RADICAL THAT DOES NOT INVOLVE FRACTIONS

1. Express the radicand in prime factored form.

2. If the exponent of any factor of the radicand is greater than or equal to the index, break up that factor into the product of a perfect power and a nonperfect power *whose exponent is less than the index.*

3. Use Rule 7.3 to rewrite the radical as a product of radicals.

4. Remove perfect powers by dividing their exponents by the index. All remaining exponents should be less than the index; factors with such exponents remain under the radical sign.

5. The simplified radical is the *product* of all factors from step 4. (Absolute value symbols may be necessary around the answer.)

6. It may be possible to reduce the order of the radical (see Section 7.2C).

Example 4 Simplify the radicals:

a. $\sqrt{27} = \sqrt{3^3}$ 	Prime factored form

$= \sqrt{3^2 \cdot 3}$ 	3^2 is a perfect power

$= \sqrt{3^2}\sqrt{3}$

$= 3\sqrt{3}$

b. $\sqrt{48} = \sqrt{2^4 \cdot 3}$

$= \sqrt{2^4}\sqrt{3}$ 	Prime factored form of 48

$= 2^2\sqrt{3}$

$= 4\sqrt{3}$

$48 = 2^4 \cdot 3$

2	48
2	24
2	12
2	6
	3

c. $\sqrt[3]{54} = \sqrt[3]{2 \cdot 3^3}$

$= \sqrt[3]{2}\,\sqrt[3]{3^3}$ 	Prime factored form of 54

$= \sqrt[3]{2}\,(3)$

$= 3\sqrt[3]{2}$

$54 = 2 \cdot 3^3$

2	54
3	27
3	9
	3

d. $\sqrt{360} = \sqrt{2^3 \cdot 3^2 \cdot 5}$

$= \sqrt{2^2 \cdot 2 \cdot 3^2 \cdot 5}$

$= 2 \cdot 3 \cdot \sqrt{2 \cdot 5} = 6\sqrt{10}$ 	Simplified form

e. $\sqrt{12x^4y^3} = \sqrt{2^2 \cdot 3 \cdot x^4 \cdot y^2 \cdot y}$

$= 2 \cdot x^2 \cdot |y|\sqrt{3y} = 2x^2|y|\sqrt{3y}$ 	Simplified form

f. $\sqrt[3]{-16a^5b^7} = \sqrt[3]{-2^4a^5b^7}$

$$= \sqrt[3]{-2^3 \cdot 2 \cdot a^3 \cdot a^2 \cdot b^6 \cdot b}$$

$$= -2 \cdot a \cdot b^2 \sqrt[3]{2 \cdot a^2 \cdot b} = -2ab^2\sqrt[3]{2a^2b}$$

g. $\sqrt[4]{96h^{11}k^3m^8} = \sqrt[4]{2^5 \cdot 3h^{11}k^3m^8}$

$$= \sqrt[4]{2^4 \cdot 2 \cdot 3 \cdot h^8 \cdot h^3 \cdot k^3 \cdot m^8}$$

$$= 2 \cdot h^2 \cdot m^2 \sqrt[4]{2 \cdot 3 \cdot h^3 \cdot k^3}$$

$$= 2h^2m^2\sqrt[4]{6h^3k^3}$$

h. $5xy^2\sqrt{28x^4y^9z^3} = 5xy^2\sqrt{2^2 \cdot 7 \cdot x^4 \cdot y^8 \cdot y \cdot z^2 \cdot z}$

$$= 5xy^2 \cdot 2 \cdot x^2 \cdot y^4 \cdot |z|\sqrt{7 \cdot y \cdot z}$$

$$= 10x^3y^6|z|\sqrt{7yz} \quad \blacksquare$$

Sometimes, finding the root of an integer can be simplified if by inspection you can see that the number has a factor that is a perfect power (see Example 5).

Example 5 Simplify the radicals:

a. $\sqrt{50} = \sqrt{25 \cdot 2} = \sqrt{25}\sqrt{2} = 5\sqrt{2}$

b. $\sqrt[3]{24} = \sqrt[3]{8 \cdot 3} = \sqrt[3]{8}\sqrt[3]{3} = 2\sqrt[3]{3}$

c. $\sqrt[4]{32} = \sqrt[4]{16 \cdot 2} = \sqrt[4]{16}\sqrt[4]{2} = 2\sqrt[4]{2} \quad \blacksquare$

EXERCISES 7.2A

Set I Simplify each radical. Assume $a \neq 0$, $b \neq 0$, and $c \neq 0$.

1. $\sqrt{4x^2}$ 2. $\sqrt{9y^2}$ 3. $\sqrt[3]{8x^3}$ 4. $\sqrt[3]{27y^3}$

5. $\sqrt[4]{16x^4y^8}$ 6. $\sqrt[4]{81u^8v^4}$ 7. $\sqrt{2^5}$ 8. $\sqrt{3^3}$

9. $\sqrt{(-2)^2}$ 10. $\sqrt{(-3)^2}$ 11. $\sqrt[3]{-3^5}$ 12. $\sqrt[3]{-2^8}$

13. $\sqrt[4]{32}$ 14. $\sqrt[4]{48}$ 15. $\sqrt[5]{-x^7}$ 16. $\sqrt[5]{-z^8}$

17. $\sqrt{8a^4b^2}$ 18. $\sqrt{20m^8u^2}$ 19. $\sqrt{18m^3n^5}$ 20. $\sqrt{50h^5k^3}$

21. $5\sqrt[3]{-24a^5b^2}$ 22. $6\sqrt[3]{-54c^4d}$ 23. $\sqrt[5]{64m^{11}p^{15}u}$

24. $\sqrt[5]{128u^4v^{10}w^{16}}$ 25. $\sqrt[3]{8(a+b)^3}$ 26. $\sqrt[3]{27(x-y)^6}$

27. $\dfrac{3}{2abc}\sqrt[3]{2^5a^8b^9c^{10}}$ 28. $\dfrac{7}{2bc}\sqrt[3]{2^6a^5b^6c^7}$

Set II Simplify each radical. Assume $a \neq 0$, $b \neq 0$, $x \neq 0$, and $y \neq 0$.

1. $\sqrt{25x^2}$ 2. $\sqrt{64a^4}$ 3. $\sqrt[6]{64y^6}$ 4. $\sqrt[5]{32b^8}$

5. $\sqrt[4]{256a^8b^{12}}$ 6. $\sqrt[4]{81x^4y^7}$ 7. $\sqrt{2^7}$ 8. $\sqrt[3]{5^4}$

9. $\sqrt{(-7)^2}$ 10. $\sqrt[5]{-3^5}$ 11. $\sqrt[3]{-2^5}$ 12. $\sqrt{(-3)^4}$

13. $\sqrt{40}$ 14. $\sqrt[5]{128}$ 15. $\sqrt[5]{-x^7}$ 16. $\sqrt[3]{a^8}$

17. $\sqrt{75x^5y^4}$ **18.** $\sqrt{48a^3b^5c}$ **19.** $\sqrt[3]{27xy^8z^5}$ **20.** $\sqrt[3]{-16x^3y^2}$

21. $3\sqrt{32x^5y^9}$ **22.** $\sqrt[3]{-27ab^2c^3}$ **23.** $\sqrt[7]{256x^9y^{15}}$ **24.** $\sqrt{21x^4y^7z^{10}}$

25. $\sqrt[3]{(a+b)^6}$ **26.** $-8\sqrt[3]{-8s^2t^7}$ **27.** $\dfrac{3}{4xy}\sqrt[3]{2^6x^5y^6z^5}$ **28.** $\dfrac{5}{2ab^2}\sqrt[3]{8a^5b^3}$

7.2B   Radicals Involving Fractions

Here is another basic rule for working with radicals:

RULE 7.4

$$\sqrt[n]{\frac{a}{b}} = \frac{\sqrt[n]{a}}{\sqrt[n]{b}} \qquad (b \neq 0)$$

if a and b are not *both* negative when n is even.

Proof: (We assume $a \geq 0$ and $b > 0$.) If we change the radicals to exponential form, we have

$$\sqrt[n]{\frac{a}{b}} = \left(\frac{a}{b}\right)^{1/n} = \frac{a^{1/n}}{b^{1/n}} = \frac{\sqrt[n]{a}}{\sqrt[n]{b}}$$

It is also true, of course, that $\dfrac{\sqrt[n]{a}}{\sqrt[n]{b}} = \sqrt[n]{\dfrac{a}{b}}$.

Rule 7.4 can be used in simplifying radicals in which the radicand is a fraction (see Example 6), and in Section 7.4 we will use it in *dividing* radicals.

A *third* condition that must be satisfied in order for a radical to be in *simplest radical form* is that the radicand cannot be a fraction.

Example 6   Simplify the radicals; assume $y \neq 0$ and $k \neq 0$.

a. $\sqrt{\dfrac{25}{36}} = \dfrac{\sqrt{25}}{\sqrt{36}} = \dfrac{5}{6}$ b. $\sqrt[3]{\dfrac{8}{27}} = \dfrac{\sqrt[3]{8}}{\sqrt[3]{27}} = \dfrac{2}{3}$

c. $\sqrt{\dfrac{x^4}{y^6}} = \dfrac{\sqrt{x^4}}{\sqrt{y^6}} = \dfrac{x^2}{|y^3|}$ d. $\sqrt{\dfrac{50h^2}{2k^4}} = \sqrt{\dfrac{\overset{25}{\cancel{50}}h^2}{\cancel{2}k^4}} = \dfrac{\sqrt{25h^2}}{\sqrt{k^4}} = \dfrac{5|h|}{k^2}$

e. $\sqrt[5]{\dfrac{32x^{10}}{y^{15}}} = \dfrac{\sqrt[5]{2^5x^{10}}}{\sqrt[5]{y^{15}}} = \dfrac{2x^2}{y^3}$ f. $\sqrt{\dfrac{3x^2}{4}} = \dfrac{\sqrt{3x^2}}{\sqrt{4}} = \dfrac{|x|\sqrt{3}}{2}$ ■

A *fourth* condition that must be satisfied if a radical is to be in *simplest radical form* is that no denominator can contain a radical. (In Example 6, each denominator happened to be a perfect power, so no radicals were left in the denominators, but that will not always be the case.)

If there is a fraction under the radical sign or if the denominator contains a radical, we may need to multiply the numerator and denominator of the fraction by some factor that will change the denominator into a rational number. This procedure is called **rationalizing the denominator** (see Example 7).

Example 7   Rationalize the denominator of each of the following fractions:

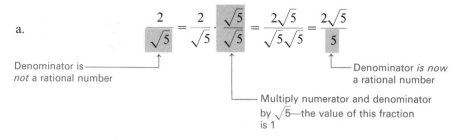

a. $\dfrac{2}{\sqrt{5}} = \dfrac{2}{\sqrt{5}} \cdot \dfrac{\sqrt{5}}{\sqrt{5}} = \dfrac{2\sqrt{5}}{\sqrt{5}\sqrt{5}} = \dfrac{2\sqrt{5}}{5}$

Denominator is *not* a rational number

Denominator *is now* a rational number

Multiply numerator and denominator by $\sqrt{5}$—the value of this fraction is 1

b. $\dfrac{6}{\sqrt[3]{2}} = \dfrac{6}{\sqrt[3]{2}} \cdot \dfrac{\sqrt[3]{2^2}}{\sqrt[3]{2^2}} = \dfrac{6\sqrt[3]{4}}{\sqrt[3]{2^3}} = \dfrac{6\sqrt[3]{4}}{2} = 3\sqrt[3]{4}$

Since we have *cube* roots, the numerator and denominator are multiplied by $\sqrt[3]{2^2}$, which makes the radicand in the denominator a perfect cube, $\sqrt[3]{2^3}$

c. Assume $y > 0$.

$\dfrac{3xy}{\sqrt[4]{y}} = \dfrac{3xy}{\sqrt[4]{y}} \cdot \dfrac{\sqrt[4]{y^3}}{\sqrt[4]{y^3}} = \dfrac{3xy\sqrt[4]{y^3}}{\sqrt[4]{y^4}} = \dfrac{3xy\sqrt[4]{y^3}}{y} = 3x\sqrt[4]{y^3}$

Multiply numerator and denominator by $\sqrt[4]{y^3}$ to make the radicand in the denominator a perfect fourth power, $\sqrt[4]{y^4}$ ∎

Rationalizing the denominator can often be combined with simplifying a radical, as Example 8 shows.

Example 8   Simplify the radicals:

a. $\sqrt{\dfrac{4}{5}}$

We can do this problem in either of two ways:

$$\sqrt{\dfrac{4}{5}} = \dfrac{\sqrt{4}}{\sqrt{5}} = \dfrac{2}{\sqrt{5}} = \dfrac{2\sqrt{5}}{\sqrt{5}\sqrt{5}} = \dfrac{2\sqrt{5}}{5}$$

See Example 7a

or

$$\sqrt{\dfrac{4}{5}} = \sqrt{\dfrac{4}{5} \cdot \dfrac{5}{5}} = \dfrac{2\sqrt{5}}{\sqrt{25}} = \dfrac{2\sqrt{5}}{5}$$

Multiply by $\dfrac{5}{5}$ in order to make the denominator a perfect square

b. $\sqrt{\dfrac{x^3}{8}} = \sqrt{\dfrac{x^3}{8} \cdot \dfrac{2}{2}} = \sqrt{\dfrac{2x^3}{16}} = \sqrt{\dfrac{2 \cdot x^2 \cdot x}{16}} = \dfrac{|x|}{4}\sqrt{2x}$ Simplified form

Multiply by $\dfrac{2}{2}$ in order to make the denominator a perfect square

c. Assume $c \neq 0$.

$$\sqrt[3]{\frac{a^4b^3}{-2c}} = \sqrt[3]{\frac{a^4b^3}{-2c} \cdot \boxed{\frac{2^2c^2}{2^2c^2}}} = \frac{\sqrt[3]{a^3ab^3 2^2 c^2}}{\sqrt[3]{-2^3c^3}} = \frac{ab\sqrt[3]{4ac^2}}{-2c} = -\frac{ab\sqrt[3]{4ac^2}}{2c}$$

— Multiply by $2^2c^2/2^2c^2$ in order to make the denominator a perfect cube

d. Assume $x \neq 0$, $y \neq 0$.

$$\sqrt[5]{\frac{24x^2y^6}{64x^4y}} = \sqrt[5]{\frac{\overset{3}{24x^2y^6}}{\underset{8}{64x^4y}}} = \sqrt[5]{\frac{3y^5}{2^3x^2} \cdot \boxed{\frac{2^2x^3}{2^2x^3}}} = \frac{\sqrt[5]{12y^5x^3}}{\sqrt[5]{2^5x^5}} = \frac{y\sqrt[5]{12x^3}}{2x}$$

Multiply by $2^2x^3/2^2x^3$ in order to make the denominator a perfect fifth power

e. Assume $x \neq 0$, $y > 0$.

$$\frac{8y}{x^4}\sqrt{\frac{5x^5y^2}{2xy^3}} = \frac{8y}{x^4}\sqrt{\frac{5x^4}{2y}} = \frac{8y}{x^4} \cdot \frac{x^2}{1}\sqrt{\frac{5}{2y} \cdot \boxed{\frac{2y}{2y}}}$$

$$= \frac{\overset{4}{8y}}{x^4} \cdot \frac{x^2}{\underset{x^2}{2y}}\sqrt{10y} = \frac{4}{x^2}\sqrt{10y} \quad \blacksquare$$

TO SIMPLIFY A RADICAL INVOLVING FRACTIONS

1. Reduce the fraction of the radicand to lowest terms.

2. Write the numerator and denominator in prime factored form.

3. Remove perfect powers by dividing their exponents by the index. (The root of a perfect power in the numerator of the radicand becomes a factor of the numerator outside the radical. The root of a perfect power in the denominator becomes a factor of the denominator outside the radical.)

4. Multiply the numerator and denominator of the remaining radicand by an expression that makes the denominator a perfect power.

5. Remove the perfect power in the denominator formed in step 4.

6. The simplified radical is the fraction formed by those factors that were removed (reduced to lowest terms) multiplied by the radical whose radicand is the product of all factors that were not removed.

EXERCISES 7.2B

Set I   Simplify each radical; assume all variables in denominators are nonzero.

1. $\sqrt{\dfrac{16}{25}}$

2. $\sqrt{\dfrac{64}{100}}$

3. $\sqrt[3]{\dfrac{-27}{64}}$

4. $\sqrt[3]{\dfrac{-8}{125}}$

5. $\sqrt[4]{\dfrac{a^4b^8}{16c^0}}$

6. $\sqrt[4]{\dfrac{c^8d^{12}}{81e^0}}$

7. $\sqrt{\dfrac{4x^3y}{xy^3}}$

8. $\sqrt{\dfrac{x^5y}{9xy^3}}$

9. $\dfrac{10}{\sqrt{5}}$

10. $\dfrac{14}{\sqrt{2}}$

11. $\dfrac{5}{\sqrt{3}}$

12. $\dfrac{8}{\sqrt{7}}$

13. $\dfrac{9}{\sqrt[3]{3}}$

14. $\dfrac{10}{\sqrt[3]{5}}$

15. $\dfrac{8}{\sqrt[5]{4}}$

16. $\dfrac{5}{\sqrt[4]{3}}$

17. $\sqrt[3]{\dfrac{m^5}{-3}}$

18. $\sqrt[3]{\dfrac{k^4}{-5}}$

19. $\dfrac{n}{2m}\sqrt[3]{\dfrac{8m^2n}{2n^3}}$

20. $\dfrac{x}{3y}\sqrt[3]{\dfrac{18xy^2}{2x^3}}$

21. $\sqrt[4]{\dfrac{3m^7}{4m^3p^2}}$

22. $\sqrt[4]{\dfrac{5a^9}{2a^5b^3}}$

23. $\sqrt[5]{\dfrac{15x^4y^7}{24x^6y^2}}$

24. $\sqrt[5]{\dfrac{30mp^8}{48m^4p^3}}$

25. $\dfrac{4x^2}{5y^3}\sqrt[3]{\dfrac{3x^2y^3}{8x^5y}}$

26. $\dfrac{3x}{4y^2}\sqrt[3]{\dfrac{2xy^5}{3x^3y}}$

27. $\dfrac{2x^3}{y}\sqrt[3]{\dfrac{5y^0z}{16x^7z^8}}$

28. $\dfrac{5c}{b}\sqrt[3]{\dfrac{b^4cd^2}{25a^0c^5}}$

Set II   Simplify each radical; assume all variables in denominators are nonzero.

1. $\sqrt{\dfrac{36}{81}}$

2. $\sqrt{\dfrac{100}{49}}$

3. $\sqrt[3]{\dfrac{-1}{27}}$

4. $\sqrt[4]{\dfrac{16}{81}}$

5. $\sqrt{\dfrac{x^6y^0}{v^8}}$

6. $\sqrt[4]{\dfrac{5^0}{a^4b^8}}$

7. $\sqrt[5]{\dfrac{x^{15}y^{10}}{-243}}$

8. $\sqrt[3]{\dfrac{6^0st^3}{s^3t^2}}$

9. $\dfrac{18}{\sqrt{3}}$

10. $\dfrac{6}{\sqrt{15}}$

11. $\dfrac{3}{\sqrt[5]{8}}$

12. $\dfrac{16}{\sqrt[3]{12}}$

13. $\dfrac{8}{\sqrt[7]{4}}$

14. $\dfrac{1}{\sqrt[3]{16}}$

15. $\dfrac{2}{\sqrt[3]{3}}$

16. $\dfrac{3}{\sqrt[3]{81}}$

17. $\sqrt[3]{\dfrac{x^7}{-2}}$

18. $\sqrt[5]{\dfrac{-y^3}{4}}$

19. $\dfrac{4}{a}\sqrt[3]{\dfrac{3a^2b}{4b^3}}$

20. $\dfrac{x}{3}\sqrt[3]{\dfrac{75x^8}{3x}}$

21. $\sqrt[3]{\dfrac{8a^4b^5}{81ab^2}}$

22. $\sqrt[3]{\dfrac{48x^3y^5}{8x^6y^2}}$

23. $\sqrt[7]{\dfrac{2xy^5}{12x^2y^2}}$

24. $\sqrt[3]{\dfrac{y^5zw^2}{4x^0z^5}}$

25. $\dfrac{3x^4}{2y^5}\sqrt[3]{\dfrac{96xy^4}{2x^2y}}$

26. $\dfrac{5x}{2y^4}\sqrt[3]{\dfrac{8xy^6}{5x^3y}}$

27. $\dfrac{7xz}{y}\sqrt[3]{\dfrac{3x}{4^0yz^2}}$

28. $\dfrac{s^3}{t^2}\sqrt[3]{\dfrac{2st^4}{8s^2t^5}}$

7.2C   Radicals in Which the Order of the Radical Can Be Reduced

In this section, we will assume that all variables represent nonnegative numbers. If we change $\sqrt[4]{x^2}$ to exponential form, we have $x^{2/4}$. But since $\frac{2}{4} = \frac{1}{2}$, $x^{2/4} = x^{1/2}$. Also, $x^{1/2} = \sqrt{x}$. Therefore, $\sqrt[4]{x^2} = \sqrt{x}$. Rewriting a radical as an *equivalent* radical with a *smaller index* is called **reducing the order** of the radical.

Whenever there is some number that is a factor of the index of the radical and also of every exponent under the radical, the order of the radical can be reduced. The easiest way to do this is to change the radical to exponential form and reduce the rational exponents; then change the expression back to radical form.

Example 9   Reduce the order of the radical:

a. $\sqrt[4]{x^2} = x^{2/4} = x^{1/2} = \sqrt{x}$

b. $\sqrt[6]{8b^3} = (2^3b^3)^{1/6} = 2^{3/6}b^{3/6} = 2^{1/2}b^{1/2} = (2b)^{1/2} = \sqrt{2b}$

c. $\sqrt[8]{16x^4y^4z^4} = (2^4x^4y^4z^4)^{1/8} = ((2xyz)^4)^{1/8}$

$$= (2xyz)^{1/2} = \sqrt{2xyz} \quad \blacksquare$$

A *fifth* condition that must be satisfied if a radical is to be in simplest form is that the *order of the radical* must be as small as possible.

Let's summarize the rules we've had so far for expressing a radical in *simplest radical form*:

A RADICAL IS IN SIMPLEST FORM IF:

1. The radicand is a positive number.

2. No prime factor of a radicand has an exponent equal to or greater than the index.

3. No radicand contains a fraction.

4. No denominator contains a radical.

5. The order of the radical cannot be reduced.

Example 10   Express the radicals in simplest radical form:

a. $\sqrt[8]{16x^{12}y^4z^{20}} = (2^4x^{12}y^4z^{20})^{1/8}$

$$= 2^{4/8}x^{12/8}y^{4/8}z^{20/8}$$

$$= 2^{1/2}x^{3/2}y^{1/2}z^{5/2} = (2x^3yz^5)^{1/2}$$

$$= \sqrt{2x^3yz^5} = xz^2\sqrt{2xyz}$$

b. $\sqrt[6]{\dfrac{8y^9}{x^3}} = \sqrt[6]{\dfrac{8y^9}{x^3}\cdot\dfrac{x^3}{x^3}} = \sqrt[6]{\dfrac{2^3y^9x^3}{x^6}} = \left(\dfrac{2^3y^9x^3}{x^6}\right)^{1/6}$

$$= \dfrac{2^{3/6}y^{9/6}x^{3/6}}{x^{6/6}} = \dfrac{2^{1/2}y^{3/2}x^{1/2}}{x} = \dfrac{(2xy^3)^{1/2}}{x}$$

$$= \dfrac{\sqrt{2xy^3}}{x} = \dfrac{y\sqrt{2xy}}{x} \quad or \quad \dfrac{y}{x}\sqrt{2xy} \quad \blacksquare$$

EXERCISES 7.2C

Set I   Express the radicals in simplest radical form; assume that all variables represent nonnegative numbers.

1. $\sqrt[6]{x^3}$ **2.** $\sqrt[6]{x^2}$ **3.** $\sqrt[8]{a^6}$ **4.** $\sqrt[8]{a^2}$

5. $\sqrt[6]{27b^3}$ **6.** $\sqrt[6]{4b^4}$ **7.** $\sqrt[6]{49a^2}$ **8.** $\sqrt[4]{144x^2}$

9. $\sqrt[8]{81x^4y^0z^{12}}$ **10.** $\sqrt[6]{27x^9y^3z^0}$ **11.** $\sqrt[6]{256x^8y^4z^{10}}$ **12.** $\sqrt[4]{64x^8y^2z^6}$

13. $\sqrt[6]{\dfrac{x^3}{27}}$ **14.** $\sqrt[6]{\dfrac{x^2}{4}}$ **15.** $\dfrac{1}{\sqrt[6]{a^3}}, a \neq 0$ **16.** $\dfrac{1}{\sqrt[4]{x^2}}, x \neq 0$

Set II   Express the radicals in simplest radical form; assume that all variables represent nonnegative numbers.

1. $\sqrt[6]{x^4}$ **2.** $\sqrt[10]{y^8}$ **3.** $\sqrt[6]{z^9}$ **4.** $\sqrt[8]{a^{10}}$

5. $\sqrt[6]{81x^4}$ **6.** $\sqrt[8]{16y^6}$ **7.** $\sqrt[4]{25y^2}$ **8.** $\sqrt[6]{64x^6y^9}$

9. $\sqrt[6]{16x^4y^0z^8w^{12}}$ **10.** $\sqrt[4]{81a^6b^8c^2}$ **11.** $\sqrt[6]{81a^6b^8c^{10}}$ **12.** $\sqrt[6]{5^0x^3y^9z^6}$

13. $\sqrt[6]{\dfrac{a^3}{64}}$ **14.** $\sqrt[6]{\dfrac{16x}{x^5}},\ x \neq 0$ **15.** $\dfrac{1}{\sqrt[8]{y^4}},\ y \neq 0$ **16.** $\dfrac{3}{\sqrt[4]{a^6}},\ a \neq 0$

7.3 Combining Radicals

Like Radicals   **Like radicals** are radicals that have the *same index* and the *same radicand*. The *coefficients* of the radicals can be different.

Example 1   Examples of like radicals:

a. $3\sqrt{5},\ 2\sqrt{5},\ -7\sqrt{5}$ Index $= 2$; radicand $= 5$

b. $2\sqrt[3]{x},\ -9\sqrt[3]{x},\ 11\sqrt[3]{x}$ Index $= 3$; radicand $= x$

c. $\dfrac{2}{3}\sqrt[4]{5ab},\ -\dfrac{1}{2}\sqrt[4]{5ab}$ Index $= 4$; radicand $= 5ab$ ∎

Unlike Radicals   **Unlike radicals** are radicals that have different indices or different radicands or both.

Example 2   Examples of unlike radicals:

a. $\sqrt{7},\ \sqrt{5}$ Different radicands

b. $\sqrt[3]{x},\ \sqrt{x}$ Different indices

c. $\sqrt[5]{2y},\ \sqrt[3]{2}$ Different indices and radicands ∎

When two or more *unlike* radicals are connected with addition or subtraction symbols, we usually cannot express the sum or difference with just one radical sign. We can find an *approximation* of the sum or difference by using a calculator.

A WORD OF CAUTION $\sqrt{a} + \sqrt{b} \neq \sqrt{a + b}$. To verify this, let $a = 9$ and $b = 16$. Then $\sqrt{9} + \sqrt{16} = 3 + 4 = 7$, but $\sqrt{9 + 16} = \sqrt{25} = 5$. Therefore, $\sqrt{9} + \sqrt{16} \neq \sqrt{9 + 16}$.   ☑

Combining Like Radicals
We can combine like radicals, as we can combine any like terms, by using the distributive property.

Example 3   Combine the like radicals:

a. $5\sqrt{2} + 3\sqrt{2} = (5 + 3)\sqrt{2} = 8\sqrt{2}$

b. $6\sqrt[3]{x} - 4\sqrt[3]{x} = (6 - 4)\sqrt[3]{x} = 2\sqrt[3]{x}$

c. $2x\sqrt[4]{5x} - x\sqrt[4]{5x} = (2x - x)\sqrt[4]{5x} = x\sqrt[4]{5x}$

d. $\dfrac{2}{3}\sqrt[5]{4xy^2} - 6\sqrt[5]{4xy^2} = \left(\dfrac{2}{3} - 6\right)\sqrt[5]{4xy^2} = -\dfrac{16}{3}\sqrt[5]{4xy^2}$ ∎

We can see from Example 3 that to combine like radicals we simply add the coefficients.

Combining Unlike Radicals

While most unlike radicals cannot be combined, some *can* be combined. Sometimes, terms that are not like radicals *become* like radicals after they have been expressed in simplest radical form; they can then be combined.

TO COMBINE UNLIKE RADICALS

1. Simplify each radical in the sum.

2. Then combine any terms that have like radicals by adding their coefficients and multiplying that sum by the like radical.

A radical expression with two or more terms is not in *simplest radical form* unless each term is in simplest radical form *and* all like terms have been combined. This condition must be added to the list of rules in Section 7.2C for expressing a radical in simplest terms.

Example 4   Express in simplest radical form; assume that all variables represent positive numbers:

a. $\sqrt{8} + \sqrt{18}$

$= \sqrt{4 \cdot 2} + \sqrt{9 \cdot 2}$

$= 2\sqrt{2} + 3\sqrt{2} = 5\sqrt{2}$

b. $\sqrt{12} + \sqrt{50}$

$= \sqrt{4 \cdot 3} + \sqrt{25 \cdot 2}$

$= 2\sqrt{3} + 5\sqrt{2}$

This expression cannot be simplified further; the radicals are not like radicals.

c. $\sqrt[4]{4} + \sqrt{2}$

$= \sqrt{2} + \sqrt{2}$

$= (1 + 1)\sqrt{2}$

$= 2\sqrt{2}$

d. $\sqrt{12x} - \sqrt{27x} + 5\sqrt{3x}$

$= \sqrt{4 \cdot 3 \cdot x} - \sqrt{9 \cdot 3 \cdot x} + 5\sqrt{3x}$

$= 2\sqrt{3x} - 3\sqrt{3x} + 5\sqrt{3x}$

$= (2 - 3 + 5)\sqrt{3x} = 4\sqrt{3x}$

e. $\sqrt[3]{24a^2} - 5\sqrt[3]{3a^5} + 2\sqrt[3]{81a^2}$

$= \sqrt[3]{2^3 \cdot 3 \cdot a^2} - 5\sqrt[3]{3 \cdot a^3 \cdot a^2} + 2\sqrt[3]{3^3 \cdot 3 \cdot a^2}$

$= 2\sqrt[3]{3a^2} - 5a\sqrt[3]{3a^2} + 2 \cdot 3\sqrt[3]{3a^2}$

$= (2 - 5a + 6)\sqrt[3]{3a^2} = (8 - 5a)\sqrt[3]{3a^2}$

f. $2\sqrt{\dfrac{1}{2}} - 6\sqrt{\dfrac{1}{8}} - 10\sqrt{\dfrac{4}{5}}$

$= \dfrac{2}{1}\sqrt{\dfrac{1}{2}\cdot\dfrac{2}{2}} - \dfrac{6}{1}\sqrt{\dfrac{1}{2^3}\cdot\dfrac{2}{2}} - \dfrac{10}{1}\sqrt{\dfrac{4}{5}\cdot\dfrac{5}{5}}$

$= \dfrac{2}{1}\cdot\dfrac{1}{2}\sqrt{2} - \dfrac{6}{1}\cdot\dfrac{1}{4}\sqrt{2} - \dfrac{10}{1}\cdot\dfrac{2}{5}\sqrt{5}$

$= \sqrt{2} - \dfrac{3}{2}\sqrt{2} - 4\sqrt{5}$

$= \left(1 - \dfrac{3}{2}\right)\sqrt{2} - 4\sqrt{5} = -\dfrac{1}{2}\sqrt{2} - 4\sqrt{5}$

g. $5\sqrt[4]{\dfrac{3x}{8}} + \dfrac{2x}{3}\sqrt[4]{\dfrac{1}{6^3x^3}}$

$= \dfrac{5}{1}\sqrt[4]{\dfrac{3x}{2^3}\cdot\dfrac{2}{2}} + \dfrac{2x}{3}\sqrt[4]{\dfrac{1}{6^3x^3}\cdot\dfrac{6x}{6x}}$

$= \dfrac{5}{2}\sqrt[4]{6x} + \dfrac{2x}{3}\cdot\dfrac{1}{6x}\sqrt[4]{6x}$

$= \dfrac{5}{2}\sqrt[4]{6x} + \dfrac{1}{9}\sqrt[4]{6x}$

$= \left(\dfrac{5}{2} + \dfrac{1}{9}\right)\sqrt[4]{6x} = \left(\dfrac{45}{18} + \dfrac{2}{18}\right)\sqrt[4]{6x} = \dfrac{47}{18}\sqrt[4]{6x}$ ∎

EXERCISES 7.3

Set I   Express in simplest radical form; assume that all variables represent positive numbers.

1. $8\sqrt{2} + 3\sqrt{2}$ 2. $12\sqrt{5} + 6\sqrt{5}$ 3. $3\sqrt{6} + \sqrt{6}$

4. $\sqrt{7} + 5\sqrt{7}$ 5. $\sqrt{15} + \sqrt{10}$ 6. $\sqrt{2} + \sqrt{14}$

7. $3\sqrt{5} - \sqrt{5}$ 8. $4\sqrt{3} - \sqrt{3}$ 9. $\sqrt{9} + \sqrt{12}$

10. $\sqrt{45} + \sqrt{25}$ 11. $\sqrt{12} - \sqrt{8}$ 12. $\sqrt{28} - \sqrt{3}$

13. $\sqrt{18} + \sqrt[4]{4}$ 14. $\sqrt{3} + \sqrt[4]{9}$ 15. $5\sqrt[3]{xy} + 2\sqrt[3]{xy}$

16. $7\sqrt[4]{ab} + 3\sqrt[4]{ab}$ 17. $2\sqrt{50} - \sqrt{32}$ 18. $3\sqrt{24} - \sqrt{54}$

19. $3\sqrt{32x} - \sqrt{8x}$ 20. $4\sqrt{27y} - 3\sqrt{12y}$

21. $\sqrt{125M} + \sqrt{20M} - \sqrt{45M}$ 22. $\sqrt{75P} - \sqrt{48P} + \sqrt{27P}$

23. $\sqrt[3]{27x} + \dfrac{1}{2}\sqrt[3]{8x}$ 24. $\dfrac{3}{4}\sqrt[3]{64a} + \sqrt[3]{27a}$

25. $\sqrt[3]{a^4} + 2a\sqrt[3]{8a}$ 26. $H\sqrt[3]{8H^2} + 3\sqrt[3]{H^5}$

27. $\sqrt[5]{x^2y^6} + \sqrt[5]{x^7y}$ 28. $\sqrt[5]{a^3b^8} + \sqrt[5]{a^8b^3}$

29. $3\sqrt{\dfrac{1}{6}} + \sqrt{12} - 5\sqrt{\dfrac{3}{2}}$ 30. $3\sqrt{\dfrac{5}{2}} + \sqrt{20} - 5\sqrt{\dfrac{1}{10}}$

31. $10\sqrt{\dfrac{5b}{4}} - \dfrac{3b}{2}\sqrt{\dfrac{4}{5b}}$ 32. $12\sqrt[3]{\dfrac{x^3}{16}} + x\sqrt[3]{\dfrac{1}{2}}$

33. $2k\sqrt[4]{\dfrac{3}{8k}} - \dfrac{1}{k}\sqrt[4]{\dfrac{2k^3}{27}} + 5k^2\sqrt[4]{\dfrac{6}{k^2}}$

34. $6\sqrt[3]{\dfrac{a^4}{54}} + 2a\sqrt[3]{\dfrac{a}{2}}$

35. $\sqrt{4x^2 + 4x + 1}$

36. $\sqrt{16a^2 + 8a + 1}$

Set II   Express in simplest radical form; assume that all variables represent positive numbers.

1. $5\sqrt{7} + 10\sqrt{7}$

2. $8\sqrt{5} + 2\sqrt{5}$

3. $9\sqrt{11} + \sqrt{11}$

4. $\sqrt{6} + \sqrt{6}$

5. $\sqrt{7} + \sqrt{2}$

6. $10\sqrt{3} + \sqrt{3}$

7. $5\sqrt{13} - 3\sqrt{13}$

8. $\sqrt{6} - \sqrt{2}$

9. $\sqrt{49} + \sqrt{28}$

10. $\sqrt{7} + \sqrt{18}$

11. $5\sqrt{50} - \sqrt{2}$

12. $3\sqrt{16} - \sqrt{2}$

13. $\sqrt{5} + \sqrt[4]{25}$

14. $\sqrt{50} + \sqrt{18}$

15. $8\sqrt[5]{5a} + \sqrt[5]{5a}$

16. $3\sqrt[3]{6x^2} - 5\sqrt[3]{6x^2}$

17. $7\sqrt{98} - 3\sqrt{50}$

18. $2\sqrt[3]{54a^2} + 4\sqrt[3]{16a^2}$

19. $8\sqrt{75x^5} + 2x\sqrt{3x^3}$

20. $3\sqrt{25} + 2\sqrt{72} - \sqrt{16}$

21. $7\sqrt{14x} - 2\sqrt{5x} + \sqrt{3x}$

22. $4\sqrt{27a^5} - a\sqrt{12a^3}$

23. $\sqrt[3]{64x} + \dfrac{1}{5}\sqrt[3]{8x}$

24. $\dfrac{1}{3}x\sqrt[4]{4x^2} + x\sqrt{8x}$

25. $\sqrt[3]{x^7} - 5x^2\sqrt[3]{x}$

26. $\sqrt{x^5y^7} + 2xy\sqrt{16xy^3} - \sqrt{xy^3}$

27. $\sqrt[6]{a^6b^3} + 6a\sqrt{a^2b^3}$

28. $\sqrt[3]{8x^5} + x\sqrt[6]{x^4} - \sqrt[3]{x}$

29. $5\sqrt{\dfrac{1}{8}} - 7\sqrt{\dfrac{1}{18}} - 5\sqrt{\dfrac{1}{50}}$

30. $8\sqrt[3]{\dfrac{a^3}{32}} + a\sqrt[3]{54}$

31. $12\sqrt{\dfrac{7z}{9}} - \dfrac{4z}{5}\sqrt{\dfrac{25}{7z}}$

32. $12\sqrt[3]{\dfrac{x^5}{24}} + 6x\sqrt[3]{\dfrac{x^2}{3}}$

33. $3h^2\sqrt[4]{\dfrac{4}{27h}} + 4h^2\sqrt[4]{\dfrac{5}{8}} - 2h^2\sqrt[4]{\dfrac{12}{h}}$

34. $\sqrt{\dfrac{x^3}{3y^3}} + xy\sqrt{\dfrac{x}{3y^5}} - \dfrac{y^2}{3}\sqrt{\dfrac{3x^3}{y^7}}$

35. $\sqrt{a^2 + 6a + 9}$

36. $\sqrt{25x^2 - 10x + 1}$

7.4 Multiplying and Dividing Radicals

7.4A Multiplying Radicals When the Indices Are the Same

To multiply two or more radicals together when the *indices* are the same, we use Rule 7.3.

TO MULTIPLY RADICALS

We assume that a and b are not both negative if n is even.

1. Replace $\sqrt[n]{a}\,\sqrt[n]{b}$ by $\sqrt[n]{a \cdot b}$ (Rule 7.3).

2. Simplify the resulting radical (Section 7.2A).

Example 1   Multiply the radicals; assume that all variables represent nonnegative numbers.

a. $\sqrt{3y}\sqrt{12y^3} = \sqrt{3y \cdot 12y^3} = \sqrt{36y^4} = 6y^2$

b. $2\sqrt[3]{2x^2} \cdot 3\sqrt[3]{4x} = 2 \cdot 3\sqrt[3]{8x^3} = 6 \cdot 2x = 12x$

c. $\sqrt[4]{8ab^3}\sqrt[4]{4a^3b^2} = \sqrt[4]{2^3ab^3 \cdot 2^2a^3b^2} = \sqrt[4]{2^5a^4b^5}$

$\qquad = \sqrt[4]{2^4 \cdot 2 \cdot a^4 \cdot b^4 \cdot b} = 2ab\sqrt[4]{2b}$

d. $(4\sqrt{3})^2 = 4\sqrt{3} \cdot 4\sqrt{3} = 16\sqrt{3 \cdot 3} = 16 \cdot 3 = 48$ ∎

We now have a final condition to be added to our list for simplest radical form:

AN ALGEBRAIC EXPRESSION IS IN SIMPLEST RADICAL FORM IF:

1. The radicand is a positive number.

2. No prime factor of a radicand has an exponent equal to or greater than the index.

3. No radicand contains a fraction.

4. No denominator contains a radical.

5. The order of the radical cannot be reduced.

6. All like radicals have been combined.

7. No term of the expression contains more than one radical sign.

The distributive property is used to multiply algebraic expressions containing two or more terms with radicals by another algebraic expression. If we need to multiply two algebraic expressions containing two terms each, we can use the FOIL method, even though the expressions are not polynomials.

Example 2   Find $\sqrt{8x}(\sqrt{8x} - 3\sqrt{2})$ and simplify. Assume $x > 0$.

$$\sqrt{8x}(\sqrt{8x} - 3\sqrt{2}) = \sqrt{8x} \cdot \sqrt{8x} - \sqrt{8x} \cdot 3\sqrt{2}$$

$$= \sqrt{64x^2} - 3\sqrt{16x}$$

$$= 8x - 3 \cdot 4\sqrt{x}$$

$$= 8x - 12\sqrt{x}$$ ∎

Example 3   Find $(\sqrt{3} - 5)(\sqrt{3} + 2)$ and simplify.

Solution Using the FOIL method, we have,

$$(\sqrt{3} - 5)(\sqrt{3} + 2) = \sqrt{3} \cdot \sqrt{3} + 2\sqrt{3} - 5\sqrt{3} - 5 \cdot 2$$

$$= 3 - 3\sqrt{3} - 10$$

$$= -7 - 3\sqrt{3}$$ ∎

Example 4   Find $(3\sqrt{5} - 4)^2$ and simplify.

We square this as we would any binomial

Solution

$$(3\sqrt{5} - 4)^2 = (3\sqrt{5})^2 - 2(3\sqrt{5})(4) + 4^2$$
$$= 9 \cdot 5 - 24\sqrt{5} + 16$$
$$= 45 - 24\sqrt{5} + 16$$
$$= 61 - 24\sqrt{5} \quad \blacksquare$$

Example 5   Find $(\sqrt[4]{x} - 1)^4$ and simplify; assume $x \geq 0$.

We use the binomial theorem here, even though $\sqrt[4]{x} - 1$ is not a binomial. The coefficients are 1, 4, 6, 4, and 1.

$$(\sqrt[4]{x} - 1)^4$$
$$= (\sqrt[4]{x})^4 - 4(\sqrt[4]{x})^3(1) + 6(\sqrt[4]{x})^2(1)^2 - 4(\sqrt[4]{x})^1(1)^3 + 1^4$$

$$(\sqrt[4]{x})^2 = \sqrt[4]{x^2} = \sqrt{x}$$

$$= x - 4\sqrt[4]{x^3} + 6\sqrt{x} - 4\sqrt[4]{x} + 1 \quad \blacksquare$$

Example 6   Find $(x^{1/3} + y^{1/3})^3$ and simplify.

We use the binomial theorem, even though $x^{1/3} + y^{1/3}$ is not a binomial. The coefficients are 1, 3, 3, and 1.

$$(x^{1/3} + y^{1/3})^3$$
$$= (x^{1/3})^3 + 3(x^{1/3})^2(y^{1/3}) + 3(x^{1/3})(y^{1/3})^2 + (y^{1/3})^3$$
$$= x + 3x^{2/3}y^{1/3} + 3x^{1/3}y^{2/3} + y \quad \blacksquare$$

EXERCISES 7.4A

Set I   In Exercises 1–38, simplify each expression. Assume that all variables represent nonnegative numbers.

1. $\sqrt{3}\sqrt{3}$

2. $\sqrt{7}\sqrt{7}$

3. $\sqrt[3]{3}\sqrt[3]{9}$

4. $\sqrt[3]{4}\sqrt[3]{16}$

5. $\sqrt[4]{9}\sqrt[4]{9}$

6. $\sqrt[4]{25}\sqrt[4]{25}$

7. $\sqrt{5ab^2}\sqrt{20ab}$

8. $\sqrt{3x^2y}\sqrt{27xy}$

9. $3\sqrt[5]{2a^3b} \cdot 2\sqrt[5]{16a^2b}$

10. $4\sqrt[5]{4cb^4} \cdot 5\sqrt[5]{8c^2b}$

11. $(5\sqrt{7})^2$

12. $(4\sqrt{6})^2$

13. $\sqrt{2}(\sqrt{2} + 1)$

14. $\sqrt{3}(\sqrt{3} + 1)$

15. $\sqrt{x}(\sqrt{x} - 3)$

16. $\sqrt{y}(4 - \sqrt{y})$

17. $\sqrt{3}(2\sqrt{3} + 1)$

18. $\sqrt{5}(3\sqrt{5} + 1)$

19. $\sqrt{3x}(\sqrt{3x} - 4\sqrt{12})$

20. $\sqrt{5a}(\sqrt{10} + 3\sqrt{5a})$

21. $(\sqrt{7} + 2)(\sqrt{7} + 3)$

22. $(\sqrt{3} + 2)(\sqrt{3} + 4)$

23. $(5 + \sqrt{3})(5 - \sqrt{3})$

24. $(\sqrt{5} + \sqrt{3})(\sqrt{5} - \sqrt{3})$

25. $(2\sqrt{3} - 5)^2$

26. $(5\sqrt{2} - 3)^2$

27. $2\sqrt{7x^3y^3} \cdot 5\sqrt{3xy} \cdot 2\sqrt{7x^3y}$

28. $3\sqrt{5xy} \cdot 4\sqrt{2x^5y^3} \cdot 5\sqrt{5x^3y^5}$

29. $(3\sqrt{2x + 5})^2$

30. $(4\sqrt{3x - 2})^2$

31. $(\sqrt{2x} + 3)(\sqrt{2x} - 3)$

32. $(\sqrt{5x} + 7)(\sqrt{5x} - 7)$

33. $(\sqrt{xy} - 6\sqrt{y})^2$ **34.** $(\sqrt{ab} + 2\sqrt{a})^2$

35. $(\sqrt[5]{x} + 1)^5$ **36.** $(1 + \sqrt[3]{y})^3$

37. $(x^{1/4} + 1)^4$ **38.** $(x^{1/2} + y^{1/2})^2$

39. Find the value of $x^4 - 1$ if $x = 1 - \sqrt{2}$.

40. Find the value of $x^3 + 1$ if $x = 1 + \sqrt{2}$.

Set II   In Exercises 1–38, simplify each expression. Assume that all variables represent nonnegative numbers.

1. $\sqrt{13}\sqrt{13}$ **2.** $\sqrt{2}\sqrt{32}$ **3.** $\sqrt[3]{5}\sqrt[3]{25}$

4. $\sqrt[5]{48}\sqrt[5]{4}$ **5.** $\sqrt[4]{49}\sqrt[4]{49}$ **6.** $\sqrt[4]{2}\sqrt[4]{8}$

7. $\sqrt[5]{4x^2y^3}\sqrt[5]{8x^3y^2}$ **8.** $\sqrt[3]{4x^2y^2}\sqrt[3]{2x^2y}$ **9.** $5\sqrt[5]{x^8y^6} \cdot 4\sqrt[5]{x^2y^4}$

10. $6\sqrt[3]{24a^4b^2} \cdot 5a\sqrt[3]{3ab^2}$ **11.** $(3\sqrt{2})^2$ **12.** $(2\sqrt{5})^3$

13. $\sqrt{5}(\sqrt{5} + 1)$ **14.** $\sqrt{8}(\sqrt{2} - 4)$ **15.** $\sqrt{z}(\sqrt{z} - 5)$

16. $\sqrt{5x}(\sqrt{5x} - 2)$ **17.** $\sqrt{7}(3\sqrt{7} + 2)$ **18.** $\sqrt{27}(4\sqrt{3} + 5)$

19. $\sqrt{2y}(10\sqrt{10y} + 2\sqrt{6})$ **20.** $\sqrt{3a}(4\sqrt{3a} + 2)$

21. $(\sqrt{11} + 2)(\sqrt{11} + 5)$ **22.** $(\sqrt{7} + 3)(\sqrt{7} - 3)$

23. $(\sqrt{6} - \sqrt{3})(\sqrt{6} + \sqrt{3})$ **24.** $(2 - \sqrt{6})(2 + \sqrt{6})$

25. $(2\sqrt{5} - 4)^2$ **26.** $(\sqrt{5} + \sqrt{3})^2$

27. $3\sqrt{5x^4y^3} \cdot 2\sqrt{15xy^5} \cdot 5\sqrt{2x^2y}$ **28.** $8\sqrt[4]{6a^3b^5} \cdot 3\sqrt[4]{2ab^3} \cdot 2\sqrt[4]{8a^2b^4}$

29. $(5\sqrt{3x} - 4)^2$ **30.** $(4\sqrt{5} - 2a)^2$

31. $(\sqrt{7x} + 3)(\sqrt{7x} - 3)$ **32.** $(8 - \sqrt{7x})(8 + \sqrt{7x})$

33. $(\sqrt{x} + 3\sqrt{y})^2$ **34.** $(3\sqrt{a} - \sqrt{2b})^2$

35. $(\sqrt[4]{x} + 2)^4$ **36.** $(\sqrt[4]{x} - \sqrt[4]{y})^4$

37. $(x^{1/3} - 1)^3$ **38.** $(x^{1/5} + 2)^5$

39. Find the value of $y^2 - 2y - 5$ if $y = 1 - \sqrt{6}$.

40. Find the value of $x^4 + 1$ if $x = 1 + \sqrt{2}$.

7.4B   Dividing Radicals When the Indices Are the Same

To divide radicals when the indices are the same, we use Rule 7.4.

TO DIVIDE RADICALS

We assume that a and b are not both negative if n is even.

1. Replace $\dfrac{\sqrt[n]{a}}{\sqrt[n]{b}}$ by $\sqrt[n]{\dfrac{a}{b}}$ (Rule 7.4).

2. Simplify the resulting radical (Section 7.2B).

Example 7   Divide the radicals; assume that all variables represent positive numbers:

a. $\dfrac{12\sqrt[3]{a^5}}{2\sqrt[3]{a^2}} = \dfrac{6}{1}\sqrt[3]{\dfrac{a^5}{a^2}} = 6\sqrt[3]{a^3} = 6a$

b. $\dfrac{5\sqrt[4]{28xy^6}}{10\sqrt[4]{7xy}} = \dfrac{1}{2}\sqrt[4]{\dfrac{28xy^6}{7xy}} = \dfrac{1}{2}\sqrt[4]{4y^5} = \dfrac{1}{2}\sqrt[4]{4y^4y} = \dfrac{y}{2}\sqrt[4]{4y}$

c. $\dfrac{\sqrt{5x}}{\sqrt{10x^2}} = \sqrt{\dfrac{5x}{10x^2}} = \sqrt{\dfrac{1}{2x}} = \sqrt{\dfrac{1}{2x}\cdot\dfrac{2x}{2x}} = \dfrac{1}{2x}\sqrt{2x}$ ∎

When the dividend contains more than one term but the divisor contains only one term, we divide *each term* of the dividend by the divisor (see Example 8). This procedure is similar to that used in dividing a polynomial by a monomial.

Example 8   Divide the radicals:

a. $\dfrac{3\sqrt{14} - \sqrt{8}}{\sqrt{2}} = \dfrac{3\sqrt{14}}{\sqrt{2}} - \dfrac{\sqrt{8}}{\sqrt{2}} = 3\sqrt{\dfrac{14}{2}} - \sqrt{\dfrac{8}{2}} = 3\sqrt{7} - \sqrt{4} = 3\sqrt{7} - 2$

b. $\dfrac{3\sqrt[5]{64a} - 9\sqrt[5]{4a^3}}{3\sqrt[5]{2a}} = \dfrac{3\sqrt[5]{64a}}{3\sqrt[5]{2a}} - \dfrac{9\sqrt[5]{4a^3}}{3\sqrt[5]{2a}} = \sqrt[5]{\dfrac{64a}{2a}} - 3\sqrt[5]{\dfrac{4a^3}{2a}}$

$= \sqrt[5]{32} - 3\sqrt[5]{2a^2} = 2 - 3\sqrt[5]{2a^2}$ ∎

Rationalizing a Denominator That Contains Two Terms

In order to discuss division problems in which the divisor contains radicals and has two terms, we need a new definition.

CONJUGATE

The **conjugate** of the algebraic expression $a + b$ is the algebraic expression $a - b$.

Example 9   Examples of conjugates:

a. The conjugate of $1 + \sqrt{3}$ is $1 - \sqrt{3}$.

b. The conjugate of $\sqrt{5} - \sqrt{3}$ is $\sqrt{5} + \sqrt{3}$.

c. The conjugate of $\sqrt{x} - \sqrt{y}$ is $\sqrt{x} + \sqrt{y}$.   ∎

If an algebraic expression contains *square roots* and has two terms, then the product of the expression and its conjugate will always be a rational number. For example, the conjugate of $1 + \sqrt{3}$ is $1 - \sqrt{3}$.

$$(1 + \sqrt{3})(1 - \sqrt{3}) = (1)^2 - (\sqrt{3})^2$$

$$= 1 - 3 = -2 \qquad \text{Rational number}$$

Because of this fact, the following procedure should be used when a denominator with two terms contains square roots.

TO RATIONALIZE A DENOMINATOR THAT
CONTAINS SQUARE ROOTS AND HAS TWO TERMS

Multiply the numerator and the denominator by the conjugate of the denominator.

Example 10   Rationalize the denominator and simplify:

a. $\dfrac{2}{1 + \sqrt{3}} = \dfrac{2}{1 + \sqrt{3}} \cdot \dfrac{1 - \sqrt{3}}{1 - \sqrt{3}} = \dfrac{2(1 - \sqrt{3})}{1 - 3} = \dfrac{2(1 - \sqrt{3})}{-2} = \sqrt{3} - 1$

Multiply numerator and denominator
by $1 - \sqrt{3}$ (the conjugate of the
denominator $1 + \sqrt{3}$)

b. $\dfrac{\sqrt{5} + \sqrt{3}}{\sqrt{5} - \sqrt{3}} = \dfrac{\sqrt{5} + \sqrt{3}}{\sqrt{5} - \sqrt{3}} \cdot \dfrac{\sqrt{5} + \sqrt{3}}{\sqrt{5} + \sqrt{3}} = \dfrac{5 + 2\sqrt{15} + 3}{5 - 3} = \dfrac{8 + 2\sqrt{15}}{2}$

$= \dfrac{2(4 + \sqrt{15})}{2} = 4 + \sqrt{15}$ ∎

Multiply numerator and
denominator by $\sqrt{5} + \sqrt{3}$ (the
conjugate of the denominator
$\sqrt{5} - \sqrt{3}$)

EXERCISES 7.4B

Set I   Simplify each expression; assume that all variables represent positive numbers.

1. $\dfrac{\sqrt{32}}{\sqrt{2}}$

2. $\dfrac{\sqrt{98}}{\sqrt{2}}$

3. $\dfrac{\sqrt[3]{5}}{\sqrt[3]{4}}$

4. $\dfrac{\sqrt[3]{7}}{\sqrt[3]{2}}$

5. $\dfrac{12\sqrt[4]{15x}}{4\sqrt[4]{5x}}$

6. $\dfrac{15\sqrt[4]{18y}}{5\sqrt[4]{3y}}$

7. $\dfrac{\sqrt[5]{128z^7}}{\sqrt[5]{2z}}$

8. $\dfrac{\sqrt[5]{3^7 b^8}}{\sqrt[5]{3b^2}}$

9. $\dfrac{\sqrt{72x^3 y^2}}{\sqrt{2xy^2}}$

10. $\dfrac{\sqrt{27x^2 y^3}}{\sqrt{3x^2 y}}$

11. $\dfrac{\sqrt{20} + 5\sqrt{10}}{\sqrt{5}}$

12. $\dfrac{2\sqrt{6} + \sqrt{18}}{\sqrt{6}}$

13. $\dfrac{6\sqrt[4]{2^5 m^2}}{2\sqrt[4]{2m^3}}$

14. $\dfrac{7\sqrt[4]{3^5 H^3}}{14\sqrt[4]{3H^4}}$

15. $\dfrac{4\sqrt[3]{8x} + 6\sqrt[3]{32x^4}}{2\sqrt[3]{4x}}$

16. $\dfrac{10\sqrt[3]{81a^7} + 15\sqrt[3]{6a}}{5\sqrt[3]{3a}}$

17. $\dfrac{6}{\sqrt{3} - 1}$

18. $\dfrac{10}{\sqrt{3} + 1}$

19. $\dfrac{\sqrt{2}}{\sqrt{3} + \sqrt{2}}$

20. $\dfrac{\sqrt{7}}{\sqrt{7} - \sqrt{2}}$

21. $\dfrac{\sqrt{7} + \sqrt{3}}{\sqrt{7} - \sqrt{3}}$

22. $\dfrac{\sqrt{11} - \sqrt{5}}{\sqrt{11} + \sqrt{5}}$

23. $\dfrac{4\sqrt{3} - \sqrt{2}}{4\sqrt{3} + \sqrt{2}}$

24. $\dfrac{\sqrt{x + 1} - \sqrt{x}}{\sqrt{x + 1} + \sqrt{x}}$

25. $\sqrt{\dfrac{a^2 + 2a - 3}{a^2 + 4a + 3}}, \ a > 1$

26. $\sqrt{\dfrac{m^2 - m - 2}{m^2 - 3m + 2}}, \ m > 2$

Set II   Simplify each expression; assume that all variables represent positive numbers.

1. $\dfrac{\sqrt{72}}{\sqrt{2}}$

2. $\dfrac{\sqrt{75}}{\sqrt{3}}$

3. $\dfrac{\sqrt[5]{3}}{\sqrt[5]{4}}$

4. $\dfrac{\sqrt[3]{x^8 y}}{\sqrt[3]{5xy^2}}$

5. $\dfrac{30\sqrt[4]{64x}}{6\sqrt[4]{4x}}$

6. $\dfrac{35\sqrt[5]{96x^5}}{7\sqrt[5]{6x^3}}$

7. $\dfrac{\sqrt{x^4 y}}{\sqrt{5y}}$

8. $\dfrac{\sqrt{m^6 n}}{\sqrt{3n}}$

9. $\dfrac{\sqrt{300a^5 b^2}}{\sqrt{3ab^2}}$

10. $\dfrac{\sqrt[4]{2xy^3}}{\sqrt[4]{27x^2 y}}$

11. $\dfrac{\sqrt{34} + 2\sqrt{6}}{\sqrt{2}}$

12. $\dfrac{3\sqrt{27} - \sqrt{2}}{\sqrt{3}}$

13. $\dfrac{6\sqrt[3]{4B^2}}{9\sqrt[3]{8B^4}}$

14. $\dfrac{5\sqrt[3]{3K^3}}{15\sqrt[3]{9K^5}}$

15. $\dfrac{30\sqrt[4]{32a^6} - 6\sqrt[4]{24a^2}}{3\sqrt[4]{2a^2}}$

16. $\dfrac{8\sqrt[3]{2x} - 4\sqrt[3]{3x^4}}{2\sqrt[3]{5x^2}}$

17. $\dfrac{8}{\sqrt{5} - 1}$

18. $\dfrac{3}{\sqrt{6} + 1}$

19. $\dfrac{\sqrt{7}}{\sqrt{3} + \sqrt{7}}$

20. $\dfrac{21}{3\sqrt{5} + 2\sqrt{6}}$

21. $\dfrac{\sqrt{5} + \sqrt{2}}{\sqrt{5} - \sqrt{2}}$

22. $\dfrac{3\sqrt{2} + \sqrt{6}}{3\sqrt{2} - \sqrt{6}}$

23. $\dfrac{5\sqrt{7} + \sqrt{3}}{5\sqrt{7} - \sqrt{3}}$

24. $\dfrac{x - 4}{\sqrt{x} + 2}$

25. $\sqrt{\dfrac{a^2 + 2ab + b^2}{a^2 - b^2}}, \ a > b$

26. $\sqrt{\dfrac{x^2 - y^2}{x^2 - 2xy + y^2}}, \ x > y$

7.4C   Multiplying and Dividing Radicals When the Indices Are Not the Same

In this section, we will assume that all variables represent positive numbers.

    If all radicands can be expressed as powers of the same base, it is possible to multiply and divide radicals even when the indices are not the same. The easiest way to do this is to (1) write any numerical coefficients in prime factored form, (2) convert the radicals to exponential form, (3) perform the indicated multiplication or division, and (4) express the answer in simplest radical form.

Example 11   Perform the indicated operations and express the answers in simplest radical form:

a. $\sqrt{x}\,\sqrt[3]{x} = x^{1/2} x^{1/3} = x^{3/6} x^{2/6} = x^{5/6} = \sqrt[6]{x^5}$

b. $\sqrt{2}\,\sqrt[3]{-32} = 2^{1/2}(-2^5)^{1/3} = -2^{1/2 + 5/3} = -2^{3/6 + 10/6} = -2^{13/6}$

$$= -2^{2 + 1/6} = -2^2 \cdot 2^{1/6} = -4\sqrt[6]{2}$$

c. $\sqrt[4]{a^3}\,\sqrt{a}\,\sqrt[3]{a^2} = a^{3/4} a^{1/2} a^{2/3} = a^{9/12} a^{6/12} a^{8/12} = a^{23/12} = a^{1 + 11/12}$

$$= a \cdot a^{11/12} = a\sqrt[12]{a^{11}}$$

d. $\dfrac{\sqrt[3]{-d^2}}{\sqrt[4]{d^3}} = \dfrac{-d^{2/3}}{d^{3/4}} = -d^{2/3 - 3/4} = -d^{8/12 - 9/12} = -d^{-1/12} = -\dfrac{1}{\sqrt[12]{d}}$

We can use fractional exponents to rationalize the denominator as follows:

$$-\frac{1}{\sqrt[12]{d}} = -\frac{1}{d^{1/12}} \cdot \frac{d^{11/12}}{d^{11/12}} = -\frac{\sqrt[12]{d^{11}}}{d}$$

Multiply by the expression that will make the exponent in the denominator a whole number, in this case, $d^{1/12} \cdot d^{11/12} = d^{12/12} = d^1$ ∎

EXERCISES 7.4C

Set I   In the exercises below, perform the indicated operations. Express the answers in simplest radical form. Assume that all variables represent positive numbers.

1. $\sqrt{a}\sqrt[4]{a}$

2. $\sqrt{b}\sqrt[3]{b}$

3. $\sqrt{8}\sqrt[3]{16}$

4. $\sqrt{27}\sqrt[3]{81}$

5. $\sqrt[3]{x^2}\sqrt[4]{x^3}\sqrt{x}$

6. $\sqrt{y}\sqrt[3]{y}\sqrt[4]{y^3}$

7. $\sqrt[3]{-8z^2}\sqrt[3]{-z}\sqrt[4]{16z^3}$

8. $\sqrt[3]{-27w}\sqrt[3]{-w^2}\sqrt[4]{16w^3}$

9. $\dfrac{\sqrt[4]{G^3}}{\sqrt[3]{G^2}}$

10. $\dfrac{\sqrt[5]{H^4}}{\sqrt{H}}$

11. $\dfrac{\sqrt[3]{-x^2}}{\sqrt[6]{x^5}}$

12. $\dfrac{\sqrt[6]{y^3}}{\sqrt[3]{-y^2}}$

Set II   In the exercises below, perform the indicated operations. Express the answers in simplest radical form. Assume that all variables represent positive numbers.

1. $\sqrt[3]{a^2}\sqrt[6]{a^2}$

2. $\sqrt[2]{x^3}\sqrt[5]{x^4}$

3. $\sqrt{2}\sqrt[6]{8}$

4. $\sqrt[5]{3}\sqrt[5]{81}$

5. $\sqrt{x}\sqrt[4]{x^3}\sqrt[8]{x^6}$

6. $\sqrt[3]{a}\sqrt[5]{a^2}\sqrt[6]{a^4}$

7. $\sqrt[3]{-5x^2}\sqrt[4]{x^5}\sqrt[3]{-25x^3}$

8. $\sqrt[3]{x}\sqrt[5]{x^3}\sqrt[4]{x^6}$

9. $\dfrac{\sqrt[4]{a^3}}{\sqrt[3]{a^5}}$

10. $\dfrac{\sqrt[3]{x^2}}{\sqrt[5]{x^6}}$

11. $\dfrac{\sqrt[3]{-x^4}}{\sqrt{x^3}}$

12. $\dfrac{\sqrt[4]{32x^3}}{\sqrt{2x}}$

7.5 Review: 7.1–7.4

Relations between Exponents and Radicals
7.1

Rule 7.1 $\sqrt[n]{x} = x^{1/n}$, if $x \geq 0$ when n is even.

Rule 7.2 $\sqrt[b]{x^a} = (\sqrt[b]{x})^a = x^{a/b}$, if $x \geq 0$ when b is even.

Simplifying Radicals
7.2

Factor the radicand and use the following formulas:

Rule 7.3 $\sqrt[n]{ab} = \sqrt[n]{a}\sqrt[n]{b}$

Rule 7.4 $\sqrt[n]{\dfrac{a}{b}} = \dfrac{\sqrt[n]{a}}{\sqrt[n]{b}}$

} if a and b are not *both* negative when n is even.

Simplified Form of a Radical Expression
7.2, 7.3, 7.4

An algebraic expression is in simplest radical form if:

1. The radicand is a positive number.

2. No prime factor of a radicand has an exponent equal to or greater than the index.

3. No radicand contains a fraction.

4. No denominator contains a radical.

5. The order of the radical cannot be reduced.

6. All like radicals have been combined.

7. No term of the expression contains more than one radical sign.

Rationalizing the Denominator
7.2B

Denominator with a single term: Multiply the numerator and denominator by an expression that will make the exponent of every factor in the radicand of the denominator exactly divisible by the index.

7.4B

Denominator with two terms: Multiply the numerator and denominator by the *conjugate* of the denominator.

Addition of Radicals
7.3

Like radicals: Add their coefficients.

Unlike radicals:

1. Simplify each radical.

2. Then combine any terms that have like radicals by adding their coefficients and multiplying their sum by the like radical.

Multiplication of Radicals
7.4A, 7.4C

Use the formula $\sqrt[n]{a}\,\sqrt[n]{b} = \sqrt[n]{ab}$ (if a and b are not both negative when n is even); then simplify.

Division of Radicals
7.4B, 7.4C

Use the formula $\dfrac{\sqrt[n]{a}}{\sqrt[n]{b}} = \sqrt[n]{\dfrac{a}{b}}$ (if a and b are not both negative when n is even); then simplify.

Review Exercises 7.5 Set I

In Exercises 1–3, rewrite each expression in an equivalent radical form. Assume $a \geq 0$ and $y \geq 0$.

1. $a^{3/4}$ **2.** $(3y)^{3/4}$ **3.** $(2x^2)^{2/5}$

In Exercises 4–6, replace each radical with an equivalent exponential expression. Assume $b \geq 0$.

4. $\sqrt[4]{b^3}$ **5.** $\sqrt[5]{8x^4}$ **6.** $\sqrt[5]{27x^3}$

In Exercises 7 and 8, evaluate each expression.

7. $(-64)^{2/3}$ **8.** $(-27)^{2/3}$

In Exercises 9 and 10, perform the indicated operations. Express the answers in exponential form, using positive exponents. Assume $R \geq 0$, $a > 0$, and $b > 0$.

9. $(P^{2/3}R^{3/4})^{2/3}$

10. $\left(\dfrac{27a^{1/3}b^{2/3}}{3b^{-1}}\right)^{-3/2}$

In Exercises 11–16, simplify each expression. Assume $y > 0$.

11. $\sqrt[3]{32}$

12. $\sqrt[3]{-125x^3}$

13. $\sqrt[4]{16y^8}$

14. $\dfrac{1}{3}\sqrt[5]{3^5 m^6 p}$

15. $\sqrt{\dfrac{20x^3}{5y}}$

16. $\dfrac{15}{\sqrt{3y}}$

In Exercises 17–28, perform the indicated operations and give your answers in simplest radical form. Assume that all variables represent positive numbers.

17. $\sqrt[3]{-2x}\,\sqrt[3]{-4x^4}$

18. $(5\sqrt{3x})^2$

19. $\dfrac{\sqrt{3}+\sqrt{7}}{\sqrt{3}-\sqrt{7}}$

20. $\dfrac{8}{\sqrt{5}+1}$

21. $(\sqrt{2}+3)(4\sqrt{2}-1)$

22. $(\sqrt{13}+\sqrt{3})^2$

23. $\sqrt[3]{16x^5}+x\sqrt[3]{54x^2}$

24. $(\sqrt{13}-2)(\sqrt{13}+2)$

25. $\sqrt[3]{-z^2}\,\sqrt[4]{z^2}$

26. $(\sqrt[4]{2}-x)^4$

27. $\dfrac{\sqrt[4]{G^2}}{\sqrt[5]{G}}$

28. $3\sqrt[4]{\dfrac{2ab}{32a^3}}-\dfrac{1}{2}\sqrt[4]{\dfrac{b}{a^2}}$

In Exercises 29 and 30, factor the expression completely.

29. $14x^{-2/3}y^{1/4}z^{1/3}-7x^{1/3}y^{-3/4}z^{-2/3}$

30. $4x^{-2}-x^{-1}-3$

Review Exercises 7.5 Set II

In Exercises 1–3, rewrite each expression in an equivalent radical form.

1. $R^{4/5}$ **2.** $(4x^2)^{3/5}$ **3.** $B^{2/3}$

1. _____

2. _____

3. _____

In Exercises 4–6, replace each radical with an equivalent exponential expression. Assume $x \geq 0$.

4. $\sqrt[3]{8y^2}$ **5.** $(\sqrt[4]{x^3})^2$ **6.** $\sqrt[5]{a^2}$

4. _____

5. _____

6. _____

In Exercises 7 and 8, evaluate each expression.

7. $(-32)^{2/5}$ **8.** $(-125)^{2/3}$

7. _____

8. _____

9. _____

In Exercises 9 and 10, perform the indicated operations. Express the answers in exponential form, using positive exponents. Assume $x > 0$ and $y \geq 0$.

9. $(x^{3/2}y^{3/4})^{2/3}$ **10.** $\left(\dfrac{27x^{-1}y^{2/3}}{3x^{1/3}}\right)^{1/2}$

10. _____

11. _____

12. _____

13. _____

In Exercises 11–16, simplify each expression. Assume $b > 0$ and $a \geq 0$.

11. $\sqrt[3]{81}$ **12.** $\sqrt[5]{32x^{10}}$ **13.** $\sqrt[3]{36x^4}$

14. _____

15. _____

16. _____

14. $3b\sqrt[4]{\dfrac{a^3}{27b}}$ **15.** $\dfrac{1}{2}\sqrt[3]{16m^4n^7}$ **16.** $\dfrac{b}{3}\sqrt[3]{\dfrac{-27a}{b^2}}$

In Exercises 17–28, perform the indicated operations and give your answers in simplest radical form. Assume all variables represent positive numbers.

17. $\sqrt[3]{-3a^2}\,\sqrt[3]{-9a^2}$

18. $\dfrac{3+\sqrt{5}}{1-\sqrt{5}}$

19. $(4+\sqrt{2x})^2$

20. $z\sqrt[3]{32z}+\sqrt[3]{4z^4}$

21. $\dfrac{3\sqrt{2}-1}{2\sqrt{2}+3}$

22. $2\sqrt[4]{\dfrac{xy}{81x^3}}-\dfrac{1}{3}\sqrt[4]{\dfrac{y^2}{x^2y}}$

23. $(\sqrt{7z}-\sqrt{3})(\sqrt{7z}+\sqrt{3})$

24. $(\sqrt[4]{x}+2)^4$

25. $(2\sqrt{3z})^3$

26. $\sqrt[3]{-M^2}\,\sqrt[6]{M^4}$

27. $\dfrac{\sqrt[6]{H^4}}{\sqrt[5]{H^3}}$

28. $(x-\sqrt{3})^2$

29. Factor $4x^{-2}-12x^{-1}+5$.

30. Factor $18a^{2/3}b^{-2/3}c^{4/5}-10a^{-1/3}b^{1/3}c^{-1/5}$.

17. _____
18. _____
19. _____
20. _____
21. _____
22. _____
23. _____
24. _____
25. _____
26. _____
27. _____
28. _____
29. _____
30. _____

7.6 Radical Equations

Radical Equations

A **radical equation** is an equation in which the variable appears in a radicand. If the index of the radical is an *even* number, then the domain of the variable is the set of all real numbers that will make the radicand greater than or equal to zero. Recall that even roots of negative numbers are not real numbers. If the index is an *odd* number, the domain is the set of all real numbers.

Example 1   Find the domain in each of these radical equations (*do not solve the equations*):

a. $\sqrt{x + 2} = 3$

$$x + 2 \geq 0 \qquad \text{The } \textit{radicand} \text{ must be } \geq 0$$

$$x \geq -2$$

The domain is $\{x | x \geq -2\}$.

b. $\sqrt[3]{x - 1} = -4$

The domain is the set of all real numbers, because the index of the radical is not an even number.

c. $\sqrt{4x + 5} - \sqrt{x - 1} = 3$

$$4x + 5 \geq 0 \qquad and \quad x - 1 \geq 0$$

$$x \geq -\frac{5}{4} \quad and \quad x \qquad \geq 1$$

The numbers that satisfy *both* conditions are those numbers ≥ 1; therefore, the domain is $\{x | x \geq 1\}$. ∎

Solving Radical Equations

In order to solve a radical equation, we must eliminate the radical signs by raising both sides of the equation to some power. *When we do this, we may introduce extraneous roots*; therefore, all apparent solutions to the equation must be checked in the original equation.

TO SOLVE A RADICAL EQUATION

1. Arrange the terms so that one term with a radical is by itself on one side of the equation.

2. Raise each side of the equation to a power equal to the index of the radical.

3. Collect like terms.

4. If a radical still remains, repeat steps 1, 2, and 3.

5. Solve the resulting equation for the variable.

6. Check apparent solutions in the original equation.

Example 2   Find the solution set for each of these equations:

a. $\sqrt{x + 2} = 3$.

The domain is $\{x \mid x \geq -2\}$.

$$(\sqrt{x + 2})^2 = 3^2 \qquad \text{Square both sides}$$

$$x + 2 = 9$$

$$x = 7$$

Check $\sqrt{7 + 2} = \sqrt{9} = 3$, and 7 is in the domain. The solution set is $\{7\}$.

b. $\sqrt[3]{x - 1} + 4 = 0$.

The domain is the set of all real numbers.

$$\sqrt[3]{x - 1} + 4 = 0$$

$$\sqrt[3]{x - 1} = -4 \qquad \text{Get the radical by itself on one side}$$

$$(\sqrt[3]{x - 1})^3 = (-4)^3 \qquad \text{Cube both sides}$$

$$x - 1 = -64$$

$$x = -63$$

Check $\sqrt[3]{x - 1} + 4 = 0$

$$\sqrt[3]{-63 - 1} + 4 \overset{?}{=} 0$$

$$\sqrt[3]{-64} + 4 \overset{?}{=} 0$$

$$-4 + 4 \overset{?}{=} 0$$

$$0 = 0$$

The solution set is $\{-63\}$.

c. $\sqrt[4]{2x + 1} = -2$.

For the domain, $2x + 1 \geq 0$, or $x \geq -\frac{1}{2}$. We know the principal root of an even-index radical must be *positive*. Therefore, this equation does not have a solution that is a real number. If you did not notice this and followed the procedure outlined for solving radical equations, the same result would be obtained. Following the procedure outlined, we have

$$\sqrt[4]{2x + 1} = -2$$

$$(\sqrt[4]{2x + 1})^4 = (-2)^4$$

$$2x + 1 = 16$$

$$2x = 15$$

$$x = \frac{15}{2}$$

Check
$$\sqrt[4]{2x + 1} = -2$$

$$\sqrt[4]{2\left(\frac{15}{2}\right) + 1} \overset{?}{=} -2$$

$$\sqrt[4]{15 + 1} \overset{?}{=} -2$$

$$\sqrt[4]{16} \overset{?}{=} -2$$

$$2 \neq -2$$

$\uparrow$ Principal root

Therefore, $\dfrac{15}{2}$ is not a solution. The solution set is $\{\ \ \}$.

A WORD OF CAUTION If one side of the equation has more than one term, squaring each term is *not* the same as squaring both sides of the equation. That is, if $a = b + c$, then $a^2 \neq b^2 + c^2$; rather, $a^2 = (b + c)^2$. The squaring of the righthand term will *always* result in a trinomial. ☑

d. $\sqrt{2x + 1} = x - 1$.

The domain is $\{x \mid x \geq -1/2\}$.

$$(\sqrt{2x + 1})^2 = (x - 1)^2$$

When squaring $(x - 1)$, do not forget this middle term

$$2x + 1 = x^2 - 2x + 1$$

$$0 = x^2 - 4x$$

$$0 = x(x - 4)$$

$$x = 0 \quad or \quad x - 4 = 0$$

$$x = 4$$

Check for $x = 0$

$$\sqrt{2x + 1} = x - 1$$

$$\sqrt{2(0) + 1} \overset{?}{=} (0) - 1$$

$$\sqrt{1} \overset{?}{=} -1 \qquad \text{The symbol } \sqrt{1} \text{ } \textit{always} \text{ stands for the } \textit{principal} \text{ square}$$

$$1 \neq -1 \qquad \text{root of 1, which is 1 } (\textit{not } -1)$$

Therefore, 0 *is not a solution of* $\sqrt{2x + 1} = x - 1$ because it does not satisfy the original equation.

Check for $x = 4$

$$\sqrt{2x + 1} = x - 1$$

$$\sqrt{2(4) + 1} \overset{?}{=} (4) - 1$$

$$\sqrt{9} \overset{?}{=} 3$$

$$3 = 3$$

Therefore, 4 *is a solution* because it does satisfy the original equation. The solution set is $\{4\}$.

e. $\sqrt{4x + 5} - \sqrt{x - 1} = 3$.

The domain is $\{x \mid x \geq 1\}$ (see Example 1c).

$$\sqrt{4x + 5} = \sqrt{x - 1} + 3 \qquad \text{Get one radical by itself on one side}$$

$$(\sqrt{4x + 5})^2 = (\sqrt{x - 1} + 3)^2$$

When squaring, don't forget this term

$$4x + 5 = x - 1 + \boxed{6\sqrt{x - 1}} + 9$$

$$3x - 3 = 6\sqrt{x - 1}$$

$$x - 1 = 2\sqrt{x - 1} \qquad \text{Divide both sides by 3}$$

$$(x - 1)^2 = (2\sqrt{x - 1})^2$$

$$x^2 - 2x + 1 = 4(x - 1)$$

$$x^2 - 6x + 5 = 0$$

$$(x - 1)(x - 5) = 0$$

$$x - 1 = 0 \quad \text{or} \quad x - 5 = 0$$

$$x = 1 \quad \text{or} \quad x = 5$$

Check for $x = 1$ *Check for $x = 5$*

$$\sqrt{4x + 5} - \sqrt{x - 1} = 3 \qquad\qquad \sqrt{4x + 5} - \sqrt{x - 1} = 3$$

$$\sqrt{4(1) + 5} - \sqrt{1 - 1} \overset{?}{=} 3 \qquad \sqrt{4(5) + 5} - \sqrt{5 - 1} \overset{?}{=} 3$$

$$\sqrt{9} - \sqrt{0} \overset{?}{=} 3 \qquad\qquad\qquad \sqrt{25} - \sqrt{4} \overset{?}{=} 3$$

$$3 = 3 \qquad\qquad\qquad\qquad 5 - 2 \overset{?}{=} 3$$

$$3 = 3$$

The solution set is $\{1, 5\}$. ∎

A similar method can be used to solve some equations that have rational exponents.

Example 3   Find the solution set for $x^{-1/4} = 2$.

Raise both sides to the -4 power

$$(x^{-1/4})^{-4} = 2^{-4}$$

$$x = 2^{-4} = \frac{1}{2^4} = \frac{1}{16}$$

Check

$$\left(\frac{1}{16}\right)^{-1/4} = (16)^{1/4} = \sqrt[4]{16} = 2$$

The solution set is $\{1/16\}$. ∎

Word Problems Involving Radical Equations

There are many applications of word problems involving radical equations in the sciences, business, engineering, and so forth.

Example 4   Find the amount of power, P, consumed if an appliance has a resistance of 5 ohms and draws 10 amps (amperes) of current, using this formula from electricity:

$$I = \sqrt{\frac{P}{R}},$$ where I, the current, is measured in amps (amperes); P, the power, is measured in watts; and R, the resistance, is measured in ohms.

Solution We must find the power, P, when $R = 5$ and $I = 10$.

$$I = \sqrt{\frac{P}{R}}$$

$$10 = \sqrt{\frac{P}{5}}$$

$$(10)^2 = \left(\sqrt{\frac{P}{5}}\right)^2$$

$$100 = \frac{P}{5}$$

$$500 = P$$

$$P = 500 \text{ watts}$$

Check

$$I = \sqrt{\frac{P}{R}}$$

$$10 \overset{?}{=} \sqrt{\frac{500}{5}}$$

$$10 \overset{?}{=} \sqrt{100}$$

$$10 = 10 \quad \blacksquare$$

EXERCISES 7.6

Set I   In Exercises 1–20, solve each equation.

1. $\sqrt{3x + 1} = 5$ **2.** $\sqrt{7x + 8} = 6$

3. $\sqrt{x + 1} = \sqrt{2x - 7}$ **4.** $\sqrt{3x - 2} = \sqrt{x + 4}$

5. $\sqrt[4]{4x - 11} - 1 = 0$ **6.** $\sqrt[4]{3x + 1} - 2 = 0$

7. $\sqrt{4x - 1} = 2x$ **8.** $\sqrt{6x - 1} = 3x$

9. $\sqrt{x + 7} = 2x - 1$ **10.** $\sqrt{2x + 1} = \sqrt{2x - 3}$

11. $\sqrt{3x + 4} - \sqrt{2x - 4} = 2$ **12.** $\sqrt{2x - 1} + 2 = \sqrt{3x + 10}$

13. $\sqrt[3]{2x + 3} - 2 = 0$ **14.** $\sqrt[3]{4x - 3} - 3 = 0$

15. $\sqrt{4u + 1} - \sqrt{u - 2} = \sqrt{u + 3}$ **16.** $\sqrt{2 - v} + \sqrt{v + 3} = \sqrt{7 + 2v}$

17. $x^{1/2} = 5$ **18.** $x^{1/3} = 3$

19. $2x^{-5/3} = 64$ **20.** $5x^{-3/2} = 40$

In Exercises 21 and 22, solve each problem for the required unknown, using the formula $I = \sqrt{\dfrac{P}{R}}$, as given in Example 4.

21. Find the amount of power, P, consumed if an appliance has a resistance of 16 ohms and draws 5 amps of current.

22. Find the amount of power, P, consumed if an appliance has a resistance of 9 ohms and draws 8 amps of current.

In Exercises 23 and 24, use this formula from statistics: $\sigma = \sqrt{npq}$, where σ (*sigma*) is the *standard deviation*, n is the number of trials, p is the probability of success, and q is the probability of failure.

23. Find the probability of success, p, if the standard deviation is $3\frac{1}{3}$, the probability of failure is $\frac{2}{3}$, and the number of trials is 50.

24. Find the probability of success, p, if the standard deviation is 12, the probability of failure is $\frac{3}{5}$, and the number of trials is 600.

Set II   In Exercises 1–20, solve each equation.

1. $\sqrt{3x - 2} = x$

2. $x = \sqrt{10 - 3x}$

3. $\sqrt{3x - 2} = \sqrt{5x + 4}$

4. $\sqrt{5x - 6} = x$

5. $\sqrt[5]{7x + 4} - 2 = 0$

6. $\sqrt{x + 4} - \sqrt{2} = \sqrt{x - 6}$

7. $x = \sqrt{12x - 36}$

8. $\sqrt{3x + 1} = \sqrt{1 - x}$

9. $\sqrt{x - 3} = x - 5$

10. $\sqrt{4x + 5} + 5 = 2x$

11. $\sqrt{v + 7} - \sqrt{v - 2} = 5$

12. $\sqrt{x} = \sqrt{x + 16} - 2$

13. $\sqrt[3]{x - 1} = 2$

14. $\sqrt{2 + x} = 1$

15. $\sqrt[5]{3x - 14} - 1 = 0$

16. $\sqrt{2x - 9} - \sqrt{4x + 3} = 0$

17. $x^{1/4} = 1$

18. $x^{1/5} = 2$

19. $x^{3/5} = 8$

20. $\sqrt{4v + 1} = \sqrt{v + 4} + \sqrt{v - 3}$

In Exercises 21 and 22, solve each problem for the required unknown, using the formula $I = \sqrt{\dfrac{P}{R}}$, as given in Example 4.

21. Find the amount of power, P, consumed if an appliance has a resistance of 25 ohms and draws 4 amps of current.

22. Find R, the resistance in ohms, for an electrical system that consumes 600 watts and draws 5 amps of current.

In Exercises 23 and 24, use this formula from statistics: $\sigma = \sqrt{npq}$, where σ (*sigma*) is the *standard deviation*, n is the number of trials, p is the probability of success, and q is the probability of failure.

23. Find the probability of success, p, if the standard deviation is 8, the probability of failure is $\frac{4}{5}$, and the number of trials is 400.

24. Find the probability of success, p, if the standard deviation is 20, the probability of failure is $\frac{5}{6}$, and the number of trials is 2,880.

7.7 The Pythagorean Theorem

Right Triangles
A triangle that has a *right angle* (90°) is called a **right triangle**. The diagonal of a rectangle divides the rectangle into two right triangles. The parts of a right triangle and a rectangle and one of its diagonals are shown in Figure 7.7.1.

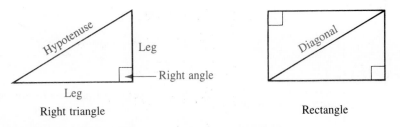

Right triangle   Rectangle

FIGURE 7.7.1.

The following theorem is proved in geometry:

THE PYTHAGOREAN THEOREM

The square of the hypotenuse of a right triangle is equal to the sum of the squares of the other sides.

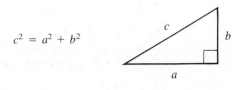

$$c^2 = a^2 + b^2$$

NOTE   The Pythagorean theorem applies only to *right triangles*.   ☑

The Pythagorean theorem can be used to find one side of a right triangle when the other two sides are known (see Example 1).

Example 1   Find x, using the Pythagorean theorem.

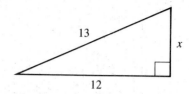

The domain is the set of all *positive* numbers, since the length of a side of a triangle must be positive.

$$c^2 = a^2 + b^2 \qquad \text{Pythagorean theorem}$$
$$13^2 = 12^2 + x^2$$
$$169 = 144 + x^2$$
$$0 = x^2 - 25$$
$$0 = (x + 5)(x - 5)$$
$$x + 5 = 0 \quad or \quad x - 5 = 0$$
$$x = -5 \quad or \qquad x = 5$$

$x = 5$ and $x = -5$ are both solutions of the original equation; however, -5 is not in the domain of the variable. Therefore, the answer is $x = 5$. ∎

Example 2   Find the hypotenuse of a right triangle with legs that are 8 and 6 units long.

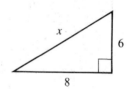

The domain is the set of all positive numbers.

$$c^2 = a^2 + b^2$$
$$x^2 = 8^2 + 6^2$$
$$x^2 = 64 + 36$$
$$x^2 = 100$$
$$x^2 - 100 = 0$$
$$(x - 10)(x + 10) = 0$$
$$x - 10 = 0 \quad or \quad x + 10 = 0$$
$$x = 10 \quad or \qquad x = -10$$

$x = 10$ and $x = -10$ are solutions of the original equation. Because -10 is not in the domain of the variable, the only solution is $x = 10$. ∎

If $k \geq 0$, we can use the following rule for solving an equation in the form $x^2 = k$.

If $x^2 = k$ and if $k \geq 0$, then $x = \sqrt{k}$ or $x = -\sqrt{k}$.

We can easily verify that $\sqrt{k}$ and $-\sqrt{k}$ are solutions of $x^2 = k$. If $k \geq 0$, then

$$\text{if } x = \sqrt{k}, \quad x^2 = (\sqrt{k})^2 = \sqrt{k}\sqrt{k} = k$$
$$\text{if } x = -\sqrt{k}, \quad x^2 = (-\sqrt{k})^2 = (-\sqrt{k})(-\sqrt{k}) = \sqrt{k}\sqrt{k} = k$$

We sometimes combine the solutions and write $x = \pm\sqrt{k}$.*

Example 3   Find x, using the Pythagorean theorem.

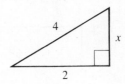

The domain is the set of positive numbers.

$$c^2 = a^2 + b^2$$
$$4^2 = 2^2 + x^2$$
$$16 = 4 + x^2$$
$$x^2 = 12$$
$$x = \sqrt{12} \text{ or } x = -\sqrt{12}$$
$$x = 2\sqrt{3} \text{ or } x = -2\sqrt{3}$$

Because $-2\sqrt{3}$ is not in the domain, $x = 2\sqrt{3}$ is the only solution. ∎

Example 4   The length of a rectangle is 2 more than its width. If the length of its diagonal is 10, find the dimensions of the rectangle.

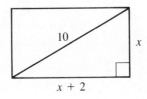

The domain is the set of all positive numbers.

Let $x = \text{width}$ $(10)^2 = (x)^2 + (x + 2)^2$

$x + 2 = \text{length}$ $100 = x^2 + x^2 + 4x + 4$

$$0 = 2x^2 + 4x - 96$$

$$0 = x^2 + 2x - 48 \qquad \text{Divide both sides by 2}$$

$$0 = (x + 8)(x - 6)$$

$$x + 8 = 0 \quad \text{or} \quad x - 6 = 0$$

Not in the domain $x = -8 \quad \text{or} \qquad x = 6 \qquad$ Width

$$x + 2 = 8 \qquad \text{Length} \quad ∎$$

---

* The symbol $\pm$ is read "plus or minus" (positive or negative). For example, ± 2 is read "plus or minus 2," and $x = \pm 2$ is read "x equals $+2$ or -2"; this means $x = +2$ or $x = -2$.

EXERCISES 7.7

Set I   In Exercises 1–6, use the Pythagorean theorem to find x in each figure.

1.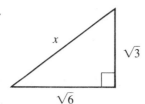

2.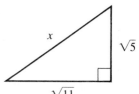

3.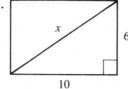

4.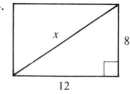

5.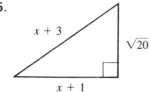

6.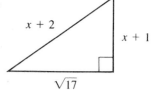

In Exercises 7–12, set up each problem algebraically, solve, and check.

7. Find the diagonal of a square with side equal to 4.

8. Find the diagonal of a square with side equal to 3.

9. Find the width of a rectangle that has a diagonal of 25 and a length of 24.

10. Find the width of a rectangle that has a diagonal of 41 and a length of 40.

11. One leg of a right triangle is 4 less than twice the other leg. If the hypotenuse is 10, how long are the two legs?

12. One leg of a right triangle is 4 more than twice the other leg. If the hypotenuse is $\sqrt{61}$, how long are the two legs?

Set II   In Exercises 1–6, use the Pythagorean theorem to find x in each figure.

1.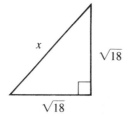

2.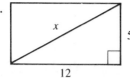

3.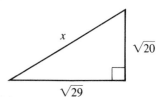

4.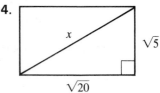

Index

5.

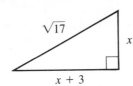

6.

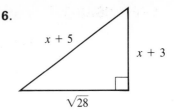

In Exercises 7–12, set up each problem algebraically, solve, and check.

7. Find the diagonal of a square with side equal to 5.

8. Find the diagonal of a rectangle if the width is 8 and the length is 11.

9. Find the width of a rectangle that has a diagonal of 17 and a length of 15.

10. One leg of a right triangle is 2 more than twice the other leg. If the hypotenuse is 2 less than three times the shorter leg, find the length of the legs and the hypotenuse of the triangle.

11. One leg of a right triangle is 3 more than twice the other leg. If the hypotenuse is $\sqrt{137}$, how long are the two legs?

12. The length of a rectangle is 3 more than its width. If the length of its diagonal is 15, find the dimensions of the rectangle.

7.8 Complex Numbers

All numbers discussed up to this point in the book have been *real* numbers. Recall that the set of real numbers is the union of the set of rational numbers with the set of irrational numbers. In this section, we discuss a new kind of number that is *not* a real number but is essential in many applications of mathematics.

7.8A Basic Definitions

In order for us to be able to solve equations such as $x^2 = -4$, we must invent, or *define*, a new set of numbers that will *not* be real numbers.

The basis for our new set of numbers is the number i, which is defined as follows:

$$i = \sqrt{-1}$$
$$i^2 = -1$$

Pure Imaginary Number

A **pure imaginary number** is a number that can be written as bi, where b is a real number and $i = \sqrt{-1}$. If b is an irrational number, sometimes the i is written first, as ib.

Example 1 Examples of pure imaginary numbers:

$$-5i, \quad -2\sqrt{3}i, \quad -\frac{2}{5}i, \quad 0.63i \quad \blacksquare$$

A WORD OF CAUTION Students often believe that $i = -1$. *This is not true!* 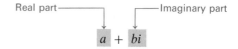 $i = \sqrt{-1}$, not -1. Also, students often write a number such as $\sqrt{5}i$ as $\sqrt{5i}$. The i should *not* be under the radical sign. (Numbers such as $\sqrt{5i}$ are discussed in higher-level courses.) $\sqrt{5}i$ can be written as $i\sqrt{5}$. ☑

Complex Numbers

A **complex number** is a number of the form $a + bi$.

Real part ⟶ ⟵ Imaginary part

$$a + bi$$

Example 2 Examples of complex numbers:

$$2 - 3i, \qquad \sqrt{5} - \frac{1}{2}i, \qquad -0.7 + 0.4i \quad \blacksquare$$

Since the set of complex numbers is a completely new set, we need definitions for equality, addition, subtraction, and so forth.

We should emphasize that the *ordering* property does not hold for complex numbers; that is, the relations "less than" and "greater than" are *not defined* for the set of complex numbers.

The definition of equality of complex numbers follows:

TWO COMPLEX NUMBERS ARE EQUAL IF:

1. Their real parts are equal.

2. Their imaginary parts are equal.

If $(a + bi) = (c + di)$, then $a = c$ (real parts equal) and $b = d$ (imaginary parts equal).

When the *real* part is zero, the complex number is a *pure imaginary number.*

$$0 + 3i = 3i$$

a is zero ⟶ ⟵ Pure imaginary number

Therefore, the set of pure imaginary numbers is a subset of the set of complex numbers.

By definition,

$$0i = 0$$

This means that zero is a pure imaginary number as well as a real number.

When the *imaginary* part is zero, the complex number is a *real number*.

$$2 + \boxed{0}\,i = \boxed{2}$$

b is zero ⎯⎯⎯⎯⎯⎯⎯⎯⎯⎯⎯ ⎿ Real number

Therefore, the set of real numbers is a subset of the set of complex numbers.

Example 3   Write the following numbers in the form $a + bi$:

a. $\sqrt{-9} = \sqrt{9(-1)} = \sqrt{9}\sqrt{-1} = 3i = 0 + 3i$

b. $\sqrt{-17} = \sqrt{17(-1)} = \sqrt{17}\sqrt{-1} = \sqrt{17}i = 0 + \sqrt{17}i$

c. $2 - \sqrt{-25} = 2 - \sqrt{25(-1)} = 2 - \sqrt{25}\sqrt{-1} = 2 - 5i$ ∎

A WORD OF CAUTION   In writing complex numbers in $a + bi$ form, we have used Rule 7.3 from Section 7.2A:

$$\sqrt[n]{ab} = \sqrt[n]{a}\sqrt[n]{b}$$

This rule does *not* apply when *both* a and b are negative.

$$\sqrt{(-4)(-9)} = \sqrt{36} = 6$$

$$\sqrt{-4}\sqrt{-9} = 2i \cdot 3i = 6i^2 = -6$$

Therefore, $\sqrt{(-4)(-9)} \neq \sqrt{-4}\sqrt{-9}$. Rule 7.3 does not apply in this case.   ☑

We can use the definition of equality of complex numbers in solving equations involving complex numbers. We simply set the two *real* parts equal to each other and solve that equation; then we set the coefficient of i from one side of the equation equal to the coefficient of i from the other side and solve *that* equation (see Example 4).

Example 4   Solve the equations:

a. If $(x - 3i) = (5 + yi)$, then

$$x = 5 \qquad \text{Real parts equal}$$

and

$$-3 = y \qquad \text{Imaginary parts equal}$$

$$y = -3$$

b. If $(3x + 7yi) = (10 - 2i)$, then

$$3x = 10 \qquad \text{Real parts equal}$$

$$x = \frac{10}{3}$$

and

$$7y = -2 \qquad \text{Imaginary parts equal}$$

$$y = -\frac{2}{7}$$ ∎

EXERCISES 7.8A

Set I   In Exercises 1–12, convert each expression to the $a + bi$ form. Express all radicals in simplest radical form.

1. $3 + \sqrt{-16}$ **2.** $4 - \sqrt{-25}$ **3.** $\sqrt{-64}$

4. $\sqrt{-100}$ **5.** $5 + \sqrt{-32}$ **6.** $6 + \sqrt{-18}$

7. $\sqrt{-36} + \sqrt{4}$ **8.** $\sqrt{9} - \sqrt{-25}$ **9.** $2i - \sqrt{9}$

10. $3i - \sqrt{16}$ **11.** 14 **12.** -7

In Exercises 13–20, solve for x and y.

13. $3 - 4i = x + 2yi$ **14.** $3x + 5i = 6 + yi$

15. $5x - 3i = 6 - 7yi$ **16.** $-3 - yi = 2x + 3i$

17. $\sqrt{3}x - yi = 2 + \sqrt{2}i$ **18.** $3 + \sqrt{5}yi = \sqrt{8}x - i$

19. $\dfrac{3}{4}x - \dfrac{1}{3}yi = \dfrac{3}{5}x + \dfrac{1}{2}yi$ **20.** $\dfrac{2}{3}x - yi = \dfrac{1}{2}x + 3yi$

Set II   In Exercises 1–12, convert each expression to the $a + bi$ form. Express all radicals in simplest radical form.

1. $5 + \sqrt{-49}$ **2.** $\sqrt{-4} - 6$ **3.** $\sqrt{-81}$

4. -16 **5.** $3 + \sqrt{-8}$ **6.** $\sqrt{7} + \sqrt{-36}$

7. $\sqrt{-100} + \sqrt{16}$ **8.** 7 **9.** $5i - \sqrt{7}$

10. $\sqrt{8} - \sqrt{-18}$ **11.** $\sqrt{50}$ **12.** $\sqrt{-27}$

In Exercises 13–20, solve for x and y.

13. $5 - yi = x + 4i$ **14.** $8x - 6i = 12 + yi$

15. $3x + 7yi = 2 + 3i$ **16.** $2x - 3yi = 5 + 2i$

17. $4 + \sqrt{2}yi = \sqrt{5}x - 3i$ **18.** $\sqrt{7}x + 2i = \sqrt{2} + 4yi$

19. $\dfrac{1}{3}x - \dfrac{3}{4}i = \dfrac{1}{2} + \dfrac{1}{5}yi$ **20.** $\dfrac{3}{5}x - \dfrac{1}{2}yi = 3 - 4i$

7.8B   Addition and Subtraction of Complex Numbers

Addition of Complex Numbers

The addition of complex numbers is defined as follows:

$$(a + bi) + (c + di) = (a + c) + (b + d)i$$

Therefore,

TO ADD COMPLEX NUMBERS

1. Add the real parts.

2. Add the imaginary parts.

3. Express the result in $a + bi$ form.

$$(a + bi) + (c + di) = (a + c) + (b + d)i$$

Example 5   Add the following complex numbers:

a. $(2 + 3i) + (-4 + 5i)$

$(\underline{2} + \underline{\underline{3i}}) + (\underline{-4} + \underline{\underline{5i}}) = (2 + [-4]) + (3 + 5)i = -2 + 8i$

b. $(7) + (-5 + 3i)$

$(\underline{7}) + (\underline{-5} + \underline{\underline{3i}}) = (7 + [-5]) + 3i = 2 + 3i$

c. $(-7 + 4i) + (6 - 3i) = \underline{-7} + \underline{\underline{4i}} + \underline{6} - \underline{\underline{3i}} = -1 + i$

d. $(\underline{8} + \underline{\underline{7i}}) + (\underline{\underline{-5i}}) + (\underline{-13} + \underline{\underline{4i}}) = -5 + 6i$ ■

Subtraction of Complex Numbers

The definition of subtraction of complex numbers is

$$(a + bi) - (c + di) = (a - c) + (b - d)i$$

Therefore,

TO SUBTRACT ONE COMPLEX NUMBER FROM ANOTHER

1. Subtract the real parts.

2. Subtract the imaginary parts.

3. Write the result in $a + bi$ form.

$$(a + bi) - (c + di) = (a - c) + (b - d)i$$

Example 6   Subtract the following complex numbers:

a. $(-5 + 2i) - (6 - 2i)$

$(\underline{-5} + \underline{\underline{2i}}) - (\underline{6} - \underline{\underline{2i}}) = (-5 - 6) + (2 - [-2])i = -11 + 4i$

b. $(-2) - (-9 - 4i)$

$(\underline{-2}) - (\underline{-9} - \underline{\underline{4i}}) = (-2 - [-9]) + (-[-4])i = 7 + 4i$

c. $(-13 + 8i) - (7 - 11i) = \underline{-13} + \underline{\underline{8i}} - \underline{7} + \underline{\underline{11i}} = -20 + 19i$

d. $(7 - i) - (6 - 10i) - (-4) = \underline{7} - \underline{\underline{i}} - \underline{6} + \underline{\underline{10i}} + \underline{4} = 5 + 9i$ ■

When complex numbers are not written in $a + bi$ form, you must change them into $a + bi$ form before you perform any operation with them.

Example 7   Add $(2 + \sqrt{-4}) + (3 - \sqrt{-9}) + (\sqrt{-16})$.

$(\underline{2} + \underline{\underline{2i}}) + (\underline{3} - \underline{\underline{3i}}) + (\underline{\underline{4i}}) = 5 + 3i$ ■

EXERCISES 7.8B

Set I   In Exercises 1–10, perform the indicated operations; write the answers in $a + bi$ form.

1. $(4 + 3i) + (5 - i)$ **2.** $(6 - 2i) + (-3 + 5i)$

3. $(7 - 4i) - (5 + 2i)$ **4.** $(8 - 3i) - (4 + i)$

5. $(2 + i) + (3i) - (2 - 4i)$ **6.** $(3 - i) + (2i) - (-3 + 5i)$

7. $(2 + 3i) - (x + yi)$ **8.** $(x - i) - (7 + yi)$

9. $(9 + \sqrt{-16}) + (2 + \sqrt{-25}) + (6 - \sqrt{-64})$

10. $(13 - \sqrt{-36}) - (10 - \sqrt{-49}) + (8 + \sqrt{-4})$

In Exercises 11–14, solve for x and y.

11. $(4 + 3i) - (5 - i) = (3x + 2yi) + (2x - 3yi)$

12. $(3 - 2i) - (x + i) = (2x - yi) - (x + 2yi)$

13. $(2 - 5i) - (5 + 3i) = (3x + 2yi) - (5x + 3yi)$

14. $(4x - 3yi) - (7x + 2yi) = (7 - 2i) - (3 + 4i)$

Set II   In Exercises 1–10, perform the indicated operations; write the answers in $a + bi$ form.

1. $(8 - 5i) + (7 + 2i)$ **2.** $(5 - 2i) - (4) - (3 + 4i)$

3. $(9 - 12i) - (7 + i)$ **4.** $(7i) - (2 + i) + (-3 - 5i)$

5. $(7 + 3i) - (2i) - (2 - 5i)$ **6.** $(8 + 3i) - (2 - i) + (-9i)$

7. $(3 - xi) - (y - 5i)$ **8.** $(3x - 4i) + (x - yi) - (3 + yi)$

9. $(3 + \sqrt{-9}) - (4 - \sqrt{-81}) + (2 - \sqrt{-1})$

10. $(5 - \sqrt{-16}) + (\sqrt{-4} - 5) - (3 - \sqrt{-25})$

In Exercises 11–14, solve for x and y.

11. $(5 - i) + (-3 + 2i) = (4x - 5yi) - (7x - 2yi)$

12. $5 - yi = x + 4i$

13. $(3 - 2i) - (x + yi) = (2x + 5i) - (4 + i)$

14. $(5 + 2i) - (3i) - (x - 3i) = (x + yi) - (3 + 2yi)$

7.8C Multiplication of Complex Numbers

Multiplication is distributive over addition for the set of complex numbers, as it is for the set of real numbers. Because of this, and because $i^2 = -1$, the definition of the multiplication of two complex numbers is

$$(a + bi)(c + di) = (ac - bd) + (ad + bc)i$$

Therefore,

TO MULTIPLY TWO COMPLEX NUMBERS

1. Multiply the numbers as you would two binomials.

2. Replace i^2 by -1.

3. Collect like terms and write the result in $a + bi$ form.

Example 8   Multiply $(4 + 3i)(-5 + 2i)$.

$$(4 + 3i) \quad (-5 + 2i)$$
$$-15i$$
$$+ 8i$$

$$= -20 - 7i + 6i^2$$

$$= -20 - 7i + 6(-1)$$

$$= -26 - 7i \qquad\qquad \text{Product in } a + bi \text{ form} \quad \blacksquare$$

Example 9   Find $(5 - 3i)^2$.

$$(5 - 3i)(5 - 3i) = 25 - 30i + 9i^2$$

$$= 25 - 30i - 9$$

$$= 16 - 30i \quad \blacksquare$$

Because $\sqrt{a}\sqrt{b} \neq \sqrt{ab}$ if a and b are *both* negative, in Example 10 we *must* express $\sqrt{-25}$ and $\sqrt{-9}$ in simplest radical form before we multiply.

Example 10   Multiply $(2 - \sqrt{-25})(-3 + \sqrt{-9})$.

$$\left. \begin{array}{l} 2 - \sqrt{-25} = 2 - 5i \\ -3 + \sqrt{-9} = -3 + 3i \end{array} \right\} \qquad \text{First convert to } a + bi \text{ form}$$

Therefore, $(2 - \sqrt{-25})(-3 + \sqrt{-9}) = (2 - 5i)(-3 + 3i)$

$$= -6 + 21i - 15i^2$$

$$= -6 + 21i + 15$$

$$= 9 + 21i \quad \blacksquare$$

Simplifying Powers of i

Any power of i can be rewritten as ± 1 or $\pm i$. Therefore, an algebraic expression is not considered to be in *simplest form* if it contains any powers of i greater than 1.

Example 11   Powers of i:

a. $i = i$

b. $i^2 = -1$

c. $i^3 = i^2 \cdot i = (-1)i = -i$

d. $i^4 = i^2 \cdot i^2 = (-1)(-1) = 1$

Each integral power of i must be one of these four values

e. $i^{13} = (i^4)^3 \cdot i = (1)^3 \cdot i = i$

f. $i^{51} = (i^2)^{25} \cdot i = (-1)^{25} \cdot i = (-1)i = -i$

g. $i^{100} = (i^4)^{25} = (1)^{25} = 1 \quad \blacksquare$

Example 12   Simplify $(1 + i)^6$.

We will use the binomial theorem. The coefficients are 1, 6, 15, 20, 15, 6, and 1. Therefore,

$$(1 + i)^6 = 1^6 + 6(1)^5 i + 15(1)^4 i^2 + 20(1)^3 i^3 + 15(1)^2 i^4 + 6(1)i^5 + i^6$$

$$= 1 + 6i + 15(-1) + 20(-i) + 15(1) + 6i + (-1)$$

$$= 0 - 8i \text{ or } -8i \quad \blacksquare$$

EXERCISES 7.8C

Set I   Perform the indicated operations. Express your answers in $a + bi$ form.

1. $(1 + i)(1 - i)$ 2. $(3 + 2i)(3 - 2i)$ 3. $(4 - i)(3 + 2i)$

4. $(5 + 2i)(2 - 3i)$ 5. $(6 - 2i)(2 - 3i)$ 6. $(4 + 7i)(3 + 2i)$

7. $(\sqrt{5} + 2i)(\sqrt{5} - 2i)$ 8. $(\sqrt{7} - 3i)(\sqrt{7} + 3i)$ 9. $5i(i - 2)$

10. $6i(2i - 1)$ 11. $(2 + 5i)^2$ 12. $(3 - 4i)^2$

13. i^{10} 14. i^{23} 15. i^{87}

16. i^{73} 17. $(3i)^3$ 18. $(2i)^3$

19. $(2i)^4$ 20. $(3i)^4$

21. $(3 - \sqrt{-4})(4 + \sqrt{-25})$ 22. $(5 + \sqrt{-64})(2 - \sqrt{-36})$

23. $(2 - \sqrt{-1})^2$ 24. $(3 + \sqrt{-1})^2$ 25. $[3 + i^6]^2$

26. $[4 - i^{10}]^2$ 27. $i^{10}(i^{23})$ 28. $i^{34}(i^{16})$

29. $i^{15} + i^7$ 30. $i^{27} + i^{14}$ 31. $[2 + (-i)^{11}]^2$

32. $[3 - (-i)^5]^2$ 33. $(1 - i)^5$ 34. $(1 + i)^4$

35. $(2 - i)^4$ 36. $(4 - i)^3$

Set II   Perform the indicated operations. Express your answers in $a + bi$ form.

1. $(8 + 5i)(3 - 4i)$ 2. $(7 - i)(3 + 2i)$ 3. $(6 - 3i)(4 + 5i)$

4. $(8 - i)(7 + 2i)$ 5. $(7 + 2i)(1 - i)$ 6. $(1 + 3i)(1 - 3i)$

7. $(4 - 2i)(4 + 2i)$ 8. $(1 + i)(1 + i)$ 9. $8i(2 - 3i)$

10. $-4i(3 - 2i)$ 11. $(-4 + 3i)^2$ 12. $(-7 - 2i)^2$

13. i^{13} 14. i^{83} 15. i^{91}

16. i^{74} 17. $(2i)^5$ 18. $(-3i)^3$

19. $(-5i)^2$ 20. $(-3i)^4$

21. $(5 + \sqrt{-36})(3 - \sqrt{-100})$ 22. $(2 - \sqrt{-49})(4 + \sqrt{-81})$

23. $(4 + \sqrt{-1})^2$ 24. $(6 - \sqrt{-25})^2$ 25. $(3 - i^{13})^2$

26. $(3 + [-i]^7)^2$ 27. $i^{24}(i^{18})$ 28. $i^{37}(i^{23})$

29. $i^{14} + i^{25}$ 30. $i^{25} - i^{17}$ 31. $[8 - (-i)^{13}]^2$

32. $[6 + 5(-i)^7]^2$ 33. $(1 + i)^5$ 34. $(1 + 2i)^4$

35. $(3 - i)^3$ 36. $(1 - i)^6$

7.8D Division of Complex Numbers

The **conjugate of a complex number** is obtained by changing the sign of its imaginary part.

The conjugate of $a + bi$ is $a - bi$
The conjugate of $a - bi$ is $a + bi$

Example 13   Examples of conjugate complex numbers:

a. The conjugate of $3 - 2i$ is $3 + 2i$.

b. The conjugate of $-5 + 4i$ is $-5 - 4i$.

c. The conjugate of $7i$ is $-7i$, because $7i = 0 + 7i$ with conjugate $0 - 7i = -7i$.

d. The conjugate of 5 is 5, because $5 = 5 + 0i$ with conjugate $5 - 0i = 5$. ■

The product of a complex number and its conjugate is a real number.

$$(a + bi)(a - bi) = a^2 - b^2i^2 = a^2 + b^2 \qquad \text{Real number}$$

In order to divide one complex number by another, we must convert the expression to the form $a + bi$; in other words, we must make the divisor (or denominator) a *real* number. Because the product of a complex number and its conjugate is a real number, we have the following rules for division of complex numbers:

TO DIVIDE ONE COMPLEX NUMBER BY ANOTHER

1. Write the division as a fraction.

2. Multiply the numerator and denominator by the conjugate of the denominator.

$$\frac{a + bi}{c + di} \cdot \frac{c - di}{c - di}$$

3. Simplify, and write the result in $a + bi$ form.

This procedure is similar to the procedure for dividing radicals when the divisor (or denominator) contains two terms.

Example 14   Division of complex numbers:

a. $\dfrac{10i}{1 - 3i} = \dfrac{10i}{1 - 3i} \cdot \dfrac{1 + 3i}{1 + 3i} = \dfrac{10i + 30i^2}{1 - 9i^2} = \dfrac{10i - 30}{1 + 9}$

$$= \frac{\overset{1}{\cancel{10}}(i - 3)}{\underset{1}{\cancel{10}}} = i - 3 = -3 + i$$

The denominator has been converted into a real number

b. $(2 + i) \div (3 - 2i) = \dfrac{2 + i}{3 - 2i} = \dfrac{2 + i}{3 - 2i} \cdot \boxed{\dfrac{3 + 2i}{3 + 2i}}$

$$= \dfrac{6 + 7i + 2i^2}{9 - 4i^2} = \dfrac{6 + 7i - 2}{9 + 4} = \dfrac{4 + 7i}{13}$$

$$= \dfrac{4}{13} + \dfrac{7}{13}i \qquad \text{Quotient in } a + bi \text{ form}$$

c. $(3 + i) \div i = \dfrac{3 + i}{i} \cdot \boxed{\dfrac{-i}{-i}} = \dfrac{-3i - i^2}{-i^2} = \dfrac{-3i + 1}{1} = 1 - 3i$

The conjugate of i is $-i$,
because $i = 0 + i$ and its
conjugate $0 - i = -i$

d. $5 \div (-2i) = \dfrac{5}{-2i} = \dfrac{5}{-2i} \cdot \boxed{\dfrac{i}{i}} = \dfrac{5i}{-2i^2} = \dfrac{5}{2}i = 0 + \dfrac{5}{2}i$

Even though the conjugate of $-2i$ is $2i$, we were able to make the denominator a real number by multiplying by i instead of by $2i$. ∎

EXERCISES 7.8D

Set I   In Exercises 1–6, write the conjugate of each complex number.

1. $3 - 2i$ **2.** $5 + 4i$ **3.** $5i$ **4.** $-7i$ **5.** 10 **6.** -8

In Exercises 7–18, perform the indicated operations and write the answers in $a + bi$ form.

7. $\dfrac{10}{1 + 3i}$ **8.** $\dfrac{5}{1 + 2i}$ **9.** $\dfrac{1 + i}{1 - i}$ **10.** $\dfrac{1 - i}{1 + i}$

11. $\dfrac{8 + i}{i}$ **12.** $\dfrac{4 - i}{i}$ **13.** $\dfrac{3}{2i}$ **14.** $\dfrac{4}{5i}$

15. $\dfrac{15i}{1 - 2i}$ **16.** $\dfrac{20i}{1 - 3i}$ **17.** $\dfrac{4 + 3i}{2 - i}$ **18.** $\dfrac{3 + 2i}{4 + 2i}$

Set II   In Exercises 1–6, write the conjugate of each complex number.

1. $5 - 3i$ **2.** $-2 + 3i$ **3.** $-3i$

4. 0 **5.** 7 **6.** $3i$

In Exercises 7–18, perform the indicated operations and write the answers in $a + bi$ form.

7. $\dfrac{8}{2 - 3i}$ **8.** $\dfrac{2 + 6i}{2 + i}$ **9.** $\dfrac{3 + i}{3 - i}$

10. $\dfrac{8 + i}{6i}$ **11.** $\dfrac{4 + 2i}{3i}$ **12.** $\dfrac{5 + 3i}{5 - 3i}$

13. $\dfrac{9}{4i}$ **14.** $\dfrac{8 - 3i}{8 + 3i}$ **15.** $\dfrac{29i}{2 + 5i}$

16. $\dfrac{3}{7i}$ **17.** $\dfrac{2i + 5}{3 + 2i}$ **18.** $\dfrac{6i - 1}{6i + 1}$

7.9 Review: 7.6–7.8

To Solve a Radical Equation
7.6

1. Arrange the terms so that one term with a radical is by itself on one side of the equation.

2. Raise each side of the equation to a power equal to the index of the radical.

3. Collect like terms.

4. If a radical still remains, repeat steps 1, 2, and 3.

5. Solve the resulting equation for the unknown letter.

6. Check apparent solutions in the original equation.

The Pythagorean Theorem
7.7

The square of the hypotenuse of a right triangle is equal to the sum of the squares of the other sides.

$$c^2 = a^2 + b^2$$

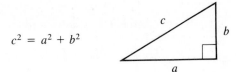

Complex Numbers
7.8

A **complex number** is a number of the form $a + bi$, where a and b are real numbers and $i = \sqrt{-1}$.

The set of complex numbers: $C = \{a + bi \mid a, b \in R, i = \sqrt{-1}\}$.

$$i = \sqrt{-1}$$
$$i^2 = -1$$

When the real part is zero, the complex number is a *pure imaginary number.*

When the imaginary part is zero, the complex number is a *real number.*

Equality of Complex Numbers
7.8A

Two complex numbers are equal if:

1. Their real parts are equal.

2. Their imaginary parts are equal.

If $(a + bi) = (c + di)$, then $a = c$ (real parts equal) and $b = d$ (imaginary parts equal).

Addition of Complex Numbers
7.8B

1. Add the real parts.

2. Add the imaginary parts.

3. Write the result in $a + bi$ form.

Subtraction of Complex Numbers
7.8B

1. Subtract the real parts.

2. Subtract the imaginary parts.

3. Write the result in $a + bi$ form.

Multiplication of Complex Numbers 7.8C

1. Multiply the numbers as you would two binomials.

2. Replace i^2 by -1.

3. Collect like terms and write the result in $a + bi$ form.

Division of Complex Numbers 7.8D

1. Write the division as a fraction.

2. Multiply the numerator and denominator by the conjugate of the denominator.

$$\frac{a + bi}{c + di} \cdot \boxed{\frac{c - di}{c - di}}$$

3. Simplify and write the result in $a + bi$ form.

Review Exercises 7.9 Set I

In Exercises 1–6, solve and check each equation.

1. $\sqrt{x - 5} = \sqrt{3x - 8}$

2. $\sqrt{3x - 5} + 3 = x$

3. $\sqrt{5x - 4} - \sqrt{2x + 1} = 1$

4. $\sqrt[5]{5x + 4} = -2$

5. $x^{5/6} = 32$

6. $x^{3/4} = 27$

In Exercises 7 and 8, solve for x and y.

7. $5 - yi = x + 6i$

8. $(2 - 5i) - (x + yi) = (x - 7i) + (4 - 2yi)$

In Exercises 9–13, perform the indicated operations and write the answers in $a + bi$ form.

9. $(3i + 2)(4 - 2i)$

10. $(5 + 2i)(3i - 7)$

11. $\dfrac{2 + i}{1 + 3i}$

12. $\dfrac{3 + i}{1 - 2i}$

13. $(4 + \sqrt{-27}) + (2 - \sqrt{-12}) - (1 - \sqrt{-3})$

In Exercises 14 and 15, set up the problem algebraically, solve, and check.

14. The length of a rectangle is 2 ft more than its width. Its diagonal is $\sqrt{34}$ ft. Find the dimensions of the rectangle.

15. The width of a rectangle is 3 m less than its length. Its diagonal is $\sqrt{45}$ m. Find the dimensions of the rectangle.

Review Exercises 7.9 Set II

NAME _____

ANSWERS

In Exercises 1–6, solve and check each equation.

1. $x = \sqrt{3x + 10}$

2. $\sqrt[3]{4x - 1} = -2$

3. $\sqrt{3x + 7} - \sqrt{x - 2} = 3$

4. $x^{3/5} = -8$

5. $x = 2\sqrt{x + 6} - 3$

6. $x^{1/3} = -2$

In Exercises 7 and 8, solve for x and y.

7. $3x - 3i = 8 - yi$

8. $(4 - 3i) - (x + 2yi) = (x + yi) - (4 - 5i)$

In Exercises 9–13, perform the indicated operations and write the answers in $a + bi$ form.

9. $(8 + 7i) - (3 - 2i) + (\sqrt{2} - 3i)$

10. $4i(6 - 2i)$

11. $\dfrac{5 - 3i}{5i}$

1. _____

2. _____

3. _____

4. _____

5. _____

6. _____

7. _____

8. _____

9. _____

10. _____

11. _____

12. $(3 - \sqrt{-50}) - (1 + \sqrt{-18}) + \sqrt{-32}$

ANSWERS

12. _____

13. _____

14. _____

15. _____

13. $\dfrac{8 + 5i}{8 - 5i}$

In Exercises 14 and 15, set up the problem algebraically, solve, and check.

14. The length of a rectangle is 7 ft more than its width. If the length of its diagonal is 13 ft, find the dimensions of the rectangle.

15. The longer leg of a right triangle is 3 in. more than the shorter leg, and the hypotenuse is 6 in. more than the shorter leg. Find the lengths of the three sides.

Chapter 7 Diagnostic Test

The purpose of this test is to see how well you understand operations with radicals and exponents. We recommend that you work this diagnostic test *before* your instructor tests you on this chapter. Allow yourself about 50 minutes.

Complete solutions for all the problems on this test, together with section references, are given in the answer section at the end of the book. For the problems you do incorrectly, study the sections cited.

In Problems 1–4, perform the indicated operations. Express the answers in exponential form with positive exponents. Assume that the variables represent positive numbers.

1. $x^{1/2}x^{-1/4}$

2. $(R^{-4/3})^3$

3. $\dfrac{a^{5/6}}{a^{1/3}}$

4. $\left(\dfrac{x^{-2/3}y^{3/5}}{x^{1/3}y}\right)^{-5/2}$

In Problems 5–9, write each expression in simplest radical form.

5. $\sqrt[3]{54x^6y^7}$

6. $\dfrac{4xy}{\sqrt{2x}}, x > 0$

7. $\sqrt[6]{a^3}$

8. $\sqrt{40} + \sqrt{9}$

9. $\sqrt{x}\sqrt[3]{x}, x \geq 0$

10. Evaluate the expression $(-27)^{2/3}$.

In Problems 11–17, perform the indicated operations. Give your answers in simplified form. Assume $x > 0$ and $y \geq 0$.

11. $4\sqrt{8y} + 3\sqrt{32y}$

12. $3\sqrt{\dfrac{5x^2}{2}} - 5\sqrt{\dfrac{x^2}{10}}$

13. $\sqrt{2x^4}\sqrt{8x^3}$

14. $\sqrt{2x}(\sqrt{8x} - 5\sqrt{2})$

15. $\dfrac{\sqrt{10x} + \sqrt{5x}}{\sqrt{5x}}$

16. $\dfrac{5}{\sqrt{7} + \sqrt{2}}$

17. $(1 - \sqrt[3]{x})^3$

In Problems 18–21, perform the indicated operations; write the answers in $a + bi$ form.

18. $(5 - \sqrt{-8}) - (3 - \sqrt{-18})$

19. $(3 + i)(2 - 5i)$

20. $\dfrac{10}{1 - 3i}$

21. $(2 - i)^3$

22. Solve and check: $x^{3/2} = 8$.

23. Solve and check: $\sqrt{x - 3} + 5 = x$.

24. Find the value of x shown in the right triangle.

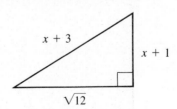

$x + 3$

$x + 1$

$\sqrt{12}$

Cumulative Review Exercises
Chapters 1–7

In Exercises 1–6, perform the indicated operations and simplify. Assume that the value(s) of the variable(s) that make the denominator zero are excluded.

1. $\dfrac{6}{a^2 - 9} - \dfrac{2}{a^2 - 4a + 3}$

2. $\dfrac{x^3 - 8}{2x^2 + x - 10} \div \dfrac{3x^3 - x^2}{6x^2 + 13x - 5}$

3. $\dfrac{\dfrac{4}{x} - \dfrac{8}{x^2}}{\dfrac{1}{x} - \dfrac{2}{x^2}}$

4. $\sqrt{5x}(\sqrt{5x} + 2),\ x \geq 0$ **5.** $(\sqrt{26} - \sqrt{10})^2$ **6.** $\dfrac{6}{2 - \sqrt{5}}$

In Exercises 7–11, solve each equation and inequality.

7. $3(4x - 1) - (3 - 2x) = 4(2x - 3)$

8. $\dfrac{3x}{4} - \dfrac{5}{6} \leq \dfrac{7x}{12}$

9. $\sqrt{2x + 2} = 1 + \sqrt{3x - 12}$

10. $\dfrac{3}{x + 2} - \dfrac{11}{2x + 4} = \dfrac{5}{2}$

11. $6x^2 + 11x = 10$

12. Solve for a in terms of the other letters:

$$\frac{1}{a} + \frac{1}{b} = \frac{1}{c}$$

13. Find the solution set for $|2x - 5| > 3$.

In Exercises 14 and 15, set up each problem algebraically, solve, and check.

14. Leroy can do a job in 5 hr. Adolph can do the same job in 6 hr. How long would it take if they work together?

15. The area of a rectangle is 54 sq. cm. Find its dimensions if its sides are in the ratio of 2 to 3.

8 Graphing and Functions

Graphs are mathematical pictures that help explain relationships between variables. In this chapter, we discuss graphs of ordered pairs and graphs of equations and inequalities in two variables. We also discuss relations, functions and their inverses, and variation.

8.1 The Rectangular Coordinate System and Mathematical Relations

Ordered Pairs
Two *ordered pairs* are not equal to each other unless they contain the same elements *in the same order*. We enclose the elements of an ordered pair in *parentheses*. Thus,

$$\{1, 4\} = \{4, 1\} \qquad (1, 4) \neq (4, 1)$$

Set   Ordered pair

Rectangular Coordinate System
The **rectangular coordinate system** in the plane usually consists of a horizontal number line, called the *horizontal axis* or *x-axis*, and a vertical number line, called the *vertical axis* or *y-axis*. These lines intersect at a point we call the *origin*. The units of measure on these two lines are usually equal, but in some cases it is best for them to be *unequal*, for example, in graphing the ordered pair (3, 200).

The two axes divide the plane into four *quadrants*. Some of the terms commonly used with a rectangular coordinate system are shown in Figures 8.1.1 and 8.1.2.

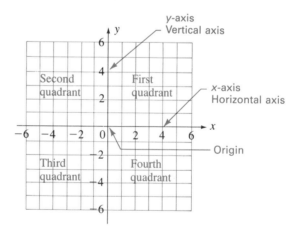

FIGURE 8.1.1   RECTANGULAR COORDINATE SYSTEM

Graph of a Point
There is exactly one point in the plane that corresponds to each ordered pair of real numbers. The origin corresponds to the ordered pair (0, 0).

The *first* number of an ordered pair tells us how far the point is from the *y*-axis. A *positive* first coordinate indicates that the point is to the *right* of the *y*-axis; a *negative* first coordinate indicates that the point is to the *left* of the *y*-axis.

The *second* number in the ordered pair tells us how far the point is from the *x*-axis. A *positive* second coordinate indicates that the point is *above* the *x*-axis; a *negative* second coordinate indicates that the point is *below* the *x*-axis.

The point (3, 2) is shown in Figure 8.1.2.

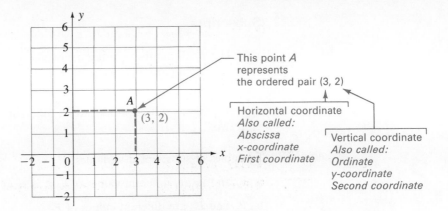

FIGURE 8.1.2 GRAPH OF AN ORDERED PAIR

NOTE   When the order is changed in an ordered pair, we get a different point. For example, (1, 4) and (4, 1) are two different points (see Figure 8.1.3).   ☑

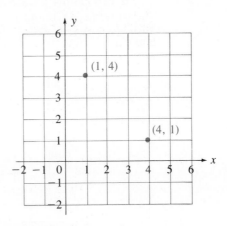

FIGURE 8.1.3

The phrase "plot the points" means the same as "graph the points."

Example 1   Plot the points $A(3, 5)$, $B(-5, 2)$, $C(-5, -4)$, $D(0, -3)$, and $E(4, -6)$.

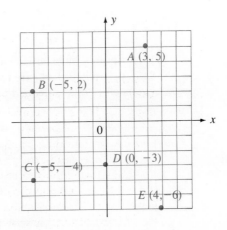

Subscripts

x_1 The small number written below and to the right of the letter is used to indicate a particular value of that letter; it is called a *subscript*. x_1 is read "x sub one."

x_2 A different subscript indicates a different value of that letter. x_2 is read "x sub two."

Example 2 Examples of subscripted variables:

a. y_1 and y_2 are different values of y. y_1 is read "y sub one"; y_2 is read "y sub two."

b. P_1 and P_2 are different values of P.

c. D_1 and D_2 are different values of D. ∎

The Distance Between Two Points

We use the notation $|PQ|$ to represent the distance between points P and Q. When discussing general points, we usually use subscripted variables; thus, (x_1, y_1) represents a point that is different from the point (x_2, y_2).

If two points have equal y-coordinates, they lie on the same *horizontal* line; therefore, (x_1, y_1) and (x_2, y_1) are two points on the same horizontal line. The distance between two such points is defined to be $|x_2 - x_1|$ (see Figure 8.1.4).

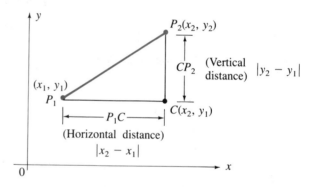

FIGURE 8.1.4

TO FIND THE DISTANCE BETWEEN POINTS
(x_1, y_1) AND (x_2, y_1)

$$|x_2 - x_1|$$

If two points have equal x-coordinates, they lie on the same *vertical* line; therefore, (x_1, y_1) and (x_1, y_2) are two points on the same vertical line. The distance between two such points is defined to be $|y_2 - y_1|$ (see Figure 8.1.4).

TO FIND THE DISTANCE BETWEEN POINTS
(x_1, y_1) AND (x_1, y_2)

$$|y_2 - y_1|$$

The formula for finding the distance, d, between the points $P_1(x_1, y_1)$ and $P_2(x_2, y_2)$ that lie *anywhere* in the plane follows:

TO FIND THE DISTANCE BETWEEN TWO POINTS
$P_1(x_1, y_1)$ AND $P_2(x_2, y_2)$

$$d = \sqrt{(x_2 - x_1)^2 + (y_2 - y_1)^2}$$

Proof: We will assume that P_1 and P_2 do not lie on the same horizontal or vertical line. Draw a horizontal line through $P_1(x_1, y_1)$ and a vertical line through $P_2(x_2, y_2)$. These lines meet at a point we will call C (see Figure 8.1.4); the coordinates of C *must* be (x_2, y_1). The triangle formed by joining points P_1, C, and P_2 is a right triangle with P_1P_2 as its hypotenuse.

The horizontal distance $|P_1C| = |x_2 - x_1|$, and the vertical distance $|CP_2| = |y_2 - y_1|$. Because $|x_2 - x_1|^2 = (x_2 - x_1)^2$ and $|y_2 - y_1|^2 = (y_2 - y_1)^2$ (you should verify this), using the Pythagorean theorem to find d gives

$$(d)^2 = (|x_2 - x_1|)^2 + (|y_2 - y_1|)^2$$
$$= (x_2 - x_1)^2 + (y_2 - y_1)^2$$

Solving for d, we have

$$d = \sqrt{(x_2 - x_1)^2 + (y_2 - y_1)^2}$$

or

$$d = -\sqrt{(x_2 - x_1)^2 + (y_2 - y_1)^2}$$

However, since d represents the length of a line segment, we reject the negative answer. Therefore,

$$d = \sqrt{(x_2 - x_1)^2 + (y_2 - y_1)^2}$$

Example 3   Find the distance between the points $(-6, 5)$ and $(6, -4)$. Let

$$P_1 = (-6, 5)$$
$$P_2 = (6, -4)$$

Then

$$d = \sqrt{(x_2 - x_1)^2 + (y_2 - y_1)^2}$$
$$= \sqrt{[6 - (-6)]^2 + [-4 - 5]^2}$$
$$= \sqrt{(12)^2 + (-9)^2} = \sqrt{144 + 81} = \sqrt{225} = 15$$

The distance is not changed if the points P_1 and P_2 are interchanged.

Let

$$P_1 = (6, -4)$$

$$P_2 = (-6, 5)$$

Then

$$d = \sqrt{[-6 - 6]^2 + [5 - (-4)]^2}$$

$$= \sqrt{(-12)^2 + (9)^2} = \sqrt{144 + 81} = \sqrt{225} = 15 \quad \blacksquare$$

Relations

A **mathematical relation** is a set of ordered pairs (x, y).

Example 4 Examples of relations:

$\mathcal{R}$ represents the relation

a. $\mathcal{R} = \{(-1, 2), (3, -4), (0, 5), (4, 3)\}$

b. $\mathcal{R} = \{(3, 5), (-5, 2), (-5, -4), (0, -3), (4, -6)\}$ $\quad \blacksquare$

*The **domain** of a relation* is the set of all the first coordinates of the ordered pairs of that relation. We represent the domain of the relation $\mathcal{R}$ by the symbol $D_{\mathcal{R}}$.

*The **range** of a relation* is the set of all the second coordinates of the ordered pairs of that relation. We represent the range of the relation $\mathcal{R}$ by the symbol $R_{\mathcal{R}}$.

The graph of a relation is the graph of all the ordered pairs of that relation.

Example 5 Find the domain, range, and graph of the relation

$$\mathcal{R} = \{(-1, 2), (3, -4), (0, 5), (4, 3)\}$$

The domain of $\{(\boxed{-1}, 2), (\boxed{3}, -4), (\boxed{0}, 5), (\boxed{4}, 3)\}$ is $\{-1, 3, 0, 4\} = D_{\mathcal{R}}$.

The range of $\{(-1, \boxed{2}), (3, \boxed{-4}), (0, \boxed{5}), (4, \boxed{3})\}$ is $\{2, -4, 5, 3\} = R_{\mathcal{R}}$.

The graph of $\{(-1, 2), (3, -4), (0, 5), (4, 3)\}$ is shown in Figure 8.1.5.

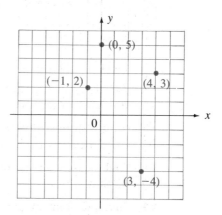

FIGURE 8.1.5

EXERCISES 8.1

Set I   **1.** Give the coordinates of each of the following points as shown in Figure 8.1.6:

a. *R*   b. *N*   c. *U*   d. *S*

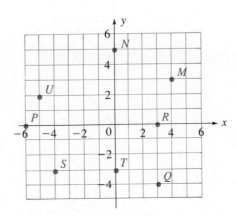

FIGURE 8.1.6

2. Give the coordinates of each of the following points as shown in Figure 8.1.6:

a. *M*   b. *P*   c. *Q*   d. *T*

3. Draw the triangle that has vertices with the following coordinates:

$A(0, 0)$, $B(3, 2)$, $C(-4, 5)$

4. Draw the triangle that has vertices with the following coordinates:

$A(-2, -3)$, $B(-2, 4)$, $C(3, 5)$

5. Find the distance between the two given points:

a. $(-2, -2)$ and $(2, 1)$ b. $(-3, 3)$ and $(3, -1)$

c. $(5, 3)$ and $(-2, 3)$ d. $(2, -2)$ and $(2, -5)$

e. $(4, 6)$ and $(0, 0)$

6. Find the distance between the two given points:

a. $(-4, -3)$ and $(8, 2)$ b. $(-3, 2)$ and $(4, -3)$

c. $(-3, -4)$ and $(-3, 2)$ d. $(-1, -2)$ and $(5, -2)$

e. $(-6, 9)$ and $(0, 0)$

7. Find the perimeter of the triangle that has vertices at $A(-2, 2)$, $B(4, 2)$, and $C(6, 8)$.

8. Find the perimeter of the triangle that has vertices at $A(0, 2)$, $B(11, 2)$, and $C(8, 6)$.

9. Use the distance formula to discover whether the triangle with vertices $A(-3, -2)$, $B(5, -1)$, and $C(3, 2)$ is or is not a right triangle.

10. Use the distance formula to discover whether the triangle with vertices $A(3, 2)$, $B(-5, 1)$, and $C(-3, -2)$ is or is not a right triangle.

11. Find the domain and range of the relation $\{(2, -1), (3, 4), (0, 2), (-3, -2)\}$ and graph it.

12. Find the domain and range of the relation $\{(-4, 0), (0, 0), (3, -2), (1, 5), (-3, -3)\}$ and graph it.

Set II

1. Give the coordinates of each of the following points as shown in Figure 8.1.7:

   a. *F*   b. *G*   c. *K*   d. *L*

2. Give the coordinates of each of the following points as shown in Figure 8.1.7:

   a. *A*   b. *B*   c. *C*   d. *D*

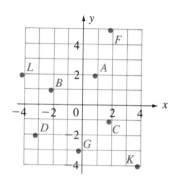

FIGURE 8.1.7

3. Draw the triangle that has vertices with the following coordinates:

   $A(4, -4)$, $B(2, 3)$, $C(-4, 1)$

4. Draw the parallelogram that has vertices with the following coordinates:

   $A(-2, -5)$, $B(3, -5)$, $C(0, 4)$, $D(5, 4)$

5. Find the distance between the two given points:

   a. $(7, -3)$ and $(15, 3)$ b. $(-14, 6)$ and $(-14, -13)$

   c. $(9, -8)$ and $(-6, -5)$ d. $(-11, -18)$ and $(-17, -18)$

   e. $(2, 12)$ and $(-6, 16)$

6. Find the distance between the two given points:

   a. $(3, 0)$ and $(-1, 4)$ b. $(3, -1)$ and $(-3, 1)$

   c. $(8, 3)$ and $(-2, 3)$ d. $(-4, 2)$ and $(3, -1)$

   e. $(7, 2)$ and $(7, -5)$

7. Find the perimeter of the triangle that has vertices at $R(4, -7)$, $S(9, 5)$, and $T(-8, -2)$.

8. Use the distance formula to discover whether the triangle with vertices $A(-2, -5)$, $B(-4, -2)$, and $C(5, 0)$ is or is not a right triangle.

9. Use the distance formula to discover whether the triangle with vertices $A(-2, -3)$, $B(2, -2)$, and $C(0, 3)$ is or is not a right triangle.

10. Do the points $P(10, -6)$, $Q(-5, 3)$, and $R(-15, 9)$ lie in a straight line? Why or why not?

11. Find the domain and range of the relation $\{(-4, 3), (-2, 0), (-3, -5), (4, -2), (4, 4)\}$ and graph it.

12. Find the domain and range of the relation $\{(-6, 3), (2, -4), (0, 5), (-1, -1)\}$ and graph it.

8.2 Graphing Straight Lines

In Section 8.1, we showed how to graph points in the real plane. In this section, we show how to graph *straight lines* in the real plane. The following statement will not be proved, but *it must be memorized*:

> In the real plane, the graph of any first-degree equation in one or two variables is a straight line.

Such equations are called **linear equations**. The general form of a linear equation is

$$Ax + By + C = 0 \qquad \text{(where } A, B, \text{ and } C \text{ are real numbers;}$$
$$A \text{ and } B \text{ are not both 0)}$$

The solution set of the equation $Ax + By + C = 0$ is a set of ordered pairs and is, therefore, a relation.

A point (x, y) will lie on the line whose equation is $Ax + By + C = 0$ if its coordinates satisfy that equation. To find a point on the line, if $B \neq 0$, we can let x have *any* value whatever and then solve the equation for y. If $A \neq 0$, we can instead let y have *any* value whatever and then solve the equation for x. We will have found a point on the line.

We can draw a straight line if we know two points that lie on that line. We could use any two points, but it is usually more convenient to choose the two points where the line crosses the coordinate axes. These two points are called the **intercepts** of the line. The **x-intercept** is the point where the line crosses the x-axis. The **y-intercept** is the point where the line crosses the y-axis. (See Figure 8.2.1.) To prevent errors, it is safest to find a third point as well.

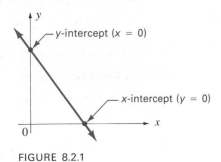

FIGURE 8.2.1

The Intercept Method of Graphing a Straight Line

Example 1   Graph the relation $4x + 3y = 12$.

x-intercept Set $y = 0$.

Then $\qquad 4x + 3y = 12$

becomes $4x + 3(0) = 12$

$$4x = 12$$

$$x = 3$$

The x-intercept is $(3, 0)$

Table of values

x	y
3	0

355

We sometimes say "the x-intercept is 3" (the x-*coordinate* of the point where the line crosses the x-axis, instead of the point itself).

y-intercept Set $x = 0$.

Then $\quad 4x + 3y = 12$

becomes $4(0) + 3y = 12$

$$3y = 12$$

$$y = 4$$

The y-intercept is $(0, 4)$

Table of values

x	y
3	0
0	4

We sometimes say "the y-intercept is 4" (the y-*coordinate* of the point where the line crosses the y-axis, instead of the point itself).

Third point Set $x = -3$.

Then $\quad 4x + 3y = 12$

becomes $4(-3) + 3y = 12$

$$3y = 24$$

$$y = 8$$

A third point is $(-3, 8)$

Table of values

x	y
3	0
0	4
-3	8

We then graph the x- and y-intercepts and the third point and note that these three points *do* appear to lie on the same straight line. See Figure 8.2.2.

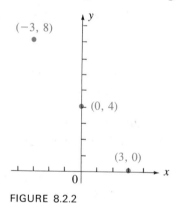

FIGURE 8.2.2

This is *not yet* the graph of $4x + 3y = 12$. There are *infinitely* many points whose coordinates satisfy the equation. Therefore, we must now connect these points with a *straight line*. The line actually extends infinitely far in both directions; to indicate this, we put arrows on both ends of it. See Figure 8.2.3.

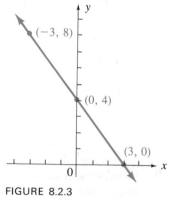

FIGURE 8.2.3

Example 2   Graph the relation $3x - 4y = 0$.

x-intercept Set $y = 0$.

Then $3x - 4y = 0$

becomes $3x - 4(0) = 0$

$$3x = 0$$

$$x = 0$$

Therefore, the *x*-intercept is $(0, 0)$—the origin. Since the line goes through the origin, the *y-intercept* is also $(0, 0)$.

We have found only one point on the line: $(0, 0)$. Therefore, we must find another point on the line. To find another point, we can set either variable equal to a number and then solve the equation for the other variable.

Second point Set $y = 3$.

Then $3x - 4y = 0$

becomes $3x - 4(3) = 0$

$$3x = 12$$

$$x = 4$$

This gives the point $(4, 3)$ on the line.

Third point Set $x = -4$.

Then $3x - 4y = 0$

becomes $3(-4) - 4y = 0$

$$-4y = 12$$

$$y = -3$$

This gives the point $(-4, -3)$. We now plot the points $(0, 0)$, $(4, 3)$, and $(-4, -3)$ and connect them with a straight line. See Figure 8.2.4.

Table of values

x	y
0	0
0	0
4	3
-4	-3

Both intercepts are the same point

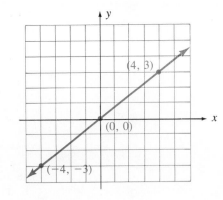

FIGURE 8.2.4

Sometimes, the *x*- and *y*-intercepts are very close together and to draw the line through them accurately would be very difficult. In this case, find another point on the line far enough away from the intercepts so that drawing an accurate line is easy. To find the other point, set either variable equal to a number, and then solve the equation for the other variable.

Some equations of a line have only one variable. Such equations have graphs that are either vertical or horizontal lines (see Examples 3 and 4).

Example 3 Graph the relation $x = 3$. (The equation $x = 3$ is equivalent to $x + 0 \cdot y = 3$ and to $x - 3 = 0$.)

The domain of the relation is $\{3\}$, since 3 is the only value that x can have. While y is not mentioned in the equation, it is understood that $x = 3$ *for all y-values.* We could make a chart of values, but x would always equal 3. We will plot the points $(3, 0)$, $(3, -2)$, and $(3, 4)$ and then connect them with a straight line. See Figure 8.2.5.

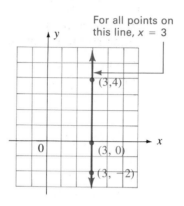

FIGURE 8.2.5

The graph of $x = k$ is always a vertical line.

Example 4 Graph the relation $y + 4 = 0$. (The equation $y + 4 = 0$ is equivalent to $y = -4$ and to $0 \cdot x + y + 4 = 0$.)

The domain of the relation is the set of all real numbers. While x is not mentioned in the equation, it is understood that $y + 4 = 0$ *for all x.* We will plot the points $(0, -4)$, $(3, -4)$, and $(-2, -4)$ and connect them with a straight line. The graph of the relation $y + 4 = 0$ is shown in Figure 8.2.6.

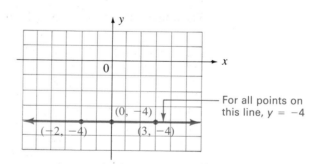

FIGURE 8.2.6

The graph of $y = k$ is always a horizontal line.

The following example illustrates the use of different scales on the two axes.

Example 5 Graph the relation $\{(x, y) \mid 50y - x = 100\}$.

The statement in set-builder notation means that the relation consists of all of the *ordered pairs* (x, y) that satisfy the equation $50y - x = 100$. Since the domain of the relation is not specified, it is the set of all real numbers. The graph of such a set of points will be a straight line.

Table of values

x	y
0	2
−100	0
50	3

It would be impractical to have the units on the two axes be of equal lengths since our graph would run off the paper. The graph of the relation is shown in Figure 8.2.7.

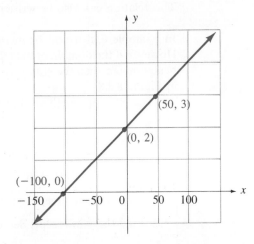

FIGURE 8.2.7 ∎

Example 6 Find the domain and range of the relation $\{(x, y)|2x + 3y = 6, x = -3, 0, 3, 6\}$ and graph it.

The domain is *not* the set of real numbers; it is $\{-3, 0, 3, 6\}$.

If $x = -3$, $2(-3) + 3y = 6$
$$-6 + 3y = 6$$
$$y = \boxed{4}$$

If $x = 0$, $2(0) + 3y = 6$
$$0 + 3y = 6$$
$$y = \boxed{2}$$

If $x = 3$, $2(3) + 3y = 6$
$$6 + 3y = 6$$
$$y = \boxed{0}$$

If $x = 6$, $2(6) + 3y = 6$
$$12 + 3y = 6$$
$$y = \boxed{-2}$$

Table of values

x	y
−3	4
0	2
3	0
6	−2

Domain —⎿   ⎾— Range

Therefore, the range $R_{\mathscr{R}} = \{4, 2, 0, -2\}$. The graph of the relation is shown in Figure 8.2.8.

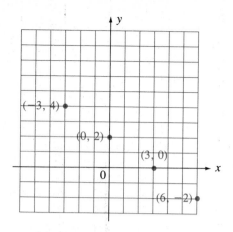

FIGURE 8.2.8

This relation can also be written $\{(-3, 4), (0, 2), (3, 0), (6, -2)\}$ ∎

In Example 6, it would be incorrect to connect the four points with a straight line. However, if the domain of the relation were changed from $\{-3, 0, 3, 6\}$ to the set of all real numbers, then the graph would be the straight line through the four points shown in Figure 8.2.8.

The intercept method of graphing a straight line is summarized in the following box:

TO GRAPH A STRAIGHT LINE (INTERCEPT METHOD)

1. Find the x-intercept: Set $y = 0$; then solve for x.

2. Find the y-intercept: Set $x = 0$; then solve for y.

3. If the line goes through the origin, another point must be chosen.

4. Find one other point.

5. Plot the three points.

6. Draw a straight line through the points.

7. The graph of $x = a$ is a vertical line that passes through $(a, 0)$.

8. The graph of $y = b$ is a horizontal line that passes through $(0, b)$.

EXERCISES 8.2

Set I   In Exercises 1–20, sketch the graph of each relation.

1. $3x + 2y = 6$ **2.** $4x - 3y = 12$ **3.** $5x - 3y = 15$

4. $2x + 5y = 10$ **5.** $9x + 5y = 18$ **6.** $6x - 11y = 22$

7. $10x = 21 + 7y$ **8.** $13y = 40 - 8x$ **9.** $9y = 25 - 7x$

10. $17x = 31 + 6y$ **11.** $8x - 41 = 14y$ **12.** $5y - 33 = -15x$

13. $6x + 11y = 0$ **14.** $3x + 2y = 0$ **15.** $4y = -8x$

16. $9x = 3y$ **17.** $x + 5 = 0$ **18.** $x = 4$

19. $y = -3$ **20.** $y - 2 = 0$

For Exercises 21–34, graph the given relation.

21. $\{(x, y)\,|\,7x + 5y = 2\}$

22. $\{(x, y)\,|\,3x + 8y = 4\}$

23. $\{(x, y)\,|\,y = \frac{1}{2}x - 1\}$

24. $\{(x, y)\,|\,y = \frac{1}{3}x + 2\}$

25. $\{(x, y)\,|\,3(x - 5) = 7y\}$

26. $\{(x, y)\,|\,4x = 3(y - 6)\}$

27. $\{(x, y)\,|\,50x + y = -100\}$

28. $\{(x, y)\,|\,x - 30y = 90\}$

29. $\{(x, y)\,|\,x = 50y\}$

30. $\{(x, y)\,|\,y = 70x\}$

31. $\{(x, y)\,|\,y = -2x, x = 1, 3, 5\}$

32. $\{(x, y)\,|\,y = 3x, x = -1, 3, 4\}$

33. $\{(x, y)\,|\,x - y = 5, x = 1, 4\}$

34. $\{(x, y)\,|\,2x - y = 3, x = 0, 2\}$

In Exercises 35 and 36, (a) graph the two relations for each exercise on the same set of axes and (b) give the coordinates of the point where the two lines cross.

35. $\begin{cases} 5x - 7y = 18 \\ 2x + 3y = -16 \end{cases}$

36. $\begin{cases} 4x + 9y = 3 \\ 2x - 5y = 11 \end{cases}$

Set II In Exercises 1–20, sketch the graph of each relation.

1. $3x + 8y = 24$

2. $4x - 12y = 24$

3. $4x - 5y = 20$

4. $x = 5$

5. $15x + 8y = 32$

6. $y = -6$

7. $7x - 28 = 9y$

8. $-2x + 5y = 10$

9. $19y = 35 - 8x$

10. $y = 3x + 4$

11. $7y = 16x - 47$

12. $y = \frac{2}{3}x + 4$

13. $5x - 13y = 0$

14. $3x = 5y$

15. $2x = 8y$

16. $y = \frac{2}{3}x - 1$

17. $x + 4 = 0$

18. $y - 6 = 0$

19. $y = 4$

20. $x + y = 0$

For Exercises 21–34, graph the given relation.

21. $\{(x, y)\,|\,11x - 4y = 2\}$

22. $\{(x, y)\,|\,x = 0\}$

23. $\{(x, y)\,|\,y = \frac{2}{5}x - 3\}$

24. $\{(x, y)\,|\,y = 0\}$

25. $\{(x, y)\,|\,4(y + 7) = 9x\}$

26. $\{(x, y)\,|\,x = -4\}$

27. $\{(x, y)\,|\,20y - x = 80\}$

28. $\{(x, y)\,|\,y = \frac{2}{3}x\}$

29. $\{(x, y)\,|\,y = 100x\}$

30. $\{(x, y)\,|\,x = \frac{2}{3}y\}$

31. $\{(x, y)\,|\,y = 4x, x = -2, 2\}$

32. $\{(x, y)\,|\,y = 5x - 2, x = 2, 4, 6\}$

33. $\{(x, y)\,|\,x - 2y = 4, x = 2, 4, 6\}$

34. $\{(x, y)\,|\,x = 5y, x = -5, 0, 5\}$

In Exercises 35 and 36, (a) graph the two relations for each exercise on the same set of axes and (b) give the coordinates of the point where the two lines cross.

35. $\begin{cases} 7x + 10y = -1 \\ 3x - 8y = -25 \end{cases}$

36. $\begin{cases} 8x - y = 4 \\ x + 2y = 9 \end{cases}$

8.3 Slopes and Equations of Straight Lines

In Section 8.2, we discussed the graph of a straight line. In this section, we discuss the slope of a line and show how to write the equation of a line given certain facts about the line.

8.3A   The Slope of a Line

If we imagine a line as representing a hill, then the slope of a line is a measure of the steepness of the hill. To measure the *slope* of a line, we choose any two points on the line, $P_1(x_1, y_1)$ and $P_2(x_2, y_2)$ (see Figure 8.3.1).

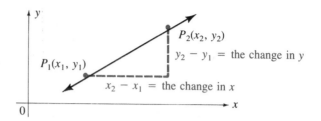

FIGURE 8.3.1

We use m to represent the slope of a line. The slope is defined as follows:

$$\text{Slope} = \frac{\text{The change in } y}{\text{The change in } x}$$

$$m = \frac{y_2 - y_1}{x_2 - x_1}$$

Example 1   Find the slope of the line through the points $(-3, 5)$ and $(6 - 1)$.

Let $P_1 = (-3, 5)$

$\quad\quad P_2 = (6, -1)$

Then $m = \dfrac{y_2 - y_1}{x_2 - x_1}$

$\quad\quad = \dfrac{-1 - 5}{6 - (-3)} = \dfrac{-6}{9} = -\dfrac{2}{3}$

The slope is not changed if the points P_1 and P_2 are interchanged.

Let $P_1 = (6, -1)$

$\quad\quad P_2 = (-3, 5)$

Then $m = \dfrac{y_2 - y_1}{x_2 - x_1}$

$\quad\quad = \dfrac{5 - (-1)}{-3 - 6} = \dfrac{6}{-9} = -\dfrac{2}{3}$

The solution is shown graphically in Figure 8.3.2.

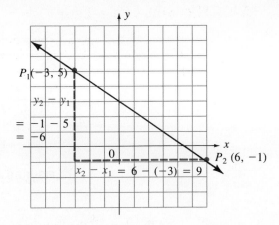

FIGURE 8.3.2

Notice that in Example 1 the slope of the line is *negative*, and that a point moving along the line in the positive x-direction *falls*.

Example 2   Find the slope of the line through the points $A(-2, -4)$ and $B(5, 1)$.

$$m = \frac{y_2 - y_1}{x_2 - x_1}$$

$$= \frac{1 - (-4)}{5 - (-2)} = \frac{5}{7}$$

The solution is shown graphically in Figure 8.3.3.

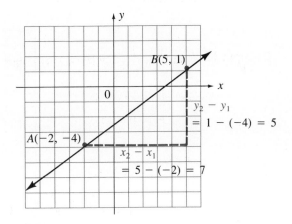

FIGURE 8.3.3

Notice that in Example 2 the slope of the line is *positive*, and that a point moving along the line in the positive x-direction *rises*.

Example 3   Find the slope of the line through the points $E(-4, -3)$ and $F(2, -3)$.

$$m = \frac{y_2 - y_1}{x_2 - x_1}$$

$$= \frac{-3 - (-3)}{2 - (-4)} = \frac{0}{6} = 0$$

Whenever the slope is zero, the line is horizontal (see Figure 8.3.4).

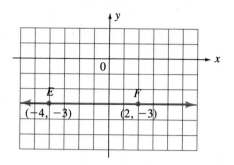

FIGURE 8.3.4

Example 4   Find the slope of the line through the points $R(4, 5)$ and $S(4, -2)$.

$$m = \frac{y_2 - y_1}{x_2 - x_1}$$

$$= \frac{-2 - 5}{4 - 4} = \frac{-7}{0}$$

Note that $\dfrac{-7}{0}$ is not a real number. Therefore, the slope does not exist when the line is vertical (see Figure 8.3.5).

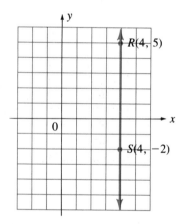

FIGURE 8.3.5

The facts about the slope of a line are summarized as follows:

The slope of a line is positive if a point moving along the line in the positive x-direction rises. (See Figure 8.3.3.)

The slope of a line is negative if a point moving along the line in the positive x-direction falls. (See Figure 8.3.2.)

The slope is zero if the line is horizontal. (See Figure 8.3.4.)

The slope does not exist if the line is vertical. (See Figure 8.3.5.)

Example 5   Graph each of the following lines and find each slope:

a. $y = -\frac{2}{3}x$

x	y
-3	2
0	0
3	-2

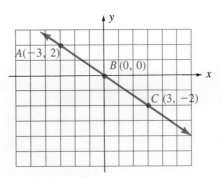

For the slope, if we use the points A and B, we have

$$m = \frac{2 - 0}{-3 - 0} = -\frac{2}{3}$$

If we use the points B and C, we have

$$m = \frac{0 - (-2)}{0 - 3} = -\frac{2}{3}$$

b. $y = -\frac{2}{3}x - 2$

x	y
-6	2
-3	0
0	-2

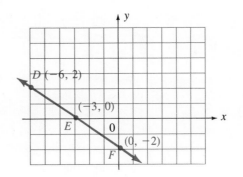

For the slope, if we use the points D and E, we have

$$m = \frac{2 - 0}{-6 - (-3)} = -\frac{2}{3}$$

If we use the points E and F, we have

$$m = \frac{-2 - 0}{0 - (-3)} = -\frac{2}{3}$$

You can verify that for each of the lines, if any other points were used, the slope would remain unchanged.

c. $y = \frac{3}{2}x$

x	y
-2	-3
0	0
2	3

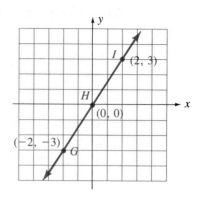

For the slope, if we use the points G and H, we have

$$m = \frac{-3 - 0}{-2 - 0} = \frac{3}{2}$$

If we use the points H and I, we have

$$m = \frac{3 - 0}{2 - 0} = \frac{3}{2}$$

d. Graph the lines from Example 5a and Example 5b on the same axes.

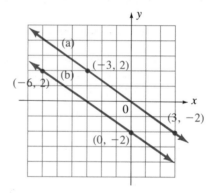

e. Graph the lines from Example 5a and Example 5c on the same axes.

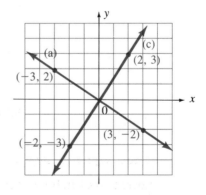

Note that in Examples 5a and 5b, $m = -\frac{2}{3}$, and that in Example 5c, $m = +\frac{3}{2}$, the negative reciprocal of $-\frac{2}{3}$. ■

The following rules are stated without proof:

Parallel lines have the same slope; conversely, any lines that have the same slope are parallel.

Perpendicular lines (if neither is vertical) have slopes whose product is -1; equivalently, if one line having slope m_1 is perpendicular to another line having slope m_2, then

$$m_1 = -\frac{1}{m_2}$$

A vertical line is parallel to any other vertical line and is perpendicular to any horizontal line.

In Examples 5a and 5b, the lines are *parallel* to each other and the *slopes* of the two lines are equal. The lines of Examples 5a and 5c appear to be perpendicular to each other, and the *product* of the slopes of these lines is -1.

Example 6   Graph the line that passes through the point $(3, 4)$ and has a slope of $-\frac{2}{3}$.

If we interpret the slope as $\dfrac{-2}{3}$, we find that the line falls 2 units for each 3 units it moves to the right. The line *falls* because the numerator is negative; it moves to the *right* because the denominator is *positive*. We know that one point the line passes through is $(3, 4)$. Therefore, the line is as shown in Figure 8.3.6.

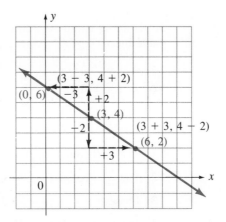

FIGURE 8.3.6

If we interpret the slope as $\dfrac{2}{-3}$, we find that the line rises 2 units for each 3 units it moves to the left. It *rises* because the numerator is *positive*; it moves to the *left* because the denominator is *negative*. We see that when we interpret the slope as $\dfrac{2}{-3}$, we simply get a different point on the same line.   ■

EXERCISES 8.3A

Set I   In Exercises 1–8, find the slope of the line through the given pair of points.

1. $(1, 4)$ and $(10, 6)$ 2. $(-3, -5)$ and $(3, 0)$

3. $(-5, -5)$ and $(1, -7)$ 4. $(-1, 0)$ and $(7, -4)$

5. $(-7, -5)$ and $(2, -5)$ 6. $(0, -2)$ and $(5, -2)$

7. $(-4, 3)$ and $(-4, -2)$ 8. $(-5, 2)$ and $(-5, 7)$

In Exercises 9 and 10, graph each of the lines on the same axes and find the slope of each line.

9. a. $y = \frac{3}{4}x$ b. $y = \frac{3}{4}x + 5$ c. $y = \frac{3}{4}x - 2$

10. a. $y = x$ b. $y = x - 3$ c. $y = x + 4$

In Exercises 11–14, graph the line described.

11. Passes through $(-1, 3)$ and has a slope of 3.

12. Passes through $(2, -4)$ and has a slope of 5.

13. Passes through $(0, 4)$ and has a slope of $-\frac{2}{5}$.

14. Passes through $(1, -3)$ and has a slope of $-\frac{5}{3}$.

Set II   In Exercises 1–8, find the slope of the line through the given pair of points.

1. $(-5, -8)$ and $(-9, 4)$ 2. $(9, 15)$ and $(-6, 3)$

3. $(-2, -11)$ and $(-7, -11)$ 4. $(14, -9)$ and $(14, -21)$

5. $(-3, 2)$ and $(4, -3)$ 6. $(8, 1)$ and $(8, 6)$

7. $(0, 5)$ and $(-3, 5)$ 8. $(4, -2)$ and $(-2, 4)$

In Exercises 9 and 10, graph each of the lines on the same axes and find the slope of each line.

9. a. $y = -\frac{1}{2}x$ b. $y = -\frac{1}{2}x + 2$ c. $y = -\frac{1}{2}x - 3$

10. a. $y = -4x$ b. $y = -4x + 3$ c. $y = -4x - 2$

In Exercises 11–14, graph the line described.

11. Passes through $(5, 0)$ and has a slope of -3.

12. Passes through $(-2, 4)$ and has a slope of $\frac{3}{5}$.

13. Passes through $(0, 0)$ and has a slope of 0.

14. Passes through $(3, -1)$ and has a slope of $-\frac{1}{4}$.

8.3B   Equations of Lines

While the graph of *any* first-degree (linear) equation in one or two variables is a straight line, three forms of the equation of a straight line are especially useful: the *general form,* the *point-slope form,* and the *slope-intercept form.*

General Form of the Equation of a Line

The general form for the equation of a line, *as used in this text*, is as follows:

GENERAL FORM OF THE EQUATION OF A LINE

$$Ax + By + C = 0$$

where A, B, and C are integers, $A \geq 0$, and A and B are not both 0.

To write the equation of a straight line in the *general form*, clear fractions and move all terms to the left of the equal sign. If A is then negative, multiply both sides of the equation by -1.

Example 7 Write $-\dfrac{2}{3}x + \dfrac{1}{2}y = 1$ in the general form.

LCD = 6

$$\frac{6}{1}\left(-\frac{2}{3}x\right) + \frac{6}{1}\left(\frac{1}{2}y\right) = \frac{6}{1}\left(\frac{1}{1}\right)$$

$$-4x \quad + \quad 3y \quad = \quad 6$$

$$4x - 3y + 6 = 0 \qquad \text{General form} \quad \blacksquare$$

Point-Slope Form of the Equation of a Line

Let $P_1(x_1, y_1)$ be a known point on the line with slope m. Let $P(x, y)$ represent *any* other point on the line (see Figure 8.3.7). Then

$$m = \frac{y - y_1}{x - x_1}$$

Therefore,

$$\frac{(x - x_1)}{1} \cdot \frac{m}{1} = \frac{(x - x_1)}{1} \cdot \frac{y - y_1}{x - x_1}$$

$$(x - x_1)m = y - y_1$$

Point-slope form

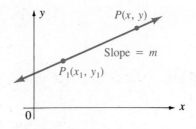

FIGURE 8.3.7

This equation is usually written as follows:

POINT-SLOPE FORM OF THE EQUATION OF A LINE

$$y - y_1 = m(x - x_1)$$

where m = slope of the line and $P_1(x_1, y_1)$ is a known point on the line.

When we are given the *slope* of a line and a *point* through which it passes, we will use the *point-slope form* of the equation of a line in order to write the equation of the line (see Example 8).

Example 8   Write the general form of the equation of the line that passes through $(-1, 4)$ and has a slope of $-\frac{2}{3}$.

Into the point-slope form, we substitute -1 for x_1, 4 for y_1, and $-\frac{2}{3}$ for m.

$$y - y_1 = m(x - x_1)$$

$$y - 4 = -\frac{2}{3}[x - (-1)] \qquad \text{Point-slope form}$$

$$3y - 12 = -2(x + 1)$$

$$3y - 12 = -2x - 2$$

$$2x + 3y - 10 = 0 \qquad \text{General form} \quad \blacksquare$$

Slope-Intercept Form of the Equation of a Line

Let $(0, b)$ be the *y-intercept* of a line with slope m (see Figure 8.3.8). Then

$$y - y_1 = m(x - x_1)$$

$$y - b = m(x - 0)$$

$$y - b = mx$$

$$y = mx + b$$

Slope ⟶   ⟶ y-intercept

Slope-intercept form

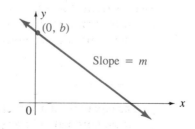

FIGURE 8.3.8

SLOPE-INTERCEPT FORM OF THE EQUATON OF A LINE

$$y = mx + b$$

where m = slope of the line, and b = y-intercept of the line

When we are given the *slope* of a line and its *y-intercept*, we may use the *slope-intercept form* of the equation of a line (see Example 9). The point-slope form could also be used.

Example 9   Write the general form of the equation of the line that has a slope of $-\dfrac{3}{4}$ and a y-intercept of -2.

Into the slope-intercept form, we substitute $-\frac{3}{4}$ for m and -2 for b.

$$y = mx + b$$

$$y = -\frac{3}{4}x - 2 \qquad \text{Slope-intercept form}$$

$$4y = -3x - 8$$

$$3x + 4y + 8 = 0 \qquad \text{General form} \quad \blacksquare$$

The Equation of a Horizontal Line

The following statement can be used in writing the equation of a horizontal line:

The equation of a horizontal line is of the form $y = k$ or $y - k = 0$, where k is the y-coordinate of every point on the line.

Example 10   Find the equation of the horizontal line that passes through $(2, -4)$.

Because the y-coordinate of the given point is -4, the equation is

$$y = -4$$

$$y + 4 = 0 \qquad \text{General form} \quad \blacksquare$$

The Equation of a Vertical Line

Since a *vertical* line has no slope, we cannot use the point-slope form or the slope-intercept form when writing its equation. In fact, the only way to write the equation of a vertical line is to memorize the following statement:

The equation of a vertical line is of the form $x = k$ or $x - k = 0$, where k is the x-coordinate of every point on the line.

Example 11   Find the equation of the vertical line through $(3, -5)$.

Since the line is vertical, we know its equation will be of the form $x = k$. Because the x-coordinate of the given point is 3, the equation is $x = 3$.   ■

Example 12 illustrates the technique of finding the equation of a line when we know two points on the line.

Example 12   Find the equation of the line that passes through the points $(-15, -9)$ and $(-5, 3)$.

Step 1 Find the slope from the two given points.

$$m = \frac{(-9) - (3)}{(-15) - (-5)} = \frac{-12}{-10} = \frac{6}{5}$$

Step 2 Use this slope with *either* given point to find the equation of the line.

Using the point $(-5, 3)$	*Using the point* $(-15, -9)$
$y - y_1 = m(x - x_1)$	$y - y_1 = m(x - x_1)$
$y - 3 = \dfrac{6}{5}[x - (-5)]$	$y - (-9) = \dfrac{6}{5}[x - (-15)]$
$5y - 15 = 6(x + 5)$	$5(y + 9) = 6(x + 15)$
$5y - 15 = 6x + 30$	$5y + 45 = 6x + 90$
$0 = 6x - 5y + 45$	$0 = 6x - 5y + 45$

Note that the same equation is obtained no matter which of the two given points is used.   ■

It is sometimes useful to change the general form of the equation of a line into the slope-intercept form (see Example 13).

Example 13   Uses of the slope-intercept form:

a. Write the general form of the equation of the line through $(-4, 7)$ and parallel to the line $2x + 3y + 6 = 0$.

Solution Parallel lines have the same slope. Therefore, the line we are trying to find has the same slope as $2x + 3y + 6 = 0$. To find the slope of $2x + 3y + 6 = 0$, write $2x + 3y + 6 = 0$ in the slope-intercept form by solving it for y.

$2x + 3y + 6 = 0$	General form
$3y = -2x - 6$	Divide both sides by 3
$y = -\dfrac{2}{3}x - 2$	Slope-intercept form

Slope ⟍

Therefore, the line we are trying to find has a slope of $-\dfrac{2}{3}$ and passes through $(-4, 7)$.

$$y - y_1 = m(x - x_1)$$

$$y - 7 = -\frac{2}{3}[x - (-4)] \qquad \text{Point-slope form}$$

$$3y - 21 = -2(x + 4)$$

$$3y - 21 = -2x - 8$$

$$2x + 3y - 13 = 0 \qquad \text{General form}$$

b. Find the y-intercept of the line $2x + 3y + 6 = 0$.

Solution In Example 13a, we found that the slope-intercept form of the equation was

$$y = -\frac{2}{3}x \boxed{-2}$$

$$\text{y-intercept}$$

Therefore, the y-intercept is -2. ∎

Example 14 Write the general form of the equation of the line through $(-4, 7)$ and perpendicular to the line $2x + 3y + 6 = 0$.

In Example 13, we found that the slope of the line $2x + 3y + 6 = 0$ was $-\frac{2}{3}$. Since the required line is to be perpendicular to that one, its slope must be the negative reciprocal of $-\frac{2}{3}$, which is

$$+\frac{1}{\frac{2}{3}} = \frac{3}{2}$$

Therefore, the line we are trying to find has a slope of $\frac{3}{2}$ and passes through $(-4, 7)$.

$$y - 7 = \frac{3}{2}(x - [-4]) \qquad \text{Point-slope form}$$

$$2(y - 7) = 3(x + 4)$$

$$2y - 14 = 3x + 12$$

$$3x - 2y + 26 = 0 \qquad \text{General form} \quad \blacksquare$$

EXERCISES 8.3B

Set I   In Exercises 1–8, write each equation in general form.

1. $5x = 3y - 7$ 　　　　 **2.** $4x = -9y + 3$ 　　　　 **3.** $\dfrac{x}{2} - \dfrac{y}{5} = 1$

4. $\dfrac{y}{6} - \dfrac{x}{7} = 1$ 　　　　 **5.** $y = -\dfrac{5}{3}x + 4$ 　　　　 **6.** $y = -\dfrac{3}{8}x - 5$

7. $4(x - y) = 11 - 2(x + 3y)$ 　　　 **8.** $15 - 6(3x + y) = 7(x - 2y)$

In Exercises 9–14, write the general form of the equation of the line that passes through the given point and has the indicated slope.

9. $(4, -3)$, $m = \dfrac{1}{5}$ **10.** $(-2, -1)$, $m = -\dfrac{5}{6}$ **11.** $(-6, 5)$, $m = \dfrac{1}{4}$

12. $(-3, -2)$, $m = -\dfrac{4}{5}$ **13.** $(-1, 3)$, $m = -4$ **14.** $(3, 0)$, $m = 2$

In Exercises 15–20, write the general form of the equation of the line that has the indicated slope and y-intercept.

15. $m = \dfrac{5}{7}$, y-intercept $= -3$ **16.** $m = -\dfrac{1}{4}$, y-intercept $= -2$

17. $m = -\dfrac{4}{3}$, y-intercept $= \dfrac{1}{2}$ **18.** $m = -\dfrac{3}{5}$, y-intercept $= \dfrac{3}{4}$

19. $m = 0$, y-intercept $= 5$ **20.** $m = 0$, y-intercept $= 7$

21. Write the equation of the horizontal line that passes through the point $(-4, 3)$.

22. Write the equation of the horizontal line that passes through the point $(2, -5)$.

23. Write the equation of the vertical line that passes through the point $(7, -2)$.

24. Write the equation of the vertical line that passes through the point $(-6, 4)$.

In Exercises 25–28, (a) write the given equation in the slope-intercept form, (b) give the slope of the line, and (c) give the y-intercept of the line.

25. $4x - 5y + 20 = 0$ **26.** $8x + 3y - 24 = 0$

27. $\dfrac{2}{3}x + 3y + 5 = 0$ **28.** $3x - \dfrac{5}{6}y - 2 = 0$

In Exercises 29–34, find the general form of the equation of the line that passes through the given points.

29. $(8, -1)$ and $(6, 4)$ **30.** $(7, -2)$ and $(5, 1)$

31. $(10, 0)$ and $(7, 4)$ **32.** $(-4, 0)$ and $(-6, -5)$

33. $(-9, 3)$ and $(-3, -1)$ **34.** $(-11, 4)$ and $(-3, -2)$

35. Write the general form of the equation of the line through $(-4, 7)$ and parallel to the line $3x - 5y = 6$.

36. Write the general form of the equation of the line through $(8, -5)$ and parallel to the line $7x + 4y + 3 = 0$.

37. Write the general form of the equation of the line through $(6, 2)$ and perpendicular to the line $2x + 4y = 3$.

38. Write the general form of the equation of the line through $(5, -1)$ and perpendicular to the line $3x - 6y = 2$.

39. Write the general form of the equation of the line that has an x-intercept of 4 and is parallel to the line $3x + 5y - 12 = 0$.

40. Write the general form of the equation of the line that has an x-intercept of -3 and is parallel to the line $9x - 14y + 6 = 0$.

41. Write the general form of the equation of the line that has an x-intercept of -6 and a y-intercept of 4.

42. Write the general form of the equation of the line that has an x-intercept of 15 and a y-intercept of -12.

Set II   In Exercises 1–8, write each equation in the general form.

1. $6y = 8 - 13x$ **2.** $8y = 2x - 4$ **3.** $\dfrac{x}{-3} - \dfrac{y}{6} = 1$

4. $5x = 2y$ **5.** $y = \frac{2}{9}x - 13$ **6.** $x = \frac{1}{5}y + 3$

7. $17 - 5(2x - y) = 8(x + 4y)$ **8.** $3x - 5(2y - 5x) = 4y + 7x - 1$

In Exercises 9–14, write the general form of the equation of the line that passes through the given point and has the indicated slope.

9. $(7, -4)$, $m = \frac{1}{6}$ **10.** $(8, 3)$, $m = -4$

11. $(-5, -8)$, $m = -\frac{3}{4}$ **12.** $(0, 0)$, $m = \frac{2}{5}$

13. $(2, -5)$, $m = -1$ **14.** $(-3, 0)$, $m = 8$

In Exercises 15–20, write the general form of the equation of the line that has the indicated slope and y-intercept.

15. $m = \frac{5}{6}$, y-intercept $= -4$ **16.** $m = -\frac{2}{9}$, y-intercept $= \frac{1}{3}$

17. $m = 0$, y-intercept $= -3$ **18.** $m = 3$, y-intercept $= 0$

19. $m = -\frac{1}{4}$, y-intercept $= 1$ **20.** $m = -5$, y-intercept $= -3$

21. Write the equation of the horizontal line that passes through the point $(-3, 7)$.

22. Write the equation of the horizontal line that passes through the point $(-9, -7)$.

23. Write the equation of the vertical line that passes through the point $(-5, -1)$.

24. Write the equation of the vertical line that passes through the point $(0, -5)$.

In Exercises 25–28, (a) write the given equation in the slope-intercept form, (b) give the slope of the line, and (c) give the y-intercept of the line.

25. $3x - 5y + 30 = 0$ **26.** $8x + 3y = 5$

27. $\frac{4}{5}x - 6y + 3 = 0$ **28.** $3x + \frac{4}{7}y - 5 = 0$

In Exercises 29–34, find the general form of the equation of the line that passes through the given points.

29. $(12, -7)$ and $(8, -9)$ **30.** $(-17, 3)$ and $(-5, -12)$

31. $(14, -6)$ and $(-1, 4)$ **32.** $(-3, 5)$ and $(-3, 2)$

33. $(4, 7)$ and $(7, 4)$ **34.** $(0, 4)$ and $(-3, 5)$

35. Write the general form of the equation of the line through $(-7, -13)$ and parallel to the line $6x - 8y = 15$.

36. Write the general form of the equation of the line through $(-7, -13)$ and parallel to the line $6y - 4x = 5$.

37. Write the general form of the equation of the line through $(0, 0)$ and perpendicular to the line $2x + 5y = 10$.

38. Write the general form of the equation of the line through $(0, 3)$ and perpendicular to the line $2y + 5x = 1$.

39. Write the general form of the equation of the line that has an x-intercept of -8 and is parallel to the line $12x - 9y - 7 = 0$.

40. Write the general form of the equation of the line that has a y-intercept of -5 and is parallel to the line $8x + 3y = 5$.

41. Write the general form of the equation of the line that has an x-intercept of -14 and a y-intercept of -6.

42. Write the general form of the equation of the line that has an x-intercept of 3 and a y-intercept of 5.

8.4 Graphing First-Degree Inequalities

Half-Planes

Any line in a plane divides that plane into two half-planes. For example, in Figure 8.4.1, the line AB divides the plane into the two half-planes shown.

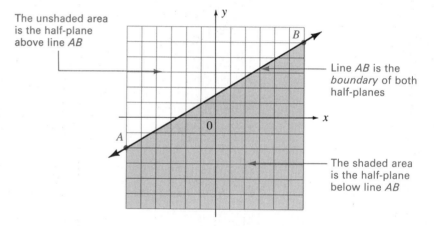

The unshaded area is the half-plane above line AB

Line AB is the *boundary* of both half-planes

The shaded area is the half-plane below line AB

FIGURE 8.4.1

The following statement will not be proved, but *it must be memorized*:

In the real plane, any first-degree inequality in one or two variables has a graph that is a half-plane.

The equation of the *boundary line* of the half-plane is obtained by replacing the inequality sign with an equal sign.

How to Determine Whether the Boundary Is a Dashed or a Solid Line The boundary line is drawn as a *solid* line and is part of the solution when the inequality symbol is $\geq$ or $\leq$. When the inequality symbol is $>$ or $<$, the boundary line is drawn as a dashed line and is not part of the solution.

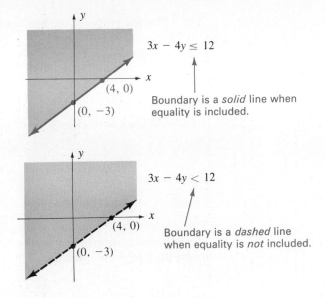

$3x - 4y \leq 12$

Boundary is a *solid* line when equality is included.

$3x - 4y < 12$

Boundary is a *dashed* line when equality is *not* included.

How to Determine the Correct Half-Plane

1. *If the boundary does not go through the origin*, substitute the coordinates of the origin $(0, 0)$ into the inequality.

   If the resulting statement is *true*, the solution is the half-plane containing $(0, 0)$.

   If the resulting statement is *false*, the solution is the half-plane *not* containing $(0, 0)$.

2. *If the boundary goes through the origin*, select a point *not* on the boundary. Substitute the coordinates of this point into the inequality.

   If the resulting statement is *true*, the solution is the half-plane containing the point selected.

   If the resulting statement is *false*, the solution is the half-plane *not* containing the point selected.

TO GRAPH A FIRST-DEGREE INEQUALITY (IN THE PLANE)

1. The boundary line is *solid* if equality is included ($\leq, \geq$).

The boundary line is *dashed* if equality is *not* included ($<, >$).

2. Graph the boundary line.

3. Select and shade the correct half-plane.

Example 1   Graph the inequality $2x - 3y < 6$.

Change $<$ to $=$:

Boundary line $2x - 3y = 6$

Step 1 The boundary is a *dashed* line because the equality is *not* included.

$$2x - 3y < 6$$

Step 2 Plot the graph of the boundary line by the intercept method.

x-intercept Set $y = 0$. Then $2x - 3(0) = 6$

$$2x = 6$$

$$x = 3$$

y-intercept Set $x = 0$. Then $2(0) - 3y = 6$

$$-3y = 6$$

$$y = -2$$

x	y
3	0
0	-2

Therefore, the boundary line goes through $(3, 0)$ and $(0, -2)$.

Step 3 Select the correct half-plane. The solution of the inequality is only one of the two half-planes determined by the boundary line. Substitute the coordinates of the origin $(0, 0)$ into the inequality:

$$2x - 3y < 6$$

$$2(0) - 3(0) < 6$$

$$0 < 6 \qquad \text{True}$$

Therefore, the half-plane containing the origin is the solution. The solution is the shaded area in Figure 8.4.2.

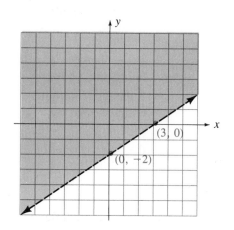

FIGURE 8.4.2

Example 2   Graph the inequality $3x + 4y \leq -12$.

Step 1 The boundary is a *solid* line because the equality is included.

$$3x + 4y \leq -12$$

Step 2 Plot the graph of the boundary line $3x + 4y = -12$ (see Figure 8.4.3).

x-intercept Set $y = 0$. Then $3x + 4(0) = -12$

$$3x = -12$$

$$x = -4$$

y-intercept Set $x = 0$. Then $3(0) + 4y = -12$

$$4y = -12$$

$$y = -3$$

x	y
-4	0
0	-3

Step 3 Select the correct half-plane. Substitute the coordinates of the origin $(0, 0)$:

$$3x + 4y \leq -12$$

$$3(0) + 4(0) \leq -12$$

$$0 \leq -12 \quad \text{False}$$

Therefore, the solution is the half-plane *not* containing $(0, 0)$.

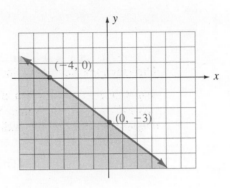

FIGURE 8.4.3

Some inequalities have equations with only one variable. Such inequalities have graphs whose boundaries are either vertical or horizontal lines (see Example 3).

Example 3   Graph the inequality $x + 4 < 0$.

Step 1 The boundary is a *dashed* line because the equality is *not* included.

$$x + 4 \boxed{<} 0$$

Step 2 Plot the graph of the boundary line $x + 4 = 0$, or $x = -4$ (see Figure 8.4.4).

Step 3 Select the correct half-plane. Substitute the coordinates of the origin $(0, 0)$:

$$x + 4 < 0$$

$$0 + 4 < 0$$

$$4 < 0 \quad \text{False}$$

Therefore, the solution is the half-plane *not* containing $(0, 0)$.

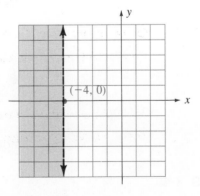

FIGURE 8.4.4

In Section 9.9A, we will discuss how to graph higher-degree inequalities in a single variable on the number line.

Example 4   Graph the inequality $2y - 5x \geq 0$.

Step 1 The boundary is a *solid* line because the equality is included.

$$2y - 5x \boxed{\geq} 0$$

Step 2 Plot the graph of the boundary line $2y - 5x = 0$ (see Figure 8.4.5).

x-intercept Set $y = 0$. Then $2(0) - 5x = 0$

$$-5x = 0$$

$$x = 0$$

y-intercept Set $x = 0$. Then $2y - 5(0) = 0$

$$2y = 0$$

$$y = 0$$

Therefore, the boundary line passes through the origin $(0, 0)$. To find another point on the line $2y - 5x = 0$, set $x = 2$.

Then $2y - 5(2) = 0$

$$2y - 10 = 0$$

$$2y = 10$$

$$y = 5$$

x	y
0	0
0	0
2	5

This gives the point $(2, 5)$ on the line.

Step 3 Select the correct half-plane. Since the boundary goes through the origin $(0, 0)$, select a point *not* on the boundary, say $(1, 0)$. Substitute the coordinates of $(1, 0)$ into $2y - 5x \geq 0$.

$$2(0) - 5(1) \geq 0$$

$$-5 \geq 0 \qquad \text{False}$$

Therefore, the solution is the half-plane *not* containing $(1, 0)$.

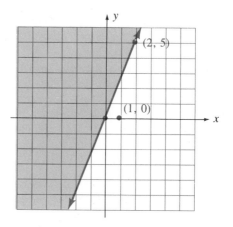

FIGURE 8.4.5   ■

EXERCISES 8.4

Set I   Graph each of the following inequalities.

1. $4x + 5y < 20$ **2.** $5x - 3y > 15$ **3.** $3x - 8y > -16$

4. $6x + 5y < -18$ **5.** $9x + 7y \leq -27$ **6.** $5x - 14y \geq -28$

7. $x \geq -1$ **8.** $y \leq -4$ **9.** $6x - 13y > 0$

10. $4x + 9y < 0$ **11.** $14x + 3y \leq 17$ **12.** $10x - 4y \geq 23$

13. $\dfrac{x}{4} - \dfrac{y}{2} > 1$ **14.** $\dfrac{x}{3} + \dfrac{y}{5} < 1$

15. $4(x + 2) + 7 \leq 3(5 - 2x)$ **16.** $3(y + 4) - 8 \geq 4(1 - 2y)$

17. $\dfrac{2x + y}{3} - \dfrac{x - y}{2} \geq \dfrac{5}{6}$ **18.** $\dfrac{4x - 3y}{5} - \dfrac{2x - y}{2} \geq \dfrac{2}{5}$

Set II Graph each of the following inequalities.

1. $3x - 4y > 12$ **2.** $7x - 2y < 14$ **3.** $8x + 11y < -24$

4. $x - 5y \geq 0$ **5.** $12x - 17y \geq -36$ **6.** $x > 3$

7. $y \leq 3$ **8.** $x + y < 0$ **9.** $5x + 8y < 0$

10. $x \leq -2$ **11.** $12x - 7y \geq 19$ **12.** $4y + 2x > 4$

13. $\dfrac{x}{2} + \dfrac{y}{6} < -1$ **14.** $\dfrac{y}{3} - \dfrac{x}{2} \geq 2$

15. $6(4 - y) + 11 \geq 5(6y + 7)$ **16.** $8(3 + x) + 2 < 3(x - 4)$

17. $\dfrac{3x - 5y}{3} - \dfrac{4x + 7y}{12} < \dfrac{3}{4}$ **18.** $\dfrac{2}{3} - \dfrac{4x - y}{2} > y$

8.5 Review: 8.1–8.4

**To Graph a Point
8.1**

An *ordered pair* of numbers is used to represent a point in the plane.

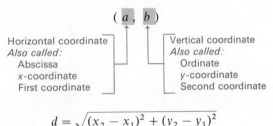

$$d = \sqrt{(x_2 - x_1)^2 + (y_2 - y_1)^2}$$

**Distance between Two
Points $P_1(x_1, y_1)$ and
$P_2(x_2, y_2)$
8.1**

**Relations
8.1**

A **mathematical relation** is a set of ordered pairs (x, y).

The domain of a relation is the set of all the first coordinates of the ordered pairs of that relation.

The range of a relation is the set of all the second coordinates of the ordered pairs of that relation.

The graph of a relation is the graph of all the ordered pairs of that relation.

**To Graph a Straight Line
(Intercept Method)
8.2**

1. Find the x-intercept: Set $y = 0$; then solve for x.

2. Find the y-intercept: Set $x = 0$; then solve for y.

3. If the line goes through the origin $(0, 0)$, another point must be chosen.

4. Find a third point.

5. Plot the three points.

6. Draw a straight line through the points.

7. The graph of $x = a$ is a vertical line that passes through $(a, 0)$.

8. The graph of $y = b$ is a horizontal line that passes through $(0, b)$.

Slope of the Line through Points $P_1(x_1, y_1)$ and $P_2(x_2, y_2)$ 8.3A

$$m = \frac{y_2 - y_1}{x_2 - x_1}$$

Parallel lines have the same slope. If two lines are perpendicular (and neither is a vertical line), the product of their slopes is -1.

Equations of a Line 8.3B

General form: $Ax + By + C = 0$, where A and B are not both 0.

Point-slope form: $y - y_1 = m(x - x_1)$, where (x_1, y_1) is a known point on the line and $m = $ slope of the line.

Slope-intercept form: $y = mx + b$, where $m = $ slope and b is the y-intercept of the line.

To Graph a First-Degree Inequality in the Plane 8.4

1. The boundary line is *solid* if equality *is* included ($\leq$, $\geq$).

   The boundary line is *dashed* if equality is *not* included ($<$, $>$).

2. Graph the boundary line.

3. Select and shade the correct half-plane.

Review Exercises 8.5 Set I

1. Find the distance between the two given points.
   a. $(-3, -4)$ and $(2, -4)$ b. $(-2, -3)$ and $(4, 1)$

2. Find the domain and range of the relation $\{(0, 5), (-2, 3), (3, -4), (0, 0)\}$.

3. Find the domain and range of $\{(x, y)|3x - 2y = 6, x = -2, 0, 6, 8\}$ and graph it.

In Exercises 4–7, graph each relation.

4. $3y + 2x = -12$

5. $x + 2y = 0$

6. $y = 2x$

7. $\dfrac{2x + 3y}{5} - \dfrac{x - 3y}{4} = \dfrac{9}{10}$

In Exercises 8 and 9, find the slope of the line through the given pair of points.

8. $(3, -5)$ and $(-2, 4)$

9. $(-6, 2)$ and $(3, 2)$

10. Write the equation of the line that passes through $(-8, 4)$ and has slope $m = -\frac{3}{4}$.

11. Write the equation of the line that has slope $m = -\frac{1}{2}$ and y-intercept $= 6$.

12. Write the equation of the line that passes through the points $(-2, -4)$ and $(1, 3)$.

13. Find the slope and y-intercept of the line $\dfrac{2x}{5} - \dfrac{3y}{2} = 3$.

In Exercises 14–16, graph each inequality in the plane.

14. $y > 3$

15. $2x - 5y > 10$

16. $3x - 2y \geq 0$

Review Exercises 8.5 Set II

NAME _____

1. Find the distance between the two given points.

   a. $(8, -6)$ and $(-12, -2)$ b. $(-7, 5)$ and $(7, -13)$

2. Find the domain and range of the relation $\{(10, 6), (-5, -2), (0, 7), (-9, -6)\}$.

3. Find the domain and range of $\{(x, y)|4x + 3y = 12, x = -3, 0, 3\}$ and graph it.

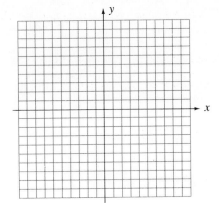

ANSWERS

1a. _____

b. _____

2. _____

_____

3. _____

_____

Use graph. _____

4. Use graph. _____

5. Use graph. _____

In Exercises 4–7, graph each relation.

4. $6x - 3y = 6$ **5.** $5x - 3y = 0$

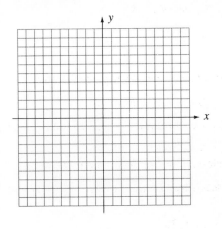
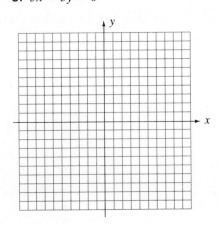

6. $\dfrac{x - 4y}{7} - \dfrac{3x - 7y}{6} = \dfrac{20}{21}$

7. $x = 5$

6. <u>Use graph.</u>

7. <u>Use graph.</u>

8. _____

9. _____

10. _____

11. _____

12. _____

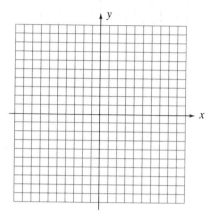

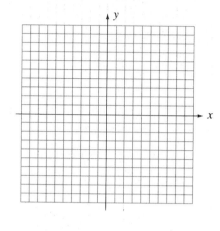

In Exercises 8 and 9, find the slope of the line through the given pair of points.

8. $(-12, 11)$ and $(-25, -28)$

9. $(-17, -14)$ and $(35, -22)$

10. Write the equation of the line that passes through $(-7, 12)$ and has a slope of $-\frac{4}{5}$.

11. Write the equation of the line that has a slope of $-\frac{7}{4}$ and a y-intercept of -6.

12. Write the equation of the line through the points $(-16, 15)$ and $(-38, -25)$.

13. Find the slope and y-intercept of the line $\dfrac{4x}{7} - \dfrac{6y}{5} = 2$.

In Exercises 14–16, graph each inequality in the plane.

14. $x + 4y \geq 0$

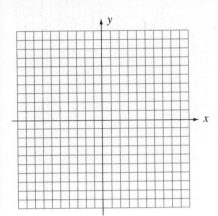

15. $y \leq -1$

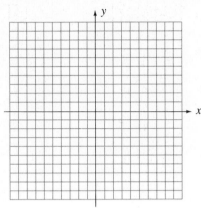

16. $3x - 9y > 9$

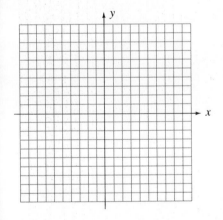

ANSWERS

13. _____

_____

14. Use graph. _____

15. Use graph. _____

16. Use graph. _____

8.6 Functions

We live in a world of functions. For example, if you are paid $5.65 an hour, your weekly salary is $S = 5.65h$, where h is the number of hours you work in the week. Your salary is a *function* of the number of hours you work. When you rent a car, you usually pay a flat rate plus mileage. If the flat rate is $12 a day and you pay 15¢ for every mile you drive, your car rental cost $C = 12 + 0.15m$, where m is the number of miles you drive. Therefore, the cost is a *function* of the miles driven.

8.6A Definition of a Function

Function
A **function** is a relation in which no two ordered pairs have the same first coordinate and different second coordinates.

No vertical line can meet the graph of a function in more than one point.

We can think of a function as a *rule* that assigns *one and only one* value to y for each value of x in the domain of the variable.

Example 1
Determine from each graph whether the relation is a function:

a.

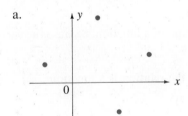

This *is* the graph of a function, because any vertical line meets the graph in no more than one point.

b.

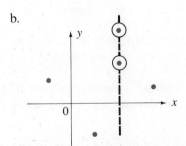

This *is not* the graph of a function, because one vertical line meets the graph in two points.

c.

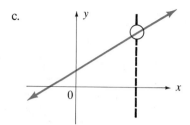

This *is* the graph of a function, because any vertical line meets the graph in no more than one point. Straight lines (other than vertical ones) are graphs of linear functions. A **linear function** is one with a formula of the form $y = mx + b$, where m and b are constants (see Section 8.3).

d.

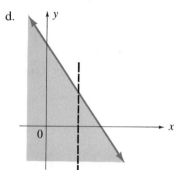

This *is not* the graph of a function, because any vertical line meets the graph in an infinite number of points. Linear inequalities are **linear relations** (see Section 8.1).

e.

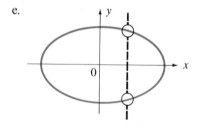

This *is not* the graph of a function, because the vertical line shown meets the graph in two points. ■

Example 2   Determine whether the relation is a function:

a. $\{(1, 7), (3, 6), (4, 7)\}$

Since no two ordered pairs have the same first coordinate, the relation *is* a function.

b. $\{(2, 8), (2, 9), (3, 7)\}$

Because $(2, 8)$ and $(2, 9)$ have the same first coordinate but different second coordinates, the relation is *not* a function. ■

Domain, Range, and Graph of a Function

Since a function is a relation, the meanings of its domain, range, and graph are the same as for a relation.

The *domain* of a function is the set of all permitted x-values. When an equation for a function is given, the domain will be the set of real numbers *unless* one of the following occurs:

1. The domain is restricted by some statement accompanying the equation.

2. There are variables in a denominator (or, equivalently, variable expressions with negative exponents).

3. Variables occur under a radical sign when the index of the radical is an even number.

4. Variable expressions with rational exponents occur where the denominator of the exponent is an even number.

To determine the domain of a function by looking at its graph, we look "right and left" to see how much of the plane is "used up."

The *range* of a function is the set of all the *y*-values. Because the value of *y* depends on the value of *x*, we often call *y* the **dependent variable** and *x* the **independent variable**. It is often more difficult to find the range of a function than to find its domain. In fact, in some cases the range cannot be found without using techniques beyond the scope of this course. If the function can be graphed, then the range can be found by examining the graph. To do this, we look "up and down" to see how much of the plane is "used up."

Example 3 Find the domain and the range for each of the following functions:

a.

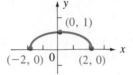

Because no part of the graph is to the *left* of $x = -2$ and no part is to the *right* of $x = 2$, the domain is $\{x \mid -2 \le x \le 2\}$. Because no part of the graph is *above* $y = 1$ and no part is below $y = 0$, the range is $\{y \mid 0 \le y \le 1\}$.

b.

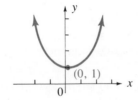

Because the graph extends infinitely far left and right, the domain is $\{x \mid x \in R\}$. Because no part of the graph is *below* $y = 1$, the range is $\{y \mid y \ge 1\}$.

c.

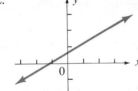

Because the graph extends infinitely far left and right, the domain is $\{x \mid x \in R\}$. Because the graph extends infinitely far up and down, the range is $\{y \mid y \in R\}$.

d.

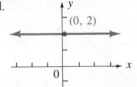

Because the graph extends infinitely far left and right, the domain is $\{x \mid x \in R\}$. Because the only *y*-value that is "used up" is $y = 2$, the range is $\{2\}$.

e.

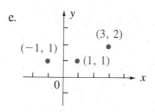

Because the only x-values that are "used up" are -1, 1, and 3, the domain is $\{-1, 1, 3\}$. Because the only y-values that are "used up" are 1 and 2, the range is $\{1, 2\}$. ■

Example 4   Find the domain and range of the function:

a. $y = 3x + 2$

Solution Since there are no denominators, no radical signs, no negative exponents, no rational exponents, and no other restrictions on the domain, the domain is the set of all real numbers. We recognize the equation as the equation of a straight line that is *not* a horizontal line; therefore, the range is also the set of all real numbers.

b. $\{(x, y)|y = 2x, x = -1, 4\}$

Solution The domain is restricted to $\{-1, 4\}$. From the equation, we see that when $x = -1$, $y = -2$, and when $x = 4$, $y = 8$. Therefore, the range is $\{-2, 8\}$.

c. $y = 7$

Solution The equation is that of a horizontal line. Therefore, the domain is $\{x|x \in R\}$, and the range is $\{7\}$.

d. $y = \sqrt{2 + x}$

Solution Because we have a square root, the radicand must be nonnegative. Therefore, $2 + x \geq 0$, or $x \geq -2$. The domain is $\{x|x \geq -2\}$. Finding the range is more difficult. We know that y can never be negative, because the principal square root is never negative. If $x = -2$, $y = \sqrt{0} = 0$; therefore, y *can* equal 0. We can see, too, that as x gets larger and larger, y gets larger and larger. Therefore, the range is $\{y|y \geq 0\}$. ■

EXERCISES 8.6A

Set I   **1.** Which of the following are graphs of functions?

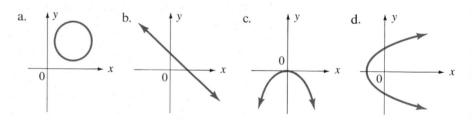

2. Which of the following are graphs of functions?

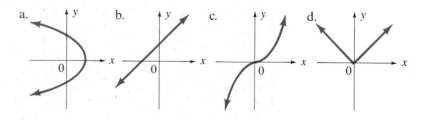

3. Find the range of the function $\{(x, y)\,|\,2x + 5y = 10, x = -5, -1, 0, 2\}$ and graph the function.

4. Find the range of the function $\{(x, y)\,|\,3x - 6 = 2y, x = -2, 0, 2, 4\}$ and graph the function.

5. Graph the function $\{(x, y)\,|\,y = 2x - 3\}$ with domain the set of real numbers.

6. Graph the function $\left\{(x, y)\,\middle|\,\dfrac{x}{2} - \dfrac{y}{3} = 1\right\}$ with domain the set of real numbers.

In Exercises 7 and 8, determine whether each relation is a function.

7. a. $\{(2, 3), (5, 3), (1, 6)\}$ **b.** $\{(-1, 6), (-1, 8)\}$

    c. $\{(x, y)\,|\,x = 7\}$ **d.** $\{(x, y)\,|\,y = 3\}$

8. a. $\{(-3, 6), (-3, -8), (4, 2)\}$ **b.** $\{(2, -8), (5, -8)\}$

    c. $\{(x, y)\,|\,y = 3x + 4\}$ **d.** $\{(x, y)\,|\,x = 0\}$

In Exercises 9 and 10, find the domain and range of the functions.

9. a. The graph is   **10. a.** The graph is

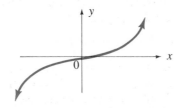   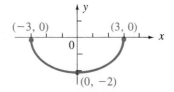

b. $y = -2x + 1$ **b.** $\{(x, y)\,|\,y = \sqrt{3 + x}\}$

c. $\{(x, y)\,|\,y = \sqrt{x - 5}\}$ **c.** $y = \dfrac{2}{3}x - 4$

d. $\{(x, y)\,|\,y = -x + 1, x = 1, 4, 7\}$ **d.** $\{(x, y)\,|\,y = 3x - 4, x = 0, 1\}$

Set II   **1.** Which of the following are graphs of functions?

    a. 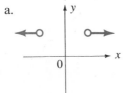   **b.**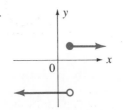

    c. 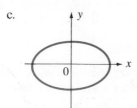   **d.**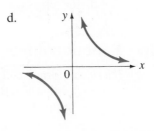

2. Which of the following are graphs of functions?

a.

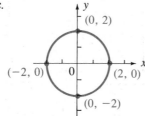

b.

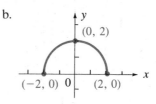

c.

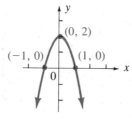

d.

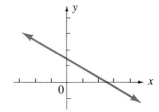

3. Find the range of the function $\{(x, y)\,|\,10x - 7y = 25, x = -1, 2, 4, 6\}$ and graph the function.

4. Find the range of the function $\{(x, y)\,|\,3x - 9y = 6, x = -1, 0, 1, 2\}$ and graph the function.

5. Graph the function $\{(x, y)\,|\,4x - 12y = 12\}$ with domain the set of real numbers.

6. Graph the function $\left\{(x, y)\,\middle|\,\dfrac{x}{2} + \dfrac{y}{5} = -1\right\}$ with domain the set of real numbers.

In Exercises 7 and 8, determine whether each relation is a function.

7. a. $\{(0, 3), (0, 7), (1, 2)\}$ b. $\{(1, 6), (2, 6)\}$

    c. $\{(x, y)\,|\,y = x\}$ d. $\{(x, y)\,|\,x = 6\}$

8. a. $\{(3, 5), (4, 5), (7, 5)\}$ b. $\{(1, 0), (1, 1)\}$

    c. $\{(x, y)\,|\,x = 3\}$ d. $\{(x, y)\,|\,y = -1\}$

In Exercises 9 and 10, find the domain and range of the functions.

9. a. The graph is

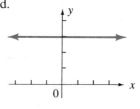

    b. $\{(x, y)\,|\,y = \sqrt{1 - x}\}$

    c. $y = 4x$

    d. $\{(x, y)\,|\,y = -x, x = -1, 2, 5\}$

10. a. The graph is

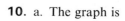

    b. $y = 3x - 2$

    c. $\{(x, y)\,|\,y = \sqrt{6 - 3x}\}$

    d. $\{(x, y)\,|\,y = \tfrac{2}{3}x - 1, x = -3, 0, 3\}$

8.6B Functional Notation

If a rule or formula relating y and x is known and if there is no more than one value of y for each value of x, then y is said to be a **function of x**. This is written $y = f(x)$ and is read as "y equals f of x." (See Figure 8.6.1.)

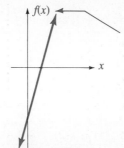

y and f(x) are two ways of writing the value of a function; the vertical coordinates of points (ordinates) can be written as f(x) as well as y, so the vertical axis can be considered the f(x)-axis

FIGURE 8.6.1

A WORD OF CAUTION   The notation $f(x)$ does *not* mean f times x. It is simply a different way of writing y when y is a function of x.   ☑

The equations $y = 5x - 7$ and $f(x) = 5x - 7$ mean the same thing, and we often combine the equations as follows:

$$y = f(x) = 5x - 7$$

Evaluating a Function

To *evaluate a function* means to determine what value y or $f(x)$ has for a particular x-value. If a function $f(x)$ is to be evaluated at $x = a$, we denote this by $f(a)$ where $f(a)$ is read as "f of a."

Example 5   If $f(x) = 5x - 7$, find $f(2)$.

Since $f(x) = 5x - 7$,

$$f(2) = 5(2) - 7 \qquad \text{Substitute 2 for } x$$
$$f(2) = 10 - 7$$
$$f(2) = 3$$

The statement $f(2) = 3$ means that $y = 3$ when $x = 2$.   ∎

Example 6   Evaluate the function $f(x) = \dfrac{2x^2 - 7x}{5x - 3}$ when $x = -2, 0, 1, h,$ and $a + b$:

$$f(x) = \frac{2(x)^2 - 7(x)}{5(x) - 3}$$

$$f(\ ) = \frac{2(\ )^2 - 7(\ )}{5(\ ) - 3}$$

a. $f(\boxed{-2}) = \dfrac{2(\boxed{-2})^2 - 7(\boxed{-2})}{5(\boxed{-2}) - 3} = \dfrac{8 + 14}{-10 - 3} = -\dfrac{22}{13}$

b. $f(\boxed{0}) = \dfrac{2(\boxed{0})^2 - 7(\boxed{0})}{5(\boxed{0}) - 3} = \dfrac{0 - 0}{0 - 3} = 0$

c. $f(\boxed{1}) = \dfrac{2(\boxed{1})^2 - 7(\boxed{1})}{5(\boxed{1}) - 3} = \dfrac{2 - 7}{5 - 3} = -\dfrac{5}{2}$

d. $f(\boxed{h}) = \dfrac{2(\boxed{h})^2 - 7(\boxed{h})}{5(\boxed{h}) - 3} = \dfrac{2h^2 - 7h}{5h - 3}$

e. $f(\boxed{a + b}) = \dfrac{2(\boxed{a+b})^2 - 7(\boxed{a+b})}{5(\boxed{a+b}) - 3} = \dfrac{2a^2 + 4ab + 2b^2 - 7a - 7b}{5a + 5b - 3}$ ∎

Example 7   Given $f(x) = 2x + 1$, evaluate $\dfrac{f(-5) - f(2)}{4}$.

$$f(x) = 2(x) + 1$$
$$f(-5) = 2(-5) + 1 = -10 + 1 = -9$$
$$f(2) = 2(2) + 1 = 4 + 1 = 5$$

Therefore, $\dfrac{f(-5) - f(2)}{4} = \dfrac{-9 - 5}{4} = \dfrac{-14}{4} = -\dfrac{7}{2}$ ■

Example 8   Given $f(x) = x^5$, find $\dfrac{f(x + h) - f(x)}{h}$ and simplify.

If $f(x) = x^5$, then $f(x + h) = (x + h)^5$. Using the binomial theorem, we have

$$(x + h)^5 = x^5 + 5x^4h + 10x^3h^2 + 10x^2h^3 + 5xh^4 + h^5$$

Therefore,

$$f(x + h) - f(x) = \overbrace{x^5 + 5x^4h + 10x^3h^2 + 10x^2h^3 + 5xh^4 + h^5}^{f(x+h)} - \overset{\underset{\uparrow}{f(x)}}{(x^5)}$$

and

$$\frac{f(x + h) - f(x)}{h} = \frac{x^5 + 5x^4h + 10x^3h^2 + 10x^2h^3 + 5xh^4 + h^5 - x^5}{h}$$

$$= \frac{5x^4h + 10x^3h^2 + 10x^2h^3 + 5xh^4 + h^5}{h}$$

$$= \frac{\overset{1}{\cancel{h}}(5x^4 + 10x^3h + 10x^2h^2 + 5xh^3 + h^4)}{\underset{1}{\cancel{h}}}$$

$$= 5x^4 + 10x^3h + 10x^2h^2 + 5xh^3 + h^4 \quad ■$$

Letters other than f can be used to name functions.

Variables other than x can be used for the independent variable.

Variables other than y can be used for the dependent variable.

Example 9   Examples of using other letters to represent functions and variables:

a. $g(x)$, $h(x)$, $F(x)$, $G(x)$

b. $f(z)$, $g(y)$, $G(t)$, $H(s)$ ■

Example 10   Graphs of functions using letters other than x, y, and f:

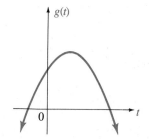
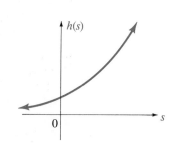

■

Example 11   Given $h(r) = 5r^2$ and $g(s) = 4s - 1$, find $h(a + 1) - g(3a)$.

$$h(r) = 5(r)^2$$
$$h(a + 1) = 5(a + 1)^2 = 5(a^2 + 2a + 1) = 5a^2 + 10a + 5$$
$$g(s) = 4(s) - 1$$
$$g(3a) = 4(3a) - 1 = 12a - 1$$

Therefore,

$$h(a + 1) - g(3a) = (5a^2 + 10a + 5) - (12a - 1)$$
$$= 5a^2 - 2a + 6 \quad \blacksquare$$

Word Problems Involving Functions

There are many applications of functions and functional notation in business, statistics, the sciences, and so on.

Example 12   If h is measured in feet and t in seconds, and if the formula for finding the height of an arrow that is shot upward from ground level is $h(t) = 64t - 16t^2$, $0 \le t \le 4$, find the height of the arrow 1 sec after it is shot into the air.

Solution We need to find h when $t = 1$. Therefore, we must find $h(1)$. $h(1) = 64(1) - 16(1^2) = 64 - 16 = 48$. The arrow is 48 feet above the ground 1 sec after it is shot upward. $\blacksquare$

Functions and Relations of More Than One Variable

All the functions and relations discussed so far in this section have been functions of *one* variable. Many functions and relations have more than one variable.

Example 13   Example of a function of more than one variable.

If you put \$100 (P) in a bank that pays $\frac{1}{2}\%$ a month interest (i) and leave it there for 24 months (n), the amount of money (A) in your account after that time is found by using the formula

$$A = P(1 + i)^n$$

This is a function of three variables: $A = f(P, i, n)$, read as "A is a function of P, i, and n." In this case, the *dependent variable* A is a function of *three independent variables* P, i, and n. $\blacksquare$

EXERCISES 8.6B

Set I   **1.** Given $f(x) = 3x - 1$, find:

a. $f(2)$ b. $f(0)$ c. $f(a - 2)$ d. $f(x + 2)$

2. Given $f(x) = 4x + 1$, find:

a. $f(3)$ b. $f(-5)$ c. $f(0)$ d. $f(x - 2)$

3. Given $f(x) = 2x^2 - 3$, evaluate $\dfrac{f(5) - f(2)}{6}$.

4. Given $f(x) = 5x^2 - 2$, evaluate $\dfrac{f(3) - f(1)}{5}$.

5. Given $f(x) = 3x^2 - 2x + 4$, find $2f(3) + 4f(1) - 3f(0)$.

6. Given $f(x) = (x + 1)(x^2 - x + 1)$, find $3f(0) + 5f(2) - f(1)$.

7. If $f(x) = x^3$ and $g(x) = \dfrac{1}{x}$, find $f(-3) - 6g(2)$.

8. If $f(x) = x^2$ and $g(x) = \dfrac{1}{x}$, find $2f(-4) - 9g(3)$.

9. If $H(x) = 3x^2 - 2x + 4$ and $K(x) = x - x^2$, find $2H(2) - 3K(3)$.

10. If $P(a) = a^2 - 4$ and $Q(a) = 2 - a$, find $3P(2) + 2Q(4)$.

11. Find the domain and range of the function $f(x) = \sqrt{x - 4}$.

12. Find the domain and range of the function $f(x) = -\sqrt{9x - 16}$.

In Exercises 13–16, find and simplify $\dfrac{f(x + h) - f(x)}{h}$ for the given functions.

13. $f(x) = x^2 - x$ **14.** $f(x) = 3x^2$ **15.** $f(x) = x^4$ **16.** $f(x) = x^3$

17. If $A(r) = \pi r^2$ and $C(r) = 2\pi r$, find $\dfrac{3A(r) - 2C(r)}{\pi r}$.

18. If $A(r) = \pi r^2$ and $C(r) = 2\pi r$, find $\dfrac{5A(r) + 3C(r)}{\pi r}$.

19. If the formula for finding the height of an arrow that was shot upward from ground level is $h(t) = 64t - 16t^2$, $0 \le t \le 4$, find the height of the arrow 2 sec after it is shot into the air.

20. If the formula for finding the height of an arrow that was shot upward from ground level is $h(t) = 128t - 16t^2$, $0 \le t \le 8$, find the height of the arrow 1 sec after it is shot into the air.

21. If the formula for finding the cost of manufacturing x number of bushings per day is $C(x) = 500 + 20x - 0.1x^2$, find the cost of manufacturing 100 bushings per day.

22. If the formula for finding the cost of manufacturing x number of brackets per day is $C(x) = 400 + 10x - 0.1x^2$, find the cost of manufacturing 100 brackets per day.

23. Evaluate the function $z = g(x, y) = 5x^2 - 2y^2 + 7x - 4y$ when $x = 3$ and $y = -4$.

24. Evaluate the function $z = h(x, y) = 2x^2 - 6xy + 5y^2$ when $x = -1$ and $y = -2$.

25. Given that $A = f(P, i, n) = P(1 + i)^n$, evaluate $f(100, 0.08, 12)$.

26. Given that $F = f(A, v) = 58.6Av^2$, evaluate $f(126.5, 634)$.

Set II   **1.** Given $f(x) = 13 - 5x$, find:

     a. $f(9)$ b. $f(-7)$ c. $f(0)$ d. $f(x - 6)$

   2. Given $f(x) = 8 + 2x$, find:

     a. $f(0)$ b. $f(-1)$ c. $f(x + 2)$ d. $f(x) + 2$

   3. Given $f(x) = 8 - 3x^2$, evaluate $\dfrac{f(4) - f(-6)}{12}$.

4. Given $f(x) = x^2 - 2$, evaluate $\dfrac{f(0) + f(2)}{3}$.

5. Given $f(x) = (3x - 5)(x^2 - 9)$, find $6f(8) - 13f(0) - f(-5)$.

6. Given $f(x) = (x - 1)(2x + 1)(x + 1)$, find $3f(0) - 7f(-1) + 2f(4)$.

7. If $f(x) = 2x^2$ and $g(x) = \dfrac{1}{x^2}$, find $\dfrac{8}{f(-6)} - 12g(4)$.

8. If $f(x) = x + 3$ and $g(x) = \sqrt{x - 1}$, find $\dfrac{1}{f(0)} + g(5)$.

9. If $h(x) = \dfrac{x}{x - 2}$ and $k(x) = x^2 + 4$, find $h(0) + 3h(3) - k(1)$.

10. If $F(e) = \dfrac{3e - 1}{e^2}$ and $G(w) = \dfrac{1}{5 - w}$, find $\dfrac{4F(-3)}{5G(4)}$.

11. Find the domain and range of the function $f(x) = \sqrt{15 - 4x}$.

12. Find the domain and range of the function $f(x) = \sqrt{5x - 2}$.

In Exercises 13–16, find and simplify $\dfrac{f(x + h) - f(x)}{h}$ for the given functions.

13. $f(x) = 5x^2 - 3$ **14.** $f(x) = 1 - x^2$

15. $f(x) = -2x^3$ **16.** $f(x) = -x^3$

17. If $h(x) = 3x^2$ and $k(x) = x^2 - 2x$, find $\dfrac{h(x) - k(x)}{x}$.

18. If $A(r) = \pi r^2$ and $C(r) = 2\pi r$, find $\dfrac{6A(r) + 3C(r)}{12\pi r}$.

19. If the formula for finding the height of an arrow that was shot upward from ground level is $h(t) = 128t - 16t^2, 0 \le t \le 8$, find the height of the arrow 3 sec after it is shot into the air.

20. If the formula for finding the height of an arrow that was shot upward from ground level is $h(t) = 64t - 16t^2, 0 \le t \le 4$, find the height of the arrow 3 sec after it is shot into the air.

21. If the formula for finding the cost of manufacturing x number of handles per day is $C(x) = 600 + 30x - 0.1x^2$, find the cost of manufacturing 100 handles per day.

22. If the formula for finding the cost of manufacturing x number of faucets per day is $C(x) = 1,000 + 20x - 0.1x^2$, find the cost of manufacturing 100 faucets per day.

23. Evaluate the function $w = f(x, y, z) = \dfrac{5xyz - x^2}{2z}$ when $x = -3, y = 4$, and

24. Evaluate the function $w = f(x, y, z) = \dfrac{3x + y^2}{z}$ when $x = -2, y = -3$, and $z = 5$.

25. Given that $A = f(P, i, n) = P(1 + i)^n$, evaluate $f(500, 0.11, 20)$.

26. Given that $w = f(x, y, z) = \dfrac{x - z}{2y}$, evaluate $f(3, -2, -4)$.

8.6C Graphing $y = |x|$, and Comparing $y = f(x) + h$ and $y = f(x + h)$ with $y = f(x)$

Example 14   Find the domain and range of the function $f(x) = |x|$ and graph the function.

There are no restrictions on x; therefore, the domain is $\{x \mid x \in R\}$. Since $y = |x|$, we know that y can never be negative. The range is $\{y \mid y \geq 0\}$.

Because $f(0) = 0$, one point on the graph will be the origin, $(0, 0)$.

By the definition of absolute value, if $x > 0$, $|x| = x$. Therefore, to the *right* of the y-axis (that is, where $x > 0$), we will graph the line $y = x$.

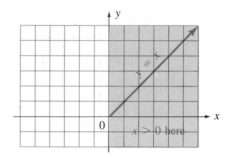

By the definition of absolute value, if $x < 0$, $|x| = -x$. To the *left* of the y-axis (that is, where $x < 0$), we will graph the line $y = -x$.

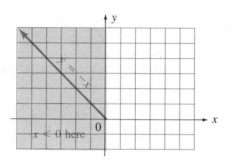

Putting these two graphs together with the point $(0, 0)$, we have the graph of $y = f(x) = |x|$.

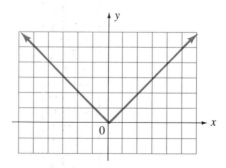

∎

In general, once we find the graph of $y = f(x)$, we can find the graph of $y = f(x) + h$ by shifting $y = f(x)$ *upward* $|h|$ units if h is positive (see Example 15) and *downward* $|h|$ units if h is negative.

Example 15   Graph $y = |x| + 3$.

The instructions above tell us to shift the graph of $y = |x|$ *upward* three units. Check by examining the table of values.

Table of values

x	y
−2	5
−1	4
0	3
1	4
2	5

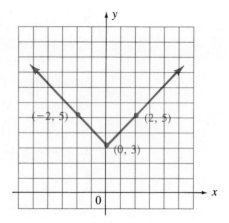

In general, the graph of $y = f(x + h)$ can be found from the graph of $y = f(x)$ by shifting $y = f(x)$ to the right or left $|h|$ units. We move to the *left* if h is positive (see Example 16) and to the *right* if h is negative.

Example 16   Graph $y = |x + 3|$.

The instructions above instruct us to shift the graph of $y = |x|$ three units to the *left* because h is positive. Check by examining the table of values.

NOTE   The graph of the function $f(x) = |ax + b|$ is shaped like a **v**. The graph of the function $f(x) = -|ax + b|$ is shaped like an upside-down **v**.   ☑

Table of values

x	y
−7	4
−6	3
−5	2
−4	1
−3	0
−2	1
−1	2
0	3
1	4

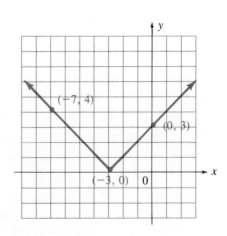

EXERCISES 8.6C

Set I   Sketch the graph of each of the functions.

1. a. $f(x) = |x| - 2$ **b.** $f(x) = |x - 2|$ **c.** $f(x) = -|x - 2|$

2. a. $f(x) = |x| + 5$ **b.** $f(x) = |x + 5|$ **c.** $f(x) = -|x + 5|$

3. a. $f(x) = -3x$ **b.** $f(x) = -3x + 2$ **c.** $f(x) = -3(x + 2)$

4. a. $f(x) = 2x$ **b.** $f(x) = 2x - 3$ **c.** $f(x) = 2(x - 3)$

Set II   Sketch the graph of each of the functions.

1. a. $f(x) = |x| + 4$ **b.** $f(x) = |x + 4|$ **c.** $f(x) = -|x + 4|$

2. a. $f(x) = |x| - 3$ **b.** $f(x) = |x - 3|$ **c.** $f(x) = -|x - 3|$

3. a. $f(x) = 4x$ **b.** $f(x) = 4x + 2$ **c.** $f(x) = 4(x + 2)$

4. a. $f(x) = -3x$ **b.** $f(x) = -3x + 2$ **c.** $f(x) = -3(x + 2)$

8.7 Inverse Relations and Functions

Inverse Relation
A relation $\mathcal{R}$ was defined as a set of ordered pairs (Section 8.1). The **inverse relation of**
$\mathcal{R}$ is defined to be the set of ordered pairs obtained by interchanging the first and
second coordinates in each ordered pair of $\mathcal{R}$.

$$\mathcal{R} = \{(3, 1), (3, -2), (2, -4)\}$$
$$\mathcal{R}^{-1} = \{(1, 3), (-2, 3), (-4, 2)\}$$

$\mathcal{R}^{-1}$ represents the inverse relation of $\mathcal{R}$

It follows from this definition of the inverse relation that the *domain* of $\mathcal{R}^{-1}$ is
$D_{\mathcal{R}^{-1}} = R_{\mathcal{R}}$ (the *range* of $\mathcal{R}$) and the *range* of $\mathcal{R}^{-1}$ is $R_{\mathcal{R}^{-1}} = D_{\mathcal{R}}$ (the *domain* of $\mathcal{R}$).

Graph of an Inverse Relation
In Figure 8.7.1, the points of $\mathcal{R}$ and the points of $\mathcal{R}^{-1}$ are plotted.

The points of $\mathcal{R}$	The points of $\mathcal{R}^{-1}$	
$A(3, 1)$	$\longrightarrow$ $A'(1, 3)$	A' is the *image* of A
$B(3, -2)$	$\longrightarrow$ $B'(-2, 3)$	B' is the *image* of B
$C(2, -4)$	$\longrightarrow$ $C'(-4, 2)$	C' is the *image* of C

Each point of the inverse relation $\mathcal{R}^{-1}$ is the *mirror image*, with respect to the line
$y = x$, of the corresponding point of the relation $\mathcal{R}$. The mirror image of a point is the
same distance behind the "mirror" (in this case, the line $y = x$) as the actual point is in
front of the mirror. Therefore, in Figure 8.7.1, $|AM_1| = |M_1A'|$, $|BM_2| = |M_2B'|$, and
$|CM_3| = |M_3C'|$.

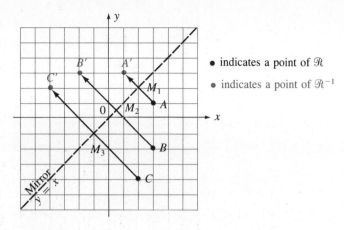

FIGURE 8.7.1

Example 1 Given $\mathcal{R} = \{(2, -3), (-3, -1), (-4, 5), (4, 0)\}$, find $\mathcal{R}^{-1}$, $D_{\mathcal{R}^{-1}}$, and $R_{\mathcal{R}^{-1}}$, and graph $\mathcal{R}$ and $\mathcal{R}^{-1}$.

$$\mathcal{R} = \{(2, -3), (-3, -1), (-4, 5), (4, 0)\} \qquad \mathcal{R} \text{ is a } function$$

$$\mathcal{R}^{-1} = \{(-3, 2), (-1, -3), (5, -4), (0, 4)\} \qquad \mathcal{R}^{-1} \text{ is a } function$$

$$D_{\mathcal{R}^{-1}} = \{-3, -1, 5, 0\} = R_{\mathcal{R}}$$

$$R_{\mathcal{R}^{-1}} = \{2, -3, -4, 4\} = D_{\mathcal{R}}$$

The graph of the relation and its inverse is shown in Figure 8.7.2.

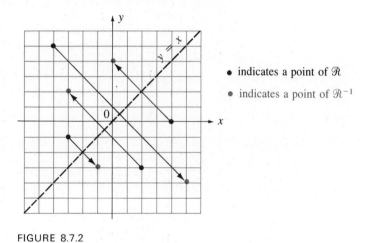

FIGURE 8.7.2 ■

Inverse Functions and Their Graphs

A function will have an inverse if for each y-value there is only one x-value. We call such a function *invertible*. Graphically, this means that a horizontal line will not touch the graph in more than one point. If $f(x)$ is invertible, the inverse of $y = f(x)$ will *also* be a function, and we will write it $y = f^{-1}(x)$.

A WORD OF CAUTION The -1 is *not* an exponent, and $f^{-1}(x) \neq \dfrac{1}{f(x)}$. ☑

To find the inverse of a function whose equation is given, substitute y for $f(x)$ if necessary, interchange x and y in the equation, and then solve the new equation for y.

The *domain* of $f(x)$ equals the *range* of $f^{-1}(x)$, and the *range* of $f(x)$ equals the *domain* of $f^{-1}(x)$, as was true for relations.

The graphs of $y = f(x)$ and $y = f^{-1}(x)$ will be the mirror images of each other with respect to the line $y = x$.

Example 2   Finding and graphing inverses of functions:

a. Find the inverse function for $y = f(x) = 2x - 3$.

Solution

$$y = 2x - 3$$

$$x = 2y - 3 \qquad \text{Interchange } x \text{ and } y$$

$$x + 3 = 2y$$

$$\left. \frac{x + 3}{2} = y \qquad \text{Solve for } y \right\}$$

$$y = f^{-1}(x) = \frac{x + 3}{2} \qquad \begin{array}{l} f^{-1}(x) \text{ is the inverse relation for} \\ f(x) = 2x + 3 \end{array}$$

b. Plot the graphs of $y = f(x) = 2x - 3$ and $y = f^{-1}(x) = \dfrac{x + 3}{2}$.

<table>
<tr><td colspan="2">Graph the function</td><td colspan="2">Graph the inverse function</td></tr>
</table>

Graph the function

$y = f(x) = 2x - 3$

x-intercept:

$y = 2x - 3$

$0 = 2x - 3$

$\frac{3}{2} = x$

x	y
$\frac{3}{2}$	0
0	-3

y-intercept:

$y = 2x - 3$

$y = 2(0) - 3 = -3$

Graph the inverse function

$y = f^{-1}(x) = \dfrac{x + 3}{2}$

x-intercept:

$y = \dfrac{x + 3}{2}$

$0 = \dfrac{x + 3}{2}$

$-3 = x$

x	y
-3	0
0	$\frac{3}{2}$

y-intercept:

$y = \dfrac{x + 3}{2}$

$y = \dfrac{0 + 3}{2} = \dfrac{3}{2}$

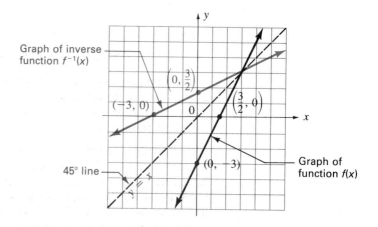

Graph of inverse function $f^{-1}(x)$

$\left(0, \frac{3}{2}\right)$

$(-3, 0)$

$\left(\frac{3}{2}, 0\right)$

$(0, -3)$

Graph of function $f(x)$

45° line

FIGURE 8.7.3

Note that it is not necessary to calculate the entries of the inverse table. Use the entries from the function table, but enter the x-values in the y-column and the y-values in the x-column. The graphs are shown in Figure 8.7.3. ∎

In Example 2, it is apparent from the graphs that $f(x)$ and $f^{-1}(x)$ are both functions (Section 8.6).

Example 3 Find the inverse function for $y = f(x) = \dfrac{5x - 1}{x}$ and find the domain and range for both functions.

$$y = \frac{5x - 1}{x}$$

$$x = \frac{5y - 1}{y} \qquad \text{Interchange } x \text{ and } y$$

$$\left. \begin{array}{c} xy = 5y - 1 \\[4pt] xy - 5y = -1 \qquad \text{Solve for } y \\[4pt] y(x - 5) = -1 \\[4pt] y = \dfrac{1}{5 - x} = f^{-1}(x) \end{array} \right\} \quad \begin{array}{l} f^{-1}(x) \text{ is the inverse function for} \\[4pt] f(x) = \dfrac{5x - 1}{x} \end{array}$$

The domain of $f(x)$ will be all real numbers except 0, since the denominator cannot equal 0. Therefore, the range of $f^{-1}(x)$ must be the set of all real numbers except 0, since the domain of $f(x)$ equals the range of $f^{-1}(x)$. We cannot determine the range of $f(x)$ by looking at its equation; however, we *can* determine that the domain of $f^{-1}(x) = \dfrac{1}{5 - x}$ is the set of all real numbers except 5. Because the range of $f(x)$ equals the domain of $f^{-1}(x)$, we now know that the range of $f(x)$ must be the set of all real numbers except 5.

In summary,

$$\text{domain of } f(x) = \{x \mid x \in R, \, x \neq 0\}$$
$$\text{range of } f(x) = \{y \mid y \in R, \, y \neq 5\}$$
$$\text{domain of } f^{-1}(x) = \{x \mid x \in R, \, x \neq 5\}$$
$$\text{range of } f^{-1}(x) = \{y \mid y \in R, \, y \neq 0\} \quad ∎$$

TO FIND THE INVERSE RELATION OR FUNCTION

1. If a relation, $\mathscr{R}$, or function, $f(x)$, is given as a set of ordered pairs:
    a. Interchange the first and second coordinates of each ordered pair.
    b. The inverse relation, $\mathscr{R}^{-1}$, or function, $f^{-1}(x)$, is the set of ordered pairs obtained in step 1a.

2. If an equation is given and if the relation is a function that is invertible:
    a. Substitute y for $f(x)$ if necessary.
    b. Interchange x and y in the equation.
    c. Solve the resulting equation for y.
    d. The inverse function, $f^{-1}(x)$, is found by substituting $f^{-1}(x)$ for y in the equation obtained in step 2c.

EXERCISES 8.7

Set I

1. Given $\mathscr{R} = \{(-10, 7), (3, -8), (-5, -4), (3, 9)\}$, find $\mathscr{R}^{-1}$, $D_{\mathscr{R}^{-1}}$, and $R_{\mathscr{R}^{-1}}$, and graph $\mathscr{R}$ and $\mathscr{R}^{-1}$. Is $\mathscr{R}$ a function? Is $\mathscr{R}^{-1}$ a function?

2. Given $\mathscr{R} = \{(9, -6), (0, 11), (3, 8), (-2, -6), (10, -4)\}$, find $\mathscr{R}^{-1}$, $D_{\mathscr{R}^{-1}}$, and $R_{\mathscr{R}^{-1}}$, and graph $\mathscr{R}$ and $\mathscr{R}^{-1}$. Is $\mathscr{R}$ a function? Is $\mathscr{R}^{-1}$ a function?

3. Find the inverse function for $y = f(x) = 5 - 2x$. Graph $y = f(x)$ and its inverse.

4. Find the inverse function for $y = f(x) = 3x - 10$. Graph $y = f(x)$ and its inverse.

5. Find the inverse function for $y = f(x) = \dfrac{4x - 3}{5}$.

6. Find the inverse function for $y = f(x) = \dfrac{2x - 7}{3}$.

7. Find the inverse function for $y = f(x) = \dfrac{5}{x + 2}$.

8. Find the inverse function for $y = f(x) = \dfrac{10}{2x - 1}$.

Set II

1. Given $\mathscr{R} = \{(-10, 2), (6, 5), (-11, -9), (1, -3), (-7, 5)\}$, find $\mathscr{R}^{-1}$, $D_{\mathscr{R}^{-1}}$, and $R_{\mathscr{R}^{-1}}$, and graph $\mathscr{R}$ and $\mathscr{R}^{-1}$. Is $\mathscr{R}$ a function? Is $\mathscr{R}^{-1}$ a function?

2.. Given $\mathscr{R} = \{(-3, 6), (5, 6), (2, 3)\}$, find $\mathscr{R}^{-1}$, $D_{\mathscr{R}^{-1}}$, and $R_{\mathscr{R}^{-1}}$, and graph $\mathscr{R}$ and $\mathscr{R}^{-1}$. Is $\mathscr{R}$ a function? Is $\mathscr{R}^{-1}$ a function?

3. Find the inverse function for $y = f(x) = \frac{1}{5}x + 2$. Graph $y = f(x)$ and its inverse.

4. Find the inverse function for $y = f(x) = \frac{2}{3}x - 4$. Graph $y = f(x)$ and its inverse.

5. Find the inverse function for $y = f(x) = \dfrac{3x - 8}{4}$.

6. Find the inverse function for $y = f(x) = \dfrac{3}{x - 2}$.

7. Find the inverse function for $y = f(x) = \dfrac{6}{4 - 3x}$.

8. Find the inverse function for $y = f(x) = \dfrac{8}{4 - x}$.

8.8 Graphing Polynomial Functions

It is shown in calculus that the graph of an equation that can be expressed in the form

$$y = a_n x^n + a_{n-1} x^{n-1} + \cdots + a_2 x^2 + a_1 x + a_0$$

is always a *smooth curve*; that is, it has *no sharp corners*. Because the right side of the above equation is a polynomial, we call the function a **polynomial function**.

Example 1 Examples of polynomial functions:

a. $f(x) = 3x - 5$ *Linear* polynomial function

b. $f(x) = x^2 - x - 2$ *Quadratic* polynomial function

c. $f(x) = x^3 - 4x$ *Cubic* polynomial function

d. $f(x) = 7x^5 - 2x^3 + 6$ *Fifth-degree* polynomial function ∎

In Section 8.2, we showed how to graph straight lines (linear polynomial functions). In this section, we show how to graph *curved* lines (polynomial functions other than linear).

Two points are all that we need to draw a straight line. To draw a curved line, however, we must find more than two points.

Example 2 Graph the function $y = f(x) = x^2$.

x	y
-3	9
-2	4
-1	1
$-\frac{1}{2}$	$\frac{1}{4}$
$-\frac{1}{4}$	$\frac{1}{16}$
0	0
$\frac{1}{4}$	$\frac{1}{16}$
$\frac{1}{2}$	$\frac{1}{4}$
1	1
2	4
3	9

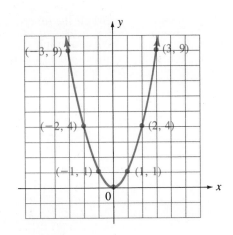

FIGURE 8.8.1

∎

In Figure 8.8.1, we graph these points and draw a smooth curve through them.

In drawing the smooth curve, start with the point in the table of values having the smallest x-value. Draw to the point having the next larger value of x. Continue in this way through all the points. The graph of the equation $y = x^2$ is called a *parabola*. A parabola is one of a family of curves of quadratic polynomial functions called *conic sections*, which are discussed in Section 9.8.

A WORD OF CAUTION   The graph in Example 2 has *no sharp corners* and thus does *not* look like this:

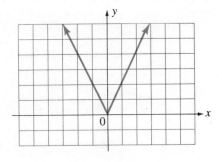

☑

Example 3 Graph the function $y = g(x) = x^2 - 2$.

We can graph $y = x^2 - 2$ by shifting the graph of Figure 8.8.1, $y = f(x) = x^2$, two units *down* (see Figure 8.8.2). We need not make a chart of values, although the curve *could* be graphed by making such a chart.

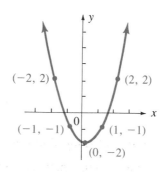

FIGURE 8.8.2 ∎

Example 4 Graph the function $y = h(x) = (x - 2)^2$.

We can graph $y = (x - 2)^2$ by shifting the graph of Figure 8.8.1, $y = f(x) = x^2$, two units *to the right* (see Figure 8.8.3).

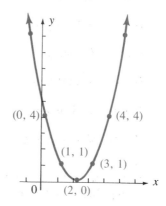

FIGURE 8.8.3 ∎

Example 5 Graph the function $y = x^2 - x - 2$.

Make a table of values by substituting values of x in the equation and finding the corresponding values for y.

x	y
-2	4
-1	0
0	-2
1	-2
2	0
3	4

If $x = -2$, then $y = (-2)^2 - (-2) - 2 = 4 + 2 - 2 = 4$

If $x = -1$, then $y = (-1)^2 - (-1) - 2 = 1 + 1 - 2 = 0$

If $x = 0$, then $y = (0)^2 - (0) - 2 = -2$

If $x = 1$, then $y = (1)^2 - (1) - 2 = 1 - 1 - 2 = -2$

If $x = 2$, then $y = (2)^2 - (2) - 2 = 4 - 2 - 2 = 0$

If $x = 3$, then $y = (3)^2 - (3) - 2 = 9 - 3 - 2 = 4$

In Figure 8.8.4, we graph these points and draw a smooth curve through them.

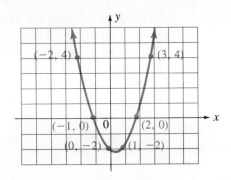

FIGURE 8.8.4

Example 6   Graph the function $y = x^3 - 4x$.

First make a table of values.

x	y
-3	-15
-2	0
-1	3
0	0
1	-3
2	0
3	15

If $x = -3$, then $y = (-3)^3 - 4(-3) = -27 + 12 = -15$

If $x = -2$, then $y = (-2)^3 - 4(-2) = -8 + 8 = 0$

If $x = -1$, then $y = (-1)^3 - 4(-1) = -1 + 4 = 3$

If $x = 0$, then $y = (0)^3 - 4(0) = 0$

If $x = 1$, then $y = (1)^3 - 4(1) = 1 - 4 = -3$

If $x = 2$, then $y = (2)^3 - 4(2) = 8 - 8 = 0$

If $x = 3$, then $y = (3)^3 - 4(3) = 27 - 12 = 15$

In Figure 8.8.5, we graph these points and then draw a smooth curve through them, taking them in order from left to right.

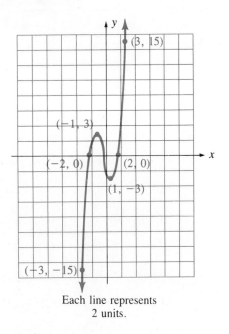

Each line represents
2 units.

FIGURE 8.8.5

Finding the Table of Values by Using Synthetic Division

Graphing polynomial functions by using synthetic division to find the y-values is often simpler than finding the y-values by direct substitution. To find y-values by synthetic division, we use the remainder theorem, which is stated below and proved in Appendix A.

THE REMAINDER THEOREM

If we divide a polynomial in x by $x - a$, the remainder is equal to the value of the polynomial when $x = a$. In symbols, if the remainder is R and the function is $y = f(x)$, then $f(a) = R$.

Example 7 Given $f(x) = 2x^4 - 11x^3 + 7x^2 - 12x + 14$, find $f(5)$.

First method Using substitution,

$$f(x) = 2x^4 - 11x^3 + 7x^2 - 12x + 14$$
$$f(5) = 2(5)^4 - 11(5)^3 + 7(5)^2 - 12(5) + 14$$
$$= 1250 - 1375 + 175 - 60 + 14 = \boxed{4}$$

Second method Using synthetic division,

$$
\begin{array}{r|rrrrr}
 & 2 & -11 & 7 & -12 & 14 \\
 & & 10 & -5 & 10 & -10 \\
\hline
5 & 2 & -1 & 2 & -2 & 4
\end{array}
$$

These products can be kept in mind and need not be written

$f(5)$ ∎

Example 8 Use synthetic division to find the table of values in Example 6.

$$y = f(x) = x^3 - 4x$$
$$= 1x^3 + 0x^2 - 4x + 0$$

$$
\begin{array}{r|rrrr}
 & 1 & 0 & -4 & 0 \\
\end{array}
$$

x				y
-3	1	-3	5	-15
-2	1	-2	0	0
-1	1	-1	-3	3
0	1	0	-4	0
1	1	1	-3	-3
2	1	2	0	0
3	1	3	5	15

To simplify the writing of this table, the products are not written

∎

EXERCISES 8.8

Set I   In Exercises 1–6, complete the table of values for each equation and draw its graph.

1. $y = x^2 + 3$

x	y
−3	
−2	
−1	
0	
1	
2	
3	

2. $y = x^2 + 1$

x	y
−3	
−2	
−1	
0	
1	
2	
3	

3. $y = (x + 1)^2$

x	y
−4	
−3	
−2	
−1	
0	
1	
2	

4. $y = (x + 3)^2$

x	y
−6	
−5	
−4	
−3	
−2	
−1	
0	

5. $y = x^2 - 2x$

x	y
−2	
−1	
0	
1	
2	
3	
4	

6. $y = 3x - x^2$

x	y
−2	
−1	
0	
1	
2	
3	
4	

7. Use integer values of x from -2 to $+4$ to make a table of values for the equation $y = 2x - x^2$. Graph the points and draw a smooth curve through them.

8. Use integer values of x from -3 to $+1$ to make a table of values for the equation $y = 2x + x^2$. Graph the points and draw a smooth curve through them.

9. Use integer values of x from -2 to $+2$ to make a table of values for the equation $y = x^3$. Graph the points and draw a smooth curve through them.

10. Use integer values of x from -2 to $+2$ to make a table of values for the equation $y = x^3 + 2$. Graph the points and draw a smooth curve through them.

11. Use integer values of x from -3 to $+1$ to make a table of values for the equation $y = (x + 1)^3$. Graph the points and draw a smooth curve through them.

12. Use integer values of x from -1 to $+3$ to make a table of values for the equation $y = (x - 1)^3$. Graph the points and draw a smooth curve through them.

13. Use synthetic division to find the range of the function $f(x) = x^3 - 2x^2 - 13x + 20$ if the domain is $\{-4, -3, -2, 0, 2, 3, 4, 5\}$.

14. Use synthetic division to find the range of the function $f(x) = x^3 - 3x^2 - 20x + 12$ if the domain is $\{-3, -2, 0, 2, 3, 4, 5, 6\}$.

Set II   In Exercises 1–6, complete the table of values for each equation and draw its graph.

1. $y = x^2 - 1$

x	y
-3	
-2	
-1	
0	
1	
2	
3	

2. $y = (x - 1)^2$

x	y
-2	
-1	
0	
1	
2	
3	
4	

3. $y = x - \frac{1}{2}x^2$

x	y
-2	
-1	
0	
1	
2	
3	
4	

4. $y = 2x^2$

x	y
-3	
-2	
-1	
0	
1	
2	
3	

5. $y = 2x^2 + 3$

x	y
-3	
-2	
-1	
0	
1	
2	
3	

6. $y = 2x^2 - 4x$

x	y
-2	
-1	
0	
1	
2	
3	
4	

7. Use integer values of x from -1 to $+4$ to make a table of values for the equation $y = 3x - x^2$. Graph the points and draw a smooth curve through them.

8. Use integer values of x from -4 to $+1$ to make a table of values for the equation $y = 3x + x^2$. Graph the points and draw a smooth curve through them.

9. Use integer values of x from -2 to $+2$ to make a table of values for the equation $y = x^3 - 1$. Graph the points and draw a smooth curve through them.

10. Use integer values of x from -2 to $+2$ to make a table of values for the equation $y = x^4$. Graph the points and draw a smooth curve through them.

11. Use integer values of x from -2 to $+2$ to make a table of values for the equation $y = x^4 - 1$. Graph the points and draw a smooth curve through them.

12. Use integer values of x from -2 to $+2$ to make a table of values for the equation $y = x^3 - 3x + 4$. Graph the points and draw a smooth curve through them.

13. Use synthetic division to find the range of the function $f(x) = x^3 + 3x^2 - x - 3$ if the domain is $\{-3, -2, -1, 0, 1, 2\}$.

14. Use synthetic division to find the range of the function $f(x) = x^3 + x^2 - 4x - 4$ if the domain is $\{-2, -1, 0, 1, 2, 3\}$.

8.9 Variation and Proportion

In this section, we will discuss direct variation and proportion, as well as inverse variation, joint variation, and combined variation.

8.9A Direct Variation and Proportion

Direct Variation

If a function can be represented by an equation of the form $y = kx^n$, where k is some constant and n is some positive number, then that function is called a **direct variation**. The constant k is called the **constant of proportionality**. In a direct variation, as one of the variables increases, the other increases also; as one of the variables decreases, the other decreases also.

Many examples of direct variation exist:

If the number of miles per gallon obtained by a certain car is a constant, then the number of miles driven in that car is directly proportional to the number of gallons of gasoline used.

If someone is working at a certain wage per hour (k), then as the number of hours (h) changes, the salary (s) changes according to the formula $s = kh$. Therefore, s is directly proportional to h, and s is a function of h.

In circles, as the diameter (D) changes, the circumference (C) changes according to the formula $C = \pi D$, where $\pi = 3.14$. In this case, π is the constant of proportionality. C is a function of D, and we can say that C varies as D, or that C is directly proportional to D.

DIRECT VARIATION

The following statements all translate into the equation

$$y = kx^n, \text{ where } n > 0:$$

Constant of proportionality

y varies directly with x^n.

y varies directly as x^n.

y is directly proportional to x^n.

y is proportional to x^n.

Example 1 Given: y varies directly with x. If $y = 10$ when $x = 2$, find k (the constant of proportionality) and find y when $x = 3$.

Solution Since y varies directly with x, our equation is $y = kx$. Substituting 10 for y and 2 for x, we have $10 = k(2)$. Therefore, $k = 5$.
The equation is now $y = 5x$. Substituting 3 for x, we have $y = 5(3) = 15$. ∎

Subscripts make it possible to indicate *corresponding values* of variables. In Example 1, we consider $y = 10$ and $x = 2$ to be a pair of corresponding values, because we are told that $y = 10$ *when* $x = 2$. To indicate by subscripted variables that these are corresponding values, we use the *same* subscript. That is,

$$\text{Condition 1} \quad x_1 = 2 \text{ and } y_1 = 10$$

In Example 1, we also consider $y = 15$ and $x = 3$ to be a pair of corresponding values. Therefore,

$$\text{Condition 2} \quad x_2 = 3 \text{ and } y_2 = 15$$

In general, for the direct variation whose equation is $y = kx$,

$$\text{Condition 1} \begin{cases} \text{If} & x = x_1 \\ \text{and } y = y_1 \end{cases} \text{ then } y_1 = kx_1 \tag{1}$$

Equation 1 results from substituting x_1 and y_1 into the formula $y = kx$.

$$\text{Condition 2} \begin{Bmatrix} \text{If} & x = x_2 \\ \text{and} & y = y_2 \end{Bmatrix} \text{ then } y_2 = kx_2 \tag{2}$$

Equation 2 results from substituting x_2 and y_2 into the formula $y = kx$.

Proportion

When an equation can be put into the form $\dfrac{a}{b} = \dfrac{c}{d}$, it is called a **proportion**. (Stated differently, a proportion is a statement that two ratios are equal.)

RELATED PROPORTIONS FOR THE DIRECT VARIATION
WHOSE EQUATION IS $y = kx^n$

$$\frac{y_1}{y_2} = \frac{x_1^n}{x_2^n} \quad \text{and} \quad \frac{y_1}{x_1^n} = \frac{y_2}{x_2^n}$$

The proportions above are derived as follows: If Equation 1 ($y_1 = kx_1^n$) is divided by Equation 2 ($y_2 = kx_2^n$), we have

$$\frac{y_1}{y_2} = \frac{\overset{1}{\cancel{k}}x_1^n}{\underset{1}{\cancel{k}}x_2^n} = \frac{x_1^n}{x_2^n}$$

Alternately, if Equations 1 and 2 are solved for k, we have $k = \dfrac{y_1}{x_1^n}$ (from Equation 1) and $k = \dfrac{y_2}{x_2^n}$ (from Equation 2). Therefore,

$$\frac{y_1}{x_1^n} = \frac{y_2}{x_2^n}$$

Because a proportion is simply a fractional equation, it can be solved by the techniques learned in Chapter 6. An alternate method of solution is based on the following fact: When we multiply both sides of the equation $\dfrac{a}{b} = \dfrac{c}{d}$ by the LCD, we obtain the new equation $ad = bc$.

Therefore, the equation $ad = bc$ is equivalent to the equation $\dfrac{a}{b} = \dfrac{c}{d}$ *except* for the domain of the variable. When we rewrite $\dfrac{a}{b} = \dfrac{c}{d}$ as $ad = bc$, we say we are *cross-multiplying*.

We can, then, cross-multiply as the first step in solving a proportion. However, since we may introduce extraneous roots when we do this, we must be sure to check all solutions in the original equation.

In solving variation problems, we can, if we wish, solve the related proportion without first finding k. This method will be designated as the alternate method in most of the examples in this section.

ALTERNATE METHOD FOR SOLVING WORD PROBLEMS INVOLVING DIRECT VARIATION

1. Represent the unknown quantity by a letter.

2. Be sure to put the units of measure next to the numbers when writing the proportion.

3. Be sure the same units occupy corresponding positions in the two ratios of the proportion.

Correct arrangements   *Incorrect arrangements*

$$\frac{\text{miles}}{\text{hours}} = \frac{\text{miles}}{\text{hours}} \qquad \frac{\text{dollars}}{\text{weeks}} = \frac{\text{weeks}}{\text{dollars}}$$

$$\frac{\text{hours}}{\text{miles}} = \frac{\text{hours}}{\text{miles}} \qquad \frac{\text{dollars}}{\text{weeks}} = \frac{\text{dollars}}{\text{days}}$$

$$\frac{\text{miles}}{\text{miles}} = \frac{\text{hours}}{\text{hours}}$$

4. Once the numbers have been correctly entered in the proportion by using the units as a guide, drop the units when cross-multiplying to solve for the unknown.

Example 2 The number of miles driven is proportional to the number of gallons of gasoline used. Sherma knows she can drive 2,220 miles on 60 gallons of gasoline. Find k, the constant of proportionality, and find how many miles she can expect to drive on 17 gallons of gasoline.

Because the number of miles (m) driven is proportional to the number of gallons (g) of gasoline, the equation of the variation is $m = kg$.

Let $m_2 =$ the number of miles on 17 gal of gasoline.

$$\text{Condition 1} \begin{cases} m_1 = 2{,}220 \text{ mi} \\ g_1 = 60 \text{ gal} \end{cases} \qquad \text{Condition 2} \begin{cases} m_2 = ? \\ g_2 = 17 \text{ gal} \end{cases}$$

From condition 1,

$$2{,}220 = k(60)$$

$$k = 37$$

From condition 2,

$$m_2 = 37(17) = 629 \text{ mi}$$

Alternate method A related proportion is

$$\frac{m_1}{g_1} = \frac{m_2}{g_2}$$

Therefore,

$$\frac{2{,}220 \text{ mi}}{60 \text{ gal}} = \frac{m_2}{17 \text{ gal}}$$

Then, cross-multiplying,

$$2{,}220(17) = 60 m_2$$

$$m_2 = 629 \text{ mi} \quad \blacksquare$$

The following theorem from geometry leads to equations involving direct variation: If two triangles are *similar*, their sides are directly proportional. (Recall that two triangles are similar if their corresponding angles are equal.) Example 3 uses this theorem and uses the alternate method only.

Example 3 If a 6-ft man casts a $4\frac{1}{2}$-ft shadow, how tall is a tree that casts a 30-ft shadow?

We use the fact that the length of a shadow is determined by the angle of a ray of the sun. (We assume that the tree and the man are both vertical; you should verify that the triangies are similar.)

NOTE   The ground does not have to be horizontal.   ✓

Let x = height of tree (in feet).

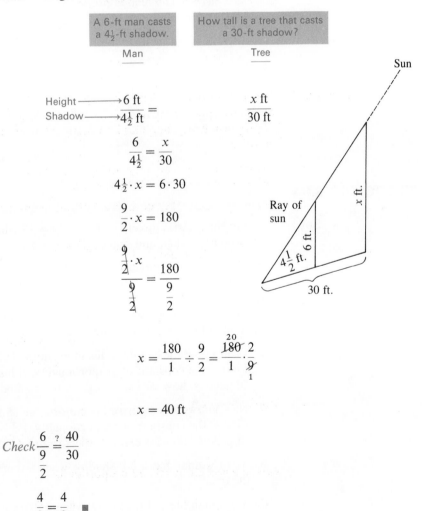

A 6-ft man casts a $4\frac{1}{2}$-ft shadow.	How tall is a tree that casts a 30-ft shadow?
Man	Tree

$$\text{Height} \longrightarrow \frac{6 \text{ ft}}{4\frac{1}{2} \text{ ft}} = \frac{x \text{ ft}}{30 \text{ ft}}$$
Shadow

$$\frac{6}{4\frac{1}{2}} = \frac{x}{30}$$

$$4\frac{1}{2} \cdot x = 6 \cdot 30$$

$$\frac{9}{2} \cdot x = 180$$

$$\frac{\frac{9}{2} \cdot x}{\frac{9}{2}} = \frac{180}{\frac{9}{2}}$$

$$x = \frac{180}{1} \div \frac{9}{2} = \frac{\overset{20}{\cancel{180}}}{1} \cdot \frac{2}{\underset{1}{\cancel{9}}}$$

$$x = 40 \text{ ft}$$

$$Check \frac{6}{\frac{9}{2}} \overset{?}{=} \frac{40}{30}$$

$$\frac{4}{3} = \frac{4}{3} \quad \blacksquare$$

415

The relationship between x and y in a direct variation need not be linear; that is, x can be raised to any positive power. Thus, $y = kx^2$ and $y = kx^3$ are also examples of direct variation.

Example 4 Given: The area (A) of a circle varies directly with the square of the radius (r). If $A = 200.96$ when $r = 8$, find k, the constant of proportionality, and find A when $r = 5$.

Because A varies directly as r^2, the equation for the variation is $A = kr^2$.

$$\text{Condition 1} \begin{cases} A_1 = 200.96 \\ r_1 = 8 \end{cases} \qquad \text{Condition 2} \begin{cases} A_2 = ? \\ r_2 = 5 \end{cases}$$

From condition 1,

$$200.96 = k(8^2)$$

$$k = \frac{200.96}{64} = 3.14$$

From condition 2,

$$A_2 = 3.14(5^2) = 78.5$$

Alternate method The related proportion is

$$\frac{A_1}{r_1^2} = \frac{A_2}{r_2^2}$$

Then

$$\frac{200.96}{8^2} = \frac{A_2}{5^2}$$

$$A_2 = 78.5 \quad \blacksquare$$

EXERCISES 8.9A

Set I

1. Given: y varies directly with x. If $y = 12$ when $x = 3$, find k, the constant of proportionality, and find y when $x = 5$.

2. Given: y varies directly with x. If $y = 10$ when $x = 4$, find k, the constant of proportionality, and find y when $x = -6$.

For Exercises 3 and 4, assume that the number of miles driven is proportional to the number of gallons of gasoline used.

3. Leon knows he can drive his motorhome 161 miles on 23 gallons of gasoline. Find k, the constant of proportionality. If his tanks are full and together hold 50 gallons, how far can he expect to drive before stopping for more gasoline?

4. Nick knows he can drive his motorhome 85 miles on 17 gallons of gasoline. Find k, the constant of proportionality. If his tanks are full and together hold 75 gallons, how far can he expect to drive before stopping for more gasoline?

5. A 5-ft woman has a 3-ft shadow when a tree casts a 27-ft shadow. How tall is the tree?

6. A 6-ft man has a 4-ft shadow when a tree casts a 22-ft shadow. How tall is the tree?

7. The circumference (C) of a circle varies directly with the radius (r). If $C = 47.1$ when $r = 7.5$, find k, and find C when $r = 4.5$.

8. The pressure (P) in water varies directly with the depth (d). If $P = 4.33$ when $d = 10$, find k, and find P when $d = 18$.

9. The area (A) of a circle varies directly with the square of the radius (r). If $A = 28.26$ when $r = 3$, find k, and find A when $r = 6$.

10. The surface area (S) of a sphere varies directly with the square of the radius (r). If $S = 50.24$ when $r = 2$, find k, and find S when $r = 4$.

11. The amount of sediment a stream will carry is directly proportional to the sixth power of its speed. If a stream carries 1 unit of sediment when the speed of the current is 2 mph, how many units of sediment will it carry when the current is 4 mph?

12. The salary John earns is directly proportional to the number of hours he works. One week he worked 18 hours, and his salary was $153.54. The next week he worked 25 hours. How much did he earn the second week?

Set II   1. Given: y varies directly with x. If $y = 3$ when $x = -6$, find k, the constant of proportionality, and find y when $x = 8$.

2. Given: y varies directly as x. If $y = 4$ when $x = -2$, find k, the constant of proportionality, and find y when $x = 7$.

For Exercises 3 and 4, assume that the number of miles driven is proportional to the number of gallons of gasoline used.

3. Ted knows he can drive his motorhome 117 miles on 13 gallons of gasoline. Find k, the constant of proportionality. If his tank is full and holds 50 gallons, how far can he expect to drive before stopping for more gasoline?

4. Jo knows she can drive her car 494 miles on 13 gallons of gasoline. Find k, the constant of proportionality. If her tank is full and holds 15 gallons, how far can she expect to drive before stopping for more gasoline?

5. A 6-ft man has a 4-ft shadow when a building casts a 24-ft shadow. How tall is the building?

6. Ruth drives 1,008 miles in $3\frac{1}{2}$ days. At this rate, how far should she be able to drive in 5 days? Assume that the number of miles driven varies directly with the number of hours.

7. The circumference (C) of a circle varies directly with the diameter (D). If $C = 9.42$ when $D = 3$, find k, and find C when $D = 15$.

8. The pressure (P) in water varies directly with the depth (d). If $P = 8.66$ when $d = 20$, find k, and find P when $d = 50$.

9. Given: y varies directly as the square of x. If $y = 20$ when $x = 10$, find k, and find y when $x = 15$.

10. The area (A) of a circle varies directly with the square of the radius (r). If $A = 13.8474$ when $r = 2.1$, find k, and find A when $r = 1.2$.

11. The distance d in miles that a person can see to the horizon from a point h ft above the surface of the earth varies approximately as the square root of the height h. If for a height of 600 ft the horizon is 30 miles distant, how far is the horizon from a point that is 1,174 ft high?

12. Given: y is directly proportional to the cube of x. If $y = 72$ when $x = 6$, find k, and find y when $x = -3$.

8.9B Inverse Variation

If a function can be represented by an equation of the form $y = \dfrac{k}{x^n}$, where k is some constant, $x \neq 0$, and n is some positive number, then that function is called an **inverse variation**. The constant k is called the *constant of proportionality*. In an inverse variation, as one of the variables increases, the other decreases.

Two examples of inverse variation:

If the amount of work to be done is held constant, then the amount of time required to do that work is inversely proportional to the rate of speed of the worker or machine.

The volume occupied by a gas under certain conditions varies inversely as the pressure.

INVERSE VARIATION

The following statements all translate into the equation

—————————Constant of proportionality

$$y = \frac{k}{x^n}, \text{ where } n > 0,\ x \neq 0:$$

y varies inversely with x^n.

y varies inversely as x^n.

y is inversely proportional to x^n.

Example 5 The amount of time necessary to complete a job is inversely proportional to the rate of speed of the worker. Ruth types at the rate of $5\frac{1}{2}$ pages per hour. If she spends 8 hours on a certain job, find k, the constant of proportionality. How long would it take Sheila, who types at the rate of $3\frac{2}{3}$ pages per hour, to do the same job?

Because *time* is inversely proportional to *rate*, the equation of the variation is $t = \dfrac{k}{r}$.

Let $t_2 = $ Sheila's time.

$$\text{Condition 1} \begin{cases} r_1 = 5\frac{1}{2} \\ t_1 = 8 \end{cases} \qquad \text{Condition 2} \begin{cases} r_2 = 3\frac{2}{3} \\ t_2 = ? \end{cases}$$

From condition 1,

$$8 = \frac{k}{5.5}$$

$$k = 44$$

From condition 2,

$$t_2 = \frac{44}{3\frac{2}{3}} = 12 \text{ hr} \quad \blacksquare$$

An alternate way to solve inverse variation problems is based on the following facts:

$$\text{Condition 1} \begin{cases} \text{If} & x = x_1 \\ \text{and} & y = y_1 \end{cases} \text{ then } y_1 = \frac{k}{x_1^n}$$

Equation 1 results from substituting x_1 and y_1 in the equation $y = \dfrac{k}{x^n}$.

$$\text{Condition 2} \begin{cases} \text{If} & x = x_2 \\ \text{and} & y = y_2 \end{cases} \text{then } y_2 = \dfrac{k}{x_2^n}$$

Equation 2 results from substituting x_2 and y_2 in the equation $y = \dfrac{k}{x^n}$. If we solve Equations 1 and 2 for k, we have $k = x_1^n y_1$ (from Equation 1) and $k = x_2^n y_2$ (from Equation 2). Therefore,

$$x_1^n y_1 = x_2^n y_2$$

We can, if we wish, use the equation $x_1^n y_1 = x_2^n y_2$ in solving problems dealing with inverse proportions. This method will be shown in the examples in this section as the alternate method.

Example 6   Under certain conditions, the pressure (P) of a gas varies inversely with the volume (V). If $P = 30$ when $V = 500$, find k, the constant of proportionality, and find P when $V = 200$.

$$\text{Condition 1} \begin{cases} P_1 = 30 \\ V_1 = 500 \end{cases} \qquad \text{Condition 2} \begin{cases} P_2 = ? \\ V_2 = 200 \end{cases}$$

Since P varies *inversely* with V, our equation is $P = \dfrac{k}{V}$. From condition 1, we have

$$30 = \frac{k}{500}, \quad \text{or} \quad k = 30(500) = 15{,}000$$

We can find P when $V = 200$:

$$P = \frac{15{,}000}{200} = 75$$

Alternate method The equation $P_1 V_1 = P_2 V_2$ can be used:

$$30(500) = P_2(200)$$
$$P_2 = 75 \quad \blacksquare$$

Example 7   Given: y varies inversely with the square of x. If $y = -3$ when $x = 4$, find k, and find y when $x = -6$.

$$\text{Condition 1} \begin{cases} x_1 = 4 \\ y_1 = -3 \end{cases} \qquad \text{Condition 2} \begin{cases} x_2 = -6 \\ y_2 = ? \end{cases}$$

Since y varies inversely with x^2, the equation of the variation is $y = \dfrac{k}{x^2}$. From condition 1, we have

$$-3 = \frac{k}{4^2}$$
$$k = -48$$

From condition 2,

$$y = \frac{-48}{(-6)^2} = \frac{-48}{36} = -\frac{4}{3}$$

Alternate method We use the equation $x_1^2 y_1 = x_2^2 y_2$. Therefore,

$$4^2(-3) = (-6)^2 y_2$$

$$y_2 = -\frac{4}{3} \quad \blacksquare$$

EXERCISES 8.9B

Set I

1. Given: y varies inversely with x. If $y = 7$ when $x = 2$, find k, the constant of proportionality, and find y when $x = -7$.

2. Given: z varies inversely with w. If $z = 4$ when $w = -12$, find k, and find z when $w = 8$.

3. Given: Pressure (P) varies inversely with volume (V). If $P = 18$ when $V = 15$, find k, and find P when $V = 10$.

4. Given: s varies inversely with t. If $s = 8$ when $t = 5$, find k, and find s when $t = 4$.

For Exercises 5 and 6, assume that time is inversely proportional to rate.

5. Machine A works for 3 hr to complete one order. It makes a certain part at the rate of 375 parts per hour. Find k, and find how long it would take Machine B, which makes the parts at the rate of 225 parts per hour, to complete the same order.

6. Machine C works for 9 hr to complete one order. It makes a certain part at the rate of 275 parts per hour. Find k, and find how long it would take Machine D, which makes the parts at the rate of 330 parts per hour, to complete the same order.

7. Given: y varies inversely with the square of x. If $y = 9$ when $x = 4$, find k, and find y when $x = 3$.

8. Given: C varies inversely with the square of v. If $C = 8$ when $v = 3$, find k, and find C when $v = 6$.

9. Given: F varies inversely with the square of d. If $F = 3$ when $d = 4$, find k, and find F when $d = 2$.

10. The intensity (I) of light received from a light source varies inversely with the square of the distance (d) from the source. If the light intensity is 15 foot-candles at a distance of 10 ft from the light source, what is the light intensity at a distance of 15 ft?

Set II

1. Given: y varies inversely with x. If $y = 5$ when $x = 4$, find k, the constant of proportionality, and find y when $x = 2$.

2. Given: u varies inversely with v. If $u = 15$ when $v = 7$, find k, and find u when $v = 3$.

3. Given: V varies inversely with P. If $V = 340$ when $P = 30$, find k, and find V when $P = 85$.

4. Given: w varies inversely with x. If $w = 38$ when $x = 8$, find k, and find w when $x = 19$.

For Exercises 5 and 6, assume that time is inversely proportional to rate.

5. Machine A works for 4 hr to complete one order. It makes a certain part at the rate of 130 parts per hour. Find k, and find how long it would take Machine B, which makes the parts at the rate of 120 parts per hour, to complete the same order.

6. Machine A, which prints negatives at the rate of 290 ft per minute, works for 3.5 hr to complete one job. Find k, the constant of proportionality. How long would it take Machine B, which prints negatives at the rate of 350 ft per minute, to do the same job?

7. Given: L varies inversely with the square of r. If $L = 9$ when $r = 5$, find k, and find L when $r = 3$.

8. Given: y varies inversely with the cube of x. If $y = 960$ when $x = 4$, find k, and find y when $x = 2$.

9. Given: x varies inversely with the cube of y. If $x = \frac{1}{4}$ when $y = 2$, find k, and find x when $y = 4$.

10. The gravitational attraction (F) between two bodies varies inversely with the square of the distance (d) separating them. If the attraction measures 36 when the distance is 4 cm, find the attraction when the distance is 80 cm.

8.9C   Joint Variation and Combined Variation

While direct and inverse variation are functions of *one* variable, variations also exist that are functions of *several* variables. We will now discuss variations of this kind.

Joint Variation

Joint variation is a type of variation that relates one variable to the *product* of two other variables.

JOINT VARIATION

The following statements translate into the equation

$$z = kx^n y^m, \text{ where } n > 0 \text{ and } m > 0:$$

Constant of proportionality

z varies jointly with x^n and y^m.

y is jointly proportional to x^n and y^m.

Example 8   Given: z varies jointly with x and y according to the formula $z = 2xy$:

a. If $x = 3$ and $y = 5$,
   then $z = 2(3)(5) = 30$

b. If $x = 4$ and $y = 5$,
   then $z = 2(4)(5) = 40$

c. If $x = 3$ and $y = 4$,
   then $z = 2(3)(4) = 24$

The value of z depends on the product xy

Note that as x *increased* from 3 to 4 while y was held constant at 5, z *increased* from 30 to 40. Also, as y *decreased* from 5 to 4 while x was held constant at 3, z *decreased* from 30 to 24. Also, when the product xy *increased* from $(3)(5) = 15$ to $(4)(5) = 20$, z *increased* from 30 to 40. ∎

Example 9   If the principal is held constant, then the amount of interest (I) earned in time (t) varies jointly with t and the interest rate (r). If a certain amount of money earns $440 in 2 years when it is invested at 5.5% interest (per year), find k, the constant of proportionality, and find I when the money is invested at 5% interest for 3 years.

$$\text{Condition 1} \begin{cases} I_1 = 440 \\ r_1 = 0.055 \\ t_1 = 2 \end{cases} \qquad \text{Condition 2} \begin{cases} I_2 = ? \\ r_2 = 0.05 \\ t_2 = 3 \end{cases}$$

Because I varies jointly with t and r, the equation of the variation is $I = krt$. From condition 1,

$$440 = k(0.055)(2)$$
$$k = 4,000$$

From condition 2,

$$I = 4,000(0.05)(3) = 600$$

Therefore, the amount of money earned at 5% for 3 years is $600. The principal is k, or $4,000. ∎

Example 10   The heat (H) generated by an electric heater is jointly proportional to R and the square of I. If $H = 1,200$ when $I = 8$ and $R = 15$, find k, and find H when $I = 5.5$ and $R = 20$.

$$\text{Condition 1} \begin{cases} I_1 = 8 \\ R_1 = 15 \\ H_1 = 1,200 \end{cases} \qquad \text{Condition 2} \begin{cases} I_2 = 5.5 \\ R_2 = 20 \\ H_2 = ? \end{cases}$$

Since H is jointly proportional to R and I^2, our formula is $H = kRI^2$. From condition 1, we have

$$1,200 = k(15)(8^2)$$
$$k = 1.25$$

Therefore, if $R = 20$ and $I = 5.5$, we have

$$H = 1.25(20)(5.5)^2 = 756.25 \quad ∎$$

Combined Variation

A variable can be *directly* proportional to some variables and at the same time *inversely* proportional to others. The equations resulting from such circumstances are called **combined variations**.

Example 11   Examples of combined variation, with k the constant of proportionality in each equation:

a. $w = \dfrac{kx}{y}$

The variable w is directly proportional to x and inversely proportional to y.

b. $R = \dfrac{kL}{d^2}$

The variable R is directly proportional to L and inversely proportional to d^2.

c. $F = \dfrac{kMm}{d^2}$

The variable F is jointly proportional to M and m and inversely proportional to d^2. ∎

Example 12   The strength (S) of a rectangular beam is jointly proportional to b and the square of d, and inversely proportional to L, where b is the breadth, d is the depth, and L is the length of the beam. If $S = 2{,}000$ when $b = 2$, $d = 10$, and $L = 15$, find k, and find S when $b = 4$, $d = 8$, and $L = 12$.

$$\text{Condition 1}\begin{cases} b_1 = 2 \\ d_1 = 10 \\ L_1 = 15 \\ S_1 = 2{,}000 \end{cases} \qquad \text{Condition 2}\begin{cases} b_2 = 4 \\ d_2 = 8 \\ L_2 = 12 \\ S_2 = ? \end{cases}$$

Since we have a combined variation, the formula is

$$S = \frac{kbd^2}{L}$$

From condition 1,

$$2{,}000 = \frac{k(2)(10^2)}{15}$$

$$k = 150$$

When $b = 4$, $d = 8$, and $L = 12$,

$$S = \frac{150(4)(8^2)}{12} = 3{,}200 \quad ∎$$

EXERCISES 8.9C

Set I   **1.** Given: z varies jointly with x and y. If $z = -36$ when $x = -3$ and $y = 2$, find k, the constant of proportionality, and find z when $x = 4$ and $y = 3$.

2. Given: A varies jointly with L and W. If $A = 120$ when $L = 6$ and $W = 5$, find k, and find A when $L = 7$ and $W = 3$.

3. The simple interest I earned in a given time t varies jointly as the principal P and the interest rate r. If $I = 115.50$ when $P = 880$ and $r = 0.0875$, find k, and find I when $P = 760$ and $r = 0.0925$.

4. If I varies jointly with P and r, and $I = 240.50$ when $P = 860$ and $r = 0.0775$, find k, and find I when $P = 1,250$ and $r = 0.0950$.

5. The wind force F on a vertical surface varies jointly as the area A of the surface and as the square of the wind velocity V. When the wind is blowing 20 mph, the force on 1 sq. ft of surface is 1.8 lb. Find the force exerted on a surface of 2 sq. ft when the wind velocity is 60 mph.

6. The pressure P in a liquid varies jointly with the depth h and density D of the liquid. If $P = 204$ when $h = 163.2$ and $D = 1.25$, find P when $h = 182.5$ and $D = 13.56$.

7. Given: z is directly proportional to x and inversely proportional to y. If $z = 12$ when $x = 6$ and $y = 2$, find k, and find z when $x = -8$ and $y = -4$.

8. The electrical resistance R of a wire is directly proportional to L and inversely proportional to the square of d. If $R = 2$ when $L = 8$ and $d = 4$, find k, and find R when $L = 10$ and $d = 5$.

9. The elongation e of a wire is jointly proportional to P and L and inversely proportional to A. If $e = 3$ when $L = 45$, $P = 2.4$, and $A = 0.9$, find k, and find e when $L = 40$, $P = 1.5$, and $A = 0.75$.

10. When a horizontal beam with rectangular cross-section is supported at both ends, its strength S varies jointly as the breadth b and the square of the depth d and inversely as the length L. A 2- by 4-in. beam 8 ft long resting on the 2-in. side will safely support 600 lb. What is the safe load when the beam is resting on the 4-in. side?

Set II

1. Given: V varies jointly with L and H. If $V = 144$ when $L = 3$ and $H = 8$, find k, the constant of proportionality, and find V when $L = 2$ and $H = 5$.

2. Given: C varies jointly with L and W. If $C = 7,500$ when $L = 25$ and $W = 20$, find k, and find C when $L = 18$ and $W = 23$.

3. The simple interest I earned in a given time t varies jointly as the principal P and the interest rate r. If $I = 255$ when $P = 1,250$ and $r = 0.0975$, find k, and find I when $P = 1,500$ and $r = 0.0825$.

4. On a certain truck line, it costs $56.80 to send 5 tons of goods 8 miles. How much will it cost to send 14 tons a distance of 15 miles? (The cost varies jointly with the weight and the distance.)

5. Given: H varies jointly with R and the square of I. If $H = 1,458$ when $R = 24$ and $I = 4.5$, find k, and find H when $R = 22$ and $I = 5.5$.

6. Given: y varies jointly with x and the square of z. If $y = 72$ when $x = 2$ and $z = 3$, find k, and find y when $x = 5$ and $z = 2$.

7. Given: z is directly proportional to x and inversely proportional to y. If $z = 2$ when $x = 4$ and $y = 10$, find k, and find z when $x = 3$ and $y = 6$.

8. Given: P is directly proportional to T and inversely proportional to V. If $P = 10$ when $T = 250$ and $V = 400$, find k, and find P when $T = 280$ and $V = 350$.

9. Given: W is jointly proportional to x and y and inversely proportional to the square of z. If $W = 1{,}200$ when $x = 8$, $y = 6$, and $z = 2$, find k, and find W when $x = 5.6$, $y = 3.8$, and $z = 1.5$.

10. The gravitational attraction F between two masses is jointly proportional to M and m and inversely proportional to the square of d. If $F = 1{,}000$ when $d = 100$, $m = 50$, and $M = 2{,}000$, find k, and find F when $d = 66$, $m = 125$, and $M = 1{,}450$.

8.10 Review: 8.6–8.9

Functions
8.6

A **function** is a relation such that no two of its ordered pairs have the *same first coordinate* and *different second coordinates*. This means that no vertical line can meet the graph of a function in more than one point.

Linear function: $\quad f(x) = mx + b$; graph is a *straight line*

Quadratic function: $\quad f(x) = ax^2 + bx + c$; graph is a *parabola*

Cubic function: $\quad f(x) = ax^3 + bx^2 + cx + d$

The value of a function: $f(a)$, read "f of a," is the value of $f(x)$ when x is replaced by a.

The Graphs of $y = f(x) + h$ and $y = f(x + h)$
8.6C

The graph of $y = f(x) + h$ can be found by shifting the graph of $y = f(x)$ upward $|h|$ units if h is positive and downward $|h|$ units if h is negative.

The graph of $y = f(x + h)$ can be found by shifting the graph of $y = f(x)$ to the left $|h|$ units if h is positive and to the right $|h|$ units if h is negative.

To Find the Inverse Relation $\mathscr{R}^{-1}$ of a Relation $\mathscr{R}$
8.7

1. If the relation is given as a set of ordered pairs, $\mathscr{R}^{-1}$ is the set of ordered pairs found by interchanging the first and second coordinates of each ordered pair in $\mathscr{R}$.

2. If the relation is given by an equation, $\mathscr{R}^{-1}$ is found by interchanging x and y in the equation and then solving the new equation for y.

The graph of the inverse relation $\mathscr{R}^{-1}$ is the mirror image of the relation $\mathscr{R}$, with the mirror being the line $y = x$.

The Inverse of a Function
8.7

If a function is invertible, that is, if for each y-value there is only one x-value, then $f^{-1}(x)$ is found by substituting y for $f(x)$ (if necessary), interchanging x and y, and then solving the new equation for y.

The graph of the inverse function $y = f^{-1}(x)$ is the mirror image of the graph of the function $y = f(x)$, with the mirror being the line $y = x$.

To Graph a Curve (Polynomial Functions Other Than Linear)
8.8

1. Use the equation to make a table of values.

2. Plot the points from the table of values.

3. Draw a smooth curve through the points, taking them in order from left to right.

Variation
8.9

The equation for "y varies directly as x^n" is $y = kx^n$.

The equation for "y varies inversely as x^n" is $y = \dfrac{k}{x^n}$.

The equation for "y varies jointly with s^n and t^m" is $y = ks^n t^m$.

The equation for "y varies directly as x^n and inversely as z^m" is $y = \dfrac{kx^n}{z^m}$.

Proportion
8.9

An equation that can be put in the form $\dfrac{a}{b} = \dfrac{c}{d}$ is called a **proportion**.

Review Exercises 8.10 Set I

1. Which of the following are graphs of functions?

   a. 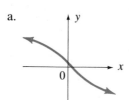   b. 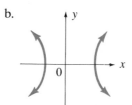   c.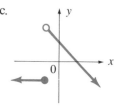

2. Which of the following are graphs of functions?

   a. 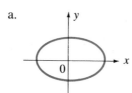   b. 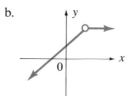   c.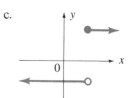

3. Given $f(x) = 3x^2 - 5x + 4$, find:

   a. $f(2)$ b. $f(0)$ c. $f(x - 1)$

4. If $F(x) = x^3 - 2x^2 + 6$ and $g(x) = 2x^2 - 7x$, find $\frac{1}{3}F(2) - 6g(4)$.

In Exercises 5–7, graph the function.

5. $y = f(x) = |x| + 1$ 6. $y = f(x) = |x| - 1$

7. $y = f(x) = |x + 1|$

8. Given $\mathcal{R} = \{(-1, -2), (-4, 4), (5, 0), (4, -2), (-5, -3)\}$, find $\mathcal{R}^{-1}$, $D_{\mathcal{R}^{-1}}$, and $R_{\mathcal{R}^{-1}}$, and graph $\mathcal{R}$ and $\mathcal{R}^{-1}$. Is $\mathcal{R}$ a function? Is $\mathcal{R}^{-1}$ a function?

In Exercises 9 and 10, find the inverse function for each function. Graph each function and its inverse. Find the domain and range for $y = f(x)$ and $y = f^{-1}(x)$.

9. $y = f(x) = \dfrac{x + 6}{3}$ 10. $y = f(x) = -\dfrac{5}{2}x + 1$

In Exercises 11 and 12, find the inverse function for each function.

11. $y = f(x) = \dfrac{9}{2 - 7x}$

12. $y = f(x) = \dfrac{11}{2(4x - 5)}$

In Exercises 13–15, complete the table of values for each equation and then draw the graph.

13. $y = \dfrac{x^2}{2}$

x	y
-4	
-2	
-1	
0	
1	
2	
4	

14. $y = \dfrac{x^2}{2} + 1$

x	y
-4	
-2	
-1	
0	
1	
2	
4	

15. $y = x^3 - 3x$

x	y
-3	
-2	
-1	
0	
1	
2	
3	

16. The variable c varies jointly with p and q and inversely with the square of t. If $c = 30$ when $p = 3$, $q = 5$, and $t = 4$, find k, and find c when $p = 7$, $q = 13$, and $t = 2$.

Review Exercises 8.10 Set II

NAME _____

1. Which of the following are graphs of functions?

a.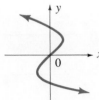

b.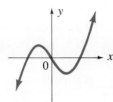

c.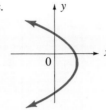

ANSWERS

1a. _____

b. _____

c. _____

2a. _____

b. _____

c. _____

3. _____

4. _____

5. __Use graph._____

6. __Use graph._____

2. Given $f(x) = 5x^2 - 12x + 16$, find:

a. $f(-1)$ b. $f(4)$ c. $f(2a - 1)$

3. If $H(x) = 5x^3 + 7$ and $g(y) = 4y - 2y^2$, find $\dfrac{5}{11} H(-2) - \dfrac{1}{6} g(5)$.

4. If $F(x) = 3x - x^2$ and $G(w) = 4 - w^2$, find $\dfrac{F(1 - c)}{G(c)}$.

In Exercises 5 and 6, graph the function.

5. $y = f(x) = |x| - 4$

6. $y = f(x) = |x - 4|$

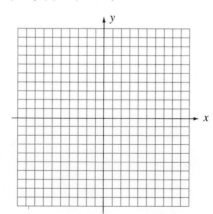

7. Given: $\mathscr{R} = \{(-2, 4), (-1, 2), (3, -1), (0, 4)\}$. Find $\mathscr{R}^{-1}$, $D_{\mathscr{R}^{-1}}$, and $R_{\mathscr{R}^{-1}}$ and graph $\mathscr{R}$ and $\mathscr{R}^{-1}$. Is $\mathscr{R}$ a function? Is $\mathscr{R}^{-1}$ a function?

7. _____

_____

_____

<u>Use graph.</u>

<u>Use graph.</u>

_____

_____

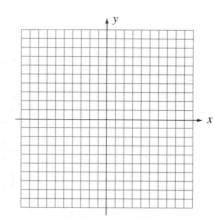

8. For $y = f(x) = \frac{4}{7}x - 2$, find the inverse function, $f^{-1}(x)$. Graph the function and its inverse on the same axes. Find the domain and range for $y = f(x)$ and $y = f^{-1}(x)$.

8. _____

<u>Use graph.</u>

_____

_____

_____

_____

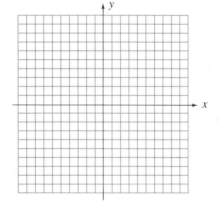

9. _____

10. _____

For Exercises 9–12, find the inverse function, $y = f^{-1}(x)$.

11. _____

9. $y = f(x) = x - 2$

10. $y = f(x) = \dfrac{x - 2}{5}$

12. _____

11. $y = f(x) = \dfrac{1}{x}$

12. $y = f(x) = \dfrac{13}{3(2x + 3)}$

In Exercises 13 and 14, complete the table of values for each equation and then draw the graph.

13. $y = \dfrac{(x + 1)^2}{2}$

x	y
−4	
−3	
−2	
−1	
0	
1	
2	

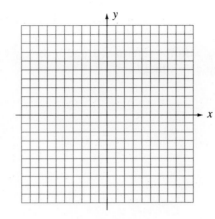

14. $y = 5x - x^3$

x	y
−3	
−2	
−1	
0	
1	
2	
3	

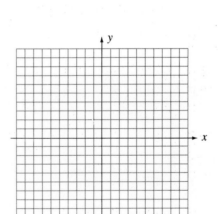

15. The variable d varies directly with e and inversely with the cube of f. If $d = 60$ when $e = 32$ and $f = 2$, find k, and find d when $e = 9$ and $f = 3$.

_____

16. The variable y varies directly with the square of x and inversely with the cube of z. If $y = \frac{4}{9}$ when $x = 2$ and $z = 3$, find k.

Chapter 8 Diagnostic Test

The purpose of this test is to see how well you understand functions and graphing. We recommend that you work this diagnostic test *before* your instructor tests you on this chapter. Allow yourself about 50 minutes.

Complete solutions for all the problems on this test, together with section references, are given in the answer section at the end of the book. For the problems you do incorrectly, study the sections cited.

1. a. Draw the triangle with vertices at $A(-4, 2)$, $B(1, -3)$, and $C(5, 3)$.

   b. Find the length of the side AB.

   c. Find the slope of the line through B and C.

   d. Write the general form of the equation of the line through A and B.

   e. Find the x-intercept of the line through A and B.

   f. Find the y-intercept of the line through A and B.

2. Find the general form of the equation of the line that has a slope of $\frac{6}{5}$ and a y-intercept of -4.

3. Graph the relation $x - 2y = 6$.

4. Complete the table of values and graph the relation $y = 1 + x - x^2$.

x	y
-2	
-1	
0	
1	
2	
3	

5. Graph the inequality $4x - 3y \le -12$.

6. Given the relation $\{(-4, -5), (2, 4), (4, -2), (-2, 3), (2, -1)\}$:

   a. Find its domain.

   b. Find its range.

   c. Draw the graph of the relation.

   d. Is this relation a function?

7. Given $f(x) = 3x^2 - 5$. Find:

   a. $f(-2)$ b. $f(4)$ c. $\dfrac{f(4) - f(-2)}{6}$

8. Given $\mathscr{R} = \{(1, 4), (-5, -3), (4, -2), (-5, 2)\}$, find $\mathscr{R}^{-1}$, $D_{\mathscr{R}^{-1}}$, and $R_{\mathscr{R}^{-1}}$, and graph $\mathscr{R}$ and $\mathscr{R}^{-1}$. Is $\mathscr{R}$ a function? Is $\mathscr{R}^{-1}$ a function?

9. Find the inverse function for $y = f(x) = -\frac{3}{2}x + 1$. Graph $y = f(x)$ and $y = f^{-1}(x)$ on the same axes.

10. Find the inverse function for $y = f(x) = \dfrac{15}{4(2 - 5x)}$. Find the domain and range for $y = f(x)$ and $y = f^{-1}(x)$.

11. The variable w varies jointly with x and y and inversely with the square of z. If $w = 20$ when $x = 8$, $y = 6$, and $z = 12$, find k, the constant of proportionality, and find w when $x = 6$, $y = 10$, and $z = 5$.

Cumulative Review Exercises
Chapters 1–8

In Exercises 1 and 2, factor completely.

1. $2x^4 - 24x^2 + 54$

2. $8a^4b - 27ab^4$

In Exercises 3 and 4, perform the indicated operations and express your answers in simplest radical form.

3. $\sqrt[3]{-4a^4} \cdot \sqrt[3]{2a}$

4. $4\sqrt{18x^4} + \sqrt{32x^5} - \sqrt{50x^4}$

In Exercises 5–7, perform the indicated operations and write the answers in $a + bi$ form.

5. $\dfrac{3 + 2i}{2 - i}$

6. $(7 - \sqrt{-16}) - (5 - \sqrt{-36})$

7. $(3 + i)^4$

8. Solve for r: $S = \dfrac{a}{1 - r}$.

9. Solve and check: $x^{-1/3} = 3$.

10. Subtract $(2x^2 - 3x + 4)$ from the sum of $(9x^2 + x - 7)$ and $(8 - 6x - 4x^2)$.

11. If $f(x) = 3x^2 - 2x + 7$, find $f(0)$ and $f(-2)$.

12. Graph $2x - y = 4$.

13. Write the equation of the straight line that passes through the points $(-3, 4)$ and $(1, -2)$.

14. The variable y varies inversely with the cube of x. If $y = 3$ when $x = -2$, find k, and find y when $x = 3$.

In Exercises 15 and 16, set up each problem algebraically, solve, and check.

15. A grocer makes up a 60-lb mixture of cashews and peanuts. If the cashews cost $7.40 a pound and the peanuts cost $2.80 a pound, how many pounds of each kind of nut must be used in order for the mixture to cost $4.18 a pound?

16. Dorothy can drive from A to B at 55 mph, but in driving from B to C, she can travel only 50 mph. B is 8 mi further from A than it is from C. If it takes her the same length of time to get from A to B as it takes her to get from B to C, what is the distance from A to B?

9 Nonlinear Equations and Inequalities

In this chapter, we discuss several methods of solving quadratic equations and inequalities. We also discuss graphing quadratic functions and conic sections. (We have already solved quadratic equations by *factoring* in Chapters 5, 6, and 7.)

9.1 Basic Definitions

Quadratic Equations

A **quadratic equation** is a polynomial equation with a *second-degree* term as its highest-degree term. Such equations are also called **second-degree equations**. The number of roots of a polynomial equation is at *most* equal to the degree of the polynomial. For this reason, we expect to get two roots when we solve quadratic equations. (Refer to the footnote on page 453.)

Example 1   Examples of quadratic equations:

a. $3x^2 + 7x + 2 = 0$

b. $\frac{1}{2}x^2 = \frac{2}{3}x - 4$

c. $x^2 - 4 = 0$

d. $5x^2 - 15x = 0$ ∎

General Form (Standard Form)   The *general form* of a quadratic equation, as used in this text, is as follows:

> THE GENERAL FORM OF A QUADRATIC EQUATION
>
> $$ax^2 + bx + c = 0$$
>
> where a, b, and c are integers and $a > 0$.

Note that a is the coefficient of x^2, b is the coefficient of x, and c is the constant.

> TO CHANGE A QUADRATIC EQUATION INTO GENERAL FORM
>
> **1.** Remove fractions by multiplying each term by the LCD.
>
> **2.** Remove grouping symbols.
>
> **3.** Combine like terms.
>
> **4.** Get all terms to one side by adding the same expression to both sides. *Only zero must remain on the other side.* Then arrange the terms in descending powers

Example 2   Change each of the following quadratic equations into the general form, and then identify a, b, and c:

a. $7x = 5 - 2x^2$

   $2x^2 + 7x - 5 = 0$ General form $\begin{cases} a = 2 \\ b = 7 \\ c = -5 \end{cases}$

b. $\qquad 5x^2 = 3$

$\qquad 5x^2 + 0x - 3 = 0$ General form $\begin{cases} a = 5 \\ b = 0 \\ c = -3 \end{cases}$

c. $\qquad 6x = 11x^2$

$\qquad 0 = 11x^2 - 6x + 0$

$\qquad 11x^2 - 6x + 0 = 0$ General form $\begin{cases} a = 11 \\ b = -6 \\ c = 0 \end{cases}$

d. $\qquad \dfrac{2}{3}x^2 - 5x = \dfrac{1}{2}$

$\qquad \text{LCD} = 6$

$\qquad \dfrac{6}{1} \cdot \dfrac{2}{3}x^2 + \dfrac{6}{1} \cdot (-5x) = \dfrac{6}{1} \cdot \dfrac{1}{2}$

$\qquad 4x^2 - 30x = 3$

$\qquad 4x^2 - 30x - 3 = 0$ General form $\begin{cases} a = 4 \\ b = -30 \\ c = -3 \end{cases}$

e. $(x + 2)(2x - 3) = 3x - 7$

$\qquad 2x^2 + x - 6 = 3x - 7$

$\qquad 2x^2 - 2x + 1 = 0$ General form $\begin{cases} a = 2 \\ b = -2 \\ c = 1 \end{cases}$ ■

EXERCISES 9.1

Set I Write each of the quadratic equations in general form; then identify a, b, and c.

1. $3x^2 + 5x = 2$ **2.** $3x + 5 = 2x^2$ **3.** $3x^2 = 4$

4. $16 = x^2$ **5.** $\dfrac{4x}{3} = 4 + x^2$ **6.** $\dfrac{3x}{2} - 5 = x^2$

7. $2 - 4x = 3x^2$ **8.** $6x - 3 = 5x^2$

9. $x(x + 2) = 4$ **10.** $4(x - 5) = x^2$

11. $3x(x - 2) = (x + 1)(x - 5)$ **12.** $7x(2x + 3) = (x - 3)(x + 4)$

Set II Write each of the quadratic equations in general form; then identify a, b, and c.

1. $2x - 5 = 6x^2$ **2.** $6 - 3x = 5x^2$ **3.** $8 = 2x^2$

4. $x^2 - 1 = 3x$ **5.** $\dfrac{x^2}{2} - 3 = 7x$ **6.** $\dfrac{3 - x^2}{4} = x$

7. $8x - x^2 = -2$ **8.** $4 - \dfrac{x}{2} = \dfrac{x^2}{4}$ **9.** $2x(3 - x) = 5$

10. $x(x - 4) = 3$

11. $5x(x + 3) = (4x - 5)(6x + 3)$

12. $(2x - 1)(3x + 5) = 2x - 1$

9.2 Incomplete Quadratic Equations

An **incomplete quadratic equation** is one in which b or c (or both) is zero. The only letter that *cannot* be zero is a. If a were zero, the equation would not be quadratic.

Example 1   Examples of incomplete quadratic equations:

a. $12x^2 + 5 = 0$ $(b = 0)$ b. $7x^2 - 2x = 0$ $(c = 0)$

c. $3x^2 = 0$ $(b$ and $c = 0)$ ■

An incomplete quadratic equation in which $c = 0$ is solved by factoring. (See Example 2.)

Example 2   Solve $12x^2 = 3x$.

$$12x^2 - 3x = 0 \qquad \text{General form}$$

$$3x(4x - 1) = 0 \qquad \text{GCF} = 3x$$

$$3x = 0 \quad or \quad 4x - 1 = 0$$

$$x = 0 \qquad\qquad 4x = 1$$

$$x = \tfrac{1}{4}$$

The check is left to the student. The solution set is $\{0, \tfrac{1}{4}\}$.   ■

A WORD OF CAUTION   In Example 2, a common mistake students make is to divide both sides of the equation by x.

$$12x^2 = 3x$$

$$12x = 3 \qquad \text{Divide both sides by } x$$

$$x = \tfrac{1}{4}$$

Using this method, we found only the solution $x = \tfrac{1}{4}$, *not* $x = 0$. By dividing both sides of the equation by x, we lost the solution $x = 0$.

   Do not divide both sides of an equation by an expression containing the variable because you may lose solutions. ☑

In Section 7.7, the following method was shown for solving an incomplete quadratic equation in which $b = 0$ *and* $k > 0$:

$$\text{If } x^2 = k, \text{ then } x = \sqrt{k} \text{ or } x = -\sqrt{k}.$$

It can be shown that this rule holds even if k is negative; therefore, we can solve an equation of the form $ax^2 + c = 0$ by the following method:

TO SOLVE A QUADRATIC EQUATION WHEN $b = 0$

1. Add $-c$ to both sides of the equation.

2. Divide both sides by the coefficient a of x^2.

3. Take the square root of both sides, putting $\pm$ in front of the constant.

4. Express the constant in simplest form.

5. When the radicand is *positive* or zero, the square roots are real numbers; when it is *negative*, the square roots are complex numbers.

Example 3   Solve $3x^2 - 5 = 0$.

$$3x^2 = 5$$

$$x^2 = \frac{5}{3}$$

$$\sqrt{x^2} = \pm\sqrt{\frac{5}{3}} = \pm\frac{\sqrt{5}}{\sqrt{3}} \cdot \frac{\sqrt{3}}{\sqrt{3}} = \pm\frac{\sqrt{15}}{3}$$

$$x = \pm\frac{\sqrt{15}}{3}$$

The check is left to the student. We can use a calculator to approximate $\sqrt{15}$ and express the answers as decimals.

$$x = \pm\frac{\sqrt{15}}{3} \doteq \pm\frac{3.873}{3} = \pm 1.291 \doteq \pm 1.29 \qquad \text{Rounded off to two decimal places}$$

The solution set is

$$\left\{\frac{\sqrt{15}}{3}, -\frac{\sqrt{15}}{3}\right\} \quad \blacksquare$$

Example 4   Solve $x^2 + 25 = 0$.

$$x^2 = -25$$

$$\sqrt{x^2} = \pm\sqrt{-25}$$

$$x = \pm 5i$$

Check

$$x^2 + 25 = 0$$

$$(\pm 5i)^2 + 25 \overset{?}{=} 0$$

$$25i^2 + 25 \overset{?}{=} 0$$

$$-25 + 25 = 0$$

The solution set is $\{5i, -5i\}$. $\blacksquare$

In Section 7.6, we solved equations with rational exponents by raising both sides of the equation to the same power. However, the problems in that section were carefully selected to ensure that the power was never a fraction with an even-number denominator. Raising both sides of an equation to a fractional power in which the *denominator* of the exponent is an *even* number is equivalent to taking an *even root* of both sides of the equation. When we do this, we must put a $\pm$ sign in front of the constant (see Example 5).

Example 5 Solve $x^{-2/3} = 4$.

$$x^{-2/3} = 2^2$$

$$(x^{-2/3})^{-3/2} = \pm(2^2)^{-3/2}$$

We raise both sides to the $-\frac{3}{2}$ power in order to make the exponent of x equal to $1 : \left(-\frac{2}{3}\right)\left(-\frac{3}{2}\right) = 1$

$$x^{(-2/3)(-3/2)} = \pm 2^{2(-3/2)}$$

$$x = \pm 2^{-3} = \pm\frac{1}{8}$$

Check for $x = \frac{1}{8}$

$$x^{-2/3} = 4$$

$$\left(\frac{1}{8}\right)^{-2/3} \overset{?}{=} 4$$

$$(2^{-3})^{-2/3} \overset{?}{=} 4$$

$$2^2 \overset{?}{=} 4$$

$$4 = 4$$

Check for $x - \frac{1}{8}$

$$x^{-2/3} = 4$$

$$\left(-\frac{1}{8}\right)^{-2/3} \overset{?}{=} 4$$

$$(-8)^{2/3} \overset{?}{=} 4$$

$$\sqrt[3]{(-8)^2} \overset{?}{=} 4$$

$$\sqrt[3]{64} \overset{?}{=} 4$$

$$4 = 4$$

The solution set is $\{-\frac{1}{8}, \frac{1}{8}\}$. ∎

EXERCISES 9.2

Set I   In Exercises 1–20, solve the equations.

1. $x^2 - 27 = 0$

2. $x^2 - 8 = 0$

3. $x^2 + 16 = 0$

4. $x^2 + 81 = 0$

5. $x^2 = 7$

6. $x^2 = 13$

7. $x^2 = -12$

8. $x^2 = -75$

9. $12x = 8x^3$

10. $9x = 12x^3$

11. $5x^2 + 4 = 0$

12. $3x^2 + 25 = 0$

13. $\dfrac{2x^2}{3} = 4x$

14. $\dfrac{3x}{5} = 6x^2$

15. $x(x - 2) = (2x + 3)x$

16. $x(x - 3) = x(2x - 8)$

17. $\dfrac{x + 2}{3x} = \dfrac{x + 1}{x}$

18. $\dfrac{3x - 2}{4x} = \dfrac{x + 1}{3x}$

19. $3x^{-2/3} = 48$

20. $x^{2/5} = 4$

In Exercises 21–24, set up each problem algebraically and solve. In Exercises 22–24, express the answer in simplest radical form.

21. The length of the diagonal of a square is $\sqrt{32}$. What is the length of a side?

22. The length of the diagonal of a square is 18. What is the length of a side?

23. A rectangle is 7 cm wide and 10 cm long. Find the length of its diagonal.

24. A rectangle is 12 cm long and 8 cm wide. Find the length of its diagonal.

Set II In Exercises 1–20, solve the equations.

1. $x^2 - 50 = 0$ **2.** $x^2 - 48 = 0$ **3.** $x^2 + 144 = 0$

4. $x^2 = -5$ **5.** $x^2 = 3$ **6.** $x^2 - 12 = 0$

7. $x^2 = -20$ **8.** $x^2 = 3x$ **9.** $8x = 10x^3$

10. $5x = 3x^2$ **11.** $3x^2 + 7 = 0$ **12.** $2x^2 = 11$

13. $\dfrac{5x}{2} = 15x^2$ **14.** $3x = \dfrac{2x^2}{5}$

15. $2x(x - 1) = 3x(2x + 1)$ **16.** $4x(3x + 2) = x(x - 5)$

17. $\dfrac{2x - 1}{3x} = \dfrac{x - 3}{x}$ **18.** $\dfrac{4x - 3}{5x} = \dfrac{2x - 1}{x}$

19. $x^{4/5} = 16$ **20.** $x^{4/3} = 81$

In Exercises 21–24, set up each problem algebraically and solve. In Exercises 21–23, express the answer in simplest radical form.

21. The length of the diagonal of a square is 100. What is the length of a side?

22. The area of a square is 75. What is the length of a side?

23. A rectangle is 12 m long and 4 m wide. Find the length of its diagonal.

24. The area of a certain square equals its perimeter. Find the length of a side of the square.

9.3 Solving Equations That Are Quadratic in Form

Sometimes, equations that are not quadratics can be solved like quadratics after an appropriate substitution is made. Equations that are quadratic in form can be recognized by noticing that the power of an expression in one term is twice the power of the same expression in another term (see Example 1).

Example 1 Recognizing equations of quadratic form:

a. $y^{-8} - 10y^{-4} + 9 = 0$ -8 is twice -4

b. $h^{-2/3} - h^{-1/3} = 0$ $-\dfrac{2}{3}$ is twice $-\dfrac{1}{3}$

c. $(x^2 - 2x)^2 - 7(x^2 - 2x)^1 + 12 = 0$ 2 is twice 1 ■

USING SUBSTITUTION TO SOLVE AN EQUATION THAT IS
WRITTEN AS $a(x^n)^2 + b(x^n)^1 + c = 0$

1. Let some different variable equal x^n.

2. Substitute that variable for x^n.

3. Solve the resulting quadratic equation.

4. Set each solution equal to x^n.

5. Solve the resulting equations for x.

6. Check all answers in the original equation.

Example 2 Solve $x^4 - 29x^2 + 100 = 0$.

$x^4 - 29x^2 + 100 = 0$ can be written as $(x^2)^2 - 29(x^2)^1 + 100 = 0$. Let $z = x^2$; then $z^2 = x^4$.

Therefore, $$x^4 - 29x^2 + 100 = 0$$

becomes $$z^2 - 29z + 100 = 0 \qquad \text{This is quadratic in } z$$

$$(z - 4)(z - 25) = 0$$

$$z - 4 = 0 \quad or \quad z - 25 = 0$$

$$z = 4 \quad or \quad z = 25$$

$$x^2 = 4 \quad or \quad x^2 = 25 \qquad \text{Replace } z \text{ with } x^2$$

$$x = \pm 2 \quad or \quad x = \pm 5$$

Check for $x = \pm 2$	_Check for_ $x = \pm 5$
$(\pm 2)^4 - 29(\pm 2)^2 + 100 \overset{?}{=} 0$	$(\pm 5)^4 - 29(\pm 5)^2 + 100 \overset{?}{=} 0$
$16 - 29(4) + 100 \overset{?}{=} 0$	$625 - 29(25) + 100 \overset{?}{=} 0$
$16 - 116 + 100 \overset{?}{=} 0$	$625 - 725 + 100 \overset{?}{=} 0$
$0 = 0$	$0 = 0$

The solution set is $\{\pm 2, \pm 5\}$. ∎

Example 3 Solve $h^{-2/3} - h^{-1/3} = 0$.

$h^{-2/3} - h^{-1/3} = 0$ can be written as $(h^{-1/3})^2 - (h^{-1/3})^1 = 0$. Let $z = h^{-1/3}$; then $z^2 = h^{-2/3}$.

Therefore,
$$h^{-2/3} - h^{-1/3} = 0$$

becomes
$$z^2 - z = 0$$

$$z(z - 1) = 0$$

$$z = 0 \quad or \quad z - 1 = 0$$

$$z = 1$$

$$h^{-1/3} = 0 \quad or \quad h^{-1/3} = 1 \qquad \text{Replace } z \text{ with } h^{-1/3}$$

$$(h^{-1/3})^{-3} = \boxed{(0)}^{-3} \quad (h^{-1/3})^{-3} = (1)^{-3}$$

$$h = 1$$

Does not exist ⟶

The solution $h = 1$ checks. (We leave the check to the student.) The solution set is $\{1\}$. ∎

Example 4   Solve $(x^2 - 2x)^2 - 11(x^2 - 2x) + 24 = 0$.

Let
$$z = x^2 - 2x; \text{ then } z^2 = (x^2 - 2x)^2.$$

Therefore,
$$(x^2 - 2x)^2 - 11(x^2 - 2x) + 24 = 0$$

becomes
$$z^2 \quad - \quad 11z \quad + 24 = 0$$

$$(z - 3)(z - 8) \qquad\qquad = 0$$

$$z - 3 = 0 \qquad or \qquad\qquad z - 8 = 0$$

$$z = 3 \qquad or \qquad\qquad z = 8$$

$$x^2 - 2x = 3 \qquad or \qquad\quad x^2 - 2x = 8 \qquad \text{Replace } z \text{ with } x^2 - 2x$$

$$x^2 - 2x - 3 = 0 \qquad or \qquad\quad x^2 - 2x - 8 = 0$$

$$(x + 1)(x - 3) = 0 \qquad or \qquad (x + 2)(x - 4) = 0$$

$$x + 1 = 0 \quad or \quad x - 3 = 0 \quad or \quad x + 2 = 0 \quad or \quad x - 4 = 0$$

$$x = -1 \quad or \qquad x = 3 \quad or \qquad x = -2 \quad or \qquad x = 4$$

All these answers check. (We leave the checks to the student.) The solution set is $\{-1, 3, -2, 4\}$. ∎

EXERCISES 9.3

Set I   In Exercises 1–12, solve by factoring, after making appropriate substitutions.

1. $x^4 - 37x^2 + 36 = 0$ 2. $y^4 - 13y^2 + 36 = 0$

3. $z^{-4} - 10z^{-2} + 9 = 0$ 4. $x^{-4} - 5x^{-2} + 4 = 0$

5. $y^{2/3} - 5y^{1/3} = -4$ 6. $x^{2/3} - 10x^{1/3} = -9$

7. $z^{-4} - 4z^{-2} = 0$ 8. $R^{-4} - 9R^{-2} = 0$

9. $K^{-2/3} + 2K^{-1/3} + 1 = 0$ 10. $M^{-1} - 2M^{-1/2} + 1 = 0$

11. $(x^2 - 4x)^2 - (x^2 - 4x) - 20 = 0$

12. $(x^2 - 2x)^2 - 2(x^2 - 2x) - 3 = 0$

In Exercises 13–16, set up each problem algebraically and solve.

13. The length of a rectangle is twice its width. If the numerical sum of its area and perimeter is 80, find the length and width.

14. The length of a rectangle is three times its width. If the numerical sum of its area and perimeter is 80, find its dimensions.

15. Bruce drives from Los Angeles to the Mexican border and back to Los Angeles, a total distance of 240 mi. His average speed returning to Los Angeles was 20 mph faster than his average speed going to Mexico. If his total driving time was 5 hr, what was his average speed driving from Los Angeles to Mexico?

16. Ruth drives from Creston to Des Moines, a distance of 90 mi. Then she continues on from Des Moines to Omaha, a distance of 120 mi. Her average speed was 10 mph faster on the second part of the journey than on the first part. If the total driving time was 6 hr, what was her average speed on the first leg of the journey?

Set II In Exercises 1–12, solve by factoring, after making appropriate substitutions.

1. $y^4 - 26y^2 + 25 = 0$

2. $x^4 + 49 = 50x^2$

3. $x^{-4} - 17x^{-2} = -16$

4. $x^{-4} - 29x^{-2} + 100 = 0$

5. $x^{2/3} - 4x^{1/3} + 4 = 0$

6. $y^{2/3} - 2y^{1/3} = 3$

7. $x^{-4} - 16x^{-2} = 0$

8. $x^4 = 16x^2$

9. $x^{-2/3} - 6x^{-1/3} + 9 = 0$

10. $x^{-2/3} + x^{-1/3} = 2$

11. $(x^2 - 6x)^2 + 17(x^2 - 6x) + 72 = 0$

12. $(x^2 + 2x)^2 - 7(x^2 + 2x) = 8$

In Exercises 13–16, set up each problem algebraically and solve.

13. The length of a rectangle is 2 more than twice its width. If its diagonal is 3 more than twice its width, what are its dimensions?

14. The tens digit of a two-digit number is 4 more than the units digit. If the product of the units digit and tens digit is 21, find the number.

15. Jeff jogged from his home to a park 15 mi away, and then he walked back home. He jogged 2 mph faster than he walked. If his total traveling time was 8 hr, how fast did he jog?

16. If the product of two consecutive even integers is increased by 4, the result is 84. Find the integers.

9.4 Completing the Square of a Quadratic Equation and the Quadratic Formula

In Section 5.7, we used *completing the square* as a method of factoring. In this section, we use completing the square to solve quadratic equations and to derive the quadratic formula. The methods we have used in this chapter so far can be used only to solve *some* quadratic equations. The quadratic formula (or completing the square) can be used to solve *any* quadratic equation.

Solving a Quadratic Equation by Completing the Square

The technique we use here for completing the square is different from the one shown in Chapter 5, because in this chapter we are working with equations. In Chapter 5, we had to add an amount *to* and then subtract it *from* a polynomial, since we were not working with an equation. Here, we will add the same number to both sides of the equation. The method is as follows:

TO SOLVE A QUADRATIC EQUATION (IN x) BY COMPLETING THE SQUARE

1. Get all the terms containing x on one side of the equal sign and the constant term on the other side.

2. Divide both sides of the equation by a, the coefficient of x^2.

3. Find the quantity that, when added to the left side, makes the left side a trinomial square. Do this by squaring one-half of the coefficient of x^1.

4. Add the number found in step 3 to both sides of the equation.

5. Factor the left side.

6. Take the square root of both sides, putting $\pm$ in front of the constant.

7. Solve the resulting first-degree (linear) equation for x.

8. Check your solutions.

Example 1   Solve $x^2 - 4x + 1 = 0$.

To find the quantity that, when added to both sides, makes the left side a trinomial square:

$$x^2 - 4x = -1$$

Take $\frac{1}{2}$ of -4: $\frac{1}{2}(-4) = -2$

Then $(-2)^2 = 4$

$$x^2 - 4x + 4 = -1 + 4$$

Add 4 to both sides to make the left side a trinomial square

$$(x - 2)^2 = 3$$

Factor the left side

$$\sqrt{(x - 2)^2} = \pm\sqrt{3}$$

Take the square root of both sides

$$x - 2 = \pm\sqrt{3}$$

Simplify the radical

$$x = 2 \pm \sqrt{3}$$

Add 2 to both sides

Check for $x = 2 + \sqrt{3}$

$$x^2 \quad - \quad 4x \quad + 1 = 0$$

$$(2 + \sqrt{3})^2 - 4(2 + \sqrt{3}) + 1 \overset{?}{=} 0$$

$$4 + 4\sqrt{3} + 3 - 8 - 4\sqrt{3} + 1 \overset{?}{=} 0$$

$$0 = 0$$

We leave the check for $x = 2 - \sqrt{3}$ to the student. ∎

Example 2   Solve $25x^2 - 30x + 11 = 0$.

$$25x^2 - 30x = -11$$

$$x^2 - \frac{30}{25}x = -\frac{11}{25} \qquad \text{Divide both sides by 25}$$

Take $\frac{1}{2}$ of $-\frac{30}{25}$: $\frac{1}{2}\left(-\frac{30}{25}\right) = -\frac{3}{5}$

Then $\left(-\frac{3}{5}\right)^2 = \frac{9}{25}$

$$x^2 - \frac{6}{5}x + \frac{9}{25} = -\frac{11}{25} + \frac{9}{25} \qquad \text{Add } \frac{9}{25} \text{ to both sides to make}$$

the left side a trinomial square

$$\left(x - \frac{3}{5}\right)^2 = -\frac{2}{25} \qquad \text{Factor the left side}$$

$$\sqrt{\left(x - \frac{3}{5}\right)^2} = \pm\sqrt{-\frac{2}{25}} \qquad \text{Take the square root of both sides}$$

$$x - \frac{3}{5} = \pm\frac{\sqrt{2}}{5}i \qquad \text{Simplify the radicals}$$

$$x = \frac{3}{5} \pm \frac{\sqrt{2}}{5}i \qquad \text{Add } \frac{3}{5} \text{ to both sides}$$

Check for $x = \dfrac{3}{5} - \dfrac{\sqrt{2}}{5}i = \dfrac{3 - i\sqrt{2}}{5}$

$$25\left(\frac{3 - i\sqrt{2}}{5}\right)^2 - \overset{6}{\cancel{30}}\left(\frac{3 - i\sqrt{2}}{\underset{1}{\cancel{5}}}\right) + 11 \overset{?}{=} 0$$

$$\overset{1}{\cancel{25}}\left(\frac{9 - 6i\sqrt{2} + 2i^2}{\underset{1}{\cancel{25}}}\right) - 6(3 - i\sqrt{2}) + 11 \overset{?}{=} 0$$

$$9 - \cancel{6i\sqrt{2}} - 2 - 18 + \cancel{6i\sqrt{2}} + 11 \overset{?}{=} 0$$

$$0 = 0$$

The check for $x = \dfrac{3}{5} + \dfrac{\sqrt{2}}{5}i$ is left to the student. ∎

Solving a Quadratic Equation by Using the Quadratic Formula

The method of completing the square can be used to solve *any* quadratic equation. We now use it to solve the *general form* of the quadratic equation and in this way derive the *quadratic formula*.

$$ax^2 + bx + c = 0 \qquad\qquad \text{General form}$$

$$ax^2 + bx = 0 - c \qquad\qquad \text{Subtract } c \text{ from both sides}$$

$$x^2 + \frac{b}{a}x = -\frac{c}{a} \qquad\qquad \text{Divide both sides by } a$$

$$\text{Take } \frac{1}{2} \text{ of } \frac{b}{a}: \frac{1}{2}\left(\frac{b}{a}\right) = \frac{b}{2a}$$

$$\text{Then } \left(\frac{b}{2a}\right)^2 = \frac{b^2}{4a^2}$$

$$x^2 + \frac{b}{a}x + \frac{b^2}{4a^2} = \frac{b^2}{4a^2} - \frac{c}{a} = \frac{b^2}{4a^2} - \frac{4ac}{4a^2} \qquad \text{Add } \frac{b^2}{4a^2} \text{ to both sides to}$$

make the left side a trinomial square

$$\left(x + \frac{b}{2a}\right)^2 = \frac{b^2 - 4ac}{4a^2} \qquad\qquad \begin{array}{l}\text{Factor the left side and} \\ \text{add fractions on the} \\ \text{right side}\end{array}$$

$$\sqrt{\left(x + \frac{b}{2a}\right)^2} = \pm\sqrt{\frac{b^2 - 4ac}{4a^2}} \qquad\qquad \begin{array}{l}\text{Take the square root of} \\ \text{both sides}\end{array}$$

$$x + \frac{b}{2a} = \pm\frac{\sqrt{b^2 - 4ac}}{\sqrt{4a^2}} = \pm\frac{\sqrt{b^2 - 4ac}}{2a} \qquad \text{Simplify radicals}$$

$$x = -\frac{b}{2a} \pm \frac{\sqrt{b^2 - 4ac}}{2a} \qquad\qquad \text{Add } -\frac{b}{2a} \text{ to both sides}$$

Therefore,
$$x = \frac{-b \pm \sqrt{b^2 - 4ac}}{2a} \qquad\qquad \textbf{Quadratic formula}$$

The procedure for using the quadratic formula can be summarized as follows:

TO SOLVE A QUADRATIC EQUATION BY FORMULA

1. Arrange the equation in general form.

$$ax^2 + bx + c = 0$$

2. Substitute the values of a, b, and c into the quadratic formula.

$$x = \frac{-b \pm \sqrt{b^2 - 4ac}}{2a} \qquad (a \neq 0)$$

3. Simplify your answers.

4. Check your answers by substituting them in the original equation.

Example 3   Solve $x^2 - 5x + 6 = 0$ by the quadratic formula.

Substitute $\begin{Bmatrix} a = 1 \\ b = -5 \\ c = 6 \end{Bmatrix}$ in the formula $x = \dfrac{-b \pm \sqrt{b^2 - 4ac}}{2a}$.

$$x = \frac{-(-5) \pm \sqrt{(-5)^2 - 4(1)(6)}}{2(1)}$$

$$x = \frac{5 \pm \sqrt{25 - 24}}{2} = \frac{5 \pm \sqrt{1}}{2}$$

$$x = \frac{5 \pm 1}{2} = \begin{cases} \dfrac{5 + 1}{2} = \dfrac{6}{2} = 3 \\[2mm] \dfrac{5 - 1}{2} = \dfrac{4}{2} = 2 \end{cases}$$

This equation can also be solved by factoring.

$$x^2 - 5x + 6 = 0$$

$$(x - 2)(x - 3) = 0$$

$$x - 2 = 0 \quad or \quad x - 3 = 0$$

$$x = 2 \quad or \quad\quad x = 3$$

The check is left to the student. ■

Solving a quadratic equation by factoring is ordinarily shorter than using the quadratic formula. Therefore, first check to see if the equation can be factored by any of the methods discussed in Chapter 5. If it cannot, use the formula.

Example 4   Solve $\dfrac{1}{4} x^2 = 1 - x$.

LCD $= 4$

$$\frac{4}{1} \cdot \frac{1}{4} x^2 = 4 \cdot (1 - x)$$

$$x^2 = 4 - 4x \qquad \text{First, change the equation to general form}$$

$$x^2 + 4x - 4 = 0$$

Substitute $\begin{Bmatrix} a = 1 \\ b = 4 \\ c = -4 \end{Bmatrix}$ into $x = \dfrac{-b \pm \sqrt{b^2 - 4ac}}{2a}$.

$$x = \frac{-(4) \pm \sqrt{(4)^2 - 4(1)(-4)}}{2(1)}$$

$$= \frac{-4 \pm \sqrt{16 + 16}}{2} = \frac{-4 \pm \sqrt{32}}{2}$$

$$= \frac{-4 \pm 4\sqrt{2}}{2} = -2 \pm 2\sqrt{2}$$

Check for $x = -2 - 2\sqrt{2}$

$$\frac{1}{4}x^2 = 1 - x$$

$$\frac{1}{4}(-2 - 2\sqrt{2})^2 \stackrel{?}{=} 1 - (-2 - 2\sqrt{2})$$

$$\frac{1}{4}(4 + 8\sqrt{2} + 8) \stackrel{?}{=} 1 + 2 + 2\sqrt{2}$$

$$\frac{1}{4}(12 + 8\sqrt{2}) \stackrel{?}{=} 3 + 2\sqrt{2}$$

$$3 + 2\sqrt{2} = 3 + 2\sqrt{2}$$

The check for $x = -2 + 2\sqrt{2}$ is left to the student. ■

Example 5 Solve $x^2 - 6x + 13 = 0$.

Substitute $\begin{cases} a = 1 \\ b = -6 \\ c = 13 \end{cases}$ into $x = \dfrac{-b \pm \sqrt{b^2 - 4ac}}{2a}$.

$$x = \frac{-(-6) \pm \sqrt{(-6)^2 - 4(1)(13)}}{2(1)}$$

$$= \frac{6 \pm \sqrt{36 - 52}}{2} = \frac{6 \pm \sqrt{-16}}{2}$$

$$= \frac{6 \pm 4i}{2} = 3 \pm 2i$$

Check for $x = 3 + 2i$

$$x^2 \quad - \quad 6x \quad + 13 = 0$$

$$(3 + 2i)^2 - 6(3 + 2i) + 13 \stackrel{?}{=} 0$$

$$9 + 12i + 4i^2 - 18 - 12i + 13 \stackrel{?}{=} 0$$

$$9 + 12i - 4 - 18 - 12i + 13 \stackrel{?}{=} 0$$

$$0 = 0$$

We leave the check for $x = 3 - 2i$ to the student. ■

Example 6 Solve $x^2 - 5x + 3 = 0$. Express the answers as decimals correct to two decimal places. Do not check the solutions.

Substitute $\begin{cases} a = 1 \\ b = -5 \\ c = 3 \end{cases}$ into $x = \dfrac{-b \pm \sqrt{b^2 - 4ac}}{2a}$.

$$x = \frac{-(-5) \pm \sqrt{(-5)^2 - 4(1)(3)}}{2(1)}$$

$$= \frac{5 \pm \sqrt{25 - 12}}{2} = \frac{5 \pm \sqrt{13}}{2} \qquad \sqrt{13} \doteq 3.606$$

$$\doteq \frac{5 \pm 3.606}{2} = \begin{cases} \dfrac{5 + 3.606}{2} = \dfrac{8.606}{2} = 4.303 \doteq 4.30 \\[2mm] \dfrac{5 - 3.606}{2} = \dfrac{1.394}{2} = 0.697 \doteq 0.70 \end{cases}$$ ■

EXERCISES 9.4

Set I   In Exercises 1–6, use the method of completing the square to solve each equation.

1. $x^2 = 6x + 11$ **2.** $x^2 = 10x - 13$ **3.** $x^2 - 13 = 4x$

4. $x^2 + 20 = 8x$ **5.** $x^2 - 2x - 2 = 0$ **6.** $4x^2 - 8x + 1 = 0$

In Exercises 7–24, use the quadratic formula to solve each equation.

7. $3x^2 - x - 2 = 0$ **8.** $2x^2 + 3x - 2 = 0$ **9.** $x^2 - 4x + 1 = 0$

10. $x^2 - 4x - 1 = 0$ **11.** $x^2 - 4x + 2 = 0$ **12.** $x^2 - 2x - 2 = 0$

13. $x^2 + x + 5 = 0$ **14.** $x^2 + x + 7 = 0$ **15.** $3x^2 + 2x + 1 = 0$

16. $4x^2 + 3x + 2 = 0$ **17.** $2x^2 = 8x - 9$ **18.** $3x^2 = 6x - 4$

19. $x + \dfrac{1}{3} = \dfrac{-1}{3x}$ **20.** $x + \dfrac{1}{4} = \dfrac{-1}{4x}$ **21.** $2x^2 - 5x = -7$

22. $3x^2 - 5x = -6$

In Exercises 23 and 24, show the check.

23. $x^2 - 4x + 5 = 0$ **24.** $x^2 - 6x + 10 = 0$

In Exercises 25–28, set up each problem algebraically and solve. Express answers in simplest radical form and use a calculator to approximate the answers correct to two decimal places.

25. The length of a rectangle is 2 more than its width. If its area is 2, find its dimensions.

26. The length of a rectangle is 4 more than its width. If its area is 6, find its dimensions.

27. The perimeter of a square is numerically 4 more than its area. Find the length of its side.

28. The area of a square is numerically 2 more than its perimeter. Find the length of its side.

Set II   In Exercises 1–6, use the method of completing the square to solve each equation.

1. $x^2 = 4x + 10$ **2.** $x^2 - 6x - 5 = 0$ **3.** $x^2 - 3 = 8x$

4. $x^2 + x = 5$ **5.** $x^2 - 3x - 3 = 0$ **6.** $3x^2 - 6x + 1 = 0$

In Exercises 7–24, use the quadratic formula to solve each equation.

7. $4x^2 = 12x - 7$ **8.** $3x^2 + 2x = -5$ **9.** $3x^2 = 4x + 1$

10. $5x^2 = 1 - 2x$ **11.** $2x^2 = 3 - 5x$ **12.** $3x = 1 - x^2$

13. $x^2 + x + 4 = 0$ **14.** $x^2 - x + 4 = 0$ **15.** $4x^2 + 3x + 1 = 0$

16. $6x^2 = 2 - x$ **17.** $x^2 + 6 = 2x$ **18.** $x^2 + 3x = -4$

19. $\dfrac{x}{2} + \dfrac{6}{x} = \dfrac{5}{2}$ **20.** $\dfrac{x}{3} + \dfrac{3}{x} = 2$ **21.** $4x^2 - 5x = -2$

22. $5x^2 - x + 3 = 0$

In Exercises 23 and 24, show the check.

23. $x^2 - x + 1 = 0$ **24.** $x^2 + x + 1 = 0$

In Exercises 25–28, set up each problem algebraically and solve. Express the answers in simplest radical form and use a calculator to approximate the answers to two decimal places.

25. The length of a rectangle is 4 more than its width. If its area is 1, find its dimensions.

26. Find the diagonal of a square with side equal to 4.

27. The area of a square is numerically 12 more than its perimeter. Find the length of its side.

28. The diagonal of a rectangle is 4, and the length of one side of the rectangle is 2. Find the length of the other side of the rectangle.

9.5 The Nature of Quadratic Roots

Of the quadratic equations solved so far, some have had real roots, some complex roots, some rational roots, and some irrational roots. Some have had equal roots, and some have had unequal roots. In this section, we will show how to determine what kinds of roots a quadratic equation has *without actually solving the equation.*

The Quadratic Discriminant

The roots of the quadratic equation $ax^2 + bx + c = 0$ are

$$x = \frac{-b \pm \sqrt{b^2 - 4ac}}{2a}$$

For the equation $5x^2 - 4x + 2 = 0$, we have $a = 5$, $b = -4$, and $c = 2$. Therefore, $b^2 - 4ac = (-4)^2 - 4(5)(2) = 16 - 40 = -24$. This means that $\sqrt{b^2 - 4ac} = \sqrt{-24}$, so the roots are complex conjugates.

If, for another equation, $\sqrt{b^2 - 4ac} = \sqrt{13}$, then its roots must be real and irrational conjugates. If, for still another equation, $\sqrt{b^2 - 4ac} = \sqrt{25} = 5$, then its roots must be real and rational. Since the value of $b^2 - 4ac$ determines the nature of the roots, $b^2 - 4ac$ is called the **quadratic discriminant**.

The information relating the quadratic discriminant to the roots of an equation is summarized in the following box:

THE RELATION BETWEEN THE QUADRATIC DISCRIMINANT AND ROOTS	
$b^2 - 4ac$	*Roots*
Positive and perfect square	Real, rational, unequal
Positive and not perfect square	Real, irrational conjugates, unequal
Zero	One real, rational root*
Negative	Complex conjugates

* When $b^2 - 4ac = 0$, the one real root is sometimes considered as two equal roots, or as a *root of multiplicity two*. This is done so that *all* quadratic equations can be considered to have two roots.

NOTE   When a, b, and c are integers, any *real, irrational* roots occur in *conjugate pairs*. This means that if $2 + \sqrt{3}$ is a root, then $2 - \sqrt{3}$ must also be a root. Also, any *complex* roots occur in conjugate pairs, so that if $2 - i$ is a root, $2 + i$ must also be a root. ☑

Example 1   Determine the nature of the roots of each of the following equations without solving the equation:

a. $2x^2 + 5x - 12 = 0$

$$\left\{\begin{array}{l} a = 2 \\ b = 5 \\ c = -12 \end{array}\right\} b^2 - 4ac = (5)^2 - 4(2)(-12) = 25 + 96 = 121 \qquad \left\{\begin{array}{l} \text{Perfect} \\ \text{square:} \\ 11^2 = 121 \end{array}\right.$$

Therefore, the roots are real, rational, and unequal.

b. $x^2 - 2x - 2 = 0$

$$\left\{\begin{array}{l} a = 1 \\ b = -2 \\ c = -2 \end{array}\right\} b^2 - 4ac = (-2)^2 - 4(1)(-2) = 4 + 8 = 12 \qquad \left\{\begin{array}{l} \textit{Not a} \\ \text{perfect} \\ \text{square} \end{array}\right.$$

Therefore, the roots are real, irrational conjugates, and unequal.

c. $9x^2 - 6x + 1 = 0$

$$\left\{\begin{array}{l} a = 9 \\ b = -6 \\ c = 1 \end{array}\right\} b^2 - 4ac = (-6)^2 - 4(9)(1) = 36 - 36 = 0$$

Therefore, there is one real, rational root.

d. $x^2 - 6x + 11 = 0$

$$\left\{\begin{array}{l} a = 1 \\ b = -6 \\ c = 11 \end{array}\right\} b^2 - 4ac = (-6)^2 - 4(1)(11) = 36 - 44 = -8$$

Therefore, the roots are complex conjugates.   ∎

Using Roots to Find the Equation

Sometimes we want to find an equation that has a given set of numbers as its roots. We do this by *reversing* the procedure used to solve an equation by factoring.

Example 2   Find a quadratic equation that has the roots -3 and 5.

If the roots are -3 and 5, then $x = -3$ and $x = 5$, so $x + 3 = 0$ and $x - 5 = 0$. Then the *product* of $x + 3$ and $x - 5$ must equal zero. Therefore, $(x + 3)(x - 5) = 0$. Removing the parentheses, we get $x^2 - 2x - 15 = 0$. Therefore, a quadratic equation that has roots -3 and 5 is $x^2 - 2x - 15 = 0$.   ∎

Example 3   Find an equation of lowest degree that has integral coefficients and that has $1 + \sqrt{2}$ as a root.

Since the coefficients are integers, we know that the *conjugate* of $1 + \sqrt{2}$ must also be a root.

$$x = 1 + \sqrt{2} \qquad\qquad x = 1 - \sqrt{2} \qquad \text{Irrational conjugate roots}$$
$$x - 1 - \sqrt{2} = 0 \qquad x - 1 + \sqrt{2} = 0$$

$$(x - 1 - \sqrt{2}) \cdot (x - 1 + \sqrt{2}) = 0$$
$$[(x - 1) - \sqrt{2}][(x - 1) + \sqrt{2}] = 0$$
$$(x - 1)^2 - (\sqrt{2})^2 = 0$$
$$x^2 - 2x + 1 - 2 = 0$$
$$x^2 - 2x - 1 = 0 \qquad \text{This equation has the given roots} \quad \blacksquare$$

Example 4 Find an equation of lowest degree that has integral coefficients and that has $2 - 3i$ as a root.

Since the coefficients are integers, complex roots occur in conjugate pairs; therefore, $2 + 3i$ must also be a root.

$$x = 2 + 3i \qquad\qquad x = 2 - 3i \qquad \text{Complex conjugate roots}$$
$$x - 2 - 3i = 0 \qquad x - 2 + 3i = 0$$

$$(x - 2 - 3i) \cdot (x - 2 + 3i) = 0$$
$$[(x - 2) - 3i][(x - 2) + 3i] = 0$$
$$(x - 2)^2 - (3i)^2 = 0$$
$$x^2 - 4x + 4 - 9i^2 = 0$$
$$x^2 - 4x + 13 = 0 \quad \blacksquare$$

Example 5 Find a *cubic* equation that has roots $\frac{1}{2}$, -3, and $\frac{2}{3}$.

$$x = \tfrac{1}{2} \qquad\qquad x = -3 \qquad\qquad x = \tfrac{2}{3}$$
$$2x - 1 = 0 \qquad x + 3 = 0 \qquad 3x - 2 = 0$$

$$(2x - 1) \cdot (x + 3) \cdot (3x - 2) = 0$$
$$(2x^2 + 5x - 3)(3x - 2) = 0$$
$$6x^3 + 11x^2 - 19x + 6 = 0 \quad \blacksquare$$

EXERCISES 9.5

Set I In Exercises 1–8, use the quadratic discriminant to determine the nature of the roots without solving the equation.

1. $x^2 - x - 12 = 0$

2. $x^2 + 3x - 10 = 0$

3. $6x^2 - 7x = 3$

4. $10x^2 - 11x = 6$

5. $x^2 - 4x = 0$

6. $x^2 + 9x = 0$

7. $9x^2 + 2 = 6x$

8. $2x^2 + 6x + 5 = 0$

In Exercises 9–18, find a quadratic equation that has the given roots.

9. 4 and -2

10. -3 and 2

11. 0 and 5

12. 6 and 0

13. $2 + \sqrt{3}$ and $2 - \sqrt{3}$

14. $3 + \sqrt{5}$ and $3 - \sqrt{5}$

15. $\frac{1}{2}$ and $\frac{2}{3}$

16. $\frac{3}{5}$ and $\frac{2}{3}$

17. $\dfrac{1 + \sqrt{3}i}{2}$ and $\dfrac{1 - \sqrt{3}i}{2}$

18. $\dfrac{1 - \sqrt{2}i}{3}$ and $\dfrac{1 + \sqrt{2}i}{3}$

In Exercises 19–22, find a cubic equation that has the given roots.

19. 1, 3, and 4

20. 2, 1, and 5

21. 3, $-2i$, and $+2i$

22. 2, $-3i$, and $+3i$

In Exercises 23–28, find and simplify the equation of lowest degree that has integral coefficients and that has the given roots.

23. $5 - i$

24. $2 + 3i$

25. $1 - 2\sqrt{5}$

26. $3 + 5\sqrt{2}$

27. 2 and $-3i$

28. -3 and $6i$

Set II   In Exercises 1–8, use the quadratic discriminant to determine the nature of the roots without solving the equation.

1. $x^2 + 25 = 10x$

2. $2x^2 + 3x = 2$

3. $x^2 - 2x = 2$

4. $x^2 - x + 1 = 0$

5. $x^2 + 4x = 0$

6. $x^2 - 8x = -16$

7. $3x^2 + 5x = 2$

8. $x^2 = 8$

In Exercises 9–18, find a quadratic equation that has the given roots.

9. 3 and -4

10. $3\sqrt{2}$ and $-3\sqrt{2}$

11. -8 and 0

12. $3 - \sqrt{5}$ and $3 + \sqrt{5}$

13. $4 - \sqrt{7}$ and $4 + \sqrt{7}$

14. $2i$ and $-2i$

15. $\frac{3}{4}$ and $\frac{1}{8}$

16. 3 and $\frac{2}{5}$

17. $\dfrac{3 + 5i}{3}$ and $\dfrac{3 - 5i}{3}$

18. $3 - \sqrt{5}i$ and $3 + \sqrt{5}i$

In Exercises 19–22, find a cubic equation that has the given roots.

19. 0, 2, and 5

20. 2, $1 + \sqrt{2}$, and $1 - \sqrt{2}$

21. 4, $5i$, and $-5i$

22. 0, $2 - 3i$, and $2 + 3i$

In Exercises 23–28, find and simplify the equation of lowest degree that has integral coefficients and that has the given roots.

23. $6 + i$

24. $2 - 4i$

25. $5 + 3\sqrt{7}$

26. 3 and $\sqrt{5}$

27. 3 and $7i$

28. 0 and i

9.6 Review: 9.1–9.5

Quadratic Equations
9.1

A **quadratic equation** is a polynomial equation that has a second-degree term as its highest-degree term.

The General Form
9.1

The general form of a quadratic equation is $ax^2 + bx + c = 0$, where a, b, and c are real numbers ($a \neq 0$). In this book, we will not consider the quadratic equation to be in general form unless a, b, and c are *integers* and a is positive.

Solving Incomplete Quadratics
9.2

When $c = 0$: Find the greatest common factor (GCF); then solve by factoring.

When $b = 0$:

1. Add $-c$ to both sides of the equation.

2. Divide both sides by the coefficient of x^2.

3. Take the square root of both sides, putting $\pm$ in front of the constant.

Using Substitution in Solving an Equation That Is Written As
$a(x^n)^2 + b(x^n)^1 + c = 0$
9.3

1. Let some different variable equal x^n.

2. Substitute that variable for x^n.

3. Solve the resulting quadratic equation.

4. Set each solution equal to x^n.

5. Solve the resulting equations for x.

6. Check all answers in the original equation.

Solving Equations That Are in Quadratic Form by the Quadratic Formula
9.4

1. Arrange in general form.

2. Substitute values of a, b, and c into

$$x = \frac{-b \pm \sqrt{b^2 - 4ac}}{2a}$$

3. Simplify the answers.

The Relation between the Quadratic Discriminant and Roots
9.5

$b^2 - 4ac > 0$ and a perfect square

The roots are real, rational, and unequal

$b^2 - 4ac > 0$ and not a perfect square

The roots are real, unequal, irrational conjugates

$b^2 - 4ac = 0$

One real, rational root

$b^2 - 4ac < 0$

The roots are complex conjugates

Using Roots to Find the Equation
9.5

Reverse the procedure used to solve an equation by factoring.

Review Exercises 9.6 Set I

In Exercises 1–14, solve the equation by any convenient method.

1. $x^2 + x = 6$

2. $x^2 = 3x + 10$

3. $x^2 - 2x - 4 = 0$

4. $x^2 - 4x + 2 = 0$

5. $x^2 - 2x + 5 = 0$

6. $x^2 - 4x + 7 = 0$

7. $\dfrac{2x}{3} = \dfrac{3}{8x}$

8. $\dfrac{3x}{5} = \dfrac{5}{12x}$

9. $\dfrac{x+2}{3} = \dfrac{1}{x-2} + \dfrac{2}{3}$

10. $\dfrac{x+2}{4} = \dfrac{2}{x+2} + \dfrac{1}{2}$

11. $(x + 5)(x - 2) = x(3 - 2x) + 2$

12. $(2x - 1)(3x + 5) = x(x + 7) + 4$

13. $(x^2 - 4x)^2 + 5(x^2 - 4x) + 4 = 0$

14. $(x^2 + 6x)^2 + 13(x^2 + 6x) + 36 = 0$

In Exercises 15 and 16, use the quadratic discriminant to determine the nature of the roots without solving the equation.

15. $x^2 - 6x + 7 = 0$

16. $x^2 - 8x + 13 = 0$

In Exercises 17–20, set up each problem algebraically and solve. If answers are not rational, express in simplest radical form and give decimal approximations rounded off to two decimal places.

17. If the product of two consecutive odd integers is decreased by 14, the result is 85. Find the integers.

18. If the product of two consecutive integers is increased by 4, the result is 60. Find the integers.

19. The length of a rectangle is 3 more than its width. If its area is 8, find its dimensions.

20. The length of one leg of a right triangle is 2 more than the other leg. If its hypotenuse is 3, find the length of each leg.

21. Find a quadratic equation that has the roots $1 - \sqrt{7}$ and $1 + \sqrt{7}$.

22. Find an equation of lowest degree that has integral coefficients and that has the roots 2 and $-\sqrt{6}i$.

Review Exercises 9.6 Set II

In Exercises 1–14, solve the equation by any convenient method.

1. $x^2 + x = 20$

2. $x^2 - 13 = 0$

3. $x^2 - 2x - 15 = 0$

4. $4x^2 + 3x = 0$

5. $x^2 - x + 7 = 0$

6. $x^2 - x = 30$

7. $\dfrac{3x}{5} = \dfrac{5}{3x}$

8. $\dfrac{5x}{2} = \dfrac{1}{x-2}$

9. $\dfrac{3}{x} - \dfrac{x}{x+2} = 2$

10. $\dfrac{2}{x} + \dfrac{x}{x+1} = 5$

11. $(x+3)(x-4) = x(3-x) + 3$

12. $(3x-4)(x-1) = x(2-4x) - 2$

13. $(x^2 - 6x)^2 + 2(x^2 - 6x) - 63 = 0$

14. $(x^2 - 3x)^2 - 14(x^2 - 3x) + 40 = 0$

In Exercises 15 and 16, use the quadratic discriminant to determine the nature of the roots without solving the equation.

15. $x^2 + x + 5 = 0$

16. $3x^2 - 5 = 0$

In Exercises 17–20, set up each problem algebraically and solve. If answers are not rational, express in simplest radical form and give decimal approximations rounded off to two decimal places.

17. If the product of two consecutive even integers is decreased by 8, the result is 40. Find the integers.

18. The area of a square is 5. Find the length of a side of the square.

19. The length of a rectangle is 4 more than its width. The area is 3. Find the width of the rectangle.

20. One leg of a right triangle is 3 units shorter than the other. The hypotenuse is $\sqrt{11}$. Find the length of each leg.

21. Find a quadratic equation that has the roots $-2 - 3i$ and $-2 + 3i$.

22. Find the equation of lowest degree that has integral coefficients and that has the roots $2i$ and $-\sqrt{5}$.

15. _____

16. _____

17. _____

_____

18. _____

19. _____

20. _____

_____

21. _____

22. _____

9.7 Graphing Quadratic Functions of One Variable

In Section 8.8, we introduced the graphing of quadratic functions of one variable. In this section, we include additional information about quadratic functions of one variable that will simplify the drawing of their graphs.

Recall that a *quadratic function* is a function that can be written in the form $y = f(x) = ax^2 + bx + c$ and that its graph is a curve called a *parabola*. For $y = f(x) = ax^2 + bx + c$, if $a > 0$, the parabola opens *upward*; if $a < 0$, the parabola opens *downward*. (See Figure 9.7.1.)

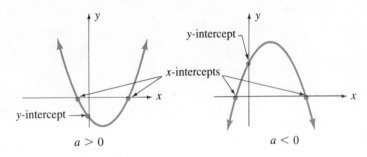

$a > 0$ $a < 0$

FIGURE 9.7.1

y-intercept

The *y-intercept* is the point at which the parabola crosses the y-axis; it is found by letting $x = 0$. For the parabola $y = f(x) = ax^2 + bx + c$, there is only one y-intercept—the point $(0, c)$.

$$y = f(x) = ax^2 + bx + c$$

$$y = f(0) = a(0)^2 + b(0) + c$$

$$y = c$$

The y-intercept of a quadratic function of one variable is *always equal to the constant term*.

x-intercepts

The *x-intercepts* are the points at which the parabola crosses the x-axis. There may be two x-intercepts, one, or none. They are found by setting $y = 0$ and then solving the resulting equation for x.

$$\boxed{y} = f(x) = ax^2 + bx + c \boxed{= 0}$$

If we do not get real values for x, then there are no x-intercepts; the graph does not cross the x-axis.

Example 1 Determine whether each parabola opens upward or downward and find all the intercepts:

a. $y = f(x) = 6 - x - x^2$

$a = -1 < 0$. Therefore, the parabola opens downward. If $x = 0$, $y = 6$; the y-intercept is $(0, 6)$. We sometimes say simply that the y-intercept is 6.

If $y = 0$, we have

$$0 = 6 - x - x^2$$
$$0 = (2 - x)(3 + x)$$
$$2 - x = 0 \text{ or } 3 + x = 0$$
$$x = 2 \text{ or } \qquad x = -3$$

The x-intercepts are $(2, 0)$ and $(-3, 0)$. We could say that the x-intercepts are 2 and -3.

b. $y = f(x) = x^2 - 2x - 1$

$a = 1 > 0$. Therefore, the parabola opens upward. If $x = 0$, $y = -1$; the y-intercept is $(0, -1)$.

Set $y = 0$.

$$\boxed{y} = f(x) = x^2 - 2x - 1 \boxed{= 0}$$

Substitute $\begin{cases} a = 1 \\ b = -2 \\ c = -1 \end{cases}$ into $x = \dfrac{-b \pm \sqrt{b^2 - 4ac}}{2a}$.

$$x = \frac{-(-2) \pm \sqrt{(-2)^2 - 4(1)(-1)}}{2(1)}$$

$$= \frac{2 \pm \sqrt{4 + 4}}{2} = \frac{2 \pm \sqrt{8}}{2}$$

$$= \frac{2 \pm 2\sqrt{2}}{2} = 1 \pm \sqrt{2}$$

The x-intercepts are $1 + \sqrt{2}$ and $1 - \sqrt{2}$. These can be approximated by using a calculator to find $\sqrt{2} \doteq 1.4$.

$$\text{Therefore } \begin{cases} 1 + \sqrt{2} \doteq 1 + 1.4 = 2.4 \\ 1 - \sqrt{2} \doteq 1 - 1.4 = -0.4 \end{cases}$$

c. $y = f(x) = x^2 - 4x + 5$

$a = 1 > 0$; the parabola opens upward. If $x = 0$, $y = 5$; the y-intercept is $(0, 5)$.

Set $y = 0$.

$$\boxed{y} = f(x) = x^2 - 4x + 5 \boxed{= 0}$$

Substitute $\begin{cases} a = 1 \\ b = -4 \\ c = 5 \end{cases}$ into $x = \dfrac{-b \pm \sqrt{b^2 - 4ac}}{2a}$.

$$x = \frac{-(-4) \pm \sqrt{(-4)^2 - 4(1)(5)}}{2(1)}$$

$$= \frac{4 \pm \sqrt{16 - 20}}{2} = \frac{4 \pm \sqrt{-4}}{2}$$

$$= \frac{4 \pm 2i}{2} = 2 \pm i$$

Since $2 \pm i$ are not real numbers, *the parabola does not cross the x-axis.* There are no x-intercepts in this case. ∎

NOTE   The graphs of the parabolas of Example 1 are shown in Figure 9.7.4 on pages 465 and 466. ☑

Symmetrical Points and the Axis of Symmetry

If two points are symmetric with respect to a line, they are equidistant from that line. The line is called the **axis of symmetry** (see Figure 9.7.2).

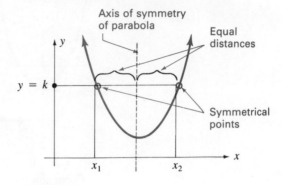

FIGURE 9.7.2

The axis of symmetry of the parabola $y = f(x) = ax^2 + bx + c$ is a *vertical* line midway between any pair of symmetrical points on that parabola. It is shown in Appendix A that the equation of the axis of symmetry for $y = f(x) = ax^2 + bx + c$ can be found as follows:

The equation of the axis of symmetry for the parabola $y = f(x) = ax^2 + bx + c$ is

$$x = -\frac{b}{2a}$$

Example 2   Find the equation of the axis of symmetry for the graph of the quadratic function $y = f(x) = 2x^2 + 7x - 4$.

$$x = -\frac{b}{2a} = -\frac{7}{2(2)} = -\frac{7}{4}$$

Therefore, $x = -\frac{7}{4}$ is the equation of the axis of symmetry.   ■

A WORD OF CAUTION   Students often say that the equation of the axis of symmetry is $-\frac{b}{2a}$. *This is incorrect*; $-\frac{b}{2a}$ is not an equation at all! An equation must have an equal sign in it. ☑

Vertex

The point at which the parabola crosses its axis of symmetry is called the **vertex** of the parabola. Its coordinates are

$$\left(-\frac{b}{2a}, f\left(-\frac{b}{2a}\right)\right)$$

If the parabola opens upward, the vertex will be the *lowest* point on the parabola, and *y* will have its *minimum* value there. If the parabola opens downward, the vertex will be the *highest* point on the parabola, and *y* will have its *maximum* value there. (See Figure 9.7.3.)

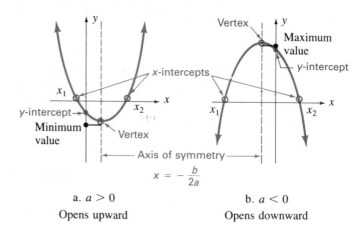

a. $a > 0$
Opens upward

b. $a < 0$
Opens downward

FIGURE 9.7.3

Example 3 Find the equation of the axis of symmetry and the coordinates of the vertex for each parabola of Example 1.

a. $y = f(x) = 6 - x - x^2$

$a = -1, b = -1, c = 6.$

The equation of the axis of symmetry is $x = -\dfrac{-1}{2(-1)}$, or $x = -\frac{1}{2}$.

$$f(-\tfrac{1}{2}) = 6 - (-\tfrac{1}{2}) - (-\tfrac{1}{2})^2 = 6 + \tfrac{1}{2} - \tfrac{1}{4} = 6\tfrac{1}{4}$$

Therefore, the vertex is $(-\frac{1}{2}, 6\frac{1}{4})$.

A WORD OF CAUTION Students often think that they can rewrite $y = 6 - x - x^2$ as $y = x^2 + x - 6$. These two equations are *not equivalent* to each other. ($0 = 6 - x - x^2$ is, however, equivalent to $0 = x^2 + x - 6$.) Multiplying both sides of $y = 6 - x - x^2$ by -1 gives $-y = x^2 + x - 6$, *not* $y = x^2 + x - 6$. ☑

b. $y = f(x) = x^2 - 2x - 1$

$a = 1, b = -2, c = -1.$

The equation of the axis of symmetry is $x = -\dfrac{-2}{2(1)}$, or $x = 1$.

$$f(1) = 1^2 - 2(1) - 1 = -2$$

Therefore, the vertex is $(1, -2)$.

c. $y = f(x) = x^2 - 4x + 5$

$a = 1, b = -4, c = 5.$

The equation of the axis of symmetry is $x = -\dfrac{-4}{2(1)}$, or $x = 2$.

$$f(2) = (2)^2 - 4(2) + 5 = 4 - 8 + 5 = 1$$

Therefore, the vertex is $(2, 1)$. ∎

Graphing Quadratic Functions of One Variable

In graphing a parabola that has two x-intercepts, we can draw a fairly accurate graph by plotting the x- and y-intercepts and the vertex and then connecting these points with a smooth curve. If the parabola has fewer than two x-intercepts, we need to find additional points on the curve. The procedure is summarized below:

TO GRAPH A QUADRATIC FUNCTION OF ONE VARIABLE

$$y = f(x) = ax^2 + bx + c$$

1. Determine whether the parabola opens upward or downward.

2. y-intercept is $(0, c)$.

3. x-intercepts: Set $y = 0$ and solve the resulting equation for x.

4. Axis of symmetry: $x = \dfrac{-b}{2a}$.

5. Vertex: $\left(-\dfrac{b}{2a}, f\left(-\dfrac{b}{2a} \right) \right)$.

6. Plot the points found in steps 2–5. Then plot the points symmetrical to those points with respect to the axis of symmetry.

7. Draw a smooth curve through the points found in steps 2–5, taking them in order from left to right. If necessary, calculate some additional points.

Example 4 Graph the parabolas from Example 1; label the intercepts and the vertex, and sketch the axis of symmetry:

a. $y = 6 - x - x^2$

b. $y = x^2 - 2x - 1$

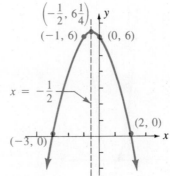

Parabola opens downward

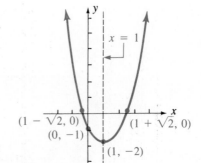

Parabola opens upward

FIGURE 9.7.4 (continued on p. 466)

c. $y = x^2 - 4x + 5$

The point symmetrical to $(0, 5)$ is $(4, 5)$.

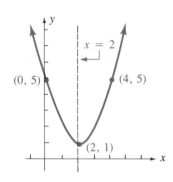

FIGURE 9.7.4   (continued)

Example 5   Discuss and graph $y = f(x) = 9x^2 - 6x + 1$.

Step 1 The parabola opens upward, since $a = 9 > 0$.

Step 2 The y-intercept is $(0, 1)$, since $c = 1$.

Step 3

$$y = f(x) = 9x^2 - 6x + 1 \boxed{= 0} \qquad \text{Set } y = 0$$
$$(3x - 1)(3x - 1) = 0$$
$$3x - 1 = 0 \text{ or } 3x - 1 = 0$$
$$x = \tfrac{1}{3} \text{ or } \qquad x = \tfrac{1}{3}$$

The x-intercepts are both the same, which means that the parabola touches the x-axis in only one point, $x = \tfrac{1}{3}$ (see Figure 9.7.5); that is, the parabola is *tangent* to the x-axis.

Step 4 The equation of the axis of symmetry is $x = -\dfrac{-6}{2(9)}$, or $x = \tfrac{1}{3}$.

Step 5 The vertex is $(\tfrac{1}{3}, 0)$.

Step 6 Plot the points found so far (see Figure 9.7.5). The point symmetrical to $(0, 1)$ is $(\tfrac{2}{3}, 1)$.

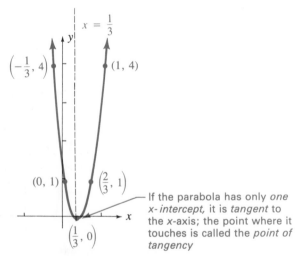

If the parabola has only *one* x-intercept, it is *tangent* to the x-axis; the point where it touches is called the *point of tangency*

FIGURE 9.7.5

Step 7 Because the three points found so far are quite close together, we might find one other point and its symmetric point. Let $x = 1$. Then $f(1) = 9(1)^2 - 6(1) + 1 = 4$. One other point, then, is $(1, 4)$, and its symmetric point is $(-\frac{1}{3}, 4)$. ∎

Example 6   Graph the function $f(x) = x^2 - x - 2$.

Step 1 The parabola opens upward, since $a = 1 > 0$.

Step 2 The y-intercept is $(0, -2)$ since $c = -2$.

Step 3 x-intercepts: $y = f(x) = x^2 - x - 2 = 0$

$$(x + 1)(x - 2) = 0$$

$$x + 1 = 0 \quad or \; x - 2 = 0$$

$$x = -1 \; or \qquad x = 2$$

Step 4 Axis of symmetry: $x = \dfrac{-b}{2a} = \dfrac{-(-1)}{2(1)} = \dfrac{1}{2}$

Step 5 Vertex:

$$x = \frac{-b}{2a} = \frac{1}{2}$$

$$y = f\left(\frac{-b}{2a}\right) = f\left(\frac{1}{2}\right) = \left(\frac{1}{2}\right)^2 - \left(\frac{1}{2}\right) - 2 = -2\frac{1}{4}$$

Vertex = $(\frac{1}{2}, -2\frac{1}{4})$

Step 6 Plot the points found so far (see Figure 9.7.6). The point symmetrical to $(0, -2)$ is $(1, -2)$.

Step 7 Calculate an additional point to help draw the graph:
Choose $x = 3$. Then $f(3) = (3)^2 - (3) - 2 = 9 - 3 - 2 = 4$. Therefore, an additional point is $(3, 4)$; its symmetrical point is $(-2, 4)$.

Draw a smooth curve through all points mentioned in steps 6 and 7, taking them in order from left to right (Figure 9.7.6).

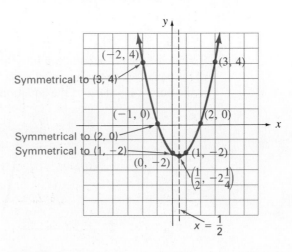

FIGURE 9.7.6

The table of values can also be found by using synthetic division as follows (see Section 8.8).

$$f(x) = x^2 - x - 2$$

$$1 \quad -1 \quad -2$$

x			$f(x) = y$
-2	1	-3	4
-1	1	-2	0
0	1	-1	-2
1	1	0	-2
2	1	1	0
3	1	2	4	■

Recall from Section 8.6C that the graph of $y = f(x) + h$ can be obtained from the graph of $y = f(x)$ by shifting the graph of $y = f(x)$ up or down, and that the graph of $y = f(x + h)$ can be obtained from the graph of $y = f(x)$ by shifting the graph of $y = f(x)$ to the right or left. Therefore, the graph of $y - k = (x - h)^2$ has the exact same *size* and *shape* as the graph of $y = x^2$; however, the *vertex* of $y - k = (x - h)^2$ is at the point (h, k) instead of at $(0, 0)$. The equation of the axis of symmetry is $x = h$.

Example 7   Graph $y - 2 = (x - 3)^2$.

Since $y - 2 = (x - 3)^2$ fits the pattern $y - k = (x - h)^2$ if $k = 2$ and $h = 3$, the vertex of the parabola will be at $(3, 2)$, and the parabola will open upward. The equation of the axis of symmetry is $x = 3$. The y-intercept is $(0, 11)$, and its symmetric point is $(6, 11)$. The curve is as follows:

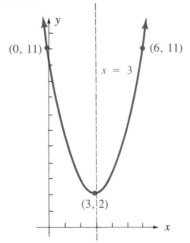

Example 8   Graph $y = (x - 4)^2 - 1$.

To change the given equation into the form $y - k = (x - h)^2$, we add 1 to both sides of the equation, obtaining $y + 1 = (x - 4)^2$. Therefore, $k = -1$ and $h = 4$. The vertex is the point $(4, -1)$, and the equation of the axis of symmetry is $x = 4$.

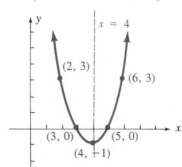

Minimum and Maximum Values

If a parabola opens upward, then the vertex will be the lowest point on the curve. In this case, the y-coordinate of the vertex is known as the **minimum value** of the function.

If a parabola opens downward, then the vertex will be the highest point on the curve, in which case the y-coordinate of the vertex is known as the **maximum value** of the function.

In other words, for the quadratic function $y = f(x) = ax^2 + bx + c$, if a is positive, the function $f(x)$ has a *minimum*, and if a is negative, $f(x)$ has a *maximum*. The minimum or maximum is $f\left(-\dfrac{b}{2a}\right)$.

Example 9   Find the maximum or minimum value of $f(x) = 3x^2 - 6x + 2$.

a is *positive*; therefore, $f(x)$ has a *minimum* value.

$$\text{Minimum value} = f\left(-\frac{b}{2a}\right) = f\left(-\frac{-6}{2(3)}\right) = f(1)$$

$$= 3(1)^2 - 6(1) + 2 = 3 - 6 + 2 = -1 \quad \blacksquare$$

Example 10   Find the maximum or minimum value of $f(x) = 5 - 2x - 4x^2$.

In general form, $f(x) = -4x^2 - 2x + 5$. a is *negative*; therefore, $f(x)$ has a *maximum* value.

$$\text{Maximum value} = f\left(-\frac{b}{2a}\right) = f\left(-\frac{-2}{2(-4)}\right) = f\left(-\frac{1}{4}\right)$$

$$= -4\left(-\frac{1}{4}\right)^2 - 2\left(-\frac{1}{4}\right) + 5 = -\frac{1}{4} + \frac{2}{4} + 5 = 5\frac{1}{4} = \frac{21}{4} \quad \blacksquare$$

EXERCISES 9.7

Set I   In Exercises 1–18, analyze and graph the functions.

1. $y = f(x) = x^2 - 2x - 3$
2. $y = f(x) = x^2 - 2x - 15$
3. $y = f(x) = x^2 - 2x - 13$
4. $y = f(x) = x^2 - 4x - 8$
5. $y = f(x) = 3 + x^2 - 4x$
6. $y = f(x) = 2x - 8 + x^2$
7. $y = f(x) = x^2 + 3x - 10$
8. $y = f(x) = 2x^2 - 7x - 4$
9. $f(x) = x^2 - 8x + 12$
10. $f(x) = x^2 - 4x - 6$
11. $f(x) = 2x - x^2 + 3$
12. $f(x) = 5 - 4x - x^2$
13. $y = f(x) = x^2 - 6x + 10$
14. $y = f(x) = x^2 - 6x + 11$
15. $y = f(x) = 4x^2 - 9$
16. $y = f(x) = 9x^2 - 4$
17. $f(x) = 6 + x^2 - 4x$
18. $f(x) = 2x - x^2 - 2$

In Exercises 19–24, find the maximum or minimum value and the vertex of each quadratic function.

19. $f(x) = x^2 - 6x + 7$
20. $f(x) = x^2 - 4x + 5$
21. $f(x) = 8x - 2x^2 - 3$
22. $f(x) = 4 + 6x - 3x^2$

23. $f(x) = -\dfrac{1}{2}x^2 + x + \dfrac{3}{2}$ **24.** $f(x) = -\dfrac{2}{3}x^2 - \dfrac{8}{3}x + \dfrac{1}{3}$

In Exercises 25–32, graph the functions.

25. $y = x^2 - 6$ **26.** $y = x^2 - 3$

27. $y - 3 = (x + 2)^2$ **28.** $y - 1 = (x + 3)^2$

29. $y + 4 = (x - 1)^2$ **30.** $y + 2 = (x - 1)^2$

31. $y = (x - 1)^2 + 3$ **32.** $y = (x - 3)^2 + 1$

Set II   In Exercises 1–18, analyze and graph the functions.

1. $y = f(x) = x^2 + x - 2$ **2.** $y = f(x) = 2 + x - x^2$

3. $y = f(x) = 2x^2 - x - 6$ **4.** $y = f(x) = 3x^2 - 3x - 6$

5. $y = f(x) = 3x^2 - 10x + 6$ **6.** $y = f(x) = 3 + 5x - 2x^2$

7. $y = f(x) = x^2 - 2x - 8$ **8.** $y = f(x) = x^2 + 4x + 4$

9. $y = f(x) = 6x^2 - 7x - 3$ **10.** $y = f(x) = x^2 + 2x + 4$

11. $y = f(x) = 2x^2 + 7x - 4$ **12.** $y = f(x) = 2x - x^2 - 1$

13. $y = f(x) = 30x - 9x^2 - 25$ **14.** $y = f(x) = 3 + 2x - x^2$

15. $y = f(x) = x^2 - 1$ **16.** $y = f(x) = 4 - x^2$

17. $f(x) = 2x^2 - 4x + 1$ **18.** $f(x) = 3x^2 - 6x + 1$

In Exercises 19–24, find the maximum or minimum value and the vertex of each quadratic function.

19. $y = f(x) = 4x^2 - 8x + 7$ **20.** $y = f(x) = x^2$

21. $y = f(x) = 5x^2 + 10x - 3$ **22.** $y = f(x) = 3x^2 - x$

23. $y = f(x) = x^2 + 2x - 8$ **24.** $y = f(x) = 5x^2 - 1$

In Exercises 25–32, graph the function.

25. $y = x^2 - 2$ **26.** $y = (x - 2)^2$

27. $y - 2 = (x + 1)^2$ **28.** $y = (x + 2)^2 - 2$

29. $y + 3 = (x - 2)^2$ **30.** $y = (x + 1)^2 - 4$

31. $y = (x - 2)^2 + 5$ **32.** $y = (x + 5)^2 - 1$

9.8 Conic Sections

Conic sections are curves formed when a plane cuts through a cone. (See Figures 9.8.1, 9.8.2, 9.8.3, and 9.8.4.) Parabolas, circles, ellipses, and hyperbolas are all conic sections. Circles, ellipses, and hyperbolas are never functions; a parabola is a function only if its axis of symmetry is a vertical line.

In this book, we will consider only those conic sections that have a vertical or horizontal axis of symmetry and only those ellipses and hyperbolas that have their centers at the origin.

The Equations of the Conic Sections

GENERAL EQUATIONS OF PARABOLAS

Vertical axis of symmetry: $y = f(x) = ax^2 + bx + c$

Horizontal axis of symmetry: $x = ay^2 + by + c$

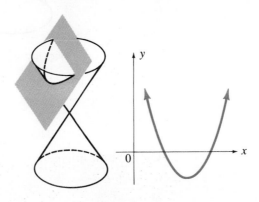

FIGURE 9.8.1   PARABOLA

GENERAL EQUATIONS OF CIRCLES

Center at the origin: $\qquad\qquad x^2 + y^2 = r^2$

Center at (h, k): $\qquad\qquad (x - h)^2 + (y - k)^2 = r^2$

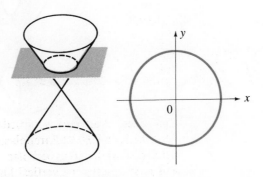

FIGURE 9.8.2   CIRCLE

GENERAL EQUATIONS OF ELLIPSES

Center at the origin: $\qquad cx^2 + dy^2 = e$

or $\qquad\qquad\qquad\qquad \dfrac{x^2}{a^2} + \dfrac{y^2}{b^2} = 1$

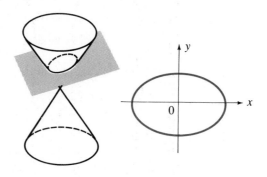

FIGURE 9.8.3   ELLIPSE

GENERAL EQUATIONS OF HYPERBOLAS

Center at the origin: $\qquad ex^2 - fy^2 = g$

or $\qquad\qquad\qquad\qquad \dfrac{x^2}{a^2} - \dfrac{y^2}{b^2} = 1$

or $\qquad\qquad\qquad\qquad \dfrac{y^2}{c^2} - \dfrac{x^2}{d^2} = 1$

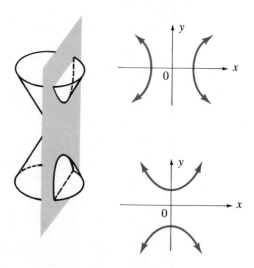

FIGURE 9.8.4   HYPERBOLA

Notice that in the equation of a parabola, either x is squared or y is squared, *but not both*. In the equations of the other conic sections, x and y are *both* squared. Both equations of the hyperbola have a *negative* sign between the x^2 term and the y^2 term, while the circle and the ellipse both have a *plus* sign there. How can you tell the equation of a circle from that of an ellipse? In the equation for a circle, the coefficients of x^2 and y^2 are equal; in the equation for an ellipse, the coefficients are *not* equal.

Example 1 Graph $x^2 + y^2 = 16$.

The equation fits the pattern $x^2 + y^2 = r^2$; therefore, the graph will be a *circle* with its center at the origin. We will find the intercepts.

x-intercepts Set $y = 0$ in $x^2 + y^2 = 16$.

$$x^2 + 0^2 = 16$$
$$x^2 = 16$$
$$x = \pm 4$$

y-intercepts Set $x = 0$ in $x^2 + y^2 = 16$.

$$0^2 + y^2 = 16$$
$$y = \pm 4$$

x	y
4	0
-4	0
0	4
0	-4

Therefore, we have a circle centered at the origin with radius $= 4$. For *any* equation of a circle, the radius equals r. The graph is as follows.

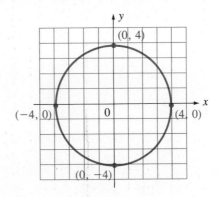

Example 2 Graph $9x^2 + 4y^2 = 36$.

The equation fits the pattern $cx^2 + dy^2 = e$; therefore, the graph will be an *ellipse* with its center at the origin. We will find the intercepts.

x-intercepts Set $y = 0$ in $9x^2 + 4y^2 = 36$.

$$9x^2 + 4(0)^2 = 36$$
$$9x^2 = 36$$
$$x^2 = 4$$
$$x = \pm 2$$

y-intercepts Set $x = 0$ in $9x^2 + 4y^2 = 36$.

$$9(0)^2 + 4y^2 = 36$$
$$4y^2 = 36$$
$$y^2 = 9$$
$$y = \pm 3$$

x	y
2	0
-2	0
0	3
0	-3

The graph is as follows.

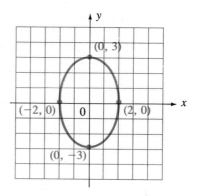

■

Example 3   Graph $y^2 = -12x$.

We notice that y is squared and x is not; therefore, this conic section must be a *parabola*. If we solve the equation for x, we have $x = -\frac{1}{12}y^2$. This fits the pattern $x = ay^2 + by + c$ (in this case, $b = 0$ and $c = 0$), which is the equation of a parabola with a *horizontal* axis of symmetry. Let's make a chart of values, letting y be the independent variable.

```
                                          ┌──── Independent variable
                                          ▼
```

x	y
-3	-6
$-\frac{1}{3}$	-2
$-\frac{1}{12}$	-1
0	0
$-\frac{1}{12}$	1
$-\frac{1}{3}$	2
-3	6

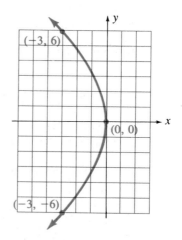

We can see from the graph and from the chart of values that the axis of symmetry is the line $y = 0$ and that the vertex is at $(0, 0)$. ■

Example 4   Graph $(x - 3)^2 + (y + 1)^2 = 16$.

The equation $(x - 3)^2 + (y + 1)^2 = 16$ fits the pattern $(x - h)^2 + (y - k)^2 = r^2$ if $h = 3$, $k = -1$, and $r = 4$. Therefore, the graph will be a *circle* of radius 4 with its center at the point $(3, -1)$.

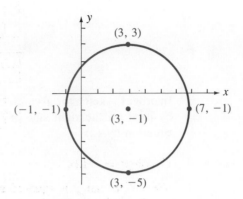

■

Asymptotes of a Hyperbola

Associated with each hyperbola are two straight lines called the **asymptotes** of the hyperbola. The hyperbola gets closer to these straight lines as the points of the graph get further from the center of the hyperbola, but the curve never touches the asymptotes. The asymptotes are helpful in sketching the graph of the hyperbola, but they are *not* part of the graph itself.

If the equation of a hyperbola can be put into the form $\dfrac{x^2}{a^2} - \dfrac{y^2}{b^2} = 1$, one asymptote passes through the origin and through the point (a, b), while the other passes through the origin and through the point $(-a, b)$. The rectangle with vertices at (a, b), $(-a, b)$, $(-a, -b)$, and $(a, -b)$ is called the *rectangle of reference* for the hyperbola $\dfrac{x^2}{a^2} - \dfrac{y^2}{b^2} = 1$; the asymptotes of the hyperbola are the diagonals of this rectangle.

If the equation of a hyperbola can be put into the form $\dfrac{y^2}{c^2} - \dfrac{x^2}{d^2} = 1$, one asymptote passes through the origin and through the point (d, c), while the other passes through the origin and through the point $(-d, c)$. The rectangle with vertices at (d, c), $(-d, c)$, $(-d, -c)$, and $(d, -c)$ is called the rectangle of reference for the hyperbola $\dfrac{y^2}{c^2} - \dfrac{x^2}{d^2} = 1$.

Example 5   Graph $3y^2 - 4x^2 = 12$.

In this equation, x and y are both squared, but there is a *negative* sign between the two squared terms; therefore, the graph will be a *hyperbola*.

x-intercepts   Set $y = 0$ in $3y^2 - 4x^2 = 12$.

$$3(0)^2 - 4x^2 = 12$$

$$x^2 = -3$$

$$x = \pm\sqrt{3}i$$

Since $\pm\sqrt{3}i$ are complex numbers, they cannot be plotted in a coordinate system in which points on both axes represent only real numbers. This means this graph does not intersect the x-axis.

y-intercepts　　Set $x = 0$ in $3y^2 - 4x^2 = 12$.

$$3y^2 - 4(0)^2 = 12$$
$$y^2 = 4$$
$$y = \pm 2$$

x	y
0	2
0	-2

In order to sketch the asymptotes, we need to use the form of the equation with $+1$ all by itself on the right side of the equation. Therefore, we divide both sides of the equation by 12:

$$\frac{3y^2 - 4x^2}{12} = \frac{12}{12}$$

$$\frac{y^2}{4} - \frac{x^2}{3} = 1$$

Our equation now fits the pattern $\dfrac{y^2}{c^2} - \dfrac{x^2}{d^2} = 1$. If $c^2 = 4$, then $c = \pm 2$, and if $d^2 = 3$, then $d = \pm\sqrt{3}$. The coordinates of the vertices of the rectangle of reference are $(\sqrt{3}, 2), (-\sqrt{3}, 2), (-\sqrt{3}, -2)$, and $(\sqrt{3}, -2)$. We can now sketch the asymptotes of the hyperbola; they are the diagonals of this rectangle (see Figure 9.8.5).

A WORD OF CAUTION　　The hyperbola does *not* pass through the points $(\sqrt{3}, 2)$, $(-\sqrt{3}, 2), (-\sqrt{3}, -2)$, and $(\sqrt{3}, -2)$. ☑

Let's find some other points on the graph. You can verify that if $x = 3$, $y = \pm 4$; therefore, the graph passes through the points $(3, 4)$ and $(3, -4)$. If $x = -3$, $y = \pm 4$; therefore, two more points on the curve are $(-3, 4)$ and $(-3, -4)$. Because we know what a hyperbola should look like (see Figure 9.8.4), we can draw the graph as shown in Figure 9.8.6.

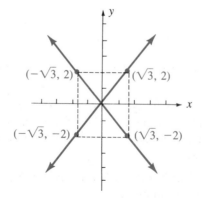

FIGURE 9.8.5

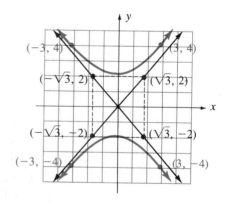

FIGURE 9.8.6

EXERCISES 9.8

Set I   Sketch and identify each conic section.

1. $x^2 + y^2 = 9$ **2.** $x^2 + y^2 = 4$

3. $y = x^2 + 2x - 3$ **4.** $y = 6 - x - x^2$

5. $3x^2 + 3y^2 = 21$ **6.** $3x^2 + 4y^2 = 12$

7. $4x^2 + 9y^2 = 36$ **8.** $16x^2 + y^2 = 16$

9. $9x^2 - 4y^2 = 36$ **10.** $x^2 - 4y^2 = 4$

11. $y^2 = 8x$ **12.** $y^2 = -4x$

13. $(x + 1)^2 + (y - 2)^2 = 4$ **14.** $(x - 2)^2 + (y + 3)^2 = 1$

Set II   Sketch and identify each conic section.

1. $x^2 + y^2 = 20$ **2.** $\dfrac{x^2}{9} + \dfrac{y^2}{4} = 1$

3. $y = 5 + 4x - x^2$ **4.** $x^2 - \dfrac{y^2}{4} = 1$

5. $2x^2 + 2y^2 = 8$ **6.** $4x^2 + y^2 = 4$

7. $9x^2 + 16y^2 = 144$ **8.** $x^2 = 6y$

9. $4y^2 - 16x^2 = 64$ **10.** $x^2 + y^2 = 9$

11. $y^2 = 4x$ **12.** $x^2 - y^2 = 9$

13. $(x + 5)^2 + (y - 2)^2 = 9$ **14.** $(x - 2)^2 + (y + 1)^2 = 16$

9.9 Solving Nonlinear Inequalities

9.9A Solving Nonlinear Inequalities in One Variable

In Chapter 2, we discussed solving first-degree inequalities with one variable and graphing their solution sets on the real number line. In this section, we discuss the solution of *nonlinear* inequalities with one variable and graph their solution sets on the real number line.

We will show two different methods of solving nonlinear inequalities in one variable.

TO SOLVE A NONLINEAR INEQUALITY IN ONE VARIABLE

1. For *either* method, temporarily substitute an equal sign for the inequality symbol.

2. Solve the resulting equation. (For *method 1*, the solutions will be the x-intercepts of the curve that will be sketched. For *method 2*, the solutions will be the *critical points* that separate the real number line into several intervals.)

3. Proceed with method 1 or method 2. (Both methods are explained in the following examples.)

Example 1   Solve $x^2 + x - 2 > 0$ and graph its solution set on the number line.

Step 1 $x^2 + x - 2 \boxed{= } 0$ Substitute = for >

Step 2
$$x^2 + x - 2 \boxed{= 0}$$ Solve the equation
$$(x + 2)(x - 1) = 0$$
$$x + 2 = 0 \; or \; x - 1 = 0$$
$$x = -2 \; or \quad x = 1$$

Step 3 We will show both methods of solution.

Method 1 We will sketch the graph of the related quadratic function $x^2 + x - 2 \boxed{= y}$ obtained by temporarily substituting $= y$ for > 0.

We know from Section 9.7 that this is the equation of a parabola that opens upward, since $a > 0$. We found in step 2 that the x-intercepts are -2 and 1. To find the y-intercept, set $x = 0$.

$$y = f(0) = 0^2 + 0 - 2 = -2$$

The intercepts $(-2, 0)$, $(1, 0)$, and $(0, -2)$ are all we need to make a rough sketch of the parabola (Figure 9.9.1).

Since we are solving the inequality $\boxed{y} = x^2 + x - 2 \boxed{> 0}$, we need only indicate which x-values make $y > 0$. That is, we must determine those x-values for which the graph is *above* the x-axis. These values are shown by the heavy arrows in Figure 9.9.1.

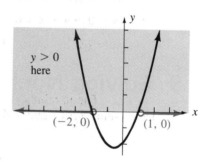

FIGURE 9.9.1

Method 2 We found the *critical points* ($x = -2$ and $x = 1$) in step 2. These are the points where the sign of the function can change. We plot these two points on the real number line; because our inequality was > and not ≥, we use *hollow* circles. We see that the points separate the number line into three intervals: the set of numbers less than -2, the set of numbers between -2 and 1, and the set of numbers greater than 1 (see Figure 9.9.2).

FIGURE 9.9.2

We now look at the sign of each of the factors of $x^2 + x - 2$. The factor $x + 2$ is negative for all $x < -2$ and positive for all $x > -2$. The factor $x - 1$ is negative for all $x < 1$ and positive for all $x > 1$. We indicate these facts on the number line as follows:

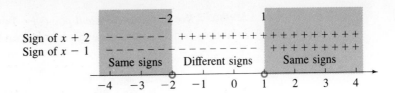

Because we're interested in the interval(s) on which the *product* of $x + 2$ and $x - 1$ is *positive*, we select the interval(s) where both signs are the *same*.

For *either* method, the final solution set is $\{x|x < -2\} \cup \{x|x > 1\}$. This means that the solution set consists of all the values of $x < -2$, *as well as* all the values of $x > 1$. The graph of the solution set is as follows:

Example 2   Find the domain of the function $y = f(x) = \sqrt{8 - 10x - 3x^2}$.

We know that the radicand must be greater than or equal to 0. Therefore, we must solve the inequality $8 - 10x - 3x^2 \geq 0$.

Step 1 $8 - 10x - 3x^2 \;\boxed{=}\; 0$ Substitute = for ≥

Step 2 $8 - 10x - 3x^2 = 0$ Solve the equation

$$(2 - 3x)(4 + x) = 0$$

$$2 - 3x = 0 \;\text{or}\; 4 + x = 0$$

$$x = \tfrac{2}{3} \;\text{or} \qquad x = -4$$

Step 3
Method 1 The parabola $y = 8 - 10x - 3x^2$ must open downward, since $a < 0$, and have x-intercepts $\tfrac{2}{3}$ and -4. To find the *y-intercept*, set $x = 0$:

$$f(0) = 8 - 10(0) - 3(0)^2 = 8$$

This means that the parabola must go through $(0, 8)$. The heavy line in Figure 9.9.3 is the graph of the solution set, $\{x| -4 \leq x \leq \tfrac{2}{3}\}$. These are the x-values that make $y \geq 0$.

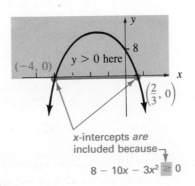

FIGURE 9.9.3

Method 2 We found the *critical points* (-4 and $\frac{2}{3}$) in step 2. We plot those points as *solid* dots because our inequality symbol ($\geq$) includes the equal sign.

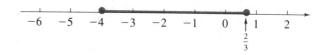

Because we want to find the interval in which the function is *positive*, we select the interval in which the signs of both factors are the *same*—the interval between -4 and $\frac{2}{3}$.

For either method, the final solution set for the inequality is $\{x \mid -4 \leq x \leq \frac{2}{3}\}$. The graph is as follows:

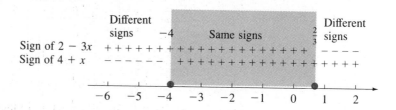

Therefore, the domain of the function $y = \sqrt{8 - 10x - 3x^2}$ is $\{x \mid -4 \leq x \leq \frac{2}{3}\}$. ∎

When a quadratic function cannot be factored, use the *quadratic formula* to find the *x*-intercepts for method 1 or the critical points for method 2.

Example 3   Solve $x^2 - 2x - 4 < 0$, and graph the solution set on the real number line.

Step 1 $x^2 - 2x - 4 \boxed{=} 0$ Substitute = for <

Step 2

$$x^2 - 2x - 4 = 0 \begin{cases} a = 1 \\ b = -2 \\ c = -4 \end{cases}$$

$$x = \frac{-b \pm \sqrt{b^2 - 4ac}}{2a} = \frac{-(-2) \pm \sqrt{(-2)^2 - 4(1)(-4)}}{2(1)}$$

$$= \frac{2 \pm \sqrt{4 + 16}}{2} = \frac{2 \pm \sqrt{20}}{2} = \frac{2 \pm 2\sqrt{5}}{2} = 1 \pm \sqrt{5}$$

$$x_1 = 1 - \sqrt{5} \doteq 1 - 2.2 = -1.2 \qquad \sqrt{5} \doteq 2.236$$

$$x_2 = 1 + \sqrt{5} \doteq 1 + 2.2 = 3.2$$

Step 3 We will show only *method 1* for this example. The parabola must open upward, since $a > 0$, and have *x*-intercepts -1.2 and 3.2. The solution set is chosen to make $y < 0$, because $x^2 - 2x - 4 \boxed{<} 0$.

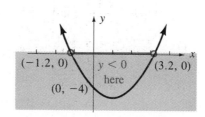

The solution set is $\{x \mid 1 - \sqrt{5} < x < 1 + \sqrt{5}\}$. The graph of the solution set is as follows:

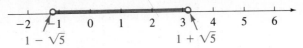

Example 4 Solve $x^3 - x^2 - 8x + 12 \geq 0$, and graph the solution set on the real number line.

Step 1 $x^3 - x^2 - 8x + 12 = 0$ Substitute = for ≥

Step 2 We must use synthetic division to factor the polynomial:

$$
\begin{array}{r|rrrr}
 & 1 & -1 & -8 & 12 \\
 &   & 2 & 2 & -12 \\
\hline
2 & 1 & 1 & -6 & \boxed{0}
\end{array}
$$

Therefore,

$$x^3 - x^2 - 8x + 12 = (x - 2)(x^2 + x - 6)$$
$$= (x - 2)(x - 2)(x + 3)$$
$$= (x - 2)^2(x + 3)$$
$$x - 2 = 0 \ or \ x + 3 = 0$$
$$x = 2 \ or \quad x = -3$$

Step 3 We will show only *method 2* for this example. The critical points are -3 and 2. We graph them with *solid* dots, since our inequality ($\geq$) includes the equal sign. We know that $(x - 2)^2$ is never negative.

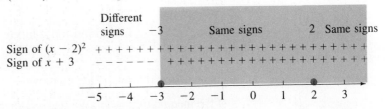

Because our inequality symbol was $\geq$, we select the interval where both signs are *the same*. The solution set, then, is $\{x \mid x \geq -3\}$. The graph of the solution is as follows:

In Examples 5 and 6, the inequality contains a denominator with variables. When the denominator contains variables, the factors of the denominator, as well as those of the numerator, must be set equal to zero in order to find critical points.

Example 5 Solve $\dfrac{x + 5}{x - 3} \leq 0$, and graph the solution set on the real number line.

Step 1 $\dfrac{x + 5}{x - 3} = 0$ Substitute = for <

Step 2 $\dfrac{x + 5}{x - 3} = 0$ Solve the equation

$$x + 5 = 0$$
$$x = -5$$

The equation has only one solution. However, when we set the denominator equal to zero, we find that 3 is a *critical point*.

Step 3 We will not use method 1, because we cannot easily graph $y = \dfrac{x + 5}{x - 3}$. Using *method 2*, we graph the critical point -5 with a *solid* dot, because the inequality symbol includes the equal sign. However, because 3 is not in the domain of the variable, we must graph 3 with a hollow circle.

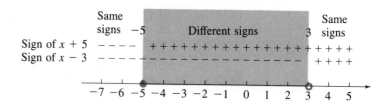

Since a fraction is negative if the numerator and denominator have different signs, we select the interval on which the signs are *different*. The solution set is $\{x \mid -5 \le x < 3\}$, and the graph of the solution set is as follows:

A WORD OF CAUTION   The solution set is *not* $\{x \mid -5 \le x \le 3\}$. The 3 *cannot* be included.   ■

Example 6   Solve $x \le \dfrac{3}{x + 2}$, and graph the solution set on the real number line.

We can solve this inequality by moving $\dfrac{3}{x + 2}$ to the left, so that we have 0 on one side of the inequality symbol. We then proceed in a manner similar to the method used in Example 5.

$$x - \frac{3}{x + 2} \le 0$$

$$\frac{x(x + 2) - 3}{x + 2} \le 0 \qquad \text{Rewrite the left side as a single fraction}$$

$$\frac{x^2 + 2x - 3}{x + 2} \le 0$$

$$\frac{(x + 3)(x - 1)}{x + 2} \le 0$$

We set each factor of the numerator *and* of the denominator equal to zero to find the critical points:

$$x + 3 = 0, \quad x - 1 = 0, \quad x + 2 = 0$$
$$x = -3, \qquad x = 1, \qquad x = -2$$

The critical points are −3, 1, and −2. We must graph −2 as a hollow circle because −2 is not in the domain of the variable.

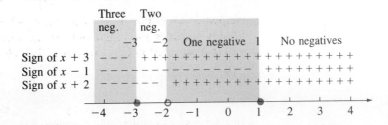

Because the fraction is to be negative or 0, we must have an *odd* number of negative signs. There is an odd number of negative signs to the left of −3 and between −2 and 1.

The solution set is $\{x \mid x \le -3\} \cup \{x \mid -2 < x \le 1\}$. This means that the solution set consists of all the values of $x \le -3$, *as well as* all values of x between −2 and 1, including 1. The graph of the solution set is as follows:

A different method of solution is shown below. To remove fractions, we usually multiply both sides by the LCD, $x + 2$. Since this is an inequality, we must multiply by $(x + 2)^2$ to make sure both sides are being multiplied by a positive number so that the sense of the inequality does not change.

$$x \le \frac{3}{x + 2}$$

$$\frac{(x + 2)^2}{1} \cdot \frac{x}{1} \le \frac{(x + 2)^2}{1} \cdot \frac{3}{(x + 2)}$$

$$x(x + 2)^2 \le 3(x + 2)$$

$$x(x + 2)^2 - 3(x + 2) \le 0 \longleftarrow (x + 2) \text{ is a common factor}$$

$$(x + 2)[x(x + 2) - 3] \le 0$$

$$(x + 2)[x^2 + 2x - 3] \le 0$$

$$(x + 2)(x + 3)(x - 1) \le 0$$

$x = -2$, $x = -3$, and $x = 1$ are the critical points.

The problem can then be finished using method 2; the results will, of course, be the same. ∎

EXERCISES 9.9A

Set I   In Exercises 1–20, solve the inequalities and graph their solution sets on the real number line.

1. $(x + 1)(x - 2) < 0$ **2.** $(x + 1)(x - 2) > 0$ **3.** $3 - 2x - x^2 \ge 0$

4. $2 - x - x^2 \le 0$ **5.** $x^2 - 3x - 4 < 0$ **6.** $x^2 + 4x - 5 > 0$

7. $x^2 + 7 > 6x$ **8.** $x^2 + 13 < 8x$ **9.** $x^2 \le 5x$

10. $x^2 \ge 3x$ **11.** $3x - x^2 > 0$ **12.** $7x - x^2 < 0$

13. $x^3 - 3x^2 - x + 3 > 0$

14. $x^3 + 2x^2 - x - 2 > 0$

15. $x^3 - 3x^2 + 4 < 0$

16. $x^3 + 3x^2 - 4 < 0$

17. $\dfrac{x - 2}{x + 3} \geq 0$

18. $\dfrac{x + 4}{x - 2} \leq 0$

19. $x < \dfrac{2}{x + 1}$

20. $x > \dfrac{4}{x + 3}$

In Exercises 21–24, find the domain of the given function.

21. $y = f(x) = \sqrt{x^2 - 4x - 12}$

22. $y = f(x) = \sqrt{x^2 + 3x - 10}$

23. $y = f(x) = \sqrt{4 + 3x - x^2}$

24. $y = f(x) = \sqrt{5 - 4x - x^2}$

Set II In Exercises 1–20, solve the inequalities and graph their solution sets on the real number line.

1. $(x + 4)(x - 1) < 0$

2. $(2x - 5)(x + 2) > 0$

3. $8 - 2x - x^2 \geq 0$

4. $x^2 - 2x \leq 3$

5. $x^2 - 5x - 6 < 0$

6. $x^3 - 7x^2 + 11x - 5 < 0$

7. $x^2 + 8 > 7x$

8. $x^2 < 9$

9. $x^2 \geq x$

10. $x^3 - 2x^2 - 7x < 4$

11. $3x - x^2 < 0$

12. $1 + 4x + 3x^2 \geq 0$

13. $x^3 + x^2 - 4x - 4 > 0$

14. $x^3 - 5x^2 + 7x - 3 < 0$

15. $x^3 + 2x^2 - 5x - 6 < 0$

16. $x^2 + 9 < 6x$

17. $\dfrac{x + 2}{x - 4} \geq 0$

18. $\dfrac{3x - 1}{2 - x} \leq 0$

19. $x < \dfrac{6}{x + 5}$

20. $x \geq \dfrac{5}{6 - x}$

In Exercises 21–24, find the domain of the given function.

21. $y = f(x) = \sqrt{x^2 + 6x - 7}$

22. $y = f(x) = \sqrt{x^2 + 4x + 3}$

23. $y = f(x) = \sqrt{8 + 2x - x^2}$

24. $y = f(x) = \sqrt{10 - x^2 + 3x}$

9.9B Solving Quadratic Inequalities in Two Variables by Graphing

A parabola separates the plane into two regions: the region "inside" the parabola and the region "outside" the parabola. Similarly, circles and ellipses separate the plane into the regions *inside* them and the regions *outside* them. In Figures 9.9.4 and 9.9.5, the regions inside a parabola and inside an ellipse are shaded in. A hyperbola separates the plane into *three* regions (see Figure 9.9.6).

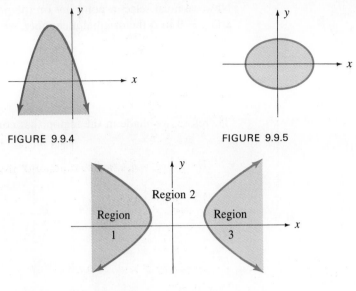

FIGURE 9.9.4   FIGURE 9.9.5

FIGURE 9.9.6

TO SOLVE A QUADRATIC INEQUALITY IN TWO
VARIABLES GRAPHICALLY

1. Temporarily substitute an equal sign for the inequality symbol and graph the resulting conic section.

2. Select any point *not* on the conic section and substitute its coordinates into the original inequality. If the statement is

   a. *true*, shade in the region of the plane that contains the point selected;

   b. *false*, shade in the region of the plane that does *not* contain the point selected.

3. The coordinates of any point that lies in the shaded region(s) will satisfy the inequality.

Example 7   Solve $y \geq x^2 - 5x - 6$.

We first sketch the graph of the equation $y = x^2 - 5x - 6$. It is a parabola that opens upward; the x-intercepts are 6 and -1, and the y-intercept is -6. We draw the graph as a *solid curve* because the equal sign is included in the original inequality.

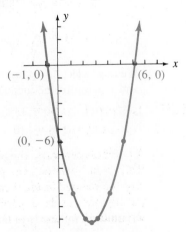

Now we must select a point *not* on the parabola. Let's use $(0, 0)$. Substituting $x = 0$ and $y = 0$ into the original inequality, we have

$$0 \geq 0^2 - 5(0) - 6$$

$$0 \geq -6 \qquad \text{A \textit{true} statement}$$

Therefore, we shade in the region that contains the point $(0, 0)$.

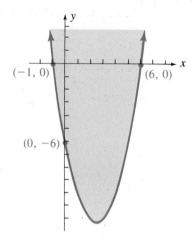

The coordinates of any point that lies in the shaded region satisfy the inequality $y \geq x^2 - 5x - 6$. ∎

Example 8 Solve $(x + 1)^2 + (y - 3)^2 > 4$.

We temporarily replace $>$ with $=$, giving $(x + 1)^2 + (y - 3)^2 = 4$. This is the equation of a circle with its center at the point $(-1, 3)$ and radius 2. Because the equal sign was *not* included in the original inequality, we sketch the circle with a *dotted line*.

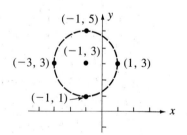

We now select any point not *on* the circle. Again, let's choose $(0, 0)$. Substituting $x = 0$ and $y = 0$ into the inequality, we have

$$(0 + 1)^2 + (0 - 3)^2 > 4$$

$$1 + 9 > 4$$

$$10 > 4 \qquad \text{A \textit{true} statement}$$

Therefore, we shade in the region that contains the point $(0, 0)$.

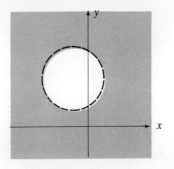

The coordinates of any point in the shaded region satisfy the inequality. ■

Example 9 Solve $x^2 - y^2 > 1$.

We temporarily replace $>$ with $=$, giving $x^2 - y^2 = 1$. This is a *hyperbola*. If $y = 0$, $x^2 = 1$. Therefore, the x-intercepts are $(1, 0)$ and $(-1, 0)$. We can see that the hyperbola separates the plane into three regions.

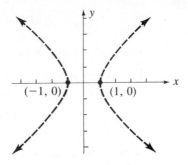

Again, let's choose $(0, 0)$ as the point to try in the inequality.

$$0^2 - 0^2 > 1$$

$$0 > 1 \quad \text{A \textit{false} statement}$$

Therefore, we shade in the portions of the plane that do *not* contain $(0, 0)$.

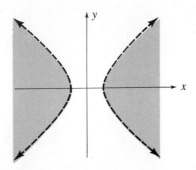

The coordinates of any point in either shaded region satisfy the inequality. (You should verify this.) ■

EXERCISES 9.9B

Set I   Solve each of the following inequalities graphically.

1. $y \le x^2 + 5x + 6$ 2. $y \le x^2 + 4x + 3$

3. $x^2 + 4y^2 > 4$ 4. $9x^2 + y^2 > 9$

5. $(x + 2)^2 + (y - 3)^2 \leq 9$

6. $(x - 1)^2 + (y + 2)^2 \leq 4$

7. $4x^2 - y^2 < 4$

8. $9x^2 - y^2 < 9$

Set II Solve each of the following inequalities graphically.

1. $y \leq x^2 + 3x + 2$

2. $(x + 1)^2 + (y + 1)^2 \leq 1$

3. $16x^2 + y^2 > 16$

4. $y < x^2 - 3x + 2$

5. $(x - 3)^2 + (y - 2)^2 \leq 16$

6. $x^2 - 9y^2 > 9$

7. $16x^2 - y^2 < 16$

8. $x^2 + 9y^2 \geq 9$

9.10 Review: 9.7–9.9

Quadratic Functions 9.7

A **quadratic function** is a function whose formula is a quadratic polynomial.

$$y = f(x) = ax^2 + bx + c \qquad \text{General form of a quadratic function}$$

Its graph is called a *parabola*.

Its *x-intercepts* are found by setting the function equal to zero and then solving the resulting quadratic equation for x.

The *y-intercept* is found by setting $x = 0$ and then solving the resulting equation for y. The y-intercept of a quadratic function of one variable is always equal to the constant term.

A *maximum value* occurs when $a < 0$.

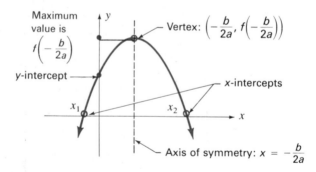

A *minimum value* occurs when $a > 0$.

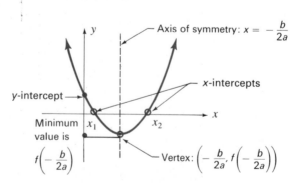

Conic Sections 9.8

Conic sections are curves formed when a plane cuts through a cone. They are the parabola, circle, ellipse, and hyperbola. A quick sketch of the conics covered in this section can usually be made by using the *intercept method*.

To Solve a Quadratic Inequality with One Variable 9.9A

1. Substitute an equal sign for the inequality symbol.

2. Solve the resulting equation. The solutions will be the x-intercepts if method 1 is used, and they will be the critical points if method 2 is used.

3. a. *Method 1.* Sketch the graph of the related function that is obtained by substituting y for 0 in the inequality. Read the solution set from the graph.
   b. *Method 2.* Separate the real number line into intervals by graphing the critical points. Determine the sign of the function in each of the intervals.

To Solve a Quadratic Inequality with Two Variables 9.9B

1. Substitute an equal sign for the inequality symbol and graph the resulting conic section.

2. Select any point *not on* the conic section, and substitute its coordinates into the *original inequality*. If the statement is
   a. *true*, shade in the region of the plane that contained the point selected;
   b. *false*, shade in the region of the plane that did *not* contain the point selected.

Review Exercises 9.10 Set I

In Exercises 1 and 2, (a) find the x-intercepts, if they exist; (b) find the y-intercept; (c) find the coordinates of the vertex; and (d) graph the function.

1. $f(x) = x^2 - 2x - 8$ **2.** $f(x) = 6x - 9 - x^2$

In Exercises 3–5, solve the inequalities.

3. $(4 - x)(2 + x) > 0$ **4.** $x + \dfrac{2}{x - 3} < 0$ **5.** $x > \dfrac{3}{x + 2}$

6. Find the domain of the function $y = f(x) = \sqrt{6 + 5x - x^2}$.

In Exercises 7–9, sketch and identify each conic section.

7. $3x^2 + 3y^2 = 27$ **8.** $4y^2 - x^2 = 16$ **9.** $9x^2 + 4y^2 = 36$

10. Solve $y \geq x^2 + 2x - 3$ graphically.

Review Exercises 9.10 Set II

NAME _____

In Exercises 1 and 2, graph the function.

1. $f(x) = 2x + 3 - x^2$

2. $f(x) = x^2 + 4x + 4$

ANSWERS

1. Use graph.

2. Use graph.

3. _____

4. _____

5. _____

6. _____

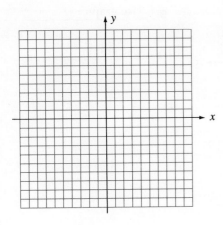

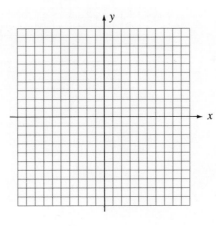

In Exercises 3–5, solve the inequalities.

3. $x^2 \leq 3x + 10$

4. $x^2 \geq 1 - 2x$

5. $x < \dfrac{4}{x + 3}$

6. Find the domain of the function $y = f(x) = \sqrt{x^2 + 7x - 8}$.

In Exercises 7–9, sketch and identify each conic section.

7. $y = x^2 + 2x - 3$

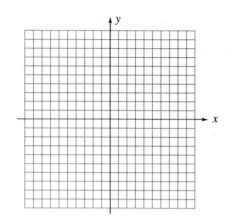

8. $x^2 + 16y^2 = 16$

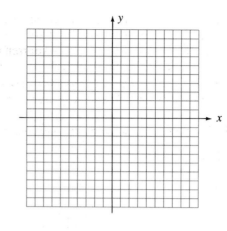

7. _Use graph._

8. _Use graph._

9. _Use graph._

10. _Use graph._

9. $x^2 - 4y^2 = 4$

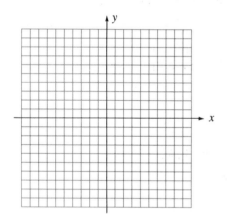

10. Solve $y \geq x^2 + 5x + 4$ graphically.

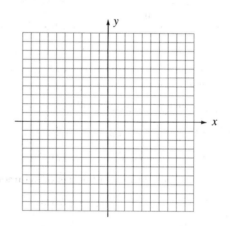

Chapter 9 Diagnostic Test

The purpose of this test is to see how well you understand nonlinear equations and inequalities. We recommend that you work this diagnostic test *before* your instructor tests you on this chapter. Allow yourself about 50 minutes.

Complete solutions for all the problems on this test, together with section references, are given in the answer section at the end of the book. For the problems you do incorrectly, study the sections cited.

In Problems 1–7, solve by any convenient method.

1. $2x^2 = 6x$

2. $2x^2 = 18$

3. $\dfrac{x-1}{2} + \dfrac{4}{x+1} = 2$

4. $2x^{2/3} + 3x^{1/3} = 2$

5. $x^2 = 6x - 7$

6. $3x^2 + 7x = 1$

7. $x^2 + 6x + 10 = 0$

8. Use the quadratic discriminant to determine the nature of the roots of the equation $25x^2 - 20x + 7 = 0$. Do *not* solve for the roots of the equation.

9. Write an equation (with integral coefficients) of least degree that has roots 3 and $2 + \sqrt{3}i$.

10. Identify and sketch the graph of the conic section whose equation is $25x^2 + 16y^2 = 400$.

11. Solve the inequality $x^2 + 5 < 6x$.

12. Solve the inequality $x^2 + 2x \geq 8$.

13. Given the quadratic function $f(x) = x^2 - 4x$, find:

   a. the equation of the axis of symmetry

   b. the coordinates of the vertex

   c. the x-intercepts (if they exist)

   Draw the graph.

Set up the following problem algebraically and solve.

14. It takes Jan 2 hr longer to do a job than it does Oscar. After Jan works on the job for 1 hr, Oscar joins her. Together they finish the job in 3 hr. How long would it take each of them working alone to do the entire job?

Cumulative Review Exercises
Chapters 1–9

1. Find the slope of the line through $(4, -1)$ and $(2, 5)$.

2. Find the general form of the equation of the line with slope $-\frac{1}{2}$ that passes through $(-2, 3)$.

3. Solve $|4 - 3x| \geq 10$.

4. Solve and check $\sqrt{2 - x} - 4 = x$.

5. Draw the graph of $4x - 2y < 8$.

6. Find the inverse relation for $y = f(x) = 2x - 3$. Graph $f(x)$ and its inverse.

In Exercises 7–9, perform the indicated operations and express the answers in exponential form with positive exponents.

7. $\left(\dfrac{x^{-3}y^4}{x^2y} \right)^{-2}$

8. $(8x^{-3/5})^{2/3}$

9. $a^{1/3} \cdot a^{-1/2}$

10. Solve $x^2 - x + 7 = 0$.

11. Solve $3x^2 + x = 3$.

12. Graph $9x^2 + 16y^2 = 144$.

13. Find the domain for $y = f(x) = \sqrt{4 - 3x - x^2}$.

In Exercises 14 and 15, set up each problem algebraically and solve.

14. The length of a rectangle is 2 more than its width. If the length of its diagonal is 10, find the dimensions of the rectangle.

15. It takes Mina 3 hr longer to do a job than it does Merwin. After Mina has worked on the job for 5 hr, Merwin joins her. Together they finish the job in 3 hr. How long would it take each of them to do the entire job working alone?

10 Systems of Equations and Inequalities

In previous chapters, we showed how to solve a single equation for a single variable. In this chapter, we show how to solve systems of two (or more) equations in two (or more) variables. We also include a brief discussion of systems of inequalities.

10.1 Basic Definitions

Two Equations in Two Variables

$\begin{cases} x + y = 6 \\ x - y = 2 \end{cases}$ is called *a system of two equations in two variables*.

A *solution* of a system of two equations in two variables is an ordered pair that, when substituted into each equation, makes each equation a true statement.

Example 1   (4, 2) is the solution for the system $\begin{cases} x + y = 6 \\ x - y = 2 \end{cases}$.

Substituting (4, 2) into each equation, we have

First equation	*Second equation*
$x + y = 6$	$x - y = 2$
$4 + 2 = 6$	$4 - 2 = 2$
True	True

Therefore, (4, 2) satisfies the system $\begin{cases} x + y = 6 \\ x - y = 2 \end{cases}$. ∎

Ordered Triple   Two ordered triples are not equal unless they contain the same three elements *in the same order*. We enclose the elements of an ordered triple in *parentheses*:

$$(1, 4, 7) \neq (4, 1, 7)$$

Ordered triple

Three Equations in Three Variables

$\begin{cases} 2x - 3y + z = 1 \\ x + 2y + z = -1 \\ 3x - y + 3z = 4 \end{cases}$ is called *a system of three equations in three variables*.

A *solution* of a system of three equations in three variables is an ordered triple that, when substituted into each equation, makes each equation a true statement.

Example 2   Verify that the ordered triple $(-3, -1, 4)$ is a solution for the system

$$\begin{cases} 2x - 3y + z = 1 \\ x + 2y + z = -1 \\ 3x - y + 3z = 4 \end{cases}$$

Substituting $(-3, -1, 4)$ into each equation, we have

First equation	*Second equation*	*Third equation*
$2x - 3y + z = 1$	$x + 2y + z = -1$	$3x - y + 3z = 4$
$2(-3) - 3(-1) + 4 \overset{?}{=} 1$	$-3 + 2(-1) + 4 \overset{?}{=} -1$	$3(-3) - (-1) + 3(4) \overset{?}{=} 4$
$-6 + 3 + 4 = 1$	$-3 - 2 + 4 = -1$	$-9 + 1 + 12 = 4$
True	True	True

Therefore, the ordered triple $(-3, -1, 4)$ satisfies the given system of equations. ∎

Linear System If each equation of a system is a first-degree equation, the system is called a **linear system**.

Quadratic System If the highest-degree equation of a system is second degree, then the system is called a **quadratic system**.

Example 3 Examples of systems of equations and inequalities:

a. $\begin{cases} x + y = 6 \\ x - y = 2 \end{cases}$ is a linear system.

b. $\begin{cases} x^2 + y^2 = 25 \\ x - y = 4 \end{cases}$ is a quadratic system.

c. $\begin{cases} 2x - 3y + z = 1 \\ x + 2y + z = -1 \\ 3x - y + 3z = 4 \end{cases}$ is a linear system.

d. $\begin{cases} 3x - 2y > 6 \\ x - 2y < 4 \end{cases}$ is a system of linear *inequalities*. ∎

Solving a System of Equations To *solve* a system of two equations in two variables means to find an ordered pair (if one exists) that satisfies *both* equations. To solve a system of three equations in three variables means to find an ordered triple (if one exists) that satisfies *all three* equations. In this text, we will consider solving only those systems with the same number of equations as variables. (We will also solve systems of four equations in four variables.)

10.2 Graphical Method for Solving a Linear System of Two Equations in Two Variables

The graphical method is not an exact method of solution for two equations in two variables, but it can sometimes be used successfully in solving such systems.

TO SOLVE A LINEAR SYSTEM OF TWO EQUATIONS
BY THE GRAPHICAL METHOD

1. Graph each equation of the system on the same set of axes.

2. There are three possibilities:

a. *The lines intersect at one point.* The solution is the ordered pair representing the point of intersection. (See Figure 10.2.1.)

b. *The lines never cross* (they are parallel). There is no solution. (See Figure 10.2.2.)

c. *Both equations have the same line for their graph.* For the line $ax + by = c$, the solution set is the set of all ordered pairs of the form $\left(t, \dfrac{c - at}{b} \right)$, where t represents some real number. (See Figure 10.2.3.)

3. If a unique solution was found in step 2, check it in *both* equations.

When the lines intersect in exactly one point, we say:

1. There is a *unique* solution for the system.

2. The system of equations is *consistent* and *independent*.

When the lines are parallel, we say:

1. There is *no* solution for the system.

2. The system of equations is *inconsistent* and *independent*.

When both equations have the same line for their graph, that is, when the lines coincide, we say:

1. There are *infinitely* many solutions for the system.

2. The system of equations is *consistent* and *dependent*.

Example 1 Solve the system $\begin{cases} x + y = 6 \\ x - y = 2 \end{cases}$ graphically.

Draw the graph of each equation on the same set of axes (see Figure 10.2.1).

Line 1 $x + y = 6$

x	y
6	0
0	6

x-intercept: If $y = 0$, then $x = 6$

y-intercept: If $x = 0$, then $y = 6$

Therefore, line 1 goes through $(6, 0)$ and $(0, 6)$.

Line 2 $x - y = 2$

x	y
2	0
0	-2

x-intercept: If $y = 0$, then $x = 2$

y-intercept: If $x = 0$, then $y = -2$

Therefore, line 2 goes through $(2, 0)$ and $(0, -2)$.

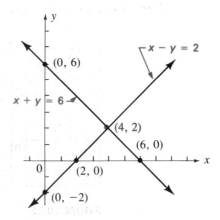

FIGURE 10.2.1

The lines appear to intersect at the point $(4, 2)$. We can check to see whether they do in fact intersect there by substituting 4 for x and 2 for y in *both* equations:

$$x + y = 6 \qquad\qquad x - y = 2$$
$$4 + 2 = 6 \quad \text{True} \qquad 4 - 2 = 2 \quad \text{True}$$

Therefore, the solution $(4, 2)$ is correct, and we can say that the lines intersect in a *unique* point, that the system of equations is *consistent* and *independent*, and that the *solution* of the system is $(4, 2)$. ∎

Example 2 Solve the system $\begin{Bmatrix} 2x - 3y = 6 \\ 6x - 9y = 36 \end{Bmatrix}$ graphically.

Draw the graph of each equation on the same set of axes (Figure 10.2.2).

Line 1 $2x - 3y = 6$ has intercepts $(3, 0)$ and $(0, -2)$.

Line 2 $6x - 9y = 36$ has intercepts $(6, 0)$ and $(0, -4)$.

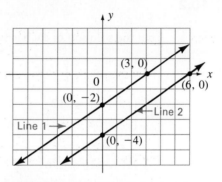

FIGURE 10.2.2

There is no solution, because the two lines never meet. We can say that the lines are parallel, the system of equations is *inconsistent* and *independent*, and there is *no solution* for the system of equations. ∎

Example 3 Solve the system $\begin{Bmatrix} 3x + 5y = 15 \\ 6x + 10y = 30 \end{Bmatrix}$ graphically.

Draw the graph of each equation on the same set of axes (Figure 10.2.3).

Line 1 $3x + 5y = 15$ has intercepts $(5, 0)$ and $(0, 3)$.

Line 2 $6x + 10y = 30$ has intercepts $(5, 0)$ and $(0, 3)$.

Since both lines go through the same two points, they must be the same line.

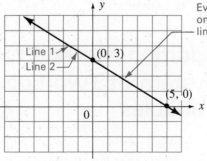

Every point of line 1 also lies on line 2; *every* point on each line is a solution

FIGURE 10.2.3

We can say that the lines *coincide*, the system of equations is *consistent* and *dependent*, and there are *infinitely many solutions* for the system of equations.

We find the solution set by substituting some variable, such as t, for x in one of the equations and then solving for y:

$$3t + 5y = 15$$

$$5y = 15 - 3t$$

$$y = \frac{15 - 3t}{5}$$

The solution set is the set of ordered pairs $\left(t, \dfrac{15 - 3t}{5} \right)$, where t is any real number.

The solution set $\left(\dfrac{15 - 5s}{3}, s \right)$, obtained by substituting s for y instead of t for x, is *also* correct. ∎

EXERCISES 10.2

Set I   Find the solution of each system graphically (if a solution exists).

1. $\begin{cases} 2x + y = 6 \\ x - y = 0 \end{cases}$

2. $\begin{cases} 2x - y = -4 \\ x + y = -2 \end{cases}$

3. $\begin{cases} x + 2y = 3 \\ 3x - y = -5 \end{cases}$

4. $\begin{cases} 5x + 4y = 12 \\ x + 3y = -2 \end{cases}$

5. $\begin{cases} x + 2y = 0 \\ 2x - y = 0 \end{cases}$

6. $\begin{cases} 2x + y = 0 \\ x - 3y = 0 \end{cases}$

7. $\begin{cases} 8x - 5y = 15 \\ 10y - 16x = 16 \end{cases}$

8. $\begin{cases} 3x + 9y = 18 \\ 2x + 6y = -24 \end{cases}$

9. $\begin{cases} 8x - 10y = 16 \\ 15y - 12x = -24 \end{cases}$

10. $\begin{cases} 14x + 30y = -70 \\ 15y + 7x = -35 \end{cases}$

Set II   Find the solution of each system graphically (if a solution exists).

1. $\begin{cases} 8x - 5y = 30 \\ 2x - 7y = -4 \end{cases}$

2. $\begin{cases} x + 2y = -5 \\ x - y = 4 \end{cases}$

3. $\begin{cases} 3x + 2y = -8 \\ 5x - 2y = -8 \end{cases}$

4. $\begin{cases} 3x - 2y = 0 \\ 2x + 5y = 0 \end{cases}$

5. $\begin{cases} 2x + 3y = -12 \\ x - y = -1 \end{cases}$

6. $\begin{cases} 3x + 8y = 9 \\ 9x + 5y = -30 \end{cases}$

7. $\begin{cases} 4x + 8y = -20 \\ 10y + 5x = 10 \end{cases}$

8. $\begin{cases} 5x + 8y = -22 \\ 4x - 3y = 20 \end{cases}$

9. $\begin{cases} 15x + 7y = -35 \\ 14y + 30x = -70 \end{cases}$

10. $\begin{cases} 5x - 8y = 14 \\ 9x - 2y = -12 \end{cases}$

10.3 Addition Method for Solving a Linear System of Two Equations in Two Variables

The graphical method for solving a system of equations has two disadvantages: (1) it is slow, and (2) it is not an exact method of solution. The method we discuss in this section has neither of these disadvantages. We need one definition before we proceed:

EQUIVALENT SYSTEMS OF EQUATIONS

Two systems of equations are said to be **equivalent systems** if they both have the same solution set.

In solving a system of two equations in two variables algebraically, our objective is to find an *equivalent* system in which one of the equations is in the form $x = a$ and the other is in the form $y = b$. That is, we hope to find an equivalent system in which each equation has only one variable.

We will be able to find such an equivalent system if the system of equations is consistent and independent. In the other two cases, *both* variables will drop out. We will be left with a *false* statement (such as $0 = 5$) if the system of equations is inconsistent and with a *true* statement (such as $0 = 0$) if the system is dependent.

In using the *addition* method of solution, we will use the following property of equality, which is stated here without proof:

$$\text{If } a = b \text{ and } c = d, \text{ then } a + c = b + d.$$

Before we use this property, however, we must first make the coefficients of one of the variables *equal numerically* but *opposite in sign*. If we then add the two equations together, we will have eliminated one variable. (This method is sometimes called the *elimination method*.) We will then have an equation with only one variable.

The complete procedure is as follows:

TO SOLVE A LINEAR SYSTEM OF TWO EQUATIONS BY THE ADDITION METHOD

1. Multiply the equations by numbers that make the coefficients of one of the variables equal numerically but opposite in sign.

2. Add the equations.

3. There are three possibilities:

   a. *One variable remains.* Solve *the resulting equation for that variable.* Then substitute this value into either equation to find the value of the other variable.

   b. *Both variables are eliminated and a false statement results.* There is no solution.

   c. *Both variables are eliminated and a true statement results.* There are infinitely many solutions. For the line $ax + by = c$, the solution set is the set of all ordered pairs of the form $\left(t, \dfrac{c - at}{b} \right)$.

4. If a unique solution is found in step 3, check it in *both* equations.

We will give examples of each type of system.

Systems That Have Only One Solution (Consistent, Independent Systems)

Example 1 Solve the system $\begin{cases} 3x + 2y = 13 \\ 3x - 4y = 1 \end{cases}$.

If we multiply the second equation by -1, the coefficients of x will be equal numerically and opposite in sign:

$$
\begin{aligned}
3x + 2y &= 13 \\
-3x + 4y &= -1
\end{aligned}
\Big\rangle \text{ Add}
$$

$$
6y = 12
$$

$$
y = 2
$$

Substituting $y = 2$ into Equation 2, we have

$$
\begin{aligned}
\text{Equation 2:} \quad 3x - 4y &= 1 \\
3x - 4(2) &= 1 \\
3x &= 9 \\
x &= 3
\end{aligned}
$$

Therefore, the solution of the system is $\begin{cases} x = 3 \\ y = 2 \end{cases}$, written (3, 2). The system $\begin{cases} x = 3 \\ y = 2 \end{cases}$ is equivalent to the system $\begin{cases} 3x + 2y = 13 \\ 3x - 4y = 1 \end{cases}$, since both systems have the same solution set.

Check

$$
\begin{array}{ll}
3x + 2y = 13 & \qquad 3x - 4y = 1 \\
3(3) + 2(2) \stackrel{?}{=} 13 & \qquad 3(3) - 4(2) \stackrel{?}{=} 1 \\
9 + 4 = 13 \quad \text{True} & \qquad 9 - 8 = 1 \quad \text{True} \quad \blacksquare
\end{array}
$$

When we have found the value of one variable, that value may be substituted into either Equation 1 or Equation 2 to find the value of the other variable. Often one equation is easier to work with than the other.

Example 2 Solve the system $\begin{cases} 3x + 4y = 6 \\ 2x + 3y = 5 \end{cases}$ (a) by eliminating the x's and (b) by eliminating the y's.

Solutions

a. Equation 1: $3x + 4y = 6$
   Equation 2: $2x + 3y = 5$

If Equation 1 is multiplied by -2 and Equation 2 is multiplied by 3, the coefficients of x will be equal numerically but opposite in sign.

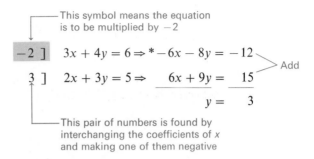

This symbol means the equation is to be multiplied by -2

$$-2 \;] \quad 3x + 4y = 6 \Rightarrow {}^{*}{-}6x - 8y = -12$$
$$3 \;] \quad 2x + 3y = 5 \Rightarrow \quad 6x + 9y = \quad 15$$

Add

$$y = \quad 3$$

This pair of numbers is found by interchanging the coefficients of x and making one of them negative

Substituting $y = 3$ into Equation 2, we have

$$2x + \; 3y \; = \quad 5$$
$$2x + 3(3) = \quad 5$$
$$2x + \quad 9 \; = \quad 5$$
$$2x = -4$$
$$x = -2$$

Therefore, the solution of the system is $\begin{cases} x = -2 \\ y = \quad 3 \end{cases}$, written $(-2, 3)$.

b.

This pair is found by interchanging the coefficients of y and making one of them negative

$$3 \;] \quad 3x + 4\,y = 6 \Rightarrow \quad 9x + 12y = \quad 18$$
$$-4 \;] \quad 2x + 3\,y = 5 \Rightarrow -8x - 12y = -20$$

Add

$$x \qquad = -\,2$$

Substituting $x = -2$ into Equation 1, we have

$$3(-2) + 4y = \; 6$$
$$-6 + 4y = \; 6$$
$$4y = 12$$
$$y = \; 3$$

Therefore, we get the same solution as before: $(-2, 3)$. (The check will not be shown.) ■

In Examples 1 and 2, we can say that the lines intersect in exactly one point and that the system of equations is consistent and independent.

---

* The symbol $\Rightarrow$, read "implies," means that the second statement is true if the first statement is true. For example,

$$x - 2 = 0 \quad \Rightarrow \quad x = 2$$

is read "$x - 2 = 0$ implies $x = 2$"

and means $x = 2$ is true if $x - 2 = 0$ is true.

We can always make the coefficients of one of the variables equal numerically by simply interchanging the coefficients. Sometimes, however, smaller numbers can be used (see Example 3).

Example 3 Consider the system $\begin{cases} 10x - 9y = 5 \\ 15x + 6y = 4 \end{cases}$.

This pair is found by interchanging the coefficients of x

$$\boxed{15}\ ]\quad \boxed{3}\ ]\quad \boxed{10}\,x - 9y = 5 \Rightarrow \boxed{30}\,x - 27y = 15$$
$$\boxed{10}\ ]\quad \boxed{2}\ ]\quad \boxed{15}\,x + 6y = 4 \Rightarrow \boxed{30}\,x + 12y = \ 8$$

This pair is found by reducing the ratio $\dfrac{15}{10}$ to $\dfrac{3}{2}$

This pair is found by interchanging the coefficients of y

$$\boxed{6}\ ]\quad \boxed{2}\ ]\quad 10x - \boxed{9}\,y = 5 \Rightarrow 20x - \boxed{18}\,y = 10$$
$$\boxed{9}\ ]\quad \boxed{3}\ ]\quad 15x + \boxed{6}\,y = 4 \Rightarrow 45x + \boxed{18}\,y = 12$$

This pair is found by reducing the ratio $\dfrac{6}{9}$ to $\dfrac{2}{3}$ ∎

Systems That Have No Solution (Inconsistent, Independent Systems)

In Section 10.2, we found that a system whose graphs are parallel lines has no solution (see Section 10.2, Example 2). Here, we show how to identify systems that have no solution by using the *addition method*.

When we attempt to solve a system of equations algebraically and *both* variables drop out and a *false statement* results, there is no solution for the system.

Example 4 Solve the system $\begin{cases} 2x - 3y = \ \ 6 \\ 6x - 9y = 36 \end{cases}$.

$$\boxed{-9}\ ]\quad \boxed{-3}\ ]\quad 2x - \boxed{3}\,y = \ \ 6 \Rightarrow -6x + \boxed{9}\,y = -18$$
$$\boxed{3}\ ]\quad \boxed{1}\ ]\quad 6x - \boxed{9}\,y = 36 \Rightarrow \ \ 6x - \boxed{9}\,y = \ \ \ 36$$
$$\underline{\hphantom{6x - 9y = 36}}$$
$$0 = \boxed{18}$$

A false statement

We can say that the lines are parallel, the system of equations is inconsistent and dependent, and there is no solution for this system of equations. ∎

Systems That Have More Than One Solution (Consistent, Dependent Systems)

In Section 10.2, we found that a system whose equations have the same graph has an infinite number of solutions (see Section 10.2, Example 3). Here, we show how to identify such systems by using the *addition method*.

When we attempt to solve a system of equations algebraically and *both* variables drop out and a *true* statement results, there are infinitely many solutions for the system.

Example 5   Solve the system $\begin{cases} 4x + 6y = 4 \\ 6x + 9y = 6 \end{cases}$.

$$-9\,]-3\,]\quad 4x + 6y = 4 \Rightarrow -12x - 18y = -12$$
$$6\,]2\,]\quad 6x + 9y = 6 \Rightarrow 12x + 18y = 12$$
$$0 = 0$$

↑
A true statement

We can say that the lines coincide and the system of equations is consistent and dependent. We can find the solution set for the system by letting $x = t$ in either equation and solving for y:

$$4t + 6y = 4$$

$$6y = 4 - 4t$$

$$y = \frac{4 - 4t}{6} = \frac{\overset{1}{\cancel{2}}(2 - 2t)}{\underset{3}{\cancel{6}}} = \frac{2 - 2t}{3}$$

Therefore, the solution set is the set of ordered pairs $\left(t, \dfrac{2 - 2t}{3} \right)$, where t is any real number. If we had let $y = s$, the solution set would have been $\left(\dfrac{2 - 3s}{2}, s \right)$. ∎

EXERCISES 10.3

Set I   Find the solution of each system by the addition method. Write "inconsistent" if no solution exists. Write "dependent" if an infinite number of solutions exist.

1. $\begin{cases} 3x - y = 11 \\ 3x + 2y = -4 \end{cases}$

2. $\begin{cases} 6x + 5y = 2 \\ 2x - 5y = -26 \end{cases}$

3. $\begin{cases} 8x + 15y = 11 \\ 4x - y = 31 \end{cases}$

4. $\begin{cases} x + 6y = 24 \\ 5x - 3y = 21 \end{cases}$

5. $\begin{cases} 7x - 3y = 3 \\ 20x - 9y = 12 \end{cases}$

6. $\begin{cases} 10x + 7y = -1 \\ 2x + y = 5 \end{cases}$

7. $\begin{cases} 6x + 5y = 0 \\ 4x - 3y = 38 \end{cases}$

8. $\begin{cases} 7x + 4y = 12 \\ 2x - 3y = -38 \end{cases}$

9. $\begin{cases} 4x + 6y = 5 \\ 8x + 12y = 7 \end{cases}$

10. $\begin{cases} 5x - 2y = 3 \\ 15x - 6y = 4 \end{cases}$

11. $\begin{cases} 7x - 3y = 5 \\ 14x - 6y = 10 \end{cases}$

12. $\begin{cases} 8x - 12y = 16 \\ 2x - 3y = 4 \end{cases}$

13. $\begin{cases} 9x + 4y = -4 \\ 15x - 6y = 25 \end{cases}$

14. $\begin{cases} 16x - 25y = -38 \\ 8x + 5y = -12 \end{cases}$

15. $\begin{cases} 9x + 10y = -3 \\ 14y = 7 - 15x \end{cases}$

16. $\begin{cases} 35x + 18y = 30 \\ 7x = 24y - 17 \end{cases}$

Set II   Find the solution of each system by the addition method. Write "inconsistent" if no solution exists. Write "dependent" if an infinite number of solutions exist.

1. $\begin{cases} 2x - 7y = 6 \\ 4x + 7y = -30 \end{cases}$

2. $\begin{cases} x - 2y = -32 \\ 7x + 8y = -4 \end{cases}$

3. $\begin{cases} 12x + 17y = 30 \\ 3x - y = 39 \end{cases}$

4. $\begin{cases} 3x - 2y = -51 \\ 2x + 3y = -21 \end{cases}$

5. $\begin{cases} 3x - 5y = -2 \\ 2x + y = 16 \end{cases}$

6. $\begin{cases} 3x - y = -14 \\ x + 2y = 7 \end{cases}$

7. $\begin{cases} 2x - y = 0 \\ 3x + 4y = -22 \end{cases}$ 　8. $\begin{cases} 2x - 5y = 15 \\ 3x + 2y = 13 \end{cases}$ 　9. $\begin{cases} 12x - 9y = 28 \\ 20x - 15y = 35 \end{cases}$

10. $\begin{cases} 7x - 2y = 4 \\ 14x - 4y = 8 \end{cases}$ 　11. $\begin{cases} 21x + 35y = 28 \\ 12x + 20y = 16 \end{cases}$ 　12. $\begin{cases} 8x - 5y = 3 \\ 24x - 15y = 6 \end{cases}$

13. $\begin{cases} 3x + 10y = 4 \\ 9x - 20y = -18 \end{cases}$ 　14. $\begin{cases} 7x + 2y = 4 \\ 2x + 3y = -11 \end{cases}$ 　15. $\begin{cases} 3x + 4y = 2 \\ 4y - 3x = 0 \end{cases}$

16. $\begin{cases} 22x - 15y = -29 \\ 33x = 10y - 11 \end{cases}$

10.4 Substitution Method for Solving a Linear System of Two Equations in Two Variables

All linear systems of two equations in two variables can be solved by the addition method shown in Section 10.3. However, you should also learn the *substitution method* of solution at this time, so that you can apply it later to solving more complicated systems (Section 10.10).

TO SOLVE A LINEAR SYSTEM OF TWO EQUATIONS
BY THE SUBSTITUTION METHOD

1. Solve one equation for one of the variables in terms of the other.

2. Substitute the expression obtained in step 1 into the other equation, and simplify both sides of the equation.

3. There are three possibilities:

   a. *One variable remains.* Solve the equation resulting from step 2 for its variable, and substitute that value into either equation to find the value of the other variable. There is a unique solution for the system.
   b. *Both variables are eliminated, and a false statement results.* There is no solution for the system.
   c. *Both variables are eliminated, and a true statement results.* There are many solutions for the system; the solution set can be found by using the method described in Section 10.3.

4. If a unique solution is found, check it in *both* equations.

Examples 1 through 3 show three ways of deciding which variable to solve for in step 1 of the substitution method.

Example 1　One of the equations is already solved for a variable:

$$\begin{cases} 2x - 5y = 4 \\ y = 3x + 7 \end{cases}$$

└─ Already solved for y　∎

Example 2   One of the variables has a coefficient of 1:

$$\begin{cases} 2x + 6y = 3 \\ \boxed{x} - 4y = 2 \end{cases} \Rightarrow \boxed{x} = 4y + 2$$

x has a coefficient of 1   ∎

Example 3   Choose the variable with the smallest coefficient:

$$\begin{cases} 11x - 7y = 10 \\ 14x + \boxed{2}\,y = 9 \end{cases} \Rightarrow y = \frac{9 - 14x}{2}$$

Smallest of the four coefficients ⎯⎯

Smallest possible denominator in this case   ∎

Systems That Have a Unique Solution (Consistent, Independent Systems)

We now give two examples of using the substitution method with systems that have a unique solution.

Example 4   Solve the system $\begin{cases} 2x - 5y = 4 \\ \quad\quad y = 3x + 7 \end{cases}$.

Step 1 Equation 2 has already been solved for y.

Step 2 Substitute $\boxed{3x + 7}$ for y in Equation 1:

$$2x - 5(\,\boxed{3x + 7}\,) = 4$$
$$2x - 15x - 35 = 4$$
$$-13x = 39$$
$$x = -3$$

Step 3 Substitute $x = -3$ into $y = 3x + 7$:

$$y = 3(-3) + 7$$
$$y = -2$$

Therefore, $(-3, -2)$ is the solution for this system.

Step 4: Check

$$2x - 5y = 4 \qquad\qquad y = 3x + 7$$
$$2(-3) - 5(-2) \overset{?}{=} 4 \qquad\qquad -2 \overset{?}{=} 3(-3) + 7$$
$$-6 + 10 = 4 \quad \text{True} \qquad -2 = -9 + 7 \quad \text{True} \quad ∎$$

Example 5   Solve the system $\begin{cases} x - 2y = 11 \\ 3x + 5y = -11 \end{cases}$.

Step 1 Solve Equation 1 for x: $x - 2y = 11$

$$x = \boxed{11 + 2y}$$

Step 2 Substitute $11 + 2y$ for x in Equation 2:

$$3x + 5y = -11$$
$$3(\,11 + 2y\,) + 5y = -11$$
$$33 + 6y + 5y = -11$$
$$11y = -44$$
$$y = -4$$

Step 3 Substitute $y = -4$ into $x = 11 + 2y$:

$$x = 11 + 2(-4)$$
$$x = 11 - 8$$
$$x = 3$$

Step 4: Check

$x - \quad 2y \quad = 11$	$3x + \quad 5y \quad = -11$
$3 - 2(-4) \overset{?}{=} 11$	$3(3) + 5(-4) \overset{?}{=} -11$
$3 + \quad 8 \quad = 11 \qquad$ True	$9 - \quad 20 \quad = -11 \qquad$ True

Therefore, $(3, -4)$ is a solution. ∎

Systems That Have No Solution (Inconsistent, Independent Systems)

We now show how to identify systems that have no solution by using the *substitution method*.

Example 6   Solve the system $\begin{Bmatrix} 2\,x - 3y = 6 \\ 6x - 9y = 36 \end{Bmatrix}$.

Smallest coefficient

Step 1 Solve Equation 1 for x:

$$2x - 3y = 6 \Rightarrow 2x = 3y + 6$$
$$x = \frac{3y + 6}{2}$$

Step 2 Substitute $\dfrac{3y + 6}{2}$ for x in Equation 2:

$$6x \qquad\quad - 9y = 36$$

$$\overset{3}{\cancel{6}} \left(\frac{3y + 6}{\underset{1}{\cancel{2}}} \right) - 9y = 36$$

$$3(3y + 6) - 9y = 36$$
$$9y + 18 - 9y = 36$$
$$18 = 36$$

A false statement

Step 3 No values for x and y can make $18 = 36$. Therefore, there is *no solution* for this system of equations. ■

Systems That Have More Than One Solution (Consistent, Dependent Systems)

We now show how to identify systems that have more than one solution by using the *substitution method*.

Example 7 Solve the system $\begin{Bmatrix} 9x + 6y = 6 \\ 6x + 4\,y = 4 \end{Bmatrix}$.

$\underset{\text{Smallest coefficient}}{\underline{\qquad\qquad}}$

Step 1 Solve Equation 2 for y:

$$6x + 4y = 4 \Rightarrow 4y = 4 - 6x$$

$$y = \frac{4 - 6x}{4}$$

$$y = \frac{\overset{1}{\cancel{2}}(2 - 3x)}{\underset{2}{\cancel{4}}}$$

$$y = \frac{2 - 3x}{2}$$

Step 2 Substitute $\dfrac{2 - 3x}{2}$ for y in Equation 1:

$$9x + 6y = 6$$

$$9x + \overset{3}{\cancel{6}}\left(\frac{2 - 3x}{\underset{1}{\cancel{2}}}\right) = 6$$

$$9x + 3(2 - 3x) = 6$$

$$9x + 6 - 9x = 6$$

$$\boxed{6 = 6}$$

$\nearrow$
A true statement

Step 3 To find the solution set, we let $x = t$. Then $y = \dfrac{2 - 3t}{2}$. Therefore, the solution set is the set of all ordered pairs of the form $\left(t, \dfrac{2 - 3t}{2}\right)$. ■

EXERCISES 10.4

Set I   Find the solution set of each system. Write "inconsistent" if no solution exists. Write "dependent" if an infinite number of solutions exist.

In Exercises 1–10, use the substitution method.

1. $\begin{Bmatrix} 7x + 4y = 4 \\ y = 6 - 3x \end{Bmatrix}$

2. $\begin{Bmatrix} 2x + 3y = -5 \\ x = y - 10 \end{Bmatrix}$

3. $\begin{cases} 5x - 4y = -1 \\ 3x + y = -38 \end{cases}$

4. $\begin{cases} 3x - 5y = 5 \\ x - 6y = 19 \end{cases}$

5. $\begin{cases} 8x - 5y = 4 \\ x - 2y = -16 \end{cases}$

6. $\begin{cases} 12x - 6y = 24 \\ 3x - 2y = -2 \end{cases}$

7. $\begin{cases} 15x + 5y = 8 \\ 6x + 2y = -10 \end{cases}$

8. $\begin{cases} 15x - 5y = 30 \\ 12x - 4y = 11 \end{cases}$

9. $\begin{cases} 20x - 10y = 70 \\ 6x - 3y = 21 \end{cases}$

10. $\begin{cases} 2x - 10y = 18 \\ 5x - 25y = 45 \end{cases}$

In Exercises 11–14, solve by any convenient method.

11. $\begin{cases} 8x + 4y = 7 \\ 3x + 6y = 6 \end{cases}$

12. $\begin{cases} 5x - 4y = 2 \\ 15x + 12y = 12 \end{cases}$

13. $\begin{cases} 4x + 4y = 3 \\ 6x + 12y = -6 \end{cases}$

14. $\begin{cases} 4x + 9y = -11 \\ 10x + 6y = 11 \end{cases}$

Set II Find the solution set of each system. Write "inconsistent" if no solution exists. Write "dependent" if an infinite number of solutions exist.

In Exercises 1–10, use the substitution method.

1. $\begin{cases} 4x + 3y = -7 \\ y = 2x - 9 \end{cases}$

2. $\begin{cases} 13y - 7x = 17 \\ 2x - y = -13 \end{cases}$

3. $\begin{cases} 12x - 16y = -3 \\ 8x - 4y = 8 \end{cases}$

4. $\begin{cases} y = x + 8 \\ 2y - 3x = 18 \end{cases}$

5. $\begin{cases} x + 4y = 1 \\ 2x + 9y = 1 \end{cases}$

6. $\begin{cases} 3x + y = 5 \\ -6x - 2y = -10 \end{cases}$

7. $\begin{cases} 3x - 9y = 15 \\ 4x - 12y = 7 \end{cases}$

8. $\begin{cases} x + 4y = 8 \\ 3y - 2x = -5 \end{cases}$

9. $\begin{cases} 8x - 2y = 26 \\ 16x - 4y = 52 \end{cases}$

10. $\begin{cases} x - 4y = 3 \\ 4y - x = 3 \end{cases}$

In Exercises 11–14, solve by any convenient method.

11. $\begin{cases} -19x + 10y = 26 \\ 12x - 5y = 2 \end{cases}$

12. $\begin{cases} 7x - 4y = 5 \\ 4y - 7x = 5 \end{cases}$

13. $\begin{cases} 3x + 2y = -1 \\ 15x + 14y = -23 \end{cases}$

14. $\begin{cases} 3x - 2y = 3 \\ 8x + 5y = 8 \end{cases}$

10.5 Higher-Order Systems

So far we have considered only systems of two equations in two variables. If a system has more than two equations and more than two variables, it is usually called a **higher-order system**. A system with three equations and three variables is called a *third-order system*, one with four equations and four variables is a *fourth-order system*, and so on.

Third-Order Systems

In solving third-order systems, we want to find, if it exists, an *equivalent* system of equations in which one of the equations is in the form $x = a$, another is in the form $y = b$, and another is in the form $z = c$. The solution set will be the ordered triple (a, b, c).

The addition method can be used to solve third-order systems, as outlined below.

TO SOLVE A THIRD-ORDER LINEAR SYSTEM BY ADDITION

1. Eliminate one variable from a pair of equations by addition.

2. Eliminate the *same* variable from a different pair of equations by addition.

3. The equation in two variables obtained in step 1 and the equation in the same two variables obtained in step 2 form a second-order system that can then be solved by addition.

Example 1 Solve the system $\begin{cases} 2x - 3y + z = 1 \\ x + 2y + z = -1 \\ 3x - y + 3z = 4 \end{cases}$.

First, eliminate z from Equations 1 and 2. (While any one of the variables can be eliminated, we choose z in this case.)

$$\begin{array}{ll}
(1) \quad \boxed{1} \;] \; 2x - 3y + z = 1 \Rightarrow 2x - 3y + z = 1 \\
(2) \quad \boxed{-1} \;] \; x + 2y + z = -1 \Rightarrow -x - 2y - z = 1 \\
\hline
(4) \qquad\qquad\qquad\qquad\qquad x - 5y \qquad = 2
\end{array} \; \text{Add}$$

Next, eliminate z from Equations 1 and 3:

$$\begin{array}{ll}
(1) \quad \boxed{3} \;] \; 2x - 3y + z = 1 \Rightarrow 6x - 9y + 3z = 3 \\
(3) \quad \boxed{-1} \;] \; 3x - y + 3z = 4 \Rightarrow -3x + y - 3z = -4 \\
\hline
(5) \qquad\qquad\qquad\qquad\qquad 3x - 8y \qquad = -1
\end{array} \; \text{Add}$$

Equations 4 and 5 form a second-order system that we solve by addition.

$$\begin{array}{ll}
(4) \quad \boxed{3} \;] \; x - 5y = 2 \Rightarrow 3x - 15y = 6 \\
(5) \quad \boxed{-1} \;] \; 3x - 8y = -1 \Rightarrow -3x + 8y = 1 \\
\hline
\qquad\qquad\qquad\qquad\qquad\qquad -7y = 7 \\
\qquad\qquad\qquad\qquad\qquad\qquad\quad y = -1
\end{array}$$

Substituting $y = -1$ into Equation 4, we have

$$\begin{array}{rl}
(4) \quad x - 5y &= 2 \\
x - 5(-1) &= 2 \\
x + 5 &= 2 \\
x &= -3
\end{array}$$

The two values found are substituted into any one of the original equations to find the value of the third variable.

Substituting $x = -3$ and $y = -1$ into Equation 2, we have

$$
\begin{array}{rcl}
(2) \quad x + 2y + z & = & -1 \\
(-3) + 2(-1) + z & = & -1 \\
-3 - 2 + z & = & -1 \\
z & = & 4
\end{array}
$$

Therefore, the solution of the system is $\left\{ \begin{array}{l} x = -3 \\ y = -1 \\ z = 4 \end{array} \right\}$, which is written $(-3, -1, 4)$.

Check The check for this solution is shown in Example 2 of Section 10.1. The solution is the ordered triple $(-3, -1, 4)$. ∎

Higher-Order Systems

The method for solving a third-order system can be extended to a fourth-order system as follows:

1. Eliminate one variable from a pair of equations. This gives one equation in three variables.

2. Eliminate the *same* variable from a different pair of equations. This gives a second equation in three variables.

3. Eliminate the *same* variable from a third different pair of equations. This gives a third equation in three variables. (Note that each equation of the system must be used in at least one pair of equations.)

4. The three equations obtained in steps 1, 2, and 3 form a third-order system that is then solved by the method given in the box on page 511 and shown in Example 1.

This same method can be extended to solve systems of *any* order. Because of the amount of work involved in solving higher-order systems, solutions are usually carried out by computer.

Some higher-order systems have no solution (inconsistent, independent systems) and others have many solutions (consistent, dependent systems), as was true for second-order systems. In this book, we consider only higher-order systems that have a single solution (consistent, independent systems).

The graph of a linear equation in three variables is a *plane* in three-dimensional space. Graphical solutions of third-order linear systems are too complicated for practical use. Graphical solutions for *higher* than third-order linear systems are not possible.

EXERCISES 10.5

Set I   Solve each system.

1. $\left\{ \begin{array}{rcr} 2x + y + z & = & 4 \\ x - y + 3z & = & -2 \\ x + y + 2z & = & 1 \end{array} \right\}$

2. $\left\{ \begin{array}{rcr} x + y + z & = & 1 \\ 2x + y - 2z & = & -4 \\ x + y + 2z & = & 3 \end{array} \right\}$

3. $\left\{ \begin{array}{rcr} x + 2y + 2z & = & 0 \\ 2x - y + z & = & -3 \\ 4x + 2y + 3z & = & 2 \end{array} \right\}$

4. $\left\{ \begin{array}{rcr} 2x + y - z & = & 0 \\ 3x + 2y + z & = & 3 \\ x - 3y - 5z & = & 5 \end{array} \right\}$

5. $\begin{cases} x \quad\quad + 2z = 7 \\ 2x - y \quad\quad = 5 \\ \quad\quad 2y + z = 4 \end{cases}$

6. $\begin{cases} x - 2y \quad\quad = 4 \\ \quad\quad y + 3z = 8 \\ 2x \quad\quad - z = 1 \end{cases}$

7. $\begin{cases} 2x + 3y + z = 7 \\ 4x \quad\quad - 2z = -6 \\ \quad\quad 6y - z = 0 \end{cases}$

8. $\begin{cases} 4x + 5y + z = 4 \\ \quad\quad 10y - 2z = 6 \\ 8x \quad\quad + 3z = 3 \end{cases}$

9. $\begin{cases} x + y + z + w = 5 \\ 2x - y + 2z - w = -2 \\ x + 2y - z - 2w = -1 \\ -x + 3y + 3z + w = 1 \end{cases}$

10. $\begin{cases} x + y + z + w = 4 \\ x - 2y - z - 2w = -2 \\ 3x + 2y + z + 3w = 4 \\ 2x + y - 2z - w = 0 \end{cases}$

11. $\begin{cases} 6x + 4y + 9z + 5w = -3 \\ 2x + 8y - 6z + 15w = 8 \\ 4x - 4y + 3z - 10w = -3 \\ 2x - 4y + 3z - 5w = -1 \end{cases}$

12. $\begin{cases} 12x + 9y + 4z - 8w = 1 \\ 6x + 15y + 2z + 4w = 2 \\ 3x + 6y + 4z + 2w = 5 \\ 4x + 4y + 4z + 4w = 3 \end{cases}$

Set II   Solve each system.

1. $\begin{cases} x + y - z = 0 \\ 2x - y + 3z = 1 \\ 3x + y + z = 2 \end{cases}$

2. $\begin{cases} 2x + y + z = -1 \\ 3x + 5y + z = 0 \\ 7x - y + 2z = 1 \end{cases}$

3. $\begin{cases} x + 2y - 3z = 5 \\ x + y + z = 0 \\ 3x + 4y + 2z = -1 \end{cases}$

4. $\begin{cases} x + 2y + z = 0 \\ 2x + 3y - 5z = 1 \\ -3x + y + 4z = -7 \end{cases}$

5. $\begin{cases} 3x \quad\quad + 2z = 0 \\ \quad\quad 5y - z = 6 \\ 2x - 3y \quad\quad = 8 \end{cases}$

6. $\begin{cases} x + 2y - \quad\quad = 0 \\ \quad\quad y - 2z = 0 \\ x \quad\quad - 4z = 0 \end{cases}$

7. $\begin{cases} 5x + y + 6z = -2 \\ \quad\quad 2y - 3z = 3 \\ 5x \quad\quad + 6z = -4 \end{cases}$

8. $\begin{cases} x + y + 2z = 7 \\ 5x - y + z = 2 \\ 3x + 3y - z = 0 \end{cases}$

9. $\begin{cases} x + y + z + w = 5 \\ 3x - y + 2z - w = 0 \\ 2x + y - z + 2w = 4 \\ 2x + y + z + 2w = 2 \end{cases}$

10. $\begin{cases} 2x + 5y + 3z - 4w = 0 \\ -x + y \quad\quad + 6w = -1 \\ 3x \quad\quad - z - 2w = 1 \\ 4x + 2y - z \quad\quad = 3 \end{cases}$

11. $\begin{cases} x + 2y + 2z + w = 0 \\ -x + y + 3z + w = 2 \\ 2x + 3y + 2z - w = -5 \\ 3x - y - 7z + w = 2 \end{cases}$

12. $\begin{cases} 3x + 2y + 4z + 5w = 5 \\ 9x \quad\quad - 8z + 10w = -4 \\ \quad\quad 6y + 12z + 5w = 5 \\ -6x - 4y \quad\quad + 15w = -1 \end{cases}$

10.6 Review: 10.1–10.5

Systems of Equations
10.1

In a linear system of equations, each equation is first degree.

In a quadratic system of equations, the highest-degree equation is second degree.

A solution of a system of two equations in two variables is an ordered pair that, when substituted into each equation, makes each equation a true statement.

A solution of a system of three equations in three variables is an *ordered triple* that, when substituted into each equation, makes each equation a true statement.

Methods of Solving a System of Linear Equations
10.2
10.3
10.4
10.5

Second-order system
1. Graphical method
2. Addition method
3. Substitution method

Higher-order systems can be solved by the addition method.

When solving a system of linear equations, there are three possibilities:

1. *There is only one solution.*
   a. Graphical method: The lines intersect at one point.
   b. Algebraic method:
      Addition $\left.\right\}$ The equations can be solved
      Substitution $\left.\right\}$ for a single ordered pair.

2. *There is no solution.*
   a. Graphical method: The lines are parallel.
   b. Algebraic method:
      Addition $\left.\right\}$ Both variables drop out and a
      Substitution $\left.\right\}$ false statement results.

3. *There are many solutions.*
   a. Graphical method: Both equations have the same line for a graph.
   b. Algebraic method:
      Addition $\left.\right\}$ Both variables drop out and a
      Substitution $\left.\right\}$ true statement results.

Review Exercises 10.6 Set I

In Exercises 1–3, solve each system graphically if a solution exists.

1. $\begin{cases} 4x + 5y = 22 \\ 3x - 2y = 5 \end{cases}$

2. $\begin{cases} 9x - 12y = 3 \\ 12x - 16y = 4 \end{cases}$

3. $\begin{cases} 2x - 3y = 3 \\ 3y - 2x = 6 \end{cases}$

In Exercises 4–10, solve each system by any convenient method. Write "inconsistent" if no solution exists. Write "dependent" if an infinite number of solutions exist.

4. $\begin{cases} 6x + 4y = 13 \\ 8x + 10y = 1 \end{cases}$

5. $\begin{cases} 4x - 8y = 4 \\ 3x - 6y = 3 \end{cases}$

6. $\begin{cases} 4x - 7y = 28 \\ 7y - 4x = 20 \end{cases}$

7. $\begin{cases} x = y + 2 \\ 4x - 5y = 3 \end{cases}$

8. $\begin{cases} 7x - 3y = 1 \\ y = x + 5 \end{cases}$

9. $\begin{cases} 2x + y - z = 1 \\ 3x - y + 2z = 3 \\ x + 2y + 3z = -6 \end{cases}$

10. $\begin{cases} x - 2y + z = -3 \\ 3x + 4y + 2z = 4 \\ 2x - 4y - z = 3 \end{cases}$

Review Exercises 10.6 Set II

NAME

In Exercises 1–3, solve each system graphically if a solution exists.

1. $\begin{cases} 2x + 3y = -5 \\ 4x - 5y = 23 \end{cases}$

2. $\begin{cases} 5y - 3x = 10 \\ 3x - 5y = 15 \end{cases}$

ANSWERS

1. _Use graph._

2. _Use graph._

3. _Use graph._

4. _____

5. _____

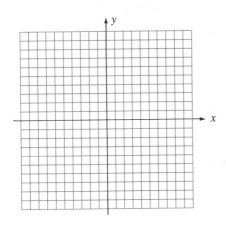

3. $\begin{cases} 7x - 8y = -9 \\ 5x + 6y = 17 \end{cases}$

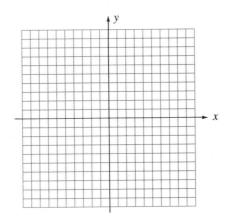

In Exercises 4–10, solve each system by any convenient method. Write "inconsistent" if no solution exists. Write "dependent" if an infinite number of solutions exist.

4. $\begin{cases} 6x + 4y = -1 \\ 4x + 6y = -9 \end{cases}$

5. $\begin{cases} 8x - 4y = 12 \\ 6x - 3y = 9 \end{cases}$

6. $\begin{cases} 3x + 2y = 1 \\ 7x + 3y = 9 \end{cases}$

7. $\begin{cases} 4x + 6y = -9 \\ 2x - 8y = 23 \end{cases}$

8. $\begin{cases} 3x - 2y = 10 \\ 5x + 4y = 24 \end{cases}$

9. $\begin{cases} 3x + 2y + z = 5 \\ 2x - 3y - 3z = 1 \\ 4x + 3y + 2z = 8 \end{cases}$

10. $\begin{cases} 4x + 3y + 2z = 6 \\ 8x + 3y - 3z = -1 \\ -4x + 6y + 5z = 5 \end{cases}$

10.7 Determinant Method for Solving a Second-Order Linear System

10.7A Second-Order Determinants

A **determinant** is a square array of numbers enclosed between two vertical bars (see Figure 10.7.1). A determinant represents the sum of certain products.

The *elements* of a determinant are the numbers in its array.

A *row* of a determinant is a *horizontal* line of its elements.

A *column* of a determinant is a *vertical* line of its elements.

The *principal diagonal* of a determinant is the line of its elements from the upper left corner to the lower right corner.

The *secondary diagonal* of a determinant is the line of elements from the lower left corner to the upper right corner.

A *second-order determinant* is a determinant that has two rows and two columns of elements (Figure 10.7.1).

The *value of a second-order determinant* is the product of the elements in its main diagonal minus the product of the elements in its secondary diagonal.

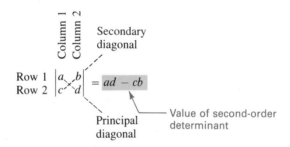

FIGURE 10.7.1   SECOND-ORDER DETERMINANT

Example 1   Find the value of each second-order determinant:

a. $\begin{vmatrix} 3 & 4 \\ 1 & 2 \end{vmatrix} = (3)(2) - (1)(4) = 6 - 4 = 2$

b. $\begin{vmatrix} -5 & -6 \\ 2 & 3 \end{vmatrix} = (-5)(3) - (2)(-6) = -15 + 12 = -3$

c. $\begin{vmatrix} 6 & -7 \\ 4 & 0 \end{vmatrix} = (6)(0) - (4)(-7) = 0 + 28 = 28$ ∎

EXERCISES 10.7A

Set I   In Exercises 1–6, find the value of each second-order determinant.

1. $\begin{vmatrix} 3 & 4 \\ 2 & 5 \end{vmatrix}$

2. $\begin{vmatrix} 4 & 3 \\ 2 & 7 \end{vmatrix}$

3. $\begin{vmatrix} 2 & -4 \\ 5 & -3 \end{vmatrix}$

4. $\begin{vmatrix} 5 & 0 \\ -9 & 8 \end{vmatrix}$

5. $\begin{vmatrix} -7 & -3 \\ 5 & 8 \end{vmatrix}$

6. $\begin{vmatrix} 2 & -4 \\ -3 & 6 \end{vmatrix}$

In Exercises 7 and 8, solve for x.

7. $\begin{vmatrix} 2 & -4 \\ 3 & x \end{vmatrix} = 20$ 　　　**8.** $\begin{vmatrix} 3 & x \\ -4 & 5 \end{vmatrix} = 27$

Set II 　In Exercises 1–6, find the value of each second-order determinant.

1. $\begin{vmatrix} 6 & 7 \\ -5 & -2 \end{vmatrix}$ 　　**2.** $\begin{vmatrix} -9 & 8 \\ -3 & 2 \end{vmatrix}$ 　　**3.** $\begin{vmatrix} 1 & -3 \\ 2 & -6 \end{vmatrix}$

4. $\begin{vmatrix} 3 & 4 \\ 1 & 5 \end{vmatrix}$ 　　**5.** $\begin{vmatrix} -1 & 4 \\ 3 & 2 \end{vmatrix}$ 　　**6.** $\begin{vmatrix} 5 & -1 \\ 6 & -2 \end{vmatrix}$

In Exercises 7 and 8, solve for x.

7. $\begin{vmatrix} -2 & 3 \\ x & 4 \end{vmatrix} = 10$ 　　**8.** $\begin{vmatrix} 2x & 5 \\ 2 & 3x \end{vmatrix} = -11x$

10.7B　General Solution of a Second-Order Linear System Using Cramer's Rule

Terms Associated with a Second-Order Linear System

$$\begin{cases} a_1 x + b_1 y = c_1 \\ a_2 x + b_2 y = c_2 \end{cases}$$

Determinant of coefficients

$$\begin{vmatrix} a_1 & b_1 \\ a_2 & b_2 \end{vmatrix} \quad \begin{matrix} c_1 \\ c_2 \end{matrix}$$

Column of constants

$$\begin{matrix} a_1 & b_1 \\ a_2 & b_2 \end{matrix}$$

Column of y-coefficients

Column of x-coefficients

Cramer's Rule

Consider the linear system $\begin{cases} a_1 x + b_1 y = c_1 \\ a_2 x + b_2 y = c_2 \end{cases}$. Solving for x by addition, we have

$$(a_1 b_2 - a_2 b_1)x = c_1 b_2 - c_2 b_1$$

$$x = \frac{c_1 b_2 - c_2 b_1}{a_1 b_2 - a_2 b_1}$$

This can be written

$$x = \frac{c_1 b_2 - c_2 b_1}{a_1 b_2 - a_2 b_1} = \frac{\begin{vmatrix} c_1 & b_1 \\ c_2 & b_2 \end{vmatrix}}{\begin{vmatrix} a_1 & b_1 \\ a_2 & b_2 \end{vmatrix}}$$

Solving for y by addition, we have

$$-a_2\,] \quad a_1 x + b_1 y = c_1 \Rightarrow -a_1 a_2 x - a_2 b_1 y = -a_2 c_1$$
$$a_1\,] \quad a_2 x + b_2 y = c_2 \Rightarrow \quad a_1 a_2 x + a_1 b_2 y = \quad a_1 c_2$$

> Add

$$(a_1 b_2 - a_2 b_1) y = a_1 c_2 - a_2 c_1$$

$$y = \frac{a_1 c_2 - a_2 c_1}{a_1 b_2 - a_2 b_1}$$

This can be written

$$y = \frac{a_1 c_2 - a_2 c_1}{a_1 b_2 - a_2 b_1} = \frac{\begin{vmatrix} a_1 & c_1 \\ a_2 & c_2 \end{vmatrix}}{\begin{vmatrix} a_1 & b_1 \\ a_2 & b_2 \end{vmatrix}}$$

The formulas derived above make up Cramer's rule.

CRAMER'S RULE

In the solution of a linear system of equations, each variable is equal to the ratio of two determinants. The denominator for *every* variable is the determinant of the coefficients. The numerator for each variable is the determinant of the coefficients with the column of coefficients for that variable replaced by the column of constants.

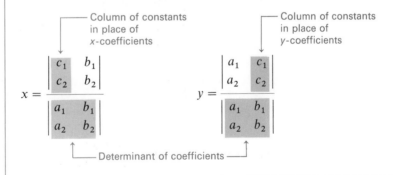

When a system of equations is solved by Cramer's rule, there are three possibilities:

1. *Only one solution (consistent, independent system)*: The determinant of the coefficients is not equal to zero.

2. *No solution (inconsistent, independent system)*: The determinant of the coefficients is equal to zero, *and* the determinants serving as numerators for the variables are not equal to zero.

3. *Many solutions (consistent, dependent system)*: The determinant of the coefficients is equal to zero, *and* the determinants serving as numerators for the variables are also equal to zero.

Example 2 Solve $\begin{cases} x + 4y = 7 \\ 3x + 5y = 0 \end{cases}$ by using Cramer's rule.

Column of constants in place of x-coefficients

$$x = \frac{\begin{vmatrix} 7 & 4 \\ 0 & 5 \end{vmatrix}}{\begin{vmatrix} 1 & 4 \\ 3 & 5 \end{vmatrix}} = \frac{(7)(5) - (0)(4)}{(1)(5) - (3)(4)} = \frac{35}{-7} = -5$$

Determinant of coefficients

Column of constants in place of y-coefficients

$$y = \frac{\begin{vmatrix} 1 & 7 \\ 3 & 0 \end{vmatrix}}{\begin{vmatrix} 1 & 4 \\ 3 & 5 \end{vmatrix}} = \frac{(1)(0) - (3)(7)}{(1)(5) - (3)(4)} = \frac{-21}{-7} = 3$$

Determinant of coefficients

Therefore, the solution is $\begin{cases} x = -5 \\ y = 3 \end{cases}$, written as $(-5, 3)$. This is a consistent, independent system. ∎

Example 3 Solve $\begin{cases} 2x - 3y = 6 \\ 6x - 9y = 36 \end{cases}$ by using Cramer's rule.

$$x = \frac{\begin{vmatrix} 6 & -3 \\ 36 & -9 \end{vmatrix}}{\begin{vmatrix} 2 & -3 \\ 6 & -9 \end{vmatrix}} = \frac{(6)(-9) - (36)(-3)}{(2)(-9) - (6)(-3)} = \frac{-54 + 108}{-18 + 18} = \frac{54}{0} \quad \text{Not possible}$$

$$y = \frac{\begin{vmatrix} 2 & 6 \\ 6 & 36 \end{vmatrix}}{\begin{vmatrix} 2 & -3 \\ 6 & -9 \end{vmatrix}} = \frac{(2)(36) - (6)(6)}{(2)(-9) - (6)(-3)} = \frac{72 - 36}{-18 + 18} = \frac{36}{0} \quad \text{Not possible}$$

This system has *no solution*. It is an inconsistent, independent system (see Example 2, Section 10.2). ∎

Example 4 Solve $\begin{cases} 3x + 5y = 15 \\ 6x + 10y = 30 \end{cases}$ by using Cramer's rule.

$$x = \frac{\begin{vmatrix} 15 & 5 \\ 30 & 10 \end{vmatrix}}{\begin{vmatrix} 3 & 5 \\ 6 & 10 \end{vmatrix}} = \frac{(15)(10) - (30)(5)}{(3)(10) - (6)(5)} = \frac{150 - 150}{30 - 30} = \frac{0}{0} \quad \text{Cannot be determined}$$

$$y = \frac{\begin{vmatrix} 3 & 15 \\ 6 & 30 \end{vmatrix}}{\begin{vmatrix} 3 & 5 \\ 6 & 10 \end{vmatrix}} = \frac{(3)(30) - (6)(15)}{(3)(10) - (6)(5)} = \frac{90 - 90}{30 - 30} = \frac{0}{0} \quad \text{Cannot be determined}$$

Therefore, the solution cannot be found by Cramer's rule. This is a consistent, dependent system. There are many solutions (see Example 3, Section 10.2). ■

The method for solving a second-order linear system by using Cramer's rule can be summarized as follows:

TO SOLVE $\begin{cases} a_1x + b_1y = c_1 \\ a_2x + b_2y = c_2 \end{cases}$ BY USING CRAMER'S RULE

The solution is

$$x = \frac{D_x}{D}, \qquad y = \frac{D_y}{D}$$

where

$D = \begin{vmatrix} a_1 & b_1 \\ a_2 & b_2 \end{vmatrix}$ Determinant of coefficients

$D_x = \begin{vmatrix} c_1 & b_1 \\ c_2 & b_2 \end{vmatrix}$ Column of constants in place of x-coefficients

$D_y = \begin{vmatrix} a_1 & c_1 \\ a_2 & c_2 \end{vmatrix}$ Column of constants in place of y-coefficients

EXERCISES 10.7B

Set I   Use Cramer's rule to solve each system. Write "inconsistent" if no solution exists. Write "dependent" if an infinite number of solutions exist.

1. $\begin{cases} 2x + y = 7 \\ x + 2y = 8 \end{cases}$

2. $\begin{cases} x + 3y = 6 \\ 2x + y = 7 \end{cases}$

3. $\begin{cases} x - 2y = 3 \\ 3x + 7y = -4 \end{cases}$

4. $\begin{cases} 5x + 7y = 1 \\ 3x + 4y = 1 \end{cases}$

5. $\begin{cases} 3x - 4y = 5 \\ 9x + 8y = 0 \end{cases}$

6. $\begin{cases} 2x + y = 0 \\ x - 3y = 0 \end{cases}$

7. $\begin{cases} x + 3y = 1 \\ 2x + 6y = 3 \end{cases}$

8. $\begin{cases} 2x - y = 2 \\ 6x - 3y = 4 \end{cases}$

9. $\begin{cases} 2x - 4y = 6 \\ 3x - 6y = 9 \end{cases}$

10. $\begin{cases} 2x - 6y = 2 \\ 3x - 9y = 3 \end{cases}$

Set II   Use Cramer's rule to solve each system. Write "inconsistent" if no solution exists. Write "dependent" if an infinite number of solutions exist.

1. $\begin{cases} 3x + y = -2 \\ 5x + 4y = -1 \end{cases}$

2. $\begin{cases} 4x + 3y = 2 \\ 3x + 5y = -4 \end{cases}$

3. $\begin{cases} 6x - 5y = -5 \\ 8x + 15y = 2 \end{cases}$

4. $\begin{cases} 15x - 10y = 30 \\ 18x - 12y = 30 \end{cases}$

5. $\begin{cases} 18x - 27y = 36 \\ 22x - 33y = 44 \end{cases}$ **6.** $\begin{cases} 4x - 5y = 6 \\ 8x - 3y = 5 \end{cases}$

7. $\begin{cases} 3x - 2y = 9 \\ 6x - 4y = 9 \end{cases}$ **8.** $\begin{cases} 3x - 2y = 0 \\ 7x - 5y = 0 \end{cases}$

9. $\begin{cases} 4x - 2y = 8 \\ 14x - 7y = 28 \end{cases}$ **10.** $\begin{cases} 6x + y = 2 \\ 12x + 2y = 3 \end{cases}$

10.8 Determinant Method for Solving a Third-Order Linear System

10.8A Third-Order Determinants

Third-Order Determinant   A **third-order determinant** is a determinant that has three rows and three columns (see Figure 10.8.1).

$$\begin{array}{c} \text{Row 1} \\ \text{Row 2} \\ \text{Row 3} \end{array} \begin{vmatrix} a_1 & b_1 & c_1 \\ a_2 & b_2 & c_2 \\ a_3 & b_3 & c_3 \end{vmatrix}$$

Column 1 Column 2 Column 3

FIGURE 10.8.1   THIRD-ORDER DETERMINANT

Minor   The **minor** of an element of a determinant is the determinant that remains after striking out the row and column in which that element appears. For example, in Figure 10.8.1, the minor of element a_2 is the determinant $\begin{vmatrix} b_1 & c_1 \\ b_3 & c_3 \end{vmatrix}$.

Cofactor   The **cofactor** of an element of a determinant is the *signed* minor of that element; in particular, the cofactor of an element in the ith row and the jth column of a determinant is $(-1)^{i+j}$ times the minor of that element. In Figure 10.8.1, the cofactor of element a_2 is

$$(-1)^{2+1}\begin{vmatrix} b_1 & c_1 \\ b_3 & c_3 \end{vmatrix} \quad \text{or} \quad (-1)\begin{vmatrix} b_1 & c_1 \\ b_3 & c_3 \end{vmatrix}$$

Example 1   Given the determinant $\begin{vmatrix} 2 & 0 & -1 \\ 5 & -4 & 6 \\ -3 & 1 & 7 \end{vmatrix}$:

a. Find the minor of 5.

$$\begin{vmatrix} 2 & 0 & -1 \\ \text{⑤} & -4 & 6 \\ -3 & 1 & 7 \end{vmatrix}$$

Strike out the row and column containing 5, leaving $\begin{vmatrix} 0 & -1 \\ 1 & 7 \end{vmatrix}$. Therefore, the minor of 5 is $\begin{vmatrix} 0 & -1 \\ 1 & 7 \end{vmatrix}$.

b. Find the cofactor of 5.

Because 5 is in the *second* row and the *first* column, the sign of its cofactor is $(-1)^{2+1}$ or -1. Therefore, the cofactor of 5 is $(-1)\begin{vmatrix} 0 & -1 \\ 1 & 7 \end{vmatrix}$.

c. Find the minor of 1.

The minor of 1 is $\begin{vmatrix} 2 & -1 \\ 5 & 6 \end{vmatrix}$ because $\begin{vmatrix} 2 & 0 & -1 \\ 5 & -4 & 6 \\ -3 & ① & 7 \end{vmatrix}$.

d. Find the cofactor of 1.

Because 1 is in the *third* row and the *second* column, the sign of its cofactor is $(-1)^{3+2}$ or -1. Therefore, the cofactor of 1 is $(-1)\begin{vmatrix} 2 & -1 \\ 5 & 6 \end{vmatrix}$.

e. Find the minor of 7.

The minor of 7 is $\begin{vmatrix} 2 & 0 \\ 5 & -4 \end{vmatrix}$ because $\begin{vmatrix} 2 & 0 & -1 \\ 5 & -4 & 6 \\ -3 & 1 & ⑦ \end{vmatrix}$.

f. Find the cofactor of 7.

Because 7 is in the *third* row and the *third* column, the sign of its cofactor is $(-1)^{3+3}$ or $+1$. Therefore, the cofactor of 7 is $\begin{vmatrix} 2 & 0 \\ 5 & -4 \end{vmatrix}$. ∎

An easier way to find the sign of the cofactor of any element is to memorize the pattern of signs shown in Figure 10.8.2. (The pattern can be extended to a determinant of any size.)

$$\begin{vmatrix} + & - & + \\ - & + & - \\ + & - & + \end{vmatrix}$$

FIGURE 10.8.2

The Value of a Third-Order Determinant   By definition, the value of the determinant

$$\begin{vmatrix} a_1 & b_1 & c_1 \\ a_2 & b_2 & c_2 \\ a_3 & b_3 & c_3 \end{vmatrix}$$

is

$$a_1 b_2 c_3 - a_1 b_3 c_2 + a_3 b_1 c_2 - a_2 b_1 c_3 + a_2 b_3 c_1 - a_3 b_2 c_1$$

The student can verify that this value could be rewritten as

$$a_1(b_2 c_3 - b_3 c_2) - a_2(b_1 c_3 - b_3 c_1) + a_3(b_1 c_2 - b_2 c_1)$$

or

$$a_1 \begin{vmatrix} b_2 & c_2 \\ b_3 & c_3 \end{vmatrix} - a_2 \begin{vmatrix} b_1 & c_1 \\ b_3 & c_3 \end{vmatrix} + a_3 \begin{vmatrix} b_1 & c_1 \\ b_2 & c_2 \end{vmatrix}$$

Notice the negative sign, and note that the cofactor of a_2 is negative

523

When we rewrite the value of a third-order determinant in this last way, we say we are *expanding by cofactors of the elements of the first column.*

We can expand a determinant by cofactors of *any* row or *any* column. To expand by cofactors of a *row*, we multiply each element in that row by its cofactor and then add the products. To expand by cofactors of a *column*, we multiply each element in that column by its cofactor and then add the products. *The same value is obtained no matter what row or column is used.*

Example 2   Find the value of $\begin{vmatrix} 1 & 3 & 2 \\ 2 & -1 & 1 \\ -4 & 1 & -3 \end{vmatrix}$ by (a) expansion by column 1 and (b) expansion

by row 2.

Solutions

a.

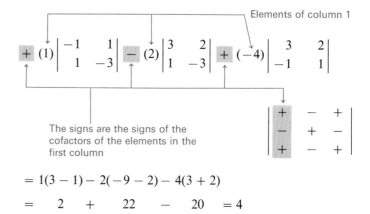

$$= 1(3-1) - 2(-9-2) - 4(3+2)$$
$$= \quad 2 \quad + \quad 22 \quad - \quad 20 \quad = 4$$

b.

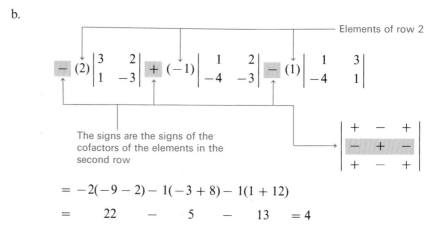

$$= -2(-9-2) - 1(-3+8) - 1(1+12)$$
$$= \quad 22 \quad - \quad 5 \quad - \quad 13 \quad = 4$$

Note that the same value, 4, was obtained from *both* expansions.   ■

EXERCISES 10.8A

Set I   **1.** For the determinant $\begin{vmatrix} 1 & 2 & 3 \\ 4 & 5 & -1 \\ -3 & -5 & 0 \end{vmatrix}$, find:

a. the minor of 2   b. the cofactor of 2

c. the minor of −5   d. the cofactor of −5

e. the minor of −3   f. the cofactor of −3

2. For the determinant $\begin{vmatrix} 2 & 0 & 1 \\ 4 & 1 & 5 \\ -3 & -2 & 4 \end{vmatrix}$, find:

    a. the minor of -3 b. the cofactor of -3

    c. the minor of 5   d. the cofactor of 5

    e. the minor of -2 f. the cofactor of -2

In Exercises 3–6, find the value of each determinant by expanding by cofactors of the indicated row or column.

3. $\begin{vmatrix} 1 & 2 & 1 \\ 3 & 1 & 2 \\ 4 & 2 & 0 \end{vmatrix}$ column 3   **4.** $\begin{vmatrix} 2 & 1 & 1 \\ 1 & 3 & 1 \\ 0 & 2 & 4 \end{vmatrix}$ column 1

5. $\begin{vmatrix} 1 & 3 & -2 \\ -1 & 2 & -3 \\ 0 & 4 & 1 \end{vmatrix}$ row 3   **6.** $\begin{vmatrix} 2 & -1 & 1 \\ 0 & 5 & -3 \\ 1 & 2 & -2 \end{vmatrix}$ row 2

In Exercises 7–10, expand by any row or column.

7. $\begin{vmatrix} 1 & -2 & 3 \\ -3 & 4 & 0 \\ 2 & 6 & 5 \end{vmatrix}$ **8.** $\begin{vmatrix} 2 & -4 & -1 \\ 5 & 0 & -6 \\ -3 & 4 & -2 \end{vmatrix}$

9. $\begin{vmatrix} 6 & 7 & 8 \\ -6 & 7 & -9 \\ 0 & 0 & -2 \end{vmatrix}$ **10.** $\begin{vmatrix} 0 & 0 & -3 \\ 5 & 6 & 9 \\ -5 & 6 & -8 \end{vmatrix}$

In Exercises 11 and 12, solve for x.

11. $\begin{vmatrix} x & 0 & 1 \\ 0 & 2 & 3 \\ 4 & -1 & -2 \end{vmatrix} = 6$ **12.** $\begin{vmatrix} 0 & x & 1 \\ -3 & 2 & 4 \\ -2 & 1 & 0 \end{vmatrix} = 17$

Set II   **1.** For the determinant $\begin{vmatrix} -3 & 1 & 2 \\ 0 & 4 & -1 \\ 5 & -2 & 6 \end{vmatrix}$, find:

    a. the minor of 4   b. the cofactor of 4

    c. the minor of 2   d. the cofactor of 2

    e. the minor of 1   f. the cofactor of 1

2. For the determinant $\begin{vmatrix} 2 & 5 & 6 \\ 1 & 8 & 4 \\ 3 & 7 & 9 \end{vmatrix}$, find:

    a. the minor of 2   b. the cofactor of 2

    c. the minor of 1   d. the cofactor of 1

    e. the minor of 7   f. the cofactor of 7

In Exercises 3–6, find the value of each determinant by expanding by cofactors of the indicated row or column.

3. $\begin{vmatrix} 2 & -1 & -3 \\ 4 & 0 & -2 \\ -5 & 2 & 3 \end{vmatrix}$ column 2   **4.** $\begin{vmatrix} 0 & 5 & -2 \\ -3 & 4 & -1 \\ 2 & -4 & 6 \end{vmatrix}$ row 1

5. $\begin{vmatrix} 3 & -2 & 4 \\ 5 & 1 & 0 \\ 0 & -1 & 2 \end{vmatrix}$ row 3   **6.** $\begin{vmatrix} 1 & 5 & -1 \\ 2 & 0 & -2 \\ 3 & 1 & -1 \end{vmatrix}$ column 2

In Exercises 7–10, expand by any row or column.

7. $\begin{vmatrix} -1 & 3 & -2 \\ -4 & 2 & 5 \\ 0 & 1 & -3 \end{vmatrix}$

8. $\begin{vmatrix} 4 & -5 & 2 \\ -2 & 0 & -3 \\ 6 & 0 & -1 \end{vmatrix}$

9. $\begin{vmatrix} 3 & -2 & 0 \\ -2 & 1 & -2 \\ 2 & -1 & 2 \end{vmatrix}$

10. $\begin{vmatrix} 3 & 0 & 5 \\ -1 & -1 & 3 \\ 2 & -3 & 1 \end{vmatrix}$

In Exercises 11 and 12, solve for x.

11. $\begin{vmatrix} 0 & -4 & 3 \\ x & 2 & 0 \\ -1 & 5 & x \end{vmatrix} = 31$

12. $\begin{vmatrix} 2 & x & 1 \\ -1 & x & 2 \\ x & 0 & 1 \end{vmatrix} = 18$

10.8B General Solution of a Third-Order Linear System Using Cramer's Rule

The following rule is stated without proof:

TO SOLVE $\begin{cases} a_1 x + b_1 y + c_1 z = d_1 \\ a_2 x + b_2 y + c_2 z = d_2 \\ a_3 x + b_3 y + c_3 z = d_3 \end{cases}$ BY USING CRAMER'S RULE

The solution is

$$x = \frac{D_x}{D}, \qquad y = \frac{D_y}{D}, \qquad z = \frac{D_z}{D},$$

where

$$D = \begin{vmatrix} a_1 & b_1 & c_1 \\ a_2 & b_2 & c_2 \\ a_3 & b_3 & c_3 \end{vmatrix} \qquad \text{Determinant of coefficients}$$

Column of constants in place of x-coefficients

$$D_x = \begin{vmatrix} d_1 & b_1 & c_1 \\ d_2 & b_2 & c_2 \\ d_3 & b_3 & c_3 \end{vmatrix}$$

Column of constants in place of y-coefficients

$$D_y = \begin{vmatrix} a_1 & d_1 & c_1 \\ a_2 & d_2 & c_2 \\ a_3 & d_3 & c_3 \end{vmatrix}$$

Column of constants in place of z-coefficients

$$D_z = \begin{vmatrix} a_1 & b_1 & d_1 \\ a_2 & b_2 & d_2 \\ a_3 & b_3 & d_3 \end{vmatrix}$$

Cramer's rule can be used to solve linear systems of any order. When a third-order linear system of equations is solved by Cramer's rule, there are three possibilities:

1. *Only one solution (consistent, independent system):* $D \neq 0$.

2. *No solution (inconsistent, independent system):* $D = 0$, and D_x, D_y, $D_z \neq 0$.

3. *Many solutions (consistent, dependent system):* $D = 0$, and $D_x = D_y = D_z = 0$.

These same criteria can be extended to linear systems of higher order.

Example 3   Solve the system $\begin{cases} x - 3y + 2z = 3 \\ 3x - 4y + 2z = -2 \\ x + 5y - z = -1 \end{cases}$ using Cramer's rule.

$$\begin{cases} x - 3y + 2z = \boxed{3} \\ 3x - 4y + 2z = \boxed{-2} \\ x + 5y - z = \boxed{-1} \end{cases}$$

Column of constants in place of coefficients of variable being solved for

$$x = \frac{\begin{vmatrix} 3 & -3 & 2 \\ -2 & -4 & 2 \\ -1 & 5 & -1 \end{vmatrix}}{\begin{vmatrix} 1 & -3 & 2 \\ 3 & -4 & 2 \\ 1 & 5 & -1 \end{vmatrix}} = \frac{D_x}{D}, \quad y = \frac{\begin{vmatrix} 1 & 3 & 2 \\ 3 & -2 & 2 \\ 1 & -1 & -1 \end{vmatrix}}{\begin{vmatrix} 1 & -3 & 2 \\ 3 & -4 & 2 \\ 1 & 5 & -1 \end{vmatrix}} = \frac{D_y}{D}, \quad z = \frac{\begin{vmatrix} 1 & -3 & 3 \\ 3 & -4 & -2 \\ 1 & 5 & -1 \end{vmatrix}}{\begin{vmatrix} 1 & -3 & 2 \\ 3 & -4 & 2 \\ 1 & 5 & -1 \end{vmatrix}} = \frac{D_z}{D}$$

$$D = \begin{vmatrix} 1 & -3 & 2 \\ 3 & -4 & 2 \\ 1 & 5 & -1 \end{vmatrix} = +(1)\begin{vmatrix} -4 & 2 \\ 5 & -1 \end{vmatrix} - (-3)\begin{vmatrix} 3 & 2 \\ 1 & -1 \end{vmatrix} + (2)\begin{vmatrix} 3 & -4 \\ 1 & 5 \end{vmatrix}$$

$$= 1(4 - 10) + 3(-3 - 2) + 2(15 + 4) = 17$$

$$D_x = \begin{vmatrix} 3 & -3 & 2 \\ -2 & -4 & 2 \\ -1 & 5 & -1 \end{vmatrix} = +(3)\begin{vmatrix} -4 & 2 \\ 5 & -1 \end{vmatrix} - (-2)\begin{vmatrix} -3 & 2 \\ 5 & -1 \end{vmatrix} + (-1)\begin{vmatrix} -3 & 2 \\ -4 & 2 \end{vmatrix}$$

$$= 3(4 - 10) + 2(3 - 10) - 1(-6 + 8) = -34$$

$$D_y = \begin{vmatrix} 1 & 3 & 2 \\ 3 & -2 & 2 \\ 1 & -1 & -1 \end{vmatrix} = -(3)\begin{vmatrix} 3 & 2 \\ 1 & -1 \end{vmatrix} + (-2)\begin{vmatrix} 1 & 2 \\ 1 & -1 \end{vmatrix} - (-1)\begin{vmatrix} 1 & 2 \\ 3 & 2 \end{vmatrix}$$

$$= -3(-3 - 2) - 2(-1 - 2) + 1(2 - 6) = 17$$

$$D_z = \begin{vmatrix} 1 & -3 & 3 \\ 3 & -4 & -2 \\ 1 & 5 & -1 \end{vmatrix} = +(3)\begin{vmatrix} 3 & -4 \\ 1 & 5 \end{vmatrix} - (-2)\begin{vmatrix} 1 & -3 \\ 1 & 5 \end{vmatrix} + (-1)\begin{vmatrix} 1 & -3 \\ 3 & -4 \end{vmatrix}$$

$$= 3(15 + 4) + 2(5 + 3) - 1(-4 + 9) = 68$$

$$x = \frac{D_x}{D} = \frac{-34}{17} = -2, \quad y = \frac{D_y}{D} = \frac{17}{17} = 1, \quad z = \frac{D_z}{D} = \frac{68}{17} = 4$$

Therefore, the solution is $(-2, 1, 4)$.   ∎

If zeros appear anywhere in a determinant, expand the determinant by the row or column containing the most zeros. This minimizes the numerical work that needs to be done in evaluating the determinant.

Example 4   Selecting the best row or column to expand the determinant by:

a. $\begin{vmatrix} -2 & 1 & 0 \\ 4 & -2 & 1 \\ 3 & -1 & 5 \end{vmatrix}$ Expand by row 1 (or column 3) because it contains a zero

Expanding by row 1:

$$= (-2)\begin{vmatrix} -2 & 1 \\ -1 & 5 \end{vmatrix} - (1)\begin{vmatrix} 4 & 1 \\ 3 & 5 \end{vmatrix} + (0)\begin{vmatrix} 4 & -2 \\ 3 & -1 \end{vmatrix}$$

$$= (-2)(-10 + 1) - 1(20 - 3) + 0 = 1$$

b. $\begin{vmatrix} -4 & 0 & -1 \\ 1 & 2 & -3 \\ -2 & 0 & 5 \end{vmatrix}$ Expand by column 2 because it contains two zeros

Expanding by column 2:

It is not necessary to write the minor when it is multiplied by zero

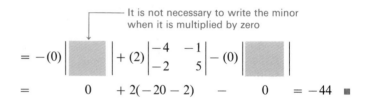

$$= -(0)\begin{vmatrix} \\ \end{vmatrix} + (2)\begin{vmatrix} -4 & -1 \\ -2 & 5 \end{vmatrix} - (0)\begin{vmatrix} \\ \end{vmatrix}$$

$$= \qquad 0 \qquad + 2(-20 - 2) \qquad - \qquad 0 \qquad = -44 \quad\blacksquare$$

EXERCISES 10.8B

Set I   Solve each system by using Cramer's rule.

1. $\begin{cases} 2x + y + z = 4 \\ x - y + 3z = -2 \\ x + y + 2z = 1 \end{cases}$

2. $\begin{cases} x + y + z = 1 \\ 2x + y - 2z = -4 \\ x + y + 2z = 3 \end{cases}$

3. $\begin{cases} 2x + 3y + z = 7 \\ 4x - 2z = -6 \\ 6y - z = 0 \end{cases}$

4. $\begin{cases} x - 2y = 4 \\ y + 3z = 8 \\ 2x - z = 1 \end{cases}$

Set II   Solve each system by using Cramer's rule.

1. $\begin{cases} x + 2z = 7 \\ 2x - y = 5 \\ 2y + z = 4 \end{cases}$

2. $\begin{cases} 4x + 5y + z = 4 \\ 10y - 2z = 6 \\ 8x + 3z = 3 \end{cases}$

3. $\begin{cases} 2x + y - 3z = 3 \\ x + 2y = 0 \\ -2x - 2y + 5z = -2 \end{cases}$

4. $\begin{cases} 3x - y + 2z = 4 \\ x - 2y - 3z = -4 \\ x + y = 2 \end{cases}$

10.9 Using Systems of Equations to Solve Word Problems

In solving word problems that involve more than one unknown, it is sometimes difficult to represent each unknown in terms of a single letter. In this section, we eliminate that difficulty by using a different variable for each unknown.

TO SOLVE A WORD PROBLEM USING A SYSTEM OF EQUATIONS

1. Read the problem completely and determine how many unknown numbers there are.

2. Draw a diagram showing the relationships in the problem whenever possible.

3. Represent each unknown number by a different variable.

4. Use word statements to write a system of equations. *There must be as many equations as variables.*

5. Solve the system of equations using one of the following:

   a. addition method (Section 10.3)
   b. substitution method (Section 10.4)
   c. determinant method (Sections 10.7 and 10.8)
   d. graphical method (Section 10.2)

Example 1 Doris has 17 coins in her purse with a total value of $1.15. If she has only nickels and dimes, how many of each are there?

Let D = number of dimes
N = number of nickels

	Doris has 17 coins.		She has only nickels and dimes.
(1)	17	$=$	$N + D$

The coins in her purse have a total value of $1.15 (115¢).

	Amount of money in dimes		Amount of money in nickels		Total amount of money
(2)	$10D$	$+$	$5N$	$=$	115

$$(1) \begin{cases} N + D = 17 \\ (2) \ 5N + 10D = 115 \end{cases}$$

Arrange the equations so that like terms are in the same column

$$N + D = 17 \Rightarrow N = 17 - D$$

$$5N + 10D = 115$$

$$5(17 - D) + 10D = 115$$

$$85 - 5D + 10D = 115$$

$$5D = 30$$

$$D = 6 \qquad \text{Number of dimes}$$

$$N = 17 - D = 17 - 6 = 11 \qquad \text{Number of nickels}$$

(The check will not be shown.) ■

Example 2   Jeff left Riverside at 5 A.M. traveling toward Stockton. His friend George left Riverside at 5:40 A.M., driving 10 mph faster than Jeff. George, also traveling toward Stockton, overtook Jeff at 9 A.M. Find the average speed of each car and the total distance traveled before they met.

Solution Note that Jeff traveled 4 hours and George traveled 3 hours, 20 minutes before they met and that 3 hours, 20 minutes can be expressed as $3\frac{1}{3}$ hours.

Let x = Jeff's average speed (in mph)

y = George's average speed

Then $4x$ = Jeff's distance $\left(x\dfrac{\text{mi}}{\text{hr}}\right)(4\text{ hr})$

$\dfrac{10}{3}y$ = George's distance $\left(y\dfrac{\text{mi}}{\text{hr}}\right)\left(\dfrac{10}{3}\text{hr}\right)$

$$(1) \begin{cases} 4x = \dfrac{10}{3}y \\ (2)\quad y = x + 10 \end{cases}$$

The distances are equal

George's speed was 10 mph faster than Jeff's

Clearing fractions in Equation 1, we have

$$12x = 10y$$

Then, substituting Equation 2 into $12x = 10y$, we have

$$12x = 10(x + 10)$$
$$12x = 10x + 100$$
$$2x = 100$$
$$x = 50 \qquad \text{Jeff's average speed}$$
$$x + 10 = 60 \qquad \text{George's average speed}$$
$$4x = 200 \qquad \text{The total distance traveled before they met}$$

Check $60 = 50 + 10$ George's speed is 10 mph more than Jeff's

$$4(50) \overset{?}{=} \frac{10}{3}(60)$$

$$200 = 200 \qquad \text{George's distance equals Jeff's distance} \quad \blacksquare$$

Example 3   If crew A works 9 hr, crew B works 4 hr, and crew C works 10 hr, then 7 cars are completed. If crew A works 3 hr and crew B works 8 hr, then 5 cars are completed. If crew B works 6 hr and crew C works 5 hr, then 4 cars are completed. How long does it take each crew, working alone, to complete 1 car?

Let crew A's rate = $a\dfrac{\text{car}}{\text{hr}}$

crew B's rate = $b\dfrac{\text{car}}{\text{hr}}$

crew C's rate = $c\dfrac{\text{car}}{\text{hr}}$

The basic idea used to solve work problems:

$$\text{Rate} \times \text{Time} = \text{Amount of work done}$$

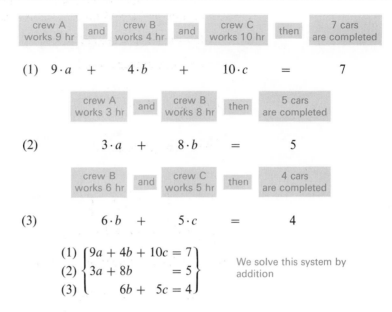

(1) $9 \cdot a + 4 \cdot b + 10 \cdot c = 7$

(2) $3 \cdot a + 8 \cdot b = 5$

(3) $6 \cdot b + 5 \cdot c = 4$

(1) $\begin{cases} 9a + 4b + 10c = 7 \\ 3a + 8b = 5 \\ 6b + 5c = 4 \end{cases}$

We solve this system by addition

Eliminate c from the pair of equations (1) and (3):

(1) $1\ ]\quad 9a + 4b + 10c = 7 \Rightarrow 9a + 4b + 10c = 7$
(3) $-2\ ]\quad\quad 6b + 5c = 4 \Rightarrow \quad\ -12b - 10c = -8$
(4) $\quad\quad\quad\quad\quad\quad 9a - 8b = -1$

Adding the pair (2) and (4):

(2) $\quad 3a + 8b = 5$
(4) $\quad 9a - 8b = -1$
$\quad\ 12a = 4$

$$a = \frac{4}{12} = \frac{1}{3}\frac{\text{car}}{\text{hr}}$$

Therefore, crew A takes 3 hr to complete 1 car.

Substitute $a = \dfrac{1}{3}$ into (2):

(2) $\quad 3a + 8b = 5$

$$3\left(\frac{1}{3}\right) + 8b = 5$$

$$1 + 8b = 5$$

$$8b = 4$$

$$b = \frac{4}{8} = \frac{1}{2}\frac{\text{car}}{\text{hr}}$$

Therefore, crew B takes 2 hr to complete 1 car.

Substitute $b = \dfrac{1}{2}$ into (3):

$$(3) \qquad 6b + 5c = 4$$

$$6\left(\dfrac{1}{2}\right) + 5c = 4$$

$$3 + 5c = 4$$

$$5c = 1$$

$$c = \dfrac{1}{5}\dfrac{\text{car}}{\text{hr}}$$

Therefore, crew C takes 5 hr to complete 1 car. (The check will not be shown.) ∎

EXERCISES 10.9

Set I   Set up each word problem algebraically, *using at least two variables*, solve, and check. Be sure to state what your variables represent.

1. The sum of two numbers is 30. Their difference is 12. What are the numbers?

2. The sum of two angles is 180°. Their difference is 70°. Find the angles.

3. Beatrice has 15 coins with a total value of $1.75. If the coins are nickels and quarters, how many of each kind are there?

4. Raul has 22 coins with a total value of $5.00. If the coins are dimes and half-dollars, how many of each kind are there?

5. A fraction has a value of two-thirds. If 10 is added to its numerator and 5 is subtracted from its denominator, the value of the fraction becomes 1. What was the original fraction?

6. A fraction has a value of one-half. If 8 is added to its numerator and 6 is added to its denominator, the value of the fraction becomes two-thirds. What was the original fraction?

7. The sum of the digits of a three-digit number is 20. The tens digit is 3 more than the units digit. The sum of the hundreds digit and the tens digit is 15. Find the number.

8. The sum of the digits of a three-digit number is 21. The units digit is 1 less than the tens digit. Twice the hundreds digit plus the tens digit is 17. Find the number.

9. Albert, Bill, and Carlos working together can do a job in 2 hr. Bill and Carlos together can do the job in 3 hr. Albert and Bill together can do the job in 4 hr. How long would it take each man to do the entire job working alone?

10. Crews A and C working together can assemble 1 machine in 3 hr. Crews A and B together take 8 hr to assemble 3 machines. Crews B and C together take 24 hr to assemble 5 machines. How long would it take each crew to assemble 1 machine?

11. A pilot takes $5\frac{1}{2}$ hr to fly 2,750 mi against the wind and only 5 hr to return with the wind. Find the average speed of the plane in still air and the average speed of the wind.

12. A pilot takes $2\frac{1}{2}$ hr to fly 1,200 mi against the wind and only 2 hr to return with the wind. Find the average speed of the plane in still air and the average speed of the wind.

13. A 90-lb mixture of two different grades of coffee costs $338.90. If grade A costs $3.85 a pound and grade B costs $3.65 a pound, how many pounds of each grade were used?

14. An 80-lb mixture of two different grades of coffee costs $305.25. If grade A costs $3.95 a pound and grade B costs $3.70 a pound, how many pounds of each grade were used?

15. The sum of the digits of a two-digit number is 12. If the digits are reversed, the new number is 54 less than the original number. Find the original number.

16. The sum of the digits of a two-digit number is 14. If the digits are reversed, the new number is 18 less than the original number. Find the original number.

17. Tom spent $7.21 on 29 stamps, buying 18¢, 22¢, and 45¢ stamps. He bought twice as many 22¢ stamps as 18¢ stamps. How many of each kind did he buy?

18. Sherma spent $5.07 on 21 stamps, buying 18¢, 22¢, and 45¢ stamps. She bought twice as many 18¢ stamps as 45¢ stamps. How many of each kind did she buy?

19. A tie and a pin cost $1.10. The tie costs $1.00 more than the pin. What is the cost of each?

20. A number of birds are resting on two limbs of a tree. One limb is above the other. A bird on the lower limb says to the birds on the upper limb, "If one of you will come down here, we will have an equal number on each limb." A bird from above replies, "If one of you will come up here, we will have twice as many up here as you have down there." How many birds are sitting on each limb?

Set II   Set up each word problem algebraically, *using at least two variables*, solve, and check. Be sure to state what your variables represent.

1. The sum of two numbers is 50. Their difference is 22. What are the numbers?

2. The sum of two angles is 90°. Their difference is 40°. Find the angles.

3. Carol has 18 coins with a total value of $3.45. If the coins are dimes and quarters, how many of each kind are there?

4. Don spent $3.70 for 22 stamps. If he bought only 15¢ stamps and 20¢ stamps, how many of each kind did he buy?

5. A fraction has a value of three-fourths. If 4 is subtracted from the numerator and 2 is added to the denominator, the value of the new fraction is one-half. What was the original fraction?

6. Several families went to a movie together. They spent $24.75 for 8 tickets. If adult tickets cost $4.50 and children's tickets cost $2.25, how many of each kind of ticket were bought?

7. The sum of the digits of a three-digit number is 15. The tens digit is 5 more than the units digit. The sum of the hundreds digit and the units digit is 9. Find the number.

8. One-third the sum of two numbers is 12. Twice their difference is 12. Find the numbers.

9. A refinery tank has one fill pipe and two drain pipes. Pipe 1 can fill the tank in 3 hr. Pipe 2 takes 6 hr longer to drain the tank than pipe 3. If it takes 12 hr to fill the tank when all three pipes are open, how long does it take pipe 3 to drain the tank alone?

10. The sum of the digits of a three-digit number is 11. The tens digit is twice the units digit. If the digits are reversed, the new number is 297 less than the original number. Find the original number.

11. Jerry takes 6 hr to ride his bicycle 30 mi against the wind. He takes 2 hr to return with the wind. Find Jerry's average riding speed in still air and the average speed of the wind.

12. A fraction has a value of two-thirds. If 5 is added to the numerator and 4 is added to the denominator, the value of the new fraction is three-fourths. What was the original fraction?

13. A 60-lb mixture of two different grades of coffee costs $218.50. If grade A costs $3.80 a pound and grade B costs $3.55 a pound, how many pounds of each grade were used?

14. Find two numbers such that 5 times the larger plus 3 times the smaller is 47, and 4 times the larger minus twice the smaller is 20.

15. The sum of the digits of a two-digit number is 11. If the digits are reversed, the new number is 27 less than the original number. Find the original number.

16. The sum of the digits of a three-digit number is 13. The tens digit is 4 times the units digit. If the digits are reversed, the new number is 99 less than the original number. Find the original number.

17. Gloria spent $6.31 on 26 stamps, buying 18¢, 22¢, and 45¢ stamps. She bought twice as many 18¢ stamps as 22¢ stamps. How many of each kind did she buy?

18. $26,000 was divided and placed in three different accounts. Twice as much was put into an account earning 7% per year as was put into an account earning 6% per year. The rest was put into an account earning 5% per year. The interest earned in one year by all three accounts together was $1,650. How much was invested at each rate?

19. Al, Chet, and Muriel are two brothers and a sister. Ten years ago, Al was twice as old as Chet was then. Three years ago, Muriel was three-fourths Chet's age at that time. In 15 years, Al will be 8 years older than Muriel is then. Find their ages now.

20. Tickets for a certain concert sold for $6, $8, and $12 each. There were 280 more $6 tickets sold than $8 and $12 tickets together, and the total revenue from 840 tickets was $6,080. How many tickets were sold at each price?

10.10 Quadratic Systems

All the systems studied in this chapter so far have been *linear systems* of equations. In this section, we discuss the solution of *quadratic systems*. A quadratic system is one that has a second-degree equation as its highest-degree equation.

The quadratic equations that appear in the quadratic systems of this section are equations of conic sections (Section 9.8). A method of graphing conic sections was discussed in Section 9.8.

Systems That Have One Quadratic Equation and One Linear Equation

---

TO SOLVE A SYSTEM THAT HAS ONE QUADRATIC AND
ONE LINEAR EQUATION

1. Solve the linear equation for one variable.

2. Substitute the expression obtained in step 1 into the quadratic equation of the system; then solve the resulting equation.

3. Substitute the solutions obtained in step 2 into the expression obtained in step 1 to solve for the remaining variable.

Example 1   Solve the quadratic system $\begin{cases} x - 2y = -4 \\ x^2 = 4y \end{cases}$.

Step 1 Solve Equation 1 for x: $x - 2y = -4$

$$x = 2y - 4$$

Step 2 Substitute $2y - 4$ for x in Equation 2:

$$x^2 = 4y$$
$$(2y - 4)^2 = 4y$$
$$4y^2 - 16y + 16 = 4y$$
$$4y^2 - 20y + 16 = 0$$
$$y^2 - 5y + 4 = 0$$
$$(y - 1)(y - 4) = 0$$
$$y - 1 = 0 \quad or \quad y - 4 = 0$$
$$y = 1 \quad or \quad y = 4$$

Step 3 If $y = 1$, then $x = 2y - 4 = 2(1) - 4 = -2$. Therefore, one solution is $(-2, 1)$.

If $y = 4$, then $x = 2y - 4 = 2(4) - 4 = 8 - 4 = 4$. Therefore, the second solution is $(4, 4)$.

When the graphs of Equations 1 and 2 are drawn on the same set of axes, we see that the two solutions, $(-2, 1)$ and $(4, 4)$, are the points where the graphs *intersect* (Figure 10.10.1). Refer to Section 8.2 for graphing $x - 2y = -4$. Refer to Section 9.8 for graphing $x^2 = 4y$.

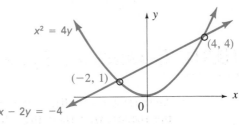

FIGURE 10.10.1

When the system has one quadratic equation and one linear equation, there are three possible cases:

1. Two points of intersection (two real solutions)

2. One point of intersection (one real solution)

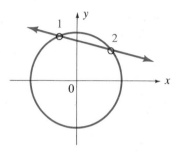

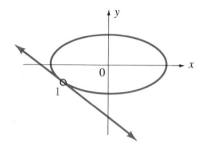

3. No point of intersection (two *complex* solutions)

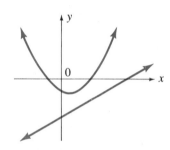

Systems That Have Two Quadratic Equations

We now discuss how to solve some systems that have two quadratic equations.

Example 2   Solve the quadratic system $\begin{cases} x^2 + y^2 = 13 \\ 2x^2 + 3y^2 = 30 \end{cases}$.

We can use the addition method because the two equations have like terms.

$$
\begin{array}{lll}
(1) & -2\ ] & x^2 + y^2 = 13 \Rightarrow -2x^2 - 2y^2 = -26 \\
(2) & 1\ ] & 2x^2 + 3y^2 = 30 \Rightarrow \underline{2x^2 + 3y^2 = 30} \\
& & y^2 = 4 \\
& & y = \pm 2
\end{array}
$$

$\rangle$ Add

Substitute $y = 2$ into Equation 1:

$$
\begin{aligned}
x^2 + y^2 &= 13 \\
x^2 + (2)^2 &= 13 \\
x^2 + 4 &= 13 \\
x^2 &= 9 \\
x &= \pm 3
\end{aligned}
$$

Therefore, two solutions are $(3, 2)$ and $(-3, 2)$.

Substitute $y = -2$ into Equation 1:

$$x^2 + y^2 = 13$$
$$x^2 + (-2)^2 = 13$$
$$x^2 + 4 = 13$$
$$x^2 = 9$$
$$x = \pm 3$$

Therefore, two more solutions are $(3, -2)$ and $(-3, -2)$.

When the graphs of Equations 1 and 2 are drawn on the same set of axes, we see that the four solutions, $(3, 2)$, $(3, -2)$, $(-3, 2)$ and $(-3, -2)$, are the points where the two graphs *intersect* (Figure 10.10.2).

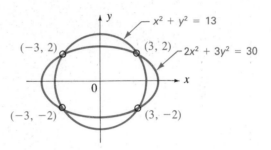

FIGURE 10.10.2

When the system has two quadratic equations, there are five possible cases:

1. No points of intersection
   (*complex* solutions)

2. One point of intersection
   (one real solution)

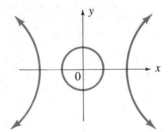

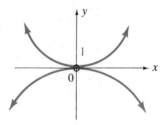

3. Two points of intersection
   (two real solutions)

4. Three points of intersection
   (three real solutions)

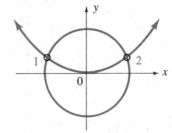

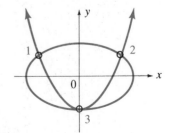

5. Four points of intersection (four real solutions)

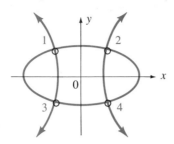

Example 3   Solve the system $\begin{cases} xy = 1 \\ x^2 + y^2 = 2 \end{cases}$.

We have not previously discussed an equation such as $xy = 1$. It is a quadratic equation, because it is of degree 2. It happens to be a *hyperbola* with the *x*- and *y*-axes as its asymptotes.

We must use the *substitution method* in solving this system of equations.

Step 1 Solve Equation 1 for *y*: $xy = 1$

$$y = \frac{1}{x}$$

Step 2 Substitute $\frac{1}{x}$ for *y* in Equation 2:

$$x^2 + y^2 = 2$$

$$x^2 + \left(\frac{1}{x}\right)^2 = 2$$

$$x^2 + \frac{1}{x^2} = 2$$

$$x^4 + 1 = 2x^2$$

$$x^4 - 2x^2 + 1 = 0$$

$$(x^2 - 1)^2 = 0$$

$$x^2 - 1 = 0$$

$$x^2 = 1$$

$$x = \pm 1$$

Step 3 If $x = 1$, $y = \frac{1}{1} = 1$. Therefore, one solution is $(1, 1)$.

If $x = -1$, $y = \frac{1}{-1} = -1$. Therefore, the second solution is $(-1, -1)$. The graph is

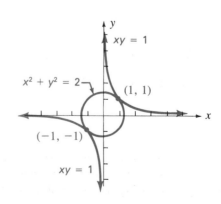

NOTE   When a quadratic equation contains an xy-term, we cannot determine which of the conic sections it is by simply looking at the equation.   ☑

EXERCISES 10.10

Set I   Solve each system of equations.

1. $\begin{cases} x^2 = 2y \\ x - y = -4 \end{cases}$

2. $\begin{cases} x^2 = 4y \\ x + 2y = 4 \end{cases}$

3. $\begin{cases} x^2 = 4y \\ x - y = 1 \end{cases}$

4. $\begin{cases} x^2 + y^2 = 25 \\ x - 3y = -5 \end{cases}$

5. $\begin{cases} xy = 4 \\ x - 2y = 2 \end{cases}$

6. $\begin{cases} xy = 3 \\ x + y = 0 \end{cases}$

7. $\begin{cases} x^2 + y^2 = 61 \\ x^2 - y^2 = 11 \end{cases}$

8. $\begin{cases} x^2 + 4y^2 = 4 \\ x^2 - 4y = 4 \end{cases}$

9. $\begin{cases} 2x^2 + 3y^2 = 21 \\ x^2 + 2y^2 = 12 \end{cases}$

10. $\begin{cases} 4x^2 - 5y^2 = 62 \\ 5x^2 + 8y^2 = 106 \end{cases}$

11. $\begin{cases} xy = -4 \\ y = 6x - 9 - x^2 \end{cases}$

12. $\begin{cases} xy = 8 \\ y = 8 + x^2 - 4x \end{cases}$

Set II   Solve each system of equations.

1. $\begin{cases} x^2 = 2y \\ 2x + y = -2 \end{cases}$

2. $\begin{cases} xy = 6 \\ x - y = 1 \end{cases}$

3. $\begin{cases} x^2 + y^2 = 25 \\ 3x + y = -5 \end{cases}$

4. $\begin{cases} 4x^2 + 9y^2 = 36 \\ 2x^2 - 9y = 18 \end{cases}$

5. $\begin{cases} 3x^2 + 4y^2 = 35 \\ 2x^2 + 5y^2 = 42 \end{cases}$

6. $\begin{cases} xy = 36 \\ y = 2x^2 - 5x - 3 \end{cases}$

7. $\begin{cases} 9x^2 + 16y^2 = 144 \\ 3x + 4y = 12 \end{cases}$

8. $\begin{cases} x^2 - y^2 = 4 \\ x^2 + y^2 = 4 \end{cases}$

9. $\begin{cases} x + y = 4 \\ y = x^2 - 4x + 4 \end{cases}$

10. $\begin{cases} 9x^2 + y^2 = 9 \\ 3x - y = -3 \end{cases}$

11. $\begin{cases} y = 3 - 2x - x^2 \\ y = x^2 + 2x + 3 \end{cases}$

12. $\begin{cases} y = 4 - x^2 \\ xy = 3 \end{cases}$

10.11 Solving a System of Inequalities in Two Variables by Graphing

10.11A Solving a System of Linear Inequalities by Graphing

So far we have discussed only systems of *equations*. In this section, we discuss solving systems of linear *inequalities*. You may wish to refer back to Section 8.4, where drawing the graph of a linear inequality was discussed in detail.

TO SOLVE A SYSTEM OF TWO LINEAR INEQUALITIES GRAPHICALLY

1. Graph the first inequality, shading the half-plane that represents its solution (Section 8.4).

2. Graph the second inequality on the same set of axes. Use a different type of shading for the half-plane that represents its solution.

3. Heavily shade in the region that contains *both* types of shading if such a region exists.

4. The coordinates of any point that lies in the heavily shaded region will satisfy *both* inequalities.

Example 1   Solve the system $\begin{cases} 2x - 3y < 6 \\ 3x + 4y \leq -12 \end{cases}$ graphically.

Step 1 Graph inequality 1: $2x - 3y < 6$

The boundary, $2x - 3y = 6$, is a *dashed* line because the equality is *not* included

$$2x - 3y < 6$$

x-intercept: Set $y = 0$. Then $2x - 3(0) = 6$
$$2x = 6$$
$$x = 3$$

y-intercept: Set $x = 0$. Then $2(0) - 3y = 6$
$$-3y = 6$$
$$y = -2$$

x	y
3	0
0	-2

Therefore, the boundary line goes through $(3, 0)$ and $(0, -2)$. Substitute the coordinates of the origin, $(0, 0)$, into inequality 1:

$$2x - 3y < 6$$
$$2(0) - 3(0) < 6$$
$$0 < 6 \qquad \text{True}$$

Therefore, the half-plane containing $(0, 0)$ is the solution (see Figure 10.11.1).

Step 2 Graph inequality 2: $3x + 4y \leq -12$

The boundary, $3x + 4y = -12$, is a *solid* line because the equality *is* included

$$3x + 4y \leq -12$$

x-intercept: Set $y = 0$. Then $3x + 4(0) = -12$
$$3x = -12$$
$$x = -4$$

y-intercept: Set $x = 0$. Then $3(0) + 4y = -12$
$$4y = -12$$
$$y = -3$$

x	y
-4	0
0	-3

Substitute the coordinates of the origin, $(0, 0)$, into inequality 2:

$$3x + 4y \leq -12$$

$$3(0) + 4(0) \leq -12$$

$$0 \leq -12 \quad \text{False}$$

Therefore, the solution is the half-plane *not* containing $(0, 0)$ (see Figure 10.11.1).

Step 3 Heavily shade in the region that contains both types of shading (see Figure 10.11.1).

Step 4 The coordinates of any point that lies in the heavily shaded region will satisfy both inequalities.

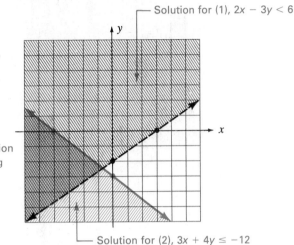

Solution for (1), $2x - 3y < 6$

Heavily shade in the region with *both* types of shading

Solution for (2), $3x + 4y \leq -12$

FIGURE 10.11.1

EXERCISES 10.11A

Set I   Solve each system of linear inequalities graphically.

1. $\begin{cases} 4x - 3y > -12 \\ y > 2 \end{cases}$ 2. $\begin{cases} x - y > -2 \\ 2x + y > 2 \end{cases}$ 3. $\begin{cases} 2x - y \leq 2 \\ x + y \geq 5 \end{cases}$

4. $\begin{cases} x - y \leq 4 \\ x + y \geq -2 \end{cases}$ 5. $\begin{cases} 2x + y < 0 \\ x - y \geq -3 \end{cases}$ 6. $\begin{cases} 3x > 6 - y \\ y + 3x \leq 0 \end{cases}$

7. $\begin{cases} 3x - 2y < 6 \\ x + 2y \leq 4 \\ 6x + y > -6 \end{cases}$ 8. $\begin{cases} 3x + 4y \leq 15 \\ 2x + y \leq 2 \\ -4 < x < 1 \\ -2 < y < 6 \end{cases}$

Set II   Solve each system of linear inequalities graphically.

1. $\begin{cases} 3x - 5y < 15 \\ x < 3 \end{cases}$ 2. $\begin{cases} 2x + 3y < 6 \\ x - 3y < 3 \end{cases}$ 3. $\begin{cases} 3x - y \geq 0 \\ 3x + 2y < 6 \end{cases}$

4. $\begin{cases} 2x \geq y - 4 \\ y - 2x > 0 \end{cases}$ 5. $\begin{cases} 3x - 2y < 6 \\ x + 2y \geq 2 \end{cases}$ 6. $\begin{cases} 4x + y \leq 4 \\ 2x - y > 2 \end{cases}$

7. $\begin{cases} 4x + 3y \geq 12 \\ y - x > 1 \\ 9x - 28y \geq 42 \end{cases}$ 8. $\begin{cases} 4x - 3y \geq 12 \\ x < 3 \end{cases}$

10.11B Solving a System of Quadratic Inequalities by Graphing

---

TO SOLVE A SYSTEM OF QUADRATIC INEQUALITIES GRAPHICALLY

1. Graph the first inequality, shading the region that represents its solution (Section 9.9B).

2. Graph the second inequality on the same set of axes. Use a different type of shading for the region that represents its solution.

3. Heavily shade in the region that contains *both* types of shading.

4. The coordinates of any point that lies in the heavily shaded region will satisfy both inequalities.

This technique also applies when one of the inequalities is linear and the other is quadratic (see Example 3).

Example 2   Solve the system $\left\{ \begin{array}{c} y \geq x^2 - 2x - 3 \\ x^2 + 4y^2 \leq 4 \end{array} \right\}$ graphically.

First, we graph the equation $y = x^2 - 2x - 3$. It is a parabola that opens upward; the x-intercepts are 3 and -1, and the y-intercept is -3. A *true* statement is obtained if we substitute $x = 0$ and $y = 0$ into the inequality. Therefore, we shade in the region that contains $(0, 0)$, using *diagonal* lines (see Figure 10.11.2).

   Next, we graph the equation $x^2 + 4y^2 = 4$. It is an ellipse; the x-intercepts are 2 and -2, and the y-intercepts are 1 and -1. A *true* statement is obtained if we substitute $x = 0$ and $y = 0$ into the inequality. Therefore, we shade in the region that contains $(0, 0)$ with *vertical* lines (see Figure 10.11.2).

   We now heavily shade in that portion of the plane that has both diagonal *and* vertical lines in it (see Figure 10.11.2).

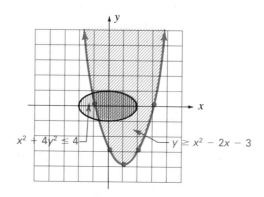

FIGURE 10.11.2

Any point that lies in the heavily shaded region is in the solution set for the system. ∎

Example 3   Solve the system $\left\{ \begin{array}{c} y \leq 4 - x^2 \\ y \leq x + 3 \end{array} \right\}$ graphically.

We will graph the inequality $y \leq 4 - x^2$ with *diagonal* lines. $y = 4 - x^2$ is a parabola that opens downward; the x-intercepts are 2 and -2, and the y-intercept is 4. Because $(0, 0)$ satisfies the inequality, we shade in the region inside the parabola (see Figure 10.11.3).

We will graph the inequality $y \leq x + 3$ with *vertical* lines. $y = x + 3$ is a *linear* equation. We graph that line and then find that $(0, 0)$ satisfies the inequality $y \leq x + 3$. Therefore, we shade in the half-plane that contains the origin (see Figure 10.11.3).

We heavily shade in that portion of the plane that contains both diagonal *and* vertical lines (see Figure 10.11.3).

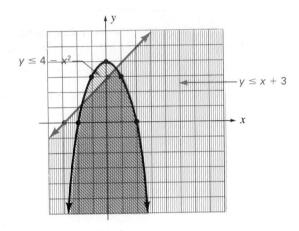

FIGURE 10.11.3

Any point that lies in the heavily shaded region is in the solution set of the system of inequalities. ■

EXERCISES 10.11B

Set I   Solve each system of inequalities graphically.

1. $\begin{cases} \dfrac{x^2}{9} + \dfrac{y^2}{4} < 1 \\ \dfrac{x^2}{4} + \dfrac{y^2}{9} < 1 \end{cases}$

2. $\begin{cases} \dfrac{x^2}{4} + y^2 \leq 1 \\ x + y < 1 \end{cases}$

3. $\begin{cases} y > 1 - x^2 \\ x^2 + y^2 < 4 \end{cases}$

4. $\begin{cases} x^2 + y^2 \geq 1 \\ x^2 + y^2 \leq 9 \end{cases}$

5. $\begin{cases} x^2 + y^2 \leq 9 \\ y \geq x - 2 \end{cases}$

Set II   Solve each system of inequalities graphically.

1. $\begin{cases} x^2 - \dfrac{y^2}{9} \leq 1 \\ \dfrac{x^2}{9} + \dfrac{y^2}{4} \leq 1 \end{cases}$

2. $\begin{cases} y \leq x^2 - 1 \\ 4x^2 + y^2 \leq 4 \end{cases}$

3. $\begin{cases} x^2 + \dfrac{y^2}{9} \leq 1 \\ y \leq 1 - x^2 \end{cases}$

4. $\begin{cases} \dfrac{x^2}{9} + y^2 \leq 1 \\ x^2 + y^2 \geq 4 \end{cases}$

5. $\begin{cases} x^2 + y^2 \leq 16 \\ x + y > 2 \end{cases}$

10.12 Review: 10.7–10.11

Cramer's Rule

Cramer's rule, using determinants, can be used in solving:

10.7   1. A second-order system

10.8   2. A third-order system

To Solve a Word Problem Using a System of Equations

10.9

1. Read the problem completely and determine how many unknown numbers there are.

2. Draw a diagram showing the relationships in the problem whenever possible.

3. Represent each unknown number by a different variable.

4. Use word statements to write a system of equations. There must be as many equations as variables.

5. Solve the system of equations using one of the following:

10.3	a. addition method
10.4	b. substitution method
10.7, 10.8	c. determinant method
10.2	d. graphical method

Methods of Solving a Quadratic System of Equations

10.10

1. *One quadratic and one linear equation*: Solve the linear equation for one variable, then substitute the expression obtained into the quadratic equation.

2. *Two quadratic equations* (with like terms): Use addition.

To Solve a System of Inequalities

10.11

1. Graph the first inequality, shading the region that represents its solution.

2. Graph the second inequality, using a different type of shading.

3. Heavily shade in the region that contains *both* types of shading.

4. Any point that lies in the heavily shaded region is in the solution set of both inequalities.

Review Exercises 10.12 Set I

In Exercises 1–3, use Cramer's rule to solve each system.

1. $\begin{cases} 3x - 2y = 8 \\ 2x + 5y = -1 \end{cases}$

2. $\begin{cases} 3x + y + 2z = 4 \\ 2x - 3y + 3z = -5 \\ 5x + 2y + 3z = 7 \end{cases}$

3. $\begin{cases} 5x + 2y = 1 \\ 7x - 6y = 8 \end{cases}$

In Exercises 4–8, solve each system by any convenient method. Write "inconsistent" if no solution exists. Write "dependent" if an infinite number of solutions exist.

4. $\begin{cases} 5x - 4y = -7 \\ -6x + 8y = 2 \end{cases}$

5. $\begin{cases} x - 3y = 15 \\ 5x + 7y = -13 \end{cases}$

6. $\begin{cases} 2x + 3y - 4z = 4 \\ 3x + 2y - 5z = 0 \\ 4x + 5y + 2z = -4 \end{cases}$

7. $\begin{cases} x - 2y = -1 \\ 2x^2 - 3y^2 = 6 \end{cases}$

8. $\begin{cases} x + 3y = -2 \\ x^2 - 2y^2 = 8 \end{cases}$

In Exercises 9–11, solve each system of inequalities graphically.

9. $\begin{cases} x + 4y \le 4 \\ 3x + 2y > 2 \end{cases}$

10. $\begin{cases} 3x + 6 \ge 2y \\ 3x + y < 3 \end{cases}$

11. $\begin{cases} y \le 12 + 4x - x^2 \\ x^2 + y^2 \le 16 \end{cases}$

In Exercises 12–16, set up algebraically and solve, using at least two variables.

12. The sum of two numbers is 6. Their difference is 40. What are the numbers?

13. A mail-order office paid $730 for a total of 80 rolls of stamps in two denominations. If one kind cost $10 per roll and the other kind cost $8 per roll, how many rolls of each kind were bought?

14. Jennifer sails 64 mi upstream in 4 hr and sails back in half the time. Find the average speed of her boat in still water and the average speed of the stream.

15. The sum of the digits of a three-digit number is 12. The hundreds digit is 3 times the units digit. The tens digit is 2 more than the units digit. Find the number.

16. The difference of two numbers is -7. The difference of their squares is 7. Find the numbers.

Review Exercises 10.12 Set II

NAME _____

ANSWERS

In Exercises 1–3, use Cramer's rule to solve each system.

1. $\begin{cases} 3x - 6y = -4 \\ -5x + 8y = 6 \end{cases}$

2. $\begin{cases} 3x - 2y = 10 \\ 5x + 4y = 24 \end{cases}$

1. _____

2. _____

3. _____

4. _____

3. $\begin{cases} x + 2y + z = 3 \\ 3x + y - 2z = -1 \\ 2x - 3y - z = 4 \end{cases}$

5. _____

6. _____

7. _____

8. _____

In Exercises 4–8, solve each system by any convenient method. Write "inconsistent" if no solution exists. Write "dependent" if an infinite number of solutions exist.

4. $\begin{cases} 7x + 3y = -1 \\ 5x + y = -5 \end{cases}$

5. $\begin{cases} 3x + 2y + z = 5 \\ 2x - 3y - 3z = 1 \\ 4x + 3y + 2z = 8 \end{cases}$

6. $\begin{cases} 4x + 3y + 2z = 6 \\ 8x + 3y - 3z = -1 \\ -4x + 6y + 5z = 5 \end{cases}$

7. $\begin{cases} x - 3y = 1 \\ x^2 = 6y - 8 \end{cases}$

8. $\begin{cases} x^2 + y^2 = 5 \\ x^2 - 3y^2 = 1 \end{cases}$

In Exercises 9–11, solve each system of inequalities graphically.

9. $\begin{cases} 5x + 2y \geq 0 \\ 5y - 6x > 15 \end{cases}$

10. $\begin{cases} y \leq x^2 - 4x + 3 \\ x^2 + 4y^2 \leq 4 \end{cases}$

ANSWERS

9. _Use graph._

10. _Use graph._

11. _Use graph._

12. _____

_____

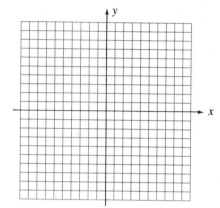

11. $\begin{cases} x^2 + y^2 \geq 4 \\ x^2 + 9y^2 \leq 9 \end{cases}$

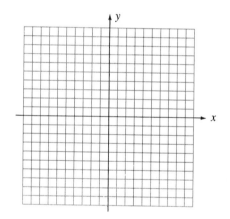

In Exercises 12–16, set up algebraically and solve, using at least two variables.

12. Half the sum of two numbers is 15. Half their difference is 8. Find the numbers.

13. Brian worked at two jobs during the week for a total of 32 hr. For this he received a total of $86.60. If he was paid $2.20 an hour as a tutor and $3.10 an hour as a waiter, how many hours did he work at each job?

14. Leticia worked at two jobs during the week for a total of 26 hr. For this she received a total of $118.25. If she was paid $4.75 an hour as a lab assistant and $4.40 an hour as a clerk-typist, how many hours did she work at each job?

15. The sum of the digits of a three-digit number is 11. The units digit is 3 more than the tens digit. The hundreds digit is 1 less than the units digit. Find the number.

16. Fausto sails 21 mi upstream in 3 hr and sails back in one-third the time. Find the average speed of the boat in still water and the average speed of the stream.

Chapter 10 Diagnostic Test

The purpose of this test is to see how well you understand systems of equations and systems of inequalities. We recommend that you work this diagnostic test *before* your instructor tests you on this chapter. Allow yourself about 50 minutes.

Complete solutions for all the problems on this test, together with section references, are given in the answer section at the end of the book. For the problems you do incorrectly, study the sections cited.

1. Solve graphically: $\begin{cases} 3x + 2y = 4 \\ x - y = 3 \end{cases}$.

In Exercises 2–7, solve the system by any convenient method. Write "inconsistent" if no solution exists. Write "dependent" if an infinite number of solutions exist.

2. $\begin{cases} 4x - 3y = 13 \\ 5x - 2y = 4 \end{cases}$

3. $\begin{cases} 5x + 4y = 23 \\ 3x + 2y = 9 \end{cases}$

4. $\begin{cases} 15x + 8y = -18 \\ 9x + 16y = -8 \end{cases}$

5. $\begin{cases} 35y - 10x = -18 \\ 4x - 14y = 8 \end{cases}$

6. $\begin{cases} x + y + z = 0 \\ 2x - 3z = 5 \\ 3y + 4z = 3 \end{cases}$

7. $\begin{cases} y^2 = 8x \\ 3x + y = 2 \end{cases}$

8. Solve the system $\begin{cases} 2x + 3y \le 6 \\ y - 2x < 2 \end{cases}$ graphically.

9. Evaluate each of the following determinants:

a. $\begin{vmatrix} 8 & -9 \\ 5 & -3 \end{vmatrix}$

b. $\begin{vmatrix} 2 & 0 & -1 \\ -3 & 1 & 4 \\ -1 & 5 & 6 \end{vmatrix}$

10. Given the system $\begin{cases} x - y - z = 0 \\ x + 3y + z = 4 \\ 7x - 2y - 5z = 2 \end{cases}$, express y as a ratio of two third-order determinants.

Set up the following problem algebraically, *using two variables*, and solve.

11. Barney sails 30 mi upstream in 2 hr and sails back in half the time. Find the average speed of his boat in still water and the average speed of the stream.

Cumulative Review Exercises
Chapters 1–10

1. Add $\dfrac{x}{xy - y^2} + \dfrac{y}{xy - x^2}$.

2. Divide $(x^3 - 5x^2 + 9x + 20)$ by $(x - 3)$.

In Exercises 3 and 4, simplify each radical.

3. $\sqrt[6]{4x^2}$

4. $\sqrt{\dfrac{3a^3b^7}{8a^5b^4}}$

5. Write the general form of the equation of the line through $(-1, 2)$ and $(2, 4)$.

6. Solve the inequality $x^2 - 8x + 12 < 0$.

In Exercises 7 and 8, solve each equation.

7. $4x^2 - 25 = 0$

8. $\dfrac{x + 2}{3} + \dfrac{5}{x - 2} = 4$

9. Use the quadratic formula to solve $x^2 - 4x + 5 = 0$.

10. Is division associative?

11. What is the additive inverse of $-\frac{3}{5}$?

12. What is the multiplicative inverse of $-\frac{3}{5}$?

In Exercises 13–15, solve the system by any convenient method. Write "inconsistent" if no solution exists. Write "dependent" if an infinite number of solutions exist.

13. $\begin{cases} 4x + 3y = 8 \\ 8x + 7y = 12 \end{cases}$

14. $\begin{cases} 2x - 3y = 3 \\ 3y - 2x = 6 \end{cases}$

15. $\begin{cases} 2x + 3y + z = 4 \\ x + 4y - z = 0 \\ 3x + y - z = -5 \end{cases}$

16. Solve the system $\begin{cases} 9x^2 + 4y^2 \geq 36 \\ 3x + 2y \geq 6 \end{cases}$ graphically.

17. Find the domain for the function $y = f(x) = \sqrt{12 - 4x - x^2}$.

In Exercises 18–20, set up the problem algebraically and solve.

18. The length of a rectangle is 7 more than its width. If the area is 60, find its dimensions.

19. It takes Darryl 2 hr longer to do a job than it does Jeannie. After Darryl has worked on the job for 1 hr, Jeannie joins him. Together they finish the job in 3 hr. How long would it take each of them to do the entire job working alone?

20. On a bicycle tour, it took Barbara 1 hr longer to ride 45 mi than it took Pat to ride 48 mi. If Pat averages 3 mph more than Barbara, find the average speed of each.

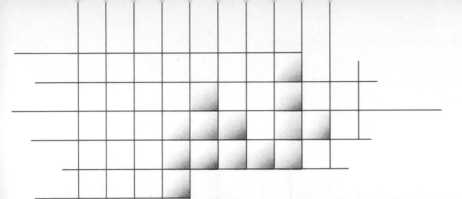

11 Exponential and Logarithmic Functions

In this chapter, we discuss exponential and logarithmic functions and some of their applications. Logarithms have many applications in mathematics and science; for example, they are used to measure the magnitude of earthquakes and the pH factor of solutions.*

11.1 Basic Definitions

11.1A The Exponential Function and Its Graph

Exponential Function

An **exponential function** is a function of the form $y = f(x) = b^x$, where b is any real number greater than zero except 1 and x is any real number.

The *domain* of the exponential function is the set of all real numbers. It is proved in higher mathematics courses that the graph of the exponential function is a smooth curve. The technique of graphing an exponential function is demonstrated in Example 1.

Example 1   Graph the exponential function $y = 2^x$. Then find the range of the function.

Calculate the value of the function for integral values of x from -2 to $+3$.

$y = 2^x$

$y = 2^{-2} = \dfrac{1}{2^2} = \dfrac{1}{4}$

$y = 2^{-1} = \dfrac{1}{2^1} = \dfrac{1}{2}$

$y = 2^0 = 1$

$y = 2^1 = 2$

$y = 2^2 = 4$

$y = 2^3 = 8$

x	y
-2	$\dfrac{1}{4}$
-1	$\dfrac{1}{2}$
0	1
1	2
2	4
3	8

Next, plot the points listed in the table of values and draw a *smooth curve* through them (taking the points in order from left to right). The graph of $y = 2^x$ is shown in Figure 11.1.1. We see from the graph that the curve never crosses the x-axis and is never below it. Therefore, the *range* of the function $y = 2^x$ is the set of all real numbers greater than 0.

---

* Note to the Instructor: In this chapter, logarithms are found by using calculators. If you prefer the use of tables, you may substitute Appendix B for Section 11.4. A section on calculations using logarithms, including an exercise set, is also included in Appendix B.

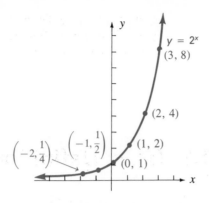

FIGURE 11.1.1

Example 2   Graph $y = \left(\dfrac{1}{3}\right)^x$. Then find the range of the function.

x	y
-2	9
-1	3
0	1
1	$\frac{1}{3}$
2	$\frac{1}{9}$

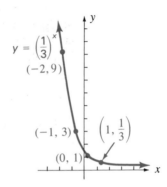

We see again that the graph *never* crosses the x-axis and is never below it. Therefore, the *range* is the set of all real numbers greater than 0. ■

If $b > 1$, the graph of $y = f(x) = b^x$ will always look like the graph in Figure 11.1.2. The curve *rises* as we move toward the right and lies entirely above the x-axis. It passes through the point (0, 1).

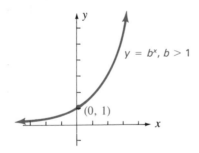

FIGURE 11.1.2

e

An *irrational number*, designated by *e*, is particularly important as a base for exponential functions.* It is so important, in fact, that special tables are made up for the function $y = f(x) = e^x$ (see Appendix C), and most scientific calculators have a

---

* An explanation of how *e* is calculated is beyond the scope of this text.

special key labeled $\boxed{e^x}$. If you press these keys, in order—$\boxed{1}$, $\boxed{e^x}$—you find that e^1 is approximately 2.7. To find e^5, press $\boxed{5}$, $\boxed{e^x}$, and so forth.

We will use two rules concerning exponential functions in this chapter. They are stated here without proof.

RULE 11.1

If $b^x = b^y$, then $x = y$.

RULE 11.2

If $a^x = b^x$, then $a = b$.

EXERCISES 11.1A

Set I   Graph each of the given functions.

1. $y = 4^x$ **2.** $y = 5^x$

3. $y = e^x$ (Use a calculator or Table 1, Appendix C, for the y-values.)

4. $y = \left(\dfrac{1}{2}\right)^x$ **5.** $y = \left(\dfrac{3}{2}\right)^x$

Set II   Graph each of the given functions.

1. $y = 6^x$ **2.** $y = -3^x$

3. $y = -e^x$ (Use a calculator or Table 1, Appendix C, for the y-values.)

4. $y = \left(\dfrac{5}{2}\right)^x$ **5.** $y = \left(\dfrac{1}{4}\right)^x$

11.1B   The Logarithmic Function and Its Graph

We can see from the graph of $y = f(x) = b^x$ (Figure 11.1.2) that for each y-value, there is only one x-value. Therefore, $y = f(x) = b^x$ must have an *inverse*. We even know what the graph of the inverse looks like, and we can find its domain and range. Its graph is the mirror image, with respect to the line $y = x$, of the graph of $y = b^x$ (see Figure 11.1.3). Its domain must be the set of all real numbers greater than 0, because

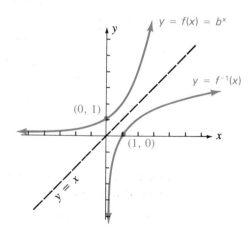

FIGURE 11.1.3

the domain of the inverse of a function equals the range of the original function. Its range must be the set of all real numbers, because the range of an inverse function equals the domain of the original function.

To find the inverse of $y = f(x) = b^x$, we first interchange x and y and write $x = b^y$. We now need to solve this new equation for y. However, we first need new notation and a definition.

Logarithm

The definition of a logarithm is as follows:

> The **logarithm** of a positive* number x is the exponent y to which the base b ($b > 0, b \neq 1$) must be raised to give x. In symbols,
>
> $$y = \log_b x$$
>
> if and only if $b^y = x$, where x is any real number greater than 0.

NOTE $y = \log_b x$ is read "y is the logarithm of x to the base b."   ☑

Argument   In the expression $\log_b x$, x is called the **argument** of the logarithmic function.

Example 3   Graph the logarithmic function $y = \log_2 x$.

We rewrite $y = \log_2 x$ in the form $x = 2^y$ and let y be the independent variable.

$x = 2^y$

$x = 2^{-3} = \dfrac{1}{2^3} = \dfrac{1}{8}$

$x = 2^{-2} = \dfrac{1}{2^2} = \dfrac{1}{4}$

$x = 2^{-1} = \dfrac{1}{2^1} = \dfrac{1}{2}$

$x = 2^0 = 1$

$x = 2^1 = 2$

$x = 2^2 = 4$

$x = 2^3 = 8$

x	y
$\frac{1}{8}$	-3
$\frac{1}{4}$	-2
$\frac{1}{2}$	-1
1	0
2	1
4	2
8	3

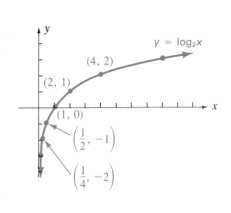

Notice that the *domain* is the set of all real numbers greater than 0 and the *range* is the set of all real numbers. ■

* The logarithm of a negative number exists, but it is a complex number. We will not discuss the logarithm of a negative number in this book.

Example 4   Graph $y = 2^x$ and $y = \log_2 x$ on the same axes.

Combining Examples 1 and 3, we get the following graph:

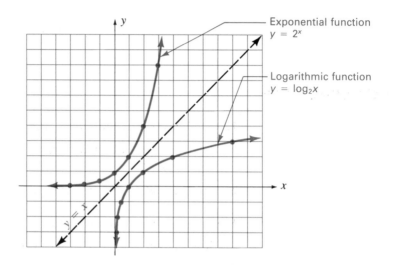

In general, the graph of any logarithmic function with a base greater than 1 has the appearance of the curve shown in Figure 11.1.4. It can also be seen in Figure 11.1.4 that:

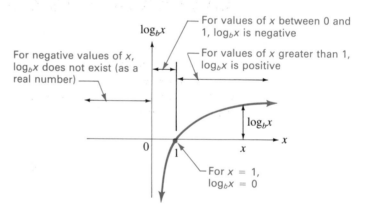

FIGURE 11.1.4

1. The logarithmic function is an *increasing function*. This means that as x gets larger, $\log_b x$ also gets larger.

2. Since $\log_b x$ is a *function*, if two numbers are equal, then their logarithms must be equal. This fact is used in solving exponential equations (Section 11.5) and is stated in symbols in Rule 11.3, which follows.

RULE 11.3

If $M = N$, then $\log_b M = \log_b N$.

Similarly, we can see the following from the graph:

RULE 11.4

If $\log_b M = \log_b N$, then $M = N$.

EXERCISES 11.1B

Set I

1. Graph $y = \log_2 x$ and $y = \log_{10} x$ on the same set of axes.

2. Graph the exponential function $y = 3^x$ and its inverse function, $y = \log_3 x$, on the same set of axes.

3. Graph $y = e^x$ and its inverse function, $y = \log_e x$, on the same set of axes.

Set II

1. Graph $y = \log_2 x$ and $y = \log_3 x$ on the same set of axes.

2. Graph $y = 4^x$ and its inverse logarithmic function on the same set of axes.

3. Graph $y = 5^x$ and its inverse function on the same set of axes.

11.2 Working with Exponential and Logarithmic Functions

11.2A Exponential and Logarithmic Forms

From the definition of logarithms, *logarithms are exponents*. Consequently, every exponential equation can be written in logarithmic form, and every logarithmic equation can be written in exponential form. In the following box, the symbol $\Leftrightarrow$ means "is equivalent to."

Exponential form		*Logarithmic form*
$b^y = x$	$\Leftrightarrow$	$y = \log_b x$

Example 1

Change $10^2 = 100$ to logarithmic form.

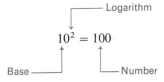

The *logarithm* is the *exponent* (2) to which the base (10) must be raised to give the number (100). This can be written $\log_{10} 100 = 2$ and is read "the logarithm of 100 to the base 10 equals 2."

Exponential form		*Logarithmic form*
$10^2 = 100$	$\Leftrightarrow$	$\log_{10} 100 = 2$ ∎

Example 2   Change each of the following to logarithmic form:

	Exponential form		Logarithmic form
a.	$5^2 = 25$	$\Leftrightarrow$	$\log_5 25 = 2$
b.	$2^3 = 8$	$\Leftrightarrow$	$\log_2 8 = 3$ ∎

Example 3   Change each of the following to exponential form:

	Logarithmic form		Exponential form
a.	$\log_4 16 = 2$	$\Leftrightarrow$	$4^2 = 16$
b.	$\log_{25} 5 = \dfrac{1}{2}$	$\Leftrightarrow$	$25^{1/2} = 5$
c.	$\log_{10} 10{,}000 = 4$	$\Leftrightarrow$	$10^4 = 10{,}000$
d.	$\log_{10} 0.01 = -2$	$\Leftrightarrow$	$10^{-2} = 0.01$ ∎

EXERCISES 11.2A

Set I   In Exercises 1–12, write each equation in logarithmic form.

1. $3^2 = 9$ **2.** $4^3 = 64$ **3.** $10^3 = 1{,}000$

4. $10^5 = 100{,}000$ **5.** $2^4 = 16$ **6.** $4^2 = 16$

7. $3^{-2} = \dfrac{1}{9}$ **8.** $2^{-3} = \dfrac{1}{8}$ **9.** $12^0 = 1$

10. $8^0 = 1$ **11.** $16^{1/2} = 4$ **12.** $8^{1/3} = 2$

In Exercises 13–24, write each equation in exponential form.

13. $\log_8 64 = 2$ **14.** $\log_2 32 = 5$ **15.** $\log_7 49 = 2$

16. $\log_4 64 = 3$ **17.** $\log_5 1 = 0$ **18.** $\log_6 1 = 0$

19. $\log_9 3 = \dfrac{1}{2}$ **20.** $\log_8 2 = \dfrac{1}{3}$ **21.** $\log_{10} 100 = 2$

22. $\log_{10} 1{,}000 = 3$ **23.** $\log_{10} 0.001 = -3$ **24.** $\log_{10} 0.01 = -2$

Set II   In Exercises 1–12, write each equation in logarithmic form.

1. $2^3 = 8$ **2.** $10^4 = 10{,}000$ **3.** $4^{-2} = \dfrac{1}{16}$

4. $5^0 = 1$ **5.** $4^{1/2} = 2$ **6.** $3^4 = 81$

7. $5^2 = 25$ **8.** $3^{-3} = \dfrac{1}{27}$ **9.** $6^{-3} = \dfrac{1}{216}$

10. $17^0 = 1$ **11.** $64^{1/3} = 4$ **12.** $2^5 = 32$

In Exercises 13–24, write each equation in exponential form.

13. $\log_4 64 = 3$ **14.** $\log_{16} 4 = \dfrac{1}{2}$ **15.** $\log_3 1 = 0$

16. $\log_7 7 = 1$ **17.** $\log_{10} 100{,}000 = 5$ **18.** $\log_b a = c$

19. $\log_2 64 = 6$ **20.** $\log_7 1 = 0$ **21.** $\log_6 36 = 2$

22. $\log_{13} 13 = 1$ **23.** $\log_{10} 0.0001 = -4$ **24.** $\log_{16} 2 = \dfrac{1}{4}$

11.2B Solving Simple Logarithmic Equations and Evaluating Logarithms

We can sometimes solve a logarithmic equation by rewriting the equation in exponential form and then solving the exponential equation.

Example 4 Solve for b: $\log_b 64 = 3$.

Logarithmic form		*Exponential form*
$\log_b 64 = 3$	$\Leftrightarrow$	$b^3 = 64$

If $b^3 = 64$, $b = \sqrt[3]{64} = 4$. Therefore, $b = 4$. ■

Example 5 Solve for N: $\log_2 N = 4$.

Logarithmic form		*Exponential form*
$\log_2 N = 4$	$\Leftrightarrow$	$2^4 = N$

If $N = 2^4$, then $N = 16$. ■

Example 6 Solve for x: $\log_2 32 = x$.

Logarithmic form		*Exponential form*
$\log_2 32 = x$	$\Leftrightarrow$	$2^x = 32$

We know that $32 = 2^5$. If $2^x = 2^5$, then by Rule 11.1, $x = 5$. ■

It is also possible to *evaluate* certain logarithms as follows: (1) let the logarithmic expression equal x, (2) rewrite the logarithmic equation in exponential form, and (3) solve the exponential equation for x.

Example 7 Find $\log_{10} 1{,}000$.

	Logarithmic form		*Exponential form*
Let	$x = \log_{10} 1{,}000$	$\Leftrightarrow$	$10^x = 1{,}000 = 10^3$
			$x = 3$

Therefore, $\log_{10} 1{,}000 = 3$. ■

Example 8   Find $\log_8 4$.

	Logarithmic form		*Exponential form*	
Let	$x = \log_8 4$	$\Leftrightarrow$	$8^x = 4$	
			$(2^3)^x = 2^2$	Write 8 and 4 as powers of 2
			$2^{3x} = 2^2$	
			$3x = 2$	Rule 11.1
			$x = \dfrac{2}{3}$	

Therefore, $\log_8 4 = \dfrac{2}{3}$. ■

Example 9   Find $\log_7\left(\dfrac{1}{49}\right)$.

	Logarithmic form		*Exponential form*
Let	$x = \log_7\left(\dfrac{1}{49}\right)$	$\Leftrightarrow$	$7^x = \dfrac{1}{49} = \dfrac{1}{7^2} = 7^{-2}$
			$x = -2$ Rule 11.1

Therefore, $\log_7\left(\dfrac{1}{49}\right) = -2$. ■

NOTE   The logarithm of a positive number can be negative, but, as was mentioned previously, the logarithm of a *negative* number is *complex* and is not discussed in this book. ☑

Example 10   Find $\log_{10} 0$.

	Logarithmic form		*Exponential form*
Let	$x = \log_{10} 0$	$\Leftrightarrow$	$10^x = 0$
			No solution because no value of x makes $10^x = 0$

Therefore, $\log_{10} 0$ does not exist. ■

The result in Example 10 can be generalized as follows:

The logarithm of 0 *to any base b* $(b > 0, b \neq 1)$ *does not exist.*

EXERCISES 11.2B

Set I   In Exercises 1–18, find the value of the unknown b, N, or x.

1. $\log_5 N = 2$ **2.** $\log_2 N = 5$ **3.** $\log_3 9 = x$

4. $\log_2 16 = x$ **5.** $\log_b 27 = 3$ **6.** $\log_b 81 = 4$

7. $\log_5 125 = x$ **8.** $\log_3 81 = x$ **9.** $\log_{10} 10^{-4} = x$

10. $\log_{10} 10^{-3} = x$ **11.** $\log_{3/2} N = 2$ **12.** $\log_{5/3} N = 3$

13. $\log_9\left(\dfrac{1}{3}\right) = x$ **14.** $\log_8\left(\dfrac{1}{64}\right) = x$ **15.** $\log_b 8 = 1.5$

16. $\log_b 125 = 1.5$ **17.** $\log_2 N = -2$ **18.** $\log_{10} N = -2$

In Exercises 19–30, find the value of each logarithm.

19. $\log_5 25$ **20.** $\log_2 16$ **21.** $\log_{10} 10{,}000$ **22.** $\log_{10} 100{,}000$

23. $\log_4 8$ **24.** $\log_{27} 9$ **25.** $\log_3 3^4$ **26.** $\log_2 2^5$

27. $\log_{16} 16$ **28.** $\log_{20} 20$ **29.** $\log_8 1$ **30.** $\log_7 1$

Set II   In Exercises 1–18, find the value of the unknown b, N, or x.

1. $\log_{25} N = 1.5$ **2.** $\log_b 9 = \dfrac{2}{3}$ **3.** $\log_{16} 32 = x$

4. $\log_{16} N = \dfrac{5}{4}$ **5.** $\log_4 8 = x$ **6.** $\log_{625} N = 0.5$

7. $\log_b\left(\dfrac{1}{2}\right) = -\dfrac{1}{3}$ **8.** $\log_b\left(\dfrac{27}{8}\right) = 3$ **9.** $\log_b 32 = \dfrac{5}{3}$

10. $\log_8 4 = x$ **11.** $\log_{1/2} N = 2$ **12.** $\log_b 32 = 5$

13. $\log_{25}\left(\dfrac{1}{5}\right) = x$ **14.** $\log_{3/4} N = -1$ **15.** $\log_b\left(\dfrac{1}{6}\right) = -1$

16. $\log_{27} 3 = x$ **17.** $\log_4 N = 0$ **18.** $\log_{25} 5 = x$

In Exercises 19–30, find the value of each logarithm.

19. $\log_4 64$ **20.** $\log_{13} 13$ **21.** $\log_4 1$ **22.** $\log_{64} 8$

23. $\log_9 27$ **24.** $\log_5 1$ **25.** $\log_{81} 3$ **26.** $\log_7 7^8$

27. $\log_{16} 4$ **28.** $\log_{16} 8$ **29.** $\log_3 1$ **30.** $\log_{49} 7$

11.3 Rules of Logarithms

Since logarithms are exponents, we can derive the rules of logarithms from the rules of exponents. We will develop several rules of logarithms by using the techniques shown in Section 11.2.

RULE 11.5

If $b > 0$ and $b \neq 1$, then the logarithm of b to the base b equals 1.

$$\log_b b = 1$$

Proof: Let $x = \log_b b$. Then $b^x = b$. We know that $b = b^1$; therefore, $b^x = b^1$. If $b^x = b^1$, $x = 1$ (by Rule 11.1). Therefore, $\log_b b = 1$.

Example 1   Find $\log_6 6$.

By Rule 11.5, $\log_6 6 = 1$.   ∎

RULE 11.6

The logarithm of 1 to any base b ($b > 0, b \neq 1$) equals 0.

$$\log_b 1 = 0$$

Proof: Let $x = \log_b 1$. Then $b^x = 1$. We know that $b^0 = 1$; therefore, $b^x = b^0$. If $b^x = b^0$, $x = 0$ (by Rule 11.1). Therefore, $\log_b 1 = 0$.

Example 2   Find $\log_5 1$.

By Rule 11.6, $\log_5 1 = 0$.   ∎

RULE 11.7

$$\log_b MN = \log_b M + \log_b N$$

Proof: Let

$$x = \log_b M \Leftrightarrow b^x = M$$

$$y = \log_b N \Leftrightarrow b^y = N$$

Then

$$MN = b^x b^y = b^{x+y} \Leftrightarrow \log_b MN = x + y$$

but

$$x + y = \log_b M + \log_b N$$

Therefore, $\log_b MN = \log_b M + \log_b N$

NOTE $\log_b MN = \log_b(MN)$, *not* $(\log_b M)N$.   ☑

A WORD OF CAUTION   A common mistake students make is to think that

$$\log_b(M + N) = \log_b M + \log_b N \qquad \text{Incorrect}$$

Since $M + N \neq MN$, $\log_b(M + N) \neq \log_b MN$. Then, since $\log_b MN = \log_b M + \log_b N$, $\log_b(M + N) \neq \log_b M + \log_b N$. WARNING: $\log_b(M + N)$ *cannot* be rewritten as a sum of terms.   ☑

RULE 11.8

$$\log_b\left(\frac{M}{N}\right) = \log_b M - \log_b N$$

Proof: Let $\qquad x = \log_b M \Leftrightarrow b^x = M$

$$y = \log_b N \Leftrightarrow b^y = N$$

Then $\qquad \dfrac{M}{N} = \dfrac{b^x}{b^y} = b^{x-y} \Leftrightarrow \log_b \dfrac{M}{N} = x - y$

but $\qquad x - y = \log_b M - \log_b N$

Therefore, $\log_b\left(\dfrac{M}{N}\right) = \log_b M - \log_b N$.

A WORD OF CAUTION $\quad \log_b(M - N) \neq \log_b M - \log_b N$.
WARNING: $\log_b(M - N)$ *cannot* be rewritten as a difference of two terms. ☑

A WORD OF CAUTION $\quad \log_b \dfrac{M}{N} \neq \dfrac{\log_b M}{\log_b N}$. The rule is $\log_b \dfrac{M}{N} = \log_b M - \log_b N$.

☑

RULE 11.9

$$\log_b N^p = p \log_b N$$

Proof: Let $\qquad y = \log_b N \Leftrightarrow b^y = N$

Then $\qquad N^p = (b^y)^p = b^{yp} \Leftrightarrow \log_b N^p = yp = py$

but $\qquad py = p \log_b N$

Therefore, $\log_b N^p = p \log_b N$.

The rules of logarithms can be summarized as follows:

THE RULES OF LOGARITHMS

11.3 If $M = N$, then $\log_b M = \log_b N$.

11.4 If $\log_b M = \log_b N$, then $M = N$.

11.5 $\log_b b = 1$

11.6 $\log_b 1 = 0$

11.7 $\log_b MN = \log_b M + \log_b N$

11.8 $\log_b\left(\dfrac{M}{N}\right) = \log_b M - \log_b N$

11.9 $\log_b N^p = p \log_b N$

where $\begin{cases} M \text{ and } N \text{ are positive real numbers} \\ b > 0, b \neq 1 \\ p \text{ is any real number} \end{cases}$

A WORD OF CAUTION   You must be careful about the use of parentheses, as usual; $\log_b(M + N) \neq \log_b M + N$.   ☑

Example 3   Transforming logarithmic expressions by using the rules of logarithms:

a. $\log_{10}(56)(107) = \log_{10} 56 + \log_{10} 107$ Rule 11.7

b. $\log_{10}\left(\dfrac{275}{89}\right) = \log_{10} 275 - \log_{10} 89$ Rule 11.8

c. $\log_{10}(37)^2 = 2 \log_{10} 37$ Rule 11.9

d. $\log_{10} \sqrt{5} = \log_{10} 5^{1/2} = \dfrac{1}{2} \log_{10} 5$ Rule 11.9

e. $\log_{10}\left[\dfrac{(57)(23)}{101}\right] = \log_{10}(57)(23) - \log_{10} 101$ Rule 11.8

$\qquad = \log_{10} 57 + \log_{10} 23 - \log_{10} 101$ Rule 11.7

f. $\log_{10}\left[\dfrac{(49)(19)^3}{(1.04)^7}\right] = \log_{10}(49)(19)^3 - \log_{10}(1.04)^7$ Rule 11.8

$\qquad = \log_{10} 49 + \log_{10}(19)^3 - \log_{10}(1.04)^7$ Rule 11.7

$\qquad = \log_{10} 49 + 3 \log_{10} 19 - 7 \log_{10} 1.04$ Rule 11.9

g. $\log_{10}\left(\dfrac{\sqrt[5]{21.4}}{(3.5)^4}\right) = \log_{10}(21.4)^{1/5} - \log_{10}(3.5)^4$ Rule 11.8

$\qquad = \dfrac{1}{5} \log_{10} 21.4 - 4 \log_{10} 3.5$ Rule 11.9   ∎

Example 4   Given $\begin{cases} \log_{10} 2 = 0.301 \\ \log_{10} 3 = 0.477 \end{cases}$ *, find:

a. $\log_{10} 6 = \log_{10}(2)(3) = \log_{10} 2 + \log_{10} 3$ Rule 11.7

$\qquad = 0.301 + 0.477 = 0.778$

b. $\log_{10} 1.5 = \log_{10}\left(\dfrac{3}{2}\right) = \log_{10} 3 - \log_{10} 2$ Rule 11.8

$\qquad = 0.477 - 0.301 = 0.176$

c. $\log_{10} 8 = \log_{10} 2^3 = 3 \log_{10} 2$ Rule 11.9

$\qquad = 3(0.301) = 0.903$

d. $\log_{10} \sqrt{3} = \log_{10} 3^{1/2} = \dfrac{1}{2} \log_{10} 3$ Rule 11.9

$\qquad = \dfrac{1}{2}(0.477) = 0.2385$

e. $\log_{10} 5 = \log_{10}\left(\dfrac{10}{2}\right) = \log_{10} 10 - \log_{10} 2$ Rule 11.8

$\qquad = 1 - 0.301 = 0.699$ ∎

The rules of logarithms can be used to simplify some algebraic expressions, as in Example 5.

---

* The methods for finding that $\log_{10} 2 = 0.301$ and $\log_{10} 3 = 0.477$ are shown in Section 11.4 and in Appendix B.

Example 5   a. $\log_b 5x + 2 \log_b x = \log_b 5x + \log_b x^2$ Rule 11.9

$$= \log_b[(5x)(x^2)]$$ Rule 11.7

$$= \log_b 5x^3$$

b. $\dfrac{1}{2} \log_b x - 4 \log_b y = \log_b x^{1/2} - \log_b y^4$ Rule 11.9

$$= \log_b\!\left(\dfrac{\sqrt{x}}{y^4}\right)$$ Rule 11.8 ■

EXERCISES 11.3

Set I   In Exercises 1–10, transform each expression by using the rules of logarithms, as was done in Example 3.

1. $\log_{10}(31)(7)$ **2.** $\log_{10}(17)(29)$ **3.** $\log_{10}\!\left(\dfrac{41}{13}\right)$

4. $\log_{10}\!\left(\dfrac{19}{23}\right)$ **5.** $\log_{10}(19)^3$ **6.** $\log_{10}(7)^4$

7. $\log_{10} \sqrt[5]{75}$ **8.** $\log_{10} \sqrt[4]{38}$

9. $\log_{10}\!\left[\dfrac{35\sqrt{73}}{(1.06)^8}\right]$ **10.** $\log_{10}\!\left[\dfrac{27\sqrt{31}}{(1.03)^{10}}\right]$

In Exercises 11–20, find the value of each logarithm, given that $\log_{10} 2 = 0.301$, $\log_{10} 3 = 0.477$, and $\log_{10} 7 = 0.845$. (Remember, $\log_{10} 10 = 1$.)

11. $\log_{10} 14$ **12.** $\log_{10} 21$ **13.** $\log_{10}\!\left(\dfrac{9}{7}\right)$

14. $\log_{10}\!\left(\dfrac{7}{4}\right)$ **15.** $\log_{10} \sqrt{27}$ **16.** $\log_{10} \sqrt{8}$

17. $\log_{10}(36)^2$ **18.** $\log_{10}(98)^2$

19. $\log_{10} 6{,}000$ **20.** $\log_{10} 1{,}400$

In Exercises 21–30, write each expression as a single logarithm and simplify.

21. $\log_b x + \log_b y$ **22.** $4 \log_b x + 2 \log_b y$

23. $2 \log_b x - 3 \log_b y$ **24.** $\dfrac{1}{2} \log_b x^4$

25. $3(\log_b x - 2 \log_b y)$ **26.** $\dfrac{1}{3} \log_b y^3$

27. $\log_b(x^2 - y^2) - 3 \log_b(x + y)$ **28.** $\log_b(x^2 - z^2) - \log_b(x - z)$

29. $2 \log_b 2xy - \log_b 3xy^2 + \log_b 3x$ **30.** $2 \log_b 3xy - \log_b 6x^2y^2 + \log_b 2y^2$

Set II   In Exercises 1–10, transform each expression by using the rules of logarithms, as was done in Example 3.

1. $\log_{10}(27)(11)$ **2.** $\log_{10}(8)(12)(4)$

3. $\log_{10}\!\left(\dfrac{5}{14}\right)$ **4.** $\log_{10}\!\left(\dfrac{83}{7}\right)$

5. $\log_{10}(24)^5$

6. $\log_{10}(18)^{-4}$

7. $\log_{10}\left[\dfrac{(17)(31)}{29}\right]$

8. $\log_{10}\left[\dfrac{(7)(11)}{13}\right]$

9. $\log_{10}\left[\dfrac{53}{(11)(19)^2}\right]$

10. $\log_{10}\left[\dfrac{29}{(31)^3(47)}\right]$

In Exercises 11–20, find the value of each logarithm, given that $\log_{10} 2 = 0.301$, $\log_{10} 3 = 0.477$, and $\log_{10} 7 = 0.845$. (Remember, $\log_{10} 10 = 1$.)

11. $\log_{10} 40$

12. $\log_{10} 90$

13. $\log_{10} \sqrt[4]{3}$

14. $\log_{10} \sqrt[5]{7}$

15. $\log_{10} 7^3$

16. $\log_{10} 32$

17. $\log_{10} \sqrt{14}$

18. $\log_{10} \dfrac{3}{7}$

19. $\log_{10} \dfrac{20}{3}$

20. $\log_{10} 8^5$

In Exercises 21–30, write each expression as a single logarithm and simplify.

21. $\log_b x - \log_b y$

22. $2(3 \log_b x - \log_b y)$

23. $\dfrac{1}{2} \log_b(x - a) - \dfrac{1}{2} \log_b(x + a)$

24. $3 \log_b v + 2 \log_b v^2 - \log_b v$

25. $\log_b\left(\dfrac{6}{7}\right) - \log_b\left(\dfrac{27}{4}\right) + \log_b\left(\dfrac{21}{16}\right)$

26. $\log_b x - \log_b y - \log_b z$

27. $5 \log_b xy^3 - \log_b x^2 y$

28. $2 \log_b x - 3 \log_b y + \log_b z$

29. $2 \log_b x + 2 \log_b y$

30. $\log_b(x^3 + y^3) - \log_b(x + y)$

11.4 Logarithms and the Calculator*

11.4A Finding Logarithms Using a Calculator

There are two systems of logarithms in widespread use:

1. Common logarithms (base 10)

2. Natural logarithms (base $e = 2.71828\ldots$)

When the logarithm of a number x is written as log x, *without* a base being specified, the base of the logarithm is understood to be 10. For example, log 8 is understood to mean $\log_{10} 8$. A special abbreviation is used for *natural* logarithms, also: ln. For example, ln 6 means $\log_e 6$.

Most scientific calculators use symbols that reflect these abbreviations. Most have a key marked $\boxed{\log}$ or $\boxed{\log x}$ that is used for common logarithms and a key marked $\boxed{\ln}$ or $\boxed{\ln x}$ for natural logarithms.

---

* Note to the Instructor: If you prefer your students to use tables, use Appendix B in place of this section.

Example 1   Using a calculator, find the logarithms of the given numbers. Round off answers to four decimal places.

a. log 2

Press these keys in this order: $\boxed{2}$ $\boxed{\log}$. When we round off the answer, we see that log 2 = 0.3010.

NOTE   Even though the logarithms found by using a calculator (or tables) are almost all approximations, it is customary to use an equal sign (rather than $\doteq$) in a logarithmic statement. $\boxed{\checkmark}$

b. log 20

Press these keys in this order: $\boxed{2}$ $\boxed{0}$ $\boxed{\log}$. When we round off the answer, we see that log 20 = 1.3010.

c. log 200

Press these keys in this order: $\boxed{2}$ $\boxed{0}$ $\boxed{0}$ $\boxed{\log}$; log 200 = 2.3010.

d. log 0.002

Press these keys in this order: $\boxed{\cdot}$ $\boxed{0}$ $\boxed{0}$ $\boxed{2}$ $\boxed{\log}$; log 0.002 = -2.6990.

e. 3 + log 0.002

3 + log 0.002 = 3 + (-2.6990) = 0.3010.

f. log 0

When we press $\boxed{0}$ $\boxed{\log}$, we get an error message. This is to be expected, since $\log_{10} 0$ does not exist.

g. log (-3)

When we press $\boxed{3}$ $\boxed{+/-}$ $\boxed{\log}$, we get an error message, because $\log_{10} (-3)$ is not a real number.   ∎

Example 2   Using a calculator, find the logarithms of the given numbers. Round off answers to four decimal places.

a. ln 2

Press these keys in this order: $\boxed{2}$ $\boxed{\ln}$. When we round off, we see that ln 2 = 0.6931.

b. ln 20

Press these keys in this order: $\boxed{2}$ $\boxed{0}$ $\boxed{\ln}$; ln 20 = 2.9957.

c. ln 0.002

When we press $\boxed{\cdot}$ $\boxed{0}$ $\boxed{0}$ $\boxed{2}$ $\boxed{\ln}$, we see that ln 0.002 = -6.2146.

d. ln 0

When we press $\boxed{0}$ $\boxed{\ln}$, we get an error message, because ln 0 does not exist.

e. ln (-5)

When we press $\boxed{5}$ $\boxed{+/-}$ $\boxed{\ln}$, we get an error message, because ln (-5) is not a real number.   ∎

EXERCISES 11.4A

Set I Find the logarithm of each given number, using a calculator. Round off all answers to four decimal places.

1. a. log 3   b. log 3,000   c. log 30

    d. ln 3   e. ln 3,000   f. ln 30

2. a. log 10   b. log 100   c. log 100,000

    d. ln 10   e. ln 100   f. ln 100,000

3. a. log 0.1   b. log 0.01   c. log 0.001

    d. ln 0.1   e. ln 0.01   f. ln 0.001

4. a. log 0.3   b. log 0.0003   c. log 0.000003

    d. ln 0.3   e. ln 0.0003   f. ln 0.000003

Set II Find the logarithm of each given number, using a calculator. Round off all answers to four decimal places.

1. a. log 5   b. log 5,000,000   c. log 500

    d. ln 5   e. ln 5,000,000   f. ln 500

2. a. log 0.5   b. log 0.000005   c. log 0.005

    d. ln 0.5   e. ln 0.000005   f. ln 0.005

3. a. log 12   b. log 120,000   c. log 0.00012

    d. ln 12   e. ln 120,000   f. ln 0.00012

4. a. log 0.16   b. log 0.0016   c. log 0.000016

    d. ln 0.16   e. ln 0.0016   f. ln 0.000016

11.4B Finding Antilogarithms Using a Calculator

Significant Digits

When we use a calculator to find a logarithm or to find a number whose logarithm is known, we almost never get an exact answer. For that reason, we will give here a brief explanation of the number of *significant digits* in a number.

To determine the number of significant digits in a number, read from left to right and start counting from the *first nonzero* digit. If the number does not have a decimal point, or if it has a decimal point but no digits to the right of the decimal point, *stop counting* when all the remaining digits are zeros. If the number has a decimal point and one or more digits to the right of the decimal point, start counting with the first nonzero digit and continue counting to the end of the number.

Example 3 Find the number of significant digits in each number.

a. 6,080,000

6,080,000 has 3 significant digits.

b. 300

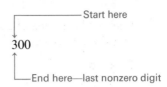

300 has 1 significant digit.

c. 300.00

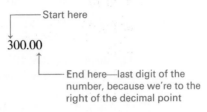

300.00 has 5 significant digits.

d. 0.00030

0.00030 has 2 significant digits. ■

Antilogarithms

In Section 11.4A, we discussed finding the logarithm of a given number by using a calculator. In this section, we discuss the inverse operation: finding the *number* when its logarithm is known.

If the logarithm of N is L, then N is the **antilogarithm** of L. In symbols,

If	$\log N = L$
then	$N = \text{antilog } L$

If a base is not mentioned, it is understood to be 10. Problems in which we need to find an antilogarithm can be worded in either of two ways:

Find antilog 3.6263. ⎫ Both statements

Find N if $\log N = 3.6263$. ⎬ mean the same thing

Example 4   Find the (common) antilogs and round off all answers to three significant digits:

a. antilog 3.6263

Press these keys in this order:

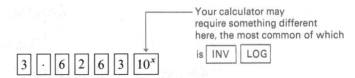

The display shows 4229.6068. When we round this off to three significant digits, we get

$$\text{antilog } 3.6263 = 4{,}230$$

NOTE   The statement "antilog $3.6263 = 4{,}230$" is equivalent to the statement "$\log 4{,}230 = 3.6263$." ✓

b. Find N if $\log N = -1.1864$.

Press these keys in this order:

$$\boxed{1}\ \boxed{\cdot}\ \boxed{1}\ \boxed{8}\ \boxed{6}\ \boxed{4}\ \boxed{+/-}\ \boxed{10^x}$$

The display is 0.0651028, which rounds off to 0.0651. Therefore, $N = 0.0651$. (The problem could have been stated this way: Find antilog (-1.1864).)   ■

Example 5   Find N if $\ln N = 0.4886$. Round off the answer to three significant digits.

Note that this time we've been given the *natural* log of N, rather than the common log of N. Therefore, we press these keys in this order:

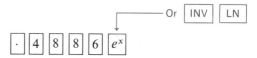

The display is 1.6300326, which rounds off to 1.63.   ■

EXERCISES 11.4B

Set I   In Exercises 1–4, find the common antilogarithms. Round off answers to three significant digits.

1. antilog 0.3711

2. antilog 0.6085

3. antilog (-0.0701)

4. antilog (-0.1221)

In Exercises 5–12, find N. Round off answers to three significant digits.

5. $\log N = 3.4082$

6. $\log N = 1.8136$

7. $\log N = -2.5143$

8. $\log N = -3.3883$

9. $\ln N = 2.7183$

10. $\ln N = 5.4366$

11. $\ln N = -2.5849$

12. $\ln N = -5.1534$

Set II   In Exercises 1–4, find the common antilogarithms. Round off answers to three significant digits.

1. antilog 1.6990

2. antilog (-1.6990)

3. antilog 4.7275

4. antilog (-2.2381)

In Exercises 5–12, find N. Round off answers to three significant digits.

5. $\log N = 2.5119$

6. $\log N = 4.5465$

7. $\log N = -2.6271$

8. $\log N = -3.2652$

9. $\ln N = 3.0204$

10. $\ln N = 5.8435$

11. $\ln N = -2.7790$

12. $\ln N = -7.0436$

11.5 Exponential and Logarithmic Equations

In this section, we discuss the application of logarithms and the rules of logarithms in the solution of exponential and logarithmic equations. Although calculating with logarithms is being replaced by the use of hand calculators and computers, the use of logarithms and the rules of logarithms will continue to be important in the solution of exponential and logarithmic equations.

Exponential Equations

An **exponential equation** is an equation in which the unknown appears in one or more exponents.

Example 1 Examples of exponential equations:

a. $3^x = 17$ b. $(5.26)^{x+1} = 75.4$ ■

It is possible to solve some exponential equations by expressing both sides as powers of the same base.

Example 2 Solve $16^x = \frac{1}{4}$.

$$16^x = \frac{1}{4}$$

$$\left.\begin{array}{c} (2^4)^x = \dfrac{1}{2^2} \\[2mm] 2^{4x} = 2^{-2} \end{array}\right\} \quad \text{Express both sides as powers of the same base, 2}$$

Therefore, $4x = -2$

$$x = -\frac{2}{4} = -\frac{1}{2} \quad ■$$

When both sides of an exponential equation *cannot* be expressed as powers of the same base, we solve the equation by taking logarithms of both sides. Rule 11.3 justifies our doing this. Most exponential equations are of this type. We can take either the *common* logarithm or the *natural* logarithm of both sides.

Example 3 Solve $3^x = 17$. Round off the answer to four significant digits.

If we take the *common* logarithm of both sides, we have

$$\log 3^x = \log 17$$

$$x \log 3 = \log 17 \qquad \text{Rule 11.9}$$

$$x = \frac{\log 17}{\log 3} = \frac{1.2304}{0.4771} \doteq 2.579$$

This division could be done by logarithms

573

A WORD OF CAUTION A common mistake students make is to think that

$$\frac{\log 17}{\log 3} = \log\left(\frac{17}{3}\right) = \log 17 - \log 3 \qquad \text{Incorrect}$$

Actually, $\dfrac{\log 17}{\log 3} = \dfrac{1.2304}{0.4771} \doteq 2.579 \longleftarrow$ ─── Unequal ─┐

whereas $\log\left(\dfrac{17}{3}\right) = \log 17 - \log 3$

$$= 1.2304 - 0.4771 = 0.7533 \longleftarrow$$

$\boxed{\checkmark}$

If we take the *natural* logarithm of both sides, we have

$$3^x = 17$$

$$\ln 3^x = \ln 17$$

$$x \ln 3 = \ln 17$$

$$x = \frac{\ln 17}{\ln 3} = \frac{2.8332}{1.0986} \doteq 2.579$$

Note that we obtained the same answer whether we took the *natural* logarithm or the *common* logarithm of both sides. ■

Example 4 Solve $e^{4x} = 7$. Round off the answer to four significant digits.

We could take the common logarithm of both sides of the equation, but because the base of the exponential function is e, we will instead take the natural logarithm of both sides:

$$e^{4x} = 7$$

$$\ln e^{4x} = \ln 7$$

$$4x \ln e = \ln 7 \qquad \ln e = \log_e e = 1$$

Therefore,

$$4x = \ln 7$$

$$x = \frac{\ln 7}{4} = \frac{1.9459101}{4} \doteq 0.4865$$

A completely different method can be used. We can rewrite the given exponential equation in logarithmic form:

$$e^{4x} = 7 \Leftrightarrow \log_e 7 = 4x$$

$$\ln 7 = 4x$$

$$x = \frac{\ln 7}{4} \doteq 0.4865 \qquad \blacksquare$$

Logarithmic Equations

A **logarithmic equation** is an equation in which the unknown appears in the argument of a logarithm. Recall from Section 11.1B that in the expression $\log_b x$, x is called the *argument* of the logarithmic function.

Example 5 Examples of logarithmic equations:

a. $\ln (2x + 1) + \ln 5 = \ln (x + 6)$

b. $\log x + \log (11 - x) = 1$ ∎

Logarithmic equations can be solved by using the rules of logarithms to simplify both sides of the equation and then using Rule 11.4; if $\log_b M = \log_b N$, then $M = N$.

Example 6 Solve $\ln(2x + 1) + \ln 5 = \ln(x + 6)$.

$$\ln(2x + 1) + \ln 5 = \ln(x + 6)$$
$$\ln(2x + 1)(5) = \ln(x + 6) \qquad \text{Rule 11.7}$$
$$(2x + 1)(5) = x + 6 \qquad \text{Rule 11.4}$$
$$10x + 5 = x + 6$$
$$9x = 1$$
$$x = \frac{1}{9}$$

Check

$$\ln(2x + 1) + \ln 5 = \ln(x + 6)$$
$$\ln\left[2\left(\frac{1}{9}\right) + 1\right] + \ln 5 \stackrel{?}{=} \ln\left(\frac{1}{9} + 6\right)$$
$$\ln\left(\frac{11}{9}\right) + \ln 5 \stackrel{?}{=} \ln\left(\frac{55}{9}\right)$$
$$\ln\left(\frac{11}{9}\right)(5) \stackrel{?}{=} \ln\left(\frac{55}{9}\right)$$
$$\ln\left(\frac{55}{9}\right) = \ln\left(\frac{55}{9}\right) \qquad \text{True}$$

Therefore, $x = \frac{1}{9}$ is a solution. ∎

Apparent solutions to logarithmic equations *must* be checked, because it is possible to obtain extraneous roots (see Example 7).

Example 7 Solve $\log(x - 1) + \log(x + 2) = \log 4$.

$$\log(x - 1) + \log(x + 2) = \log 4$$
$$\log(x - 1)(x + 2) = \log 4$$
$$(x - 1)(x + 2) = 4 \qquad \text{Rule 11.4}$$
$$x^2 + x - 2 = 4$$
$$x^2 + x - 6 = 0$$
$$(x - 2)(x + 3) = 0$$
$$x - 2 = 0 \text{ or } x + 3 = 0$$
$$x = 2 \text{ or } \qquad x = -3$$

Check for $x = 2$

$$\log(x - 1) + \log(x + 2) = \log 4$$

$$\log(2 - 1) + \log(2 + 2) \overset{?}{=} \log 4$$

$$\log 1 + \log 4 \overset{?}{=} \log 4$$

$$0 + \log 4 \overset{?}{=} \log 4$$

$$\log 4 = \log 4 \qquad \text{True}$$

Therefore, $x = 2$ *is* a solution.

Check for $x = -3$

$$\log(x - 1) + \log(x + 2) = \log 4$$

$$\log(-3 - 1) + \log(-3 + 2) \overset{?}{=} \log 4$$

$$\log(-4) + \log(-1) \neq \log 4$$

Logarithms of negative numbers are not real numbers

Therefore, $x = -3$ *is not* a solution (-3 is an extraneous root). ∎

Example 8   Solve $\log(2x + 3) - \log(x - 1) = 0.73$.

We must first write 0.73 as a logarithm; that is, we must find antilog 0.73. Antilog $0.73 = 5.370318 \doteq 5.370$. Therefore, $0.73 = \log 5.370$. We then have

$$\log(2x + 3) - \log(x - 1) = \log 5.370$$

$$\log\left(\frac{2x + 3}{x - 1}\right) = \log 5.370$$

$$\frac{2x + 3}{x - 1} = 5.370 \qquad \text{Rule 11.4}$$

$$2x + 3 = 5.370(x - 1)$$

$$2x + 3 = 5.370x - 5.370$$

$$8.370 = 3.370x$$

$$\frac{8.370}{3.370} = x$$

$$x \doteq 2.484$$

Check for $x \doteq 2.484$

$$\log(2x + 3) - \log(x - 1) = 0.73$$

$$\log[2(2.484) + 3] - \log[2.484 - 1] \overset{?}{=} 0.73$$

$$\log 7.968 - \log 1.484 \overset{?}{=} 0.73$$

$$0.9013 - 0.1714 \overset{?}{=} 0.73$$

$$0.7299 \doteq 0.73 \qquad \text{True}$$

Therefore, $x \doteq 2.484$ *is* a solution. ∎

EXERCISES 11.5

Set I   In Exercises 1–6, solve by expressing each side as a power of the same base.

1. $27^x = \dfrac{1}{9}$ **2.** $8^x = \dfrac{1}{16}$ **3.** $4^x = \dfrac{1}{8}$

4. $125^x = \dfrac{1}{25}$ **5.** $25^{2x+3} = 5^{x-1}$ **6.** $27^{3x-1} = 9^{x+2}$

In Exercises 7–16, solve by taking the logarithm of both sides of the equation. **Round off the answers to three significant digits.**

7. $2^x = 3$ **8.** $5^x = 4$

9. $e^x = 8$ **10.** $e^x = 20$

11. $(7.43)^{x+1} = 9.55$ **12.** $(5.14)^{x-1} = 7.08$

13. $(8.71)^{2x+1} = 8.57$ **14.** $(9.55)^{3x-1} = 3.09$

15. $e^{3x+4} = 5$ **16.** $3^{2x-1} = 23$

In Exercises 17–26, solve and check each logarithmic equation.

17. $\log(3x - 1) + \log 4 = \log(9x + 2)$

18. $\log(2x - 1) + \log 3 = \log(4x + 1)$

19. $\ln(x + 4) - \ln 3 = \ln(x - 2)$

20. $\ln(2x + 1) - \ln 5 = \ln(x - 1)$

21. $\log(5x + 2) - \log(x - 1) = 0.7782$

22. $\log(8x + 11) - \log(x + 1) = 0.9542$

23. $\log x + \log(7 - x) = \log 10$

24. $\log x + \log(11 - x) = \log 10$

25. $\ln x + \ln(x - 3) = \ln 4$

26. $\ln x + \ln(x + 2) = \ln 8$

Set II   In Exercises 1–6, solve by expressing each side as a power of the same base.

1. $2^{-3x} = \dfrac{1}{8}$ **2.** $9^x = \dfrac{1}{3^{-2}}$ **3.** $5^{3x-2} = 25^x$

4. $4^{3x} = 8$ **5.** $27^{5x} = 9^2$ **6.** $25^x = \dfrac{1}{125}$

In Exercises 7–16, solve by taking the logarithm of both sides of the equation. **Round off the answers to three significant digits.**

7. $3^x = 50$ **8.** $8^x = 17$ **9.** $e^x = 29$ **10.** $e^x = 14$

11. $(4.6)^{x+1} = 100$ **12.** $(34.7)^{2x} = (12.5)^{3x-2}$

13. $(13.5)^{4x-2} = 7.12$ **14.** $(2.03)^{2x-1} = 142$

15. $e^{2x-3} = 60$ **16.** $3^{3x+5} = 25$

In Exercises 17–26, solve and check each logarithmic equation.

17. $\log(x + 4) - \log 10 = \log 6 - \log x$

18. $\log(x - 2) - \log 5 = \log 3 - \log x$

19. $\ln(5x - 7) = \ln(2x - 3) + \ln 3$

20. $\ln x + \ln(x + 4) = \ln 21$

21. $\log(2x + 1) = \log 1 + \log(x + 2)$

22. $2 \log(x + 3) = \log(7x + 1) + \log 2$

23. $\log x = \log(7x + 12) - \log(x + 3)$

24. $\log 2x + \log(x + 2) = \log(12 - x)$

25. $\ln(2x + 3) - \ln(x - 2) = \ln 5$

26. $\ln x + \ln(3x + 8) = \ln 3$

11.6 Word Problems Involving Exponential and Logarithmic Functions

Many applications of exponential and logarithmic functions exist in the real world. The formulas for calculating bacterial growth and radioactive decay contain exponential functions, as do the formulas for calculating compound interest in business. Many formulas from the sciences, including the social sciences, earth science, and astronomy, require the ability to solve exponential and logarithmic equations.

We have selected just a few applications for this section. Listed below are the formulas we will use. In formulas 1–3, P is the amount originally invested, r is the interest rate in decimal form, t is the number of years, A is the amount in the account at the end of t years, and k is the number of times per year the interest is compounded.

1. $A = P(1 + r)^t$ Interest compounded annually

2. $A = P\left(1 + \dfrac{r}{k}\right)^{kt}$ Interest compounded k times a year

3. $A = Pe^{rt}$ Interest compounded continuously ($e \doteq 2.71828$)

4. $y = Ce^{kt}$ Exponential growth of bacteria

   where

       C = the amount initially present
       t = the time
       k = some positive constant (it varies from one bacteria to another)
       y = the amount present after time t

5. $y = Ce^{-kt}$ Radioactive decay

   where

       C = the amount initially present
       t = the time
       k = some positive constant
       y = the amount present after time t

Example 1 $1,000 is invested at $5\frac{1}{4}\%$ interest. Find the amount that will be in the account after ten years if the interest is compounded:

a. annually   b. monthly   c. daily   d. continuously

(Round off answers to the nearest cent.)

Solutions

a. We will use the formula $A = P(1 + r)^t$, letting $P = \$1,000$, $r = 0.0525$ ($5\frac{1}{4}\%$ changed to a decimal), and $t = 10$.

$$A = \$1,000(1 + 0.0525)^{10}$$

$$= \$1,000(1.0525)^{10}$$ On the calculator,
$(1.0525)^{10}$ is $\boxed{1.0525}$ $\boxed{x^y}$ $\boxed{10}$

$$= \$1,000(1.6680960)$$

$$= \$1,668.10 \text{ (to the nearest cent)}$$

b. We will use the formula $A = P\left(1 + \dfrac{r}{k}\right)^{kt}$, letting $P = \$1,000$, $r = 0.0525$, $k = 12$, and $t = 10$.

$$A = \$1,000\left(1 + \frac{0.0525}{12}\right)^{(12)(10)}$$

$$= \$1,000(1 + 0.004375)^{120}$$

$$= \$1,000(1.004375)^{120}$$ On the calculator,
$(1.004375)^{120}$ is $\boxed{1.004375}$ $\boxed{x^y}$ $\boxed{120}$

$$= \$1,000(1.6885242)$$

$$= \$1,688.52$$

c. We will use the same formula as for Example 1b and the same values for P, r, and t; k will be 365.

$$A = \$1,000\left(1 + \frac{0.0525}{365}\right)^{(365)(10)}$$

$$= \$1,000(1 + 0.000143836)^{3650}$$

$$= \$1,000(1.000143836)^{3650}$$

$$= \$1,000(1.6903949)$$

$$= \$1,690.39$$

d. We will use the formula $A = Pe^{rt}$, with P, r, and t the same as in Examples 1a, 1b, and 1c. Therefore,

$$A = \$1,000e^{0.0525(10)}$$

$$= \$1,000e^{0.525}$$ On the calculator,
$e^{0.525}$ is $\boxed{.525}$ $\boxed{e^x}$

$$= \$1,000(1.6904588)$$

$$= \$1,690.46$$

Therefore, the amount in the account at the end of ten years will be $1,668.10 if the interest is compounded annually, $1,688.52 if it is compounded monthly, $1,690.39 if it is compounded daily, and $1,690.46 if it is compounded continuously. ■

Example 2 $1,000 is invested at $5\frac{1}{4}\%$ annual interest, compounded continuously. How long will it take for the money to double? Round off the answer to three significant digits.

We will use the formula $A = Pe^{rt}$. $P = \$1,000$, $r = 0.0525$, and $A = \$2,000$. We must find t. Therefore,

$$\$2,000 = \$1,000e^{0.0525t} \qquad \text{Divide both sides by \$1,000}$$

$$2 = e^{0.0525t}$$

There are two ways to finish the problem:

Method 1	*Method 2*
We can take the natural logarithm of both sides:	We can rewrite the equation in exponential form:

$$\ln 2 = \ln e^{0.0525t}$$

$$0.693147 = 0.0525t(\ln e)$$

$$0.693147 = 0.0525t$$

$$\log_e 2 = 0.0525t$$

$$\ln 2 = 0.0525t$$

$$0.693147 = 0.0525t$$

Then $$\frac{0.693147}{0.0525} = t$$

or $t = 13.2$ years   ∎

Example 3   Suppose a certain culture of bacteria increases according to the formula $y = Ce^{0.04t}$. How many hours will it take for the bacteria to grow from 1,000 to 4,000? Round off the answer to four significant digits.

We will substitute $C = 1,000$ and $y = 4,000$ into the formula $y = Ce^{0.04t}$. Solving for t,

$$4,000 = 1,000e^{0.04t}$$

$$4 = e^{0.04t}$$

Method 1	*Method 2*

$$\ln 4 = \ln e^{0.04t}$$

$$1.3862944 = 0.04t(\ln e)$$

$$1.3862944 = 0.04t$$

$$\log_e 4 = 0.04t$$

$$1.3862944 = 0.04t$$

Then $$t = \frac{1.3862944}{0.04}$$

or $t = 34.66$ hours   ∎

EXERCISES 11.6

Set I   In the exercises below, round off each answer to the nearest cent if it is an amount of money. Otherwise, round it off to four significant digits.

1. $1,250 is invested at $5\frac{1}{2}\%$ annual interest. Find the amount that will be in the account after 20 years if the interest is compounded:

    a. annually   b. monthly   c. daily   d. continuously

2. $2,500 is invested at $5\frac{3}{4}\%$ annual interest. Find the amount that will be in the account after 10 years if the interest is compounded:

    a. annually   b. monthly   c. daily   d. continuously

3. $1,500 is invested at $5\frac{3}{4}\%$ annual interest. How long will it take for the money to grow to $2,000 if the interest is compounded continuously?

4. $2,500 is invested at $5\frac{1}{2}\%$ annual interest. How long will it take for the money to grow to $4,000 if the interest is compounded continuously?

5. It is known that a certain type of bacteria grows according to the formula $y = Ce^{0.035t}$.

    a. How many bacteria will there be after 3 hours if 500 bacteria were present initially?

    b. How many hours will it take for the bacteria count to grow from 500 to 800?

6. It is known that a certain type of bacteria grows according to the formula $y = Ce^{0.025t}$.

    a. How many bacteria will there be after 2 hours if 900 bacteria were present initially?

    b. How many hours will it take for the bacteria count to grow from 900 to 1,600?

7. A certain radioactive material decomposes according to the formula $y = Ce^{-0.3t}$. How many years will it take for 100 g to decompose to 80 g?

8. A certain radioactive material decomposes according to the formula $y = Ce^{-0.4t}$. How many years will it take for 150 g to decompose to 110 g?

Set II   In the exercises below, round off each answer to the nearest cent if it is an amount of money. Otherwise, round it off to four significant digits.

1. $2,000 is invested at $5\frac{1}{4}\%$ annual interest. Find the amount that will be in the account after 8 years if the interest is compounded:

    a. annually   b. monthly   c. daily   d. continuously

2. The formula from physics for measuring sound intensity, N, in decibels is

$N = 10 \log\left(\dfrac{I}{I_0}\right)$, where I_0 is a constant and I is the power of the sound being measured. Find the number of decibels in a sound whose power is 3×10^{-10}, if $I_0 = 10^{-16}$.

3. $2,000 is invested at $5\frac{1}{2}\%$ annual interest. How long will it take for the money to grow to $2,800 if the interest is compounded continuously?

4. In chemistry, the number pH is a measure of the acidity or alkalinity of a solution. If $(H+)$ is the hydronium ion concentration measured in moles per liter, then $pH = -\log(H+)$. Find the pH of a solution with a hydronium ion concentration of 4.0×10^{-3}.

5. It is known that a certain type of bacteria grows according to the formula $y = Ce^{0.04t}$.

    a. How many bacteria will there be after 4 hours if 800 bacteria were present initially?

    b. How many hours will it take for the bacteria count to grow from 800 to 1,100?

6. The magnitude, M, of an earthquake, as measured on the Richter scale, is calculated as follows: $M = \log \dfrac{a}{a_0}$, where a_0 is a constant and a is the amplitude of the seismic wave. If $a_0 = 10^{-3}$, find:

   a. the amplitude of the seismic wave if the magnitude of the earthquake is 6

   b. the amplitude of the seismic wave if the magnitude of the earthquake is 5

7. A certain radioactive material decomposes according to the formula $y = Ce^{-0.3t}$. How many years will it take for 120 g to decompose to 100 g?

8. The formula for finding the monthly payment on a homeowner's mortgage is

$$R = \frac{Ai(1 + i)^n}{(1 + i)^n - 1}$$

   where R = monthly payment
   $\quad i$ = interest rate per month expressed as a decimal
   $\quad n$ = number of months
   $\quad A$ = original amount of mortgage

   Find the monthly payment on a 25-year, \$40,000 loan at 12% interest.

11.7 Change of Base

In some applications, logarithms to a base different from 10 are given. To find such logarithms, we must be able to *change the base* of a logarithm.

Let $x = \log_b N \Leftrightarrow b^x = N$.

Then
$$\log_a b^x = \log_a N \qquad \text{Take logarithms of both sides to the base } a$$

$$x \log_a b = \log_a N \qquad \text{Rule 11.9}$$

$$x = \frac{\log_a N}{\log_a b}$$

Therefore, $\log_b N = \dfrac{\log_a N}{\log_a b}$ because $x = \log_b N$.

RULE 11.10

To find a logarithm with base b,

$$\log_b N = \frac{\log_a N}{\log_a b}$$

Rule 11.10 makes it possible to use any table of logarithms available to find the logarithm of a number to a different base.

Example 1   Find $\log_5 51.7$.

$$\log_b N = \frac{\log_a N}{\log_a b} \qquad \text{Rule 11.10}$$

$$\log_5 51.7 = \frac{\log_{10} 51.7}{\log_{10} 5} \qquad \text{By setting} \begin{cases} b = 5 \\ a = 10 \\ N = 51.7 \end{cases}$$

$$\log_5 51.7 = \frac{1.7135}{0.6990} \doteq 2.451 \quad \blacksquare$$

Example 2   Find $\log_e 51.7$ ($e \doteq 2.7183$).

$$\log_b N = \frac{\log_a N}{\log_a b} \qquad \text{Rule 11.10}$$

$$\log_e 51.7 = \frac{\log_{10} 51.7}{\log_{10} 2.7183} = \frac{1.7135}{0.4343} \doteq 3.945 \quad \blacksquare$$

EXERCISES 11.7

Set I   Find each logarithm.

1. $\log_2 156$ 2. $\log_3 231$ 3. $\log_{12} 7.54$ 4. $\log_{20} 9.75$

5. $\log_e 3.04$ 6. $\log_e 4.08$ 7. $\log_{6.8} 0.507$ 8. $\log_{8.3} 0.0304$

Set II   Find each logarithm.

1. $\log_5 29.8$ 2. $\log_e 53.7$ 3. $\log_{14} 0.842$ 4. $\log_{5.2} 0.926$

5. $\log_e 16.1$ 6. $\log_e 0.076$ 7. $\log_8 12$ 8. $\log_3 0.333$

11.8 Review: 11.1–11.7

Exponential Functions
11.1A

An **exponential function** is a function of the form $y = f(x) = b^x$, where $b > 0$, $b \neq 1$, and $x =$ any real number.

Rules of exponents:

11.1 If $b^x = b^y$, then $x = y$.

11.2 If $a^x = b^x$, then $a = b$.

Logarithmic Functions
11.1B

A **logarithmic function** is a function of the form $y = f(x) = \log_b x$, where $b > 0$, $b \neq 1$, and $x > 0$.

The logarithm of a number x *is the exponent* y *to which the base* b $(b > 0, b \neq 1)$ must be raised to give x. The logarithm of a number can be found either by using a calculator (Section 11.4) or by using tables (Appendix B).

Exponential and
Logarithmic Form
11.2

Logarithmic form	*Exponential form*
$y = \log_b x$	$x = b^y$

Rules of Logarithms
11.3

11.3   If $M = N$, then $\log_b M = \log_b N$.

11.4   If $\log_b M = \log_b N$, then $M = N$.

11.5 $\log_b b = 1$

11.6 $\log_b 1 = 0$

11.7 $\log_b MN = \log_b M + \log_b N$

11.8 $\log_b\left(\dfrac{M}{N}\right) = \log_b M - \log_b N$

11.9 $\log_b N^p = p \log_b N$

11.10 $\log_b N = \dfrac{\log_a N}{\log_a b}$ Change of base (Section 11.7)

Exponential Equations
11.5

An **exponential equation** is an equation in which the unknown appears in one or more exponents.

To solve an exponential equation:

Method I

1. Express both sides as powers of the same base (if possible).

2. Equate the exponents.

3. Solve the resulting equation for the unknown.

Method II

1. Take the logarithm of both sides.

2. Use Rule 11.9 to rewrite the equation with no exponents.

3. Solve the resulting equation for the unknown.

Logarithmic Equations
11.5

A **logarithmic equation** is an equation in which the unknown appears in the argument of a logarithm.

To solve a logarithmic equation:

1. Use the rules of logarithms to write each side as the logarithm of a single expression.

2. Equate the expressions found in step 1.

3. Solve the resulting equation for the unknown.

4. Check apparent solutions in the given logarithmic equation.

Review Exercises 11.8 Set I

1. Write $3^4 = 81$ in logarithmic form.

2. Write $\log_4 0.0625 = -2$ in exponential form.

In Exercises 3–7, find the value of the unknown b, N, or x.

3. $\log_{10} 1{,}000 = x$ **4.** $\log_{10} 0.01 = x$

5. $\log_9 N = \dfrac{3}{2}$ **6.** $\log_b\left(\dfrac{1}{8}\right) = -3$

7. $\log_{10} 145.6 = x$

In Exercises 8–10, write each expression as a single logarithm and simplify.

8. $\dfrac{1}{5} \log x^5 + 3 \log x^4$ **9.** $\log\left(\dfrac{3}{5}\right) + \log\left(\dfrac{5}{3}\right)$

10. $\log x^4 y^4 - \log 6x + \log 3 - 4 \log xy$

In Exercises 11–14, find each logarithm.

11. $\log 25.48$ **12.** $\log 0.0008005$

13. $\ln 0.0342$ **14.** $\ln 5{,}300$

In Exercises 15 and 16, find each antilogarithm.

15. antilog 3.4072 **16.** Find N if $\ln N = 2.4849$.

In Exercises 17 and 18, solve each equation.

17. $81^{x-1} = \dfrac{1}{9}$

18. $\log 2 + \log(3x - 1) = \log(4x + 1)$

19. Find $\log_4 75$.

20. Graph $y = 6^x$ and its inverse logarithmic function on the same set of axes.

21. $2,000$ is invested at 5.8% interest. How long will it take for the money to grow to $2,500$ if the interest is compounded continuously? Round off the answer to two significant digits.

Review Exercises 11.8 Set II

NAME _____

ANSWERS

1. Write $4^2 = 16$ in logarithmic form.

2. Write $\log_{1.3} 1.69 = 2$ in exponential form.

In Exercises 3–7, find the value of the unknown b, N, or x.

3. $\log_{10} 0.001 = x$

4. $\log_{27} N = \dfrac{2}{3}$

5. $\log_b\left(\dfrac{1}{16}\right) = -4$

6. $\log_7 N = 0$

7. $\log_b\left(\dfrac{1}{16}\right) = -2$

In Exercises 8–10, write each expression as a single logarithm and simplify.

8. $\dfrac{1}{4} \log x^4 + 2 \log x^2$

9. $\log\left(\dfrac{14}{3}\right) - \log\left(\dfrac{7}{3}\right)$

10. $\log(x^2 - x - 12) - \log(x - 4)$

1. _____

2. _____

3. _____

4. _____

5. _____

6. _____

7. _____

8. _____

9. _____

10. _____

In Exercises 11–14, find each logarithm correct to four decimal places.

11. log 28.25

12. log 0.0003684

13. ln 0.00235

14. ln 12

In Exercises 15 and 16, find each antilogarithm correct to two decimal places.

15. antilog 2.6551

16. Find N if ln $N = 2.70805$.

In Exercises 17 and 18, solve each equation.

17. $(4.55)^{x+1} = 8.45$

Round off to three decimal places.

18. $\log(x + 3) + \log(x - 2) = \log 6$

19. Find $\log_6 148$ correct to three decimal places.

20. Graph $y = 3^x$ and its inverse logarithmic function on the same set of axes.

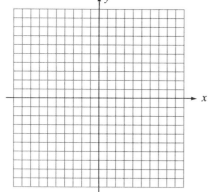

21. $1,600 is invested at 5.7% interest. How long will it take for the money to grow to $2,000 if the interest is compounded continuously? Round off the answer to two significant digits.

ANSWERS

11. _____

12. _____

13. _____

14. _____

15. _____

16. _____

17. _____

18. _____

19. _____

20. __Use graph.__

21. _____

Chapter 11 Diagnostic Test

The purpose of this test is to see how well you understand exponential and logarithmic functions. We recommend that you work this diagnostic test *before* your instructor tests you on this chapter. Allow yourself about 50 minutes.

Complete solutions for all the problems on this test, together with section references, are given in the answer section at the end of the book. For the problems you do incorrectly, study the sections cited.

1. Write $2^4 = 16$ in logarithmic form.

2. Write $\log_{2.5} 6.25 = 2$ in exponential form.

In Problems 3–7, find the value of the unknown b, N, or x.

3. $\log_4 N = 3$

4. $\log_{10} 10^{-2} = x$

5. $\log_b 6 = 1$

6. $\log_5 1 = x$

7. $\log_{0.5} N = -2$

In Problems 8–10, write each expression as a single logarithm.

8. $\log x + \log y - \log z$

9. $\dfrac{1}{2} \log x^4 + 2 \log x$

10. $\log(x^2 - 9) - \log(x - 3)$

11. Use the rules of logarithms to solve $\log(3x + 5) - \log 7 = \log(x - 1)$.

12. Use the rules of logarithms to solve $\log(x + 8) + \log(x - 2) = \log 11$.

In Problems 13 and 14, express the answer correct to three significant digits.

13. Use logarithms to solve $e^{3x-4} = 8$.

14. Find $\log_2 718$.

15. Graph $y = 7^x$ and its inverse logarithmic function on the same set of axes.

16. Suppose a certain culture of bacteria increases according to the formula $y = Ce^{0.05t}$. If there were initially 1,500 bacteria, find:

a. the number of bacteria present after 2 hours (round off your answer to four significant digits)

b. the number of hours it will take for the bacteria to triple (round off your answer to two significant digits)

Cumulative Review Exercises
Chapters 1–11

In Exercises 1 and 2, perform the indicated operations and simplify.

1. $\dfrac{7}{x^2 - x - 12} - \dfrac{3}{x^2 - 5x + 4}$

2. $\dfrac{\dfrac{2}{x} - \dfrac{2}{y}}{\dfrac{y^2 - x^2}{xy}}$

In Exercises 3 and 4, graph each equation.

3. $2x - 7y = 7$

4. $y = x^2 - 2x - 3$

In Exercises 5–8, solve each equation or inequality.

5. $\dfrac{2x}{3} - 1 \le \dfrac{x + 2}{5}$

6. $\sqrt{1 - 4x} = x + 5$

7. $\log(5x + 2) + \log 3 = \log(12x + 15)$

8. $e^{3x} = 5$ (Round off the answer to three significant digits.)

In Exercises 9 and 10, solve each system.

9. $\begin{cases} 2x + 4y = 0 \\ 5x - 3y = 13 \end{cases}$

10. $\begin{cases} 2x + y = 3 \\ y^2 = 3x \end{cases}$

11. Find the distance between $(3, -4)$ and $(1, 2)$.

12. Write the general form of the equation of the line that has an x-intercept of -14 and a y-intercept of -6.

13. Write the general form of the equation of the line that passes through $(9, -13)$ and is parallel to the line $10x - 6y + 15 = 0$.

14. What is the multiplicative identity element?

15. What is the multiplicative inverse of -3?

16. Write $2^7 = 128$ in logarithmic form.

17. Find $\log 0.0312$.

18. Find N if $\ln N = 4.276666$.

In Exercises 19 and 20, set up each problem algebraically and solve.

19. $3,000 is invested at 5.6% interest. How long will it take for the money to grow to $5,000 if the interest is compounded continuously?

20. How many liters of water must be added to $5\,\ell$ of a 60% solution of alcohol to make a 40% solution?

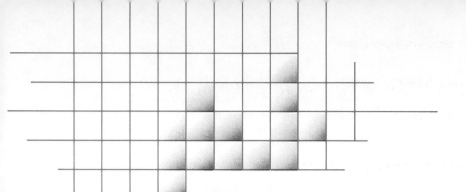

12 Sequences and Series

In this chapter, we introduce *sequences* and *series*. There are many applications of sequences and series in the sciences and in the mathematics of finance. For example, formulas for the calculation of interest, annuities, and mortgage loans are derived using series. The numbers in the logarithm tables in this book were calculated using series. This chapter is just a brief introduction to a very extensive and important part of mathematics.

12.1 Basic Definitions

Sequences

When you look at the following set of numbers, do you know what number comes next?

$$30, 40, 50, 60, 70, \ldots$$

What number comes next in the following set of numbers?

$$7, 10, 13, 16, \ldots$$

These sets of numbers are examples of sequences of numbers. A **sequence** of numbers is a set of numbers arranged in a definite order. The numbers that make up the sequence are called the **terms** of the sequence.

A sequence is usually written

$$a_1, a_2, a_3, \ldots, a_n, \ldots$$

where

$a_1 =$ first term

$a_2 =$ second term

$a_3 =$ third term

$\vdots$

$a_n = n$th term   It is also called the *general term* of the sequence

$\vdots$

The *subscript* of each term represents the *term number*.

If in counting the terms of a sequence the counting comes to an end, the sequence is called a *finite* sequence. The last term of a finite sequence is represented by the symbol a_n or l.

If in counting the terms of a sequence the counting never comes to an end, the sequence is called an *infinite* sequence. The symbol a_n represents the nth term of *any* sequence.

Example 1   Examples of finite and infinite sequences:

a. 0, 1, 2, 3, 4, 5, 6, 7, 8, 9.

The period indicates that the sequence ends here

The set of digits is a *finite* sequence. Each succeeding term is found by adding 1 to the preceding term. This sequence could also be written $0, 1, 2, \ldots, 9$.

b. 0, 1, 2, 3, ...

The 3 dots indicate that the sequence never ends

The set of whole numbers is an *infinite* sequence. Each term is found by adding 1 to the preceding term.

c. 15, 10, 5, 0, -5, -10.

The sequence ends here

This is a *finite* sequence. Each term is found by adding -5 to the preceding term. ■

In the sequences discussed so far, it is possible to discover each succeeding term *by inspection*. For many sequences, this is not the case.

Sometimes each term of a sequence is a function of n, where n is the term number; n is a natural number.

$$a_n = f(n)$$

This means that a sequence can be thought of as a *function* with domain the set of natural numbers.

Example 2   Examples of functional sequences:

a. If $\quad a_n = f(n) = \dfrac{n}{2}$,

$\quad$ then $a_1 = \dfrac{(1)}{2} = \dfrac{1}{2}$

$\quad a_2 = \dfrac{(2)}{2} = 1$

$\quad a_3 = \dfrac{(3)}{2} = \dfrac{3}{2}$

$\quad \vdots$

b. $a_n = f(n) = \dfrac{n+1}{4}$

$\quad a_1 = \dfrac{(1)+1}{4} = \dfrac{2}{4} = \dfrac{1}{2}$

$\quad a_2 = \dfrac{(2)+1}{4} = \dfrac{3}{4}$

$\quad \vdots$

$\quad a_{11} = \dfrac{(11)+1}{4} = \dfrac{12}{4} = 3$

$\quad \vdots$ ■

Series

A **series** is the indicated *sum* of a finite or infinite sequence of terms. It is a *finite* or an *infinite series* according to whether the number of terms is finite or infinite.

An infinite series is usually written

$$a_1 + a_2 + a_3 + \cdots + a_n + \cdots$$

A *partial sum of a series* is the sum of a finite number of consecutive terms of the series, beginning with the first term.

$\qquad S_1 = a_1 \qquad$ *First* partial sum

$\qquad S_2 = a_1 + a_2 \qquad$ *Second* partial sum

$\qquad S_3 = a_1 + a_2 + a_3 \qquad$ *Third* partial sum

$\qquad \vdots$

$\qquad S_n = a_1 + a_2 + \cdots + a_n \qquad$ *n*th partial sum

$\qquad \vdots$

Given the infinite *sequence*, $f(n) = \dfrac{1}{n}$:

The *sequence* is $\dfrac{1}{1}, \dfrac{1}{2}, \dfrac{1}{3}, \ldots$

The *series for this sequence* is: $1 + \dfrac{1}{2} + \dfrac{1}{3} + \cdots$

The *partial sums* are

$$S_1 = 1 \qquad\qquad = 1$$

$$S_2 = 1 + \frac{1}{2} \qquad = \frac{3}{2}$$

$$S_3 = 1 + \frac{1}{2} + \frac{1}{3} = \frac{11}{6}$$

$$\vdots$$

EXERCISES 12.1

In Exercises 1–4, for each given sequence determine the next three terms by inspection.

1. 10, 15, 20, __, __, __, $\cdots$

2. 8, 11, 14, __, __, __, $\cdots$

3. 15, 13, 11, __, __, __, $\cdots$

4. $1, \dfrac{4}{3}, \dfrac{5}{3}, $__, __, __, $\cdots$

In Exercises 5–10, use the given general term to write the terms specified.

5. $a_n = f(n) = n + 4;$ first three terms

6. $a_n = f(n) = 2n + 1;$ first four terms

7. $a_n = \dfrac{1 - n}{n};$ first four terms

8. $a_n = \dfrac{n(n - 1)}{2};$ first three terms

9. $a_n = n^2 - 1;$ first three terms

10. $a_n = n^3 + 1;$ first four terms

In Exercises 11–14, find the indicated partial sum by using the given general term.

11. Given $a_n = 2n - 3$, find S_4.

12. Given $a_n = \dfrac{2n - 1}{5 - n}$, find S_4.

13. Given $a_n = \dfrac{n - 1}{n + 1}$, find S_3.

14. Given $a_n = 3^n + 2$, find S_3.

Set II   In Exercises 1–4, for each given sequence determine the next three terms by inspection.

1. 20, 16, 12, __, __, __, ...

2. $\frac{1}{2}, \frac{3}{4}, 1,$ __, __, __, ...

3. 17, 19, 21, __, __, __, ...

4. $4\frac{2}{3}, 4, 3\frac{1}{3},$ __, __, __, ...

In Exercises 5–10, use the given general term to write the terms specified.

5. $a_n = f(n) = 1 - 2n$;   first four terms

6. $a_n = \frac{n}{1 - 2n}$;   first three terms

7. $a_n = f(n) = 3n - 1$;   first four terms

8. $a_n = f(n) = 1 - n$;   first four terms

9. $a_n = f(n) = n^2 + 1$;   first four terms

10. $a_n = \frac{2 - n}{1 + n^2}$;   first three terms

In Exercises 11–14, find the indicated partial sum by using the given general term.

11. Given $a_n = 4 - n$, find S_5.

12. Given $a_n = \frac{1 - 2^n}{3}$, find S_4.

13. Given $a_n = \frac{2n - 1}{n}$, find S_3.

14. Given $a_n = \frac{n^2 - 1}{2^n}$, find S_3.

12.2 Arithmetic Sequences and Series

Arithmetic Sequences

An **arithmetic progression (arithmetic sequence)** is a sequence in which each term after the first is found by *adding* the same fixed number to the preceding term. The fixed number added is called the *common difference, d*. Arithmetic progression is abbreviated AP.

Example 1   Write the first five terms of the infinite arithmetic progression having first term $a_1 = 3$ and common difference $d = 2$.

$$a_1 = 3$$

$$a_2 = 3 + 2 = 5 \qquad \text{Add common difference (2) to first term (3)}$$

$$a_3 = 5 + 2 = 7 \qquad \text{Add common difference (2) to second term (5)}$$

$$a_4 = 7 + 2 = 9 \qquad \text{And so on}$$

$$a_5 = 9 + 2 = 11$$

Therefore, the AP is 3, 5, 7, 9, 11, ... ■

Example 2 Write a six-term arithmetic progression having first term $a_1 = 15$ and common difference $d = -7$.

$$a_1 = 15$$
$$a_2 = 15 + (-7) = 8$$
$$a_3 = 8 + (-7) = 1$$
$$a_4 = 1 + (-7) = -6$$
$$a_5 = -6 + (-7) = -13$$
$$a_6 = -13 + (-7) = -20$$

Therefore, the AP is 15, 8, 1, -6, -13, -20. ■

Example 3 Determine which of the sequences below are arithmetic progressions:

Method Subtract each term from the following term. If every difference found this way is the same, the sequence is an AP.

a. -8, -3, 2, 7, 12

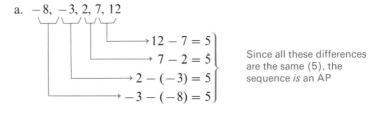

$$12 - 7 = 5$$
$$7 - 2 = 5$$
$$2 - (-3) = 5$$
$$-3 - (-8) = 5$$

Since all these differences are the same (5), the sequence *is* an AP

b. 1, 5, 9, 12, 16

$$16 - 12 = 4$$
$$12 - 9 = 3$$

Since these differences are *not* the same, the sequence is *not* an AP

c. $(5x - 3)$, $(7x - 4)$, $(9x - 5)$, ...

$$(9x - 5) - (7x - 4) = 2x - 1$$
$$(7x - 4) - (5x - 3) = 2x - 1$$

AP because differences are the same $(2x - 1)$ ■

In general, an arithmetic progression with first term a_1 and common difference d has the following terms:

$$a_1 = a_1$$
$$a_2 = a_1 + 1d$$
$$a_3 = (a_1 + d) + d = a_1 + 2d$$
$$a_4 = (a_1 + 2d) + d = a_1 + 3d$$
$$\vdots$$
$$a_n = ?$$

a_n is found in the following way:

Coefficient of d is always 1 less than term number

Term number:	1	2	3	4	$\cdots$	n

Term: $a_1, \quad a_1 + 1d, \quad a_1 + 2d, \quad a_1 + 3d, \ldots, \quad a_1 + (n-1)d$

Therefore,

THE nth TERM OF AN AP

$$a_n = a_1 + (n-1)d$$

Example 4   Find the twenty-first term of the AP having $a_1 = 23$ and $d = -2$.

$$a_n = a_1 + (n-1)d$$
$$a_{21} = 23 + (21-1)(-2)$$
$$a_{21} = 23 + (-40) = -17 \quad \blacksquare$$

Example 5   Given an AP with $a_7 = -10$ and $a_{12} = 5$, find a_1 and d.

If $n = 7$, $a_n = -10$. Therefore, $-10 = a_1 + 6d$. If $n = 12$, $a_n = 5$. Therefore, $5 = a_1 + 11d$. We now multiply both sides of the first equation by -1 and then add the two equations:

$$-a_1 - 6d = 10$$
$$\underline{a_1 + 11d = 5}$$
$$5d = 15$$
$$d = 3$$

Substitute $d = 3$ into Equation 1:

$$a_1 + 6d = -10$$
$$a_1 + 6(3) = -10$$
$$a_1 = -28 \quad \blacksquare$$

Arithmetic Series

An **arithmetic series** is the sum of the terms of an arithmetic progression. An infinite arithmetic series can be written

$$a_1 + (a_1 + d) + (a_1 + 2d) + \cdots + a_n + \cdots$$

For a finite arithmetic series of n terms, the sum of those terms, S_n, is

$$S_n = a_1 + (a_1 + d) + (a_1 + 2d) + \cdots + (a_n - 2d) + (a_n - d) + a_n$$

Subtract d from the last term
to give the preceding term

A formula for S_n can be found by adding the reverse of S_n to itself. Before we attempt to find a general formula for the sum of an arithmetic series, however, let us consider a specific example.

Example 6   Find the sum of the first 100 integers.

The story is told that the famous German mathematician, Carl Friedrich Gauss, at the age of ten very quickly solved this problem when it was first presented in his arithmetic class.

We are to find

$$
\begin{array}{ccccc}
\text{1st} & \text{2nd} & \text{3rd} & & \text{100th} \\
\text{term} & \text{term} & \text{term} & & \text{term} \\
\downarrow & \downarrow & \downarrow & & \downarrow
\end{array}
$$

$$S_{100} = 1 \; + 2 \; + 3 \; + \cdots + 98 + 99 + 100$$

If we choose to, we can, of course, write the equation as follows:

$$S_{100} = 100 + 99 + 98 + \cdots + 3 + 2 + 1$$

Now let us add the two equations together, adding the right sides term by term. We then have

$$
\begin{array}{ccccc}
\text{1st} & \text{2nd} & \text{3rd} & & \text{100th} \\
\text{term} & \text{term} & \text{term} & & \text{term} \\
\downarrow & \downarrow & \downarrow & & \downarrow
\end{array}
$$

$$S_{100} + S_{100} = \underbrace{101 + 101 + 101 + \cdots + 101 + 101 + 101}_{\text{100 terms}}$$

Therefore, $2S_{100} = 101(100)$

$$S_{100} = \frac{101(100)}{2} = 5{,}050 \quad \blacksquare$$

Using the same reasoning as in Example 6, we have in the general case

$$
\begin{array}{cccccc}
\text{1st} & \text{2nd} & \text{3rd} & (n-2)\text{nd} & (n-1)\text{st} & n\text{th} \\
\text{term} & \text{term} & \text{term} & \text{term} & \text{term} & \text{term} \\
\downarrow & \downarrow & \downarrow & \downarrow & \downarrow & \downarrow
\end{array}
$$

$$S_n = a_1 + (a_1 + d) + (a_1 + 2d) + \cdots + (a_n - 2d) + (a_n - d) + a_n$$
$$S_n = a_n + (a_n - d) + (a_n - 2d) + \cdots + (a_1 + 2d) + (a_1 + d) + a_1$$

Adding the two equations term by term, we have

$$2S_n = \underbrace{(a_1 + a_n) + (a_1 + a_n) + (a_1 + a_n) + \cdots + (a_1 + a_n) + (a_1 + a_n) + (a_1 + a_n)}_{n \text{ terms}}$$

The right side of the last equation has n terms of $(a_1 + a_n)$, so

$$2S_n = n(a_1 + a_n)$$

Therefore,

THE SUM OF n TERMS OF AN AP

$$S_n = \frac{n(a_1 + a_n)}{2}$$

Example 7 Find the sum of the first 100 natural numbers by using the formula for S_n.

$$
\left.
\begin{array}{l}
a_1 = 1 \\[2em]
a_n = 100 \\[2em]
n = 100
\end{array}
\right\}
\quad
\begin{array}{l}
S_n = \dfrac{n(a_1 + a_n)}{2} \\[2em]
S_{100} = \dfrac{\overset{50}{\cancel{100}}(1 + 100)}{\cancel{2}} = 50(101) = 5{,}050 \quad \blacksquare
\end{array}
$$

Example 8 Given an AP having $a_1 = -8$, $a_n = 20$, and $S_n = 30$, find d and n.

(1) $a_n = a_1 + (n-1)d \Rightarrow 20 = -8 + (n-1)d$

(2) $S_n = \dfrac{n(a_1 + a_n)}{2} \Rightarrow 30 = \dfrac{n(-8 + 20)}{2} \Rightarrow 30 = 6n$

$$5 = n$$

Substitute $n = 5$ into Equation 1: $20 = -8 + (n-1)d$

$$20 = -8 + (5-1)d$$
$$20 = -8 + 4d$$
$$28 = 4d$$
$$7 = d$$

Therefore, $n = 5$ and $d = 7$. $\blacksquare$

EXERCISES 12.2

Set I In Exercises 1–8, determine whether each sequence is an AP. If it is, find the common difference.

1. 3, 8, 13, 18 **2.** 7, 11, 15, 19

3. 7, 4, 1, -2, ... **4.** 9, 4, -1, -6, ...

5. 4, $5\frac{1}{2}$, 7, 9 **6.** 3, $4\frac{1}{4}$, $5\frac{1}{2}$, $6\frac{1}{2}$

7. $2x - 1$, x, 1, $-x + 2$ **8.** $3 - 2x$, $2 - x$, 1, x

9. Write the first four terms of the AP for which $a_1 = 5$ and $d = -7$.

10. Write the first five terms of the AP for which $a_1 = 4$ and $d = -5$.

11. Write the AP with five terms for which $a_1 = 7$ and $a_5 = 31$.

12. Write the AP with six terms for which $a_1 = 6$ and $a_6 = 51$.

13. Write the thirty-first term of the AP: -8, -2, 4, ...

14. Write the forty-first term of the AP: -5, -1, 3, ...

15. Write the eleventh term of the AP: x, $2x + 1$, $3x + 2$, ...

16. Write the ninth term of the AP: $2z + 1$, $3z$, $4z - 1$, ...

17. Find the sum of the even integers from 2 to 100, inclusive.

18. Find the sum of the odd integers from 1 to 99, inclusive.

19. Given an AP with $a_6 = 15$ and $a_{12} = 39$, find a_1 and d.

20. Given an AP with $a_5 = 12$ and $a_{14} = 57$, find a_1 and d.

In Exercises 21–26, certain elements of an arithmetic progression are given. Solve for the indicated elements.

21. $a_1 = -5, d = 3, a_n = 16$; find n and S_n.

22. $a_1 = -7, d = 4, a_n = 25$; find n and S_n.

23. $a_1 = 5, a_n = 17, S_n = 44$; find d and n.

24. $a_1 = 3, a_n = 42, S_n = 180$; find d and n.

25. $d = \dfrac{3}{2}, n = 9, S_n = -\dfrac{9}{4}$; find a_1 and a_n.

26. $d = \dfrac{3}{4}, n = 7, S_n = \dfrac{21}{4}$; find a_1 and a_n.

27. A rock dislodged by a mountain climber falls approximately 16 ft during the first second, 48 ft during the second second, 80 ft during the third second, and so on. Find the distance it falls during the tenth second and the total distance it falls during the first 12 sec.

28. A college student's young son saves 10¢ on the first of May, 12¢ on the second, 14¢ on the third, and so on. If he continues saving in this manner, how much does he save during the month of May?

Set II In Exercises 1–8, determine whether each sequence is an AP. If it is, find the common difference.

1. $-41, -24, -7, 10$

2. $13, 5, -3, -11, \ldots$

3. $-1, \dfrac{1}{2}, 1, 2\frac{1}{2}$

4. $-2 + x, -1 - x, -3x, 1 - 5x, \ldots$

5. $8, 4, 2, 1, \ldots$

6. $17, 14, 11, 8, \ldots$

7. $-9, -5, -1, 3, \ldots$

8. $\dfrac{13}{16}, \dfrac{1}{2}, \dfrac{3}{16}, -\dfrac{1}{8}, \ldots$

9. Write the first four terms of the AP for which $a_1 = -17$ and $d = -3$.

10. Write the first four terms of the AP for which $a_1 = 19$ and $d = -24$.

11. Write the first four terms of the AP for which $a_1 = 83$ and $a_6 = 48$.

12. Write the first five terms of the AP for which $a_1 = 7$ and $a_7 = -11$.

13. Write the twenty-ninth term of the AP: $-26, -22, -18, \ldots$.

14. Write the eighty-third term of the AP: $28, 34, 40, \ldots$.

15. Write the seventh term of the AP: $-x, x + 3, 3x + 6, \ldots$.

16. Write the eighth term of the AP: $-5x + 1, -3x - 1, -x - 3, \ldots$.

17. Find the sum of the even integers from 100 to 200, inclusive.

18. Find the sum of the odd integers from 101 to 201, inclusive.

19. Given an AP with $a_5 = 46$ and $a_9 = 74$, find a_1 and d.

20. Given an AP with $a_7 = 11$ and $a_{13} = 29$, find a_1 and d.

In Exercises 21–26, certain elements of an arithmetic progression are given. Solve for the indicated elements.

21. $a_1 = 18, d = -3, a_n = -6$; find n and S_n.

22. $a_1 = -37, d = 4, a_n = 7$; find n and S_n.

23. $a_1 = 13$, $a_n = 49$, $S_n = 217$; find d and n.

24. $a_1 = 17$, $d = -12$, $a_n = -103$; find n and S_n.

25. $a_1 = 7$, $a_n = -83$, $S_n = -722$; find d and n.

26. $d = \dfrac{2}{3}$, $n = 15$, $S_n = 35$; find a_1 and a_n.

27. If we put one penny on the first square of a chessboard, three pennies on the second square, five pennies on the third square, and continue in this way until all the squares are covered, how much money will there be on the board? Note that a chessboard has 64 squares.

28. Jason saves $1 the first week of the year, $2 the second week of the year, $3 the third week of the year, and so on. If he continues saving in this manner, how much does he save during one year?

12.3 Geometric Sequences and Series

Geometric Sequences

A **geometric progression (geometric sequence)** is a sequence in which each term after the first is found by *multiplying* the preceding term by the same fixed number, called the *common ratio, r*. Geometric progression is abbreviated GP.

Example 1   Write the first four terms of the geometric progression having first term $a_1 = 5$ and common ratio $r = 2$.

$$a_1 = 5$$

$$a_2 = 5(2) = 10 \qquad \text{Multiply first term (5) by common ratio (2)}$$

$$a_3 = 10(2) = 20 \qquad \text{Multiply second term (10) by common ratio (2)}$$

$$a_4 = 20(2) = 40 \qquad \text{Multiply third term (20) by common ratio (2)}$$

Therefore, the GP is 5, 10, 20, 40. ■

Example 2   Determine which of the sequences below are geometric progressions:

Method Divide each term by the preceding term. If every ratio found this way is the same, the sequence is a GP.

a. $24, -12, 6, -3$

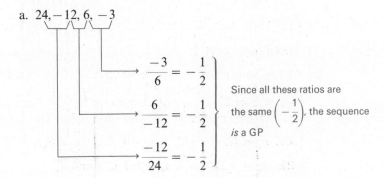

Since all these ratios are the same $\left(-\dfrac{1}{2}\right)$, the sequence *is* a GP

$$\frac{-3}{6} = -\frac{1}{2}$$

$$\frac{6}{-12} = -\frac{1}{2}$$

$$\frac{-12}{24} = -\frac{1}{2}$$

b. 36, 9, 3, 1

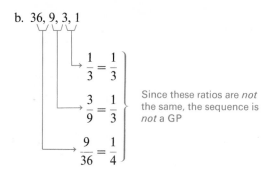

$$\frac{1}{3} = \frac{1}{3}$$

$$\frac{3}{9} = \frac{1}{3}$$

$$\frac{9}{36} = \frac{1}{4}$$

Since these ratios are *not* the same, the sequence is *not* a GP

c. $-\dfrac{3x}{y^2}, \dfrac{9x^2}{y}, -27x^3, \ldots$

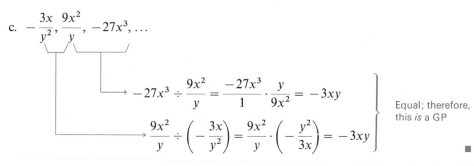

$$-27x^3 \div \frac{9x^2}{y} = \frac{-27x^3}{1} \cdot \frac{y}{9x^2} = -3xy$$

$$\frac{9x^2}{y} \div \left(-\frac{3x}{y^2}\right) = \frac{9x^2}{y} \cdot \left(-\frac{y^2}{3x}\right) = -3xy$$

Equal; therefore, this *is* a GP

■

In general, a geometric progression with first term a_1 and common ratio r has the following terms:

$$a_1 = a_1$$
$$a_2 = a_1 r$$
$$a_3 = (a_1 r)r = a_1 r^2$$
$$a_4 = (a_1 r^2)r = a_1 r^3$$
$$\vdots$$
$$a_n = ?$$

a_n is found in the following way:

> Exponent of r is always 1 less than term number

Term number: 1   2   3   4   ... n

Term: $a_1, \quad a_1 r^1, \quad a_1 r^2, \quad a_1 r^3, \quad \ldots, \quad a_1 r^{n-1}$

Therefore,

> THE nth TERM OF A GP
>
> $$a_n = a_1 r^{n-1}$$

Example 3 Find the fifth term of the GP having $a_1 = 18$ and $r = -\dfrac{1}{3}$.

$$a_n = a_1 r^{n-1}$$

$$a_5 = 18\left(-\frac{1}{3}\right)^4$$

$$a_5 = \frac{18}{1} \cdot \frac{1}{81} = \frac{2}{9} \quad \blacksquare$$

Example 4 Given a GP with $a_2 = 12$ and $a_5 = 96$, find a_1 and r.

$$a_n = a_1 r^{n-1}$$

(1) $\quad a_5 = 96 = a_1 r^4$ $\Big\}$ Therefore, $\dfrac{96}{12} = \dfrac{a_1 r^4}{a_1 r}$
(2) $\quad a_2 = 12 = a_1 r^1$

$$8 = r^3$$

$$2 = r$$

Substitute $r = 2$ into Equation 2: $12 = a_1 r^1$

$$12 = a_1(2)$$

$$6 = a_1$$

Therefore, $a_1 = 6$ and $r = 2$. $\quad \blacksquare$

Geometric Series

A **geometric series** is the sum of the terms of a geometric progression. An infinite geometric series can be written

$$a_1 + a_1 r^1 + a_1 r^2 + \cdots + a_1 r^{n-1} + \cdots$$

For a finite geometric series of n terms, the sum of those terms, S_n, is

(1) $$S_n = a_1 + a_1 r^1 + a_1 r^2 + \cdots + a_1 r^{n-1}$$

Another formula for S_n can be found as follows: Multiply both sides of Equation 1 by r; then subtract the resulting equation from Equation 1.

(1) $$S_n = a_1 + a_1 r^1 + a_1 r^2 + \cdots + a_1 r^{n-1}$$

$$rS_n = \qquad a_1 r^1 + a_1 r^2 + \cdots + a_1 r^{n-1} + a_1 r^n$$

$$\overline{S_n - rS_n = a_1 \qquad\qquad\qquad\qquad\qquad\qquad - a_1 r^n}$$

$$(1 - r)S_n = a_1(1 - r^n) \qquad \text{By factoring both sides}$$

$$S_n = \frac{a_1(1 - r^n)}{1 - r}$$

Therefore,

THE SUM OF n TERMS OF A GP

$$S_n = \frac{a_1(1 - r^n)}{1 - r}, \, r \neq 1$$

Example 5   Find the sum of the first six terms of a GP having $a_1 = 24$ and $r = \dfrac{1}{2}$.

$$S_n = \frac{a_1(1 - r^n)}{1 - r}$$

$$S_6 = \frac{24\left[1 - \left(\dfrac{1}{2}\right)^6\right]}{1 - \dfrac{1}{2}} = \frac{24\left[1 - \left(\dfrac{1}{64}\right)\right]}{\dfrac{1}{2}} = \frac{24\left[\dfrac{63}{64}\right]}{\dfrac{1}{2}} = \frac{189}{4} \quad \blacksquare$$

Example 6   Given a GP having $r = -2$, $a_n = 80$, and $S_n = 55$, find a_1 and n.

We will need to use the formula for a_n *and* the formula for S_n. Let's start with the formula for S_n, substituting 55 for S_n and -2 for r.

$$S_n = \frac{a_1(1 - r^n)}{1 - r}$$

$$55 = \frac{a_1(1 - [-2]^n)}{1 - [-2]}$$

(1) $$55 = \frac{a_1 - a_1[-2]^n}{3}$$

We see now that we need to know what $a_1[-2]^n$ equals. Let's turn to the formula for a_n, substituting 80 for a_n and -2 for r.

$$a_n = a_1 r^{n-1}$$

(2) $$80 = a_1(-2)^{n-1}$$

If we multiply $(-2)^{n-1}$ by -2, we will have $(-2)^n$, which is what we need for Equation 1. Therefore, we will multiply both sides of Equation 2 by -2:

$$(-2)(80) = a_1(-2)^{n-1}(-2)$$

(3) $$-160 = a_1(-2)^n$$

We will now substitute -160 for $a_1(-2)^n$ in Equation 1:

$$55 = \frac{a_1 - [-160]}{3}$$

$$165 = a_1 + 160$$

$$a_1 = 5$$

Substitute $a_1 = 5$ into Equation 3:

$$-160 = 5(-2)^n$$

$$-32 = (-2)^n$$

$$(-2)^5 = (-2)^n$$

$$5 = n$$

Therefore, $a_1 = 5$ and $n = 5$. $\blacksquare$

EXERCISES 12.3

Set I   In Exercises 1–8, determine whether each sequence is a GP. If it is, find the common ratio.

1. 4, 12, 36, 108

2. 7, 14, 28, 56

3. $-5, 15, -45, 135, \ldots$

4. $-6, 24, -96, 384, \ldots$

5. $2, \dfrac{1}{2}, \dfrac{1}{8}, \dfrac{1}{16}$

6. $3, \dfrac{1}{2}, \dfrac{1}{8}, \dfrac{1}{48}$

7. $5x, 10xy, 20xy^2, 40xy^3, \ldots$

8. $4xz, 12xz^2, 36xz^3, 108xz^4, \ldots$

9. Write the first five terms of the GP for which $a_1 = 12$ and $r = \dfrac{1}{3}$.

10. Write the first four terms of the GP for which $a_1 = 8$ and $r = \dfrac{3}{2}$.

11. Write the GP with five terms for which $a_1 = \dfrac{2}{3}$ and $a_5 = 54$. You will get two answers.

12. Write the GP with five terms for which $a_1 = \dfrac{3}{25}$ and $a_5 = 75$. You will get two answers.

13. Write the seventh term of the GP: $-9, -6, -4, \ldots$.

14. Write the eighth term of the GP: $-12, -18, -27, \ldots$.

15. Write the eighth term of the GP: $16x, 8xy, 4xy^2, \ldots$.

16. Write the seventh term of the GP: $27y, 9x^2y, 3x^4y, \ldots$.

17. Given a GP with $a_5 = 80$ and $r = \dfrac{2}{3}$, find a_1 and S_5.

18. Given a GP with $a_7 = 320$ and $r = 2$, find a_1 and S_5.

19. Given a GP with $a_3 = 28$ and $a_5 = \dfrac{112}{9}$, find a_1, r, and S_5. You will get two answers.

20. Given a GP with $a_2 = 384$ and $a_4 = 24$, find a_1, r, and S_4. You will get two answers.

21. Given a GP having $r = \dfrac{1}{2}$, $a_n = 3$, and $S_n = 189$, find a_1 and n.

22. Given a GP having $r = \dfrac{1}{3}$, $a_n = 4$, and $S_n = 160$, find a_1 and n.

23. A woman invested a certain amount of money that earned $1\frac{1}{5}$ times as much in the second year as in the first year, $1\frac{1}{5}$ times as much in the third year as in the second year, and so on. If the investment earned her $22,750 in the first 3 years, how much would it earn her in the fifth year?

24. A man invested a certain amount of money that earned $1\frac{1}{4}$ times as much in the second year as in the first year, $1\frac{1}{4}$ times as much in the third year as in the second year, and so on. If the investment earned him $9,760 in the first 3 years, how much would it earn him in the fifth year?

25. Suppose you took a job that pays 1¢ the first day, 2¢ the second day, and 4¢ the third day, with the pay continuing to increase in this manner for a month of 31 days.

    a. How much would you make on the tenth day?

    b. How much would you make on the thirty-first day?

    c. What would be your total earnings for the month?

Set II   In Exercises 1–8, determine whether each sequence is a GP. If it is, find the common ratio.

1. $-11, -44, -176, -704$ **2.** $-6, 30, -150, 750, \ldots$

3. $1, -\dfrac{1}{2}, -\dfrac{1}{4}, -\dfrac{1}{8}$ **4.** $20ab, -5a^3b, \dfrac{5}{4}a^5b, -\dfrac{5}{16}a^7b, \ldots$

5. $36, 18, 9, \dfrac{9}{2}, \ldots$ **6.** $-16, -8, 0, 8, \ldots$

7. $12x^5, 4x^3, \dfrac{4}{3}x, \dfrac{4}{9x}, \ldots$ **8.** $2x^4, -8x^3, 16x^2, -32x, \ldots$

9. Write the first five terms of the GP for which $a_1 = 4$ and $r = 3$.

10. Write the first four terms of the GP for which $a_1 = -9$ and $r = -\dfrac{1}{3}$.

11. Write the GP with five terms for which $a_1 = -\dfrac{3}{4}$ and $a_5 = -12$. You will get two answers.

12. Write the GP with five terms for which $a_1 = \dfrac{1}{4}$ and $a_5 = 4$. You will get two answers.

13. Write the seventh term of the GP: $-\dfrac{25}{54}, \dfrac{5}{18}, -\dfrac{1}{6}, \ldots$

14. Write the ninth term of the GP: $-16, -8, -4, \ldots$

15. Write the eighth term of the GP: $\dfrac{24}{hk}, -\dfrac{12k}{h}, \dfrac{6k^3}{h}, \ldots$

16. Write the seventh term of the GP: $-32, -8x, -2x^2, \ldots$

17. Given a GP with $a_5 = 40$ and $r = -\dfrac{2}{3}$, find a_1 and S_5.

18. Given a GP with $a_4 = -\dfrac{10}{3}$ and $r = -\dfrac{1}{3}$, find a_1 and S_5.

19. Given a GP with $a_3 = 16$ and $a_5 = 9$, find a_1, r, and S_5. You will get two answers.

20. Given a GP with $a_7 = 192$ and $a_4 = 24$, find a_1, r, and S_5.

21. Given a GP with $a_n = 972$, $r = 3$, and $S_n = 1,456$, find a_1 and n.

22. Given a GP having $r = -\dfrac{1}{2}$, $a_n = 5$, and $S_n = 55$, find a_1 and n.

23. If it takes 1 sec for a certain type of microbe to split into two microbes, how long will it take a colony of 1,500 such microbes to exceed 6 million?

24. If we put one penny on the first square of a chessboard, two pennies on the second square, four pennies on the third square, and continue in this way until all squares are covered, how much money will there be on the board? Recall that a chessboard has 64 squares.

25. Suppose you took a job that pays 1¢ the first day, 3¢ the second day, and 9¢ the third day, with the pay continuing to increase in this manner for a month of 31 days.

   a. How much would you make on the eighth day?

   b. How much would you make on the thirty-first day?

   c. What would be your total earnings for the month?

12.4 Infinite Geometric Series

Consider the formula derived in Section 12.3 for the sum of n terms of a geometric series:

$$S_n = \frac{a_1(1 - r^n)}{1 - r}, r \neq 1$$

If $|r| < 1$, then r^n gets smaller and smaller as n gets larger. Suppose $r = \frac{1}{2}$. Then

$$\left(\frac{1}{2}\right)^1 = \frac{1}{2} \qquad = 0.5$$

$$\left(\frac{1}{2}\right)^2 = \frac{1}{4} \qquad = 0.25$$

$$\left(\frac{1}{2}\right)^3 = \frac{1}{8} \qquad = 0.125$$

$$\vdots$$

$$\left(\frac{1}{2}\right)^{10} = \frac{1}{1,024} \doteq 0.001$$

$$\vdots$$

$$\left(\frac{1}{2}\right)^{20} \doteq 0.000001$$

$$\vdots$$

$$\left(\frac{1}{2}\right)^{100} \doteq 8 \times 10^{-31}$$

$\left(\frac{1}{2}\right)^n$ gets closer and closer to zero as n gets larger and larger

Therefore, $S_{100} \doteq \frac{1}{2} + \frac{1}{4} + \frac{1}{8} + \cdots + \frac{1}{1,024} + \cdots + 0 + 0 + 0$. In general, $S_n = a_1 + a_1r + a_1r^2 + a_1r^3 + \cdots + 0 + 0 + 0$ as n gets larger and larger if $|r| < 1$. That is, if $|r| < 1$, r^n is so close to zero that it contributes essentially nothing to the sum S_n when many terms are taken.

Therefore, the formula for S_n becomes

This term contributes essentially nothing when n becomes infinitely large if $|r| < 1$

$$S_n = \frac{a_1(1 - r^n)}{1 - r} \doteq \frac{a_1}{1 - r}$$

The symbol S_∞ represents S_n when n becomes infinitely large. Therefore,

---

THE SUM OF AN INFINITE GEOMETRIC SERIES

$$S_\infty = \frac{a_1}{1 - r}, \; |r| < 1$$

Example 1 Evaluate $1 + \dfrac{1}{2} + \dfrac{1}{4} + \cdots$.

$$1, \frac{1}{2}, \frac{1}{4}, \cdots$$

$$\frac{1}{2} \div 1 = \frac{1}{2} = r$$

$$S_\infty = \frac{a_1}{1 - r} = \frac{1}{1 - \dfrac{1}{2}} = \frac{1}{\dfrac{1}{2}} = 2 \quad \blacksquare$$

Example 2 Evaluate $6 - 4 + \dfrac{8}{3} - + \cdots$.

$$6, -4, \frac{8}{3}, \cdots$$

$$\frac{-4}{6} = -\frac{2}{3} = r$$

$$S_\infty = \frac{a_1}{1 - r} = \frac{6}{1 - \left(-\dfrac{2}{3}\right)} = \frac{6}{\dfrac{5}{3}} = \frac{18}{5} \quad \blacksquare$$

Example 3 Write the repeating decimal $0.252525\ldots$ as a fraction.

$$0.252525\ldots = 0.25 + 0.0025 + 0.000025 + \cdots$$

$$\frac{0.0025}{0.25} = 0.01 = r$$

$$S_\infty = \frac{a_1}{1 - r} = \frac{0.25}{1 - 0.01} = \frac{0.25}{0.99} = \frac{25}{99} \quad \blacksquare$$

The reason $|r|$ is restricted to less than 1 is that if $|r| > 1$, the absolute value of succeeding terms in the geometric series becomes larger and larger. Therefore, S_∞ would be infinitely large.

EXERCISES 12.4

Set I In Exercises 1–6, find the sum of each geometric series.

1. $3 + 1 + \dfrac{1}{3} + \cdots$

2. $9 - 1 + \dfrac{1}{9} - \cdots$

3. $\dfrac{4}{3} + 1 + \dfrac{3}{4} + \cdots$

4. $10^{-1} + 10^{-2} + 10^{-3} + \cdots$

5. $-6 - 4 - \dfrac{8}{3} - \cdots$

6. $-49 - 35 - 25 - \cdots$

In Exercises 7–12, write each repeating decimal as a fraction.

7. $0.2222\ldots$

8. $0.2121\ldots$

9. $0.05454\ldots$

10. $0.03939\ldots$

11. $8.6444\ldots$

12. $5.2666\ldots$

13. A rubber ball is dropped from a height of 9 ft. Each time it strikes the floor, it rebounds to a height that is two-thirds the height from which it last fell. Find the total distance the ball travels before coming to rest.

14. A ball bearing is dropped from a height of 10 ft. Each time it strikes the metal floor, it rebounds to a height that is three-fifths the height from which it last fell. Find the total distance the bearing travels before coming to rest.

15. The first swing of a pendulum is 12 in. Each succeeding swing is nine-tenths as long as the preceding one. Find the total distance traveled by the pendulum before it comes to rest.

Set II In Exercises 1–6, find the sum of each geometric series.

1. $5 - 1 + \dfrac{1}{5} - \cdots$

2. $10^{-2} + 10^{-4} + 10^{-6} + \cdots$

3. $\dfrac{6}{5} + 1 + \dfrac{5}{6} + \cdots$

4. $\dfrac{1}{4} + \dfrac{1}{8} + \dfrac{1}{16} + \cdots$

5. $2 - \dfrac{2}{3} + \dfrac{2}{9} - \cdots$

6. $4 + 2 + 1 + \cdots$

In Exercises 7–12, write each repeating decimal as a fraction.

7. $0.262626\ldots$

8. $0.0143143143\ldots$

9. $0.707070\ldots$

10. $0.1212\ldots$

11. $0.00136136136\ldots$

12. $3.7656565\ldots$

13. When Bob stops his car suddenly, the 3-ft radio antenna oscillates back and forth. Each swing is three-fourths as great as the previous one. If the initial travel of the antenna tip is 4 in., how far will the tip travel before it comes to rest?

14. If a rabbit moves 10 yd in the first second, 5 yd in the second second, and continues to move one-half as far in each succeeding second as he did in the preceding second:

a. How many yards does the rabbit travel before he comes to rest?

b. What is the total time the rabbit is moving?

15. The first swing of a pendulum is 10 in. Each succeeding swing is eight-ninths as long as the preceding one. Find the total distance traveled by the pendulum before it comes to rest.

12.5 Review: 12.1–12.4

Sequences
12.1

A **sequence** of numbers is a set of numbers arranged in a definite order. The numbers that make up the sequence are called the *terms* of the sequence. If in counting the terms of a sequence the counting comes to an end, the sequence is a *finite sequence*; if the counting never ends, the sequence is an *infinite sequence*.

Series
12.1

A **series** is the indicated sum of a finite or infinite sequence of terms. It is a finite or an infinite series according to whether the number of terms is finite or infinite. The *partial sum of a series* is the sum of a finite number of consecutive terms of the series, beginning with the first term.

Arithmetic Progressions
12.2

An **AP** is a sequence in which each term after the first is found by *adding* the same fixed number to the preceding term. The fixed number added is called the *common difference, d*; d can be found by subtracting any term from the term that follows it.

The nth term of an AP: $\qquad a_n = a_1 + (n - 1)d$

The sum of n terms of an AP: $\quad S_n = \dfrac{n(a_1 + a_n)}{2}$

Geometric Progressions
12.3

A **GP** is a sequence in which each term after the first is found by *multiplying* the preceding term by the same fixed number, called the *common ratio, r*. The common ratio can be found by dividing any term by the term that precedes it.

The nth term of a GP: $\qquad a_n = a_1 r^{n-1}$

The sum of n terms of a GP: $\quad S_n = \dfrac{a_1(1 - r^n)}{1 - r}, r \neq 1$

The Sum of an Infinite Geometric Series
12.4

$$S_\infty = \dfrac{a_1}{1 - r}, |r| < 1$$

Review Exercises 12.5 Set I

In Exercises 1–5, determine which of the sequences are arithmetic progressions, which are geometric progressions, and which are neither.

1. $7, 5, 3, \ldots$

2. $-2, -6, -18, \ldots$

3. $\dfrac{1}{2}, \dfrac{1}{4}, \dfrac{1}{6}, \ldots$

4. $\dfrac{3}{5}, -\dfrac{1}{5}, \dfrac{1}{15}, \ldots$

5. $3x - 2, 2x - 1, x, \ldots$

6. Write the first four terms of the AP for which $a_n = 2n - 6$. Then find d, a_{30}, and S_{30}.

7. Write the first three terms of the GP for which $a_n = \left(\dfrac{1}{2}\right)^n$. Then find S_5 and S_∞.

8. Given an AP with $a_1 = -5$, $a_n = 7$, and $S_n = 16$, find d and n.

9. Given an AP with $d = \dfrac{3}{2}$, $n = 7$, and $S_n = \dfrac{7}{2}$, find a_1 and a_n.

10. Given a GP with $a_3 = \dfrac{9}{4}$ and $r = -\dfrac{2}{3}$, find a_1 and S_6.

11. Given a GP with $a_3 = 8$ and $a_5 = \dfrac{32}{9}$, find a_1, r, and S_5. You will get two answers.

12. Write $3.2845845845\ldots$ as a fraction.

13. A rubber ball is dropped from a height of 8 ft. Each time it strikes the floor, it rebounds to a height that is three-fourths the height from which it last fell. Find the total distance the ball travels before coming to rest.

Review Exercises 12.5 Set II

NAME _____

In Exercises 1–5, determine which of the sequences are arithmetic progressions, which are geometric progressions, and which are neither.

1. _____

1. $23, 4, -15, \ldots$ **2.** $-5, -35, -245, \ldots$

2. _____

3. _____

4. _____

3. $\dfrac{1}{15}, \dfrac{1}{20}, \dfrac{1}{25}, \ldots$ **4.** $\dfrac{10}{3}, -5, \dfrac{15}{2}, \ldots$

5. _____

6. _____

5. $6 - x, 3, x, \ldots$

_____

_____

_____

6. Write the first four terms of the AP for which $a_n = 5n - 2$. Then find d, a_{25}, and S_{25}.

_____

_____

7. Write the first three terms of the GP for which $a_n = \left(\dfrac{2}{5}\right)^n$. Then find S_5 and S_∞.

7. _____

_____

_____

8. Given an AP with $a_1 = 2$, $a_n = -1$, and $S_n = 2\frac{1}{2}$, find d and n.

_____

_____

8. _____

9. Given an AP with $d = -\dfrac{4}{3}$, $n = 7$, and $S_n = 7$, find a_1 and a_n.

_____

9. _____

_____

10. Given a GP with $a_4 = 27$ and $r = -\dfrac{3}{2}$, find a_1 and S_6.

11. Given a GP with $a_3 = 18$ and $a_5 = 32$, find a_1, r, and S_5. You will get two answers.

12. Write 2.9048048048... as a fraction.

13. A mine's output in the first month was $10,000 in gold. If each succeeding monthly output is $\dfrac{9}{10}$ the previous month's output, what is the most this mine's total output can be?

Chapter 12 Diagnostic Test

The purpose of this test is to see how well you understand sequences and series. We recommend that you work this diagnostic test *before* your instructor tests you on this chapter. Allow yourself about 50 minutes.

Complete solutions for all the problems on this test, together with section references, are given in the answer section at the end of the book. For the problems you do incorrectly, study the sections cited.

1. Given $a_n = \dfrac{2n - 1}{n}$, find S_4.

2. Determine whether each of the following sequences is an AP, a GP, or neither. If an AP, give d. If a GP, give r.

   a. $8, -20, 50, \ldots$

   b. $\dfrac{1}{2}, \dfrac{3}{4}, 1, \dfrac{5}{4}, \dfrac{3}{2}, \ldots$

   c. $2x - 1, 3x, 4x + 2, \ldots$

   d. $\dfrac{c^4}{16}, -\dfrac{c^3}{8}, \dfrac{c^2}{4}, \ldots$

3. Write the first five terms of the AP: for which $a_1 = x + 1$ and $d = x - 1$.

4. Write the AP with five terms for which $a_1 = 2$ and $a_5 = -2$.

5. Write the fifteenth term of the AP: $1 - 6h, 2 - 4h, 3 - 2h, \ldots$.

6. Given an AP with $a_3 = 1$ and $a_7 = 2$, find a_1 and d.

7. Given an AP with $a_1 = 10$, $a_n = -8$, and $S_n = 7$, find d and n.

8. Write the first five terms of the GP for which $a_1 = \dfrac{c^4}{16}$ and $r = -\dfrac{2}{c}$.

9. Given a GP with $a_2 = -18$ and $a_4 = -8$, find a_1, r, and S_4.

10. Given a GP with $r = -\dfrac{2}{3}$, $a_n = -16$, and $S_n = 26$, find a_1 and n.

11. Find the sum of $8, -4, 2, -1, \ldots$.

12. Write $3.0333\ldots$ as a fraction.

13. A ball bearing dropped from a height of 6 ft rebounds to a height that is two-thirds the height from which it fell. Find the total distance the ball bearing travels vertically before it comes to rest.

Cumulative Review Exercises
Chapters 1–12

1. Solve $\left| \dfrac{x}{2} + 3 \right| < 4$.

2. Solve $x^2 - 4x = 8$.

In Exercises 3 and 4, find the value of the unknown.

3. $\log_5 \frac{1}{25} = x$

4. $\log_b 4 = \frac{1}{2}$

5. Use the rules of logarithms to solve $\log 4 + \log(x + 3) = 2 \log x$.

6. Use the rules of logarithms to solve $\log(x + 10) - \log 3 = \log 2x$.

In Exercises 7 and 8, graph each equation.

7. $x^2 + 4y^2 = 16$

8. $y = \log_3 x$

9. Solve the system $\begin{cases} 2x - 5y \geq 10 \\ 5x + y < 5 \end{cases}$ graphically.

10. Factor $x^3 + 2x^2 - x - 2$ completely, or write "Not factorable."

In Exercises 11–13, perform the indicated operations.

11. $\dfrac{x}{x - 3} - \dfrac{9}{x + 3} - \dfrac{1}{2x^2 - 18}$

12. $(x^4 + 3x^3 - 6x^2 - 2x + 1) \div (x^2 - x + 1)$

13. $\dfrac{x + 1}{3x^2 + 14x - 5} \div \dfrac{2x^2 - x - 3}{6x^2 - 11x + 3}$

14. Is $1, -4, 16, \ldots$ an arithmetic progression, a geometric progression, or neither?

15. Given an AP with $a_1 = -7$, $a_n = 11$, and $S_n = 10$, find d and n.

16. Given an AP with $d = \frac{2}{3}$, $n = 9$, and $S_n = 6$, find a_1 and a_n.

17. Given a GP with $a_4 = -1$ and $r = -\frac{2}{7}$, find a_1 and S_5.

18. Write the first three terms of the expansion of $(\sqrt{x} - 3y)^{12}$.

19. The distance (s) an object falls (in a vacuum) varies directly with the square of the time (t) it takes to fall. If an object falls 64 ft in 2 sec, how far will it fall in 4 sec?

In Exercises 20–22, set up the problem algebraically and solve.

20. Find three consecutive integers such that the product of the first two is 10 more than 4 times the third.

21. (Use two variables for this problem.) A fraction has the value $\dfrac{3}{5}$. If 4 is added to the numerator and 5 is added to the denominator, the value of the fraction becomes $\dfrac{5}{8}$. What is the original fraction?

22. A certain culture of bacteria increases according to the formula $y = Ce^{0.03t}$. How many hours will it take for the bacteria to grow from 1,000 to 5,000? (Round off the answer to four significant digits.)

Appendixes

Appendix A   Proofs

Rule 1.7b $\dfrac{1}{x^{-n}} = x^n$ (page 53)

Proof

$$\frac{1}{x^{-n}} = \frac{1}{\dfrac{1}{x^n}} = 1 \div \frac{1}{x^n} = 1 \times \frac{x^n}{1} = x^n \quad \blacksquare$$

Rule 1.7c $\left(\dfrac{x}{y}\right)^{-n} = \left(\dfrac{y}{x}\right)^{n}$ (page 53)

Proof

$$\left(\frac{x}{y}\right)^{-n} = \frac{1}{\left(\dfrac{x}{y}\right)^n} = 1 \div \left(\frac{x}{y}\right)^n = 1 \div \frac{x^n}{y^n} = 1 \times \frac{y^n}{x^n} = \frac{y^n}{x^n} = \left(\frac{y}{x}\right)^n \quad \blacksquare$$

Rule 2.1   If $a \geq 0$ and if $|N| = a$, then $N = a$ or $N = -a$, where N is any algebraic expression. (page 99)

Proof   Case I, $N \geq 0$.
If $N \geq 0$, $|N| = N$. Then $|N| = a \Rightarrow N = a$.

Proof   Case II, $N < 0$.
If $N < 0$, $|N| = -N$. Then $|N| = a \Rightarrow -N = a$. But if $-N = a$, $N = -a$.

The final answer is the *union* of the solution sets of cases I and II. Therefore, if $|N| = a$, then $N = a$ or $N = -a$.   ∎

Rule 2.2   If a is a positive real number,

1. if $|N| < a$, then $-a < N < a$, and

2. if $|N| \leq a$, then $-a \leq N \leq a$,

   where N is any algebraic expression.   (page 100)

Proof of 1   Case I, $N \geq 0$.
If $N \geq 0$, $|N| = N$. Therefore, $|N| < a \Rightarrow N < a$. We must find the intersection between $N \geq 0$ and $N < a$. Because $a > 0$, the intersection is $0 \leq N < a$. On the number line:

Proof of 1   Case II, $N < 0$.
If $N < 0$, $|N| = -N$. Therefore, $|N| < a \Rightarrow -N < a$. If $-N < a$, then $N > -a$. We must find the intersection between $N < 0$ and $N > -a$. Because $a > 0$, the intersection is $-a < N < 0$. On the number line:

The final answer is the *union* of the solution sets of Cases I and II, which is $-a < N < a$. On the number line:

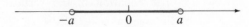

The proof of 2 is similar to the proof of 1 and will not be shown.

Rule 2.3   If a is a positive real number,

1. if $|N| > a$, then $N > a$ or $N < -a$, and

2. if $|N| \geq a$, then $N \geq a$ or $N \leq -a$,

   where N is any algebraic expression.   (page 101)

Proof of 1   Case I, $N \geq 0$.
    If $N \geq 0$, $|N| = N$. Therefore, $|N| > a \Rightarrow N > a$. We must find the intersection between $N \geq 0$ and $N > a$. Since $a > 0$, the intersection is $N > a$. On the number line:

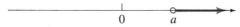

Proof of 1   Case II, $N < 0$.
    If $N < 0$, $|N| = -N$. Therefore, $|N| > a \Rightarrow -N > a$. If $-N > a$, then $N < -a$. We must find the intersection between $N < 0$ and $N < -a$. Because $a > 0$, the intersection is $N < -a$. On the number line:

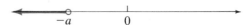

    The final answer is the *union* between the solution sets for Cases I and II: $\{N > a\} \cup \{N < -a\}$ is: $N > a$ or $N < -a$. On the number line:

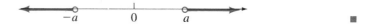

The proof of 2 is similar to the proof of 1 and will not be shown.

The Remainder Theorem   If $f(x)$ is divided by $(x - a)$, then the remainder equals $f(a)$.   (page 408)

Proof   Let us call the quotient $q(x)$ and the remainder R. Then if $f(x)$ is a polynomial of degree n, $q(x)$ is a polynomial of degree $n - 1$, and "$f(x) = (x - a)q(x) + R$" must be a true statement for all x. Let $x = a$. We then have

$$f(a) = (a - a)q(a) + R$$

But since $a - a = 0$, $f(a) = R$. Therefore, if $f(x)$ is divided by $x - a$, $R = f(a)$.   ∎

Axis of Symmetry   The equation of the axis of symmetry of the parabola $y = ax^2 + bx + c$ is $x = -\dfrac{b}{2a}$.   (page 463)

Proof   For simplicity, let us assume that the parabola crosses the x-axis. The x-intercepts are $\dfrac{-b + \sqrt{b^2 - 4ac}}{2a}$ and $\dfrac{-b - \sqrt{b^2 - 4ac}}{2a}$. The axis of symmetry passes through a point whose x-coordinate is the average of these two values—that is, the x-coordinate of the axis of symmetry is

$$\frac{\dfrac{-b + \sqrt{b^2 - 4ac}}{2a} + \dfrac{-b - \sqrt{b^2 - 4ac}}{2a}}{2} = \frac{\dfrac{-2b}{2a}}{2} = -\frac{b}{2a}$$

The equation of the vertical line that passes through the point $\left(-\dfrac{b}{2a}, 0\right)$ is $x = -\dfrac{b}{2a}$.   ∎

Appendix B   The Use of Tables for Logarithms; Computations with Logarithms

B.1 Common Logarithms: The Characteristic

We first consider logarithms of powers of 10. *The logarithm of a number is the exponent to which the base must be raised to give that number.*

$\log_{10} 10^{\boxed{3}} = \boxed{3}$ The base 10 must be raised to the exponent 3 to give the number 10^3

$\log_{10} 10^{\boxed{2}} = \boxed{2}$ The base 10 must be raised to the exponent 2 to give the number 10^2

$\log_{10} 10^{\boxed{1}} = \boxed{1}$ And so on

$\log_{10} 10^{\boxed{0}} = \boxed{0}$

$\log_{10} 10^{\boxed{-1}} = \boxed{-1}$

$\log_{10} 10^{\boxed{-2}} = \boxed{-2}$

$\vdots$

In general,

$$\log_{10} 10^k = k$$

The logarithm of a number that is *not* an integral power of 10 is made up of two parts:

1. *An integer part called the characteristic.* The characteristic is the exponent of 10 when the number is written in scientific notation.

2. *A decimal part called the mantissa* (found in Table II, Appendix C). The mantissa is the logarithm of the number between 1 and 10 when the number is written in scientific notation. (See Section B.2.)

Finding the Characteristic

While the characteristic is the exponent of 10 when the number is written in scientific notation, it is better for computational purposes to write *negative* characteristics as the *difference* of two numbers, as shown in Examples 1b, 1c, 1d, and 1f.

Example 1   Examples of writing the characteristic of the logarithm of a number:

Number	Characteristic	Written
a. 7 ∧ 6.3 →	1	1. ▭
b. 0.5 ← ∧ 06	−1	9. ▭ − 10
c. 0.09 ← ∧ 32	−2	8. ▭ − 10
d. 0.000004 ← ∧ 79	−6	4. ▭ − 10
e. 1.83×10^4	4	4. ▭
f. 2.36×10^{-7}	−7	3. ▭ − 10

Mantissa goes here ■

EXERCISES B.1

Set I   Write the characteristic of the logarithm of each number.

1. 386   **2.** 27   **3.** 5.67   **4.** 30.4

5. 0.516   **6.** 0.089   **7.** 93,000,000   **8.** 186,000

9. 0.0000806   **10.** 0.000777   **11.** 78,000   **12.** 1,400

13. 2.06×10^5 **14.** 3.55×10^4 **15.** 7.14×10^{-3} **16.** 8.96×10^{-5}

Set II   Write the characteristic of the logarithm of each number.

1. 784   **2.** 8.99   **3.** 0.314   **4.** 0.000578

5. 2.56×10^4 **6.** 3.14×10^{-3} **7.** 7.0005   **8.** 0.000109

9. 3,480   **10.** 0.00437   **11.** 2,300,000   **12.** 8.32

13. 2.78×10^3 **14.** 8.62×10^6 **15.** 3.58×10^{-4} **16.** 9.51×10^{-2}

B.2 Common Logarithms: The Mantissa

In this section, we discuss common logarithms and the use of the Table of Common Logarithms (Table II, Appendix C).

Finding the Mantissa

Hereafter, *when the logarithm of a number is written without giving the base, the base is understood to be* 10. We write log N instead of $\log_{10} N$.

Example 2   Find the mantissa for log 5.74. (Figure B.1 is part of Table II, Appendix C.)

N	0	1	2	3	4	5	6	7	8	9
5ˏ5	0.7404	0.7412	0.7419	0.7427	0.7435	0.7443	0.7451	0.7459	0.7466	0.7474
5ˏ6	0.7482	0.7490	0.7497	0.7505	0.7513	0.7520	0.7528	0.7536	0.7543	0.7551
5ˏ7	0.7559	0.7566	0.7574	0.7582	0.7589	0.7597	0.7604	0.7612	0.7619	0.7627
5ˏ8	0.7634	0.7642	0.7649	0.7657	0.7664	0.7672	0.7679	0.7686	0.7694	0.7701
5ˏ9	0.7709	0.7716	0.7723	0.7731	0.7738	0.7745	0.7752	0.7760	0.7767	0.7774
6ˏ0	0.7782	0.7789	0.7796	0.7803	0.7810	0.7818	0.7825	0.7832	0.7839	0.7846
6ˏ1	0.7853	0.7860	0.7868	0.7875	0.7882	0.7889	0.7896	0.7903	0.7910	0.7917

Third digit of 5.7 **4**

— *First two digits* of **5.7** 4

— 0.7589 is the *mantissa* of log 5.74

FIGURE B.1

Example 3   Find log 8,360.

$$\log 8 \overset{\wedge}{\underset{\longrightarrow}{360.}} \Rightarrow \text{characteristic} = 3$$

N	0	1	2	3	4	5	6	7	8	9
7∧8	0.8921	0.8927	0.8932	0.8938	0.8943	0.8949	0.8954	0.8960	0.8965	0.8971
7∧9	0.8976	0.8982	0.8987	0.8993	0.8998	0.9004	0.9009	0.9015	0.9020	0.9025
8∧0	0.9031	0.9036	0.9042	0.9047	0.9053	0.9058	0.9063	0.9069	0.9074	0.9079
8∧1	0.9085	0.9090	0.9096	0.9101	0.9106	0.9112	0.9117	0.9122	0.9128	0.9133
8∧2	0.9138	0.9143	0.9149	0.9154	0.9159	0.9165	0.9170	0.9175	0.9180	0.9186
8∧3	0.9191	0.9196	0.9201	0.9206	0.9212	0.9217	0.9222	0.9227	0.9232	0.9238
8∧4	0.9234	0.9248	0.9253	0.9258	0.9263	0.9269	0.9274	0.9279	0.9284	0.9289

Mantissa

Therefore, log 8,360 = 3 . 9222

Characteristic   ■

Example 4   Find $\log_{10} 727$.

The characteristic is 2, because $727 = 7.27 \times 10^2$. The mantissa is 0.8615 (from Table II). Therefore, $\log_{10} 727 = 2.8615$.   ■

Example 5   Find $\log_{10} 0.0438$.

The characteristic is -2, because $0.0438 = 4.38 \times 10^{-2}$. However, we will write -2 as 8. -10 . The mantissa (from Table II) is 0.6415. Therefore, $\log_{10} 0.0438 = 8.6415 - 10$.   ■

The *characteristic* may be positive, negative, or zero, but the mantissas in the table are *never* negative.   ☑

Example 6   Find log 0.0000429.

The characteristic is -5, which we will write as 5. -10 . The mantissa is 0.6325. Therefore, log 0.0000429 = 5.6325 − 10.   ■

EXERCISES B.2

Set I   Find each logarithm.

1. log 754
2. log 186
3. log 17
4. log 29
5. log 3,350
6. log 4,610
7. log 7,000
8. log 200
9. log 0.0604
10. log 0.0186
11. $\log(5.64 \times 10^3)$
12. $\log(2.14 \times 10^{-4})$

Set II   Find each logarithm.

1. log 0.905
2. log 0.306
3. log 58.9
4. log 36.7
5. $\log(5.77 \times 10^{-4})$
6. $\log(3.96 \times 10^3)$
7. log 15,000
8. log 0.0123
9. log 0.0013
10. log 5
11. $\log(3.16 \times 10^5)$
12. $\log(4.1 \times 10^{-3})$

B.3 Natural Logarithms

A special abbreviation, ln, is used for logarithms to the base e. That is, $\ln x = \log_e x$.

A brief table of natural logarithms is given in Table III, Appendix C. Natural logarithms do not have a characteristic or a mantissa. To find the natural logarithm of a number in Table III, we look for that number under the column headed n. If we find the desired number in that column, we read the value of its logarithm directly from the table, under the column headed $\log_e n$. If we do *not* find the desired number in the column headed n, we must use the laws of logarithms before we proceed (see Example 8).

Example 7   Find ln 4.7.

Figure B.2 is part of Table III, Appendix C. We *do* find 4.7 in the table under the column headed n. Therefore, we read $\ln 4.7 = 1.5476$.

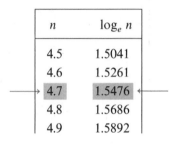

n	$\log_e n$
4.5	1.5041
4.6	1.5261
4.7	1.5476
4.8	1.5686
4.9	1.5892

FIGURE B.2

Example 8   Find ln 2,000.

We do *not* find 2,000 in the column headed n. We can, however, rewrite 2,000 as 20(100). Then

$$\ln 2{,}000 = \ln 20(100)$$
$$= \ln 20 + \ln 100$$
$$= 2.9957 + 4.6052$$
$$= 7.6009$$

We could, instead, write 2,000 as $2(10^3)$. The result is the same. ∎

EXERCISES B.3

Set I   Find the logarithms.

1. ln 3.6   **2.** ln 5.2   **3.** ln 8.1   **4.** ln 7.5

5. ln 83   **6.** ln 62   **7.** ln 0.002   **8.** ln 0.006

Set II   Find the logarithms.

1. ln 2.8   **2.** ln 7.6   **3.** ln 1.6   **4.** ln 140

5. ln 78   **6.** ln 14,000   **7.** ln 0.008   **8.** ln 0.035

B.4 Interpolation

Sometimes we want the logarithm of a number that lies *between* two consecutive numbers in Table II. The process of finding such a number is called **interpolation**.

Example 9   Find log 29.38.

2ˌ9.38 lies *between* 2ˌ9.3 and 2ˌ9.4.

N	0	1	2	3	4	5	6	7	8	9
2ˌ8	0.4472	0.4487	0.4502	0.4518	0.4533	0.4548	0.4564	0.4579	0.4594	0.4609
2ˌ9	0.4624	0.4639	0.4654	0.4669	0.4683	0.4698	0.4713	0.4728	0.4742	0.4757
3ˌ0	0.4771	0.4786	0.4800	0.4814	0.4829	0.4843	0.4857	0.4871	0.4886	0.4900
3ˌ1	0.4914	0.4928	0.4942	0.4955	0.4969	0.4983	0.4997	0.5011	0.5024	0.5038
3ˌ2	0.5051	0.5065	0.5079	0.5092	0.5105	0.5119	0.5132	0.5145	0.5159	0.5172
3ˌ3	0.5185	0.5198	0.5211	0.5224	0.5237	0.5250	0.5263	0.5276	0.5289	0.5302
3ˌ4	0.5315	0.5328	0.5340	0.5353	0.5366	0.5378	0.5391	0.5403	0.5416	0.5428

Mantissa for 2ˌ9.38 lies
between 0.4669 and 0.4683

We generally arrange the work as follows:

$$10 \left\{ \begin{array}{l} \text{log } 29.30 = 1.4669 \\[4pt] \quad _8\!\searrow \text{log } 29.38 = \\[4pt] \text{log } 29.40 = 1.4683 \end{array} \right\} \; 0.0014$$

Since 29.38 is eight-tenths of the way from 29.30 to 29.40, we assume that log 29.38 is eight-tenths of the way from 1.4669 to 1.4683. We first subtract 1.4669 from 1.4683, getting 0.0014. Next we find $\frac{8}{10}$ of 0.0014, which is 0.00112. We round that answer off to four decimal places (to 0.0011) and then add 0.0011 to 1.4669 (the smaller number). It is customary to omit the decimal point and the zeros and to show the work as follows:

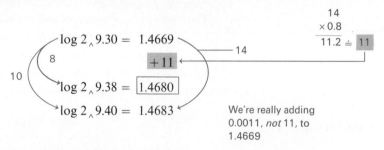

$$10 \left\{ \begin{array}{l} \text{log } 2_{\wedge}9.30 = 1.4669 \\[4pt] \quad _8\!\searrow \text{log } 2_{\wedge}9.38 = \boxed{1.4680} \\[4pt] \text{log } 2_{\wedge}9.40 = 1.4683 \end{array} \right.$$

$$\boxed{+11} \leftarrow 14$$

$$\begin{array}{r} 14 \\ \times 0.8 \\ \hline 11.2 \doteq \boxed{11} \end{array}$$

We're really adding
0.0011, *not* 11, to
1.4669

Therefore, log 29.38 = 1.4680.

The number to be added can also be found by solving a proportion. (We again omit the decimal point and the zeros.)

$$10 \left\{ \begin{array}{l} \text{log } 29.30 = 1.4669 \\[4pt] \quad _8\!\searrow \text{log } 29.38 = \\[4pt] \text{log } 29.40 = 1.4683 \end{array} \right\} \begin{array}{l} x \\ 14 \end{array}$$

$$\frac{8}{10} = \frac{x}{14}$$

$$10x = 112$$

$$x = 11.2 \doteq 11 \quad \blacksquare$$

When a four-place log table is used, the mantissa is rounded off to four decimal places.

Example 10   Find log 0.002749.

$2_\wedge 749$ lies *between* $2_\wedge 740$ and $2_\wedge 750$.

N	0	1	2	3	4	5	6	7	8	9
$2_\wedge 0$	0.3010	0.3032	0.3054	0.3075	0.3096	0.3118	0.3139	0.3160	0.3181	0.3201
$2_\wedge 1$	0.3222	0.3243	0.3263	0.3284	0.3304	0.3324	0.3345	0.3365	0.3385	0.3404
$2_\wedge 2$	0.3424	0.3444	0.3464	0.3483	0.3502	0.3522	0.3541	0.3560	0.3579	0.3598
$2_\wedge 3$	0.3617	0.3636	0.3655	0.3674	0.3692	0.3711	0.3729	0.3747	0.3766	0.3784
$2_\wedge 4$	0.3802	0.3820	0.3838	0.3856	0.3874	0.3892	0.3909	0.3927	0.3945	0.3962
$2_\wedge 5$	0.3979	0.3997	0.4014	0.4031	0.4048	0.4065	0.4082	0.4099	0.4116	0.4133
$2_\wedge 6$	0.4150	0.4166	0.4183	0.4200	0.4216	0.4232	0.4249	0.4265	0.4281	0.4298
$2_\wedge 7$	0.4314	0.4330	0.4346	0.4362	0.4378	0.4393	0.4409	0.4425	0.4440	0.4456

Mantissa for $2_\wedge 749$ lies
between 0.4378 and 0.4393

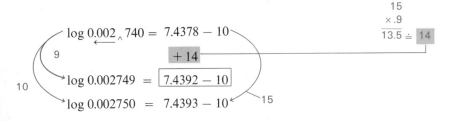

Therefore, log 0.002749 = 7.4392 − 10. ■

Tables of common logarithms come in different accuracies. The mantissa of the logarithm of a number is usually a never-ending decimal. Some tables have mantissas rounded off to four places, others to five places, and so on. Table II is a four-place table. If you use other than a four-place table to solve the problems in this chapter, you may get slightly different answers.

We will follow the customary practice of using the equal sign ($=$) instead of the approximately equal sign ($\doteq$) when writing logarithms of numbers.

The logarithms of numbers can be found by means of a calculator (with a $\boxed{\text{LOG}}$ key) as well as by using tables. If you have a calculator with a $\boxed{\text{LOG}}$ key, we suggest that you use your calculator to check logarithms found by using the tables. One difference between logarithms obtained by calculator and those obtained from Table II occurs when the characteristic of the logarithm is negative. In Example 10,

$$\log 0.002749 = 7.4392 - 10$$

was found by using Table II. If this same logarithm were found by depressing the $\boxed{\text{LOG}}$ key of a calculator, we would get

$$\log 0.002749 = -2.5608$$

But

$$7.4392 - 10 = -2.5608$$

EXERCISES B.4

Set I   Find each logarithm.

1. log 23.35   **2.** log 27.85   **3.** log 3.062

4. log 4.098   **5.** log 0.06644   **6.** log 0.5839

7. log 150.7   **8.** log 20.88   **9.** $\log(8.375 \times 10^6)$

10. $\log(3.875 \times 10^{-5})$ **11.** log 324.38   **12.** log 75.062

Set II   Find each logarithm.

1. log 186,300   **2.** log 92,840,000   **3.** log 0.8006

4. log 0.07093   **5.** log 0.004003   **6.** $\log(1.756 \times 10^{-6})$

7. log 62.34   **8.** log 0.005326   **9.** log 2,168

10. log 0.0003152   **11.** $\log(1.425 \times 10^4)$ **12.** $\log(4.257 \times 10^{-3})$

B.5 Finding Common Antilogarithms

NOTE   Finding N when ln N (its natural logarithm) is known is discussed in Section 11.4B. ☑

In the preceding sections, we discussed finding the logarithm of a given number.

Number → Logarithm

Given N,   find   log N

The two statements that follow are equivalent:

$$\log N = L$$
$$N = \text{antilog } L$$

Example 11   If log $N = 3.6263$, find N.

1. Locate the mantissa (0.6263) in the body of Table II, and find the number 4 ∧ 23 by the method shown on page 628.

2. Use the characteristic (3) to locate the actual decimal point. Therefore,

$$N = 4 {\scriptstyle\wedge} \underset{3}{\underrightarrow{230.}} = 4{,}230$$

Third digit of N

N	0	1	2	3	4	5	6	7	8	9
4,0	0.6021	0.6031	0.6042	0.6053	0.6064	0.6075	0.6085	0.6096	0.6107	0.6117
4,1	0.6128	0.6138	0.6149	0.6160	0.6170	0.6180	0.6191	0.6201	0.6212	0.6222
4,2	0.6232	0.6243	0.6253	0.6263	0.6274	0.6284	0.6294	0.6304	0.6314	0.6325
4,3	0.6335	0.6345	0.6355	0.6365	0.6375	0.6385	0.6395	0.6405	0.6415	0.6425
4,4	0.6435	0.6444	0.6454	0.6464	0.6474	0.6484	0.6493	0.6503	0.6513	0.6522

First two digits of N — Mantissa

Example 12 If $N = \text{antilog}(7.8675 - 10)$, find N.

$$\log N = 7.8675 - 10$$

1. Locate the mantissa (0.8675) in the body of Table II, and find the number 7,37 by the method shown in the figure below.

2. Use the characteristic ($7 - 10 = -3$) to locate the actual decimal point. (Recall that the characteristic is the exponent of 10 when the number is in scientific notation.) Therefore,

$$N = 0.007\,_{\wedge}37 = 0.00737$$

N	0	1	2	3	4	5	6	7	8	9
7,0	0.8451	0.8457	0.8463	0.8470	0.8476	0.8482	0.8488	0.8494	0.8500	0.8506
7,1	0.8513	0.8519	0.8525	0.8531	0.8537	0.8543	0.8549	0.8555	0.8561	0.8567
7,2	0.8573	0.8579	0.8585	0.8591	0.8597	0.8603	0.8609	0.8615	0.8621	0.8627
7,3	0.8633	0.8639	0.8645	0.8651	0.8657	0.8663	0.8669	0.8675	0.8681	0.8686
7,4	0.8692	0.8698	0.8704	0.8710	0.8716	0.8722	0.8727	0.8733	0.8739	0.8745

Mantissa

When the mantissa falls between two consecutive numbers in Table II, we must *interpolate*. (See Examples 13 and 14.)

Example 13 Find antilog 4.7129.

Let $N = \text{antilog } 4.7129$. Then $\log N = 4.7129$.

N	0	1	2	3	4	5	6	7	8	9
5,0	0.6990	0.6998	0.7007	0.7016	0.7024	0.7033	0.7042	0.7050	0.7059	0.7067
5,1	0.7076	0.7084	0.7093	0.7101	0.7110	0.7118	0.7126	0.7135	0.7143	0.7152
5,2	0.7160	0.7168	0.7177	0.7185	0.7193	0.7202	0.7210	0.7218	0.7226	0.7235
5,3	0.7243	0.7251	0.7259	0.7267	0.7275	0.7284	0.7292	0.7300	0.7308	0.7316
5,4	0.7324	0.7332	0.7340	0.7348	0.7356	0.7364	0.7372	0.7380	0.7388	0.7396

Mantissa 0.7129 lies *between* 0.7126 and 0.7135

Locate the mantissa (0.7129) *between* 0.7126 and 0.7135. The mantissa 0.7126 has antilog 5∧16, and mantissa 0.7135 has antilog 5∧17 (attach a fourth digit, 0).

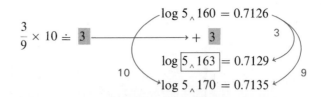

$$\frac{3}{9} \times 10 \doteq 3$$

$$\begin{array}{l} \log 5_\wedge 160 = 0.7126 \\ + \;3 \\ \log \boxed{5_\wedge 163} = 0.7129 \\ \log 5_\wedge 170 = 0.7135 \end{array}$$

Since mantissa 0.7129 is three-ninths of the way from 0.7126 to 0.7135, we assume that N is three-ninths of the way from 5∧160 to 5∧170. Therefore, we add $\frac{3}{9} \times 10 \doteq 3$ to the last place of 5∧160 and get 5∧163. Then

$$N = 5_\wedge 1630. = 51,630$$

4
↑
└── Characteristic

Therefore, antilog 4.7129 = 51,630. ∎

Example 14 Find antilog(8.7385 − 10).

$$\log N = 8.7385 - 10$$

Locate the mantissa (0.7385) between 0.7380 and 0.7388. The mantissa 0.7380 has antilog 5∧47, and mantissa 0.7388 has antilog 5∧48 (attach a fourth digit, 0).

$$\frac{5}{8} \times 10 = 6.25$$
$$\doteq 6$$

$$\begin{array}{l} \log 5_\wedge 470 = 0.7380 \\ + 6 \\ \log 5_\wedge 476 = 0.7385 \\ \log 5_\wedge 480 = 0.7388 \end{array}$$

Therefore,

$$N = 0.05_\wedge 476 = 0.05476$$

−2
↑
└── Characteristic = 8 − 10 = −2 ∎

The antilogarithms of numbers can be found with a calculator by using the $\boxed{10^x}$ key or $\boxed{\text{INV}}$ $\boxed{\text{LOG}}$ keys.

EXERCISES B.5

Set I In Exercises 1–12, find each antilogarithm.

1. antilog 3.5478

2. antilog 2.4409

3. antilog 0.9605

4. antilog 0.8848

5. antilog(9.2529 − 10)

6. antilog(8.1271 − 10)

7. antilog 3.5051   **8.** antilog 2.6335

9. antilog 4.0588   **10.** antilog 3.0846

11. antilog$(6.9900 - 10)$ **12.** antilog$(7.9596 - 10)$

In Exercises 13–16, find N.

13. $\log N = 7.7168 - 10$ **14.** $\log N = 4.9410 - 10$

15. $\log N = 1.7120$ **16.** $\log N = 4.9873$

Set II   In Exercises 1–12, find each antilogarithm.

1. antilog$(7.6117 - 10)$ **2.** antilog$(6.6010 - 10)$

3. antilog 1.1685   **4.** antilog 2.5470

5. antilog$(8.6908 - 10)$ **6.** antilog$(9.7995 - 10)$

7. antilog 4.7388   **8.** antilog$(7.6096 - 10)$

9. antilog 2.0486   **10.** antilog$(8.8136 - 10)$

11. antilog$(6.2963 - 10)$ **12.** antilog 6.0925

In Exercises 13–16, find N.

13. $\log N = 3.4084$ **14.** $\log N = 0.5011$

15. $\log N = 0.6860$ **16.** $\log N = 8.0367 - 10$

B.6   Calculating with Logarithms

Logarithms can be used to perform arithmetic calculations. In this chapter, we assume that all numbers given in examples and exercises are *exact* numbers. Answers are rounded off to the accuracy of Table II (four decimal places).

Example 15   Multiply $(37.5)(0.00842)$.
Let

$$N = (37.5)(0.00842)$$

$$\log N = \log(37.5)(0.00842)$$

$$= \log 37.5 + \log 0.00842 \qquad \text{Rule 11.7}$$

$$= 1.5740 + 7.9253 - 10 \qquad \begin{array}{l} 1.5740 \\ 7.9253 - 10 \\ \hline 9.4993 - 10 \end{array}$$

$$\log N = 9.4993 - 10 \longleftarrow$$

$$N = 0.3\,{}_{\wedge}157 = 0.3157$$

Before any calculating is done, it is helpful to analyze the problem and make an outline of the procedure to be followed. ∎

Example 16   Divide $\dfrac{6.74}{0.0391}$.

Let

$$N = \frac{6.74}{0.0391}$$

$$\log N = \log \frac{6.74}{0.0391}$$

$$= \log 6.74 - \log 0.0391 \qquad \text{Rule 11.8}$$

The characteristic 0 is written as $10 - 10$
to help with the subtraction

Blank Outline of Procedure	*Actual Calculations*
$\log 6.74 =$	$\log 6.74 = \boxed{10}\ .8287\ \boxed{-10}$
$\log 0.0391 = \underline{\hspace{2cm}} \Big]\,(-)$	$\log 0.0391 = \underline{8\ .5922\ -10} \Big]\,(-)$
$\log N =$	$\log N = \quad 2\ .2365$
$N =$	$N = \quad 1\,{}_{\wedge}72.4 = 172.4 \quad\blacksquare$

Example 17   Find $(1.05)^{10}$.

Let

$$N = (1.05)^{10}$$

$$\log N = \log(1.05)^{10}$$

$$= 10 \log 1.05 \qquad \text{Rule 11.9}$$

Blank Outline	*Actual Calculations*
$\log 1.05 =$	$\log 1.05 = 0.0212$
$\log N = 10 \log 1.05 =$	$\log N = 10 \log 1.05 = 0.2120$
$N =$	$N = 1.629$
	$= 1.629 \quad\blacksquare$

Example 18   Find $\sqrt[3]{0.506}$.

Let

$$N = \sqrt[3]{0.506} = (0.506)^{1/3}$$

$$\log N = \log(0.506)^{1/3}$$

$$= \tfrac{1}{3} \log 0.506 \qquad \text{Rule 11.9}$$

Blank Outline	*Actual Calculations*
$\log 0.506 =$	$\log 0.506 = 9.7042 - 10$
$\log N = \tfrac{1}{3} \log 0.506 =$	$= \boxed{29}\ .7042\ \boxed{-30}$
$N =$	$\log N = \tfrac{1}{3} \log 0.506 = 9.9014 - 10$
	$N = 0.7\,{}_{\wedge}968$
	$= 0.7968 \quad\blacksquare$

The characteristic $9 - 10$
is written as $29 - 30$ so
that the second term, -30,
is exactly divisible by 3

The method for calculating with logarithms can be summarized as follows:

TO CALCULATE WITH LOGARITHMS

1. Analyze the problem and make a blank outline.

2. Write all the characteristics in the blank outline.

3. Use Table II to find all the mantissas, and then write them in the blank outline.

4. Carry out the calculations indicated in the outline.

Example 19   Find $N = \dfrac{(1.16)^5(31.7)}{\sqrt{481(0.629)}}$.

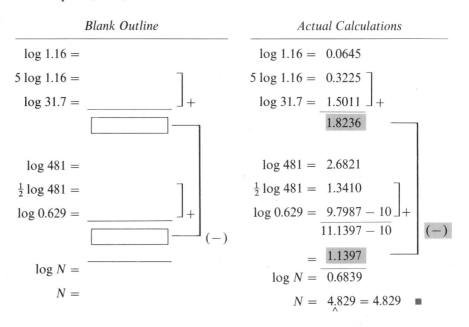

	Blank Outline		*Actual Calculations*
log 1.16 =		log 1.16 =	0.0645
5 log 1.16 =		5 log 1.16 =	0.3225
log 31.7 =	] +	log 31.7 =	1.5011] +
			1.8236
log 481 =		log 481 =	2.6821
½ log 481 =		½ log 481 =	1.3410
log 0.629 =	] +	log 0.629 =	9.7987 − 10] +
	(−)		11.1397 − 10 (−)
log N =		=	1.1397
N =		log N =	0.6839
		N =	4.829 = 4.829 ■

EXERCISES B.6

In the exercises (in both sets) that follow, use logarithms to perform the calculations. Assume that all the given numbers are *exact* numbers. Round off answers to the accuracy of Table II (four decimal places). We suggest that you use a calculator to verify the results obtained by the logarithmic calculations. There may be a slight difference in the answers obtained by using a calculator and those found by using the table because of their different levels of accuracy.

Set I

1. 74.3×0.618

2. 0.314×14.9

3. $\dfrac{562}{21.4}$

4. $\dfrac{651}{30.6}$

5. $(1.09)^5$

6. $(3.4)^4$

7. $\sqrt[3]{0.444}$

8. $\sqrt[4]{0.897}$

9. $2.863 + \log 38.46$

10. $\dfrac{\log 7.86}{\log 38.4}$

11. $\sqrt[5]{\dfrac{(5.86)(17.4)}{\sqrt{450}}}$

12. $\dfrac{(5.65)\sqrt[6]{175}}{(2.4)^4}$

Set II

1. $\dfrac{(4.92)(25.7)}{388}$

2. $\dfrac{(2.04)^5}{(5.9)(0.66)}$

3. $\log 786.4 + 3.154$

4. $\sqrt[3]{0.564}$

5. $\dfrac{\log 58.4}{\log 2.50}$

6. $\sqrt[4]{\dfrac{(39.4)(7.86)}{\sqrt[3]{704}}}$

7. $\sqrt{0.00378}$

8. $\dfrac{1.26}{(0.0245)(0.00143)}$

9. $(2.87)^{12}$

10. $\sqrt{0.792}$

11. $\dfrac{\sqrt{4.63}}{\sqrt{0.0732}}$

12. $\dfrac{\log 1.25}{\log 1.05}$

Appendix C   Tables

Table I   Exponential Functions

x	e^x	e^{-x}	x	e^x	e^{-x}
0.00	1.0000	1.0000	1.5	4.4817	0.2231
0.01	1.0101	0.9901	1.6	4.9530	0.2019
0.02	1.0202	0.9802	1.7	5.4739	0.1827
0.03	1.0305	0.9705	1.8	6.0496	0.1653
0.04	1.0408	0.9608	1.9	6.6859	0.1496
0.05	1.0513	0.9512	2.0	7.3891	0.1353
0.06	1.0618	0.9418	2.1	8.1662	0.1225
0.07	1.0725	0.9324	2.2	9.0250	0.1108
0.08	1.0833	0.9231	2.3	9.9742	0.1003
0.09	1.0942	0.9139	2.4	11.023	0.0907
0.10	1.1052	0.9048	2.5	12.182	0.0821
0.11	1.1163	0.8958	2.6	13.464	0.0743
0.12	1.1275	0.8869	2.7	14.880	0.0672
0.13	1.1388	0.8781	2.8	16.445	0.0608
0.14	1.1503	0.8694	2.9	18.174	0.0550
0.15	1.1618	0.8607	3.0	20.086	0.0498
0.16	1.1735	0.8521	3.1	22.198	0.0450
0.17	1.1853	0.8437	3.2	24.533	0.0408
0.18	1.1972	0.8353	3.3	27.113	0.0369
0.19	1.2092	0.8270	3.4	29.964	0.0334
0.20	1.2214	0.8187	3.5	33.115	0.0302
0.21	1.2337	0.8106	3.6	36.598	0.0273
0.22	1.2461	0.8025	3.7	40.447	0.0247
0.23	1.2586	0.7945	3.8	44.701	0.0224
0.24	1.2712	0.7866	3.9	49.402	0.0202
0.25	1.2840	0.7788	4.0	54.598	0.0183
0.30	1.3499	0.7408	4.1	60.340	0.0166
0.35	1.4191	0.7047	4.2	66.686	0.0150
0.40	1.4918	0.6703	4.3	73.700	0.0136
0.45	1.5683	0.6376	4.4	81.451	0.0123
0.50	1.6487	0.6065	4.5	90.017	0.0111
0.55	1.7333	0.5769	4.6	99.484	0.0101
0.60	1.8221	0.5488	4.7	109.95	0.0091
0.65	1.9155	0.5220	4.8	121.51	0.0082
0.70	2.0138	0.4966	4.9	134.29	0.0074
0.75	2.1170	0.4724	5.0	148.41	0.0067
0.80	2.2255	0.4493	5.5	244.69	0.0041
0.85	2.3396	0.4274	6.0	403.43	0.0025
0.90	2.4596	0.4066	6.5	665.14	0.0015
0.95	2.5857	0.3867	7.0	1096.6	0.0009
1.0	2.7183	0.3679	7.5	1808.0	0.0006
1.1	3.0042	0.3329	8.0	2981.0	0.0003
1.2	3.3201	0.3012	8.5	4914.8	0.0002
1.3	3.6693	0.2725	9.0	8103.1	0.0001
1.4	4.0552	0.2466	10.0	22026.0	0.00005

Table II Common Logarithms

N	0	1	2	3	4	5	6	7	8	9
1.0	0.0000	0.0043	0.0086	0.0128	0.0170	0.0212	0.0253	0.0294	0.0334	0.0374
1.1	0.0414	0.0453	0.0492	0.0531	0.0569	0.0607	0.0645	0.0682	0.0719	0.0755
1.2	0.0792	0.0828	0.0864	0.0899	0.0934	0.0969	0.1004	0.1038	0.1072	0.1106
1.3	0.1139	0.1173	0.1206	0.1239	0.1271	0.1303	0.1335	0.1367	0.1399	0.1430
1.4	0.1461	0.1492	0.1523	0.1553	0.1584	0.1614	0.1644	0.1673	0.1703	0.1732
1.5	0.1761	0.1790	0.1818	0.1847	0.1875	0.1903	0.1931	0.1959	0.1987	0.2014
1.6	0.2041	0.2068	0.2095	0.2122	0.2148	0.2175	0.2201	0.2227	0.2253	0.2279
1.7	0.2304	0.2330	0.2355	0.2380	0.2405	0.2430	0.2455	0.2480	0.2504	0.2529
1.8	0.2553	0.2577	0.2601	0.2625	0.2648	0.2672	0.2695	0.2718	0.2742	0.2765
1.9	0.2788	0.2810	0.2833	0.2856	0.2878	0.2900	0.2923	0.2945	0.2967	0.2989
2.0	0.3010	0.3032	0.3054	0.3075	0.3096	0.3118	0.3139	0.3160	0.3181	0.3201
2.1	0.3222	0.3243	0.3263	0.3284	0.3304	0.3324	0.3345	0.3365	0.3385	0.3404
2.2	0.3424	0.3444	0.3464	0.3483	0.3502	0.3522	0.3541	0.3560	0.3579	0.3598
2.3	0.3617	0.3636	0.3655	0.3674	0.3692	0.3711	0.3729	0.3747	0.3766	0.3784
2.4	0.3802	0.3820	0.3838	0.3856	0.3874	0.3892	0.3909	0.3927	0.3945	0.3962
2.5	0.3979	0.3997	0.4014	0.4031	0.4048	0.4065	0.4082	0.4099	0.4116	0.4133
2.6	0.4150	0.4166	0.4183	0.4200	0.4216	0.4232	0.4249	0.4265	0.4281	0.4298
2.7	0.4314	0.4330	0.4346	0.4362	0.4378	0.4393	0.4409	0.4425	0.4440	0.4456
2.8	0.4472	0.4487	0.4502	0.4518	0.4533	0.4548	0.4564	0.4579	0.4594	0.4609
2.9	0.4624	0.4639	0.4654	0.4669	0.4683	0.4698	0.4713	0.4728	0.4742	0.4757
3.0	0.4771	0.4786	0.4800	0.4814	0.4829	0.4843	0.4857	0.4871	0.4886	0.4900
3.1	0.4914	0.4928	0.4942	0.4955	0.4969	0.4983	0.4997	0.5011	0.5024	0.5038
3.2	0.5051	0.5065	0.5079	0.5092	0.5105	0.5119	0.5132	0.5145	0.5159	0.5172
3.3	0.5185	0.5198	0.5211	0.5224	0.5237	0.5250	0.5263	0.5276	0.5289	0.5302
3.4	0.5315	0.5328	0.5340	0.5353	0.5366	0.5378	0.5391	0.5403	0.5416	0.5428
3.5	0.5441	0.5453	0.5465	0.5478	0.5490	0.5502	0.5514	0.5527	0.5539	0.5551
3.6	0.5563	0.5575	0.5587	0.5599	0.5611	0.5623	0.5635	0.5647	0.5658	0.5670
3.7	0.5682	0.5694	0.5705	0.5717	0.5729	0.5740	0.5752	0.5763	0.5775	0.5786
3.8	0.5798	0.5809	0.5821	0.5832	0.5843	0.5855	0.5866	0.5877	0.5888	0.5899
3.9	0.5911	0.5922	0.5933	0.5944	0.5955	0.5966	0.5977	0.5988	0.5999	0.6010
4.0	0.6021	0.6031	0.6042	0.6053	0.6064	0.6075	0.6085	0.6096	0.6107	0.6117
4.1	0.6128	0.6138	0.6149	0.6160	0.6170	0.6180	0.6191	0.6201	0.6212	0.6222
4.2	0.6232	0.6243	0.6253	0.6263	0.6274	0.6284	0.6294	0.6304	0.6314	0.6325
4.3	0.6335	0.6345	0.6355	0.6365	0.6375	0.6385	0.6395	0.6405	0.6415	0.6425
4.4	0.6435	0.6444	0.6454	0.6464	0.6474	0.6484	0.6493	0.6503	0.6513	0.6522
4.5	0.6532	0.6542	0.6551	0.6561	0.6571	0.6580	0.6590	0.6599	0.6609	0.6618
4.6	0.6628	0.6637	0.6646	0.6656	0.6665	0.6675	0.6684	0.6693	0.6702	0.6712
4.7	0.6721	0.6730	0.6739	0.6749	0.6758	0.6767	0.6776	0.6785	0.6794	0.6803
4.8	0.6812	0.6821	0.6830	0.6839	0.6848	0.6857	0.6866	0.6875	0.6884	0.6893
4.9	0.6902	0.6911	0.6920	0.6928	0.6937	0.6946	0.6955	0.6964	0.6972	0.6981
5.0	0.6990	0.6998	0.7007	0.7016	0.7024	0.7033	0.7042	0.7050	0.7059	0.7067
5.1	0.7076	0.7084	0.7093	0.7101	0.7110	0.7118	0.7126	0.7135	0.7143	0.7152
5.2	0.7160	0.7168	0.7177	0.7185	0.7193	0.7202	0.7210	0.7218	0.7226	0.7235
5.3	0.7243	0.7251	0.7259	0.7267	0.7275	0.7284	0.7292	0.7300	0.7308	0.7316
5.4	0.7324	0.7332	0.7340	0.7348	0.7356	0.7364	0.7372	0.7380	0.7388	0.7396
N	0	1	2	3	4	5	6	7	8	9

Table II *Continued*

N	0	1	2	3	4	5	6	7	8	9
5$_\wedge$5	0.7404	0.7412	0.7419	0.7427	0.7435	0.7443	0.7451	0.7459	0.7466	0.7474
5$_\wedge$6	0.7482	0.7490	0.7497	0.7505	0.7513	0.7520	0.7528	0.7536	0.7543	0.7551
5$_\wedge$7	0.7559	0.7566	0.7574	0.7582	0.7589	0.7597	0.7604	0.7612	0.7619	0.7627
5$_\wedge$8	0.7634	0.7642	0.7649	0.7657	0.7664	0.7672	0.7679	0.7686	0.7694	0.7701
5$_\wedge$9	0.7709	0.7716	0.7723	0.7731	0.7738	0.7745	0.7752	0.7760	0.7767	0.7774
6$_\wedge$0	0.7782	0.7789	0.7796	0.7803	0.7810	0.7818	0.7825	0.7832	0.7839	0.7846
6$_\wedge$1	0.7853	0.7860	0.7868	0.7875	0.7882	0.7889	0.7896	0.7903	0.7910	0.7917
6$_\wedge$2	0.7924	0.7931	0.7938	0.7945	0.7952	0.7959	0.7966	0.7973	0.7980	0.7987
6$_\wedge$3	0.7993	0.8000	0.8007	0.8014	0.8021	0.8028	0.8035	0.8041	0.8048	0.8055
6$_\wedge$4	0.8062	0.8069	0.8075	0.8082	0.8089	0.8096	0.8102	0.8109	0.8116	0.8122
6$_\wedge$5	0.8129	0.8136	0.8142	0.8149	0.8156	0.8162	0.8169	0.8176	0.8182	0.8189
6$_\wedge$6	0.8195	0.8202	0.8209	0.8215	0.8222	0.8228	0.8235	0.8241	0.8248	0.8254
6$_\wedge$7	0.8261	0.8267	0.8274	0.8280	0.8287	0.8293	0.8299	0.8306	0.8312	0.8319
6$_\wedge$8	0.8325	0.8331	0.8338	0.8344	0.8351	0.8357	0.8363	0.8370	0.8376	0.8382
6$_\wedge$9	0.8388	0.8395	0.8401	0.8407	0.8414	0.8420	0.8426	0.8432	0.8439	0.8445
7$_\wedge$0	0.8451	0.8457	0.8463	0.8470	0.8476	0.8482	0.8488	0.8494	0.8500	0.8506
7$_\wedge$1	0.8513	0.8519	0.8525	0.8531	0.8537	0.8543	0.8549	0.8555	0.8561	0.8567
7$_\wedge$2	0.8573	0.8579	0.8585	0.8591	0.8597	0.8603	0.8609	0.8615	0.8621	0.8627
7$_\wedge$3	0.8633	0.8639	0.8645	0.8651	0.8657	0.8663	0.8669	0.8675	0.8681	0.8686
7$_\wedge$4	0.8692	0.8698	0.8704	0.8710	0.8716	0.8722	0.8727	0.8733	0.8739	0.8745
7$_\wedge$5	0.8751	0.8756	0.8762	0.8768	0.8774	0.8779	0.8785	0.8791	0.8797	0.8802
7$_\wedge$6	0.8808	0.8814	0.8820	0.8825	0.8831	0.8837	0.8842	0.8848	0.8854	0.8859
7$_\wedge$7	0.8865	0.8871	0.8876	0.8882	0.8887	0.8893	0.8899	0.8904	0.8910	0.8915
7$_\wedge$8	0.8921	0.8927	0.8932	0.8938	0.8943	0.8949	0.8954	0.8960	0.8965	0.8971
7$_\wedge$9	0.8976	0.8982	0.8987	0.8993	0.8998	0.9004	0.9009	0.9015	0.9020	0.9025
8$_\wedge$0	0.9031	0.9036	0.9042	0.9047	0.9053	0.9058	0.9063	0.9069	0.9074	0.9079
8$_\wedge$1	0.9085	0.9090	0.9096	0.9101	0.9106	0.9112	0.9117	0.9122	0.9128	0.9133
8$_\wedge$2	0.9138	0.9143	0.9149	0.9154	0.9159	0.9165	0.9170	0.9175	0.9180	0.9186
8$_\wedge$3	0.9191	0.9196	0.9201	0.9206	0.9212	0.9217	0.9222	0.9227	0.9232	0.9238
8$_\wedge$4	0.9243	0.9248	0.9253	0.9258	0.9263	0.9269	0.9274	0.9279	0.9284	0.9289
8$_\wedge$5	0.9294	0.9299	0.9304	0.9309	0.9315	0.9320	0.9325	0.9330	0.9335	0.9340
8$_\wedge$6	0.9345	0.9350	0.9355	0.9360	0.9365	0.9370	0.9375	0.9380	0.9385	0.9390
8$_\wedge$7	0.9395	0.9400	0.9405	0.9410	0.9415	0.9420	0.9425	0.9430	0.9435	0.9440
8$_\wedge$8	0.9445	0.9450	0.9455	0.9460	0.9465	0.9469	0.9474	0.9479	0.9484	0.9489
8$_\wedge$9	0.9494	0.9499	0.9504	0.9509	0.9513	0.9518	0.9523	0.9528	0.9533	0.9538
9$_\wedge$0	0.9542	0.9547	0.9552	0.9557	0.9562	0.9566	0.9571	0.9576	0.9581	0.9586
9$_\wedge$1	0.9590	0.9595	0.9600	0.9605	0.9609	0.9614	0.9619	0.9624	0.9628	0.9633
9$_\wedge$2	0.9638	0.9643	0.9647	0.9652	0.9657	0.9661	0.9666	0.9671	0.9675	0.9680
9$_\wedge$3	0.9685	0.9689	0.9694	0.9699	0.9703	0.9708	0.9713	0.9717	0.9722	0.9727
9$_\wedge$4	0.9731	0.9736	0.9741	0.9745	0.9750	0.9754	0.9759	0.9763	0.9768	0.9773
9$_\wedge$5	0.9777	0.9782	0.9786	0.9791	0.9795	0.9800	0.9805	0.9809	0.9814	0.9818
9$_\wedge$6	0.9823	0.9827	0.9832	0.9836	0.9841	0.9845	0.9850	0.9854	0.9859	0.9863
9$_\wedge$7	0.9868	0.9872	0.9877	0.9881	0.9886	0.9890	0.9894	0.9899	0.9903	0.9908
9$_\wedge$8	0.9912	0.9917	0.9921	0.9926	0.9930	0.9934	0.9939	0.9943	0.9948	0.9952
9$_\wedge$9	0.9956	0.9961	0.9965	0.9969	0.9974	0.9978	0.9983	0.9987	0.9991	0.9996
N	0	1	2	3	4	5	6	7	8	9

Table III   Natural Logarithms

n	$\log_e n$	n	$\log_e n$	n	$\log_e n$
	*	4.5	1.5041	9.0	2.1972
0.1	7.6974	4.6	1.5261	9.1	2.2083
0.2	8.3906	4.7	1.5476	9.2	2.2192
0.3	8.7960	4.8	1.5686	9.3	2.2300
0.4	9.0837	4.9	1.5892	9.4	2.2407
0.5	9.3069	5.0	1.6094	9.5	2.2513
0.6	9.4892	5.1	1.6292	9.6	2.2618
0.7	9.6433	5.2	1.6487	9.7	2.2721
0.8	9.7769	5.3	1.6677	9.8	2.2824
0.9	9.8946	5.4	1.6864	9.9	2.2925
1.0	0.0000	5.5	1.7047	10	2.3026
1.1	0.0953	5.6	1.7228	11	2.3979
1.2	0.1823	5.7	1.7405	12	2.4849
1.3	0.2624	5.8	1.7579	13	2.5649
1.4	0.3365	5.9	1.7750	14	2.6391
1.5	0.4055	6.0	1.7918	15	2.7081
1.6	0.4700	6.1	1.8083	16	2.7726
1.7	0.5306	6.2	1.8245	17	2.8332
1.8	0.5878	6.3	1.8405	18	2.8904
1.9	0.6419	6.4	1.8563	19	2.9444
2.0	0.6931	6.5	1.8718	20	2.9957
2.1	0.7419	6.6	1.8871	25	3.2189
2.2	0.7885	6.7	1.9021	30	3.4012
2.3	0.8329	6.8	1.9169	35	3.5553
2.4	0.8755	6.9	1.9315	40	3.6889
2.5	0.9163	7.0	1.9459	45	3.8067
2.6	0.9555	7.1	1.9601	50	3.9120
2.7	0.9933	7.2	1.9741	55	4.0073
2.8	1.0296	7.3	1.9879	60	4.0943
2.9	1.0647	7.4	2.0015	65	4.1744
3.0	1.0986	7.5	2.0149	70	4.2485
3.1	1.1314	7.6	2.0281	75	4.3175
3.2	1.1632	7.7	2.0412	80	4.3820
3.3	1.1939	7.8	2.0541	85	4.4427
3.4	1.2238	7.9	2.0669	90	4.4998
3.5	1.2528	8.0	2.0794	100	4.6052
3.6	1.2809	8.1	2.0919	110	4.7005
3.7	1.3083	8.2	2.1041	120	4.7875
3.8	1.3350	8.3	2.1163	130	4.8676
3.9	1.3610	8.4	2.1282	140	4.9416
4.0	1.3863	8.5	2.1401	150	5.0106
4.1	1.4110	8.6	2.1518	160	5.0752
4.2	1.4351	8.7	2.1633	170	5.1358
4.3	1.4586	8.8	2.1748	180	5.1930
4.4	1.4816	8.9	2.1861	190	5.2470

* Subtract 10 for $n < 1$. Thus, $\log_e 0.1 = 7.6974 - 10 = -2.3026$.

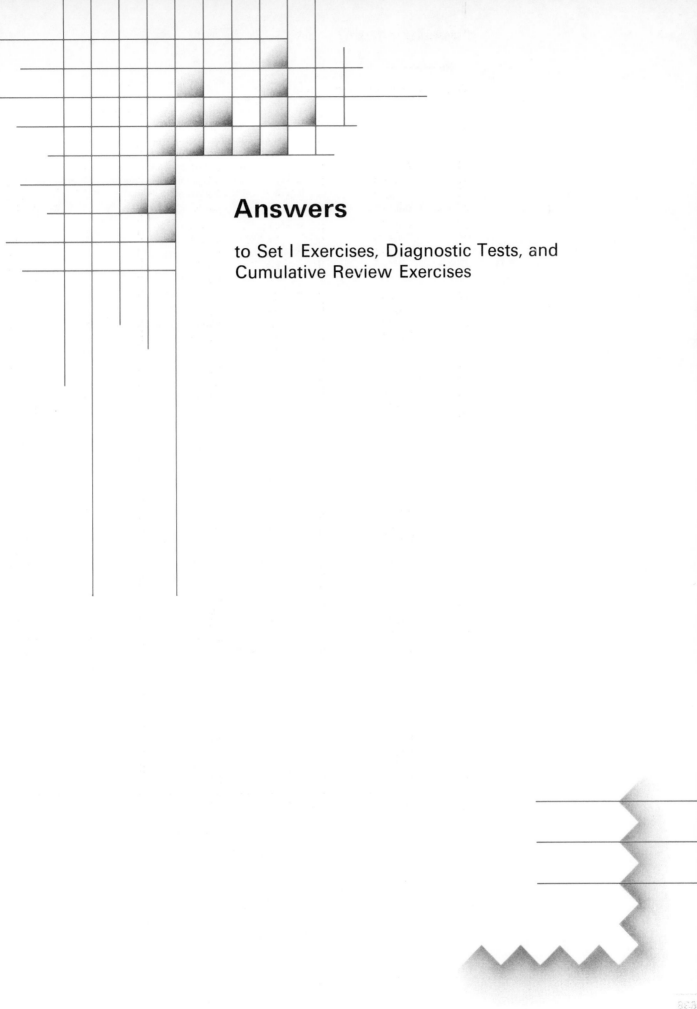

Answers

to Set I Exercises, Diagnostic Tests, and
Cumulative Review Exercises

Exercises 1.1A (page 5)

1a. True; a set is a collection of things
b. False; $\{1, 2, 3\} \neq \{1, 2, 3, \ldots\}$ **c.** True
d. False; "23" is not a set   **e.** False; 0 is *not* a natural number
f. False; $\{2\}$ is a *set*, not an element   **g.** True
h. True; $\{\ \}$ is a subset of every set   **i.** False; 10 is not a digit
j. False; the empty set has *no* elements   **k.** True
l. True; it is the empty set

2a. True   **b.** False   **c.** True   **d.** True   **e.** False   **f.** False
g. True   **h.** True   **i.** True   **j.** False   **k.** True   **l.** True

3a. Infinite   **b.** Finite   **c.** Finite

4a. Infinite   **b.** Finite   **c.** Finite

5. $\{\ \}, \{a\}, \{b\}, \{c\}, \{a, b\}, \{a, c\}, \{b, c\}, \{a, b, c\}$

6. $\{\ \}, \{1\}, \{2\}, \{1, 2\}$

7a. False, $12 \in B$ but $12 \notin A$
b. True, because the elements of C are also elements of B
c. False, because all elements of C are also elements of A

8a. True   **b.** False   **c.** True

9a. $\{0, 2, 4, 6, 8\}$ **b.** $\{5, 10, 15, \ldots\}$

10a. $\{1, 3, 5, \ldots\}$ **b.** $\{11, 22, 33, \ldots\}$

11a. $\{x \mid x$ is one of the first 5 letters of the alphabet$\}$
b. $\{x \mid x$ is a multiple of 4 and $x \in N$ and x is less than 13$\}$
c. $\{x \mid x$ is a natural number divisible by 10$\}$

12a. $\{x \mid x$ is a digit divisible by 2$\}$
b. $\{x \mid x$ is one of the last three letters of the alphabet$\}$
c. $\{x \mid x$ is a natural number divisible by 5$\}$

Exercises 1.1B (page 8)

1a. $\{1, 2, 3, 4, 5\}$ **b.** $\{2, 4\}$ **c.** $\{1, 2, 3, 4, 5\}$ **d.** $\{2, 4\}$

2a. $\{\ \}$ or $\varnothing$ **b.** $\{2, 5, 6, 7, 8, 9, 12\}$ **c.** $\{\ \}$ or $\varnothing$
d. $\{2, 5, 6, 7, 8, 9, 12\}$

3a. $\{5, 11\}$ **b.** $\{0, 3, 4, 5, 6, 7, 11, 13\}$ **c.** $\{6\}$ **d.** $\{\ \}$ or $\varnothing$
e. $\{2, 5, 6, 7, 11, 13\}$ **f.** $\{0, 3, 4, 5, 6, 7, 11, 13\}$
g. $\{5, 11\} \cap \{0, 3, 4, 6\} = \{\ \}$ **h.** $\{2, 5, 6, 11\} \cap \{\ \} = \{\ \}$
i. $\{2, 5, 6, 7, 11, 13\} \cup \{0, 3, 4, 6\} = \{0, 2, 3, 4, 5, 6, 7, 11, 13\}$
j. $\{2, 5, 6, 11\} \cup \{0, 3, 4, 5, 6, 7, 11, 13\} = \{0, 2, 3, 4, 5, 6, 7, 11, 13\}$

4a. $\{4, b\}$ **b.** $\{a, b, m, 4, 6, 7\}$ **c.** $\{a, b, n, t, 3, 4, 5, 7\}$
d. $\{\ \}$ or $\varnothing$ **e.** $\{\ \}$ or $\varnothing$ **f.** $\{b, m, n, t, 3, 4, 5, 6\}$
g. $\{\ \}$ or $\varnothing$ **h.** $\{\ \}$ or $\varnothing$ **i.** $\{a, b, m, n, t, 3, 4, 5, 6, 7\}$
j. $\{a, b, m, n, t, 3, 4, 5, 6, 7\}$

Exercises 1.2 (page 12)

1.

a. All are real   **b.** $7, -5, 10$ **c.** $7, 10$ **d.** $2.449489734\ldots$
e. $7, -5, 10, -\dfrac{3}{4}, 0.222\ldots$

2.

a. All   **b.** $-11, 4$ **c.** 4 **d.** $-2.64575131\ldots$
e. $-11, 1.666\ldots, \dfrac{5}{6}, 3\dfrac{1}{3}, 4$

3a. $\subseteq$ **b.** $\in$ **c.** $\subseteq$ **d.** $\in$ **e.** $\in$ **f.** $\subseteq$

4a. $\subseteq$ **b.** $\subseteq$ **c.** $\in$ **d.** $\in$ **e.** $\subseteq$ **f.** $\subseteq$

5a. False, because irrationals are real   **b.** True, because $J \subseteq R$
c. False; fractions are real numbers but not whole numbers
d. True; 3 is an element of the integers
e. False; 3 is not an irrational number
f. True; the irrational numbers are a subset of the real numbers
g. True; a nonrepeating, nonterminating decimal is irrational
h. True, because a nonrepeating decimal is real

6a. True   **b.** False   **c.** False   **d.** True   **e.** True   **f.** True   **g.** False
h. True

Exercises 1.3A (page 15)

1a. 3   **b.** x, y **2a.** $4, -2$ **b.** y, z

3a. Three terms   **b.** $5F$ **c.** $E, 1$

4a. Three terms   **b.** $2T$ **c.** $R, 1$

5a. Two terms   **b.** $-2(x + y)$ **c.** $(R + S), 1$

6a. Two terms   **b.** $-5(W + V)$ **c.** $(A + 2B), 1$

7a. Two terms   **b.** 4   **c.** $3, X, Y, Z$

8a. Two terms   **b.** $3x$ **c.** $4, a, b$

9a. Two terms   **b.** $\dfrac{3B - C}{DE}$ **c.** $2, A$

10a. Two terms   **b.** $\dfrac{w + z}{xyz}$ **c.** $3, s, t$

11a. 2   **b.** RT **12a.** 4   **b.** xy **13a.** -1 **b.** y **14a.** -1 **b.** b

Exercises 1.3B (page 18)

1a. $|7| = 7$ **b.** $|-5| = -(-5) = 5$ **c.** $-|-12| = -(12) = -12$

2a. 34   **b.** -5 **c.** -3 **3a.** $<$ **b.** $<$ **c.** $>$ **d.** $<$

4a. $>$ **b.** $<$ **c.** $>$ **d.** $<$

5a. Valid ($3 < 5$, $5 < 10$, and $3 < 10$ are all true)
b. Invalid ($-2 > 7$, $1 > 7$, and $-2 > 1$ are false statements)
c. Invalid (one "$<$" and one "$>$")
d. Valid ($8 > 3$, $3 > -1$, and $8 > -1$ are all true)
e. Invalid (one "$<$" and one "$>$")
f. Invalid ($0 > 8$, $3 > 8$, and $0 > 3$ are false statements)

6a. Valid   **b.** Invalid (one "$<$" and one "$>$")
c. Invalid (one "$<$" and one "$>$")   **d.** Valid
e. Invalid ($4 > 7$, $7 > 11$, and $4 > 11$ are false)
f. Invalid ($5 < 0$, $0 < -2$, and $5 < -2$ are false)

7. False   **8.** True

Exercises 1.4 (page 24)

1. $-(|-9|-|5|) = -(9-5) = -4$ **2.** -3

3. $-(|-12|+|-7|) = -(12+7) = -19$ **4.** $-\dfrac{5}{4}$

5. $-\left(\left|-\dfrac{7}{12}\right|+\left|-\dfrac{1}{6}\right|\right) = -\left(\dfrac{7}{12}+\dfrac{1}{6}\right) = -\dfrac{9}{12} = -\dfrac{3}{4}$

6. $-\dfrac{9}{8}$ or $-1\dfrac{1}{8}$ **7.** $\dfrac{21}{4}+\left(\dfrac{-5}{2}\right) = \dfrac{21}{4}+\left(\dfrac{-10}{4}\right) = \dfrac{11}{4}$ **8.** $1\dfrac{7}{10}$

9. $-13.5+8.06 = -5.44$ **10.** -0.37 **11.** $2.4+13 = 15.4$

12. 96.2 **13.** $\dfrac{1}{3}+\dfrac{1}{2} = \dfrac{5}{6}$ **14.** $26\dfrac{1}{6}$

15. $\left(-5\dfrac{3}{4}\right)+\left(-2\dfrac{2}{4}\right) = -7\dfrac{5}{4} = -8\dfrac{1}{4}$ **16.** -11.26

17. $\begin{array}{r}16.71\\+18.90\\\hline 35.61\end{array}$ **18.** 12.61 **19.** -3 **20.** 0

21. 260 (When the signs are the same, the product is positive)

22. 7.7 **23.** $\dfrac{\overset{1}{\cancel{8}}}{\underset{2}{\cancel{8}}}\cdot\dfrac{\overset{-1}{\cancel{-4}}}{\underset{3}{\cancel{9}}} = -\dfrac{1}{6}$ (Unlike signs give a negative product)

24. -15 **25.** $-\dfrac{1}{3}$ **26.** $\dfrac{5}{2}$ or $2\dfrac{1}{2}$ **27.** $\left(\dfrac{15}{2}\right)\cdot\left(\dfrac{-2}{1}\right) = -15$

28. Not possible

29. 0 (0 divided by a nonzero number *is* possible, and the answer is 0)

30. Cannot be determined   **31.** $\left(-\dfrac{5}{4}\right)\left(-\dfrac{8}{3}\right) = \dfrac{10}{3}$ or $3\dfrac{1}{3}$

32. 250 **33.** $-8-(-3) = -8+3 = -5$ **34.** -1.56

35. $5+\dfrac{2}{3} = 5\dfrac{2}{3}$ **36.** -7 **37.** $10+25 = 35$ **38.** -7

39. $-3(4) = -12$ **40.** 11

Exercises 1.5 (page 28)

1. True; commutative property of addition (order of numbers changed)
2. True; commutative property of addition
3. True; commutative property of addition and commutative property of multiplication
4. True; commutative property of addition and commutative property of multiplication
5. True; distributive property   **6.** True; distributive property
7. False   **8.** False   **9.** False   **10.** False   **11.** False
12. False   **13.** True; commutative property of multiplication
14. True; commutative property of addition and commutative property of multiplication
15. True; 0 is the additive identity
16. True; 0 is the additive identity
17. True; addition is associative   **18.** False
19. False; any number times 0 is 0   **20.** False
21. True; distributive property   **22.** True; distributive property
23. True; 1 is the multiplicative identity

24. True; 1 is the multiplicative identity   **25.** False
26. True; addition is commutative
27. True; additive inverse property
28. True; additive inverse property

Exercises 1.6 (page 31)

1. $4\cdot4\cdot4 = 64$ **2.** 49 **3.** $(-3)(-3)(-3)(-3) = 81$
4. 16 **5.** $-2^4 = -(2\cdot2\cdot2\cdot2) = -16$ **6.** -81 **7.** 0
8. 0 **9.** -1; an odd power of a negative number is negative

10. 1 **11.** $\left(\dfrac{1}{2}\right)\left(\dfrac{1}{2}\right)\left(\dfrac{1}{2}\right)\left(\dfrac{1}{2}\right) = \dfrac{1}{16}$ **12.** $\dfrac{49}{64}$

13. $(-0.1)(-0.1)(-0.1) = -0.001$ **14.** 0.0001

15. $\left(\dfrac{1}{10}\right)\left(\dfrac{1}{10}\right)\left(\dfrac{1}{10}\right) = \dfrac{1}{1000}$ **16.** 299.29

17. $(9.2)(9.2)(9.2) = 778.688$ **18.** 5.0625
19. $(-2.5)(-2.5)(-2.5)(-2.5) = 39.0625$ **20.** -148.877

Exercises 1.7A (page 32)

1. -6 **2.** 7 **3.** -5 **4.** 8 **5.** -10 **6.** -12 **7.** 9
8. 11 **9.** -16 **10.** -4

Exercises 1.7B (page 33)

1. 458 **2.** 624 **3.** 3.464 **4.** 4.123 **5.** 13.565
6. 13.820 **7.** 1.673 **8.** 3.063

Exercises 1.7C (page 34)

1. 2 **2.** 1 **3.** -3 **4.** -2 **5.** -4 **6.** -3 **7.** -2
8. -4 **9.** -10 **10.** -6 **11.** $-(\sqrt[5]{-32}) = -(-2) = 2$
12. 5

Exercises 1.8 (page 37)

1. $16-9-4 = (16-9)-4 = 7-4 = 3$ **2.** 9
3. $12\div6\div2 = (12\div6)\div2 = 2\div2 = 1$ **4.** 2
5. $10\div2(-5) = (10\div2)(-5) = 5(-5) = -25$ **6.** -9
7. $3\times16 = 48$ **8.** 45 **9.** $8+6\cdot5 = 8+30 = 38$ **10.** 11

11. $7+\dfrac{5}{3} = 8\dfrac{2}{3}$ **12.** $6\dfrac{1}{2}$ **13.** $10-3\cdot2 = 10-6 = 4$

14. 4 **15.** $10(225)-64 = 2250-64 = 2186$ **16.** 32

17. $\dfrac{1}{2}-0.02\times10^3 = \dfrac{1}{2}-20 = -19\dfrac{1}{2}$ **18.** $-3\dfrac{2}{3}$ or $-\dfrac{11}{3}$

19. $(100)(4)(5) = 2{,}000$ **20.** $1{,}500$
21. $2+3\cdot100\div25 = 2+300\div25 = 2+12 = 14$ **22.** 53
23. $28+14/7 = 28+2 = 30$ **24.** 42
25. $2(3)(8-5) = 6\times3 = 18$ **26.** 240
27. $(-18)\div(-3)(-6) = 6(-6) = -36$ **28.** -8
29. $-1000-5(100)(-3) = -1000+1500 = 500$
30. $10{,}100$ **31.** $20-[5-(-3)] = 20-[8] = 12$ **32.** 3

33. $-\dfrac{5}{5} = -1$ **34.** -4

35. $8-[5(-8)-4] = 8-[-40-4] = 8-[-44] = 52$

36. -12

37. $(3 \times 25 - 5) \div (-7) = (75 - 5) \div (-7) = 70 \div (-7) = -10$

38. -20

39. $15 - \{4 - [2 - 3(2)]\} = 15 - \{4 - [2 - 6]\} = 15 - \{4 - [-4]\}$
$= 15 - \{4 + 4\} = 15 - 8 = 7$

40. 10

Exercises 1.9 (page 40)

1. Prime; $\pm 1, \pm 5$ **2.** Composite; $\pm 1, \pm 2, \pm 4, \pm 8$

3. Prime; $\pm 1, \pm 13$ **4.** Composite; $\pm 1, \pm 3, \pm 5, \pm 15$

5. Composite; $\pm 1, \pm 2, \pm 3, \pm 4, \pm 6, \pm 12$ **6.** Prime; $\pm 1, \pm 11$

7. Composite; $\pm 1, \pm 3, \pm 17, \pm 51$

8. Composite; $\pm 1, \pm 2, \pm 3, \pm 6, \pm 7, \pm 14, \pm 21, \pm 42$

9. Composite; $\pm 1, \pm 3, \pm 37, \pm 111$ **10.** Prime; $\pm 1, \pm 101$

11.
$$\begin{array}{r|r} 2 & 28 \\ 2 & 14 \\ & 7 \end{array}$$
$28 = 2^2 \cdot 7$

12. $2 \cdot 3 \cdot 5$

13.
$$\begin{array}{r|r} 2 & 32 \\ 2 & 16 \\ 2 & 8 \\ 2 & 4 \\ & 2 \end{array}$$
$32 = 2^5$

14. $3 \cdot 11$

15. 43 is prime   **16.** $5 \cdot 7$

17.
$$\begin{array}{r|r} 2 & 84 \\ 2 & 42 \\ 3 & 21 \\ & 7 \end{array}$$
$84 = 2^2 \cdot 3 \cdot 7$

18. $3 \cdot 5^2$

19.
$$\begin{array}{r|r} 2 & 144 \\ 2 & 72 \\ 2 & 36 \\ 2 & 18 \\ 3 & 9 \\ & 3 \end{array}$$
$144 = 2^4 \cdot 3^2$

20. $2^2 \cdot 3^2 \cdot 5$

21.
$$\begin{array}{r|r} 2 & 156 \\ 2 & 78 \\ 3 & 39 \\ & 13 \end{array}$$
$156 = 2^2 \cdot 3 \cdot 13$

22. $13 \cdot 17$ **23.** $144 = 2^4 \cdot 3^2;\ 360 = 2^3 \cdot 3^2 \cdot 5$
$\text{LCM} = 2^4 \cdot 3^2 \cdot 5 = 16 \cdot 9 \cdot 5 = 720$ **24.** 420

25. $270 = 2 \cdot 3^3 \cdot 5$ **26.** $2{,}940$
$900 = 2^2 \cdot 3^2 \cdot 5^2$
$75 = 3 \cdot 5^2$
$\text{LCM} = 2^2 \cdot 3^3 \cdot 5^2 = 2{,}700$

Review Exercises 1.10 (page 45)

1. Infinite   **2.** Finite   **3.** $\{0, 1, 2, 3, 4\}$ **4.** No

5a. $\{2, 5, 7, 8\}$ **b.** $\{5, 7\}$ **c.** $\{\ \}$ or $\varnothing$
  d. No, because 2 is not an element of A

6a. All are real numbers   **b.** -2 and 0 are integers
  c. None are natural numbers
  d. $2.6457513\ldots$ is an irrational number
  e. $-2, 4.53, 0.161616\ldots, \dfrac{2}{3}$, and 0 are rational numbers

7. 4   **8.** 0   **9.** 10   **10.** 36   **11.** $-(5)(5) = -25$ **12.** 0

13. Not possible (we cannot divide by 0)   **14.** 0

15. $6 + 2 \cdot 4 - 8 = 6 + 8 - 8 = 6$ **16.** 34

17. $6 + 18 \div 6 \div 3 = 6 + 3 \div 3 = 6 + 1 = 7$

18a. $\pm 1, \pm 2, \pm 4, \pm 7, \pm 14, \pm 28$ **b.** $2^2 \cdot 7$ **c.** $2^3 \cdot 3 \cdot 7$
  d. $2^3 \cdot 3 \cdot 7 = 168$

19. Yes   **20.** No; $1 > 5$, $5 > 7$, and $1 > 7$ are false

21. No; the inequalities are not both $>$ or both $<$ **22.** False

23. True; multiplicative identity

24. True; associative property of addition

25. True; additive inverse   **26.** False

27. True; additive identity

28. True; commutative property of addition   **29.** False

30. True; distributive property

Exercises 1.11A (page 51)

1. $10^{2+4} = 10^6$ **2.** 2^5 **3.** $x^2 \cdot x^5 = x^{2+5} = x^7$ **4.** y^9

5. Cannot be simplified   **6.** Cannot be simplified   **7.** 2^{x+y}

8. 3^{m+n} **9.** $a^{8-3} = a^5$ **10.** x^3 **11.** Cannot be simplified

12. Cannot be simplified   **13.** $10^{3 \cdot 2} = 10^6$ **14.** 5^8

15. $3^{a \cdot b} = 3^{ab}$ **16.** 2^{mn} **17.** $x^5 y^5$ **18.** $u^4 v^4$

19. $2^6 x^6$ or $64 x^6$ **20.** $3^4 x^4$ **21.** Cannot be simplified

22. Cannot be simplified   **23.** $3^{4x} \cdot 3^{7x} = 3^{4x+7x} = 3^{11x}$ **24.** 5^{4x}

25. a^{x-y} **26.** x^{a-b}

27. $\dfrac{x^4}{y^2}$ cannot be simplified because the bases are different

28. $\dfrac{a^5}{b^3}$ **29.** $\dfrac{x^3}{y^3}$ **30.** $\dfrac{u^7}{v^7}$ **31.** $\dfrac{3^4}{x^4}$ or $\dfrac{81}{x^4}$ **32.** $\dfrac{x^2}{25}$

Exercises 1.11B (page 56)

1. $\dfrac{1}{a^3}$ **2.** $\dfrac{1}{x^2}$ **3.** $\dfrac{1}{10^3}$ or $\dfrac{1}{1{,}000}$ **4.** $\dfrac{1}{10^5}$ **5.** $\dfrac{5}{b^7}$ **6.** $\dfrac{3}{y^2}$

7. $\dfrac{1}{(5b)^2} = \dfrac{1}{5^2 b^2} = \dfrac{1}{25 b^2}$ **8.** $\dfrac{1}{9 y^2}$ **9.** $\dfrac{1}{x^3} \cdot \dfrac{y^2}{1} \cdot 1 = \dfrac{y^2}{x^3}$ **10.** $\dfrac{r^3}{s^4}$

11. $\dfrac{x}{1} \cdot \dfrac{1}{y^2} \cdot \dfrac{1}{z^3} \cdot 1 = \dfrac{x}{y^2 z^3}$ **12.** $\dfrac{b}{z^4 c^5}$ **13.** $a^3 \cdot \dfrac{b^4}{1} = a^3 b^4$

14. $c^4 d^5$ **15.** $\dfrac{1}{x^3} \cdot \dfrac{y^2}{1} = \dfrac{y^2}{x^3}$ **16.** $\dfrac{Q^4}{P^2}$ **17.** $x^{-7} = \dfrac{1}{x^7}$ **18.** $\dfrac{1}{y^5}$

19. $a^{3(-2)} = a^{-6} = \dfrac{1}{a^6}$ **20.** $\dfrac{1}{b^8}$ **21.** $x^{8+(-2)} = x^6$ **22.** a^2

23. $x^{2a(-3)} = x^{-6a} = \dfrac{1}{x^{6a}}$ **24.** $\dfrac{1}{y^{6c}}$ **25.** $y^{3-(-2)} = y^5$ **26.** x^{12}

27. $x^{3a-(-a)} = x^{4a}$ **28.** a^{6x} **29.** 1   **30.** 1   **31.** $5 \cdot 1 = 5$

32. 2   **33.** $\dfrac{1}{x^3} + \dfrac{1}{x^5}$ **34.** $\dfrac{1}{y^2} + \dfrac{1}{y^6}$ **35.** $x^7 - \dfrac{1}{x^5}$

36. $y^{10} - \dfrac{1}{y^3}$ **37.** $1 + 1 = 2$ **38.** 3   **39.** 1   **40.** 1

41. $10^{5+(-2)} = 10^3 = 1{,}000$ **42.** 4   **43.** $3^{(-2)(-2)} = 3^4 = 81$

44. $1{,}000$ **45.** $(1)^5 = 1$ **46.** 1

47. $10^{2+(-1)-(-3)} = 10^{2-1+3} = 10^4 = 10{,}000$ **48.** 8   **49.** $x^{-3} y$

50. xy^{-2} **51.** $a^4 x$ **52.** $m^2 n^3$ **53.** $x^4 y^{-3} z^2$ **54.** $a^{-1} b^3 c^4$

Exercises 1.11C (page 59)

1. $\dfrac{1}{(5x)^3} = \dfrac{1}{5^3 x^3} = \dfrac{1}{125 x^3}$ **2.** $\dfrac{1}{16 y^2}$ **3.** $\dfrac{7}{1} \cdot \dfrac{1}{x^2} = \dfrac{7}{x^2}$ **4.** $\dfrac{3}{y^4}$

5. $\dfrac{27}{x^3}$ **6.** $\dfrac{7^2}{y^2}$ or $\dfrac{49}{y^2}$ **7.** $\dfrac{8^2}{z}$ or $\dfrac{64}{z}$ **8.** $\dfrac{8}{x}$ **9.** $a^{2 \cdot 2} b^{3 \cdot 2} = a^4 b^6$

10. $x^{12}y^{15}$ **11.** $m^{(-2)4}n^{1\cdot 4} = m^{-8}n^4 = \dfrac{n^4}{m^8}$ **12.** $\dfrac{r^5}{p^{15}}$

13. $x^{(-2)(-4)}y^{3(-4)} = x^8 y^{-12} = \dfrac{x^8}{y^{12}}$ **14.** $\dfrac{w^6}{z^8}$ **15.** $k^{(-4)(-2)} = k^8$

16. z^{10} **17.** $2^{1\cdot 3}x^{2\cdot 3}y^{(-4)3} = 8x^6 y^{-12} = \dfrac{8x^6}{y^{12}}$ **18.** $\dfrac{9b^{10}}{a^2}$

19. $5^{1(-2)}m^{(-3)(-2)}n^{5(-2)} = 5^{-2}m^6 n^{-10} = \dfrac{m^6}{25n^{10}}$ **20.** $\dfrac{y^2}{8x^8}$

21. $\dfrac{x^{1\cdot 2}y^{4\cdot 2}}{z^{2\cdot 2}} = \dfrac{x^2 y^8}{z^4}$ **22.** $\dfrac{a^9 b^3}{c^6}$ **23.** $\dfrac{M^{(-2)4}}{N^{3\cdot 4}} = \dfrac{M^{-8}}{N^{12}} = \dfrac{1}{M^8 N^{12}}$

24. $R^{15}S^{12}$ **25.** $\dfrac{x^{(-5)(-2)}}{y^{4(-2)}z^{(-3)(-2)}} = \dfrac{x^{10}}{y^{-8}z^6} = \dfrac{x^{10}y^8}{z^6}$ **26.** $\dfrac{a^{12}b^6}{c^{15}}$

27. 1   **28.** 1   **29.** $\dfrac{3^{1\cdot 2}x^{2\cdot 2}}{y^{3\cdot 2}} = \dfrac{9x^4}{y^6}$ **30.** $\dfrac{16a^{16}}{b^8}$

31. $\dfrac{4^{1(-1)}a^{(-2)(-1)}}{b^{3(-1)}} = \dfrac{4^{-1}a^2}{b^{-3}} = \dfrac{a^2 b^3}{4}$ **32.** $25m^8 n^6$

33. $(x^{-1-4}y^2)^{-2} = (x^{-5}y^2)^{-2} = x^{(-5)(-2)}y^{2(-2)} = x^{10}y^{-4} = \dfrac{x^{10}}{y^4}$

34. $u^{12}v^3$ **35.** $(x^{3n+2n-4n})^2 = (x^n)^2 = x^{2n}$ **36.** $x^{2n-2}y^{2n-4}$

37. $(2)(-3)(x^5\cdot x^4)(y^2) = -6x^9 y^2$ **38.** $-28a^2 b^5$

39. $(-4x^{-2}y^3)(-2xy^{-1}) = (-4)(-2)(x^{-2}xy^3 y^{-1}) = 8x^{-1}y^2 = \dfrac{8y^2}{x}$

40. $\dfrac{10b}{a}$

41. $(2)(3)(-1)(s^3\cdot s\cdot s)(1)(u^{-4}\cdot u^3) = -6s^{3+1+1}u^{-4+3}$
$$= -6s^5 u^{-1} = -6s^5\cdot\dfrac{1}{u} = \dfrac{-6s^5}{u}$$

42. $\dfrac{-8x^4}{z}$

Exercises 1.12 (page 61)

1. $28.56 = 2_{\curvearrowright}8.56 = 2.856 \times 10^1$ **2.** 3.754×10^2

3. $0.06184 = 0.06_{\curvearrowleft\wedge}184 = 6.184 \times 10^{-2}$ **4.** 3.056×10^{-3}

5. $7_{\curvearrowright\wedge}8000 = 7.8 \times 10^4$ **6.** 1.4×10^3

7. $.2_{\curvearrowright\wedge}006 = 2.006 \times 10^{-1}$ **8.** 9.5×10^{-5}

9. $0.362 \times 10^{-2} = (3.62 \times 10^{-1}) \times 10^{-2} = 3.62 \times 10^{-3}$

10. 6.314×10^{-4} **11.** $(2.452 \times 10^2) \times 10^{-5} = 2.452 \times 10^{-3}$

12. 3.17×10^{-3} **13.** 1.288×10^{10} **14.** 3×10^{-9}

15. 1.6×10^{-3} **16.** 9×10^{-4}

Exercises 1.13A (page 64)

1. $2(-6)^2 + 3(5) = 2(36) + 15 = 72 + 15 = 87$ **2.** 5

3. $(-5) - 12\left(\dfrac{1}{3}\right)^2 = -5 - 12\left(\dfrac{1}{9}\right) = -5 - \dfrac{4}{3} = -\dfrac{19}{3} = -6\dfrac{1}{3}$

4. $-\dfrac{26}{3}$ or $-8\dfrac{2}{3}$ **5.** $(-5^2) - 4(5)(-6) = 25 - (-120) = 145$

6. 61   **7.** $(5 + [-6])^2 = (-1)^2 = 1$ **8.** 36

9. $(5)^2 + 2(5)(-6) + (-6)^2 = 25 - 60 + 36 = 1$ **10.** 36

11. $5^2 + (-6)^2 = 25 + 36 = 61$ **12.** 26

13. $\dfrac{3(0)}{5 + (-15)} = \dfrac{0}{-10} = 0$ **14.** 0

15. $2(-1) - [5 - (0 - 5(-15))] = -2 - [5 - (75)]$ **16.** -32
$$= -2 - [-70] = 68$$

17. $-(-1) - \sqrt{(-1)^2 - 4(-4)(5)} = 1 - \sqrt{1 + 80}$
$$= 1 - \sqrt{81} = 1 - 9 = -8$$

18. 12   **19.** $5b^2 - 4b + 8$ **20.** $4c + 3$

21. $2(x^2 - 4x)^2 - 3(x^2 - 4x) + 7$ **22.** $(y^4 + 2)^2 - 2(y^4 + 2)$

Exercises 1.13B (page 65)

1. $q = \dfrac{DQ}{H} = \dfrac{5(420)}{30} = 70$ **2.** 125

3. $A = P(1 + rt) = 500[1 + 0.09(2.5)]$
$$= 500(1 + 0.225) = 500(1.255) = 612.50$$

4. 498   **5.** $A = P(1 + i)^n = 600(1.085)^2 = 600(1.177225) \doteq 706.34$

6. $808.9375 \doteq 808.94$

7. $C = \dfrac{5}{9}(F - 32) = \dfrac{5}{9}(-10 - 32) = \dfrac{5}{9}(-42) = -23\dfrac{1}{3}$ **8.** $-21\dfrac{2}{3}$

8. $-21\dfrac{2}{3}$ **9.** $S = \dfrac{1}{2}gt^2 = \dfrac{1}{2}(32)\left(8\dfrac{1}{2}\right)^2 = (16)\left(\dfrac{17}{2}\right)^2 = 1{,}156$

10. 361   **11.** $Z = \dfrac{Rr}{R + r} = \dfrac{22(8)}{22 + 8} = \dfrac{176}{30} = 5\dfrac{13}{15} \doteq 5.87$

12. $17\dfrac{3}{16}$

13. $S = 2\pi r^2 + 2\pi rh = 2(3.14)(3)^2 + 2(3.14)(3)(20)$
$$= 2(3.14)(9) + 376.8 = 56.52 + 376.8 = 433.32$$

14. 602.88

Exercises 1.14A (page 67)

1. $2x^{2/2} = 2x$ **2.** $3y$ **3.** $m^{4/2}n^{2/2} = m^2 n$ **4.** $u^5 v^3$

5. $5a^{4\div 2}b^{2\div 2} = 5a^2 b^1$ **6.** $10b^2 c$ **7.** $x^{10\div 2}y^{4\div 2} = x^5 y^2$

8. $x^6 y^4$ **9.** $10a^{10\div 2}y^{2\div 2} = 10a^5 y^1$ **10.** $11a^{12}b^2$

11. $9m^{8\div 2}n^{16\div 2} = 9m^4 n^8$ **12.** $7c^9 d^5$

Exercises 1.14B (page 68)

1. $(3a)(6) + (3a)(x)$ **2.** $35b + 5by$
$= 18a + 3ax$

3. $(x)(-4) + (-5)(-4)$ **4.** $-5y + 10$
$= -4x + 20$

5. $(-3)(x) - (-3)(2y) + (-3)(2)$ **6.** $-2x + 6y - 8$
$= -3x - (-6y) + (-6)$
$= -3x + 6y - 6$

7. $(x)(xy) - (x)(3)$ **8.** $a^2 b - 4a$
$= x^2 y - 3x$

9. $(3a)(ab) + (3a)(-2a^2)$ **10.** $12x^2 - 8xy^2$
$= 3a^2 b - 6a^3$

11. $(3x^3)(-2xy) + (-2x^2 y)(-2xy) + (y^3)(-2xy)$
$= -6x^4 y + 4x^3 y^2 - 2xy^4$

12. $-8yz^4 + 2y^2 z^3 + 2y^4 z$ **13.** $(-2)(3)(6)(a\cdot a^2\cdot a)(b\cdot b\cdot b)(c^3)$
$$= -36a^4 b^3 c^3$$

14. $-30x^4 y^5 z^2$

15. $(4xy^2)(3x^3 y^2) - (4xy^2)(2x^2 y^3) + (4xy^2)(5xy^4)$
$= 12x^4 y^4 - 8x^3 y^5 + 20x^2 y^6$

16. $-10x^6 y^1 + 4x^5 y^2 + 6x^3 y^3$

17. $(3mn^2)(-2m^2n)(5m^2) + (3mn^2)(-2m^2n)(-n^2)$
$= (3)(-2)(5)m^{1+2+2}n^{2+1} + (3)(-2)(-1)m^{1+2}n^{2+1+2}$
$= -30m^5n^3 + 6m^3n^5$

18. $-36a^5b^3 + 18a^3b^5$

19. $-8x^3y^2z[3xy - 2xz + 5yz]$
$= (-8x^3y^2z)(3xy) - (-8x^3y^2z)(2xz) + (-8x^3y^2z)(5yz)$
$= -24x^4y^3z - (-16x^4y^2z^2) + (-40x^3y^3z^2)$
$= -24x^4y^3z + 16x^4y^2z^2 - 40x^3y^3z^2$

20. $21a^4b^3 - 14a^3b^4 - 7a^3b^3c$ 21. $7x + 3y - 2x^2$

22. $3a - b - 4c$

Exercises 1.14C (page 71)

1. $10 + 4x - y$ 2. $8 + 3a - b$

3. $7 - (-4R - S) = 7 - 1(-4R - S) = 7 + 4R + S$

4. $9 + 3m + n$ 5. $6 - 2a + 6b$ 6. $12 - 6R + 3S$

7. $3 - 2x^2 + 8xy$ 8. $2 - 10x^2 + 15xy$ 9. $-x + y + 2 - a$

10. $-a + b + x - 3$ 11. $2a - 2b - 6$ 12. $3x - 3y - 5$

13. $x - [a + y - b] = x - a - y + b$ 14. $y - m - x + n$

15. $5 - 3[a - 8x + 4y] = 5 - 3a + 24x - 12y$

16. $7 - 5x + 30a - 15b$

17. $2 - [a - 1(b - c)] = 2 - 1[a - b - c] = 2 - a + b - c$

18. $5 - x + y + z$

19. $9 - 2[-3a - 8x + 4y]$ 20. $P - x + y - 4 + z$
$= 9 + 6a + 16x - 8y$

Exercises 1.14D (page 72)

1. $-2x$ 2. $-a$ 3. $6x^2y$ 4. $7ab^2$ 5. $6xy^2 + 8x^2y$

6. $5a^2b - 4ab^2$ 7. $-2xy$ 8. $4mn$ 9. $5xyz^2 - 2x^2y^2z^2$

10. $3a^3b^3c^3 - 4abc^3$ 11. $0xyz^2 = 0$ 12. $1a^2bc$ or a^2bc

13. $3x^2y - 2xy^2$ 14. $2xy^2 - 5x^2y$ 15. $2ab - a + b$

16. $6xy - x - y$ 17. $2x^3 - 2x^2 - 2x$ 18. $-3y^3 + 5y^2 - 2y$

19. $2x - 9y + 11$ 20. $-7a - 2b - 5$

21. $-2a^2b + (-ab) + 7ab^2 = -2a^2b - ab + 7ab^2$

22. $-4x^2y + 4xy^2 + y$

Exercises 1.14E (page 74)

1. $6h^3 - 2hk - hk + 3k^4 = 6h^3 - 3hk + 3k^4$

2. $11xy^2 - 14x^2$

3. $3x - 4 - 5x = -2x - 4$ 4. $-3x - 7$

5. $(-5x)(3x) - (-5x)(4) = -15x^2 + 20x$ 6. $-40x^2 + 56x$

7. $2 + 3x$ 8. $5 + 8y$

9. $3x - [5y - 2x + 4y] = 3x - [9y - 2x] = 3x - 9y + 2x = 5x - 9y$

10. $5x - 9y$ 11. $-10[-6x + 10 + 17] - 4x$ 12. $115x - 640$
$= -10[-6x + 27] - 4x$
$= 60x - 270 - 4x$
$= 56x - 270$

13. $8 - 2(x - y + 3x) = 8 - 2(4x - y) = 8 - 8x + 2y$

14. $9 - 12u + 4t$ 15. $8x + 10x^2 - 4x$ 16. $4y + 25y^2$
$= 4x + 10x^2$

17. $3u - v - \{2u - 10 + v - 20\} - 8v$
$= 3u - v - \{2u + v - 30\} - 8v$
$= 3u - v - 2u - v + 30 - 8v = u - 10v + 30$

18. $-5x - 2y + 23$ 19. $50 - \{-2t - [5t - 6 + 2t]\} + 7^0$
$= 50 - \{-2t - [7t - 6]\} + 1$
$= 50 - \{-2t - 7t + 6\} + 1$
$= 50 - \{-9t + 6\} + 1$
$= 50 + 9t - 6 + 1 = 45 + 9t$

20. $22 + 11x$ 21. $100v - 3\{-4[8 + 2v - 5v]\}$
$= 100v - 3\{-4[8 - 3v]\}$
$= 100v - 3\{-32 + 12v\}$
$= 100v + 96 - 36v$
$= 64v + 96$

22. $72z + 96$ 23. $w^4 - 4w^2 + 4w^2 - 16 = w^4 - 16$

24. $x^4 - 81$ 25. $(3)(5)(4)(2)(x \cdot x^2 \cdot x^3) = 120x^6$ 26. $60y^8$

27. $5X^{-4+6} + 3(1) = 5X^2 + 3$ 28. $3Y^2 + 2$

29. $3(x + 2y) - 5(3x - y)$ 30. $-2x + 10y$
$= 3x + 6y - 15x + 5y = -12x + 11y$

31. $2[(3)(x + 2y) - (3x - y)]$ 32. $42x - 21y$
$= 2[3x + 6y - 3x + y] = 2(7y) = 14y$

Review Exercises 1.15 (page 76)

1. $x^{3+5} = x^8$ 2. $x^4 + x^2$ 3. $N^{2\cdot3} = N^6$ 4. $s^6 - s^2$

5. $a^{5-2} = a^3$ 6. $\dfrac{x^6}{y^4}$ 7. $\dfrac{2^3a^3}{(b^2)^3} = \dfrac{8a^3}{b^6}$ 8. $\dfrac{x^4}{y^2}$

9. $\left(\dfrac{x^{-4}y}{x^{-2}}\right)^{-1} = \left(\dfrac{x^2y}{x^4}\right)^{-1} = \left(\dfrac{y}{x^2}\right)^{-1} = \dfrac{y^{-1}}{x^{-2}} = \dfrac{x^2}{y}$ 10. 2   11. 1

12. xy^4 13. $3c^4d^2 - 12c^3d^3$ 14. $8 - 6x + 2y$

15. $(-10)(-8)(-1)(x^2x^3x)(y^3y^2)(z^4) = -80x^6y^5z^4$

16. $-8x^4 - 4x^2 + 2xy$ 17. $5 - 2[3 - 5x + 5y + 4x - 6]$
$= 5 - 2[-3 - x + 5y]$
$= 5 + 6 + 2x - 10y$
$= 11 + 2x - 10y$

18. $4x^3 - y$ 19. $1\,\underset{\wedge}{48.6} = 1.486 \times 10^2$ 20. 0.00317

21. $A = P(1 + rt) = 550[1 + (0.09)(2.5)]$ 22. $C = 40$
$= 550(1 + 0.225)$
$= 550(1.225) = 673.73$

23. $S = R\left[\dfrac{(1 + i)^n - 1}{i}\right] = 750\left[\dfrac{(1.09)^3 - 1}{0.09}\right] = 2458.575 \doteq 2458.58$

24. 472.5

Chapter 1 Diagnostic Test (page 81)

Following each problem number is the textbook section number (in parentheses) where that kind of problem is discussed.

1. (1.1, 1.2, 1.3, 1.4, 1.5)
   a. True   b. True   c. True   d. True   e. True
   f. False; division by 0 is not permitted
   g. False; it illustrates the associative property of multiplication
   h. False   i. False; 0 is a digit, but it is not a natural number
   j. True   k. True   l. True
   m. False; irrational numbers are real but not rational
   n. False; one is "<" and the other is ">"
   o. False; $3 \cdot (7 \cdot 2) = 3 \cdot 14 = 42$; $(3 \cdot 7)(3 \cdot 2) = (21)(6) = 126$

2. (1.1) $\{0, 2, 4, 6, \ldots\}$ 3. (1.1)   a. False; $y \notin A$ b. True

4. (1.1)   a. All   b. $-3, 0, 5$ c. 5   d. $2.8652916\ldots$

   e. $-3, 2.4, 0, 5, \dfrac{1}{2}, 0.18181818\ldots$

5. (1.1)   a. $\{r, s, w, x, y, z\}$ b. $\{\ \}$ c. $\{x, w\}$ d. $\{x, y, w, r, s\}$

6. (1.3) $|-17| = 17$ 7. (1.6) $(-5)^2 = (-5)(-5) = 25$

8. (1.4) $30 \div (-5) = -6$

9. (1.4) $(-35) - (2) = -35 + (-2) = -37$

10. (1.4) $(-27) - (-17) = -27 + (+17) = -10$

11. (1.4) $(-9)(-8) = 72$ **12.** (1.4) $(-19)(0) = 0$

13. (1.4) $\dfrac{-40}{-8} = 5$ **14.** (1.4) $(-9) + (-13) = -22$

15. (1.6) $-6^2 = -6 \cdot 6 = -36$ **16.** (1.11) $(-2)^0 = 1$

17. (1.3) $-|-3| = -(3) = -3$ **18.** (1.7) $\sqrt[3]{-27} = -3$

19. (1.7) $\sqrt[4]{16} = 2$ **20.** (1.11) $(3^{-2})^{-1} = 3^2 = 9$

21. (1.11) $10^{-3} \cdot 10^5 = 10^2 = 100$

22. (1.11) $\dfrac{2^{-4}}{2^{-7}} = 2^{-4-(-7)} = 2^{-4+7} = 2^3 = 8$

23. (1.8) $16 \div 4 \cdot 2 = 4 \cdot 2 = 8$

24. (1.8) $2\sqrt{9} - 5 = 2 \cdot 3 - 5 = 6 - 5 = 1$

25. (1.7) $\sqrt{81} = 9$ **26.** (1.12) $0.000316 = 3.16 \times 10^{-4}$

27. (1.9) **a.** $2 \underline{\,|\, 78}$ $78 = 2 \cdot 3 \cdot 13$ **b.** $5 \underline{\,|\, 65}$ $65 = 5 \cdot 13$
$\quad 3 \underline{\,|\, 39}$ $\quad 13$
13

c. LCM $= 2 \cdot 3 \cdot 5 \cdot 13 = 390$

28. (1.11) $x^2 \cdot x^{-5} = x^{2+(-5)} = x^{-3} = \dfrac{1}{x^3}$

29. (1.11) $(N^2)^4 = N^{2 \cdot 4} = N^8$ **30.** (1.11) $\left(\dfrac{2X^3}{Y}\right)^2 = \dfrac{2^2 X^6}{Y^2} = \dfrac{4X^6}{Y^2}$

31. (1.11) $\left(\dfrac{xy^{-2}}{y^{-3}}\right)^{-1} = \dfrac{x^{-1}y^2}{y^3} = \dfrac{1}{xy}$ **32.** (1.11) $\dfrac{1}{a^{-3}} = a^3$

33. (1.11) $\left(\dfrac{x^{-a}}{2}\right)^{-3} = \dfrac{x^{3a}}{2^{-3}} = 2^3 x^{3a}$ or $8x^{3a}$

34. (1.13)
$$S = \frac{a(1 - r^n)}{1 - r} = \frac{-8[1 - (3)^2]}{1 - (3)} = \frac{-8[1 - 9]}{1 - 3} = \frac{-8[-8]}{-2} = \frac{64}{-2} = -32$$

35. (1.14) $7x - 2(5 - x) + \sqrt{81x^2} = 7x - 10 + 2x + 9x$
$\phantom{7x - 2(5 - x) + \sqrt{81x^2}} = 18x - 10$

36. (1.14) $6x(2xy^2 - 3x^3) - 3x^2(2y^2 - 6x^2)$
$ = 12x^2y^2 - 18x^4 - 6x^2y^2 + 18x^4$
$ = 6x^2y^2$

37. (1.14) $7x - 2\{6 - 3[8 - 2(x - 3) - 2(6 - x)]\}$
$ = 7x - 2\{6 - 3[8 - 2x + 6 - 12 + 2x]\}$
$ = 7x - 2\{6 - 3[2]\}$
$ = 7x - 2\{6 - 6\} = 7x - 2\{0\} = 7x - 0 = 7x$

Exercises 2.1 (page 89)

Checks will not always be shown.

1. $4x + 3(4 + 3x) = -1$ *Check for x = −1*
$\quad 4x + 12 + 9x = -1$
$\quad\quad 13x + 12 = -1$ $4(-1) + 3(4 + 3[-1]) \overset{?}{=} -1$
$\quad\quad\quad 13x = -13$ $-4 + 3(4 + [-3]) \overset{?}{=} -1$
$\quad\quad\quad\quad\quad\quad\quad\quad\quad -4 + 3(1) \overset{?}{=} -1$
$\quad\quad\quad\quad x = -1$ $-1 = -1$

Solution set: $\{-1\}$; graph:

2. $\{-2\}$; graph:

3. $7y - 2(5 + 4y) = 8$
$\quad 7y - 10 - 8y = 8$
$\quad\quad\quad\quad -y = 18$
$\quad\quad\quad\quad\quad y = -18$

Solution set: $\{-18\}$; graph:

4. $\{-15\}$; graph:

5. $4x + 12 = 2(6 + 2x)$ **6.** Identity—solution set is R
$\quad 4x + 12 = 12 + 4x$
$\quad\quad\quad\; 12 = 12 \leftarrow$ True
Identity—solution set is R

7. $3[5 - 2(5 - z)] = 2(3z + 7)$
$\quad 3[5 - 10 + 2z] = 6z + 14$
$\quad\quad 3[-5 + 2z] = 6z + 14$
$\quad\quad\; -15 + 6z = 6z + 14$
$\quad\quad\quad\; -15 \;\;= \;\;14 \leftarrow$ False
No solution—solution set is $\{\ \}$

8. No solution—solution set is $\{\ \}$

9. $\dfrac{x}{3} - \dfrac{x}{6} = 18$ (LCM is 6)   *Check for x = 180*

$(6)\left(\dfrac{x}{3} - \dfrac{x}{6}\right) = (6)(18)$ $\dfrac{108}{3} - \dfrac{108}{6} \overset{?}{=} 18$

$(\overset{2}{\cancel{6}})\left(\dfrac{x}{\underset{1}{\cancel{3}}}\right) - (\overset{1}{\cancel{6}})\left(\dfrac{x}{\underset{1}{\cancel{6}}}\right) = 108$ $36 - 18 = 18$

$2x - x = 108$
$x = 108$

$\{108\}$; graph:

10. $\{128\}$; graph:

11. LCD $= 40$

$$\overset{5}{\cancel{40}}\left(\frac{y + 3}{\underset{1}{\cancel{8}}}\right) - \overset{10}{\cancel{40}}\left(\frac{3}{\underset{1}{\cancel{4}}}\right) = \overset{4}{\cancel{40}}\left(\frac{y + 6}{\underset{1}{\cancel{10}}}\right)$$

$\quad 5y + 15 - 30 = 4y + 24$
$\quad\quad\;\; 5y - 15 = 4y + 24$
$\quad\quad\quad\quad\quad\; y = 39$

$\{39\}$; graph:

12. $\{-25\}$; graph:

13. $5z - 3(2 + 3z) = 6$ **14.** No solution—$\{\ \}$
$\quad 5z - 6 - 9z = 6$
$\quad\quad\; -6 - 4z = 6$
$\quad\quad\quad\; -4z = 12$
$\quad\quad\quad\quad\; z = -3$
$-3 \notin N$—no solution—$\{\ \}$

15. $7x - 2(5 + 4x) = 8$
$\quad 7x - 10 - 8x = 8$
$\quad\quad\quad\quad -x = 18$
$\quad\quad\quad\quad\; x = -18$
$\quad\quad\quad\quad\; x \in J$

$\{-18\}$; graph:

16. {0}

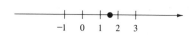
$-2 \quad -1 \quad 0 \quad 1 \quad 2$

17. $2(3x - 6) - 3(5x + 4) = 5(7x - 8)$
$6x - 12 - 15x - 12 = 35x - 40$
$-9x - 24 = 35x - 40$
$16 = 44x$
$x = \dfrac{16}{44} = \dfrac{4}{11}$

$\dfrac{4}{11} \notin J$ —no solution—{ }

18. No solution—{ }

19. LCD = 10

$$\dfrac{\overset{2}{\cancel{10}}}{1} \cdot \dfrac{2(y-3)}{\underset{-1}{\cancel{5}}} - \dfrac{\overset{5}{\cancel{10}}}{1} \cdot \dfrac{3(y+2)}{\underset{1}{\cancel{2}}} = \dfrac{\overset{1}{\cancel{10}}}{1} \cdot \dfrac{7}{\cancel{10}}$$

$4y - 12 - 15y - 30 = 7$
$-11y = 49$
$y = \dfrac{-49}{11} \text{ or } 4\dfrac{5}{11}$

$\left\{-4\dfrac{5}{11}\right\}$

$-6 \quad -5 \quad -4 \quad -3 \quad -2 \quad -1$

20. $\dfrac{81}{11}$ or $7\dfrac{4}{11}$

$5 \quad 6 \quad 7 \quad 8 \quad 9 \quad 10$

21. $6.23x + 2.5(3.08 - 8.2x) = -14.7$
$6.23x + 7.7 - 20.5x = -14.7$
$-14.27x + 7.7 = -14.7$
$-14.27x = -22.4$
$x \doteq 1.57$

$-1 \quad 0 \quad 1 \quad 2 \quad 3$

22. $\{\doteq 0.968\}$

$-1 \quad 0 \quad 1 \quad 2$

Exercises 2.2 (page 93)

1. $3x - 1 < 11$
$3x < 12$
$x < 4$

$1 \quad 2 \quad 3 \quad 4 \quad 5$

2. $x < 6$

$3 \quad 4 \quad 5 \quad 6 \quad 7$

3. $17 \geq 2x - 9$
$26 \geq 2x$
$13 \geq x$
$x \leq 13$

$11 \quad 13 \quad 15$

4. $x \geq -7$

$-9 \quad -7 \quad -5$

5. $\begin{array}{r} 2y - 16 > 17 + 5y \\ -2y \qquad -2y \\ \hline -16 > 17 + 3y \\ -33 > 3y \\ -11 > y \\ y < -11 \end{array}$

$-13 \qquad -11$

6. $y > -5$

$-5 \qquad -3$

7. $\begin{array}{r} 4z - 22 < \quad 6(z - 7) \\ 4z - 22 < \quad 6z - 42 \\ -4z \qquad -4z \\ \hline -22 < \quad 2z - 42 \\ 20 < 2z \\ 10 < z \text{ or } z > 10 \end{array}$

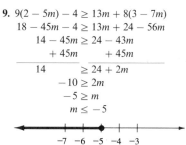
$9 \quad 10 \quad 11 \quad 12 \quad 13$

8. $a < -2$

$-4 \quad -3 \quad -2 \quad -1 \quad 0$

9. $9(2 - 5m) - 4 \geq 13m + 8(3 - 7m)$
$18 - 45m - 4 \geq 13m + 24 - 56m$
$14 - 45m \geq 24 - 43m$
$+45m \qquad +45m$
$\overline{14 \qquad \geq 24 + 2m}$
$-10 \geq 2m$
$-5 \geq m$
$m \leq -5$

$-7 \quad -6 \quad -5 \quad -4 \quad -3$

10. $k \leq 1$

$-1 \quad 0 \quad 1 \quad 2 \quad 3$

11. $10 - 5x > 2[3 - 5(x - 4)]$
$10 - 5x > 2[3 - 5x + 20]$
$10 - 5x > 2[23 - 5x]$
$10 - 5x > 46 - 10x$
$10 + 5x > 46$
$5x > 36$
$x > \dfrac{36}{5} \text{ or } x > 7\dfrac{1}{5}$

$5 \quad 6 \quad 7 \quad 8 \quad 9$

12. $y < -6$

$-8 \quad -7 \quad -6 \quad -5 \quad -4$

13. LCD = 12

$$\dfrac{\overset{4}{\cancel{12}}}{1} \cdot \dfrac{z}{\underset{1}{\cancel{3}}} > \dfrac{12}{1} \cdot \dfrac{7}{1} - \dfrac{\overset{3}{\cancel{12}}}{1} \cdot \dfrac{z}{\underset{1}{\cancel{4}}}$$

$4z > 84 - 3z$
$7z > 84$
$z > 12$

$10 \quad 11 \quad 12 \quad 13 \quad 14$

14. $t > 15$

15. LCD = 15

$$\frac{\overset{5}{\cancel{15}}}{1}\cdot\frac{1}{\cancel{3}} + \frac{\overset{3}{\cancel{15}}}{1}\cdot\frac{(w+2)}{\cancel{5}} \geq \frac{\overset{5}{\cancel{15}}}{1}\cdot\frac{(w-5)}{\cancel{3}}$$

$$5 + 3w + 6 \geq 5w - 25$$
$$11 \geq 2w - 25$$
$$36 \geq 2w$$
$$18 \geq w \text{ or } w \leq 18$$

16. $u \geq 6$

17. $14.73(2.65x - 11.08) - 22.51x \geq 13.94x(40.27)$
$39.0345x - 163.2084 - 22.51x \geq 561.3638x$
$$-544.8393x \geq 163.2084$$
$$x \leq -0.300 \text{ (approx.)}$$

18. $x \geq 0.7233$ (approx.)

19. $x + 3 < 10$
$\quad\quad x < 7$
$x \in N$
The natural numbers <7 are $\{1, 2, 3, 4, 5, 6\}$

20. $\{1, 2\}$

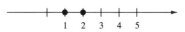

21. $2(x + 3) \leq 11$
$\quad 2x + 6 \leq 11$
$\quad\quad 2x \leq 5$
$\quad\quad\quad x \leq 5/2$
The natural numbers $\leq 5/2$ are 1 and 2; $\{1, 2\}$

22. $\{1, 2, 3, 4\}$

23. $\{x \mid x \geq 1\}$ **24.** $\{x \mid x \geq -2\}$ **25.** $\{x \mid x < 4\}$
26. $\{x \mid x < 6\}$

Exercises 2.3 (page 97)

1. $\{x \mid 0 \leq x < 3\}$ **2.** $\{x \mid 1 < x \leq 4\}$ **3.** $\{x \mid x \leq 2\}$
4. $\{x \mid x \leq 3\}$ **5.** $\{x \mid -1 \leq x \leq 1\}$ **6.** $\{x \mid 1 \leq x \leq 2\}$
7. $\{x \mid x > 1\}$ **8.** $\{x \mid x > 2\}$

9.
$$\begin{array}{ccc} 5 > & x - 2 & \geq \quad 3 \\ +2 & +2 & +2 \\ \hline 7 > & x & \geq \quad 5 \end{array}$$
or $5 \leq x \quad < \quad 7$

10. $10 > x \geq 7$
or $7 \leq x < 10$

11. $-5 \geq x - 3 \geq 2$ **12.** $\{\ \}$ or $\varnothing$ (no graph)
"$-5 \geq 2$" is false
$\{\ \}$ or $\varnothing$ (no graph)

13.
$$\begin{array}{ccc} -4 < & 3x - 1 & \leq \quad 7 \\ +1 & +1 & +1 \\ \hline \frac{-3}{3} < & \frac{3x}{3} & \leq \quad \frac{8}{3} \\ -1 < & x & \leq \quad \frac{8}{3} \end{array}$$

14. $-1 < x \leq \dfrac{7}{4}$

15.
$$\begin{array}{cc} x - 1 > & 3 \text{ or } x - 1 < -3 \\ +1 \quad +1 & +1 \quad +1 \\ \hline x \quad > \quad 4 & \text{ or } x \quad < -2 \end{array}$$

16. $x > 7$ or $x < -3$

17.
$$\begin{array}{cc} 2x + 1 \geq \quad 3 & \text{ or } \quad 2x + 1 \leq -3 \\ -1 \quad -1 & -1 \quad -1 \\ \hline \frac{2x}{2} \geq \frac{2}{2} & \text{ or } \frac{2x}{2} \leq \frac{-4}{2} \\ x \geq \quad 1 & \text{ or } \quad x \leq -2 \end{array}$$

18. $x \geq 7/3$ or $x \leq -1$

19.

20. $x < -1$

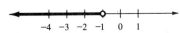

21. $x > 4$ or $x \geq 2$

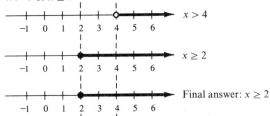

$x > 4$

$x \geq 2$

Final answer: $x \geq 2$

22. $x < 3$

23. $-5 \leq x - 3 \leq 2$

$\quad +3 \qquad +3 \quad +3$

$\overline{-2 \leq x \qquad \leq \quad 5}$, but $x \in N$. Therefore, $\{1, 2, 3, 4, 5\}$.

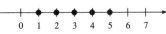

24. $\{1, 2, 3, 4, 5, 6\}$

25. $\quad 4 \geq x - 3 > -5$

$\quad +3 \qquad +3 \quad +3$

$\overline{\quad 7 \geq x \qquad > -2}$, but $x \in J$

Therefore, $\{-1, 0, 1, 2, 3, 4, 5, 6, 7\}$

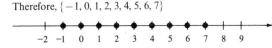

26. $\{-1, 0, 1, 2, 3, 4, 5, 6, 7, 8\}$

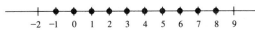

27. $-3 \leq 2x + 1 \leq 7$

$\quad -1 \qquad -1 \quad -1$

$\dfrac{-4}{2} \leq \dfrac{2x}{2} \qquad \leq \dfrac{6}{2}$

$-2 \leq x \qquad \leq 3$, but $x \in N$. Therefore, $\{1, 2, 3\}$.

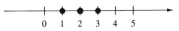

28. $\{1\}$

Exercises 2.4 (page 103)

1. $|x| = 3$

$x = 3$ or $x = -3$

$\{3, -3\}$

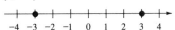

2. $\{5, -5\}$

3. $|3x| = 12$

$\quad 3x = 12$ or $3x = -12$

$\quad x = 4$ or $x = -4$

$\{4, -4\}$

4. $\{5, -5\}$

5. $|x| < 2$

$-2 < x < 2$

6. $\{x \mid -7 < x < 7\}$

7. $\qquad |4x| < 12$

$-12 < 4x < 12$

$\quad -3 < x < 3$

$\{x \mid -3 < x < 3\}$

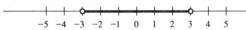

8. $\{x \mid -3 < x < 3\}$

9. $\qquad |5x| \leq 25$

$-25 \leq 5x \leq 25$

$\quad -5 \leq x \leq 5 \quad \{x \mid -5 \leq x \leq 5\}$

10. $\{x \mid -1 \leq x \leq 1\}$

11. $|x| > 2$

$x > 2$ or $x < -2$

$\{x \mid x > 2$ or $x < -2\}$

12. $\{x \mid x > 3$ or $x < -3\}$

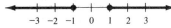

13. $|3x| \geq 3$

$\quad 3x \geq 3$ or $3x \leq -3$

$\quad x \geq 1$ or $x \leq -1 \quad \{x \mid x \geq 1$ or $x \leq -1\}$

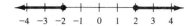

14. $\{x \mid x \geq 2$ or $x \leq -2\}$

15. $|x + 2| = 5$
$\quad x + 2 = 5$ or $x + 2 = -5$
$\quad\quad x = 3$ or $\quad\quad x = -7$
$\quad\quad \{3, -7\}$

16. $\{4, -10\}$

17. $\quad |x - 3| < 2$
$\quad -2 < x - 3 < 2$
$\quad \dfrac{3}{1} < \dfrac{3}{x} \quad \dfrac{3}{< 5}$
$\quad \{x | 1 < x < 5\}$

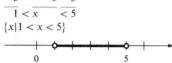

18. $\{x | 3 < x < 5\}$

19. $-3 \le x + 4 \le \quad 3$
$\quad \dfrac{-4}{-7 \le x} \quad \dfrac{-4}{\le -1} \quad \{x | -7 \le x \le -1\}$

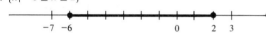

20. $\{x | -6 \le x \le 2\}$

21. $|x + 1| > \quad 3$
$\quad x + 1 > \quad 3$ or $x + 1 < -3$
$\quad \dfrac{-1}{x} \quad \dfrac{-1}{> 2}$ or $\dfrac{-1}{x} \quad \dfrac{-1}{< -4}$
$\quad \{x | x > 2$ or $x < -4\}$

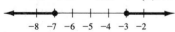

22. $\{x | x > 6$ or $x < -2\}$

23. $|x + 5| \ge \quad 2$
$\quad x + 5 \ge \quad 2$ or $x + 5 \le -2$
$\quad\quad x \ge -3$ or $\quad\quad x \le -7$ $\quad \{x | x \le -7$ or $x \ge -3\}$

24. $\{x | x \ge -3$ or $x \le -5\}$

25. $|3x + 4| = \quad 3$
$\quad 3x + 4 = \quad 3$ or $3x + 4 = -3$
$\quad\quad 3x = -1$ or $\quad\quad 3x = -7$
$\quad\quad\quad x = -\dfrac{1}{3}$ or $\quad\quad x = -\dfrac{7}{3}$
$\left\{-\dfrac{1}{3}, -\dfrac{7}{3}\right\}$

26. $\left\{-2, \dfrac{1}{2}\right\}$

27. $-4 < 2x - 3 < 4$
$\quad \dfrac{3}{-1 < 2x} \quad \dfrac{3}{< 7}$
$\quad -\dfrac{1}{2} < \quad x \quad\quad < \dfrac{7}{2} \quad \left\{x \left| -\dfrac{1}{2} < x < \dfrac{7}{2}\right.\right\}$

28. $\{x | -4/3 < x < 2\}$

29. $|3x - 5| \ge \quad 6$
$\quad 3x - 5 \ge \quad 6$ or $3x - 5 \le -6$
$\quad\quad 3x \ge 11$ or $\quad\quad 3x \le -1$
$\quad\quad\quad x \ge \dfrac{11}{3}$ or $\quad\quad x \le -\dfrac{1}{3}$

30. $\{x | x \ge 1$ or $x \le -1/2\}$

31. $\quad |1 - 2x| \le \quad 5$
$\quad -5 \le \quad 1 - 2x \le \quad 5$
$\quad \dfrac{-1}{-6 \le} \quad \dfrac{-1}{-2x \le} \quad \dfrac{-1}{4}$
$\quad 3 \ge \quad\quad x \ge -2$
$\quad \{x | -2 \le x \le 3\}$

32. $\{x | -2/3 < x < 2\}$

33. $|2 - 3x| > \quad 4$
$\quad 2 - 3x > \quad 4$ or $2 - 3x < -4$
$\quad\quad -3x > \quad 2 \quad\quad -3x < -6$
$\quad\quad\quad x < -\dfrac{2}{3}$ or $\quad\quad x > 2 \quad\quad \{x | x < -\dfrac{2}{3}$ or $x > 2\}$

34. $\{x \mid x \le -1/2 \text{ or } x \ge 11/2\}$

35. $\left|\dfrac{5x + 2}{3}\right| \ge 2$

$$\dfrac{5x + 2}{3} \ge \quad 2 \text{ or } \dfrac{5x + 2}{3} \le -2$$

$$5x + 2 \ge \quad 6 \text{ or } 5x + 2 \le -6$$

$$\underline{\quad -2 \quad\quad -2 \quad\quad\quad -2 \quad -2\quad}$$

$$5x \quad \ge \quad 4 \text{ or } 5x \quad\quad \le -8$$

$$x \ge \dfrac{4}{5} \text{ or } \qquad x \le -\dfrac{8}{5}$$

$\{x \mid x \ge 4/5 \text{ or } x \le -8/5\}$

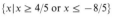

36. $\{x \mid x \ge 3 \text{ or } x \le -9/2\}$

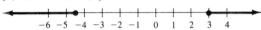

37. $-1 < \dfrac{3x - 4}{5} < 1$

$$-5 < 3x - 4 < 5$$

$$\underline{\quad 4 \qquad\quad 4 \quad 4\quad}$$

$$-1 < 3x \quad\quad < 9$$

$$-\dfrac{1}{3} < \quad x \quad\quad < 3 \qquad \{x \mid -1/3 < x < 3\}$$

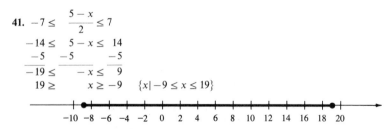

38. $\{x \mid -3/5 < x < 1\}$

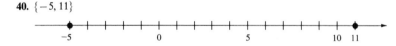

39. $\left|\dfrac{1 - x}{2}\right| = 6$

$$\dfrac{1 - x}{2} = \quad 6 \text{ or } \dfrac{1 - x}{2} = -6$$

$$1 - x = 12 \qquad 1 - x = -12$$

$$-x = 11 \qquad\quad -x = -13$$

$$x = -11 \text{ or } \quad x = 13 \qquad \{-11, 13\}$$

40. $\{-5, 11\}$

41. $-7 \le \dfrac{5 - x}{2} \le 7$

$$-14 \le \quad 5 - x \le \quad 14$$

$$\underline{\quad -5 \qquad -5 \qquad\quad -5\quad}$$

$$-19 \le \quad -x \le \quad 9$$

$$19 \ge \qquad x \ge -9 \qquad \{x \mid -9 \le x \le 19\}$$

42. $\{x \mid -5 \le x \le 13\}$

43. $\left|3 - \dfrac{x}{2}\right| > 4$

$$3 - \dfrac{x}{2} > 4 \quad \text{or} \quad 3 - \dfrac{x}{2} < -4$$

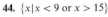

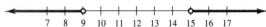

$$6 - x > 8 \quad \text{or} \quad 6 - x < -8$$
$$-x > 2 \quad \text{or} \quad -x < -14$$
$$x < -2 \quad \text{or} \quad x > 14$$

44. $\{x \mid x < 9 \text{ or } x > 15\}$

45. $-3 < 4 - \dfrac{x}{2} < 3$

$$-6 < 8 - x < 6$$
$$\underline{-8 \qquad -8 \qquad -8}$$
$$-14 < -x < -2$$
$$14 > x > 2 \quad \{x \mid 2 < x < 14\}$$

46. $\{x \mid 9 < x < 21\}$

Review Exercises 2.5 (page 105)

1. $7 - 2(M - 4) = 5$
$7 - 2M + 8 = 5$
$-2M + 15 = 5$
$\dfrac{-2M}{-2} = \dfrac{-10}{-2}$
$M = 5 \quad \{5\}$

2. No solution—$\{\ \}$

3. LCD = 12
$\dfrac{\overset{3}{\cancel{12}}}{1} \cdot \dfrac{3(x+3)}{\underset{1}{\cancel{4}}} - \dfrac{\overset{4}{\cancel{12}}}{1} \cdot \dfrac{2(x-3)}{\underset{1}{\cancel{3}}} = \dfrac{12}{1} \cdot 1$
$9(x+3) - 8(x-3) = 12$
$9x + 27 - 8x + 24 = 12$
$x = -39 \quad \{-39\}$

4. Identity—$\{x \mid x \in R\}$

5. $2[-7y - 3(5 - 4y) + 10] = 10y - 12$
$2[-7y - 15 + 12y + 10] = 10y - 12$
$2[5y - 5] = 10y - 12$
$10y - 10 = 10y - 12$
$0 \neq -2 \quad \text{No solution} \quad \{\ \}$

6. $x \leq \dfrac{1}{3}$

7. LCD = 30
$\dfrac{\overset{6}{\cancel{30}}}{1} \cdot \dfrac{3z}{\underset{1}{\cancel{5}}} + \dfrac{\overset{10}{\cancel{30}}}{1} \cdot \dfrac{-2z}{\underset{1}{\cancel{3}}} < \dfrac{\overset{15}{\cancel{30}}}{1} \cdot \dfrac{1}{\underset{1}{\cancel{2}}}$
$18z - 20z < 15$
$-2z < 15$
$z > -\dfrac{15}{2}$

8. $w > -3\dfrac{1}{2}$

9. LCD = 20
$\dfrac{\overset{2}{\cancel{20}}}{1} \cdot \dfrac{2(x+6)}{\underset{1}{\cancel{10}}} + \dfrac{\overset{1}{\cancel{20}}}{1} \cdot \dfrac{3x}{\underset{1}{\cancel{20}}} < \dfrac{20}{1} \cdot \dfrac{3}{1}$
$4(x+6) + 3x < 60$
$4x + 24 + 3x < 60$
$7x < 36$
$x < 5\dfrac{1}{7}$

10. $x > -9\dfrac{1}{11}$

11. $3x + 2 = 11$
$3x = 9$
$x = 3$

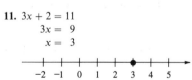

12. $\{3, -3\}$

13. $\{x \mid -3 \leq x \leq 3)$

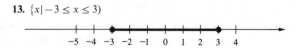

14. $\{x \mid x \geq 2\} \cup \{x \mid x \leq -2\}$

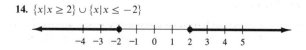

15. $|6 - 2x| = 10$

$$
\begin{array}{l|l}
6 - 2x = 10 & 6 - 2x = -10 \\
-2x = 4 & -2x = -16 \\
x = -2 & x = 8
\end{array}
$$

16. $\{x | 0 \le x \le 4\}$

17. $\quad 2|x - 3| \le 4$
$\quad\quad |x - 3| \le 2$
$\quad -2 \le x - 3 \le 2$
$\quad \dfrac{3}{} \quad\quad \dfrac{3}{} \quad \dfrac{3}{}$
$\quad \overline{1 \le x} \quad \overline{\le 5} \quad \{x | 1 \le x \le 5\}$

18. $\{x | -1 < x < 9/2\}$

19. $-2 < x + 1 < \quad 0$
$\quad \dfrac{-1}{} \quad \dfrac{-1}{} \quad \dfrac{-1}{}$
$\quad \overline{-3 < x} \quad\quad < \overline{-1}$
$\{x | -3 < x < -1, x \in J\} = \{-2\}$

20. $\{x | -2 < x < 1/3\}$

21. $-3 < x - 1 < \quad 0$
$\quad \dfrac{+1}{} \quad \dfrac{+1}{} \quad \dfrac{+1}{}$
$\quad \overline{-2 < x} \quad\quad < \overline{1} \quad \{x | -2 < x < 1, x \in J\} = \{-1, 0\}$

22. $\{3\}$

23. $\quad \dfrac{3(x - 1)}{4} + \dfrac{x}{8} = 1$

$\quad\quad 6(x - 1) + x = 8$
$\quad\quad 6x - 6 + x = 8$
$\quad\quad\quad\quad 7x - 6 = 8$
$\quad\quad\quad\quad\quad 7x = 14$
$\quad\quad\quad\quad\quad x = 2; \quad \{2\}$

24. $\{x | 3 \le x \le 9\}$

25. $\left|\dfrac{2x-4}{3}\right| \ge 2$

$$\dfrac{2x-4}{3} \ge 2 \qquad\qquad \dfrac{2x-4}{3} \le -2$$

$$\dfrac{1}{1}\cdot\dfrac{2x-4}{\cancel{3}} \ge \dfrac{3}{1}\cdot\dfrac{2}{1} \quad\Big|\quad \dfrac{1}{1}\cdot\dfrac{2x-4}{\cancel{3}} \le \dfrac{3}{1}\cdot\dfrac{-2}{1}$$

$$2x-4 \ge 6 \qquad\qquad 2x-4 \le -6$$

$$2x \ge 10 \qquad\qquad 2x \le -2$$

$$x \ge 5 \qquad\qquad x \le -1$$

$\{x \mid x \ge 5 \text{ or } x \le -1\}$

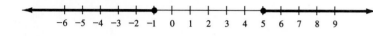

26. $\{x \mid x < 1\}$ **27.** $\{x \mid -3 < x \le 1\}$ **28.** $\{x \mid x \ge 4\}$

Chapter 2 Diagnostic Text (page 109)

Following each problem number is the textbook section number (in parentheses) where that kind of problem is discussed.

1. (2.1) $8x - 4(2+3x) = 12$ *Check*
$8x - 8 - 12x = 12$
$\qquad\qquad 8x - 4(2+3x) = 12$
$-4x = 20$
$\qquad 8(-5) - 4[2+3(-5)] \overset{?}{=} 12$
$x = -5$
$\qquad -40 - 4[2-15] \overset{?}{=} 12$
$\qquad\qquad -40 - 4[-13] \overset{?}{=} 12$
$\qquad\qquad -40 + 52 \overset{?}{=} 12$
$\qquad\qquad 12 = 12$

2. (2.1) $3(x-6) = 5(1+2x) - 7(x-4)$
$3x - 18 = 5 + 10x - 7x + 28$
$3x - 18 = 3x + 33$
$-18 \ne 33$ No solution

3. (2.1) LCD is 12
$12\left\{\dfrac{x}{6} - \dfrac{x+2}{4}\right\} = 12\left\{\dfrac{1}{3}\right\}$
$2x - 3(x+2) = 4$ *Check* $12\left\{\dfrac{-10}{6} - \dfrac{-10+2}{4}\right\} \overset{?}{=} 12\left\{\dfrac{1}{3}\right\}$
$2x - 3x - 6 = 4$
$\qquad\qquad 12\left\{\dfrac{-5}{3} - \dfrac{-8}{4}\right\} \overset{?}{=} 4$
$-x = 10$
$\qquad\qquad 12\left\{\dfrac{-20+24}{12}\right\} \overset{?}{=} 4$
$x = -10$
$\qquad\qquad 4 = 4$

4. (2.1) $2[7x - 4(1+3x)] = 5(3-2x) - 23$
$2[7x - 4 - 12x] = 15 - 10x - 23$
$2[-4 - 5x] = -10x - 8$
$-8 - 10x = -8 - 10x$
$0 = 0$ Identity

5. (2.2) $5w + 2 \le 10 - w$
$6w \le 8$
$w \le \dfrac{8}{6}$
$w \le \dfrac{4}{3}$

6. (2.2) $13h - 4(2+3h) \ge 0$
$13h - 8 - 12h \ge 0$
$h \ge 8$

7. (2.2) $2[-5y - 6(y-7)] < 6 + 4y$
$2[-5y - 6y + 42] < 6 + 4y$
$2[-11y + 42] < 6 + 4y$
$-22y + 84 < 6 + 4y$
$78 < 26y$
$3 < y \text{ or } y > 3$

8. (2.3) $\{x \mid -3 < x+1 < 5,\, x \in J\}$
$-3 < x+1 < 5$
$\dfrac{-1 \qquad -1 \qquad -1}{-4 < x \qquad < 4}$
Solution set $= \{x \mid -4 < x < 4,\, x \in J\}$
$\qquad\qquad = \{-3, -2, -1, 0, 1, 2, 3\}$

9. (2.3) $\{x \mid 4 \ge 3x + 7 > -2,\, x \in R\}$
$-3 \ge 3x > -9$
$-1 \ge x > -3,\, x \in R$
Solution set $= \{x \mid -3 < x \le -1,\, x \in R\}$

10. (2.2) $\left\{x \mid \dfrac{5(x-2)}{3} + \dfrac{x}{4} \le 12,\, x \in R\right\}$
$\dfrac{\cancel{20}^4}{1}\cdot\dfrac{5(x-2)}{\cancel{3}} + \dfrac{\cancel{20}^3}{1}\cdot\dfrac{x}{\cancel{4}} \le \dfrac{12}{1}\cdot\dfrac{12}{1}$
$20(x-2) + 3x \le 144$
$20x - 40 + 3x \le 144$
$23x \le 184$
$x \le 8,\, x \in R$
$\{x \mid x \le 8,\, x \in R\}$

11. (2.4) $\left\{x \mid \left|\dfrac{2x+3}{5}\right| = 1\right\}$
$\dfrac{2x+3}{5} = 1 \qquad\Big|\qquad \dfrac{2x+3}{5} = -1$
$2x + 3 = 5 \qquad\Big|\qquad 2x + 3 = -5$
$2x = 2 \qquad\qquad\Big|\qquad 2x = -8$
$x = 1 \qquad\qquad\Big|\qquad x = -4$
Solution set $= \{-4, 1\}$

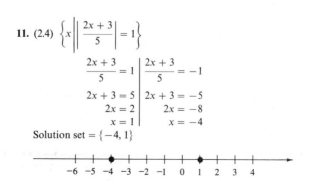

12. (2.4) $|3x - 1| > 2$

$$3x - 1 > 2 \text{ or } \quad 3x - 1 < -2$$

$$\overline{3x} \;\; > \overline{3} \text{ or } \quad \overline{3x} \;\; < \overline{-1}$$

$$x > 1 \text{ or } \qquad x < -\frac{1}{3}$$

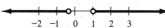

13. (2.4) $|7 - 3x| \geq 6$

$7 - 3x \geq 6$	$7 - 3x \leq -6$
$7 \geq 3x + 6$	$7 \leq 3x - 6$
$1 \geq 3x$	$13 \leq 3x$
$\dfrac{1}{3} \geq x$	$\dfrac{13}{3} \leq x$

Solution set $= \left\{x \mid x \geq 4\dfrac{1}{3}\right\} \cup \left\{x \mid x \leq \dfrac{1}{3}\right\}$

14. (2.4) $\left|\dfrac{5x + 1}{2}\right| \leq 7$

$$-7 \leq \dfrac{5x + 1}{2} \leq 7$$

$$-14 \leq 5x + 1 \leq 14$$

$$\dfrac{-1 \qquad -1 \quad -1}{-15 \leq 5x \quad\; \leq 13}$$

$$-3 \leq x \quad\; \leq \dfrac{13}{5}$$

15. (2.4) $\{x \mid |2x - 5| < 11\}$

$$-11 < 2x - 5 < 11$$

$$-6 < 2x \qquad < 16$$

$$-3 < x \qquad\;\; < 8$$

Solution set $= \{x \mid -3 < x < 8\}$

Cumulative Review Exercises:
Chapters 1 and 2 (page 110)

1. $(-14) - (-22) = (-14) + (22) = 8$ **2.** 48 **3.** -1

4. -14 **5.** $(-2)^4 = (-2)(-2)(-2)(-2) = 16$ **6.** 8

7. Not possible **8.** 0 **9.** $\dfrac{|-20|}{-5} = \dfrac{20}{-5} = -4$ **10.** -25

11. -4 **12.** -36 **13.** -5 **14.** 0 **15.** -1 **16.** 1000

17. 1 **18.** 8 **19.** $-3 - 4 \cdot 6 = -3 - 24 = -27$ **20.** 11

21. 4 **22.** -28 **23.** 0 **24.** 9 **25.** 3 **26.** 13

27. Cannot be determined **28.** 1

29. $y - 2(x - y) - 3(1 - y) - \sqrt{4y^2}$ **30.** $x^3 - 3x^2 + 4x$
$= y - 2x + 2y - 3 + 3y - 2y$
$= 4y - 2x - 3$

31. $6(3x - 5) + 7 = 9(3 + 2x) - 1$ **32.** $\{x \mid x \geq -11/3\}$
$18x - 30 + 7 = 27 + 18x - 1$
$18x - 23 = 18x + 26$
$-23 = 26 \leftarrow$ False
No solution

33. $\quad 2x + 3 = 2(2x + 5)$ **34.** $\{5\}$
$\quad 2x + 3 = \;\; 4x + 10$
$\dfrac{-2x - 10 \quad -2x - 10}{\quad -7 = \quad 2x}$
$\quad \dfrac{-7}{2} = x$

$\{-7/2\}$

35. $-5 < x + 4 \leq 3$ **36.** Identity
$\dfrac{-4 \qquad -4 \quad -4}{-9 < x \quad\; \leq -1}$
$\{x \mid -9 < x \leq -1\}$

37. $|2x + 3| > 1 \Rightarrow 2x + 3 > \quad 1 \text{ or } 2x + 3 < -1$
$2x > -2 \text{ or } \quad 2x < -4$
$x > -1 \text{ or } \qquad x < -2$
$\{x \mid x > -1 \text{ or } x < -2\}$

38. $\{x \mid 1 \leq x \leq 7\}$

Exercises 3.1 (page 115)

Note: The checks for these exercises will not be shown.

1. Let x = Unknown number **2.** 9

$2x + 7 = 23$

$2x = 16$

$x = 8$

3. Let x = Unknown number

$4x - 7 = 25$

$4x = 32$

$x = 8$

4. 11 **5.** Let x = Unknown number **6.** 24

$x - 7 = \frac{1}{2}x$

$2(x - 7) = 2\left(\frac{1}{2}x\right)$

$2x - 14 = x$

$x = 14$

7. Let x = Number of cm in second piece of string

$3x$ = Number of cm in first piece of string

$x + 3x = 12$

$4x = 12$

$x = 3$ Number of cm in second piece of string

$3x = 9$ Number of cm in first piece of string

8. 8 m, 4 m **9.** Let

x = First integer

$x + 1$ = Second integer

$x + 2$ = Third integer

$x + (x + 1) + (x + 2) = 19$

$3x + 3 = 19$

$3x = 16$

$x = \frac{16}{3}$ Not an integer

No solution

10. No solution

11. Let x = Length of second piece

$x + 8$ = Length of first piece

$x + (x + 8) = 42$

$2x + 8 = 42$

$2x = 34$

$x = 17$ cm Second piece

$x + 8 = 25$ cm First piece

12. 28 m, 22 m **13.** Let

x = First integer

$x + 1$ = Second integer

$x + 2$ = Third integer

$x + (x + 1) - (x + 2) = 10$

$x + x + 1 - x - 2 = 10$

$x - 1 = 10$

$x = 11$ First integer

$x + 1 = 12$ Second integer

$x + 2 = 13$ Third Integer

14. 18, 19, and 20

15. Let x = First odd integer **16.** No solution

$x + 2$ = Second odd integer

$x + 4$ = Third odd integer

$3[(x + 2) + (x + 4)] = 40 + 5(x)$

$3(2x + 6) = 40 + 5x$

$6x + 18 = 40 + 5x$

$x = 22$

22 is not an odd integer—no solution

17. Let x = Number of cans of peas

$x + 4$ = Number of cans of corn

$3x$ = Number of cans of green beans

$x + (x + 4) + (3x) = 24$

$5x + 4 = 24$

$5x = 20$

$x = 4$ Number of cans of peas

$x + 4 = 8$ Number of cans of corn

$3x = 12$ Number of cans of green beans

18. 3 cans of pears, 9 cans of peaches, 9 cans of cherries

19. Let x = Unknown number

$3(8 + x) = 2(x + 7)$

$24 + 3x = 2x + 14$

$x = -10$

20. 7 **21.** Let x = Unknown number **22.** 2

$8x - 2(5 + x) = 4(8 + 2x)$

$8x - 10 - 2x = 32 + 8x$

$-42 = 2x$

$-21 = x$

$x = -21$

23. Let x = First even integer

$x + 2$ = Second even integer

$x + 4$ = Third even integer

$21 < x + (x + 2) + (x + 4) < 45$

$21 < \qquad\quad 3x + 6 < 45$

$15 < \qquad\qquad 3x < 39$

$5 < \qquad\qquad\quad x < 13$

The even integers between 5 and 13 are 6, 8, 10, and 12.

Therefore, the answers are: 6, 8, and 10; 8, 10, and 12; 10, 12, and 14; and 12, 14, and 16.

24. 26, 28, and 30; and 28, 30, and 32

25. Let x = Score needed **26.** 136 to 200

$x \leq 200$

$560 \leq \quad 396 + x \leq \quad 640$

$-396 \quad -396 \qquad\quad -396$

$\overline{164 \leq \quad x \qquad\quad \leq \quad 244}$

but $x \leq 200$ so,

$164 \leq x \leq 200$

Exercises 3.2 (page 120)

1. Let $4x$ = smaller number

$5x$ = larger number

$\frac{4x}{5x} = \frac{4}{5}$ $4x + 5x = 81$

$9x = 81$

$x = 9$

Smaller number = $4x = 4(9) = 36$

Larger number = $5x = 5(9) = 45$

$\overline{81}$ Check

2. Smaller number = 21

Larger number = 56

3. Let $3x$ = First side The perimeter is 108
  $4x$ = Second side $3x + 4x + 5x = 108$
  $5x$ = Third side $12x = 108$
  $x = 9$

$3x = 27$
$4x = 36$
$5x = 45$; 27, 36, 45

4. 32, 40, 48

5. Let $4x$ = Study hours
  $2x$ = Class hours
  $3x$ = Work hours

$54 = 4x + 2x + 3x$
$54 = 9x$
$6 = x$

Therefore, Study hours = $4x = 4(6) = 24$
  Class hours = $2x = 2(6) = 12$
  Work hours = $3x = 3(6) = 18$
  $\overline{54}$ Check

6. Study hours = 16
  Class hours = 8
  Work hours = 24

7. Let $7x$ = Length of rectangle
  $6x$ = Width of rectangle

$2(7x) + 2(6x) = 78$
$14x + 12x = 78$
$26x = 78$
$x = 3$
$7x = 21$ Length
$6x = 18$ Width
Check Perimeter is $2(21) + 2(18)$
  $= 42 + 36 = 78$

8. Width = 35, length = 63

9. Let $7x$ = One number
  $6x$ = Other number

$143 = 7x + 6x$
$143 = 13x$
$x = 11$
$7x = 77$ One number
$6x = 66$ Other number
$\overline{143}$ Check

10. 136, 85

11. Let $4x$ = One side
  $5x$ = Second side
  $6x$ = Third side
  $0 < 4x + 5x + 6x < 60$
  $0 < 15x < 60$
  $0 < x < 4$
  $0 < 4x < 16$

The shortest side must be between 0 and 16.

12. The shortest side must be between 0 and 24.

Exercises 3.3 (page 124)

Note: The checks for these exercises will not be shown.

1. Let x = Speed of Malone car
  $x + 9$ = Speed of King car

	d	= r	$\cdot t$	
Malone car	$6x$	x	6	$d = r \cdot t$ $d = x \cdot 6 = 6x$
King car	$5(x + 9)$	$x + 9$	5	$d = r \cdot t$ $d = (x + 9)5 = 5(x + 9)$

Since both cars travel the same distance,
  $6x = 5(x + 9)$
  $6x = 5x + 45$

a. $x = 45$ mph Speed of Malone car
  $x + 9 = 45 + 9$
  $= 54$ mph Speed of King car

b. $45 \times 6 = 54 \times 5$
  $= 270$ miles Distance traveled

2a. Duran car—40 mph; Silva car—50 mph **b.** 400 miles

3. Let x = Hours required to return from lake
  $x + 3$ = Hours required to hike to lake

	d	= r	$\cdot$	t	
Going to lake	$2(x + 3)$	2		$x + 3$	$d = r \cdot t$ $d = 2(x + 3)$
Returning from lake	$5x$	5		x	$d = r \cdot t$ $d = 5x$

$5x = 2(x + 3)$
$5x = 2x + 6$
$3x = 6$
$x = 2$

a. $x + 3 = 5$ hr required to hike to lake

b. $d = rt$
  $= 2(5) = 10$ miles Distance to lake

4a. 3 hours **b.** 6 miles

5. Let x = Fran's speed
  $\frac{4}{5}x$ = Ron's speed

	d	= r	$\cdot$	t	
Fran	$3x$	x		3	$d = rt$ $d = (x)3 = 3x$
Ron	$3\left(\frac{4}{5}x\right)$	$\frac{4}{5}x$		3	$d = rt$ $d = \left(\frac{4}{5}x\right)3 = 3\left(\frac{4}{5}x\right)$

$\left(\begin{array}{c}\text{Distance}\\\text{traveled by Fran}\end{array}\right) + \left(\begin{array}{c}\text{Distance}\\\text{traveled by Ron}\end{array}\right) = 54$ miles

$3x + 3\left(\frac{4}{5}x\right) = 54$

$LCD = 5$
$\frac{5}{1}\left(\frac{3}{1}x\right) + \frac{5}{1}\left(\frac{3}{1}\right)\left(\frac{4}{5}x\right) = \frac{5}{1}\left(\frac{54}{1}\right)$
  $15x + 12x = 270$
  $27x = 270$
  $x = 10$ mph Fran's speed
  $\frac{4}{5}x = \frac{4}{5}(10)$
  $= 8$ mph Ron's speed

6. Tran, 9 mph; Atour, 6 mph

7. Let x = Speed of boat in still water
$x + 2$ = Speed of boat downstream
$x - 2$ = Speed of boat upstream

	d	$=$	r	$\cdot$	t	
Upstream	$5(x - 2)$		$x - 2$		5	$d = rt$ $d = (x - 2)5$
Downstream	$3(x + 2)$		$x + 2$		3	$d = rt$ $d = (x + 2)3$

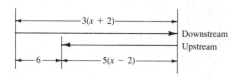

$$\frac{\text{Distance traveled}}{\text{downstream}} = 6 + \frac{\text{Distance traveled}}{\text{upstream}}$$

$$3(x + 2) = 6 + 5(x - 2)$$
$$3x + 6 = 6 + 5x - 10$$
$$10 = 2x$$
$$x = 5 \text{ mph} \quad \text{Speed in still water}$$
$$3(x + 2) = 3(5 + 2) = 3(7) = 21 \text{ miles} \quad \text{Traveled downstream}$$

8. 3 mph in still water;   16 miles downstream

9. Let t = Time with a headwind
$10 - t$ = Time with a tailwind

	d	$=$	r	$\cdot$	t	
With headwind	$80t$		$\frac{80}{100 - 20}$		t	$d = rt$ $d = 80t$
With tailwind	$(10 - t)120$		$\frac{120}{100 + 20}$		$10 - t$	$d = rt$ $d = 120(10 - t)$

$80t = 120(10 - t)$ because the distances are =
$80t = 1200 - 120t$
$200t = 1200$
$t = 6$ hr

$d = rt$
$d = 80(6) \quad = 480$ mi
$\quad$ or $120 \cdot 4 = 480$ mi

10. 6 miles

Exercises 3.4 (page 128)

Note: The checks for these exercises will not be shown.

1. Let x = Number of pounds of Colombian coffee
$100 - x$ = Number of pounds of Brazilian coffee
$3.90x + 3.60(100 - x) = 3.72(100)$
$390x + 360(100 - x) = 37,200$
$39x + 3600 - 36x = 3720$
$3x = 120$
$x = 40$ pounds of Colombian coffee
$100 - x = 60$ pounds Brazilian coffee

2. 16 pounds of cashews, 34 pounds of peanuts

3. Let x = Number of pounds of almonds
$10 - x$ = Number of pounds of walnuts
$3.00x + 4.50(10 - x) = 39.72$
$300x + 450(10 - x) = 3972$
$300x + 4500 - 450x = 3972$
$\qquad -150x = -528$
$\qquad x = 3.52$ pounds of almonds
$\qquad 10 - x = 6.48$ pounds of walnuts

4. 1.5 pounds of apple chunks, 4.5 pounds of granola

5. There are two unknown numbers: the number of nickels and the number of dimes.

Let D = Number of dimes
$17 - D$ = Number of nickels

Each dime is worth 10¢; therefore, D dimes are worth $10D$¢.
Each nickel is worth 5¢; therefore, $(17 - D)$ nickels are worth $5(17 - D)$¢.

$$\frac{\text{Amount of}}{\text{money in dimes}} + \frac{\text{Amount of}}{\text{money in nickels}} = 115¢$$

$$10D + 5(17 - D) = 115$$
$$10D + 85 - 5D = 115$$
$$5D = 30$$
$$D = 6 \text{ dimes}$$
$$17 - D = 17 - 6 = 11 \text{ nickels}$$

Check   6 dimes = 6(10) =   60¢
$\qquad$ 11 nickels = 11(5) =   55¢
$\qquad\qquad\qquad\qquad\quad \overline{115¢} = \$1.15$

6. 11 quarters, 6 dimes

7. Let x = Number of quarters
$x + 7$ = Number of dimes
$3x$ = Number of nickels
$0.25x + 0.10(x + 7) + 0.05(3x) = 3.20$
$25x + 10(x + 7) + 5(3x) = 320$
$25x + 10x + 70 + 15x = 320$
$50x = 250$
$x = 5$ quarters
$x + 7 = 12$ dimes
$3x = 15$ nickels

8. 6 dimes, 11 nickels, 12 quarters

9. Let x = Number of pounds of peanut brittle
$6.60(15) + 4.20x = 5.10(15 + x)$
$66(15) + 42x = 51(15 + x)$
$990 + 42x = 765 + 51x$
$225 = 9x$
$x = 25$ pounds of peanut brittle

10. 16 pounds

11. Let x = Number of children's tickets
$23 - x$ = Number of adult's tickets

Each children's ticket is worth $3.50, so the total value = $3.50x$
Each adult's ticket is worth $5.25, so the total value = $5.25(23 - x)$

$$\frac{\text{Total value}}{\text{of child's}} + \frac{\text{Total value}}{\text{of adult's}} = \text{Total cost}$$

$$3.50x + 5.25(23 - x) = 108.50$$
$$350x + 525(23 - x) = 10,850$$
$$350x + 12,075 - 525x = 10,850$$
$$-175x = -1225$$
$$x = 7 \text{ children's tickets}$$
$$23 - x = 16 \text{ adult's tickets}$$

Check $7(3.50) + 16(5.25) \stackrel{?}{=} 108.50$
$\qquad\qquad \$24.50 + \$84.00 = \$108.50$

12. 27 22-cent stamps;   18 18-cent stamps

Exercises 3.5 (page 131)

Note: The checks for these exercises will not be shown.

1. Let x = Number of ml of water

$$0.40(500) + 0x = 0.25(500 + x)$$
$$40(500) = 25(500 + x)$$
$$20{,}000 = 12{,}500 + 25x$$
$$7500 = 25x$$
$$x = 300 \text{ ml of water}$$

2. 5 liters

3. Let x = Number of liters of pure alcohol

$$0.20(10) + x = 0.50(10 + x)$$
$$2(10) + 10x = 5(10 + x)$$
$$20 + 10x = 50 + 5x$$
$$5x = 30$$
$$x = 6 \text{ liters of pure alcohol}$$

4. 500 ml

5. Let x = Number of cc of 20% solution

$$0.20x + 0.50(100) = 0.25(100 + x)$$
$$20x + 50(100) = 25(100 + x)$$
$$20x + 5000 = 2500 + 25x$$
$$2500 = 5x$$
$$x = 500 \text{ cc of 20\% solution}$$

6. 20 pt

7. Let x = Number of gal of 30% solution
$100 - x$ = Number of gal of 90% solution

$$.30(x) + .90(100 - x) = 100(.75)$$
$$30x + 90(100 - x) = 7500$$
$$30x + 9000 - 90x = 7500$$
$$-60x = -1500$$
$$x = 25 \text{ gal of 30\% solution}$$
$$100 - x = 75 \text{ gal of 90\% solution}$$

8. 400 grams of 65% alloy;   800 grams of 20% alloy

9. Let x = Number of ℓ of 40% solution
$10 - x$ = Number of ℓ of 90% solution

$$.40x + .90(10 - x) = .50(10)$$
$$40x + 90(10 - x) = 50(10)$$
$$40x + 900 - 90x = 500$$
$$-50x = -400$$
$$x = 8 \text{ liters of 40\% solution}$$
$$10 - x = 2 \text{ liters of 90\% solution}$$

10. 1200 ml

Exercises 3.6 (page 133)

1. Let x = Units digit
$13 - x$ = Tens digit

Original number: *Number with digits reversed*:
$10(13 - x) + x$ $10x + (13 - x)$

$$10(13 - x) + x + 27 = 10x + (13 - x)$$
$$130 - 10x + x + 27 = 10x + 13 - x$$
$$-9x + 157 = 9x + 13$$
$$144 = 18x$$
$$8 = x$$
$$x = 8 \quad \text{Units digit}$$
$$13 - x = 13 - 8 = 5 \quad \text{Tens digit}$$

Therefore, the original number is 58.

Check   Sum of digits = $5 + 8 = 13$
Original number 58
Increased by $\underline{\quad 27 \quad}$
                        85   Number with digits reversed

2. 52

3. Let $2x$ = Units digit
x = Hundreds digit
$6 - x - 2x$ = Tens digit (Sum of the digits is 6)

Original Number   *Digits Reversed*
$100x + 10(6 - 3x) + 2x$ $100(2x) + 10(6 - 3x) + x$

$$100(2x) + 10(6 - 3x) + x = 198 + 100x + 10(6 - 3x) + 2x$$
$$200x + 60 - 30x + x = 198 + 100x + 60 - 30x + 2x$$
$$171x + 60 = 72x + 258$$
$$99x = 198$$
$$x = 2 \qquad \text{Hundreds digit}$$
$$2x = 4 \qquad \text{Units digit}$$
$$6 - 3x = 0 \qquad \text{Tens digit}$$

Therefore, the original number is 204.

Check   Sum of digits = $2 + 0 + 4 = 6$
Original number   204
Increased by $\underline{\quad 198 \quad}$
                            402   Number with digits reversed

4. 326

5. The original 20 lb copper-nickel alloy

40% nickel
40% of 20 lb = 8 lb nickel
60% copper
60% of 20 lb = 12 lb copper

Let x = Number of pounds of pure copper added.

$$\frac{x + 12}{8} = \frac{3}{1} \quad \text{Required ratio is 3 to 1}$$
$$x + 12 = 24$$
$$x = 12 \quad \text{pounds of pure copper}$$

(The check will not be shown.)

6. 42

7. Let x = Amount invested at 5.75%
$13{,}000 - x$ = Amount invested at 5.25%

$$0.0575x + 0.0525(13{,}000 - x) = 702.50$$
$$575x + 525(13{,}000 - x) = 7{,}025{,}000$$
$$575x + 6{,}825{,}000 - 525x = 7{,}025{,}000$$
$$50x = 200{,}000$$
$$x = \$4000 \text{ invested at 5.75\%}$$
$$13{,}000 - x = \$9000 \text{ invested at 5.25\%}$$

Check $\$4000(0.0575) = \$230.00$
$\$9000(0.0525) = \underline{\$472.50}$
Sum: $\$702.50$

8. $600 at 6.25%; $800 at 5.75%

9. Let x = Price of cheaper camera
$x + 48$ = Price of expensive camera
$18x$ = Total price paid for cheaper cameras
$10(x + 48)$ = Total price paid for expensive cameras

$$18x = 10(x + 48)$$
$$18x = 10x + 480$$
$$8x = 480$$
$$x = \$60 \text{ for each cheaper camera}$$
$$x + 48 = \$108 \text{ for each expensive camera}$$

Check $18(\$60) = \$1{,}080$
$10(\$108) = \$1{,}080$ } Same expenditure

10. $70 per stereo for less expensive stereos; $125 per stereo for the others

Review Exercises 3.7 (page 135)

Note: The checks for these exercises will not be shown.

1. Let x = Unknown number   **2.** No solution

$$\frac{28 - 5x}{3} = 3x$$

$$\frac{1}{1}\left(\frac{28 - 5x}{\cancel{3}}\right) = \frac{3}{1}(3x)$$

$$28 - 5x = 9x$$
$$28 = 14x$$
$$x = 2$$

3. Let $3x$ = First side   The perimeter is less than 36
$7x$ = Second side $0 < 3x + 7x + 8x < 36$
$8x$ = Third side $0 < \qquad 18x < 36$
$\qquad\qquad 0 < \qquad\quad x < 2$
$\qquad\qquad 0 < \qquad\quad 3x < 6$

The shortest side must be between 0 and 6

4. 5 quarters, 8 dimes, 3 nickels

5. Let $\quad x$ = Number of lb at \$2.20   **6.** 840 cc
$15 - x$ = Number of lb at \$2.60
$2.20x + 2.60(15 - x) = 2.36(15)$
$220x + 260(15 - x) = 236(15)$
$220x + 3900 - 260x = 3540$
$\qquad\qquad -40x = -360$
$\qquad\qquad\qquad x = 9$ lb at \$2.20
$\qquad\quad 15 - x = 6$ lb at \$2.60

7. Let x = Speed returning from work

	d	=	r	$\cdot$	t
Going to work	$\frac{1}{2}(x + 10)$		$x + 10$		30 min = $\frac{1}{2}$ hr
Returning from work	$\frac{3}{4}(x)$		x		45 min = $\frac{3}{4}$ hr

$$\frac{\text{Distance going}}{\text{to work}} = \frac{\text{Distance returning}}{\text{from work}}$$

$$\frac{1}{2}(x + 10) = \frac{3}{4}(x)$$

$$\frac{1}{2}x + 5 = \frac{3}{4}x$$

$$5 = \frac{1}{4}x$$

$$x = 20 \text{ mph}$$

$$\text{Distance} = rt = 20\left(\frac{3}{4}\right) = 15 \text{ mi}$$

8. 83   **9.** Let $\quad x$ = Amount invested at 12%
$27,000 - x$ = Amount invested at 8%
$.12x + .08(27,000 - x) = 2780$
$12x + 8(27,000 - x) = 278,000$
$12x + 216,000 - 8x = 278,000$
$\qquad\qquad 4x = 62,000$
$\qquad\qquad\quad x = \$15,500$ at 12%
$\quad 27,000 - x = \$11,500$ at 8%

Chapter 3 Diagnostic Test (page 139)

Following each problem number is the textbook section number (in parentheses) where that kind of problem is discussed. The checks will not be shown.

1. (3.1) Let x = Unknown number

When 23 is added to   four times an   the sum is   31 .
$\qquad\qquad\qquad\qquad$ unknown number
$\quad 23 \qquad + \qquad 4 \cdot x \qquad\qquad = \qquad 31$
$\qquad\qquad\qquad\qquad 23 + 4x = 31$
$\qquad\qquad\qquad\qquad\qquad 4x = 8$
$\qquad\qquad\qquad\qquad\qquad\quad x = 2$

2. (3.1) Let x = First integer   Their sum is 55 .
$x + 1$ = Second integer $x + (x + 1) = 55$
$\qquad\qquad\qquad\qquad x + x + 1 = 55$
$\qquad\qquad\qquad\qquad\qquad 2x = 54$
$\qquad\qquad\qquad\qquad\qquad\quad x = 27$ First integer
$\qquad\quad x + 1 = 27 + 1 = 28$ Second integer

3. (3.2) Let $5x$ = Length
$\qquad\qquad 4x$ = Width
Perimeter is 90
$2(5x) + 2(4x) = 90$
$\qquad 10x + 8x = 90$
$\qquad\qquad 18x = 90$
$\qquad\qquad\quad x = 5$
$\qquad\qquad 5x = 25$ Length
$\qquad\qquad 4x = 20$ Width

4. (3.4) Let x = Number of dimes $\Rightarrow$ Value of dimes = $10x$
$14 - x$ = Number of quarters $\Rightarrow$ Value of
$\qquad\qquad\qquad\qquad\qquad\qquad$ quarters = $25(14 - x)$
Value of dimes + Value of quarters = Total value \$2.15
$\quad 10x \qquad + \qquad 25(14 - x) \qquad = \qquad 215$
$\qquad\qquad 10x + 350 - 25x = 215$
$\qquad\qquad\qquad\qquad -15x = -135$
$\qquad\qquad\qquad\qquad\quad x = 9$ dimes
$\qquad\qquad\qquad 14 - x = 5$ quarters

5. (3.4) Let x = Number of pounds of cashews
$60 - x$ = Number of pounds of peanuts

	Cashews	Peanuts	Mixture
Unit cost	7.40	2.80	4.18
Amount	x	$60 - x$	60
Total cost	$7.40x$	$2.80(60 - x)$	$4.18(60)$

$7.40x + 2.80(60 - x) = 4.18(60)$
$\quad 740x + 280(60 - x) = 418(60)$
$740x + 16,800 - 280x = 25,080$
$\qquad\qquad\qquad 460x = 8280$
$\qquad\qquad\qquad\quad x = 18$ pounds of cashews
$\qquad\qquad 60 - x = 42$ pounds of peanuts

6. (3.5) Let $x =$ Number of cc of water
Then $600 + x =$ Number of cc in mixture

| Amount of potassium | | Amount of potassium |
| chloride in 20% solution | $=$ | chloride in 15% solution |

$$0.20(600) = 0.15(600 + x)$$

$$20(600) = 15(600 + x)$$
$$12{,}000 = 9000 + 15x$$
$$3000 = 15x$$
$$x = 200 \text{ cc of water}$$

7. (3.6) Let $x =$ Tens digit
$2x =$ Units digit

| Value of original number | $+ \; 27 \; =$ | Value of number with digits reversed |
| $10(x) + 1(2x)$ | $+ \; 27 \; =$ | $10(2x) + 1(x)$ |

$$12x + 27 = 21x$$
$$27 = 9x$$
$$x = 3 \quad \text{Tens digit}$$
$$2x = 6 \quad \text{Units digit}$$

Therefore, the original number is 36

8. (3.4) Let $x =$ Amount invested at 10%
$23{,}000 - x =$ Amount invested at 8%
$$0.10x + 0.08(23{,}000 - x) = 2170$$
$$10x + 8(23{,}000 - x) = 217{,}000$$
$$10x + 184{,}000 - 8x = 217{,}000$$
$$2x = 33{,}000$$
$$x = \$16{,}500 \text{ invested at } 10\%$$
$$23{,}000 - x = \$6500 \text{ invested at } 8\%$$

9. (3.3) Let $t =$ Time to hike from lake
$t + 2 =$ Time to hike to lake

	d	$= r \cdot$	t
To lake	$3(t + 2)$	3	$t + 2$
From lake	$5t$	5	t

Distance to lake $=$ Distance from lake
$$5t = 3(t + 2)$$
$$5t = 3t + 6$$
$$2t = 6$$

a. $\begin{cases} t = 3 \text{ hr to hike from lake} \\ t + 2 = 5 \text{ hr to hike to lake} \end{cases}$

b. Distance $=$ (Rate)(Time) $= 3 \cdot 5 = 15$ miles

Cumulative Review Exercises: Chapters 1–3 (page 140)

1a. 10   **b.** All   **c.** $-2, \dfrac{1}{2}, 4.5, 10, 0,$ and $0.234234234\ldots$

d. $-2, 10, 0$ **e.** $1.4142136\ldots$

2. $\dfrac{a^6}{b^2}$ **3.** $S = \dfrac{1}{2} gt^2$ **4.** $2x^2y^2 - 10x^2y + 7xy$

$$= \dfrac{1}{2}(32)(2)^2$$

$$= \dfrac{1}{2}(32)(4) = 64$$

5. $6 - \{4 - [3x - 2(5 - 3x)]\}$ **6.** $x = -1$
$= 6 - \{4 - [3x - 10 + 6x]\}$
$= 6 - \{4 - [9x - 10]\}$
$= 6 - \{4 - 9x + 10\}$
$= 6 - \{14 - 9x\}$
$= 6 - 14 + 9x = 9x - 8$

7. $12 - 3(4x - 5) \geq 9(2 - x) - 6$ **8.** $-2 < x < 2$
$12 - 12x + 15 \geq 18 - 9x - 6$
$27 - 12x \geq 12 - 9x$
$-3x \geq -15$
$$\dfrac{-3x}{-3} \leq \dfrac{-15}{-3}$$
$$x \leq 5$$

9. $\left| \dfrac{2x - 6}{4} \right| = 1$ **10.** $-2 < x < 3$

$\dfrac{2x - 6}{4} = 1$	$\dfrac{2x - 6}{4} = -1$
$2x - 6 = 4$	$2x - 6 = -4$
$2x = 10$	$2x = 2$
$x = 5$	$x = 1$

11. Let $7x =$ Length of rectangle
$4x =$ Width of rectangle
$$2(7x) + 2(4x) = 66$$
$$14x + 8x = 66$$
$$22x = 66$$
$$x = 3$$
$$7x = 21 \quad \text{Length}$$
$$4x = 12 \quad \text{Width}$$
(The check will not be shown.)

12. \$7500 at 7.4%; \$4500 at 6.8%

Exercises 4.1 (page 144)

1. 2nd degree   **2.** 2nd degree
3. Not a polynomial because the exponents are not positive integers
4. Not a polynomial   **5.** 0 degree   **6.** 0 degree
7. Not a polynomial because the variable is in the denominator
8. Not a polynomial   **9.** 1st degree   **10.** 1st degree
11. Not a polynomial because the variable is under a radical sign
12. Not a polynomial
13. Not a polynomial because the variable is in the denominator
14. Not a polynomial   **15.** 6th degree   **16.** 6th degree
17. $8x^5 + 7x^3 - 4x - 5;$ 8   **18.** $-3y^5 - 2y^3 + 4y^2 + 10;$ -3
19. $-y^5 + y^3 + 3x^2y + 8x^3;$ -1 **20.** $6y^3 - 4y^2 + y + 7x^2;$ 6

Exercises 4.2 (page 146)

1. $-3x^4 - 2x^3 + 5 + 2x^4 + x^3 - 7x - 12 = -x^4 - x^3 - 7x - 7$
2. $-2y^3 + 3y^2 - 4y + 4$
3. $7 - 8v^3 + 9v^2 + 4v - 9v^3 - 6 + 8v^2 - 4v = -17v^3 + 17v^2 + 1$
4. $13x^3 - 4x^2 + 8x - 7$ **5.** $6x^3 + 2x^2 - 2$
6. $-2y^4 + 8y + 4$ **7.** $\underline{4x^3} + 6 + x - 6 - \underline{3x^5} + \underline{\underline{4x^2}}$
$\qquad\qquad\qquad = -3x^5 + 4x^3 + 4x^2 + x$
8. $4x^4 - 2x^3 - 3x$
9. $2y^4 + 4y^3 + 8 - 3y^4 - 2y^3 + 5y = -y^4 + 2y^3 + 5y + 8$
10. $5y^3 + 8y^2 - 5y - 4$ **11.** $-5x^4 - 7x^3 + x^2 + 4x - 2$
12. $-2x^4 + x^3 + 5x^2 - 2x + 6$ **13.** $7x^3 + 4x^2 + 7x - 11$
14. $7x^3 - 2x^2 - x - 12$
15. $\underline{6m^2n^2} - \underline{\underline{8mn}} + \underline{\underline{\underline{9}}} - \underline{10m^2n^2} + \underline{\underline{18mn}} - \underline{\underline{\underline{11}}} + \underline{3m^2n^2} - \underline{\underline{2mn}} + \underline{\underline{\underline{7}}}$
$\qquad = -m^2n^2 + 8mn + 5$
16. $27u^2v + 4uv^2 + 17$

17. $[5 + xy^2 + x^3y - 6 - 3xy^2 + 4x^3y]$
$$\qquad\qquad - [x^3y + 3xy^2 - 4 + 2x^3y - xy^2 + 5]$$
$= [-1 - 2xy^2 + 5x^3y] - [3x^3y + 2xy^2 + 1]$
$= -1 - 2xy^2 + 5x^3y - 3x^3y - 2xy^2 - 1$
$= 2x^3y - 4xy^2 - 2$

18. $6m^2n + 6$

19. $8.586x^2 - 9.030x + 6.976 - 1.946x^2 + 41.45x + 7.468 - 3.914x^2$
$= 2.726x^2 + 32.42x + 14.444$

20. $-40.06x^2 - 117.32x + 88.55$

Exercises 4.3A (page 150)

1. $(x)(x) + 4x + 5x + (5)(4) = x^2 + 9x + 20$ **2.** $y^2 + 10y + 21$

3. $(y)(y) - 9y + 8y - 72 = y^2 - y - 72$ **4.** $z^2 + 7z - 30$

5. $(3x)(2x) - 15x + 8x + (4)(-5) = 6x^2 - 7x - 20$

6. $8y^2 + 14y - 15$

7. $(4x)(4x) - 20xy + 20xy + (5y)(-5y) = 16x^2 - 25y^2$

8. $s^2 - 4t^2$

9. $(2x)(5x) - 2xy - 15xy + (-3y)(-y) = 10x^2 - 17xy + 3y^2$

10. $18u^2 - 27uv + 4v^2$

11. $(7z)(8w) + 21z - 16w + (-2)(3) = 56wz + 21z - 16w - 6$

12. $36xz + 45z - 4x - 5$

13. $(8x)(8x) + 72xy - 72xy + (-9y)(9y) = 64x^2 - 81y^2$

14. $49w^2 - 4x^2$

15. $(2s^2)(s) + 2s^2 + 5s + (5)(1) = 2s^3 + 2s^2 + 5s + 5$

16. $3u^3 + 3u^2 + 2u + 2$

17. $(2x)(2x) - 2xy - 2xy + (-y)(-y) = 4x^2 - 4xy + y^2$

18. $25z^2 - 10wz + w^2$

19. $(2x)(3y) - 8x + 9y + 3(-4) = 6xy - 8x + 9y - 12$

20. $12uv - 20u - 6v + 10$

21. $(7x^2)(7x^2) - 21x^2 - 21x^2 + (-3)(-3) = 49x^4 - 42x^2 + 9$

22. $16x^4 - 40x^2 + 25$

23. $(3x)(2x^2) + 15x - 8x^2 + (-4)(5) = 6x^3 - 8x^2 + 15x - 20$

24. $15y^3 - 6y^2 + 5y - 2$

25. $3x[(2x)x - 2x - 4x + 4] = 3x[2x^2 - 6x + 4]$
$$\qquad\qquad\qquad\qquad\qquad\qquad = 6x^3 - 18x^2 + 12x$$

26. $14x^3 + 7x^2 - 105x$

Exercises 4.3B (page 151)

1.
$$
\begin{array}{r}
4h^2 - 5h + 7 \\
2h - 3 \\
\hline
-12h^2 + 15h - 21 \\
8h^3 - 10h^2 + 14h \\
\hline
8h^3 - 22h^2 + 29h - 21
\end{array}
$$

2. $10k^3 + 23k^2 - 57k + 18$

3.
$$
\begin{array}{r}
a^4 + 3a^2 - 2a + 4 \\
a + 3 \\
\hline
3a^4 \qquad + 9a^2 - 6a + 12 \\
a^5 \qquad + 3a^3 - 2a^2 + 4a \\
\hline
a^5 + 3a^4 + 3a^3 + 7a^2 - 2a + 12
\end{array}
$$

4. $b^5 - 7b^4 + 10b^3 + 3b^2 - 20b + 25$

5.
$$
\begin{array}{r}
- 3z^3 + z^2 - 5z + 4 \\
- z + 4 \\
\hline
-12z^3 + 4z^2 - 20z + 16 \\
3z^4 - z^3 + 5z^2 - 4z \\
\hline
3z^4 - 13z^3 + 9z^2 - 24z + 16
\end{array}
$$

6. $v^4 - 4v^3 + 5v + 6$

7.
$$
\begin{array}{r}
3u^2 - u + 5 \\
2u^2 + 4u - 1 \\
\hline
- 3u^2 + u - 5 \\
12u^3 - 4u^2 + 20u \\
6u^4 - 2u^3 + 10u^2 \\
\hline
6u^4 + 10u^3 + 3u^2 + 21u - 5
\end{array}
$$

8. $10w^4 - w^3 - 40w^2 + 20w + 7$

9. $(-2xy)(-3x^2y) + (-2xy)(xy^2) + (-2xy)(-4y^3)$
$= 6x^3y^2 - 2x^2y^3 + 8xy^4$

10. $12x^2y^3 + 3x^3y^2 - 9x^4y$

11. $-5a^2b(a^3) + (-5a^2b)(-3a^2b) + (-5a^2b)(3ab^2)$
$$\qquad + (-5a^2b)(-b^3) = -5a^5b + 15a^4b^2 - 15a^3b^3 + 5a^2b^4$$

12. $-4m^4p^2 + 12m^3p^3 - 12m^2p^4 + 4mp^5$

13.
$$
\begin{array}{r}
x^2 + 2x + 3 \\
x^2 + 2x + 3 \\
\hline
3x^2 + 6x + 9 \\
2x^3 + 4x^2 + 6x \\
x^4 + 2x^3 + 3x^2 \\
\hline
x^4 + 4x^3 + 10x^2 + 12x + 9
\end{array}
$$

14. $z^4 - 6z^3 + z^2 + 24z + 16$

15.
$$
\begin{array}{r|r}
x^2 - xy + y^2 & x^2 + xy + y^2 \\
x + y & x - y \\
\hline
x^2y - xy^2 + y^3 & - x^2y - xy^2 - y^3 \\
x^3 - x^2y + xy^2 & x^3 + x^2y + xy^2 \\
\hline
x^3 \qquad + y^3 & x^3 \qquad - y^3
\end{array}
$$

This shows that:
$[(x + y)(x^2 - xy + y^2)][(x - y)(x^2 + xy + y^2)]$
$= [x^3 + y^3][x^3 - y^3]$
Then
$$
\begin{array}{r}
x^3 + y^3 \\
x^3 - y^3 \\
\hline
- x^3y^3 - y^6 \\
x^6 + x^3y^3 \\
\hline
x^6 \qquad - y^6
\end{array}
$$

16. $a^6 - 1$

Exercises 4.4A (page 152)

1. $(2u)^2 - (5v)^2 = 4u^2 - 25v^2$ **2.** $9m^2 - 49n^2$

3. $(2x^2)^2 - (9)^2 = 4x^4 - 81$ **4.** $100y^4 - 9$

5. $(x^5)^2 - (y^6)^2 = x^{10} - y^{12}$ **6.** $a^{14} - b^8$

7. $(7mn)^2 - (2rs)^2 = 49m^2n^2 - 4r^2s^2$ **8.** $64h^2k^2 - 25e^2f^2$

9. $(12x^4y^3)^2 - (u^7v)^2 = 144x^8y^6 - u^{14}v^2$ **10.** $121a^{10}b^4 - 81c^6d^{12}$

11. $(a + b)^2 - (2)^2 = (a + b)(a + b) - 4 = a^2 + 2ab + b^2 - 4$

12. $x^2 + 2xy + y^2 - 25$

13. $([x^2 + y] + 5)([x^2 + y] - 5)$
$= [x^2 + y]^2 - 5^2 = [x^2 + y][x^2 + y] - 25$
$= x^4 + 2x^2y + y^2 - 25$

14. $u^4 - 2u^2v + v^2 - 49$ **15.** $7x(x^2 - 1) = 7x^3 - 7x$

16. $12y^3 - 75y$

Exercises 4.4B (page 154)

1. $(2x)^2 + 2(2x)(3) + 3^2 = 4x^2 + 12x + 9$

2. $36x^2 + 60x + 25$

3. $(5x)^2 - 2(5x)(3) + 3^2 = 25x^2 - 30x + 9$

4. $81x^2 - 108x + 36$

5. $(7x)^2 - 2(7x)(10y) + (10y)^2 = 49x^2 - 140xy + 100y^2$

6. $16u^2 - 72uv + 81v^2$

7. $(u + v)^2 + 2(u + v)(7) + (7)^2 = u^2 + 2uv + v^2 + 14u + 14v + 49$

8. $s^2 + 2st + t^2 + 8s + 8t + 16$

9. $[2x - y]^2 - 2[2x - y][3] + 3^2$
$= (2x)^2 - 2(2x)(y) + y^2 - 12x + 6y + 9$
$= 4x^2 - 4xy + y^2 - 12x + 6y + 9$

10. $9z^2 - 6zw + w^2 - 42z + 14w + 49$

11. $x^2 + 2x(u + v) + (u + v)^2 = x^2 + 2xu + 2xv + u^2 + 2uv + v^2$

12. $s^2 + 2sy + 4s + y^2 + 4y + 4$

13. $y^2 - 2y[x - 2] + [x - 2]^2 = y^2 - 2xy + 4y + x^2 - 4x + 4$

14. $x^2 - 2xz + 10x + z^2 - 10z + 25$

15. $5[x^2 - 2(x)(3) + 3^2] = 5(x^2 - 6x + 9) = 5x^2 - 30x + 45$

16. $7x^2 + 14x + 7$

Exercises 4.4C (page 160)

1. $x^5 + 5x^4y + \dfrac{5 \cdot 4}{1 \cdot 2}x^3y^2 + \dfrac{5 \cdot 4 \cdot 3}{1 \cdot 2 \cdot 3}x^2y^3 + 5xy^4 + y^5$
$= x^5 + 5x^4y + 10x^3y^2 + 10x^2y^3 + 5xy^4 + y^5$

2. $r^4 + 4r^3s + 6r^2s^2 + 4rs^3 + s^4$

3. $x^5 - 5x^4(2) + \dfrac{5 \cdot 4}{1 \cdot 2}x^3(2)^2 - \dfrac{5 \cdot 4 \cdot 3}{1 \cdot 2 \cdot 3}x^2(2)^3 + 5x(2)^4 - (2)^5$
$= x^5 - 10x^4 + 40x^3 - 80x^2 + 80x - 32$

4. $y^4 - 12y^3 + 54y^2 - 108y + 81$

5. $(3r + s)^6 = (3r)^6 + 6(3r)^5s + \dfrac{6 \cdot 5}{1 \cdot 2}(3r)^4s^2 + \dfrac{6 \cdot 5 \cdot 4}{1 \cdot 2 \cdot 3}(3r)^3s^3$
$\qquad + 15(3r)^2s^4 + 6(3r)s^5 + s^6$
$= 729r^6 + 1458r^5s + 1215r^4s^2 + 540r^3s^3$
$\qquad + 135r^2s^4 + 18rs^5 + s^6$

6. $64x^6 + 192x^5y + 240x^4y^2 + 160x^3y^3 + 60x^2y^4 + 12xy^5 + y^6$

7. $(x + y^2)^4 = x^4 + 4x^3(y^2) + 6x^2(y^2)^2 + 4x(y^2)^3 + (y^2)^4$
$= x^4 + 4x^3y^2 + 6x^2y^4 + 4xy^6 + y^8$

8. $u^5 + 5u^4v^2 + 10u^3v^4 + 10u^2v^6 + 5uv^8 + v^{10}$

9. $(2x)^5 + 5(2x)^4\left(-\dfrac{1}{2}\right) + \dfrac{5 \cdot 4}{1 \cdot 2}(2x)^3\left(-\dfrac{1}{2}\right)^2 + 10(2x)^2\left(-\dfrac{1}{2}\right)^3$
$\qquad + 5(2x)\left(-\dfrac{1}{2}\right)^4 + \left(-\dfrac{1}{2}\right)^5$
$= 32x^5 - 40x^4 + 20x^3 - 5x^2 + \dfrac{5}{8}x - \dfrac{1}{32}$

10. $81x^4 - 36x^3 + 6x^2 - \dfrac{4}{9}x + \dfrac{1}{81}$

11. $\left(\dfrac{x}{3}\right)^4 + 4\left(\dfrac{x}{3}\right)^3\left(\dfrac{3}{2}\right) + \dfrac{4 \cdot 3}{1 \cdot 2}\left(\dfrac{x}{3}\right)^2\left(\dfrac{3}{2}\right)^2 + 4\left(\dfrac{x}{3}\right)\left(\dfrac{3}{2}\right)^3 + \left(\dfrac{3}{2}\right)^4$
$= \dfrac{x^4}{81} + \dfrac{2x^3}{9} + \dfrac{3x^2}{2} + \dfrac{9x}{2} + \dfrac{81}{16}$

12. $\dfrac{x^4}{625} + \dfrac{2x^3}{25} + \dfrac{3x^2}{2} + \dfrac{25x}{2} + \dfrac{625}{16}$

13. $(4x^2 - 3y^2)^5 = (4x^2)^5 + 5(4x^2)^4(-3y^2) + 10(4x^2)^3(-3y^2)^2$
$\qquad + 10(4x^2)^2(-3y^2)^3 + 5(4x^2)(-3y^2)^4 + (-3y^2)^5$
$= 1024x^{10} - 3840x^8y^2 + 5760x^6y^4$
$\qquad - 4320x^4y^6 + 1620x^2y^8 - 243y^{10}$

14. $243x^{10} - 810x^8y^3 + 1080x^6y^6 - 720x^4y^9 + 240x^2y^{12} - 32y^{15}$

15. $(x + x^{-1})^4 = (x)^4 + 4(x)^3(x^{-1}) + 6(x)^2(x^{-1})^2$
$\qquad + 4(x)(x^{-1})^3 + (x^{-1})^4$
$= x^4 + 4x^2 + 6 + 4x^{-2} + x^{-4}$
$= x^4 + 4x^2 + 6 + \dfrac{4}{x^2} + \dfrac{1}{x^4}$

16. $\dfrac{1}{x^4} - \dfrac{4}{x^2} + 6 - 4x^2 + x^4$

17. $(x)^{10} + 10(x)^9(2y^2) + \dfrac{10 \cdot 9}{1 \cdot 2}(x)^8(2y^2)^2 + \dfrac{10 \cdot 9 \cdot 8}{1 \cdot 2 \cdot 3}(x)^7(2y^2)^3 + \cdots$
$= x^{10} + 20x^9y^2 + 180x^8y^4 + 960x^7y^6 + \cdots$

18. $x^8 + 24x^7y^2 + 252x^6y^4 + 1512x^5y^6 + \cdots$

19. $(x - 3y^2)^{10} = (x)^{10} + 10(x)^9(-3y^2) + \dfrac{10 \cdot 9}{1 \cdot 2}(x)^8(-3y^2)^2$
$\qquad + \dfrac{10 \cdot 9 \cdot 8}{1 \cdot 2 \cdot 3}(x)^7(-3y^2)^3 + \cdots$
$= x^{10} - 30x^9y^2 + 405x^8y^4 - 3240x^7y^6 + \cdots$

20. $x^{11} - 22x^{10}y^3 + 220x^9y^6 - 1320x^8y^9 + \cdots$

Exercises 4.5A (page 161)

1. $\dfrac{18x^5}{6x^2} + \dfrac{-24x^4}{6x^2} + \dfrac{-12x^3}{6x^2} = 3x^3 - 4x^2 - 2x$

2. $-4y^2 + 9y - 5$ 　　**3.** $\dfrac{55a^4b^3}{-11ab} + \dfrac{-33ab^2}{-11ab} = -5a^3b^2 + 3b$

4. $-2mn^3 + 4m^2$ 　　**5.** $\dfrac{-15x^2y^2z^2}{-5xyz} + \dfrac{-30xyz}{-5xyz} = 3xyz + 6$

6. $3abc + 2$

7. $\dfrac{13x^3y^2 - 26x^5y^3 + 39x^4y^6}{13x^2y^2} = \dfrac{13x^3y^2}{13x^2y^2} + \dfrac{-26x^5y^3}{13x^2y^2} + \dfrac{39x^4y^6}{13x^2y^2}$
$= x - 2x^3y + 3x^2y^4$
$= 3x^2y^4 - 2x^3y + x$

8. $3n - 5m - 2mn^3$

Exercises 4.5B (page 165)

Note: The checks for these exercises will not be shown.

1.
$$
\begin{array}{r}
x + 3 \\
x + 7\overline{)\,x^2 + 10x - 5} \\
\underline{x^2 + 7x} \\
3x - 5 \\
\underline{3x + 21} \\
-26
\end{array}
$$
Answer: $x + 3 - \dfrac{26}{x + 7}$

2. $x + 5 - \dfrac{25}{x + 4}$

3.
$$
\begin{array}{r}
2z^2 - z - 3 \\
3z - 5\overline{)\,6z^3 - 13z^2 - 4z + 15} \\
\underline{6z^3 - 10z^2} \\
-3z^2 - 4z \\
\underline{-3z^2 + 5z} \\
-9z + 15 \\
\underline{-9z + 15} \\
0
\end{array}
$$
Answer: $2z^2 - z - 3$

4. $3y^2 - y - 4$

5.
$$
\begin{array}{r}
v^3 - 4v^2 - 4v - 5 \\
v + 1\overline{)\,v^4 - 3v^3 - 8v^2 - 9v - 5} \\
\underline{v^4 + v^3} \\
-4v^3 - 8v^2 \\
\underline{-4v^3 - 4v^2} \\
-4v^2 - 9v \\
\underline{-4v^2 - 4v} \\
-5v - 5 \\
\underline{-5v - 5} \\
0
\end{array}
$$
Answer: $v^3 - 4v^2 - 4v - 5$

6. $w^3 - 4w^2 - 4w - 5$

7.
$$-x+2\overline{)-4x^3 \qquad +8x+10}$$
quotient: $4x^2 + 8x + 8$

$\underline{-4x^3 + 8x^2}$

$-8x^2 + 8x$

$\underline{-8x^2 + 16x}$

$-8x + 10$

$\underline{-8x + 16}$

-6

Answer: $4x^2 + 8x + 8 - \dfrac{6}{2-x}$

8. $x^2 + 3x - 3 + \dfrac{-6}{3-x}$

9.
$$3x - 2y\overline{)12x^3 - 11x^2y + 17xy^2 - 10y^3}$$
quotient: $4x^2 - xy + 5y^2$

$\underline{12x^3 - 8x^2y}$

$-3x^2y + 17xy^2$

$\underline{-3x^2y + 2xy^2}$

$15xy^2 - 10y^3$

$\underline{15xy^2 - 10y^3}$

0

Answer: $4x^2 - xy + 5y^2$

10. $5x^2 - xy - 4y^2$

11.
$$x - 2\overline{)x^4 + 0x^3 + 0x^2 - 7x + 6}$$
quotient: $x^3 + 2x^2 + 4x + 1$

$\underline{x^4 - 2x^3}$

$2x^3 + 0x^2$

$\underline{2x^3 - 4x^2}$

$4x^2 - 7x$

$\underline{4x^2 - 8x}$

$x + 6$

$\underline{x - 2}$

8

Answer: $x^3 + 2x^2 + 4x + 1 + \dfrac{8}{x-2}$

12. $x^3 + x^2 + x + 7 + \dfrac{10}{x-1}$

13.
$$4x^2 + x + 1\overline{)4x^4 - 3x^3 + 8x^2 + x + 2}$$
quotient: $x^2 - x + 2$

$\underline{4x^4 + x^3 + x^2}$

$-4x^3 + 7x^2 + x$

$\underline{-4x^3 - x^2 - x}$

$8x^2 + 2x + 2$

$\underline{8x^2 + 2x + 2}$

0

Answer: $x^2 - x + 2$

14. $x^2 - x + 5$

15.
$$x^2 + 2\overline{)2x^4 + 0x^3 + 7x^2 + 0x + 5}$$
quotient: $2x^2 + 0x + 3$ R -1

$\underline{2x^4 \qquad + 4x^2}$

$3x^2 \qquad + 5$

$\underline{3x^2 \qquad + 6}$

-1

Answer: $2x^2 + 3 - \dfrac{1}{x^2+2}$

16. $3x^2 + 2 + \dfrac{-5}{x^2+3}$

17.
$$2x^3 + 3\overline{)2x^5 + 0x^4 - 10x^3 + 3x^2 + 0x - 15}$$
quotient: $x^2 \qquad - 5$

$\underline{2x^5 \qquad\qquad + 3x^2}$

$-10x^3 \qquad\qquad - 15$

$\underline{-10x^3 \qquad\qquad - 15}$

0

Answer: $x^2 - 5$

18. $x^2 - 2$

19.
$$3x^2 - x + 1\overline{)3x^4 + 14x^3 + 2x^2 + 3x + 2}$$
quotient: $x^2 + 5x + 2$

$\underline{3x^4 - \quad x^3 + \quad x^2}$

$15x^3 + \quad x^2 + 3x$

$\underline{15x^3 - 5x^2 + 5x}$

$6x^2 - 2x + 2$

$\underline{6x^2 - 2x + 2}$

0

Answer: $x^2 + 5x + 2$

20. $x^2 + 7x - 2$

Exercises 4.6 (page 169)

Note: The checks for these exercises will not be shown.

1.

	1	2	-18
		3	15
3	1	5	-3

Answer: $x + 5 - \dfrac{3}{x-3}$

2. $x + 6 + \dfrac{2}{x-2}$

3.

	1	3	-5	6
		-4	4	4
-4	1	-1	-1	10

Answer: $x^2 - x - 1 + \dfrac{10}{x+4}$

4. $x^2 + x - 1 + \dfrac{-2}{x+5}$

5.

	1	6	0	-1	-4
		-6	0	0	6
-6	1	0	0	-1	2

Answer: $x^3 + 0x^2 + 0x - 1 + \dfrac{2}{x+6}$

6. $2x^3 - x^2 + 3x + 1 + \dfrac{-5}{x+3}$

7.

	1	0	0	0	-16
		2	4	8	16
2	1	2	4	8	0

Answer: $x^3 + 2x^2 + 4x + 8$

8. $x^6 + x^5 + x^4 + x^3 + x^2 + x + 1$

9.

	1	-3	0	0	-2	3	5
		3	0	0	0	-6	-9
3	1	0	0	0	-2	-3	-4

Answer: $x^5 + 0x^4 + 0x^3 + 0x^2 - 2x - 3 + \dfrac{-4}{x-3}$

10. $x^5 + 2x^4 + x^3 + 2x^2 + 4x + 1$

11.

	3	-1	9	0	-1
		1	0	3	1
$\frac{1}{3}$	3	0	9	3	0

Answer: $3x^3 + 0x^2 + 9x + 3$

12. $3x^3 - 6x^2 + 3x - 3$

13.

	1	1	-45	-45	324	324
		-3	6	117	-216	-324
-3	1	-2	-39	72	108	0

Answer: $x^4 - 2x^3 - 39x^2 + 72x + 108$

14. $x^4 - 5x^3 - 15x^2 + 45x + 54$

15.

$$\begin{array}{r|rrrrr} & 4 & 0 & -45 & 3 & 100 \\ & & 8 & 16 & -58 & -110 \\ \hline 2 & 4 & 8 & -29 & -55 & -10 \end{array}$$

Answer: $4x^3 + 8x^2 - 29x - 55 + \dfrac{-10}{x-2}$

16. $9x^3 + 9x^2 - 4x - 2 + \dfrac{4}{x-1}$

17.

$$\begin{array}{r|rrrr} & 2.6 & 0 & 1.8 & -6.4 \\ & & 3.9 & 5.85 & 11.475 \\ \hline 1.5 & 2.6 & 3.9 & 7.65 & 5.075 \end{array}$$

Answer: $2.6x^2 + 3.9x + 7.65 + \dfrac{5.075}{x-1.5}$

18. $3.8x^2 + 8.1x + 20.25 + \dfrac{26.725}{x-2.5}$

19.

$$\begin{array}{r|rrrr} & 2.7 & 0 & -1.6 & 3.289 \\ & & 3.24 & 3.888 & 2.7456 \\ \hline 1.2 & 2.7 & 3.24 & 2.288 & 6.0346 \end{array}$$

Answer: $2.7x^2 + 3.24x + 2.288 + \dfrac{6.0346}{x-1.2}$

20. $3x^2 + 6x + 9.6 + \dfrac{13.86}{x-1.6}$

Review Exercises 4.7 (page 171)

1. 3rd degree   **2.** Not a polynomial

3. Not a polynomial because the variable is under a radical sign

4. Not a polynomial

5. $\underset{\sim}{13x} - \underline{6x^3} + \underline{\underline{14}} - \underline{15x^2} - \underline{\underline{17}} - \underline{23x^2} + \underline{4x^3} + \underset{\sim}{\underline{11x}}$
$= -2x^3 - 38x^2 + 24x - 3$

6. $9x^2y + xy^2 + 2y^2 - 12$ **7.** $-2x^3 - 2x^2 - 5x + 7$

8. $x^4 - x^3 + x^2 - x + 1$

9. $(2k^3 - 7k + 11) + (4k^3 + k^2 - 9k) - (3k^2 - 5k - 6)$
$= 2k^3 - \underline{7k} + \underline{\underline{11}} + 4k^3 + k^2 - \underset{\sim}{9k} - 3k^2 + \underline{5k} + \underline{\underline{6}}$
$= 6k^3 - 2k^2 - 11k + 17$

10. $-15a^3b^3 - 9a^2b^2 + 6ab^2c$

11. $(5x)(7x) - 10xy - 28xy + (-4y)(-2y) = 35x^2 - 38xy + 8y^2$

12. $x^8 + 12x^6 + 54x^4 + 108x^2 + 81$

13.

$$\begin{array}{r} 4x^2 - 5x + 1 \\ 2x^2 + x - 3 \\ \hline -12x^2 + 15x - 3 \\ 4x^3 - 5x^2 + x \\ 8x^4 - 10x^3 + 2x^2 \\ \hline 8x^4 - 6x^3 - 15x^2 + 16x - 3 \end{array}$$

14. $49x^2 - 25$

15. $(2x^2)^5 + 5(2x^2)^4\left(\dfrac{1}{2}\right)^1 + \dfrac{5\cdot4}{1\cdot2}(2x^2)^3\left(\dfrac{1}{2}\right)^2$
$+ 10(2x^2)^2\left(\dfrac{1}{2}\right)^3 + 5(2x^2)^1\left(\dfrac{1}{2}\right)^4 + \left(\dfrac{1}{2}\right)^5$
$= 32x^{10} + 40x^8 + 20x^6 + 5x^4 + \dfrac{5x^2}{8} + \dfrac{1}{32}$

16. $x^2 + 2xy + y^2 + 6x + 6y + 9$

17. $a^2 - 2(a)(5) + 5^2 = a^2 - 10a + 25$ **18.** $z^3 + 27$

19.

$$\begin{array}{r} a + b + 4 \\ a + b + 4 \\ \hline 4a + 4b + 16 \\ ab + 4b + b^2 \\ a^2 + ab + 4a \\ \hline a^2 + 2ab + 8a + 8b + 16 + b^2 \end{array}$$

20. $\dfrac{1}{z^8} + \dfrac{4}{z^4} + 6 + 4z^4 + z^8$

21. $4x([x^2]^2 - [y^2]^2) = 4x(x^4 - y^4) = 4x^5 - 4xy^4$

22. $\dfrac{1}{81} + \dfrac{4x^2}{9} + 6x^4 + 36x^6 + 81x^8$

23. $\dfrac{-15a^2b^3}{-5ab} + \dfrac{20a^4b^2}{-5ab} + \dfrac{-10ab}{-5ab} = 3ab^2 - 4a^3b + 2$ **24.** $3x + \dfrac{10}{2x-3}$

25.

$$\begin{array}{r} 2a + 5b \\ 5a - b\overline{)10a^2 + 23ab - 5b^2} \\ 10a^2 - 2ab \\ \hline 25ab - 5b^2 \\ 25ab - 5b^2 \\ \hline 0 \end{array}$$

Answer: $2a + 5b$

26. $x^2 - 1 + \dfrac{-10}{3x^2 - 2x + 5}$

27.

$$\begin{array}{r} x^3 - 3x^2 + 9x - 27 \\ x + 3\overline{)x^4 + 0x^3 + 0x^2 + 0x - 81} \\ x^4 + 3x^3 \\ \hline -3x^3 + 0x^2 \\ -3x^3 - 9x^2 \\ \hline 9x^2 + 0x \\ 9x^2 + 27x \\ \hline -27x - 81 \\ -27x - 81 \\ \hline 0 \end{array}$$

Answer: $x^3 - 3x^2 + 9x - 27$

28. $3x^4 + x^3 - 2x^2 + \dfrac{4}{x+2}$

29.

$$\begin{array}{r|rrrrrr} & 5 & -2 & 10 & -4 & 0 & 2 \\ & & 2 & 0 & 4 & 0 & 0 \\ \hline \dfrac{2}{5} & 5 & 0 & 10 & 0 & 0 & 2 \end{array}$$

Answer: $5x^4 + 10x^2 + \dfrac{2}{x - \dfrac{2}{5}}$

30. $2x^4 + 1 + \dfrac{2}{x+3}$

Chapter 4 Diagnostic Test (page 175)

Following each problem number is the textbook section number (in parentheses) where that kind of problem is discussed.

1. (4.1)   **a.** Degree of $-\dfrac{1}{3}x^1y^1$ is $1 + 1 = 2$

   b. Degree of a polynomial is degree of highest-degree term: degree of $2x^2y^3$ is $2 + 3 = 5$

2. (4.2)

$$\begin{array}{r} -4x^3 - 3x^2 + 5 \\ 2x^2 + 6x - 10 \\ 3x^3 - 2x + 8 \\ \hline -x^3 - x^2 + 4x + 3 \end{array}$$

3. (4.2)

$$\begin{array}{r} 3x^4 - x^3 + x - 2 \\ 5x^4 + x^3 + x^2 - 3x - 5 \\ \hline -2x^4 - 2x^3 - x^2 + 4x + 3 \end{array}$$

4. (4.2) $(-3z^2 - 6z + 8) - (8 - z + 4z^2)$
$= \underline{-3z^2} - \underset{\sim}{6z} + \underline{\underline{8}} - \underline{\underline{8}} + \underset{\sim}{z} - \underline{4z^2}$
$= -7z^2 - 5z$

5. (4.2) $\underline{3ab^2} - \underline{\underline{5ab}} - a^3 - \underset{\sim}{2ab} + \underline{\underline{4ab}} - \underline{7ab^2}$
$= -4ab^2 - 3ab - a^3$

6. (4.3) $-3ab(6a^2 - 2ab^2 + 5b)$
$= (-3ab)(6a^2) + (-3ab)(-2ab^2) + (-3ab)(5b)$
$= -18a^3b + 6a^2b^3 - 15ab^2$

7. (4.3)

$$\begin{array}{r} x^2 + 2x + 4 \\ x - 2 \\ \hline -2x^2 - 4x - 8 \\ x^3 + 2x^2 + 4x \\ \hline x^3 - 8 \end{array}$$

8. (4.3)

$$m^2 - 2m + 5$$
$$m^2 - 2m + 5$$
$$\overline{5m^2 - 10m + 25}$$
$$-2m^3 + 4m^2 - 10m$$
$$m^4 - 2m^3 \quad 5m^2$$
$$\overline{m^4 - 4m^3 + 14m^2 - 20m + 25}$$

9. (4.4A) $(2x^4 + 3)(2x^4 - 3) = (2x^4)^2 - (3)^2 = 4x^8 - 9$

10. (4.3A) $(5m - 2)(3m + 4) = (5m)(3m) + 20m - 6m - 8$
$$= 15m^2 + 14m - 8$$

11. (4.4B) $(3R^2 - 5)^2 = (3R^2)^2 + 2(3R^2)(-5) + (-5)^2$
$$= 9R^4 - 30R^2 + 25$$

12. (4.4C) $(2x + 1)^5 = (2x)^5 + 5(2x)^4(1) + \dfrac{5 \cdot 4}{1 \cdot 2}(2x)^3(1)^2$
$$+ \dfrac{5 \cdot 4}{1 \cdot 2}(2x)^2(1)^3 + 5(2x)(1)^4 + 1^5$$
$$= 32x^5 + 80x^4 + 80x^3 + 40x^2 + 10x + 1$$

13. (4.5A) $\dfrac{9z^3w + 6z^2w^2 - 12zw^3}{3zw} = \dfrac{9z^3w}{3zw} + \dfrac{6z^2w^2}{3zw} - \dfrac{12zw^3}{3zw}$
$$= 3z^2 + 2zw - 4w^2$$

14. (4.5B)

$$\begin{array}{r} 4y - 4 \\ 3y + 2 \overline{)12y^2 - 4y + 1} \\ 12y^2 + 8y \\ \hline -12y + 1 \\ -12y - 8 \\ \hline 9 \end{array}$$

Answer: $4y - 4 + \dfrac{9}{3y + 2}$

15. (4.5B)

$$\begin{array}{r} 3x^2 + 0x - 5 \\ 2x^2 - x + 4 \overline{)6x^4 - 3x^3 + 2x^2 + 5x - 7} \\ 6x^4 - 3x^3 + 12x^2 \\ \hline -10x^2 + 5x - 7 \\ -10x^2 + 5x - 20 \\ \hline 13 \end{array}$$

Answer: $3x^2 - 5 + \dfrac{13}{2x^2 - x + 4}$

16. (4.6) $2x^4 + 3x^3 - 7x^2 + 0x - 5$

$$\begin{array}{r|rrrrr} & 2 & 3 & -7 & 0 & -5 \\ & & -6 & 9 & -6 & 18 \\ \hline -3 & 2 & -3 & 2 & -6 & 13 \end{array}$$

Answer: $2x^3 - 3x^2 + 2x - 6 + \dfrac{13}{x + 3}$

Cumulative Review Exercises: Chapters 1–4 (page 176)

1. $10 - (-3 - 25) = 10 - (-28) = 10 + 28 = 38$ **2.** $\dfrac{1}{x^2y^3}$

3.

$$\begin{array}{r|r} 2 & 108 \\ \hline 2 & 54 \\ \hline 3 & 27 \\ \hline 3 & 9 \\ \hline & 3 \end{array} \quad 108 = 2^2 \cdot 3^3$$

$$\begin{array}{r|r} 2 & 360 \\ \hline 2 & 180 \\ \hline 2 & 90 \\ \hline 3 & 45 \\ \hline 3 & 15 \\ \hline & 5 \end{array} \quad 360 = 2^3 \cdot 3^2 \cdot 5$$

LCM $= 2^3 \cdot 3^3 \cdot 5 = 1080$

4. $6a - 3$ **5.** $4(x - 3) = 4 - (x + 6)$ **6.** $x \geq 3$
$$4x - 12 = 4 - x - 6$$
$$5x - 12 = 4 - 6$$
$$5x - 12 = -2$$
$$5x = 10$$
$$x = 2$$

7. $|5 - x| = 6$ **8.** $x > 4$ or $x < -\dfrac{2}{3}$
$$5 - x = 6 \text{ or } 5 - x = -6$$
$$-x = 1 \text{ or } -x = -11$$
$$x = -1 \text{ or } x = 11$$

9. $|2x - 1| \leq 4$ **10.** $3x^5 + 6x^4 + 7x^3 + 12x^2 - 4x$
$$-4 \leq 2x - 1 \leq 4$$
$$\dfrac{1}{-3} \leq \dfrac{1}{2x} \leq \dfrac{1}{5}$$
$$-\dfrac{3}{2} \leq x \leq \dfrac{5}{2}$$

11. $x^6 - 6x^5 + \dfrac{6 \cdot 5}{1 \cdot 2}x^4 - \dfrac{6 \cdot 5 \cdot 4}{1 \cdot 2 \cdot 3}x^3 + 15x^2 - 6x + 1$
$$= x^6 - 6x^5 + 15x^4 - 20x^3 + 15x^2 - 6x + 1$$

12. $x^2 - 2x - 5 + \dfrac{4}{x + 4}$

13. Let $2x = $ Length of shortest side   **14.** 4.5 pounds
$$4x = \text{Length of middle side}$$
$$5x = \text{Length of longest side}$$
$$2x + 4x + 5x = 88$$
$$11x = 88$$
$$x = 8$$
$$2x = 16 \quad \text{Shortest side}$$
$$4x = 32 \quad \text{Middle side}$$
$$5x = 40 \quad \text{Longest side}$$
$$Check \quad \overline{88} \quad \text{Perimeter}$$

15. Let $x = $ Speed of stream   (Note that 40 minutes $= \dfrac{2}{3}$ hours)

$30 + x = $ Speed downstream   Distance downstream $= \dfrac{2}{3}(30 + x)$

$30 - x = $ Speed upstream   Distance upstream $= \dfrac{2}{3}(30 - x)$

$$\dfrac{2}{3}(30 + x) = \dfrac{2}{3}(30 - x) + 4$$
$$20 + \dfrac{2}{3}x = 20 - \dfrac{2}{3}x + 4$$
$$\dfrac{4}{3}x = 4$$
$$x = 3 \quad \text{(The check will not be shown.)}$$

Exercises 5.1 (page 181)

1. GCF $= 18xy$ **2.** $15ab^2c(15b^3 - 7a^2c^5)$
$$54x^3yz^4 - 72xy^3$$
$$= 18xy(3x^2z^4 - 4y^2)$$

3. $4x(4x^2 - 2x + 1)$ **4.** $3a(9a^3 - 3a + 1)$ **5.** Not factorable

6. Not factorable   **7.** $3(2my + 5mz - 3n)$ **8.** $4(nx + 2ny + 3z)$

9. $-5r^7s^5(7t^4 + 11rs^4u^4 - 8p^8r^2s^3)$
or $5r^7s^5(-7t^4 - 11rs^4u^4 + 8p^8r^2s^3)$

10. $-40a^4c^3(3a^4b^7c^2 - d^9 + 2ac^2)$
or $40a^4c^3(-3a^4b^7c^2 + d^9 - 2ac^2)$

11. Not factorable   **12.** Not factorable

13. $-12x^4y^3(2x^4 + x^3y - 4xy^2 - 5y^3)$

14. $16y^4z^5(4y^5 + 3y^4z - y^3z^2 - 5z^3)$

15. GCF $= (a + b)$ **16.** $(a - 2b)(3a + 2)$
$m(a + b) + n(a + b)$
$= (a + b)(m + n)$

17. GCF $= (y + 1)$ **18.** $(3e - f)(2e - 3)$
$x(y + 1) - (y + 1)$
$= (y + 1)(x - 1)$

19. GCF $= (x - y)$ **20.** $(a + b)(4 - a - b)$
$5(x - y) - (x - y)^2$
$= (x - y)[5 - (x - y)]$
$= (x - y)(5 - x + y)$

21. $8x(y^2 + 3z)^2 - 6x^4(y^2 + 3z)$
$= 2x(y^2 + 3z)[4(y^2 + 3z) - 3x^3]$
$= 2x(y^2 + 3z)(4y^2 + 12z - 3x^3)$

22. $3a^2(b - 2c^5)^2(4ab - 8ac^5 - 5)$

23. $5(x + y)^2(a + b)^5([x + y] + 3[a + b])$
$= 5(x + y)^2(a + b)^5(x + y + 3a + 3b)$

24. $7(s + t)^4(u + v)^6(2u + 2v + s + t)$

Exercises 5.2 (page 184)

1. $x(m - n) - y(m - n)$ **2.** $(h - k)(a - b)$
$= (m - n)(x - y)$

3. $x(y + 1) - 1(y + 1)$ **4.** $(a - 1)(d + 1)$
$= (y + 1)(x - 1)$

5. $3a(a - 2b) + 2(a - 2b)$ **6.** $(h - 3k)(2h + 5)$
$= (a - 2b)(3a + 2)$

7. $2e(3e - f) - 3(3e - f)$ **8.** $(2m - n)(4m - 3)$
$= (3e - f)(2e - 3)$

9. $x^2(x + 3) - 2(x + 3)$ **10.** $(a - 1)(a^2 - 2)$
$= (x + 3)(x^2 - 2)$

11. $b^2(b + 4) + 5(b - 4)$ **12.** Not factorable
Not factorable

13. $2a^2(a + 4) - 3(a + 4)$ **14.** $(y - 2)(5y^2 + 2)$
$= (a + 4)(2a^2 - 3)$

15. $c[am + bm + an + bn]$ **16.** $k(u + v)(c + d)$
$= c[m(a + b) + n(a + b)]$
$= c(a + b)(m + n)$

17. $\underbrace{a^2x + 2ax + 5x} + \underbrace{a^2y + 2ay + 5y}$ **18.** $(x^2 + 3x + 7)(a + b)$

$= x(a^2 + 2a + 5) + y(a^2 + 2a + 5)$
$= (a^2 + 2a + 5)(x + y)$

19. $x(s^2 - s + 4) + y(s^2 - s + 4)$ **20.** $(t^2 - t + 3)(a + b)$
$= (s^2 - s + 4)(x + y)$

21. $\underbrace{ax^2 + ax + a} - \underbrace{x^2 - x - 1}$ **22.** $(y^2 + y + 2)(x - 1)$

$= a(x^2 + x + 1) - (x^2 + x + 1)$
$= (x^2 + x + 1)(a - 1)$

Exercises 5.3 (page 187)

1. $2x^2 - 8y^2$ **2.** $3(x + 3y)(x - 3y)$
$= 2(x^2 - 4y^2)$
$= 2(x - 2y)(x + 2y)$

3. $2(49u^4 - 36v^4)$ **4.** $3(9m^3 + 10n^2)(9m^3 - 10n^2)$
$= 2(7u^2 + 6v^2)(7u^2 - 6v^2)$

5. $(x^2 + y^2)(x^2 - y^2)$ **6.** $(a^2 + 4)(a + 2)(a - 2)$
$= (x^2 + y^2)(x + y)(x - y)$

7. Not factorable   **8.** Not factorable

9. $(2h^2k^2 + 1)(2h^2k^2 - 1)$ **10.** $(3x^2 + 1)(3x^2 - 1)$

11. $a^2b^2(25a^2 - b^2)$ **12.** $x^2y^2(y + 10x)(y - 10x)$
$= a^2b^2(5a + b)(5a - b)$

13. $8x(2x + 1)$ **14.** $5y(5y + 1)$ **15.** Not factorable

16. Not factorable

17. $[(x + y) + 2][(x + y) - 2] = (x + y + 2)(x + y - 2)$

18. $(a + b + 3)(a + b - 3)$ **19.** $(a + b)[x^2 - y^2]$
$= (a + b)(x + y)(x - y)$

20. $(x + y)(a + b)(a - b)$ **21.** Not factorable

22. Not factorable   **23.** $(x + 3y)(x - 3y) + (x - 3y)$
$= (x - 3y)([x + 3y] + 1)$
$= (x - 3y)(x + 3y + 1)$

24. $(x - y)(x + y + 1)$ **25.** $(x + 2y) + (x + 2y)(x - 2y)$
$= (x + 2y)(1 + x - 2y)$

26. $(a + b)(1 + a - b)$

Exercises 5.4A (page 191)

1. Not factorable   **2.** Not factorable   **3.** $(m + 1)(m + 12)$

4. $(x + 14)(x + 1)$ **5.** Not factorable   **6.** Not factorable

7. $(t - 3)(t + 10)$ **8.** $(m + 2)(m - 15)$ **9.** $x^2 + 10x$
$= x(x + 10)$

10. $y(y + 10)$ **11.** $u^4 - 15u^2 + 14$
$= (u^2 - 14)(u^2 - 1)$
$= (u^2 - 14)(u - 1)(u + 1)$

12. $(y - 1)(y + 1)(y^2 - 15)$ **13.** $(u - 4)(u + 16)$

14. $(v + 2)(v - 32)$ **15.** $x^2 + 3x + 2 = (x + 2)(x + 1)$

16. $(a + 5)(a + 2)$ **17.** $x^2(x^2 - 6x + 2)$ **18.** $y^2(y^4 - 2y^2 + 2)$

19. $(x + 2y)(x - y)$ **20.** $(x + 3y)^2$

21. $[(a + b) + 2][(a + b) + 4]$ **22.** $(m + n + 1)(m + n + 8)$
$= (a + b + 2)(a + b + 4)$

23. $[(x + y) + 2][x + y) - 15]$ **24.** $(x + y + 2)(x + y - 12)$
$= (x + y + 2)(x + y - 15)$

Exercises 5.4B (page 199)

1. $(x + 1)(5x + 4)$ **2.** $(5x + 2)(x + 2)$

3. $(7 - b)(1 - 3b)$ or $(3b - 1)(b - 7)$

4. $(1 - u)(7 - 3u)$ or $(3u - 7)(u - 1)$

5. Not factorable   **6.** Not factorable

7. $MP = (3)(-5) = -15$ **8.** $(3n + 5)(n - 1)$
$-15 = -1 \cdot 15; (-1) + (+15) = +14$
$\underbrace{3n^2 - n} + \underbrace{15n - 5}$
$= n(3n - 1) + 5(3n - 1)$
$= (3n - 1)(n + 5)$

9. $(3t + z)(t - 6z)$ **10.** $(3x + 2y)(x - 3y)$

11. Not factorable   **12.** Not factorable

13. $4(2 + 3z - 2z^2) = 4(1 + 2z)(2 - z)$ **14.** $3(1 + 3z)(3 - 2z)$

15. $(2a)^2 + 2(2a)(1) + (1)^2$ **16.** $(3b + 1)^2$

$(2a + 1)^2$

17. $2x^2 - 18$
$= 2(x^2 - 9)$
$= 2(x - 3)(x + 3)$

18. $5(y + 4)(y - 4)$

19. $4 + 7h^2 - 11h$
$= 7h^2 - 11h + 4$
$= (7h - 4)(h - 1)$

20. $(h - 2)(7h - 2)$

21. $2(36x^2 + 12xy + y^2)$

Then
$$36x^2 + 12xy + y^2$$
$$(\,6x\,)^2 + 2(6x)(y) + (\,y\,)^2$$

$$(\,6x\, + \,y\,)^2$$

Therefore, $24xy + 72x^2 + 2y^2 = 2(6x + y)^2$

22. $2(4x + y)^2$

23. Not factorable **24.** Not factorable

25. $2y(x^2 + 4xy + 4y^2)$
$$2y[(\,x\,)^2 + 2(x)(y) + (\,2y\,)^2]$$

$$2y(\,x\, + \,2y\,)^2$$

26. $3x(x + y)^2$

27. $(3e^2 + 4)(2e^2 - 5)$ **28.** $(5f^2 + 3)(2f^2 - 7)$

29. $3x^2(4x^2 - 25y^2) = 3x^2(2x + 5y)(2x - 5y)$

30. $4x^2(3x + 2y)(3x - 2y)$

31. $(\,a^2\,)^2 + 2(a^2)(b^2) + (\,b^2\,)^2$

$$(\,a^2\, + \,b^2\,)^2$$

32. $(x^2 + 3y^2)^2$

33. Let $(a + b) = x$
Then $2(a + b)^2 + 7(a + b) + 3 = 2x^2 + 7x + 3$
$MP = 2(+3) = +6$
$6 = 1 \cdot 6$ $(+1) + (+6) = +7$
$$\underbrace{2x^2 + x}_{} + \underbrace{6x + 3}_{}$$
$= x(2x + 1) + 3(2x + 1)$
$= (2x + 1)(x + 3)$
Therefore, $2x^2 + 7x + 3 = (2x + 1)(x + 3)$
But, since $x = (a + b)$
$2(a + b)^2 + 7(a + b) + 3 = [2(a + b) + 1][(a + b) + 3]$
$= (2a + 2b + 1)(a + b + 3)$

34. $(3a - 3b + 1)(a - b + 2)$

35. Let $(x - y) = a$
Then $4(x - y)^2 - 8(x - y) - 5 = 4a^2 - 8a - 5$
$= (2a + 1)(2a - 5)$
But, since $a = (x - y)$
$4(x - y)^2 - 8(x - y) - 5 = (2[x - y] + 1)(2[x - y] - 5)$
$= (2x - 2y + 1)(2x - 2y - 5)$

36. $(2x + 2y + 1)(2x + 2y - 3)$

37. $5x^2 + 10xy + 5y^2 = 5(x^2 + 2xy + y^2) = 5(x + y)^2$
and $-21x - 21y = -21(x + y)$
Therefore, $5x^2 + 10xy + 5y^2 - 21x - 21y + 4$
$= 5(x + y)^2 - 21(x + y) + 4$. Let $a = (x + y)$
Then $5(x + y)^2 - 21(x + y) + 4 = 5a^2 - 21a + 4$
$= (5a - 1)(a - 4)$
But, since $a = (x + y)$
$5(x + y)^2 - 21(x + y) + 4 = (5[x + y] - 1)([x + y] - 4)$
$= (5x + 5y - 1)(x + y - 4)$

38. $(5x - 5y - 2)(x - y - 2)$

39. $(2x - y)^2 - (3a + b)^2 \leftarrow$ Difference of two squares
$= [(2x - y) + (3a + b)][(2x - y) - (3a + b)]$
$= (2x - y + 3a + b)(2x - y - 3a - b)$

40. $(2x + 3y + a - b)(2x + 3y - a + b)$

41. $\underbrace{x^2 + 10xy + 25y^2}_{} - 9$
$= (x + 5y)^2 - 9$
$= (x + 5y - 3)(x + 5y + 3)$

42. $(x + 4y + 5)(x + 4y - 5)$

43.
$$a^2 - 4x^2 - 4xy - y^2 = a^2 - \overbrace{(4x^2 + 4xy + y^2)}^{\text{Perfect square trinomial}}$$
$$= a^2 - \underbrace{(2x + y)^2}_{\text{Difference of two squares}}$$
$$= (a + [2x + y])(a - [2x + y])$$
$$= (a + 2x + y)(a - 2x - y)$$

44. $(x + 3a + b)(x - 3a - b)$

45. $4x^4 - 13x^2 + 9$
$= (4x^2 - 9)(x^2 - 1)$
$= (2x - 3)(2x + 3)(x - 1)(x + 1)$

46. $(3x - 2)(3x + 2)(x + 1)(x - 1)$

47. $3x^2 - 7xy - 6y^2 = (3x + 2y)(x - 3y)$
$-x + 3y = -(x - 3y)$
Therefore, $3x^2 - 7xy - 6y^2 - x + 3y$
$= (3x + 2y)(x - 3y) - (x - 3y)$
$= (x - 3y)([3x + 2y] - 1)$
$= (x - 3y)(3x + 2y - 1)$

48. $(3t + z)(t - 6z - 1)$

49. $\underbrace{3n^2 + 2mn - 5m^2}_{} + \underbrace{3n + 5m}_{}$
$= (3n + 5m)(n - m) + (3n + 5m)$
$= (3n + 5m)(n - m + 1)$

50. $(3n - m)(n + 5m + 1)$

Review Exercises 5.5 (page 201)

1. $13xy(5xy^2 - 3y^3 - 1)$ **2.** Not factorable

3. GCF $= 3x$
$$3x^3 + 9x^2 - 12x$$
$= 3x(x^2 + 3x - 4)$
$= 3x(x + 4)(x - 1)$

4. Not factorable   **5.** $(x + 5)(x + 8)$ **6.** $(x - 4)(x + 5)$

7. Not factorable   **8.** $(x - 9)(x - 2)$ **9.** $(x - 16)(x + 16)$

10. $(x - 13)(x - 1)$ **11.** $(3x - 7)(x + 2)$ **12.** $(2x + 5)(x - 8)$

13. $3xy + 12x + 2y + 8$ (Factor by grouping)
$= 3x(y + 4) + 2(y + 4) \leftarrow y + 4$ is the common factor
$= (y + 4)(3x + 2)$

14. $(x + 5)(x + 1)(x - 1)$ **15.** Not factorable

16. Not factorable   **17.** GCF $= 2x$
$$2x(4x^2 - 1)$$
$= 2x(2x - 1)(2x + 1)$

18. Not factorable   **19.** $(4x - 1)(x + 3)$ **20.** $(8a - 5)(a + 2)$

Exercises 5.6 (page 207)

1. $(x)^3 - (2)^3$
$= (x - 2)[(x)^2 + (2)(x) + (2)^2]$
$= (x - 2)(x^2 + 2x + 4)$

2. $(x - 3)(x^2 + 3x + 9)$

3. $(4)^3 + (a)^3$
$= (4 + a)[(4)^2 - (4)(a) + (a)^2]$
$= (4 + a)(16 - 4a + a^2)$

4. $(2 + b)(4 - 2b + b^2)$

5. $(5)^3 - x^3$
$= (5 - x)[(5)^2 + (5)(x) + (x)^2]$
$= (5 - x)(25 + 5x + x^2)$

6. $(1 - a)(1 + a + a^2)$

Difference of two squares

7. $2x(4x^2 - 1) = 2x(2x - 1)(2x + 1)$

8. $3x(3x + 1)(3x - 1)$

9. $c^3 - (3ab)^3$

$= (c - 3ab)[(c)^2 + (c)(3ab) + (3ab)^2]$
$= (c - 3ab)(c^2 + 3abc + 9a^2b^2)$

10. $(c - 4ab)(c^2 + 4abc + 16a^2b^2)$

11. $8x^3y^6 + 27 = (2xy^2)^3 + (3)^3$

$= (2xy^2 + 3)[(2xy^2)^2 - (2xy^2)(3) + (3)^2]$
$= (2xy^2 + 3)(4x^2y^4 - 6xy^2 + 9)$

12. $(4a^2b + 5)(16a^4b^2 - 20a^2b + 25)$

13. Not factorable   **14.** Not factorable

15. $a^4 + ab^3 = a[a^3 + b^3]$ **16.** $y(x + y)(x^2 - xy + y^2)$

$= a[(a)^3 + (b)^3]$
$= a(a + b)[(a)^2 - (a)(b) + (b)^2]$
$= a(a + b)(a^2 - ab + b^2)$

17. $81 - 3x^3$ **18.** $5(2 - b)(4 + 2b + b^2)$

$= 3(27 - x^3)$
$= 3(3 - x)[(3)^2 + (3)(x) + (x)^2]$
$= 3(3 - x)(9 + 3x + x^2)$

19. $(x + y)^3 + (1)^3$

$= [(x + y) + (1)][(x + y)^2 - (x + y)(1) + (1)^2]$
$= (x + y + 1)(x^2 + 2xy + y^2 - x - y + 1)$

20. $(1 + x - y)(1 - x + y + x^2 - 2xy + y^2)$

21. $64x^3 - y^6$ **22.** $(5w - v^2)(25w^2 + 5wv^2 + v^4)$

$= (4x)^3 - (y^2)^3$
$= (4x - y^2)[(4x)^2 + (4x)(y^2) + (y^2)^2]$
$= (4x - y^2)(16x^2 + 4xy^2 + y^4)$

23. $4(a^3b^3 + 27c^6)$

$= 4[(ab)^3 + (3c^2)^3]$
$= 4[ab + 3c^2][(ab)^2 - (ab)(3c^2) + (3c^2)^2]$
$= 4(ab + 3c^2)(a^2b^2 - 3abc^2 + 9c^4)$

24. $5(xy^2 + 2z^3)(x^2y^4 - 2xy^2z^3 + 4z^6)$

25. $x^6 - 729$ A binomial that is both the difference of two squares and the difference of two cubes should be treated *first* as the difference of two squares.

$= (x^3 - 27)(x^3 + 27)$
$= (x - 3)(x^2 + 3x + 9)(x + 3)(x^2 - 3x + 9)$
$= (x - 3)(x + 3)(x^2 + 3x + 9)(x^2 - 3x + 9)$

26. $(y - 2)(y^2 + 2y + 4)(y + 2)(y^2 - 2y + 4)$

27. $(x + 1)^3 - (y - z)^3$

$= [(x + 1) - (y - z)][(x + 1)^2 + (x + 1)(y - z) + (y - z)^2]$
$= (x + 1 - y + z)$
    $\cdot (x^2 + 2x + 1 + xy - xz + y - z + y^2 - 2yz + z^2)$

28. $(x - y - a - b)$
    $\cdot (x^2 - 2xy + y^2 + ax + bx - ay - by + a^2 + 2ab + b^2)$

Exercises 5.7 (page 211)

Note: Steps 1–3 will not be shown.

1. $x^4 + 3x^2 + 4$ **2.** $(x^2 + x + 3)(x^2 - x + 3)$

Try $(x^2 + 2)^2$
Add and subtract x^2
$x^4 + 3x^2 + x^2 + 4 - x^2$
$x^4 + 4x^2 + 4 - x^2$
$(x^2 + 2)^2 - x^2$
$(x^2 + 2 - x)(x^2 + 2 + x)$
$(x^2 - x + 2)(x^2 + x + 2)$

3. $4m^4 + 3m^2 + 1$ **4.** $(3u^2 + u + 1)(3u^2 - u + 1)$

Try $(2m^2 + 1)^2$
Add and subtract m^2
$4m^4 + 3m^2 + m^2 + 1 - m^2$
$(4m^4 + 4m^2 + 1) - m^2$
$(2m^2 + 1)^2 - m^2$
$(2m^2 + 1 - m)(2m^2 + 1 + m)$
$(2m^2 - m + 1)(2m^2 + m + 1)$

5. $64a^4 + b^4$

Add and subtract $16a^2b^2$
$64a^4 + 16a^2b^2 + b^4 - 16a^2b^2$
$[(8a^2 + b^2)^2 - 16a^2b^2]$
$(8a^2 + b^2 - 4ab)(8a^2 + b^2 + 4ab)$
$(8a^2 - 4ab + b^2)(8a^2 + 4ab + b^2)$

6. $(a^2 + 2ab + 2b^2)(a^2 - 2ab + 2b^2)$

7. $x^4 - 3x^2 + 9$ **8.** $(x^2 + 3x + 4)(x^2 - 3x + 4)$

Add and subtract $9x^2$
$x^4 - 3x^2 + 9x^2 + 9 - 9x^2$
$x^4 + 6x^2 + 9 - 9x^2$
$(x^2 + 3)^2 - 9x^2$
$(x^2 + 3 - 3x)(x^2 + 3 + 3x)$
$(x^2 - 3x + 3)(x^2 + 3x + 3)$

9. $a^4 - 17a^2b^2 + 16b^4$ **10.** $(a + 1)(a - 1)(a + 6)(a - 6)$

Add and subtract $9a^2b^2$
$a^4 - 17a^2b^2 + 9a^2b^2 + 16b^4 - 9a^2b^2$
$a^4 - 8a^2b^2 + 16b^4 - 9a^2b^2$
$(a^2 - 4b^2)^2 - 9a^2b^2$
$(a^2 - 4b^2 - 3ab)(a^2 - 4b^2 + 3ab)$
$(a^2 - 3ab - 4b^2)(a^2 + 3ab - 4b^2)$
$(a - 4b)(a + b)(a + 4b)(a - b)$

11. Not factorable   **12.** Not factorable

13. $a^4 - 3a^2b^2 + 9b^4$

Add and subtract $9a^2b^2$
$a^4 - 3a^2b^2 + 9a^2b^2 + 9b^4 - 9a^4b^2$
$(a^4 + 6a^2b^2 + 9b^4) - 9a^2b^2$
$(a^2 + 3b^2)^2 - 9a^2b^2$
$(a^2 + 3b^2 - 3ab)(a^2 + 3b^2 + 3ab)$
$(a^2 - 3ab + 3b^2)(a^2 + 3ab + 3b^2)$

14. $(a^2 + 5ab + 5b^2)(a^2 - 5ab + 5b^2)$

15. Not factorable   **16.** Not factorable

17. $50x^4 - 12x^2y^2 + 2y^4$ **18.** $2(4x^2 + 3xy + y^2)(4x^2 - 3xy + y^2)$

$2(25x^4 - 6x^2y^2 + y^4)$
Add and subtract $16x^2y^2$
$2[25x^4 - 6x^2y^2 + 16x^2y^2 + y^4 - 16x^2y^2]$
$2[25x^4 + 10x^2y^2 + y^4 - 16x^2y^2]$
$2[(5x^2 + y^2)^2 - 16x^2y^2]$
$2[(5x^2 + y^2 - 4xy)(5x^2 + y^2 + 4xy)]$
$2(5x^2 - 4xy + y^2)(5x^2 + 4xy + y^2)$

19. $8m^4n + 2n^5$ **20.** $3m(m^2 + 2mn + 2n^2)(m^2 - 2mn + 2n^2)$

$2n(4m^4 + n^4)$
Add and subtract $4m^2n^2$
$2n[(4m^4 + n^4 + 4m^2n^2) - 4m^2n^2]$
$2n[(2m^2 + n^2)^2 - 4m^2n^2]$
$2n(2m^2 + 2mn + n^2)(2m^2 - 2mn + n^2)$

21. $50x^4y + 32x^2y^3 + 8y^5$ **22.** $3x(4x^2 + xy + y^2)(4x^2 - xy + y^2)$

$2y(25x^4 + 16x^2y^2 + 4y^4)$
Add and subtract $4x^2y^2$
$2y(25x^4 + 16x^2y^2 + 4y^4 + 4x^2y^2 - 4x^2y^2)$
$2y(25x^4 + 20x^2y^2 + 4y^4 - 4x^2y^2)$
$2y[(5x^2 + 2y^2)^2 - 4x^2y^2]$
$2y(5x^2 + 2xy + 2y^2)(5x^2 - 2xy + 2y^2)$

Exercises 5.8 (page 215)

1. Factors of the constant term are $\pm 1, \pm 3$

$$
\begin{array}{c|cccc}
 & 1 & 1 & 1 & -3 \\
 &   & 1 & 2 & 3 \\
\hline
\text{Divide by } 1 & 1 & 2 & 3 & 0 \\
\end{array}
$$

Remainder is zero; therefore, $(x - 1)$ is a factor

$x^2 + 2x + 3$ Will not factor

Therefore, $x^3 + x^2 + x - 3 = (x - 1)(x^2 + 2x + 3)$

2. $(x - 2)(x^2 + 3x + 1)$

3. Factors of the constant term are $\pm 1, \pm 2, \pm 3, \pm 4, \pm 6, \pm 12$

$$
\begin{array}{c|cccc}
 & 1 & -3 & -4 & 12 \\
 &   & 2 & -2 & -12 \\
\hline
\text{Divide by } 2 & 1 & -1 & -6 & 0 \\
\end{array}
$$

Remainder is zero; therefore, $(x - 2)$ is a factor

$x^2 - x - 6$ Quotient is another factor

$(x - 3)(x + 2)$ Factors of quotient

Therefore, $x^3 - 3x^2 - 4x + 12 = (x - 2)(x - 3)(x + 2)$

4. $(x - 1)(x + 2)(x - 3)$

5. $2(x^3 - 4x^2 + x + 6)$

We now factor $x^3 - 4x^2 + x + 6$

Factors of the constant term are $\pm 1, \pm 2, \pm 3, \pm 6$

$$
\begin{array}{c|cccc}
 & 1 & -4 & 1 & 6 \\
 &   & 1 & -3 & -2 \\
\hline
\text{Divide by } 1 & 1 & -3 & -2 & 4 \\
\end{array}
$$

Remainder is not zero; therefore, $(x - 1)$ is not a factor

$$
\begin{array}{c|cccc}
 & 1 & -4 & 1 & 6 \\
 &   & -1 & 5 & -6 \\
\hline
\text{Divide by } -1 & 1 & -5 & 6 & 0 \\
\end{array}
$$

Remainder is zero; therefore, $(x + 1)$ is a factor

$x^2 - 5x + 6$ Quotient is another factor

$(x - 2)(x - 3)$ Factors of quotient

Therefore, $x^3 - 4x^2 + x + 6 = (x + 1)(x - 2)(x - 3)$

and $2x^3 - 8x^2 + 2x + 12 = 2(x + 1)(x - 2)(x - 3)$

6. $2(x + 1)(x + 2)(x + 3)$

7. Factors of the constant term are $\pm 1, \pm 2, \pm 4$

$$
\begin{array}{c|cccc}
 & 6 & -13 & 0 & +4 \\
 &   & 12 & -2 & -4 \\
\hline
\text{Divide by } 2 & 6 & -1 & -2 & 0 \\
\end{array}
$$

Remainder is zero; therefore $(x - 2)$ is a factor

Therefore, $6x^3 - 13x^2 + 4 = (x - 2)(6x^2 - x - 2)$
$= (x - 2)(3x - 2)(2x + 1)$

8. $(x + 1)(x + 2)(x - 3)$

9. Factors of the constant term are $\pm 1, \pm 2, \pm 4$

$$
\begin{array}{c|ccccc}
 & 1 & 0 & -3 & 4 & 4 \\
 &   & -2 & 4 & -2 & -4 \\
\hline
\text{Divide by } -2 & 1 & -2 & 1 & 2 & 0 \\
\end{array}
$$

Remainder is zero; therefore, $(x + 2)$ is a factor

$x^3 - 2x^2 + x + 2$ Quotient is another factor; it does not factor

Therefore, $x^4 - 3x^2 + 4x + 4 = (x + 2)(x^3 - 2x^2 + x + 2)$

10. $(x + 2)(x^3 - 3x^2 + x + 3)$

11. Factors of the constant term are $\pm 1, \pm 2, \pm 4$

$$
\begin{array}{c|ccccc}
 & 1 & 2 & -3 & -8 & -4 \\
 &   & 1 & 3 & 0 & -8 \\
\hline
\text{Divide by } 1 & 1 & 3 & 0 & -8 & -12 \\
\end{array}
$$

Remainder is not zero; therefore, $(x - 1)$ is not a factor

$$
\begin{array}{c|ccccc}
 & 1 & 2 & -3 & -8 & -4 \\
 &   & 2 & 8 & 10 & 4 \\
\hline
\text{Divide by } 2 & 1 & 4 & 5 & 2 & 0 \\
\end{array}
$$

Remainder is zero; therefore, $(x - 2)$ is a factor

We *now* work with the coefficients 1, 4, 5, 2

Factors of the constant term are ± 1 and ± 2. However, since $+1$

did not work for the original coefficients, it will not work for the new ones. We must try $+2$ a second time:

$$
\begin{array}{c|cccc}
 & 1 & 4 & 5 & 2 \\
 &   & 2 & 12 & 34 \\
\hline
\text{Divide by } 2 & 1 & 6 & 17 & 36 \\
\end{array}
$$

Remainder is not zero; therefore, $(x - 2)$ is not a factor of $x^3 + 4x^2 + 5x + 2$

$$
\begin{array}{c|cccc}
 & 1 & 4 & 5 & 2 \\
 &   & -1 & -3 & -2 \\
\hline
\text{Divide by } -1 & 1 & 3 & 2 & 0 \\
\end{array}
$$

Remainder is zero; therefore, $(x + 1)$ is a factor

Therefore, $x^4 + 2x^3 - 3x^2 - 8x - 4$
$= (x - 2)(x + 1)(x^2 + 3x + 2)$
$= (x - 2)(x + 1)(x + 1)(x + 2)$ or
$= (x - 2)(x + 1)^2(x + 2)$

12. $(x - 1)(x + 1)(x + 2)^2$

13. Factors of the constant term are ± 1. We may also have to try $\pm 1/3$.

$$
\begin{array}{c|ccccc}
 & 3 & -4 & 0 & 0 & -1 \\
 &   & 3 & -1 & -1 & -1 \\
\hline
\text{Divide by } 1 & 3 & -1 & -1 & -1 & -2 \\
\end{array}
$$

Remainder is not zero; therefore, $(x - 1)$ is not a factor

$$
\begin{array}{c|ccccc}
 & 3 & -4 & 0 & 0 & -1 \\
 &   & -3 & 7 & -7 & 7 \\
\hline
\text{Divide by } -1 & 3 & -7 & 7 & -7 & 6 \\
\end{array}
$$

Remainder is not zero; therefore, $(x + 1)$ is not a factor

$$
\begin{array}{c|ccccc}
 & 3 & -4 & 0 & 0 & -1 \\
 &   & 1 & -1 & -1/3 & -1/9 \\
\hline
\text{Divide by } 1/3 & 3 & -3 & -1 & -1/3 & -10/9 \\
\end{array}
$$

Remainder is not zero; therefore, $(x - 1/3)$ is not a factor

$$
\begin{array}{c|ccccc}
 & 3 & -4 & 0 & 0 & -1 \\
 &   & -1 & 5/3 & -5/9 & 5/27 \\
\hline
\text{Divide by } -1/3 & 3 & -5 & 5/3 & -5/9 & -22/27 \\
\end{array}
$$

Remainder is not zero; therefore, $(x + 1/3)$ is not a factor

Since none of the possible factors work, the expression is not factorable.

14. Not factorable

15. Factors of the constant term are $\pm 1, \pm 2, \pm 3, \pm 4, \pm 6, \pm 8, \pm 12, \pm 24$

$$
\begin{array}{c|ccccc}
 & 1 & -4 & -7 & 34 & -24 \\
 &   & 1 & -3 & -10 & 24 \\
\hline
\text{Divide by } 1 & 1 & -3 & -10 & 24 & 0 \\
\end{array}
$$

Remainder is zero; therefore $(x - 1)$, is a factor

$$
\begin{array}{c|cccc}
 & 1 & -3 & -10 & 24 \\
 &   & 2 & -2 & -24 \\
\hline
\text{Divide by } 2 & 1 & -1 & -12 & 0 \\
\end{array}
$$

Remainder is zero; therefore, $(x - 2)$ is a factor

Therefore, $x^4 - 4x^3 + 34x - 7x^2 - 24$
$= (x - 1)(x - 2)(x^2 - x - 12)$
$= (x - 1)(x - 2)(x - 4)(x + 3)$

16. $(x - 2)(x + 1)(x + 3)(x + 4)$

17. Factors of the constant term are $\pm 1, \pm 2, \pm 3, \pm 6$. (We may also have to try fractions whose denominators are factors of 6.)

$$
\begin{array}{c|cccc}
 & 6 & 1 & -11 & -6 \\
 &   & 6 & 7 & -4 \\
\hline
\text{Divide by } 1 & 6 & 7 & -4 & -10 \\
\end{array}
$$

Remainder is not zero; therefore, $(x - 1)$ is not a factor

$$
\begin{array}{c|cccc}
 & 6 & 1 & -11 & -6 \\
 &   & 12 & 26 & 30 \\
\hline
\text{Divide by } 2 & 6 & 13 & 15 & 24 \\
\end{array}
$$

Remainder is not zero; therefore, $(x - 2)$ is not a factor

$$
\begin{array}{c|cccc}
 & 6 & 1 & -11 & -6 \\
 &   & -6 & 5 & 6 \\
\hline
\text{Divide by } -1 & 6 & -5 & -6 & 0 \\
\end{array}
$$

Remainder is zero; therefore, $(x + 1)$ is a factor

Therefore, $6x^3 + x^2 - 11x - 6 = (x + 1)(6x^2 - 5x - 6)$
$= (x + 1)(2x - 3)(3x + 2)$

18. $(x - 3)(3x - 2)(2x + 1)$

Exercises 5.9 (page 217)

1. $(4e - 5)(3e + 7)$ **2.** $(6f + 7)(5f - 3)$

3. $6ac - 6bd + 6bc - 6ad$ Common factor
$= 6(ac - bd + bc - ad)$ Grouping
$= 6[a(c - d) + b(c - d)]$ Common factor
$= 6(a + b)(c - d)$

4. $(2c + d)(5y - 3z)$

5. $2xy^3 - 4xy^2 - 30xy$ Common factor
$= 2xy(y^2 - 2y - 15)$ Trinomial
$= 2xy(y + 3)(y - 5)$ Leading coefficient $= 1$

6. $3yz(z - 4)(z + 2)$

7. $3x^3 + 24h^3$ Common factor
$= 3(x^3 + 8h^3)$ Sum of 2 cubes
$= 3(x + 2h)(x^2 - 2xh + 4h^2)$

8. $2(3f - g)(9f^2 + 3fg + g^2)$

9. $9e^2 - 30ef + 25f^2$ Trinomial square
$= (3e - 5f)^2$

10. $(4m + 7p)^2$

11. $x^3 + 3x^2 - 4x - 12$ Grouping
$= x^2(x + 3) - 4(x + 3)$
$= (x + 3)(x^2 - 4)$ Difference of 2 squares
$= (x + 3)(x + 2)(x - 2)$

12. $(a - 2)(a + 3)(a - 3)$

13. $a^2 - b^2 - a + b$ Grouping
$= (a + b)(a - b) - 1(a - b)$
$= (a - b)(a + b - 1)$

14. $(x + y)(x - y - 1)$

15. Not factorable   **16.** Not factorable

17.

$x^3 - 8y^3 + x^2 - 4y^2$

$= (x - 2y)(x^2 + 2xy + 4y^2) + (x - 2y)(x + 2y)$
$= (x - 2y)([x^2 + 2xy + 4y^2] + [x + 2y])$
$= (x - 2y)(x^2 + 2xy + 4y^2 + x + 2y)$

18. $(a - b)(a^2 + ab + b^2 + a + b)$

19. $3x^3 + x^2 + 3x + 5$ Synthetic division

	3	1	3	5
		-3	2	-5
-1	3	-2	5	0

$(x + 1)(3x^2 - 2x + 5)$

20. $(x - 2)(5x^2 + 3x - 1)$

21. $4 + K^4$ Add and subtract $4K^2$
$4 + 4K^2 + K^4 - 4K^2$
$= (2 + K^2)^2 - (2K)^2$ Difference of two squares
$= [(2 + K^2) + 2K][(2 + K^2) - 2K]$
$= (K^2 + 2K + 2)(K^2 - 2K + 2)$

22. $(8 + 4a + a^2)(8 - 4a + a^2)$

23. Not factorable   **24.** Not factorable

25. $x^2 - 4xy + 4y^2 = (x - 2y)^2$
$-5x + 10y = -5(x - 2y)$
Therefore, $x^2 - 4xy + 4y^2 - 5x + 10y + 6$
$= (x - 2y)^2 - 5(x - 2y) + 6$
Let $a = (x - 2y)$
Then $(x - 2y)^2 - 5(x - 2y) + 6 = a^2 - 5a + 6$
$= (a - 2)(a - 3)$
But, since $a = (x - 2y)$,
$(a - 2)(a - 3) = ([x - 2y] - 2)([x - 2y] - 3)$
Therefore, $x^2 - 4xy + 4y^2 - 5x + 10y + 6$
$= (x - 2y - 2)(x - 2y - 3)$

26. $(x - 3y - 3)(x - 3y - 5)$

27. $x^2 - 6xy + 9y^2 - 25$ Group first three terms
$(x^2 - 6xy + 9y^2) - 25$ Trinomial perfect square
$(x - 3y)^2 - 25$ Difference of two squares
$(x - 3y - 5)(x - 3y + 5)$

28. $(a - 4b + 1)(a - 4b - 1)$

Exercises 5.10 (page 222)

1. $3x(x - 4) = 0$
$3x = 0 \mid x - 4 = 0$
$x = 0 \mid x = 4$

2. $\{0, -6\}$

3. $4x^2 - 12x = 0$
$4x(x - 3) = 0$
$4x = 0 \mid x - 3 = 0$
$x = 0 \mid x = 3$

4. $\{0, 3/2\}$

5. $x^2 - 4x = 12$
$x^2 - 4x - 12 = 0$
$(x - 6)(x + 2) = 0$
$x - 6 = 0 \mid x + 2 = 0$
$x = 6 \mid x = -2$

6. $\{-3, 5\}$

7. $2x^3 + x^2 = 3x$
$2x^3 + x^2 - 3x = 0$
$x(2x^2 + x - 3) = 0$
$x(x - 1)(2x + 3) = 0$
$x = 0 \mid x - 1 = 0 \mid 2x + 3 = 0$
$x = 1 \mid 2x = -3$
$2x = -3$
$x = \dfrac{-3}{2}$

8. $\{0, -5, 1/2\}$

9. $2x^2 + 7x - 15 = 0$
$(2x - 3)(x + 5) = 0$
$2x - 3 = 0 \mid x + 5 = 0$
$2x = 3 \mid x = -5$
$x = \dfrac{3}{2}$

10. $\{2/3, -5\}$

11. $4x^2 + 9 = 12x$
$4x^2 - 12x + 9 = 0$
$(2x - 3)(2x - 3) = 0$
$2x - 3 = 0$
$2x = 3$
$x = \dfrac{3}{2}$

12. $\{2/5\}$

13. $18x^3 - 21x^2 - 60x = 0$
$3x(6x^2 - 7x - 20) = 0$
$3x(2x - 5)(3x + 4) = 0$
$3x = 0 \mid 2x - 5 = 0 \mid 3x + 4 = 0$
$x = 0 \mid 2x = 5 \mid 3x = -4$
$x = \dfrac{5}{2} \mid x = -\dfrac{4}{3}$

14. $\left\{0, \dfrac{3}{5}, \dfrac{5}{3}\right\}$

15. $4x(2x - 1)(3x + 7) = 0$
$4x = 0 \mid 2x - 1 = 0 \mid 3x + 7 = 0$
$x = 0 \mid 2x = 1 \mid 3x = -7$
$x = \dfrac{1}{2} \mid x = -\dfrac{7}{3}$

16. $\left\{0, \dfrac{3}{4}, \dfrac{6}{7}\right\}$

17. $x^3 + 3x^2 - 4x - 12 = 0$
$x^2(x + 3) - 4(x + 3) = 0$
$(x + 3)(x^2 - 4) = 0$
$(x + 3)(x + 2)(x - 2) = 0$
$x + 3 = 0 \mid x + 2 = 0 \mid x - 2 = 0$
$x = -3 \mid x = -2 \mid x = 2$

18. $\{-3, 3, -1\}$

19.

$$\begin{array}{r|rrrr} & 1 & -2 & -13 & -10 \\ & & -1 & 3 & 10 \\ \hline -1 & 1 & -3 & -10 & \underline{|\ 0} \end{array}$$

$$(x + 1)(x^2 - 3x - 10) = 0$$
$$(x + 1)(x - 5)(x + 2) = 0$$

$$\begin{array}{c|c|c} x + 1 = 0 & x - 5 = 0 & x + 2 = 0 \\ x = -1 & x = 5 & x = -2 \end{array}$$

20. $\{-3, -2, 1\}$

21.

$$x^4 - 10x^2 + 9 = 0$$
$$\text{Then}\quad (x^2 - 9)(x^2 - 1) = 0$$
$$(x - 3)(x + 3)(x - 1)(x + 1) = 0$$

$$\begin{array}{c|c|c|c} x - 3 = 0 & x + 3 = 0 & x - 1 = 0 & x + 1 = 0 \\ x = 3 & x = -3 & x = 1 & x = -1 \end{array}$$

22. $\{2, -2, 3, -3\}$

23.

$$(x + 3)^3 = x^3 + 63$$
$$x^3 + 3x^2(3) + 3x(3^2) + 3^3 = x^3 + 63$$
$$x^3 + 9x^2 + 27x + 27 = x^3 + 63$$
$$9x^2 + 27x - 36 = 0$$
$$9(x^2 + 3x - 4) = 0$$
$$9(x + 4)(x - 1) = 0$$

$$\begin{array}{c|c|c} 9 \neq 0 & x + 4 = 0 & x - 1 = 0 \\ & x = -4 & x = 1 \end{array}$$

24. $\{3, -4\}$

25. $(x + 3)^4 = x^4 + 108x + 81$
$$x^4 + 12x^3 + 54x^2 + 108x + 81 = x^4 + 108x + 81$$
$$12x^3 + 54x^2 = 0$$
$$6x^2(2x + 9) = 0$$

$$\begin{array}{c|c} 6x^2 = 0 & 2x + 9 = 0 \\ x = 0 & x = \dfrac{-9}{2} \end{array}$$

26. $\{0, -3\}$

Exercises 5.11 (page 224)

Note: The checks for these exercises usually will not be shown.

1. Let $x =$ First even integer
$x + 2 =$ Second even integer
$x + 4 =$ Third even integer

$$x(x + 2) = 38 + (x + 4)$$
$$x^2 + 2x = 38 + x + 4$$
$$x^2 + x - 42 = 0$$
$$(x - 6)(x + 7) = 0$$

$$\begin{array}{c|c} x - 6 = 0 & x + 7 = 0 \\ x = 6 & x = -7 \leftarrow \text{Not an even integer} \end{array}$$

$x + 2 = 8$
$x + 4 = 10$

2. 7, 9, and 11

3. Let
$3x =$ Length
$2x =$ Width
$$A = lw$$
$$150 = (3x)(2x)$$
$$150 = 6x^2$$
$$25 = x^2$$
$$25 - x^2 = 0$$
$$(5 - x)(5 + x) = 0$$

$$\begin{array}{c|c} 5 - x = 0 & 5 + x = 0 \\ 5 = x & x = -5 \leftarrow \text{Not in the domain} \end{array}$$

$3x = 15 =$ Length
$2x = 10 =$ Width

4. Width is 12; length is 16

5. Let $x =$ Length of a side of cube
Then $x =$ Height of box
$x + 3 =$ Width of box
$4x =$ Length of box
$x^3 =$ Volume of cube
$$x(x + 3)(4x) = \text{Volume of box}$$
$$x(x + 3)(4x) = 8x^3$$
$$4x^3 + 12x^2 = 8x^3$$
$$12x^2 = 4x^3$$
$$0 = 4x^3 - 12x^2$$
$$0 = 4x^2(x - 3)$$

$$\begin{array}{c|c|c} 4 \neq 0 & x^2 = 0 & x - 3 = 0 \\ & x = 0 & x = 3 \\ & \uparrow & \end{array}$$

Not in the domain

Height of box is 3; width is 6; length is 12. Volume of cube is $3^3 = 27$.

6. Height of box is 5; width is 10; length is 15. Volume of cube is 125.

7. Let $x =$ Length
$x - 5 =$ Width
$$A = P + 46$$
$$x(x - 5) = 4x - 10 + 46$$
$$x^2 - 5x = 4x + 36$$
$$x^2 - 9x - 36 = 0$$
$$(x - 12)(x + 3) = 0$$

$$\begin{array}{c|c} x - 12 = 0 & x + 3 = 0 \\ x\ \ = 12 & x\ \ = -3 \\ & \uparrow \end{array}$$

Not in the domain
Length = 12 m
Width = 7 m

8. Length is 10 m; width is 3 m

9. Let $h =$ Height (altitude)
$7 + h =$ Base

$$\frac{1}{2}h(7 + h) = \text{Area} \qquad \frac{1}{2}h(7 + h) = 39$$
$$h(7 + h) = 78$$
$$h^2 + 7h - 78 = 0$$
$$(h + 13)(h - 6) = 0$$

$$\begin{array}{c|c} h + 13 = 0 & h - 6 = 0 \\ h = -13 \quad \text{Not in} & h = 6 \text{ cm} \quad \text{Height} \\ \text{the domain} & 7 + h = 13 \text{ cm} \quad \text{Base} \end{array}$$

10. Height is 8 m; base is 12 m

11. Let $x =$ Side of shorter square
$x + 6 =$ Side of longer square
Area of smaller square $= x^2$
Area of larger square $= (x + 6)^2$
$$9x^2 = (x + 6)^2$$
$$9x^2 = x^2 + 12x + 36$$
$$8x^2 - 12x - 36 = 0$$
$$4(2x^2 - 3x - 9) = 0$$
$$2x^2 - 3x - 9 = 0$$
$$(2x + 3)(x - 3) = 0$$

$$\begin{array}{c|c} 2x + 3 = 0 & x - 3 = 0 \\ x\ \ = -\dfrac{3}{2} & x\ \ = 3 \\ \uparrow & \end{array}$$

Not in the domain

Side of smaller square $= 3$ cm
Side of larger square $= 9$ cm

12. Side of larger square = 8 cm; side of smaller square = 4 cm

13. Let x = Length of side of smaller cube
$x + 3$ = Length of side of larger cube
x^3 = Volume of smaller cube
$(x + 3)^3$ = Volume of larger cube

$$(x + 3)^3 = 63 + x^3$$
$$x^3 + 9x^2 + 27x + 27 = 63 + x^3$$
$$9x^2 + 27x - 36 = 0$$
$$9(x^2 + 3x - 4) = 0$$
$$9(x + 4)(x - 1) = 0$$

$9 \neq 0$ | $x + 4 = 0$ | $x - 1 = 0$ Length of side
         $x = -4$ Not in | $x = 1$ cm   of smaller cube
              the domain | Length of side
                                 $x + 3 = 4$ cm   of larger cube

14. Length of side of smaller cube is 3 cm; length of side of larger cube is 4 cm

15. Let x = Width
(Length)(Width)(Depth) = Volume

$$(x + 3)(x)(2) = 80$$
$$(x + 3)(x) = 40$$
$$x^2 + 3x - 40 = 0$$
$$(x + 8)(x - 5) = 0$$

$x + 8 = 0$ | $x - 5 = 0$
   $x = -8$ | $x = 5$ in.   Width
     ↑ | $x + 3 = 8$ in.   Length

Not in the domain

a. The dimensions of the metal sheet are 9 in. by 12 in.
b. The dimensions of the box are: Depth = 2 in., Width = 5 in., Length = 8 in.

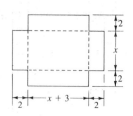

16a. 8 inches by 11 inches   **b.** 2 inches by 5 inches by 3 inches

17. Let x = Width of rectangular room
$2x - 3$ = Length of rectangular room

$$x(2x - 3) = 35$$
$$2x^2 - 3x = 35$$
$$2x^2 - 3x - 35 = 0$$
$$(2x + 7)(x - 5) = 0$$

$2x + 7 = 0$ | $x - 5 = 0$
     $x = -\dfrac{7}{2}$ | $x = 5$
       ↑

Not in the domain
   Width = 5 yd
   Length = 7 yd

18. 6 yards by 9 yards

Review Exercises 5.12 (page 228)

1. $3uv(5u - 1)$ **2.** $(3n + 1)(n + 5)$

3. $4xy(x - 2y + 1)$ **4.** $(5x + 1)(x + 2)$

5. $5u^2 + 17u - 12$
    $= (5u - 3)(u + 4)$ **6.** $(1 + 5x)(4 + x)$

7. $3uv(2u^2v - 3v^2 - 4)$ **8.** $15(a + 2b)(a - b)$

9. $9(9 - m^2) = 9(3 - m)(3 + m)$ **10.** Not factorable

11. $(2x + 3y)(5x - 8y)$ **12.** $(4x - 3y)(7x + 2y)$

13. $(2a)^3 - (3b)^3$
    $= (2a - 3b)[(2a)^2 + (2a)(3b) + (3b)^2]$
    $= (2a - 3b)(4a^2 + 6ab + 9b^2)$

14. $(4h - 5k)(16h^2 + 20hk + 25k^2)$

15. $(1)^2 + 2(1)(2y) + (2y)^2$ **16.** $(2 + 3x)^2$

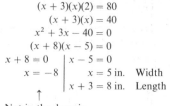

$$(1 + 2y)^2$$

17. $(x)^3 + (2y)^3$
    $= (x + 2y)[(x)^2 - (x)(2y) + (2y)^2]$
    $= (x + 2y)(x^2 - 2xy + 4y^2)$

18. $(3x + y)(9x^2 - 3xy + y^2)$

19. $x^2 - y^2 + x - y$
    $= (x + y)(x - y) + 1(x - y)$
    $= (x - y)(x + y + 1)$

20. $(x - y)(x + y - 1)$

21.
$$
\begin{array}{r|rrrr}
 & 1 & -2 & -4 & 3 \\
 &   & 3 & 3 & -3 \\
\hline
3 & 1 & 1 & -1 & \underline{0}
\end{array}
$$
$(x - 3)(x^2 + x - 1)$

22. Not factorable

23. $2(4a^2 - 4ab + b^2)$
    $2[(2a)^2 - 2(2a)(b) + (b)^2]$
                     $2(2a - b)^2$

24. $2(3h - k)^2$

25. $x^2(x - 4) - 4(x - 4)$
    $= (x - 4)(x^2 - 4)$
    $= (x - 4)(x + 2)(x - 2)$

26. $(3x^2 + 2x + 2)(3x^2 - 2x + 2)$

27.
$$
\begin{array}{r|rrrr}
 & 1 & -5 & 8 & -4 \\
 &   & 2 & -6 & 4 \\
\hline
2 & 1 & -3 & 2 & \underline{0}
\end{array}
$$
$(x - 2)(x^2 - 3x + 2) = (x - 2)(x - 2)(x - 1)$
                            $= (x - 2)^2(x - 1)$

28. $(x - 2)(x + 3)(x - 3)$

29. $4x^4 - 5x^2 + 25$
Add and subtract $25x^2$
$$4x^4 - 5x^2 + 25 + 25x^2 - 25x^2$$
$$4x^4 + 20x^2 + 25 - 25x^2$$
$$(2x^2 + 5)^2 - 25x^2$$
$$(2x^2 + 5 - 5x)(2x^2 + 5 + 5x)$$
$$(2x^2 - 5x + 5)(2x^2 + 5x + 5)$$

30. $(x + 4 + 5y)(x + 4 - 5y)$

31. Let $a = (2x + 3y)$
Then
$$(2x + 3y)^2 + (2x + 3y) - 6 = a^2 + a - 6$$
$$a^2 + a - 6 = (a + 3)(a - 2)$$
But, since $a = (2x + 3y)$,
$$(a + 3)(a - 2) = ([2x + 3y] + 3)([2x + 3y] - 2)$$
Therefore,
$$(2x + 3y)^2 + (2x + 3y) - 6 = (2x + 3y + 3)(2x + 3y - 2)$$

32. $(a + 3b - 3)(a + 3b - 4)$

33. $x^2 + 4xy + 4y^2 = (x + 2y)^2$; $-5x - 10y = -5(x + y)$
Therefore,
$$x^2 + 4xy + 4y^2 - 5x - 10y + 6 = (x + 2y)^2 - 5(x + 2y) + 6$$
Let $a = (x + 2y)$
Then $(x + 2y)^2 - 5(x + 2y) + 6 = a^2 - 5a + 6$
$$a^2 - 5a + 6 = (a - 2)(a - 3)$$
But, since $a = (x + 2y)$,
$$(a - 2)(a - 3) = ([x + 2y] - 2)([x + 2y] - 3)$$
Therefore,
$$x^2 + 4xy + 4y^2 - 5x - 10y + 6 = (x + 2y - 2)(x + 2y - 3)$$

34. $\{1, 7/5\}$ **35.**
$$x^2 = 18 + 3x$$
$$x^2 - 3x - 18 = 0$$
$$(x - 6)(x + 3) = 0$$
$x - 6 = 0$ | $x + 3 = 0$
   $x = 6$ | $x = -3$

36. $\{0, 36\}$

ANSWERS

37.
$$6x^2 = 13x + 5$$
$$6x^2 - 13x - 5 = 0$$
$$(3x + 1)(2x - 5) = 0$$

$$3x + 1 = 0 \quad | \quad 2x - 5 = 0$$
$$x = -\frac{1}{3} \quad \Big| \quad x = \frac{5}{2}$$

38. $\{5/3. 9/4\}$

39. $x^3 + 3x^2 - 18x - 40 = 0$

$$
\begin{array}{r|rrrr}
 & 1 & 3 & -18 & -40 \\
 & & 4 & 28 & 40 \\
\hline
4 & 1 & 7 & 10 & \underline{}\ 0
\end{array}
$$

$$(x - 4)(x^2 + 7x + 10) = 0$$
$$(x - 4)(x + 2)(x + 5) = 0$$

$$x - 4 = 0 \quad | \quad x + 2 = 0 \quad | \quad x + 5 = 0$$
$$x = 4 \quad \Big| \quad x = -2 \quad \Big| \quad x = -5$$

40. $\{2, 3, -3\}$

41.
$$(x + 3)^3 = x^3 + 27$$
$$x^3 + 3x^2(3) + 3x(3^2) + 3^3 = x^3 + 27$$
$$x^3 + 9x^2 + 27x + 27 = x^3 + 27$$
$$9x^2 + 27x = 0$$
$$9x(x + 3) = 0$$

$$9 \neq 0 \quad | \quad x = 0 \quad x + 3 = 0$$
$$x = -3$$

42. $\{-2, -2/5\}$

43. $(x + 3)^4 = x^4 + 12x^3 + 81$
$$x^4 + 12x^3 + 54x^2 + 108x + 81 = x^4 + 12x^3 + 81$$
$$54x^2 + 108x = 0$$
$$54x(x + 2) = 0$$

$$54 \neq 0 \quad | \quad x = 0 \quad | \quad x + 2 = 0$$
$$x = -2$$

44. $\{0, -4/3\}$

45. Let $x =$ First odd integer
$x + 2 =$ Second odd integer
$x + 4 =$ Third odd integer
$$x(x + 4) = 5 + 8(x + 2)$$
$$x^2 + 4x = 5 + 8x + 16$$
$$x^2 - 4x - 21 = 0$$
$$(x - 7)(x + 3) = 0$$

$$x - 7 = 0 \quad | \quad x + 3 = 0$$
$$x = 7 \quad \Big| \quad x = -3$$
$$x + 2 = 9 \quad \Big| \quad x + 2 = -1$$
$$x + 4 = 11 \quad \Big| \quad x + 4 = 1$$

Therefore, one set of such numbers is 7, 9, and 11; another is -3, -1, and 1.

46. Height is 8, base is 10

47. Let $5x =$ Length
$3x =$ Width
$$A = lw$$
$$240 = 5x(3x)$$
$$240 = 15x^2$$
$$0 = 15x^2 - 240$$
$$= 15(x^2 - 16)$$
$$0 = x^2 - 16$$
$$0 = (x - 4)(x + 4)$$

$$x - 4 = 0 \quad | \quad x + 4 = 0$$
$$x = 4 \quad \Big| \quad x = -4 \quad \text{Not in the domain}$$

Length $= 5x = 20$
Width $= 3x = 12$

48. 6 by 13

49. Let $x =$ Length of side of smaller cube
$x + 4 =$ Length of side of larger cube
$x^3 =$ Volume of smaller cube
$(x + 4)^3 =$ Volume of larger cube
$$(x + 4)^3 = 316 + x^3$$
$$x^3 + 12x^2 + 48x + 64 = 316 + x^3$$
$$12x^2 + 48x - 252 = 0$$
$$12(x^2 + 4x - 21) = 0$$
$$12(x + 7)(x - 3) = 0$$

$$12 \neq 0 \quad \Big| \quad x + 7 = 0 \quad \Big| \quad x - 3 = 0$$
$$\qquad\qquad x = -7 \quad \Big| \quad x = 3 \text{ cm} \quad \text{Length of side of smaller cube}$$
$$\qquad \text{Not in the} \quad \Big| \quad x + 4 = 7 \text{ cm} \quad \text{Length of side of larger cube}$$
$$\qquad \text{domain}$$

50. Length of side of smaller square is 1 cm; length of side of larger square is 4 cm

Chapter 5 Diagnostic Test (page 233)

Following each problem number is the textbook section number (in parentheses) where that kind of problem is discussed.

1. (5.1, 5.3) $\quad 4x - 16x^3 = 4x(1 - 4x^2) = 4x(1 - 2x)(1 + 2x)$

2. (5.1) $\quad 43 + 7x^2 + 6$
$7x^2 + 49$
$7(x^2 + 7)$

3. (5.4B) $\quad 7x^2 + 23x + 6$

$$7 = 7 \cdot 1 \quad (7x + 2)(x + 3) \quad 6 = 1 \cdot 6$$
$$= 2 \cdot 3$$

$$
\begin{array}{c}
2x \\
\underline{21x} \\
23x
\end{array}
$$

4. (5.3) $\quad x^2 + 81$ is a sum of two squares and cannot be factored

5. (5.1) $\quad 2x^3 + 4x^2 + 16x = 2x(x^2 + 2x + 8)$

6. (5.4B) $\quad 6x^2 - 5x - 6$

$$6 = 2 \cdot 3 \quad (3x + 2)(2x - 3) \quad 6 = 2 \cdot 3$$

$$
\begin{array}{c}
+4x \\
\underline{-9x} \\
-5x
\end{array}
$$

7. (5.6) $\quad y^3 - 1 = (y)^3 - (1)^3 = (y - 1)(y^2 + y + 1)$

8. (5.2) $\quad 3ac + 6bc - 5ad - 10bd$
$$= 3c(a + 2b) - 5d(a + 2b)$$
$$= (a + 2b)(3c - 5d)$$

9. (5.7) $\quad x^4 + 5x^2 + 9 \qquad\qquad$ Factor by completing the square
$$\underline{\quad + \ x^2 \qquad - x^2} \qquad \text{Add and subtract } x^2$$
$$x^4 + 6x^2 + 9 - x^2$$

$$(x^2 + 3)^2 - (x)^2 \qquad \text{Difference of two squares}$$
$$[(x^2 + 3) + x][(x^2 + 3) - x] \text{ or } [x^2 + x + 3][x^2 - x + 3]$$

10. (5.8) $\qquad x^3 - 8x + 3 \qquad$ Use synthetic division
$$1x^3 + 0x^2 - 8x + 3$$

$$
\begin{array}{r|rrrr}
 & 1 & 0 & -8 & 3 \\
 & & -3 & 9 & -3 \\
\hline
-3 & 1 & -3 & 1 & \underline{}\ 0
\end{array}
$$

Remainder is zero; therefore $(x + 3)$ is a factor

$$x^2 - 3x + 1 \qquad \text{Quotient is another factor}$$

Therefore, $x^3 - 8x + 3 = (x + 3)(x^2 - 3x + 1)$

11. (5.3) $\quad 4x^2 + 4x + 1 - y^2 \quad$ Factor by grouping
$$= (2x + 1)^2 - y^2$$
$$= ([2x + 1] + y)([2x + 1] - y)$$
$$= (2x + 1 + y)(2x + 1 - y)$$

673

12. (5.10) $2x^2 + x - 15 = 0$
$(x + 3)(2x - 5) = 0$

$x + 3 = 0$	$2x - 5 = 0$
$x = -3$	$x = \dfrac{5}{2}$

$\{-3, 5/2\}$

13. (5.10)
$8y^2 = 4y$
$8y^2 - 4y = 0$
$4y(2y - 1) = 0$

$4 \neq 0$	$y = 0$	$2y - 1 = 0$
		$y = 1/2$

$\{0, 1/2\}$

14. (5.10)
$6x^2 - 15 = 27x$
$6x^2 - 27x - 15 = 0$
$3(2x^2 - 9x - 5) = 0$
$3(2x + 1)(x - 5) = 0$

$3 \neq 0$	$2x + 1 = 0$	$x - 5 = 0$
	$x = -\dfrac{1}{2}$	$x = 5$

$\{-1/2, 5\}$

15. (5.10) $(x + 1)^3 = x^3 + 1$
$x^3 + 3x^2 + 3x + 1 = x^3 + 1$
$3x^2 + 3x = 0$
$3x(x + 1) = 0$

$3 \neq 0$	$x = 0$	$x + 1 = 0$
		$x = -1$

$\{0, -1\}$

16. (5.11)   Let x = First even integer
$x + 2$ = Second even integer
$x + 4$ = Third even integer
$x(x + 2) = 68 + (x + 4)$
$x^2 + 2x = 68 + x + 4$
$x^2 + x - 72 = 0$
$(x + 9)(x - 8) = 0$

$x + 9 = 0$	$x - 8 = 0$
$x = -9$ Not an even	$x = 8$
integer	$x + 2 = 10$
	$x + 4 = 12$

17. (5.11)   Let x = Height
$x + 8$ = Base
$\dfrac{1}{2}x(x + 8)$ = Area
$\dfrac{1}{2}x(x + 8) = 64$
$x(x + 8) = 128$
$x^2 + 8x - 128 = 0$
$(x + 16)(x - 8) = 0$

$x + 16 = 0$	$x - 8 = 0$	
$x = -16$ Not in the	$x = 8$ cm	Height
domain	$x + 8 = 16$ cm	Base

Cumulative Review Exercises: Chapters 1–5 (page 234)

1. $18 \div 2\sqrt{9} - 4^2 \cdot 3$
$= 18 \div 2 \cdot 3 - 16 \cdot 3$
$= 9 \cdot 3 - 16 \cdot 3$
$= 27 - 48 = -21$

2. 32

3. $2(x - 3) - 5 = 6 - 3(x + 4)$
$2x - 6 - 5 = 6 - 3x - 12$
$2x - 11 = -3x - 6$
$5x = 5$
$x = 1$

4. $-1 < x < 3$

5. $|2x - 3| \geq 7$
$2x - 3 \geq 7$ or $2x - 3 \leq -7$
$2x \geq 10$ or $2x \leq -4$
$x \geq 5$ or $x \leq -2$
$\{x \,|\, x \geq 5$ or $x \leq -2\}$

6. All are real numbers

7. $2x^2 = 9x + 5$
$2x^2 - 9x - 5 = 0$
$(2x + 1)(x - 5) = 0$
$x = -\dfrac{1}{2}$ or $x = 5$

8. $3(x + 3)(x^2 - 3x + 9)$

9. Using synthetic division:

```
          1    6    6    5
              -5   -5   -5
      -5 | 1    1    1 |  0
```

$x^3 + 6x^2 + 6x + 5 = (x + 5)(x^2 + x + 1)$

10. $6x^2 + x + 13$

11. $(a - 4)(a^2 - 2a + 5)$
$a^3 - 2a^2 + 5a - 4a^2 + 8a - 20$
$a^3 - 6a^2 + 13a - 20$

12. $9x^2 + 30x + 25$

13. $(2x - 1)^5$
$= (2x)^5 - 5(2x)^4(1) + \dfrac{5 \cdot 4}{1 \cdot 2}(2x)^3(1^2)$
$- \dfrac{5 \cdot 4}{1 \cdot 2}(2x)^2(1^3) + 5(2x)(1^4) - (1)^5$
$= 32x^5 - 80x^4 + 80x^3 - 40x^2 + 10x - 1$

14. $x^2 - 4x + 2 + \dfrac{4}{x + 2}$

15. Let x = Number of qt of antifreeze added
$.20(10) + 1.00(x) = 0.50(10 + x)$
$20(10) + 100(x) = 50(10 + x)$
$200 + 100x = 500 + 50x$
$50x = 300$
$x = 6$ qt of antifreeze

16. 6 miles

Exercises 6.1 (page 240)

1. All real numbers except -4 **2.** All real numbers except 5

3. No number can make the denominator zero. The domain is the set of all real numbers.

4. All real numbers except 0

5. All real numbers except 5 and -5

6. All real numbers except 3 and -2

7. Since $c^4 - 13c^2 + 36 = (c^2 - 4)(c^2 - 9)$
$= (c + 2)(c - 2)(c + 3)(c - 3)$,
$c = -2, c = 2, c = -3$, and $c = 3$ must be excluded. Therefore, the domain is the set of all real numbers except $-2, 2, -3$, and 3.

8. All real numbers except $-3, 3$, and 5

9. Yes; $\dfrac{1}{2y} = \dfrac{3 \div 3}{6y \div 3}$ **10.** Yes   **11.** No   **12.** No

13. Yes   **14.** Yes

15. $-\dfrac{+5}{+8} = \dfrac{+}{} \dfrac{+5}{-8}$. The missing term is -8.   **16.** 6

17. $+\dfrac{-x}{+5} = +\dfrac{+x}{-5}$. The missing term is -5 **18.** -6

19. $+\dfrac{+(8-y)}{+(4y-7)} = +\dfrac{-(8-y)}{-(4y-7)} = \dfrac{y-8}{7-4y}$ The missing term is $7-4y$

20. $2-w$

21. $+\dfrac{+(u-v)}{+(a-b)} = +\dfrac{-(u-v)}{-(a-b)} = \dfrac{v-u}{b-a}$ The missing term is $b-a$

22. $x-2$

23. $+\dfrac{+(a-b)}{[+(3a+2b)][+(a-5b)]} = +\dfrac{-(a-b)}{[+(3a+2b)][-(a-5b)]}$
$= \dfrac{b-a}{(3a+2b)(5b-a)}$ The missing term is $b-a$

24. $f-2e$

Exercises 6.2 (page 244)

1. $3m^2$ **2.** $-\dfrac{k^3}{4}$ **3.** $-\dfrac{3a^3c}{7b^2}$ **4.** $\dfrac{5f}{2e^2g^2}$

5. $\dfrac{8x(5-x)}{5x(x+2)} = \dfrac{8(5-x)}{5(x+2)}$ **6.** $\dfrac{2y^2}{3}$

7. Cannot be reduced; $\dfrac{c^2-4}{4}$ or $\dfrac{c^2}{4}-1$

8. Cannot be reduced; $\dfrac{9+d^2}{9}$ or $1+\dfrac{d^2}{9}$

9. $\dfrac{\cancel{8}wx^3(3w-2x)}{\cancel{6}w^2x(3w-2x)} = \dfrac{4x^2}{3w}$ **10.** $\dfrac{3c^3}{2d^2}$

11. $\dfrac{(x+4)(x-4)}{(x-4)(x-5)} = \dfrac{x+4}{x-5}$ **12.** $\dfrac{x-5}{x-3}$

13. $\dfrac{(2x+y)(x-y)}{(y-3x)(y-x)} = \dfrac{(2x+y)(-1)(y-x)}{(y-3x)(y-x)} = -\dfrac{2x+y}{y-3x}$ or $\dfrac{2x+y}{3x-y}$

14. $\dfrac{2k+5h}{4k-3h}$

15. $\dfrac{(x-3)(2x+3)}{(4-x)(3-x)} = \dfrac{(-1)(3-x)(2x+3)}{(4-x)(3-x)} = -\dfrac{2x+3}{4-x}$ or $\dfrac{2x+3}{x-4}$

16. $\dfrac{3+2y}{1-4y}$

17. $\dfrac{(2y-3x)(y+2x)}{(3x-2y)(x+y)} = \dfrac{-(3x-2y)(y+2x)}{(3x-2y)(x+y)} = -\dfrac{2x+y}{x+y}$

18. $-\dfrac{3x+2y}{2x+3y}$

19. $\dfrac{(2x+1)(x-5)}{(2x+3)(x+1)}$ Not reducible   **20.** Not reducible

21. $\dfrac{(a-1)(a^2+a+1)}{(1-a)(1+a)} = \dfrac{(a-1)(a^2+a+1)}{(-1)(a-1)(a+1)} = -\dfrac{a^2+a+1}{a+1}$

22. $\dfrac{x^2-xy+y^2}{y-x}$ **23.** $\dfrac{x^2+4}{(x+2)^2}$ Not reducible   **24.** Not reducible

25. $\dfrac{(2x^2+2xy+y^2)(2x^2-2xy+y^2)}{3(2x^2+2xy+y^2)} = \dfrac{2x^2-2xy+y^2}{3}$
$= \dfrac{1}{3}(2x^2-2xy+y^2)$

26. $\dfrac{1}{2}(x^2+xy+y^2)$

27. $\dfrac{x^3+8}{x^3-3x^2+6x-4} = \dfrac{(x+2)(x^2-2x+4)}{(x-1)(x^2-2x+4)} = \dfrac{x+2}{x-1}$

Factor by synthetic division

28. $\dfrac{x+1}{x-3}$

29. $\dfrac{13x^3y^2}{13x^2y^2} + \dfrac{-26xy^3}{13x^2y^2} + \dfrac{39xy}{13x^2y^2} = x - \dfrac{2y}{x} + \dfrac{3}{xy}$ or $\dfrac{x^2y-2y^2+3}{xy}$

30. $3n - 5m - \dfrac{2}{mn}$ or $\dfrac{3mn^2-5m^2n-2}{mn}$

31. $\dfrac{6a^2bc^2}{6abc} + \dfrac{-4ab^2c^2}{6abc} + \dfrac{12bc}{6abc} = ac - \dfrac{2bc}{3} + \dfrac{2}{a}$ or $\dfrac{3a^2c-2abc+6}{3a}$

32. $2a^2b - a - \dfrac{5}{2b}$ or $\dfrac{4a^2b^2-2ab-5}{2b}$

Exercises 6.3 (page 248)

1. $\dfrac{27x^4y^3}{22x^5yz} \cdot \dfrac{55x^2z^2}{9y^3z} = \dfrac{15x}{2y}$ **2.** $\dfrac{5c}{18a^2}$

3. $\dfrac{mn^3}{18n^2} \div \dfrac{5m^4}{24m^3n} = \dfrac{mn^3}{18n^2} \cdot \dfrac{24m^3n}{5m^4} = \dfrac{4n^2}{15}$ **4.** $-\dfrac{36}{5h^2}$

5. $\dfrac{3u(5-2u)}{10u^2} \cdot \dfrac{5u^3}{7(5-2u)} = \dfrac{9u^2}{14}$ **6.** $-\dfrac{4v}{15}$

7. $\dfrac{-15c^4}{40c^3-24c^2} \div \dfrac{35c}{35c^2-21c} = \dfrac{-15c^4}{8c^2(5c-3)} \cdot \dfrac{7c(5c-3)}{35c} = -\dfrac{3c^2}{8}$

8. 20

9. $\dfrac{d^2e^2-d^3e}{12e^2d} \div \dfrac{d^2e^2-de^3}{3e^2d+3e^3} = \dfrac{d^2e(e-d)}{12e^2d} \cdot \dfrac{3e^2(d+e)}{de^2(d-e)} = -\dfrac{d+e}{4e}$

10. $-\dfrac{15(3m+n)}{8m}$ **11.** $\dfrac{(w-4)(w+2)}{6(w-4)} \cdot \dfrac{5w^2}{(w+2)(w-5)} = \dfrac{5w^2}{6(w-5)}$

12. $\dfrac{3k}{8}$

13. $\dfrac{4a^2+8ab+4b^2}{a^2-b^2} \div \dfrac{6ab+6b^2}{b-a} = \dfrac{4(a+b)(a+b)}{(a+b)(a-b)} \cdot \dfrac{(b-a)}{6b(a+b)}$
$= -\dfrac{2}{3b}$

14. $-\dfrac{1}{u}$

15. $\dfrac{4-2a}{2a+2} \div \dfrac{2a^3-16}{a^2+2a+1} = \dfrac{2(2-a)}{2(a+1)} \cdot \dfrac{(a+1)(a+1)}{2(a-2)(a^2+2a+4)}$
$= \dfrac{(2-a)(a+1)}{2(a-2)(a^2+2a+4)}$
$= \dfrac{(-1)(a-2)(a+1)}{2(a-2)(a^2+2a+4)}$
$= -\dfrac{a+1}{2(a^2+2a+4)}$

16. $-\dfrac{6}{a^2 - 3a + 9}$

17. $\dfrac{x^3 + y^3}{2x - 2y} \div \dfrac{x^2 - xy + y^2}{x^2 - y^2} = \dfrac{(x+y)(x^2 - xy + y^2)}{2(x-y)} \cdot \dfrac{(x+y)(x-y)}{(x^2 - xy + y^2)}$

$= \dfrac{(x+y)^2}{2}$

18. $\dfrac{(x-y)^2}{3}$ 19. $\dfrac{(e+5f)(e+5f)}{(e+5f)(e-5f)} \cdot \dfrac{3(e-f)}{(f-e)} \cdot \dfrac{(5f-e)}{(e+5f)} = 3$

20. 1 21. $\dfrac{(x+y)(x+y+1)}{(x-y)(x-y-1)} \cdot \dfrac{(x-y)(x-y)}{(x+y)(x+y)} \cdot \dfrac{x+y}{x-y} = \dfrac{x+y+1}{x-y-1}$

22. $\dfrac{c-d}{a+b}$

Factored by completing the square

23. $\dfrac{(m^2 + 2m + 2)(m^2 - 2m + 2)}{(m+2)(m-2)} \cdot \dfrac{m+2}{m^2 - 2m + 2} = \dfrac{m^2 + 2m + 2}{m-2}$

24. $\dfrac{R^2 + R + 3}{R + 3}$

Exercises 6.4 (page 250)

1. (1) $5^2 \cdot a^3; 3 \cdot 5 \cdot a$ Denominators in factored form 2. $36b^4$
 (2) $3, 5, a$ All the different bases
 (3) $3^1, 5^2, a^3$ Highest power of each base
 (4) LCD $= 3^1 \cdot 5^2 \cdot a^3 = 75a^3$

3. (1) $2^2 \cdot 3 \cdot 5 \cdot h \cdot k^3; 2 \cdot 3^2 \cdot 5 \cdot h^2 \cdot k^4$
 (2) $2, 3, 5, h, k$
 (3) $2^2, 3^2, 5, h^2, k^4$
 (4) LCD $= 2^2 \cdot 3^2 \cdot 5 \cdot h^2 \cdot k^4 = 180h^2k^4$

4. $294x^3y^2$ (or $147x^3y^2$ if fractions were reduced first)

5. (1) $2(w-5); 2^2w$ 6. $8m^2(m-6)$
 (2) $2, w, (w-5)$
 (3) $2^2, w^1, (w-5)^1$
 (4) LCD $= 2^2 \cdot w^1 \cdot (w-5)^1 = 4w(w-5)$

7. (1) $(3b+c)(3b-c); (3b-c)^2$ 8. $(2e+5f)(2e-5f)^2$
 (2) $(3b+c), (3b-c)$
 (3) $(3b+c)^1, (3b-c)^2$
 (4) LCD $= (3b+c)(3b-c)^2$

9. (1) $2 \cdot g^3; (g-3)^2; 2^2 \cdot g \cdot (g-3)$ (The LCD is $2g^3(g-3)$
 (2) $2, g, (g-3)$ if fractions were
 (3) $2^2, g^3, (g-3)^2$ reduced first)
 (4) LCD $= 2^2 \cdot g^3 \cdot (g-3)^2 = 4g^3(g-3)^2$

10. $9y^2(y-6)^2$ (LCD is $9y^2(y-6)$ if fractions were reduced first)

11. (1) $2 \cdot (x-4)^2; (x-4) \cdot (x+5)$ 12. $5(k+7)(k-3)^2$
 (2) $2, (x-4), (x+5)$
 (3) $2^1, (x-4)^2, (x+5)^1$
 (4) LCD $= 2(x-4)^2(x+5)$

13. (1) $3 \cdot e^2; (e+3)(e-3); 2^2(e-3)$ 14. $24u^3(u+3)(u-8)$
 (2) $2, 3, e, (e+3)(e-3)$
 (3) $2^2, 3^1, e^2, (e+3)^1, (e-3)^1$
 (4) LCD $= 2^2 \cdot 3^1 \cdot e^2 \cdot (e+3)(e-3) = 12e^2(e+3)(e-3)$

15. (1) $2^2 \cdot 3 \cdot x^2 \cdot (x+2); (x-2)^2; (x+2)(x-2)$
 (2) $2, 3, x, (x+2), (x-2)$
 (3) $2^2, 3^1, x^2, (x+2)^1, (x-2)^2$
 (4) LCD $= 2^2 \cdot 3 \cdot x^2 \cdot (x+2) \cdot (x-2)^2 = 12x^2(x+2)(x-2)^2$

16. $8y(y+3)^2(y-3)$

Exercises 6.5 (page 256)

1. $\dfrac{5a}{a+2} + \dfrac{10}{a+2} = \dfrac{5a+10}{a+2} = \dfrac{5(a+2)}{(a+2)} = 5$ 2. 6

3. $\dfrac{8m}{2m-3n} - \dfrac{12n}{2m-3n} = \dfrac{8m-12n}{2m-3n} = \dfrac{4(2m-3n)}{(2m-3n)} = 4$ 4. 7

5. $\dfrac{-15w}{1-5w} - \dfrac{3}{5w-1} = \dfrac{15w}{5w-1} - \dfrac{3}{5w-1} = \dfrac{15w-3}{5w-1} = \dfrac{3(5w-1)}{(5w-1)} = 3$

6. 5 7. $\dfrac{7z}{8z-4} + \dfrac{6-5z}{4-8z} = \dfrac{7z}{8z-4} + \dfrac{5z-6}{8z-4} = \dfrac{7z+5z-6}{8z-4}$

$= \dfrac{12z-6}{8z-4} = \dfrac{6(2z-1)}{4(2z-1)} = \dfrac{3}{2}$

8. 2 9. $\dfrac{12x-31}{12x-28} - \dfrac{18x-39}{28-12x} = \dfrac{12x-31}{12x-28} + \dfrac{18x-39}{12x-28}$ 10. 2

$= \dfrac{30x-70}{12x-28} = \dfrac{10(3x-7)}{4(3x-7)} = \dfrac{5}{2}$

11. LCD $= 75a^3$ $\dfrac{9}{25a^3} + \dfrac{7}{15a} = \dfrac{9}{25a^3} \cdot \dfrac{3}{3} + \dfrac{7}{15a} \cdot \dfrac{5a^2}{5a^2}$ 12. $\dfrac{26b^2}{36}$

$= \dfrac{27}{75a^3} + \dfrac{35a^2}{75a^3} = \dfrac{27 + 35a^2}{75a^3}$

13. LCD $= 180h^2k^4$ $\dfrac{49}{60h^2k^2} - \dfrac{71}{90hk^4} = \dfrac{49}{60h^2k^2} \cdot \dfrac{3k^2}{3k^2} - \dfrac{71}{90hk^4} \cdot \dfrac{2h}{2h}$

$= \dfrac{147k^2}{180h^2k^4} - \dfrac{142h}{180h^2k^4}$

$= \dfrac{147k^2 - 142h}{180h^2k^4}$

14. $\dfrac{154x - 135y}{147x^3y^2}$ 15. LCD $= t(t-4)$ $\dfrac{5}{t} + \dfrac{2t}{t-4} = \dfrac{5}{t} \cdot \dfrac{t-4}{t-4} + \dfrac{2t}{t-4}$

$= \dfrac{5t-20}{t(t-4)} + \dfrac{2t^2}{t(t-4)}$

$= \dfrac{2t^2 + 5t - 20}{t(t-4)}$

16. $\dfrac{6r^2 - 11r + 88}{r(r-8)}$

17. $\dfrac{3k}{8k-4} - \dfrac{7}{6k} = \dfrac{3k}{4(2k-1)} - \dfrac{1}{6k}$ LCD $= 12k(2k-1)$

$\dfrac{9k^2}{12k(2k-1)} - \dfrac{7 \cdot 2(2k-1)}{12k(2k-1)} = \dfrac{9k^2}{12k(2k-1)} - \dfrac{28k-14}{12k(2k-1)}$

$= \dfrac{9k^2 - 28k + 14}{12k(2k-1)}$

18. $\dfrac{2(3j^2 + 3j + 2)}{9j(3j+2)}$

19. LCD $= x(x-3)$

$\dfrac{x^2}{1} - \dfrac{3}{x} + \dfrac{5}{x-3} = \dfrac{x^2\,(x)(x-3)}{1\,(x)(x-3)} - \dfrac{-3\,(x-3)}{x\,(x-3)} + \dfrac{5\,(x)}{(x-3)\,(x)}$

$= \dfrac{x^4 - 3x^3 - 3x + 9 + 5x}{x(x-3)}$

$= \dfrac{x^4 - 3x^3 + 2x + 9}{x(x-3)}$

20. $\dfrac{y^4 - 5y^3 + y + 10}{y(y - 5)}$

21. LCD $= b(2a - 3b)$ $\dfrac{2a + 3b}{b} + \dfrac{b}{2a - 3b}$ **22.** $\dfrac{9x^2 - 24y^2}{y(3y + 5)}$
$= \dfrac{(2a + 3b)(2a - 3b)}{b(2a - 3b)} + \dfrac{b^2}{b(2a - 3b)} = \dfrac{4a^2 - 9b^2}{b(2a - 3b)} + \dfrac{b^2}{b(2a - 3b)}$
$\qquad\qquad\qquad\qquad\qquad\qquad = \dfrac{4a^2 - 8b^2}{b(2a - 3b)} = \dfrac{4(a^2 - 2b^2)}{b(2a - 3b)}$

23. LCD $= (a + 3)(a - 1)$
$\dfrac{2\ (a - 1)}{(a + 3)(a - 1)} + \dfrac{-4\ (a + 3)}{(a - 1)(a + 3)} = \dfrac{2a - 2 - 4a - 12}{(a + 3)(a - 1)}$
$\qquad\qquad\qquad\qquad\qquad = \dfrac{-2a - 14}{(a + 3)(a - 1)}$ or $\dfrac{14 + 2a}{(3 + a)(1 - a)}$

24. $\dfrac{2b + 26}{(b - 2)(b + 4)}$

25. LCD $= (x - 3)(x - 2)$
$\dfrac{(x + 2)(x - 2)}{(x - 3)(x - 2)} + \dfrac{-(x + 3)(x - 3)}{(x - 2)(x - 3)}$
$= \dfrac{x^2 - 4}{(x - 3)(x - 2)} + \dfrac{-(x^2 - 9)}{(x - 3)(x - 2)} = \dfrac{x^2 - 4 - x^2 + 9}{(x - 3)(x - 2)}$
$= \dfrac{5}{(x - 3)(x - 2)}$

26. $\dfrac{20}{(x + 6)(x + 4)}$

27. $\dfrac{\overset{1}{(x + 2)}}{(x - 1)(x + 2)} + \dfrac{3}{(x + 1)(x - 1)}$ LCD $= (x + 1)(x - 1)$

$\dfrac{1\ (x + 1)}{(x - 1)(x + 1)} + \dfrac{3}{(x + 1)(x - 1)} = \dfrac{x + 1 + 3}{(x + 1)(x - 1)} = \dfrac{x + 4}{x^2 - 1}$

28. $\dfrac{x + 7}{(x + 2)(x - 2)}$

29. LCD $= (x - 3)(x + 3)$
$\dfrac{2x\ (x + 3)}{(x - 3)(x + 3)} + \dfrac{-2x\ (x - 3)}{(x + 3)(x - 3)} + \dfrac{36}{(x + 3)(x - 3)}$
$\qquad = \dfrac{2x^2 + 6x - 2x^2 + 6x + 36}{(x - 3)(x + 3)} = \dfrac{12x + 36}{(x - 3)(x + 3)}$
$\qquad = \dfrac{12(x + 3)}{(x - 3)(x + 3)} = \dfrac{12}{x - 3}$

30. $\dfrac{12}{6 - m}$

31. $\dfrac{x - 2}{x^2 + 4x + 4} - \dfrac{x - 1}{x^2 - 4} = \dfrac{x - 2}{(x + 2)(x + 2)} - \dfrac{x + 1}{(x + 2)(x - 2)}$
LCD $= (x + 2)^2(x - 2)$
$\dfrac{x - 2}{(x + 2)(x + 2)} \cdot \dfrac{x - 2}{x - 2} - \dfrac{x + 1}{(x + 2)(x - 2)} \cdot \dfrac{x + 2}{x + 2}$
$\qquad = \dfrac{x^2 - 4x + 4}{(x + 2)^2(x - 2)} - \dfrac{x^2 + 3x + 2}{(x + 2)^2(x - 2)}$
$\qquad = \dfrac{x^2 - 4x + 4 - x^2 - 3x - 2}{(x + 2)^2(x - 2)} = \dfrac{2 - 7x}{(x + 2)^2(x - 2)}$

32. $\dfrac{1 - 5x}{(x + 1)(x - 1)^2}$

33. $\dfrac{4}{x^2 + 2x + 4} + \dfrac{x - 2}{x + 2}$ LCD $= (x^2 + 2x + 4)(x + 2)$
$\dfrac{4\ (x + 2)}{(x^2 + 2x + 4)(x + 2)} + \dfrac{(x - 2)(x^2 + 2x + 4)}{(x + 2)(x^2 + 2x + 4)}$
$\qquad = \dfrac{4x + 8}{(x^2 + 2x + 4)(x + 2)} + \dfrac{x^3 - 8}{(x^2 + 2x + 4)(x + 2)}$
$\qquad = \dfrac{4x + x^3}{(x^2 + 2x + 4)(x + 2)}$

34. $\dfrac{x^3 + 3x}{(x - 9)(x^2 - 3x + 9)}$

35. $\dfrac{5}{2g^3} - \dfrac{3g - 9}{g^2 - 6g + 9} + \dfrac{12g}{4g^2 - 12g} = \dfrac{5}{2g^3} - \dfrac{3(g - 3)}{(g - 3)(g - 3)} + \dfrac{12g}{4g(g - 3)}$
$\qquad\qquad\qquad\qquad = \dfrac{5}{2g^3} - \dfrac{3}{g - 3} + \dfrac{3}{g - 3} = \dfrac{5}{2g^3}$

36. $\dfrac{7}{9y^2}$

37. LCD $= 2(x - 4)^2(x + 5)$
$\dfrac{(2x - 5)(x + 5)}{2(x - 4)^2(x + 5)} + \dfrac{(4x + 7)\ (2)(x - 4)}{(x + 5)(x - 4)(2)(x - 4)}$
$\qquad = \dfrac{(2x - 5)(x + 5) + 2(4x + 7)(x - 4)}{2(x - 4)^2(x + 5)}$
$\qquad = \dfrac{2x^2 + 5x - 25 + 8x^2 - 18x - 56}{2(x - 4)^2(x + 5)} = \dfrac{10x^2 - 13x - 81}{2(x - 4)^2(x + 5)}$

38. $\dfrac{23k^2 - 10k + 53}{5(k - 3)^2(k + 7)}$

39. LCD $= 12e^2(e + 3)(e - 3)$
$\dfrac{35\ (4)(e + 3)(e - 3)}{3e^2\ (4)(e + 3)(e - 3)} - \dfrac{2e\ (12e^2)}{(e + 3)(e - 3)(12e^2)}$
$\qquad - \dfrac{3\ (3e^2)(e + 3)}{4(e - 3)(3e^2)(e + 3)}$
$= \dfrac{140(e^2 - 9) - 2e(12e^2) - 9e^2(e + 3)}{12e^2(e + 3)(e - 3)}$
$= \dfrac{140e^2 - 1260 - 24e^3 - 9e^3 - 27e^2}{12e^2(e + 3)(e - 3)} = \dfrac{-33e^3 + 113e^2 - 1260}{12e^2(e + 3)(e - 3)}$
$= -\dfrac{33e^3 - 113e^2 + 1260}{12e^2(e + 3)(e - 3)}$

40. $\dfrac{164u^4 + 4u^3 + 23u^2 + 45u + 216}{24u^3(u + 3)(8 - u)}$

41. $\dfrac{x^2 + 1}{12x^3 + 24x^2} - \dfrac{4x + 3}{x^2 - 4x + 4} - \dfrac{1}{x^2 - 4}$
$= \dfrac{x^2 + 1}{12x^2(x + 2)} - \dfrac{4x + 3}{(x - 2)^2} - \dfrac{1}{(x - 2)(x + 2)}$
$\qquad\qquad\qquad\qquad\qquad$ LCD $= 12x^2(x - 2)^2(x + 2)$
$= \dfrac{(x^2 + 1)(x - 2)^2 - (4x + 3)(12x^2)(x + 2) - 12x^2(x - 2)}{12x^2(x - 2)^2(x + 2)}$
$= \dfrac{x^4 - 4x^3 + 5x^2 - 4x + 4 - 48x^4 - 132x^3 - 72x^2 - 12x^3 + 24x^2}{12x^2(x - 2)^2(x + 2)}$
$= \dfrac{-47x^4 - 148x^3 - 43x^2 - 4x + 4}{12x^2(x - 2)^2(x + 2)}$
$= -\dfrac{47x^4 + 148x^3 + 43x^2 + 4x - 4}{12x^2(x - 2)^2(x + 2)}$

42. $\dfrac{72y^3 + 149y^2 - 186y - 99}{8y(y+3)^2(y-3)}$

43. LCD $= 3y(y+4)^2(y^2-4y+16)$

$\dfrac{7}{3y(y^2-4y+16)} + \dfrac{y^2+4}{(y+4)(y^2-4y+16)} - \dfrac{y}{(y+4)^2}$

$= \dfrac{7}{3y(y^2-4y+16)}\cdot\dfrac{(y+4)^2}{(y+4)^2}$

$\quad + \dfrac{(y^2+4)(3y)(y+4)}{3y\,(y^2-4y+16)(y+4)\,(y+4)}$

$\quad - \dfrac{y\,(3y)(y^2-4y+16)}{3y(y^2-4y+16)\,(y+4)^2}$

$= \dfrac{7(y^2+8y+16)+3y(y^3+4y^2+4y+16)-3y^2(y^2-4y+16)}{3y(y+4)^2(y^2-4y+16)}$

$= \dfrac{24y^3-29y^2+104y+112}{3y(y+4)^2(y^2-4y+16)}$

44. $\dfrac{12x^3+5x^2+84x+45}{2x(x+3)^2(x^2-3x+9)}$

45. $\dfrac{x-1}{x^2(x+1)-9(x+1)} - \dfrac{x+3}{x^2(x-3)-(x-3)}$

$= \dfrac{x-1}{(x+1)(x^2-9)} - \dfrac{x+3}{(x-3)(x^2-1)}$

$= \dfrac{x-1}{(x+1)(x+3)(x-3)} - \dfrac{x+3}{(x-3)(x+1)(x-1)}$

$\qquad\qquad\qquad\text{LCD} = (x+1)(x-1)(x+3)(x-3)$

$= \dfrac{(x-1)\,(x-1)}{(x+1)(x+3)(x-3)\,(x-1)}$

$\quad - \dfrac{(x+3)\,(x+3)}{(x-3)(x+1)(x-1)\,(x+3)}$

$= \dfrac{(x^2-2x+1)-(x^2+6x+9)}{(x+1)(x+3)(x-3)(x-1)}$

$= \dfrac{x^2-2x+1-x^2-6x-9}{(x+1)(x+3)(x-3)(x-1)}$

$= \dfrac{-8x-8}{(x+1)(x+3)(x-3)(x-1)}$

$= \dfrac{-8(x+1)}{(x+1)(x+3)(x-3)(x-1)}$

$= \dfrac{-8}{(x+3)(x-3)(x-1)}$

46. $\dfrac{6x+3}{(x+1)(x-1)(x+2)(x-2)}$

47. LCD $= (x-1)^2(x+3)^2$

$= \dfrac{x+1}{(x-1)(x+3)^2} - \dfrac{x-3}{(x-1)^2(x+3)}$

$= \dfrac{(x+1)\,(x-1)}{(x-1)\,(x-1)(x+3)^2} - \dfrac{(x-3)(x+3)}{(x-1)^2(x+3)\,(x+3)}$

$= \dfrac{x^2-1-(x^2-9)}{(x-1)^2(x+3)^2} = \dfrac{x^2-1-x^2+9}{(x-1)^2(x+3)^2}$

$= \dfrac{8}{(x-1)^2(x+3)^2}$

48. $\dfrac{-21}{(x+2)^2(x-5)^2}$

Exercises 6.6 (page 261)

1. $\dfrac{21m^3n}{14mn^2} \div \dfrac{20m^2n^2}{8mn^3} = \dfrac{21m^3n}{14mn^2}\cdot\dfrac{8mn^3}{20m^2n^2} = \dfrac{3m}{5}$ **2.** $\dfrac{8}{3ab}$

3. $\dfrac{15h-6}{18h} \div \dfrac{30h^2-12h}{8h} = \dfrac{3(5h-2)}{18h}\cdot\dfrac{8h}{6h(5h-2)} = \dfrac{2}{9h}$

4. $\dfrac{3k}{5}$

5. LCD $= d^2$ $\dfrac{d^2\cdot\left(\frac{c}{d}+2\right)}{d^2\cdot\left(\frac{c^2}{d^2}-4\right)} = \dfrac{d^2\left(\frac{c}{d}\right)+d^2(2)}{d^2\left(\frac{c^2}{d^2}\right)-d^2(4)}$

$\qquad = \dfrac{cd+2d^2}{c^2-4d^2} = \dfrac{d(c+2d)}{(c-2d)(c+2d)} = \dfrac{d}{c-2d}$

6. $\dfrac{x+y}{y}$

7. $\dfrac{a+2-\dfrac{9}{a+2}}{a+1+\dfrac{a-7}{a+2}} = \dfrac{\dfrac{(a+2)}{1}\cdot\dfrac{(a+2)}{1}+\dfrac{(a+2)}{1}\left(\dfrac{-9}{a+2}\right)}{\dfrac{(a+2)}{1}\cdot\dfrac{(a+1)}{1}+\dfrac{(a+2)}{1}\left(\dfrac{a-7}{a+2}\right)}$

$\qquad = \dfrac{a^2+4a+4-9}{a^2+3a+2+a-7} = \dfrac{a^2+4a-5}{a^2+4a-5} = 1$

8. $\dfrac{x+3}{x+5}$

9. $\dfrac{\dfrac{x+y}{y}+\dfrac{y}{x-y}}{\dfrac{y}{x-y}} = \dfrac{\dfrac{y(x-y)}{1}\cdot\dfrac{(x+y)}{y}+\dfrac{y(x-y)}{1}\cdot\dfrac{y}{x-y}}{\dfrac{y(x-y)}{1}\cdot\dfrac{y}{x-y}}$

$\qquad = \dfrac{x^2-y^2+y^2}{y^2} = \dfrac{x^2}{y^2}$

10. $-\dfrac{1}{a}$

11. $\dfrac{\dfrac{x}{x+1}+\dfrac{4}{x}}{\dfrac{x}{x+1}-2} = \dfrac{\dfrac{x(x+1)}{1}\cdot\dfrac{x}{x+1}+\dfrac{x(x+1)}{1}\cdot\dfrac{4}{x}}{\dfrac{x(x+1)}{1}\cdot\dfrac{x}{x+1}+\dfrac{x(x+1)}{1}\cdot\dfrac{(-2)}{1}}$

$\qquad = \dfrac{x^2+4x+4}{x^2-2x^2-2x} = \dfrac{(x+2)(x+2)}{-x(x+2)} = -\dfrac{x+2}{x}$

12. $\dfrac{2x+1}{4x}$

13. $\dfrac{\dfrac{x+4}{x}-\dfrac{3}{x-1}}{x+1+\dfrac{2x+1}{x-1}} = \dfrac{\dfrac{x(x-1)}{1}\cdot\dfrac{(x+4)}{x}+\dfrac{x(x-1)}{1}\cdot\left(-\dfrac{3}{x-1}\right)}{\dfrac{x(x-1)}{1}\cdot\dfrac{(x+1)}{1}+\dfrac{x(x-1)}{1}\cdot\left(\dfrac{2x+1}{x-1}\right)}$

$\qquad = \dfrac{x^2+3x-4-3x}{x^3-x+2x^2+x}$

$\qquad = \dfrac{x^2-4}{x^3+2x^2} = \dfrac{(x+2)(x-2)}{x^2(x+2)} = \dfrac{x-2}{x^2}$

14. $\dfrac{x-2}{(x-6)(x-4)}$

15. $\dfrac{4x^{-2} - y^{-2}}{2x^{-1} + y^{-1}} = \dfrac{\dfrac{4}{x^2} - \dfrac{1}{y^2}}{\dfrac{2}{x} + \dfrac{1}{y}} = \dfrac{\dfrac{x^2 y^2}{1} \cdot \dfrac{4}{x^2} + \dfrac{x^2 y^2}{1}\left(-\dfrac{1}{y^2}\right)}{\dfrac{x^2 y^2}{1} \cdot \dfrac{2}{x} + \dfrac{x^2 y^2}{1} \cdot \dfrac{1}{y}}$

$= \dfrac{4y^2 - x^2}{2xy^2 + x^2 y} = \dfrac{(2y + x)(2y - x)}{xy(2y + x)} = \dfrac{2y - x}{xy}$

16. $\dfrac{3x + y}{xy}$

17. $\dfrac{\dfrac{x-2}{x+2} - \dfrac{x+2}{x-2}}{\dfrac{x-2}{x+2} + \dfrac{x+2}{x-2}}$

18. $\dfrac{m^2 + 9}{6m}$

$= \dfrac{\dfrac{(x+2)(x-2)}{1}\left(\dfrac{x-2}{x+2}\right) - \dfrac{(x+2)(x-2)}{1}\left(\dfrac{x+2}{x-2}\right)}{\dfrac{(x+2)(x-2)}{1}\left(\dfrac{x-2}{x+2}\right) + \dfrac{(x+2)(x-2)}{1}\left(\dfrac{x+2}{x-2}\right)}$

$= \dfrac{(x-2)(x-2) - (x+2)(x+2)}{(x-2)(x-2) + (x+2)(x+2)}$

$= \dfrac{x^2 - 4x + 4 - (x^2 + 4x + 4)}{x^2 - 4x + 4 + x^2 + 4x + 4} = \dfrac{-8x}{2x^2 + 8} = -\dfrac{4x}{x^2 + 4}$

19. $\dfrac{\dfrac{2x+y}{x} + \dfrac{3x+y}{y-x}}{\dfrac{x+y}{y} + \dfrac{2(x+y)}{x-y}}$

20. $\dfrac{a}{b}$

$= \dfrac{\dfrac{xy(x-y)}{1} \cdot \dfrac{2x+y}{x} - \dfrac{xy(x-y)}{1} \cdot \dfrac{3x+y}{(x-y)}}{\dfrac{xy(x-y)}{1} \cdot \dfrac{x+y}{y} + \dfrac{xy(x-y)}{1} \cdot \dfrac{2(x+y)}{(x-y)}}$

$= \dfrac{y(x-y)(2x+y) - xy(3x+y)}{x(x+y)(x-y) + 2xy(x+y)}$

$= \dfrac{y[(x-y)(2x+y) - x(3x+y)]}{x(x+y)[(x-y) + 2y]}$

$= \dfrac{y[2x^2 - xy - y^2 - 3x^2 - xy]}{x(x+y)(x+y)}$

$= \dfrac{-y[x^2 + 2xy + y^2]}{x(x+y)^2} = \dfrac{-y(x+y)^2}{x(x+y)^2} = -\dfrac{y}{x}$

21. $\dfrac{1}{x + \dfrac{1}{x + \dfrac{1}{x+x}}} = \dfrac{1}{x + \dfrac{1}{x + \dfrac{1}{2x}}} = \dfrac{1}{x + \dfrac{1(2x)}{\left(x + \dfrac{1}{2x}\right)(2x)}}$

$= \dfrac{1}{x + \dfrac{2x}{2x^2 + 1}} = \dfrac{1(2x^2 + 1)}{\left(x + \dfrac{2x}{2x^2 + 1}\right)(2x^2 + 1)}$

$= \dfrac{2x^2 + 1}{x(2x^2 + 1) + 2x}$

$= \dfrac{2x^2 + 1}{2x^3 + x + 2x} = \dfrac{2x^2 + 1}{2x^3 + 3x}$

22. $\dfrac{2y^2 + 2}{y^3 + 3y}$

23. $\dfrac{x + \dfrac{1}{2 + \dfrac{x}{3}}}{x - \dfrac{3}{4 + \dfrac{x}{2}}} = \dfrac{x + \dfrac{1(3)}{\left(2 + \dfrac{x}{3}\right)(3)}}{x - \dfrac{3(2)}{\left(4 + \dfrac{x}{2}\right)(2)}} = \dfrac{x + \dfrac{3}{6 + x}}{x - \dfrac{6}{8 + x}}$

$= \dfrac{\left(x + \dfrac{3}{6+x}\right)(6+x)(8+x)}{\left(x - \dfrac{6}{8+x}\right)(6+x)(8+x)}$

$= \dfrac{x(48 + 14x + x^2) + 3(8 + x)}{x(48 + 14x + x^2) - 6(6 + x)}$

$= \dfrac{48x + 14x^2 + x^3 + 24 + 3x}{48x + 14x^2 + x^3 - 36 - 6x}$

$= \dfrac{x^3 + 14x^2 + 51x + 24}{x^3 + 14x^2 + 42x - 36}$

24. $\dfrac{x^3 + 8x^2 + 22x + 60}{x^3 + 8x^2 - 24}$

Review Exercises 6.7 (page 264)

1.
$$20 - 45a^2 = 0$$
$$5(4 - 9a^2) = 0$$
$$5(2 + 3a)(2 - 3a) = 0$$
$$2 + 3a = 0 \text{ or } 2 - 3a = 0$$
$$a = -\dfrac{2}{3} \text{ or } \quad a = \dfrac{2}{3}$$

The domain is the set of all real numbers except $-\dfrac{2}{3}$ and $\dfrac{2}{3}$

2. All real numbers except 6 and $-5/2$

3. $\dfrac{\overset{2}{\cancel{4}}z(z^2 + z - 6)}{\underset{1}{\cancel{2}}(z^2 + 2z - 3)}$

4. $\dfrac{2k(k+1)}{k+4}$

$= \dfrac{2z(z + 3)(z - 2)}{(z + 3)(z - 1)} = \dfrac{2z(z - 2)}{z - 1}$

5. $\dfrac{(a - 3b)(a^2 + 3ab + 9b^2)}{(a - 3b)(a + 2)} = \dfrac{a^2 + 3ab + 9b^2}{a + 2}$

6. $\dfrac{x^2 + 2x + 2}{4}$

7. $\dfrac{-\overset{5}{\cancel{35}}mn^2 p^2}{\underset{2}{\cancel{14}}m^3 p^3} \cdot \dfrac{\overset{1}{\cancel{13}}m^4 n}{\underset{4}{\cancel{52}}n^3 p} = -\dfrac{5m^2}{8p^2}$

8. $-\dfrac{4c^2}{3ab^3}$

9. $\dfrac{z^2 + 3z + 2}{z^2 + 2z + 1} \div \dfrac{z^2 + 2z - 3}{z^2 - 1}$

10. 1

$= \dfrac{(z + 2)(z + 1)}{(z + 1)(z + 1)} \cdot \dfrac{(z + 1)(z - 1)}{(z + 3)(z - 1)} = \dfrac{z + 2}{z + 3}$

11. $\dfrac{(x + y)(x^2 - xy + y^2)}{3(x^2 - xy + y^2)} \cdot \dfrac{(x + 2y)(x - y)}{(x + y)(x - y)} \cdot \dfrac{\overset{3}{\cancel{15}}x^2 y}{\cancel{5}xy(x + 2y)} = x$

12. 2

13. $\dfrac{20y - 7}{6y - 8} - \dfrac{17 + 2y}{6y - 8} = \dfrac{20y - 7 - 17 - 2y}{6y - 8}$

14. -2

$= \dfrac{18y - 24}{6y - 8} = \dfrac{\overset{3}{\cancel{6}}(3y - 4)}{\underset{1}{\cancel{2}}(3y - 4)} = 3$

15. LCD $= 90e^3f^2$ $\quad \dfrac{11}{30e^3f} \cdot \dfrac{3f}{3f} - \dfrac{7}{45e^2f^2} \cdot \dfrac{2e}{2e} = \dfrac{33f - 14e}{90e^3f^2}$

16. $\dfrac{30u^2 - 49v}{280u^4v^2}$

17. $\dfrac{a+1}{(a+1)(a-2)} - \dfrac{a-2}{(a+3)(a-2)} = \dfrac{1}{a-2} - \dfrac{1}{a+3}$

LCD $= (a-2)(a+3)$

$\dfrac{(a+3)}{(a+3)} \cdot \dfrac{1}{a-2} + \dfrac{(a-2)}{(a-2)} \cdot \dfrac{-1}{a+3} = \dfrac{a+3-a+2}{(a-2)(a+3)}$

$= \dfrac{5}{(a-2)(a+3)}$

18. $\dfrac{3}{(x-1)(x+2)}$

19. $\dfrac{\overset{3}{\cancel{15}}x}{\cancel{5}x(x+4)} - \dfrac{7}{3x^2} - \dfrac{3(\cancel{x+4})}{(x+4)^{\cancel{2}}} = \dfrac{3}{\cancel{x+4}} - \dfrac{7}{3x^2} - \dfrac{3}{\cancel{x+4}} = -\dfrac{7}{3x^2}$

20. $-\dfrac{5}{11y^3}$

21. $\dfrac{\dfrac{y+1}{1} \cdot \dfrac{x}{y+1} + 2}{\dfrac{y+1}{1} \cdot \dfrac{x}{y+1} - 2} = \dfrac{\left(\dfrac{y+1}{1}\right)\left(\dfrac{x}{y+1}\right) + \left(\dfrac{y+1}{1}\right)\left(\dfrac{2}{1}\right)}{\left(\dfrac{y+1}{1}\right)\left(\dfrac{x}{y+1}\right) + \left(\dfrac{y+1}{1}\right)\left(\dfrac{-2}{1}\right)}$

$= \dfrac{x + (y+1)(2)}{x + (y+1)(-2)} = \dfrac{x + 2y + 2}{x - 2y - 2}$

22. $\dfrac{3b - a + 6}{2b + a + 4}$

23. $\dfrac{\dfrac{R^3T^3}{1} \cdot \dfrac{8}{R^3} + \dfrac{1}{T^3}}{\dfrac{R^3T^3}{1} \cdot \dfrac{4}{R^2} - \dfrac{1}{T^2}} = \dfrac{\dfrac{R^3T^3}{1} \cdot \dfrac{8}{R^3} + \dfrac{R^3T^3}{1}\left(\dfrac{1}{T^3}\right)}{\dfrac{R^3T^3}{1} \cdot \dfrac{4}{R^2} + \dfrac{R^3T^3}{1}\left(-\dfrac{1}{T^2}\right)}$

$= \dfrac{8T^3 + R^3}{4RT^3 - R^3T} = \dfrac{(\cancel{2T+R})(4T^2 - 2RT + R^2)}{RT(\cancel{2T+R})(2T - R)}$

$= \dfrac{4T^2 - 2RT + R^2}{RT(2T - R)}$

24. $\dfrac{mn(n + 4m)}{n^2 + 4mn + 16m^2}$

Exercises 6.8 (page 272)

Note: The checks for these exercises usually will not be shown.

1. LCD $= 4k(k - 5)$

$\dfrac{4k(\cancel{k-5})}{1} \cdot \dfrac{2}{\cancel{k-5}} - \dfrac{4\cancel{k}(k-5)}{1} \cdot \dfrac{5}{\cancel{k}} = \dfrac{4\cancel{k}(k-5)}{1} \cdot \dfrac{3}{\cancel{4k}}$

$4k(2) - 20(k - 5) = (k - 5)3$

$8k - 20k + 100 = 3k - 15$

$-15k = -115$

$k = \dfrac{115}{15} = \dfrac{23}{3}$

$\left\{ \dfrac{23}{3} \right\}$

2. $\left\{ -\dfrac{35}{4} \right\}$

3. LCD $= x - 2$

$\dfrac{x\cancel{-2}}{1} \cdot \dfrac{x}{x\cancel{-2}} = \dfrac{x\cancel{-2}}{1} \cdot \dfrac{2}{x\cancel{-2}} + \dfrac{x - 2}{1} \cdot 5$

$x = 2 + 5x - 10$

$8 = 4x$

$x = 2$

Not in the domain; solution set: $\{\ \}$

4. $\{\ \}$

5. LCD $= 2m - 3$

$\dfrac{2m\cancel{-3}}{1} \cdot \dfrac{12m}{2m\cancel{-3}} = \dfrac{2m - 3}{1} \cdot \dfrac{6}{1} + \dfrac{2m\cancel{-3}}{1} \cdot \dfrac{18}{2m\cancel{-3}}$

$12m = (2m - 3)6 + 18$

$12m = 12m - 18 + 18$

$12m = 12m$

$0 = 0$ Identity

Solution set: all real numbers except $\dfrac{3}{2}$

6. Identity; solution set: all real numbers except $-\dfrac{6}{5}$

7. $\dfrac{2y}{7y + 5} = \dfrac{1}{3y}$

$2y(3y) = 7y + 5$

$6y^2 = 7y + 5$

$6y^2 - 7y - 5 = 0$

$(2y + 1) \ | \ (3y - 5) = 0$

$2y + 1 = \ 0 \ | \ 3y - 5 = 0$

$y = -\dfrac{1}{2} \ \Bigg| \ y = \dfrac{5}{3}$

$\left\{ -\dfrac{1}{2}, \dfrac{5}{3} \right\}$

8. $\left\{ \dfrac{1}{2}, -\dfrac{3}{2} \right\}$

9. $\dfrac{3e - 5}{4e} = \dfrac{e}{2e + 3}$

$(3e - 5)(2e + 3) = 4e(e)$

$6e^2 - e - 15 = 4e^2$

$2e^2 - e - 15 = 0$

$(e - 3)(2e + 5) = 0$

$e - 3 = 0 \ | \ 2e + 5 = \ 0$

$e = 3 \ \Bigg| \ e = -\dfrac{5}{2}$ Solution set: $\left\{ 3, -\dfrac{5}{2} \right\}$

10. $\left\{ 1, -\dfrac{7}{4} \right\}$

11. $\dfrac{1}{2} - \dfrac{1}{x} = \dfrac{4}{x^2}$ LCD $= 2x^2$

$\cancel{2}x^2 \cdot \dfrac{1}{\cancel{2}} - 2x^{\cancel{2}} \cdot \dfrac{1}{\cancel{x}} = 2\cancel{x}^{\cancel{2}} \cdot \dfrac{4}{\cancel{x^2}}$

$x^2 - 2x = 8$

$x^2 - 2x - 8 = 0$

$(x - 4)(x + 2) = 0$

$x - 4 = 0 \ | \ x + 2 = 0$

$x = 4 \ | \ x = -2$

$\{4, -2\}$

12. $\left\{ 3, -\dfrac{4}{7} \right\}$

13. LCD $= 15x(x + 1)$

$\dfrac{15x(\cancel{x+1})}{1} \cdot \dfrac{4}{\cancel{x+1}} = \dfrac{15x(x + 1)}{1} \cdot \dfrac{3}{x} + \dfrac{\cancel{15}x(x + 1)}{1} \cdot \dfrac{1}{\cancel{15}}$

$60x = 45x + 45 + x^2 + x$

$0 = x^2 - 14x + 45$

$0 = (x - 5)(x - 9)$

$x - 5 = 0 \ | \ x - 9 = 0$

$x = 5 \ | \ x = 0$

Solution set: $\{5, 9\}$

14. $\{-2, -3\}$

15. LCD $= x(x + 3)(x + 4)$

$$\frac{x(x+3)(x+4)}{1} \cdot \frac{6}{x+4} = \frac{x(x+3)(x+4)}{1} \cdot \frac{5}{x+3}$$
$$+ \frac{x(x+3)(x+4)}{1} \cdot \frac{4}{x}$$

$$x(x+3)6 = x(x+4)5 + (x+3)(x+4)4$$
$$6x^2 + 18x = 5x^2 + 20x + 4x^2 + 28x + 48$$
$$0 = 3x^2 + 30x + 48$$
$$0 = 3(x^2 + 10x + 16)$$
$$0 = 3(x + 2)(x + 8)$$

$$x + 2 = 0 \mid x + 8 = 0$$
$$x = -2 \mid \quad x = -8$$
$$\{-2, -8\}$$

16. $\left\{2, -\dfrac{5}{4}\right\}$

17. LCD $= 5(x + 3)(x - 3)$

$$\frac{5(x+3)(x-3)}{1} \cdot \frac{6}{x^2-9} + \frac{5(x+3)(x-3)}{1} \cdot \frac{1}{5}$$
$$= \frac{5(x+3)(x-3)}{1} \cdot \frac{1}{x-3}$$

$$30 + x^2 - 9 = 5x + 15$$
$$x^2 - 5x + 6 = 0$$
$$(x - 2)(x - 3) = 0$$
$$x - 2 = 0 \mid x - 3 = 0$$
$$x = 2 \mid \quad x = 3 \quad \text{Not a root (it makes a denominator}$$
$$\text{zero and is therefore an excluded value)}$$

Check for $x = 2$
$$\frac{6}{x^2-9} + \frac{1}{5} = \frac{1}{x-3}$$
$$\frac{6}{2^2-9} + \frac{1}{5} \overset{?}{=} \frac{1}{2-3}$$
$$-\frac{6}{5} + \frac{1}{5} \overset{?}{=} -1$$
$$-1 = -1$$

Solution set: $\{2\}$

18. $\left\{\dfrac{7}{3}\right\}$

19. LCD $= (x + 2)(x - 2)$

Domain: all real numbers except 2 and -2.

$$(x+2)(x-2)\left(\frac{x+2}{x-2} - \frac{x-2}{x+2}\right) = (x+2)(x-2)\left(\frac{16}{x^2-4}\right)$$

$$(x+2)(x-2)\left(\frac{x+2}{x-2}\right) - (x+2)(x-2)\left(\frac{x-2}{x+2}\right) = 16$$

$$(x+2)(x+2) - (x-2)(x-2) = 16$$
$$x^2 + 4x + 4 - (x^2 - 4x + 4) = 16$$
$$x^2 + 4x + 4 - x^2 + 4x - 4 = 16$$
$$8x = 16$$
$$x = 2$$

But 2 is not in the domain of the variable. Therefore, the solution set is $\{\ \}$.

20. $\{\ \}$

21. LCD $= (x + 3)(x + 2)(x - 5)$

Domain: all real numbers except -3, -2, and 5

$$(x+3)(x+2)(x-5)\left(\frac{2}{(x+2)(x+3)} + \frac{3}{(x+2)(x-5)}\right)$$

$$= (x+3)(x+2)(x-5)\left(\frac{5x-1}{(x+3)(x+2)(x-5)}\right)$$

$$2(x-5) + 3(x+3) = 5x - 1$$
$$2x - 10 + 3x + 9 = 5x - 1$$
$$5x - 1 = 5x - 1$$
$$-1 = -1 \quad \text{Identity}$$

Solution set: all real numbers except -3, -2, and 5

22. All real numbers except -5, -1, and 3

23. $\dfrac{1}{(2x-5)(x-3)} + \dfrac{x-1}{(2x-5)(x+3)} = \dfrac{-4}{(x+3)(x-3)}$

LCD $= (2x - 5)(x - 3)(x + 3)$

$$(2x-5)(x-3)(x+3)\left(\frac{1}{(2x-5)(x-3)} + \frac{x-1}{(2x-5)(x+3)}\right)$$

$$= (2x-5)(x-3)(x+3)\left(\frac{-4}{(x+3)(x-3)}\right)$$

$$(x+3) + (x-3)(x-1) = (2x-5)(-4)$$
$$x + 3 + x^2 - 4x + 3 = -8x + 20$$
$$x^2 + 5x - 14 = 0$$
$$(x + 7)(x - 2) = 0$$
$$x + 7 = 0 \mid x - 2 = 0$$
$$x = -7 \mid \quad x = 2$$
$$\{2, -7\}$$

24. $\{1, 10\}$

25. LCD $= (x + 4)(x^2 - 4x + 16)(x - 4)$

Domain: all real numbers except -4 and 4

$$(x+4)(x^2-4x+16)(x-4)\left(\frac{8}{(x+4)(x^2-4x+16)} + \frac{3}{x^2-16}\right)$$

$$= (x+4)(x^2-4x+16)(x-4)\left(\frac{-1}{x^2-4x+16}\right)$$

$$8(x-4) + 3(x^2 - 4x + 16) = -1(x+4)(x-4)$$
$$8x - 32 + 3x^2 - 12x + 48 = -(x^2 - 16)$$
$$3x^2 - 4x + 16 = -x^2 + 16$$
$$4x^2 - 4x = 0$$
$$4x(x - 1) = 0$$
$$4x = 0 \text{ or } x - 1 = 0$$
$$x = 0 \text{ or } \quad x = 1$$

Solution set: $\{0, 1\}$ (The check will not be shown.)

26. $\{2\}$

Exercises 6.9 (page 276)

1. $2(3x - y) = xy - 12$
$$6x - 2y = xy - 12$$
$$6x + 12 = xy + 2y$$
$$6(x + 2) = (x + 2)y$$
$$\frac{6(x+2)}{(x+2)} = y$$
$$6 = y$$
$$y = 6$$

2. $x = -2$

3. $\dfrac{z}{1} = \dfrac{x-m}{s}$
$$zs = x - m$$
$$m = x - zs$$

4. $N = \dfrac{n - s^2}{1 - s^2}$

5. $\dfrac{2x}{5yz} = z + x$

$(5yz)\!\left(\dfrac{2x}{5yz}\right) = (5yz)(z + x)$

$2x = 5yz^2 + 5xyz$

$2x - 5xyz = 5yz^2$

$x(2 - 5yz) = 5yz^2$

$x = \dfrac{5yz^2}{2 - 5yz}$

6. $y = \dfrac{xz}{x - z}$

7. $\dfrac{C}{1} = \dfrac{5(F - 32)}{9}$

$9C = 5(F - 32)$

$9C = 5F - 160$

$9C + 160 = 5F$

$\dfrac{9C + 160}{5} = F$

$F = \dfrac{9C + 160}{5}$

8. $B = \dfrac{2A - hb}{h}$

9. $s = c\!\left(1 + \dfrac{a}{c}\right)$

$s = c + \dfrac{\cancel{c}a}{\cancel{c}}$

$s = c + a$

$s - a = c$

$c = s - a$

10. $R = \dfrac{rZ}{r - Z}$

11. $A = P(1 + rt)$

$A = P + Prt$

$A - P = Prt$

$\dfrac{A - P}{Pt} = r$

$r = \dfrac{A - P}{Pt}$

12. $t = \dfrac{2S + g}{2g}$

13. LCD $= ra$

$\dfrac{ra}{1} \cdot \dfrac{v^2}{1} = \dfrac{\cancel{r}a}{1} \cdot \dfrac{2}{\cancel{r}} - \dfrac{r\cancel{a}}{1} \cdot \dfrac{1}{\cancel{a}}$

$rav^2 = 2a - r$

$r = 2a - rav^2$

$r = a(2 - rv^2)$

$\dfrac{r}{2 - rv^2} = a$

$a = \dfrac{r}{2 - rv^2}$

14. $s = \dfrac{p}{1 - p}$

15. $S = \dfrac{a}{1 - r}$

$S(1 - r) = a$

$S - Sr = a$

$S - a = Sr$

$\dfrac{S - a}{S} = r$

$r = \dfrac{S - a}{S}$

16. $R = \dfrac{E - Ir}{I}$

17. $\dfrac{1}{F} = \dfrac{1}{u} + \dfrac{1}{v}$

$Fuv\!\left(\dfrac{1}{F}\right) = Fuv\!\left(\dfrac{1}{u} + \dfrac{1}{v}\right)$

$uv = Fuv\!\left(\dfrac{1}{u}\right) + Fuv\!\left(\dfrac{1}{v}\right)$

$uv = Fv + Fu$

$uv = F(v + u)$ or $F(u + v) = uv$

$F = \dfrac{uv}{u + v}$

18. $b = \dfrac{ac}{a - c}$

19. $L = a + (n - 1)d$

$L = a + nd - d$

$L - a + d = nd$

$\dfrac{L - a + d}{d} = n$

$n = \dfrac{L - a + d}{d}$

20. $h = \dfrac{A - 2\pi r^2}{2\pi r}$

21. $C = \dfrac{a}{1 + \dfrac{a}{\pi A}}$

$C = \dfrac{\pi A \cdot a}{\pi A \cdot 1 + \dfrac{\cancel{\pi A}}{1} \cdot \dfrac{a}{\cancel{\pi A}}}$

$\dfrac{C}{1} = \dfrac{\pi Aa}{\pi A + a}$

$C(\pi A + a) = \pi Aa$

$C\pi A + Ca = \pi Aa$

$C\pi A = \pi Aa - Ca$

$C\pi A = a(\pi A - C)$

$\dfrac{C\pi A}{\pi A - C} = a$

$a = \dfrac{C\pi A}{\pi A - C}$

22. $v = \dfrac{c^2(R - V)}{c^2 - RV}$

Exercises 6.10 (page 280)

1. Henry's rate $= \dfrac{1 \text{ house}}{5 \text{ days}} = \dfrac{1}{5}$ house per day

Jim's rate $= \dfrac{1 \text{ house}}{4 \text{ days}} = \dfrac{1}{4}$ house per day

Let $x =$ Number of days to paint the house

$$\underset{\text{Henry paints}}{\text{Amount}} + \underset{\text{Jim paints}}{\text{Amount}} = \underset{\text{painted together}}{\text{Amount}}$$

$$\dfrac{x}{5} \quad + \quad \dfrac{x}{4} \quad = \quad 1 \qquad \text{One house painted}$$

LCD $= 20$; $\dfrac{20}{1} \cdot \dfrac{x}{5} + \dfrac{20}{1} \cdot \dfrac{x}{4} = \dfrac{20}{1} \cdot 1$

$4x + 5x = 20$

$9x = 20$

$x = \dfrac{20}{9} = 2\dfrac{2}{9}$ days

2. $3\dfrac{3}{5}$ days

3. Let $x =$ Time it takes David to type 80 pages

Abby's rate $= \dfrac{100 \text{ pages}}{3 \text{ hours}} = \dfrac{100}{3}$ pages per hr

David's rate $= \dfrac{80 \text{ pages}}{x \text{ hours}} = \dfrac{80}{x}$ pages per hr

Since they both type for 10 hr to produce 500 pages

$$\underset{\text{Abby types}}{\text{Amount}} + \underset{\text{David types}}{\text{Amount}} = \underset{\text{typed together}}{\text{Amount}}$$

$$\dfrac{100}{3}(10) \quad + \quad \dfrac{80}{x}(10) \quad = \quad 500$$

LCD $= 3x$; $\dfrac{3x}{1} \cdot \dfrac{1000}{3} + \dfrac{3x}{1} \cdot \dfrac{800}{x} = \dfrac{3x}{1} \cdot \dfrac{500}{1}$

$1000x + 2400 = 1500x$

$2400 = 500x$

$x = \dfrac{2400}{500} = \dfrac{24}{5} = 4\dfrac{4}{5}$ hr

4. $49\dfrac{1}{2}$ min

5. Machine A rate $= \dfrac{1 \text{ job}}{36 \text{ hr}} = \dfrac{1}{36}$ job per hr

Machine B rate $= \dfrac{1 \text{ job}}{24 \text{ hr}} = \dfrac{1}{24}$ job per hr

Let $x =$ Number of hours both machines are running together. Since machine A runs for 12 hr before machine B is turned on, machine A runs for $x + 12$ hr.

$$\begin{array}{c} \text{Amount of job} \\ \text{done by machine A} \end{array} + \begin{array}{c} \text{Amount of job} \\ \text{done by machine B} \end{array} = \begin{array}{c} 1 \\ \text{job} \end{array}$$

$$\dfrac{1}{36}(x + 12) \quad + \quad \dfrac{1}{24}(x) \quad = 1$$

LCD $= 72$

$$\dfrac{72}{1} \cdot \dfrac{x + 12}{36} + \dfrac{72}{1} \cdot \dfrac{x}{24} = 72 \cdot 1$$

$$2x + 24 + 3x = 72$$
$$5x = 48$$
$$x = \dfrac{48}{5} = 9\dfrac{3}{5} \text{ hr}$$

6. $6\dfrac{9}{11}$ hr

7. Let $x =$ Smaller number
$x + 8 =$ Larger number

$$\begin{array}{c} \text{One-fourth the} \\ \text{larger number} \end{array} \text{ is } \begin{array}{c} \text{one more} \\ \text{than} \end{array} \begin{array}{c} \text{one-third the} \\ \text{smaller number} \end{array}$$

$$\dfrac{1}{4}(x + 8) \quad = \quad 1 \quad + \quad \dfrac{1}{3}(x)$$

LCD $= 12$

$$\dfrac{12}{1} \cdot \dfrac{x + 8}{4} = \dfrac{12}{1} \cdot 1 + \dfrac{12}{1} \cdot \dfrac{x}{3}$$

$$3x + 24 = 12 + 4x$$
$$12 = x$$
$$x = 12 \qquad \text{Smaller number}$$
$$x + 8 = 12 + 8 = 20 \quad \text{Larger number}$$

8. Smaller number is -20; larger number is -14

9. Let $d =$ distance

	d	$=$	r	$\cdot$	t
Slow plane	d		400		$\dfrac{d}{400}$
Fast plane	d		500		$\dfrac{d}{500}$

$$\begin{array}{c} \text{Slow plane's} \\ \text{time} \end{array} - \begin{array}{c} \text{Fast plane's} \\ \text{time} \end{array} = \dfrac{1}{2} \text{ hr}$$

$$\dfrac{d}{400} - \dfrac{d}{500} = \dfrac{1}{2}$$

LCD $= 2000$

$$\dfrac{2000}{1} \cdot \dfrac{d}{400} - \dfrac{2000}{1} \cdot \dfrac{d}{500} = \dfrac{2000}{1} \cdot \dfrac{1}{2}$$

$$5d - 4d = 1000$$
$$d = 1000 \text{ miles}$$

10. 6 miles

11. Let $x =$ number of qt of antifreeze to be drained and replaced
$$.45(14) - .45(x) + 1.00x = .50(14)$$
$$6.3 + .55x = 7$$
$$630 + 55x = 700$$
$$55x = 70$$
$$x = \dfrac{70}{55} = \dfrac{14}{11} = 1\dfrac{3}{11} \text{ qt}$$

12. $3\dfrac{3}{7}$ qt

13. Let $u =$ Units digit
$u + 1 =$ Tens digit

$$\begin{array}{c} \text{Product} \\ \text{of digits} \end{array} \begin{array}{c} \text{divided} \\ \text{by} \end{array} \begin{array}{c} \text{sum} \\ \text{of digits} \end{array} \text{ is } \dfrac{6}{5}$$

$$(u + 1)u \quad \div \quad (u + 1 + u) = \dfrac{6}{5}$$

$$\dfrac{(u + 1)u}{u + 1 + u} = \dfrac{6}{5}$$

$$\dfrac{u^2 + u}{2u + 1} = \dfrac{6}{5}$$

$$5(u^2 + u) = 6(2u + 1)$$
$$5u^2 + 5u = 12u + 6$$
$$5u^2 - 7u - 6 = 0$$
$$(u - 2)(5u + 3) = 0$$

$$u - 2 = 0 \mid 5u + 3 = 0$$
$$u = 2 \qquad\quad u = -\dfrac{3}{5} \text{ Not in the domain}$$
$$u + 1 = 3$$

The number is 32

14. 34

15. Let $x =$ Hours for pipe 1 to fill tank
$x + 1 =$ Hours for pipe 2 to fill tank

Pipe 1 rate $= \dfrac{1 \text{ tank}}{x \text{ hr}} = \dfrac{1}{x}$ tank per hr

Pipe 2 rate $= \dfrac{1 \text{ tank}}{(x + 1)\text{hr}} = \dfrac{1}{x + 1}$ tank per hr

Pipe 3 rate $= \dfrac{1 \text{ tank}}{2 \text{ hr}} = \dfrac{1}{2}$ tank per hr

$$\begin{array}{c} \text{Amount 1} \\ \text{does in 3 hr} \end{array} + \begin{array}{c} \text{Amount 2} \\ \text{does in 3 hr} \end{array} - \begin{array}{c} \text{Amount 3} \\ \text{does in 3 hr} \end{array} = 1 \text{ full tank}$$

$$\dfrac{1}{x}(3) \quad + \quad \dfrac{1}{x + 1}(3) \quad - \quad \dfrac{1}{2}(3) \quad = \quad 1$$

$$\dfrac{2x(x + 1)}{1} \cdot \dfrac{3}{x} + \dfrac{2x(x + 1)}{1} \cdot \dfrac{3}{x + 1} - \dfrac{2x(x + 1)}{1} \cdot \dfrac{3}{2}$$
$$= \dfrac{2x(x + 1)}{1} \cdot \dfrac{1}{1}$$

$$6(x + 1) + 6x - 3x(x + 1) = 2x(x + 1)$$
$$6x + 6 + 6x - 3x^2 - 3x = 2x^2 + 2x$$
$$5x^2 - 7x - 6 = 0$$
$$(x - 2)(5x + 3) = 0$$

$$x - 2 = 0 \mid 5x + 3 = 0$$
$$x = 2 \text{ hr} \mid x = -\dfrac{3}{5}$$

Not in the domain

16. 2 hr

17. Let x = Number of hours for Sandra to proofread 60 pages

$$\text{Ruth's rate} = \frac{230 \text{ pages}}{4 \text{ hr}}$$

$$\text{Sandra's rate} = \frac{60 \text{ pages}}{x \text{ hr}}$$

$$\begin{array}{ccc} \text{Number of pages} & & \text{Number of pages} \\ \text{Ruth reads in 6 hr} & + & \text{Sandra reads in 6 hr} \end{array} = \frac{525}{\text{pages}}$$

$$\left(\frac{230}{4}\right)(6) \quad + \quad \left(\frac{60}{x}\right)(6) \quad = \quad 525 \quad \text{(LCD is } x\text{)}$$

$$x\left(345 + \frac{360}{x}\right) = 525\, x$$

$$345x + 360 = 525x$$

$$360 = 180x$$

$$x = 2 \quad \text{hours for Sandra} \\ \text{to proofread 60 pages}$$

18. 28 hours

19. Let x = Number of minutes for machine B to process 4300 feet of film

$$\text{Rate of machine A} = \frac{5700 \text{ ft}}{60 \text{ min}}$$

$$\text{Rate of machine B} = \frac{4300 \text{ ft}}{x \text{ min}}$$

Amount of film done by machine A in 50 min		Amount of film done by machine B in 50 min	Amount of film = done together in 50 min
$\frac{5700}{60} \cdot (50)$	$+$	$\frac{4300}{x} \cdot (50)$	$= \quad 15{,}500$
4750	$+$	$\frac{215{,}000}{x}$	$= \quad 15{,}500$
$4750x$	$+$	$215{,}000$	$= \quad 15{,}500x$
		$215{,}000$	$= \quad 10{,}750x$
		x	$= \quad 20 \text{ min}$

20. 30 min

Review Exercises 6.11 (page 282)

1. $\dfrac{7}{2z+5} = \dfrac{13}{3z}$

$7(3z) = (2z+5)13$

$21z = 26z + 65$

$-5z = 65$

$z = -13$

2. $\{-8\}$

3.
$$\frac{5a-4}{6a} = \frac{-2}{3a+10}$$
$$(5a-4)(3a+10) = (6a)(-2)$$
$$15a^2 + 38a - 40 = -12a$$
$$15a^2 + 50a - 40 = 0$$
$$3a^2 + 10a - 8 = 0$$
$$(a+4)(3a-2) = 0$$
$$a + 4 = 0 \;\bigg|\; 3a - 2 = 0$$
$$a = -4 \;\bigg|\; a = \frac{2}{3}$$

4. $\left\{2, \dfrac{7}{5}\right\}$

5. LCD $= 4x^2$; $\dfrac{4x^2}{1} \cdot \dfrac{3}{x} + \dfrac{4x^2}{1} \cdot \dfrac{-8}{x^2} = \dfrac{4x^2}{1} \cdot \dfrac{1}{4}$

$$12x - 32 = x^2$$
$$0 = x^2 - 12x + 32$$
$$0 = (x-4)(x-8)$$
$$x - 4 = 0 \;\bigg|\; x - 8 = 0$$
$$x = 4 \;\bigg|\; x = 8$$

6. $\left\{-2, \dfrac{4}{5}\right\}$

7. $\dfrac{9}{x+1} = \dfrac{4}{x} + \dfrac{1}{x-1}$ \quad LCD $= x(x+1)(x-1)$

$$\frac{x(x+1)(x-1)}{1} \cdot \frac{9}{(x+1)} = \frac{x(x+1)(x-1)}{1} \cdot \frac{4}{x}$$

$$+ \frac{x(x+1)(x-1)}{1} \cdot \frac{1}{(x-1)}$$

$$9x(x-1) = 4(x+1)(x-1) + x(x+1)$$
$$9x^2 - 9x = 4x^2 - 4 + x^2 + x$$
$$4x^2 - 10x + 4 = 0$$
$$2(2x^2 - 5x + 2) = 0$$
$$2(x-2)(2x-1) = 0$$
$$x - 2 = 0 \;\bigg|\; 2x - 1 = 0$$
$$x = 2 \;\bigg|\; x = \frac{1}{2}$$

8. $\left\{1, -\dfrac{1}{5}\right\}$

9. $5(x - 2y) = 14 + 3(2x - y)$

$$5x - 10y = 14 + 6x - 3y$$
$$5x - 6x = 10y - 3y + 14$$
$$-x = 7y + 14$$
$$-14 - x = 7y$$
$$y = \frac{-x-14}{7} = -\frac{x+14}{7}$$

10. $x = \dfrac{y-6}{7}$

11.
$$\frac{R}{1} = \frac{R_1 R_2}{R_1 + R_2}$$
$$R(R_1 + R_2) = R_1 R_2$$
$$RR_1 + RR_2 = R_1 R_2$$
$$RR_2 = R_1 R_2 - RR_1$$
$$RR_2 = R_1(R_2 - R)$$
$$\frac{RR_2}{R_2 - R} = R_1$$
$$R_1 = \frac{RR_2}{R_2 - R}$$

12. $v = \dfrac{uF}{u - F}$

13. A's rate $= \dfrac{1 \text{ job}}{20 \text{ hr}} = \dfrac{1}{20}$ job per hr

B's rate $= \dfrac{1 \text{ job}}{15 \text{ hr}} = \dfrac{1}{15}$ job per hr

Let x = Hours worked together

Since tractor A starts working 5 hr before tractor B starts, the time tractor A works is $x + 5$

$$\begin{array}{ccc} \text{Amount} & + & \text{Amount} \\ \text{A does} & & \text{B does} \end{array} = \frac{1}{\text{job}}$$

$$\frac{1}{20}(x+5) + \frac{1}{15}(x) = 1$$

LCD $= 60$ \quad $\dfrac{60}{1} \cdot \dfrac{x+5}{20} + \dfrac{60}{1} \cdot \dfrac{x}{15} = 60 \cdot 1$

$$3x + 15 + 4x = 60$$
$$7x = 45$$
$$x = \frac{45}{7} = 6\frac{3}{7} \text{ hr}$$

14. $5\dfrac{1}{7}$ min

15. Let $\left.\begin{array}{l} x = \text{Numerator} \\ x + 10 = \text{Denominator} \end{array}\right\}$ Original fraction $= \dfrac{x}{x + 10}$

If one is added to both the numerator and denominator the value of the new fraction is $\dfrac{2}{3}$

$$\dfrac{(x) + 1}{(x + 10) + 1} = \dfrac{2}{3}$$

LCD $= 3(x + 11)$ $\dfrac{x + 1}{x + 11} = \dfrac{2}{3}$

$$\dfrac{3(x + 11)}{1} \cdot \dfrac{x + 1}{(x + 11)} = \dfrac{3(x + 11)}{1} \cdot \dfrac{2}{3}$$

$$3(x + 1) = (x + 11)2$$
$$3x + 3 = 2x + 22$$
$$x = 19$$
$$x + 10 = 29$$

Therefore, the original fraction $= \dfrac{19}{29}$

16. $4\dfrac{8}{13}$ hours

Chapter 6 Diagnostic Test (page 287)

Following each problem number is the textbook section number (in parentheses) where that kind of problem is discussed.

1. (6.1)

a. $\dfrac{2x + 3}{x^2 - 4x}$

The values that make the denominator zero must be excluded:
$$x^2 - 4x = 0$$
$$x(x - 4) = 0$$
$$x = 0 \mid x - 4 = 0$$
$$ x = 4 \quad \text{Exclude: 0 and 4}$$

Therefore, the domain is the set of all real numbers except 0 and 4

b.
$$3y^2 - y - 10 = 0$$
$$(3y + 5)(y - 2) = 0$$
$$3y + 5 = 0 \mid y - 2 = 0$$
$$y = -\dfrac{5}{3} \mid y = 2 \quad \text{Exclude:} -\dfrac{5}{3} \text{ and } 2$$

Therefore, the domain is the set of all real numbers except $-\dfrac{5}{3}$ and 2

2. (6.1)

a. Starting with $\dfrac{4}{-h}$, change the signs of the numerator and denominator

$$\dfrac{4}{-h} = \dfrac{-4}{-(-h)} = \dfrac{-4}{h}$$

b. Starting with $\dfrac{-3}{k - 2}$, change the signs of the numerator and denominator

$$\dfrac{-3}{k - 2} = \dfrac{-(-3)}{-(k - 2)} = \dfrac{3}{2 - k}$$

3. (6.2)

a. $\dfrac{f^2 + 5f + 6}{f^2 - 9} = \dfrac{(f + 2)(f + 3)}{(f - 3)(f + 3)} = \dfrac{f + 2}{f - 3}$

b. $\dfrac{x^4 - 2x^3 + 5x^2 - 10x}{x^3 - 8} \begin{array}{l} \leftarrow \text{Grouping} \\ \leftarrow \text{Difference of two cubes} \end{array}$

$$= \dfrac{x^3(x - 2) + 5x(x - 2)}{(x - 2)(x^2 + 2x + 4)}$$

$$= \dfrac{(x - 2)(x^3 + 5x)}{(x - 2)(x^2 + 2x + 4)} = \dfrac{x(x^2 + 5)}{x^2 + 2x + 4}$$

4. (6.3) $\dfrac{z}{(2z + 1)(z - 3)} \cdot \dfrac{3(2z + 1)(z - 2)}{6z^2} = \dfrac{z - 2}{2z(z - 3)}$

5. (6.3) $\dfrac{\overset{1}{\cancel{(x + 4)}}\overset{1}{\cancel{(x - 6)}}}{\cancel{(x - 6)}\cancel{(x + 6)}} \cdot \dfrac{\overset{1}{\cancel{(x + 1)}}\overset{1}{\cancel{(x + 6)}}}{(x - 3)\cancel{(x + 4)}} \cdot \dfrac{1}{\cancel{(x + 1)}(x^2 - x + 1)}$

$$= \dfrac{1}{(x - 3)(x^2 - x + 1)}$$

6. (6.3) $\dfrac{3\overset{1}{\cancel{(m + n)}}}{(m - n)\cancel{(m^2 + mn + n^2)}} \cdot \dfrac{\overset{1}{\cancel{(m^2 + mn + n^2)}}}{\cancel{(m + n)}(m - n)} = \dfrac{3}{(m - n)^2}$

7. (6.5) $\dfrac{20a + 27b}{12a - 20b} + \dfrac{44a - 13b}{20b - 12a}$

$$= \dfrac{20a + 27b}{12a - 20b} + \dfrac{13b - 44a}{12a - 20b}$$

$$= \dfrac{20a + 27b + 13b - 44a}{12a - 20b}$$

$$= \dfrac{-24a + 40b}{12a - 20b} = \dfrac{-\overset{2}{\cancel{8}}(3a - 5b)^{1}}{\underset{1}{\cancel{4}}(3a - 5b)^{1}} = -2$$

8. (6.5) $\dfrac{x}{(x + 4)} \cdot \dfrac{(x - 4)}{(x - 4)} - \dfrac{x}{(x - 4)} \cdot \dfrac{(x + 4)}{(x + 4)} - \dfrac{32}{(x - 4)(x + 4)}$

$$= \dfrac{x(x - 4) - x(x + 4) - 32}{(x + 4)(x - 4)} = \dfrac{x^2 - 4x - x^2 - 4x - 32}{(x + 4)(x - 4)}$$

$$= \dfrac{-8x - 32}{(x + 4)(x - 4)} = \dfrac{-8\overset{1}{\cancel{(x + 4)}}}{\underset{1}{\cancel{(x + 4)}}(x - 4)}$$

$$= \dfrac{-8}{x - 4} \quad \text{or} \quad -\dfrac{8}{x - 4}$$

$$\text{or} \quad \dfrac{8}{4 - x}$$

9. (6.5) $\dfrac{3}{(x - 2)(x + 3)} \cdot \dfrac{(x + 2)}{(x + 2)} - \dfrac{2}{(x - 2)(x + 2)} \cdot \dfrac{(x + 3)}{(x + 3)}$

$$- \dfrac{3}{(x + 2)(x + 3)} \cdot \dfrac{(x - 2)}{(x - 2)}$$

$$= \dfrac{3(x + 2) - 2(x + 3) - (3)(x - 2)}{(x - 2)(x + 3)(x + 2)}$$

$$= \dfrac{3x + 6 - 2x - 6 - 3x + 6}{(x - 2)(x + 3)(x + 2)} = \dfrac{-2x + 6}{(x - 2)(x + 3)(x + 2)}$$

10. (6.6) $\dfrac{\frac{8h^4}{5k}}{\frac{4h^2}{15k^3}} = \dfrac{8h^4}{5k} \div \dfrac{4h^2}{15k^3} = \dfrac{\overset{2}{\cancel{8}}h^4}{\cancel{5}k} \cdot \dfrac{\overset{3}{\cancel{15}}k^3}{\cancel{4}h^2}$

$$= \dfrac{6h^2k^2}{1} = 6h^2k^2$$

11. (6.6)
$$\frac{6 - \dfrac{4}{w}}{\dfrac{3w}{w-2} + \dfrac{1}{w}} \cdot \frac{w(w-2)}{w(w-2)} = \frac{\dfrac{6}{1}\cdot\dfrac{w(w-2)}{1} - \dfrac{4}{\cancel{w}}\cdot\dfrac{\cancel{w}(w-2)}{1}}{\dfrac{3w}{\cancel{w-2}}\cdot\dfrac{w(\cancel{w-2})}{1} + \dfrac{1}{\cancel{w}}\cdot\dfrac{\cancel{w}(w-2)}{1}}$$

$$= \frac{6w(w-2) - 4(w-2)}{3w^2 + w - 2}$$

$$= \frac{2(w-2)(3w-2)}{(w+1)(3w-2)} = \frac{2(w-2)}{w+1}$$

12. (6.8)
$$\frac{(3a+5)(a-2)}{1} \cdot \frac{2}{3a+5} - \frac{(3a+5)(a-2)}{1} \cdot \frac{6}{a-2}$$

$$= \frac{(3a+5)(a-2)}{1} \cdot \frac{3}{1}$$

$$(a-2)2 - (3a+5)6 = (3a^2 - a - 10)3$$
$$2a - 4 - 18a - 30 = 9a^2 - 3a - 30$$
$$0 = 9a^2 + 13a + 4$$
$$0 = (9a+4)(a+1)$$

$$9a + 4 = 0 \quad \big| \quad a + 1 = 0$$
$$a = -\frac{4}{9} \quad \big| \quad a = -1$$

$$\left\{-\frac{4}{9}, -1\right\}$$

13. (6.8) The domain is the set of all real numbers except -7.
$$(x+7)\left(\frac{x}{x+7}\right) = (x+7)\left(3 - \frac{7}{x+7}\right)$$
$$x = (x+7)(3) - (x+7)\left(\frac{7}{x+7}\right)$$
$$x = 3x + 21 - 7$$
$$x = 3x + 14$$
$$-14 = 2x$$
$$x = -7, \text{ but } -7 \text{ is not in the domain}$$
of the variable. Therefore, there is no solution. The solution set is $\{\ \ \}$.

14. (6.8)
$$\frac{\overset{3}{\cancel{6}z^2}}{1} \cdot \frac{3}{\underset{1}{\cancel{2}z}} + \frac{\overset{3}{\cancel{6}\cancel{z}}}{1} \cdot \frac{3}{\cancel{z}} = \frac{\cancel{6}z^2}{1}\left(-\frac{1}{\cancel{6}}\right)$$
$$9z + 18 = -z^2$$
$$z^2 + 9z + 18 = 0$$
$$(z+3)(z+6) = 0$$
$$z + 3 = 0 \quad \big| \quad z + 6 = 0$$
$$z = -3 \quad \big| \quad z = -6$$
$$\{-3, -6\}$$

15. (6.9)
$$I = \frac{E}{R+r}$$
$$I(R+r) = E$$
$$IR + Ir = E$$
$$Ir = E - IR$$
$$r = \frac{E - IR}{I}$$

16. (6.10) Let $x =$ Number of hours Ruben takes to make 8 bushings

$$\text{Sidney's rate} = \frac{24 \text{ bushings}}{8 \text{ hr}} = \frac{3}{1} \text{ bushings per hr}$$

$$\text{Ruben's rate} = \frac{8 \text{ bushings}}{x \text{ hr}} = \frac{8}{x} \text{ bushings per hr}$$

$$\frac{3}{1}(4) + \frac{8}{x}(4) = 14$$

$$\frac{x}{1}\cdot\frac{12}{1} + \frac{x}{1}\cdot\frac{32}{x} = \frac{x}{1}\cdot\frac{14}{1}$$

$$12x + 32 = 14x$$
$$32 = 2x$$
$$16 = x$$

It takes Ruben 16 hr to make 8 bushings

Cumulative Review Exercises: Chapters 1–6 (page 288)

1. $\left(\dfrac{x^4 y^{-3}}{x^{-2}}\right)^{-2} = (x^{4-(-2)}y^{-3})^{-2} = (x^6 y^{-3})^{-2}$ **2.** $x = -9$

$$= x^{6(-2)}y^{-3(-2)} = x^{-12}y^6 = \frac{y^6}{x^{12}}$$

3. $9 - 2(m-6) \le 3(4-m) + 5$ **4.** $2x^3 - 13x^2 + 26x - 15$
$\quad 9 - 2m + 12 \le 12 - 3m + 5$
$\quad\quad 21 - 2m \le 17 - 3m$
$\quad\quad\quad\quad m \le -4$

5.
$$\begin{array}{r} 4a - 3 \quad\text{R } 10 \\ 2a+3\overline{)8a^2 + 6a + 1} \\ \underline{8a^2 + 12a} \\ -6a + 1 \\ \underline{-6a - 9} \\ +10 \end{array}$$

Answer: $4a - 3 + \dfrac{10}{2a+3}$

6. $x^6 - 12x^5 + 60x^4 - 160x^3 + 240x^2 - 192x + 64$

7. $\dfrac{x+3}{2x^2+3x-2} \cdot \dfrac{2x^2-9x+4}{3x^2+10x+3} \div \dfrac{x-4}{x+2}$

$$= \frac{\overset{1}{\cancel{x+3}}}{\underset{1}{(2x-1)}(x+2)} \cdot \frac{\overset{1}{(2x-1)}\overset{1}{(x-4)}}{(3x+1)\underset{1}{(x+3)}} \cdot \frac{\overset{1}{x+2}}{\underset{1}{x-4}} = \frac{1}{3x+1}$$

8. $\dfrac{3x^2 - 5x + 28}{(2x+1)(x+7)(x-3)}$

9. $\dfrac{a-3}{a^3+27} - \dfrac{1}{a^2-9}$ LCD is $(a+3)(a^2-3a+9)(a-3)$

$$= \frac{a-3}{(a+3)(a^2-3a+9)} - \frac{1}{(a+3)(a-3)}$$

$$= \frac{(a-3)(a-3)}{(a+3)(a^2-3a+9)(a-3)} + \frac{-1(a^2-3a+9)}{(a+3)(a^2-3a+9)(a-3)}$$

$$= \frac{a^2 - 6a + 9 - a^2 + 3a - 9}{(a+3)(a^2-3a+9)(a-3)}$$

$$= \frac{-3a}{(a+3)(a^2-3a+9)(a-3)}$$

10. $(2x+3y)(5x-6y)$ **11.** $x^4 - x^2 - 12$
$\quad\quad\quad\quad\quad\quad\quad\quad\quad = (x^2+3)(x^2-4)$
$\quad\quad\quad\quad\quad\quad\quad\quad\quad = (x^2+3)(x-2)(x+2)$

12. $(x-2)(x^2+2x+4)$ **13.** $6ax + 3bx - 2ay - by$
$\quad\quad\quad\quad\quad\quad\quad\quad\quad\quad = 3x(2a+b) - y(2a+b)$
$\quad\quad\quad\quad\quad\quad\quad\quad\quad\quad = (2a+b)(3x-y)$

14. Length $= 12$ in.; Width $= 5$ in.

15. Let $x =$ Number of 20-cent stamps
$\quad 50 - x =$ Number of 18-cent stamps
$\quad 20x + 18(50 - x) = 970$
$\quad 20x + 900 - 18x = 970$
$\quad\quad\quad\quad\quad 2x = 70$
$\quad\quad\quad\quad\quad\quad x = 35 \quad$ 20-cent stamps
$\quad\quad\quad 50 - x = 15 \quad$ 18-cent stamps

Exercises 7.1A (page 292)

1. $5^{1/2}$ **2.** $7^{1/2}$ **3.** $z^{1/3}$ **4.** $x^{1/4}$ **5.** $x^{3/4}$ **6.** $y^{2/5}$

7. $(x^{2/3})^2 = x^{4/3}$ **8.** $x^{3/2}$ **9.** $x^{2n/n} = x^2$ **10.** y^5 **11.** $\sqrt{7}$

12. $\sqrt[3]{5}$ **13.** $\sqrt[5]{a^3}$ **14.** $\sqrt[3]{b^2}$ **15.** $\sqrt[n]{x^m}$ **16.** $x\sqrt[a]{x^b}$

17. $(2^3)^{1/3} = 2^1 = 2$ **18.** 3   **19.** $[(-3)^3]^{2/3} = (-3)^2 = 9$

20. 4   **21.** $4^{3/2} = (\sqrt{4})^3 = 2^3 = 8$ **22.** 27

23. $(\sqrt[4]{-16})^3$ This is an even index root of a negative radicand; it is not a real number.

24. Not a real number

Exercises 7.1B (page 294)

1. $x^{1/2 + 3/2} = x^{4/2} = x^2$ **2.** y^2 **3.** $a^{3/4 + (-1/2)} = a^{3/4 - 2/4} = a^{1/4}$

4. $b^{1/2}$ **5.** $z^{-1/2}z^{2/3} = z^{-3/6}z^{4/6} = z^{1/6}$ **6.** $N^{5/12}$

7. $H^{(3/4)(2)} = H^{3/2}$ **8.** $s^{5/2}$ **9.** $(x^{-3/4})^{1/3} = x^{-1/4} = \dfrac{1}{x^{1/4}}$

10. $\dfrac{1}{y^{1/3}}$ **11.** $a^{3/4 - 1/2} = a^{3/4 - 2/4} = a^{1/4}$ **12.** $b^{1/2}$

13. $\dfrac{x^{1/2}}{x^{-1/3}} = x^{1/2 - (-1/3)} = x^{3/6 + 2/6} = x^{5/6}$ **14.** $z^{7/12}$

15. $x^{2/3}xx^{-1/2} = x^{4/6}x^{6/6}x^{-3/6} = x^{4/6 + 6/6 - 3/6} = x^{7/6}$ **16.** $x^{17/12}$

17. $(x^{-1/2})^3(x^{2/3})^2 = x^{-3/2}x^{4/3} = x^{-9/6 + 8/6} = x^{-1/6} = \dfrac{1}{x^{1/6}}$

18. $\dfrac{1}{x^{1/2}}$

19. $\dfrac{u^{1/2}v^{-2/3}}{u^{-1/4}v^{-1}} = u^{1/2 - (-1/4)}v^{-2/3 - (-1)} = u^{2/4 + 1/4}v^{-2/3 + 1} = u^{3/4}v^{1/3}$

20. $uv^{2/5}$

21. $(16x^{-2/5}y^{4/9})^{3/2} = (2^4)^{3/2}(x^{-2/5})^{3/2}(y^{4/9})^{3/2}$
$$= 2^6 x^{-3/5}y^{2/3} = \dfrac{64y^{2/3}}{x^{3/5}}$$

22. $\dfrac{4x^{3/4}}{y^{1/2}}$ **23.** $\dfrac{a^{6 \cdot 7/3}d^{0 \cdot 7/3}}{b^{-9 \cdot 7/3}c^{3 \cdot 7/3}} = \dfrac{a^{14}d^0}{b^{-21}c^7} = \dfrac{a^{14}b^{21}}{c^7}$

24. $\dfrac{y^{14}w^{21}}{z^7}$ **25.** $\left(\dfrac{x^3y^0z^{-1}}{32x^{-1}z^2}\right)^{2/5} = \left(\dfrac{x^4}{2^5z^3}\right)^{2/5} = \dfrac{x^{8/5}}{2^2z^{6/5}} = \dfrac{x^{8/5}}{4z^{6/5}}$

26. $\dfrac{a^{10/3}}{4b^{10/3}}$ **27.** $\dfrac{(x^{-1})^{-3/5}(y^{2/3})^{-3/5}}{(z^{-5})^{-3/5}} = \dfrac{x^{3/5}y^{-2/5}}{z^3} = \dfrac{x^{3/5}}{y^{2/5}z^3}$

28. $\dfrac{b^{2/3}}{a^{1/2}c^{4/3}}$

29. $\left(\dfrac{9x^{-2/3}y^{2/9}}{x^{-2}}\right)^{-3/2} = (3^2x^{-2/3 - (-2)}y^{2/9})^{-3/2}$
$$= 3^{2(-3/2)}x^{4/3(-3/2)}y^{2/9(-3/2)}$$
$$= 3^{-3}x^{-2}y^{-1/3} = \dfrac{1}{27x^2y^{1/3}}$$

30. $\dfrac{1}{9SR^{2/5}}$ **31.** $(2^3)^{-2/3} = 2^{3(-2/3)} = 2^{-2} = \dfrac{1}{2^2} = \dfrac{1}{4}$ **32.** $\dfrac{1}{9}$

33. $(2^2)^{1/2}(3^2)^{-3/2} = 2(3^{-3}) = \dfrac{2}{27}$ **34.** $\dfrac{1}{32}$

35. $(10^2)^{-1/2}(-2^{3(1/3)}) = 10^{-1}(-2) = -\dfrac{2}{10} = -\dfrac{1}{5}$ **36.** $-\dfrac{3}{100}$

37. $3x^{2/3}y^{1/6}(y - 3x)$ **38.** $4a^{3/4}b^{3/8}(3a - 2b)$

39. $3x^{1/2}y^{1/3}(6x^2 + 7y)$ **40.** $6x^{3/5}y^{1/4}(6y + 5x)$

41. $(5v^{-1})^2 - 17(v^{-1}) + 6 = (5v^{-1} - 2)(v^{-1} - 3)$

42. $(5v^{-1} - 6)(v^{-1} - 1)$ **43.** $(5k^{-2} - 1)(7k^{-2} - 1)$

44. $(3k^{-2} - 1)(6k^{-2} - 1)$ **45.** $a^{-3/4}b^{-8/3}(2a - b^3)$

46. $x^{-2/5}y^{-1/3}(3y - 5x)$ **47.** $4c^{-3/4}d^{-2/3}e^{-4/5}(2e + 3cd)$

48. $5x^{-1/2}y^{-1/3}(3x + 2y)$

Exercises 7.2A (page 300)

1. $2|x|$ **2.** $3|y|$ **3.** $2x$ **4.** $3y$

5. $\sqrt[4]{2^4x^4y^8} = 2 \cdot |x| \cdot y^2 = 2|x|y^2$ **6.** $3u^2|v|$

7. $\sqrt{2^4 \cdot 2} = 2^2\sqrt{2} = 4\sqrt{2}$ **8.** $3\sqrt{3}$ **9.** $\sqrt{(-2)^2} = |-2| = 2$

10. $\sqrt{(-3)^2} = |-3| = 3$

11. $\sqrt[3]{-3^3 \cdot 3^2} = -3\sqrt[3]{3^2} = -3\sqrt[3]{9}$

12. $-4\sqrt[3]{4}$ **13.** $\sqrt[4]{2^5} = \sqrt[4]{2^4 \cdot 2} = 2\sqrt[4]{2}$

14. $2\sqrt[4]{3}$ **15.** $\sqrt[5]{-x^5 x^2} = -x\sqrt[5]{x^2}$ **16.** $-z\sqrt[5]{z^3}$

17. $\sqrt{2^3a^4b^2} = \sqrt{2^2 \cdot 2 \, a^4b^2} = 2a^2|b|\sqrt{2}$ **18.** $2m^4|u|\sqrt{5}$

19. $\sqrt[3]{3^2 \cdot 2 \, m^2 \, m \, n^4 \, n} = 3|m|n^2\sqrt[3]{2mn}$ **20.** $5h^2|k|\sqrt{2hk}$

21. $5\sqrt[3]{-2^3 \cdot 3a^5b^2} = 5\sqrt[3]{-2^3 \cdot 3 \, a^3 \, a^2b^2} = 5(-2a)\sqrt[3]{3a^2b^2}$
$$= -10a\sqrt[3]{3a^2b^2}$$

22. $-18c\sqrt[3]{2cd}$ **23.** $\sqrt[5]{2^5 \cdot 2 \, m^{10} \, m \, p^{15} \, u} = 2m^2p^3\sqrt[5]{2mu}$

24. $2v^2w^3\sqrt[5]{4u^4w}$ **25.** $\sqrt[3]{2^3(a + b)^3} = 2(a + b)$

26. $3(x - y)^2$

27. $\dfrac{3}{2abc}\sqrt[3]{2^3 \cdot 2^2a^6a^2b^9c^9c} = \dfrac{3}{2abc}(2a^2b^3c^3)\sqrt[3]{2^2a^2c} = 3ab^2c^2\sqrt[3]{4a^2c}$

28. $14abc\sqrt[3]{a^2c}$

Exercises 7.2B (page 303)

1. $\dfrac{\sqrt{16}}{\sqrt{25}} = \dfrac{4}{5}$ **2.** $\dfrac{4}{5}$ **3.** $\dfrac{\sqrt[3]{-27}}{\sqrt[3]{64}} = -\dfrac{3}{4}$ **4.** $-\dfrac{2}{5}$

5. $\dfrac{\sqrt[4]{a^4b^8}}{\sqrt[4]{16}} = \dfrac{|a|b^2}{2}$ **6.** $\dfrac{c^2|d^3|}{3}$

7. $\sqrt{\dfrac{4x^3y}{xy^3}} = \sqrt{\dfrac{4x^2}{y^2}} = \dfrac{\sqrt{4x^2}}{\sqrt{y^2}} = \left|\dfrac{2x}{y}\right|$ **8.** $\dfrac{x^2}{3|y|}$

9. $\dfrac{10}{\sqrt{5}} \cdot \dfrac{\sqrt{5}}{\sqrt{5}} = \dfrac{10\sqrt{5}}{\sqrt{5}\sqrt{5}} = \dfrac{10\sqrt{5}}{5} = 2\sqrt{5}$ **10.** $7\sqrt{2}$

11. $\dfrac{5}{\sqrt{3}} \cdot \dfrac{\sqrt{3}}{\sqrt{3}} = \dfrac{5\sqrt{3}}{\sqrt{3}\sqrt{3}} = \dfrac{5\sqrt{3}}{3}$ **12.** $\dfrac{8\sqrt{7}}{7}$

13. $\dfrac{9}{\sqrt[3]{3}} \cdot \dfrac{\sqrt[3]{3^2}}{\sqrt[3]{3^2}} = \dfrac{9\sqrt[3]{3^2}}{\sqrt[3]{3^3}} = \dfrac{9\sqrt[3]{9}}{3} = 3\sqrt[3]{9}$ **14.** $2\sqrt[3]{25}$

15. $\dfrac{8}{\sqrt[5]{4}} \cdot \dfrac{\sqrt[5]{2^3}}{\sqrt[5]{2^3}} = \dfrac{8\sqrt[5]{2^3}}{\sqrt[5]{2^5}} = \dfrac{8\sqrt[5]{8}}{2} = 4\sqrt[5]{8}$ **16.** $\dfrac{5\sqrt[4]{27}}{3}$

17. $\sqrt[3]{\dfrac{m^3m^2}{-3} \cdot \dfrac{3^2}{3^2}} = \sqrt[3]{\dfrac{m^3m^29}{-3^3}} = \dfrac{m\sqrt[3]{9m^2}}{\sqrt[3]{-3^3}} = -\dfrac{m\sqrt[3]{9m^2}}{3}$ **18.** $-\dfrac{k\sqrt[3]{25k}}{5}$

19. $\dfrac{n}{2m}\sqrt[3]{\dfrac{8m^2n}{2n^3}} = \dfrac{n}{2m}\sqrt[3]{\dfrac{4m^2n}{n^3}} = \dfrac{n}{2m} \cdot \dfrac{1}{n}\sqrt[3]{4m^2n} = \dfrac{1}{2m}\sqrt[3]{4m^2n}$

20. $\dfrac{1}{3y}\sqrt[3]{9xy^2}$

21. $\sqrt[4]{\dfrac{3m^7}{4m^3p^2}} = \sqrt[4]{\dfrac{3m^4}{2^2p^2} \cdot \dfrac{2^2p^2}{2^2p^2}} = \dfrac{\sqrt[4]{12m^4p^2}}{\sqrt[4]{2^4p^4}} = \dfrac{|m|\sqrt[4]{12p^2}}{|2p|}$

22. $\dfrac{|a|\sqrt[4]{40b}}{|2b|}$

23. $\sqrt[5]{\dfrac{15x^4y^7}{24x^6y^2}} = \sqrt[5]{\dfrac{5y^5}{2^3x^2} \cdot \dfrac{2^2x^3}{2^2x^3}} = \dfrac{\sqrt[5]{20x^3y^5}}{\sqrt[5]{2^5x^5}} = \dfrac{y\sqrt[5]{20x^3}}{2x}$

24. $\dfrac{p\sqrt[5]{20m^2}}{2m}$

25. $\dfrac{4x^2}{5y^3}\sqrt[3]{\dfrac{3x^2y^3}{8x^5y}} = \dfrac{4x^2}{5y^3}\sqrt[3]{\dfrac{3y^2}{8x^3}} = \dfrac{4x^2}{5y^3}\cdot\dfrac{1}{2x}\sqrt[3]{3y^2} = \dfrac{2x}{5y^3}\sqrt[3]{3y^2}$

26. $\dfrac{1}{4y}\sqrt[3]{18xy}$

27. $\dfrac{2x^3}{y}\cdot\sqrt[3]{\dfrac{5y^0z}{16x^7z^8}} = \dfrac{2x^3}{y}\cdot\sqrt[3]{\dfrac{5}{2^4x^6xz^6z}} = \dfrac{2x^3}{y}\cdot\dfrac{\sqrt[3]{5}}{2x^2z^2\sqrt[3]{2xz}}$

$= \dfrac{x\sqrt[3]{5}}{yz^2\sqrt[3]{2xz}}\cdot\dfrac{\sqrt[3]{2^2x^2z^2}}{\sqrt[3]{2^2x^2z^2}} = \dfrac{x\sqrt[3]{20x^2z^2}}{yz^2\cdot 2xz} = \dfrac{\sqrt[3]{20x^2z^2}}{2yz^3}$

28. $\dfrac{\sqrt[3]{5bc^2d^2}}{c}$

Exercises 7.2C (page 305)

1. $x^{3/6} = x^{1/2} = \sqrt{x}$ **2.** $\sqrt[3]{x}$ **3.** $a^{6/8} = a^{3/4} = \sqrt[4]{a^3}$ **4.** $\sqrt[4]{a}$

5. $(3^3b^3)^{1/6} = 3^{3/6}b^{3/6} = 3^{1/2}b^{1/2} = (3b)^{1/2} = \sqrt{3b}$ **6.** $\sqrt[3]{2b^2}$

7. $\sqrt[6]{49a^2} = (7^2a^2)^{1/6} = 7^{2/6}a^{2/6} = (7a)^{1/3} = \sqrt[3]{7a}$ **8.** $2\sqrt[3]{3x}$

9. $\sqrt[8]{81x^4y^0z^{12}} = (3^4x^4z^{12})^{1/8} = 3^{1/2}x^{1/2}z^{3/2} = \sqrt{3xz^3} = z\sqrt{3xz}$

10. $x\sqrt{3xy}$

11. $\sqrt[6]{256x^8y^4z^{10}} = (2^8x^8y^4z^{10})^{1/6} = 2^{8/6}x^{8/6}y^{4/6}z^{10/6}$
$= 2^{4/3}x^{4/3}y^{2/3}z^{5/3}$
$= 2^{3/3}\cdot 2^{1/3}\cdot x^{3/3}\cdot x^{1/3}\cdot y^{2/3}\cdot z^{3/3}z^{2/3}$
$= 2xz(2xy^2z^2)^{1/3} = 2xz\sqrt[3]{2xy^2z^2}$

12. $2x^2z\sqrt{2yz}$

13. $\left(\dfrac{x^3}{3^3}\right)^{1/6} = \dfrac{x^{1/2}}{3^{1/2}} = \sqrt{\dfrac{x}{3}} = \sqrt{\dfrac{x(3)}{3(3)}} = \dfrac{\sqrt{3x}}{3}$ **14.** $\dfrac{\sqrt[3]{4x}}{2}$

15. $\dfrac{1}{\sqrt[6]{a^3}} = \dfrac{1}{a^{3/6}} = \dfrac{1}{a^{1/2}} = \dfrac{1}{\sqrt{a}} = \dfrac{1}{\sqrt{a}}\dfrac{\sqrt{a}}{\sqrt{a}} = \dfrac{\sqrt{a}}{a}$ **16.** $\dfrac{\sqrt{x}}{x}$

Exercises 7.3 (page 308)

1. $11\sqrt{2}$ **2.** $18\sqrt{5}$ **3.** $4\sqrt{6}$ **4.** $6\sqrt{7}$ **5.** $\sqrt{15} + \sqrt{10}$

6. $\sqrt{2} + \sqrt{14}$ **7.** $2\sqrt{5}$ **8.** $3\sqrt{3}$ **9.** $3 + 2\sqrt{3}$

10. $5 + 3\sqrt{5}$ **11.** $2\sqrt{3} - 2\sqrt{2}$ **12.** $2\sqrt{7} - \sqrt{3}$

13. $3\sqrt{2} + \sqrt{2} = 4\sqrt{2}$ **14.** $2\sqrt{3}$ **15.** $7\sqrt[3]{xy}$ **16.** $10\sqrt[4]{ab}$

17. $2\sqrt{25\cdot 2} - \sqrt{16\cdot 2} = 2\cdot 5\sqrt{2} - 4\sqrt{2} = 10\sqrt{2} - 4\sqrt{2} = 6\sqrt{2}$

18. $3\sqrt{6}$ **19.** $3\sqrt{32x} - \sqrt{8x} = 3\sqrt{16\cdot 2x} - \sqrt{4\cdot 2x}$
$= 12\sqrt{2x} - 2\sqrt{2x}$
$= 10\sqrt{2x}$

20. $6\sqrt{3y}$

21. $\sqrt{25\cdot 5M} + \sqrt{4\cdot 5M} - \sqrt{9\cdot 5M} = 5\sqrt{5M} + 2\sqrt{5M} - 3\sqrt{5M}$
$= 4\sqrt{5M}$

22. $4\sqrt{3P}$

23. $\sqrt[3]{27x} + \dfrac{1}{2}\sqrt[3]{8x} = 3\sqrt[3]{x} + \dfrac{2}{2}\sqrt[3]{x} = 3\sqrt[3]{x} + \sqrt[3]{x} = 4\sqrt[3]{x}$

24. $6\sqrt[3]{a}$ **25.** $\sqrt[3]{a^4} + 2a\sqrt[3]{8a}$ **26.** $5H\sqrt[3]{H^2}$
$= \sqrt[3]{a^3\cdot a} + 2a\sqrt[3]{8\cdot a}$
$= a\sqrt[3]{a} + 4a\sqrt[3]{a}$
$= 5a\sqrt[3]{a}$

27. $\sqrt[5]{x^2y^5y} + \sqrt[5]{x^5x^2y} = y\sqrt[5]{x^2y} + x\sqrt[5]{x^2y} = (y + x)\sqrt[5]{x^2y}$

28. $(b + a)\sqrt[5]{a^3b^3}$

29. $\dfrac{3}{1}\sqrt{\dfrac{1}{6}\cdot\dfrac{6}{6}} + \sqrt{4\cdot 3} - \dfrac{5}{1}\sqrt{\dfrac{3}{2}\cdot\dfrac{2}{2}} = \dfrac{3}{6}\sqrt{6} + 2\sqrt{3} - \dfrac{5}{2}\sqrt{6}$
$= \left(\dfrac{3}{6} - \dfrac{5}{2}\right)\sqrt{6} + 2\sqrt{3}$
$= -2\sqrt{6} + 2\sqrt{3}$

30. $\sqrt{10} + 2\sqrt{5}$

31. $\dfrac{10}{2}\sqrt{5b} - \dfrac{3b}{2}\sqrt{\dfrac{4}{5b}\cdot\dfrac{5b}{5b}} = 5\sqrt{5b} - \dfrac{3b}{2}\cdot\dfrac{2}{5b}\sqrt{5b}$
$= 5\sqrt{5b} - \dfrac{3}{5}\sqrt{5b} = \left(5 - \dfrac{3}{5}\right)\sqrt{5b}$
$= \left(\dfrac{25}{5} - \dfrac{3}{5}\right)\sqrt{5b} = \dfrac{22}{5}\sqrt{5b}$

32. $\dfrac{7x}{2}\sqrt[3]{4}$

33. $\dfrac{2k}{1}\sqrt[4]{\dfrac{3}{2^3k}\cdot\dfrac{2k^3}{2k^3}} - \dfrac{1}{k}\sqrt[4]{\dfrac{2k^3}{3^3}\cdot\dfrac{3}{3}} + \dfrac{5k^2}{1}\sqrt[4]{\dfrac{6}{k^2}\cdot\dfrac{k^2}{k^2}}$

$= \dfrac{2k}{1}\cdot\dfrac{1}{2k}\sqrt[4]{6k^3} - \dfrac{1}{k}\cdot\dfrac{1}{3}\sqrt[4]{6k^3} + \dfrac{5k^2}{1}\cdot\dfrac{1}{k}\sqrt[4]{6k^2}$

$= \sqrt[4]{6k^3} - \dfrac{1}{3k}\sqrt[4]{6k^3} + 5k\sqrt[4]{6k^2} = \left(1 - \dfrac{1}{3k}\right)\sqrt[4]{6k^3} + 5k\sqrt[4]{6k^2}$

$= \left(\dfrac{3k}{3k} - \dfrac{1}{3k}\right)\sqrt[4]{6k^3} + 5k\sqrt[4]{6k^2} = \dfrac{3k - 1}{3k}\sqrt[4]{6k^3} + 5k\sqrt[4]{6k^2}$

34. $2a\sqrt[3]{4a}$ **35.** $\sqrt{(2x + 1)^2} = 2x + 1$ **36.** $4a + 1$

Exercises 7.4A (page 311)

1. $\sqrt{3\cdot 3} = 3$ **2.** 7 **3.** $\sqrt[3]{3\cdot 9} = \sqrt[3]{3^3} = 3$ **4.** 4

5. $\sqrt[4]{9\cdot 9} = \sqrt[4]{3^4} = 3$ **6.** 5

7. $\sqrt{100a^2b^3} = \sqrt{10^2a^2b^2b} = 10ab\sqrt{b}$ **8.** $9xy\sqrt{x}$

9. $3\cdot 2\sqrt[5]{2a^3b\cdot 2^4a^2b} = 6\sqrt[5]{2^5a^5b^2} = 6\cdot 2a\sqrt[5]{b^2} = 12a\sqrt[5]{b^2}$

10. $40b\sqrt[5]{c^3}$ **11.** $5\sqrt{7}\cdot 5\sqrt{7} = 25\sqrt{7\cdot 7} = 25\cdot 7 = 175$

12. 96 **13.** $\sqrt{2}\cdot\sqrt{2} + \sqrt{2}\cdot 1 = 2 + \sqrt{2}$ **14.** $3 + \sqrt{3}$

15. $\sqrt{x}\cdot\sqrt{x} - \sqrt{x}\cdot 3 = x - 3\sqrt{x}$ **16.** $4\sqrt{y} - y$

17. $\sqrt{3}\cdot 2\sqrt{3} + \sqrt{3}\cdot 1 = 2\cdot 3 + \sqrt{3} = 6 + \sqrt{3}$ **18.** $15 + \sqrt{5}$

19. $\sqrt{3x}\cdot\sqrt{3x} - \sqrt{3x}\cdot 4\sqrt{12} = \sqrt{3x\cdot 3x} - 4\sqrt{6^2x}$
$= 3x - 4\cdot 6\sqrt{x} = 3x - 24\sqrt{x}$

20. $5\sqrt{2a} + 15a$

21. $(\sqrt{7} + 2)(\sqrt{7} + 3) = 7 + 3\sqrt{7} + 2\sqrt{7} + 6 = 13 + 5\sqrt{7}$

22. $11 + 6\sqrt{3}$ **23.** $5^2 - (\sqrt{3})^2$ **24.** 2
$= 25 - 3$
$= 22$

25. $(2\sqrt{3})^2 + 2(2\sqrt{3})(-5) + (-5)^2 = 12 - 20\sqrt{3} + 25$
$= 37 - 20\sqrt{3}$

26. $59 - 30\sqrt{2}$

27. $2\cdot 5\cdot 2\sqrt{3\cdot 7^2x^6xy^4y} = 20\cdot 7x^3y^2\sqrt{3xy} = 140x^3y^2\sqrt{3xy}$

28. $300x^4y^4\sqrt{2xy}$ **29.** $3^2(\sqrt{2x + 5})^2 = 9(2x + 5) = 18x + 45$

30. $|48x - 32|$ **31.** $(\sqrt{2x})^2 - (3)^2 = 2x - 9$ **32.** $5x - 49$

33. $(\sqrt{xy})^2 - 2(\sqrt{xy})(6\sqrt{y}) + (6\sqrt{y})^2 = xy - 12y\sqrt{x} + 36y$

34. $ab + 4a\sqrt{b} + 4a$

(The binomial formula must be used in 35–40.)

35. $(\sqrt[5]{x})^5 + 5(\sqrt[5]{x})^4 + 10(\sqrt[5]{x})^3 + 10(\sqrt[5]{x})^2 + 5\sqrt[5]{x} + 1$

$= x + 5\sqrt[5]{x^4} + 10\sqrt[5]{x^3} + 10\sqrt[5]{x^2} + 5\sqrt[5]{x} + 1$

36. $1 + 3\sqrt[3]{y} + 3\sqrt[3]{y^2} + y$

37. $(x^{1/4})^4 + 4(x^{1/4})^3 + 6(x^{1/4})^2 + 4(x^{1/4})^1 + 1$

$= x + 4x^{3/4} + 6x^{1/2} + 4x^{1/4} + 1$

38. $x + 2x^{1/2}y^{1/2} + y$ or $x + 2\sqrt{xy} + y$

39. If $x = 1 - \sqrt{2}$, then the value of $x^4 - 1$ is

$(1 - \sqrt{2})^4 - 1$

$= [1 - 4\sqrt{2} + 6(\sqrt{2})^2 - 4(\sqrt{2})^3 + (\sqrt{2})^4] - 1$

$= 1 - 4\sqrt{2} + 6(2) - 4(2)\sqrt{2} + 4 - 1$

$= -4\sqrt{2} + 12 - 8\sqrt{2} + 4 = 16 - 12\sqrt{2}$

40. $8 + 5\sqrt{2}$

Exercises 7.4B (page 314)

1. $\sqrt{\dfrac{32}{2}} = \sqrt{16} = 4$ **2.** 7

3. $\sqrt[3]{\dfrac{5}{2^2} \cdot \dfrac{2}{2}} = \sqrt[3]{\dfrac{10}{2^3}} = \dfrac{\sqrt[3]{10}}{2}\left(\text{or }\dfrac{1}{2}\sqrt[3]{10}\right)$ **4.** $\dfrac{\sqrt[3]{28}}{2}\left(\text{or }\dfrac{1}{2}\sqrt[3]{28}\right)$

5. $\dfrac{3}{1}\sqrt[4]{\dfrac{15x}{5x}} = 3\sqrt[4]{3}$ **6.** $3\sqrt[4]{6}$

7. $\sqrt[5]{\dfrac{128z^7}{2z}} = \sqrt[5]{64z^6} = \sqrt[5]{2^6z^6} = 2z\sqrt[5]{2z}$ **8.** $3b\sqrt[5]{3b}$

9. $\sqrt{\dfrac{72x^3y^2}{2xy^2}} = \sqrt{36x^2} = 6x$ **10.** $3y$

11. $\dfrac{\sqrt{20}}{\sqrt{5}} + \dfrac{5\sqrt{10}}{\sqrt{5}} = \sqrt{\dfrac{20}{5}} + 5\sqrt{\dfrac{10}{5}} = \sqrt{4} + 5\sqrt{2} = 2 + 5\sqrt{2}$

12. $2 + \sqrt{3}$ **13.** $3\sqrt[4]{\dfrac{2^5m^2}{2m^3}} = 3\sqrt[4]{\dfrac{2^4}{m} \cdot \dfrac{m^3}{m^3}} = 3\sqrt[4]{\dfrac{2^4m^3}{m^4}} = \dfrac{6\sqrt[4]{m^3}}{m}$

14. $\dfrac{3\sqrt[4]{H^3}}{2H}$

15. $\dfrac{4\sqrt[3]{8x}}{2\sqrt[3]{4x}} + \dfrac{6\sqrt[3]{32x^4}}{2\sqrt[3]{4x}} = 2\sqrt[3]{\dfrac{8x}{4x}} + 3\sqrt[3]{\dfrac{32x^4}{4x}}$

$= 2\sqrt[3]{2} + 3\sqrt[3]{8x^3} = 2\sqrt[3]{2} + 3 \cdot 2x$

$= 2\sqrt[3]{2} + 6x$

16. $6a^2 + 3\sqrt[3]{2}$

17. $\dfrac{6}{\sqrt{3}-1} \cdot \dfrac{\sqrt{3}+1}{\sqrt{3}+1} = \dfrac{6(\sqrt{3}+1)}{(\sqrt{3})^2 - 1^2} = \dfrac{6(\sqrt{3}+1)}{3-1} = \dfrac{6(\sqrt{3}+1)}{2}$

$= 3(\sqrt{3}+1) = 3\sqrt{3} + 3$

18. $5\sqrt{3} - 5$

19. $\dfrac{\sqrt{2}}{\sqrt{3}+\sqrt{2}} \cdot \dfrac{\sqrt{3}-\sqrt{2}}{\sqrt{3}-\sqrt{2}} = \dfrac{\sqrt{2}(\sqrt{3}-\sqrt{2})}{(\sqrt{3})^2 - (\sqrt{2})^2} = \dfrac{\sqrt{6}-2}{3-2} = \sqrt{6} - 2$

20. $\dfrac{7+\sqrt{14}}{5}$

21. $\dfrac{\sqrt{7}+\sqrt{3}}{\sqrt{7}-\sqrt{3}} \cdot \dfrac{\sqrt{7}+\sqrt{3}}{\sqrt{7}+\sqrt{3}} = \dfrac{(\sqrt{7})^2 + 2\sqrt{7}\sqrt{3} + (\sqrt{3})^2}{(\sqrt{7})^2 - (\sqrt{3})^2}$

$= \dfrac{7 + 2\sqrt{21} + 3}{7 - 3} = \dfrac{10 + 2\sqrt{21}}{4}$

$= \dfrac{\overset{1}{2}(5 + \sqrt{21})}{\underset{2}{4}} = \dfrac{5 + \sqrt{21}}{2}$

22. $\dfrac{8 - \sqrt{55}}{3}$

23. $\dfrac{4\sqrt{3}-\sqrt{2}}{4\sqrt{3}+\sqrt{2}} \cdot \dfrac{4\sqrt{3}-\sqrt{2}}{4\sqrt{3}-\sqrt{2}} = \dfrac{(4\sqrt{3}-\sqrt{2})^2}{(4\sqrt{3})^2 - (\sqrt{2})^2} = \dfrac{48 - 8\sqrt{6} + 2}{48 - 2}$

$= \dfrac{50 - 8\sqrt{6}}{46} = \dfrac{2(25 - 4\sqrt{6})}{46}$

$= \dfrac{25 - 4\sqrt{6}}{23}$

24. $2x - 2\sqrt{x^2 + x + 1}$

25. $\sqrt{\dfrac{(a+3)(a-1)}{(a+3)(a+1)}} = \sqrt{\dfrac{a-1}{a+1} \cdot \dfrac{a+1}{a+1}} = \dfrac{\sqrt{a^2-1}}{\sqrt{(a+1)^2}} = \dfrac{\sqrt{a^2-1}}{a+1}$

26. $\dfrac{\sqrt{m^2-1}}{m-1}$

Exercises 7.4C (page 316)

1. $a^{1/2}a^{1/4} = a^{1/2+1/4} = a^{3/4} = \sqrt[4]{a^3}$ **2.** $\sqrt[6]{b^5}$

3. $(2^3)^{1/2}(2^4)^{1/3} = 2^{3/2}2^{4/3} = 2^{3/2+4/3} = 2^{17/6}$ **4.** $9\sqrt[6]{243}$

$= 2^{2+5/6} = 2^2 \cdot 2^{5/6} = 4\sqrt[6]{32}$

5. $x^{2/3}x^{3/4}x^{1/2} = x^{8/12+9/12+6/12} = x^{23/12}$ **6.** $y\sqrt[12]{y^7}$

$= x^{1+11/12} = x^1x^{11/12} = x\sqrt[12]{x^{11}}$

7. $(-2^3z^2)^{1/3}(-z)^{1/3}(2^4z^3)^{1/4} = 2^1z^{2/3}z^{1/3}2^1z^{3/4}$ **8.** $6w\sqrt[4]{w^3}$

$= 2^2z^{1+3/4} = 4z\sqrt[4]{z^3}$

9. $\dfrac{G^{3/4}}{G^{2/3}} = G^{3/4-2/3} = G^{9/12-8/12} = G^{1/12} = \sqrt[12]{G}$ **10.** $\sqrt[10]{H^3}$

11. $\dfrac{-x^{2/3}}{x^{5/6}} = -x^{2/3-5/6} = -x^{4/6-5/6} = -x^{-1/6}$

$= -\dfrac{1}{x^{1/6}} = -\dfrac{1}{x^{1/6}} \cdot \dfrac{x^{5/6}}{x^{5/6}} = -\dfrac{x^{5/6}}{x^{6/6}} = -\dfrac{\sqrt[6]{x^5}}{x}$

12. $-\dfrac{\sqrt[6]{y^5}}{y}$

Review Exercises 7.5 (page 317)

1. $\sqrt[4]{a^3}$ **2.** $\sqrt[4]{3^3y^3}$ or $\sqrt[4]{27y^3}$ **3.** $\sqrt[5]{2^2x^4}$ or $\sqrt[5]{4x^4}$

4. $b^{3/4}$ **5.** $(8x^4)^{1/5}$ or $8^{1/5}x^{4/5}$ **6.** $(27x^3)^{1/5}$ or $27^{1/5}x^{3/5}$

7. $(\sqrt[3]{-64})^2 = (-4)^2 = 16$ **8.** 9

9. $P^{2/3(2/3)}R^{3/4(2/3)} = P^{4/9}R^{1/2}$ **10.** $\dfrac{1}{27a^{1/2}b^{5/2}}$

11. $\sqrt[3]{32} = \sqrt[3]{2^3 \cdot 4} = 2\sqrt[3]{4}$ **12.** $-5x$

13. $\sqrt[4]{16y^8} = (2^4y^8)^{1/4} = 2y^2$ **14.** $m\sqrt[5]{mp}$

15. $\sqrt{\dfrac{4x^2x}{y} \cdot \dfrac{y}{y}} = \dfrac{2x\sqrt{xy}}{y}$ **16.** $\dfrac{5\sqrt{3y}}{y}$,   **17.** $\sqrt[3]{8x^3x^2} = 2x\sqrt[3]{x^2}$

18. $75x$

19. $\dfrac{\sqrt{3}+\sqrt{7}}{\sqrt{3}-\sqrt{7}}\cdot\dfrac{\sqrt{3}+\sqrt{7}}{\sqrt{3}+\sqrt{7}}=\dfrac{3+\sqrt{21}+\sqrt{21}+7}{(\sqrt{3})^2-(\sqrt{7})^2}$

$\qquad\qquad =-\dfrac{10+2\sqrt{21}}{4}=-\dfrac{5+\sqrt{21}}{2}$

20. $2\sqrt{5}-2$

21. $\sqrt{2}\cdot4\sqrt{2}+11\sqrt{2}-3=8+11\sqrt{2}-3=5+11\sqrt{2}$

22. $16+2\sqrt{39}$

23. $\sqrt[3]{8\cdot2\cdot x^3x^2}+x\sqrt[3]{27\cdot2x^2}=2x\sqrt[3]{2x^2}+x\cdot3\sqrt[3]{2x^2}=5x\sqrt[3]{2x^2}$

24. 9

25. $\sqrt[3]{-z^2}\,\sqrt[4]{z^2}=-z^{2/3}\cdot z^{1/2}=-z^{4/6+3/6}$

$\qquad\qquad =-z^{7/6}=-z^{1+1/6}=-z\sqrt[6]{z}$

26. $2-4\sqrt[4]{8}x+6\sqrt{2}x^2-4\sqrt[4]{2}x^3+x^4$

27. $\dfrac{\sqrt[4]{G^2}}{\sqrt[5]{G}}=\dfrac{G^{2/4}}{G^{1/5}}=G^{1/2-1/5}=G^{5/10-2/10}=G^{3/10}=\sqrt[10]{G^3}$

28. $\dfrac{\sqrt[4]{a^2b}}{a}$ **29.** $7x^{-2/3}y^{-3/4}z^{-2/3}(2yz-x)$

30. $(4x^{-1}+3)(x^{-1}-1)$

Exercises 7.6 (page 325)

1. $\sqrt{3x+1}=5$ *Check* $\sqrt{3x+1}=5$ **2.** $\{4\}$

$\quad(\sqrt{3x+1})^2=5^2 \qquad\quad \sqrt{3(8)+1}\overset{?}{=}5$

$\qquad\quad 3x+1=25 \qquad\qquad\quad \sqrt{25}\overset{?}{=}5$

$\qquad\qquad 3x=24 \qquad\qquad\qquad\quad 5=5$

$\qquad\qquad\quad x=8$

3. $\sqrt{x+1}=\sqrt{2x-7}$ *Check* $\sqrt{x+1}=\sqrt{2x-7}$ **4.** $\{3\}$

$\quad(\sqrt{x+1})^2=(\sqrt{2x-7})^2 \qquad \sqrt{8+1}\overset{?}{=}\sqrt{16-7}$

$\qquad\quad x+1=2x-7 \qquad\qquad\quad \sqrt{9}=\sqrt{9}$

$\qquad\qquad 8=x$

$\qquad\qquad x=8$

5. $\sqrt[4]{4x-11}-1=0$ *Check* $\sqrt[4]{4x-11}-1=0$ **6.** $\{5\}$

$\quad(\sqrt[4]{4x-11})^4=(1)^4 \qquad\qquad \sqrt[4]{4(3)-11}-1\overset{?}{=}0$

$\qquad\quad 4x-11=1 \qquad\qquad\qquad\qquad \sqrt[4]{1}-1\overset{?}{=}0$

$\qquad\qquad 4x=12 \qquad\qquad\qquad\qquad\quad 1-1=0$

$\qquad\qquad x=3$

7. $\sqrt{4x-1}=2x$ *Check* $\sqrt{4x-1}=2x$ **8.** $\left\{\dfrac{1}{3}\right\}$

$\quad(\sqrt{4x-1})^2=(2x)^2 \qquad\quad \sqrt{4\left(\dfrac{1}{2}\right)-1}\overset{?}{=}2\left(\dfrac{1}{2}\right)$

$\qquad\quad 4x-1=4x^2$

$\qquad\qquad 0=4x^2-4x+1 \qquad\quad \sqrt{2-1}\overset{?}{=}1$

$\qquad\qquad 0=(2x-1)(2x-1) \qquad\quad 1=1$

$\qquad\quad 2x-1=0$

$\qquad\qquad\quad x=\dfrac{1}{2}$

9. $\sqrt{x+7}=2x-1$ *Check for $x=2$*

$\quad(\sqrt{x+7})^2=(2x-1)^2 \qquad\qquad \sqrt{x+7}=2x-1$

$\qquad\quad x+7=4x^2-4x+1 \qquad\qquad \sqrt{2+7}\overset{?}{=}4-1$

$\qquad\qquad 0=4x^2-5x-6 \qquad\qquad\qquad 3=3$

$\qquad\qquad 0=(x-2)(4x+3)$

$\quad x-2=0\mid4x+3=0 \qquad\qquad$ *Check for $x=-\dfrac{3}{4}$*

$\qquad x=2\mid \quad x=-\dfrac{3}{4} \qquad\qquad\qquad \sqrt{x+7}=2x-1$

$\qquad\qquad\qquad\qquad\qquad\qquad\qquad \sqrt{-\dfrac{3}{4}+7}\overset{?}{=}2\left(-\dfrac{3}{4}\right)-1$

$\qquad\qquad\qquad\qquad\qquad\qquad\qquad\qquad \sqrt{\dfrac{25}{4}}\overset{?}{=}-\dfrac{3}{2}-1$

$\qquad\qquad\qquad\qquad\qquad\qquad\qquad\qquad\quad \dfrac{5}{2}\neq-\dfrac{5}{2}$

Therefore, the solution set is $\{2\}$

10. No solution

11. $\sqrt{3x+4}-\sqrt{2x-4}=2$

$\qquad (\sqrt{3x+4})^2=(\sqrt{2x-4}+2)^2$

$\qquad\quad 3x+4=2x-4+4\sqrt{2x-4}+4$

$\qquad\qquad x+4=4\sqrt{2x-4}$

$\qquad (x+4)^2=(4\sqrt{2x-4})^2$

$\quad x^2+8x+16=32x-64$

$\quad x^2-24x+80=0$

$\quad (x-4)(x-20)=0$

$\quad x-4=0\mid x-20=0$

$\qquad x=4\mid \quad x=20$

Check for $x=4$ $\qquad \sqrt{3(4)+4}-\sqrt{2(4)-4}\overset{?}{=}2$

$\qquad\qquad\qquad\qquad\qquad\qquad \sqrt{16}-\sqrt{4}\overset{?}{=}2$

$\qquad\qquad\qquad\qquad\qquad\qquad\quad 4-2=2$

Check for $x=20$ $\quad \sqrt{3(20)+4}-\sqrt{2(20)-4}\overset{?}{=}2$

$\qquad\qquad\qquad\qquad\qquad\qquad \sqrt{64}-\sqrt{36}\overset{?}{=}2$

$\qquad\qquad\qquad\qquad\qquad\qquad\quad 8-6=2$

12. $\{5,13\}$

13. $\sqrt[3]{2x+3}-2=0$ *Check* $\sqrt[3]{2\left(\dfrac{5}{2}\right)+3}-2\overset{?}{=}0$

$\quad(\sqrt[3]{2x+3})^3=(2)^3 \qquad\qquad \sqrt[3]{5+3}-2\overset{?}{=}0$

$\qquad\quad 2x+3=8 \qquad\qquad\qquad\quad \sqrt[3]{8}-2\overset{?}{=}0$

$\qquad\qquad 2x=5 \qquad\qquad\qquad\qquad 2-2=0$

$\qquad\qquad\quad x=\dfrac{5}{2}$

14. $\left\{\dfrac{15}{2}\right\}$

15. $\qquad\qquad\qquad \sqrt{4u+1}-\sqrt{u-2}=\sqrt{u+3}$

$\qquad\qquad\qquad (\sqrt{4u+1}-\sqrt{u-2})^2=(\sqrt{u+3})^2$

$\quad 4u+1-2\sqrt{4u+1}\sqrt{u-2}+u-2=u+3$

$\qquad\qquad\qquad\qquad 4u-4=2\sqrt{(4u+1)(u-2)}$

$\qquad\qquad\qquad (2u-2)^2=(\sqrt{(4u+1)(u-2)})^2$

$\qquad\qquad\qquad 4u^2-8u+4=4u^2-7u-2$

$\qquad\qquad\qquad\qquad\qquad -u=-6$

$\qquad\qquad\qquad\qquad\qquad\quad u=6$

Check $\sqrt{4(6)+1}-\sqrt{(6)-2}\overset{?}{=}\sqrt{(6)+3}$

$\qquad\qquad\qquad \sqrt{25}-\sqrt{4}\overset{?}{=}\sqrt{9}$

$\qquad\qquad\qquad\quad 5-2=3$

16. $\{1\}$ **17.** $x^{1/2} = 5$ *Check* $(25)^{1/2} \overset{?}{=} 5$ **18.** $\{27\}$
$(x^{1/2})^2 = 5^2$ $(5^2)^{1/2} \overset{?}{=} 5$
$x = 25$ $5 = 5$

19. $2x^{-5/3} = 64$ **20.** $\{1/4\}$
$x^{-5/3} = 32$
$(x^{-5/3})^{-3/5} = (32)^{-3/5}$
$x = (2^5)^{-3/5} = 2^{-3} = \dfrac{1}{2^3}$ or $\dfrac{1}{8}$

Solution set: $\left\{\dfrac{1}{8}\right\}$

(The check will not be shown.)

21. $R = 16, I = 5$ **22.** 576 **23.** $n = 50, \sigma = 3\dfrac{1}{3} = \dfrac{10}{3}$

$5 = \sqrt{\dfrac{P}{16}}$ $\dfrac{10}{3} = \sqrt{50\left(\dfrac{2}{3}\right)p}$

$25 = \dfrac{P}{16}$ $\dfrac{10}{3} = \sqrt{\dfrac{100}{3}p}$

$P = 400$ $\dfrac{100}{9} = \dfrac{100}{3}p$

$p = \dfrac{1}{3}$

24. $\dfrac{2}{5}$

Exercises 7.7 (page 330)

1. $x^2 = (\sqrt{6})^2 + (\sqrt{3})^2$ **2.** 4
$x^2 = 6 + 3$
$x^2 = 9$
$x = \pm\sqrt{9} = \pm 3$
$x = 3$ (-3 is not in the domain)

3. $10^2 + 6^2 = x^2$ **4.** $4\sqrt{13}$
$100 + 36 = x^2$
$136 = x^2$
$x = \pm\sqrt{136} = \pm\sqrt{4 \cdot 34} = \pm 2\sqrt{34}$
$x = 2\sqrt{34}$ ($-2\sqrt{34}$ is not in the domain)

5. $(x + 1)^2 + (\sqrt{20})^2 = (x + 3)^2$ **6.** 7
$x^2 + 2x + 1 + 20 = x^2 + 6x + 9$
$12 = 4x$
$x = 3$

7. Let x = Length of diagonal

$x^2 = 4^2 + 4^2$
$x^2 = 16 + 16$
$x^2 = 32$
$\sqrt{x^2} = \pm\sqrt{32} = \pm\sqrt{16 \cdot 2} = \pm 4\sqrt{2}$
$x = 4\sqrt{2}$

($-4\sqrt{2}$ is not in the domain)

8. $3\sqrt{2}$

9. Let W = Width

$(24)^2 + W^2 = (25)^2$
$576 + W^2 = 625$
$W^2 = 49$
$\sqrt{W^2} = \pm\sqrt{49} = \pm 7$
$W = 7$ (-7 is not in the domain)

10. 9

11. Let x = Length of one leg

$2x - 4$ = Length of other leg
$(10)^2 = (2x - 4)^2 + x^2$
$100 = 4x^2 - 16x + 16 + x^2$
$0 = 5x^2 - 16x - 84$
$0 = (5x + 14)(x - 6)$
$5x + 14 = 0$ $x - 6 = 0$
$x = -\dfrac{14}{5}$ $x = 6$ Length of one leg
  $2x - 4 = 12 - 4$
Not in the domain $= 8$ Length of other leg

12. $\dfrac{9}{5}, \dfrac{38}{5}$

Exercises 7.8A (page 333)

1. $3 + \sqrt{16}\sqrt{-1} = 3 + 4i$ **2.** $4 - 5i$

3. $0 + \sqrt{64}\sqrt{-1} = 0 + 8i$ **4.** $0 + 10i$

5. $5 + \sqrt{16}\sqrt{2}\sqrt{-1} = 5 + 4\sqrt{2}i$ **6.** $6 + 3\sqrt{2}i$

7. $\sqrt{36}\sqrt{-1} + 2 = 6i + 2 = 2 + 6i$ **8.** $3 - 5i$

9. $2i - 3 = -3 + 2i$ **10.** $-4 + 3i$ **11.** $14 + 0i$

12. $-7 + 0i$ **13.** $3 - 4i = x + 2yi$ **14.** $x = 2, y = 5$
$3 = x$ $-4 = 2y$
$x = 3$ $y = -2$
Real parts equal and imaginary parts equal

15. $5x - 3i = 6 - 7yi$ **16.** $x = -3/2, y = -3$
$5x = 6$ $-3 = -7y$
$x = \dfrac{6}{5}$ $y = \dfrac{-3}{-7} = \dfrac{3}{7}$

17. $\sqrt{3}x - yi = 2 + \sqrt{2}i$ **18.** $x = \dfrac{3\sqrt{2}}{4}, y = -\dfrac{\sqrt{5}}{5}$
$\sqrt{3}x = 2$ $-y = \sqrt{2}$
$x = \dfrac{2}{\sqrt{3}} = \dfrac{2\sqrt{3}}{3}$ $y = -\sqrt{2}$

19. $\dfrac{3}{4}x - \dfrac{1}{3}yi = \dfrac{3}{5}x + \dfrac{1}{2}yi$ **20.** $x = 0, y = 0$
$\dfrac{3}{4}x = \dfrac{3}{5}x$ $-\dfrac{1}{3}y = \dfrac{1}{2}y$
$15x = 12x$ $-2y = 3y$
$3x = 0$ $-5y = 0$
$x = 0$ $y = 0$

Exercises 7.8B (page 335)

1. $4 + 3i + 5 - i = 9 + 2i$ **2.** $3 + 3i$

3. $(7 - 4i) - (5 + 2i) = 7 - 4i - 5 - 2i = 2 - 6i$ **4.** $4 - 4i$

5. $(2 + i) + (3i) - (2 - 4i) = 2 + i + 3i - 2 + 4i = 8i = 0 + 8i$

6. $6 - 4i$

7. $(2 + 3i) - (x + yi) = 2 + 3i - x - yi = (2 - x) + (3 - y)i$

8. $(x - 7) + (-1 - y)i$

9. $9 + \sqrt{16}\sqrt{-1} + 2 + \sqrt{25}\sqrt{-1} + 6 - \sqrt{64}\sqrt{-1}$
$= 9 + 4i + 2 + 5i + 6 - 8i$
$= (9 + 2 + 6) + (4 + 5 - 8)i$
$= 17 + i$

10. $11 + 3i$

11. $(4 + 3i) - (5 - i) = (3x + 2yi) + (2x - 3yi)$
$4 + 3i - 5 + i = 3x + 2yi + 2x - 3yi$
$-1 + 4i = 5x - yi$
Therefore, $5x = -1 \mid -y = 4$
$x = -\dfrac{1}{5} \mid y = -4$

12. $x = \dfrac{3}{2}, y = 1$

13. $(2 - 5i) - (5 + 3i) = (3x + 2yi) - (5x + 3yi)$
$2 - 5i - 5 - 3i = 3x + 2yi - 5x - 3yi$
$-3 - 8i = -2x - yi$
$-3 = -2x \mid -8 = -y$
$x = \dfrac{3}{2} \mid y = 8$

14. $x = -4/3, y = 6/5$

Exercises 7.8C (page 338)

1. $1^2 - i^2 = 1 - (-1) = 1 + 1 = 2 = 2 + 0i$ **2.** $13 + 0i$

3. $12 + 5i - 2i^2 = 12 + 5i + 2 = 14 + 5i$ **4.** $16 - 11i$

5. $12 - 22i + 6i^2 = 12 - 22i - 6 = 6 - 22i$ **6.** $-2 + 29i$

7. $(\sqrt{5})^2 - (2i)^2 = 5 - (-4) = 5 + 4 = 9 = 9 + 0i$ **8.** $16 + 0i$

9. $5i^2 - 10i = -5 - 10i$ **10.** $-12 - 6i$

11. $(2)^2 + 2(2)(5i) + (5i)^2 = 4 + 20i + 25i^2$ **12.** $-7 - 24i$
$= 4 + 20i - 25 = -21 + 20i$

13. $i^{10} = i^8 \cdot i^2 = 1 \cdot (-1) = -1 = -1 + 0i$ **14.** $0 - i$

15. $i^{87} = (i^4)^{21}i^3 = (1)(-i) = -i = 0 - i$ **16.** $0 + i$

17. $(3i)^3 = 3^3i^2i = 27(-1)i = -27i = 0 - 27i$ **18.** $0 - 8i$

19. $2^4i^4 = 16(1) = 16 + 0i$ **20.** $81 + 0i$

21. $(3 - 2i)(4 + 5i) = 12 + 7i - 10i^2 = 12 + 7i + 10 = 22 + 7i$

22. $58 - 14i$ **23.** $(2 - i)^2 = 4 - 4i + (i)^2 = 4 - 4i - 1 = 3 - 4i$

24. $8 + 6i$ **25.** $[3 + i^6]^2 = [3 - 1]^2 = 2^2 = 4 + 0i$ **26.** $25 + 0i$

27. $i^{10}(i^{23}) = i^{33} = (i^4)^8 \cdot i = 1 \cdot i = 0 + i$ **28.** $-1 + 0i$

29. $i^{15} + i^7 = -i + (-i) = 0 - 2i$ **30.** $-1 - i$

31. $[2 + (-i)^{11}]^2 = [2 + i]^2 = 4 + 4i + i^2 = 4 + 4i - 1 = 3 + 4i$

32. $8 + 6i$

33. $(1 - i)^5$ (The binomial theorem must be used.)
$= 1 - 5i + 10i^2 - 10i^3 + 5i^4 - i^5 = 1 - 5i - 10 + 10i + 5 - i$
$= -4 + 4i$

34. $-4 + 0i$

35. $(2 - i)^4 = 2^4 - 4(2^3)i + 6(2^2)i^2 - 4(2)i^3 + i^4$
$= 16 - 32i - 24 + 8i + 1 = -7 - 24i$

36. $52 - 47i$

Exercises 7.8D (page 340)

1. $3 + 2i$ **2.** $5 - 4i$ **3.** $-5i$ **4.** $7i$ **5.** 10 **6.** -8

7. $\dfrac{10}{1 + 3i} \cdot \dfrac{1 - 3i}{1 - 3i} = \dfrac{10(1 - 3i)}{1 - 9i^2} = \dfrac{10(1 - 3i)}{1 + 9} = \dfrac{10(1 - 3i)}{10} = 1 - 3i$

8. $1 - 2i$

9. $\dfrac{1 + i}{1 - i} \cdot \dfrac{1 + i}{1 + i} = \dfrac{1 + 2i + i^2}{1 - i^2} = \dfrac{1 + 2i - 1}{1 - (-1)} = \dfrac{2i}{2} = i = 0 + i$

10. $0 - i$ **11.** $\dfrac{8 + i}{i} \cdot \dfrac{-i}{-i} = \dfrac{-8i - i^2}{-i^2} = \dfrac{-8i - (-1)}{-(-1)} = 1 - 8i$

12. $-1 - 4i$ **13.** $\dfrac{3}{2i} \cdot \dfrac{i}{i} = \dfrac{3i}{2i^2} = \dfrac{3i}{-2} = 0 - \dfrac{3}{2}i$ **14.** $0 - \dfrac{4}{5}i$

15. $\dfrac{15i}{1 - 2i} \cdot \dfrac{1 + 2i}{1 + 2i} = \dfrac{15i + 30i^2}{1 - 4i^2} = \dfrac{15i - 30}{1 + 4}$ **16.** $-6 + 2i$
$= \dfrac{15i - 30}{5} = \dfrac{5(3i - 6)}{5} = -6 + 3i$

17. $\dfrac{4 + 3i}{2 - i} \cdot \dfrac{2 + i}{2 + i} = \dfrac{8 + 10i + 3i^2}{4 - i^2} = \dfrac{8 + 10i - 3}{4 - (-1)}$ **18.** $\dfrac{4}{5} + \dfrac{i}{10}$
$= \dfrac{5 + 10i}{5} = \dfrac{5(1 + 2i)}{5} = 1 + 2i$

Review Exercises 7.9 (page 342)

1. $\sqrt{x - 5} = \sqrt{3x + 8}$ **2.** 7
Domain: $\{x|x - 5 \geq 0\} \cap \{x|3x + 8 \geq 0\} = \{x|x \geq 5\}$
$(\sqrt{x - 5})^2 = (\sqrt{3x + 8})^2$
$x - 5 = 3x + 8$
$-13 = 2x$
$x = -\dfrac{13}{2}$ Not in the domain

Therefore, no solution

3. $\sqrt{5x - 4} - \sqrt{2x + 1} = 1$
$(\sqrt{5x - 4})^2 = (\sqrt{2x + 1} + 1)^2$
$5x - 4 = 2x + 1 + 2\sqrt{2x + 1} + 1$
$3x - 6 = 2\sqrt{2x + 1}$
$9x^2 - 36x + 36 = 4(2x + 1)$
$9x^2 - 44x + 32 = 0$
$(x - 4)(9x - 8) = 0$
$x - 4 = 0 \mid 9x - 8 = 0$
$x = 4 \mid x = \dfrac{8}{9}$

Check for $x = 4$
$\sqrt{5x - 4} - \sqrt{2x + 1} = 1$
$\sqrt{5(4) - 4} - \sqrt{2(4) + 1} \overset{?}{=} 1$
$4 - 3 = 1$
4 is a solution

Check for $x = \dfrac{8}{9}$
$\sqrt{5x - 4} - \sqrt{2x + 1} = 1$
$\sqrt{5\left(\dfrac{8}{9}\right) - 4} - \sqrt{2\left(\dfrac{8}{9}\right) + 1} \overset{?}{=} 1$
$\sqrt{\dfrac{40 - 36}{9}} - \sqrt{\dfrac{16 + 9}{9}} \overset{?}{=} 1$
$\dfrac{2}{3} - \dfrac{5}{3} \overset{?}{=} 1$
$-1 \neq 1$

$\dfrac{8}{9}$ is not a solution

4. $-\dfrac{36}{5}$ **5.** $x^{5/6} = 32$ **6.** 81
$(x^{5/6})^{6/5} = 32^{6/5}$
$x = (2^5)^{6/5}$
$= 2^6$ or 64

7. $5 - yi = x + 6i$ Real parts equal **8.** $x = -1, y = -2$
$5 = x \mid -y = 6$ and imaginary parts
$x = 5 \mid y = -6$ equal

9. $(3i + 2)(4 - 2i) = 12i + 8 - 6i^2 - 4i$ **10.** $-41 + i$
$= \underline{12i} + \underline{8} + \underline{6} - \underline{4i} = 14 + 8i$

11. $\dfrac{2 + i}{1 + 3i} \cdot \dfrac{1 - 3i}{1 - 3i} = \dfrac{2 - 3i^2 - 5i}{1 - 9i^2} = \dfrac{5 - 5i}{10} = \dfrac{1}{2} - \dfrac{1}{2}i$

12. $\dfrac{1}{5} + \dfrac{7}{5}i$

13. $(4 + \sqrt{9 \cdot 3(-1)}) + (2 - \sqrt{4 \cdot 3(-1)}) - (1 - \sqrt{3(-1)})$
$= (4 + 3\sqrt{3}i) + (2 - 2\sqrt{3}i) - (1 - \sqrt{3}i)$
$= 4 + 3\sqrt{3}i + 2 - 2\sqrt{3}i - 1 + \sqrt{3}i$
$= 5 + 2\sqrt{3}i$

14. Width $= 3$; length $= 5$

15. Let $x = $ Width
$x + 3 = $ Length
$$x^2 + (x + 3)^2 = (\sqrt{45})^2$$
$$x^2 + x^2 + 6x + 9 = 45$$
$$2x^2 + 6x - 36 = 0$$
$$2(x + 6)(x - 3) = 0$$
$2 \neq 0 \;\Big|\; x + 6 = 0 \;\Big|\; x - 3 = 0$
$ x = -6 \;\Big|\; x = 3$ Width
 Not in the $\;\Big|\; x + 3 = 6$ Length
 domain

$Check \quad 3^2 + 6^2 \overset{?}{=} (\sqrt{45})^2$
$ 9 + 36 = 45$

Chapter 7 Diagnostic Test (page 345)

Following each problem number is the textbook section number (in parentheses) where that kind of problem is discussed.

1. (7.1) $\quad x^{1/2}x^{-1/4} = x^{1/2 - 1/4} = x^{1/4}$

2. (7.1) $\quad (R^{-4/3})^3 = R^{(-4/3)(3)} = R^{-4} = \dfrac{1}{R^4}$

3. (7.1) $\quad \dfrac{a^{5/6}}{a^{1/3}} = a^{5/6 - 1/3} = a^{3/6} = a^{1/2}$

4. (7.1) $\quad \left(\dfrac{x^{-2/3}y^{3/5}}{x^{1/3}y}\right)^{-5/2} = (x^{-2/3 - 1/3}y^{3/5 - 1})^{-5/2} = (x^{-1}y^{-2/5})^{-5/2}$
$ = x^{(-1)(-5/2)}y^{(-2/5)(-5/2)} = x^{5/2}y$

5. (7.2) $\quad \sqrt[3]{54x^6y^7} = \sqrt[3]{2(27)x^6y^6y} = 3x^2y^2\sqrt[3]{2y}$

6. (7.2) $\quad \dfrac{4xy}{\sqrt{2x}} = \dfrac{4xy}{\sqrt{2x}} \cdot \dfrac{\sqrt{2x}}{\sqrt{2x}} = \dfrac{4xy\sqrt{2x}}{2x} = 2y\sqrt{2x}$

7. (7.2) $\quad \sqrt[6]{a^3} = a^{3/6} = a^{1/2} = \sqrt{a}$

8. (7.3) $\quad \sqrt{40} + \sqrt{9} = 2\sqrt{10} + 3$

9. (7.4) $\quad \sqrt{x}\sqrt[3]{x} = x^{1/2}x^{1/3} = x^{1/2 + 1/3} = x^{5/6} = \sqrt[6]{x^5}$

10. (7.1) $\quad (-27)^{2/3} = [(-3)^3]^{2/3} = (-3)^{3(2/3)} = (-3)^2 = 9$

11. (7.3) $\quad 4\sqrt{8y} + 3\sqrt{32y} = 4\sqrt{4 \cdot 2y} + 3\sqrt{16 \cdot 2y}$
$ = 4(2)\sqrt{2y} + 3(4)\sqrt{2y} = 20\sqrt{2y}$

12. (7.3) $\quad 3\sqrt{\dfrac{5x^2}{2}} - 5\sqrt{\dfrac{x^2}{10}} = 3\sqrt{\dfrac{5x^2}{2} \cdot \dfrac{2}{2}} - 5\sqrt{\dfrac{x^2}{10} \cdot \dfrac{10}{10}}$
$ = 3\sqrt{\dfrac{10x^2}{4}} - 5\sqrt{\dfrac{10x^2}{100}}$
$ = \dfrac{3x\sqrt{10}}{2} - \dfrac{5x\sqrt{10}}{10}$
$ = \dfrac{3}{2}x\sqrt{10} - \dfrac{1}{2}x\sqrt{10} = x\sqrt{10}$

13. (7.4) $\quad \sqrt{2x^4}\sqrt{8x^3} = \sqrt{16x^6x} = 4x^3\sqrt{x}$

14. (7.4) $\quad \sqrt{2x}(\sqrt{8x} - 5\sqrt{2}) = \sqrt{2x}\sqrt{8x} + \sqrt{2x}(-5\sqrt{2})$
$ = \sqrt{16x^2} - 5\sqrt{4x} = 4x - 10\sqrt{x}$

15. (7.4) $\quad \dfrac{\sqrt{10x} + \sqrt{5x}}{\sqrt{5x}} = \dfrac{\sqrt{10x}}{\sqrt{5x}} + \dfrac{\sqrt{5x}}{\sqrt{5x}} = \sqrt{\dfrac{10x}{5x}} + 1 = \sqrt{2} + 1$

16. (7.4) $\quad \dfrac{5}{\sqrt{7} + \sqrt{2}} = \dfrac{5}{\sqrt{7} + \sqrt{2}} \cdot \dfrac{(\sqrt{7} - \sqrt{2})}{(\sqrt{7} - \sqrt{2})}$
$ = \dfrac{5(\sqrt{7} - \sqrt{2})}{7 - 2} = \sqrt{7} - \sqrt{2}$

17. (7.4) $\quad (1 - \sqrt[3]{x})^3 = (1)^3 + 3(1)^2(-\sqrt[3]{x}) + 3(1)(-\sqrt[3]{x})^2 + (-\sqrt[3]{x})^3$
$ = 1 - 3\sqrt[3]{x} + 3\sqrt[3]{x^2} - x$

18. (7.8)
$(5 - \sqrt{-8}) - (3 - \sqrt{-18}) = 5 - \sqrt{4 \cdot 2(-1)} - 3 + \sqrt{9 \cdot 2(-1)}$
$\phantom{(5 - \sqrt{-8}) - (3 - \sqrt{-18})} = 5 - 2\sqrt{2}i - 3 + 3\sqrt{2}i = 2 + \sqrt{2}i$

19. (7.8) $\quad (3 + i)(2 - 5i) = 6 - 15i + 2i - 5i^2$
$ = 6 - 13i - 5(-1) = 6 - 13i + 5$
$ = 11 - 13i$

20. (7.8) $\quad \dfrac{10}{1 - 3i} = \dfrac{10}{1 - 3i} \cdot \dfrac{1 + 3i}{1 + 3i} = \dfrac{10(1 + 3i)}{1 - 9i^2}$
$ = \dfrac{10(1 + 3i)}{10} = 1 + 3i$

21. (7.7) $\quad (2 - i)^3 = 2^3 - 3(2^2)i + 3(2)i^2 - i^3$
$ = 8 - 12i + 6(-1) - (-i)$
$ = 8 - 6 - 12i + i$
$ = 2 - 11i$

22. (7.6) $\quad x^{3/2} = 8 \qquad\qquad Check \quad x^{3/2} = 8$
$ (x^{3/2})^{2/3} = 8^{2/3} = (2^3)^{2/3} \qquad (4)^{3/2} \overset{?}{=} 2^3$
$ x = 2^2 \qquad\qquad\qquad (2^2)^{3/2} \overset{?}{=} 2^3$
$ x = 4 \qquad\qquad\qquad\quad 2^3 = 2^3$

23. (7.6) $\quad \sqrt{x - 3} + 5 = x$
$ (\sqrt{x - 3})^2 = (x - 5)^2$
$ x - 3 = x^2 - 10x + 25$
$ 0 = x^2 - 11x + 28$
$ 0 = (x - 4)(x - 7)$
$ x - 4 = 0 \;\Big|\; x - 7 = 0$
$ x = 4 \;\Big|\; x = 7$

$Check\ for\ x = 4 \qquad Check\ for\ x = 7$
$\sqrt{x - 3} + 5 = x \qquad \sqrt{x - 3} + 5 = x$
$\sqrt{4 - 3} + 5 \overset{?}{=} 4 \qquad \sqrt{7 - 3} + 5 \overset{?}{=} 7$
$\sqrt{1} + 5 \overset{?}{=} 4 \qquad\quad \sqrt{4} + 5 \overset{?}{=} 7$
$1 + 5 \neq 4 \qquad\qquad 2 + 5 = 7$
Therefore, 4 is $\qquad$ Therefore, 7 is
not a solution $\qquad$ a solution

24. (7.7) $\quad (x + 3)^2 = (x + 1)^2 + (\sqrt{12})^2$
$ x^2 + 6x + 9 = x^2 + 2x + 1 + 12$
$ 4x = 4$
$ x = 1$

Cumulative Review Exercises: Chapters 1–7 (page 346)

1. LCD $= (a + 3)(a - 3)(a - 1)$

$\dfrac{6}{(a + 3)(a - 3)} \cdot \dfrac{a - 1}{a - 1} \div \dfrac{2}{(a - 3)(a - 1)} \cdot \dfrac{a + 3}{a + 3}$

$= \dfrac{6a - 6}{(a + 3)(a - 3)(a - 1)} - \dfrac{2a + 6}{(a + 3)(a - 3)(a - 1)}$

$= \dfrac{6a - 6 - 2a - 6}{(a + 3)(a - 3)(a - 1)} = \dfrac{4a - 12}{(a + 3)(a - 3)(a - 1)}$

$= \dfrac{4(a - 3)}{(a + 3)(a - 3)(a - 1)} = \dfrac{4}{(a + 3)(a - 1)}$

2. $\dfrac{x^2 + 2x + 4}{x^2}$

3. $\dfrac{\dfrac{4}{x}\cdot\dfrac{x^2}{1}-\dfrac{8}{x^2}\cdot\dfrac{x^2}{1}}{\dfrac{1}{x}\cdot\dfrac{x^2}{1}-\dfrac{2}{x^2}\cdot\dfrac{x^2}{1}}=\dfrac{4x-8}{x-2}=\dfrac{4(x-2)}{x-2}=4$ 4. $5x+2\sqrt{5x}$

5. $(\sqrt{26})^2-2\sqrt{26}\,\sqrt{10}+(\sqrt{10})^2$
$\quad=26-2\sqrt{2^2\cdot13\cdot5}+10$
$\quad=36-4\sqrt{65}$

6. $-12-6\sqrt{5}$

7. $3(4x-1)-(3-2x)=4(2x-3)$
$\qquad 12x-3-3+2x=8x-12$
$\qquad\quad 14x-6=8x-12$
$\qquad\qquad\quad 6x=-6$
$\qquad\qquad\quad\ x=-1$

8. $x\le 5$

9.
$\qquad\sqrt{2x+2}=1+\sqrt{3x-12}$
$\qquad(\sqrt{2x+2})^2=(1+\sqrt{3x-12})^2$
$\qquad 2x+2=1+2(1)(\sqrt{3x-12})+3x-12$
$\qquad 2x+2=3x-11+2\sqrt{3x-12}$
$\qquad -x+13=2\sqrt{3x-12}$
$\qquad(-x+13)^2=(2\sqrt{3x-12})^2$
$\qquad x^2-26x+169=4(3x-12)$
$\qquad x^2-26x+169=12x-48$
$\qquad x^2-38x+217=0$
$\qquad(x-7)(x-31)=0$
$\qquad\qquad x-7=0\mid x-31=0$
$\qquad\qquad\quad x=7\mid\quad x=31$

$\quad Check\ for\ x=7\quad \sqrt{2x+2}=1+\sqrt{3x-12}$
$\qquad\qquad\qquad\sqrt{2(7)+2}\overset{?}{=}1+\sqrt{3(7)-12}$
$\qquad\qquad\qquad\quad\sqrt{16}\overset{?}{=}1+\sqrt{9}$
$\qquad\qquad\qquad\qquad 4=1+3$
$\quad Check\ for\ x=31\quad \sqrt{2x+2}=1+\sqrt{3x-12}$
$\qquad\qquad\qquad\sqrt{2(31)+2}\overset{?}{=}1+\sqrt{3(31)-12}$
$\qquad\qquad\qquad\quad\sqrt{64}\overset{?}{=}1+\sqrt{81}$
$\qquad\qquad\qquad\qquad 8\ne1+9$

Therefore, the only solution is $x=7$.

10. $x=-3$

11. $6x^2+11x=10$
$\quad 6x^2+11x-10=0$
$\quad(3x-2)(2x+5)=0$
$\quad 3x-2=0\mid 2x+5=0$
$\quad\quad 3x=2\mid\quad 2x=-5$
$\quad\quad x=\dfrac{2}{3}\mid\quad x=-\dfrac{5}{2}$

12. $a=\dfrac{bc}{b-c}$

13. $|2x-5|>3$

$\quad 2x-5>3$ or $2x-5<-3$
$\quad\ 2x>8$ or $\quad\ 2x<\ \ 2$
$\quad\ \ x>4$ or $\quad\ \ x<\ \ 1$

14. $\dfrac{30}{11}$ hr $=2\dfrac{8}{11}$ hr

15. Let $2x=$ Number of cm in width
$\quad$ Let $3x=$ Number of cm in length
$\quad(2x)(3x)=54$
$\qquad\quad 6x^2=54$
$\qquad\quad\ x^2=9$
$\qquad\quad\ \ x=\pm3$
$\quad-3$ is not in the domain; $x=3$
$\quad 2x=6$ cm in width
$\quad 3x=9$ cm in length
$\quad Check\quad(6$ cm$)(9$ cm$)=54$ sq cm

Exercises 8.1 (page 353)

1a. $(3,0)$ b. $(0,5)$ c. $(-5,2)$ d. $(-4,-3)$
2a. $(4,3)$ b. $(-6,0)$ c. $(3,-4)$ d. $(0,-3)$

3.
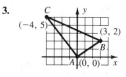

4.
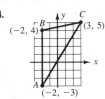

5a. Let $P_1=(-2,-2)$ and $P_2=(2,1)$
$\quad$ Then $d=\sqrt{[2-(-2)]^2+[1-(-2)]^2}$
$\qquad\qquad=\sqrt{4^2+3^2}=\sqrt{16+9}=\sqrt{25}=5$
  b. Let $P_1=(-3,3)$ and $P_2=(3,-1)$
$\quad$ Then $d=\sqrt{[3-(-3)]^2+[-1-3]^2}$
$\qquad\qquad=\sqrt{36+16}=\sqrt{52}=\sqrt{4\cdot13}=2\sqrt{13}$
  c. $|-2-5|=|-7|=7$ d. $|-2-(-5)|=|3|=3$
  e. $d=\sqrt{(4-0)^2+(6-0)^2}=\sqrt{16+36}=\sqrt{52}$
$\qquad=\sqrt{4\cdot13}=2\sqrt{13}$

6a. 13 b. $\sqrt{74}$ c. 6 d. 6 e. $3\sqrt{13}$

7. $|AB|=\sqrt{[4-(-2)]^2+(2-2)^2}=\sqrt{6^2}=6$
$\quad|BC|=\sqrt{(6-4)^2+(8-2)^2}=\sqrt{4+36}=\sqrt{40}$
$\qquad\quad=\sqrt{4\cdot10}=2\sqrt{10}$
$\quad|AC|=\sqrt{[6-(-2)]^2+(8-2)^2}=\sqrt{64+36}=\sqrt{100}=10$
$\quad$ Perimeter $=6+2\sqrt{10}+10=16+2\sqrt{10}$

8. $16+4\sqrt{5}$

9. $\quad|AB|=\sqrt{[5-(-3)]^2+[-1-(-2)]^2}=\sqrt{64+1}=\sqrt{65}$
$\quad|BC|=\sqrt{(3-5)^2+[2-(-1)]^2}=\sqrt{4+9}=\sqrt{13}$
$\quad|AC|=\sqrt{[3-(-3)]^2+[2-(-2)]^2}=\sqrt{36+16}=\sqrt{52}$
$\quad(|AB|)^2\overset{?}{=}(|BC|)^2+(|AC|)^2$
$\quad(\sqrt{65})^2\overset{?}{=}(\sqrt{13})^2+(\sqrt{52})^2$
$\qquad\ 65=13+52$
$\quad$ Therefore, the triangle is a right triangle

10. The triangle is a right triangle

11. Domain $=\{2,3,0,-3\}$
$\quad$ Range $=\{-1,4,2,-2\}$

12. Domain $=\{-4,0,3,1,-3\}$
$\quad$ Range $=\{0,-2,5,-3\}$

Exercises 8.2 (page 360)

1. $\quad 3x+2y=6$
$\quad 3x+2(0)=6$
$\qquad\qquad x=2$
$\quad 3(0)+2y=6$
$\qquad\qquad y=3$

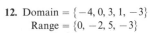

x	y
2	0
0	3
4	-3

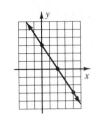

2.

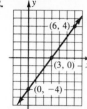

(6, 4)
(3, 0)
(0, −4)

3. $5x - 3y = 15$
$5x - 3(0) = 15$
$x = 3$
$5(0) - 3y = 15$
$y = -5$

x	y
3	0
0	−5
6	5

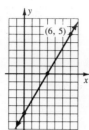

(6, 5)

8.

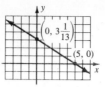

$\left(0, 3\frac{1}{13}\right)$
(5, 0)

9. $9y = 25 - 7x$
$9(0) = 25 - 7x$
$x = 3\frac{4}{7}$
$9y = 25 - 7(0)$
$y = 2\frac{7}{9}$

x	y
$3\frac{4}{7}$	0
0	$2\frac{7}{9}$
2	$1\frac{2}{9}$

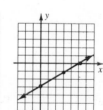

10.

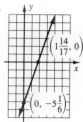

$\left(1\frac{14}{17}, 0\right)$
$\left(0, -5\frac{1}{6}\right)$

4.

(−5, 4)
(0, 2)
(5, 0)

5. $9x + 5y = 18$
$9x + 5(0) = 18$
$x = 2$
$9(0) + 5y = 18$
$y = 3\frac{3}{5}$

x	y
2	0
0	$3\frac{3}{5}$
4	$-3\frac{3}{5}$

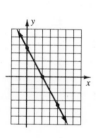

11. $8x - 41 = 14y$
$8x - 41 = 14(0)$
$x = 5\frac{1}{8}$
$8(0) - 41 = 14y$
$-2\frac{13}{14} = y$

x	y
$5\frac{1}{8}$	0
0	$-2\frac{13}{14}$
3	$-1\frac{3}{14}$

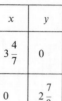

12.

(0, 6.6)
(2.2, 0)

6.

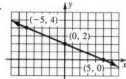

(0, −2)
$\left(3\frac{2}{3}, 0\right)$

7. $10x = 21 + 7y$
$10x = 21 + 7(0)$
$x = 2\frac{1}{10}$
$10(0) = 21 + 7y$
$-3 = y$

x	y
$2\frac{1}{10}$	0
0	−3
4	$2\frac{5}{7}$

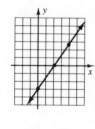

13. $6x + 11y = 0$
Both intercepts are (0, 0)
Set $y = 3$: $6x + 11(3) = 0$
$6x + 33 = 0$
$x = -5\frac{1}{2}$

x	y
0	0
$-5\frac{1}{2}$	3
2	$-1\frac{1}{11}$

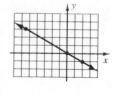

14.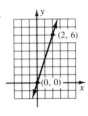

15. $4y = -8x$

x	y
0	0
1	-2
-1	2

16.

17. $x = -5$; x is always -5 no matter what y is. Vertical line

18.

19. $y = -3$; y is always -3, no matter what x is. Horizontal line

20.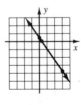

21. $7x + 5y = 2$
$7x + 5(0) = 2$
$x = \dfrac{2}{7}$
$7(0) + 5y = 2$
$y = \dfrac{2}{5}$

x	y
$\dfrac{2}{7}$	0
0	$\dfrac{2}{5}$
3	$-3\dfrac{4}{5}$

22. $\left(0, \dfrac{1}{2}\right)$ $\left(1\dfrac{1}{3}, 0\right)$ $(4, -1)$

23. $2y = x - 2$
$2(0) = x - 2$
$2 = x$
$2y = (0) - 2$
$y = -1$

x	y
2	0
0	-1
-2	-2

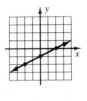

24.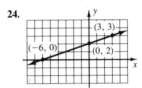

25. $3x - 15 = 7y$
$3x - 15 = 7(0)$
$x = 5$
$3(0) - 15 = 7y$
$-2\dfrac{1}{7} = y$

x	y
5	0
0	$-2\dfrac{1}{7}$
3	$-\dfrac{6}{7}$

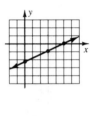

26. $(0, 6)$ $\left(-4\dfrac{1}{2}, 0\right)$

In Exercises 27–30, it is best if the units on the two axes are not the same.

27. $50x + y = -100$
Set $y = 0$: $50x + 0 = -100$
$x = -2$
Set $x = 0$: $50(0) + y = -100$

$(-2, 0)$ $(-1, -50)$ $(0, -100)$

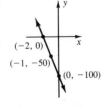

x	y
0	-100
-2	0
-1	-50

28.

(−90, −6) (0, −3) (90, 0)

29. $x = 50y$

Both intercepts are (0, 0)

Set $x = 50$: $50 = 50y$

$y = 1$

x	y
0	0
50	1
−50	−1

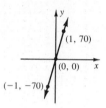

(50, 1)
(−50, −1)

30.

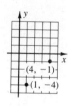

(1, 70)
(0, 0)
(−1, −70)

31. $y = -2x;\ x = 1, 3, 5$

x	y
1	−2
3	−6
5	−10

(1, −2)
(3, −6)
(5, −10)

32.

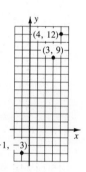

(4, 12)
(3, 9)
(−1, −3)

33. $x - y = 5;\ x = 1, 4$

(4, −1)
(1, −4)

34.

(2, 1)
(0, −3)

35a. $5x - 7y = 18$ $2x + 3y = -16$ **b.** $(-2, -4)$

x	y
$3\frac{3}{5}$	0
0	$-2\frac{4}{7}$

x	y
−8	0
0	$-5\frac{1}{3}$

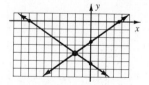

36a.

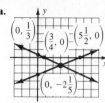

$\left(0, \frac{1}{3}\right)$ $\left(\frac{3}{4}, 0\right)$ $\left(5\frac{1}{2}, 0\right)$ $\left(0, -2\frac{1}{5}\right)$

b. $(3, -1)$

Exercises 8.3A (page 368)

1. $m = \dfrac{6 - 4}{10 - 1} = \dfrac{2}{9}$ **2.** $\dfrac{5}{6}$

3. $m = \dfrac{(-7) - (-5)}{1 - (-5)} = \dfrac{-7 + 5}{1 + 5} = \dfrac{-2}{6} = \dfrac{-1}{3}$ **4.** $-\dfrac{1}{2}$

5. $m = \dfrac{(-5) - (-5)}{2 - (-7)} = \dfrac{0}{9} = 0$ **6.** 0

7. $m = \dfrac{-2 - 3}{-4 - (-4)} = \dfrac{-5}{0}$ **8.** Does not exist

Not a real number; m does not exist

9a. $y = \dfrac{3}{4}x$ **b.** $y = \dfrac{3}{4}x + 5$ **c.** $y = \dfrac{3}{4}x - 2$

x	y
0	0
4	3
−4	−3

x	y
0	5
4	8
−4	2

x	y
0	−2
4	1
8	4

$m = \dfrac{3 - 0}{4 - 0} = \dfrac{3}{4}$ $m = \dfrac{8 - 5}{4 - 0} = \dfrac{3}{4}$ $m = \dfrac{1 - [-2]}{4 - 0} = \dfrac{3}{4}$

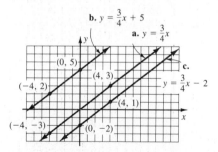

b. $y = \frac{3}{4}x + 5$
a. $y = \frac{3}{4}x$
c. $y = \frac{3}{4}x - 2$

(0, 5) (4, 3) (−4, 2) (4, 1) (−4, −3) (0, −2)

10a. $m = 1$ **b.** $m = 1$ **c.** $m = 1$ **11.**

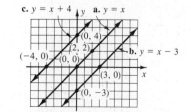

c. $y = x + 4$ **a.** $y = x$
(0, 4) (2, 2) (−4, 0) (0, 0) **b.** $y = x - 3$ (3, 0) (0, −3)

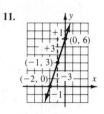

(0, 6) (−1, 3) (−2, 0)

12.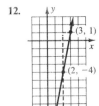

13.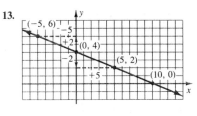

14.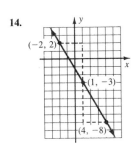

Exercises 8.3B (page 373)

1. $5x - 3y + 7 = 0$ **2.** $4x + 9y - 3 = 0$

3. $\dfrac{\cancel{10}^{5} \; x}{1 \; \cancel{2}} - \dfrac{\cancel{10}^{2} \; y}{1 \; \cancel{5}} = \dfrac{10}{1} \cdot \dfrac{1}{1}$ **4.** $6x - 7y + 42 = 0$

$5x - 2y = 10$
$5x - 2y - 10 = 0$

5. $\dfrac{3}{1} \cdot \dfrac{y}{1} = -\dfrac{\cancel{5}}{1} \cdot \dfrac{5}{\cancel{3}} x + \dfrac{3}{1} \cdot \dfrac{4}{1}$ **6.** $3x + 8y + 40 = 0$

$3y = -5x + 12$
$5x + 3y - 12 = 0$

7. $4x - 4y = 11 - 2x - 6y$ **8.** $25x - 8y - 15 = 0$
$6x + 2y - 11 = 0$

9. $y - y_1 = m(x - x_1)$ **10.** $5x + 6y + 16 = 0$
$y - (-3) = \dfrac{1}{5}(x - 4)$
$5y + 15 = x - 4$
$0 = x - 5y - 19$

11. $y - 5 = \dfrac{1}{4}[x - (-6)]$ **12.** $4x + 5y + 22 = 0$
$4y - 20 = x + 6$
$0 = x - 4y + 26$

13. $y - 3 = -4(x - [-1])$ **14.** $2x - y - 6 = 0$
$y - 3 = -4x - 4$
$4x + y + 1 = 0$

15. $y = mx + b$ **16.** $x + 4y + 8 = 0$
$y = \dfrac{5}{7}x - 3$
$7y = 5x - 21$
$0 = 5x - 7y - 21$

17. $y = -\dfrac{4}{3}x + \dfrac{1}{2}$ **18.** $12x + 20y - 15 = 0$
$6y = -8x + 3$
$8x + 6y - 3 = 0$

19. $y = 0x + 5$ **20.** $y - 7 = 0$
$y - 5 = 0$

21. Because the line is horizontal, every point on the line must have $y = 3$. Therefore, $y - 3 = 0$.

22. $y + 5 = 0$

23. Because the line is vertical, every point on the line must have $x = 7$. Therefore, $x - 7 = 0$.

24. $x + 6 = 0$

25a. $-5y = -4x - 20$
$y = \dfrac{-4x - 20}{-5}$
$y = \dfrac{4}{5}x + 4$

b. $m = \dfrac{4}{5}$

c. y-intercept $= 4$

26a. $y = -\dfrac{8}{3}x + 8$ **b.** $-\dfrac{8}{3}$ **c.** 8

27. $2x + 9y + 15 = 0$
$9y = -2x - 15$

a. $y = -\dfrac{2}{9}x - \dfrac{5}{3}$

b. $m = -\dfrac{2}{9}$

c. y-intercept $= -\dfrac{5}{3}$

28a. $y = \dfrac{18}{5}x - \dfrac{12}{5}$ **b.** $\dfrac{18}{5}$ **c.** $-\dfrac{12}{5}$

29. Use the two points to find the slope; then use m and one point to find the equation of the line
$m = \dfrac{4 - (-1)}{6 - 8} = \dfrac{5}{-2}$
$y - y_1 = m(x - x_1)$
$y - 4 = \dfrac{-5}{2}(x - 6)$
$2y - 8 = -5x + 30$
$5x + 2y - 38 = 0$

30. $3x + 2y - 17 = 0$ **31.** $m = \dfrac{4 - 0}{7 - 10} = \dfrac{4}{-3}$
$y - y_1 = m(x - x_1)$
$y - 0 = \dfrac{-4}{3}(x - 10)$
$3y = -4x + 40$
$4x + 3y - 40 = 0$

32. $5x - 2y + 20 = 0$ **33.** $m = \dfrac{(-1) - 3}{(-3) - (-9)} = \dfrac{-4}{6} = \dfrac{-2}{3}$
$y - y_1 = m(x - x_1)$
$y - (-1) = \dfrac{-2}{3}[x - (-3)]$
$3y + 3 = -2x - 6$
$2x + 3y + 9 = 0$

34. $3x + 4y + 17 = 0$

35. It must have the same slope as $3x - 5y = 6$
$-5y = -3x + 6$ $y - y_1 = m(x - x_1)$
$y = \dfrac{3}{5}x - \dfrac{6}{5}$ $y - 7 = \dfrac{3}{5}[x - (-4)]$
$m = \dfrac{3}{5}$ $5y - 35 = 3x + 12$
$0 = 3x - 5y + 47$

36. $7x + 4y - 36 = 0$

37. Slope of $2x + 4y = 3$: $\quad 4y = -2x + 3$

$y = -\dfrac{1}{2}x + \dfrac{3}{4}\quad$ Slope is $-\dfrac{1}{2}$

Slope of required line is 2.

$$y - 2 = 2(x - 6)$$
$$y - 2 = 2x - 12$$
$$2x - y - 10 = 0$$

38. $2x + y - 9 = 0$

6.

$\left(\dfrac{-28}{5}, 0\right)$ — $(0, 2)$

39. Same slope as $3x + 5y - 12 = 0$

$$5y = -3x + 12$$
$$y = \dfrac{-3}{5}x + \dfrac{12}{5}$$
$$m = \dfrac{-3}{5}$$

40. $9x - 14y + 27 = 0$

x-intercept $= (4, 0)$

$$y - 0 = \dfrac{-3}{5}(x - 4)$$
$$5y = -3x + 12$$
$$3x + 5y - 12 = 0$$

41. x-intercept $= (-6, 0)$
y-intercept $= (0, 4)$

$$m = \dfrac{4 - 0}{0 - (-6)} = \dfrac{4}{6} = \dfrac{2}{3}$$
$$y - 4 = \dfrac{2}{3}(x - 0)$$
$$3y - 12 = 2x$$
$$0 = 2x - 3y + 12$$

42. $4x - 5y - 60 = 0$

7. $x \geq -1$
Boundary line: $x = -1$
Solid line because $=$ is included in $\geq$
Half-plane includes $(0, 0)$ because:
$0 \geq -1\quad$ True

8.

$(0, -4)$

Exercises 8.4 (page 380)

1. $4x + 5y < 20$
Boundary line: $4x + 5y = 20$
Boundary line is dashed because $=$ is not included in $<$
Half-plane includes $(0, 0)$ because:
$4(0) + 5(0) < 20$
$\quad\quad 0 < 20\quad$ True

9. $6x - 13y > 0$
Boundary line: $6x - 13y = 0$
Dashed line because $=$ is not included in $>$
Both intercepts are at $(0, 0)$
Find one other point:
Set $x = 6$: $6(6) - 13y = 0$
$$y = 2\dfrac{10}{13}$$

Half-plane does not include $(1, 1)$ because:
$6(1) - 13(1) > 0$
$\quad\quad -7 > 0\quad$ False

x	y
5	0
0	4

2.

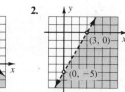

$(3, 0)$
$(0, -5)$

x	y
0	0
6	$2\dfrac{10}{13}$

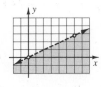

3. $3x - 8y > -16$
Boundary line: $3x - 8y = -16$
Dashed line because $=$ is not included in $>$. Half-plane includes $(0, 0)$ because:

$3(0) - 8(0) > -16$
$\quad\quad 0 > -16\quad$ True

x	y
$-5\dfrac{1}{3}$	0
0	2

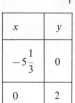

10.

$(0, 0)$
$\left(2, \dfrac{-8}{9}\right)$

11. $14x + 3y \leq 17$
Boundary line: $14x + 3y = 17$
Solid line because $=$ is included in $\leq$
Half-plane includes $(0, 0)$ because:
$14(0) + 3(0) \leq 17$
$\quad\quad 0 \leq 17\quad$ True

4.

$(-3, 0)$
$\left(0, \dfrac{-18}{5}\right)$

5. $9x + 7y \leq -27$
Boundary line: $9x + 7y = -27$
Solid line because $=$ is included in $\leq$
Half-plane does not include $(0, 0)$ because:
$9(0) + 7(0) \leq -27$
$\quad\quad 0 \leq -27\quad$ False

x	y
-3	0
0	$-3\dfrac{6}{7}$

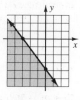

x	y
$1\dfrac{3}{14}$	0
0	$5\dfrac{2}{3}$
1	1

$\left(0, 5\dfrac{2}{3}\right)$
$(1, 1)$
$\left(1\dfrac{3}{14}, 0\right)$

12.

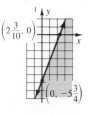

$\left(2\dfrac{3}{10}, 0\right)$
$\left(0, -5\dfrac{3}{4}\right)$

13. $\dfrac{x}{4} - \dfrac{y}{2} > 1$

$x - 2y > 4$

Boundary line: $x - 2y = 4$

Dashed line because $=$ is not included in $>$

Half-plane does not include $(0, 0)$ because:

$(0) - 2(0) > 4$

$\qquad 0 > 4 \quad$ False

x	y
4	0
0	-2

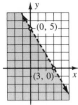

14.

15. $4x + 8 + 7 \le 15 - 6x$

$\qquad 10x \le 0$

$\qquad x \le 0$

Boundary line: $x = 0$

Solid line because $=$ is included in $\le$

Half-plane does not include $(1, 0)$ because:

$1 \le 0 \quad$ False

16.

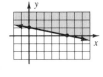

17. LCD $= 6$

$\overset{2}{\cancel{6}}\left(\dfrac{2x + y}{\cancel{3}}\right) + \overset{3}{\cancel{6}}\left(\dfrac{-(x - y)}{\cancel{2}}\right) \ge \overset{1}{\cancel{6}}\left(\dfrac{5}{\cancel{6}}\right)$

$\qquad 4x + 2y - 3x + 3y \ge 5$

$\qquad\qquad\qquad x + 5y \ge 5$

Boundary line: $x + 5y = 5$

Solid line because $=$ is included in $\ge$

Half-plane does not include $(0, 0)$ because:

$(0) + 5(0) \ge 5$

$\qquad\qquad 0 \ge 5 \quad$ False

x	y
0	1
5	0

18.

Review Exercises 8.5 (page 382)

1a. Let $P_1 = (-3, -4)$

$\qquad P_2 = (2, -4)$

$\qquad d = \sqrt{[2 - (-3)]^2 + [-4 - (-4)]^2}$

$\qquad\quad = \sqrt{5^2 + 0^2}$

$\qquad\quad = 5$

b. Let $P_1 = (-2, -3)$

$\qquad P_2 = (4, 1)$

$\qquad d = \sqrt{[4 - (-2)]^2 + [1 - (-3)]^2}$

$\qquad\quad = \sqrt{6^2 + 4^2}$

$\qquad\quad = \sqrt{36 + 16} = \sqrt{52} = \sqrt{4 \cdot 13} = 2\sqrt{13}$

2. Domain is $\{0, -2, 3\}$; range is $\{5, 3, -4, 0\}$

3. Domain is $\{-2, 0, 6, 8\}$; range is $\{-6, -3, 6, 9\}$

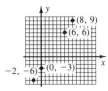

4.

5. $x + 2y = 0$

$\qquad x = -2y$

x	y
0	0
-4	2

6.

7. LCD $= 20$

$20\left(\dfrac{2x + 3y}{5}\right) + 20\left(\dfrac{-(x - 3y)}{4}\right) = 20\left(\dfrac{9}{10}\right)$

$\qquad 4(2x + 3y) + 5(-x + 3y) = 2(9)$

$\qquad\quad 8x + 12y - 5x + 15y = 18$

$\qquad\qquad\qquad 3x + 27y = 18$

$\qquad\qquad\qquad\quad x + 9y = 6$

x	y
0	$\dfrac{2}{3}$
6	0
-3	1

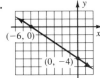

8. $-\dfrac{9}{5}$

9. $m = \dfrac{2 - 2}{3 - (-6)} = \dfrac{0}{9} = 0$

10. $3x + 4y + 8 = 0$

11.

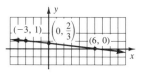

$\qquad\qquad y = mx + b$

$\qquad\qquad y = -\dfrac{1}{2}x + 6$

$\qquad\qquad 2y = -x + 12$

$\qquad x + 2y - 12 = 0$

12. $7x - 3y + 2 = 0$

13. $10\left(\dfrac{2x}{5} - \dfrac{3}{2}y\right) = 3(10)$

$4x - 15y = 30$

$\dfrac{15y}{15} = \dfrac{4x - 30}{15}$

$y = \dfrac{4}{15}x - 2$

$m = \dfrac{4}{15}$, y-intercept $= -2$

14.

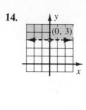

15. $2x - 5y > 10$

Boundary line:

$2x - 5y = 10$

x	y
0	-2
5	0

16.

Exercises 8.6A (page 390)

1. b and c **2.** $b, c,$ and d

3. If $x = -5, 2(-5) + 5y = 10$

$\qquad 5y = 20$

$\qquad y = 4$

If $x = -1, 2(-1) + 5y = 10$

$\qquad 5y = 12$

$\qquad y = \dfrac{12}{5}$

If $x = 0, \qquad 2(0) + 5y = 10$

$\qquad y = 2$

If $x = 2, \qquad 2(2) + 5y = 10$

$\qquad 5y = 6$

$\qquad y = \dfrac{6}{5}$

Range $= \left\{4, \dfrac{12}{5}, 2, \dfrac{6}{5}\right\}$

x	y
-5	4
-1	$\dfrac{12}{5}$
0	2
2	$\dfrac{6}{5}$

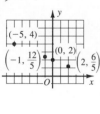

4. Range $= \{-6, -3, 0, 3\}$

x	y
-2	-6
0	-3
2	0
4	3

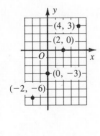

5. $y = 2x - 3$

x	y
0	-3
3	3

6.

7a. Yes   **b.** No   **c.** No   **d.** Yes

8a. No   **b.** Yes   **c.** Yes   **d.** No

9a. The domain is the set of all real numbers. (The curve extends infinitely far to the left and to the right.) The range is the set of all real numbers. (The curve extends infinitely far up and down.)

b. The domain is the set of all real numbers, and so is the range. (The equation is the equation of a straight line which is not a horizontal or vertical line.)

c. For the domain: $x - 5 \geq 0 \Rightarrow x \geq 5$. Therefore, the domain is $\{x \mid x \geq 5\}$. For the range, we know that the square root sign has an understood $+$ sign in front of it. Therefore, y cannot be negative. As x gets larger and larger, so does $x - 5$, and so does $\sqrt{x - 5}$. Therefore, the range is $\{y \mid y \geq 0\}$.

d. The domain is $\{1, 4, 7\}$. If $x = 1, y = 0$. If $x = 4, y = -3$. If $x = 7$, $y = -6$. Therefore, the range is $\{0, -3, -6\}$.

10a. Domain: $\{x \mid -3 \leq x \leq 3\}$ Range: $\{y \mid -2 \leq y \leq 0\}$

b. Domain: $\{x \mid x \geq -3\}$ Range: $\{y \mid y \geq 0\}$

c. Domain: $\{x \mid x \in R\}$ Range: $\{y \mid y \in R\}$

d. Domain: $\{0, 1\}$ Range: $\{-4, -1\}$

Exercises 8.6B (page 395)

1a. $f(2) = 3(2) - 1 = 6 - 1 = 5$

b. $f(0) = 3(0) - 1 = -1$

c. $f(a - 2) = 3(a - 2) - 1 = 3a - 6 - 1 = 3a - 7$

d. $f(x + 2) = 3(x + 2) - 1 = 3x + 6 - 1 = 3x + 5$

2a. $f(3) = 13$

b. $f(-5) = -19$

c. $f(0) = 1$

d. $f(x - 2) = 4x - 7$

3. $f(5) = 2(5)^2 - 3 = 50 - 3 = 47$ **4.** 8

$f(2) = 2(2)^2 - 3 = 5$

Therefore, $\dfrac{f(5) - f(2)}{6} = \dfrac{47 - 5}{6} = \dfrac{42}{6} = 7$

5. $f(3) = 3(3)^2 - 2(3) + 4 = 27 - 6 + 4 = 25$ **6.** 46

$f(1) = 3(1)^2 - 2(1) + 4 = 3 - 2 + 4 = 5$

$f(0) = 3(0)^2 - 2(0) + 4 = 4$

Therefore, $2f(3) + 4f(1) - 3f(0)$

$= 2(25) + 4(5) - 3(4)$

$= 50 + 20 - 12 = 58$

7. $f(-3) = (-3)^3 = -27$ **8.** 29

$6g(x) = 6\left(\dfrac{1}{x}\right)$

$6g(2) = 6\left(\dfrac{1}{2}\right) = 3$

Therefore, $f(-3) - 6g(2)$

$= -27 - 3$

$= -30$

9. $H(2) = 3(2)^2 - 2(2) + 4 = 12 - 4 + 4 = 12$ **10.** -4

$K(3) = (3) - (3)^2 = 3 - 9 = -6$

Therefore, $2H(2) - 3K(3)$

$= 2(12) - 3(-6)$

$= 24 + 18 = 42$

11. $D_f = \{x \mid x \geq 4\}$ because $\sqrt{x-4}$ will not have a real value when
$$x - 4 < 0 \text{ or } x < 4$$
$R_f = \{y \mid y \geq 0\}$ because $y = \sqrt{x-4}$, and the principal square root cannot be negative

12. $D_f = \left\{x \mid x \geq \dfrac{16}{9}\right\}; R_f = \{y \mid y \leq 0\}$

13.
$$f(x + h) = (x + h)^2 - (x + h)$$
$$= x^2 + 2xh + h^2 - x - h$$
$$\frac{f(x+h) - f(x)}{h} = \frac{x^2 + 2xh + h^2 - x - h - x^2 + x}{h}$$
$$= \frac{2xh + h^2 - h}{h} = \frac{2xh}{h} + \frac{h^2}{h} + \frac{-h}{h} = 2x + h - 1$$

14. $6x + 3h$

15. $f(x) = x^4$ ┌─Binomial theorem must be used
$$\frac{f(x+h) - f(x)}{h} = \frac{(x+h)^4 - x^4}{h}$$
$$= \frac{\cancel{x^4} + 4x^3h + 6x^2h^2 + 4xh^3 + h^4 - \cancel{x^4}}{h}$$
$$= \frac{4x^3h + 6x^2h^2 + 4xh^3 + h^4}{h}$$
$$= \frac{\overset{1}{\cancel{h}}(4x^3 + 6x^2h + 4xh^2 + h^3)}{\underset{1}{\cancel{h}}}$$
$$= 4x^3 + 6x^2h + 4xh^2 + h^3$$

16. $3x^2 + 3xh + h^2$

17. $A(r) = \pi r^2 \qquad C(r) = 2\pi r$ **18.** $5r + 6$
Then $\dfrac{3A(r) - 2C(r)}{\pi r}$
$$= \frac{3\pi r^2 - 2(2\pi r)}{\pi r}$$
$$= \frac{3\pi r^2}{\pi r} + \frac{-4\pi r}{\pi r} = 3r - 4$$

19. $h(2) = 64(2) - 16(2)^2 = 128 - 64 = 64$ **20.** 112

21. $C(100) = 500 + 20(100) - 0.1(100^2)$ **22.** 400
$$= 500 + 2000 - 0.1(10,000)$$
$$= 2500 - 1000$$
$$= 1500$$

23. $g(3, -4) = 5(3)^2 - 2(-4)^2 + 7(3) - 4(-4)$
$$= 45 - 32 + 21 + 16 = 50$$

24. $z = h(-1, -2) = 10$

25. $f(100, 0.08, 12) = 100(1 + 0.08)^{12} = 100(1.08)^{12}$
$$\doteq 251.82$$
Found by calculator

26. 2,979,659,632

Exercises 8.6C (page 400)

1. **a.** 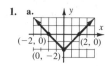 **b.**

c.

2. **a.** **b.**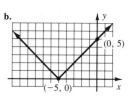

c.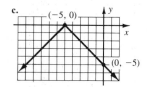

3. **a.** **b.** 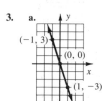 **c.**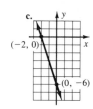

4. **a.** **b.** **c.**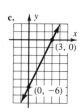

Exercises 8.7 (page 404)

1. $\mathcal{R} = \{(-10, 7), (3, -8), (-5, -4), (3, 9)\}$
$$\mathcal{R}^{-1} = \{(7, -10), (-8, 3), (-4, -5), (9, 3)\}$$
$$D_{\mathcal{R}^{-1}} = \{7, -8, -4, 9\} = R_{\mathcal{R}}$$
$$R_{\mathcal{R}^{-1}} = \{-10, 3, -5, 3\} = D_{\mathcal{R}}$$
$\mathcal{R}$ is *not* a function
$\mathcal{R}^{-1}$ is a function

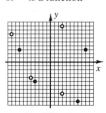

○ point of $\mathcal{R}$
● point of $\mathcal{R}^{-1}$

2. $\mathcal{R}^{-1} = \{(-6, 9), (11, 0), (8, 3), (-6, -2), (-4, 10)\}$
$$D_{\mathcal{R}^{-1}} = \{-6, 11, 8, -4\} = R_{\mathcal{R}}$$
$$R_{\mathcal{R}^{-1}} = \{9, 0, 3, -2, 10\} = D_{\mathcal{R}}$$
$\mathcal{R}$ is a function
$\mathcal{R}^{-1}$ is *not* a function

○ point of $\mathcal{R}$
● point of $\mathcal{R}^{-1}$

3. $x = 5 - 2y$

$\quad f(x) \qquad\qquad f^{-1}(x)$

$y = \dfrac{5-x}{2} = f^{-1}(x) \qquad\qquad y = \dfrac{5-x}{2}$

$\qquad\qquad\qquad y = 5 - 2x \qquad 2y = 5 - x$

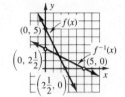

x	y
$2\dfrac{1}{2}$	0
0	5

x	y
5	0
0	$2\dfrac{1}{2}$

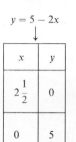

4. $f^{-1}(x) = \dfrac{x+10}{3}$

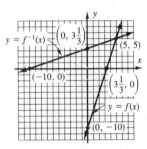

5. $\qquad y = f(x) = \dfrac{4x-3}{5}$

$\qquad\qquad x = \dfrac{4y-3}{5}$

$\qquad\qquad 5x = 4y - 3$

$\qquad\qquad 5x + 3 = 4y$

$\qquad\qquad y = \dfrac{5x+3}{4} = f^{-1}(x)$

6. $f^{-1}(x) = \dfrac{3x+7}{2}$

7. $\qquad y = f(x) = \dfrac{5}{x+2}$

$\qquad\qquad x = \dfrac{5}{y+2}$

$\qquad\qquad x(y+2) = 5$

$\qquad\qquad xy + 2x = 5$

$\qquad\qquad xy = 5 - 2x$

$\qquad\qquad y = \dfrac{5-2x}{x} = f^{-1}(x)$

8. $f^{-1}(x) = \dfrac{x+10}{2x}$

Exercises 8.8 (page 409)

1. $y = (-3)^2 + 3 = 9 + 3 = 12$

$\quad y = (-2)^2 + 3 = 4 + 3 = 7$

$\quad y = (-1)^2 + 3 = 1 + 3 = 4$

$\quad y = 0^2 + 3 = 3$

$\quad y = 1^2 + 3 = 1 + 3 = 4$

$\quad y = 2^2 + 3 = 4 + 3 = 7$

$\quad y = 3^2 + 3 = 9 + 3 = 12$

x	y
-3	12
-2	7
-1	4
0	3
1	4
2	7
3	12

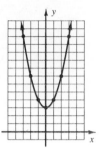

2.

x	y
-3	10
-2	5
-1	2
0	1
1	2
2	5
3	10

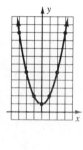

3. $y = (-4+1)^2 = (-3)^2 = 9$

$\quad y = (-3+1)^2 = (-2)^2 = 4$

$\quad y = (-2+1)^2 = (-1)^2 = 1$

$\quad y = (-1+1)^2 = 0^2 = 0$

$\quad y = (0+1)^2 = 1^2 = 1$

$\quad y = (1+1)^2 = 2^2 = 4$

$\quad y = (2+1)^2 = 3^2 = 9$

x	y
-4	9
-3	4
-2	1
-1	0
0	1
1	4
2	9

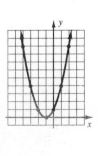

4.

x	y
-6	9
-5	4
-4	1
-3	0
-2	1
-1	4
0	9

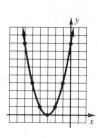

5. $y = (-2)^2 - 2(-2) = 4 + 4 = 8$

$y = (-1)^2 - 2(-1) = 1 + 2 = 3$

$y = 0^2 - 2(0) = 0$

$y = 1^2 - 2(1) = -1$

$y = 2^2 - 2(2) = 0$

$y = 3^2 - 2(3) = 3$

$y = 4^2 - 2(4) = 8$

x	y
-2	8
-1	3
0	0
1	-1
2	0
3	3
4	8

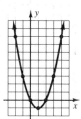

6.

x	y
-2	-10
-1	-4
0	0
1	2
2	2
3	0
4	-4

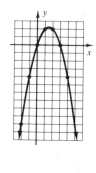

7. $y = 2(-2) - (-2)^2 = -4 - 4 = -8$

$y = 2(-1) - (-1)^2 = -2 - 1 = -3$

$y = 2(0) - 0^2 = 0$

$y = 2(1) - (1^2) = 2 - 1 = 1$

$y = 2(2) - (2^2) = 4 - 4 = 0$

$y = 2(3) - (3^2) = 6 - 9 = -3$

$y = 2(4) - (4^2) = 8 - 16 = -8$

x	y
-2	-8
-1	-3
0	0
1	1
2	0
3	-3
4	-8

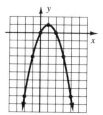

8.

x	y
-3	3
-2	0
-1	-1
0	0
1	3

9. $y = (-2)^3 = -8$

$y = (-1)^3 = -1$

$y = 0^3 = 0$

$y = 1^3 = 1$

$y = 2^3 = 8$

x	y
-2	-8
-1	-1
0	0
1	1
2	8

10.

x	y
-2	-6
-1	1
0	2
1	3
2	10

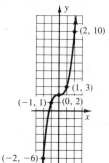

11. $y = ([-3] + 1)^3 = (-2)^3 = -8$
$y = ([-2] + 1)^3 = (-1)^3 = -1$
$y = ([-1] + 1)^3 = (0)^3 = 0$
$y = (0 + 1)^3 = (1)^3 = 1$
$y = (1 + 1)^3 = (2)^3 = 8$

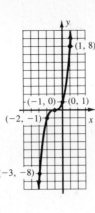

x	y
-3	-8
-2	-1
-1	0
0	1
1	8

12.

x	y
-1	-8
0	-1
1	0
2	1
3	8

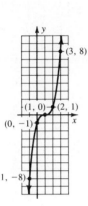

13. $f(x) = x^3 - 2x^2 - 13x + 20$

x	1	-2	-13	20 $f(x)$
-4	1	-6	11	-24
-3	1	-5	2	14
-2	1	-4	-5	30
0	1	-2	-13	20
2	1	0	-13	-6
3	1	1	-10	-10
4	1	2	-5	0
5	1	3	2	30

Range $= \{-24, 14, 30, 20, -6, -10, 0\}$

14. $\{18, 32, 12, -32, -48, -52, -38, 0\}$

Exercises 8.9A (page 416)

1. $y = kx$ Alternate method:
$12 = k(3)$
$k = 4$ Condition 1 $\begin{cases} x_1 = 3 \\ y_1 = 12 \end{cases}$ $\dfrac{y_1}{y_2} = \dfrac{x_1}{x_2}$
$y = 4(5)$
$y = 20$ Condition 2 $\begin{cases} x_2 = 5 \\ y_2 = ? \end{cases}$ $\dfrac{12}{y_2} = \dfrac{3}{5}$
$3y_2 = (5)(12)$
$y_2 = \dfrac{(5)(12)}{3} = 20$

2. $k = 2.5$
$y = -15$

3. Let $m =$ Number of miles on 50 gallons of gasoline
$m = kg$
$161 = k(23)$ Alternate method:
$k = 7$ $\dfrac{161 \text{ miles}}{23 \text{ gal}} = \dfrac{m \text{ miles}}{50 \text{ gal}}$
$m = 7(50) = 350$ miles $23m = (161)(50)$
$m = 350$ miles

4. $k = 5$
$m = 375$

5. Let $x =$ height of tree   **6.** 33 feet
$\dfrac{5 \text{ ft}}{3 \text{ ft}} = \dfrac{x \text{ ft}}{27 \text{ ft}}$
$3x = 5(27)$
$x = 45$ ft

7. $C = kr$ Alternate method: **8.** $k = 0.433$
$47.1 = k(7.5)$ $\dfrac{47.1}{C} = \dfrac{7.5}{4.5}$ $P = 7.794$
$k = 6.28$
$C = 6.28(4.5)$ $7.5C = (47.1)(4.5)$
$C = 28.26$ $7.5C = 211.95$
$C = 28.26$

9. $A = kr^2$ Alternate method:
$28.26 = k(3)^2$ $\dfrac{28.26}{A} = \dfrac{3^2}{6^2}$
$k = \dfrac{28.26}{9} = 3.14$ $A = \dfrac{(28.26)(36)}{9} = 113.04$
$A = 3.14(6)^2 = 113.04$

10. $k = 12.56$; $S = 200.96$

11. Let $S =$ Amount of sediment carried by current   **12.** \$213.25
     $s =$ Speed of current

Condition 1 $\begin{cases} S_1 = 1 \\ s_1 = 2 \end{cases}$ $\dfrac{S_1}{S_2} = \dfrac{s_1^6}{s_2^6}$

Condition 2 $\begin{cases} S_2 = ? \\ s_2 = 4 \end{cases}$ $\dfrac{1}{S_2} = \dfrac{2^6}{4^6}$

$S_2 = \dfrac{4^6}{2^6} = \dfrac{(2^2)^6}{2^6} = \dfrac{2^{12}}{2^6} = 2^{12-6} = 2^6 = 64$

This shows that when the speed of the current is doubled, its destructive power becomes 64 times as great.

Exercises 8.9B (page 420)

1. $y = \dfrac{k}{x}$ **2.** $k = -48$ **3.** $P = \dfrac{k}{V}$
$7 = \dfrac{k}{2}$ $z = -6$
$k = 14$ $18 = \dfrac{k}{15}$
$y = \dfrac{14}{-7} = -2$ $k = 270$
                           $P = \dfrac{270}{10} = 27$

4. $k = 40$ **5.** Let $t =$ Time for machine B to complete an order
$S = 10$ $t = \dfrac{k}{r}$
                  $3 = \dfrac{k}{375}$
                  $k = 1125$
                  $t = \dfrac{1125}{225} = 5$ hours

6. $k = 2475$ **7.** $y = \dfrac{k}{x^2}$ **8.** $k = 72$
$t = 7.5$ hours $C = 2$
                 $9 = \dfrac{k}{4^2}$
                 $k = 9(16) = 144$
                 $y = \dfrac{144}{3^2} = \dfrac{144}{9} = 16$

9. $F = \dfrac{k}{d^2}$ **10.** $6\dfrac{2}{3}$

$3 = \dfrac{k}{4^2}$

$k = 48$

$F = \dfrac{48}{2^2} = 12$

Exercises 8.9C (page 423)

1. $z = kxy$
$-36 = k((-3)(2)$
$k = 6$
$z = (6)(4)(3) = 72$

2. $k = 4$
$A = 84$

3. $I = kPr$
$115.50 = k(880)(0.0875)$
$k = 1.5$
$I = (1.5)(760)(0.0925)$
$= 105.45$

4. $k \doteq 3.6084$
$I \doteq 428.50$

5. $F = kAV^2$
$1.8 = k(1)(20^2)$
$k = 0.0045$
$F = 0.0045(2)(60^2)$
$= 32.4$

6. $P = 2474.7$

7. $z = \dfrac{kx}{y}$
$12 = \dfrac{k(6)}{2}$
$k = 4$
$z = \dfrac{(4)(-8)}{-4} = 8$

8. $k = 4$
$R = 1.6$

9. $e = \dfrac{kPL}{A}$
$3 = \dfrac{k(2.4)(45)}{0.9}$
$k = 0.025$
$e = \dfrac{0.025(1.5)(40)}{0.75}$
$= 2$

10. 300 pounds

Review Exercises 8.10 (page 426)

1. a and c **2.** b and c

3a. $f(2) = 3(2)^2 - 5(2) + 4$
$= 12 - 10 + 4 = 6$

4. -22

b. $f(0) = 3(0)^2 - 5(0) + 4$
$= 0 - 0 + 4 = 4$

c. $f(x-1) = 3(x-1)^2 - 5(x-1) + 4$
$= 3(x^2 - 2x + 1) - 5x + 5 + 4$
$= 3x^2 - 11x + 12$

5.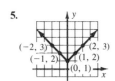

6.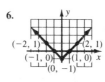

7.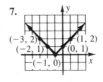

8. $\mathscr{R}^{-1} = \{(-2, -1), (4, -4), (0, 5), (-2, 4), (-3, -5)\}$
$D_{\mathscr{R}^{-1}} = \{-2, 4, 0, -3\} = R_{\mathscr{R}}$
$R_{\mathscr{R}^{-1}} = \{-1, -4, 5, 4, -5\} = D_{\mathscr{R}}$
$\mathscr{R}$ is a function
$\mathscr{R}^{-1}$ is *not* a function

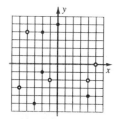

○ point of $\mathscr{R}$
● point of $\mathscr{R}^{-1}$

9. $y = f(x) = \dfrac{x + 6}{3}$
$3y = x + 6$
$3x = y + 6$
$y = 3x - 6 = f^{-1}(x)$

$y = \dfrac{x + 6}{3}$
$\downarrow$

x	y
-6	0
0	2

$y = 3x - 6$
$\downarrow$

x	y
2	0
0	-6

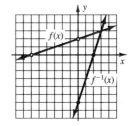

The domain is the set of all real numbers for $y = f(x)$ and for $y = f^{-1}(x)$. The range is the set of all real numbers for $y = f(x)$ and for $y = f^{-1}(x)$.

10. $f^{-1}(x) = \dfrac{2 - 2x}{5}$

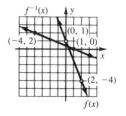

The domain is the set of all real numbers for $y = f(x)$ and for $y = f^{-1}(x)$. The range is the set of all real numbers for $y = f(x)$ and for $y = f^{-1}(x)$.

11. $y = f(x) = \dfrac{9}{2 - 7x}$
$x(2 - 7y) = 9$
$2x - 7xy = 9$
$2x - 9 = 7xy$
$y = \dfrac{2x - 9}{7x} = f^{-1}(x)$

12. $f^{-1}(x) = \dfrac{10x + 11}{8x}$

13.

x	y
-4	8
-2	2
-1	$\dfrac{1}{2}$
0	0
1	$\dfrac{1}{2}$
2	2
4	8

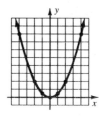

ANSWERS

14.

x	y
−4	9
−2	3
−1	$\frac{3}{2}$
0	1
1	$\frac{3}{2}$
2	3
4	9

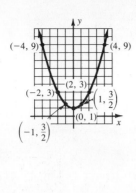

15. $y = x^3 - 3x$

$y = (-3)^3 - (3)(-3) = -27 + 9 = -18$

$y = (-2)^3 - 3(-2) = -8 + 6 = -2$

$y = (-1)^3 - 3(-1) = -1 + 3 = 2$

$y = 0^3 - 3(0) = 0$

$y = 1^3 - 3(1) = -2$

$y = 2^3 - 3(2) = 2$

$y = 3^3 - 3(3) = 18$

x	y
−3	−18
−2	−2
−1	2
0	0
1	−2
2	2
3	18

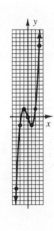

16. $k = 32$
$c = 728$

Chapter 8 Diagnostic Test (page 433)

Following each problem number is the textbook section number (in parentheses) where that kind of problem is discussed.

1a. (8.1)

b. (8.1) $A(-4, 2), B(1, -3)$
$(|AB|)^2 = [1 - (-4)]^2 + (-3 - 2)^2 = 25 + 25 = 50$
$|AB| = \sqrt{50} = \sqrt{25 \cdot 2} = 5\sqrt{2}$

c. (8.3A) $B(1, -3), C(5, 3)$
$m = \frac{3 - (-3)}{5 - 1} = \frac{6}{4} = \frac{3}{2}$

d. (8.3B) $A(-4, 2), B(1, -3)$
$m = \frac{-3 - 2}{1 - (-4)} = \frac{-5}{5} = -1$
$y - y_1 = m(x - x_1)$
$y - (-3) = -1(x - 1)$
$x + y + 2 = 0$

e. (8.3)   If $y = 0$: $x + y + 2 = 0$
$x + 0 + 2 = 0$
$x = -2$

f. (8.3)   If $x = 0$: $x + y + 2 = 0$
$0 + y + 2 = 0$
$y = -2$

2. (8.3B) $y = mx + b$
$y = \frac{6}{5}x - 4$
$5y = 6x - 20$
$0 = 6x - 5y - 20$

3. (8.2) $x - 2y = 6$
If $x = 0$: $0 - 2y = 6$
$y = -3$
If $y = 0$: $x - 2(0) = 6$
$x = 6$

x	y
0	−3
6	0

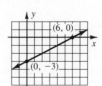

707

4. (8.8) $y = 1 + x - x^2$

$y = 1 + (-2) - (-2)^2 = -5$

$y = 1 + (-1) - (-1)^2 = -1$

$y = 1 + (0) - (0)^2 = 1$

$y = 1 + (1) - (1)^2 = 1$

$y = 1 + (2) - (2)^2 = -1$

$y = 1 + (3) - (3)^2 = -5$

x	y
-2	-5
-1	-1
0	1
1	1
2	-1
3	-5

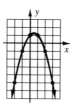

5. (8.4) $4x - 3y \leq -12$

Boundary line: $4x - 3y = -12$

If $x = 0$, $4(0) - 3y = -12$

$y = 4$

If $y = 0$, $4x - 3(0) = -12$

$x = -3$

Boundary line is solid because equality is included

Test point: $(0, 0)$ $4x - 3y \leq -12$

$4(0) - 3(0) \leq -12$

$0 \leq -12$ False

x	y
0	4
-3	0

6. (8.1, 8.6)   **a.** $\{(-4, -5), (2, 4), (4, -2), (-2, 3), (2, -1)\}$

Domain: $\{-4, 2, 4, -2\}$

b. $\{(-4, -5), (2, 4), (4, -2), (-2, 3), (2, -1)\}$

Range: $\{-5, 4, -2, 3, -1\}$

c.

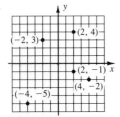

d. The relation *is not* a function because $(2, 4)$ and $(2, -1)$ have the same first coordinate and different second coordinates

7. (8.6)

$f(x) = 3(x)^2 - 5$

a. $f(-2) = 3(-2)^2 - 5$

$= 12 - 5 = 7$

b. $f(4) = 3(4)^2 - 5$

$= 48 - 5 = 43$

c. $\dfrac{f(4) - f(-2)}{6} = \dfrac{43 - 7}{6}$

$= \dfrac{36}{6} = 6$

8. (8.1, 8.6) $\mathcal{R} = \{(1, 4), (-5, -3), (4, -2), (-5, 2)\}$

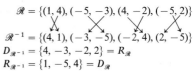

$\mathcal{R}^{-1} = \{(4, 1), (-3, -5), (-2, 4), (2, -5)\}$

$D_{\mathcal{R}^{-1}} = \{4, -3, -2, 2\} = R_{\mathcal{R}}$

$R_{\mathcal{R}^{-1}} = \{1, -5, 4\} = D_{\mathcal{R}}$

$\mathcal{R}$ is *not* a function

$\mathcal{R}^{-1}$ *is* a function

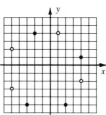

○ point of $\mathcal{R}$
● point of $\mathcal{R}^{-1}$

9. (8.7)

$y = f(x) = -\dfrac{3}{2}x + 1$

$x = -\dfrac{3}{2}y + 1$

$2x = -3y + 2$

$3y = 2 - 2x$

$y = \dfrac{2 - 2x}{3} = f^{-1}(x)$

$y = -\dfrac{3}{2}x + 1$ $y = \dfrac{2 - 2x}{3}$

$2y = -3x + 2$ $3y = 2 - 2x$

x	y
$\dfrac{2}{3}$	0
0	1
4	-5

x	y
1	0
0	$\dfrac{2}{3}$
-5	4

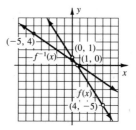

10. (8.9) $y = f(x) = \dfrac{15}{4(2 - 5x)}$

$\mathcal{D}_{f(x)} = $ all real numbers except $\dfrac{2}{5} = R_{f^{-1}(x)}$

$x = \dfrac{15}{4(2 - 5y)}$

$4x(2 - 5y) = 15$

$8x - 20xy = 15$

$y = \dfrac{8x - 15}{20x} = f^{-1}(x)$

$\mathcal{D}_{f^{-1}(x)} = $ all real numbers except $0 = R_{f(x)}$

11. (8.9) $w = \dfrac{kxy}{z^2}$

$20 = \dfrac{k(8)(6)}{(12)^2}$

$k = 60$

$w = \dfrac{(60)(6)(10)}{(5)^2}$

$= 144$

Cumulative Review Exercises: Chapters 1–8 (page 435)

1. $2x^4 - 24x^2 + 54$
$= 2(x^4 - 12x^2 + 27)$
$= 2(x^2 - 3)(x^2 - 9)$
$= 2(x^2 - 3)(x + 3)(x - 3)$

2. $ab(2a - 3b)(4a^2 + 6ab + 9b^2)$

3. $\sqrt[3]{-4a^4} \cdot \sqrt[3]{2a} = \sqrt[3]{-8a^5} = \sqrt[3]{-2^3 a^3 a^2} = -2a\sqrt[3]{a^2}$

4. $7x^2\sqrt{2} + 4x^2\sqrt{2x}$

5. $\dfrac{3 + 2i}{2 - i} \cdot \dfrac{2 + i}{2 + i} = \dfrac{6 + 7i + 2i^2}{4 - i^2} = \dfrac{6 + 7i - 2}{4 - (-1)} = \dfrac{4 + 7i}{5} = \dfrac{4}{5} + \dfrac{7}{5}i$

6. $2 + 2i$

7. $(3 + i)^4 = 3^4 + 4(3^3)i + 6(3^2)i^2 + 4(3)i^3 + i^4$
$= 81 + 108i + 54(-1) + 12(-i) + 1$
$= 81 - 54 + 1 + (108 - 12)i = 28 + 96i$

8. $r = \dfrac{S - a}{S}$

9. $x^{-1/3} = 3$
$(x^{-1/3})^{-3} = (3)^{-3}$
$x = \dfrac{1}{3^3} = \dfrac{1}{27}$
$\left\{ \dfrac{1}{27} \right\}$

10. $3x^2 - 2x - 3$

11. $f(0) = 3(0)^2 - 2(0) + 7 = 7$
$f(-2) = 3(-2)^2 - 2(-2) + 7 = 3(4) + 4 + 7 = 12 + 11 = 23$

12.

(2, 0)
(0, −4)

13. $m = \dfrac{4 - (-2)}{-3 - 1} = \dfrac{6}{-4} = -\dfrac{3}{2}$

$y - 4 = -\dfrac{3}{2}(x - [-3])$

$2(y - 4) = -3(x + 3)$

$2y - 8 = -3x - 9$

$3x + 2y + 1 = 0$

14. $k = -24$

$y = -\dfrac{8}{9}$

---

15. Let $x = $ Number of pounds of cashews
$60 - x = $ Number of pounds of peanuts
$7.40x + 2.80(60 - x) = 4.18(60)$
$740x + 280(60 - x) = 418(60)$
$74x + 28(60 - x) = 418(6)$
$74x + 1680 - 28x = 2508$
$46x = 828$
$x = 18$ pounds of cashews
$60 - x = 42$ pounds of peanuts
Check 18 lb @ \$7.40 = \$133.20
42 lb @ \$2.80 = \$117.60
$\overline{\$250.80}$
60 lb @ \$4.18 = \$250.80

16. 88 miles

Exercises 9.1 (page 439)

1. $3x^2 + 5x - 2 = 0 \begin{cases} a = & 3 \\ b = & 5 \\ c = & -2 \end{cases}$ **2.** $2x^2 - 3x - 5 = 0 \begin{cases} a = & 2 \\ b = & -3 \\ c = & -5 \end{cases}$

3. $3x^2 + 0x - 4 = 0 \begin{cases} a = & 3 \\ b = & 0 \\ c = & -4 \end{cases}$ **4.** $x^2 + 0x - 16 = 0 \begin{cases} a = & 1 \\ b = & 0 \\ c = & -16 \end{cases}$

5. $\dfrac{4x}{3} = 4 + x^2$
$4x = 12 + 3x^2 \begin{cases} a = & 3 \\ b = & -4 \\ c = & 12 \end{cases}$
$3x^2 - 4x + 12 = 0$

6. $2x^2 - 3x + 10 = 0 \begin{cases} a = & 2 \\ b = & -3 \\ c = & 10 \end{cases}$ **7.** $3x^2 + 4x - 2 = 0 \begin{cases} a = & 3 \\ b = & 4 \\ c = & -2 \end{cases}$

8. $5x^2 - 6x + 3 = 0 \begin{cases} a = & 5 \\ b = & -6 \\ c = & 3 \end{cases}$ **9.** $x^2 + 2x - 4 = 0 \begin{cases} a = & 1 \\ b = & 2 \\ c = & -4 \end{cases}$

10. $x^2 - 4x + 20 = 0 \begin{cases} a = & 1 \\ b = & -4 \\ c = & 20 \end{cases}$

11. $3x(x - 2) = (x + 1)(x - 5) \begin{cases} a = & 2 \\ b = & -2 \\ c = & 5 \end{cases}$
$3x^2 - 6x = x^2 - 4x - 5$
$2x^2 - 2x + 5 = 0$

12. $13x^2 + 20x + 12 = 0 \begin{cases} a = 13 \\ b = 20 \\ c = 12 \end{cases}$

Exercises 9.2 (page 442)

1. $x^2 = 27$
$x = \pm\sqrt{27} = \pm 3\sqrt{3}$

2. $\{\pm 2\sqrt{2}\}$ **3.** $x^2 = -16$
$x = \pm\sqrt{-16}$
$x = \pm 4i$

4. $\{\pm 9i\}$ **5.** $x^2 = 7$
$\sqrt{x^2} = \pm\sqrt{7}$
$x = \pm\sqrt{7}$ **6.** $\{\pm\sqrt{13}\}$ **7.** $x^2 = -12$
$\sqrt{x^2} = \pm\sqrt{-12}$
$x = \pm 2\sqrt{3}i$

8. $\{\pm 5\sqrt{3}i\}$

9. $0 = 8x^3 - 12x$

$0 = 4x(2x^2 - 3)$

$4x = 0 \mid 2x^2 - 3 = 0$

$x = 0 \mid \quad 2x^2 = 3$

$x^2 = \dfrac{3}{2}$

$x = \pm\sqrt{\dfrac{3}{2}}$

$x = \pm\sqrt{\dfrac{3}{2} \cdot \dfrac{2}{2}} = \pm\dfrac{\sqrt{6}}{2}$

$\left\{0, \pm\dfrac{\sqrt{6}}{2}\right\}$

10. $\left\{0, \dfrac{\sqrt{3}}{2}, -\dfrac{\sqrt{3}}{2}\right\}$

11. $x^2 = -\dfrac{4}{5}$

$\sqrt{x^2} = \pm\sqrt{-\dfrac{4}{5}}$

$x = \pm\dfrac{2i}{\sqrt{5}} = \pm\dfrac{2i}{\sqrt{5}} \cdot \dfrac{\sqrt{5}}{\sqrt{5}}$

$x = \pm\dfrac{2\sqrt{5}}{5}i$

$\left\{\pm\dfrac{2\sqrt{5}}{5}i\right\}$

12. $\left\{\pm\dfrac{5\sqrt{3}}{3}i\right\}$

13. $\dfrac{2x^2}{3} = \dfrac{4x}{1}$

$2x^2 = 12x$

$2x^2 - 12x = 0$

$2x(x - 6) = 0$

$2x = 0 \mid x - 6 = 0$

$x = 0 \mid \quad x = 6$

$\{0, 6\}$

14. $\left\{0, \dfrac{1}{10}\right\}$

15. $x(x - 2) = (2x + 3)x$

$x^2 - 2x = 2x^2 + 3x$

$x^2 + 5x = 0$

$x(x + 5) = 0$

$x = 0 \text{ or } x = -5$

$\{0, -5\}$

16. $\{0, 5\}$

17. $3x(x + 1) = x(x + 2)$

$3x^2 + 3x = x^2 + 2x$

$2x^2 + x = 0$

$x(2x + 1) = 0$

$x = 0 \quad \mid \quad 2x + 1 = 0$

Not in the | $x = -\dfrac{1}{2}$

the

domain

$\left\{-\dfrac{1}{2}\right\}$

18. $\{2\}$

19. $x^{-2/3} = 16$

$(x^{-2/3})^{-3/2} = \pm 16^{-3/2}$

$x = \pm\dfrac{1}{16^{3/2}}$

$= \pm\dfrac{1}{(\sqrt{16})^3} = \pm\dfrac{1}{4^3} = \pm\dfrac{1}{64}$

$\left\{\dfrac{1}{64}, -\dfrac{1}{64}\right\}$ (both check)

20. $\{32, -32\}$

21. Let x = Length of one side

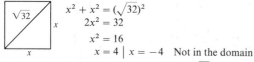

$x^2 + x^2 = (\sqrt{32})^2$

$2x^2 = 32$

$x^2 = 16$

$x = 4 \mid x = -4$ Not in the domain

22. $9\sqrt{2}$

23. Let x = Length of diagonal

$7^2 + 10^2 = x^2$

$49 + 100 = x^2$

$\sqrt{149} = x$

$x = -\sqrt{149}$ is not the domain.

24. $4\sqrt{13}$

Exercises 9.3 (page 445)

1. $x^4 - 37x^2 + 36 = 0$

Let $z = x^2$: $z^2 - 37z + 36 = 0$

$(z - 36)(z - 1) = 0$

$z - 36 = 0 \text{ or} \qquad z - 1 = 0$

$z = 36 \text{ or} \qquad z = 1$

$x^2 = 36 \text{ or} \qquad x^2 = 1$

$x^2 - 36 = 0 \text{ or} \qquad x^2 - 1 = 0$

$(x - 6)(x + 6) = 0 \text{ or } (x - 1)(x + 1) = 0$

$x = 6 \quad x = -6 \quad x = 1 \quad x = -1$

$\{-6, -1, 1, 6\}$

2. $\{-3, -2, 2, 3\}$

3. $z^{-4} - 10z^{-2} + 9 = 0$

Let $y = z^{-2}$: $y^2 - 10y + 9 = 0$

$(y - 9)(y - 1) = 0$

$y - 9 = 0 \quad \text{or } y - 1 = 0$

$y = 9 \quad \text{or} \quad y = 1$

$z^{-2} = 9 \quad \text{or} \quad z^{-2} = 1$

$\dfrac{1}{z^2} = 9 \quad \text{or} \quad \dfrac{1}{z^2} = 1$

$9z^2 = 1 \quad \text{or} \quad z^2 = 1$

$z = \pm\dfrac{1}{3} \text{ or} \quad z = \pm 1$

$\left\{1, -1, \dfrac{1}{3}, -\dfrac{1}{3}\right\}$ (all check)

4. $\left\{1, -1, \dfrac{1}{2}, -\dfrac{1}{2}\right\}$

5. $y^{2/3} - 5y^{1/3} = -4$

Let $a = y^{1/3}$: $a^2 - 5a + 4 = 0$

$(a - 4)(a - 1) = 0$

$a - 4 = 0 \quad \text{or } a - 1 = 0$

$a = 4 \quad \text{or} \qquad a = 1$

$y^{1/3} = 4 \quad \text{or} \quad y^{1/3} = 1$

$(y^{1/3})^3 = 4^3 \text{ or } (y^{1/3})^3 = 1^3$

$y = 64 \text{ or} \qquad y = 1$

$\{1, 64\}$

6. $\{1, 729\}$

7. $z^{-4} - 4z^{-2} = 0$

Let $\qquad a = z^{-2}$

$a^2 - 4a = 0$

$a(a - 4) = 0$

$a = 0 \qquad\qquad a = 4$

$z^{-2} = 0 \qquad\quad z^{-2} = 4$

$\dfrac{1}{z^2} = 0 \qquad\quad \dfrac{1}{z^2} = \dfrac{4}{1}$

$\qquad\qquad\qquad 4z^2 = 1$

$1 = 0 \qquad 4z^2 - 1 = 0$

False $\mid (2z - 1)(2z + 1) = 0$

$z = \dfrac{1}{2} \quad z = -\dfrac{1}{2}$

$\left\{\dfrac{1}{2}, -\dfrac{1}{2}\right\}$

8. $\left\{\dfrac{1}{3}, -\dfrac{1}{3}\right\}$

9. $K^{-2/3} + 2K^{-1/3} + 1 = 0$

Let $a = K^{-1/3}$

$a^2 = K^{-2/3}$

$a^2 + 2a + 1 = 0$

$(a + 1)(a + 1) = 0$

Same answer for | $a + 1 = 0$

both factors | $a = -1$

$K^{-1/3} = -1$

$(K^{-1/3})^{-3} = (-1)^{-3} = \dfrac{1}{(-1)^3} = \dfrac{1}{-1} = -1$

$K = -1$

10. $\{1\}$

11. $(x^2 - 4x)^2 - (x^2 - 4x) - 20 = 0$

Let $a = (x^2 - 4x)$

$a^2 = (x^2 - 4x)^2$

$a^2 - a - 20 = 0$

$(a + 4)(a - 5) = 0$

$a + 4 = 0 \qquad\qquad a - 5 = 0$

$a = -4 \text{ or} \qquad a = 5$

$x^2 - 4x = -4 \text{ or} \qquad x^2 - 4x = 5$

$x^2 - 4x + 4 = 0 \quad\Big|\quad x^2 - 4x - 5 = 0$

$(x - 2)(x - 2) = 0 \quad\Big|\quad (x - 5)(x + 1) = 0$

$x - 2 = 0 \;\Big|\; x - 5 = 0 \;\Big|\; x + 1 = 0$

$x = 2 \;\Big|\qquad x = 5 \;\Big|\qquad x = -1$

Solution set: $\{-1, 2, 5\}$ (all check)

12. $\{-1, 1, 3\}$

13. Let $W =$ Width

$A = w(2w) = 2w^2$

$P = 2w + 2(2w) = 6w$

$2w^2 + 6w = 80$

$2w^2 + 6w - 80 = 0$

$w^2 + 3w - 40 = 0$

$(w + 8)(w - 5) = 0$

$w = -8 \quad\Big|\quad w = 5 \quad$ Width

Not in the domain $\Big|\; 2w = 10 \quad$ Length

14. Width $= 4$;

length $= 12$

15. Let $r =$ Speed from Los Angeles to Mexico

$r + 2 =$ Speed returning

	d	$=$	r	$\cdot$	t
Going	120		r		$\dfrac{120}{r}$
Returning	120		$r + 20$		$\dfrac{120}{r + 20}$

Time to go $+$ Time to return $= 5$ hr

$\dfrac{120}{r} + \dfrac{120}{r + 20} = 5$

$\dfrac{24}{r} + \dfrac{24}{r + 20} = 1$

LCD $= r(r + 20)$

$\dfrac{r(r + 20)}{1} \cdot \dfrac{24}{r} + \dfrac{r(r + 20)}{1} \cdot \dfrac{24}{r + 20} = \dfrac{r(r + 20)}{1} \cdot 1$

$24r + 480 + 24r = r^2 + 20r$

$r^2 - 28r - 480 = 0$

$(r + 12)(r - 40) = 0$

$r + 12 = 0 \quad\Big|\quad r - 40 = 0$

$r = -12 \quad\Big|\quad r = 40 \text{ mph}$

Not in the domain $\Big|\quad$ Rate going

16. 30 mph

Exercises 9.4 (page 452)

1. $x^2 = 6x + 11$

$x^2 - 6x = 11$

$x^2 - 6x + 9 = 9 + 11$

$(x - 3)^2 = 20$

$\sqrt{(x - 3)^2} = \pm\sqrt{20}$

$x - 3 = \pm\sqrt{4 \cdot 5}$

$x = 3 \pm 2\sqrt{5}$

$\{3 \pm 2\sqrt{5}\}$

2. $\{5 \pm 2\sqrt{3}\}$

3.

$x^2 - 13 = 4x$

$x^2 - 4x = 13$

$x^2 - 4x + 4 = 13 + 4$

$(x - 2)^2 = 17$

$x - 2 = \pm\sqrt{17}$

$x = 2 \pm\sqrt{17}$

4. $\{4 \pm 2i\}$

5. $x^2 - 2x - 2 = 0$

$x^2 - 2x = 2$

$x^2 - 2x + 1 = 2 + 1$

$(x - 1)^2 = 3$

$x - 1 = \pm\sqrt{3}$

$x = 1 \pm\sqrt{3}$

6. $\left\{\dfrac{2 \pm \sqrt{3}}{2}\right\}$

7. $3x^2 - x - 2 = 0$ $\begin{cases} a = 3 \\ b = -1 \\ c = -2 \end{cases}$

$x = \dfrac{-(-1) \pm \sqrt{(-1)^2 - 4(3)(-2)}}{2(3)}$

$= \dfrac{1 \pm \sqrt{1 + 24}}{6} = \dfrac{1 \pm \sqrt{25}}{6}$

$= \dfrac{1 \pm 5}{6} = \begin{cases} \dfrac{1 + 5}{6} = \dfrac{6}{6} = 1 \\ \dfrac{1 - 5}{6} = \dfrac{-4}{6} = -\dfrac{2}{3} \end{cases}$

$\left\{1, -\dfrac{2}{3}\right\}$

8. $\left\{\dfrac{1}{2}, -2\right\}$

9. $x^2 - 4x + 1 = 0$ $\begin{cases} a = 1 \\ b = -4 \\ c = 1 \end{cases}$

$x = \dfrac{-(-4) \pm \sqrt{(-4)^2 - 4(1)(1)}}{2(1)}$

$= \dfrac{4 \pm \sqrt{16 - 4}}{2(1)} = \dfrac{4 \pm \sqrt{12}}{2}$

$= \dfrac{4 \pm 2\sqrt{3}}{2} = 2 \pm \sqrt{3}$

$\{2 \pm \sqrt{3}\}$

10. $\{2 \pm \sqrt{5}\}$

11. $x^2 - 4x + 2 = 0$ $\begin{cases} a = 1 \\ b = -4 \\ c = 2 \end{cases}$

$x = \dfrac{+4 \pm \sqrt{(-4)^2 - 4(1)(2)}}{2(1)}$

$x = \dfrac{4 \pm \sqrt{16 - 8}}{2} = \dfrac{4 \pm \sqrt{8}}{2} = \dfrac{4 \pm 2\sqrt{2}}{2}$

$x = 2 \pm \sqrt{2}$

$\{2 \pm \sqrt{2}\}$

12. $\{1 \pm \sqrt{3}\}$

13. $x^2 + x + 5 = 0$ $\begin{cases} a = 1 \\ b = 1 \\ c = 5 \end{cases}$

$x = \dfrac{-(1) \pm \sqrt{(1)^2 - 4(1)(5)}}{2(1)} = \dfrac{-1 \pm \sqrt{1 - 20}}{2}$

$= \dfrac{-1 \pm \sqrt{-19}}{2} = \dfrac{-1 \pm \sqrt{19}i}{2}$

$\left\{\dfrac{-1 \pm i\sqrt{19}}{2}\right\}$

14. $\left\{\dfrac{-1 \pm 3\sqrt{3}i}{2}\right\}$

15. $3x^2 + 2x + 1 = 0$ $\begin{cases} a = 3 \\ b = 2 \\ c = 1 \end{cases}$

$x = \dfrac{-2 \pm \sqrt{(2)^2 - 4(3)(1)}}{2(3)}$

$= \dfrac{-2 \pm \sqrt{4 - 12}}{6} = \dfrac{-2 \pm \sqrt{-8}}{6}$

$= \dfrac{-2 \pm 2\sqrt{2}i}{6} = \dfrac{-1 \pm \sqrt{2}i}{3}$

$\left\{ \dfrac{-1 \pm i\sqrt{2}}{3} \right\}$

16. $\left\{ \dfrac{-3 \pm \sqrt{23}i}{8} \right\}$

17. $2x^2 - 8x + 9 = 0$ $\begin{cases} a = 2 \\ b = -8 \\ c = 9 \end{cases}$

$x = \dfrac{-(-8) \pm \sqrt{(-8)^2 - 4(2)(9)}}{2(2)}$

$= \dfrac{8 \pm \sqrt{64 - 72}}{4} = \dfrac{8 \pm \sqrt{-8}}{4} = \dfrac{8 \pm 2\sqrt{2}i}{4}$

$= \dfrac{\overset{1}{\cancel{2}}(4 \pm \sqrt{2}i)}{\underset{2}{\cancel{4}}} = \dfrac{4 \pm \sqrt{2}i}{2}$

$\left\{ \dfrac{4 \pm i\sqrt{2}}{2} \right\}$

18. $\left\{ \dfrac{3 \pm \sqrt{3}i}{3} \right\}$

19. $3x\left(x + \dfrac{1}{3}\right) = 3x\left(\dfrac{-1}{3x}\right)$

$3x^2 + x = -1$

$3x^2 + x + 1 = 0$ $\begin{cases} a = 3 \\ b = 1 \\ c = 1 \end{cases}$

$x = \dfrac{-1 \pm \sqrt{1^2 - 4(3)(1)}}{2(3)}$

$= \dfrac{-1 \pm \sqrt{1 - 12}}{6} = \dfrac{-1 \pm \sqrt{-11}}{6} = \dfrac{-1 \pm \sqrt{11}i}{6}$

Solutions must be checked, since we multipled both sides by $3x$.

The check for $x = \dfrac{-1 - \sqrt{11}i}{6}$ is left to the student

Check for $x = \dfrac{-1 + \sqrt{11}i}{6}$:

$\dfrac{-1 + \sqrt{11}i}{6} + \dfrac{1}{3} \overset{?}{=} \dfrac{-1}{3\left(\dfrac{-1 + \sqrt{11}i}{6}\right)}$

$\dfrac{-1 + \sqrt{11}i + 2}{6} \overset{?}{=} \dfrac{-2}{-1 + \sqrt{11}i}$

$\dfrac{1 + \sqrt{11}i}{6} \overset{?}{=} \dfrac{-2(-1 - \sqrt{11}i)}{(-1 + \sqrt{11}i)(-1 - \sqrt{11}i)}$

$\dfrac{1 + \sqrt{11}i}{6} \overset{?}{=} \dfrac{2 + 2\sqrt{11}i}{1 + 11}$

$\dfrac{1 + \sqrt{11}i}{6} \overset{?}{=} \dfrac{2(1 + \sqrt{11}i)}{12}$

$\dfrac{1 + \sqrt{11}i}{6} = \dfrac{1 + \sqrt{11}i}{6}$

$\left\{ \dfrac{-1 \pm i\sqrt{11}}{6} \right\}$

20. $\left\{ \dfrac{-1 \pm i\sqrt{15}}{8} \right\}$

21. $2x^2 - 5x = -7$

$2x^2 - 5x + 7 = 0$ $\begin{cases} a = 2 \\ b = -5 \\ c = 7 \end{cases}$

$x = \dfrac{-(-5) \pm \sqrt{(-5)^2 - 4(2)(7)}}{2(2)}$

$= \dfrac{5 \pm \sqrt{25 - 56}}{4} = \dfrac{5 \pm \sqrt{-31}}{4}$

$= \dfrac{5 \pm \sqrt{31}i}{4}$

$\left\{ \dfrac{5 \pm \sqrt{31}i}{4} \right\}$

22. $\left\{ \dfrac{5 \pm i\sqrt{47}}{6} \right\}$

23. $x^2 - 4x + 5 = 0$ $\begin{cases} a = 1 \\ b = -4 \\ c = 5 \end{cases}$

$x = \dfrac{-(-4) \pm \sqrt{(-4)^2 - 4(1)(5)}}{2(1)}$

$= \dfrac{4 \pm \sqrt{16 - 20}}{2} = \dfrac{4 \pm \sqrt{-4}}{2} = \dfrac{4 \pm 2i}{2} = 2 \pm i$

Check for $x = 2 - i$:

$x^2 - 4x + 5 = 0$

$(2 - i)^2 - 4(2 - i) + 5 \overset{?}{=} 0$

$4 - 4i + i^2 - 8 + 4i + 5 \overset{?}{=} 0$

$4 - 4i - 1 - 8 + 4i + 5 \overset{?}{=} 0$

$9 - 9 + 4i - 4i \overset{?}{=} 0$

$0 = 0$

The check for $x = 2 + i$ is left to the student

24. $\{3 \pm i\}$

25. Let W = Width

Area $= LW = (W + 2)W = 2$

$W^2 + 2W = 2$

$W^2 + 2W - 2 = 0$ $\begin{cases} a = 1 \\ b = 2 \\ c = -2 \end{cases}$

$W = \dfrac{-(2) \pm \sqrt{(2)^2 - 4(1)(-2)}}{2(1)} = \dfrac{-2 \pm \sqrt{4 + 8}}{2}$

$= \dfrac{-2 \pm \sqrt{12}}{2} = \dfrac{-2 \pm 2\sqrt{3}}{2}$

$= -1 \pm \sqrt{3} = \begin{cases} -1 + \sqrt{3} \doteq -1 + 1.732 \\ -1 - \sqrt{3} \doteq -1 - 1.732 \end{cases}$

$\doteq \begin{cases} 0.732 \doteq 0.73 \text{ Width} \\ -2.732 \doteq -2.73 \text{ Not in the domain} \end{cases}$

$W + 2 = -1 + \sqrt{3} + 2 = 1 + \sqrt{3} \doteq 2.73$

26. Width $= -2 + \sqrt{10} \doteq 1.16$

Length $= 2 + \sqrt{10} \doteq 5.16$

27. Let x = Length of a side

$P = 4x \quad A = x^2$

$4x = 4 + x^2$

$x^2 - 4x + 4 = 0$

$(x - 2)(x - 2) = 0$

$x = 2.00$

28. Side $= 2 + \sqrt{6} \doteq 4.45$

Exercises 9.5 (page 455)

1. $x^2 - x - 12 = 0$ $\begin{cases} a = 1 \\ b = -1 \\ c = -12 \end{cases}$ **2.** Real, rational, and unequal

$b^2 - 4ac = (-1)^2 - 4(1)(-12)$
$= 1 + 48 = 49$ Perfect square
Therefore, roots are real, rational, and unequal

3. $6x^2 - 7x - 3 = 0$ $\begin{cases} a = 6 \\ b = -7 \\ c = -3 \end{cases}$ **4.** Real, rational, and unequal

$b^2 - 4ac = (-7)^2 - 4(6)(-3)$
$= 49 + 72 = 121$ Perfect square
Therefore, roots are real, rational, and unequal

5. $x^2 - 4x = 0$ $\begin{cases} a = 1 \\ b = -4 \\ c = 0 \end{cases}$ **6.** Real, rational, and unequal

$b^2 - 4ac = (-4)^2 - 4(1)(0)$
$= 16$ Perfect square
Therefore, roots are real, rational, and unequal

7. $9x^2 - 6x + 2 = 0$ $\begin{cases} a = 9 \\ b = -5 \\ c = 2 \end{cases}$ **8.** Complex conjugates

$b^2 - 4ac = (-6)^2 - 4(9)(2)$
$= 36 - 72 = -36$
Therefore, roots are complex conjugates

9.
$\begin{array}{c|c} x = 4 & x = -2 \\ x - 4 = 0 & x + 2 = 0 \end{array}$ **10.** $x^2 + x - 6 = 0$
$(x - 4) \cdot (x + 2) = 0$
$x^2 - 2x - 8 = 0$

11.
$\begin{array}{c|c} x = 0 & x = 5 \\ x = 0 & x - 5 = 0 \end{array}$ **12.** $x^2 - 6x = 0$
$x \cdot (x - 5) = 0$
$x^2 - 5x = 0$

13.
$\begin{array}{c|c} x = 2 + \sqrt{3} & x = 2 - \sqrt{3} \\ x - 2 - \sqrt{3} = 0 & x - 2 + \sqrt{3} = 0 \end{array}$
$[(x - 2) - \sqrt{3}][(x - 2) + \sqrt{3}] = 0$
$(x - 2)^2 - (\sqrt{3})^2 = 0$
$x^2 - 4x + 4 - 3 = 0$
$x^2 - 4x + 1 = 0$

14. $x^2 - 6x + 4 = 0$

15.
$\begin{array}{c|c} x = \dfrac{1}{2} & x = \dfrac{2}{3} \\ 2x = 1 & 3x = 2 \\ 2x - 1 = 0 & 3x - 2 = 0 \end{array}$ **16.** $15x^2 - 19x + 6 = 0$
$(2x - 1)(3x - 2) = 0$
$6x^2 - 7x + 2 = 0$

17.
$\begin{array}{c|c} x = \dfrac{1 + \sqrt{3}i}{2} & x = \dfrac{1 - \sqrt{3}i}{2} \\ 2x = 1 + \sqrt{3}i & 2x = 1 - \sqrt{3}i \\ 2x - 1 - \sqrt{3}i = 0 & 2x - 1 + \sqrt{3}i = 0 \end{array}$
$[(2x - 1) - \sqrt{3}i][(2x - 1) + \sqrt{3}i] = 0$
$(2x - 1)^2 - (\sqrt{3}i)^2 = 0$
$4x^2 - 4x + 1 + 3 = 0$
$4x^2 - 4x + 4 = 0$
$x^2 - x + 1 = 0$

18. $3x^2 - 2x + 1 = 0$

19.
$\begin{array}{c|c|c} x = 1 & x = 3 & x = 4 \\ x - 1 = 0 & x - 3 = 0 & x - 4 = 0 \end{array}$
$(x - 1)(x - 3)(x - 4) = 0$
$(x^2 - 4x + 3)(x - 4) = 0$
$x^3 - 8x^2 + 19x - 12 = 0$

20. $x^3 - 8x^2 + 17x - 10 = 0$

21. $(x - 3)(x + 2i)(x - 2i) = 0$ **22.** $x^3 - 2x^2 + 9x - 18 = 0$
$(x - 3)(x^2 + 4) = 0$
$x^3 - 3x^2 + 4x - 12 = 0$

23. If $5 - i$ is a root, $5 + i$ is a root   **24.** $x^2 - 4x + 13 = 0$
$x = 5 - i$ or $x = 5 + i$
$x - 5 + i = 0$ or $x - 5 - i = 0$
$([x - 5] + i)([x - 5] - i) = 0$
$[x - 5]^2 - i^2 = 0$
$x^2 - 10x + 25 - (-1) = 0$
$x^2 - 10x + 26 = 0$

25. If $1 - 2\sqrt{5}$ is a root, $1 + 2\sqrt{5}$ is a root.
$x = 1 - 2\sqrt{5}$ or $x = 1 + 2\sqrt{5}$
$x - 1 + 2\sqrt{5} = 0$ or $x - 1 - 2\sqrt{5} = 0$
$([x - 1] + 2\sqrt{5})([x - 1] - 2\sqrt{5}) = 0$
$[x - 1]^2 - (2\sqrt{5})^2 = 0$
$x^2 - 2x + 1 - 20 = 0$
$x^2 - 2x - 19 = 0$

26. $x^2 - 6x - 41 = 0$

27. If $-3i$ is a root, $+3i$ is a root.
$\begin{array}{c|c|c} x = 2 & x = -3i & x = 3i \\ x - 2 = 0 & x + 3i = 0 & x - 3i = 0 \end{array}$
$(x - 2)(x + 3i)(x - 3i) = 0$
$(x - 2)(x^2 + 9) = 0$
$x^3 - 2x^2 + 9x - 18 = 0$

28. $x^3 + 3x^2 + 36x + 108 = 0$

Review Exercises 9.6 (page 458)

1.
$x^2 + x - 6 = 0$ **2.** $\{5, -2\}$
$(x + 3)(x - 2) = 0$
$\begin{array}{c|c} x + 3 = 0 & x - 2 = 0 \\ x = -3 & x = 2 \end{array}$

3. $x^2 - 2x - 4 = 0$ $\begin{cases} a = 1 \\ b = -2 \\ c = -4 \end{cases}$ **4.** $\{2 \pm \sqrt{2}\}$

$x = \dfrac{-(-2) \pm \sqrt{(-2)^2 - 4(1)(-4)}}{2(1)}$

$= \dfrac{2 \pm \sqrt{4 + 16}}{2} = \dfrac{2 \pm \sqrt{20}}{2} = \dfrac{2 \pm 2\sqrt{5}}{2} = 1 \pm \sqrt{5}$

5. $x^2 - 2x + 5 = 0$ $\begin{cases} a = 1 \\ b = -2 \\ c = 5 \end{cases}$ **6.** $\{2 \pm \sqrt{3}i\}$

$x = \dfrac{-(-2) \pm \sqrt{(-2)^2 - 4(1)(5)}}{2(1)}$

$= \dfrac{2 \pm \sqrt{-16}}{2} = \dfrac{2 \pm 4i}{2} = 1 \pm 2i$

7. $\dfrac{2x}{3} = \dfrac{3}{8x}$ **8.** $\left\{ \pm \dfrac{5}{6} \right\}$
$16x^2 = 9$
$x^2 = \dfrac{9}{16}$
$x = \pm \dfrac{3}{4}$

9. LCD $= 3(x - 2)$

$$\frac{\cancel{3}(x - 2)}{1} \cdot \frac{(x + 2)}{\cancel{3}} = \frac{3(x - 2)}{1} \cdot \frac{1}{(x - 2)} + \frac{\cancel{3}(x - 2)}{1} \cdot \frac{2}{\cancel{3}}$$

$$(x - 2)(x + 2) = 3 + 2(x - 2)$$
$$x^2 - 4 = 3 + 2x - 4$$
$$x^2 - 2x - 3 = 0$$
$$(x - 3)(x + 1) = 0$$
$$x - 3 = 0 \mid x + 1 = 0$$
$$x = 3 \mid \quad x = -1$$
$$\{3, -1\}$$

10. $\{-4, 2\}$

11. $(x + 5)(x - 2) = x(3 - 2x) + 2$
$$x^2 + 3x - 10 = 3x - 2x^2 + 2$$
$$3x^2 = 12$$
$$x^2 = 4$$
$$\sqrt{x^2} = \pm\sqrt{4}$$
$$x = \pm 2$$
$$\{2, -2\}$$

12. $\left\{\pm\dfrac{3\sqrt{5}}{5}\right\}$

13. (1) $(x^2 - 4x)^2 + 5(x^2 - 4x) + 4 = 0$
Let $z = (x^2 - 4x)$; then $z^2 = (x^2 - 4x)^2$
Equation (1)
becomes $\quad z^2 + 5z + 4 = 0$
$$(z + 4)(z + 1) = 0$$
$$(x^2 - 4x + 4)(x^2 - 4x + 1) = 0$$
$$(x - 2)(x - 2)(x^2 - 4x + 1) = 0$$
$$x - 2 = 0 \mid x^2 - 4x + 1 = 0$$
$$x = 2 \mid$$
$$\qquad\qquad x = \frac{-(-4) \pm \sqrt{16 - 4}}{2(1)}$$
$$\qquad\qquad x = 2 \pm \sqrt{3}$$
$$\{2, 2 \pm \sqrt{3}\}$$

14. $\{-3, -3 + \sqrt{5}, -3 - \sqrt{5}\}$

15. $x^2 - 6x + 7 = 0 \begin{cases} a = 1 \\ b = -6 \\ c = 7 \end{cases}$

$b^2 - 4ac = 36 - 28 = 8 > 0$
Therefore, roots are real, irrational conjugates

16. Real, irrational conjugates

17. Let $x =$ first odd integer $\quad (x)(x + 2) - 14 = 85$
$x + 2 =$ second odd integer $\quad x^2 + 2x - 99 = 0$
$$(x + 11)(x - 9) = 0$$
$$x = -11 \mid x = 9$$
$$x + 2 = -9 \mid x + 2 = 11$$

18. 7 and 8, or -8 and -7

19. Let $x =$ Width
$x + 3 =$ Length
$$x(x + 3) = 8$$
$$x^2 + 3x - 8 = 0$$
$$x = \frac{-3 \pm \sqrt{9 + 32}}{2} = \frac{-3 \pm \sqrt{41}}{2} \doteq \frac{-3 \pm 6.403}{2}$$
$$= \begin{cases} -4.70 \quad \text{Not possible} \\ 1.70 \end{cases}$$

Therefore, Width $= x = (-3 + \sqrt{41})/2 \doteq 1.70$;

Length $= x + 3 = \dfrac{3 + \sqrt{41}}{2} \doteq 4.70$

20. One leg is $\dfrac{-2 + \sqrt{14}}{2} \doteq 0.87$

The other leg is $\dfrac{2 + \sqrt{14}}{2} \doteq 2.87$

21.
$$x = 1 - \sqrt{7} \qquad x = 1 + \sqrt{7}$$
$$x - 1 + \sqrt{7} = 0 \qquad x - 1 - \sqrt{7} = 0$$
$$(x - 1 + \sqrt{7})(x - 1 - \sqrt{7}) = 0$$
$$([x - 1] + \sqrt{7})([x - 1] - \sqrt{7}) = 0$$
$$([x - 1]^2 - [\sqrt{7}]^2 = 0$$
$$x^2 - 2x + 1 - 7 = 0$$
$$x^2 - 2x - 6 = 0$$

22. $x^3 - 2x^2 + 6x - 12 = 0$

Exercises 9.7 (page 469)

1. Set $y = 0$
$$x^2 - 2x - 3 = 0$$
$$(x - 3)(x + 1) = 0$$
$$x - 3 = 0 \mid x + 1 = 0$$
$$x = 3 \mid \quad x = -1$$
x-intercepts are -1 and 3
y-intercept is -3

axis of symmetry is $x = \dfrac{-(-2)}{2} = 1$

$f(1) = 1^2 - 2(1) - 3 = 1 - 2 - 3 = -4$
vertex is at $(1, -4)$; opens upward

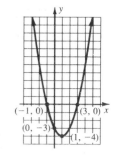

2. x-intercepts are -3 and 5
y-intercept is -15
axis of symmetry is $x = 1$
vertex is at $(1, -16)$; opens upward

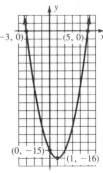

3. Set $y = 0$ Then $x^2 - 2x - 13 = 0$
Use formula:

$$x = \frac{-(-2) \pm \sqrt{(-2)^2 - 4(1)(-13)}}{2(1)}$$

$$= \frac{2 \pm \sqrt{4 + 52}}{2} = \frac{2 \pm \sqrt{56}}{2} = \frac{2 \pm \sqrt{4 \cdot 14}}{2}$$

$$= \frac{2 \pm 2\sqrt{14}}{2} = 1 \pm \sqrt{14}$$

x-intercepts are $1 + \sqrt{14}$ and $1 - \sqrt{14}$
y-intercept is -13

axis of symmetry is $x = \dfrac{-(-2)}{2} = 1$

$f(1) = 1^2 - 2(1) - 13 = -14$
vertex is at $(1, -14)$; opens upward

$(1 - \sqrt{14}, 0) \qquad (1 + \sqrt{14}, 0)$

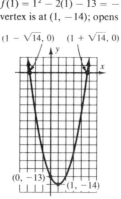

4. x-intercepts are $2 + 2\sqrt{3}$ and $2 - 2\sqrt{3}$
y-intercept is -8
axis of symmetry is $x = 2$
vertex is at $(2, -12)$; opens upward

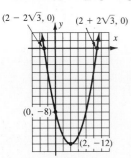

5. Set $\qquad y = 0$
$\quad x^2 - 4x + 3 = 0$
$\quad (x - 3)(x - 1) = 0$
$x - 1 = 0 \mid x - 3 = 0$
$\quad x = 1 \mid \quad x = 3$
x-intercepts are 1 and 3
y-intercept is -3

axis of symmetry is $x = \dfrac{-(-4)}{2} = 2$

$f(2) = 2^2 - 4(2) + 3 = -1$
vertex is at $(2, -1)$; opens upward

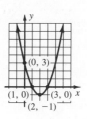

6. x-intercepts are 2 and -4
y-intercept is -8
axis of symmetry is $x = -1$
vertex is at $(-1, -9)$; opens upward

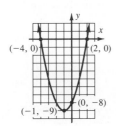

7. Set $\qquad y = 0$
$\quad x^2 + 3x - 10 = 0$
$\quad (x - 2)(x + 5) = 0$
$\qquad x = 2 \mid x = -5$
x-intercepts are 2 and -5
y-intercept is -10

axis of symmetry is $x = -\dfrac{3}{2}$

$f\left(-\dfrac{3}{2}\right) = \left(-\dfrac{3}{2}\right)^2 + 3\left(-\dfrac{3}{2}\right) - 10 = -\dfrac{49}{4}$

vertex is at $\left(-\dfrac{3}{2}, -\dfrac{49}{4}\right)$; opens upward

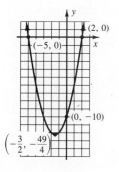

8. x-intercepts are 4 and $-\dfrac{1}{2}$
y-intercept is -4

axis of symmetry is $x = \dfrac{7}{4}$

vertex is at $\left(\dfrac{7}{4}, -\dfrac{81}{8}\right)$; opens upward

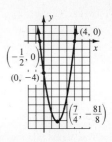

9. y-intercept is 12
$y = f(x) = x^2 - 8x + 12$
Set $y = 0$
$\quad 0 = (x - 2)(x - 6)$
x-intercepts are 2 and 6

axis of symmetry is $x = -\dfrac{-8}{2} = 4$

$f(4) = 4^2 - 8(4) + 12$
$\qquad = 16 - 32 + 12$
$\qquad = -4$
vertex is at $(4, -4)$; opens upward

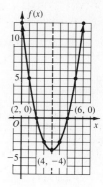

10. x-intercepts are $2 \pm \sqrt{10}$
y-intercept is -6
axis of symmetry is $x = 2$
vertex is at $(2, -10)$; opens upward

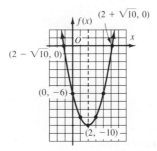

11. y-intercept is 3
Set $y = 0$
$\quad 0 = 3 + 2x^2 - x^2$
$\quad 0 = (3 - x)(1 + x)$
$3 - x = 0 \mid 1 + x = 0$
$\quad x = 3 \mid \quad x = -1$
x-intercepts are 3 and -1

axis of symmetry is $x = -\dfrac{2}{2(-1)} = 1$

$f(1) = 2(1) - 1^2 + 3 = 4$
vertex is at $(1, 4)$; opens downward

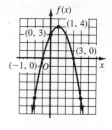

12. x-intercepts are -5 and 1
y-intercept is 5
axis of symmetry is $x = -2$
vertex is at $(-2, 9)$; opens downward

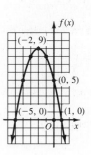

13. $y = f(x) = x^2 - 6x + 10$

Set $y = 0$ Then $x^2 - 6x + 10 = 0$

$$x = \frac{-(-6) \pm \sqrt{(-6)^2 - 4(1)(10)}}{2(1)}$$

$$= \frac{6 \pm \sqrt{36 - 40}}{2} = \frac{6 \pm \sqrt{-4}}{2}$$

$$= \frac{6 \pm 2i}{2} = 3 \pm i$$

This means that the curve does not cross the x-axis

y-intercept is 10

axis of symmetry is $x = -\dfrac{-6}{2} = 3$

vertex is at $(3, 1)$; opens upward

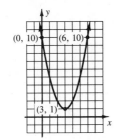

14. no x-intercepts

y-intercept is 11

axis of symmetry is $x = 3$

vertex is at $(3, 2)$; opens upward

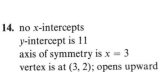

15. y-intercept is -9

Set $y = 0$

$0 = 4x^2 - 9$

$9 = 4x^2$

$x^2 = \dfrac{9}{4}$

$x = \pm\sqrt{\dfrac{9}{4}} = \pm\dfrac{3}{2}$

x-intercepts are $\pm\dfrac{3}{2}$

axis of symmetry is $x = \dfrac{-0}{2(4)} = 0$

$f(0) = -9$

vertex is at $(0, -9)$; opens upward

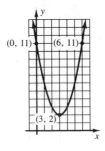

16. x-intercepts are $\pm\dfrac{2}{3}$

y-intercept is -4

axis of symmetry is $x = 0$

vertex is at $(0, -4)$; opens upward

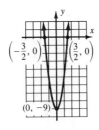

17. $y = f(x) = x^2 - 4x + 6$ If we set $y = 0$, there are no real solutions. (No x-intercepts)

y-intercept is 6

axis of symmetry is $x = -\dfrac{-4}{2} = 2$

vertex is at $(2, 2)$; opens upward

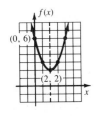

18. No x-intercepts

y-intercept is -2

axis of symmetry is $x = 1$

vertex is at $(1, -1)$; opens downward

19. $f(x) = x^2 - 6x + 7$

$a > 0$

$f(x)$ has a minimum

$$\text{Minimum} = f\left(-\frac{b}{2a}\right)$$

$$= f\left(-\frac{-6}{2(1)}\right) = f(3)$$

$$f(3) = (3)^2 - 6(3) + 7$$

$$= 9 - 18 + 7 = -2$$

$$= -2 \quad \text{Minimum}$$

Vertex: $(3, -2)$

20. Minimum = 1

Vertex: $(2, 1)$

21. $y = -2x^2 + 8x - 3$

$a < 0$

$f(x)$ has a maximum

$$x = \frac{-8}{2(-2)} = 2$$

$$f(2) = -2(4) + 8(2) - 3 = 5 \quad \text{Maximum}$$

Vertex: $(2, 5)$

22. Maximum = 7

Vertex: $(1, 7)$

23. $f(x) = -\dfrac{1}{2}x^2 + x + \dfrac{3}{2}$

$a < 0$

$f(x)$ has a maximum

$$f\left(-\frac{b}{2a}\right) = f\left(-\frac{1}{2\left(-\frac{1}{2}\right)}\right) = f(1)$$

$$f(1) = -\frac{1}{2}(1)^2 + (1) + \frac{3}{2} = 2 \quad \text{Maximum}$$

Vertex: $(1, 2)$

24. Maximum = 3

Vertex: $(-2, 3)$

25. $y = x^2 - 6$ is equivalent to $y + 6 = x^2$; the graph has the same size and shape as $y = x^2$. The vertex is at $(0, -6)$.

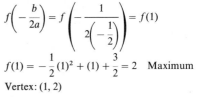

26.

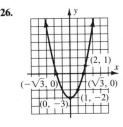

27. The graph has the same size and shape as the graph of $y = x^2$. The vertex is at $(-2, 3)$.

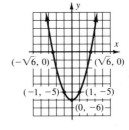

28.

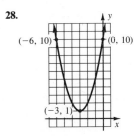

29. The graph has the same size and shape as the graph of $y = x^2$. The vertex is at $(1, -4)$.

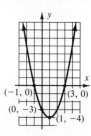

30.

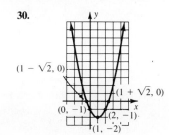

31. $y = (x - 1)^2 + 3$ is equivalent to $y - 3 = (x - 1)^2$; the graph has the same size and shape as the graph of $y = x^2$. The vertex is at $(1, 3)$.

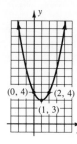

32.

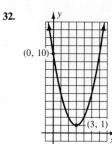

Exercises 9.8 (page 477)

1. $x^2 + y^2 = 9$
Circle
x-intercepts: $x^2 + 0^2 = 9$
$\qquad\qquad\quad x^2 = 9$
$\qquad\qquad\quad x = \pm 3$
y-intercepts: $0^2 + y^2 = 9$
$\qquad\qquad\quad y^2 = 9$
$\qquad\qquad\quad y = \pm 3$

x	y
3	0
-3	0
0	3
0	-3

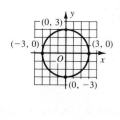

2. Circle

3. $y = x^2 + 2x - 3$
Parabola
x-intercepts: $0 = x^2 + 2x - 3$
$\qquad\qquad\quad 0 = (x + 3)(x - 1)$
$\qquad\qquad\quad x = -3 \quad$ or $\quad x = 1$
y-intercept: $y = 0 + 0 - 3$
$\qquad\qquad\quad = -3$

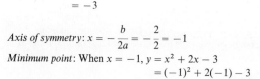

Axis of symmetry: $x = -\dfrac{b}{2a} = -\dfrac{2}{2} = -1$
Minimum point: When $x = -1$, $y = x^2 + 2x - 3$
$\qquad\qquad\qquad\qquad\qquad\quad = (-1)^2 + 2(-1) - 3$
$\qquad\qquad\qquad\qquad\qquad\quad = -4$

Vertex is at $(-1, -4)$

4. Parabola

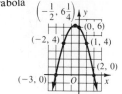

5. $3x^2 + 3y^2 = 21$
$\quad x^2 + y^2 = 7$
Circle
x-intercepts: $x^2 + 0^2 = 7$
$\qquad\qquad\quad x^2 = 7$
$\qquad\qquad\quad x = \pm\sqrt{7} \doteq \pm 2.6$
y-intercepts: $0^2 + y^2 = 7$
$\qquad\qquad\quad y = \pm\sqrt{7} \doteq \pm 2.6$

6. Ellipse

7. $4x^2 + 9y^2 = 36$
Ellipse
x-intercepts: $4x^2 + 9(0)^2 = 36$
$\qquad\qquad\qquad\quad 4x^2 = 36$
$\qquad\qquad\qquad\quad x^2 = 9$
$\qquad\qquad\qquad\quad x = \pm 3$
y-intercepts: $4(0)^2 + 9y^2 = 36$
$\qquad\qquad\qquad\quad 9y^2 = 36$
$\qquad\qquad\qquad\quad y^2 = 4$
$\qquad\qquad\qquad\quad y = \pm 2$

8. Ellipse

9. $9x^2 - 4y^2 = 36$

Hyperbola

x-intercepts: $9x^2 - 4(0)^2 = 36$

$9x^2 = 36$

$x^2 = \pm 4$

$x = \pm 2$

y-intercepts: $9(0)^2 - 4y^2 = 36$

$y^2 = -9$

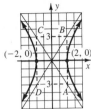

$y = \pm 3i$ (Graph does not intercept y-axis)

The rectangle of reference has vertices at $(2, 3)$ $(2, -3)$ $(-2, 3)$, and $(-2, -3)$

10. Hyperbola

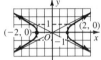

11. $y^2 = 8x$

Parabola

When $x = 1$, $y^2 = 8$

$y = \pm\sqrt{8} \doteq \pm 2.8$

When $x = 2$, $y^2 = 16$

$y = \pm 4$

When $x = 0$, $y^2 = 0$

$y = 0$

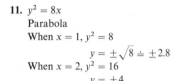

12. Parabola

13. $(x + 1)^2 + (y - 2)^2 = 4$ is in the form $(x - h)^2 + (y - k)^2 = r^2$, where $h = -1, k = 2$, and $r = 2$. The conic is a circle with its center at $(-1, 2)$ and with a radius of 2.

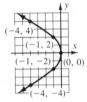

14. Circle; center at $(2, -3)$, radius is 1

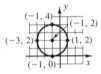

Exercises 9.9A (page 483)

(*Note*: Some exercises are shown with method 1 and some with method 2.)

1. $(x + 1)(x - 2) < 0$

Let $f(x) = (x + 1)(x - 2) = 0$

Then $x + 1 = 0 \quad | \quad x - 2 = 0$

$x = -1 \quad | \quad x = 2$

The x-intercepts are -1 and 2

$f(x) = (x + 1)(x - 2)$

$f(0) = (1)(-2) = -2$

The curve goes through $(0, -2)$

Solution set: $\{x | -1 < x < 2\}$

2. $\{x | x < -1\} \cup \{x | x > 2\}$

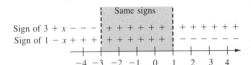

3. $3 - 2x - x^2 \geq 0$

Let $f(x) = (3 + x)(1 - x) = 0$

Then $3 + x = 0 \quad | \quad 1 - x = 0$

$x = -3 \quad | \quad x = 1$

The critical points are -3 and 1

Our inequality was $\geq$. We select the interval on which both signs are the same. The graph is:

Solution set: $\{x | -3 \leq x \leq 1\}$

4. $\{x | x \leq -2\} \cup \{x | x \geq 1\}$

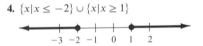

5. $x^2 - 3x - 4 < 0$

Let $f(x) = x^2 - 3x - 4 = 0$

Then $(x - 4)(x + 1) = 0$

x-intercepts: 4 and -1

$f(0) = 0 - 0 - 4 = -4$

The curve goes through $(0, -4)$

Solution set: $\{x | -1 < x < 4\}$

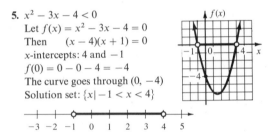

6. $\{x | x < -5\} \cup \{x | x > 1\}$

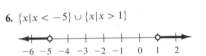

7. $x^2 + 7 > 6x$

$x^2 - 6x + 7 > 0$

Let $f(x) = x^2 - 6x + 7 = 0$

$x = \dfrac{-(-6) \pm \sqrt{36 - 28}}{2} = \dfrac{6 \pm \sqrt{8}}{2}$

$= \dfrac{6 \pm 2\sqrt{2}}{2} = 3 \pm \sqrt{2}$

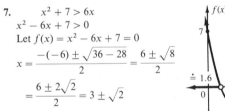
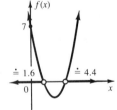

x-intercepts: $3 - \sqrt{2}$ and $3 + \sqrt{2} \doteq 1.6$ and 4.4

$f(0) = 0 - 0 + 7 = 7$

The graph goes through $(0, 7)$

Solution set: $\{x | x < 3 - \sqrt{2}\} \cup \{x | x > 3 + \sqrt{2}\}$

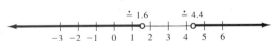

8. $\{x | 4 - \sqrt{3} < x < 4 + \sqrt{3}\}$

9. $x^2 \le 5x$

Let $f(x) = x^2 - 5x = 0$

Then $\quad x(x - 5) = 0$

x-intercepts: 0 and 5

$f(1) = 1 - 5 = -4$

The graph goes through $(1, -4)$

Solution set: $\{x \mid 0 \le x \le 5\}$

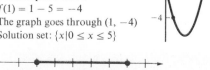

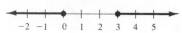

10. $\{x \mid x \le 0\} \cup \{x \mid x \ge 3\}$

11. $3x - x^2 > 0$

Let $f(x) = x(3 - x) = 0$

Critical points are 0 and 3

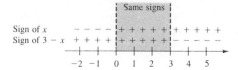

We select the interval on which both signs are the same. The graph is:

Solution set: $\{x \mid 0 < x < 3\}$

12. $\{x \mid x < 0\} \cup \{x \mid x > 7\}$

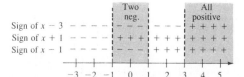

13. $x^3 - 3x^2 - x + 3 > 0$

Let $f(x) = x^3 - 3x^2 - x + 3 = 0$

Factoring by grouping or by synthetic division, we have

$x^3 - 3x^2 - x + 3 = (x - 3)(x + 1)(x - 1)$

Critical points are -1, 1, and 3

We select the intervals on which there are an *even* number of negative signs or where all the signs are positive. The graph is:

Solution set: $\{x \mid -1 < x < 1\} \cup \{x \mid x > 3\}$

14. $\{x \mid -2 < x < -1\} \cup \{x \mid x > 1\}$

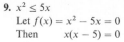

15. $x^3 - 3x^2 + 4 < 0$

Let $f(x) = x^3 - 3x^2 + 4 = 0$

Factoring by synthetic division, we have $(x + 1)(x - 2)^2 = 0$

Critical points are -1 and 2

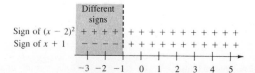

We select the interval on which the signs are different. The graph is:

Solution set: $\{x \mid x < -1\}$

16. $\{x \mid x < 1\}$

17. $\dfrac{x - 2}{x + 3} \ge 0$

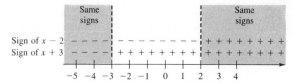

We select the interval on which the signs are the same. (Remember that x cannot equal -3.) The graph is:

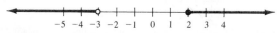

Solution set: $\{x \mid x < -3\} \cup \{x \mid x \ge 2\}$

18. $\{x \mid -4 \le x < 2\}$

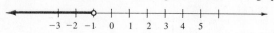

19. Multiply by $(x + 1)^2$, which is positive. This clears fractions and does not change the sense of the inequality

$$\frac{(x + 1)^2}{1} \cdot \frac{x}{1} < \frac{(x + 1)^2}{1} \cdot \frac{2}{x + 1}$$

$(x + 1)^2 x < 2(x + 1)$

$(x + 1)^2 x - 2(x + 1) < 0$

$(x + 1)[(x + 1)x - 2] < 0$

$(x + 1)(x^2 + x - 2) < 0$

$(x + 1)(x + 2)(x - 1) < 0$

Let $f(x) = (x + 1)(x + 2)(x - 1) = 0$

Critical points are -2, -1, and 1

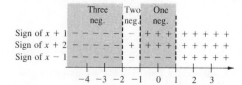

We select the interval on which there are an *odd* number of negative signs. The graph is:

Solution set: $\{x \mid x < -2\} \cup \{x \mid -1 < x < 1\}$

20. $\{x|-4 < x < -3\} \cup \{x|x > 1\}$

21. We must solve $x^2 - 4x - 12 \geq 0$. Let $y = f(x) = x^2 - 4x - 12 = 0$.

$(x - 6)(x + 2) = 0$

$x - 6 = 0 \mid x + 2 = 0$

$\quad x = 6 \mid \quad x = -2$

Critical points are 6 and -2

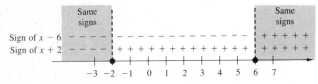

We select the interval on which the signs are the same. The graph is:

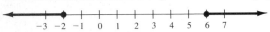

Solution set: $\{x|x \leq -2\} \cup \{x|x \geq 6\}$

22. $\{x|x \leq -5\} \cup \{x|x \geq 2\}$

23. To find the domain of $y = f(x) = \sqrt{4 + 3x - x^2}$, we must solve $4 + 3x - x^2 \geq 0$. Let $y = f(x) = (4 - x)(1 + x) = 0$.
Critical points are 4 and -1.

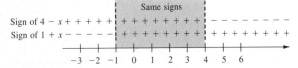

We select the interval on which the signs are the same. The graph is:

Solution set: $\{x|-1 \leq x \leq 4\}$

24. $\{x|-5 \leq x \leq 1\}$

Exercises 9.9B (page 487)

1. $y \leq x^2 + 5x + 6$. We first graph $y = x^2 + 5x + 6$; x-intercepts are -2 and -3; y-intercept is 6. We try $(0, 0)$ in the inequality: $0 \leq 0^2 + 0 + 6$ is true. Therefore, we shade in the region that contains $(0, 0)$.

2.

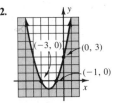

3. $x^2 + 4y^2 > 4$. We first graph $\dfrac{x^2}{4} + \dfrac{y^2}{1} = 1$, using a dotted line. It is an ellipse with x-intercepts 2 and -2 and y-intercepts 1 and -1. Then we try $(0, 0)$ in the inequality: $0^2 + 4(0^2) > 4$ is a false statement. Therefore, we shade in the region that does not contain $(0, 0)$.

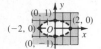

4.

5. We first graph $(x + 2)^2 + (y - 3)^2 = 9$; this is a circle with its center at $(-2, 3)$ and with a radius of 3. Then we try $(0, 0)$ in the inequality:
$(0 + 2)^2 + (0 - 3)^2 \leq 9$ is a false statement. Therefore, we shade in the region that does not contain $(0, 0)$.

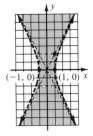

6.

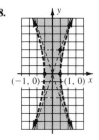

7. $4x^2 - y^2 < 4$. We first graph $4x^2 - y^2 = 4$, using a dotted line. It is a hyperbola with x-intercepts 1 and -1. We try $(0, 0)$ in the inequality:
$4(0^2) - 0^2 < 4$ is a true statement. We shade in the region that contains $(0, 0)$.

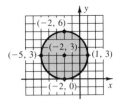

8.

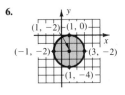

Review Exercises 9.10 (page 489)

1a. Letting $f(x) = 0$, we have
$x^2 - 2x - 8 = 0$
$(x - 4)(x + 2) = 0$
$x - 4 = 0 \quad$ or $\quad x + 2 = 0$
$\quad x = 4 \quad$ or $\qquad x = -2$
x-intercepts are 4 and -2

b. $f(0) = 0^2 - 2(0) - 8 = -8$;
y-intercept is -8

c. Axis of symmetry: $x = -\dfrac{-2}{2} = 1$
$f(1) = 1^2 - 2(1) - 8 = -9$
vertex is at $(1, -9)$

d.

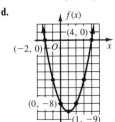

2a. x-intercept is 3
b. y-intercept is -9
c. Vertex is at $(3, 0)$
d.

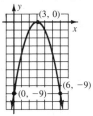

3. $(4 - x)(2 + x) > 0$

Let $f(x) = (4 - x)(2 + x) = 0$

$$4 - x = 0 \mid 2 + x = 0$$
$$x = 4 \mid x = -2$$

x-intercepts are -2 and 4

$f(0) = (4)(2) = 8$

The curve goes through $(0, 8)$

Solution set: $\{x \mid -2 < x < 4\}$

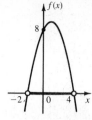

4. $\{x \mid x < 1\} \cup \{x \mid 2 < x < 3\}$

5. $\qquad x > \dfrac{3}{x + 2}$

$$x - \dfrac{3}{x + 2} > 0$$
$$\dfrac{x^2 + 2x - 3}{x + 2} > 0$$
$$\dfrac{(x + 3)(x - 1)}{x + 2} > 0$$

Critical points are -3, 1, and -2

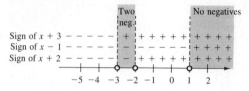

We select the interval on which there are an even number of negative signs or no negative signs. The graph is:

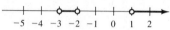

Solution set: $\{x \mid -3 < x < -2\} \cup \{x \mid x > 1\}$

6. $\{x \mid -1 \leq x \leq 6\}$

7. $3x^2 + 3y^2 = 27$

This is a circle with its center at the origin and a radius of 3.

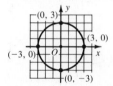

8. Hyperbola

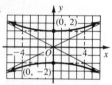

9. $9x^2 + 4y^2 = 36$ Ellipse

x-intercepts: $9x^2 + 4(0)^2 = 36$
$$9x^2 = 36$$
$$x = \pm 2$$

y-intercepts: $9(0)^2 + 4y^2 = 36$
$$4y^2 = 36$$
$$y = \pm 3$$

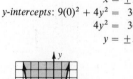

10.

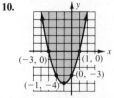

Chapter 9 Diagnostic Test (page 493)

Following each problem number is the textbook section number (in parentheses) where that kind of problem is discussed.

1. (9.2) $\qquad 2x^2 = 6x$
$$2x^2 - 6x = 0$$
$$2x(x - 3) = 0$$
$$2x = 0 \mid x - 3 = 0$$
$$x = 0 \mid x = 3$$

2. (9.2) $\qquad 2x^2 = 18$
$$2x^2 - 18 = 0$$
$$2(x^2 - 9) = 0$$
$$2(x + 3)(x - 3) = 0$$
$$x + 3 = 0 \mid x - 3 = 0$$
$$x = -3 \mid x = 3$$

3. (9.3) $\quad \dfrac{x - 1}{2} + \dfrac{4}{x + 1} = 2 \quad$ LCD $= 2(x + 1)$

$$\dfrac{2(x + 1)}{1} \cdot \dfrac{(x - 1)}{2} + \dfrac{2(x + 1)}{1} \cdot \dfrac{4}{x + 1} = \dfrac{2(x + 1)}{1} \cdot \dfrac{2}{1}$$
$$(x + 1)(x - 1) + 2 \cdot 4 = 4(x + 1)$$
$$x^2 - 1 + 8 = 4x + 4$$
$$x^2 - 4x + 3 = 0$$
$$(x - 1)(x - 3) = 0$$
$$x - 1 = 0 \mid x - 3 = 0$$
$$x = 1 \mid x = 3$$

Check for $x = 1$

$$\dfrac{x - 1}{2} + \dfrac{4}{x + 1} = 2$$
$$\dfrac{(1) - 1}{2} + \dfrac{4}{(1) + 1} \overset{?}{=} 2$$
$$0 + 2 = 2$$

Check for $x = 3$

$$\dfrac{x - 1}{2} + \dfrac{4}{x + 1} = 2$$
$$\dfrac{(3) - 1}{2} + \dfrac{4}{(3) + 1} \overset{?}{=} 2$$
$$1 + 1 = 2$$

Both 1 and 3 are solutions

4. (9.3) (1) $2x^{2/3} + 3x^{1/3} = 2$

Let $z = x^{1/3}$; then $z^2 = x^{2/3}$

Equation (1) becomes $2z^2 + 3z - 2 = 0$
$$(z + 2)(2z - 1) = 0$$

$z + 2 = 0$
$$z = -2$$
$$x^{1/3} = -2$$
$$(x^{1/3})^3 = (-2)^3$$
$$x = -8$$

$2z - 1 = 0$
$$z = \dfrac{1}{2}$$
$$x^{1/3} = \dfrac{1}{2}$$
$$(x^{1/3})^3 = \left(\dfrac{1}{2}\right)^3$$
$$x = \dfrac{1}{8}$$

Check for $x = -8$
$$2(-8)^{2/3} + 3(-8)^{1/3} \overset{?}{=} 2$$
$$2(4) + 3(-2) \overset{?}{=} 2$$
$$8 - 6 = 2 \; True$$

Check for $x = \dfrac{1}{8}$
$$2\left(\dfrac{1}{8}\right)^{2/3} + 3\left(\dfrac{1}{8}\right)^{1/3} \overset{?}{=} 2$$
$$2\left(\dfrac{1}{4}\right) + 3\left(\dfrac{1}{2}\right) \overset{?}{=} 2$$
$$\dfrac{1}{2} + \dfrac{3}{2} = 2 \; True$$

Both -8 and $\dfrac{1}{8}$ are solutions

5. (9.4) $\qquad x^2 = 6x - 7$

$x^2 - 6x + 7 = 0$ will not factor; we use the quadratic formula

$$x = \dfrac{-(-6) \pm \sqrt{(-6)^2 - 4(7)}}{2(1)} = \dfrac{6 \pm \sqrt{36 - 28}}{2}$$
$$= \dfrac{6 \pm \sqrt{8}}{2} = \dfrac{6 \pm 2\sqrt{2}}{2} = 3 \pm \sqrt{2}$$

6. (9.4) $3x^2 + 7x = 1$ will not factor; we use the quadratic formula

$$3x^2 + 7x - 1 = 0 \begin{cases} a = 3 \\ b = 7 \\ c = -1 \end{cases}$$

$$x = \frac{-7 \pm \sqrt{7^2 - 4(3)(-1)}}{2(3)} = \frac{-7 \pm \sqrt{49 + 12}}{6}$$

$$= \frac{-7 \pm \sqrt{61}}{6}$$

7. (9.4) $x^2 + 6x + 10 = 0$ will not factor; we use the quadratic formula

$a = 1, b = 6, c = 10$

$$x = \frac{-6 \pm \sqrt{6^2 - 4(1)(10)}}{2(1)}$$

$$= \frac{-6 \pm \sqrt{36 - 40}}{2}$$

$$= \frac{-6 \pm \sqrt{-4}}{2}$$

$$= \frac{-6 \pm 2i}{2}$$

$$= \frac{-6}{2} \pm \frac{2i}{2}$$

$$= -3 \pm i$$

8. (9.5) $25x^2 - 20x + 7 = 0 \begin{cases} a = 25 \\ b = -20 \\ c = 7 \end{cases}$

$b^2 - 4ac = (-20)^2 - 4(25)7$
$\qquad = 400 - 700 = -300$
Roots are complex conjugates

9. (9.5)   If $2 + i\sqrt{3}$ is a root, $2 - i\sqrt{3}$ is also a root
$x = 2 + i\sqrt{3}, x = 2 - i\sqrt{3}$, and $x = 3$
$x - 2 - i\sqrt{3} = 0, x - 2 + i\sqrt{3} = 0$, and $x - 3 = 0$, and so
$(x - 2 - i\sqrt{3})(x - 2 + i\sqrt{3})(x - 3) = 0$
$([x - 2] - i\sqrt{3})([x - 2] + i\sqrt{3})(x - 3) = 0$
$([x - 2]^2 - [i\sqrt{3}]^2)(x - 3) = 0$
$(x^2 - 4x + 4 - 3i^2)(x - 3) = 0$
$(x^2 - 4x + 4 + 3)(x - 3) = 0$
$(x^2 - 4x + 7)(x - 3) = 0$
$x^3 - 7x^2 + 19x - 21 = 0$

10. (9.8) $25x^2 + 16y^2 = 400$ Ellipse
x-intercepts: Set $y = 0$ in $25x^2 + 16y^2 = 400$
$\qquad\qquad\qquad 25x^2 + 16(0)^2 = 400$
$\qquad\qquad\qquad\qquad\quad 25x^2 = 400$
$\qquad\qquad\qquad\qquad\qquad x^2 = 16$
$\qquad\qquad\qquad\qquad\qquad\; x = \pm 4$
y-intercepts: Set $x = 0$ in $25x^2 + 16y^2 = 400$
$\qquad\qquad\qquad 25(0)^2 + 16y^2 = 400$
$\qquad\qquad\qquad\qquad\quad 16y^2 = 400$
$\qquad\qquad\qquad\qquad\qquad y^2 = 25$
$\qquad\qquad\qquad\qquad\qquad\; y = \pm 5$

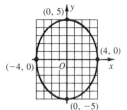

11. (9.9) $x^2 + 5 < 6x$
$\qquad\quad x^2 - 6x + 5 < 0$
$\qquad\quad (x - 1)(x - 5) < 0$
Let $f(x) = (x - 1)(x - 5) = 0$
Then $x - 1 = 0 \mid x - 5 = 0$
$\qquad\qquad x = 1 \mid \qquad x = 5$
The *x*-intercepts are 1 and 5
$f(x) = (x - 1)(x - 5)$
$f(0) = (-1)(-5) = 5$
The curve goes through $(0, 5)$
Solution set: $\{x \mid 1 < x < 5\}$

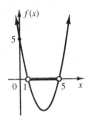

12. (9.9) $x^2 + 2x \geq 8$
$\qquad\quad x^2 + 2x - 8 \geq 0$
$\qquad\quad (x + 4)(x - 2) \geq 0$
Let $f(x) = (x + 4)(x - 2) = 0$
Then $x + 4 = 0 \mid x - 2 = 0$
$\qquad\quad x = -4 \mid \quad x = 2$
The *x*-intercepts are -4 and 2
$f(x) = (x + 4)(x - 2)$
$f(0) = (4)(-2) = -8$
The curve goes through $(0, -8)$
Solution set: $\{x \mid x \leq -4\} \cup \{x \mid x \geq 2\}$

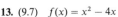

13. (9.7) $f(x) = x^2 - 4x$

a. Equation of axis of symmetry: $x = -\dfrac{b}{2a} = \dfrac{-4}{2(1)} = 2$

b. Vertex: $f(2) = (2)^2 - 4(2)$
$\qquad\qquad\qquad = 4 - 8 = -4$
Vertex: $(2, -4)$

c. *x*-intercepts: $f(x) = x(x - 4) = 0$
$\qquad\qquad\qquad\quad x = 0 \mid x - 4 = 0$
$\qquad\qquad\qquad\qquad\qquad\quad x = 4$
x-intercepts: 0 and 4

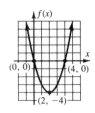

14. (9.3)   Let x = Number of hours for Oscar to do the job

$\qquad\qquad$ Oscar does $\dfrac{1}{x}$ of the work each hour

$x + 2$ = Number of hours for Jan to do the job

$\qquad\qquad$ Jan does $\dfrac{1}{x + 2}$ of the work each hour

Jan works a total of 4 hr and Oscar works 3 hr to do the complete job

$$\begin{array}{c} \text{Work done} \\ \text{by Jan} \end{array} + \begin{array}{c} \text{Work done} \\ \text{by Oscar} \end{array} = \begin{array}{c} \text{Total work done} \\ \text{(the complete job)} \end{array}$$

$$4\left(\frac{1}{x + 2}\right) + 3\left(\frac{1}{x}\right) = 1$$

$$\frac{4}{x + 2} + \frac{3}{x} = 1$$

LCD $= x(x + 2)$

$$\frac{x(x + 2)}{1} \cdot \frac{4}{x + 2} + \frac{x(x + 2)}{1} \cdot \frac{3}{x} = \frac{x(x + 2)}{1} \cdot \frac{1}{1}$$

$$4x + (x + 2)3 = x(x + 2)$$
$$4x + 3x + 6 = x^2 + 2x$$
$$0 = x^2 - 5x - 6$$
$$0 = (x - 6)(x + 1)$$
$$x - 6 = 0 \mid x + 1 = 0$$
$$x = 6 \mid \quad x = -1$$
$$\mid \text{Not in the domain}$$

$x = 6$ hours for Oscar to do the job
$x + 2 = 8$ hours for Jan to do the job

Cumulative Review Exercises: Chapters 1–9 (page 494)

1. $m = \dfrac{-1-5}{4-2} = \dfrac{-6}{2} = -3$ **2.** $x + 2y - 4 = 0$

3. $|4 - 3x| \geq 10$

$4 - 3x \geq 10$	$4 - 3x \leq -10$
$-3x \geq 6$	$-3x \leq -14$
$\dfrac{-3x}{-3} \leq \dfrac{6}{-3}$	$\dfrac{-3x}{-3} \geq \dfrac{-14}{-3}$
$x \leq -2$	$x \geq \dfrac{14}{3}$

$\{x \mid x \leq -2\} \cup \left\{x \geq \dfrac{14}{3}\right\}$

4. $\{-2\}$

5. $4x - 2y < 8$
Boundary line: $4x - 2y = 8$
Boundary line is dashed because = is not included in <
Half-plane includes $(0, 0)$ because
$4(0) - 2(0) < 8$
$0 < 8$ True

x	y
2	0
0	−4

6. $f^{-1}(x) = \dfrac{x+3}{2}$

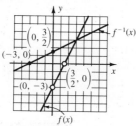

7. $\left(\dfrac{x^{-3}y^4}{x^2y}\right)^{-2} = (x^{-3-2}y^{4-1})^{-2} = (x^{-5}y^3)^{-2} = x^{10}y^{-6} = \dfrac{x^{10}}{y^6}$

8. $\dfrac{4}{x^{2/5}}$

9. $a^{1/3} \cdot a^{-1/2} = a^{1/3+(-1/2)} = a^{2/6+(-3/6)} = a^{-1/6} = \dfrac{1}{a^{1/6}}$

10. $\left\{\dfrac{1 + 3i\sqrt{3}}{2}, \dfrac{1 - 3i\sqrt{3}}{2}\right\}$

11. $3x^2 + x - 3 = 0 \begin{cases} a = 3 \\ b = 1 \\ c = -3 \end{cases}$

$x = \dfrac{-1 \pm \sqrt{1^2 - 4(3)(-3)}}{2(3)}$

$x = \dfrac{-1 \pm \sqrt{1 + 36}}{6}$

$x = \dfrac{-1 \pm \sqrt{37}}{6}$

12.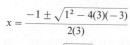

13. We must solve $4 - 3x - x^2 \geq 0$. Solving $4 - 3x - x^2 = 0$, we have $(4 + x)(1 - x) = 0$. Critical points are -4 and 1.

Sign of $4 + x$ $- - - -$ | $+ + + + + + + + +$ | $+ + +$
Sign of $1 - x$ $+ + + +$ | $+ + + + + + + + +$ | $- - -$

$-6\ -5\ -4\ -3\ -2\ -1\ \ 0\ \ 1\ \ 2$

The domain of $y = f(x) = \sqrt{4 - 3x - x^2}$ is $\{x \mid -4 \leq x \leq 1\}$.

14. Length = 8; width = 6

15. Let x = Hours for Merwin Merwin does $\dfrac{1}{x}$ of the work each hour

$x + 3$ = Hours for Mina Mina does $\dfrac{1}{x+3}$ of the work each hour

Mina works a total of 8 hr and Merwin works 3 hr

$$\begin{matrix} \text{Work done} \\ \text{by Mina} \end{matrix} + \begin{matrix} \text{Work done} \\ \text{by Merwin} \end{matrix} = \begin{matrix} \text{Total work done} \\ \text{(the complete job)} \end{matrix}$$

$$8\left(\dfrac{1}{x+3}\right) + 3\left(\dfrac{1}{x}\right) = 1$$

LCD $= x(x + 3)$

$$\dfrac{x(x+3)}{1} \cdot \dfrac{8}{x+3} + \dfrac{x(x+3)}{1} \cdot \dfrac{3}{x} = \dfrac{x(x+3)}{1} \cdot 1$$

$$8x + 3x + 9 = x^2 + 3x$$
$$x^2 - 8x - 9 = 0$$
$$(x - 9)(x + 1) = 0$$

$x + 1 = 0$	$x - 9 = 0$	
$x = -1$	$x = 9$	Hours for Merwin to do the job
Not in the domain	$x + 3 = 12$	Hours for Mina to do the job

Exercises 10.2 (page 500)

1. (1) $2x + y = 6$
Intercepts: $(3, 0)$, $(0, 6)$

(2) $x - y = 0$
Intercepts: $(0, 0)$
If $x = 5$, then $y = 5$, so (2) goes through $(5, 5)$

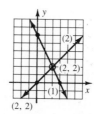

2.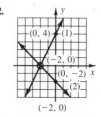

3. (1) $x + 2y = 3$
Intercepts:
$(3, 0)$, $\left(0, \dfrac{3}{2}\right)$

(2) $3x - y = -5$
Intercepts:
$\left(-\dfrac{5}{3}, 0\right)$, $(0, 5)$

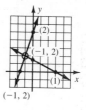

4.

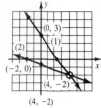

(4, −2)

5. (1) $x + 2y = 0$
Intercept: (0, 0)
Additional point: (6, −3)
(2) $2x − y = 0$
Intercept: (0, 0)
Additional point: (3, 6)

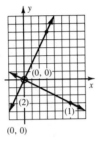

(0, 0)

6.

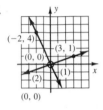

(0, 0)

7. (1) $8x − 5y = 15$
Intercepts: $\left(1\frac{7}{8}, 0\right)$, (0, −3)
(2) $10y − 16x = 16$
Intercepts: $(−1, 0)$, $\left(0, 1\frac{3}{5}\right)$

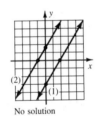

No solution

8.

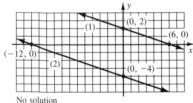

No solution

9. (1) $8x − 10y = 16$
Intercepts: (2, 0), $\left(0, −1\frac{3}{5}\right)$
(2) $15y − 12x = −24$
Intercepts: (2, 0), $\left(0, −1\frac{3}{5}\right)$
Since both lines have the same intercepts, they are the same line

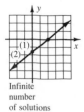

Infinite
number
of solutions

10.

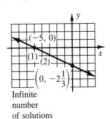

Infinite
number
of solutions

Exercises 10.3 (page 505)

1. $-1]$ $3x − y = 11 \Rightarrow −3x + y = −11$ **2.** $(−3, 4)$
 $3x + 2y = −4 \Rightarrow \underline{3x + 2y = −4}$
$ 3y = −15$
$\phantom{-1]\quad 3x + 2y = −4 \Rightarrow } y = −5$

Substitute $y = −5$ in (1):
(1) $3x − y = 11$
 $3x − (−5) = 11$
 $3x + 5 = 11$
 $3x = 6$
 $x = 2$
Solution: $(2, −5)$

3. $4]$ $1]$ $8x + 15y = 11 \Rightarrow 8x + 15y = 11$ **4.** $(6, 3)$
 $−8]$ $−2]$ $4x − y = 31 \Rightarrow \underline{−8x + 2y = −62}$
$ 17y = −51$
$ y = −3$

Substitute $y = −3$ in (2):
(2) $4x − y = 31$
 $4x − (−3) = 31$
 $4x + 3 = 31$
 $4x = 28$
 $x = 7$
Solution: $(7, −3)$

5. $9]$ $3]$ $7x − 3y = 3 \Rightarrow 21x − 9y = 9$
 $−3]$ $−1]$ $20x − 9y = 12 \Rightarrow \underline{−20x + 9y = −12}$
$\phantom{5.\quad −3] −1] 20x − 9y = 12 \Rightarrow } x = −3$

Substitute $x = −3$ in (1):
(1) $7x − 3y = 3$
 $7(−3) − 3y = 3$
 $−21 − 3y = 3$
 $−3y = 24$
 $y = −8$
Solution: $(−3, −8)$

6. $(9, −13)$

7. $4]$ $2]$ $6x + 5y = 0 \Rightarrow 12x + 10y = 0$
 $−6]$ $−3]$ $4x − 3y = 38 \Rightarrow \underline{−12x + 9y = −114}$
$\phantom{7.\quad −6] −3] 4x − 3y = 38 \Rightarrow } 19y = −114$
$\phantom{7.\quad −6] −3] 4x − 3y = 38 \Rightarrow } y = −6$

Substitute $y = −6$ in (1):
(1) $6x + 5y = 0$
 $6x + 5(−6) = 0$
 $6x − 30 = 0$
 $6x = 30$
 $x = 5$
Solution: $(5, −6)$

8. $(−4, 10)$

9. $−2]$ $4x + 6y = 5 \Rightarrow −8x − 12y = −10$
 $8x + 12y = 7 \Rightarrow \underline{8x + 12y = 7}$
$ 0 = −3$ A *false* statement

Inconsistent; solution: { }

10. Inconsistent: solution: { }

11. $−2]$ $7x − 3y = 5 \Rightarrow −14x + 6y = −10$
 $14x − 6y = 10 \Rightarrow \underline{14x − 6y = 10}$
$ 0 = 0$ A *true* statement

Dependent; $\left(t, \dfrac{7t − 5}{3}\right)$

12. Dependent; $\left(t, \dfrac{2t − 4}{3}\right)$

13.

$$\begin{array}{ll} 6\,]\ 3] & 9x + 4y = -4 \Rightarrow 27x + 12y = -12 \\ 4\,]\ 2] & 15x - 6y = 25 \Rightarrow 30x - 12y = 50 \end{array}$$
$$\overline{57x = 38}$$
$$x = \frac{38}{57} = \frac{2}{3}$$

Substitute $x = \dfrac{2}{3}$ in (1):

(1) $\quad 9x + 4y = -4$

$$\overset{3}{\cancel{9}}\left(\frac{2}{\cancel{3}}\right) + 4y = -4$$
$$6 + 4y = -4$$
$$4y = -10$$
$$y = \frac{-10}{4} = -\frac{5}{2}$$

Solution: $\left(\dfrac{2}{3}, -\dfrac{5}{2}\right)$

14. $\left(-\dfrac{7}{4}, \dfrac{2}{5}\right)$

15. Add $15x$ to both sides of equation (2) so that like terms are in the same column:

$$\begin{array}{ll} 15\,] & 5] & 9x + 10y = -3 \Rightarrow 45x + 50y = -15 \\ -9\,] & -3] & 15x + 14y = 7 \Rightarrow -45x - 42y = -21 \end{array}$$
$$\overline{8y = -36}$$
$$y = -\frac{36}{8} = -\frac{9}{2}$$

Substitute $y = -\dfrac{9}{2}$ in (1):

(1) $\quad 9x + 10y = -3$

$$9x + \overset{5}{\cancel{10}}\left(-\frac{9}{\cancel{2}}\right) = -3$$
$$9x - 45 = -3$$
$$9x = 42$$
$$x = \frac{42}{9} = \frac{14}{3}$$

Solution: $\left(\dfrac{14}{3}, -\dfrac{9}{2}\right)$

16. $\left(\dfrac{3}{7}, \dfrac{5}{6}\right)$

Exercises 10.4 (page 509)

1. (1) $\quad 7x + 4y = 4$

(2) $\qquad y = 6 - 3x$

Substitute $6 - 3x$ for y in (1):

(1) $\qquad 7x + 4y = 4$
$$7x + 4(6 - 3x) = 4$$
$$7x + 24 - 12x = 4$$
$$-5x = -20$$
$$x = 4$$

Substitute $x = 4$ in $y = 6 - 3x$

$$y = 6 - 3(4)$$
$$y = 6 - 12 = -6$$

Solution: $(4, -6)$

2. $(-7, 3)$

3. (1) $\quad 5x - 4y = -1$

(2) $\quad 3x + y = -38 \Rightarrow y = -3x - 38$

Substitute $-3x - 38$ for y in (1):

(1) $\qquad 5x - 4y = -1$
$$5x - 4(-3x - 38) = -1$$
$$5x + 12x + 152 = -1$$
$$17x = -153$$
$$x = -9$$

Substitute $x = -9$ in $y = -3x - 38$

$$y = -3(-9) - 38$$
$$y = 27 - 38 = -11$$

Solution: $(-9, -11)$

4. $(-5, -4)$

5. (1) $\quad 8x - 5y = 4$

(2) $\quad x - 2y = -16 \Rightarrow x = 2y - 16$

Substitute $2y - 16$ for x in (1):

(1) $\quad 8(2y - 16) - 5y = 4$
$$16y - 128 - 5y = 4$$
$$11y = 132$$
$$y = 12$$

Substitute $y = 12$ in $x = 2y - 16$

$$x = 2(12) - 16$$
$$x = 24 - 16 = 8$$

Solution: $(8, 12)$

6. $(10, 16)$

7. (1) $\quad 15x + 5y = 8$

(2) $\quad 6x + 2y = -10 \Rightarrow y = -3x - 5$

(1) $\quad 15x + 5(-3x - 5) = 8$
$$15x - 15x - 25 = 8$$
$$-25 = 8 \quad \text{A false statement}$$

Inconsistent; solution: $\{\ \}$

8. Inconsistent; solution: $\{\ \}$

9. (1) $\quad 20x - 10y = 70$

(2) $\quad 6x - 3y = 21 \Rightarrow y = 2x - 7$

(1) $\quad 20x - 10(2x - 7) = 70$
$$20x - 20x + 70 = 70$$
$$70 = 70 \quad \text{A true statement}$$

Dependent; $(t, 2t - 7)$

10. Dependent

$(5s + 9, s)$

11. (1) $\quad 8x + 4y = 7$

(2) $\quad 3x + 6y = 6 \Rightarrow 3x = 6 - 6y$

$$x = \frac{6 - 6y}{3} = 2 - 2y$$

Substitute $2 - 2y$ for x in (1):

(1) $\qquad 8x + 4y = \quad 7$

$\qquad 8(\, 2 - 2y \,) + 4y = \quad 7$

$\qquad 16 - 16y + 4y = \quad 7$

$$-12y = -9 \Rightarrow y = \frac{3}{4}$$

Substitute $y = \dfrac{3}{4}$ in $x = \, 2 - 2y$

$$x = 2 - 2\left(\frac{3}{4}\right) = \frac{1}{2}$$

Solution: $\left(\dfrac{1}{2}, \dfrac{3}{4}\right)$

12. $\left(\dfrac{3}{5}, \dfrac{1}{4}\right)$

13. (1) $\quad 4x + \quad 4y = \quad 3 \Rightarrow 4x = \, 3 - 4y \Rightarrow x = \dfrac{3 - 4y}{4}$

(2) $\quad 6x + 12y = -6$

Substitute $\dfrac{3 - 4y}{4}$ for x in (2):

(2) $\qquad\qquad 6x + 12y = -6$

$$\overset{3}{\cancel{6}} \left(\frac{3 - 4y}{\underset{2}{\cancel{4}}}\right) + 12y = -6$$

LCD $= 2$

$$\frac{\cancel{2}}{1} \cdot 3\left(\frac{3 - 4y}{\cancel{2}}\right) + 2(12y) = 2(-6)$$

$$9 - 12y + 24y = -12$$

$$12y = -21$$

$$y = -\frac{21}{12} = -\frac{7}{4} = -1\frac{3}{4}$$

Substitute $y = -\dfrac{7}{4}$ in $x = \dfrac{3 - 4y}{4}$

$$x = \frac{3 - 4\left(-\dfrac{7}{4}\right)}{4} = \frac{3 + 7}{4} = \frac{10}{4} = 2\frac{1}{2}$$

Solution: $\left(2\dfrac{1}{2}, -1\dfrac{3}{4}\right)$

14. $\left(2\dfrac{1}{2}, -2\dfrac{1}{3}\right)$

Exercises 10.5 (page 512)

1. (1) $\quad 2x + y + \quad z = \quad 4$

(2) $\quad\; x - y + 3z = -2$

(3) $\quad\; x + y + 2z = \quad 1$

(1) + (2): $\quad 3x \qquad + 4z = \quad 2$

(2) + (3): $\quad 2x \qquad + 5z = -1$

Next, eliminate x:

$\quad 2 \,]\;\; 3x + 4z = \quad 2 \Rightarrow \quad 6x + \quad 8z = \quad 4$

$-3 \,]\;\; 2x + 5z = -1 \Rightarrow -6x \quad - 15z = \quad 3$

$\qquad\qquad\qquad\qquad\qquad\qquad\overline{\qquad\qquad - 7z = \quad 7}$

$\qquad\qquad\qquad\qquad\qquad\qquad\qquad\qquad\quad z = -1$

Substitute $z = -1$ in $3x + 4z = 2$

$$3x - 4 = 2$$

$$3x = 6$$

$$x = 2$$

Substitute $x = 2$ and $z = -1$ in (3):

(3) $\quad x + y + 2z = 1$

$\qquad 2 + y - 2 = 1$

$\qquad\qquad\quad y = 1$

The solution is $(2, 1, -1)$

2. $(1, -2, 2)$

3. $\qquad$ (1) $\quad\; x + 2y + 2z = \quad 0$

$\qquad$ (2) $\quad 2x - \quad y + \quad z = -3$

$\qquad$ (3) $\quad 4x + 2y + 3z = \quad 2$

(1) + 2(2): $\;\; 5x \qquad + 4z = -6 \quad$ (4)

2(2) + (3): $\;\; 8x \qquad + 5z = -4$

$-5 \,]\; 5x + \; 4z = -6 \Rightarrow -25x - 20z = \quad 30$

$\;\;\,4 \,]\; 8x + \; 5z = -4 \Rightarrow \quad 32x + 20z = -16$

$\qquad\qquad\qquad\qquad\qquad\overline{\qquad 7x \qquad\quad = \quad 14}$

$\qquad\qquad\qquad\qquad\qquad\qquad\qquad\;\; x = \quad 2$

Substitute $x = 2$ in (4):

(4) $\quad 5x + 4z = \quad -6$

$\qquad 5(2) + 4z = \quad -6$

$\qquad\qquad\;\; 4z = -16$

$\qquad\qquad\quad z = \quad -4$

Substitute $x = 2$ and $z = -4$ in (1):

(1) $\quad x + 2y + 2z = 0$

$\qquad 2 + 2y + 2(-4) = 0$

$\qquad\qquad\qquad 2y = 6$

$\qquad\qquad\qquad\; y = 3$

The solution is $(2, 3, -4)$

4. $(3, -4, 2)$

5. $\qquad$ (1) $\quad\;\; x \qquad\; + 2z = \quad 7$

$\qquad$ (2) $\quad 2x - \;\; y \qquad\;\; = \quad 5$

$\qquad$ (3) $\qquad\quad 2y + \quad z = \quad 4$

2(2) + (3): $\;\; 4x \qquad + \quad z = 14 \quad$ (4)

(1): $\qquad\;\; x \qquad\; + 2z = \quad 7$

$2 \,]\; 4x + 1z = 14 \Rightarrow \quad 8x + 2z = \quad 28$

$-(1) \qquad\qquad\qquad\;\;\; -x - 2z = -7$

$\qquad\qquad\qquad\overline{\qquad 7x \qquad\quad = \quad 21}$

$\qquad\qquad\qquad\qquad\qquad x = \quad 3$

Substitute $x = 3$ in (4):

(4) $\quad 4x + z = 14$

$\qquad 4(3) + z = 14$

$\qquad\qquad\;\; z = 2$

Substitute $z = 2$ in (3):

(3) $\quad 2y + z = 4$

$\qquad 2y + 2 = 4$

$\qquad\quad 2y = 2$

$\qquad\quad\; y = 1$

The solution is $(3, 1, 2)$

6. $(2, -1, 3)$

7.

$$
\begin{array}{ll}
(1) & 2x + 3y + z = 7 \\
(2) & 4x - 2z = -6 \\
(3) & 6y - z = 0 \\
\end{array}
$$

$$
\begin{array}{ll}
2(3): & 12y - 2z = 0 \\
(2): & 4x - 2z = -6 \\
\end{array}
$$

$$
\begin{array}{lll}
2(3) - (2): & -4x + 12y = 6 & (4) \\
(1) + (3): & 2x + 9y = 7 & (5) \\
\end{array}
$$

$$
\tfrac{1}{2}(4): \quad -2x + 6y = 3
$$

$$
(5) + \tfrac{1}{2}(4): \quad 15y = 10
$$

$$
y = \frac{2}{3}
$$

Substitute $y = \dfrac{2}{3}$ in (3):

$$
\begin{array}{ll}
(3) & 6y - z = 0 \\
& 6\left(\dfrac{2}{3}\right) - z = 0 \\
& 4 - z = 0 \Rightarrow z = 4
\end{array}
$$

Substitute $y = \dfrac{2}{3}$ and $z = 4$ in (1):

$$
\begin{array}{ll}
(1) & 2x + 3y + z = 7 \\
& 2x + 3\left(\dfrac{2}{3}\right) + 4 = 7 \\
& 2x + 2 + 4 = 7 \\
& 2x = 1 \\
& x = \dfrac{1}{2}
\end{array}
$$

The solution is $\left(\dfrac{1}{2}, \dfrac{2}{3}, 4\right)$.

8. $\left(\dfrac{3}{4}, \dfrac{2}{5}, -1\right)$

9.

$$
\begin{array}{ll}
(1) & x + y + z + w = 5 \\
(2) & 2x - y + 2z - w = -2 \\
(3) & x + 2y - z - 2w = -1 \\
(4) & -x + 3y + 3z + w = 1 \\
\end{array}
$$

$$
\begin{array}{lll}
(1) + (2): & 3x + 3z = 3 & (5) \\
2(1) + (3): & 3x + 4y + z = 9 & (6) \\
(2) + (4): & x + 2y + 5z = -1 & (7) \\
\end{array}
$$

$$
\begin{array}{ll}
(6): & 3x + 4y + z = 9 \\
-2(7): & -2x - 4y - 10z = 2 \\
\end{array}
$$

$$
\begin{array}{lll}
& x - 9z = 11 \\
-\tfrac{1}{3}(5): & -x - z = -1 & (8) \\
\hline
& -10z = 10 \\
& z = -1
\end{array}
$$

Substitute $z = -1$ in $-1(8)$:

$$
\begin{array}{ll}
-1(8) & x + z = 1 \\
& x + (-1) = 1 \\
& x = 2
\end{array}
$$

Substitute $x = 2$ and $z = -1$ in (7):

$$
\begin{array}{ll}
(7) & x + 2y + 5z = -1 \\
& 2 + 2y - 5 = -1 \\
& 2y = 2 \\
& y = 1
\end{array}
$$

Substitute $x = 2$, $y = 1$, and $z = -1$ in (1):

$$
\begin{array}{ll}
(1) & x + y + z + w = 5 \\
& 2 + 1 - 1 + w = 5 \\
& w = 3
\end{array}
$$

The solution is $(2, 1, -1, 3)$.

10. $(1, 2, 3, -2)$

11.

$$
\begin{array}{ll}
(1) & 6x + 4y + 9z + 5w = -3 \\
(2) & 2x + 8y - 6z + 15w = 8 \\
(3) & 4x - 4y + 3z - 10w = -3 \\
(4) & 2x - 4y + 3z - 5w = -1 \\
\end{array}
$$

$$
\begin{array}{lll}
(1) + (4): & 8x + 12z = -4 & (5) \\
2(1) + (3): & 16x + 4y + 21z = -9 & (6) \\
(2) + 3(4): & 8x - 4y + 3z = 5 & (7) \\
\end{array}
$$

$$
\begin{array}{lll}
(5): & 8x + 12z = -4 \\
(6) + (7): & 24x + 24z = -4 & (8) \\
\hline
3(5) - (8): & 12z = -8 \\
& z = -\dfrac{2}{3}
\end{array}
$$

Substitute $z = -\dfrac{2}{3}$ in (5):

$$
\begin{array}{ll}
(5) & 8x + 12z = -4 \\
& 8x + 12\left(-\dfrac{2}{3}\right) = -4 \\
& 8x - 8 = -4 \\
& x = \dfrac{4}{8} = \dfrac{1}{2}
\end{array}
$$

Substitute $x = \dfrac{1}{2}$ and $z = -\dfrac{2}{3}$ in (7):

$$
\begin{array}{ll}
(7) & 8x - 4y + 3z = 5 \\
& 8\left(\dfrac{1}{2}\right) - 4y + 3\left(-\dfrac{2}{3}\right) = 5 \\
& 4 - 4y - 2 = 5 \\
& -4y = 3 \\
& y = -\dfrac{3}{4}
\end{array}
$$

Substitute $x = \dfrac{1}{2}$, $y = -\dfrac{3}{4}$, and $z = -\dfrac{2}{3}$ in (4):

$$
\begin{array}{ll}
(4) & 2x - 4y + 3z - 5w = -1 \\
& 2\left(\dfrac{1}{2}\right) - 4\left(-\dfrac{3}{4}\right) + 3\left(-\dfrac{2}{3}\right) - 5w = -1 \\
& 1 + 3 - 2 - 5w = -1 \\
& -5w = -3 \\
& w = \dfrac{3}{5}
\end{array}
$$

Solution: $\left(\dfrac{1}{2}, -\dfrac{3}{4}, -\dfrac{2}{3}, \dfrac{3}{5}\right)$

12. $\left(-\dfrac{5}{6}, \dfrac{1}{3}, \dfrac{3}{2}, -\dfrac{1}{4}\right)$

Review Exercises 10.6 (page 514)

1.
$$
\begin{array}{ll}
(1) & 4x + 5y = 22 \\
(2) & 3x - 2y = 5
\end{array}
$$

(1) Intercepts: $\left(5\dfrac{1}{2}, 0\right)$ and $\left(0, 4\dfrac{2}{5}\right)$

(2) Intercepts: $\left(1\dfrac{2}{3}, 0\right)$ and $\left(0, -2\dfrac{1}{2}\right)$

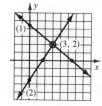

$(3, 2)$

2.

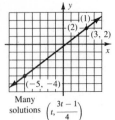

Many solutions $\left(t, \dfrac{3t-1}{4}\right)$

3. (1) $2x - 3y = 3$
(2) $3y - 2x = 6$

(1) Intercepts: $\left(1\dfrac{1}{2}, 0\right)$ and $(0, -1)$

(2) Intercepts: $(-3, 0)$ and $(0, 2)$

No solution

4. $\left(4\dfrac{1}{2}, -3\dfrac{1}{2}\right)$

5. $-3]\ 4x - 8y = 4 \Rightarrow -12x + 24y = -12$
$4]\ 3x - 6y = 3 \Rightarrow \underline{\quad 12x - 24y = \quad 12}$
$\qquad\qquad\qquad\qquad\qquad 0 = \quad 0$

Dependent (many solutions)

$\left(t, \dfrac{t-1}{2}\right)$

6. Inconsistent; solution set: $\{\ \ \}$

7. (1) $x = y + 2$
(2) $4x - 5y = 3$

Substitute $y + 2$ in place of x in (2):

(2) $\quad 4x - 5y = \quad 3$
$\quad 4(y + 2) - 5y = \quad 3$
$\quad 4y + 8 - 5y = \quad 3$
$\qquad\qquad -y = -5$
$\qquad\qquad\ y = \quad 5$

Substitute $y = 5$ in $x = y + 2$
$\qquad\qquad x = \ 5 + 2 = 7$

Solution: $(7, 5)$

8. $(4, 9)$

9.
(1) $2x + y - z = \quad 1$
(2) $3x - y + 2z = \quad 3$
(3) $x + 2y + 3z = -6$

$(1) + (2)$: $5x \quad\ + z = \quad 4$ (4)
$2(2) + (3)$: $7x \quad\ + 7z = \quad 0$ (5)

$\dfrac{1}{7}\,(5)$: $x \quad\ + z = \quad 0$ (6)

(4): $5x \quad\ + z = \quad 4$ (4)
$(4) - (6)$: $\underline{4x \qquad\qquad = \quad 4}$
$\qquad\qquad\qquad x = \quad 1$

Substitute $x = 1$ in (6) $\Rightarrow z = -1$
Substitute $x = 1$ and $z = -1$ in (1) $\Rightarrow y = -2$
The solution is $(1, -2, -1)$

10. $(2, 1, -3)$

Exercises 10.7A (page 517)

1. $\begin{vmatrix} 3 & 4 \\ 2 & 5 \end{vmatrix} = (3)(5) - (2)(4) = 15 - 8 = 7$ **2.** 22

3. $\begin{vmatrix} 2 & -4 \\ 5 & -3 \end{vmatrix} = 2(-3) - 5(-4) = -6 + 20 = 14$ **4.** 40

5. $\begin{vmatrix} -7 & -3 \\ 5 & 8 \end{vmatrix} = (-7)(8) - (5)(-3) = -56 - (-15)$
$\qquad\qquad\qquad = -56 + 15 = -41$

6. 0   **7.** $\begin{vmatrix} 2 & -4 \\ 3 & x \end{vmatrix} = 20$ **8.** 3

$2x - (3)(-4) = 20$
$2x + 12 = 20$
$2x = \quad 8$
$x = \quad 4$

Exercises 10.7B (page 521)

1. $2x + \ y = 7$
$\quad x + 2y = 8$

$x = \dfrac{\begin{vmatrix} 7 & 1 \\ 8 & 2 \end{vmatrix}}{\begin{vmatrix} 2 & 1 \\ 1 & 2 \end{vmatrix}} = \dfrac{(7)(2) - (8)(1)}{(2)(2) - (1)(1)} = \dfrac{14 - 8}{4 - 1} = \dfrac{6}{3} = 2$

$y = \dfrac{\begin{vmatrix} 2 & 7 \\ 1 & 8 \end{vmatrix}}{\begin{vmatrix} 2 & 1 \\ 1 & 2 \end{vmatrix}} = \dfrac{(2)(8) - (1)(7)}{(2)(2) - (1)(1)} = \dfrac{16 - 7}{3} = \dfrac{9}{3} = 3$

The solution is $(2, 3)$

2. $(3, 1)$

3. $x - 2y = \quad 3$
$\quad 3x + 7y = -4$

$x = \dfrac{\begin{vmatrix} 3 & -2 \\ -4 & 7 \end{vmatrix}}{\begin{vmatrix} 1 & -2 \\ 3 & 7 \end{vmatrix}} = \dfrac{(3)(7) - (-4)(-2)}{(1)(7) - (3)(-2)} = \dfrac{13}{13} = 1$

$y = \dfrac{\begin{vmatrix} 1 & 3 \\ 3 & -4 \end{vmatrix}}{\begin{vmatrix} 1 & -2 \\ 3 & 7 \end{vmatrix}} = \dfrac{(1)(-4) - (3)(3)}{(1)(7) - (3)(-2)} = \dfrac{-13}{13} = -1$

The solution is $(1, -1)$

4. $(3, -2)$

5. $3x - 4y = 5$
$\quad 9x + 8y = 0$

$x = \dfrac{\begin{vmatrix} 5 & -4 \\ 0 & 8 \end{vmatrix}}{\begin{vmatrix} 3 & -4 \\ 9 & 8 \end{vmatrix}} = \dfrac{(5)(8) - (0)(-4)}{(3)(8) - (9)(-4)} = \dfrac{40}{60} = \dfrac{2}{3}$

$y = \dfrac{\begin{vmatrix} 3 & 5 \\ 9 & 0 \end{vmatrix}}{\begin{vmatrix} 3 & -4 \\ 9 & 8 \end{vmatrix}} = \dfrac{(3)(0) - (9)(5)}{(3)(8) - (9)(-4)} = \dfrac{-45}{60} = -\dfrac{3}{4}$

The solution is $\left(\dfrac{2}{3}, -\dfrac{3}{4}\right)$

6. $(0, 0)$

7. $x + 3y = 1$
$\quad 2x + 6y = 3$

$x = \dfrac{\begin{vmatrix} 1 & 3 \\ 3 & 6 \end{vmatrix}}{\begin{vmatrix} 1 & 3 \\ 2 & 6 \end{vmatrix}} = \dfrac{6 - 9}{6 - 6} = \dfrac{-3}{0}$ Not possible

$y = \dfrac{\begin{vmatrix} 1 & 1 \\ 2 & 3 \end{vmatrix}}{\begin{vmatrix} 1 & 3 \\ 2 & 6 \end{vmatrix}} = \dfrac{3 - 2}{6 - 6} = \dfrac{1}{0}$ Not possible

Inconsistent (no solution)

8. Inconsistent (no solution)

9. $2x - 4y = 6$
$3x - 6y = 9$

$$x = \frac{\begin{vmatrix} 6 & -4 \\ 9 & -6 \end{vmatrix}}{\begin{vmatrix} 2 & -4 \\ 3 & -6 \end{vmatrix}} = \frac{(6)(-6) - (9)(-4)}{(2)(-6) - (3)(-4)} = \frac{-36 + 36}{-12 + 12} = \frac{0}{0}$$

Cannot be determined

$$y = \frac{\begin{vmatrix} 2 & 6 \\ 3 & 9 \end{vmatrix}}{\begin{vmatrix} 2 & -4 \\ 3 & -6 \end{vmatrix}} = \frac{(2)(9) - (3)(6)}{(2)(-6) - (3)(-4)} = \frac{18 - 18}{-12 + 12} = \frac{0}{0}$$

Cannot be determined

Dependent (an infinite number of solutions)

10. Dependent (an infinite number of solutions)

Exercises 10.8A (page 524)

1a. $\begin{vmatrix} 4 & -1 \\ -3 & 0 \end{vmatrix}$ **b.** $-\begin{vmatrix} 4 & -1 \\ -3 & 0 \end{vmatrix}$ **c.** $\begin{vmatrix} 1 & 3 \\ 4 & -1 \end{vmatrix}$ **d.** $-\begin{vmatrix} 1 & 3 \\ 4 & -1 \end{vmatrix}$

e. $\begin{vmatrix} 2 & 3 \\ 5 & -1 \end{vmatrix}$ **f.** $\begin{vmatrix} 2 & 3 \\ 5 & -1 \end{vmatrix}$

2a. $\begin{vmatrix} 0 & 1 \\ 1 & 5 \end{vmatrix}$ **b.** $\begin{vmatrix} 0 & 1 \\ 1 & 5 \end{vmatrix}$ **c.** $\begin{vmatrix} 2 & 0 \\ -3 & -2 \end{vmatrix}$ **d.** $-\begin{vmatrix} 2 & 0 \\ -3 & -2 \end{vmatrix}$

e. $\begin{vmatrix} 2 & 1 \\ 4 & 5 \end{vmatrix}$ **f.** $-\begin{vmatrix} 2 & 1 \\ 4 & 5 \end{vmatrix}$

3. $\begin{vmatrix} 1 & 2 & 1 \\ 3 & 1 & 2 \\ 4 & 2 & 0 \end{vmatrix} = (1)\begin{vmatrix} 3 & 1 \\ 4 & 2 \end{vmatrix} - (2)\begin{vmatrix} 1 & 2 \\ 4 & 2 \end{vmatrix} + (0)\begin{vmatrix} 1 & 2 \\ 3 & 1 \end{vmatrix}$ **4.** 18

$\qquad = 1(6 - 4) - 2(2 - 8) + 0 = 2 + 12 = 14$

5. $\begin{vmatrix} 1 & 3 & -2 \\ -1 & 2 & -3 \\ 0 & 4 & 1 \end{vmatrix} = 0\begin{vmatrix} 3 & -2 \\ 2 & -3 \end{vmatrix} - 4\begin{vmatrix} 1 & -2 \\ -1 & -3 \end{vmatrix} + 1\begin{vmatrix} 1 & 3 \\ -1 & 2 \end{vmatrix}$

$\qquad = 0 - 4(-3 - 2) + 1(2 + 3)$
$\qquad = 0 + 20 + 5 = 25$

6. -10

7. $\begin{vmatrix} 1 & -2 & 3 \\ -3 & 4 & 0 \\ 2 & 6 & 5 \end{vmatrix} = (3)\begin{vmatrix} -3 & 4 \\ 2 & 6 \end{vmatrix} - (0)\begin{vmatrix} \\ \end{vmatrix} + (5)\begin{vmatrix} 1 & -2 \\ -3 & 4 \end{vmatrix}$

$\qquad = 3(-18 - 8) - 0 + 5(4 - 6)$
$\qquad = 3(-26) + 5(-2) = -78 - 10 = -88$

8. -84 **9.** $\begin{vmatrix} 6 & 7 & 8 \\ -6 & 7 & -9 \\ 0 & 0 & -2 \end{vmatrix} = 0\begin{vmatrix} \\ \end{vmatrix} - 0\begin{vmatrix} \\ \end{vmatrix} - 2\begin{vmatrix} 6 & 7 \\ -6 & 7 \end{vmatrix}$

$\qquad = 0 - 0 - 2(42 + 42) = -168$

10. -180 **11.** $\begin{vmatrix} x & 0 & 1 \\ 0 & 2 & 3 \\ 4 & -1 & -2 \end{vmatrix} = 6$ **12.** -2

$\qquad x\begin{vmatrix} 2 & 3 \\ -1 & -2 \end{vmatrix} + 1\begin{vmatrix} 0 & 2 \\ 4 & -1 \end{vmatrix} = 6$

$\qquad x(-1) + 1(-8) = 6$
$\qquad -x - 8 = 6$
$\qquad x = -14$

Exercises 10.8B (page 528)

1. $2x + y + z = 4$
$x - y + 3z = -2$
$x + y + 2z = 1$

$$D = \begin{vmatrix} 2 & 1 & 1 \\ 1 & -1 & 3 \\ 1 & 1 & 2 \end{vmatrix} = (2)\begin{vmatrix} -1 & 3 \\ 1 & 2 \end{vmatrix} - (1)\begin{vmatrix} 1 & 3 \\ 1 & 2 \end{vmatrix} + (1)\begin{vmatrix} 1 & -1 \\ 1 & 1 \end{vmatrix}$$

$\qquad = 2(-5) - 1(2 - 3) + 1(1 + 1)$
$\qquad = -10 + 1 + 2 = -7$

$$D_x = \begin{vmatrix} 4 & 1 & 1 \\ -2 & -1 & 3 \\ 1 & 1 & 2 \end{vmatrix}$$

$\qquad = (4)\begin{vmatrix} -1 & 3 \\ 1 & 2 \end{vmatrix} - (-2)\begin{vmatrix} 1 & 1 \\ 1 & 2 \end{vmatrix} + (1)\begin{vmatrix} 1 & 1 \\ -1 & 3 \end{vmatrix}$

$\qquad = 4(-5) + 2(1) + 1(4)$
$\qquad = -20 + 2 + 4 = -14$

$$D_y = \begin{vmatrix} 2 & 4 & 1 \\ 1 & -2 & 3 \\ 1 & 1 & 2 \end{vmatrix}$$

$\qquad = (2)\begin{vmatrix} -2 & 3 \\ 1 & 2 \end{vmatrix} - (4)\begin{vmatrix} 1 & 3 \\ 1 & 2 \end{vmatrix} + (1)\begin{vmatrix} 1 & -2 \\ 1 & 1 \end{vmatrix}$

$\qquad = 2(-7) - 4(-1) + 1(3)$
$\qquad = -14 + 4 + 3 = -7$

$$D_z = \begin{vmatrix} 2 & 1 & 4 \\ 1 & -1 & -2 \\ 1 & 1 & 1 \end{vmatrix},$$

$\qquad = (2)\begin{vmatrix} -1 & -2 \\ 1 & 1 \end{vmatrix} - (1)\begin{vmatrix} 1 & -2 \\ 1 & 1 \end{vmatrix} + (4)\begin{vmatrix} 1 & -1 \\ 1 & 1 \end{vmatrix}$

$\qquad = 2(1) - 1(3) + 4(2)$
$\qquad = 2 - 3 + 8 = 7$

$x = \dfrac{D_x}{D} = \dfrac{-14}{-7} = 2, \ y = \dfrac{D_y}{D} = \dfrac{-7}{-7} = 1, \ z = \dfrac{D_z}{D} = \dfrac{7}{-7} = -1$

The solution is $(2, 1, -1)$

2. $(1, -2, 2)$

3. $2x + 3y + z = 7$ **4.** $(2, -1, 3)$
$4x \qquad - 2z = -6$
$\qquad 6y - z = 0$

$$D = \begin{vmatrix} 2 & 3 & 1 \\ 4 & 0 & -2 \\ 0 & 6 & -1 \end{vmatrix}$$

$\qquad = (0)\begin{vmatrix} \\ \end{vmatrix} - (6)\begin{vmatrix} 2 & 1 \\ 4 & -2 \end{vmatrix} + (-1)\begin{vmatrix} 2 & 3 \\ 4 & 0 \end{vmatrix}$

$\qquad = -6(-8) - 1(-12)$
$\qquad = 48 + 12 = 60$

$$D_x = \begin{vmatrix} 7 & 3 & 1 \\ -6 & 0 & -2 \\ 0 & 6 & -1 \end{vmatrix}$$

$\qquad = (0)\begin{vmatrix} \\ \end{vmatrix} - (6)\begin{vmatrix} 7 & 1 \\ -6 & -2 \end{vmatrix} + (-1)\begin{vmatrix} 7 & 3 \\ -6 & 0 \end{vmatrix}$

$\qquad = 0 - 6(-8) - 1(18) = 30$

$$D_y = \begin{vmatrix} 2 & 7 & 1 \\ 4 & -6 & -2 \\ 0 & 0 & -1 \end{vmatrix} = +(-1)\begin{vmatrix} 2 & 7 \\ 4 & -6 \end{vmatrix} = -1(-40) = 40$$

$$D_z = \begin{vmatrix} 2 & 3 & 7 \\ 4 & 0 & -6 \\ 0 & 6 & 0 \end{vmatrix} = -(6)\begin{vmatrix} 2 & 7 \\ 4 & -6 \end{vmatrix} = -6(-40) = 240$$

$x = \dfrac{D_x}{D} = \dfrac{30}{60} = \dfrac{1}{2}, \ y = \dfrac{D_y}{D} = \dfrac{40}{60} = \dfrac{2}{3}, \ z = \dfrac{D_z}{D} = \dfrac{240}{60} = 4$

The solution is $\left(\dfrac{1}{2}, \dfrac{2}{3}, 4\right)$

Exercises 10.9 (page 532)

Note: The checks for these exercises will not be shown.

1. Let x = One number   (1) $x + y = 30$
      y = The other number   (2) $x - y = 12$

$$\underline{\hspace{2cm}}$$
$$2x \quad\quad = 42$$
$$x \quad\quad = 21$$

Substitute $x = 21$ in (1) $\Rightarrow 21 + y = 30 \Rightarrow y = 9$

2. $125°$ and $55°$

3. Let x = Number of nickels   **4.** 15 dimes, 7 half-dollars
    y = Number of quarters
  (1) $x + y = 15$
  (2) $5x + 25y = 175$
Solving (1) for x, we have:
  (1) $x + y = 15 \Rightarrow x = 15 - y$

Substitute $15 - y$ for x in (2):
  (2) $5x + 25y = 175$
     $5(15 - y) + 25y = 175$
     $75 - 5y + 25y = 175$
           $20y = 100$
           $y = 5$ quarters

Substitute $y = 5$ in $x = 15 - y$
       $x = 15 - 5 = 10$ nickels

5. Let x = Numerator
     y = Denominator
  (1) $\dfrac{x}{y} = \dfrac{2}{3}$
  (2) $\dfrac{x + 10}{y - 5} = 1$
  (1) $\dfrac{x}{y} = \dfrac{2}{3} \Rightarrow 3x = 2y$
  (2) $\dfrac{x + 10}{y - 5} = 1 \Rightarrow x + 10 = y - 5 \Rightarrow x = y - 15$

Substitute $y - 15$ for x in $3x = 2y$
         $3(y - 15) = 2y$
         $3y - 45 = 2y$
           $y = 45$
Substitute $y = 45$ in $x = y - 15$
       $x = 45 - 15 = 30$
Original fraction was $\dfrac{30}{45}$

6. $\dfrac{12}{24}$

7. Let u = Units digit   **8.** 498
    t = Tens digit
    h = Hundreds digit
     (1) $h + t + u = 20$
     (2) $t - u = 3$
     (3) $h + t \quad = 15$
(1) + (2) $\overline{h + 2t \quad\quad = 23}$ (4)
     (3) $h + t \quad\quad = 15$
(4) − (3) $\overline{\quad t \quad\quad = 8}$
Substitute $t = 8$ in (3) $\Rightarrow h = 7$
Substitute $t = 8$ in (2) $\Rightarrow u = 5$
The number is 785

9. Let a = Hours for A to do job
    b = Hours for B to do job
    c = Hours for C to do job
Then in 1 hr A does $\dfrac{1}{a}$ of the job, B does $\dfrac{1}{b}$ of the job, and C does $\dfrac{1}{c}$ of the job

  (1) $\dfrac{2}{a} + \dfrac{2}{b} + \dfrac{2}{c} = 1$
  (2) $\dfrac{3}{b} + \dfrac{3}{c} = 1$
  (3) $\dfrac{4}{a} + \dfrac{4}{b} \quad\quad = 1$

$$\underline{\hspace{3cm}}$$
  (1) $\dfrac{2}{a} + \dfrac{2}{b} + \dfrac{2}{c} = 1$
$\dfrac{1}{2}$ (3) $\dfrac{2}{a} + \dfrac{2}{b} \quad\quad = \dfrac{1}{2}$
$$\underline{\hspace{3cm}}$$
$(1) - \dfrac{1}{2}$ (3) $\dfrac{2}{c} = \dfrac{1}{2} \Rightarrow c = 4$ hr

Substitute $c = 4$ in (2) $\Rightarrow b = 12$ hr
Substitute $b = 12$ in (3) $\Rightarrow a = 6$ hr

10. A: 4 hr;   B: 8 hr;   C: 12 hr

11. Let x = Average speed of plane in still air
     y = Average speed of wind
  $x - y$ = Average speed flying against the wind
  $x + y$ = Average speed flying with the wind
         Formula to use: $rt = d$

  (1) $2\,]\;(x - y)\dfrac{11}{2} = 2750 \Rightarrow 11(x - y) = 2(2750)$
  (2) $(x + y)(5) = 2750 \Rightarrow 5(x + y) = 2750$
  (1) $1/11\,]\;\; 11x - 11y = 5500 \Rightarrow\; x - y = \;500$
      $1/5\,]\;\;\; 5x + 5y = 2750 \Rightarrow\; x + y = \;550$ Add
$$\underline{\hspace{4cm}}$$
            $2x \quad\quad = 1050$
            $x \quad\quad = 525$ mph, speed of
                      plane in still air
        $525 + y = 550$
            $y = 25$ mph,
               speed of wind

12. 540 mph = speed of plane; 60 mph = speed of wind

13. Let x = Number of pounds of grade A coffee
     y = Number of pounds of grade B coffee
  (1) $x + y = 90 \;\Rightarrow\; -365\,] \;\; x + y = 90$
  (2) $100\,]\; 3.85x + 3.65y = 338.90 \Rightarrow \quad 385x + 365y = 33890$
$$\underline{\hspace{5cm}}$$
                   $-365x - 365y = -32850$
                   $385x + 365y = \;\;33890$
$$\underline{\hspace{5cm}}$$
                     $20x \quad\quad = 1040$
                     $x \quad\quad = 52$ lb of grade A coffee
                $52 + y = 90$
                    $y = 38$ lb of grade B coffee

14. 37 lb of grade A coffee; 43 lb of grade B coffee

15. Let u = Units digit   **16.** 86
     t = Tens digit
    (1) $t + u = 12$
    (2) $(10t + u) - (10u + t) = 54$
    (2) $10t + u - 10u - t = 54$
    (2) $9t - 9u = 54$
$\dfrac{1}{9}$ (2) $t - u = 6$
    (1) $t + u = 12$
$(1) + \dfrac{1}{9}$ (2) $2t \quad\quad = 18$
                $t \quad = 9$

Substitute $t = 9$ in (1) $\Rightarrow 9 + u = 12 \Rightarrow u = 3$
The number is 93

17. Let x = Number of 18-cent stamps
    y = Number of 22-cent stamps
    z = Number of 45-cent stamps
(1) $\qquad x + y + z = 29$
(2) $\quad 18x + 22y + 45z = 721$
(3) $\qquad\qquad y = 2x$
Substitute (3) into (1) and into (2):
(4) $\qquad x + 2x + z = 29 \Rightarrow 3x + z = 29$
(5) $\quad 18x + 44x + 45z = 721 \Rightarrow 62x + 45z = 721$
$-45(4)\quad -135x - 45z = -1305$
(5) $\qquad\underline{\quad 62x + 45z = \quad 721}$
$\qquad\qquad\quad -73x \quad = -584$
$\qquad\qquad\qquad x = 8 \quad$ 18-cent stamps
Substitute $x = 8$ into (3):
$\qquad\quad y = 2(8) = 16 \quad$ 22-cent stamps
Substitute $x = 8$ and $y = 16$ into (1):
$\quad 8 + 16 + z = 29 \Rightarrow z = 5 \quad$ 45-cent stamps

18. 6   18-cent stamps; 12   22-cent stamps; 3   45-cent stamps

19. Let t = Cost of tie
    p = Cost of pin
(1) $\;t + p = 110$
(2) $\;t = 100 + p$
Substitute $100 + p$ for t in (1):
(1) $\qquad\qquad t + p = 110$
$\qquad 100 + p + p = 110$
$\qquad\qquad\quad 2p = 10$
$\qquad\qquad\quad p = 5$
$\qquad\quad t = 100 + p = 100 + 5 = 105$
The pin costs 5¢, and the tie costs $1.05

20. 7 on upper branch; 5 on lower branch

Exercises 10.10 (page 539)

1. (1) $\qquad x^2 = 2y$
(2) $\;x - y = -4$
$\qquad\qquad y = x + 4$
Substitute $x + 4$ for y in (1):
(1) $\qquad\qquad x^2 = 2y$
$\qquad\qquad x^2 = 2(x + 4)$
$\qquad\qquad x^2 = 2x + 8$
$\qquad x^2 - 2x - 8 = 0$
$\qquad (x - 4)(x + 2) = 0$
$\quad x - 4 = 0 \mid x + 2 = 0$
$\qquad x = 4 \mid \qquad x = -2$
Substitute $x = 4$ in $y = x + 4$
$\qquad\qquad y = 8$
Substitute $x = -2$ in $y = x + 4$
$\qquad\qquad y = 2$
The solutions are $(4, 8)$ and $(-2, 2)$

2. $(2, 1)$ and $(-4, 4)$

3. (1) $\qquad x^2 = 4y$
(2) $\;x - y = 1$
Solve (2) for y:
$\;x - y = 1$
$\qquad y = x - 1$

4. $(-5, 0)$ and $(4, 3)$

Substitute $x - 1$ for y in (1):
(1) $\qquad\qquad x^2 = 4y$
$\qquad\qquad x^2 = 4(x - 1)$
$\qquad\qquad x^2 = 4x - 4$
$\qquad x^2 - 4x + 4 = 0$
$\qquad (x - 2)(x - 2) = 0$
Therefore, $x = 2$
Substitute $x = 2$ in (2):
(2) $\;x - y = 1$
$\quad 2 - y = 1 \Rightarrow y = 1$
There is only one solution, $(2, 1)$.

5. (1) $\qquad xy = 4$
(2) $\;x - 2y = 2$
Solve (2) for x:
$\;x - 2y = 2$
$\qquad x = 2y + 2$
Substitute $2y + 2$ for x in (1):
(1) $\qquad\qquad xy = 4$
$\qquad\quad (2y + 2)y = 4$
$\qquad 2y^2 + 2y - 4 = 0$
$\qquad\; y^2 + y - 2 = 0$
$\qquad (y + 2)(y - 1) = 0$
$\;y + 2 = 0 \mid y - 1 = 0$
$\quad y = -2 \mid \quad y = 1$
Substitute $y = -2$ in $xy = 4$
$\qquad\qquad x(-2) = 4$
$\qquad\qquad\quad x = -2$
Substitute $y = 1$ in $xy = 4$
$\qquad\qquad x(1) = 4$
$\qquad\qquad\; x = 4$
The solutions are $(-2, -2)$ and $(4, 1)$

6. $(-\sqrt{3}i, \sqrt{3}i)$ and $(\sqrt{3}i, -\sqrt{3}i)$

7. (1) $\quad x^2 + y^2 = 61$
(2) $\quad\underline{x^2 - y^2 = 11}$
(1) + (2): $\; 2x^2 \qquad = 72$
$\qquad\qquad x^2 = 36$
$\qquad\qquad x = \pm 6$
Substitute $x = \pm 6$ in (1):
(1) $\qquad x^2 + y^2 = 61$
$\qquad (\pm 6)^2 + y^2 = 61$
$\qquad\quad 36 + y^2 = 61$
$\qquad\qquad\quad y^2 = 25$
$\qquad\qquad\quad y = \pm 5$
The solutions are $(6, 5), (6, -5), (-6, 5),$ and $(-6, -5)$

8. $(2, 0), (-2, 0),$ and $(0, -1)$

9. (1) $\;2x^2 + 3y^2 = 21$
(2) $\;x^2 + 2y^2 = 12$
$-1]\;\; 2\;\; x^2 + 3y^2 = 21 \Rightarrow -2x^2 - 3y^2 = -21$
$2]\;\; 1\;\; x^2 + 2y^2 = 12 \Rightarrow \underline{\;\; 2x^2 + 4y^2 = \quad 24}$
$\qquad\qquad\qquad\qquad\qquad\quad y^2 = \quad 3$
$\qquad\qquad\qquad\qquad\qquad\; y = \pm\sqrt{3}$
Substitute $y = \pm\sqrt{3}$ in (2):
(2) $\qquad x^2 + 2y^2 = 12$
$\qquad x^2 + 2(\pm\sqrt{3})^2 = 12$
$\qquad\qquad x^2 + 6 = 12$
$\qquad\qquad\quad x^2 = 6$
$\qquad\qquad\quad x = \pm\sqrt{6}$
The solutions are
$(\sqrt{6}, \sqrt{3}), (\sqrt{6}, -\sqrt{3}), (-\sqrt{6}, \sqrt{3}), (-\sqrt{6}, -\sqrt{3})$

10. $(3\sqrt{2}, \sqrt{2}), (3\sqrt{2}, -\sqrt{2}), (-3\sqrt{2}, \sqrt{2})$, and $(-3\sqrt{2}, -\sqrt{2})$

11. (1) $xy = -4$
(2) $y = 6x - 9 - x^2$
Solve (1) for y:
(1) $xy = -4$
$$y = \frac{-4}{x}$$
Substitute $\dfrac{-4}{x}$ for y in (2):
$$\frac{-4}{x} = 6x - 9 - x^2$$
$$-4 = 6x^2 - 9x - x^3$$
$$x^3 - 6x^2 + 9x - 4 = 0$$

$\begin{array}{r|rrrr} & 1 & -6 & 9 & -4 \\ & & 1 & -5 & 4 \\ \hline 1 & 1 & -5 & 4 & 0 \end{array}$ Factor using synthetic division

$(x - 1)(x^2 - 5x + 4) = 0$

$\begin{array}{l|l} x - 1 = 0 & x^2 - 5x + 4 = 0 \\ x = 1 & (x - 1)(x - 4) = 0 \\ & x = 1 \mid x - 4 = 0 \\ & x = 4 \end{array}$

$\begin{array}{l|l} \textit{When } x = 1 \textit{ in (1):} & \textit{When } x = 4 \textit{ in (1):} \\ (1) \quad xy = -4 & (1) \quad xy = -4 \\ (1)y = -4 & (4)y = -4 \\ y = -4 & y = -1 \end{array}$

The solutions are $(1, -4)$ and $(4, -1)$

12. Real solution: $(2, 4)$
Complex solutions:
$(1 + \sqrt{3}i, 2 - 2\sqrt{3}i), (1 - \sqrt{3}i, 2 + 2\sqrt{3}i)$

Exercises 10.11A (page 541)

1. (1) $4x - 3y > -12$
(2) $\qquad y > 2$
Boundary line for (1): $4x - 3y = -12$
Intercepts:

x	y
0	4
-3	0

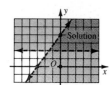

Both lines are dashed lines
because equality is not included

The origin is in the correct half-plane for (1) because
$4(0) - 3(0) > -12$
$0 > -12$ *True*

2.

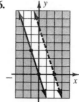

3. (1) $2x - y \le 2$
(2) $\quad x + y \ge 5$
Boundary line for (1): $2x - y = 2$
Intercepts:

x	y
0	-2
1	0

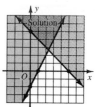

Both lines are solid
because equality is included

Boundary line for (2): $x + y = 5$
Intercepts:

x	y
0	5
5	0

The origin is in the correct half-plane for (1), but not for (2)

4.

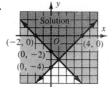

5. (1) $2x + y < 0$
(2) $\quad x - y \ge -3$
Boundary line for (1): $2x + y = 0$
Points on line:

x	y
0	0
-1	2

The boundary line for (1) is
dashed because equality is
not included; the boundary line
for (2) is solid because equality
is included

The point $(-1, 0)$ is in the correct half-plane
Boundary line for (2): $x - y = -3$
Points on line:

x	y
0	3
-3	0

The origin is in the correct half-plane

6.

No solution

7. (1) $3x - 2y < 6$
   (2) $x + 2y \le 4$
   (3) $6x + y > -6$
Boundary line for (1): $3x - 2y = 6$
Intercepts:

x	y
2	0
0	-3

Shaded area is solution

The boundary lines for (1) and (3) are dashed because equality is not included; the boundary line for (2) is solid because equality is included

The half-plane includes $(0, 0)$ because $3(0) - 2(0) < 6$
Boundary line for (2): $x + 2y = 4$
Intercepts:

x	y
4	0
0	2

The half-plane includes $(0, 0)$ because $(0) + 2(0) \le 4$
Boundary line for (3): $6x + y = -6$
Intercepts:

x	y
-1	0
0	-6

The half-plane includes $(0, 0)$ because $6(0) + (0) > -6$

8.

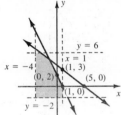

Shaded area is solution

Exercises 10.11B (page 543)

1. Boundary for $\dfrac{x^2}{9} + \dfrac{y^2}{4} < 1$ is $\dfrac{x^2}{9} + \dfrac{y^2}{4} = 1$, which is an ellipse with intercepts $(\pm 3, 0)$ and $(0, \pm 2)$. Boundary for $\dfrac{x^2}{4} + \dfrac{y^2}{9} < 1$ is $\dfrac{x^2}{4} + \dfrac{y^2}{9} = 1$, which is an ellipse with intercepts $(\pm 2, 0)$ and $0, \pm 3)$. Both boundaries must be graphed as dashed curves. Substituting $(0, 0)$ in both inequalities gives true statements.

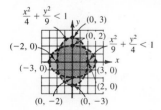

2.

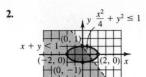

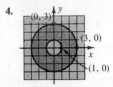

3. Boundary for $y > 1 - x^2$ is $y = 1 - x^2$, which is a parabola with intercepts $(\pm 1, 0)$ and $(0, 1)$. Boundary for $x^2 + y^2 < 4$ is $x^2 + y^2 = 4$, which is a circle with intercepts $(\pm 2, 0)$ and $(0, \pm 2)$. Both curves must be graphed as dashed curves. Substituting $(0, 0)$ in $y > 1 - x^2$ gives a false statement; we must shade in the region that does not contain the origin. Substituting $(0, 0)$ in $x^2 + y^2 < 4$ gives a true statement; we must shade in the region that contains the origin. The final answer is heavily shaded.

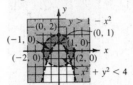   **4.**

5. Boundary for $x^2 + y^2 \le 9$ is $x^2 + y^2 = 9$, which is a circle of radius 3 with its center at the origin; it must be graphed with a solid line. Boundary for $y \ge x - 2$ is a straight line with intercepts $(2, 0)$ and $(0, -2)$; it must be graphed with a solid line. Substituting $(0, 0)$ in $x^2 + y^2 \le 9$ gives a true statement; we shade in the region that contains the origin (the region *inside* the circle). Substituting $(0, 0)$ in $y \ge x - 2$ gives a true statement; we shade in the half-plane that contains the origin. The final answer is heavily shaded in.

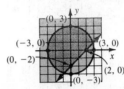

Review Exercises 10.12 (page 544)

1. $3x - 2y = 8$
   $2x + 5y = -1$

$$x = \frac{D_x}{D} = \frac{\begin{vmatrix} 8 & -2 \\ -1 & 5 \end{vmatrix}}{\begin{vmatrix} 3 & -2 \\ 2 & 5 \end{vmatrix}} = \frac{40 - 2}{15 + 4} = \frac{38}{19} = 2$$

$$y = \frac{D_y}{D} = \frac{\begin{vmatrix} 3 & 8 \\ 2 & -1 \end{vmatrix}}{\begin{vmatrix} 3 & -2 \\ 2 & 5 \end{vmatrix}} = \frac{-3 - 16}{15 + 4} = \frac{-19}{19} = -1$$

The solution is $(2, -1)$

2. $(-1, 3, 2)$

3. $5x + 2y = 1$
   $7x - 6y = 8$

$$x = \frac{D_x}{D} = \frac{\begin{vmatrix} 1 & 2 \\ 8 & -6 \end{vmatrix}}{\begin{vmatrix} 5 & 2 \\ 7 & -6 \end{vmatrix}} = \frac{-6 - 16}{-30 - 14} = \frac{-22}{-44} = \frac{1}{2}$$

$$y = \frac{D_y}{D} = \frac{\begin{vmatrix} 5 & 1 \\ 7 & 8 \end{vmatrix}}{\begin{vmatrix} 5 & 2 \\ 7 & -6 \end{vmatrix}} = \frac{40 - 7}{-30 - 14} = \frac{33}{-44} = -\frac{3}{4}$$

The solution is $\left(\dfrac{1}{2}, -\dfrac{3}{4}\right)$

4. $(-3, -2)$

ANSWERS

5.
$$\begin{aligned} -5\,] \quad 1\ x - 3y &= 15 \Rightarrow -5x + 15y = -75 \\ 1\,] \quad 5\ x + 7y &= -13 \Rightarrow \underline{\quad 5x + 7y = -13\quad} \\ 22y &= -88 \\ y &= -4 \end{aligned}$$

Substitute $y = -4$ in (1):
(1) $\qquad x - 3y = 15$
$\qquad x - 3(-4) = 15$
$\qquad x + 12 = 15$
$\qquad\qquad x = 3$
Solution: $(3, -4)$

7. (1) $\quad x - 2y = -1$
(2) $\quad 2x^2 - 3y^2 = 6$
Solve (1) for x:
(1) $\quad x - 2y = -1$
$\qquad\qquad x = 2y - 1$
Substitute $2y - 1$ for x in (2):
(2) $\qquad\qquad 2x^2 - 3y^2 = 6$
$\qquad 2(2y - 1)^2 - 3y^2 = 6$
$\qquad 2(4y^2 - 4y + 1) - 3y^2 = 6$
$\qquad 8y^2 - 8y + 2 - 3y^2 = 6$
$\qquad\qquad 5y^2 - 8y - 4 = 0$
$\qquad\qquad (y - 2)(5y + 2) = 0$
$\qquad y - 2 = 0 \mid 5y + 2 = 0$
$\qquad\quad y = 2 \mid \quad 5y = -2$
$\qquad\qquad\qquad\qquad y = -\dfrac{2}{5}$

Substitute $y = 2$ in $x = 2y - 1$:
$\qquad x = 2(2) - 1 = 3$
$(3, 2)$ is a solution
Substitute $y = -\dfrac{2}{5}$ in $x = 2y - 1$:
$$x = 2\left(-\frac{2}{5}\right) - 1 = -\frac{4}{5} - 1 = -\frac{9}{5}$$
$\left(-\dfrac{9}{5}, -\dfrac{2}{5}\right)$ is a solution

8. $(4, -2)$ and $\left(-\dfrac{20}{7}, \dfrac{2}{7}\right)$

9. (1) $\quad x + 4y \le 4$
(2) $\quad 3x + 2y > 2$
Boundary line for (1): $x + 4y = 4$
Points on line:

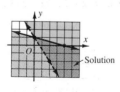

x	y
0	1
4	0

The origin is in the correct half-plane
Boundary line for (2): $3x + 2y = 2$
Points on line:

x	y
0	1
2	-2

The origin is not in the correct half-plane

6. $(-3, 2, -1)$

10.

11. Boundary for $y \le 12 + 4x - x^2$ is $y = 12 + 4x - x^2$, which is a parabola. Its intercepts are $(-2, 0)$, $(6, 0)$, and $(0, 12)$, and its vertex is at $(2, 16)$; it is graphed with a solid line. Boundary for $x^2 + y^2 \le 16$ is $x^2 + y^2 = 16$, which is a circle of radius 4 with its center at the origin; it must be graphed with a solid line. Substituting $(0, 0)$ in $y \le 12 + 4x - x^2$ gives a true statement; we shade in the region that contains the origin (the region "inside" the parabola). Substituting $(0, 0)$ in $x^2 + y^2 \le 16$ gives a true statement; we shade in the region that contains the origin (the region *inside* the circle). The final answer is heavily shaded in.

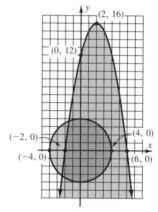

12. $23, -17$

13. Let $x =$ Number of \$10 rolls
$\qquad y =$ Number of \$8 rolls
(1) $\quad x + y = 80$
(2) $\quad 10x + 8y = 730$
(1) $\quad x + y = 80 \Rightarrow x = 80 - y$
Substitute $80 - y$ for x in (2):
(2) $\qquad\qquad 10x + 8y = 730$
$\qquad 10(80 - y) + 8y = 730$
$\qquad 800 - 10y + 8y = 730$
$\qquad\qquad -2y = -70$
$\qquad\qquad y = 35 \quad$ \$8 rolls
Substitute $y = 35$ in $x = 80 - y$:
$x = 80 - 35 = 45 \quad$ \$10 rolls

14. 24 mph is the average speed of Jennifer's boat. 8 mph is the average speed of the stream.

15. Let $u =$ Units digit
$\qquad t =$ Tens digit
$\qquad h =$ Hundreds digit
(1) $\quad u + t + h = 12$
(2) $\qquad\qquad h = 3u$
(3) $\qquad\qquad t = 2 + u$
Substitute (2) and (3) into (1):
$u + (2 + u) + 3u = 12$
$\qquad\qquad 5u + 2 = 12$
$\qquad\qquad 5u = 10$
$\qquad\qquad u = 2$
Substitute $u = 2$ into (2) and (3): $h = 3(2) = 6$
$\qquad\qquad\qquad\qquad\qquad t = 2 + 2 = 4$

The number is 642

16. One pair is $-4, 3$, and another is $-3, 4$

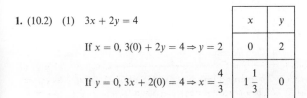

ANSWERS

Chapter 10 Diagnostic Test (page 551)

Following each problem number is the textbook section number (in parentheses) where that kind of problem is discussed.

1. (10.2) (1) $3x + 2y = 4$

If $x = 0$, $3(0) + 2y = 4 \Rightarrow y = 2$

If $y = 0$, $3x + 2(0) = 4 \Rightarrow x = \dfrac{4}{3}$

x	y
0	2
$1\frac{1}{3}$	0

(2) $x - y = 3$

If $x = 0$, $0 - y = 3 \Rightarrow y = -3$

If $y = 0$, $x - 0 = 3 \Rightarrow x = 3$

x	y
0	-3
3	0

Solution: $(2, -1)$

2. (10.3) $-2]\ 4x - 3y = 13 \Rightarrow -8x + 6y = -26$
$3]\ 5x - 2y = 4 \Rightarrow \dfrac{15x - 6y = 12}{7x \qquad = -14}$
$$x = -2$$

Substitute $x = -2$ into (2):

(2)
$$5x - 2y = 4$$
$$5(-2) - 2y = 4$$
$$-10 - 2y = 4$$
$$-2y = 14$$
$$y = -7$$

Solution: $(-2, -7)$

3. (10.3 or 10.4) (1) $5x + 4y = 23$
(2) $3x + 2y = 9 \Rightarrow 2y = 9 - 3x$
$$y = \dfrac{9 - 3x}{2}$$

Substitute $\dfrac{9 - 3x}{2}$ in place of y in (1):

(1)
$$5x + 4y = 23$$
$$5x + \overset{2}{\cancel{4}}\left(\dfrac{9 - 3x}{\underset{1}{\cancel{2}}}\right) = 23$$
$$5x + 2(9 - 3x) = 23$$
$$5x + 18 - 6x = 23$$
$$-x = 5$$
$$x = -5$$

Substitute $x = -5$ in $y = \dfrac{9 - 3x}{2} = \dfrac{9 - 3(-5)}{2}$
$$= \dfrac{9 + 15}{2} = \dfrac{24}{2} = 12$$

Solution: $(-5, 12)$

4. (10.3) $16]\quad 2]\ 15x + 8y = -18 \Rightarrow 30x + 16y = -36$
$-8]\ -1]\ 9x + 16y = -8 \Rightarrow \dfrac{-9x - 16y = +8}{21x \qquad = -28}$
$$x = \dfrac{-28}{21}$$
$$= \dfrac{-4}{3}$$

Substitute $x = \dfrac{-4}{3}$ in (1):

(1)
$$15x + 8y = -18$$
$$\overset{5}{\cancel{15}}{}_{1}\left(\dfrac{-4}{\underset{1}{\cancel{3}}}\right) + 8y = -18$$
$$-20 + 8y = -18$$
$$8y = 2$$
$$y = \dfrac{2}{8} = \dfrac{1}{4}$$

Solution: $\left(\dfrac{-4}{3}, \dfrac{1}{4}\right)$

5. (10.5) $4]\ 2]\ -10x + 35y = -18 \Rightarrow -20x + 70y = -36$
$10]\ 5]\quad 4x - 14y = 8 \Rightarrow \dfrac{20x - 70y = 40}{0 = 4}$
$$\text{False}$$

No solution

6. (10.5) (1) $x + y + z = 0$
(2) $2x \qquad - 3z = 5$
(3) $\qquad 3y + 4z = 3$
$2(1) - (2)\ \dfrac{\qquad}{2y + 5z = -5}$ (4)
(3) $\qquad 3y + 4z = 3$
$3(4) - 2(3)\ \dfrac{\qquad}{7z = -21}$
$$z = -3$$

Substitute $z = -3$ in (2):
$2x - 3(-3) = 5 \Rightarrow x = -2$
Substitute $z = -3$ in (3):
$3y + 4(-3) = 3 \Rightarrow y = 5$
Solution: $(-2, 5, -3)$

7. (10.10) (1) $y^2 = 8x$
(2) $3x + y = 2 \Rightarrow y = 2 - 3x$

Substitute $2 - 3x$ for y in (1):

(1)
$$y^2 = 8x$$
$$(2 - 3x)^2 = 8x$$
$$4 - 12x + 9x^2 = 8x$$
$$9x^2 - 20x + 4 = 0$$
$$(x - 2)(9x - 2) = 0$$
$$x - 2 = 0 \mid 9x - 2 = 0$$
$$x = 2 \qquad x = \dfrac{2}{9}$$

If $x = 2$, $y = 2 - 3x = 2 - 3(2) = -4$

One solution is $(2, -4)$

If $x = \dfrac{2}{9}$, $y = 2 - 3\left(\dfrac{2}{9}\right) = \dfrac{4}{3}$

A second solution is $\left(\dfrac{2}{9}, \dfrac{4}{3}\right)$

8. (10.11) (1) $2x + 3y \leq 6$

Boundary line $2x + 3y = 6$ is solid
because equality is included

x	y
3	0
0	2

If $y = 0$, $2x + 3(0) = 6 \Rightarrow x = 3$

If $x = 0$, $2(0) + 3y = 6 \Rightarrow y = 2$

Substitute $(0, 0)$ in (1):
$2(0) + 3(0) \leq 6$
$\qquad 0 \leq 6$ *True*
The half-plane containing $(0, 0)$ is the solution of (1)
(2) $y - 2x < 2$

Boundary line $y - 2x = 2$ is dashed
because equality is *not* included

x	y
−1	0
0	2

If $y = 0$, $0 - 2x = 2 \Rightarrow x = -1$

If $x = 0$, $y - 2(0) = 2 \Rightarrow y = 2$

Substitute $(0, 0)$ in (2):
$0 - 2(0) < 2$
$\qquad 0 < 2$ *True*
The half-plane containing $(0, 0)$ is a solution of (2)

9. (10.7)

a. $\begin{vmatrix} 8 & -9 \\ 5 & -3 \end{vmatrix} = (8)(-3) - (5)(-9) = -24 + 45 = 21$

b. $\begin{vmatrix} 2 & 0 & -1 \\ -3 & 1 & 4 \\ -1 & 5 & 6 \end{vmatrix}$

$= +(2)\begin{vmatrix} 1 & 4 \\ 5 & 6 \end{vmatrix} - (0)\begin{vmatrix} -3 & 4 \\ -1 & 6 \end{vmatrix} + (-1)\begin{vmatrix} -3 & 1 \\ -1 & 5 \end{vmatrix}$

$= 2(6 - 20) - 0 - 1(-15 + 1) = -14$

10. (10.8) $\begin{aligned} 1x - 1y - 1z &= 0 \\ 1x + 3y + 1z &= 4 \\ 7x - 2y - 5z &= 2 \end{aligned}$

$D = \begin{vmatrix} 1 & -1 & -1 \\ 1 & 3 & 1 \\ 7 & -2 & -5 \end{vmatrix}$

$y = \dfrac{\begin{vmatrix} 1 & 0 & -1 \\ 1 & 4 & 1 \\ 7 & 2 & -5 \end{vmatrix}}{\begin{vmatrix} 1 & -1 & -1 \\ 1 & 3 & 1 \\ 7 & -2 & -5 \end{vmatrix}}$

11. (10.9) Let b = Speed of boat
$\qquad\qquad\quad c$ = Speed of stream

	d	$=$	r	$\cdot$	t
Upstream	30		$b - c$		2
Downstream	30		$b + c$		1

$2(b - c) = 30 \Rightarrow b - c = 15$ (1)
$\quad b + c = 30 \Rightarrow b + c = 30$ (2)
$\qquad\qquad\qquad\qquad \overline{\quad 2b \qquad = 45}$ (1) + (2)

$\qquad b = 22\dfrac{1}{2}$ mph   Boat speed

$\qquad 2c = 15$ (2) − (1)

$\qquad c = 7\dfrac{1}{2}$ mph   Stream speed

Cumulative Review Exercises: Chapters 1–10 (page 552)

1. $\dfrac{x}{y(x-y)} + \dfrac{y}{x(y-x)} = \dfrac{x}{y(x-y)} \cdot \dfrac{x}{x} + \dfrac{-y}{x(x-y)} \cdot \dfrac{y}{y}$

$\qquad = \dfrac{x^2 - y^2}{xy(x-y)} = \dfrac{(x+y)(x-y)}{xy(x-y)} = \dfrac{x+y}{xy}$

2. $x^2 - 2x + 3 + \dfrac{29}{x - 3}$

3. $(2^2 x^2)^{1/6} = 2^{2/6} x^{2/6} = 2^{1/3} x^{1/3} = \sqrt[3]{2x}$ **4.** $\dfrac{|b|}{4|a|} \sqrt{6b}$

5. $\quad m = \dfrac{4 - 2}{2 - (-1)} = \dfrac{2}{3}$ **6.** $\{x | 2 < x < 6\}$

$y - y_1 = m(x - x_1)$

$y - 2 = \dfrac{2}{3}[x - (-1)]$

$3(y - 2) = 2(x + 1)$

$3y - 6 = 2x + 2$

$\quad 0 = 2x - 3y + 8$

7. $4x^2 = 25$ **8.** $\{5, 7\}$

$x^2 = \dfrac{25}{4}$

$x = \pm \sqrt{\dfrac{25}{4}}$

$x = \pm \dfrac{5}{2}$

9. $x^2 - 4x + 5 = 0 \begin{cases} a = 1 \\ b = -4 \\ c = 5 \end{cases}$ **10.** No   **11.** $\dfrac{3}{5}$ **12.** $-\dfrac{5}{3}$

$x = \dfrac{-(-4) \pm \sqrt{(-4)^2 - 4(1)(5)}}{2(1)} = \dfrac{4 \pm \sqrt{-4}}{2}$

$\quad = \dfrac{4 \pm 2i}{2} = 2 \pm i$

13. $-2] \; 4x + 3y = 8 \Rightarrow -8x - 6y = -16$ **14.** No solution
$\qquad\quad 8x + 7y = 12 \Rightarrow \underline{\quad 8x + 7y = \quad 12}$
$\qquad\qquad\qquad\qquad\qquad\qquad\qquad y = \; -4$

$4x + 3(-4) = 8$
$\quad 4x - 12 = 8$
$\qquad\quad 4x = 20$
$\qquad\quad x = 5$

$(5, -4)$

15.

$$
\begin{array}{ll}
(1) & 2x + 3y + z = 4 \\
(2) & x + 4y - z = 0 \\
(3) & 3x + y - z = -5
\end{array}
$$

$$
\begin{array}{lll}
(1) + (2) & 3x + 7y = 4 & (4) \\
(1) + (3) & 5x + 4y = -1 & (5)
\end{array}
$$

$$
\begin{array}{ll}
5 \,]\ 3x + 7y = 4 \Rightarrow & 15x + 35y = 20 \quad (6) \\
-3 \,]\ 5x + 4y = -1 \Rightarrow & -15x - 12y = 3 \quad (7)
\end{array}
$$

$$
\begin{array}{ll}
(6) + (7) & 23y = 23 \\
& y = 1
\end{array}
$$

Substituting $y = 1$ in Equation 4, we have $3x + 7(1) = 4$

$$
\begin{array}{r}
3x = -3 \\
x = -1
\end{array}
$$

Substituting $y = 1$ and $x = -1$ in Equation 1, we have

$$
\begin{array}{l}
2(-1) + 3(1) + z = 4 \\
-2 + 3 + z = 4 \\
z = 3
\end{array}
$$

The solution is $(-1, 1, 3)$. (The check is left to the student.)

16.

17. To find the domain for the function $y = f(x) = \sqrt{12 - 4x - x^2}$, we must solve the inequality $12 - 4x - x^2 \geq 0$. Let $y = f(x) = (6 + x)(2 - x) = 0$. Critical points are -6 and 2.

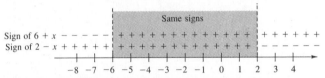

We select the interval on which both signs are the same. The graph is:

Solution set: $\{x \mid -6 \leq x \leq 2\}$.

18. Length: 12; width: 5

19. Let $x =$ Number of hours for Jeannie to do the job alone

$x + 2 =$ Number of hours for Darryl to do the job alone

Then $\dfrac{1}{x} =$ Jeannie's rate

$\dfrac{1}{x + 2} =$ Darryl's rate

$$
\left(\frac{1}{x}\right)(3) + \left(\frac{1}{x + 2}\right)(4) = 1
$$

$$
\frac{3}{x} + \frac{4}{x + 2} = 1
$$

$$
x(x + 2)\left(\frac{3}{x} + \frac{4}{x + 2}\right) = 1(x)(x + 2)
$$

$$
3(x + 2) + 4x = x^2 + 2x
$$

$$
3x + 6 + 4x = x^2 + 2x
$$

$$
7x + 6 = x^2 + 2x
$$

$$
0 = x^2 - 5x - 6
$$

$$
0 = (x - 6)(x + 1)
$$

$$
\begin{array}{l|l}
x - 6 = 0 & x + 1 = 0 \\
x = 6 & x = -1 \quad \text{(Not in the domain)} \\
x + 2 = 8 &
\end{array}
$$

8 hours for Darryl; 6 hours for Jeannie

20. Barbara's average speed: 9 mph; Pat's average speed: 12 mph

Exercises 11.1A (page 556)

1. $y = 4^x$

	x	y
$y = 4^{-2} = \dfrac{1}{16}$	-2	$\dfrac{1}{16}$
$y = 4^{-1} = \dfrac{1}{4}$	-1	$\dfrac{1}{4}$
$y = 4^0 = 1$	0	1
$y = 4^1 = 4$	1	4
$y = 4^2 = 16$	2	16

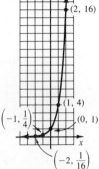

2.

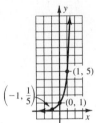

3. $y = e^x$

	x	y
$y = e^{-2} = 0.1$	-2	0.1
$y = e^{-1} = 0.4$	-1	0.4
$y = e^0 = 1$	0	1
$y = e^1 = 2.7$	1	2.7
$y = e^2 = 7.4$	2	7.4

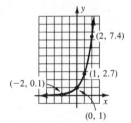

4.

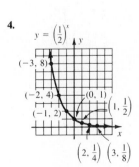

5.

x	y
-3	$\dfrac{8}{27}$
-2	$\dfrac{4}{9}$
-1	$\dfrac{2}{3}$
0	1
1	$\dfrac{3}{2}$
2	$\dfrac{9}{4}$
3	$\dfrac{27}{8}$
4	$\dfrac{81}{16}$
5	$\dfrac{243}{32}$

$y = \left(\dfrac{3}{2}\right)^x$

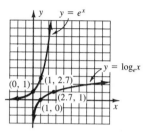

Exercises 11.1B (page 559)

1. The exponential form for $y = \log_2 x$ is $x = 2^y$
The exponential form for $y = \log_{10} x$ is $x = 10^y$

$x = 2^y$

x	y
$\dfrac{1}{4}$	-2
$\dfrac{1}{2}$	-1
1	0
2	1
4	2
8	3

$x = 10^y$

x	y
0.01	-2
0.1	-1
1	0
10	1

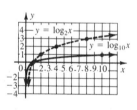

2.

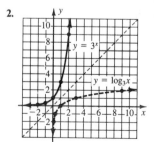

3.

$y = e^x$	
x	y
-1	0.4
0	1
1	2.7
2	7.4

$y = \log_e x$	
x	y
0.4	-1
1	0
2.7	1
7.4	2

Exercises 11.2A (page 560)

1. $\log_3 9 = 2$ **2.** $\log_4 64 = 3$ **3.** $\log_{10} 1000 = 3$
4. $\log_{10} 100{,}000 = 5$ **5.** $\log_2 16 = 4$ **6.** $\log_4 16 = 2$
7. $\log_3\left(\dfrac{1}{9}\right) = -2$ **8.** $\log_2\left(\dfrac{1}{8}\right) = -3$ **9.** $\log_{12} 1 = 0$
10. $\log_8 1 = 0$ **11.** $\log_{16} 4 = \dfrac{1}{2}$ **12.** $\log_8 2 = \dfrac{1}{3}$
13. $8^2 = 64$ **14.** $2^5 = 32$ **15.** $7^2 = 49$ **16.** $4^3 = 64$
17. $5^0 = 1$ **18.** $6^0 = 1$ **19.** $9^{1/2} = 3$ **20.** $8^{1/3} = 2$
21. $10^2 = 100$ **22.** $10^3 = 1000$ **23.** $10^{-3} = \dfrac{1}{10^3} = \dfrac{1}{1000} = 0.001$
24. $10^{-2} = 0.01$

Exercises 11.2B (page 562)

1. $N = 5^2 = 25$ **2.** 32 **3.** $3^x = 9 = 3^2$ **4.** 4
$\qquad\qquad\qquad\qquad\qquad\qquad\quad x = 2$
5. $b^3 = 27 = 3^3$ **6.** 3 **7.** $5^x = 125 = 5^3$ **8.** 4
$\qquad b = 3$ $\qquad\qquad\qquad\qquad x = 3$
9. $10^x = 10^{-4}$ **10.** -3 **11.** $\left(\dfrac{3}{2}\right)^2 = N;\ N = \dfrac{9}{4}$ **12.** $\dfrac{125}{27}$
$\quad x = -4$
13. $\quad 9^x = \dfrac{1}{3}$ **14.** -2 **15.** $\quad b^{1.5} = 8 = 2^3$
$\quad (3^2)^x = 3^{-1}$ $\qquad\qquad\qquad\qquad b^{3/2} = 2^3$
$\quad 3^{2x} = 3^{-1}$ $\qquad\qquad\qquad (b^{3/2})^{2/3} = (2^3)^{2/3}$
$\quad 2x = -1$ $\qquad\qquad\qquad\qquad b = 2^2 = 4$
$\quad x = -\dfrac{1}{2}$
16. 25 **17.** $2^{-2} = N;\ N = \dfrac{1}{2^2};\ N = \dfrac{1}{4}$ **18.** 0.01
19. Let $x = \log_5 25 \Leftrightarrow 5^x = 25 = 5^2$ **20.** 4
$\qquad\qquad\qquad\qquad\qquad\qquad x = 2$
$\quad \log_5 25 = 2$
21. Let $x = \log_{10} 10{,}000 \Leftrightarrow 10^x = 10{,}000 = 10^4$ **22.** 5
$\qquad\qquad\qquad\qquad\qquad\qquad\qquad\qquad x = 4$
$\quad \log_{10} 10{,}0000 = 4$

23. Let $x = \log_4 8 \Leftrightarrow \quad 4^x = 8$
$$(2^2)^x = 2^3$$
$$2^{2x} = 2^3$$
$$2x = 3$$
$$x = \frac{3}{2}$$

$$\log_4 8 = \frac{3}{2}$$

24. $\dfrac{2}{3}$

25. Let $x = \log_3 3^4 \Leftrightarrow 3^x = 3^4$
$$x = 4$$
$$\log_3 3^4 = 4$$

26. 5

27. Let $x = \log_{16} 16 \Leftrightarrow 16^x = 16$
$$x = 1$$
$$\log_{16} 16 = 1$$

28. 1

29. Let $x = \log_8 1 \Leftrightarrow 8^x = 1 = 8^0$
$$x = 0$$
$$\log_8 1 = 0$$

30. 0

Exercises 11.3 (page 567)

1. $\log_{10} 31 + \log_{10} 7$ **2.** $\log_{10} 17 + \log_{10} 29$

3. $\log_{10} 41 - \log_{10} 13$ **4.** $\log_{10} 19 - \log_{10} 23$ **5.** $3 \log_{10} 19$

6. $4 \log_{10} 7$ **7.** $\log_{10} 75^{1/5} = \dfrac{1}{5} \log_{10} 75$ **8.** $\dfrac{1}{4} \log_{10} 38$

9. $\log_{10} 35\sqrt{73} - \log_{10}(1.06)^8 = \log_{10} 35 + \dfrac{1}{2}\log_{10} 73 - 8 \log_{10} 1.06$

10. $\log_{10} 27 + \dfrac{1}{2}\log_{10} 31 - 10 \log_{10} 1.03$

11. $\log_{10}(2)(7) = \log_{10} 2 + \log_{10} 7$
$$= 0.301 + 0.845 = 1.146$$

12. 1.322

13. $\log_{10} 9 - \log_{10} 7$
$$= \log_{10} 3^2 - \log_{10} 7$$
$$= 2 \log_{10} 3 - \log_{10} 7$$
$$= 2(0.477) - 0.845$$
$$= 0.954 - 0.845 = 0.109$$

14. 0.243

15. $\log_{10}(27)^{1/2} = \log_{10}(3^3)^{1/2}$
$$= \log_{10} 3^{3/2} = \dfrac{3}{2}\log_{10} 3$$
$$= (1.5)(0.477) = 0.7155 \doteq 0.716$$

16. $0.4515 \doteq 0.452$

17. $\log_{10}(6^2)^2 = \log_{10} 6^4 = 4 \log_{10} 6$
$$= 4[\log_{10} 2 + \log_{10} 3]$$
$$= 4[0.301 + 0.477]$$
$$= 4(0.778) = 3.112$$

18. 3.982

19. $\log_{10}(2)(3)(10^3) = \log_{10} 2 + \log_{10} 3 + 3 \log_{10} 10$
$$= 0.301 + 0.477 + 3 = 3.778$$

20. 3.146   **21.** $\log_b xy$ **22.** $\log_b x^4 y^2$

23. $2 \log_b x - 3 \log_b y = \log_b x^2 - \log_b y^3$
$$= \log_b\left(\dfrac{x^2}{y^3}\right)$$

24. $2 \log_b x$

25. $3(\log_b x - 2 \log_b y) = 3 \log_b x - 6 \log_b y$
$$= \log_b x^3 - \log_b y^6 = \log_b\left(\dfrac{x^3}{y^6}\right)$$

26. $\log_b y$

27. $\log_b(x^2 - y^2) - \log_b(x + y)^3 = \log_b\left[\dfrac{x^2 - y^2}{(x + y)^3}\right]$
$$= \log_b\left[\dfrac{(x + y)(x - y)}{(x + y)^3}\right] = \log_b\left[\dfrac{(x - y)}{(x + y)^2}\right]$$

28. $\log_b(x + z)$

29. $\log_b(2xy)^2 - \log_b 3xy^2 + \log_b 3x$
$$= \log_b 4x^2 y^2 - \log_b 3xy^2 + \log_b 3x$$
$$= \log_b\left(\dfrac{4x^2 y^2 3x}{3xy^2}\right) = \log_b 4x^2 = \log_b(2x)^2 = 2 \log_b 2x$$

30. $\log_b 3y^2$

Exercises 11.4A (page 570)

1a. 0.4771   **b.** 3.4771   **c.** 1.4771   **d.** 1.0986   **e.** 8.0064   **f.** 3.4012

2a. 1.0000   **b.** 2.0000   **c.** 5.0000   **d.** 2.3026   **e.** 4.6052   **f.** 11.5129

3a. -1.0000 **b.** -2.0000 **c.** -3.0000 **d.** -2.3026 **e.** -4.6052
f. -6.9078

4a. -0.5229 **b.** -3.5229 **c.** -5.5229 **d.** -1.2040 **e.** -8.1117
f. -12.7169

Exercises 11.4B (page 572)

1. 2.35   **2.** 4.06   **3.** 0.851   **4.** 0.755   **5.** 2,560   **6.** 65.1

7. 0.00306   **8.** 0.000409   **9.** 15.2   **10.** 230   **11.** 0.0754

12. 0.00578

Exercises 11.5 (page 577)

1. $(3^3)^x = \dfrac{1}{3^2}$ **2.** $-\dfrac{4}{3}$ **3.** $(2^2)^x = \dfrac{1}{2^3}$ **4.** $-\dfrac{2}{3}$
$$3^{3x} = 3^{-2} \qquad\qquad 2^{2x} = 2^{-3}$$
$$3x = -2 \qquad\qquad 2x = -3$$
$$x = -\dfrac{2}{3} \qquad\qquad x = -\dfrac{3}{2}$$

5. $(5^2)^{2x+3} = 5^{x-1}$ **6.** 1   **7.** $\quad 2^x = 3$
$$5^{4x+6} = 5^{x-1} \qquad\qquad\qquad \log 2^x = \log 3$$
$$4x + 6 = x - 1 \qquad\qquad\qquad x \log 2 = \log 3$$
$$3x = -7 \qquad\qquad\qquad x = \dfrac{\log 3}{\log 2} \doteq \dfrac{0.4771}{0.3010} \doteq 1.59$$
$$x = -\dfrac{7}{3} \qquad\qquad\qquad\text{(1.58 if log 3 and log 2 are not rounded off)}$$

8. 0.861   **9.** $\quad e^x = 8$ **10.** 3.00
$$\ln e^x = \ln 8$$
$$x \ln e = 2.079$$
$$x = 2.08$$

11. $\quad (7.43)^{x+1} = 9.55$ **12.** 2.20
$$\log(7.43)^{x+1} = \log 9.55$$
$$(x + 1) \log 7.43 = \log 9.55$$
$$x + 1 = \dfrac{\log 9.55}{\log 7.43} = \dfrac{0.9800}{0.8710}$$
$$x + 1 \doteq 1.125$$
$$x \doteq 0.125$$

13. $\quad (8.71)^{2x+1} = 8.57$ **14.** 0.500
$$\log(8.71)^{2x+1} = \log 8.57$$
$$(2x + 1) \log 8.71 = \log 8.57$$
$$2x + 1 = \dfrac{\log 8.57}{\log 8.71} = \dfrac{0.93298}{0.94002}$$
$$2x + 1 \doteq 0.99251$$
$$x \doteq -0.00375$$
$$(-0.00372 \text{ if tables are used})$$

15. $\quad e^{3x+4} = 5$ **16.** 1.93
$$\ln e^{3x+4} = \ln 5$$
$$(3x + 4)\ln e = 1.609$$
$$3x + 4 = 1.609$$
$$3x = -2.391$$
$$x = -0.797$$

17. $\log(3x - 1) + \log 4 = \log(9x + 2)$ **18.** 2
$$\log(3x - 1)4 = \log(9x + 2)$$
$$(3x - 1)4 = 9x + 2$$
$$12x - 4 = 9x + 2$$
$$3x = 6$$
$$x = 2$$
Check for $x = 2$
$$\log[3(2) - 1] + \log 4 \overset{?}{=} \log[9(2) + 2]$$
$$\log 5 + \log 4 \overset{?}{=} \log 20$$
$$\log(5)(4) \overset{?}{=} \log 20$$
$$\log 20 = \log 20$$
2 is a solution

19. $\ln(x + 4) - \ln 3 = \ln(x - 2)$ **20.** 2
$$\ln \frac{x + 4}{3} = \ln(x - 2)$$
$$\frac{x + 4}{3} = x - 2$$
$$x + 4 = 3(x - 2)$$
$$x + 4 = 3x - 6$$
$$10 = 2x$$
$$x = 5$$
Check $\ln(5 + 4) - \ln 3 \overset{?}{=} \ln(5 - 2)$
$$\ln \frac{9}{3} \overset{?}{=} \ln 3$$
$$\ln 3 = \ln 3$$

21. $\log(5x + 2) - \log(x - 1) = 0.7782$ **22.** 2.00
$$\log\left(\frac{5x + 2}{x - 1}\right) = 0.7782$$
Let $N = \dfrac{5x + 2}{x - 1}$
Then $\log N = 0.7782$
$$N = 6.000$$
$$\frac{5x + 2}{x - 1} \doteq 6$$
$$5x + 2 \doteq 6x - 6$$
$$8 \doteq x$$
Check for $x = 8$
$$\log(5x + 2) - \log(x - 1) = 0.7782$$
$$\log[5(8) + 2] - \log(8 - 1) \overset{?}{=} 0.7782$$
$$\log 42 - \log 7 \overset{?}{=} 0.7782$$
$$\log\left(\frac{42}{7}\right) \overset{?}{=} 0.7782$$
$$\log 6 \overset{?}{=} \log 0.7782$$
$$0.7782 = 0.7782$$
8 is a solution

23. $\log x + \log(7 - x) = \log 10$
$$\log x(7 - x) = \log 10$$
$$x(7 - x) = 10$$
$$7x - x^2 = 10$$
$$x^2 - 7x + 10 = 0$$
$$(x - 2)(x - 5) = 0$$
$$x - 2 = 0 \mid x - 5 = 0$$
$$x = 2 \mid \quad x = 5$$
Check for $x = 2$
$$\log 2 + \log(7 - 2) \overset{?}{=} \log 10$$
$$\log(2)(5) \overset{?}{=} \log 10$$
$$\log 10 = \log 10$$
Check for $x = 5$
$$\log 5 + \log(7 - 5) \overset{?}{=} \log 10$$
$$\log(5)(2) \overset{?}{=} \log 10$$
$$\log 10 = \log 10$$
Both 2 and 5 are solutions

24. 1 and 10

25.
$$\ln x + \ln(x - 3) = \ln 4$$
$$\ln x(x - 3) = \ln 4$$
$$x(x - 3) = 4$$
$$x^2 - 3x = 4$$
$$x^2 - 3x - 4 = 0$$
$$(x - 4)(x + 1) = 0$$
$$x - 4 = 0 \mid x + 1 = 0$$
$$x = 4 \mid \quad x = -1$$
Check for $x = 4$
$$\ln 4 + \ln(4 - 3) \overset{?}{=} \ln 4$$
$$\ln 4 + \ln 1 \overset{?}{=} \ln 4$$
$$\ln 4 + 0 \overset{?}{=} \ln 4$$
$$\ln 4 = \ln 4$$
Check for $x = -1$
$$\ln(-1) + \ln(-1 - 3) = \ln 4$$
Not real numbers
-1 *is not* a solution; 4 is the only solution

26. 2

Exercises 11.6 (page 580)

Note: Your calculator displays may vary from those shown below.

1. $P = \$1250, r = 0.055, t = 20$
a. $A = P(1 + r)^t$
$$A = \$1250(1 + 0.055)^{20}$$
$$= \$1250(1.055)^{20}$$
$$= \$1250(2.917757)$$
$$= \$3647.20$$
b. $A = P\left(1 + \dfrac{r}{k}\right)^{kt}; \quad k = 12$
$$A = \$1250\left(1 + \frac{0.055}{12}\right)^{12(20)}$$
$$= \$1250(1 + 0.00458333)^{240}$$
$$= \$1250(1.00458333)^{240}$$
$$= \$1250(2.9966255)$$
$$= \$3745.78$$
c. $A = P\left(1 + \dfrac{r}{k}\right)^{kt}; \quad k = 365$
$$A = \$1250\left(1 + \frac{0.055}{365}\right)^{365(20)}$$
$$= \$1250(1 + 0.000150685)^{7300}$$
$$= \$1250(1.000150685)^{7300}$$
$$= \$1250(3.0039164)$$
$$= \$3754.90$$
d. $A = Pe^{rt}$
$$A = \$1250e^{0.055(20)}$$
$$= \$1250e^{1.1}$$
$$= \$1.250(3.0041660)$$
$$= \$3755.21$$

2a. 4372.64 **b.** 4436.73 **c.** 4442.62 **d.** 4442.83

3. We use $A = Pe^{rt}$, where $P = \$1500, r = 0.0575, A = \$2000$
$$\$2000 = \$1500e^{0.0575t}$$
$$1.3333333 = e^{0.0575t} \quad \leftarrow \text{Write in log form}$$
$$\log_e 1.3333333 = 0.0575t$$
$$0.2876821 = 0.0575t$$
$$t = 5.003 \text{ years}$$

4. 8.546 years

5. The formula is $y = Ce^{0.035t}$

   a. $C = 500, t = 3$ $y = 500e^{0.035(3)}$
$$= 500e^{0.105}$$
$$= 500(1.110711)$$
$$= 555.4$$

   b. $y = 800; C = 500$
$$800 = 500e^{0.035t}$$
$$1.6 = e^{0.035t} \quad \leftarrow \text{Take ln of both sides}$$
$$\ln 1.6 = \ln e^{0.035t}$$
$$0.4700036 = 0.035t \ln e \quad \text{But } \ln e = \log_e e = 1$$
$$0.035t = 0.4700036$$
$$t = 13.43 \text{ hours}$$

6a. 946.1   **b.** 23.01

7. The formula is $y = Ce^{-0.3t}$. $y = 80; C = 100$.
$$80 = 100e^{-0.3t}$$
$$0.8 = e^{-0.3t} \quad \leftarrow \text{Take ln of both sides}$$
$$\ln 0.8 = \ln e^{-0.3t}$$
$$-0.223144 = -0.3t \ln e \quad (\ln e = 1)$$
$$-0.3t = -0.223144$$
$$t = 0.7438 \text{ years}$$

8. 0.7754 years

Exercises 11.7 (page 583)

1. $\log_2 156 = \dfrac{\log_{10} 156}{\log_{10} 2} = \dfrac{2.1931}{0.3010} \doteq 7.286$ **2.** 4.954

3. $\log_{12} 7.54 = \dfrac{\log_{10} 7.54}{\log_{10} 12} = \dfrac{0.8774}{1.0792} \doteq 0.8130$ **4.** 0.7602

5. $\log_e 3.04 = \dfrac{\log_{10} 3.04}{\log_{10} 2.718} = \dfrac{0.4829}{0.4343} \doteq 1.112$ **6.** 1.406

7. $\log_{6.8} 0.507 = \dfrac{\log 0.507}{\log 6.8} = \dfrac{-0.2950}{0.8325} = -0.3544$ **8.** -1.651

Review Exercises 11.8 (page 584)

1. $\log_3 81 = 4$ **2.** $4^{-2} = 0.0625$

3. $\log_{10} 1000 = x \Leftrightarrow 10^x = 1000$ **4.** -2
$$10^x = 10^3$$
$$x = 3$$

5. $\log_9 N = \dfrac{3}{2} \Leftrightarrow 9^{3/2} = N$ **6.** 2
$$(3^2)^{3/2} = 3^3$$
$$= 27 = N$$

7. $10^x = 145.6$ **8.** $13 \log x$
$$\log 10^x = \log 145.6$$
$$x \log 10 = \log 145.6 \quad (\log 10 = 1)$$
$$x = 2.1632$$

9. $\log\left(\dfrac{3}{5}\right) + \log\left(\dfrac{5}{3}\right) = \log\left(\dfrac{3}{5}\right)\left(\dfrac{5}{3}\right) = \log 1 = 0$ **10.** $-\log 2x$

11. 1.4062   **12.** -3.0966 **13.** -3.3755 **14.** 8.5755

15. 2554   **16.** 12.0   **17.** $(3^4)^{x-1} = \dfrac{1}{3^2}$ **18.** $\dfrac{3}{2}$
$$3^{4x-4} = 3^{-2}$$
$$4x - 4 = -2$$
$$4x = 2$$
$$x = \dfrac{1}{2}$$

19. $\log_4 75 = \dfrac{\log_{10} 75}{\log_{10} 4} = \dfrac{1.8751}{0.6021} \doteq 3.114$

20. The inverse function of $y = 6^x$ is $y = \log_6 x$

      $y = 6^x$ $y = \log_6 x$

x	y	x	y
-2	$\dfrac{1}{36}$	$\dfrac{1}{36}$	-2
-1	$\dfrac{1}{6}$	$\dfrac{1}{6}$	-1
0	1	1	0
1	6	6	1
2	36	36	2

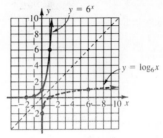

21. We use $A = Pe^{rt}$, where $A = \$2500, P = \$2000, r = 0.058$
$$2500 = 2000e^{0.058t}$$
$$1.25 = e^{0.058t}$$
$$\ln 1.25 = \ln e^{0.058t} \quad \text{Take ln of both sides}$$
$$0.223144 = 0.058t \ln e \quad (\ln e = 1)$$
$$0.058t = 0.223144$$
$$t = 3.8 \text{ years}$$

Chapter 11 Diagnostic Test (page 589)

Following each problem number is the textbook section number (in parentheses) where that kind of problem is discussed.

1. (11.2)   *Exponential form*   *Logarithmic form*
           $2^4 = 16$ $\Leftrightarrow$ $\log_2 16 = 4$

2. (11.2)   *Logarithmic form*   *Exponential form*
           $\log_{2.5} 6.25 = 2$ $\Leftrightarrow$ $(2.5)^2 = 6.25$

3. (11.2) $\log_4 N = 3 \Leftrightarrow 4^3 = N$
           Therefore, $N = 64$

4. (11.2) $\log_{10} 10^{-2} = x \Leftrightarrow 10^x = 10^{-2}$
           Therefore, $x = -2$

5. (11.2) $\log_b 6 = 1 \Leftrightarrow b^1 = 6$
           Therefore, $b = 6$

6. (11.2) $\log_5 1 = x \Leftrightarrow 5^x = 1 = 5^0$
           Therefore, $x = 0$

7. (11.2) $\log_{0.5} N = -2 \Leftrightarrow (0.5)^{-2} = N$
$$\left(\dfrac{1}{2}\right)^{-2} = N$$
$$\dfrac{1^{-2}}{2^{-2}} = N$$
$$2^2 = N$$
$$N = 4$$

8. (11.3) $\log x + \log y - \log z = \log\left(\dfrac{xy}{z}\right)$

9. (11.3) $\dfrac{1}{2}\log x^4 + 2\log x = \log(x^4)^{1/2} + 2\log x$
$\qquad\qquad\qquad\qquad = \log x^2 + 2\log x$
$\qquad\qquad\qquad\qquad = 2\log x + 2\log x$
$\qquad\qquad\qquad\qquad = 4\log x$

10. (11.3) $\log(x^2 - 9) - \log(x - 3)$
$\qquad = \log(x + 3)(x - 3) - \log(x - 3)$
$\qquad = \log(x + 3) + \log(x - 3) - \log(x - 3)$
$\qquad = \log(x + 3)$

11. (11.5) $\log(3x + 5) - \log 7 = \log(x - 1)$
$\qquad\qquad \log\left[\dfrac{(3x + 5)}{7}\right] = \log(x - 1)$
$\qquad\qquad\qquad \dfrac{3x + 5}{7} = \dfrac{x - 1}{1}$
$\qquad\qquad$ LCD $= 7$
$\qquad\qquad \dfrac{\cancel{7}}{1} \cdot \dfrac{3x + 5}{\cancel{7}} = \dfrac{7}{1} \cdot \dfrac{x - 1}{1}$
$\qquad\qquad\qquad 3x + 5 = 7x - 7$
$\qquad\qquad\qquad\qquad 12 = 4x$
$\qquad\qquad\qquad\qquad\ x = 3$
$\qquad$ *Check*
$\qquad\quad \log(3x + 5) - \log 7 = \log(x - 1)$
$\qquad\quad \log[3(3) + 5] - \log 7 \overset{?}{=} \log(3 - 1)$
$\qquad\qquad\quad \log 14 - \log 7 \overset{?}{=} \log 2$
$\qquad\qquad\quad \log(2 \cdot 7) - \log 7 \overset{?}{=} \log 2$
$\qquad\quad \log 2 + \log 7 - \log 7 \overset{?}{=} \log 2$
$\qquad\qquad\qquad\qquad \log 2 = \log 2$

12. (11.5) $\log(x + 8) + \log(x - 2) = \log 11$
$\qquad\qquad \log(x + 8)(x - 2) = \log 11$
$\qquad\qquad\qquad x^2 + 6x - 16 = 11$
$\qquad\qquad\qquad x^2 + 6x - 27 = 0$
$\qquad\qquad\qquad (x - 3)(x + 9) = 0$
$\qquad\ x - 3 = 0 \mid x + 9 = 0$
$\qquad\qquad x = 3 \mid\qquad x = -9$
$\qquad$ *Check for* $x = 3$
$\qquad \log(3 + 8) + \log(3 - 2) \overset{?}{=} \log 11$
$\qquad\qquad \log 11 + \log 1 \overset{?}{=} \log 11$
$\qquad\qquad\qquad\qquad \log 11 = \log 11$
$\qquad x = 3$ is a solution

$\qquad$ *Check for* $x = -9$
$\qquad \log(-9 + 8) = \log(-1)$
$\qquad$ which is not permitted

13. (11.5) $\qquad e^{3x - 4} = 8$
$\qquad\qquad \ln e^{3x - 4} = \ln 8$
$\qquad\quad (3x - 4)\ln e = 2.0794415$
$\qquad\qquad\quad 3x - 4 = 2.0794415$
$\qquad\qquad\qquad\quad 3x = 6.0794415$
$\qquad\qquad\qquad\quad\ x = 2.03$

14. (11.7) Find $\log_2 718$
$\qquad\quad \log_2 N = \dfrac{\log_{10} N}{\log_{10} 2}$

$\qquad \log_2 718 = \dfrac{\log 718}{\log 2} = \dfrac{2.8561}{0.3010} \doteq 9.49$

15. (11.1) The inverse function of $y = 7^x$ is $y = \log_7 x$.
We find points on the curve $y = 7^x$ by giving x-values and solving for y:

$y = 7^x$	x	y
$y = 7^{-2} = \dfrac{1}{49}$	-2	$\dfrac{1}{49}$
$y = 7^{-1} = \dfrac{1}{7}$	-1	$\dfrac{1}{7}$
$y = 7^0 = 1$	0	1
$y = 7^1 = 7$	1	7
$y = 7^2 = 49$	2	49

We find points on the curve $y = \log_7 x$ by plotting points on the equivalent exponential curve $x = 7^y$. In this case, we give y-values and solve for x:

$x = 7^y$	x	y
$x = 7^{-2} = \dfrac{1}{49}$	$\dfrac{1}{49}$	-2
$x = 7^{-1} = \dfrac{1}{7}$	$\dfrac{1}{7}$	-1
$x = 7^0 = 1$	1	0
$x = 7^1 = 7$	7	1
$x = 7^2 = 49$	49	2

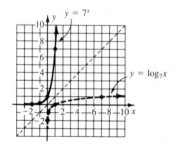

16. (11.6) The formula is $y = Ce^{0.05t}$. $C = 1500$.
$\qquad$ **a.** $t = 2 \qquad y = 1500e^{0.05(2)}$
$\qquad\qquad\qquad\qquad y = 1500e^{0.1}$
$\qquad\qquad\qquad\qquad y = 1500(1.1051709)$
$\qquad\qquad\qquad\qquad y = 1658 \quad$ (to 4 significant digits)

$\qquad$ **b.** $C = 1500; y = 4500$
$\qquad\qquad\quad 4500 = 1500e^{0.05t}$
$\qquad\qquad\qquad\quad 3 = e^{0.05t} \quad \leftarrow$ Take ln of both sides
$\qquad\qquad\quad \ln 3 = \ln e^{0.05t}$
$\qquad 1.0986123 = 0.05t \ln e \qquad (\ln e = 1)$
$\qquad\qquad 0.05t = 1.0986123$
$\qquad\qquad\qquad\ t = 22 \text{ hours} \quad$ (to 2 significant digits)

Cumulative Review Exercises: Chapters 1–11 (page 590)

1. $\dfrac{7}{(x-4)(x+3)(x-1)} \cdot \dfrac{(x-1)}{} - \dfrac{3}{(x-4)(x-1)(x+3)} \cdot \dfrac{(x+3)}{}$

$= \dfrac{7x-7-3x-9}{(x-4)(x+3)(x-1)} = \dfrac{4x-16}{(x-4)(x+3)(x-1)}$

$= \dfrac{4(x-4)}{(x-4)(x+3)(x-1)} = \dfrac{4}{(x+3)(x-1)}$

2. $\dfrac{2}{y+x}$

3. $2x - 7y = 7$
$2x - 7(0) = 7$
$x = \dfrac{7}{2}$
$2(0) - 7y = 7$
$y = -1$

x	y
$3\frac{1}{2}$	0
0	-1

4.

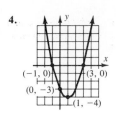

$(-1, 0)$ $(3, 0)$
$(0, -3)$
$(1, -4)$

5. $LCD = 15$
$\dfrac{15}{1} \cdot \dfrac{2x}{3} - \dfrac{15}{1} \cdot \dfrac{1}{1} \le \dfrac{15}{1} \cdot \dfrac{x+2}{5}$
$10x - 15 \le 3x + 6$
$7x \le 21$
$x \le 3$

6. $\{-2\}$

7. $\log(5x + 2) + \log 3 = \log(12x + 15)$
$\log(5x + 2)3 = \log(12x + 15)$
$(5x + 2)3 = (12x + 15)$
$15x + 6 = 12x + 15$
$3x = 9$
$x = 3$

Check
$\log(5x + 2) + \log 3 = \log(12x + 15)$
$\log[5(3) + 2] + \log 3 \overset{?}{=} \log[12(3) + 15]$
$\log 17 + \log 3 \overset{?}{=} \log 51$
$\log(17)(3) \overset{?}{=} \log 51$
$\log 51 = \log 51 \quad True$
3 is a solution

8. 0.536

9. $3]\quad 2x + 4y = 0 \Rightarrow 6x + 12y = 0$
$4]\quad 5x - 3y = 13 \Rightarrow 20x - 12y = 52$
$\overline{\qquad\qquad 26x \qquad\quad = 52}$

$2x + 4y = 0$
$2(2) + 4y = 0$
$4 + 4y = 0$
$4y = -4$
$y = -1$
Solution: $(2, -1)$

10. $(3, -3)$ and $\left(\dfrac{3}{4}, \dfrac{3}{2}\right)$

11. $d = \sqrt{[1-3]^2 + [2-(-4)]^2}$
$= \sqrt{4 + 36} = \sqrt{40} = 2\sqrt{10}$

12. $3x + 7y + 42 = 0$

13. $10x - 6y + 15 = 0 \Leftrightarrow y = \dfrac{5}{3}x + \dfrac{5}{2}$. We must write the equation of the line which passes through $(9, -13)$ and which has a slope of $\dfrac{5}{3}$.

$y - (-13) = \dfrac{5}{3}(x - 9)$
$3(y + 13) = 5(x - 9)$
$3y + 39 = 5x - 45$
$5x - 3y - 84 = 0$

14. 1 **15.** $-\dfrac{1}{3}$ **16.** $\log_2 128 = 7$ **17.** -1.5058 **18.** 72.0

19. We use $A = Pe^{rt}$, where $A = \$5000$, $P = \$3000$, $r = 0.056$
$\$5000 = \$3000e^{0.056t}$
$1.6666667 = e^{0.056t} \quad \leftarrow$ Take ln of both sides
$\ln 1.6666667 = \ln e^{0.056t}$
$0.5108256 = 0.056t \ln e$
$0.056t = 0.5108256$
$t = 9.122$ years

20. $2\dfrac{1}{2}$ liters

Exercises 12.1 (page 594)

1. 25, 30, 35
Add 5 to preceding term

2. 17, 20, 23

3. 9, 7, 5
Add -2 to preceding term

4. $2, \dfrac{7}{3}, \dfrac{8}{3}$

5. $a_n = n + 4$
$a_1 = 1 + 4 = 5$
$a_2 = 2 + 4 = 6$
$a_3 = 3 + 4 = 7$
The first three terms are 5, 6, 7

6. 3, 5, 7, 9

7. $a_n = \dfrac{1 - n}{n}$
$a_1 = \dfrac{1 - (1)}{(1)} = 0$
$a_2 = \dfrac{1 - (2)}{(2)} = -\dfrac{1}{2}$
$a_3 = \dfrac{1 - (3)}{(3)} = -\dfrac{2}{3}$
$a_4 = \dfrac{1 - (4)}{(4)} = -\dfrac{3}{4}$
The first four terms are $0, -\dfrac{1}{2}, -\dfrac{2}{3}, -\dfrac{3}{4}$

8. 0, 1, 3

9. $a_n = n^2 - 1$
$a_1 = 1^2 - 1 = 0$
$a_2 = 2^2 - 1 = 3$
$a_3 = 3^2 - 1 = 8$
The first three terms are 0, 3, 8

10. 2, 9, 28, 65

11. $a_n = 2n - 3$
$a_1 = 2(1) - 3 = -1$
$a_2 = 2(2) - 3 = 1$
$a_3 = 2(3) - 3 = 3$
$a_4 = 2(4) - 3 = 5$
$S_4 = a_1 + a_2 + a_3 + a_4$
$= -1 + 1 + 3 + 5 = 8$

12. $10\dfrac{3}{4}$

13. $a_n = \dfrac{n-1}{n+1}$

$a_1 = \dfrac{1-1}{1+1} = 0$

$a_2 = \dfrac{2-1}{2+1} = \dfrac{1}{3}$

$a_3 = \dfrac{3-1}{3+1} = \dfrac{1}{2}$

$S_3 = 0 + \dfrac{1}{3} + \dfrac{1}{2} = \dfrac{5}{6}$

14. 45

19. $a_6 = a_1 + (6-1)d \Rightarrow a_1 + 5d = 15$ (1)
$a_{12} = a_1 + (12-1)d \Rightarrow a_1 + 11d = 39$ (2)

$\overline{ 6d = 24}$
$ d = 4$

Substitute $d = 4$ in (1):
$a_1 + 5(4) = 15$
$a_1 + 20 = 15$
$ a_1 = -5$

20. $d = 5$
$ a_1 = -8$

21. $16 = -5 + (n-1)(3)$
$21 = 3n - 3 \Rightarrow 3n = 24 \Rightarrow n = 8$
$S_8 = \dfrac{8}{2}(-5+16) = 4(11) = 44$

22. $n = 9$
$ S_9 = 81$

23. $S_n = \dfrac{n}{2}(a_1 + a_n)$

$44 = \dfrac{n}{2}(5+17)$

$44 = \dfrac{n}{2}(22) \Rightarrow n = 4$

$a_4 = 5 + 3d = 17$
$ 3d = 12 \Rightarrow d = 4$

24. $n = 8$

$d = \dfrac{39}{7}$

Exercises 12.2 (page 599)

1. 3, 8, 13, 18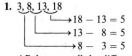
$ \rightarrow 18 - 13 = 5$
$ \rightarrow 13 - 8 = 5$
$ \rightarrow 8 - 3 = 5$
AP, because all the differences are 5

2. AP; $d = 4$

3. 7, 4, 1, −2
$ \rightarrow -2 - 1 = -3$
$ \rightarrow 1 - 4 = -3$
$ \rightarrow 4 - 7 = -3$
AP, because all the differences are −3

4. AP, $d = -5$

5. 4, $5\dfrac{1}{2}$, 7, 9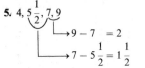
$ \rightarrow 9 - 7 = 2$
$ \rightarrow 7 - 5\dfrac{1}{2} = 1\dfrac{1}{2}$
Not an AP, because the differences are not all the same

6. Not an AP

7. $2x - 1, x, 1, -x + 2$
$ \rightarrow -x + 2 - 1 = -x + 1$
$ \rightarrow 1 - x = -x + 1$
$ \rightarrow x - (2x - 1) = -x + 1$
AP, because all the differences are $-x + 1$

8. AP; $d = x - 1$

9. $a_1, a_1 + d, a_1 + 2d, a_1 + 3d$
$5, 5 + (-7), 5 + 2(-7), 5 + 3(-7)$
$5, -2, -9, -16$

10. $4, -1, -6, -11, -16$

11. $a_5 = a_1 + (5-1)d$
$31 = 7 + 4d$
$24 = 4d$
$ d = 6$
AP: $7, 7 + 6, 7 + 2(6), 7 + 3(6), 7 + 4(6)$
$7, 13, 19, 25, 31$

12. 6, 15, 24, 33, 42, 51

13. $-8, -2, 4, \ldots$
$ \rightarrow 4 - (-2) = 6 = d$
$ \rightarrow -2 - (-8) = 6$
$a_{31} = a_1 + (31-1)d$
$a_{31} = -8 + 30(6)$
$a_{31} = 172$

14. 155

15. $x, 2x + 1, 3x + 2, \ldots$
$d = (2x + 1) - x = x + 1$
$a_{11} = a_1 + (11-1)d = x + 10(x + 1)$
$a_{11} = 11x + 10$

16. $10z - 7$

17. $2 + 4 + \cdots + 100$
$S_{50} = \dfrac{50}{2}(2 + 100) = 2550$

18. 2500

25. $a_n = a_1 + 8\left(\dfrac{3}{2}\right) \Rightarrow a_n = a_1 + 12$

$S_n = \dfrac{n}{2}(a_1 + a_n)$

$-\dfrac{9}{4} = \dfrac{9}{2}(a_1 + a_n)$

Substitute $a_1 + 12$ for a_n

$-\dfrac{9}{4} = \dfrac{9}{2}(a_1 + a_1 + 12)$

$-\dfrac{9}{4} = \dfrac{9}{2}(2a_1 + 12)$

$-\dfrac{9}{4} = 9a_1 + 54$

$-9 = 36a_1 + 216 \Rightarrow a_1 = -\dfrac{25}{4}$

Substitute $a_1 = -\dfrac{25}{4}$ in $a_n = a_1 + 12$

$a_n = -\dfrac{25}{4} + \dfrac{48}{4} = \dfrac{23}{4}$

26. $a_1 = -\dfrac{3}{2}$
$ a_n = a_7 = 3$

27. $\left.\begin{array}{l} a_1 = 16 \\ a_2 = 48 \\ a_3 = 80 \\ \vdots \end{array}\right\}\; d = 48 - 16 = 32$

$a_{10} = a_1 + 9d = 16 + 9(32)$
$a_{10} = 16 + 288 = 304$ ft
$a_{12} = 304 + 64 = 368$ ft
$S_{12} = \dfrac{12}{2}(16 + 368) = 6(384) = 2304$ ft

28. $12.40

Exercises 12.3 (page 605)

1. 4, 12, 36, 108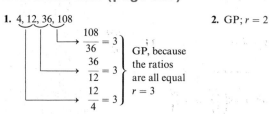
$ \rightarrow \dfrac{108}{36} = 3$
$ \rightarrow \dfrac{36}{12} = 3$
$ \rightarrow \dfrac{12}{4} = 3$
GP, because the ratios are all equal $r = 3$

2. GP; $r = 2$

3. $-5, 15, -45, 135, \ldots$

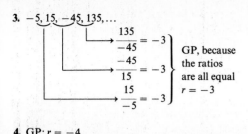

$\dfrac{135}{-45} = -3$
$\dfrac{-45}{15} = -3$
$\dfrac{15}{-5} = -3$

$\left.\right\}$ GP, because the ratios are all equal $r = -3$

4. GP; $r = -4$

5. $2, \dfrac{1}{2}, \dfrac{1}{8}, \dfrac{1}{16}$

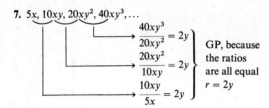

$\dfrac{1}{16} \div \dfrac{1}{8} = \dfrac{1}{16} \cdot \dfrac{8}{1} = \dfrac{1}{2}$
$\dfrac{1}{8} \div \dfrac{1}{2} = \dfrac{1}{8} \cdot \dfrac{2}{1} = \dfrac{1}{4}$

$\left.\right\}$ *Not* GP, because all ratios are not equal

6. Not GP

7. $5x, 10xy, 20xy^2, 40xy^3, \ldots$

$\dfrac{40xy^3}{20xy^2} = 2y$
$\dfrac{20xy^2}{10xy} = 2y$
$\dfrac{10xy}{5x} = 2y$

$\left.\right\}$ GP, because the ratios are all equal $r = 2y$

8. GP; $r = 3z$

9. $a_1 = 12$

$a_2 = 12\left(\dfrac{1}{3}\right) = 4$

$a_3 = 4\left(\dfrac{1}{3}\right) = \dfrac{4}{3}$

$a_4 = \dfrac{4}{3}\left(\dfrac{1}{3}\right) = \dfrac{4}{9}$

$a_5 = \dfrac{4}{9}\left(\dfrac{1}{3}\right) = \dfrac{4}{27}$

$12, 4, \dfrac{4}{3}, \dfrac{4}{9}, \dfrac{4}{27}$

10. $8, 12, 18, 27$

11. $a_5 = a_1 r^4$

$54 = \dfrac{2}{3} r^4$

$81 = r^4$

$r = \pm 3$

There are two answers
One answer: $r = 3$
$\dfrac{2}{3}, 2, 6, 18, 54$
Second answer: $r = -3$
$\dfrac{2}{3}, -2, 6, -18, 54$

12. *One answer:* $r = 5$
$\dfrac{3}{25}, \dfrac{3}{5}, 3, 15, 75$
Second answer: $r = -5$
$\dfrac{3}{25}, -\dfrac{3}{5}, 3, -15, 75$

13. $-9, -6, -4, \ldots$

$r = \dfrac{-4}{-6} = \dfrac{2}{3}$

$a_7 = a_1 r^6 = -9\left(\dfrac{2}{3}\right)^6 = -\dfrac{64}{81}$

14. $-\dfrac{6561}{32}$

15. $16x, 8xy, 4xy^2, \ldots$

$\dfrac{8xy}{16x} = \dfrac{y}{2} = r$

$a_8 = a_1 r^7 = 16x\left(\dfrac{y}{2}\right)^7 = \dfrac{xy^7}{8}$

16. $\dfrac{x^{12}y}{27}$

17. $a_5 = a_1 r^4$

$80 = a_1\left(\dfrac{2}{3}\right)^4$

$80 = \dfrac{16}{81} a_1$

$a_1 = 405$

$S_5 = \dfrac{a_1(1 - r^5)}{1 - r}$

$= \dfrac{405\left[1 - \left(\dfrac{2}{3}\right)^5\right]}{1 - \dfrac{2}{3}} = \dfrac{405\left[1 - \dfrac{32}{243}\right]}{\dfrac{1}{3}} = \dfrac{405}{1}\left(\dfrac{211}{243}\right)\dfrac{3}{1} = 1055$

18. $a_1 = 5$
$S_5 = 155$

19. (2) $a_5 = a_1 r^4 = \dfrac{112}{9}$
(1) $a_3 = a_1 r^2 = 28$

$\left.\right\}$ $r^2 = \dfrac{112}{9} \div 28 = \dfrac{112}{9} \cdot \dfrac{1}{28} = \dfrac{4}{9}$

$r = \pm \dfrac{2}{3}$

$r_1 = \dfrac{2}{3}$:

(1) $a_1\left(\dfrac{2}{3}\right)^2 = 28$

$\dfrac{4}{9} a_1 = 28$

$a_1 = 63$

$S_5 = \dfrac{63\left[1 - \left(\dfrac{2}{3}\right)^5\right]}{1 - \dfrac{2}{3}} = \dfrac{63 - \dfrac{224}{27}}{\dfrac{1}{3}}$

$= \dfrac{1477}{27} \cdot \dfrac{3}{1} = \dfrac{1477}{9}$

$r_2 = -\dfrac{2}{3}$:

(1) $a_1\left(-\dfrac{2}{3}\right)^2 = 28$

$a_1 = 63$

$S_5 = \dfrac{63\left[1 - \left(-\dfrac{2}{3}\right)^5\right]}{1 - \left(-\dfrac{2}{3}\right)} = \dfrac{63 - \left(-\dfrac{224}{27}\right)}{\dfrac{5}{3}}$

$= \dfrac{1925}{27} \cdot \dfrac{3}{5} = \dfrac{385}{9}$

20. $\begin{cases} r_1 = \dfrac{1}{4} \\ a_1 = 1536 \\ S_4 = 2040 \end{cases}$

$\begin{cases} r_2 = -\dfrac{1}{4} \\ a_1 = -1536 \\ S_4 = -1224 \end{cases}$

21.

$a_n = a_1 r^{n-1}$

$3 = a_1\left(\frac{1}{2}\right)^{n-1}$

(1) $\frac{3}{2} = a_1\left(\frac{1}{2}\right)^n$

$S_n = \frac{a_1(1-r^n)}{1-r}$

$189 = \frac{a_1\left[1-\left(\frac{1}{2}\right)^n\right]}{1-\frac{1}{2}} = \frac{a_1 - a_1\left(\frac{1}{2}\right)^n}{\frac{1}{2}}$

$189 = \frac{a_1 - \frac{3}{2}}{\frac{1}{2}} = 2a_1 - 3$ ← From (1)

$192 = 2a_1$

$a_1 = 96$

Substitute $a_1 = 96$ in (1):

$\frac{3}{2} = 96\left(\frac{1}{2}\right)^n$

$\left(\frac{1}{2}\right)^6 = \left(\frac{1}{2}\right)^n$

$6 = n$

22. $a_1 = 108$

$n = 4$

23. $S_3 = \frac{a_1\left(1-\left[\frac{6}{5}\right]^3\right)}{1-\frac{6}{5}}$

$= a_1\left(-\frac{91}{125}\right)\left(-\frac{5}{1}\right) = \frac{91}{25}a_1$

$\frac{91}{25}a_1 = 22{,}750$

$a_1 = \$6250$

$a_5 = a_1 r^4$

$= 6250\left(\frac{6}{5}\right)^4 = 6250\left(\frac{1296}{625}\right)$

$= \$12{,}960$

24. $6250

25.

$a_n = a_1 r^{n-1}$

a. $a_{10} = 1(2)^9 = 512¢ = \$5.12$

b. $a_{31} = 1(2)^{30} = 1{,}073{,}741{,}824¢ = \$10{,}737{,}418.24$

or $\log a_{31} = 30 \log 2 = 30(0.3010) = 9.0300$

$a_{31} = \text{antilog } 9.0300 \doteq 1{,}072{,}000{,}000¢ = \$10{,}720{,}000$

c. $S_{31} = \frac{a_1(1-r^n)}{1-r} = \frac{1(1-2^{31})}{1-2} = 2^{31} - 1$

$= 2{,}147{,}483{,}646¢ = \$21{,}474{,}836.46$

If logs are used: $21{,}430{,}000.

Exercises 12.4 (page 609)

1. $3 + 1 + \frac{1}{3} + \cdots$

$\frac{1}{3} = r$

$S_\infty = \frac{a_1}{1-r} = \frac{3}{\frac{2}{3}} = \frac{9}{2}$

2. $\frac{81}{10}$

3. $\frac{4}{3} + 1 + \frac{3}{4} + \cdots$

$\frac{\frac{3}{4}}{1} = \frac{3}{4} = r$

$S_\infty = \frac{a_1}{1-r} = \frac{\frac{4}{3}}{1-\frac{3}{4}} = \frac{\frac{4}{3}}{\frac{1}{4}} = \frac{16}{3}$

4. $\frac{1}{9}$

5. $-6 - 4 - \frac{8}{3} - \cdots$

$\frac{-4}{-6} = \frac{2}{3} = r$

$S_\infty = \frac{a_1}{1-r} = \frac{-6}{1-\frac{2}{3}} = \frac{-6}{\frac{1}{3}} = -18$

6. $-\frac{343}{2}$

7. $0.2222\ldots$

$= 0.2 + 0.02 + 0.002 + 0.0002 + \cdots$

$\frac{0.02}{0.2} = 0.1$

$S_\infty = \frac{a_1}{1-r} = \frac{0.2}{1-0.1} = \frac{0.2}{0.9} = \frac{2}{9}$

8. $\frac{7}{33}$

9. $0.05454\ldots$

$= 0.054 + 0.00054 + \cdots$

$\frac{0.00054}{0.054} = 0.01 = r$

$S_\infty = \frac{a_1}{1-r} = \frac{0.054}{1-0.01} = \frac{0.054}{0.99} = \frac{3}{55}$

10. $\frac{13}{330}$

11. $8.6444\ldots$

$= 8.6 + 0.04 + 0.004 + 0.0004 + \cdots$

$r = 0.1, \ S_\infty = \frac{0.04}{1-0.1} = \frac{0.04}{0.9} = \frac{2}{45}$

$8.6444\ldots = \frac{8}{1} + \frac{6}{10} + \frac{2}{45}$

$= \frac{720}{90} + \frac{54}{90} + \frac{4}{90} = \frac{778}{90} = \frac{389}{45}$

12. $\frac{79}{15}$

13.

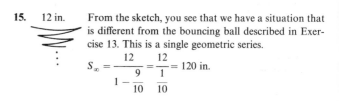

9 ft 6 …

The geometric series of the heavy lines is

$6 + 4 + \frac{8}{3} + \cdots$

$S_\infty = \frac{a_1}{1-r} = \frac{6}{1-\frac{2}{3}} = \frac{6}{\frac{1}{3}} = 18$ ft

This distance is doubled to include all but the first drop: $2(18) = 36$

The total distance traveled $= 9 + 36 = 45$ ft

14. 40 ft

15. 12 in.

From the sketch, you see that we have a situation that is different from the bouncing ball described in Exercise 13. This is a single geometric series.

$S_\infty = \frac{12}{1-\frac{9}{10}} = \frac{12}{\frac{1}{10}} = 120$ in.

Review Exercises 12.5 (page 610)

1. 7, 5, 3, $\cdots$

$3 - 5 = -2$

$5 - 7 = -2$

AP, because -2 is the common difference

2. GP

3. $\dfrac{1}{2}, \dfrac{1}{4}, \dfrac{1}{6}, \ldots$

$\left.\begin{array}{l}\dfrac{1}{6} - \dfrac{1}{4} = -\dfrac{1}{12} \\[2mm] \dfrac{1}{4} - \dfrac{1}{2} = -\dfrac{1}{4}\end{array}\right\}$ Therefore, *not an AP*

$\dfrac{1}{2}, \dfrac{1}{4}, \dfrac{1}{6}, \ldots$

$\left.\begin{array}{l}\dfrac{\frac{1}{6}}{\frac{1}{4}} = \dfrac{2}{3} \\[4mm] \dfrac{\frac{1}{4}}{\frac{1}{2}} = \dfrac{1}{2}\end{array}\right\}$ Therefore, *not a GP*

Neither

4. GP

5. $3x - 2, 2x - 1, x$
$(2x - 1) - (3x - 2) = -x + 1$
$\quad x - (2x - 1) = -x + 1$
AP

6. $-4, -2, 0, 2$
$d = 2$
$a_{30} = 54$
$S_{30} = 750$

7. $a_n = \left(\dfrac{1}{2}\right)^n$ $\qquad S_n = \dfrac{a_1(1 - r^n)}{1 - r}$

$a_1 = \left(\dfrac{1}{2}\right)^1 = \dfrac{1}{2}$

$a_2 = \left(\dfrac{1}{2}\right)^2 = \dfrac{1}{4}$ $\qquad S_5 = \dfrac{\frac{1}{2}\left(1 - \frac{1}{32}\right)}{\frac{1}{2}} = \dfrac{31}{32}$

$a_3 = \left(\dfrac{1}{2}\right)^3 = \dfrac{1}{8}$ $\qquad S_\infty = \dfrac{a_1}{1 - r} = \dfrac{\frac{1}{2}}{1 - \frac{1}{2}} = 1$

8. $n = 16$

$d = \dfrac{4}{5}$

9. $a_n = a_1 + 6\left(\dfrac{3}{2}\right) = a_1 + 9$

$S_n = \dfrac{n(a_1 + a_n)}{2}$

$\dfrac{7}{2} = \dfrac{7(2a_1 + 9)}{2}$

$1 = 2a_1 + 9$
$-8 = 2a_1$
$-4 = a_1$
$a_n = a_7 = -4 + 9 = 5$

10. $a_1 = \dfrac{81}{16}$

$S_6 = \dfrac{133}{48}$

11. $a_5 = \dfrac{32}{9} = a_1 r^4 \quad (1)$

$a_3 = \quad 8 = a_1 r^2 \quad (2)$

$\dfrac{4}{9} = r^2$ $\quad$ Divide (1) by (2)

$\pm \dfrac{2}{3} = r$

If $r = \dfrac{2}{3}$: $\quad a_3 = a_1 r^2$

$8 = a_1 \cdot \dfrac{4}{9}$

$18 = a_1$

$S_5 = \dfrac{a_1(1 - r^5)}{1 - r} = \dfrac{18\left[1 - \left(\frac{2}{3}\right)^5\right]}{1 - \frac{2}{3}} = \dfrac{18\left(1 - \frac{32}{243}\right)}{\frac{1}{3}} = \dfrac{18}{1}\left(\dfrac{211}{243}\right) \cdot \dfrac{3}{1}$

$= \dfrac{422}{9}$

If $r = -\dfrac{2}{3}$: $\quad a_3 = a_1 r^2$

$8 = a_1 \cdot \dfrac{4}{9}$

$18 = a_1$

$S_5 = \dfrac{18\left[1 - \left(-\frac{2}{3}\right)^5\right]}{1 - \left(-\frac{2}{3}\right)} = \dfrac{18\left(1 + \frac{32}{243}\right)}{\frac{5}{3}} = \dfrac{18}{1}\left(\dfrac{275}{243}\right) \cdot \dfrac{3}{5}$

$= \dfrac{110}{9}$

12. $\dfrac{32{,}813}{9990}$

13. 8 ft $\sqrt[6]{}\bigwedge\bigwedge$ $\cdots$ Heavy lines: $6 + \dfrac{9}{2} + \cdots$

$S_\infty = \dfrac{6}{1 - \frac{3}{4}} = \dfrac{6}{\frac{1}{4}} = 24$ ft

Total distance $= 8 + 2(24) = 56$ ft

Chapter 12 Diagnostic Test (page 615)

Following each problem number is the textbook section number (in parentheses) where that kind of problem is discussed.

1. (12.1) $a_n = \dfrac{2n - 1}{n}$ (The sequence is not arithmetic and it is not geometric)

$S_4 = \dfrac{2(1) - 1}{1} + \dfrac{2(2) - 1}{2} + \dfrac{2(3) - 1}{3} + \dfrac{2(4) - 1}{4}$

$= 1 + \dfrac{3}{2} + \dfrac{5}{3} + \dfrac{7}{4} = \dfrac{71}{12}$

2. (12.2, 12.3) **a.** $8, -20, 50, - + \cdots$

$\left.\begin{array}{l}\dfrac{50}{-20} = -\dfrac{5}{2} \\[3mm] \dfrac{-20}{8} = -\dfrac{5}{2}\end{array}\right\}$ GP $\quad r = -\dfrac{5}{2}$

b. $\dfrac{1}{2}, \dfrac{3}{4}, 1, \dfrac{5}{4}, \dfrac{3}{2}, \ldots$

$\left.\begin{array}{l}1 - \dfrac{3}{4} = \dfrac{1}{4} \\[3mm] \dfrac{3}{4} - \dfrac{1}{2} = \dfrac{1}{4}\end{array}\right\}$ $\begin{array}{l}\text{AP} \\[3mm] d = \dfrac{1}{4}\end{array}$

c. $2x - 1, 3x, 4x + 2, \ldots$

$\left.\begin{array}{l}4x + 2 - 3x = x + 2 \\ 3x - (2x - 1) = x + 1\end{array}\right\}$ Therefore, *not an AP*

$\left.\begin{array}{l}\dfrac{4x + 2}{3x} \neq \dfrac{3x}{2x - 1}\end{array}\right\}$ Therefore, *not a GP*

d. $\dfrac{c^4}{16}, -\dfrac{c^3}{8}, \dfrac{c^2}{4}, - + \cdots$

$\left.\begin{array}{l}\dfrac{c^2}{4} \div \left(-\dfrac{c^3}{8}\right) = \dfrac{c^2}{4} \cdot \left(-\dfrac{8}{c^3}\right) = -\dfrac{2}{c} \\[3mm] -\dfrac{c^3}{8} \div \dfrac{c^4}{16} = -\dfrac{c^3}{8} \cdot \dfrac{16}{c^4} = -\dfrac{2}{c}\end{array}\right\}$ $\begin{array}{l}\text{GP} \\[3mm] r = -\dfrac{2}{c}\end{array}$

3. (12.2) $x + 1, (x + 1) + (x − 1), (x + 1) + 2(x − 1),$
$(x + 1) + 3(x − 1), (x + 1) + 4(x − 1)$
$= x + 1, 2x, 3x − 1, 4x − 2, 5x − 3$

4. (12.2) $a_5 = a_1 + 4d$ | $2, 2 + (−1), 2 + 2(−1), 2 + 3(−1), 2 + 4(−1)$
$−2 = 2 + 4d$
$−4 = 4d$ | $= 2, \quad 1, \quad\quad 0, \quad\quad −1, \quad\quad −2$
$−1 = d$

5. (12.2) $1 − 6h, 2 − 4h, 3 − 2h, \ldots$

$(2 − 4h) − (1 − 6h) = 1 + 2h = d$
$a_{15} = a_1 + 14d = (1 − 6h) + 14(1 + 2h) = 15 + 22h$

6. (12.2) $a_7 = a_1 + 6d \Rightarrow 2 = a_1 + 6d$ (1)
$a_3 = a_1 + 2d \Rightarrow 1 = a_1 + 2d$ (2)
$\overline{\hspace{2.5em} 1 = \hspace{2em} 4d}$ Subtract (2) from (1)
$\dfrac{1}{4} = d$

Substitute $d = \dfrac{1}{4}$ in (2):

$1 = a_1 + 2\left(\dfrac{1}{4}\right)$

$1 = a_1 + \dfrac{1}{2}$

$\dfrac{1}{2} = a_1$

7. (12.2) $S_n = \dfrac{n}{2}(a_1 + a_n)$ $\qquad a_n = a_1 + (n − 1)d$
$\hspace{12em} −8 = 10 + 6d$
$7 = \dfrac{n}{2}(10 − 8) \qquad −18 = 6d$
$7 = n \hspace{8em} −3 = d$

8. (12.3) $\dfrac{c^4}{16}, \dfrac{c^4}{16}\left(−\dfrac{2}{c}\right), \dfrac{c^4}{16}\left(−\dfrac{2}{c}\right)^2, \dfrac{c^4}{16}\left(−\dfrac{2}{c}\right)^3, \dfrac{c^4}{16}\left(−\dfrac{2}{c}\right)^4$

$= \dfrac{c^4}{16}, \quad −\dfrac{c^3}{8}, \quad \dfrac{c^2}{4}, \quad −\dfrac{c}{2}, \quad 1$

9. (12.3) $a_4 = a_1 r^3 \Rightarrow −8 = a_1 r^3$ (1)
$a_2 = a_1 r \Rightarrow −18 = a_1 r$ (2)
$\overline{\hspace{3em} \dfrac{8}{18} = \hspace{1em} r^2}$ Divide (1) by (2)
$\pm \dfrac{2}{3} = r$

If $r = \dfrac{2}{3}$:

Substitute $r = \dfrac{2}{3}$ in (2):

$−18 = a_1\left(\dfrac{2}{3}\right) \Rightarrow a_1 = −27$

$S_4 = \dfrac{a_1(1 − r^4)}{1 − r} = \dfrac{27\left(1 − \dfrac{16}{81}\right)}{1 − \left(−\dfrac{2}{3}\right)}$

$S_4 = \dfrac{−27\left(\dfrac{65}{81}\right)}{\dfrac{1}{3}} = −65$

If $r = −\dfrac{2}{3}$:

Substitute $r = −\dfrac{2}{3}$ in (2):

$−18 = a_1\left(−\dfrac{2}{3}\right) \Rightarrow a_1 = 27$

$S_4 = \dfrac{a_1(1 − r^4)}{1 − r} = \dfrac{27\left(1 − \dfrac{16}{81}\right)}{1 − \left(−\dfrac{2}{3}\right)}$

$S_4 = \dfrac{27\left(\dfrac{65}{81}\right)}{\dfrac{5}{3}} = \dfrac{65}{5} = 13$

10. (12.3) $a_n = a_1 r^{n−1}$
$a_n r = a_1 r^n$
$−16\left(−\dfrac{2}{3}\right) = a_1\left(−\dfrac{2}{3}\right)^n$

(1) $\dfrac{32}{3} = a_1\left(−\dfrac{2}{3}\right)^n$

$S_n = \dfrac{a_1(1 − r^n)}{1 − r}$

$26 = \dfrac{a_1\left[1 − \left(−\dfrac{2}{3}\right)^n\right]}{1 − \left(−\dfrac{2}{3}\right)}$

From (1)

$26 = \dfrac{a_1 − a_1\left(−\dfrac{2}{3}\right)^n}{\dfrac{5}{3}} = \dfrac{a_1 − \dfrac{32}{3}}{\dfrac{5}{3}}$

$26 = \dfrac{3a_1 − 32}{5}$

$130 = 3a_1 − 32$
$54 = a_1$

Substitute $a_1 = 54$ in (1):

$\dfrac{32}{3} = 54\left(−\dfrac{2}{3}\right)^n$

$\dfrac{16}{81} = \left(−\dfrac{2}{3}\right)^n \Rightarrow \left(\dfrac{2}{3}\right)^4 = \left(−\dfrac{2}{3}\right)^n$

$4 = n$

11. (12.4) $8, −4, 2, −1, \ldots$

$\left.\begin{array}{l} \dfrac{−1}{2} = −\dfrac{1}{2} \\[1em] \dfrac{2}{−4} = −\dfrac{1}{2} \\[1em] \dfrac{−4}{8} = −\dfrac{1}{2} \end{array}\right\}$ GP, $r = −\dfrac{1}{2}$

$S_\infty = \dfrac{a_1}{1 − r} = \dfrac{8}{1 − \left(−\dfrac{1}{2}\right)} = \dfrac{8}{\dfrac{3}{2}} = \dfrac{16}{3}$

12. (12.4) $3.0333\ldots = 3 + 0.0333\ldots$

$0.0333\ldots = 0.03 + 0.003 + 0.0003 + \cdots$

$$\frac{0.0003}{0.003} = \frac{1}{10} = r$$

$$0.0333\ldots = \frac{0.03}{1 - \dfrac{1}{10}} = \frac{0.03}{0.9} = \frac{1}{30}$$

$$3.0333\ldots = 3 + \frac{1}{30} = \frac{91}{30}$$

13. (12.4)

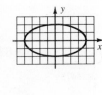

6 ft

The series of heavy lines:

$$S_\infty = \frac{4}{1 - \dfrac{2}{3}} = \frac{4}{\dfrac{1}{3}} = 12 \text{ ft}$$

Total distance $= 6 + 2(12) = 6 + 24 = 30$ ft

Cumulative Review Exercises: Chapters 1–12 (page 616)

1. $\left|\dfrac{x}{2} + 3\right| < 4$ **2.** $\{2 \pm 2\sqrt{3}\}$

$-4 < \dfrac{x}{2} + 3 < 4$

$-7 < \dfrac{x}{2} \qquad < 1$

$-14 < x \qquad < 2$

3. $\log_5 \dfrac{1}{25} = x \Rightarrow 5^x = \dfrac{1}{25} = \dfrac{1}{5^2} = 5^{-2}$ **4.** $b = 16$

$x = -2$

5. $\log 4 + \log(x + 3) = 2 \log x$

$\log 4(x + 3) = \log x^2$

$4x + 12 = x^2$

$0 = x^2 - 4x - 12$

$0 = (x - 6)(x + 2)$

$x - 6 = 0 \mid x + 2 = 0$

$x = 6 \mid \qquad x = -2$

Check for $x = 6$:   *Check for $x = -2$:*

$\log 4 + \log(6 + 3) \overset{?}{=} 2 \log 6$ $\log 4 + \log(-2 + 3) \overset{?}{=} 2 \log(-2)$

$\log(4)(9) \overset{?}{=} \log 6^2$ Not real number $\longrightarrow$

$\log 36 = \log 36$ -2 is *not* a solution

6 is a solution

6. $x = 2$

7. $x^2 + 4y^2 = 16$ Ellipse

x-intercepts: $x^2 + 4(0)^2 = 16$

$x^2 = 16$

$x = \pm 4$

y-intercepts: $0^2 + 4y^2 = 16$

$4y^2 = 16$

$y^2 = 4$

$y = \pm 2$

8.

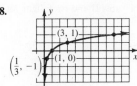

9. (1) $2x - 5y \geq 10$

(2) $5x + y < 5$

Boundary line for (1): $2x - 5y = 10$

Intercepts:

x	y
0	-2
5	0

Origin is the correct half-plane for (2), but not for (1)

Boundary line for (2): $5x + y = 5$

Intercepts:

x	y
0	5
1	0

10. $(x + 2)(x + 1)(x - 1)$

11. LCD $= 2(x - 3)(x + 3)$

$$\frac{x}{x - 3} = \frac{x\,(2)(x + 3)}{(x - 3)\,(2)(x + 3)}$$

$$\frac{9}{x + 3} = \frac{9\,(2)(x - 3)}{(x + 3)\,(2)(x - 3)}$$

$$\frac{1}{2x^2 - 18} = \frac{1}{2(x - 3)(x + 3)}$$

$$\frac{x}{x - 3} - \frac{9}{x + 3} - \frac{1}{2x^2 - 18} = \frac{2x^2 + 6x - 18(x - 3) - 1}{2(x - 3)(x + 3)}$$

$$= \frac{2x^2 + 6x - 18x + 54 - 1}{2(x - 3)(x + 3)}$$

$$= \frac{2x^2 - 12x + 53}{2x^2 - 18}$$

12. $x^2 + 4x - 3 + \dfrac{-9x + 4}{x^2 - x + 1}$

13. $\dfrac{x + 1}{(3x - 1)(x + 5)} \cdot \dfrac{(3x - 1)(2x - 3)}{(2x - 3)(x + 1)} = \dfrac{1}{x + 5}$

14. GP

15. $S_n = \dfrac{n(a_1 + a_n)}{2}$

$10 = \dfrac{n(-7 + 11)}{2}$

$10 = 2n$

$5 = n$

$a_n = a_1 + (n - 1)d$

$11 = -7 + 4d$

$18 = 4d$

$\dfrac{9}{2} = d$

16. $a_1 = -2$

$a_9 = \dfrac{10}{3}$

17. $a_4 = a_1 r^3$

$$-1 = a_1 \left(-\frac{2}{7}\right)^3$$

$$\frac{343}{8} = a_1$$

$$S_5 = \frac{a_1(1 - r^5)}{1 - r} = \frac{\dfrac{343}{8}\left[1 - \left(-\dfrac{2}{7}\right)^5\right]}{1 - \left(-\dfrac{2}{7}\right)} = \frac{\dfrac{343}{8}\left[1 + \dfrac{32}{16,807}\right]}{\dfrac{9}{7}}$$

$$= \frac{7}{9}\left(\frac{343}{8}\right)\left(\frac{16,839}{16,807}\right) = \frac{1871}{56}$$

18. $x^6 - 36x^5 y\sqrt{x} + 594x^5 y^2 - \cdots$

19. $s = kt^2$

$64 = k(2)^2$

$k = \dfrac{64}{4} = 16$

$s = 16(4)^2 = 256$ ft

20. Two answers: 6, 7, and 8 or -3, -2, and -1

21. Let x = Numerator

y = Denominator

$$\frac{x}{y} = \frac{3}{5}$$

$$\frac{x + 4}{y + 5} = \frac{5}{8}$$

$$\left\{ \begin{array}{l} 5x = 3y \\ 8(x + 4) = 5(y + 5) \end{array} \right\}$$

$$\left\{ \begin{array}{ll} 5x - 3y = 0 & \text{Equation 1} \\ 8x - 5y = -7 & \text{Equation 2} \end{array} \right.$$

$\begin{array}{rrrl} 5] & 5x - 3y = & 0 \Rightarrow & 25x - 15y = 0 \\ -3] & 8x - 5y = -7 \Rightarrow & & \underline{-24x + 15y = 21} \\ & & & x = 21 \end{array}$

$3y = 5(21)$

$y = 35$

The original fraction is $\dfrac{21}{35}$. (The check is left to the student.)

22. 53.65 hours

Exercises B.1 (page 622)

1. $3{\scriptstyle\wedge}86$ Characteristic is 2   **2.** 1   **3.** $5{\scriptstyle\wedge}67$ Characteristic is 0

4. 1   **5.** $0.5{\scriptstyle\wedge}16$ Characteristic is -1, written as $9 - 10$

6. -2, written as $8 - 10$ **7.** $9{\scriptstyle\wedge}3000000$ Characteristic is 7

8. 5   **9.** $0.00008{\scriptstyle\wedge}06$ Characteristic is -5, written as $5 - 10$

10. -4, written as $6 - 10$

11. $7{\scriptstyle\wedge}8000$ Characteristic is 4   **12.** 3

13. 5 (same as exponent of 10)   **14.** 4

15. -3 (same as exponent of 10), written as $7 - 10$

16. -5, written as $5 - 10$

Exercises B.2 (page 623)

1. $\log 7{\scriptstyle\wedge}54. = 2.8774$ **2.** 2.2695   **3.** $\log 1{\scriptstyle\wedge}7. = 1.2304$

4. 1.4624   **5.** $\log 3{\scriptstyle\wedge}350. = 3.5250$ **6.** 3.6637

7. $\log 7{\scriptstyle\wedge}000. = 3.8451$ **8.** 2.3010

9. $\log 0.06{\scriptstyle\wedge}04 = 8.7810 - 10$

10. $8.2695 - 10$ **11.** $\log(5.64 \times 10^3) = 3.7513$

12. $6.3304 - 10$

Exercises B.3 (page 624)

1. 1.2809   **2.** 1.6487   **3.** 2.0919   **4.** 2.0149   **5.** 4.4189

6. 4.1271   **7.** -6.21467 **8.** -5.1160

Exercises B.4 (page 627)

1.
$\log 23.30 = 1.3674$
$\log 23.35 = \boxed{1.3683}$
$\log 23.40 = 1.3692$
$\quad 5 \quad 9 \quad 10 \quad 18$
$\times 0.5$
$\overline{9.0}$
   2. 1.4448

3.
$\log 3.060 = 0.4857$
$\log 3.062 = \boxed{0.4860}$
$\log 3.070 = 0.4871$
$\quad 2 \quad 3 \quad 10 \quad 14$
$\times 0.2$
$\overline{2.8} \doteq 3$
   4. 0.6126

5.
$\log 0.06{\scriptstyle\wedge}640 = 8.8222 - 10$
$\log 0.06644 = \boxed{8.8224 - 10}$
$\log 0.06650 = 8.8228 - 10$
$\quad 4 \quad 2 \quad 10 \quad 6$
$\times 0.4$
$\overline{2.4} \doteq 2$

6. $9.7663 - 10$

7.
$\log 1{\scriptstyle\wedge}50.0 = 2.1761$
$\log 150.7 = \boxed{2.1781}$
$\log 151.0 = 2.1790$
$\quad 7 \quad 20 \quad 10 \quad 29$
$\times 0.7$
$\overline{20.3} \doteq 20$
   8. 1.3197

9.
$\log 8.370 \times 10^6 = 6.9227$
$\log 8.375 \times 10^6 = \boxed{6.9230}$
$\log 8.380 \times 10^6 = 6.9232$
$\quad 5 \quad 3 \quad 10 \quad 5$
$\times 0.5$
$\overline{2.5} \doteq 3$
   10. $5.5883 - 10$

11. Because we are using a four-place table, we first round off 324.38 to 324.4
$\log 3{\scriptstyle\wedge}24.0 = 2.5105$
$\log 324.4 = \boxed{2.5111}$
$\log 325.0 = 2.5119$
$\quad 4 \quad 6 \quad 10 \quad 14$
$\times 0.4$
$\overline{5.6} \doteq 6$
   12. 1.8754

Exercises B.5 (page 629)

1. $\log N = 3 \, . \, 5478$

Characteristic / Mantissa

Locate mantissa 0.5478 in body of Table II and read digits for N: $3{\scriptstyle\wedge}53$

$N = 3{\scriptstyle\wedge}530. = 3530$

Characteristic

2. 276

3. $\log N = 0.9605$

Mantissa — (pointing up arrow)
Characteristic — (pointing up arrow)

Locate mantissa 0.9605 in body of Table II and read digits for N:
$9_\wedge 13$
$N = 9.13$ (characteristic is 0)

4. 7.67

5. $\log N = 9.2529 - 10$
Locate mantissa 0.2529 in body of Table II and read digits for N:
$1_\wedge 79$
$N = 0.1_\wedge 79 = 0.179$ because characteristic is $9 - 10 = -1$

6. 0.0134

7. $\log N = 3.5051$
Locate mantissa 0.5051 in body of Table II and read digits for N:
$3_\wedge 20$
Characteristic is 3; $N = 3_\wedge \underset{3}{200.} = 3200$

8. 430

9. $\log N = 4.0588$

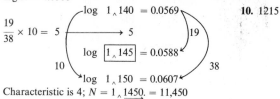

$\frac{19}{38} \times 10 = 5$

$\log\ 1_\wedge 140 = 0.0569$
$\log\ \boxed{1_\wedge 145} = 0.0588$
$\log\ 1_\wedge 150 = 0.0607$

Characteristic is 4; $N = 1_\wedge \underset{4}{1450.} = 11,450$

10. 1215

11. $\log N = 6.9900 - 10$

$\frac{1}{4} \times 10 = 2.5 \doteq 3$

$\log\ 9_\wedge 770 = 0.9899$
$\log\ \boxed{9_\wedge 773} = 0.9900$
$\log\ 9_\wedge 780 = 0.9903$

Characteristic is -4; $N = 0.0009_{\underset{-4}{\wedge}} 773 = 0.0009773$

12. 0.009112

13. $\log N = 7.7168 - 10$
Locate mantissa 0.7168 in body of Table II and read digits for N:
$5_\wedge 21$
Characteristic is $7 - 10 = -3$; $N = 0.005_{\underset{-3}{\wedge}} 21 = 0.00521$

14. 0.00000873

15. $\log N = 1.7120$

$\frac{2}{8} \times 10 = 2.5 \doteq 3$

$\log\ 5_\wedge 150 = 0.7118$
$\log\ \boxed{5_\wedge 153} = 0.7120$
$\log\ 5_\wedge 160 = 0.7126$

Characteristic is 1; $N = 5_\wedge \underset{1}{1}.53 = 51.53$

16. 97,120

3. Let $N = \dfrac{562}{21.4}$

$\begin{array}{l} \log 562 = 2.7497 \\ \log 21.4 = 1.3304 \end{array} \Big] (-)$
$\log N = 1.4193$
$N = 26.26$

4. 21.28

5. Let $N = (1.09)^5$
$\log N = 5 \log 1.09$
$\quad \log 1.09 = 0.0374$
$\log N = 5 \log 1.09 = 0.1870$
$\quad\quad N = 1.538$

6. 133.7

7. Let $\quad N = \sqrt[3]{0.444} = (0.444)^{1/3}$
Then $\log N = \frac{1}{3} \log 0.444$

$\log 0.444 = 9.6474 - 10$
$\quad\quad\quad = 29.6474 - 30$

$\frac{1}{3} \log 0.444 = 3\underline{|29.6474 - 30}$
$\log N = 9.8825 - 10$
$N = 0.7_\wedge 630 = 0.7630$

8. 0.9732

9. $2.863 + \log 38.46 = 2.863 + 1.5850 = 4.4480$

10. 0.5652

11. Let $\quad N = \sqrt[5]{\dfrac{(5.86)(17.4)}{\sqrt{450}}}$

$\begin{array}{l} \log 5.86 = 0.7679 \\ \log 17.4 = 1.2405 \end{array} \Big] (+)$
$\quad\quad\quad\quad 2.0084$
$\log 450 = 2.6532$
$\frac{1}{2} \log 450 = 1.3266 \Big] (-)$

$\log N = \frac{1}{5} (0.6818)$
$\quad\quad = 0.1364$
$\quad\quad N = 1.369$

12. 0.4027

Exercises B.6 (page 632)

1. Let $N = (74.3)(0.618)$
$\begin{array}{l} \log 74.3 = 1.8710 \\ \log 0.618 = 9.7910 - 10 \end{array} \Big] (+)$
$\log N = 11.6620 - 10$
$\quad\quad = 1.6620$
$\quad\quad N = 45.92$

2. 4.679